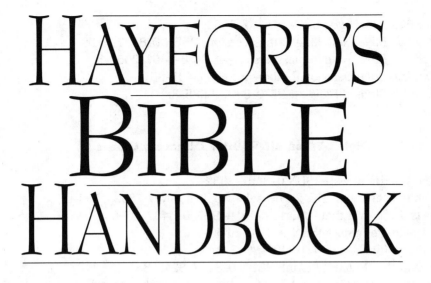

HAYFORD'S BIBLE HANDBOOK

Other Spirit-Filled Life™ Titles Available
From Thomas Nelson Publishers:

Living the Spirit-Filled Life—ISBN 0–8407–8353–1
Spirit-Filled Life Bible, New King James Version—ISBN 0–8407–1800–4
Spirit-Filled Life Bible, King James Version—ISBN 0–8407–2050–5
Spirit-Filled Life Daily Devotional Bible—ISBN 0–8407–8511–9
Spirit-Filled Life Student Bible—ISBN 0–8407–0935–8

Spirit-Filled Life™ Bible Discovery Guides

Beyond the Veil (Hebrews)—ISBN 0–8407–2082–3
Fearless Faith (Galatians, 1 & 2 Thessalonians)—ISBN 0–7852–1134–9
His Name Is Jesus (Matthew, Mark, Luke)—ISBN 0–8407–2090–4
Kingdom Living (Romans)—ISBN 0–8407–8350–7
Kingdom Power (Acts)—ISBN 0–8407–8345–0
Living Beyond the Ordinary (John)—ISBN 0–8407–8349–3
Milestones to Maturity (Exodus, Leviticus, Numbers, Deuteronomy)
   —ISBN 0–8407–8513–5
Pathways to Pure Power (1 Corinthians)—ISBN 0–8407–8514–3
Prisoner of Joy (Ephesians, Philippians, Colossians, Philemon)
   —ISBN 0–8407–8512–7
Promises and Beginnings (Genesis)—ISBN 0–8407–8515–1
Redemption and Restoration (Ruth, Esther)—ISBN 0–7852–1133–0
Singing from the Heart (Psalms)—ISBN 0–8407–8347–7
Twelve Voices for Truth (Minor Prophets)—ISBN 0–8407–2093–9
Until the End of Time (Daniel, Revelation)—ISBN 0–8407–2081–5

Spirit-Filled Life™ Kingdom Dynamics Guides

Answering the Call to Evangelism—ISBN 0–8407–2096–3
Appointed to Leadership—ISBN 0–8407–2083–1
Bible Ministries for Women—ISBN 0–8407–8519–4
Focusing on the Future—ISBN 0–8407–8517–8
God's Way to Wholeness—ISBN 0–8407–8430–9
Kingdom Warfare—ISBN 0–8407–8433–3
Life in the Kingdom—ISBN 0–8407–8432–5
People of the Covenant—ISBN 0–8407–8520–8
People of the Spirit—ISBN 0–8407–8431–7
Power Faith—ISBN 0–8407–2904–7
Praying in the Spirit—ISBN 0–7852–1141–1
Race and Reconciliation—ISBN 0–7852–1131–4
The Spirit-Filled Family—ISBN 0–8407–2085–8
Toward More Glorious Praise—ISBN 0–8407–8519–4

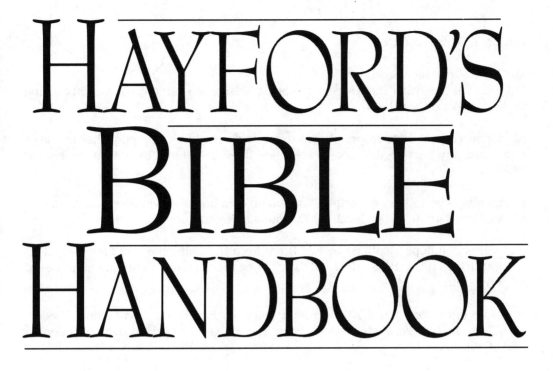

HAYFORD'S BIBLE HANDBOOK

JACK W. HAYFORD
General Editor

THOMAS NELSON PUBLISHERS
Nashville • Atlanta • London • Vancouver

Hayford's Bible Handbook

© 1995 by Thomas Nelson, Inc.
Published in Nashville, Tennessee, by Thomas Nelson, Inc., and distributed in Canada
by Nelson/Word Canada.

Unless otherwise indicated, Scripture quotations are from the *New King James Version
of the Bible,* © 1979, 1980, 1982, 1990, Thomas Nelson, Inc.

Scripture quotations identified by NASB are from the *New American Standard Bible,*
© 1960, 1962, 1963, 1968, 1971, 1973, 1975 by the Lockman Foundation, and used
by permission.

Scripture quotations noted NIV are from *The Holy Bible: New International Version,*
© 1978 by the New York International Bible Society. Used by permission of Zondervan
Bible Publishers.

Survey portions (except for notes in shaded boxes) are based on material written by
Lawrence O. Richards. Used by permission of Word, Inc., Dallas, Texas. All Rights
Reserved.

Visual Survey of the Bible, by Kenneth D. Boa and Mylan W. Lorenzen, © 1985, Thomas
Nelson, Inc. Minor adaptations were made by Jack W. Hayford for use in this
Handbook.

Artwork which accompanies the Encyclopedic Dictionary entries "Soul" and "Spirit"
are copyright by Jack W. Hayford, reproduced by permission, from *A Reader on the
Holy Spirit,* © 1993 by the International Church of the Foursquare Gospel.

Library of Congress Cataloging-in-Publication Data

Hayford's Bible Handbook.
     p. cm.
   Includes bibliographical references.
   ISBN 0–8407–8359–0
   1. Bible—Handbooks, manuals, etc.   I. Thomas Nelson Publishers.
BS417.H39   1995   95–11898
220.6'1—dc20   CIP

Printed in the United States of America

1 2 3 4 5 6 7 8—00 99 98 97 96 95

CONTENTS

EDITOR'S PREFACE

There is a central heartbeat to God's Word. This Handbook has been conceived in the hope of capturing its pulse.

That pulsebeat flows from the heart of divine love—from the God who "so loved, He gave." In giving us His Son, the God of all glory and grace at once achieved two things: the fulfillment of His plan of redemption, and the possibility of His plan for restoration. This means that our Father has more in mind than simply making us "heaven-ready." His desire is to make us "ever-ready"—readied with His Spirit's power to effectively deliver the gospel of the kingdom to a world strained and pained by the void of that order of life God intended every person to know.

The study tool in your hands has been prepared with scholarly carefulness, but it isn't intended as a tool for scholars: it's for *workers.* By the Bible's own description, to *study* God's Word is to be called a "worker," and in the design, development, and delivery of our Handbook, the publishers and I had in mind "uncommonly common" people.

You are probably one of these, the "uncommon" who have a deep desire to know the Bible and grow in understanding of it, yet still a "common" person in terms of your "everyday-ness."

There are millions of us today—and by reason of the swelling tide of God's wave of blessing which is sweeping the earth, the number is increasing daily. We are "everyday" people in our approach to the Bible for two reasons:

(1) We are not called to the mission of the advanced scholar, though we value depth of insight; and

(2) We desire the *practical* and the *workable* in the Word of God.

In short, we aren't interested in speculation or expansive elaboration. We want to get to the core of the truth, first to see how it applies to our lives, then to see how we can minister that truth to others. That idea—*ministry*—is what has guided the preparation of this Handbook. Let me explain.

This Handbook is focused on ministry —yours!

My whole life centers on the conviction that *every believer* is intended to become a fully qualified minister, not in the professional sense of the word, but in the most practical way. If the Bible teaches anything about the salvation God has provided us in His Son Jesus, it's that "being saved" isn't an end in itself. Through faith in Christ, we *have* been saved, to be sure! We're forgiven and destined for eternal glory—Hallelujah! But the objective of our salvation *in* Christ is the replication *of* Christ in us—and *through* us daily, in ways the Holy Spirit enables us to "minister" His grace, goodness, and gifts with power.

This points to the distinctive of this Handbook: It is intended as a study aid *not* simply to provide *information* but to lead to *incarnation.* In its preparation I was guided by a single passion—that the user of this resource would become more "kingdom-minded." When that is realized in any of us who love the Lord, a threefold fact results:

(1) We become more aware of the *purpose* of God's Word,

(2) We become more filled with the *Holy Spirit* of God's Word, and,

(3) We begin to minister more of *Christ,* the Living Word.

To be kingdom-minded is to have a heart set on the desire of spreading God's kingdom to share, teach, give, or spread the love of Jesus Christ in the power of the Holy Spirit. It is to realize He has given us His Spirit in order that we might be fully qualified not only to *live* His life, but to *give* it too—by His power and for His glory!

I suspect that if you're reading these words, I've just described you! I dare say you're already serious about experiencing more than the incredible blessing of *knowing* God, but you've decided you want to live in the joy of *showing* Him and His beauty to others.

And *that's the real purpose for knowing God's Word!* Bible study was never intended to be a mere accumulation of information, only an intellectual pursuit. God gave His Word so that we might be transformed by it and equipped with it!

So, you'll find this Handbook focused on ministry—yours! Whatever your vocation—sales clerk, schoolteacher, gas station attendant, software salesperson, corporate executive, housewife, charity volunteer, college student, or pastor, youth worker, or other professional church leader—here's a key intended to unlock new doorways in kingdom living and ministry.

These words of introduction are also words of dedication—for my efforts are designed to serve you, and thereby indicate my dedication to you, a servant of our Lord Jesus who wants to become more in Him and more for Him.

Partnered with you, serving Him,

Jack W. Hayford

EDITOR'S ACKNOWLEDGMENTS

Hayford's Bible Handbook was so named by Thomas Nelson Publishers' leadership. When they informed me of their desire to use this name, I was at once amazed, humbled, and overwhelmed. Having from my earliest days of in-depth Bible study been blessed by the handbooks prepared by far greater men and women than I, with their names often attached to the handbooks that resulted from their labors, I was stunned to think I could ever be remotely considered worthy of such an honor.

While there are distinct traits and facets of this work that are my own contribution, there is no way this marvelous tool could have come into being through my limited efforts alone. First, I am indebted to the nearly two dozen scholars, pastors, and spiritual leaders whose contributions to the *Spirit-Filled Life*™ *Bible* are included here.

Reuben P. Anderson	Larry Lea
Charles E. Blake	Freda Lindsay
Jamie Buckingham	Dick Mills
Larry Christenson	Gilbert E. Patterson
Glen Cole	Oral Roberts
Dick Eastman	James Robison
Charles Green	Demos Shakarian
Jack Hayford III	Charles Simpson
Marilyn Hickey	Nathaniel M. Van Cleave
Roy Hicks, Sr.	Paul Walker

The rearrangement here of their excellent work provides a special access and convenience that users of that work will appreciate.

Second, the tremendous body of newly developed and edited-for-ministry-mindedness material herein required the dedicated and academically qualified talents of several gifted men—Scott Bauer, Perry Geue, Dan Hicks, and Herman Rosenberger—who brought a special quality to this Handbook carrying my name. Theirs should be included—with gratitude to God for their commitment to the Word of God and for their skill in mining its Holy Spirit-empowered insights.

Third, a body of existing material from the resources of Thomas Nelson Publishers was available for adaptation to the Spirit-Filled Life™ focus of this Handbook. Though these materials have often been revised extensively, I would be remiss if I did not honor by acknowledgment those who labored before me in those endeavors cited elsewhere. Charts, articles, and encyclopedic entries, as well as a considerable portion of the survey section of this Handbook, were first fashioned by others whose dedication equalled that of those who helped me personally. We stood on their shoulders and thus were allowed to reach heights we could not have without their earlier work.

Finally, I want to thank others who deserve special mention: the Biblical Reference editorial and production staff at Thomas Nelson, where Mark Roberts supervised and Lee Hollaway coordinated the project, and Rebecca Bauer, my eldest daughter, whose spiritual sensitivity and editorial skill has time and time again helped me in my writing efforts.

Beyond all, may God be praised! The goal of setting forth the eternal glories and the present possibilities of His kingdom has been central to our pursuits. May the Holy Spirit, whose anointing brings the power of kingdom life to each of us who open fully to His working, attend your use of this Handbook. He is the Author of THE BOOK! May He bless this one.

J.W.H.

THE ESSENTIAL MESSAGE OF GOD'S WORD

by Jack W. Hayford

Each time a person picks up a Bible, he or she opens the grandest message ever given to earth. Nothing has ever come to the hands of humankind that even approaches the completeness and clarity or the love and grace presented in God's Word.

Exceeding any of its other superlative qualities is the Bible's unique, multi-dimensional power. The Bible breathes with truth that is proven in its power to set human beings free. The Bible transforms individual men and women trapped in any and every order of human failure, lifting them from selfishness and sin to dignity and destiny by the power of the grace it reveals. And the Bible heals the human soul through its unparalleled ability to communicate and infuse love into and through human nature by the power of the Holy Spirit.

Truth, grace, and love abound here—but the power that attends and actuates them is the dynamic difference in the Bible's message. Of all the writings that have affected human thought and behavior, the Word of God stands alone in this respect: received in faith, it is "a word with power."

The central theme of the Bible focuses on power, but not in the sense that human reason or institutions pursue it. Fallen man tends to think of power only in terms of self-serving possessiveness or dominating control. Power in human hands, apart from God's transforming grace in the life, is self-centered, manipulative, and inevitably destructive.

But the power the Bible reveals differs radically at every point. The power that flows through and from the Word of God finds its fountain in the heart of God's love and its foundation in the wisdom of God's purposes. By understanding His heart and His purposes for us, we can approach the Bible clearly and properly. Its essential message expresses His heart and aims at fulfilling His purposes. The quickest summary of the Bible's message might be made with a three-word outline: revelation, redemption, and restoration.

The Bible's *revelation* helps us understand two fundamental facts: (1) God's orig-

> **God's plan is to bring humanity into renewed relationship and active partnership with Him.**

inal and benevolent order and design for humankind on earth, and (2) humanity's distortion of that design through refusing God's order.

Redemption in the Bible reveals God's pathway to recovering His intended order and design for humankind. It is taught in two parts: (1) In the Old Testament, the pathway to recovery is introduced through the sacrificial system of blood atonement, forecasting a future plan of final redemption. (2) In the New Testament, the promised redemption is accomplished in the person of Jesus Christ, through His life, death, and resurrection. Placed in Christ by God's grace, humanity experiences redemption now in part and shall experience it in full in the future.

God offers the promise and the possibilities of *restoration* to all who receive His redemption in Jesus Christ. Restoration aims at two goals: (1) to return human beings to the personal relationship, intimacy, and companionship with God that He intended from the beginning; and (2) to return redeemed men and women to their original place of rulership over all things under God, experiencing the privilege and joy of partnership with Him.

These three points make clear the whole flow of God's dealings in the Bible—in both redemption and restoration. His program of salvation can be seen as a twofold plan, intended to bring mankind both into a renewed relationship with Him and into an active partnership. The more clearly we see God's intention in the salvation He has given us, the greater will be our expectation and thus our readiness to respond to the Father's fullest purpose for us. Indeed, clearly perceiving God's revealed plan of redemption and restoration lies at the core of the great breakthrough taking place in the global church today.

A Holy Spirit-begotten dynamic has invaded the whole church within this century. What began with the holy quest of a few individuals seeking to unlock the secret to the early church's power has led to a century-long awakening to the work, ministry, and gifting of the Holy Spirit. The dramatic impact has invited comparisons with the turnaround seen in the church during the Reformation over four hundred years earlier. This expanding, ongoing work of renewal by God's Spirit within His church has caused many to recognize that humankind's salvation has a "kingdom" objective: first, the *recovery* of a former rebel (man) through divine forgiveness, for renewed fellowship with God; and second, the *reinstatement* of a former ruler (man) to obedience and rulership under God.

The idea of the kingdom of God, then, runs through the whole of Scripture. It reaches its culmination in Jesus' declaration and ministry of "the gospel of the kingdom" and His commissioning and enabling the church to proclaim and demonstrate that message throughout the world by the power of the Holy Spirit. Until believers grasp the full meaning of "the gospel of the kingdom," they may miss the fullness of God's intention for the redeemed. Too many see their salvation as involving only their forgiveness for sins in their past, their call to holy living in the present, and their hope of eternal joy in heaven in the future. As blessedly true and fully meaningful as these dimensions of salvation are, if salvation is limited to these, believers neglect another crucial dimension: the divine intent to restore man's original "ruling" or "dominion" aspect—the rulership (ministry in the Spirit's power) intended to be joined with our fellowship (renewed intimacy and companionship with the Father).

The Bible's "power" theme thus has a positive and negative aspect. The power of God Almighty, who created all things and then placed man in dominion over the earth, is recognized as the fountainhead of all power. The power of sin to break man's relationship with God—and thereby cause his loss of "ruling" ability—is acknowledged as the corruption of power. Not only has man misused and forfeited his rule through disobedience, but by submitting to sin he surrendered his rule to the Serpent, who then seized the temporal control of this present world order.

The purpose of Jesus' coming was not only to bring saving forgiveness to sinful man, but also to break the power of the Serpent's usurped control. And the purpose of Christ in His church is to extend the ministry He began: (1) extending the message of kingdom grace and forgiveness to lost sinners, that they might be restored to fellowship; and (2) extending the message of kingdom authority and dominion—ministering with love and power through the Holy Spirit's fullness in their lives to break the bonds of evil, heal human brokenness and need, and begin again to partner in the rule of God toward the full restoration of His kingdom.

Every believer is called both to be forgiven and to be filled with the Holy Spirit. Salvation's forgiveness opens the door to joyous fellowship and holy communion with our Creator-Father through the work of Christ. Then, salvation's fullness opens the door to responsible growth in partnership with our Redeemer-Savior through the power of the Holy Spirit. At that point "the gospel of the kingdom" has found its fullest expression in our open hearts. As in Jesus' parable of the sower, the seed of truth multiplies as it falls on hearts that are completely open to all that redemption affords us in Christ Jesus.

HOW TO USE HAYFORD'S BIBLE HANDBOOK

Hayford's Bible Handbook has been designed as a useful companion to the *Spirit-Filled Life Bible*, although you will find it helpful with any Bible you may have. General Editor Jack W. Hayford and the team of contributors have worked to highlight those elements within the Scripture that magnify and clarify the Spirit-filled life. His perspective is expressed in his Preface (p. vii) and Introduction (p. x), as well as the Dictionary entry "Gospel of the Kingdom."

Two major segments fill most of this volume. The opening section—the Handbook proper—covers the entire Bible in its normal sequence, book by book, Genesis through Revelation. The treatment of most Bible books begins with a two-page Kingdom Keys article (see sample below). Here you will find a Kingdom Key, Timeline Key, Master Key, Power Key, and Word-Text Key, plus a footer crossing the pages and pointing to a major theme of the book.

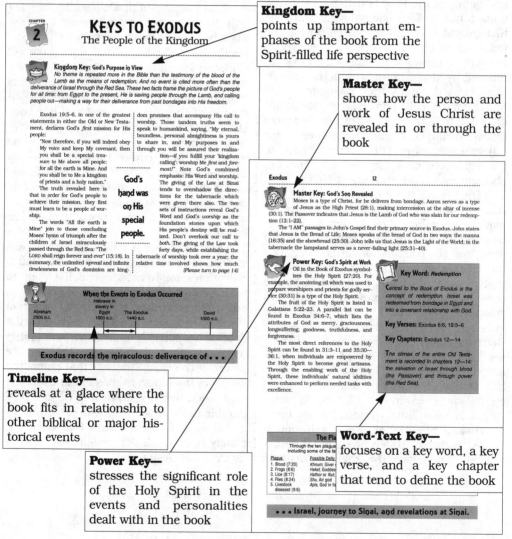

Kingdom Key— points up important emphases of the book from the Spirit-filled life perspective

Master Key— shows how the person and work of Jesus Christ are revealed in or through the book

Timeline Key— reveals at a glace where the book fits in relationship to other biblical or major historical events

Power Key— stresses the significant role of the Holy Spirit in the events and personalities dealt with in the book

Word-Text Key— focuses on a key word, a key verse, and a key chapter that tend to define the book

Introducing
EXODUS

Author. Moses, whose name means "Drawn Out," is the central figure of Exodus. He is the Hebrew prophet who led the Israelites out of Egypt. Exodus is traditionally attributed to Moses. Four passages in Exodus lend strong support to Moses' authorship of at least most of it (17:14; 24:4, 7; 34:27). Through various events and face-to-face encounters with God, Moses received the revelation of those things God wanted to be known. Then, through the process of Holy Spirit inspiration, Moses communicated this revealed information to the Hebrew people both orally and in written form.

Date. Conservative tradition dates Moses' death sometime around 1400 B.C., so the Book of Exodus was likely compiled during the forty years preceding, while in the wilderness.

Background. Exodus is the continuation of the Genesis account, dealing with the development of a small family group of people into a large nation of millions. In the years the Hebrews lived in Egypt, many times in bondage. Exodus records the development, their trip from Egypt, Sinai to receive God's law, and Sinai to the building of the tions on the construction of the as a dwelling place for God.

Content. The Book of Exodus into three major sections: deliverance of Israel (1:1—19 uous journey to Sinai (13: the miraculous revelations 40:38).

Section one (1:1—13: Hebrews being oppressed. Like any group under res complained. Their compl not only to their capto (2:23–25). God heard th motion a plan to del plished this prophet named

Delivera neously; it v amount of ti gain the Pharaoh's gr

Kingdom Key *continued from page 11*

more slowly humankind consents to the sur...
render worship requires, compared w...
study God's Word deserves.

As Genesis reveals humankind's...

dom" potential, Exodus unveils the fact that only in living to worship God can we find the ... the promises and fulfill the ...

Surveying
EXODUS

I. THE MIRACULOUS DELIVE ISRAEL 1:1—13:16. During n 430 years in Egypt, the Isr enslaved by the pharaohs. God, chosen Israel to be His people performs many mighty acts th way for His people's departur Egypt and thus their deli bondage.

A. Oppression of the Israe (1:1–22). The family of Israel tile district (Goshen) in the ea Nile. Within several generat tion of Israel grows so gr Pharaoh perceives them devises ways of decreas (7–14). Eventually, he con tians to drown all Hebrew river (15–22; see Feared).

B. The birth and early l 4:31). A son is born to To hide him, the infant's in a floating basket al river. He is discovered b who adopts the boy as (3–10).

As an adult, Mos beating a Hebrew, wh of his own people. Pha for the deed (11–15) where he marries an While ...

10:27). Pharaoh had hardened his heart for so long, the Lord now was using Pharaoh's own will to further His purposes.

The plague of hail (9:13–33) defeats the goddess of life and the god who protected the crops.

The plague of locusts (10:1–20) destroys Egypt's remaining source of food.

> **"that you may know that I am the Lord"**
>
> (10:1–20). God's twofold purpose in confronting Pharaoh was to gain Israel's release and to magnify His own name. His signs and mighty works in Egypt bore witness to His overruling power in nature, His dominion over all creation, and His power over the kingdom of Satan. Today we can expect signs and mighty works to accompany Christ's faithful witnesses in the world so that men may know that He is the Lord and that they might be released from their bondage to sin (see Mark 15:15–16; Acts 5:12; 14:1 Cor. 12:7–11).

The plague of darkness (Ex. 10:21–29) is a frontal assault on the most sacred religious symbol in Egypt, the sun.

The plague of death (11:1–10) makes known that the God of the Hebrews is greater than the Egyptian giver of life.

D. The Exodus event (1... dience to God's departure ...

II. THE MIRACULOUS JOURNEY TO SINAI 13:17—19:27. Although God acts to deliver, sustain, and protect them from any enemies, Israel regularly reacts them with fear, disbelief, and murmuring.

A. Deliverance at the Red Sea (13:17— 15:21). God leads Israel out of Egypt "by way of the wilderness of the Red Sea" (13:18), making His presence known by guiding Israel with pillars of cloud and fire (21–22). But Pharaoh realizes that he is losing his slave labor force and marshals a chariot army to recapture Israel (14:1–9).

God executes a dramatic twofold deliverance for Israel: (1) Israel passes through the parted waters of the sea to safety, and (2) Pharaoh's army is drowned as they presumptuously follow Israel into the sea (10–31).

> **"I will sing to the Lord, for He has triumphed gloriously"**
>
> (15:1–21). Witnessing the Lord's victory over the Egyptians (14:21–31) the Israelites break forth in exuberant praise, expressing to God (1) great gratitude for the crossing of the Red Sea (no ... tion of the Land of promise) ... because the Lord has he ... ously on our behalf (see 2 ... 3–18), we walk the pathway ... ed wonders. Personal vic ... and small, should exc ... spiritual song—a pr ... Spirit's fullness in our ...

TRUTH-IN-ACTION through EXODUS

Truth Exodus Teaches	Action Exodus Invites
1 Four Keys to Understanding God Successful Christian living begins with knowing who God is. In Exodus, God reveals part of His nature and character. Knowing God in truth will affect our behavior. Exodus gives four keys to make our lives more faithful and fruitful.	**3:14, 15** *Understand* that God is! His Name is "I AM WHO I AM." Rest on this foundation. Be grounded and established in Him. **15:25, 26** *Receive* God as "The Lord Who Heals You." To heal is His nature; His will is to make us whole. **17:15** *Rely* upon God who is "The Lord Your Banner." As you surrender to Him—your Victory, Miracle, and Protection— in truth will attend. **31:13** *Pursue* God who is "the Lord Who Makes You Holy." His life in us makes our holiness possible.
2 Steps to Holiness God calls us to be holy, "set apart to Him and His purposes." God intends His people to be distinguished in nature and in character from the world—different in the way we think, act, and live. This difference will be visible and bring God glory.	**7:1—11:10** *Know* that God deals differently with us than with the world (see 8:23; 9:26; 10:23; 11:7). **12:7** Rely on the blood of Jesus to protect you from all evil (see 1 Pet. 1:18, 19). **19:5** *Obey* God's Word and you will become His "special treasure." **21:5** *Be* Jesus' bondslave. He will open your ears to hear His voice clearly and understand His Word. **32:26–29** *Be zealous* for God's holiness. He honors those who honor Him.
3 Guidelines to Godly Living Godly living is living with God in your life and His Life in you. He gives guidelines to help us build our lives on His precepts. God calls us to acts of faith that build godliness. Without faith, our acts become vain religion. Godliness embraces godly practice and shuns vain religious acts.	**3:3** *Stay* alert to seek out God's working. It often comes in a way we do not expect. **12:15, 19, 20; 13:3, 6, 7** *Participate* regularly in the Lord's Supper. We thus share in His deliverance and life. **14:13, 14** *Be* still as God works. You will see His deliverance. **16:4** *Be careful* to apply God's Word. He wants us to follow His instructions. **23:16; 34:22** *Celebrate* God's blessings to you. **25:8; 33:15** *Dwell* in and esteem God's Presence. It distinguishes us from everyone else. **31:12–17; 33:14** *Rest* in God's Sabbath. His rest gives us rest from our own works (see Heb. 4:10, 11).
4 Keys to Wise Living God calls His people to wisdom. Wisdom is knowing how to apply truth. Exodus gives principles that teach us how to live wisely and please God. It also teaches us certain wise practices. The Holy Spirit will train us to practice wisdom as a discipline that will lead to the fullness of life.	**19:8; 24:3, 7** *Do* not trust yourself to obey God's Word. Depend upon His Holy Spirit. **20:1–17** *Meditate* on the Ten Commandments regularly to learn God's moral nature and character. **20:20** *Learn* reverence for the Lord; it will keep you from sinning. **23:2, 3** *Suspect* majority opinion that proposes deviance. Evil is often popular but disobeys God. **23:15** *Give* every time you gather with God's people for worship. It shows faith that He provides for you. **32:1** *Do* not become impatient with God. It leads to sin. **32:... ** *Recognize* that any skill or ability you have is God's

---

Following the Kingdom Keys is an Introduction of the Bible book that reviews such details as the date of writing, authorship, other background information, a summary of the content, and a personal application of the book's teaching to the Christian's daily life.

The Survey of each Bible book looks at the content passage by passage, briefly describing what is contained in each one. The Kingdom Life Insights™, a special feature of this section, appear in tinted boxes. These offer Spirit-filled life perspectives on individual verses. An index of all biblical references accompanied by Kingdom Life Insights™ can be found in the back of the Handbook.

Throughout the Survey, several kinds of cross-references help you deepen your study. Related Scripture verses or passages are given in parenthesis. When you look these up in the Bible you may find: (1) additional background information; (2) a parallel historical account; (3) a complementary teaching of a principle; (4) a prophecy concerning the incident you are studying; or (5) a promise or prophecy fulfilled. Turning to the Survey section for the cited passage, you will find further insights into the purpose and significance of those verses.

Also in parenthesis are citations pointing to entries or Kingdom Dynamics articles found in the Encyclopedic Dictionary section of the Handbook. Within the main text an asterisk (*) has been placed in front of key words to indicate that an entry on that word appears in the Encyclopedic Dictionary.

A Truth-in-Action chart at the end of each Bible book study directs your attention to practical principles contained in the book and specific actions that might grow out of those principles within your Christian life. A list of all such charts and their page number is included in the Index.

At the back of the Handbook is the Encyclopedic Dictionary, containing more than 1,300 entries arranged alphabetically. These entries fall into three categories, each marked by a different icon. The open Bible icon 📖 marks entries that explain important biblical or doctrinal terms. The sword icon 🗡 marks Word Wealth entries, providing brief word studies of key Greek and Hebrew words in the original text. The dove icon 🕊 marks entries that bring together hundreds of Kingdom Dynamics features from the *Spirit-Filled Life Bible* into twenty-two full-length articles, such as "The Kingdom of God." Indexes related to Word Wealth entries and Kingdom Dynamics articles also appear at the very back of the Handbook.

Tucked in between the two major sections are three special reference features designed to strengthen your overall approach to Bible study: Visual Survey of the Bible; The Intertestamental Period; and Important Archaeological Discoveries and the Bible. The final few pages of the Handbook include the indexes cited above and a bibliography of many additional volumes worth examining for further study.

How you use these many resources will vary according to the nature of your study. If your focus is on a particular Scripture passage, you will want to begin by reading it carefully in the Bible. Then read the Survey material related to it, and trace any references to other verses or key words. Look back at the Kingdom Keys and Introduction for the book to see how your passage relates to the overall emphases of the book. Finally, check the Truth-in-Action chart at the back of the Survey section of the book for pointers on applying the passage in your life.

If your study is topical, you will want to start with an entry in the Encyclopedic Dictionary. Frequently the entry will also direct you to other related articles in this section or to Scripture passages that support or illumine the topic.

HANDBOOK
TO THE
BOOKS OF THE BIBLE

Keys to the Scriptures

At the beginning of each Bible book study—which includes an introduction to the book as well as a chapter-by-chapter survey—the reader will find a two-page section entitled "Keys to (the name of the book)." This highlight of Hayford's Bible Handbook not only gives a concise, focused overview of each book, but also includes a brief analysis of the concept of the kingdom of God revealed in that book. In a few cases some of the shorter books have been clustered together, so there are fifty-two such two-page spreads. Within each spread are five "keys" to help the reader grasp the practical, spiritual thrust of the book:

The Kingdom Key: The General Editor's assessment of each book;

The Timeline Key: Places the events of each book in the chronological context of history and the whole of Scripture;

The Master Key: Spotlights the central personality of every book in the Bible: the Lord Jesus Christ (He is our Lord and Master—and all study profits most when He is found, worshiped, and obeyed);

The Power Key: Focuses on the Holy Spirit's action and activities in the Word; and

The Word-Text Key: In most books, includes (1) a key verse, (2) a key chapter, and (3) key words that define the book and recur often in the text.

The combination of these keys, taken together as a team of blended Bible study features, distills each book's Keynote Thrust: Its place in the whole of the Word, work, and will of God's kingdom, its place in the span of time the Bible covers, its place in presenting the Person of Christ, its place in unveiling the power of the Holy Spirit, and its place in communicating essential truth to us.

KEYS TO GENESIS
The Precepts of the Kingdom

Kingdom Key: God's Purpose in View

Every major theme of God's plan and purpose for humankind is introduced in Genesis, including the founding precepts of "the kingdom of God." Two underlying concepts appear in chapter 1: (1) The sovereign God is the fountain of all life and power, whose kingdom embraces all that is; and (2) He has created humankind to share dominion with Him within His kingdom.

We must see these two grand facts from the start of our study of the Bible. God's sovereignty and human significance are not opposing ideas, though both the secular and religious communities often pit them against each other. Unless we discern God's original design, created dignity, and intended destiny for humanity at the outset, we will misread His motive and manner in carrying out His plan of redemption.

The "kingdom" key to Genesis is wrapped in the truth that God created humankind as *partners*, not as peons (i.e., not serfs, drudges, or pawns). While infinitely less than equal with God, humankind was nonetheless created for partnership with Him. Though that high purpose was frustrated by the Fall of man through disobedience and sin, it is still firm in the Creator's redemptive plan. Thus,

> God is the fountain of all life and power.

God's program for redeeming humanity will be more than restoring the relationship which sin has broken. He also will seek to bring this fallen creature back to the place of destiny and dominion He chose for humankind from the beginning.

Genesis 1:26 establishes these essential precepts: (a) humankind is "made in God's image" (granted qualities unique and elevated in the created order) and (b) given "dominion" (granted the status of a king whose decisions and actions will determine the course of this new world being placed under his rule). (*See* Kingdom of God, which expands this concept as it unfolds in the Book of Genesis. The reader also should have read the introductory articles to this study feature on pages xii–xiv and 1.)

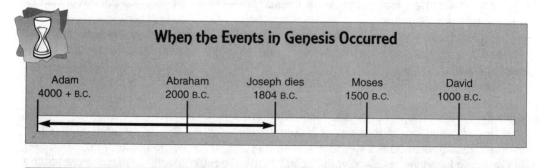

When the Events in Genesis Occurred

Adam	Abraham	Joseph dies	Moses	David
4000 + B.C.	2000 B.C.	1804 B.C.	1500 B.C.	1000 B.C.

Genesis is wrapped in the truth that God

Master Key: God's Son Revealed

The preexistent Christ, the living Word, was very much involved in the creation. "All things were made through Him, and without Him nothing was made that was made" (John 1:3). Jesus' ministry is anticipated in Genesis 3:15, suggesting that the "Seed" of the woman who will bruise the Serpent's (Satan's) head is Jesus Christ, the "Seed" of Abraham mentioned by Paul in Galatians 3:16. Melchizedek is the mysterious king-priest of Genesis 14. The Letter to the Hebrews identifies him as a type of Jesus Christ, our King and High Priest (Heb. 6:20).

The greatest revelation of Christ in Genesis is found in God's covenant with Abraham in chapters 15 and 17. The promises God made to Abraham are fulfilled in Jesus, as Paul explains in detail in Galatians. Much of the Bible is built upon the Abrahamic covenant and its flowering in Jesus Christ.

Abraham's willingness to sacrifice his son Isaac at God's command bears a startling similarity to the crucial event of the New Testament. "Take . . . your only son Isaac, whom you love . . . and offer him there as a burnt offering" (22:2) reminds us of God's sacrifice of *His* only Son for the sins of the world.

Finally, Jacob's blessing upon Judah anticipates the coming of "Shiloh," to be identified as the Messiah. "And to Him shall be the obedience of the people" (49:10).

Power Key: God's Spirit at Work

"The Spirit of God was hovering over the face of the waters" (1:2). Thus we find the Spirit involved in creation. The Holy Spirit also worked in Joseph, a fact obvious to Pharaoh: "Can we find such a one as this, a man in whom is the Spirit of God?" (41:38).

Although the Holy Spirit is not mentioned again in Genesis, we see His work in drawing the animals from the four corners of the earth into Noah's ark. We also perceive His working in the lives of the patriarchs, protecting them and their families and blessing them materially. All sorts of difficulties and impossible situations threatened to frustrate the fulfillment of God's promises to Abraham, but the Spirit of God supernaturally resolved every challenge.

Key Word: *Beginnings*

Genesis gives the beginning of almost everything, including the beginning of the universe, life, humanity, sabbath, death, marriage, sin, redemption, family, literature, cities, art, language, and sacrifice.

Key Verses: Genesis 3:15; 12:3

Key Chapter: Genesis 15

Central to all of Scripture is the Abrahamic covenant, which is given in 12:1–3 and ratified in 15:1–21. Israel receives three specific promises: (1) the promise of a great land—*"from the river of Egypt to the great river, the River Euphrates"* (15:18); (2) the promise of a great nation—*"and I will make your descendants as the dust of the earth"* (13:16); and (3) the promise of a great blessing—*"I will bless you and make your name great; and you shall be a blessing"* (12:2).

---

created humankind as partners, not as peons.

Introducing
GENESIS

Author: Jewish tradition lists Moses as the author of Genesis and of the next four books. Together these books are called the Pentateuch. Jesus said, "If you believed Moses, you would believe Me; for he wrote about Me" (John 5:46). The Pentateuch itself depicts Moses as having written extensively. (*See* Ex. 17:14; 24:4; Deut. 31:24.) Acts 7:22 tells us that "Moses was learned in all the wisdom of the Egyptians." In the notes accompanying the text we observe a number of loanwords from Egyptian that are found in Genesis, a fact which suggests that the original author had his roots in Egypt, as did Moses.

Date: The traditional date of the Exodus from Egypt is the mid-fifteenth century B.C. First Kings 6:1 states that Solomon began building the temple "in the four hundred and eightieth year after the children of Israel had come out of the land of Egypt." Solomon is thought to have begun construction about 960 B.C., dating the Exodus about 1440 B.C. So Moses wrote Genesis after 1440 B.C., during the forty years in the wilderness.

Content: Genesis opens with the formation of the solar system, the preparation of the land for habitation, and the creation of life on the earth. All of the eight acts of creation are accomplished in six days.

The subsequent ten chapters explain the origins of many mysterious qualities of life: human sexuality, marriage, sin, sickness, pain in childbearing, death, the wrath of God, man's enmity toward man, and the dispersion of races and languages throughout the earth.

Genesis, beginning in chapter 12, recounts the call of Abraham and the inauguration of God's covenant with him—a glorious, eternal covenant renewed with Isaac and Jacob. Genesis is remarkable for its exquisite narrative, highlighted by the inspiring account of Joseph and the divine preservation and multiplication of the people of God in Egypt. It is a lesson in divine election, as Paul recounts in Romans 9.

Genesis in many ways anticipates the New Testament: the very personal God, the Trinity, the institution of marriage, the seriousness of sin, divine judgment, and righteousness by faith. The Tree of Life, lost in Genesis, is restored in Revelation 22.

Genesis concludes with the blessing of Jacob upon Judah, from whose tribe was to come the Messiah: "The scepter shall not depart from Judah, nor a lawgiver from between his feet, until Shiloh comes; and to Him shall be the obedience of the people" (49:10). Many centuries and many struggles will follow before this prophecy finds it fulfillment in Jesus Christ.

Personal Application: Genesis immediately brings into question many secular world views, so serious Genesis students must become accustomed to thinking differently. We must perceive the world and its history as the ancient biblical authors reveal it. For example, the narratives of chapters 1—3 are not to be understood allegorically but as actual history. The Word of God must always stand above the word of man; we are not to judge His Word, but rather, it judges us. Therefore, ancient Hebrews should not be thought of as primitive simply because they relate reality differently. Rationalized Greek thinking about world realities may be our heritage, but it is not always true.

Genesis teaches many other lessons as well: Abraham is our example of faith (15:6; Gal. 3:7); Joseph's life is an exquisite sermon for all who suffer unfairly and is a challenge to faithfulness in this age of undisciplined permissiveness.

Finally, we understand human nature properly only as we grasp the truth of "original sin." When Adam sinned, all of us not only sinned but inherited a resident sin nature (8:21; Rom. 5:19; 7:18). Only a Savior can deal effectively with this inherited natural corruption.

Surveying
GENESIS

I. THE EARLY HISTORY OF *MAN 1:1—11:32.
On the foundation of creation, the Bible constructs its unique view of life, death, sin, redemption, history, and the future triumph of good over evil. The first part of Genesis (chs. 1—11) presents the personal nature of God's creation and His relationship with human beings; the second part (chs. 12—50), the purposive nature of God's creation, revealed through the covenant promises He makes to Abraham.

A. The creation narratives (1:1—2:25). Against ancient creation myths and modern scientific theories of creation, Genesis presents an all-powerful Creator who calls the universe into being and whose personal action explains all beginnings.

1. Creation of the heavens, the earth, and life upon the earth (1:1—2:3). Over a dark, formless void, God's Spirit moves, and by His word God creates heaven and earth. On days one and two (3–8), God lays the foundation for life on earth as light is *created and the waters are divided. The organization of the earth for habitation takes place on days three and four (9–19). The population of the earth occurs on days five and six (20–31), starting with the creation of all sorts of creatures. To this point, God's evaluation of His workmanship is "it was good" (10, 12, 18, 21, 25). God then shapes human beings "in His own image" (27) and gives them dominion over His creation (26, 28). Now God pronounces His work as "very good" (31; *see* Blood, The; Family Life; Human Worth; Kingdom of God; Manhood), and on day seven He rests (2:2–3; *see* Stewardship).

2. Creation of man (2:4–25). Chapter 2 reviews the creation of humankind. God forms a human (Heb. *adam*) from the dust of the ground (Heb. *adamah*) and breathes life into him (7); God also forms "a helper comparable to him" (18, 21–22). The identity shared by woman (Heb. *ishshah*) and man (*ish*), not the differences between them, is stressed in Adam's words (23). God designs an environment (Eden) in which provisions are made for the first humans to develop their full potential: natural resources to use, opportunities to exercise creativity, meaningful work to do, another person with whom to share God's good gifts, and an opportunity for moral development ("the tree of the knowledge of good and evil," v. 9).

B. The Fall (3:1–24). Sin enters into God's creation, and there are consequences. The serpent injects doubt into the first humans' understanding of their relationship to God. God's word is questioned (1), His motives and love subtly denied (5), and His warnings flatly contradicted. Moral and psychological consequences accompany the act of sin. The man and the woman are crushed by guilt and shame (7) and try to hide their deed from God. The just Lord must pronounce judgment upon them, but He begins with hope: here is given the first proclamation of what Jesus will eventually come to do (15; *see* Angels; Blood, The; Human Worth; Kingdom of God; Manhood; Messianic Promises; Restoration).

> **"He shall bruise your *head"**
> (3:15). This statement is the inaugural declaration that God will triumph over Satan. Seen prophetically, God declares that one would come from a woman to ful-

fill this sentence of death on the devil. All believers participate in the working out of the overthrow of the works of darkness by believing the gospel of Jesus, thus being united with Him in His victory over Satan. Believers also demonstrate this overthrow with each work of power the Holy Spirit performs through them.

The impact of sin upon human life, upon the relationship between men and women, and upon nature is explained (16–19). Suffering is a natural consequence of sin. Sin disrupts the relationship between the Creator and His creatures, and the humans are banished from Eden (23–24).

C. The pre-Flood world (4:1—5:32). The dark shadows of sin and death are cast upon the human race. Cain, angry because God accepted Abel's animal sacrifice and not his own, murders his brother (4:2–10; *see* Blood, The; Brotherly Love). Cain deserves execution but is protected (11–15). Cain's line produces another murderer, Lamech (23); but there is hope in another line (that of Seth and his son) who calls "on the name of the Lord" (25–26; *see* Women). It is through this line that the genealogy of Adam is recorded (5:1–32).

D. Noah and the Flood (6:1—9:29). Wickedness permeates the pre-Flood generations (6:5; *see* Restoration). Although it grieves God to do so (6–7), He will act in judgment if human suffering fails to bring repentance. God explains the moral basis of the coming flood to Noah, the single exception during the generations of depravity (9–22). The earth is corrupt and full of violence (11, 13), so God purges it of wicked humanity by means of the Flood.

The Flood accomplishes God's purpose of judgment (7:17–24). Humanity is given a new start through Noah and his family. Saved from destruction by God, the survivors express thanks by sacrificial offerings (8:1–20; *see* Blood, The). God's decision not to destroy the earth by flood again is revealed to Noah in the form of a covenant, a promise which reveals God's firm intention (8:21—9:17; *see* Faith, Seed; Human Worth; Kingdom of God).

Sin, however, remains viable and Ham, the father of Canaan, engages in some sort of sexual perversity (9:21–22) and is cursed by Noah. Ham's immoral actions are projected and the future of one of his sons, Canaan, described. Indeed, the Canaanites became known as a sexually and religiously degraded people. Thus, the descendants of Ham will serve the descendants of Shem and Japheth (25–27).

E. The table of nations (10:1–32).
This genealogy lists the descendants of Noah's sons.

F. The confusion of languages (11:1–9).
Until this time, the nations were united by a common language (1, 6). Noah's descendants attempt to build a unified culture in a city known as Babel (lit., "confusion"). They construct a "tower" as symbol and seal of their common identity (4). The tower was probably a ziggurat, a vast construction of clay bricks (3), on which certain Babylonian peoples housed the shrines of their city's gods. God does not tolerate this outbreak of idolatry: He confuses the languages of the people and scatters them, thereby making unity impossible (7–9).

G. Genealogy of Abram (Abraham) (11:10–32).
The genealogy of Shem (10) is continued to Terah, who had three sons: Abram, Nahor, and Haran (27). This list would serve to confirm the roots of the people of Israel, as well as the claim that the workings of Israel's God can be traced back to creation.

II. THE CHOSEN PATRIARCHS 12:1—50:26.
The first part of Genesis depicts God's dealings with humankind as a whole from creation to Abraham, a period lasting thousands of years. The second part (chs. 12—50) concentrates on only four generations and less than four centuries. God no longer deals with the whole human race, but with a single family, that of Abraham, through whom God intends ultimately to bring salvation to all. Beginning here (Genesis 12), the remainder of the Old Testament focuses on the chosen people, Israel, through whom God will work out His purposes.

A. Abram (Abraham) (12:1—23:20).
The heart of Genesis is the covenant God makes with Abraham. The covenant embodies promises which reveal the purposes of God throughout all of salvation history.

1. Abraham's call (12:1—13:18). In Abraham's day (c. 2000 B.C.), several mature civilizations (e.g., Egyptian, Hittite, Hurrian, and Assyrian) bordered the Land of Promise (modern day Palestine), which was at that time the land of the Canaanites and Amorites.

Abraham was born in Ur, a city in lower Mesopotamia (later known as Babylonia). Abraham probably worshiped idols in his home city; his father did in Haran (see Josh. 24:2), where Terah had settled his family (Gen. 11:31; see Families).

God reveals himself to Abraham, commanding him to leave his country, people, and relations, to travel to the land God would make known (12:1). God makes specific promises (2–3; see Kingdom of God; Leadership, Spiritual) to Abraham, which will be expanded upon and explained further (see Genesis chs. 15, 17). The faithful Abraham departs from Haran, taking his wife, his nephew (Lot), and their possessions (4–5). While Abraham is traveling in Canaan, God appears to him and states that this is the land to be given to his descendants (7). Abraham abandons the land because of famine and journeys to Egypt; there, he asks Sarah to conceal their relationship (10–20; see ch. 55 of this Handbook, §3.5.b).

Upon his return to Canaan, Abraham permits Lot to choose a portion of the land in which to dwell. Abraham remains in Canaan (13:12); Lot settles in the plain of Jordan (11).

2. The battle of the kings (14:1–24). Raiding kings from the east come to war against a local coalition of city states in the region where Lot settled (1–12; see ch. 55, §3.5.a). Abraham rescues Lot (16). Melchizedek, king of Salem (later called Jerusalem) and "priest of God *Most High," greets Abraham with a banquet and blesses him. (See ch. 55, §3.6.b.)

3. God's covenant with Abraham (15:1—21:34). Abraham is concerned about who will inherit his property since he is childless (see ch. 55, §3.5.b). God repeats the promises of Genesis 12. Abraham's own son will be heir, and his descendants will be beyond counting. The nature of faith is clearly stated: Abraham "believed in the Lord, and He *accounted it to him for righteousness" (6).

> ### "And he believed in the Lord"
> (15:3–6). Without any supporting evidence from his physical circumstances, Abraham believed that God would fulfill His promise (see Num. 23:19). God was pleased by Abraham's trust in His word and counts this response as righteous (v. 6). In Romans 4:19–21 the apostle Paul cites the faith (or belief) of Abraham as an example for us to follow. Our trust in God that He will save us as He has promised to do (mixing faith with the promise) produces assurance within us (see Rom. 10:9). In fact, our faith in God as faithful to His promises makes "all things" possible (see Mark 9:23). Believe God today for the apparently impossible situations in your life.

God confirms His promise by a formal oath, marked by the blood of slain animals. (See Blood, The.) God binds Himself alone, without condition, to fulfill His promise (9–17). Although the descendants of Abraham will possess the land, not every generation will live there (14–16).

Sarah bids Abraham to conceive a child with her maidservant, Hagar. This course was without God's direction, and led to much conflict within the household (16:1–6; see Women; ch. 55, §3.5.b). Abraham's descendants through the line of Ishmael will also be countless (10).

God again appears and expresses His *covenant purposes. Abraham is to be father of many peoples, which is reflected in the name God gives him ("father of many nations"), and his offspring will possess the land of Canaan (17:1–8; see Faith's Confession). Circumcision is established as "a sign of the covenant" (11; see Blood, The), and is intended to identify the individual with the people of God. God states that the covenant relationship is to be transmitted through a son of Abraham's wife, Sarah (15–21).

God's impending judgment of two cities in which sin dominated is revealed to Abraham. Abraham intercedes (see Prayer) on behalf of the righteous in Sodom and Gomorrah who would be destroyed along with the wicked. Only one who might be considered even slightly righteous is found, so God spares Lot and his family (18:1—19:29). The descendants born to Lot by his daughters, known as Moabites and Ammonites (19:30–38), will be a bane to Abraham's descendants.

Abraham's faith is replaced by fear in the land of Gerar (ch. 20; see ch. 55 of this Handbook, §3.5.b). Again the Lord works mightily on behalf of Abraham and Sarah.

"And God healed Abimelech"
(20:17–18). Abraham hid his relationship with Sarah, his wife (vv. 2, 5), and Abimelech unknowingly sinned by taking Sarah into his household (v. 3). But God dealt graciously with both men. Abraham's wife was restored to him (v. 14), and when Abraham prayed for Abimelech, God healed him, his wife, and his female servants (v. 17). Abimelech's healing predates the Healing Covenant of Exodus 15:25–26, which reveals that it has always been God's nature to heal. Today He remains "the Lord who heals" (see v. 26; Heb. 13:8). Let us look to Him for the healing of our physical, as well as our spiritual, ills.

God is faithful to His promise, and Sarah bears a son, Isaac, who will carry on the covenant line (21:1–5, 12). So that there might be no misunderstanding about the line through which covenant rights obtain, God commands Abraham to cut off Ishmael (12). But God does not abandon Ishmael, and from him a great nation (the Arab peoples) will emerge (13–21).

4. Abraham's test (22:1–24). Abraham's supreme act of faith is his obedience to God's command that he sacrifice his beloved *son Isaac (1–10; see Blood, The). The experience demonstrates to all Abraham's conviction that God is trustworthy and keeps His word. In Isaac's hearing, the covenant promise is reconfirmed (16–18).

"God will provide"
(22:1–14). The Hebrew for "The-Lord-Will-Provide" carries the idea that God will provide where He sees a need. Abraham needed a sacrificial lamb. In faith he said to Isaac, "God will provide for Himself the lamb for a burnt offering" (v. 8). God saw the need and provided a lamb that spared Isaac's life. All humankind needs a savior. That need has been met in Christ, the Lamb of God, who died for our sins (see John 1:29, 34–36; 3:16). The greater truth is that Christ's redemptive work on the Cross also provides for all our needs (see Rom. 8:32). Receive from His unlimited provision today.

---

5. The death of Sarah (23:1–20). After Sarah's death, Abraham bargains with the Hittites for a burial site near Hebron.

B. Isaac (24:1—26:35). Israel's identity and her title deed to her land are dependent upon God's having made a covenant with the forefathers. The guarantee of Israel's genealogical claim to covenant relationship with God is illustrated in God's selection from among Abraham's descendants of the second generation.

1. Isaac's bride from Mesopotamia (24:1–67). Abraham sends a servant back to his home country (Haran) to find a bride for Isaac in an apparent attempt to maintain the purity of bloodline (24:2–4). Abraham and the servant depend upon God's guidance, and Rebekah is shown to be the proper bride for Isaac (7–67; see Women; ch. 55 of this Handbook, §3.6.b).

2. Abraham's death (25:1–11). Abraham is buried in that part of the Promised Land which he legally owned (25:9–10). Isaac remains in Canaan; Abraham's other sons are sent eastward (to Arabia).

3. Ishmael, Esau, and Jacob (25:12–34). The genealogies of Abraham's other sons are given (1–4, 12–18), but God ordains that the covenant promise be transmitted through Isaac's line. According to custom, the older of Isaac's twin sons, Esau, would be heir; according to God's plan (23), however, the younger son, Jacob, will retain the "birthright" and the claim to the covenant promise (29–34).

4. God's affirmation of His covenant with Isaac (26:1–35). Fear leads Isaac to lie, as did Abraham. During famine and conflict over water rights (1–31), God reassures Isaac and reaffirms the covenant (3–4, 24; *see* Kingdom of God; Swore; ch. 55, §3.5.b).

C. Jacob (27:1—35:29). God had already revealed His choice of Jacob as inheritor of the covenant line. Deceit and scheming lead to conflict among the third generation descendants of Abraham.

1. Jacob's deception of his father (27:1–46). The aged and nearly blind Isaac is tricked into giving Jacob his blessing, an acknowledgement of him as heir. Upon learning of the deception, Isaac does not withdraw the blessing but confirms it (33). Esau plots to kill his younger brother (41), and to hide Jacob from Esau's fury, Rebekah sends Jacob to her brother (42–46). (*See* ch. 55, §3.5.b.)

2. Jacob's flight to Haran (28:1–10). Isaac blesses Jacob again, now specifically in terms of the covenant God made with Abraham (3–4). Isaac wants Jacob to marry a woman from Haran, not Canaan (1–2).

3. God's affirmation of His covenant with Jacob (28:11–22). As Jacob journeys to his mother's homeland, God confronts him and confirms the covenant (11–15).

4. Jacob's marriage in Haran (29:1–30:43). For twenty years, Jacob stays in Haran and works for his wily, deceptive uncle Laban, who changes Jacob's wages repeatedly (*see* 29:21–28; 30:31–38). Jacob marries two of Laban's daughters (Leah and Rachel), and eleven of Jacob's twelve sons are born (29:16—30:24; *see* Praise; Son; ch. 55, §3.5.b). Before Jacob returns to Canaan, God provides him an abundance of wealth from among Laban's riches (30:25–43), which leads to conflict.

5. Jacob's return to Canaan (31:1—35:29). Jacob and Laban resolve their differences (31:1–55; *see* ch. 55, §3.5.b). Jacob fears that a greater threat awaits him—Esau: he prays for deliverance and prepares gifts for Esau (32:9–21). After his midnight struggle with God's messenger, Jacob's name is changed to Israel ("he struggles with God"), the name by which the covenant people of God will be known.

Jacob and Esau are reconciled (33:1–16). Jacob buys land near Shechem (19), but he must move on to Bethel after his sons kill the Shechemites, at whose hands their sister is defiled (34:1–31).

At Bethel, Jacob directs his family members to destroy all of their idols (35:1–4). God appears to Jacob, personally changes Jacob's name, and reaffirms the covenant (9–15). Jacob buries Rachel, who died giving birth to Benjamin (16–20). Reuben commits an indiscretion that will cost him his birthright (22).

D. Esau (36:1–43). The descendants of Esau (the Edomites) are listed, which serves as a reminder of the brotherhood of Esau and Jacob and their respective nations. (*See* ch. 55, §3.5.a.)

E. Joseph (37:1–50:26). All twelve of Jacob's sons are in the covenant line (*see* 35:23–26). From this point, the covenant people of God will be referred to frequently as "children of Israel" (or "Israelites"). The rest of Genesis focuses on one of Jacob's sons, Joseph. God told Abraham that his family would reside in Egypt for 400 years before being given the Promised Land (Gen. 15:13), and Joseph is the instrument by which He moves Abraham's family to Egypt.

1. The sale of Joseph into slavery (37:1—40:23). Hated by his brothers because of their father's favoritism, Joseph deepens the antagonism when he tells of dreams that suggest the family will one day "bow down" to him (37:6–10). The brothers plot to kill him but compromise by selling Joseph to travelling merchants, who resell him to a high government official in Egypt (12–36). The immorality of Judah (38:1–30) highlights by contrast Joseph's moral choices in Egypt.

Joseph demonstrates administrative genius as overseer of Potiphar's household, and the Lord enhances his success (39:2, 4). Joseph's good looks attract his master's wife, who attempts incessantly to seduce Joseph. When Joseph refuses her, she accuses him of rape and he is imprisoned (6–20). In prison, Joseph's talents gain him a trusted position (39:21—40:23).

2. Joseph's exaltation (41:1–57). When Pharaoh is troubled by nightmares, his chief cupbearer recalls that Joseph had interpreted dreams in prison. Joseph accurately interprets Pharaoh's prophetic dream (1–37). Pharaoh gives Joseph a high office and wide-ranging authority, as well as a wife, who bears two sons (39–52; *see* Restoration).

The predicted famine ravages Egypt and the entire region, but Egypt has bread because of Joseph's foresight and planning (53–57).

3. Joseph's dealings with his brothers (42:1—45:28). Canaan also is famine stricken, so Jacob sends his sons to Egypt to buy grain (42:1–5). Joseph recognizes his brothers but conceals his identity, putting them through a series of tests in which they must make difficult choices (42:7—44:34). Joseph's elaborate ruse provides the occasion for his brothers' admission of guilt in their sin against Joseph years earlier (42:21–22); their attitude toward Benjamin indicates that they have been chastened by that experience (42:37; 43:8–9; 44:18–34).

Joseph reveals his identity to his brothers, and they are reconciled (45:1–15; *see* Brotherly Love). Joseph interprets all that happened to him as God's plan (5–8) and makes provisions for the entire family to come to Egypt for the duration of the famine (9–28).

4. Jacob's move to Egypt (46:1—48:22). As Jacob departs for Egypt, God reassures him that He will keep His covenant promise (46:2–4). The seventy who enter Egypt will become a great multitude (*see* Ex. 12:37).

Joseph's handling of affairs during the famine years makes Pharaoh owner of nearly all the land, establishes a vast tax revenue, and strengthens the Egyptian government (47:13–26).

Jacob tells Joseph of God's promise (48:3–4) and blesses Joseph's sons, Manasseh and Ephraim.

5. Jacob's blessing and burial (49:1—50:21). Jacob's prophetic final words to his sons are a blessing for some and a curse for others. The best blessings are reserved for Judah (49:8–12; *see* Shiloh) and Joseph (22–26); indeed, their descendants became the most dominant tribes in Israel (Judah in the south; Ephraim and Manasseh in the north). Jesus is from the line of Judah (*see* Matt. 1:3; Luke 3:33).

After Jacob's death, Joseph takes his father's body to Canaan and places it in Abraham's tomb (50:1–13). Back in Egypt, Joseph's brothers ask his forgiveness, and Joseph provides for them (15–21).

> **"But God meant it for good"**
> (50:19–21). Joseph reassures his brothers that, although they plotted evil against him, God transformed their evil for His divine purpose to save a family and nation. Despite years of unjust suffering, Joseph neither harbored unforgiveness nor succumbed to bitterness and resentment; instead he exhibits great love and kindness toward his brothers—weeping upon the request for forgiveness (v. 17), calming their fear (v. 19), and caring for their need (v. 21). These spiritual graces are not self-produced—they arise as we yield to the Spirit's release of forgiving love in our hearts.

6. Joseph's final days (50:22–26). Before his death, Joseph predicts that "God will surely visit" Israel and bring them out of Egypt (24). Joseph is buried in Egypt, but his last request to the children of Israel was that they carry his bones away from there (25–26).

Thus ends the age of the patriarchs. Genesis leaves the children of Israel in Egypt, where they will remain for hundreds of years as strangers and slaves in a foreign land. Joseph, the most powerful child of Israel in Egypt, gives testimony to God's covenant with His people, and his last words sound the note of Israel's deliverance by God's hand.

TRUTH-IN-ACTION through GENESIS

Truth Genesis Teaches	**Action** Genesis Invites
1 Keys to Understanding God God is Creator, and only He has self-existence. We are created beings. God created all living things to reproduce *after their own kinds*.	**1:1—2:25** *Understand* that as a creature, you are ultimately accountable to the Creator. *Understand* you can reproduce only what you are. Therefore, *pursue* Christlikeness. **22:14** *Understand* that God's nature is to provide for His creation. He reveals Himself as "The LORD Who Provides."
2 Guidelines to Avoiding Sin Man fell by choice. The tempter is the father of lies (John 8:44), deceiving and seducing us to sin.	**3:1–5** *Do not challenge* God's Word. *Ask* instead, "What does God's Word mean to me? How can I apply it to my life?" *(continued)*

Truth Genesis Teaches	**Action** Genesis Invites
2 Guidelines to Avoiding Sin *(continued)* The Lie questions God's Word, giving our opinion absolute authority. Our opinions are easy prey to Satan's deception.	**3:6** *Suspect* urgings that come from carnal appetites, visual enticements that invite acquisition, and things that tug at personal ambition (*see* 1 John 2:16).
3 Steps in Hating Sin God hates sin perfectly, and thus it must be judged and punished. Civilizations have been judged for sin and collapsed as a result. Genesis teaches that faithfulness to God means hatred for sin.	**6:1–7** *Avoid* ungodliness (life that is unconscious of God). God destroyed the earth with a flood because of it. **11:1–9** *Turn away* from appeals to personal power and recognition. God confused human speech because of it. **19:1–28** *Flee* from immorality and impurity. Because of them, God destroyed Sodom and Gomorrah.
4 Key Lessons in Faith Abraham is the father of faith and the faithful. Through his life, faith is exemplified. From this "friend of God" (James 2:23), we learn that faith is not perfect character or integrity. Rather, it is simply taking God at His word. By doing so, Abraham became the model of faith for the believer. His life demonstrates how we benefit from believing what God says despite evidence to the contrary.	**12:1–9** *Do not fear* when God's direction takes a turn you do not understand. He knows what He is doing. **15:6** *Believe* God's promises to you. He knows how to bring them to pass although you may not. **16:1–4** *Avoid* striving to fulfill God's promises by yourself. Doing so always backfires and produces undesired results. **22:1–14** *Trust* that God will provide as He promises. His nature is to provide. *Remember:* God's provisions are strategically located along the pathway of faithful obedience.
5 Keys to Generous Living The lives of the patriarchs richly illustrate that encounters with God unavoidably result in men and women who are generous with God and with others. Later codified in the Law, tithing (giving a tenth) began as an act of faithful devotion to God to acknowledge that He alone is our resource.	**14:18–24** *Tithe* as a basic expression of trust in and allegiance to God. Thus did Abraham lift up his hand (that is, show allegiance) "to the LORD, God Most High, the Possessor of heaven and earth." **28:18–22** *Understand* that to the patriarchs, to tithe was an expression of loyalty to and faith in God; also it is an expression of covenant relationship with God.
6 Steps to Realize Fulfilled Vision Joseph was faithful to a vision. His life proves that vision restrains people from sin (Prov. 29:18). Because he believed what God had shown him, he remained steadfastly faithful and loyal in all his relationships, especially with God. Individuals who are faithful to God's vision will enjoy favor with Him and with others and will succeed in their endeavors. In the end they will realize their vision, experiencing vindication in spite of any adversity they may have faced.	**37:5–10** *Hold fast* to the vision God gives you early in life. *Do not divert from it.* God can bring it to pass. **39:4, 21** *Expect* God's favor in the sight of others. He grants favor and success to the faithful. **39:9** *Remain faithful* to God in all you do. *Do not compromise,* especially when your vision is slow in coming. **41:14–57** *Believe* that God is sufficient. He has given you the gifts you need to realize His purpose through you. **45:7; 50:20** *Trust* in God's sovereign providence. He causes all things to work for your good as you remain faithful to His calling and purpose for you.

KEYS TO EXODUS
The People of the Kingdom

Kingdom Key: God's Purpose in View
No theme is repeated more in the Bible than the testimony of the blood of the Lamb as the means of redemption. And no event is cited more often than the deliverance of Israel through the Red Sea. These two facts frame the picture of God's people for all time: from Egypt to the present, He is saving *people through the Lamb, and* calling *people out—making a way for their deliverance from past bondages into His freedom.*

Exodus 19:5–6, in one of the greatest statements in either the Old or New Testament, declares God's *first* mission for His people:

"Now therefore, if you will indeed obey My voice and keep My covenant, then you shall be a special treasure to Me above all people; for all the earth is Mine. And you shall be to Me a kingdom of priests and a holy nation."

The truth revealed here is that in order for God's people to achieve their mission, they first must learn to be a people of worship.

The words "All the earth is Mine" join to those concluding Moses' hymn of triumph after the children of Israel miraculously passed through the Red Sea: "The LORD shall reign forever and ever" (15:18). In summary, the unlimited *spread* and infinite *timelessness* of God's dominion are king-

> God's hand was on His special people.

dom promises that accompany His call to worship. Those tandem truths seem to speak to humankind, saying, "My eternal, boundless, personal almightiness is yours to share in, and My purposes in and through you will be assured their realization—if you fulfill your 'kingdom calling': worship Me *first* and *foremost!*" Note God's combined emphasis: His Word and worship. The giving of the Law at Sinai tends to overshadow the directions for the tabernacle which were given there also. The two sets of instructions reveal *God's Word* and *God's worship* as the foundation stones upon which His people's destiny will be realized. Don't overlook our call to *both.* The giving of the Law took forty days, while establishing the tabernacle of worship took over a year; the relative time involved shows how much

(Please turn to page 14.)

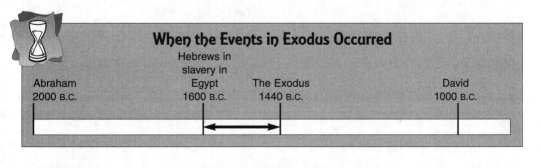

When the Events in Exodus Occurred

Abraham 2000 B.C.	Hebrews in slavery in Egypt 1600 B.C.	The Exodus 1440 B.C.	David 1000 B.C.

Exodus records the miraculous: deliverance of • • •

Master Key: God's Son Revealed

Moses is a type of Christ, for he delivers from bondage. Aaron serves as a type of Jesus as the High Priest (28:1), making intercession at the altar of incense (30:1). The Passover indicates that Jesus is the Lamb of God who was slain for our redemption (12:1–22).

The "I AM" passages in John's Gospel find their primary source in Exodus. John states that Jesus is the Bread of Life; Moses speaks of the bread of God in two ways: the manna (16:35) and the showbread (25:30). John tells us that Jesus is the Light of the World; in the tabernacle the lampstand serves as a never-failing light (25:31–40).

Power Key: God's Spirit at Work

Oil in the Book of Exodus symbolizes the Holy Spirit (27:20). For example, the anointing oil which was used to prepare worshipers and priests for godly service (30:31) is a type of the Holy Spirit.

The fruit of the Holy Spirit is listed in Galatians 5:22–23. A parallel list can be found in Exodus 34:6–7, which lists the attributes of God as mercy, graciousness, longsuffering, goodness, truthfulness, and forgiveness.

The most direct references to the Holy Spirit can be found in 31:3–11 and 35:30—36:1, when individuals are empowered by the Holy Spirit to become great artisans. Through the enabling work of the Holy Spirit, these individuals' natural abilities were enhanced to perform needed tasks with excellence.

Key Word: *Redemption*

Central to the Book of Exodus is the concept of redemption. Israel was redeemed from bondage in Egypt and into a covenant relationship with God.

Key Verses: Exodus 6:6; 19:5–6

Key Chapters: Exodus 12—14

The climax of the entire Old Testament is recorded in chapters 12—14: the salvation of Israel through blood (the Passover) and through power (the Red Sea).

The Plagues of God vs. the Gods of Egypt

Through the ten plagues God demonstrated His superiority over false pagan deities, including some of the favorite gods of Egypt (*see* 7:5; 8:10, 22; 9:14, 29; 10:2; 12:12).

Plague	Possible Deity	Plague	Possible Deity
1. Blood (7:20)	*Khnum,* Giver of the Nile	6. Boils (9:10)	*Sekhmet,* Goddess of sickness
2. Frogs (8:6)	*Heket,* Goddess with frog's head	7. Hail (9:23)	*Aker* or *Geb,* Earth-gods
3. Lice (8:17)	*Hathor* or *Nut,* Sky goddesses	8. Locusts (10:13)	*Serapis,* Protector from locusts
4. Flies (8:24)	*Shu,* Air god	9. Darkness (10:22)	*Ra,* God of sun
5. Livestock diseased (9:6)	*Apis,* God in form of bull	10. Death of firstborn (12:29)	*Selket,* Guardian of life

---

• • • Israel, journey to Sinai, and revelations at Sinai.

Introducing
EXODUS

Author. Moses, whose name means "Drawn Out," is the central figure of Exodus. He is the Hebrew prophet who led the Israelites out of Egypt. Exodus is traditionally attributed to him. Four passages in Exodus lend strong support to Moses' authorship of at least most of it (17:14; 24:4, 7; 34:27). Through various events and face-to-face encounters with God, Moses received the revelation of those things God wanted to be known. Then, through the process of Holy Spirit inspiration, Moses communicated this revealed information to the Hebrew people both orally and in written form.

Date. Conservative tradition dates Moses' death sometime around 1400 B.C., so the Book of Exodus was likely compiled during the forty years preceding, while in the wilderness.

Background. Exodus is the continuation of the Genesis account, dealing with the development of a small family group of seventy people into a large nation of millions. For 430 years the Hebrews lived in Egypt, most of the time in bondage. Exodus records Moses' development, Israel's deliverance from their bondage, their trip from Egypt to Mount Sinai to receive God's law, and His instructions on the building of the tabernacle. It ends with the construction of the tabernacle as a dwelling place for God.

Content. The Book of Exodus can be divided into three major sections: the miraculous deliverance of Israel (1:1—13:16), the miraculous journey to Sinai (13:17—18:27), and the miraculous revelations at Sinai (19:1—40:38).

Section one (1:1—13:16) opens with the Hebrews being oppressed in Egypt (1:10–14). Like any group under restraint, the Hebrews complained. Their complaint was made known not only to their captors, but to their God (2:23–25). God heard their plea and put in motion a plan to deliver them. He accomplished this deliverance through selecting a prophet named Moses (3:1–10).

Deliverance did not occur instantaneously; it was a process. A considerable amount of time and ten plagues were used to gain the release of the Hebrews from Pharaoh's grip. The plagues accomplished two important things: first, they demonstrated the superiority of the Hebrew God over Egyptian gods and, second, they brought freedom to the Hebrews.

The second division recounts the miraculous journey to Sinai (13:17—18:27). Four major events occur in this section. First, the Hebrews witness God's miraculous delivering power (13:17—15:21). Second, they experience firsthand God's ability to provide for His children (15:22—17:7). Third, they receive protection from their enemy, the Amalekites (17:8–16). Fourth, ruling elders are established to keep peace among the people (18:1–27). These four major events teach one major concept: God had His hand on the lives of His special people. Since they witnessed His presence and knew the way God worked in their behalf, they could adjust their lives to His way in order to continue receiving His blessings.

The final section deals with the miraculous revelations at Sinai (19:1—40:38). God's deliverance of the people is for the specific purpose of developing a covenant people. This section has three major components. First is the giving of the Ten Commandments and those instructions that explain in great detail how these commandments are to be expressed in the lives of God's covenant people (19:1—23:19). The results of living outside this covenant structure are demonstrated by the incident involving the golden calf (32:1–35). Second are instructions concerning the building of a tabernacle and its furniture (25:1—31:18). Third is the actual construction of the tabernacle, its furnishings, and the dwelling of God's presence in the completed structure (35:4—40:33).

Personal Application. The first concept to be gleaned from the Book of Exodus is that God blesses those who remain in a covenant relationship with Him. He is their God and they become His holy people.

Second, God explains in great detail what is acceptable to Him.

Third, God delivers those who find themselves in bondage. The deliverance may not come instantaneously, but it will come to those who wait and make preparation for His deliverance. That deliverance is based upon obedience to God's expressed will and upon moving when He says to move. The children of Israel had to wait until after the Passover meal and the angel of death had passed over; after that, God gave the command to go. Thus, we also must wait, but be ready to move when God commands.

Kingdom Key *continued from page 11*

more slowly humankind consents to the *surrender* worship requires, compared with the *study* God's Word deserves.

As Genesis reveals humankind's "kingdom" potential, Exodus unveils the fact that only in living to *worship* God can we find the way to possess the promises and fulfill the purposes He has for each person.

Surveying

EXODUS

I. THE MIRACULOUS DELIVERANCE OF ISRAEL 1:1—13:16.
During much of their 430 years in Egypt, the Israelites were enslaved by the pharaohs. God, however, had chosen Israel to be His people. He therefore performs many mighty acts that prepare the way for His people's departure (exodus) from Egypt and thus their deliverance from bondage.

A. Oppression of the Israelites in Egypt (1:1–22).
The family of Israel settled in a fertile district (Goshen) in the eastern delta of the Nile. Within several generations, the population of Israel grows so great that the new Pharaoh perceives them as a threat and devises ways of decreasing their number (7–14). Eventually, he commands the Egyptians to drown all Hebrew male children in the river (15–22; *see* Feared).

B. The birth and early life of Moses (2:1—4:31).
A son is born to Levite parents (2:1–2). To hide him, the infant's mother conceals him in a floating basket along the banks of the river. He is discovered by Pharaoh's daughter, who adopts the boy and names him Moses (3–10).

As an adult, Moses kills an Egyptian for beating a Hebrew, whom Moses regards as one of his own people. Pharaoh wants Moses killed for the deed (11–15), but he flees to Midian, where he marries and has a son (16–25).

While Moses is in Midian, God appears to him near Mount Horeb (the Heb. name of Mount Sinai), stating that He has heard (*see* Know) the cries of His people and that He will deliver them (3:8). Although Moses lacks confidence (3:11) and makes excuses (4:10), he is chosen as God's instrument to deliver Israel (3:10).

Equipped with God's name, authenticating signs (4:3–9), and an accomplished spokesperson (Aaron, 4:14), Moses journeys back to Egypt (18). When God's message is delivered to the elders of Israel, the children of Israel believe and worship (29–31).

C. The deliverance process (5:1—11:10).
In his first audience with Pharaoh, Moses states clearly God's demand: "Let My people go" (5:1; *see* 6:11; 7:16; 8:1, 20; 9:1, 13; 10:3). Pharaoh sneers his contemptuous refusal (5:2) and increases Israel's workload. The Israelites, beaten and driven by their taskmasters, lose heart and turn against Moses (19–21). Moses turns to God (22–23), who answers with a promise (6:1–8).

God sends Moses and Aaron to Pharaoh, but Pharaoh hardens his heart (7:22; 8:15; 8:19; 8:32; 9:7; 9:35). Multiplied signs and wonders soon will show all of Egypt who God is (7:1–5). The first sign performed by Aaron is duplicated by Pharaoh's magicians (7:8–13).

> **"But Aaron's rod swallowed up their rods"**
> (7:10–12). The replicating of God's signs by the magicians serves to alert us that Satan is powerful in his deceptions. But Satan eventually must bow to the power of the Spirit of God. What may appear as a success on the part of the Enemy is only a short-range victory in the presence of the Almighty.

The ensuing ten plagues not only bring God's judgment against Pharaoh and ruin to the nation itself, but each plague also directly defeats one after another of Egypt's pantheon of gods (*see* 12:12).

The plague on the Nile (7:14–24) pollutes the sacred river with blood.

The plague of frogs (8:1–15) defeats the goddess of fertility.

The plague of lice (8:16–19) brings Pharaoh's magicians to admit the superiority of the Hebrew God.

The plague of flies (8:20–30) brings Pharaoh to offer a compromise, but he goes back on his word when the flies disappear.

The plague on livestock (9:1–7) attacks the mother-goddess of Egypt, who was often portrayed in the form of a cow.

The plague of boils (9:8–12) defeats Pharaoh's magicians. It is after this plague that Scripture for the first time says that *the Lord* hardened Pharaoh's heart (9:12; 10:20;

10:27). Pharaoh had hardened his heart for so long, the Lord now was using Pharaoh's own will to further His purposes.

The plague of hail (9:13–33) defeats the goddess of life and the god who protected the crops.

The plague of locusts (10:1–20) destroys Egypt's remaining source of food.

"That you may know that I am the LORD"

(10:1–2). God's twofold purpose in confronting Pharaoh was to gain Israel's release and to magnify His own name. His signs and mighty works in Egypt bore witness to His overruling power in nature, His dominion over all creatures, and His power over the kingdom of Satan. Today we can expect signs and mighty works to accompany Christ's faithful witnesses in the world so that men may know that He is the Lord and that they might be released from their bondage to sin (see Mark 16:15–18; Acts 5:12, 14; 1 Cor. 12:7–11).

The plague of darkness (Ex. 10:21–29) is a frontal assault on the most sacred religious symbol in Egypt, the sun.

The plague of death (11:1–10) makes known that the God of the Hebrews is greater than the Egyptian giver of life.

D. The Exodus event (12:1—13:16). In obedience to God's command, Israel prepares for departure. But first, God institutes the Passover—a tangible sign of God's presence and protection. Each family is to select and prepare a lamb to be eaten as part of the Passover meal. On this night, the blood of the sacrificial lamb is to be sprinkled on the doorposts of the homes. Inside, the families are to eat the roasted meat hurriedly—dressed for the journey and ready for departure. The messenger of death, seeing the blood on the doorposts, will pass over the Israelites' homes (12:1–13; see Blood, The).

Blood sacrifice is seen as the means of deliverance for the individual, the family, and the nation. A feast of hope and life, the Passover represents deliverance and new beginnings; in many of its elements, it is a type of Christ our Redeemer, the Lamb of God (see Spirit-Filled Life Bible note on 12:1–11 and Kingdom Dynamics for 12:13).

Personally affected by this plague of death, Pharaoh finally urges Israel to leave Egypt. After 430 years, the Israelites are on their way to the land promised to them by God in His covenant (12:29–42; see also Gen. 12:7).

II. THE MIRACULOUS JOURNEY TO SINAI 13:17—18:27. Although God acts to deliver, sustain, and protect them from new enemies, Israel regularly reacts with fear, disbelief, and murmuring.

A. Deliverance at the Red Sea (13:17—15:21). God leads Israel out of Egypt "by way of the wilderness of the Red Sea" (13:18), making His presence known by guiding Israel with pillars of cloud and fire (21–22). But Pharaoh realizes that he is losing his slave labor force and marshals a chariot army to recapture Israel (14:1–9).

God executes a dramatic twofold deliverance for Israel: (1) Israel passes through the parted waters of the sea to safety, and (2) Pharaoh's army is drowned as they presumptuously follow Israel into the sea (10–31).

"I will sing to the LORD, for He has triumphed gloriously!"

(15:1–21). Witnessing the Lord's victory over the Egyptians (14:21–31) the Israelites break forth in exuberant praise, expressing to God (1) great gratitude for the miraculous crossing of the Red Sea (vv. 1–13), and (2) expectant faith concerning the possession of the Land of Promise (15:14–17). Because the Lord has triumphed victoriously on our behalf (see 2 Cor. 2:14; Col. 2:15), we walk the pathway of continuous praise, expressing through song His works and wonders. Personal victories, both large and small, should occasion spontaneous spiritual song—a primary effect of the Spirit's fullness in our lives (Eph. 5:18–19).

B. Provisions provided (15:22—17:7). For forty years Israel will be completely dependent upon God to provide food and water. Here, the Lord makes the bitter water sweet in spite of the grumbling of the people (15:22–26; see Faith, Seed; Healing, Divine).

"For I am the LORD who *heals you"

(15:26). Often referred to as the Old Testament Healing Covenant, this verse also set forth these conditions for physical healing: Israel was to listen to the Lord's voice, live righteous lives, hear His commandments, and keep all His decrees. In

continued on next page

continued from preceding page
the New Testament the sick person is to call for the church elders, letting them pray over him, anointing him with oil (James 5:14–16). When we obey the Scriptures, we are assured of healing.

The Israelites continue to murmur against Moses about food (16:1–36) and water (17:3). God miraculously provides both (16:31; 17:1–7; *see* Rested). The "bread," some type of white seed that tasted like honey wafers, is called "manna."

C. Protection from Amalekites (17:8-16).
The Israelites encounter and defeat a wandering tribe of Amalekites.

"I will stand on the top of the hill with the rod of God in my hand" (17:8–13). The rod of God had summoned the plagues of Egypt, and under it Israel came out from Egyptian bondage. Now in the hand of Moses, the rod is an appeal to God for help and a reminder to the army that the battle is the Lord's (Is. 51:9–10). Remembering our past God-given victories will encourage us (Ps. 77:10–12), and looking to Jesus for renewed faith and victory will win the battle (Heb. 12:2; 1 Cor. 15:57).

D. Establishment of ruling elders (18:1-27).
Moses' wife, sons, and father-in-law (Jethro) now join with him as Israel camps at Mount Sinai. While Jethro is there, he sees the heavy burden that Moses is under as judge in settling disputes, and as teacher imparting what he knows of God's statutes and laws (15–16). Jethro advises Moses to continue to teach Israel God's way, but suggests that he delegate authority for settling small disputes to God-fearing men who will judge various-sized groups (17–23).

III. THE MIRACULOUS REVELATIONS AT SINAI 19:1—40:38.
God now begins to shape this people into a nation capable of taking the Promised Land and holding it. The rest of Exodus provides an overview of the Law through which God will guide His people toward life as a holy community.

A. Arrival at Sinai and God's appearing (19:1-25).
Encamped at the Wilderness of Sinai, the people of Israel are terrified by a cloud-shrouded, quaking mountain—the place where God reveals Himself to Moses (*see* Went Up) and all of Israel. God directs Moses to announce His covenant to the children of Israel: If Israel obeys God's voice and keeps His covenant, they will be treasured by God above all other people (19:5) and will be to Him a "kingdom of priests and a holy nation" (6; *see* Kingdom of God).

B. The Ten Commandments (20:1-21).
God's commands to Israel are brief statements of principles that reveal God's moral character and embody the values He seeks to inculcate in His people. These commandments lay the moral foundation of the holy community.

The first four commands speak of how the people of Israel are to relate to God. God identifies Himself as "the LORD your God," the One who delivered Israel (20:2). He demands exclusive allegiance (3) and forbids worship of idols (4–6). God's name is neither meaningless nor empty; therefore His name is not to be used in a manner that denies the reality of God's presence and power (7). The Sabbath command, modeled upon the Creator's pattern of work and rest, involves desisting from the everyday activities of life and honoring God (8–11).

The last six commands speak of how the children of Israel are to relate to one another. Respect for parents preserves the integrity of the family, an institution that is basic to a healthy and holy community (12). Taking the life of others is prohibited (13). Respect for the life of others is protected. Adultery violates the holiness of marriage and destroys the relationship between husband and wife (14). Respect for other persons extends to their property (15). The reputations of others are to be guarded as carefully as their property (16). Even the possessions of others are not to be desired (17).

C. The Book of the Covenant (20:22—23:19).
The "Book of the Covenant" is a collection of incidents which illustrate and serve as precedents for applying the basic laws (Ten Commandments) just given. This code pictures life in the Promised Land and shows that the whole life of the community—political, social, economic, and religious—is governed by God. In sharp contrast to other such law codes of that era, this one places greater emphasis on the value of persons rather than on the value of property.

The rights of servants are discussed first (21:1–11). The sanctity of human life is evident in the laws concerning violence and accidental injury (12–36). These are followed by civil laws on the misuse of property (22:1–15), regulations upholding moral and ceremonial principles (16–31), provisions to protect the poor and aliens (23:1–9), and religious regulations for the Sabbath and for annual feasts (10–19;

see Keep a Feast; ch. 55 of this Handbook, §3.1).

D. God's angel of protection (23:20–33). God promises to send His special messenger to prepare the Land of Promise for His people and to protect them from the inhabitants of the land. God specifically demands that all inhabitants of the land be driven out (23:31–33).

E. Israel accepts the Covenant (24:1–18). Moses records God's words and reads them to the people of Israel (24:4, 7). Israel promises to do "all that the LORD has said" (3, 7).

F. Directions concerning the tabernacle (25:1—31:18). God tells Moses to collect an offering from the children of Israel for the construction of a sanctuary (25:1–8) so that God "may dwell among them" (v. 8; *see* Cherubim).

Aaron and his sons are to be set apart for special service as priests (28:1; *see* Leadership, Spiritual). The priesthood is charged with the tasks of serving at the tabernacle and leading the worship of God (*see* Continually). As high priest, Aaron is the chief representative of Israel to God and of God to Israel.

Detailed instructions are given for the assembling of both the tabernacle and the priestly garments, and Moses is charged to make everything exactly as it was shown to him. Later, the writer of Hebrews tells us that this tabernacle was a "copy and shadow of the heavenly things" which would ultimately be fulfilled in Jesus (Hebrews 8:5).

G. The golden calf (32:1–35). Ironically, even as Moses receives God's revelation—as recorded on tablets of stone by God Himself (31:18)—the people of Israel grow impatient and break the first commandment. Having brought precious items to Aaron, the children of Israel persuade him to fashion a calf, which is proclaimed to be the god "that brought [Israel] out of the *land of Egypt" (32:1–4). Moses turns God's anger (7–14; *see* Prayer), but in his own anger Moses breaks the tablets containing God's revelation upon seeing Israel break the Law those tablets contain (15–19). The Levites rally at Moses' call and kill the idolaters (26–28). The next day, a plague kills all the rest who sinned (29–35). God's Law provides a standard, and with it a basis for judgment: No longer will Israel sin with impunity.

H. Repentance and renewal of covenant (33:1—35:3). Despite their sin, God intends for the Israelites to continue on their journey to the Land of Promise, but now without His presence in their midst (33:3). Moses pitches his tent far from the people, and there God makes His presence known (7–11).

God does not grant Moses' request to see His "glory" (lit., "weight"—the inner reality of who God is), but He does provide a more complete definition of His name (33:12—34:7; *see* Give Rest). God rewrites the tablets containing His revelation to Israel and renews His covenant with them (34:10–28; *see* Made).

I. Building the tabernacle (35:4—40:33). At God's command, offerings for building the tabernacle are brought by the people of Israel (35:4–29), who give in abundance (36:2–7). Skilled craftsmen take pains to follow God's design. The worship system of Israel will be focused around the tabernacle until it is superseded by the temple built by Solomon.

The term "tabernacle of meeting" (35:21) captures the significance of this portable worship structure in the experience of Israel. God's people needed an avenue by which they might approach Him for forgiveness. The tabernacle, with its sacrifices and priesthood, became that place of meeting—where a sinful people might come to meet their holy God. A visible presence in the camp of Israel, the tabernacle is a constant reminder of God's presence among His people. (*See* Ephod; Memorial; Tribe.)

"He has filled him with the Spirit of God, in wisdom and understanding" (35:30–35). The verse cited for this section contains a phrase later used by Isaiah (Is. 11:2) in his description of Messiah. Remarkably, the supernatural gifts of God are to function naturally, as in Bezaleel and the others and in Messiah. These verses show the connection between supernatural gifts and a God-ordained opportunity for their use. Whatever the serving opportunity may be, it is important to expect the Holy Spirit to dispense His gifts as He wills (1 Cor. 12:10).

The furnishings of the tabernacle are all pictures of Jesus and the blessings He poured out on the lives of believers through His death and resurrection.

—The Ark of the Covenant (Ex. 37:1–9; *see* 25:10–22) was the place of the mercy seat, where once a year the priest would offer the blood of the sacrifice to atone for the sins of Israel. It also contained God's commandments to Israel. The ark of the covenant is a picture of Jesus' sacrifice for us that covered over the Law, offered us God's mercy in its place, and atoned for our sins.

—The Table (37:10–16; *see* 25:23–30) was

made for the daily display of fresh loaves of bread. It foreshadows Jesus' words in John 6:35, "I am the bread of life"—the One who satisfies our hunger for relationship with and restoration to God.

—The Gold Lampstand (37:17–24; *see* 25:31–40), a seven-branched oil lamp, provided light in the tabernacle. "I am the light of the world," declared Jesus in John 9:5. The lampstand is a picture of the light Jesus blazed into the darkness of sin, drawing all people to Himself.

—The Altar of Incense (37:25–28; *see* 30:1–10), which symbolized daily prayer to God, was a type of Christ as our Intercessor (Heb. 7:25).

—Animal sacrifices were made at the bronze Altar of Burnt Offering (38:1–7; *see* 27:1–8), and pictured Christ's sacrificial death for us.

—The Bronze Laver (38:8; *see* 30:17–21) was a basin in which the priests purified themselves for service, picturing the cleansing from impurity that is ours through Christ.

Moses inspects the tabernacle and blesses the people of Israel for obeying God's instructions (39:42–43). Just one year after Israel's departure from Egypt, the tabernacle is erected on the first day of the first month. Israel is poised to celebrate the second Passover feast in freedom, under God's Law, with a place for sacrifice and worship. However, the tabernacle is useless without God's presence.

J. The glory of the Lord filling the tabernacle (40:34–38). The Book of Exodus, which began with the people of Israel in slavery, ends with God's glory filling the tabernacle. God is now personally present in the midst of His people, and God will be present with "the house of Israel, throughout all their journeys" (40:38).

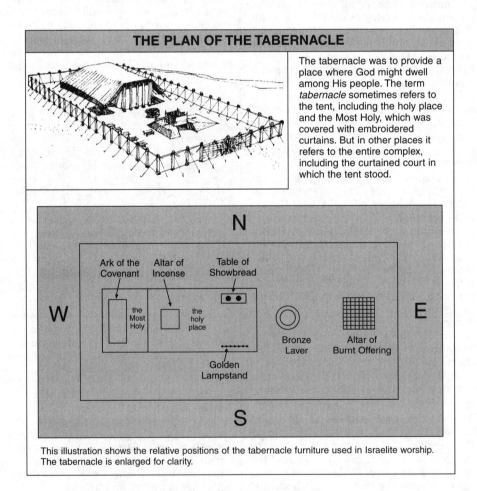

THE PLAN OF THE TABERNACLE

The tabernacle was to provide a place where God might dwell among His people. The term *tabernacle* sometimes refers to the tent, including the holy place and the Most Holy, which was covered with embroidered curtains. But in other places it refers to the entire complex, including the curtained court in which the tent stood.

N

Ark of the Covenant

Altar of Incense

Table of Showbread

W

the Most Holy

the holy place

Bronze Laver

Altar of Burnt Offering

E

Golden Lampstand

S

This illustration shows the relative positions of the tabernacle furniture used in Israelite worship. The tabernacle is enlarged for clarity.

TRUTH-IN-ACTION through EXODUS

Truth Exodus Teaches	**Action** Exodus Invites
1 Four Keys to Understanding God Successful Christian living begins with knowing who God is. In Exodus, God reveals part of His nature and character. Knowing God in truth will affect our behavior. Exodus gives four keys to make our lives more faithful and fruitful.	**3:14, 15** *Understand* that God <u>is</u>! His Name is "I AM WHO I AM." *Rest* on this foundation. *Be grounded* and established in Him. **15:25, 26** *Receive* God as "The Lord Who Heals You." To heal is His nature; His will is to make us whole. **17:15** *Rely upon* God who is "The Lord Your Banner." As you surrender to Him—your Victory, Miracle, and Protection—your battle against the flesh will succeed. **31:13** *Pursue* God who is "The Lord Who Makes You Holy." His life in us makes our holiness possible.
2 Steps to Holiness God calls us to be holy, "set apart to Him and His purposes." God intends His people to be distinguished in nature and in character from the world—different in the way we think, act, and live. This difference will be visible and bring God glory.	**7:1—11:10** *Know* that God deals differently with us than with the world (see 8:23; 9:26; 10:23; 11:7). **12:7** *Rely* on the blood of Jesus to protect you from all evil (see 1 Pet. 1:18, 19). **19:5** *Obey* God's Word and you will become His "special treasure." **21:5** *Be Jesus' bondslave.* He will open your ears to hear His voice clearly and understand His Word. **32:26–29** *Be zealous* for God's holiness. He honors those who honor Him.
3 Guidelines to Godly Living Godly living is living with God in your life and His Life in you. He gives guidelines to help us build our lives on His precepts. God calls us to acts of faith that build godliness. Without faith, our acts become vain religion. Godliness embraces godly practice and shuns vain religious acts.	**3:3** *Stay alert* to seek out God's working. It often comes in a way we do not expect. **12:15, 19, 20; 13:3, 6, 7** *Participate* regularly in the Lord's Supper. We thus share in His deliverance and life. **14:13, 14** *Be still* as God works. You will see His deliverance. **16:4** *Be careful* to apply God's Word. He wants us to follow His instructions. **23:16; 34:22** *Celebrate* God's blessings to you. **25:8; 33:15** *Dwell in* and *esteem* God's Presence. It distinguishes us from everyone else. **31:12–17; 33:14** *Rest* in God's Sabbath. His rest gives us rest from our own works (see Heb. 4:10, 11).
4 Keys to Wise Living God calls His people to wisdom. Wisdom is knowing how to apply truth. Exodus gives principles that teach us how to live wisely and please God. It also teaches us certain wise practices. The Holy Spirit will train us to practice wisdom as a discipline that will lead to the fullness of life.	**19:8; 24:3, 7** *Do not trust* yourself to obey God's Word. Depend upon His Holy Spirit. **20:1–17** *Meditate* on the Ten Commandments regularly to learn God's moral nature and character. **20:20** *Learn* reverence for the Lord; it will keep you from sinning. **23:2, 3** *Suspect* majority opinion that proposes deviance. Evil is often popular but disobeys God. **23:15** *Give* every time you gather with God's people for worship. It shows faith that He provides for you. **32:1** *Do not become impatient* with God. It leads to sin. **35:30–35** *Recognize* that any skill or ability you have is God's gift. *Be grateful* for His gifts, avoiding pride.
5 Keys to Understanding Authority God rules His people through delegated authority. All authority is from God (see Rom. 13). To distrust those He places over us is to distrust Him. God calls His people to a submissive attitude toward His leaders. He cautions us to be careful how we speak about them.	**16:8; 22:28** *Do not grumble* against spiritual leadership. You thus grumble against the Lord and rebel. **22:18** *Avoid* and *shun* the occult. To seek out spiritual direction from evil leads to death. **35:20–29** *Listen* to those God sends to speak to and lead us. *Do not rebel* against their leadership. To disregard godly leaders is to disregard Him.

KEYS TO LEVITICUS
The Priesthood of the Kingdom

Kingdom Key: God's Purpose in View
The Book of Leviticus continues God's revelation to His redeemed of how to function as "kingdom people." In Exodus 19:6 the Lord had established two things: (1) His people are to be a people of worship ("a kingdom of priests"), and (2) He has called them to holiness ("you shall be . . . a holy nation").

Contrary to traditionalized ideas about holiness, the tone of Leviticus communicates that "kingdom living"—even its worship forms—is an intensely practical way of life. Worship is blended with daily life in Leviticus, teaching us that worship was never meant to be seen as mystical, impractical, or occasional. Not only is *daily* worship taught here, but note that all "holiness" commands are essentially guidelines for healthy, life-nurturing practices.

While the *legal* aspect of this book is no longer binding, the *regal* guidelines for godliness which it presents are still applicable. First Peter 2:5 and 9 reassert the abiding call—God's people are to be a priestly people of *worship* who live a life of *practical* holiness: "You also, as living stones, are being built up a spiritual house, a holy priesthood, to offer up spiritual sacrifices acceptable to God through Jesus Christ. . . .

....

**Holiness
—being
set apart
for
fellowship
with God.**

....

You are a chosen generation, a royal [kingly] priesthood, a holy nation, His own special people, that you may proclaim the praises of Him who called you out of darkness into His marvelous light."

The word "holy" occurs nearly one hundred times in Leviticus, far more than in any other book of the Bible. As a "kingdom of priests," destined to extend God's dominion of love to the nations of the world, God's people must learn the three elements of holiness: priority, purity, and practicality. The *priority* of being holy means we are to be solely the Lord's, that is, "sanctified" unto Him—His *alone*. The *purity* of being holy relates to our obedience in observing those ways which keep us clean, and avoiding those which pollute our character. The *practicality* of being holy is that it produces happy, whole relationships, and all of life is enriched and ennobled by this

Months and Feasts of the Jewish Sacred Year

Nisan[1, 2, 3]	Iyar	Sivan[4]	Tammuz	Ab	Elul
First Month	Second Month	Third Month	Fourth Month	Fifth Month	Sixth Month
(Mar.–Apr.)	(Apr.–May)	(May–June)	(June–July)	(July–Aug.)	(Aug.–Sept.)

[1] Passover—evening of the fourteenth day of Nisan (Ex. 12:1–28, 43–49; Lev. 23:5; Num. 28:16; Deut. 16:1–8)
[2] Feast of Unleavened Bread*—began on fifteenth day of Nisan, continued one week (Ex. 12:15–20; 13:3–10; Lev. 23:6–8; Num. 28:17–25; Deut. 16:3–8)
[3] Day of Firstfruits—the day after the Sabbath of Passover week (Lev. 23:9–14)
[4] Feast of Pentecost (or Weeks)*—fiftieth day after the Day of Firstfruits (Lev. 23:15–22; Num. 28:26–31; Deut. 16:9–12)

God's people are to be a priestly people of

higher standard. Leviticus is full of concepts which can benefit today's New Testament "priesthood" (i.e., every believer). "Kingdom living" is enhanced when holiness is seen for the beauty and health it affords, rather than as a rigid, pietistic separatism.

Master Key: God's Son Revealed

Christ is not specifically mentioned in Leviticus. However, the sacrificial system and the high priest in the Book of Leviticus are types that picture the work of Christ. The Book of Hebrews describes Christ as the High Priest and uses the text of Leviticus as a basis for illustrating His work. Some have resorted to extreme symbolism in order to reveal Christ in Leviticus; however, this method of Bible interpretation should be used cautiously in order to preserve the book's original historical and cultural meaning. The Book of Leviticus focuses on the life and the worship of ancient Israel.

Power Key: God's Spirit at Work

Though the term "Holy Spirit" is never mentioned in the Book of Leviticus, God's presence is felt throughout. The holiness of God's character is constantly referred to as a standard in designating the people's actions and worship as holy. He is not seen as were the unresponsive pagan idols, but He is in the midst of His people as they worship Him. They must be holy even as He is holy.

Key Word: *Holiness*

Leviticus centers around the concept of the holiness of God, and how an unholy people can acceptably approach Him and then remain in continued fellowship.

Key Verses: Leviticus 17:11; 20:7–8

Key Chapter: Leviticus 16

The Day of Atonement ("Yom Kippur") was the most important single day in the Hebrew calendar as it was the only day the high priests entered into the Most Holy Place to "make atonement for you, to cleanse you, that you may be clean from all your sins before the LORD" (16:30).

Tishri[5, 6, 7]	Heshvan	Chislev[8]	Tebeth	Shebat	Adar[9]
Seventh Month	Eighth Month	Ninth Month	Tenth Month	Eleventh Month	Twelfth Month
(Sept.–Oct.)	(Oct.–Nov.)	(Nov.–Dec.)	(Dec.–Jan.)	(Jan.–Feb.)	(Feb.–Mar.)

[5] Day of Trumpets (*Rosh Hashanah*)—first day of Tishri (Lev. 23:23–25; Num. 10:10; 29:1–6)

[6] Day of Atonement (*Yom Kippur*)—tenth day of Tishri (Lev. 16; 23:26–32; Num. 29:7–11)

[7] Feast of Tabernacles (or Booths or Ingathering)*—fifteenth through twenty-first day of Tishri (Lev. 23:33–43; Num. 29:12–38; Deut. 16:13–17)

[8] Dedication (or Lights or *Hanukkah*)—began on twenty-fifth day of Chislev, continued eight days (mentioned in John 10:22; begun after 165 B.C.)

[9] Purim (Lots) — the fourteenth and fifteenth day of Adar (Esth. 9:18–32; begun after the return from the Exile in Babylon)

* In Deuteronomy 16:16, God commanded all of Israel's males to attend the Feast of Unleavened Bread, the Feast of Weeks, and the Feast of Tabernacles every year "in the place which the LORD chooses."

worship who live a life of *practical* holiness.

Introducing
LEVITICUS

Author. The Book of Leviticus is the third book ascribed to Moses from the Hebrew Scriptures of the Old Testament. In 1:1, the text refers to the word of the Lord, which was spoken to Moses from the tabernacle of meeting; this forms the basis for this entire book of Scripture. The priests and Levites have preserved its contents.

Date. Scholars have dated the Book of Leviticus from the time of Moses' activities (earlier dating in the fifteenth century B.C. and the later alternative dating in the twelfth century B.C.) to the time of Ezra during the return (sixth century B.C.). Acceptance of Mosaic authorship for Leviticus would date its writing to about 1440 B.C. The book describes the sacrificial system and worship that precedes the time of Ezra and recalls the institution of the sacrificial system. The book contains little historical information that would give an exact date.

Background. The theology of the Book of Leviticus links the idea of holiness to everyday life. It goes beyond the issue of sacrifice though the sacrificial worship and the work of the priests are explained with great care. The concept of holiness affects not only the relationship that each individual has with God, but also the relationship of love and respect that each person must have for his neighbor. The code of holiness permeates the work because each individual must be pure even as God Himself is pure and because the purity of each individual is the foundation of the holiness of the entire covenant community. The teaching of Jesus Christ, "Therefore, whatever you want men to do to you, do also to them, for this is the Law and the Prophets" (Matt. 7:12), reflects the text of Leviticus 19:18, "Love your neighbor as yourself."

Content. In Hebrew the Book of Leviticus was named *Vayikra*, which means "And He Called." The Hebrew title is taken from the first word of the book, which was a customary way of naming ancient works. The English title "Leviticus" is derived from the Greek version of the work and means "Matters Pertaining to the Levites." The title is somewhat misleading because the book deals with many more issues relating to purity, holiness, the whole priesthood, the sanctity of God, and holiness in everyday life. The word "holy" appears more than eighty times in the book.

Sometimes the Book of Leviticus has been viewed as a difficult work to grasp; however, according to early tradition, in Jewish education it was the first book to be taught to children. It deals with God's character and will, especially in matters of holiness, which the Jewish sages considered to be of primary importance. They felt that before proceeding to other biblical texts, children should first be educated concerning the sanctity of God and the responsibility of each individual to live a holy life. Holiness (Hebrew *kedushah*) is a key word in Leviticus, describing the sanctity of the divine presence. Holiness is being set apart from the profane, and holy is the opposite of the common or secular.

Another major theme of the Book of Leviticus is the sacrificial system. The Burnt Sacrifice (Hebrew *olah*) refers to the only sacrifice that is entirely consumed upon the altar, and therefore it is sometimes called the whole offering. The Grain Offering (Hebrew *minchah*) is a tribute offering made in order to secure or maintain the divine favor, indicating that the fruits of a person's labor should be dedicated to God. The Peace Offering (Hebrew *shelamim*) is designed to provide expiation and permits the one who makes the offering to eat the meat of the sacrifice. It was often given on a joyous occasion. The Sin Offering (Hebrew *chatta't*) is employed to remove impurity from the sanctuary. The Trespass Offering (Hebrew *asham*), also referred to as the Guilt Offering or the Offering of Reparation, is prepared for violation of the sanctity of the property of God or of another person, usually by use of a false oath. The trespass had desecrated the sanctity of God and an offering is required.

In addition to the sacrifices, the liturgical calendar holds a significant place in the Book of Leviticus. The Sabbatical year refers to the emancipation of Israelite slaves, and people in debt, as well as the redemption of the land (*see* also Ex. 21:2–6; 23:10–11; Deut. 15:1–11, 12–18). The Jubilee Year refers to the fact that the land of Israel, as well as the people, belongs to God and not to any individual. The land, therefore, must have rest after each period of forty-nine years (Lev. 25:8–17), which teaches God's ownership. The entire Book of Leviticus is permeated with the sanctity of God, the holiness of His character, and the necessity of the congregation to approach Him in purity of heart and mind.

Personal Application. The Book of Leviticus has a powerful contemporary and personal application for the life of the church today. The sanctity of God and His great desire for fellowship with His people are clearly seen in the descriptions of the sacrificial system. Holiness, being set apart for a saintly life in fellowship with God, is the primary issue for the people of ancient Israel as it is for the people of God today.

Surveying
LEVITICUS

I. THE DESCRIPTION OF THE SACRIFICIAL SYSTEM 1:1—7:38.

The Book of Leviticus records God's instructions to Moses concerning how the children of Israel shall worship their God. After God delivered the Israelites from bondage in Egypt, He called the entire nation into a covenant relationship (Ex. 19:5–6). Thus, the regulations and stipulations in Leviticus do not pertain solely to the activities of Israel's priests (Levites). The Book of Leviticus—with its descriptions of offerings, sacrifices, holy days and feasts—defines holiness, and it delineates the boundaries between the sacred and the profane, between purity and impurity. In so doing, it links the concept of holiness to the everyday lives of the children of Israel (19:2).

In the Book of Leviticus, which covers the period from the erection of the tabernacle (Ex. 40:17) to the departure from Sinai (Num. 10:11–12), the children of Israel learn that their deliverance requires that they be a separate people dedicated to the God who delivered them from Egypt.

The first section provides God's detailed instructions concerning offerings to be made at the tabernacle. Some of the offerings are voluntary, others are compulsory, but all are gifts brought to God in worship. Approaching God and being accepted by Him comes through worship, and worship has a cost—offering and sacrifice.

A. The burnt offering (1:1–17). The offerer, according to his wealth, is to bring either a bull (3–9), a male sheep or goat (10–13), or turtledoves or young pigeons (14–17). This voluntary offering is to be burned in its entirety (except the skin) on the altar; hence it is also called the whole burnt offering. The purpose of the burnt offering is to atone for sin in general (4) and to signify complete dedication and consecration to God. The stipulation that the animal be "without blemish" (3) means that what is offered to God in sacrifice should be the best the offerer has.

B. The grain offering (2:1–16). This voluntary offering accompanies all the burnt offerings, and it signifies the offerer's homage and thanksgiving to God. The main ingredients of this offering, which may be cooked in several ways (4–7, 14), are fine flour and oil (2). A memorial portion is to be burnt on the altar (2, 9, 16); the remainder is given to the priests (3, 10).

C. The peace offering (3:1–17). This is a voluntary offering by which the offerer expresses gratitude to God for some blessing or deliverance. Depending upon the person's wealth, unblemished animals from the herd (1–5) or flock (6–16) are presented to the priest for a burnt sacrifice. The fatty parts are burned and the blood is sprinkled on the altar. God's command that His people "shall eat neither fat nor blood" (17) is a dietary regulation that sets Israel apart from other peoples.

D. The sin offering (4:1—5:13). The purpose of the sin offering, a compulsory one, is to atone for sins committed unknowingly. Any violation of God's commandments (see Guilty) disrupts the covenant relationship with Him. Stipulations for the sin offering—the animal to be brought and the manner in which it is to be sacrificed—are given for anointed priests (4:3–12; see Priest), the congregation of Israel as a whole (13–21), a ruler (22–26), or a common individual (27–35).

E. The trespass offering (5:14—6:7). In instances where someone has trespassed against God's sacred property (5:14–19) or against a neighbor's property (6:1–7), animals must be offered for sacrifice and restitution made.

F. Other instructions (6:8—7:38). Specific instructions concerning the offerings and sacrifices are now given to the priests, who are responsible for the sacrificial system. The instruction about each offering is introduced with the phrase "This is the law [Heb. torah] of. . . ."

These sections identify the priests' share of the offerings. Since the priests were dependent on these offerings for their livelihood, the priests could monitor the spiritual condition of the children of Israel; if the offerings slacken, the priests will know and can summon Israel to commitment. God reiterates that no one, priest or otherwise, shall eat either the fat portion or the blood of the sacrificed animal, or that person will be "cut off from his people" (7:22–27).

II. THE SERVICE OF THE PRIESTS IN THE SANCTUARY 8:1—10:20.

The priests are divinely appointed leaders who are set apart to perform designated tasks in the worship of God in the tabernacle.

A. Ordination of Aaron and his sons (8:1–36). Israel's priests are to be taken only from the family of Aaron, who is of the tribe of Levi. Moses purifies the priests with water, clothes them in the priestly garments (see Exodus 28—30), and anoints them with oil (Lev. 8:6–13). Although the priests are set apart from others in this way, they share in the need for forgiveness, and thus a sin offering is necessary (14–36).

B. The priests take office (9:1–24). The leaders of the people bring offerings (*see* Sin Offering), and Aaron and his sons make sacrifices at the tabernacle altar in the manner prescribed by Moses (1–16). God Himself lights the altar fire (24) to indicate His acceptance of their sacrifices.

C. The sin of Nadab and Abihu (10:1–11). God desires obedience more than sacrifice (1 Sam. 15:22); and in the giving of the ordinances and principles of worship, He expected Israel to obey. When two of Aaron's sons offer incense in a fire which has not been kindled from the altar, they themselves are consumed in flame (Lev. 10:1–2). Aaron accepts God's explanation and His charge: Priests are to "distinguish between holy and unholy, and between *unclean and clean" (10), and they are to teach others God's commandments (11).

D. The sin of Eleazar and Ithamar (10:12–20). When two sons of Aaron inadvertently burn all of an offering, part of which was to have been saved for food, their unintentional error is forgiven. God does not demand absolute perfection, but He will not tolerate rebellion.

III. THE LAW OF IMPURITIES 11:1–16:34. Ritual cleanness and uncleanness, which emphasizes approach to God as a unique and special experience, set Israel apart from all other peoples. Some unavoidable and natural occurrences (e.g., childbirth, burying the dead) can make a person ritually unclean. Therefore, uncleanness is not to be equated with "evil" in a moral sense. The root of ritual cleanness and uncleanness is religious, not "moral" or "hygienic"; but the lesson to be learned is that humankind at their best can still never be "clean" enough to stand before God on their own.

A. Animal impurities (11:1–47). Diet regulations serve as a daily reminder that the Israelites are set apart from other peoples. Israel is to live out her consecration to God in everyday life, as well as in special times of worship.

B. Childbirth impurities (12:1–8). Women who give birth are ceremonially unclean. This does not mean that there is anything sinful about the sexual act or childbirth. An important aspect of ritual cleanness and uncleanness is introduced: purification. God always provides a way for those excluded to be returned to Him. An unclean individual must be purified before being restored to fellowship. In this case, the procedures for purification include periods of seclusion (2, 4–5) and both

burnt and sin offerings (6–8; *see* Luke 2:22–24).

C. Skin impurities (13:1—14:57). The word "leprosy" refers to a variety of skin disorders, e.g., infections (2), ulcers (7–8), boils (19), scabs (30), and general eczema (38–40). A person with any of these symptoms is to appear before the priest to be judged as clean or unclean. If deemed unclean, the person is sent out of the camp until healed.

Objects also can be ritually unclean. Molds and fungus on clothing are discussed here (13:47–59).

When the symptoms of the disorder disappear, a priest is to be called. If his examinations determine a healthy state, purification ceremonies are prescribed (14:1–32; *see* Cleansed).

D. Discharge impurities (15:1–33). Ritual uncleanness may result from the discharges or secretions of male and female sexual organs. These include abnormal (1–15; 25–33) and normal (16–18; 19–24) emissions. Bathing is sufficient to remove uncleanness if the emission is normal (18, 21), but offering and sacrifice are necessary if the emission is abnormal (14–15, 29–30).

A person may become ritually unclean directly (in the case of his or her own bodily discharge), but uncleanness can also be transmitted or contracted by touch. Purification rites for direct uncleanness typically last seven days and involve sacrifice (13–15, 24, 28–30). Uncleanness contracted by touch lasts only until evening, and only requires purification by water (5–11, 16–23, 27).

E. Moral impurities (16:1–34). Atonement is a central theme in Leviticus. The Hebrew word for atonement, *kippur,* comes from a verb which has as its primary meaning "to cover," but also carries with it the sense of "to make reconciliation, to pacify or appease, to clear or purge or cleanse." On the Day of Atonement (*Yom Kippur*), which is the tenth day of the seventh month (29), a special sacrifice is made: a sin offering on behalf of all the people of Israel (17, 21, 30, 34; *see* Assembly) for their uncleanness, transgressions, and sins (16). The objective of this sacrificial ceremony is clear: cleansing (30).

A striking feature of the ceremony on *Yom Kippur* is the scapegoat. The sins of Israel are symbolically laid on the goat, which is taken outside the camp and released in the wilderness (10, 20–22).

IV. THE HOLINESS CODE 17:1—26:46. In this section, there is a shift away from an emphasis on sacrifice and atonement to an emphasis on sanctification and holiness. The

Hebrew word for holiness, *qadosh*, means "set apart, dedicated to sacred purposes; holy, sacred, pure, clean, morally or ceremonially pure." The holiness code instructs the Israelites on the manner of life that is proper for a people called to be in special relationship to God, a people God intends to be set apart as holy.

A. Killing for food (17:1–16). These regulations concern hunting and sacrifice, but the most significant restriction is dietary. Prior to consumption, the *blood of a slaughtered animal must be drained (6, 10–11). The people of Israel, unlike those in other cultures, are not to "eat blood" (10, 12, 14). God's explanation for this strict command also provides insight into the relationship between blood and atonement: "For the life of the flesh is in the blood, and I have given it to you upon the altar to make atonement for your souls; for it is the blood that makes atonement for the soul" (11; *see* also v. 14; Blood, The).

B. On being holy (18:1—20:27). Each moral issue discussed in this section rests on the intimate relationship between God and the people He calls to holiness: Israel shall be *holy, for God is holy (19:2).

Proper sexual conduct means that a person shall not have sexual intercourse (expressed in the phrase "to uncover nakedness") with their next of kin (18:6–18), with a woman when "she is in her customary impurity" (19), or with a neighbor's spouse (20). In addition to incest and adultery, homosexuality (22) and bestiality (23) are prohibited. By all these immoral practices other nations are defiled (24–25), and the children of Israel are "not [to] commit any of these abominable customs" (30).

Other statutes are pronounced by God for the purpose of setting His people apart from all others (19:1–37). The children of Israel are to distinguish themselves in their dealings with their family and neighbors, with the poor and foreigners, as well as in their manner of worship and in their business practices. Many of these statutes are summed up in God's command that the Israelites are to love their neighbors (18) and the stranger who lives among them (34; *see* Brotherly Love) as themselves.

The penalties for disobedience are severe (20:1–27). The worship of Molech, a Phoenician deity, often involved child sacrifice, sexual deviations, and the consultation of mediums, and it is forbidden absolutely (2–6).

The purpose of the holiness code is stated clearly: God wants His people to be separate from the people who dwell in the Land of Promise (22–26). The people of Israel are to be "set apart" (holy), for their God is holy.

C. Laws for priests and sacrifices (21:1—22:33). While all Israel is set apart to the Lord, a higher standard of holiness is established for the priests because they present offerings on behalf of the rest of Israel. The priesthood is limited to Aaron and those of his sons who meet God's requirements.

D. Holy days and religious feasts (23:1–44). The feasts and holy days instituted by God are intended to provide times of rest and opportunities for Israel to contemplate her redemption history. As such, the holy days are a vital part of the education of each new generation, as well as a constant reminder to everyone of Israel's role as a holy nation, set apart by God.

The foundation of all annual feasts is the Sabbath, which God declared as a day "of solemn rest" (3). The Sabbath establishes the principle that certain times are sacred, devoted to the Lord (3–4).

The Feast of Passover (5) is held on the fourteenth day of the first month (Nisan, or Abib [March/April]). The next day, the Feast of Unleavened Bread (6–8), begins a one-week period during which bread without yeast is to be eaten, which serves as a reminder of Israel's hurried departure from Egypt (*see* Exodus 12).

The Feast of Firstfruits (Lev. 23:9–14; *see* Blemish), celebrated on the day after the Sabbath of Passover (March/April), is intended as a dedication and consecration of the firstfruits of the barley harvest.

The Feast of Weeks (15–22), held the day after the seventh Sabbath following the Feast of Firstfruits (May/June), is the occasion for dedicating and consecrating the firstfruits of the wheat harvest.

The Feast of Trumpets (23–25) is known as *Rosh Hashanah* and occurs on the first day of the seventh month (Tishri [September/October]), an especially significant month in Israel's liturgical year. The sound of trumpets heralds this day of rest and offering.

The Day of Atonement (26–32) comes on the evening of the ninth day of Tishri. *Yom Kippur* is a most holy day of rest, ordained by God as the time at which the children of Israel are to make atonement before the Lord their God (28; *see* ch. 16).

The Feast of Tabernacles (or Booths; Hebrew *Sukkot*) begins the fifteenth of Tishri and ends on the twenty-first (33–43). During this week, all of Israel is to live outdoors in shelters made of palm branches or the boughs of other trees. The children of Israel are to do no work on these days, but are to commemorate God's deliverance of His people from Egypt and to relive their time of travel through the wilderness to the Land of Promise. The eighth day of this festival serves as a climax to all the festivals and feasts.

E. Laws for holy elements of worship (24:1-9). Statutes are given to regulate two items in the tabernacle which require perpetual care. Pure oil must be used to keep the lamps of the gold lampstand burning continually (2-4), and the twelve loaves of bread on the table of showbread, representing the twelve tribes of Israel, must be replaced with fresh bread each Sabbath (5-9).

F. Punishment for blasphemy (24:10-23). The punishment for blaspheming "the name of the LORD" (11, 16) is established in this narrative interlude, and the punishment is severe—death by stoning (16, 23). The principle of "eye for eye, tooth for tooth" (*lex talionis*) is instituted to restrict excessive retaliation for injury and loss (17-22). Other cultures allowed for the killing of one who caused injury and damage; the Mosaic covenant limits retaliation.

G. The Sabbath and Jubilee years (25:1-55). In addition to the annual feasts, Israel's religious calendar includes two other sacred times and events. Every seventh year is to be a Year of Sabbath, a year of rest for the land, during which it shall lie fallow (1-7, 18-22). The harvests in the Land of Promise will be so great that the land will not need to be worked in the seventh year. This statute prevents the ruin of the land (*see* also Ex. 23:10-11 and Deut. 15:1-11).

The Year of Jubilee follows the seventh cycle of Sabbath Years (Lev. 25:8-17, 23-34). The Jubilee Year is to be consecrated as a year of release, of setting free, a year in which Israel is to "proclaim *liberty throughout all the land to all its inhabitants" (10). If an Israelite family sold the tract of land allotted to it upon entering Canaan, during the Jubilee Year that land is to revert back to the original family. If an Israelite found it necessary to sell himself or herself as a hired servant, during the Jubilee Year that person is to be freed to return to his or her family. These statutes prevent the ruin of impoverished and indebted people.

God's concern for the poor is illustrated in His command that no Israelite is to lend money to a compatriot at interest (35-38), and that no Israelite who becomes a hired servant is to be treated as a slave (39-55).

H. Blessing for obedience and punishment for disobedience (26:1-46). God rehearses tenets of His covenant with the people He led out of Egypt. The people of Israel are to lead holy and consecrated lives before the Lord, and there are only two options: obedience to God's statutes and commandments, which invites God's blessing (1-13), and disobedience, which elicits God's severe wrath and results in terrible punishment (14-39). Even if the people of Israel are chastised because of iniquity, God provides for their restoration if they confess and repent (40-45). No matter what, God will never completely destroy His people, and He "will remember the covenant of their ancestors" (44-45).

V. GIFTS TO THE SANCTUARY 27:1-34. This section of the Levitical code discusses gifts dedicated to the tabernacle and offerings consecrated to the Lord, as well as the circumstances and conditions that permit the redemption of those gifts and offerings. These regulations stand as a preventive against making foolish vows and as a warning against forsaking vows made to God, and they cover commitments made with respect to persons (2-8), animals (9-13), houses (14-15), land (16-24), and tithes (30-33). The penalty for reclaiming that which has been dedicated to God is set at the value of the item plus twenty percent (13, 15, 19, 27, 31). Vows made to God are not to be taken lightly.

The commandments and statutes recorded in Leviticus are for the people of Israel not only during their sojourn in the wilderness, but also when they enter and possess the Land of Promise. As the moment of entering Canaan draws near, God instructs the children of Israel that they are to consecrate themselves to Him, that they are to be a separate and holy people, even as their God, the One who delivered them from Egypt, is holy—and then the people of Israel will be the people of God.

TRUTH-IN-ACTION through LEVITICUS

Truth Leviticus Teaches	**Action** Leviticus Invites
1 Steps to Dynamic Devotion God wants our devotion for Him to guide the way we live. The Bible suggests many ways to build a life that expresses zealous devotion for God. A devoted life focuses on knowing and pleasing God.	**3:1** *Know* that fellowship with God requires time, energy, and resources we would normally use otherwise. **6:12, 13** *Be constant* in your zeal for the Lord and His kingdom. Half-hearted devotion is unworthy (see Rev. 3:16).
2 Keys to Effective Service Leviticus is a book on service. It has much to say to the believer about how God wants all spiritual ministry to be conducted. Since every believer is called to be a ministering person (see Eph. 4:11–16), these guidelines are highly important.	**1:3** *Serve* the Lord with the best of your efforts. *Make sure* that your ministry is without the defects of pride, selfish ambition, or a personal lack of holiness. **2:1** *Soak* all ministry with continuous prayer (incense) and *be filled* with the Holy Spirit (oil) while engaged in any ministry activity. **19:19** *Avoid* mixing Spirit-filled and fleshly activity in the conduct of your ministry. God abhors such a mixture. **19:23–25** *Do not urge* the immature to enter ministry prematurely. Long-term fruitfulness may be limited. **24:1–4** *Be ready* constantly to bear witness to your faith in Jesus as Lord and Savior. **25:46** Leaders, *minister* with meekness, gentleness, and humility. Harsh, overbearing leadership misrepresents God's character and nature.
3 Keys to Moral Purity Moral impurity is extremely destructive to spiritual life and personal relationships. Sexual unfaithfulness is often an analogy for idolatry and unfaithfulness in the OT. Impurity compromises the integrity of our minds, hearts, and bodies. God tells us to flee from it because of its evil power.	**11:47; 15:31** *Avoid* all spiritual and moral uncleanness. It will corrupt and defile every aspect of your life. **18:1–30** *Know* what God's Word says about sexual conduct. *Flee* from and *avoid* every form of sexual and moral uncleanness. **20:13** *Know* God's attitude about homosexuality. It is a serious perversion. Though He offers grace to the homosexual offender, He rejects his conduct.
4 Guidelines for Godly Living Though often concerned with the types of Hebrew ceremonial and ritual laws, Leviticus can prove helpful for any believer who is serious about learning to live a life that is godly in Christ Jesus. Leviticus makes it clear that godliness is not optional for those who want to live in a way that pleases their Lord.	**4:2, 13, 22, 27** *Acknowledge* that you are inclined to sin by your very nature. **7:6, 28–36** *Honor* God's servants with adequate financial support. **19:32** *Honor* your parents. *Shun* the kind of disregard for elderly parents that the world promotes. **26:1–46** *Study* and *know* God's Word. *Practice* it faithfully. God blesses obedience, but considers unfaithfulness <u>hostility</u> to Him. **27:1–8** *Know* that God puts special value on everyone He has redeemed.
5 Keys to Dealing with Sin Like cancer, sin can spread quickly and defile a whole church or nation. God commands that we deal with sin forthrightly and thoroughly. Only through confronting sin can we ever be saved from its power. God cannot look upon sin because of His holiness, so we should not overlook it or deal with it lightly.	**5:1; 19:17** *Do not conceal* wrongdoing you are aware of. *Confront* sin. **5:2–4** *Know* that you are accountable even for sins you are not aware of. *Be sensitive* to the Holy Spirit's conviction of sin, and *repent* when convicted. **5:5; 26:40** *Confess* your sins quickly, frankly, and openly. Hiding them will only harden your heart. **6:5** Whenever possible, *make restitution* for sins you have committed against others, as a part of genuine repentance.

KEYS TO NUMBERS
The Pathway to the Kingdom

Kingdom Key: God's Purpose in View

Israel's journey toward their Promised Land is a study in how God's people—ordained to a kingdom—move forward to realize their destiny. Numbers illustrates how the Lord guides and corrects His redeemed as they move toward fulfilling His purposes for them. While segments of this book are occupied with priestly duties, details of civil law, and a register of tribal populations and boundaries, a full fourteen chapters (9—14, 16—17, 20—25) provide kingdom lessons.

Here are landmark events that illustrate lessons for today's New Testament believers:

- In your pursuits, only make moves which follow God's leading (9:15–23).
- Organization is a key to effective forward movement. Its disciplines are not a hindrance to freedom; when the structure is given by God, it releases the fullest possibilities of growth and grace (10:1–36, and throughout).
- The spirit of complaint and murmuring can never be satisfied. Don't give it a place in your heart or mouth (11:1–35)!
- Jealousy and self-seeking quests for position will inevitably bring shame and decay (12:1–16).
- Unbelief born of rebellion misses the best God-ordained opportunities and delays the fulfilling of His intended promise for our lives (14:1–45).

> **There is no victory or conquest without struggle and warfare.**

- Rebellion against God's appointed leaders brings death and the end of potential promise (chs. 16–17).
- Leaders who lose patience with their people embarrass themselves, reflect poorly on God, and block their own future effectiveness (20:1–29).

The primary kingdom lesson in chapters 20—25 is that there is no victory or conquest without struggle and warfare. The people of the kingdom do not merely "believe," but their faith takes action. When faith's action moves into faith's warfare, God's hand works wonders and wins impossible victories. Examples: (1) Israel's testimony for centuries to come would be how mightily God overthrew the kingdoms of Og and Sihon

When the Events in Numbers Occurred

		The Exodus 1440 B.C.	Death of Moses 1400 B.C.		David 1000 B.C.
Abraham 2000 B.C.					

(21:21–35; Pss. 135:11; 136:20). Their overthrow illustrates how New Testament spiritual warfare—prayer, service, and witness—may still overthrow godless forces at work in a society and drive back hell's boundaries. (2) God's confounding of Balak's schemes against God's people and Balaam's greedy conspiracy reminds us of the kingdom promise: "'No weapon formed against you shall prosper, and every tongue which rises against you in judgment you shall condemn. This is the heritage of the servants of the LORD, and their righteousness is from Me,' says the LORD" (Is. 54:17).

Master Key: God's Son Revealed

Jesus Christ is pictured in Numbers as the Provider. The apostle Paul writes that Christ was the spiritual Rock that followed the Israelites through the wilderness and gave them spiritual drink (1 Cor. 10:4). The rock that gave water occurs twice in the story of the wilderness (ch. 20; Exodus 17). Paul emphasizes Christ's provision for the needs of His people whom He has delivered from bondage.

A kingly Messiah is prophesied by Balaam in 24:17: "I see Him, but not now; I behold Him, but not near; a Star shall come out of Jacob; a Scepter shall rise out of Israel." Jewish tradition interpreted this verse messianically, as attested by the Qumran texts. Jesus Christ is the Messiah, according to the uniform witness of the New Testament, and the true King about whom Balaam speaks.

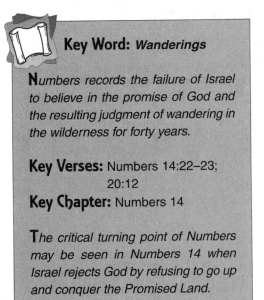

Key Word: *Wanderings*

Numbers records the failure of Israel to believe in the promise of God and the resulting judgment of wandering in the wilderness for forty years.

Key Verses: Numbers 14:22–23; 20:12

Key Chapter: Numbers 14

The critical turning point of Numbers may be seen in Numbers 14 when Israel rejects God by refusing to go up and conquer the Promised Land.

Power Key: God's Spirit at Work

The Holy Spirit is spoken of directly in chapter 11. There the Spirit is depicted as performing two functions: anointing for leadership and inspiring prophecy. In verse 16 Moses is asking the Lord for help in his leadership duties. The response is that Yahweh will take the Spirit that is upon Moses (identified in v. 29 as the Lord's Spirit) and pass it to his assistants. Even a leader like Moses needed Spirit-gifted people to help him perform his task.

His redeemed toward fulfilling His purposes.

Introducing

NUMBERS

Author. Authorship is traditionally ascribed to Moses, the central personality of the book. Numbers 33:2 makes specific reference to Moses writing down points about the wilderness journey.

The English title *Numbers* is taken from its title (*arithmoi*) in the Greek translation of the Old Testament (the Septuagint), followed by the Latin Vulgate (*numeri*). In the Hebrew text the name of the book is *In the Wilderness*, taken from the opening line, "The LORD spoke to Moses in the Wilderness of Sinai."

Date. Assuming Mosaic authorship, it was likely written about 1400 B.C., shortly before his death. Events in the book span about 40 years, beginning shortly after the Exodus in 1440 B.C.

Content. The division of the opening books of the Old Testament into five books or scrolls, (called "The Pentateuch," meaning "Five Scrolls"), should not obscure the point that each of the five books is a continuation of the preceding. Moses, whose birth is recounted in Exodus 2 and whose death is narrated in Deuteronomy 34, is the figure who unites the story from Exodus through Deuteronomy.

The Book of Numbers continues the account of the Mosaic period, which begins in Exodus. It begins with Israel still at Sinai. The Israelites' entry into the Wilderness of Sinai is recorded in Exodus 19:1. Israel leaves Sinai at Numbers 10:11.

Numbers has two major divisions: (1) the section containing instructions while still at Sinai (1:1—10:10); (2) the wilderness journey, which covers the itinerary from Sinai to the plains of Moab across the Jordan from the Promised Land (10:11—36:13). The instructions at Sinai deal with the preparation for the journey, and the rest of the book tells of the journey itself.

The instructions at Sinai (1:1—10:10) cover a variety of topics, but those dealing with the preparation for the journey dominate. Chapters 1—4 deal with a series of instruc-tions to number (take a census of) various groups followed by a report of the compliance with the command. Chapters 5 and 6 deal with ritual uncleanness, marital unfaithfulness, and Nazirites. In chapter 7 the leaders of the people bring offerings for the tabernacle. Chapter 8 deals with the consecration of the Levites. Chapter 9 deals with Passover and the cloud and fire; the preparation motif is reconsidered in 10:1–10, where the instructions are given for signal trumpets to be made.

The section of Numbers that deals with the journey (10:11—36:13) has two major parts. First, 10:11—25:18 describes the perishing of the generation that experienced Yahweh's deliverance from Egypt. The key points in this part are the accounts of the complaints, rebellions, and disobedience of the first generation, which led to their deaths.

The second subsection (26—36) narrates the preparation of the second generation for entry into the Promised Land. It begins with a new census (compare ch. 1), noting that the entire first generation, except Joshua, Caleb, and Moses, had died in the wilderness. This section ends with the apportionment of the land among the tribes after they have entered the Promised Land.

Personal Application. One of the most familiar events in Numbers is the negative report of the ten spies, as opposed to the positive one of Joshua and Caleb (13:25–33). This resulted in severe chastisement (14:20–38). From this we learn the profound consequences that can sometimes develop from being faithless and negative. When God speaks a promise, we need to respond with optimism, not pessimism.

The repeated grumblings of the Israelites, even in light of God's continuous provision, show us the need to maintain an attitude of thankfulness to God, even when we have great needs (Phil. 4:6).

Numbers also shows us the side of God that He is slow to reveal—His anger (14:20–38). Though He is loving and merciful, He is also just. When mankind repeatedly rejects Him, He must issue judgment (Heb. 9:27); when His children repeatedly disobey, He must chastise, sometimes severely (Heb. 12:3–11).

Surveying

NUMBERS

I. INSTRUCTIONS FOR THE JOURNEY FROM SINAI 1:1—10:10.

A. Account of census taking (1:1—4:49).

1. Military census (1:1—2:34). One month after completing the tabernacle, a census is taken of men over twenty, able to serve in the army. The result shows 603,550, indicating that the total population of Israel was probably between two and two and a half million.

This number is given in a number of Old

Testament texts (Ex. 12:37; 38:26; Num. 1:46; 2:32; 11:21; and 26:51). The tribe of Levi is not included in the military census (1:47).

Moses arranges the camp (2:1–34). The tribes are placed where their tents will be set up on the journey. Recent archaeological studies have shown that the square design of the encampment was used by the Egyptians in the time of Rameses II. (*See* chart, page 35.)

2. Nonmilitary census: Levites (3:1—4:49). The Levites are assigned ministries. Chapter 4 records the assignments of the clans of the tribe of Levi. There is work for every Levite between the ages of thirty and fifty.

B. Further instructions and accounts (5:1—10:10). The events in this section are not in chronological sequence. They report what led up to the first anniversary celebration of Passover, celebrated at Sinai two weeks before the census. But the reported order of the events is significant. It demonstrates the purity of the camp as Israel joins in a culminating time of worship on the plains before Mount Sinai.

1. Five instructions (5:1—6:27). The rules for ritual cleanness given in Leviticus are observed (5:1–31).

Nazirite vows are established (6:1–21). Regulations for a special vow of separation and personal dedication are given.

Included here are words with which the priests are to bless the people of God (6:22–27).

> **"This is the way you shall bless"** (6:24–26). The Aaronic benediction captures the essential purpose of priestly ministry—to bless the people with God's presence and provision. The blessing is God's Person, who shines upon the recipient—just as Moses' "face shone" after being in God's presence (Ex. 34:29). The New Testament identifies this as God's glory—which we behold with "unveiled face"—reflected as the Spirit transforms us into His image (2 Cor. 3:18). In our ministry as priests, we portray and pronounce the blessing of Christ's shining nature—His fullness—to each other, that God's glorious face might leave its radiant impression upon all.

2. Leaders' offerings (7:1–89). Each tribal group presents offerings following dedication of the tabernacle.

3. Dedicating Levites (8:1–26). After reviewing the design of the tabernacle lampstand with Moses (8:1–4), the Lord gives instructions concerning the dedication of the Levitical tribe, whose members are specially set aside to serve God (8:5–26).

4. Second Passover (9:1–14). On the first anniversary of leaving Egypt the people keep the Passover. Throughout history each Jew is expected to relive and affirm God's salvation through this annual celebration. (*See* Appointed Time.)

5. Guidance by cloud and fire (9:15–23). As Israel is about to move on, the writer focuses on the cloudy/fiery pillar suspended over the tabernacle.

As Israel sets out on her journey from Sinai, it becomes clear that there has been no real change in the people. The Law given at Sinai has not modified their character; they continue in their sinful course. What changes is God's response to Israel's behavior! Now God acts to discipline whenever Israel sins.

6. The silver trumpets (10:1–10). A blast on silver trumpets will call Israel to assembly. (*See* Spiritual Warfare.)

II. ACCOUNT OF THE JOURNEY FROM SINAI 10:11—36:13.

A. Rebellion and punishment of first generation (10:11—25:18).

1. Account of first march from Sinai (10:11–36; see Settled Down). Israel leaves the Sinai encampment, traveling in marching order (14–28).

> **"Come with us, and we will treat you well"** (10:29). Moses invited his father-in-law to continue with Israel as they moved from Sinai toward Canaan. He could serve as their guide (v. 31), and he would be treated well, for the Lord had promised good things to Israel (*see* Deut. 8:7–9). The gentle, loving concern that Moses showed should be an encouragement for us today. Believers bound for the heavenly Canaan should lead and encourage their families and friends to go with them, for the Lord has promised good things to all believers (*see* John 14:1–3; Rev. 21:1–7, 9–23; 22:1–5).

2. Complaining of the people (11:1–3). Complaint against God is judged immediately as the Lord's anger produces fire at the edge of the camp.

3. Craving for meat (11:4–35). The people crave meat and yearn for the foods they ate before their redemption from Egypt. God brings great flocks of quail that provide the meat demanded. But with meat comes a plague that strikes down thousands.

> ### "Oh that all the LORD's people were prophets and that the LORD would put His Spirit upon them!"
> (11:24–29). It is necessary to read this entire chapter in order to establish the context for these selected verses. Clearly, the gift of prophecy is demonstrated and encouraged as a gift for "all the Lord's people." It is important to recognize the sense of "burden" (17) which is associated with this gift and the connection to its pastoral function as seen in Moses. The gifts of the Spirit are not designed to operate in a vacuum; they function best in relationship to others. Moses was burdened with his pastoral charge to shepherd the people of God. God's response to Moses' burden was to distribute a prophetic gift among the seventy to assist him in shepherding the people of God.

4. Challenge to Moses (12:1–16). The brother and sister of Moses are jealous of his preeminence. They speak against him and receive God's discipline. (*See* Healing, Divine.)

> ### "The man Moses was very humble"
> (12:3–7). The high accolade given to Moses is poignantly displayed in his response to insubordination (vv. 1–2). In the face of sharp criticism, Moses reveals true meekness—he says nothing, and does not defend himself, but allows the Lord to speak for him. Humility expresses absolute dependence upon God; the truly meek entrust themselves to God alone. By yielding to the Spirit of God, who forms Christ's nature within us, we can take the high road of submission and suffering, following the example of our Lord "who . . . committed Himself to Him who judges righteously" (1 Pet. 2:23).

> ### "Please heal her, O God, I pray!"
> (12:10–15). When Miriam and Aaron revolted against Moses (vv. 1–2), God was quick to vindicate His appointed leader (vv. 5–9). In His anger, Miriam was stricken with leprosy. Aaron repented for both of them, pleading with Moses to intercede in

Miriam's behalf. God heard Moses' cry and Miriam was healed. We are assured today that when we confess our sins to one another and pray for one another, God will heal us (*see* James 5:16).

5. Refusal to enter the Promised Land (13:1—14:45). We come now to the turning point in this generation's experience. God leads Israel to the border of Canaan. He commands the people to enter the land, but they are terrified at the prospect of war and refuse to obey. The New Testament returns to this event often to illustrate the hard-heartedness of God's people, and to demonstrate the relationship between faith and obedience (Hebrews 3, 4; *see* Leadership, Spiritual).

A representative from each tribe is selected to explore the Promised Land and bring a report (Num. 13:1–25). All twelve agree that the land is rich. But ten of the scouts fearfully talk about the power of the giant inhabitants (vv. 26–33; *see* Able; Faith's Confession).

Rebellion (14:1–10)! All night long the agitated Israelites discuss and grumble. By morning they are agreed. They will choose a new leader and return to Egypt!

Moses intercedes (14:11–25; *see* Clears). The people are suddenly cowed as the glory of the Lord appears in the tabernacle. God is angry enough to strike down the whole nation, but Moses' prayer of intercession is a model for all time. He can say nothing good about Israel, but he can plead the character of God! God announces His decision: Israel will be spared, but not one of the rebels who treated God with contempt will live to enter the Promised Land.

The death sentence is given to a generation (14:26–38). Not one person over twenty years of age (29) who witnessed God's miracles in Egypt will survive forty years of wandering in the desert.

Frightened at the judgment which Moses announces, the people decide to invade Canaan after all. But this is simply another act of disobedience! God has told them to turn back to the wilderness (14:39–45). The attack fails, and a stricken, cowed Israel retreats into the desert.

Little is told in Scripture of the years spent in the wilderness. The following events reported in chapters 15—19 are not arranged chronologically.

6. Instruction concerning offerings (15:1–41). Moses gives instructions for offerings. In spite of defeat and disobedience, God will keep His promise to the covenant people. (*See* Atonement [Make].)

7. Challenges to Aaron's authority (16:1—18:32).
Korah, a Levite, insolently challenges Moses' and Aaron's spiritual authority and leadership and begins a rebellion (16:1–50).

As a test, Korah and his followers are told to present themselves before the tabernacle, bringing incense to offer the Lord. Suddenly fire from the Lord lashes out to destroy those bringing the unauthorized offerings. At the same instant, the ground opens to swallow the possessions and the families of the rebels (16:28–35).

Amazingly, the very next day the congregation accuses Moses of having "killed the people of the LORD" (16:41). Only the leader's intervention stops a resulting plague after it had striken 14,700 of the people.

Aaron's staff buds (17:1–13). To demonstrate once for all that it is God who has chosen Aaron's family for the priesthood, a wooden staff is brought by each tribe to the tabernacle. The next morning Aaron's staff has sprouted and actually produced fruit. The staff is placed in the tabernacle as a witness to God's calling.

8. Laws of purification (19:1–22).
Regulations for priests and Levites are reviewed, and the offerings which will support them are reaffirmed.

Regulations for purification from ritual uncleanness (*see* Leviticus 11—15) after touching a dead body are developed (Num. 19:1–22). This instruction is necessary because, as Israel journeys, a whole generation will die in the desert.

9. Death of Miriam and Aaron (20:1–29).
Moses disobeys at Kadesh (20:1–13). On returning to Kadesh, Israel finds the springs dry. God tells Moses to speak to the rock he struck years before to produce water (Exodus 17). Angry at the people's complaints, Moses strikes the rock and speaks as if his own effort plays a part in supplying the waters that now gush out (*see* 27:12–14; Deut. 32:38–52). This fails to honor God or display trust, so Moses is told he will not enter Canaan. Also, Miriam dies while they are at Kadesh.

Moses confronts Edom (20:14–20). An ancient, well-known route known as the Kings' Highway stretched from Kadesh to Canaan, crossing the land of Edom. Moses asks permission to travel the established highway to Canaan, promising not to stray off it into the land. The request is rejected, and Edom sets a powerful army across the roadway. Israel turns away.

Aaron dies (20:22–29). The high priesthood passes to his son.

10. From Mount Hor to the plains of Moab (21:1–35).
The people complain against Moses. In judgment the Lord sends venomous snakes. When the people finally exhibit repentance (21:7), Moses makes a bronze snake and lifts it up on a pole in the center of the camp. All who are bitten can travel to the center of camp, look at the bronze serpent, and live. (*See* Healing, Divine; Praise.)

> **"So Moses prayed for the people"** (21:7–9). Because of Israel's murmuring against God and against Moses, God sent fiery serpents among the people (v. 6). When they repented, Moses prayed for them and, in answer to his prayer, God provided for their healing. As they looked at the bronze serpent on the pole, they were healed. The bronze serpent typified Christ's dying on the Cross for our redemption, which provides both spiritual and physical healing for us today (*see* John 3:14–15; Is. 53:4–5; Matt. 8:16–17; 1 Pet. 2:24).

To reach Canaan, Israel must cross the land of the Amorites. Request for free passage is made and refused (Num. 21:23). Israel goes to battle, taking possession of Transjordan, the lands east of the Jordan river. A policy of total destruction of the enemy is established by God.

11. Balak and Balaam (22:1—25:18).
Israel is now camped on the plains below Moab, just across the Jordan river from Canaan. Although Moab is not threatened, the king and people are terrified. So Balak, the king of Moab, sends for a soothsayer. The Hebrew here is specific: Balaam is not a "prophet" (*navi'*) but a "trafficker in magic" (*hakkisim*). Balak intends to have Balaam, known for supernatural powers, curse Israel. He believes the curse will weaken Israel's power.

The summons to Balaam (22:1–20). Balak's invitation is rejected, for God tells Balaam not to go. Another embassy is sent. Balaam receives permission to go but is warned to say only what God commands. Balaam, however, is determined to gain the wealth promised by Balak.

To convince Balaam he must speak only what God commands, an angel is sent to confront him along the way. Balaam's life is preserved only because the donkey avoids the angel, who stands with drawn sword, blocking the way (22:21–41).

Balaam declares five oracles (23:1—24:25). Balaam directs the king to make sacrifices, promising to tell him whatever the Lord reveals in response. The message is disappointing. God refuses to curse Israel and instead actually blesses them. Balak tries again and again, hoping that God will permit Balaam to curse Israel. But each time the seer is forced to announce a blessing. The furious Balak banishes Balaam to his home. Before Balaam leaves, he is forced to pronounce the coming destruction of Moab at the hands of Israel, and to announce Israel's ultimate ascendancy.

Balaam has been unable to curse God's people. But after returning home, he devises a plan he believes will strip Israel of God's protection (see Rev. 2:14); he will entice Israel to sin!

Balaam's plan is to pollute Israel so that God will be forced to curse His people. Instead, God destroys the guilty (see Deut. 4:3–4), and spares the others, thus purifying His people and preserving their holy character (Num. 25:1–18).

B. Preparation of the new generation (26:1—36:13). The original generation has been replaced during the years of wandering. There has been no loss of strength.

1. A new census (26:1–65). Men of military age still number over 600,000. This census is taken as a basis for distribution of land in Canaan.

2. Instructions concerning inheritance, offerings, and vows (27:1—30:16). The five daughters of Zelophehad demand the right to inherit in their father's name, since he left no sons (27:1–10; see Women).

Joshua commissioned by Moses (27:12–23). As Moses' life draws to a close, God tells him to commission Joshua to lead the people when he is gone.

> **"Take Joshua . . . a man in whom is the Spirit"**
> (27:18). Joshua, who was to succeed Moses in the leadership of Israel, was indwelled by the Spirit of the Lord. No doubt he had been filled with the Spirit at the time the seventy elders all received the Spirit (Num. 11:16–17, 24–25). The expression "a man in whom is the Spirit," connotes possession of discernment and wisdom (Deut. 34:9). The Spirit-filled believer today possesses spiritual discernment (1 Cor.

> 2:14–15) and wisdom (Acts 6:3, 10) to lead in ministry as did Joshua and the other elders in Israel.

Offerings (see Grain Offering), festivals, and vows are reviewed (28:1—30:16).

3. Vengeance on the Midianites (31:1–54). Midianites had taken the lead in carrying out Balaam's plot to corrupt Israel. Now Moses is commanded to attack that people. All in the area are wiped out—including Balaam—and not a single Israelite soldier is lost (49)! This time, although the Midianites are killed, their property is saved and divided among the soldiers and the community, with a proper share to the priesthood.

4. The Transjordanian tribes (32:1–42). Two of the tribes of Israel are impressed with the richness of the land east of Jordan. It seems ideal for their large flocks and herds. They ask it as their inheritance, but promise to lead the armies that cross the Jordan and stay until the Promised Land has been occupied and divided.

5. Itinerary from Egypt to Moab (33:1–49). The stages of the journey from Egypt to the plains of Moab are listed. (See map next page.)

6. Instructions for the occupation of Canaan (33:50—36:13). The inheritance in Canaan is carefully outlined.

The Levites have been set apart to serve God (35:1–8). They will not be given a tribal land in Canaan. Instead, they are to be given towns and pasture land within the inheritance of the other tribes (see Lev. 25:32–34; Joshua 21).

Cities of refuge established (35:9–33). The structure of Israel as a nation made no provision for a federal police or justice system. In this system, murder was to be avenged by the community. Often the lead would be taken by the murder victim's relatives, called the "avengers of blood."

God has previously announced the death penalty for murder (see Gen. 9:6; Ex. 21:12). But now a clear distinction is made between manslaughter (accidental killing without hostility) and premeditated murder (hostility-motivated killing). Through the cities of refuge, provision is made to protect the individual who kills another accidentally.

The daughters of Zelophehad (ch. 27) are instructed to marry within their clans, so that when their land passes to their children it will remain part of the tribal inheritance (36:1–13; see Judgments).

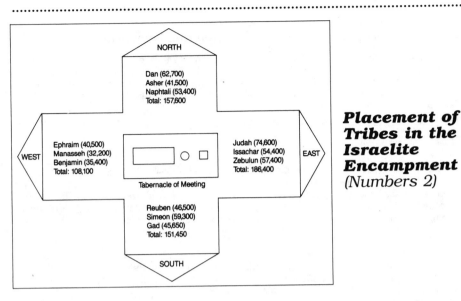

Placement of Tribes in the Israelite Encampment
(Numbers 2)

NORTH

Dan (62,700)
Asher (41,500)
Naphtali (53,400)
Total: 157,600

WEST

Ephraim (40,500)
Manasseh (32,200)
Benjamin (35,400)
Total: 108,100

Tabernacle of Meeting

Judah (74,600)
Issachar (54,400)
Zebulun (57,400)
Total: 186,400

EAST

Reuben (46,500)
Simeon (59,300)
Gad (45,650)
Total: 151,450

SOUTH

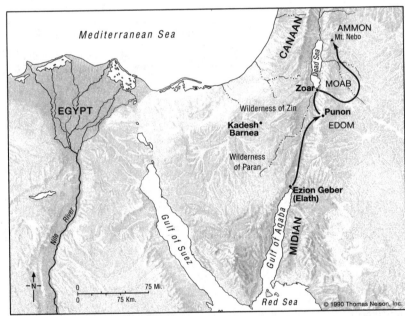

From the Wilderness to Canaan
(Numbers 33)

This map reviews Israel's journeys from the Exodus through their encampment on the plains of Moab, poised to enter Canaan.

TRUTH-IN-ACTION through NUMBERS

Truth Numbers Teaches	**Action** Numbers Invites
1 Keys to Knowing God and His Ways Numbers reveals much about the character and ways of God. Moses' prayer in Exodus 33:13 should be dominant in the heart of every believer. Much can be learned about God and His ways as we observe His dealings with Israel.	**22:32** *Know* that not all restraint or opposition is from the Devil. God will often oppose those whose ways are reckless before Him. **23:19** *Understand* that God is immutable, never changing in nature, character, or in what He says (see Heb. 13:8). **23:23; 24:10** *Know* that God is for you. He will even turn curses into blessings and use evil shaped against you for your good (see Rom. 8:28).

Truth Numbers Teaches	**Action** Numbers Invites
2 Steps to Dynamic Devotion The devotion God desires from His people is a theme that continues in Numbers. The Nazirite Law and the lives of Caleb and Joshua provide outstanding examples of the devotion God honors. They stand in bold contrast to Israel's general unfaithfulness.	**6:1–8** *Commit yourself* to be wholly devoted to the Lord. God calls all His people to live lives fully separated unto Him. **14:6–9, 24, 30** *Allow* the Lord to develop in you the spirit of Caleb and Joshua. *Follow* the Lord wholeheartedly.
3 Guidelines for Growing in Godliness Numbers gives several important guidelines for building a life that increases its capacity for God. Becoming godly does not happen automatically through exposure to religious exercise. Rather, it is the result of a conscious pursuit of God. From the way we regard the community of God to the way we embrace the truths of our redemption, every aspect of godly living is important.	**1:49–51** *Honor* the gifts of ministry the Lord has given to the church (see Eph. 4:10–13). **2:2, 17** *Gather* frequently with God's people. *Make* the gathering of God's people a central part of your life in Christ. **9:2, 3** *Set apart* certain regular times to celebrate God's redemptive acts on your behalf. *Celebrate* with all of your heart. **21:8** *Look to* Jesus' sacrifice (see John 3:14, 15). *Trust* His death as sufficient to cover all your sin. **23:9** *Live* so that others will know that you do not consider yourself as one of the worldly.
4 Steps to Dealing with Sin Numbers reiterates that it is important for God's people to know how to deal with sin. The seducing Midianites and the fiery serpents are among the analogies that show sin's vicious and virulent nature. God deals with sin ruthlessly and calls His people to deal with it similarly in their own personal lives. Sin must not be allowed to remain, but must be eradicated wherever possible.	**5:5–8** *Confess* your sins, and *make restitution*. Your restitution also belongs to God. **19:1–22** *Confess* your sin quickly, and *avail yourself* often of God's provision for us to be purified from all our sin (see 1 John 1:7, 9). **25:16–18** *Deal ruthlessly* with your own sin. *Search* it out in your own heart, and *repent* from it. *Give it no place* to stay or grow in you. **33:55, 56** *Deal thoroughly* with sin. Any sin you fail to deal with may well be your undoing.
5 Keys to Contentment Numbers underlines that God's people are to be contented with God's provision. Discontent reveals a lack of faith in God. He knows what we need and will meet that need in His perfect time. Faith is willing to wait for that time and rest in His present provision.	**2:1–34** *Accept* where God has placed you in His body. *Rest* in the fact that He has placed you just where He wants you to be (see 1 Col. 12:18). **11:1** *Do not complain* because of hardships. God designs them to train us for maturity. **18:20** *Rejoice! Know* that the Lord is your inheritance because He has given you His Son and eternal life.
6 Lessons for Leaders Numbers presents a number of crucial lessons for His leaders. Because leaders serve as examples, His Word has much to say about them specifically. All of God's people can learn from these passages and profit through their application.	**11:14–25** *Share* the load of ministry with others God has put under your charge in order to increase, rather than limit, the ministry. **20:7–12** *Honor* the Lord as holy among His people. *Never take credit* for something God has done through you. **27:15–23** *Remember* that you are responsible to raise up successors to your leadership (see 2 Tim. 2:2).
7 Keys to Relating Authority Numbers says much about relationship to those who bear God's delegated authority. Some of God's most severe judgments come for Israel's rebellion against Moses and Aaron. These incidents present clear lessons for believers today.	**12:1, 2** *Do not talk* against God's appointed leadership. It will bring His judgment and chastisement. **16:1–50** *Never align* in rebellion against God's appointed leadership. He hates and deals severely with this offense. Such rebellion often results in judgment on the rebellious community.

KEYS TO DEUTERONOMY
The Principles of the Kingdom

Kingdom Key: God's Purpose in View

The children of Israel have now experienced four decades as people of a kingdom, destined for dominion, and the Book of Deuteronomy reflects their maturing. What they had learned earlier—through obedience, worship, and warfare—had brought them to the brink of Jordan. Now Moses reviews the Law. Scattered throughout this book are principles of (1) tithing, (2) domestic duties, (3) compassion for others, (4) generosity to the poor, (5) avoiding idolatry, (6) doing battle in faith, (7) maintaining sexual morality, and (8) living in ways which assure blessing and avoid exposure to sin's curses. Our response today to these timeless principles will determine our potential for success in "kingdom living."

Consider the exalted destiny for His people which God beautifully describes: "Today the LORD has proclaimed you to be His special people, just as He promised you, that you should keep all His commandments, and that He will set you high above all nations which He has made, in praise, in name, and in honor, and that you may be a holy people to the LORD your God, just as He has spoken" (26:18–19). Then mark the blessings He promises (*study* Deut. 28:1–14). These Scriptures reveal the grand possibilities God has for His people in every era.

For a proper understanding of the "kingdom life" promised us today, always remember: God's promises of prosperity and position are *never* given as

> **God has grand possibilities for His people in every era.**

promises for social status or political dominance. Neither are they guarantees of lavish financial reward for our obedience. Rather, all blessing abides upon the church today for the same reason it did then: that God's covenant promise might be fulfilled—"In you all the families of the earth shall be blessed" (Gen. 12:3). Nations may be blessed through the people of the kingdom—revealing the character of God in their upright conduct and generosity.

God's Law is given to kingdom people to guide them to blessing more than to control them. As they are obedient to God, their lives will in turn bless others.

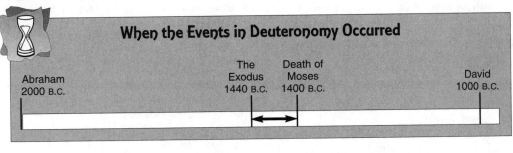

When the Events in Deuteronomy Occurred

| Abraham 2000 B.C. | The Exodus 1440 B.C. | Death of Moses 1400 B.C. | David 1000 B.C. |

Deuteronomy is a plea to obey God based • • •

Master Key: God's Son Revealed

Moses was the first to prophesy the coming of the Messiah, a prophet like Moses himself (18:15). Notably, Moses is the only person with whom Jesus ever compared Himself. "For if you believed Moses, you would believe Me; for he wrote about Me. But if you do not believe his writings, how will you believe My words?" (John 5:46–47). Jesus often quoted from Deuteronomy. When asked to name the most important commandment, He responded with Deuteronomy 6:5. When confronted by Satan at His temptation, He quoted exclusively from Deuteronomy (8:3; 6:16; 6:13; and 10:20). How significant that Christ, who was perfectly obedient to the Father, even unto death, used this book on obedience to demonstrate His submission to the Father's will!

Power Key: God's Spirit at Work

The unifying theme throughout the Bible is the redemptive activity of God. Deuteronomy reminds the people that the Spirit of God had been with them from the time of their deliverance from Egypt and that He would continue to guide and protect them if they would be obedient to the covenant.

Second Peter 1:21 clearly describes Moses: "Holy men of God spoke *as they were moved* by the Holy Spirit." Moses demonstrated the presence of the Holy Spirit as he prophesied to the people. Several of his most significant prophecies included the coming of the Messiah (Deut. 18:15), the dispersion of Israel (30:1), the repentance (v. 2) and restoration (v. 5) of Israel, Israel's future national restoration and conversion (vv. 5–6), and Israel's national prosperity (v. 9).

Key Word: *Covenant*

The primary theme of the entire Book of Deuteronomy is the renewal of the covenant.

Key Verses: Deuteronomy 10:12–13; 30:19–20

Key Chapter: Deuteronomy 27

The formal ratification of the covenant occurs in Deuteronomy 27, as Moses, the priests, the Levites, and all of Israel "take heed and listen, O Israel: This day you have become the people of the LORD your God" (27:9).

Deuteronomy as a Treaty

Meredith Kline maintains that the whole Book of Deuteronomy, plus the Ten Commandments and passages such as Joshua 24, are written in the form of an ancient covenant, or treaty, between a monarch and his subjects. In this case the Monarch was God and His subjects were the Israelites. Kline details five parts in his *Treaty to the Great King.* Whether or not Deuteronomy was actually designed in this pattern, material very similar to these parts occurs in the book:

1. Preamble, identifying the suzerain, or lord (Deut. 1:1-5).
2. Prologue, describing previous history or relationships (Deut. 1:6—3:29).
3. Stipulations and demands of the suzerain (Deut. 4—26).

4. Ratifications, or swearing allegiance, with benefits for keeping the treaty and curses for breaking it (Deut. 27—30).
5. Witnesses and instructions for implementing the covenant (Deut. 31—34).

• • • upon the twin motives of love and fear.

Introducing
DEUTERONOMY

Author. Deuteronomy identifies the book's content with Moses: "These are the words which Moses spoke to all Israel" (1:1). "Moses wrote this law and delivered it to the priests" (31:9) may well refer to his writing of the entire book as well. Moses' name appears nearly forty times in the volume, and the book clearly reflects Moses' personality. The first person pronoun used freely throughout its pages further supports Mosaic authorship.

Both Jewish and Samaritan tradition are unanimous in identifying Moses as the author. Christ expressly acknowledges Moses as the author of the book's content, as do Peter and Stephen (Matt. 19:7–8; Mark 10:3–4; Acts 3:22; 7:37).

The last chapter, which contains the account of Moses' death, was probably written by his intimate friend Joshua.

Date. Moses and the Israelites began the Exodus from Egypt about 1440 B.C. They arrived on the plains of Moab where Deuteronomy was likely written about 1400 B.C. on the occasion of the speaking of its content to the people "in the eleventh month, on the first day of the month," of the fortieth year of their wilderness wandering (1:3). This was just before Moses' death and Joshua's leading of the Israelites into Canaan. Deuteronomy therefore covers less than a two-month period, which includes the thirty days of mourning for Moses' death.

Background. Moses was now 120 years old and the Promised Land lay ahead. He had led the Israelites out of captivity from Egypt and through the wilderness to receive God's Law at Mount Sinai. Because of Israel's disobedience in refusing to enter the land of Canaan, which God had promised them, they had wandered aimlessly in the desert for thirty-eight years. Now they were camped on the eastern border of Canaan, in the valley opposite Beth Peor in the uplands of Moab overlooking Jericho and the plain of Jordan. As the Israelites prepared to enter the Promised Land, they faced a turning point in their history—new foes, new temptations, and new leadership. Moses called the people together to remind them of the Lord's faithfulness and to challenge them to be faithful and obedient to their God as they possessed the Promised Land.

Content. Deuteronomy is a series of farewell addresses by Moses to the Israelites as he prepares to die and as they make ready to enter the Promised Land. Although God had forbidden him to enter Canaan, Moses experiences a strong sense of anticipation for the people. What God had promised Abraham, Isaac, and Jacob centuries before is about to come true. Deuteronomy is the proclamation of a second chance for Israel. Israel's lack of faith and disloyalty had prevented the conquest of Canaan earlier. The majority of the people with Moses at the threshold of the Promised Land had not witnessed the scenes at Sinai; they had been born and reared in the wilderness. Thus Moses exhorts them thirty-five times to "go in and possess" the land. Thirty-four times he reminds them that this is the land that the Lord is giving them.

As this new generation of Israelites poised to enter the Promised Land, Moses vividly recalls with them God's faithfulness throughout their history and reminds them of their unique covenant relationship with the Lord. Moses realizes that the Israelites' greatest temptation in the new land will be to forsake God and to take up the worship of the Canaanite idols. Thus he is concerned for the perpetuation of the covenant relationship. To prepare the nation for life in the new land, Moses expounds the commandments and statutes God had given in His covenant. Obedience to God is equated with life, blessing, health, and prosperity. Disobedience is equated with death, cursing, disease, and poverty. The covenant showed God's children the way to live in fellowship with Him and with each other. So powerful is Deuteronomy's message that it is quoted over eighty times in the New Testament.

Personal Application. Deuteronomy is characterized by a strong sense of urgency. Even to the contemporary reader the challenge is decisive: "I have set before you life and death, blessing and cursing; therefore choose life, that both you and your descendants may live" (30:19). The decision is ours.

Deuteronomy teaches that the relation of God to His people is far more than law. The indispensable conditions of our covenant relationship with God are obedience and loyalty. Our love, affection, and devotion to the Lord must be the true foundation of all our actions. Loyalty to God is the essence of true piety and holiness. Success, victory, prosperity, and happiness all depend upon our obedience to the Father. The book is a plea for our obedience to God based upon the motives of love and fear. "What does the LORD your God require of you, but to fear the LORD your God, to walk in all His ways and to love Him, to serve the LORD your God with all your heart and with all your soul, *and* to keep the commandments of the LORD and His statutes" (10:12–13).

Surveying
DEUTERONOMY

I. MOSES' FIRST MESSAGE 1:1—4:43.

A. Introduction (1:1-5). This brief editorial insert tells us that it is the eleventh month of the fortieth year after leaving Egypt (3) that Moses gathers the people of Israel to hear his final *words. He now expounds the Law (5) as an impassioned preacher.

The plains on which Israel stands to listen are only eleven days' journey from Mount Horeb (the name Deuteronomy gives Mount Sinai). The unbelief of the first generation has stretched an eleven-day hike into forty years!

The treaty form on which Deuteronomy is patterned begins with a historical review of relationships between ruler and subjects. Here Moses recreates a series of incidents which sum up God's experiences with the generation He brought out of Egypt.

B. The past remembered (1:6—3:29). The call to possess the land (1:6-25). After the Law was given on Sinai, God called Israel to move toward Canaan, to take possession of the land God promised the forefathers. The camp was organized and the scouts sent out to view the Promised Land. The report of the scouts was unanimous: "it is a good land which the LORD our God is giving us" (25).

Rebellion is recalled (1:26-46). But Israel failed to trust God, even though He "carried [them], as a man carries his son" (31). They rebelled and refused to enter the land.

The years spent wandering were punishment for sin. Still God guarded His people (2:1-25). For the entire time, Moses recalled, "the LORD your God has been with you; you have lacked nothing" (2:7).

Then Israel again approached Canaan. This time Israel did fight, and the Lord gave total victory over the nations who chose to be their enemies. The Lord even gave the lands east of Jordan to two tribes as their possession: it was His action that gave victory, and He gave the land (2:26—3:20; see ch. 55 of this Handbook, §3.5.a).

Joshua is commissioned (3:21-29). Moses, too, disobeyed God and was not permitted to enter Canaan. But God appointed Joshua as the leader who would lead the people across and would "cause them to inherit the land" (28). The promise made of old will be kept now.

C. A call of obedience given (4:1-40). In a deeply moving chapter, Moses applies the lessons of recent history and makes an impassioned plea for allegiance to God. This is to be expressed by obedience (1-14), by rejecting idolatry (15-31), and by always remembering who the Lord is (32-40). Woven into Moses' exhortation is a distinctive exposition of the love bond between the Lord and His people. Only love will move them to become a holy community.

D. Cities of refuge appointed (4:41-43).

II. MOSES' SECOND MESSAGE 4:44—26:19.

A. Exposition of the Ten Commandments (4:44—11:32). The Ten Commandments, first given at Sinai, are repeated for the new generation. These lay the foundation for life under the Mosaic covenant. The commandments are in two sections. The first (commands 1-4) speak of relationship with God. Israel is to guard her allegiance to the Lord by acknowledging His identity, nature, name, and day. The second (commands 5-10) speak of relationship with others. In a holy community, each is to care for others by respecting life, person, property, and reputation. Both Jesus and the New Testament epistles point out that these commands can be summed up in love (Matt. 22:34-40; Rom. 13:8-10; Gal. 5:13-14).

Many see chapter 6 as an exposition of the first commandment (vv. 1-5; see One). It includes warnings against forgetting God when prosperity comes (10-12), against the dangers of serving idols, and against testing God (13-19). He is Lord and is to be honored and obeyed (20-25). Two themes in the chapter are special. First, Israel is called to "love the LORD your God with all your heart, with all your soul, and with all your strength" (5). The commands of God can never be understood apart from the deep love that is to motivate each party to covenant relationship. Second, much attention is paid to the training of children (1-2, 6-9, 20-25). Both Law, and God's motivation in giving it ("for our good always, that He might preserve us alive," 24), are to be taught.

Moses then explains that total allegiance to God will involve being His instrument in war against the peoples of Canaan (7:1-26). These are to be totally destroyed (1-6). These people need not be feared—even though they seem stronger—for "the LORD your God, the great and awesome God, is among you" (21). Along with the command to destroy the enemy and their worship centers is a promise of the blessings that full allegiance to God will bring.

> **"And the LORD will take away from you all sickness"**
> (7:15). The word "deuteronomy" means "the repetition of the Law." The Book of Deuteronomy tells of a new generation of

Israelites who had grown up since the Law was given at Mount Sinai. So that they might learn how God deals with His people, Moses rehearses the Law, which includes the healing covenant, to this new generation. God's Word must be taught to every new generation if it is to know God's commandments and experience healing for all its diseases. Today many believers have not been taught that Jesus Christ heals and, as a result, they endure illnesses unnecessarily. God would have them know His full provision so that they might enjoy wholeness and healing (see Acts 20:27).

Once in the land, Israel will have the prosperity promised in God's covenant. Then they will need to recall the years in the wilderness, remembering both God's discipline and His supply. Wealth must not lead to pride or self-reliance. It must stimulate remembrance of God, thanksgiving, and obedience (8:1–20; see Possess; Power; Word of God).

"Then you shall bless the LORD your God"
(8:10). Entrance into the good Land of Promise would mean abundant provision (vv. 7–10). Cautioning against the pride and self-sufficiency that could arise in prosperity (vv. 11–17), Moses links praise to remembrance: The people's duty to "bless the LORD" would help them not to "forget the LORD" (vv. 10–11). Thankful remembrance would keep the people God-focused (v. 18). All the pathways of God's goodness in our lives lead back to the Cross of Christ—the fountainhead of blessing. Because of His completed Cross work, He has given us His Spirit to remind us continually of His words and works (John 14:26; 15:26). For this purpose the Spirit ignites praise in our heart as we join Him in glorifying Christ (John 16:14; Eph. 5:18–19).

Why has God loved Israel? Deuteronomy 7 introduces both the question and a warning. Israel may try to explain her relationship with God by some supposed merit in the people (7:7). But actually, God simply *chose* to love Israel, and He delivered the people from Egypt because He is faithful to His commitments (9:1—10:11).

Chapter 9 suggests another reason Israel might later grasp for as explanation. Possess-

ing the Law, they might say, "Because of my righteousness the LORD has brought me in to possess this land" (4). This is exactly the attitude of the Jews of the apostle Paul's day (see Rom. 2:17–29)! Moses rejects this explanation, and as evidence of Israel's unrighteousness recalls the incident of the golden calf (Exodus 32). Only Moses' intercessory prayer turned aside God's anger (23–29). The real explanation is found solely in God's character: in His free choice to love Abraham's descendants, and in His faithfulness to that commitment.

Moses now applies his message (10:12–22). How are the people of the Lord to respond to God's great love? Moses' answer is to reverence the Lord, walk in His ways, love Him, and serve Him in complete commitment (12).

Moses has demonstrated from history the reality of God's love for His people (Deuteronomy 9). Now he calls on Israel to return that love and shows how love for God finds practical expression (11:1–32; see Tread). This generation has witnessed God's acts on Israel's behalf (11:1–7). Now they are to "observe all the commands" of the Law Moses has given. Their faithful obedience will bring great blessings, as the Lord enriches Canaan (11:8–15). But Israel must not turn away from the Lord to worship other gods (11:16–21). Thus Moses sets two ways before Israel: a way of blessing, if they love God and walk in His ways; and a way of discipline and judgment, if a generation should turn its back on God and move away in disobedience.

B. Exposition of the ceremonial laws (12:1—16:17). Canaanite worship featured many places of worship, often on hilltops or in groves of trees. Moses instructs Israel that God is not to be worshiped in that pagan way (12:1–32). Instead the Lord will choose a central location in the Promised Land, and only there may sacrifices and offerings be made. Not until David, some five hundred years later, was that place selected: Jerusalem, the ancient site of Abraham's offering of Isaac (Genesis 22).

Judgments made concerning idolaters (13:1–18). The command to worship only God is essential to covenant life. It is so vital that the entire community must take personal responsibility for obedience. Any prophet or spiritualist who tries to lead anyone to worship other gods is to be executed.

Rules of evidence under the Law require at least two witnesses to any crime, so individuals were protected from false accusations.

Dietary regulations from Leviticus are repeated (14:1–21).

Tithing is required (14:22–29). Establishment of a worship center may make it difficult for distant families to follow some laws given in the wilderness. Moses explains modifications of tithing principles for the settled life in the land. He affirms how the tithes will support the Levites, who serve God at the temple and are landless. Old Testament giving supported those who served God.

God's release of Israel from slavery provides the basis for His call to Israel to cancel personal debts every seventh year (15:1–6), to freely lend to the poor (15:7–11), and to release those bound to service (15:12–18).

Three annual pilgrimages are directed (16:1–17). Three of the annual feasts which enrich Israel's worship cycle require that God's people leave their homes and gather at the central sanctuary. (See Sacrifice.)

C. Exposition of the civil law (16:18—18:22). Several different kinds of leaders emerged during Israel's history. Here Moses looks ahead and gives regulations as to how different leaders will function.

Judges were placed (16:18–17:7). These seem to have been leaders of local councils of elders, to exist in "all your gates," meaning in "each of your tribes in every town" (16:18). They are to settle local differences and decide justly, without perverting justice, showing partiality, or taking bribes (v. 19).

Whenever an accusation is made, the judges are to investigate carefully (17:4). The testimony of at least two witnesses is required for proof (v. 6). God's Law is the standard by which judgment is to be made (2).

Priests and Levites are to serve as a court of appeals to which more difficult cases can be brought (17:8–13). This court is to sit at the sanctuary location (ch. 12), and its verdict must be accepted.

Moses here predicts a future time when Israel will demand a king (17:14–20). When that happens, the people are to anoint one whom God selects. The passage describes a number of additional safeguards the king and people are to follow. Solomon's failure to live by this passage caused his personal decline (see 1 Kings 11).

When a king took the throne, Moses ordained that he should be given a personal copy of God's Law. Israel's king ruled under the overarching authority of the Great King, God Himself. Like his brothers, the king was to accept his place as a subject of *Yahweh.*

The organization of priests and Levites is outlined for when Israel inhabits the Promised Land (18:1–8; see Name).

The office of prophet, vital to covenant life, is introduced, and his role explained (18:9–22; see Messianic Promises).

D. Exposition of the criminal laws (19:1—21:9). Regulations concerning unintentional killing are repeated (19:1–13), and rules of evidence for legal cases are laid down (14–21).

When Israel goes to war, a priest is to encourage the army to trust the Lord (20:1–4). Officers are to release anyone newly married or with an undedicated house or one who is fearful (20:5–9). Cities that are attacked are to be given an opportunity to surrender (20:10–15), and trees around a besieged city are not to be cut down (20:19–20). But the peoples of Canaan are to be destroyed completely, "lest they teach you to do according to all their abominations which they have done for their gods, and you sin against the LORD your God" (v. 18).

E. Exposition of the social laws (21:10—26:19). One major theme of chapters 21—24 is marriage practices and violations. These regulations (22:13–30; 24:1–5) are primarily concerned with purity and faithfulness. This is particularly important for Israel, surrounded as it was by licentious pagan cultures. The dedicated family is not only vital to the health of the society; it is also the primary communicator of faith (see Deut. 6:5–7; 11:16–22).

A liturgy is provided for the celebration of firstfruits and for the paying of the third year tithe (26:1–19; see 14:28–29; Special).

III. MOSES' THIRD MESSAGE 27:1—30:20.

A. Ratification ceremony (27:1–26). The Law covenant was not an unconditional announcement of what God was committed to perform. Instead, it was a treaty, defining relationships between the Lord as Ruler and the Israelites as subjects. The first generation accepted the covenant of Law at Sinai. Now the second generation is given instructions for a ceremony of covenant renewal. Particularly important is the response of Amen ["so be it"] that the people are to make as each stipulation is stated in the ceremony. This constitutes the voluntary commitment of that generation to the covenant of Law, by which this generation existentially "became" (27:9) God's people.

A similar ceremony of renewal later held for the third generation is reported in Joshua 24.

B. Covenant sanctions (28:1–68). Moses lists the blessings and the curses associated with keeping or breaking the covenant. During Israel's centuries in Canaan (Palestine), each blessing and each curse was experienced by different generations. God is faithful to His word—both to His promises of good and His warnings about the consequences which will follow sin. (*See* Prophecy.)

C. The covenant oath (29:1—30:20). This brief, final sermon recapitulates the covenant established between God and His people and records Moses' impassioned plea to Israel to obey God and so to choose life.

Moses exhorts Israel to commit to covenant life (29:1–15), based on all God has done.

No individual dares make merely a verbal commitment (29:16–29). Commitment must be from the heart, or judgment will surely follow.

Forgiveness is promised (30:1–10). Even should Israel be scattered by judgment, God will accept His people when they return to Him with their whole hearts, and He will restore all the lost blessings.

The choice Israel always has before her is the choice between life and death (30:11–20). What is at stake is the experience of blessings during this life, on the land God gives His people. It is not difficult to find the way to blessing. All Israel need do is to love God, to listen to His voice, and to cling only to Him (20).

IV. MOSES' FINAL WORDS AND DEATH 31:1—34:12.

A. Perpetuation of the covenant (31:1–29). The Book of Deuteronomy, and the Pentateuch, closes with a description of Moses' final days and of his death.

Joshua presented to the people (31:1–8). Moses has been told earlier that Joshua will succeed him as leader. Now Joshua is officially presented to Israel.

Covenant readings are ordained (31:9–13). Every seven years the Law which Moses has written down (9; *see* Wrote) is to be publicly read in solemn ceremony at the Feast of Tabernacles.

Moses predicts rebellion (31:14–29). Moses has no illusions about Israel. He predicts that whatever commitments the people

now make, their children will turn to the gods of the land, abandon the Lord, and become corrupt. Because they will do evil, disaster will follow.

B. The song of witness (31:30—32:47). The song which Moses now teaches to Israel has an important purpose. It will serve as a testimony and a witness against the people (31:19). The Law itself might seem long and complicated, but poetry set to music will be learned and passed on as a folk song from generation to generation. (*See* Safety.)

"I make alive; . . . and I heal" (32:39). God's nature is unchanging (*see* Mal. 3:6); therefore, He will always be the God who heals. Because He is sovereign, however, He will *judge those who rebel against Him—"I kill; . . . I wound"* (Deut. 32:39). Those who turn to Him in repentance and faith are promised healing, deliverance, restoration of sight, and liberation from spiritual bondage (*see* Luke 4:18). All areas of our being—spiritual, physical, mental, and emotional—are provided for. We were once dead; now we are alive in Christ (*see* Rom. 6:11; 1 Cor. 15:22).

C. Moses' blessing on Israel (32:48—33:29). Having suffered with Israel for forty years, Moses is well acquainted with distinctive tribal traits. As prototype prophet (18:15; 34:10), Moses is able to look ahead and share information God revealed to him. (*See* Favor.)

D. Moses' death and successor (34:1–12). Deuteronomy closes with a sensitive report of Moses' death. God leads him, alone, into the mountains overlooking Canaan. Peering together across the Jordan, God shows Moses the Promised Land. Moses dies there, and God buries His faithful servant in a secret grave.

Moses is gone. But the new leader, Joshua, is about to bring Israel into her heritage.

TRUTH-IN-ACTION through DEUTERONOMY

Truth Deuteronomy Teaches	**Action** Deuteronomy Invites
1 Steps to Knowing God and His Ways Deuteronomy focuses on how God brings His people to maturity. He will not allow us to skip any of the steps in the process and will	**2:14** *Know* that God will always bring you back to face any area of growth you have tried to skip. **7:22** *Do not despise* small advances. The process toward maturity is made up mostly of small steps, rather than major ones.

(continued)

Truth Deuteronomy Teaches	**Action** Deuteronomy Invites
1 Steps to Knowing God and His Ways *(continued)* make sure we complete it.	**32:11, 12** *Rest* in God's nurturing care. *Know* that He has committed Himself to care for you, guide you, and bring you to maturity.
2 Steps to Dynamic Devotion Deuteronomy adds much to our understanding of being devoted to God with all of our heart and soul. It emphasizes the need for whole-hearted commitment. God calls His people to pursue Him with all of their strength.	**1:42** *Seek out* and *depend upon* God's presence. Without it, victory is unlikely, if not impossible. **4:1, 2, 6–8** *Study* God's Word faithfully and carefully. *Apply* it to all you think and do. God will show His goodness and greatness. **4:29; 6:4, 5** *Seek* God's face continually. *Do not neglect* prayer and Scripture meditation.
3 Steps to Holiness Holiness means being separated from and distinct from the world. Deuteronomy gives much insight into the positive disciplines for building lives that are fully dedicated to God.	**11:18–21** *Practice* Scripture memorization and meditation to fix God's Word in your consciousness and allow it to change your behavior. **12:25, 28, 32** *Seek out* from the Scriptures the ways God wants you to live, and *practice them* so that your life will be pleasing to Him. **30:15–20** *Understand* that when you choose any action, you choose its consequences as well. God cannot bless and prosper disobedience and unfaithfulness.
4 Guidelines for Growing in Godliness Deuteronomy gives much attention to the practices that will help you live with a continual God-consciousness, making more and more room for Him in your life. Godly people are careful to maintain proper attitudes and disciplines in their relationships. Deuteronomy also explores how to maintain a proper regard for the authority God's Word has in life and conduct.	**8:10–20** *Guard against* pride amid God's blessings. *Know* that prosperity often brings arrogance, causing us to forget that God is the source of all blessing. **12:4, 8, 13** *Measure* your conduct and attitudes regularly according to God's Word. **13:1–5; 18:21, 22** *Test* all ministry by God's Word. *Reject* any ministry that does not measure up to the Bible. **21:18–21** *Give attention* to proper parental discipline. Rebellious children bring shame to their parents and dishonor the Lord.
5 Steps to Dealing with Sin It is important to deal with sins of heart and attitude before they fester, poisoning our lives and resulting in hateful actions.	**29:18** *Guard against* bitterness in your own heart and among God's people. It most often causes people to turn away from God. **31:5–8** *Turn away* from fear, faint-heartedness, and discouragement. All unbelief is sin. *Trust* in God's presence. He promises to be with you always to keep you from fear. **31:29** *Remain mindful* of your proneness to sin and turning away from God. *Acknowledge* and *rely* on God's strength and abundant provision.
6 Keys to Moral Purity Deuteronomy reiterates that moral and sexual purity are essential to covenant loyalty to God. God's standards cannot be compromised and are usually in stark contrast to social standards of those among whom God's people dwell.	**22:13–21** *Value* virginity; *do not be ashamed* of it. *Shun* today's casual attitude toward sexual relationships. *Realize* that God places a high premium on sexual purity. **22:22** *Flee from* and *detest* adultery, and *honor* marital fidelity. *Understand* that God rejects adultery and will always judge it severely.
7 Guidelines to Gaining Victory Many scriptures point to our involvement in active spiritual combat, in which we must conduct ourselves as good soldiers. No wonder, then, that learning how to gain victory in this warfare is so important.	**3:21, 22** *Remember,* the battle is the Lord's. *Trust* your battles to Him, and *rest* in His victory. He will fight for you. **30:11–14** *Be confident* that God will supply the dynamic for all He demands. *Understand* that our life in Christ is a life of faith. *Depend* upon His constant provision.

KEYS TO JOSHUA
Warfare and the Kingdom

CHAPTER 6

Kingdom Key: God's Purpose in View

To apply Joshua's lessons today, we must remember that the New Testament concept of the kingdom of God never advocates earthly governmental control or the political dominance of the church over any kingdom (John 18:36). Thus, the concept of "warfare and the kingdom" essentially relates to the moral and spiritual struggle of God's people as they actively confront and overthrow evil through their prayers and intercession, their godly influence and witness. Our struggle is not a quest for dominance which employs a political or military means (Eph. 6:10–20).

Still, spiritual warfare is real and intense. Old Testament characters and events prophetically illustrate the order of warfare in which "kingdom" people are to enter. The Book of Joshua indicates the kind of warfare which New Testament believers are to wage in a spiritual and moral sense (1 Tim. 2:1–4).

Joshua's God-ordained commission—to possess the land, evict the Canaanites, and establish God's order—provides a clear picture. (1) The Canaanite culture was saturated with evil, both human and demonic. (2) The Israelite troops were led by God (5:13–15), were promised power and victory by His presence (1:1–9) and His miracles (3:1–17), and were obedient to God and gave Him praise (6:1–16).

In the New Testament, the church is

> **Spiritual warfare is real and intense.**

promised the same dominion over evil (Matt. 16:16–19) and is called to extend God's kingdom by the same means: by the presence of the Lord (Matt. 28:18–20), by His miracle power (Mark 16:15–20), and by the spirit of praise and obedience (2 Cor. 10:3–5). In this respect, Joshua depicts our call to:

- See and believe there is an inheritance of divine promise to be possessed (1:2–4);
- Be unafraid, not limiting God to a former generation, but knowing that He is active in the present as He was in the past (1:5).

Joshua models for today our mission in casting down demonic powers which manipulate mankind, advancing God's rule over evil, not over governments. History

(Please turn to page 47.)

When the Events in Joshua Occurred

Death of Moses 1400 B.C.	Death of Joshua 1375 B.C.	David 1000 B.C.	Ezra 458 B.C.

Joshua: fulfillment of God's promises of blessing ● ● ●

Master Key: God's Son Revealed

Christ is revealed in the Book of Joshua in three ways: by direct revelation, by types, and by illuminating aspects of His nature.

In 5:13–15, the triune God appeared to Joshua as the "Commander of the army of the LORD." By His appearance, Joshua was made aware that God Himself was in charge. It was Joshua's task, as it is ours, not so much to follow the Commander's plans as to know the Commander. We need to be on His side even more than having Him on ours.

A type is a symbol or a parallel that provides an object lesson. Types can be found in a person, in a religious ritual, even in a historical event. Joshua himself was a type of Christ. Joshua's name, which means "Yahweh Is Salvation," is a Hebrew equivalent of the Greek "Jesus." Joshua led the Israelites into the possession of their promised inheritance, just as Christ leads us into possession of eternal life.

The scarlet cord in Rahab's window (2:18, 21) is another type, one which suggests Christ's redemptive work on the Cross. The blood-red cloth hanging in the window saved Rahab and her household from death. So, too, Christ shed His blood and hung on the Cross to save us from eternal death.

One aspect of Christ's nature illuminated in Joshua involves God's fulfillment of His promises. At the end of his life, Joshua testified, "Not one thing has failed of all the good things which the LORD your God spoke concerning you" (23:14). God, in His grace and faithfulness, had sustained and preserved His people by bringing them out of the wilderness and into the Land of Promise.

Key Word: *Conquest*

The entire Book of Joshua describes the entering, conquering, and occupying of the land of Canaan.

Key Verses: Joshua 1:8; 11:23

Key Chapter: Joshua 24

Joshua reviews for the people God's fulfillment of His promises and then challenges them to review their commitment to the covenant (24:24–25), which is the foundation for all successful national life.

God will do the same and more for us through Christ, who is the Promise.

Power Key: God's Spirit at Work

The Holy Spirit's work flows consistently through the Book of Joshua. The Spirit's presence initially surfaces in 1:5, where God, knowing the overwhelming task of leading the nation Israel, provided Joshua with the promise of His ever-present Spirit.

The work of the Holy Spirit is the same now as it was then: He draws people into a saving relationship with God, and He accomplishes the purposes of the Father. God's objective in Joshua, as in all the Old Testament, was the salvation of Israel, for it was through this nation that God chose to save the world (Is. 63:7–9).

Several characteristics of the Spirit's work can be seen in Joshua. The Holy Spirit's work is *continual.* "I will not leave you nor forsake you" (1:5). The Holy Spirit is committed

(Please turn to page 48.)

• • • depends on cooperation, obedience, and faith.

Introducing
JOSHUA

Author. The author of the Book of Joshua cannot be determined from the Scripture. Use of the pronouns "we" and "us" in 5:1, 6 supports the theory that the author must have been an eyewitness to some of the events that occurred during this period. Joshua 24:26 suggests that the author of at least large sections was Joshua himself.

Other passages, however, could not have been written by Joshua. His death is recorded in the final chapter (24:29–32). Several other events are mentioned that did not occur until after his death: Caleb's conquest of Hebron (14:6–15); Othniel's victory (15:13–17); and the Danite migration (19:47). Parallel passages in Judges 1:10–16 and Judges 18 confirm that these events occurred after Joshua's death.

It is most probable that the book was composed in its final form by a later scribe or editor, but was founded on recorded documents written by Joshua.

Date. The Book of Joshua covers some twenty-five years of Israel's history under the leadership of Joshua, Moses' assistant and successor.

The commonly accepted date of Joshua's death is about 1375 B.C. Therefore, the book covers Israel's history between 1400 B.C. and 1375 B.C. and was likely compiled shortly thereafter.

Background. The book opens at the doorstep of Israel's entrance into Canaan. Politically, Canaan was divided into many city-states, each with its own autocratic government and all feuding with each other. Morally, the people were depraved; lawlessness and brutality were commonplace. Canaanite religion emphasized fertility and sex, serpent worship, and child sacrifice. The stage was set and the land ripe for conquest.

By contrast, the people of Israel had been without a homeland for four hundred years (Gen. 15:13). They had lived in bondage to Egyptian pharaohs, then had wandered aimlessly in the desert for over forty years. Yet they remained faithful, though imperfectly, to the one true God and clung to the promise He had made to their forefather, Abraham. Centuries before, God had promised to make Abraham and his descendants into a great nation and to give them Canaan as a homeland on the condition that they remain faithful and obedient to Him (Genesis 17). Now, they were at the threshold of experiencing the fulfillment of that promise.

Content. The Book of Joshua is the sixth book of the Old Testament and the first in a group of books called the Former Prophets. Collectively, these books trace the development of God's kingdom in the Promised Land until the Babylonian captivity—a period of some nine hundred years. Joshua chronicles the period from Israel's entrance into Canaan through the conquest, division, and settlement of the Promised Land.

Personal Application. The Book of Joshua teaches that the fulfillment of God's promises of blessing to Israel depend on their cooperation. The blessings of victory, inheritance, abundant provision, peace, and rest all came to the people of God as they obeyed Him. Faithful meditation on His Word and faithful obedience to His commands are the key to blessing and abundance (1:8). Near the end of his book, also, Joshua called the people to a life of obedience and faith (22:5).

Today, this abiding trust provides a clear foundation for our growth and blessing. As surely as blessing follows obedience, judgment follows disobedience. Achan's sin reveals the principle that no man lives to himself (ch. 7), but the sin of one affects the lives of many. God hates sin and is just as faithful to punish the disobedient as He is to bless the steadfast. These principles of blessing and cursing are object lessons for us on our pathway to maturity. Joshua's life and leadership demonstrated that spiritual maturity is not independence from God, but responsive dependence on God. To be victorious, we must surrender to Him; to lead others, we must follow Him.

The Book of Joshua provides other valuable lessons: attitudes essential for God-given victory; principles of leadership; the fatal result of pride; the relevance of memorials; God's faithfulness to His Word; and examples of His miracle power.

Kingdom Key *continued from page 45*

gives ample lessons of the tragic loss of spiritual power that ensues whenever the church seeks political control. Jesus said His servants did not physically fight for Him because "My kingdom is not of this world" (John 18:36).

Power Key *continued from page 46*

to accomplishing the task, no matter how long it takes. We need His continued presence for God's plan to succeed in our lives. The Holy Spirit's work is *mutual.* "Only be strong and very courageous, that you may observe to do according to all the law which Moses My servant commanded you; do not turn from it to the right hand or to the left, that you may prosper wherever you go" (1:7). It has been said, "Without Him, we cannot; without us, He will not." Cooperation with the Holy Spirit is essential to victory. He empowers *us* to fulfill our calling and complete the task at hand. The Holy Spirit's work is *supernatural.* The fall of Jericho was wrought by the miraculous destruction of its walls (6:20). Victory was attained at Gibeon when the Spirit stayed the sun (10:12–13). No true work of God, whether deliverance from bondage or possession of blessing, is accomplished without the Spirit's help.

Surveying
JOSHUA

I. PREPARING FOR THE INHERITANCE 1:1—5:15.

A. Through choosing the army's leader (1:1-18).

1. Joshua hears the call (1:1–9). On Moses' death, God meets with Joshua. God will be with the new leader; no enemy will stand against Israel (vv. 5, 9). Joshua is to count on this promise and "be *strong and very coura-geous," being careful to obey (7; *see* Manhood).

2. Joshua gives the command (1:10–15). Joshua does not hesitate. Israel is commanded to prepare to cross the Jordan.

3. Joshua receives encouragement (1:16–18). The people promise to obey the new leader: "Only the LORD your God be with you, as He was with Moses" (17).

B. Through readying the army for battle (2:1—5:15).

1. By searching out the enemy's morale (2:1–24). Joshua sends spies to examine Jericho. This walled city controls the passes into central Canaan. The spies are discovered but are hidden by a woman named Rahab. Rahab tells of the demoralization of the Canaanites, who fear Israel's God. She wins a promise that her family will be spared when Israel destroys Jericho, and she helps the spies escape over the city wall.

2. By positioning the people for battle (3:1—5:1). God now demonstrates conclusively that He is with Joshua. Joshua has priests carrying the ark of God (*see* Exodus 37) lead the people into the Jordan. (*See* Passed.)

"And the people crossed over opposite Jericho"
(3:9–17). Forty years earlier, Israel failed to go in and possess Canaan because of unbelief (*see* Num. 13:31–33; 14:34). Now, at the Jordan River, their faith would be tested again. At the Red Sea God honored Moses by parting the waters before Israel when their enemy was in hot pursuit (*see* Ex. 14:22–23), but at the Jordan He would part the waters with their enemy confronting them. However the enemy may posture himself, as we walk in obedience to God, He will always enable us to "cross over" into new areas of growth and ministry.

In the spring, the Jordan is in flood (Josh. 3:15; 4:18). Yet when the feet of the priests touch the stream, the waters stop and pile up "in a heap" as far as the town Adam (3:16).

Joshua immediately shifts the focus from himself to the Lord (4:1–24). Twelve stones from the place the priests stood in the middle of the Jordan are carried to Gilgal, Israel's first camp in Canaan. The stones are set up as a memorial—a sign to future generations, who can bring their children to see the stones and tell the story of what the Lord did.

When the people are all across, the priests move to the Canaan shore. Immediately the Jordan returns to flood stage (18). Joshua is now held in awe by Israel (14), and there is new evidence of God's power to feed the fear of the peoples of the land (24; *see* Hand).

3. By strengthening the troops for war (5:2–12). Gilgal lies in the valley between the Jordan and Jericho. It now becomes the base of operations for conquest. But first, three important events take place. The men of Israel are circumcised, a rite apparently neglected in the desert (*see* Genesis 17); the Passover Feast is kept on the fortieth anniversary of the first Passover, held in Egypt (see Exodus 12); and the manna which God has supplied as food for the wilderness journey ceases as Israel eats the produce of Canaan (see Ex. 16:14–22). The new era has begun, and a deeper faith relationship with God is developing.

4. *By convincing a leader to serve (5:13–15).* The Lord reveals His presence with Israel.

II. POSSESSING THE INHERITANCE 6:1–12:24.

A. The central territory (6:1—8:35).
Rugged highlands overlook the Dead Sea and Jordan valley. Several passes lead up through the mountainous ridge into the heart of Palestine. These passes were controlled in Joshua's day by the walled city of Jericho, where there was also a vital fresh water supply. Today, too, Jericho is watered by the ancient springs—an agricultural oasis in a barren region of Israel.

Militarily, Joshua and Israel have to conquer this strong point and quickly establish control of the passes. Delay could be fatal to the conquest.

There is also a spiritual necessity facing Israel. The people must realize that it is the Lord who brings them victory. And they must learn the importance of obedience. These themes are emphasized as the author of

Central and Southern Campaigns
(Joshua 6—10)

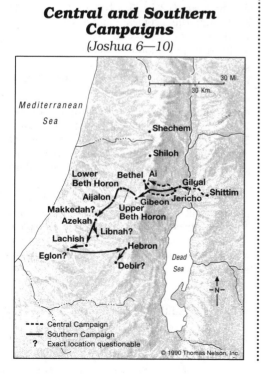

---- Central Campaign
—— Southern Campaign
? Exact location questionable

© 1990 Thomas Nelson, Inc.

Joshua tells the story of the central campaign, during which the military objectives are achieved, and the spiritual lessons are dramatically underlined.

1. *Obedience brings conquest—Jericho (6:1–27).* Jericho must be taken quickly. But the city is shut up, prepared for a siege.

The people follow the strange orders which Joshua relays. For six days they march in complete silence around the walls of Jericho and return to camp. The seventh day they circle the city seven times. When the last circuit is completed, as a signal trumpet sounds, Israel shouts—and the walls of the city tumble outward! All except those who have taken refuge in Rahab's house are destroyed, while all silver, gold, and bronze objects are set aside for the Lord's treasury. (See Faith's Confession.)

2. *Sin brings defeat—Achan (7:1–26).* Not everyone obeyed the command to surrender Jericho's spoil. When Joshua sends a few thousand men up one of the passes to take the small settlement of Ai, Israel is defeated, and thirty–six men are killed! It is clear that God has withheld victory.

A shaken Joshua turns immediately to God (vv. 6–9); God commands Joshua to gather all the people. Defeat has come because of disobedience: the sin must be purged before Israel will be able to stand against her enemies (13).

Achan is identified from all the tribes, clans, and families of Israel, and he confesses his sin. He has taken from Jericho a Babylonian robe, with silver and gold, in direct disobedience to God. The hiding place, "in his tent, with the silver under it" (21–22) makes it clear the whole family is involved and thus shares Achan's responsibility. Achan and his family are condemned to death, and all his possessions are burned.

The twin lessons of Jericho and Ai are particularly vital in this initial stage of the conquest: Obedience will bring continued victory; disobedience will bring defeat.

3. *Repentance brings victory—Ai (8:1–29).* God sends the Israelites to take Ai. Joshua's classic strategy is to lure the enemy away from the city and then set an ambush (3–8). The city is taken and destroyed. It is possible that the fighting men of Bethel were involved in this battle. Joshua 12:9 identifies Ai as "beside Bethel," and implies Bethel might have been taken early in the campaign.

4. *The law brings blessing—Mount Ebal and Mount Gerizim (8:30–35).* Moses has commanded that when Israel enters Canaan, the Law is to be written on plastered stones,

erected atop Mount Ebal (Deut. 27:1–26). Now the people stand between the peaks of 3,080-foot Mount Ebal and 2,891-foot Mount Gerizim and hear the words of Moses' Law read to them.

B. The southern territory (9:1—10:43).

1. Deception brings bondage—Gibeonites (9:1–27). Gibeon is the major city of a minority people in Canaan, the Hivites. The other Canaanites unite to resist Israel (1–2), but the Gibeonites are convinced resistance is futile: they have been told how "the LORD . . . commanded His servant Moses to give [Israel] all the land, and to destroy all the inhabitants" (24). Now they send a delegation to Joshua dressed in worn clothes and carrying molded bread. Though they are only a day's march from Gilgal (10:9), they pretend to have come a great distance, and urge a quick treaty. The leaders of Israel fail to inquire of the Lord (9:14), and hurriedly swear an oath of peace. When the deception is discovered, Joshua feels committed by the oath Israel has sworn in God's name.

Joshua consigns the Gibeonites to menial work. They still lived in Canaan some four hundred years later, in David's time.

2. Miracles bring deliverance—Amorites (10:1–43). Northern and southern Canaan have now been separated by Israeli forces. In a series of battles Joshua crushes the southern coalition, and then turns to demolish the north. Not every city in Canaan is destroyed in Joshua's campaign. Each Israelite tribe is left with enemies to mop up after they settle in, but all effective opposition is crushed.

The angry Canaanites lay siege to Gibeon, to punish them for their treaty with Israel. An all night march brings Joshua and his army to the rescue. The enemy forces are caught in the open and destroyed. God's actions for Israel are stressed in the report. He sends hailstones to strike the enemy (11). And, in a unique miracle, God answers Joshua's prayer and prolongs daylight (13–14) so that destruction of the enemy can be complete. Surely "the LORD fought for Israel" (14; *see* Prayer; ch. 55 of this Handbook, §3.7).

C. The northern territory (11:1–15). A

northern coalition is formed, led by Hazor, a city of some forty thousand people. The united army is huge and also has war chariots, the tanks of the biblical world. But again it is Joshua who launches the sudden attack (7). The enemy army is destroyed, and their cities are taken. Only Hazor is burned. Israelites will populate the other towns.

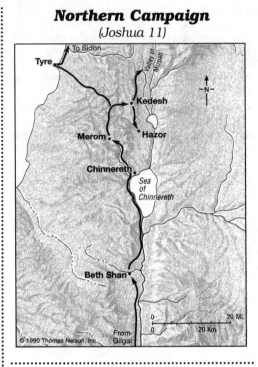

Northern Campaign
(Joshua 11)

D. Reviewing the conquered territories (11:16—12:24).

1. The territories (11:16–23).

2. The kings (12:1–24). Chapter 12 lists the kings and the peoples that Israel has conquered west of the Jordan. With all possibility of effective opposition removed, the people can go about distributing the land.

III. PARTAKING OF THE INHERITANCE 13:1—22:34.

A. Distributing the inheritance (13:1—21:45). Organized resistance is destroyed. So Israel now divides the land among her tribes by lot. Great care is taken to record the geographical boundaries of each tribe's inheritance.

1. Portions yet unconquered (13:1–7). The land allotted still contains Canaanite settlements. Now each tribe is to be responsible to expand its own territory, trusting the Lord's promise that He will fight for them (6). Later, reasons are given for this principle: the Canaanites are left to test the faith of Israel (Judg. 2:22), to keep Israel familiar with war (Judg. 3:2), and to keep the cultivated lands from reverting to wilderness.

2. Portions for Reuben, Gad, and Manasseh (13:8–33).

3. *Dividing the portions west of the Jordan (14:1–5).*

4. *A portion for Caleb (14:6–15).* Caleb, with Joshua, is the only person from Egyptian days to survive the wilderness journey (Num. 14:20–25). Now he asks for hill country around Hebron which is held by the Anakim. He immediately goes up and drives them out.

5. *A portion for Judah (15:1–63).*

6. *A portion for Ephraim and Manasseh (16:1–17:18).* The Ephraimites complain they are not given enough land. Joshua tells them to take what they need from the Canaanites. But the people of Ephraim hesitate: "all the Canaanites who dwell in the land of the valley have chariots of iron" (17:12–19).

7. *Portions for the remaining tribes (18:1—19:48).*

8. *A portion for Joshua (19:49–51).*

9. *Cities for refuge and the Levites (20:1—21:42).* The tribe of Levi has been set apart to serve God and is supported by the Lord's offerings. Now cities and pasture land scattered within the lands of the other tribes are provided for Levi, and a number of the towns are designated as cities of refuge (cf. Ex. 13:1–14; Num. 3:40–51; 13:8–32; 35:1–8).

10. *Epilogue (21:43–45).*

B. Discussing the future (22:1–34). The battle for Canaan, which is covered so briefly in the Book of Joshua, has taken seven years!

1. *A blessing for the eastern tribes (22:1–9).* Now, at last, the men whose families have settled on the east side of Jordan can return home (2–4; *see* Possession).

2. *A clarification of the altar (22:10–34).* As the men from the eastern tribes (*see* Congregation) return home, they pause to erect an imposing altar near the Jordan! This appears to the others as apostasy, for Mosaic Law requires that sacrifices be made only at the tabernacle, by Aaronic priests. Phinehas heads a fact-finding mission, which discovers that the easterners have not really turned away from God. Instead, the altar, constructed on the same design as the altar of sacrifice, is intended as a witness to the unity of all Israel, demonstrating that the eastern peoples share a common heritage and Lord with those of the west. The explanation is accepted, and civil war is averted.

IV. JOSHUA'S FINAL DISCOURSE AND DEATH 23:1—24:33.

A. Joshua counsels the leaders (23:1–16). About 1390 B.C. Joshua, now nearly 110 (24:29), calls the leaders of the tribes together. He exhorts them to follow the Lord without turning "to the right hand or to the left" (23:6). He reminds them of the victories won. As long as this generation of leaders lives, Israel will serve God (24:31; Judg. 2:6–7).

B. Joshua challenges the people (24:1–28). Joshua's final public act is to lead the people, and the new generation represented, in a ceremony of covenant renewal. This important act of personal commitment bound the individual and the community to be faithful to God, and recognized the Lord's right to discipline and to bless according to the Mosaic Law (*see* Exodus 19; Deuteronomy 27).

C. Joshua dies (24:29–33).

TRUTH-IN-ACTION through JOSHUA

Truth Joshua Teaches	**Action** Joshua Invites
1 Keys to Knowing God and His Ways Joshua shows much about how God responds to godly lives. Proverbs 16:7 says, "When a man's ways please the LORD, He makes even his enemies to be at peace with him." Joshua reveals many benefits of knowing the ways of God with men whose ways please Him.	**2:8–11, 24; 3:7** *Expect* God's favor when you follow His Word and the Spirit's direction and when your ways please Him. **4:19–24** *Know* that you will encounter no obstacle God cannot work in and through you to overcome. **21:45; 23:14** *Rest* in the confidence that God will never fail to fulfill His promises to you when your ways please Him.
2 Steps to Dynamic Devotion Joshua continues to call God's people to devote themselves completely to the Lord. In a day when so many follow the Lord with only partial devotion, Joshua and	**9:14** *Seek* the Lord prayerfully for every decision you make. *Know* that you cannot consistently make good decisions without His Word and Spirit. **14:8, 9, 14** *Follow* God wholeheartedly and be devoted to Him. Doing so will yield a rich inheritance. *(continued)*

Truth Joshua Teaches	**Action** Joshua Invites
2 Steps to Dynamic Devotion *(continued)* Caleb "who wholly followed the LORD" provide challenging examples of the life the Lord honors.	**22:5; 23:6** *Be careful* faithfully to apply all of God's Word to all of your life. *Follow* Him with all of your heart and soul.
3 Steps to Holiness Joshua continually exhorts God's people to live holy lives. God's holy people will live <u>unto</u> Him and <u>apart from</u> the world. Joshua demonstrates that our failure to live in holiness can and will have dire consequences.	**6:18, 19** *Do not covet* this world's goods. *Understand* that things we strive to get for ourselves will seriously weaken our walk with God. **23:7** *Be careful* to not adopt this world's way of thinking and behavior. *Hold fast*, rather, to God's ways and serve Him wholeheartedly. **24:23** *Reject* and *turn away* from this world and its ways. *Be assured* that you will thus be free to fully yield your heart to God.
4 Guidelines for Growing in Godliness Growing in godliness through knowing and applying God's Word is a recurring theme in Joshua. Simply knowing God's Word is not enough. We must know God's Word well enough to apply it to life's situations. God promises that this kind of faithfulness to His Word will result in a successful and prosperous life.	**1:7, 8** *Practice regularly* Scripture memorization and meditation. Then *determine beforehand* to put it into practice. This promises sure success. **4:4–7** *Establish memorials* in your spiritual journey. *Keep a record* of your experiences with God. *Share* these to instruct and encourage others. **5:2–9** As God's people were circumcised for a sign, *be baptized*. *Rehearse* baptism's meaning and benefits (Col. 2:11–15). *Know* that this is a key to spiritual victory. **8:34, 35** *Incorporate* regular Scripture reading as a part of personal and corporate worship.
5 Keys to Wise Living Good theology must always impact the way we live. Knowing God's Word but not knowing how to apply it is foolish and futile. Joshua helps us apply faithfully what we know about God's Word.	**1:6, 7, 9** *Rely* on God's strength and wisdom, not your own. *Allow* God's abiding presence to give you courage: *Know* that Jesus' promise to be ever with you will keep you from terror and discouragement. **15:63; 16:10; 17:12** *Do not rely* on your own strength and wisdom when dealing with sin. *Be assured* that without God you will have no success.
6 Steps to Dealing with Sin The failure to detect and deal with sin caused Israel's defeat at Ai. Past successes can cause us to be less careful about sin. None of us can afford to drop our guard, for even one person's sins can weaken the life of a whole church.	**7:10–13** *Understand* that individual sin weakens the whole church. *Deal with sin* quickly and forthrightly. **11:11** *Leave* no sin unconfessed or undealt with. *Be aware* that unconfessed sin will become a snare.
7 Guidelines to Gaining Victory Joshua is a type of Christ who always leads His people in victory and triumph. Our victories result from surrendering to Jesus' lordship and allowing Him to work through us to overcome our obstacles and adversities.	**5:14, 15** *Submit yourself* continually to Jesus' lordship in your life. *Acknowledge* that He comes as the Captain of His army to lead us to victory (see Ex. 17:14, 15). **17:18** *Be assured* that regardless of the strength of the enemy, God can and will enable you to prevail.

KEYS TO JUDGES
Lawlessness and the Kingdom

Kingdom Key: God's Purpose in View

The Book of Judges is a study in what happens to God's people when He gives the dimensions for kingdom rule but the disciplines of His kingdom order are disregarded, when humans through pride, lust, and worldly wisdom choose to discount and disobey that order. In the Old Testament God's laws were not given in order to bully and dominate His people, but to bless and protect, direct and enrich them. Similarly, New Testament believers are called to heed all His ways and disciplines (Matt. 11:28–30; 1 John 5:3).

No sooner had the tribes of Israel taken hold of their inheritance than they began to grow lax and indulgent regarding the disciplines of warfare. Judges 3:1–5 reveals God's intent that the hostile neighbors remaining in the land would keep His people dependent on Him and keep ensuing generations battle-ready. By failing to follow God's commands, Israel turned their back on their Commanding King, who alone could promise victory.

The kingdom key to Judges is to learn from Israel's mistakes and realize that no season of life will be without the need for the discipline of constant readiness for spiritual battle.

God's laws and disciplines are "geared" for man's benefit, and obedience to them brings God's blessing. Obedience to God aligns us with the divinely arranged structures of blessing which have been established since

> **The Lord**
>
> **is our**
>
> **Judge and**
>
> **our**
>
> **Deliverer.**

creation. When we heed God's laws and disciplines, life succeeds; when we violate them, whether through ignorance, disobedience, rebellion, or perversion, failure inevitably ensues. First Corinthians 6:9–11 specifically mentions lifestyles that will not "inherit the kingdom of God"— that is, will *not* receive the intended blessing of God's willed purposes for humanity.

The Book of Judges is a sobering reminder that our entry into partnership with God, as instruments of His kingdom, never grants us a license for selfish, carnal, or spiritual indulgence. Gideon (chs. 6—8) and Samson (chs. 13—16) are examples of (1) how God's Spirit will appoint and anoint a human instrument to accomplish God's purpose; and yet (2) how a surrender to pride or presumption can bring a ruinous end.

When the Events in Judges Occurred

Moses 1500 B.C.	Death of Joshua 1375 B.C.	Coronation of Saul 1050 B.C.	David 1000 B.C.	Ezra 458 B.C.

Judges: God uses consecrated men and women, • • •

Master Key: God's Son Revealed

The Book of Judges graphically portrays the character of the Lord in His dealings with the children of Israel. In His righteousness, the Lord punished them for their sin; in His love and mercy, the Lord delivered them in response to their penitent cry. Though the judges are called the deliverers or saviors of the people of Israel, God ultimately is their Savior. "God is the Judge" (Ps. 75:7). He is "a just God and a Savior" (Is. 45:21).

The Book of Judges emphasizes humanity's need of a divine deliverer or savior. Throughout history, God's people have sinned. God, the Lord of history, has always delivered His people from oppression when they repented and turned their hearts toward Him. In the fullness of time, God in His love sent forth His Son Jesus Christ as our Deliverer, our Savior, to redeem us from the bondage of sin and death. Our Lord is a righteous Judge (2 Tim. 4:8) who will one day "judge the world in righteousness" (Acts 17:31).

Power Key: God's Spirit at Work

The Spirit of the Lord is clearly at work in the charismatic leaders in the Book of Judges. The heroic deeds of Othniel, Gideon, Jephthah, and Samson are attributed to the Spirit of the Lord:

1. The Spirit of the Lord came upon Othniel (3:10) and enabled him to deliver the Israelites from the hand of Cushan-Rishathaim, king of Mesopotamia.

2. Through the personal presence of the Spirit of the Lord, Gideon (6:34) delivered God's people from the oppression of the Midianites. Literally, the Spirit of the Lord clothed Himself with Gideon. The Spirit empowered this divinely appointed leader and acted through him to accomplish God's saving act on behalf of His people.

3. The Spirit of the Lord equipped Jephthah (11:29) with leadership skills in his military campaign against the Ammonites. Jephthah's victory over the Ammonites was the Lord's act of deliverance on behalf of Israel.

4. The Spirit of the Lord empowered Samson to perform extraordinary deeds. He began to stir Samson (13:25), and the Spirit of the Lord came mightily upon him on several

(Please turn to page 56.)

Key Word: *Cycles*

The Book of Judges is written primarily on a thematic rather than a chronological basis (16—21 actually preceed 3—15). The author uses the accounts of the various judges to prove the utter failure of living out the closing verse of Judges: "Everyone did what was right in his own eyes." To accomplish this, the author uses a five-point cycle to recount the repeated spiral of disobedience, destruction, and defeat. The five parts are: (1) sin, (2) servitude, (3) supplication, (4) salvation, and (5) silence.

Key Verses: Judges 2:20–21; 21:25

Key Chapter: Judges 2

The second chapter of Judges is a miniature of the whole book as it records the transition of the godly to the ungodly generation, the format of the cycles, and the purpose of God in not destroying the Canaanites.

• • • empowered with His Spirit, to deliver His people.

Introducing
JUDGES

Author. The author of Judges is unknown. The Talmud ascribes the Book of Judges to Samuel. He may have written portions of the book, for it is recorded that he was a writer (1 Sam. 10:25). The inspired author carefully selected oral and written sources to provide a history of Israel with theological import.

Date. The Book of Judges covers the period between Joshua's death and the rise of the monarchy. The actual date of composition is unknown. Internal evidence, however, indicates that it was written during the early part of the monarchy following Saul's coronation but prior to David's conquest of Jerusalem, about 1050 to 1000 B.C. This date is supported by two facts: (1) The words "In those days there was no king in Israel" (17:6) were penned from a period when Israel did have a king and (2) the declaration that "the Jebusites dwell with the children of Benjamin in Jerusalem to this day" (1:21) points to a time before David conquered the city (2 Sam. 5:6–7).

Background. The Book of Judges covers a chaotic period in Israel's history from about 1380 to 1050 B.C. Under the leadership of Joshua, Israel had generally conquered and occupied the land of Canaan, but large areas remained yet to be possessed by the individual tribes. Israel did evil in the sight of the Lord continually and "there was no king in Israel; everyone did what was right in his own eyes" (21:25). By deliberately serving foreign gods, the people of Israel broke their covenant with the Lord. As a result, the Lord delivered them into the hands of various oppressors. Each time the people cried out to the Lord, He faithfully raised up a judge to bring deliverance to His people. These judges whom the Lord chose and anointed with His Spirit were military and civil leaders. The Book of Judges not only looks back to the conquest of Canaan led by Joshua and records the conditions in Canaan during the period of the judges, but it also anticipates the establishment of the monarchy in Israel. (*See* map, page 60.)

Purpose. The purpose of the Book of Judges is threefold: (1) historical, (2) theological, and (3) spiritual. Historically, the book describes the events that transpired during a specific period in Israel's history and provides a link between the conquest of Canaan and the monarchy. Theologically, the book underscores the principle established in the Law that obedience to the Law brings peace and life, and disobedi-ence brings oppression and death. Moreover, the book points to the need for a centralized hereditary monarchy in Israel. Israel's disobedience of the Lord's kingship throughout the time of the inspired leadership of the judges resulted in apostasy and anarchy, which consequently demonstrated the need for a permanent, centralized, hereditary monarchy through which the Lord would continue to exert His kingship over the nation of Israel. Spiritually, the book serves to show the faithfulness of the Lord to His covenant. Whenever His people repented and turned from their evil ways, the Lord always forgave them and raised up Spirit-empowered leaders to deliver them from their oppressors.

Content. The Book of Judges is divided into three main sections: (1) a prologue (1:1—3:6); (2) a main body (3:7—16:31); and (3) an epilogue (17:1—21:25). The first part of the prologue (1:1—2:5) establishes the historical scene for the narratives that follow. It describes Israel's incomplete conquest of the Promised Land (1:1–36) and the Lord's rebuke for her unfaithfulness to His covenant (2:1–5). The second part of the prologue (2:6—3:6) provides an overview of the main body of the book. It portrays Israel's rebellious ways during the first centuries in the Promised Land and shows how the Lord dealt with her in that period, a time characterized by a recurring cycle of apostasy, oppression, repentance, and deliverance.

The main body of the book (3:7—16:31) illustrates this recurring pattern within Israel's early history. The Israelites did evil in the sight of the Lord (apostasy); the Lord delivered them into the hands of enemies (oppression); the people of Israel cried out to the Lord (repentance); and in response to their cry, the Lord raised up deliverers whom He empowered with His Spirit (deliverance). Six individuals—Othniel, Ehud, Deborah, Gideon, Jephthah, and Samson—whose role as deliverers is related in some detail are classified as the "major" judges. Six others who are only briefly mentioned—Shamgar, Tola, Jair, Ibzan, Elon, and Abdon—are referred to as the "minor" judges. The thirteenth individual, Abimelech, is supplemental to the story of Gideon.

Two stories are appended to the Book of Judges (17:1—21:25) in the form of an epilogue. The purpose of these appendices is not to establish an end to the period of the judges but to depict the religious and moral corruption that existed during this period. The first story illustrates the corruption in Israel's religion. Micah established in Ephraim a paganized form of worship of the Lord, which was adopted by the Danites when they abandoned their appointed inheritance and migrated into northern Israel. The second story in the epilogue illustrates Israel's moral corruption by relating the unfortunate experience of a Levite at Gibeah in Benjamin and the ensuing Benjamite War. Apparently, the purpose of this concluding section of the book is to illustrate the consequences of Israel's apostasy and anarchy when "there was no king in Israel."

Personal Application. The Book of Judges illustrates the disastrous consequences of breaking fellowship with God through idolatrous worship. Sin separates from God. The Lord requires commitment from His people.

When we commit sin, the Lord in His love chastises us until we come to full repentance. When we cry out to Him, the Lord faithfully responds to us. He forgives us, brings deliverance to us, and restores fellowship with us.

The Lord is our Judge—our Deliverer. He is able to do impossible things. Just as He appointed deliverers and empowered them with His Spirit to do exploits, He is able to endue us with His Holy Spirit and to use us to bring deliverance to those who are bound in sin and despair. He responds to the cry of a penitent heart. The Lord is faithful and His love is constant.

Power Key *continued from page 54*

occasions. Samson tore a lion apart with his bare hands (14:6). At one time he killed thirty Philistines (14:19), and at another time he freed himself from ropes that bound his hands and then killed a thousand Philistines with the jawbone of a donkey (15:14–15).

The same Holy Spirit who enabled these deliverers to perform these exploits and fulfill

the Lord's purposes is at work today. God desires to move upon His people so that they too can do seemingly impossible things. The Lord wants to bring deliverance to His people, and He is looking for consecrated men and women whom He can empower with His Holy Spirit.

Surveying
JUDGES

I. PROLOGUE: CONDITIONS IN CANAAN AFTER THE DEATH OF JOSHUA 1:1—3:6.
The days of the judges were so disastrous that it is necessary to explain how God's chosen people could be crushed. The answer: sin. God proved Himself faithful in the conquest; now Israel proves herself unfaithful.

A. Continuing conquests by Israelite tribes (1:1–26). While the Israelites continue to win victories over the remaining Canaanites (vv. 1–6), enemies settled in the plains scare them with wooden war chariots outfitted with iron—a metal new to them. The Israelites hesitate to attack (19). Doubt is the first hesitant step toward decline.

B. Incomplete conquests of the land (1:27–36). Some Canaanite tribes are defeated but not destroyed; others are not even defeated (27–33). In merely putting these under forced labor (28, 30, 33, 35), Israel disobeys God directly (Deut. 20:16–18).

C. Covenant of the Lord broken (2:1–5). God's special messenger confronts Israel with her disobedience and with judgment: God will

not drive out the remaining Canaanites; instead, they will be "thorns" and a "snare" to Israel (3).

D. Introduction to the period of the judges (2:6—3:6). The causes of Israel's decline are explained further. Although Israel remained faithful to the Lord throughout the days of Joshua and the elders (2:7), subsequent generations, without personal knowledge of what God had done for His covenant people, are unfaithful and disobedient. Because Israel disobeys God's command to drive out the Canaanites, numerous generations of Israelites are now tempted to participate in the false religion and moral depravity of the people (3:3, 5) who live among them in the land.

Israelites now pursue idol worship (2:11–13) and intermarry (3:6), both of which are forbidden in Mosaic Law. Israel forsakes God and serves "Baal and the Ashtoreths" (2:13). "Baal" (often referred to in the plural, "Baals" [2:11], because each locality had its own Baal) is the designation for the Canaanites' fertility and nature deities. "Ashtoreth" refers to their female deities (also associated with fertility), such as Ashtoreth and Asherah.

A cyclical pattern of events (*see* 2:11–23), which is to characterize Israel's history during the eight hundred-year period of the judges, is described: *rebellion*—Israel turns to idol worship and deserts the way of life prescribed in the Law of Moses; *retribution*—God punishes Israel at the hands of foreign nations; *repentance*—Israel, under intense oppression, repents and cries out to God for deliverance; *restoration*—God hears, pities His people, and sends a *judge, who delivers Israel from her oppressors; *rest*—the judge keeps the people faithful to God. But after the judge dies, rather than learn from previous events, Israel reverts back to her sinful ways, which kindles God's anger, and the cyclical pattern begins again.

II. HISTORY OF OPPRESSIONS AND DELIVERANCES DURING THE PERIOD OF THE JUDGES 3:7—16:31.

The dreary picture of Israel's apostasy and oppression is brightened only by the stories of the judges God sent to Israel as deliverers. The Hebrew word translated as "judge" is *shaphat*, which means "one who judges, governs, passes down divine judgment, pronounces sentence, and decides matters." Judges were leaders with executive, legislative, military, and judicial power. They were divinely appointed and anointed by the Spirit to lead God's people against their enemies. Six deliverers (Othniel, Ehud, Deborah, Gideon, Jephthah, and Samson) are considered "major" judges because their stories are told in more detail than the other six "minor" judges (Shamgar, Tola, Jair, Ibzan, Elon, and Abdon).

A. Mesopotamian oppression and deliverance by Othniel (3:7–11). The cyclical pattern of events that characterizes the period of the judges is clearly evident here. Rebellion (v. 7) leads to retribution (8), which occasions repentance (9), and is followed by restoration (9–10), and rest (11). The oppressors are the Mesopotamians from the distant north; the deliverer is Othniel.

B. Moabite oppression and deliverance by Ehud (3:12–30). The Moabite oppressors under "Eglon king of Moab" (12) represent a threat to the south and east. "The City of Palms" (13) probably refers to the Jericho oasis (*see* 1:16). Ehud, a left-handed man from the tribe of Benjamin, uses trickery—concealing his dagger and pretending to pay tribute—to kill the king of Moab. Ehud leads an uprising that cuts off the army occupying southern Israel.

C. Philistine oppression and deliverance by Shamgar (3:31).

D. Canaanite oppression and deliverance by Deborah and Barak (4:1—5:31). Attention shifts to the north. Resurgent Canaanites, equipped with nine hundred iron chariots, establish a new power base at Hazor. Now oppression comes from within the land, from enemies Israel should have driven out a century before. Israel's new deliverer, Deborah, is widely recognized as a prophetess (4:4) and has been serving as a judge (4:4–5; *see* Women).

> **"Now Deborah, a prophetess . . . was judging Israel at that time"** (4:4). The main function of Old Testament prophets was to speak to men and women with words from God. Deborah is unique—a woman who functions in the office of a judge and with the gift of prophecy. God uses women in ministry today, as well.

Deborah summons Barak to muster an army. A great victory is won when the Canaanite chariots are mired in the overflow of the River Kishron, about ninety miles north of Bethel. Deborah's credit for the victory is due to Barak's lack of trust in the Lord (4:8).

> **"Then Deborah and Barak . . . sang on that day"** (5:1). "Deborah's song" (5:1–31; *see* Perish; Sing) celebrated the Israelites' God-given military victory over Jabin, Sisera, and the Canaanites (4:2–24). In a beautiful poetic expression, Deborah praises the Lord, highlighting the details of victory and cheering the enemy's destruction. As believers who enjoy God-given victory over sin and death through Christ's redemptive work on the Cross, we too celebrate in songs of praise and worship (*see* Rom. 7:24—8:3; 1 Cor. 15:53–57; Rev. 1:5–6), as the Holy Spirit fills us with Christ's mighty presence and ignites victorious song deep within our hearts (Eph. 5:18–19).

E. Midianite oppression and deliverance by Gideon (6:1—8:35). Israel is now oppressed by several eastern peoples, led by the Midianites, who overrun Israel, plundering crops and livestock (6:1–5). A prophet reminds Israel of her past deliverances from oppressions and of her disobediences (7–10). God's special messenger appears to Gideon, who is stunned to hear that he has been chosen to deliver Israel. Gideon balks and offers two reasons: a dearth of miracles indicates that the Lord has forsaken Israel; Gideon himself is the least in the least tribe of Israel (11–15). After a sign from the Angel of the Lord, Gideon erects an altar to the Lord ("The-Lord-Is-Peace," Heb. *Yahweh Shalom*) and then tears down the city's altar to Baal (17–28). The city's angry reaction shows how completely Israel is polluted by idolatry (29–35; *see* Leadership, Spiritual).

> ### "The LORD said to him . . . tear down the altar of Baal"
>
> (6:25–32). This instruction to Gideon came from the Lord Himself. God, who said He would have no other gods before Him, will not tolerate the presence of idolatry in His children. Because God has such high purpose for each of His children, the Holy Spirit will orchestrate the destruction and removal of any false god or idol from their lives. The partnership of man with God at such moments spells certain defeat for Satan and advance for the kingdom.

> ### "But the Spirit of the LORD came upon Gideon"
>
> (6:34). In Hebrew this literally means "the Spirit of the Lord clothed Himself with Gideon." Gideon needed to be empowered by the Spirit so that he might win the battles that lay ahead of him. Today we need the Spirit's power (*see* Acts 1:8) and the armor of God *(see* Eph. 6:11–18) so that we might stand against the wiles of the devil (v. 11). Through the power of the Spirit, Gideon won every battle (Judges 7—8). Empowered by the Spirit, we can do the same.

Still unable to see himself as Israel's deliverer, Gideon proposes his famous series of tests with a wool fleece (6:36–40). Empowered by the Spirit, Gideon assembles an army to battle the sizable Midianite forces, but God reduces Gideon's ranks from thirty-two thousand to three hundred so that Israel cannot claim the glory for victory (7:1–8).

> ### "The sword of the LORD and of Gideon!"
>
> (7:9–23). While secretly exploring the camp of the Midianites with his companion, Gideon's faith increased as he overheard a Midianite soldier say, "This is nothing else but the sword of Gideon" (vv. 13–15). Gideon knew it was more than just his own sword: It was the sword of the Lord *and* of Gideon that would bring victory over the Midianites (v. 18). Today, as we use the sword of the Spirit—the Word of God—to meet daily challenges, our faith increases and we are victorious over the enemy *(see* Rom. 10:17; Eph. 6:17; Matt. 4:1–11).

Gideon and his men undertake a crafty night maneuver, and the enemy flees in terror (Judg. 7:15–25). Gideon's other victories are more deadly (8:1–21). Although the Israelites credit Gideon with victory and urge him to be their king, Gideon refuses because only "the LORD shall rule over" Israel (22–23; *see* Leadership, Spiritual). However, Gideon's act of erecting a golden ephod becomes a snare to his people (24–27), and Israel soon returns to her idolatrous Baal worship (33–35).

F. Brief reign of Abimelech (9:1–57). Gideon's son, Abimelech ("My father is king"), murders all of his brothers except Jotham and, with the aid of the citizens of Shechem, sets himself up as king (1–6). Jotham exposes Abimelech's worthlessness and predicts impending enmity between Abimelech and the Shechemites (7–20), a curse which comes to pass after only three years (22–57; *see* Leadership, Spiritual).

G. Tola's judgeship (10:1–2). The judgeships of Tola and the several other "minor" judges who succeed him seem to have been confined to maintaining and administering the Law in Israel.

H. Jair's judgeship (10:3–5). The judgeship of Jair, who was from Gilead (east of the Jordan), anticipates that of the next "major" judge, Jephthah, also from Gilead.

I. Ammonite oppression and deliverance by Jephthah (10:6–12:7). The people of Israel again forsake the Lord and serve many deities in addition to the Baals and Ashtoreths (10:6). Thus, "the *anger of the LORD was hot against Israel" (7), so hot that two formidable opponents, the Philistines and the Ammonites, oppress Israel for eighteen years (8). After the people of Israel cry out and confess their sin, God recalls to them past deliverances and declares that He will deliver them no more (10–15). The people are left to seek for themselves a deliverer, and they find one in the person of Jephthah, an illegitimate son of Gilead, who won a military reputation by leading a band of raiders outside Israel's settled area (11:1–3). Although Jephthah attempts a tactful diplomatic negotiation by presenting Israel's territorial claim to the king of Ammon (12–18), war is inevitable. Jephthah's vow reflects a tragic misunderstanding of God's ways, for His Law forbids human sacrifice (Deut. 12:31; 18:10).

> ### "Then the Spirit of the LORD came upon Jephthah"
>
> (11:29). Though despised and rejected by his family (vv. 1–2), Jephthah was not

rejected by God. Because Jephthah was leader of the Gileadites, the Spirit of the Lord came upon him, and he led his people to victory over the Ammonites (vv. 6, 29, 32). The Holy Spirit still uses the despised and insignificant today to accomplish His purposes (*see* 1 Cor. 1:26–31). As we are filled with the Spirit, we too can defeat the enemy who would try to take back that which Christ has gained for us (Judg. 11:13, 21–23; *see* John 10:10).

Jephthah's next opponent arises from within Israel: Civil war breaks out, and Jephthah must squelch the Ephraimite rebellion (12:1–7).

J. Ibzan's judgeship (12:8–10). Ibzan of Bethlehem, a man of wealth and status, judges Israel for seven years.

K. Elon's judgeship (12:11–12). Elon (from Zebulun) judges Israel for ten years.

L. Abdon's judgeship (12:13–15). Abdon, a man of wealth and status from Ephraim, judges Israel for eight years.

M. Philistine oppression and the exploits of Samson (13:1—16:31). Israel reenters a phase of sin, and God uses the Philistines to reprove His people. The Philistines, who arrive in Canaan during the invasion of the "Sea Peoples" around 1200 B.C., oppress Israel for forty years (and will be Israel's foe through the days of Saul and David). One reason for the Philistines' dominance is the superiority they maintained in weaponry (smelted from iron). The Lord raises up Samson, from the tribe of Dan, to deliver Israel. Set apart from birth for his divinely appointed mission (13:3–24; *see* Angels; Wondrous Thing [Did A]), Samson is endowed with amazing physical strength, but he remains morally weak. A slave to his physical appetites, Samson betrays his calling. He begins to compromise his Nazarite vow and the Law by desiring a Philistine wife (14:1–20); he violates his Nazarite vow by touching part of a dead animal, the jawbone of a donkey, to kill one thousand Philistines (15:15).

"Then the Spirit of the LORD came mightily upon him"
(15:14–15). Samson was freed from his restraints when the Spirit of the Lord came upon him (v. 14). Then, by the power of the Spirit, he was able to kill one thousand Philistines with the jawbone of a donkey (v. 15). Today, the Holy Spirit comes with power to free us from the restraints of fear, addictions, traumas caused by rejection or abuse, hurts caused by broken relationships, etc. Freed and empowered by the Spirit, we are then able to minister according to God's designs for us (*see* John 8:36; Rom. 8:2; 2 Cor. 3:17).

Samson is beguiled by Delilah (16:4–21), and God finally revokes his judgeship (20), whereupon the Philistines subdue him and blind him. God allows Samson one more feat of strength at a pagan temple (23–30).

"O Lord GOD, remember me, I pray!"
(16:25–30). The tragedy of this story is the disgrace that was brought through Samson; he did not finish well. Yet, in spite of his failures, he understood enough to call out to God for help. Dagon, the god of the Philistines, was being praised and, in essence, the God of Samson was being mocked. The story shows that wherever God can find a willing instrument, He will vindicate His name. In spiritual warfare, remember that God will be victorious regardless of how bad things seem to be.

Samson's individual victories disrupted Philistine dominance over Israel, but he never liberated Israel during his judgeship of twenty years.

III. EPILOGUE: CONDITIONS ILLUSTRATING THE PERIOD OF THE JUDGES 17:1—21:25. Two stories are appended to illustrate the consequences of Israel's apostasy and the anarchy that reigned when Israel turned from God. The first story tells of depravity in Israel's religious practices; the second, of immorality in one of Israel's tribes. Society crumbles when knowledge of God is corrupted.

A. Apostasy: The idolatry of Micah and the migration of the Danites (17:1—18:31). An Ephraimite named Micah steals silver from his mother, but returns it after hearing her curse. The mother dedicates the silver "to the LORD" to be made into an idol! Micah erects the idol in the family shrine, makes one of his sons priest, and then enlists a Levite as priest (17:1–13). Scouts from the small tribe of Dan pass Micah's house as they search for land to settle. Later, they return with their army, steal Micah's household gods, and offer the Levite a position as priest of the whole tribe. When

Micah complains, the Danites threaten him with death (18:1–31).

B. Immorality: The atrocity at Gibeah and the Benjamite War (19:1—21:25). A Levite from Ephraim chooses a concubine (a slave or mistress who is a secondary wife) from Bethlehem. During the course of a journey, the Levite refuses to stay in Jerusalem, which is still occupied by Jebusites. Refused hospitality by the Benjamites, the Levite and his party stay in Gibeah at the house of an old man, also from Ephraim. The house is surrounded by citizens who demand that the Levite be surrendered for homosexual rape (19:1–22). To avoid assault, the Levite gives his concubine to the "perverted men" (22), who rape her until she dies at dawn (23–26).

The twelve tribes of Israel are gathered to deal with the perpetrators of the atrocity, who were Benjamites (20:1–13). The Benjamites refuse to hand over the criminals, and this occasions a destructive civil war in which the Benjamites are nearly wiped out (14–48). When only six hundred men of Benjamin remain, the other tribes relent, lest one of the twelve tribes be destroyed (21:1–6).

Judges depicts Israel's political and spiritual decline as she deserts not only the moral and spiritual values upon which her life is based, but also her faith in God, upon which morality must ultimately rest. The next stage in Israel's history will see the emergence of a monarchy, in which one person is responsible to command obedience. The final verse (25) restates the apostate condition of Israel during the days in which "there was no king in Israel."

The Judges of Israel

© 1990 Thomas Nelson, Inc.

TRUTH-IN-ACTION through JUDGES

Truth Judges Teaches	**Action** Judges Invites
1 Guidelines for Growing in Godliness Judges emphasizes the necessity of trusting God's presence and divine resources rather than our own. Even those talents and abilities we have from birth are corrupted by sin and must be	**6:14, 16** *Believe* that God strengthens those He calls and commissions. *Trust* in the promise of His abiding presence **10:13, 14** *Heed God's warning: Do not* continue to *rely* upon your fleshly wisdom and ability lest God limit you to those resources rather than releasing His wisdom and power through you. *(continued)*

Truth Judges Teaches	**Action** Judges Invites
1 Guidelines for Growing in Godliness (continued) energized by the Holy Spirit to bear fruit for God.	
2 Keys to Wise Living Wisdom is knowing how to apply what you know to be true. Therefore, wisdom demands that you ascertain the Lord's direction and leadings for your life. Also, Judges warns against assuming that all leadings are true. Self-righteousness and religious sentiment can be a source of serious deception.	**6:36–40** *Test* and *confirm* any sense of divine leading. *Refuse* to move impulsively. *Be certain* of God's direction; it results in greater confidence. **17:3** *Know that* God rejects any idolatry, regardless how religious or sincere one's sentiment may be. *Be wary* of religious deception.
3 Steps to Dealing with Sin Sin presents a constant struggle with which we must deal or risk downfall. When we resist sin, we often feel the battle is over only to be tempted by the same sin again and again. Sin never goes away, and so we must constantly be on guard against it. However, even when we are overcome with sin, we have hope. God always gives another chance to turn from sin and back to Him.	**2:2, 3** *Understand* that sins not dealt with radically and ruthlessly ultimately weaken and may cause downfall. **14:17** *Persist* for victory in your struggle against sin. **16:4–22** *Guard* against the seductions of the world and the flesh. *Understand* that compromise will eventually weaken and wear you out, giving the Evil One an occasion to overpower you. **16:28** *Repent quickly* when overcome by sin. *Be confident* that God is faithful to honor all truly heartfelt repentance.
4 Lessons for Leaders Good leadership is a key to the triumph of God's purposes. Judges underlines the need for godly leaders who speak with prophetic, anointed voices. When there is a lack of such leadership among God's people, the people lead unrestrained lives guided by their own opinions rather than God's Word and godly wisdom.	**2:10–15** *Know* that a lack of godly leadership will cause God's people to become worldly and incur God's judgment. *Strive* to become godly in your leadership. **17:6; 18:1; 19:1; 21:25** *Pursue* a prophetic dimension in your ministry.
5 Key Lessons in Faith Faith sees beyond trials and obstacles, knowing that God is sovereign over such and uses them to shape us and strengthen us for future battles. Faith also relies on an ever-present God to bring the necessary answer and supply the present need.	**2:22; 3:2–4** *Accept* adversity and *welcome* opposition. *Believe* that God will use them to train you in obedience and strengthen you in spiritual warfare. **4:9** *Avoid* relying upon men due to a lack of confidence in God's presence. Faith in God honors Him and results in your receiving what He intends for you.
6 Steps in Developing Humility Judges stresses that humility is acknowledging that any good or righteous acts we accomplish result from God's working through us. We often think of humility as a weak self-abasement when, in fact, it is a bold confidence in a faithful God.	**7:1–8** *Understand* that God's spiritual victory does not depend upon natural strength or ability. *Rely totally* upon God's enablement and strength. **8:27** *Refuse* to build any monuments to your successes or victories. *Know* that they will likely become an occasion of stumbling for yourself and others.

KEYS TO RUTH
Redemption and the Kingdom

Kingdom Key: God's Purpose in View
This brief book presents one of the grandest displays of the redemptive ways of Salvation's King. Ruth reveals how redemption not only recovers loss, but how it also enriches individuals and enables them to advance God's kingdom plans despite their human limitations. Ruth's experience is a dramatic example of this:

- She is the recipient of unusual mercy. As a Gentile (Moabitess, 1:4), Ruth had no place in God's covenant, but her hunger for the Living God redeemed her (1:16; 2:12).

- She possesses a submitted spirit. Ruth's responsiveness to Boaz's gracious overtures and Naomi's practical guidance illustrate how believers are to yield to the Holy Spirit and submit to Christ (2:1—3:8).

- She receives a new potential. Boaz's actions as the kinsman-redeemer not only made Ruth one of the people of God, they afforded her a place of security, propriety, and fulfillment (3:9—4:12).

- She becomes an instrument of the kingdom to come. Ruth's divinely ordained place in the line of King David's ancestry, and thereby her place in the Messiah's line (4:13–22), illustrates how God uses those

whom He redeems to accomplish His purposes.

Ruth's mother-in-law provides us with a contrast between human presuppositions and faith. The Naomi of chapter 1 is an image of doubt born of blindness to God's true nature. The Naomi of chapters 2—4 reflects the faith born of a vision of the God who redeems our lost circumstances.

In Boaz we see a picture of Jesus as our Redeemer. Just as Boaz's literal relationship with the family at loss encourages his readiness to act, so Jesus coming as "the Word made flesh"—as one with us in our human condition—reveals His complete sensitivity to our need (see Heb. 4:14–16). He fully understands our pain and responds to our cry.

The Book of Ruth unveils the kingdom way by which we are brought *to* Christ, and by which the Holy Spirit acts to restore and

> **God can overthrow the difficulties into which we fall.**

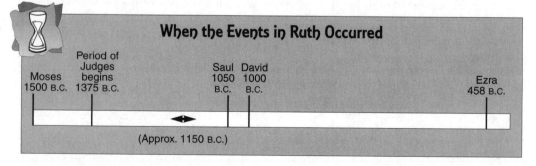

When the Events in Ruth Occurred

Moses 1500 B.C.	Period of Judges begins 1375 B.C.	Saul 1050 B.C.	David 1000 B.C.	Ezra 458 B.C.

(Approx. 1150 B.C.)

Ruth: God's redemption recovers loss and enables individuals

enrich our lives, making us avenues *through* which the kingdom is advanced—now and in the future.

Master Key: God's Son Revealed

Boaz is a memorable, dramatic figure in the Old Testament, one who foreshadows the redeeming work of Jesus Christ. By assuming the role of the "kinsman-redeemer," Boaz brings about Ruth's personal restoration. His actions bring about her enfranchisement in the blessings of Israel and bring her into the family line of the Messiah (Eph. 2:19). Here is a magnificent foreshadowing of Christ's redemptive grace centuries in advance. As our "Kinsman," Messiah becomes flesh—comes as a man (John 1:14; Phil. 2:5–8). Just as Boaz assumed responsibility for his family, Christ in His willingness to identify with the human family has redeemed us from our plight. Ruth's inability to do anything to alter her state typifies absolute human helplessness (Rom. 5:6); Boaz's willingness to pay the complete price (4:9) foreshadows Christ's full payment for our salvation (1 Cor. 6:20; Gal. 3:13; 1 Pet. 1:18–19).

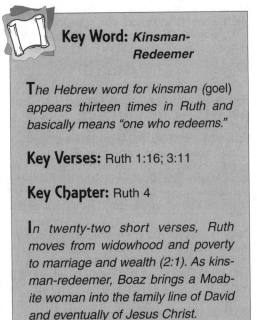

Key Word: *Kinsman-Redeemer*

The Hebrew word for kinsman (goel) appears thirteen times in Ruth and basically means "one who redeems."

Key Verses: Ruth 1:16; 3:11

Key Chapter: Ruth 4

In twenty-two short verses, Ruth moves from widowhood and poverty to marriage and wealth (2:1). As kinsman-redeemer, Boaz brings a Moabite woman into the family line of David and eventually of Jesus Christ.

Power Key: God's Spirit at Work

There is no direct reference to the Holy Spirit in this book. An interesting analogy to the Holy Spirit is suggested, however, by how Naomi expresses concern for Ruth as she guides her through the process of establishing a relationship with Boaz. Although Naomi's perception of God's dealings in her own life was limited, she nonetheless typifies the Holy Spirit's work in our lives. Naomi is seen as a gracious and tender woman who navigates great difficulties with an abiding fidelity. At the point of Ruth's first encounter with Boaz, Naomi's guidance may be seen as representative of the way in which the Holy Spirit prompts, directs, brings people to Christ (John 16:8; Rom. 2:4), and then leads them to experience God's blessing (John 16:13–15; Gal. 5:5, 16–18, 22–25).

A Distinguished Descendant

Even though Ruth was a Gentile, she became part of the family line which led to David and Jesus. More detailed genealogies appear in Ruth 4:18-22, Matthew 1:6-16, and Luke 3:32-38.

Boaz and Ruth ⟶ Obed ⟶ Jesse ⟶ David ⟶ Christ

to advance His plans despite human limitations.

Introducing
RUTH

Author and Date. Scholars differ regarding the date of the book's writing, but its historical setting is obvious. Ruth occurs during the period of the judges, as a part of those events that occur between the death of Joshua and the rise of Samuel's influence (probably between 1150 and 1100 B.C.).

Rabbinic tradition holds that Samuel wrote the book in the latter half of the eleventh century B.C. While more recent criticism suggests a much later postexilic date (about 500 B.C.), there is sufficient evidence in the language of the book, as well as its references to unique customs dating to the twelfth century B.C., to recommend acceptance of the earlier date. It is also reasonable to suppose that Samuel, who witnessed the decline of Saul's rule and was directed by God to anoint David as God's heir-apparent to the throne, could have penned this himself. The lovely story would already have attracted oral retelling among the people of Israel, and the concluding genealogy would have secured a link with the patriarchs—thus giving a ready answer to all in Israel who would desire their king's family background.

Purpose. Almost every commentator observes the Book of Ruth as a study in the sovereignty of God, emphasizing the sustaining mercy of God, which brings a fruitful end to a story that begins with famine, death, and loss. Unfortunately, such observations are often made on the basis of the recurrent laments of Naomi as she proposes "the hand of the LORD" as having been against her (1:13, 20–21). Twice, in her lamentations, Naomi uses the name "the Almighty" with reference to God, emphasizing His irresistible might and sovereign power against her. However, it is not necessary to presume that Naomi's viewpoint is meant to be understood as a spiritual revelation intended as doctrine. Rather, her words are perhaps best understood as the historical record of what she said in her bewilderment.

This adjustment in viewing her words seems pivotal to a sound understanding. It does not seem consistent with the revelation of the whole of the Scripture and its disclosure of the nature of God to presume that the disastrous things in this book were either intended or initiated by God. The famine (1:1) was the natural by-product of sin, a judgment imposed by the people upon themselves through their disobedience. The Lord had previously warned that the land itself would turn against them if they were unfaithful to Him (Deut. 28:15–16,

23–24, 38–40). Further, Elimelech's choice to move his family to the country of Moab (1:2) is not evidenced as being God's direction but simply his own decision. Why suggest that the events that follow (his and his sons' deaths) are something of God's direct providence? There is more reason to propose that these unfortunate happenings, while not outside God's omniscience, are not direct divine judgments, but rather the natural result of exposure to circumstances outside the canopy of divine promise. God's protective canopy is to those who remain obedient to Him in the land of His appointment.

Naomi, therefore, represents more of a folklore theology. Though obviously a sincere and believing woman, she nonetheless reveals vulnerability to the practice common throughout history—the blaming or assigning to God's will those things that steal away, kill, and destroy His people and over which unaided mankind has no power. But the revelation of the *whole* of Scripture shows that such besetting events are not directly brought by God on people. Instead, these are either (1) the fruit of the general curse resulting from man's fall; (2) the product of the flesh when having given place to its own will, however innocent or malicious the intent; or (3) the direct and assailing efforts of our adversary, the devil (John 10:10).

That Ruth is a book demonstrating the sovereignty of God is not minimized by these observations; rather, what is underscored is the objective of God's sovereign grace and power. His almightiness is not revealed as man's opponent but rather as man's deliverer. He overthrows the restrictive or damning difficulties or devices into which we fall as the result of our sin, the flesh, or the devil.

Content. Johann Wolfgang von Goethe, the German writer-poet, described Ruth as "the loveliest complete work on a small scale." This poignant, fascinating, emotionally gripping, and historically significant narrative might be called the Crown Jewel of the Old Testament. Herein is not only a literary masterpiece, but a record of the genealogy of David, the crowned king of Israel appointed by God to sire the line leading to the Messiah's royal and endless rule.

Personal Application. The messages of Ruth transcend the immediately obvious purpose of providing King David's genealogy. Ruth presents several grand themes which merit exploration and elaboration. (1) The Book of Ruth introduces the *universal* scope of redemption's purposes. The inclusion of the Moabitess, Ruth, as a Gentile participant in Israel's kingly line pictures God's love as it reaches out to all the nations of the world. He not only incorporates Gentiles in His salvation, but employs non-Jewish people as instruments in His redemptive program. Ruth's message dissolves tendencies toward exclusivism, whether potential in Israel at that time or realized in any group's traditions in our time. (2) The Book of Ruth ennobles the beauty of *commitment and friendship* and underscores the values of family commitment. Both values are obviously important and need to be reinforced in our time. Ruth's acceptance of her daughter-servant role under the aging Naomi, Naomi's preoccupation with Ruth's best interest, and Boaz's self-effacing will to see the endowment of a foreign maid with what will bring her a promising future, all are worthy of examination in this regard.

(3) Ruth is a book of glorious *redemptive imagery.* The principle God proposed through the tradition of the levirate marriage (Deut. 25:5–10) dramatically reveals His intent that human loss always be recoverable and that we are to work with Him in extending such possibilities to those in need. While technically speaking no levirate marriage occurs in the Book of Ruth, this principle motivates Boaz's actions and illustrates the Spirit of God's redemptive ways.

Surveying
RUTH

I. A HEBREW FAMILY IN MOAB 1:1–22.
Ruth provides important balance to the dreary picture of decline drawn in Judges 17—21. Here we see that there are still pockets of faith in Israel; that in spite of general apostasy, some still live out God's Law. The conversion of Ruth the Moabitess to the God of Israel shows what might have been, had all Israel wholly followed the Lord. (*See* Women.)

A. Naomi's heartbreak (1:1–5). When a famine strikes Israel, the family of Elimelech and Naomi move to Moab. There, in violation of Mosaic Law, their two sons marry Moabite women. There too the father and sons die.

B. Ruth's devotion and vow (1:6–18). Ruth refuses to leave her mother-in-law. (*See* People.)

C. Return to Bethlehem (1:19–22). When Naomi hears that the Lord is again blessing Israel, she decides to return with Ruth.

II. A HUMBLE GLEANER 2:1–23.

A. Ruth in the field of Boaz (2:1–3). The two women have no means of support, so Ruth goes into the fields during the harvest season to glean. Mosaic Law requires that the poor be permitted to follow the harvesters and gather grain that falls to the ground when the sheaves are gathered up (Deut. 24:19–21).

B. Boaz's provision and protection (2:4–17). Boaz notices the young woman. Knowing of her faithfulness to Naomi and good reputation (11–12), he tells her to return to his fields and promises her protection (9). Privately Boaz tells his workers to leave some stalks in the fields for her to find.

C. God's favor recognized by Naomi (2:18–23). Naomi urges Ruth to return to Boaz's fields. One reason—a grim reminder of the moral condition of Israel—is that she feels Ruth will be relatively safe from being assaulted there.

But Naomi has another reason. Boaz is a relative of her family, and thus a potential "kinsman-redeemer." This phrase refers to a provision of Old Testament Law especially for women whose husbands die and leave them childless. To preserve the family line and the family land, a relative is permitted to marry the widow. The first boy will be counted as son of the dead husband, and the line will thus be preserved.

III. A PLANNED MARRIAGE 3:1–18.

A. Naomi's instruction (3:1–5).

B. Ruth's obedience (3:6–13). Ruth's request in 3:9 is no invitation to an immoral relationship; it is an appeal to Boaz to marry her and perform the duty of a kinsman-redeemer.

> **"You have shown more kindness at the end than at the beginning"**
> (3:10–11). Ruth willingly places herself under Boaz's protection, her near kinsman, allowing for the redemption of her deceased husband's inheritance and the securing of her future. Her act of kindness (Hebrew *chesed*, also "covenant faithfulness") is faithfulness-in-action, flowing from a commitment to Yahweh (1:16). It becomes the basis of her submission to Naomi's instructions and the key to personal redemption. By remaining faithfully committed to our relationships with one another and our covenant relationship
> *continued on next page*

continued from preceding page
with the Lord, the Spirit can lead us to perform many acts of kindness—whereby we posture ourselves for His redemption and blessing.

C. Reward of obedience (3:14–18). Boaz promises to resolve Ruth's situation.

IV. A KINSMAN-REDEEMER 4:1–22.

A. Boaz, God's chosen redeemer (4:1–12). Boaz is willing to exercise his responsibility, but there is a nearer relative, who has prior claim. When the nearer relation realizes that taking over the land of the deceased (2–4) will also mean marrying Ruth, he surrenders his claim to Boaz (5–6). This transaction, witnessed by the city elders, is concluded by taking off a sandal and passing it to Boaz. Archaeology has corroborated this way of concluding a contract. Boaz immediately announces his intention to take Ruth as his wife and guard the land for her offspring.

B. The marriage of Boaz to Ruth (4:13).

C. God's blessing upon Naomi (4:14–17). The first son of Ruth and Boaz, Obed, is raised by Naomi as her own. (*See* Restore.)

D. The genealogy of David (4:18–22). Obed becomes the grandfather of David, Israel's greatest king.

TRUTH-IN-ACTION through RUTH

Truth Ruth Teaches	**Action** Ruth Invites
1 Keys to Godly Relationships Ruth is replete with principles of righteous and godly relationships. Ruth is a supreme example of someone who prioritizes personal relationships. She exemplifies loyalty, servanthood, diligence, and moral righteousness. Much grief can be avoided when we learn to relate to one another in love and understand what this really implies about our relationships.	**1:10** *Do not* make commitments too hastily. *Wait* until you understand the full implications of any commitment you make to another. **1:16** *Practice* loyalty, and *understand* that a loyal person prioritizes his relationships over personal advantage or comfort. *Do not back out* of a commitment you make to a friend, even if it means personal sacrifice. **2:2** *Learn* servanthood. *Know* that God calls us to serve those we love. *Believe* that God will honor those with a servant's heart.
2 Guidelines for Growing in Godliness Hospitality means showing kindness and generosity to strangers. Most will treat friends well, but godly persons treat strangers as they would treat friends.	**2:8** *Practice* hospitality to strangers. *Do not withhold* blessings from those unfamiliar to you. *Know* that God rewards and honors such unselfishness.
3 Keys to Relating to Authority Proper relationship to authority is characteristic of godly people. Faithful, loving obedience is a key characteristic of such a right response to authority.	**3:5** *Obey* legitimate authority. *Believe* that God will bless such obedience in ways you cannot expect.

KEYS TO 1 SAMUEL
Carnality and the Kingdom

Kingdom Key: God's Purpose in View

The establishment of the monarchy, with Saul being anointed as Israel's first king (chs. 8—12), begins an era from which we can draw dramatic lessons concerning the kingdom of God as revealed in Scripture. The essence of the "kingdom" concept—that God's redemptive plan intends both (1) the rescue of man from sin's penalty, and (2) the restoration of man's role as a ruler-in-life under God—is thoroughly illustrated throughout this Bible history.

Saul's beginnings as king indicate "what might be" when an individual receives the Spirit's anointing for serving God's purpose in His power: (1) See how privilege is offered to a person given rule over a specific section of God's larger realm, a person who participates in an inheritance (10:1); and (2) see how the Holy Spirit enables and equips a person for the task of "kingdom" rule (10:6–12). In Saul, we see at his outset how a humble candidate for "kingdom" life (10:21–22) may be given God-ordained assistance (10:26) and is promised God's blessing (12:13–14).

However, this finest of beginnings rapidly and tragically dissolves to the worst imaginable outcome. The history of Saul's rule becomes an awesome warning of the disastrous results which ensue when carnality dominates the soul of a per-

> Men look on outward appearances, but God looks on the heart.

son whom God intended to serve His high "kingdom" purpose. As ones "seated" to rule with Christ (Eph. 2:6), we would do well to learn from Saul. When Saul indulges his self-will, Samuel has to announce that what might have been can no longer be (13:13–14). The lessons for today's "kingdom" people are obvious: Let us take warning from Saul's (1) violation of obedient worship before God (13:9–11); (2) his motivation by a self-defending, self-promoting spirit (13:3–8); and (3) his outright self-serving disobedience (15:1–10). The consequence for Saul was God's outright rejection of his privileged rule. Saul eventually lost his kingdom (15:10–28) when his carnal ways led to murderous jealousy and consorting with demons (28:3–25). The story of David's rise and response (chs. 16—31) provides a *(Please turn to page 68.)*

When the Events in First Samuel Occurred

Moses	Period of Judges begins	Samuel born	Death of Saul David anointed		Ezra
1500 B.C.	1375 B.C.	1150 B.C.	1010 B.C.		458 B.C.

First Samuel shows God at work in Israel's transition • • •

Kingdom Key *continued from page 67*

contrast to Saul's violation of the terms of "kingdom dominion." This story continues into 2 Samuel and tells of how David learned to be a responsible ruler.

Master Key: God's Son Revealed

The similarities between the boy Jesus and the boy Samuel are striking. Both were children of promise. Both were dedicated to God before birth. Both were the bridges of transition from one stage in Israel's history to another. Samuel combined the offices of prophet and priest; Christ is Prophet, Priest, and King.

The tragic end of Saul illustrates the ultimate end of earthly kingdoms. The only hope is a kingdom of God on earth, ruled by God Himself. In David, an earthly king, the lineage of God's King begins. In Christ, God comes as King, and He will come again as King of kings.

David, the simple shepherd boy, prefigures Christ, the Good Shepherd. Jesus becomes the ultimate Shepherd-King.

Power Key: God's Spirit at Work

First Samuel contains remarkable instances of the coming of the Holy Spirit. The Spirit comes upon the prophets, as well as upon Saul and his servants. The Holy Spirit comes upon Saul (10:6), who prophesies and is "turned into another man," that is, he is equipped by the Spirit to fulfill God's calling.

> ### Key Word: *Transition*
>
> **F**irst Samuel records the critical transition in Israel from the rule of God through the judges to His rule through the kings.
>
> ### Key Verses: First Samuel 13:14; 15:22
> ### Key Chapter: First Samuel 15
>
> **F**irst Samuel 15 records the tragic transition of kingship from Saul to David.

After David is anointed by Samuel, "the Spirit of the LORD came upon David from that day forward" (16:13).

The phenomenon of the Spirit inspiring worship occurs in chapter 10 and again in 19:20. This was not the emotionalized raving of the pagans; it was true, Spirit-inspired worship and praise of God, not unlike what happened on the Day of Pentecost (Acts 2).

In the uses of the ephod, and the Urim, and the Thummim, we look forward to the time when the "Spirit of truth" will guide us into "all truth," tell us of "things to come," and "take of what is Mine [Jesus'] and declare it to you" (John 16:13–14).

• • • from a theocracy to an earthly kingdom.

Introducing

1 SAMUEL

Author. The author of 1 Samuel is not named in this book, but it is likely that Samuel either wrote or supplied the information for 1:1—25:1, which covers his life and ministry until his death. (*See* map, page 184.) The authorship of the rest of 1 Samuel cannot certainly be determined, but some suppose that Abiathar the priest wrote it.

Date. Because of the references to the city of Ziklag, which "has belonged to the kings of Judah to this day" (27:6) and other references to Judah and Israel, we know that it was written after the division of the nation in 931 B.C. Also, since there is no mention of the fall of Samaria in 722 B.C., it should be dated before this event. The Book of 1 Samuel covers a period of about 140 years, beginning with the birth of Samuel at about 1150 B.C., and ending with the death of Saul at about 1010 B.C.

Content. Israel had been governed by judges whom God raised up at crucial times in the nation's history; however, the nation had degenerated both morally and politically. It had been under the merciless onslaught of the Philistines. The temple at Shiloh had been desecrated and the priesthood is corrupt and immoral. Into this religious and political confusion steps Samuel, the miraculous son of Hannah. In a remarkable way the renewal and joy that his birth brought to his mother prefigures the same for the nation.

Samuel's own sons do not share his godly character. The people do not have confidence in his sons' abilities; as Samuel grows old, they press him to give them a king. Reluctantly, he does so. Saul, a handsome and charismatic man, is chosen to become Israel's first king. His ego is as large as his stature. He impatiently steps into the office of priest, rather than wait for Samuel. After rejecting God's commands, he is rejected by God. After this rejection Saul becomes a tragic figure, consumed with jealousy and fear, gradually losing his sanity. His final years are spent relentlessly chasing David through the wilderness backcountry of his kingdom in an effort to kill him. David, however, has found an ally in Saul's son, Jonathan, who warns David of his father's plots to kill him. Ultimately, when both Saul and Jonathan are killed in battle, the stage is set for David to become the second king of Israel.

Personal Application. It is clear in 1 Samuel that God is at work in history. Even the most sinful and rebellious occurrences can be used by Him to continue His divine plan. The corruption of Eli's sons and his unwillingness to deal with them becomes the schooling environment for the child Samuel. The rejection of God and the demand for a king by Israel become the basis for the establishment of an earthly royal line that will bring forth the entrance of God into human history in the person of the Messiah. Finally, Saul, who had such a wonderful beginning, ends his life in tragedy and suicide. Yet, because of Saul's insanity, David is brought from the sheepfold into the courts of the king. Saul's senseless jealousy and enraged pursuit of David provide the backdrop against which the greatest king of Israel, the "man after God's own heart," comes to the throne.

But it is not only in the broad sweeps of history that God's hand is obvious. The following lessons are also evident in 1 Samuel. God steps into the pain and misery of Hannah to give her, not only a son, but three sons and two daughters (2:21). Though men look on the outward appearance, God looks on the heart (16:7). Obedience is better than sacrifice (15:22–23), indicating that God is concerned about men's hearts as well as their actions. God does not spare even those in high position when they have sinned, but He is still a God of patience and forgiveness.

Surveying

1 SAMUEL

I. RENEWAL UNDER SAMUEL 1:1—7:17.

A. Birth and childhood of Samuel (1:1—2:36).

1. Birth and dedication of Samuel (1:1—2:11). During one of Elkanah's times of service in the tabernacle, his childless wife, Hannah, vows to dedicate her first child to the Lord if only God opens her womb (1:11). This prayer is answered. Hannah has a son, who is named Samuel ("heard by God"). When Samuel is weaned at three, he is brought to Shiloh to the resident high priest, Eli. There Samuel is to serve the Lord at the tabernacle "his whole life."

2. Growth of Samuel and the corruption of Eli's sons (2:12–36). Eli's two sons, who carry on the worship rituals, are "wicked men" (12). Their immorality is a known scandal, as is their contempt for the worship regulations they are supposed to follow. Young Samuel's character stands in marked contrast to these adults among whom he grows up.

Judgment prophesied (2:27–36). A curse is placed on Eli's line, but God will raise up a man who will be faithful to all that is in God's heart and mind.

B. Beginning of Samuel's prophetic ministry (3:1—4:1).

1. *His call from God (3:1–9).*

2. *His word for Eli (3:10–18).* The prophecy against Eli's family is confirmed when the Lord speaks directly to Samuel (11).

3. *His ministry to all Israel (3:19—4:1).* As Samuel matures he is widely recognized as a *prophet, for the Lord "let none of his words fall to the ground."

C. Samuel's ministry as judge (4:2—7:17).

1. *The capture of the ark by the Philistines (4:2–11).* This battle against the Philistines is fought in two phases. After an initial defeat, the Israelites send to Shiloh for the ark of God. It is supposed to stay in the tabernacle, but now is superstitiously brought to the battleground. In the second phase of the battle Israel suffers a crushing defeat and the ark of God is captured.

2. *Death of Eli (4:12–22).* Eli's two evil sons die in the battle. When Eli hears, he falls and breaks his neck. The death of this man, who has led Israel for forty years, plus the capture of the ark, completely demoralizes the Israelites (21–22) and ends organized resistance to the Philistines.

3. *Recovery of the ark by Israel (5:1—7:1).* The people of the ancient world credited victories to the superiority of their gods over the gods of the enemy. The Philistines make this mistake, and view the Lord as a defeated enemy. But when their god is found face down before the ark and the people begin to suffer a plague of tumors, they begin to fear. In panic the Philistines return the ark to the Israelites.

4. *Samuel's call for repentance (7:2–6).* In the two decades since the defeat at Aphek, Samuel has become Israel's acknowledged leader. He also has moved the people to a fresh commitment to God (3–4).

5. *Defeat of the Philistines (7:7–17).* When all Israel gathers at Mizpah for fasting and commitment, the Philistines attack, seeking to break up what they view as a dangerous unity movement in the subjugated people. The Philistines are fought and defeated, as the Lord battles for Israel (10–12).

II. THE REIGN OF SAUL 8:1—15:35.

A. Saul's establishment as king (8:1—12:25).

1. *Israel's demand for a king (8:1–22).* When Samuel is old, the elders of Israel come to him and demand a king. Samuel takes this as a personal affront, but the people are really rejecting God, Israel's true ruler (7). Samuel tries to warn Israel of the disadvantages of an absolute ruler (10–18), but the people will not listen.

2. *Saul chosen and anointed as king (9:1—12:25).* Saul meets Samuel while searching for lost donkeys. God identifies him to the prophet (*see* Seer) as the chosen king (9:16–17). The humble Saul is stunned when Samuel honors him, and then anoints him with oil (9:18—10:1). The detailed prediction of what will happen on Saul's way home is important: it confirms to Saul that Samuel does speak for God in this call to the kingship (10:2–13).

"Then the Spirit of God came upon him, and he prophesied among them"
(10:5–11). In this situation, Saul is moved by the Spirit of God to prophesy. Given the severe consequences of being identified as a false prophet in the Old Testament, for one to speak prophetically would require a definite move of God's Spirit. Saul did not function in the office of a prophet, though as Israel's leader and king, he might have served the nation better if he had. This incident seems to establish that God was willing to give the gift to Saul for such a purpose.

Saul proclaimed and confirmed (10:14–25). Saul is presented to the people by Samuel as God's choice for king. When the Ammonites besiege Jabesh Gilead, Saul calls Israel out, and falls on the enemy camp at dawn (11:1–11). The total victory won firmly establishes Saul in his office (11:12–15).

"Then the Spirit of God came upon Saul"
(11:6–7). When Saul learned of the Ammonite's inhuman threat to the inhabitants of Jabesh Gilead, the Spirit of God came upon him, and he became angry (vv. 1–6). He mustered an army of 300,000 with which he went out and destroyed the enemy forces (vv. 8, 11). No matter how great the enemy's threat against the church today, when God's people unite and move under Spirit-empowered leadership, the church will defeat the enemy and realize the victory (2 Cor. 10:4).

Samuel's farewell speech (12:1–25). Samuel is now ready to withdraw completely from leadership. In a last great oration he warns Israel against turning from God.

B. Saul's wars (13:1—14:52). Saul ruled in Israel for two years (13:1), but soon he began to demonstrate serious flaws, which led to his rejection by God.

Fear (13:1–22). Early in Saul's reign, a skirmish with the Philistines at Geba leads to a major invasion. The Israelites are terrified at the size of the forces that come against them. Saul is at Gilgal, sent there by Samuel with instructions to wait for him seven days. Then the aged prophet and priest will come to pray for victory.

As his forces dwindle, a desperate Saul determines to offer up the sacrifice himself, an act forbidden to anyone who is not a priest. Samuel appears just as the sacrifice is finished. Furious, he tells Saul that God will not permit a son of his to inherit the throne.

Battle won (14:1–52).

C. Saul's rejection by God (15:1–35). God's rejection of Saul is confirmed as the king again disobeys. Sent to destroy an ancient enemy, Saul permits the people to keep the best of the cattle for themselves and destroys only what is worthless. Samuel confronts Saul and announces God's judgment.

III. SAUL'S DECLINE AND DAVID'S RISE 16:1—31:13.

A. David's increasing prominence (16:1—17:58).

1. His anointing by Samuel (16:1–13). Samuel is now sent to Bethlehem to make a sacrifice with the hidden purpose of anointing another to replace Saul on the throne (1). The youngest son of a man named Jesse is selected, and David is anointed with oil in a private family ceremony.

> **"The Spirit of the LORD came upon David"**
> (16:13). This was the first of three anointings David experienced. The second was as king over Judah (*see* 2 Sam. 2:4), and the third as king over all Israel (*see* 5:3). At his first anointing the Spirit came upon David to equip him and direct him in the details of his life and rulership. In like manner, the Spirit who abides in us anoints us today, teaching, equipping, and directing in the details of our lives and ministries (*see* Acts 11:12; 16:6–7; 1 Cor. 12:7–11; 1 John 2:27).

2. His singing before Saul (16:14–23). Saul's

emotional instability now expresses itself in deep depressions (14–15). David is recommended to help him, and comes to Gibeah to play his harp. This brings Saul some relief (23). David is liked and given the honor of serving as one of Saul's armor bearers.

> **"David would take a harp and play it . . . then Saul would become refreshed and well, and the distressing spirit would depart from him"**
> (16:22–23). The profound impact of music as an instrument of spiritual warfare is demonstrated in this passage. David made this declaration for his own life in Psalm 32. Incorporating worship in song as a part of warfare will both drive back the enemy and invigorate the believer's soul.

3. His defeat of Goliath (17:1–58). The Philistines again assemble an invasion army. But now they send a giant warrior, over nine feet tall, with a challenge to single combat.

David, apparently still too young to serve in combat, visits the army with food from home for his brothers. He is shocked that no one will face this pagan who defies "the armies of the living God" (26). When someone reports David's reaction, he is called before Saul. There David volunteers to fight Goliath himself. David's faith in God is well founded. He kills the giant with his shepherd's sling, and the demoralized Philistines flee.

> **"I come to you in the name of the LORD of hosts, the God of the armies of Israel . . . this day the LORD will deliver you into my hand"**
> (17:38–51). With great faith in our Lord we can meet any challenge with courage, even in the face of insurmountable odds. David was skilled in the use of the sling but his trust was in the Lord, who had shown David His delivering power during past crises (vv. 34–37). The "good fight of faith" (1 Tim. 6:12) entails a bold yet balanced approach to life's challenges: As human abilities are made available to the Lord, He empowers those who completely trust Him and works great exploits for His kingdom.

B. Saul's decreasing influence (18:1—31:13).

1. Saul's persecution of David (18:1—27:12). David is rewarded with a military position. For a decade David carries out all his duties so successfully that he advances rapidly (5). Saul becomes jealous of David's success and popularity (8–9). Recognizing that the Lord is with David, Saul begins to fear him (12–16, 28–29). These emotions harden to implacable enmity. Saul now determines to kill David, who has become his son-in-law. After some ten years in Saul's court, David is forced to flee for his life (19:14–21).

David and Saul's son Jonathan are now close friends. Back in Gibeah, Jonathan angrily confronts his father, then carries a warning to David. The two swear everlasting friendship in the Lord's name, and each makes a commitment to care for the other's descendants (20:42), whichever of them survives.

David now faces a jolting change in status (*see* chs. 21—30). For a decade he has been a respected military hero. Suddenly he is a lone fugitive.

David and the priests (21:1–9; 22:1–23). David flees, weaponless and hungry, to Nob, where the tabernacle rests. There Ahimelech, the priest, assuming David is on a mission for Saul, gives him food and a sword. Later an Edomite, Doeg, informs Saul that the priest has helped his enemy. In spite of Ahimelech's protests of innocence, Saul puts him and eighty-five other priests, with their families, to death. Psalm 52 and possibly 53 were written by David out of this tragic experience.

David flees to Gath (21:10–15). David has only two choices: he can find a hiding place in Israel, or leave the country. At first David goes to Philistia, where he is recognized. Afraid for his life, David pretends madness. Psalms 56 and 34 flow from this experience, revealing David's inner torment.

David at Adullam (22:1–5). David returns to Israel and hides in a cave about fifteen miles from his Bethlehem home. He is joined by his family and others alienated by Saul's increasingly erratic behavior. Psalm 142 shares David's thoughts at this time.

David saves Keilah, and is betrayed (23:1–29). David's emotions at this betrayal are shared in Psalm 54.

David twice spares Saul's life (24:1—26:25). Now Saul dedicates himself to hunting David down. On two occasions David has the opportunity to kill Saul—but will not. God has made Saul king. David will not lift his hand against God's anointed, even though his own life is threatened. The story of David and Abigail (25:1–44) is related here.

Even though David made the godly choice in refusing to touch Saul, he is deeply discouraged, as Psalm 57 reveals.

David's despair (27:1–12). David leads his men back to Philistia. There he enlists as a mercenary soldier with Achish, the king of Gath. He is given the town of Ziklag.

2. Saul's visit to a medium (28:1–25). As the Philistines assemble to fight against Israel, Saul looks desperately for help. Samuel has died, but Saul goes to a spiritualist and demands she contact the dead prophet. The woman is amazed when Samuel actually does appear (12–14). Samuel announces that Saul and his three sons will be killed in the battle the next day and that Israel will be defeated.

3. David's conflicts with the Philistines and the Amalekites (29:1—30:31). David and his men raid Israel's old enemies, but mislead Achish, who believes that they are raiding southern Israel. When war again threatens between Israel and the Philistines, the rulers of the other plains cities will not trust David among their forces. He is sent back to Ziklag, where he discovers that his own town has been raided and stripped by Amalekites (30:1–2). David pursues, and thus is far away when the decisive battle between Israel and the Philistines is fought.

4. Saul's death (31:1–13). In that battle, Saul is struck by an enemy arrow and wounded. To avoid being taken alive, Saul falls on his own sword and dies. The tragic rule of Saul has ended at last.

TRUTH-IN-ACTION through 1 SAMUEL

Truth 1 Samuel Teaches	**Action** 1 Samuel Invites
1 Guidelines for Growing in Godliness As parents, we have much to do with our children's destiny. Give them over to God's purposes and continue to train them to become fruitful in godly living.	**8:3ff.** *Raise* godly children. *Understand* that a failure to do so can result in greater ungodliness. **1:22, 28** *Dedicate* your children to the Lord. *Remember* that they are an inheritance and gift from the Lord.

Truth 1 Samuel Teaches	**Action** 1 Samuel Invites
2 Steps to Holiness Holiness is saying "No!" to the world and its expectations and "Yes!" to God.	**10:19** *Rely upon* God's wisdom, strength, and ingenuity rather than that of people.
3 Key Lessons in Faith Belief results in obedience; what we practice provides evidence of our faith. Faith is not merely a propositional affirmation. It determines action, produces obedience, and through overcoming, becomes fruitful.	**3:10** *Be ready to obey* the words the Lord speaks to you. *Know* that God only continues to speak to those who do what He says. **15:8–35** *Understand* that incomplete obedience is the same as disobedience. *Obey the Lord completely* and do not turn away from Him. **15:22, 23** *Do not substitute* religion for obedience to God's Word. *Know* that disobedience and rebellion are as witchcraft in God's sight. *Understand* that to hear God's Word and not to practice it (obey) is to reject it. **17:45–50** *Do not fear* opposition even when it seems stronger or better supported. *Be assured* that God can use your minimal resources, when accompanied by great faith, to overcome whatever obstacles you face.
4 Keys to Wise Living Wisdom is in large measure understanding the principles by which God governs the moral universe. To gain wisdom means to learn to think God's thoughts after Him, esteeming the things He esteems and despising the things He despises. Learning wisdom is gaining the perspective that results from adopting God's values and rejecting the values this world espouses.	**8:22** *Be aware* that if you persist in ungodly or unwise prayer, God may give you what you ask as a form of discipline, which would have been unnecessary otherwise. **14:6** *Do not overvalue* size. *Remember,* the Lord accomplishes great things through small numbers. **16:7** *Know* that God looks on the heart, not the outward appearance. *Do not judge* based upon what you see. **17:34–37** *Do not despise* small opportunities. *Understand* that they prepare us for bigger battles.
5 Keys to Relating to Authority Learning to relate properly to God-ordained authority is an important part of spiritual maturity. Because our nature is sinful—in rebellion against God—we do not automatically know how to relate properly to authority. It is something we must be trained in and something for which we will experience much discipline from the Lord.	**8:7, 8** *Receive* God-appointed authority, but *do not honor them above* God or His Word. *Know* that to do so is idolatry. **14:7** *Practice loyalty* to God-appointed leaders in order to enhance their effectiveness on your behalf. **24:6–22; 26:9–25** *Do not speak against* or take up a cause against God-ordained leaders even if they seem to be wrong. *Leave* them to God's judgment and *intercede* for them. Each one of us must answer to God for our actions.
6 Lessons for Leaders Spiritual leadership differs radically from this world's ideas about how to lead. God's leaders must realize that they represent Him in their role, since He has given them their authority. In order to honor God, His servants must be faithful both to Him and to His people.	**12:23** Leaders, *pray* for those whom you lead. Not to do so is to sin against God. **13:13, 14** Leaders, *do not act presumptuously.* Obedience will establish your authority. **22:2** Leaders, *do not despise* anyone the Lord brings to you. God is able to raise up even the lowliest through godly leadership. **30:23–31** Leaders, *honor all ministry equally.* Those who support others are equally important to God.
7 Steps to Dealing with Sin Sin must be dealt with or it will become our downfall.	**3:13** *Understand* that God holds us accountable for sins we know about but do not confront as we are able.
8 How to Tame the Tongue Taming the tongue involves knowing that things you should not say to men may often be said to God.	**1:7, 10–16** *Voice* any complaints *only* to the Lord. *Remember* that vindication comes only from the Lord.

KEYS TO 2 SAMUEL
Humility and the Kingdom

Kingdom Key: God's Purpose in View

David first appears in Scripture (1 Samuel 16) as both chosen and anointed for God-ordained rule (vv. 1, 3, 13). From the outset of God's dealings with David, he shines as a man after God's own heart (1 Sam. 13:14). The hallmark of David's character is humility, a trait recurrently manifest in his unpresumptuous behavior during the concluding days of Saul's reign. Though David was preferred by God, he deferred to Saul (1 Sam. 24:10) and honored the anointing of God's Spirit which had once rested upon the failing leader. Even at Saul's death, David humbly honors the fallen king, rather than revelling in the demise of his adversary or the opportunity this gave him to assume the throne (2 Samuel 1; also see 9:1–13).

See how even in his struggles against his adversaries, David reveres God's justice, and he never exalts himself (chs. 2—4). See how he waits on the Lord for timing and direction in his actions (5:22–25, etc.). Since David's *passion* for God clearly puts the *worship* of God above all else, he seeks *God's* enthronement in Jerusalem beyond his own (ch. 6). Note the humility and childlike quality of David's praise to God as the ark is returned (6:13–23), as well as David's humble amazement at God's covenant with him, which promises that the Messiah will be of his seed (7:1–29). Even in his drastic failure (chs. 11—12), David humbly accepts rebuke, seeks the Lord, and yields to the prophet's word and the law of God (*see* also

Humility is a hallmark of godly character.

Psalm 51). Further, when he is assailed by his own son, and as mockers join the attack (chs. 15—16), David appeals to the Lord for justice rather than seeking to vindicate himself. This is the *heart* of kingdom rulership: a heart to love God and to serve people, a heart which refrains from self-exaltation even though God has chosen to ennoble and advance his or her lot.

When we assess the grace of humility demonstrated so consistently in David's life, we must look for the source of this quality. David's brokenness before God results from (1) his consciousness of personal failure and (2) a sensitivity gained through communion with the Almighty. Regular fellowship with God has caused

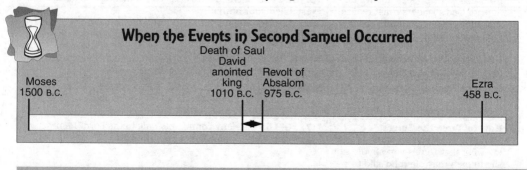

When the Events in Second Samuel Occurred

	Death of Saul / David anointed king	Revolt of Absalom	
Moses 1500 B.C.	1010 B.C.	975 B.C.	Ezra 458 B.C.

In 2 Samuel David learns to be a responsible

him to develop a finely tuned awareness of God's greatness and holiness.

David's humility also grows out of his abiding commitment to worship as a lifestyle. Those who would learn this kingdom quality must worship, like David, in a way that transcends mere formality and moves into deep, personal openness before God and high praise in His presence. David models worship characterized by a constant transparency before the Lord and a sincere, childlike abandon marked by free expressions of joy and awe.

Master Key: God's Son Revealed

David and his reign point toward the coming of the Messiah. Chapter 7 especially anticipates the future King. God intercepts David's plans to build a house for the ark. God explains that while David cannot build Him a house, He is building David a house, that is, a lineage that will last forever.

In his victory over all of Israel's enemies, his humility and commitment to the Lord, his zeal for the house of God, his combining of the offices of prophet, priest, and king, David is a forerunner of the Root of Jesse, Jesus Christ.

Power Key: God's Spirit at Work

Jesus explained the work of the Spirit in John 16:8: "And when He has come, He will convict the world of sin, and of righteousness, and of judgment." We clearly see that the Holy Spirit works in these ways in 2 Samuel. The Spirit functioned most often through the priest. The Spirit works as counselor in the many instances when David would "inquire of the LORD" through the priest and the ephod.

Key Word: *David*

The central character of Second Samuel is David, around whom the entire book is written.

Key Verses: Second Samuel 7:12–13; 22:21

Key Chapter: Second Samuel 11

The eleventh chapter of 2 Samuel is pivotal for the entire book. This chapter records the tragic sins of David regarding Bathsheba and her husband Uriah. All of the widespread blessings on David's family and his kingdom are quickly removed as God chastises His anointed one.

The convincing or convicting work of the Spirit is evident when Nathan the prophet confronts David about his sin with Bathsheba against Uriah. David's sin is laid bare, righteousness is demanded, and the judgment is spelled out. This incident is a microcosm which illustrates the broad working of the Holy Spirit in the world through the Spirit-empowered church.

ruler, "a man after God's own heart."

Introducing

2 SAMUEL

Author. The two books that now make up 1 and 2 Samuel were originally one book called "The Book of Samuel." The actual author is unknown. Samuel undoubtedly had written a great deal about this time in Israel's history. However, other materials had been collected from which the actual writer could draw. Three of these are mentioned in 1 Chronicles 29:29, namely: "the book of Samuel the seer," "the book of Nathan the prophet," and "the book of Gad the seer." Both Gad and Abiathar had access to the court events of David's reign and one or both may have given us these two books.

Date. The book has to be dated after the division of the kingdoms following Solomon's reign, 931 B.C., because of the comment in 1 Samuel 27:6, "Ziklag has belonged to the kings of Judah to this day." Though a distinction was often drawn between Israel and Judah, and though David reigned in Judah for seven and one-half years before unifying the kingdom, there were no kings in Judah before this date.

There is no mention or reference to the fall of Samaria in 722 B.C., which makes a date after that event unlikely.

Content. Second Samuel deals with the ascendance of David to the throne of Israel and the forty years of his reign. He is the focal point of the book.

The book begins with the death of Saul and Jonathan at the battlefield on Mt. Gilboa. David is then anointed king over Judah, his own tribe. There is a power play by the house of Saul in the persons of Ishbosheth, Saul's son, and Abner, Saul's commander in chief of the armies. Though the rebellion is quelled, this summary statement describes the seven and one-half years before the nation is unified under David: "Now there was a long war between the house of Saul and the house of David. But David grew stronger and stronger, and the house of Saul grew weaker and weaker" (3:1).

David unifies both the political and religious life of the nation by bringing the ark of the covenant from the house of Abinadab, where it had rested since its return from the Philistines (6:1—7:1).

The theme of the coming King, the Messiah, is introduced as God establishes an everlasting covenant with David and his kingdom, "Your throne shall be established forever" (7:16).

David successfully defeats the enemies of Israel, and a time of stability and prosperity begins to emerge. Sadly however, his vulnerability and weakness lead him into his sin with Bathsheba and his murder of Uriah, her husband.

Though David repents after being confronted by the prophet Nathan, the consequences of his actions are spelled out: "The sword shall never depart from your house" (12:10).

David's son Absalom, after a long estrangement from his father, instigates a rebellion against the king, and David flees from Jerusalem. The rebellion ends when Absalom, hanging by his hair from a tree, is killed by Joab.

There is a quarrel between Israel and Judah concerning bringing the king back to Jerusalem. The rebel Sheba rouses Israel to desert David and go back to their homes. Although David makes a series of unfortunate and unwise decisions, the rebellion is quelled and David once again is established in Jerusalem.

The book ends with two beautiful poems, a list of David's mighty men, and David's sin in numbering the fighting men of Israel. David repents, buys the threshing floor of Araunah, and presents offerings to the Lord on the altar he builds there.

Personal Application. This book unfolds God's working in history. Although human beings were sinful and must sometimes be punished by Him, God still worked through them to accomplish His redemptive purpose, fully realized in Jesus Christ, the Messiah and King of kings. (See Rev. 22:16.)

Likewise, God has left the church in the world as the body of Christ to witness for Him and to carry out His purposes on the earth today.

Surveying
2 SAMUEL

I. THE TRIUMPHS OF DAVID 1:1—10:19.

A. The political triumphs of David (1:1—5:25).

1. Reign of David in Hebron (1:1—4:12). Initially David is recognized as king only by his own tribe of Judah. The others remain loyal to Saul's remaining son, Ishbosheth.

Report of Saul's death (1:1–27). The lament for Saul and Jonathan communicates David's surprising appreciation for the feats of his old persecutor (19–27).

David anointed king of Judah (2:1–7). The tribe from which David springs now recognizes him as king.

War between David and Saul's family (2:1—3:5). Abner, Saul's army commander, apparently holds off Ishbosheth's coronation for some years (cf. 2 Sam. 2:10 with 5:5). A long war simmers, with David growing stronger while his rival grows weaker.

During these years of strife between David and Ishbosheth a blood feud develops between Abner and David's commander, Joab.

Abner turns to David (3:6–39). Ishbosheth accuses Abner of having sexual relations with one of Saul's concubines. The angry Abner determines to bring all Israel over to David. Abner makes his peace with David but is assassinated by Joab on the way home. David mourns publicly, making it clear he does not condone the murder, but without Abner the weak Ishbosheth clearly is doomed.

Ishbosheth murdered (4:1–12). Amid the plotting and bloodshed, David alone seems to have kept perspective and acted morally.

2. Reign of David in Jerusalem (5:1–25).

David crowned (5:1–5). David is acknowledged as king of a united Israel. He will rule over the united kingdom for thirty-three years.

David takes Jerusalem (5:6–9). The city of Jerusalem has been Jebusite territory since before the Exodus (Josh. 18:16, 28). David leads an attack against the favorably located city. It becomes his capital, and it belongs to neither the rival north or south. By taking it from an enemy, David avoids any show of favoritism. It is mountainous, easily defended, and has a good water supply. The Jebusites jeer when David attacks, shouting that blind and lame men could hold their city. David urges his men on to take the citadel and to destroy the "lame and blind" defenders! (*See* map on page 80.)

David defeats the Philistines (5:17–25). The Philistines now attack Israel in force, hoping to catch David and kill him. Both 2 Samuel and Chronicles carefully report David's attitude going into battle. He "inquires of God" and is careful to follow the Lord's directions. The Philistines are defeated.

B. The spiritual triumphs of David (6:1—7:29).

1. Moving the ark (6:1–23). David now determines to bring the ark to Jerusalem. He brings thirty thousand warriors to escort the ark to Jerusalem. They put it on a cart for transport. On the way, when one of David's men reaches out to steady the ark, he is struck dead. David is both angry and afraid, and leaves the ark when the incident happens.

David is angry, but the incident has underlined the holiness and majesty of God. David now discovers regulations in the Law of Moses instructing how the ark is to be moved (Num. 1:47–52). Reassured, David assembles priests and Levites and joyfully brings the ark to Jerusalem. First Chronicles 15 details David's careful preparations to continue the journey and his explanation of why God's anger broke out earlier (11–15).

David leads in worship (6:12–23). As David brings the ark into Jerusalem, he is caught up in worship, dancing before the Lord in the streets. His wife Michal, Saul's daughter, watches contemptuously. She apparently despises David as a religious fanatic.

2. God's covenant with David (7:1–29). David is troubled. Why should he live in a palace, when the ark of God is covered only by a tent? So David determines to build God a temple. But God gives Nathan the prophet a message for David. David is not to build God a *house; instead God will build David's "house." This is a reference to the line, or family, of David. The right to Israel's throne will pass from generation to generation of David's descendants, forever.

David's prayer of response (2 Sam. 7:18–29).

C. The military triumphs of David (8:1—10:19).

1. Triumphs over his enemies (8:1–12).

2. David's righteous rule (8:13—9:13). David's civil government (8:15–18; *see* Reigned). David organizes a powerful military machine and reorganizes Israel's worship. He also establishes a central governmental system for the collection of taxes, storage of supplies, and supervision of agriculture.

David and Mephibosheth (9:1–13). David searches for any descendants of his friend Jonathan. One man has survived, who is crippled from childhood. David restores Saul's land to him and shows him great kindness.

2 Samuel

"Is there still anyone who is left . . . that I may show him kindness?"
(9:1–7). David's desire to show kindness to a descendent of Saul is motivated by his commitment to a previous covenant with Jonathan (*see* 1 Sam. 20:12–15). "Kindness" (Hebrew *chesed*) can also be translated "covenant faithfulness," indicating that David's care for Mephibosheth is based on a commitment to a friend: David is being a promise-keeper. The Holy Spirit produces in our lives the fruit of kindness (Gal. 5:22)—an action rooted in commitment to relationship—when we are faithful to our covenant with Christ Jesus and are committed to the people around us.

3. Triumphs over Ammon and Syria (10:1–19). The record of David's conquest in this section of the sacred history concludes with a report of war with the Ammonites. The war stems from a tragic misinterpretation of David's expression of sympathy on the death of the Ammonite king. In the war that results, the Ammonites enlist a mercenary army of Arameans. David defeats the combined powers, and then immediately invades Aramea, to prevent future coalitions forming against him.

II. THE TRANSGRESSIONS OF DAVID 11:1–27.

A. The sin of adultery (11:1–5). David's most notorious sin involves his adultery with Bathsheba.

B. The sin of murder (11:6–27).

1. Uriah's loyalty to David (11:6–13).

2. David's command to murder Uriah (11:14–25). David arranges for the death of Bathsheba's husband, Uriah, in battle. This action is even more despicable because Uriah is one of his old companions (*see* 1 Chr. 11:41).

3. David and Bathsheba's marriage (11:26–27).

III. THE TROUBLES OF DAVID 12:1–24:25.

A. Troubles in David's house (12:1–13:36).

1. Prophecy by Nathan (12:1–14). Nathan the prophet is sent to confront David. David immediately confesses his sin and humbles himself before the Lord.

2. Death of David's son (12:15–25).

3. Joab's loyalty to David (12:26–31).

4. Incest in David's house (13:1–20). David, like others in his day, has many wives. Many of his problems stem from conflicts which develop within his household, between half-brothers and half-sisters. One son, Amnon, rapes his half-sister, Tamar.

5. Absalom's murder of Amnon (13:21–36). Tamar's brother, Absalom, arranges to kill Amnon in revenge.

B. Troubles in David's kingdom (13:37–24:25).

1. Rebellion of Absalom (13:37—17:29). Absalom sets out to win the loyalty of the northern tribes (Israel) away from his father (ch. 15). He even wins the support of some of David's oldest associates! Finally Absalom is ready for open rebellion.

David is forced to flee Jerusalem (15:13–37). On that bitter journey he is even cursed by a distant relative of Saul's named Shimei. David's feelings at this time are expressed in Psalms 3 and 4.

Not all of David's old friends have turned against him. He succeeds in placing an advisor in Absalom's camp, who delays pursuit until David can raise an army from loyal Judah (16:15—17:29).

2. Joab's murder of Absalom (18:1–33). By the time Absalom has gathered a larger army and pursues his father, David's commanders are ready. The supporters of Absalom are defeated and the young man is killed (18:1–18).

3. David restored as king (19:1—20:26). The civil war is not ended. As David is returning to Jerusalem, a "troublemaker" named Sheba (from one of the northern tribes) shouts, in effect, "Let's go home!" and the Israelites desert David again! It takes no civil war to reestablish David now. Joab, his military commander, simply follows Sheba and sees to it he is killed (ch. 20).

4. Commentary of the reign of David (21:1—24:25).
> Gibeonites avenged (21:1–14).
> Philistine wars reviewed (21:15–22).
> David's praise for deliverance (22:1–23:7). The psalms (*See* Word.) of praise recorded here tell David's feelings as success comes to him as king.

"I will give thanks to You . . . and sing praises to Your name"
(22:47–50). In this poetic song, David thanks and praises the Lord for His deliverance from all enemies and the hand of Saul (v. 1). Without inhibition or hesitation, he offers praise even among the Gentiles (v. 50). In the same manner, we give thanks

for our deliverance through Christ (Col. 1:12–13; 1 Thess. 1:10); and being empowered and inspired by the Spirit to witness through words of praise (Acts 1:8; 2:11, 47; 4:21), without hesitation we offer our thanksgiving among the "Gentiles"—the unconverted—which the Spirit uses to draw them to Christ for their own deliverance.

"The *Spirit of the LORD spoke by me"

(23:1–7). Here David prophesies about the kind of king who will ultimately lead Israel. Only the Messiah—and not David—would fulfill this description (*see* also Is. 42:1–4). David acknowledges that he falls short of governing in this way (v. 5), yet he affirms God's faithfulness to keep His covenant nonetheless. We may assure ourselves similarly that God's gifts and calling flow

from His abundant grace, not from our merit (Rom. 11:29).

The second psalm (23:1–7), written later, continues the theme, and is the final testimony of Israel's great king.

David's mighty men (23:8–39).

David counts his people (24:1–25). David takes a census. This is viewed even by David's military commanders as a sin, possibly because the act suggests confidence in numbers rather than the Lord. God judges this sin, but gives David a choice of national punishments. The plague which David chooses is stopped just outside Jerusalem. There David builds an altar and offers sacrifices. (*See* Faith, Seed.)

This place will become the site of Solomon's temple and all other temples built in Jerusalem. It is the same place where Abraham was about to offer up Isaac (Genesis 22). It is the place where prophecy says a rebuilt temple will stand in Messiah's day (Ezekiel 40—48).

TRUTH-IN-ACTION through **2 SAMUEL**

Truth 2 Samuel Teaches	**Action** 2 Samuel Invites
1 Guidelines for Growing in Godliness Godliness is living by God's Spirit, in the fear of God, under the eye of God, according to the will of God, with an uninterrupted consciousness of God's indwelling presence. Living this way will keep us from much trouble and tragedy.	**14:14** *Continually practice forgiveness,* as this imitates the ways of God. **9:1** *Be careful* to honor past vows and promises you have made. *Be assured* the Lord has heard them. **11:1** *Be certain* that you are always where God wants you to be or you put yourself in jeopardy.
2 Steps to Dynamic Devotion God highly values His people's devotion in worship. David's humility in worship and Uzzah's presumption, along with Michal's criticism regarding worship, have much to teach us. Worship and praise must be our very highest priority.	**22:1—23:7** *Learn to praise God* for all victories and spiritual gains. *Understand* that this increases your chances for further victories. **6:14** *Worship* the Lord with your whole being as an appropriate response to His presence. **6:16, 23** *Be careful* not to criticize forms of worship unfamiliar to you. To do so may cause future unfruitfulness.
3 Steps to Dealing with Sin The story of David and Bathsheba provides a negative, albeit poignant, object lesson on the importance of avoiding, repenting of, and forsaking sin. Its witness is consistent with the whole counsel of God: Confess and forsake sin quickly or it will prove to be your undoing.	**11:3–17** *Confess* known sins. *Do not hide* them. Doing so usually leads to greater sin. *Understand* that continued refusal to deal with sin can lead to serious, even fatal consequences. **12:5–14** *Learn* to see sin as God does. *Seek to develop* within yourself a godly hatred for sin.

Truth 2 Samuel Teaches	**Action** 2 Samuel Invites
4 Keys to Relating to Authority Since all authority comes from God (Rom. 13), how we relate to God-ordained and God-appointed authority can reveal much to us about how we, in fact, are relating to God. Whether we submit or rebel will test our true character.	**1:11, 12** *Honor* leadership. *Know* that the fall of any Christian leader is a defeat and shame for the whole church. **1:14–16** *Understand* that taking up a cause against any leader is a serious offense. *Know* that God has His ways of dealing with His leaders. **15:1ff.** *Be diligent in loyalty. Refuse* to cultivate a following from those of another's ministry. *Understand* that doing so promotes disunity and division.
5 Lessons for Leaders Spiritual leadership is a sacred trust. How Christian leaders conduct themselves impacts far more than their own lives. This is why they will be more severely judged (see James 3: 1). Also, godly leadership should grow and become stronger through its transmission to subsequent generations.	**21:15–22** Leaders, *know* that you must eventually delegate a large measure of your authority to those you have raised up into ministry. **24:1–17** Leaders, *be careful* not to overvalue the importance of numbers. **12:14** Leaders, *understand* that sins you persist in can cause God's enemies to show utter contempt to the Lord and His people. **6:7** Leaders, *regard* ministry as holy. *Do not act* presumptuously in carrying out assigned responsibilities.
6 Keys to Moral Purity One pattern of attack on our moral purity comes through the improper glance that lodges in the mind.	**11:2–4** *Guard* your eyes! *Be warned* that a lustful gaze will often lead to lustful thoughts and can result in immoral action.
7 Steps in Developing Humility Humility is a premium spiritual virtue. The humble man is not necessarily self-effacing; rather, he refuses to take credit for accomplishments, knowing that any good in his life has resulted from God's working through him.	**15:34; 17:14** *Pray* that the Lord will confuse and frustrate the advice of wicked and ungodly counsel. *Trust* that He will thwart them. *Know* that counsel against God's people originates from hell and is part of the Enemy's strategies against you.
8 Keys to Generous Living Sacrificial giving flows out of a godly and generous heart.	**24:24** *Follow* David's example. *Learn* to give sacrificially.

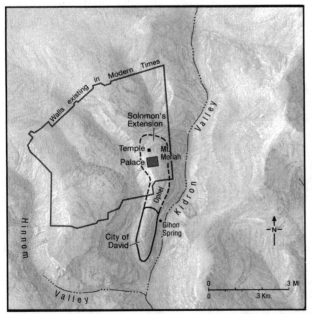

Jerusalem: David's City

David took the fortress city of Jebus and renamed it the "City of David." This established his military and political kingship. He established his religious leadership when he moved the ark of the covenant to Jerusalem.

KEYS TO 1 KINGS
God's Sovereign Will

Kingdom Key: God's Purpose in View
The transition from David's rule to Solomon's is a study in movement from grace to glory—from God's favor *bestowed upon us to God's* majesty *dwelling in our midst. Chapters 1—9 recount the building and dedication of the temple, which underscores the kingdom-life principle that worship must come first among God's people.*

The remaining chapters of 1 Kings testify to God's sovereignty, demonstrating that whatever man does—either in partnership with God or in rebellion against Him—God's purposes will prevail. For example, see how God disciplines Solomon when he strays (11:1–25).

All too often, God's sovereignty is taken to mean that He so overrules in human affairs that human actions have no consequence or at least cannot affect God's purposes. Examining God's dealings with Solomon can help us avoid this kind of "sanctified fatalism."

When Solomon turns from the Lord's ways (11:2), God declares His overruling will (11:11). Difficulties with a neighboring nation also are seen as the result of God's sovereign action (11:14). The Word does not reveal that God foreordained Solomon's failures (fatalism) but that His disci-

....

Whether man acts in partnership with God or in rebellion, God's purposes will prevail.

....

plining grace and wisdom intervened to sustain the testimony of His holy character and eternal will (sovereignty). This same evidence of God's sovereign dealings is seen in 11:26—14:31, as the Lord sustains His purposes for David's royal seed despite the revolt of the ten northern tribes.

God's sovereign ways are displayed further in the prophetic ministries of Elijah and Elisha. Though sinful kings arise in both the north and the south, Ahab and Jezebel's rule in Samaria reveals just how thoroughly self, sin, and Satan may invade a setting, even God's appointed and anointed realm. Even so, God's sovereignty shines in the midst of Israel's darkest hours. Whatever man's influence as he "rules under God," we see God's hand ultimately controlling the final outcome (chs. 15—22).

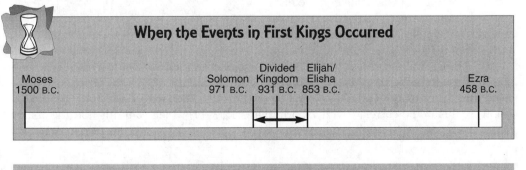

When the Events in First Kings Occurred

| Moses 1500 B.C. | | Solomon 971 B.C. | Divided Kingdom 931 B.C. | Elijah/ Elisha 853 B.C. | | Ezra 458 B.C. |

First Kings demonstrates that obedience to • • •

Master Key: God's Son Revealed

The failure of the prophets, priests, and kings emphasizes the necessity of a Messiah. Christ Himself is the ideal combination of these three offices. As a prophet, Christ's Word far surpasses that of the prophet Elijah (Matt. 17:1–5). Many of Jesus' miracles call to mind the wonders God did through Elijah and Elisha. In addition, Christ as a priest is superior to any of those recorded in Kings (Heb. 7:22–27). First Kings illustrates our need for Christ as our King. When asked if He was King of the Jews, Jesus affirmed that He was (Matt. 27:11). However, Christ is a king "greater than Solomon" (Matt. 12:42). The name "Solomon" means "Peace"; Christ is the "Prince of Peace," and there will be no end to His peace (Is. 9:6). Solomon was noted for his wisdom, but Christ is the "wisdom of God" (1 Cor. 1:25, 29). Solomon's reign was temporary, but Christ will reign on the throne of David forever (1 Chr. 17:14; Is. 9:7). He is "KING OF KINGS AND LORD OF LORDS" (Rev. 19:16). For a further study of allusions to Christ during the time of 1 Kings, read Keys to 1 Chronicles: Master Key and Keys to 2 Chronicles: Master Key.

Power Key: God's Spirit at Work

First Kings 18:12 is the only direct reference to the Holy Spirit in 1 Kings, where He is called the "Spirit of the LORD." Obadiah here indicates that the Holy Spirit sometimes transported Elijah from one location to another (*see* also 2 Kin. 2:16). Acts 8:39–40 describes Philip having a similar experience.

There is an allusion in 18:46 ("the hand of the LORD") to the Holy Spirit's enabling Elijah to perform miracles. The formula "hand of the LORD" referred to the inspiration of the prophets by the Spirit of God (*see* 2 Kin. 3:15 and Ezek. 1:3; compare with 1 Sam. 10:6, 10 and 19:20, 23). Here "the hand of the LORD" refers to the Spirit of God, who endowed Elijah with supernatural strength to do an amazing feat (for similar examples, *see* Judg. 14:6, 19; and 15:14).

Key Word: *Division of the Kingdom*

The theme of 1 Kings centers on the fact that the welfare of Israel and Judah depends upon the faithfulness of the people and their king to the covenant. The two books of Kings trace the monarchy from the point of its greatest prosperity under Solomon to its demise and destruction in the Assyrian and Babylonian captives. Observance of God's law produces blessing, but apostasy is rewarded by judgment.

Key Verses: First Kings 9:4–5; 11:11

Key Chapter: First Kings 12

The critical turning point in 1 Kings occurs in chapter 12, when the united kingdom becomes the divided kingdom upon the death of Solomon.

First Kings 22:24 (*see* 2 Chr. 18:23) may also refer to the Holy Spirit. This verse mentions a "spirit from the LORD" (*see* note on 22:24) and may indicate that the prophets understood that their ability to prophesy came by the Spirit of God (*see* 1 Sam. 10:6, 10; 19:20, 23). If so, this would correlate with 1 Corinthians 12:7–11, which confirms that the ability

(Please turn to page 84.)

• • • **God is necessary and disobedience is painful.**

Introducing
1 KINGS

Author. Since 1 and 2 Kings were originally one book (*see* "Content" below), then this work had to be compiled some time after the capture of Judah by the Babylonians in 586 B.C. (*see* 2 Kings 25). The book gives the impression that it is the product of one author and that this author was an eyewitness to the fall of Jerusalem. Though the authorship cannot be known with certainty, several suggestions have been made. Some have nominated Ezra as the compiler, while others point to Isaiah as the editor. Compare 2 Kings 18:19–20 with Isaiah 36—39. A number of scholars say that the writer of 1 and 2 Kings was an unknown prophet or a Jewish captive in Babylon at about 550 B.C. Because Josephus (a prominent Jewish historian of the first century A.D.) ascribes Kings to "the prophets," many have abandoned the search for a specific author. However, the most probable position is that the prophet Jeremiah was author of 1 and 2 Kings. The early Jewish tradition of the Talmud states that Jeremiah wrote Kings. This famous prophet preached in Jerusalem before and after its fall, and 2 Kings 24 and 25 appear in Jeremiah 39—42; 52. Jeremiah could have written all but the contents of the last appendix (2 Kin. 25:27–30), which were probably added by one of his disciples.

Date. Though the precise date for the composition of 1 and 2 Kings is uncertain, it is believed to have come into its final compilation sometime in the late sixth century B.C. The last event recorded in 2 Kings is the release of King Jehoiachin of Judah from imprisonment in Babylon. Since Jehoiachin was imprisoned in 597 B.C. (*see* 2 Kin. 24:8–17) and released thirty-seven years later (*see* 2 Kin. 25:27), then Kings must have been written after 560 B.C. to include this information. It is almost certain that the writer of Kings would have mentioned something as significant as the fall of Babylon to Persia in 538 B.C. had he known of these events. Since there is no mention of this prominent event in Kings, it is then concluded that 1 and 2 Kings probably was written before 538 B.C. Therefore the date of 1 and 2 Kings is fixed between 560 and 538 B.C., though the events recorded in 1 Kings occurred some three hundred years earlier.

Background. The events covered in 1 Kings span a period of about one hundred and twenty years. First Kings records the turbulent experiences of God's people from the death of David around 971 B.C., to the reign of Jehoshaphat (the fourth king in the southern kingdom of Judah) and the reign of Ahaziah (the ninth king in the northern kingdom of Israel) around 853 B.C. This was a difficult period in the history of God's people, a time of great change and upheaval. There was struggle from within and pressure from without. The result was a dark moment in which the stable kingdom under a strong leader split in two.

Occasion and Purpose. Contemplating the horror of the exile of God's people, the author compiles 1 and 2 Kings to answer the looming question of why both the northern kingdom of Israel and the southern kingdom of Judah had been taken captive. He writes with a prophetic message, showing that this punishment by captivity to foreign pagan nations was the inevitable consequence of the persistent violation of God's covenant with them. Kings was written to move the exiles to reflect on their history and return to the Lord. Perhaps this prophetic perspective is one reason why it was included in the "earlier prophets" in the Hebrew Bible.

Content. First and 2 Kings were originally one unbroken book, which formed a sequel to 1 and 2 Samuel. The composers of the Greek Old Testament (the Septuagint, or LXX) divided the work into "3 and 4 Kingdoms" (1 and 2 Samuel were "1 and 2 Kingdoms"). The title "Kings" is derived from Jerome's Latin translation (the Vulgate) and is appropriate because of the emphasis of these books on the kings who reigned during this period.

The books of 1 and 2 Kings take up recording the historical events of God's people where the books of 1 and 2 Samuel leave off. However, Kings is more than just a compilation of the politically important or socially significant happenings in Israel and Judah. In fact, it is not as detailed a history as might be expected (four hundred years in only forty-seven chapters). Instead, 1 and 2 Kings is a selective history, one with a theological purpose. Therefore, the author selects and emphasizes the people and events that are morally and religiously significant. First and 2 Kings present God as the Lord of history. From history, these books establish God's providential working in and through the lives of His people for His redemptive purpose. They demonstrate the necessity of obedience to God's covenant and the painful consequence of disobedience. Therefore, the books of 1 and 2 Kings are not to be viewed as mere history, but as theology and lessons from history.

The united work of 1 and 2 Kings naturally divides into three main sections. The "Unified Kingdom" under Solomon in 1 Kings 1—11; the "Divided Kingdom" in 1 Kings 12—2 Kings 17; and finally, 2 Kings 18—25 focuses on the surviving "Kingdom of Judah."

The first half of 1 Kings records the glory of Solomon's reign, his wealth, wisdom, and the monumental accomplishment of the building of the temple. However, his disobedience in marrying foreign wives led him into idolatry, and the stage was set for the division of the kingdom. The king with a divided heart would leave behind a divided kingdom. On his death, those in the northern part of the empire rebelled and established their own nation, known as Israel. In the south, those who remained faithful to the house of David and Solomon formed the nation known as Judah.

In the second half of 1 Kings, which describes the divided kingdom, the narrative is difficult to follow. The author switches back and forth between the northern kingdom of Israel and the southern kingdom of Judah, tracing their histories simultaneously. There were nineteen regents in Israel, all of them bad. In Judah, there were twenty rulers, only eight of them good. First Kings records the first nine rulers in Israel and the first four kings in Judah. Some of these thirteen regents are only mentioned in a few verses, while whole chapters are devoted to others. Major attention is directed to those who either serve as a model of uprightness, or to those who illustrate why these nations eventually collapsed. When 1 Kings closes, Jehoshaphat is the king in Judah, and Ahaziah is on the throne in Israel.

Personal Application. The message of 1 and 2 Kings is as relevant today as when it was written. God still controls human affairs. The nation, leader, or person who responds to and obeys the Lord will enjoy the benefits of a relationship with Him. Those who refuse and rebel will experience God's discipline. Though people are sinful, God is the author of redemption, and He graciously forgives those who will repent and return to Him.

Power Key *continued from page 82*

to prophesy is indeed a manifestation of the Holy Spirit.

For more on the Holy Spirit in the king-dom period, read Keys to 2 Kings: Power Key and Keys to 2 Chronicles: Power Key.

Surveying
1 KINGS

I. THE KINGDOM UNITED 1:1—11:43.

A. The establishment of Solomon as king (1:1—2:46). Competition for the throne (1:1–27). David is old and feeble. Still he hesitates to confirm the succession of Solomon, which he has promised to do. Another son, Adonijah, invites key supporters to a feast, intending to make himself king. Other advisors warn David that unless he acts both he and Solomon will likely be killed!

David makes Solomon co-regent (1:28–53). David acts with his old decisiveness. He proclaims Solomon king, and all Jerusalem breaks out in spontaneous demonstration. When the news is brought to Adonijah, his supporters slip away, and Adonijah begs Solomon for his life. The request is granted—so long as this brother of Solomon keeps his place.

David's charge to Solomon (2:1–12). David is near death. He gives his final instructions to his son. David underlines the need to keep all of God's commandments wholeheartedly (2–4). David also instructs Solomon to deal with several of his old enemies (5–9).

Solomon's control established (2:13–46). After David dies Adonijah maneuvers for another try at the throne. He asks to marry one of David's concubines (13–17). By custom a king's concubines are part of the inheritance of his heir (*see* 2 Sam. 16:21). Such a marriage would provide basis for a later claim to Solomon's throne by the popular (1 Kin. 2:15) Adonijah. Solomon immediately puts Adonijah to death for treason. There is no indication Solomon harmed other brothers.

B. The elevation of Solomon as king (3:1—8:66). Request for wisdom (3:1–15). Solomon acts quickly as king. He strengthens his relations with other states and shows love for God, first by obedience, and second by his worship. God then appears to Solomon and instructs him to request whatever he wishes. Solomon asks for wisdom and knowledge needed to "lead this great people of yours."

Wisdom demonstrated (3:16–28). Solomon's wise decision helps establish him in the eyes of his people.

Solomon's administration (4:1–19).
Solomon's finances (4:20–28).

Solomon's intellectual achievements (4:29–34). Solomon's knowledge and his wisdom are "greater than the wisdom of all the men of the East." With all his other activities, Solomon finds time to add thousands of proverbs and over a thousand songs to the literary heritage of Israel.

The great achievement of Solomon's reign is construction of the temple of Jerusalem. These chapters (5—7) tell of its construction and the massive effort required. There are thirty thousand laborers conscripted just to cut timber, and another 150,000 needed for other tasks. The temple is built of stone, paneled with cedar, and overlaid with gold. The gold alone, figured at the old price of thirty-five dollars an ounce, is worth almost three billion dollars. Here Israel will now come to worship and keep the annual festivals, for here is Israel's true treasure: not the gold, but God.

The ark brought to the temple (8:1–11). The ark was constructed in the days of Moses, and was the focus of God's presence with His people.

Solomon's sermon (8:12–21).

Solomon's prayer of dedication (8:22–61; see Heaven). Solomon's prayer of dedication is a model Old Testament petition. In it the king affirms who God is and bases his requests on promises made and principles laid down in the written Law. The prayer concludes with a blessing on Israel and a call to the people to commitment.

Two weeks of worship (8:62–66).

C. The error of Solomon as king (9:1—11:43).
God's response to Solomon's prayer (9:1–9). God tells the young king that his prayer has been heard. God has consecrated the temple by His very presence. But Solomon is exhorted to "walk before Me . . . in integrity of heart and in uprightness" (9:4).

Solomon's many projects (9:10–28). The first twenty years of Solomon's rule are productive and active. In all his projects Solomon is a great success. During these years Solomon's reputation spreads worldwide.

The Queen of Sheba (10:1–13).

Solomon's splendor (10:14–29). A summary is given of the wealth that flows into Israel from Solomon's various ventures. However, Solomon accumulates chariots and horses (10:26), which is strictly forbidden to Israel's kings (Deut. 17:14–20). This is the first indication that in his later years Solomon will drift away from his early commitment to God. (See ch. 55 of this Handbook, §3.3.)

Solomon's wives (11:1–13). The law concerning kings also forbids multiple wives, and the general law strictly prohibits taking foreign wives. But Solomon makes many political alliances, and these involve marriages between royal houses. However wise this course seems, it leads Solomon into serious trouble and involves him in direct disobedience to the Lord.

Solomon's love for God is gradually replaced by his love for these women. As he grows older "his wives turned his heart after other gods" (11:4). Now the Lord appears to Solomon a third time, but this time to announce judgment!

Enemies arise (11:14–40). Hadad, of the royal family of Edom, and Rezon, who will launch a dynasty in Syria, begin movements which will lead to the rebellion of these subject lands. One of Solomon's own officials, Jeroboam, rebels against the king. This ambitious and talented young man is told by the prophet Ahijah that on Solomon's death he will become king over the northern tribes. (See Chose.)

Solomon's death (11:41–43).

II. THE KINGDOM DIVIDED 12:1—22:53.

A. The revolt and reign of Jeroboam in Israel (12:1—14:20).
On Solomon's death, the northern tribes demand that his son lighten the taxes and the forced labor levies that Solomon imposed. Rehoboam threatens to make the load even heavier. Israel immediately rebels. Only the intervention of the prophet Shemaiah prevents civil war between Israel and the still-faithful Judah.

False worship system (12:25–33). Solomon's old enemy Jeroboam is made king of Israel (Jeroboam I, 930–909 B.C.). He must now break the strands which link his new nation to Judah. Most serious is the common faith of Judah and Israel, for all Israelites are to come to Jerusalem for worship and sacrifice. Jeroboam devises a false worship system that imitates the system given by God. He sets up two worship centers, consecrates a new priesthood, and institutes festivals that mimic the Old Testament festivals but are held in different months. This apostasy sets the spiritual direction of the northern kingdom.

Judgment announced (13:1–6). An unnamed prophet is sent from Judah to the Bethel worship center to confront Jeroboam.

"The man of God entreated the LORD, and the king's hand was restored" (13:6). King Jeroboam's hand extended against the unnamed "man of God" withers because he withstands God Himself. Yet

continued on next page

continued from preceding page
intercession by the man of God prompts the Lord's restoration and healing, and Jeroboam's hand is made completely whole. Here miraculous healing results not from sinful man's repentance, but God's favor invoked through intercession. It pleases God today when His people ask for His mercy, not only for themselves, but also for those who directly oppose them.

Obedience demanded (13:7–34).

Jeroboam I as king (14:1–20). Secular sources tell us that Jeroboam lost much territory during his twenty-two-year reign. But most serious is the fact that Jeroboam leads Israel into the detestable practices of the nations the Lord had driven out of Palestine (9).

B. The reign of Rehoboam in Judah (14:21–31). Rehoboam has border skirmishes with Jeroboam of Israel during his seventeen-year reign. But his nation grows stronger, as those who are faithful to the Law and the Jerusalem temple migrate to the tribal areas of Judah and Benjamin.

C. The reign of Abijam in Judah (15:1–8). Abijah's brief reign is not marked by a return to piety. It is marked, however, by a significant victory over an invasion force from Israel.

D. The reign of Asa in Judah (15:9–24). Asa is one of only eight kings of Judah who are said to have been good in God's eyes. Not one king of Israel is so praised. Each of them "did evil." Asa purges the land of idolatrous worship centers and repairs the temple altar at Jerusalem.

E. The reign of Nadab of Israel (15:25–32). Nadab is the son of Jeroboam. As the prophet Ahijah has foretold (1 Kings 14), he is assassinated.

F. The reign of Baasha in Israel (15:33—16:7). Baasha has replaced Jeroboam's dynasty, but he follows the apostate system set up by that king. (*See* Anger.)

G. The reign of Elah in Israel (16:8–14).

H. The reign of Zimri in Israel (16:15–20).

I. The reign of Omri in Israel (16:21–28). A civil war between supporters of Tibni and Omri is settled by the death of Tibni. Little is said of Omri in the Old Testament, but other records of that era give us a picture of his significant reign. He established a new capital at Samaria (1 Kin. 16:24), built to be a defensive stronghold. From the Moabite Stone, a monument found in A.D. 1898, we know that "Omri,

King of Israel" conquered Moab and imposed tribute. The marriage of his son Ahab to Jezebel, a Phoenician princess, shows he made an important alliance with that coastal power. Final evidence of the resurgence of Israel under this vigorous though evil king is found in inscriptions from several Assyrian rulers, which over a century later still identify Israel as the "land of Omri."

J. The reign of Ahab in Israel (16:29—22:40). No king of the divided kingdoms is given so much space in the Old Testament as Ahab. This is due to the significant religious struggle that developed during his reign.

Jezebel, Ahab's Phoenician wife, was not satisfied with the coexistence of pagan worship and worship of Jehovah. She introduced the Baal cult of her people and sought to have it completely replace the faith of Israel. Like other Canaanite religions, this cult was morally degrading and included religious prostitution. God sent the prophet Elijah to Israel to confront the king and to stand against the new pagan religion (*see* map, page 184). The biblical record focuses on the religious conflict.

Ahab as king (16:29–34). The basic evaluation of Ahab is that he did more evil in the eyes of the Lord than any of those before him (30).

Elijah and the famine (17:1–24). Elijah is called to confront Ahab and announce a severe drought in Israel. God cares for the prophet during the terrible three-year famine that settles on the land. (See Faith, Seed.)

"The LORD heard the voice of Elijah; and the soul of the child came back to him"
(17:17–24). Often we do not understand the reason for sickness. Here the son of the widow of Zarephath becomes sick and dies (v. 17). Zarephath is in Sidon, outside of Israel, in the regions of Baal worship. But the widow has shown faith in the Lord and kindness to Elijah. She questions Elijah's responsibility (v. 18); Elijah questions God's reasonableness (v. 20); then lying prostrate on the child, he cries out in intercession to the Lord (v. 21)—and resurrection is the result. God is pleased to demonstrate His power even in Baal's territory (*see* Luke 4:24–26). Healing comes as we move from reasoning over questions of *why* and begin responding to *how* the Lord works through faith-filled prayer. The Lord desires to heal.

Elijah reappears (18:1–15). Elijah now returns to Israel. He meets a devout believer who is one of Ahab's administrators. This man's fear, and the fact he has been forced to hide a number of prophets because Jezebel "was killing off the prophets of the Lord," gives us some insight into the fierce battle between religious faiths going on at that time.

On Mount Carmel (18:16–46). Elijah confronts Ahab and the people of Israel. The people must choose whom they will worship. In a contest held on Mount Carmel, the 450 prophets of Baal call on their impotent god all day. When Elijah prays, fire falls from heaven to consume a water-soaked sacrifice. The prophets of Baal are killed, and a great rain comes to break the drought.

"Elijah said to Ahab, 'Go up, eat and drink; for there is the sound of abundance of rain' . . . then he bowed down on the ground, and put his face between his knees"
(18:41–46). Elijah's prophetic declaration of promised rain is followed by intense intercession. Great faith is evident here (1) in Elijah's *confidence to speak forth* the imminent fulfillment of promise; and (2) in Elijah's *commitment to pray persistently* until the promise is realized. Elijah's example is later used to illustrate how "the effective fervent prayer of a righteous man avails much" (*see* James 5:16–18). Like Elijah, we are all candidates to exercise the earnest prayer of faith in actuating God's word of promise.

Elijah's fear (19:1–9). The furious queen, Jezebel, grimly promises to kill Elijah.

Strangely, Elijah is suddenly terrified and flees.

God appears to Elijah (19:9–21). Finally God speaks to Elijah, who has fallen into deep depression. God comforts His prophet and provides Elijah a companion who will become his successor.

Ben-Hadad attacks Samaria (20:1–43; *see* Listen).

Naboth's vineyard (21:1–29). Ahab decides he wants a vineyard that belongs to a man named Naboth. Naboth will not sell, for family inheritances of land are not to be transferred (4). Jezebel bribes two men to accuse Naboth of treason and blasphemy, and he is executed. The moral character of the king and queen, and of their religion, is clearly revealed in this terrible incident.

Elijah finds Ahab at Naboth's vineyard and announces God's judgment on this king.

Micaiah prophesies against Ahab (22:1–40). Ahab makes a treaty with Judah against the Aramaeans. False prophets promise victory, but Jehoshaphat of Judah insists on asking "a prophet of the Lord." Ahab calls Micaiah, who tells him that Israel will lose the battle and Ahab will be killed.

Micaiah's words are from the Lord. In the battle Ahab is killed, and thus the reign of one of the most evil men produced in Israel comes to an end.

K. The reign of Jehoshaphat in Judah (22:41–50). Jehoshaphat is the second good king of Judah. He battles the penetration of Baal worship in Judah.

L. The reign of Ahaziah in Israel (22:51–53). The son of Ahab succeeds him, but he rules only two years.

TRUTH-IN-ACTION through 1 KINGS

Truth 1 Kings Teaches	**Action** 1 Kings Invites
1 Guidelines for Growing in Godliness The godly person has confidence that God cares about his character, faithfulness, and integrity and that He rewards those who walk faithfully with Him.	**1:29** *Remember* and *carry out* vows and promises you make. *Be assured* the Lord has heard and will enable you to do so. **2:3** *Remember* that the Lord prospers and grants success to those who walk in His ways.
2 Steps to Holiness Holiness implies a life that is separate from the world. Taking even small steps across this line too easily makes room for greater compromise.	**3:3** *Avoid* even small compromises in holiness, purity, and worship. *Understand* that even the slightest deviations from what you know to be right may eventually become major transgressions.

Truth 1 Kings Teaches	**Action** 1 Kings Invites
3 Steps in Developing Humility Humility refuses to promote or exalt itself, trusting the Lord to bring advancement. It quickly acknowledges the Lord when anything it does is recognized, knowing that all accomplishments are realized through God.	**1:5, 29** *Avoid* self-promotion. *Rely* upon the Lord to bring promotion to you. *Remember:* He who exalts himself will be humbled (see Matt. 23:12). **8:27** *Be aware* that your life is only a conduit for or a reflection of God's life. *Know* that even the greatest thing you build will manifest only a small facet of God's glory.
4 Keys to Wise Living God is the only source of true wisdom, and He promises to give it to anyone who asks for it. Wisdom begins with the fear of the Lord and finds its fulfillment in love for others.	**3:7–14** *Do not presume* to know how to do what the Lord has called you to do. *Cleave* to the Lord. *Depend* upon him for wisdom. **3:16–28** *Choose to believe* that God will give wisdom to all who ask for it (see James 1:5). **8:39, 40** *Be assured* that only God knows the hearts of men; we cannot. *Allow* this to cause you to reverence God.
5 Steps to Dynamic Devotion Make no mistake about it: God gives special recognition to those whose hearts are wholly His. To believe that casual devotion to God is as blessed as whole-hearted devotion is self-deception.	**8:61** *Be assured* that the Lord's promises are for those whose hearts are fully committed to Him and His ways. *Examine* yourself for any lukewarmness you need to confess. **11:1–8** *Be very careful* not to let those for whom you have affection lead you away from full devotion to the Lord.
6 Lessons for Leaders God's leaders serve Him on the people's behalf, not vice versa. Confusion on this point has caused many a tragedy among God's people. The kings who sought to please the people rather than God opened the way for great sin and received a bad report. What an important lesson in a day when popularity has become such an idol to many! God's leaders are encouraged to follow His Word closely and to be careful regarding other sources of advice.	**12:6–11** Leaders, *be wise* and *seek counsel* from other seasoned and fruitful leaders. *Avoid* the exclusive counsel of untried leaders who have borne little fruit. **12:28; 13:34; 22:14–28** Leaders, *be faithful* to God's Word. What you say may not always be popular, but it must measure up to the standards of Scripture. Otherwise, your ministry may promote idolatry. **15:3, 11** Leaders, *pattern your lives* and ministries after leaders who have God's approval and follow His Word closely. *Avoid* patterns that, although successful by worldly standards, contradict God's Word.
7 Steps to Dealing with Sin Deception begins when we forget that all of us are inclined to sin.	**8:46** *Be assured* that there is no one who does not sin. *Let God search your heart daily* to guard you against sin, which you might not notice.
8 Key Lessons in Faith Believe that where the Lord leads, He feeds. Where He guides, He provides. Faith does not let a threat of privation alter the course the Lord has set.	**17:1–9** *Do not allow* the threat of reduced income to cause you to disobey the Lord's direction for your life. *Choose to believe* that the Lord knows how to care for His servants.

KEYS TO 2 KINGS
God's Sovereign Judgment

Kingdom Key: God's Purpose in View

The opening chapters of 2 Kings (1—9) are full of accounts of prophetic ministry, including the dramatic climax of Elijah's witness and the awesome power of Elisha's. God's kingdom power is most clearly demonstrated, however, in His judgment executed upon the house of Israel. The fall of the northern kingdom shows that there is no "kingdom power" without "kingdom obedience." Israel's continuous violations of God's ways, revealed in the leadership and lifestyle of every one of the northern kings, exhausted the seemingly endless patience of the loving, yet holy, God Almighty.

Second Kings 17:5–23 offers a plaintive, heart-rending analysis of Israel's fall. God's holiness required the capital punishment of nations, though the text makes it clear that the Almighty took no delight in this. This passage both (1) vindicates God's action, and (2) describes those things that will invite similar judgment anywhere, anytime. They are:

1. Refusal of God's ways (17:7–8): "[They] walked in the statutes of the nations whom the LORD had cast out."

2. Running to evil excesses (17:9–12): "[They] secretly did against the LORD their God things that were not right."

3. Rejection of prophetic warnings (17:13–15): "The LORD testified . . . by all of His prophets . . . saying, 'Turn from your evil ways.'"

4. Rebellion unto demonic worship (17:16–18): "[They] worshiped all the host of heaven, and served Baal . . . practiced witchcraft and soothsaying and sold themselves to do evil."

These four "Rs" of apostasy invoke certain judgment. Chapter 17:19–23 introduces a fifth—*Removal:* The Lord was very angry and "cast them from His sight." Kingdom living offers great promise and blessing, but it never allows for selfish, carnal, or evil pursuit. Persistence in what *offends* God *ends* the enjoyment of His blessings and mercies.

Second Kings abounds with material which shows how kingdom people are *not* to live. Kingdom living requires a constant availability to correction: "If we would judge ourselves, we would not be judged" (1 Cor. 11:31). This book reveals the price of neglecting that discipline.

....

No kingdom power without kingdom obedience.

....

When the Events in Second Kings Occurred

		Elisha begins ministry 853 B.C.	Israel falls to Assyria 722 B.C.	Judah falls to Babylon 586 B.C.	Ezra 458 B.C.
Moses 1500 B.C.					

2 Kings: continuous refusal, running, rejection, • • •

Master Key: God's Son Revealed

When prophets, priests, and kings all fall short, the need for a messiah becomes clear. Jesus Christ became the ideal combination of these three offices. As a prophet, He far surpassed the great prophet Elijah (Matt. 17:1–5). Many of His miracles were reminiscent of the wonders God did through Elijah and Elisha. In addition, no priest recorded in Kings or elsewhere in human history could measure up to Christ (Heb. 7:22–27). Second Kings also illustrates our need for Christ as our reigning King. When asked if He was King of the Jews, Jesus affirmed that He was (Matt. 27:11), but Christ is a King far superior to their greatest king (Matt. 12:42). The reign of each of the twenty-six rulers came to an end, but Christ will reign forever (1 Chr. 17:14; Is. 9:7), for He is "KING OF KINGS AND LORD OF LORDS" (Rev. 19:16). For further study of allusions to Christ during the time of 2 Kings, read Keys to 2 Chronicles: Master Key.

Power Key: God's Spirit at Work

The words of the prophets (2:16) indicate that the Holy Spirit (the "Spirit of the LORD") sometimes transported Elijah from one location to another (see 1 Kin. 18:12). The early church witness, Philip, is described as having a similar experience in Acts 8:39–40.

An indirect reference to the Holy Spirit in the phrase "spirit of Elijah" is found in 2:9, 15 (see the text and note on 1 Kin. 2:9–16). Here Elisha is seeking to receive the same empowerment Elijah had in order to carry on Elijah's prophetic ministry. The energizing spirit or power that enabled Elijah to prophesy was the Spirit of God (see 1 Sam. 10:6, 10 and 19:20, 23).

Second Kings 2:9–16 provides an interesting Old Testament parallel to Acts 1:4–9 and 2:1–4. After Elijah went into heaven, Elisha sought the empowerment to carry on his master's ministry, and received it. In a similar way, Jesus ascended, the disciples prayed and waited, and the Holy Spirit empowered them to carry on the work that their Lord began.

A final allusion to the Holy Spirit is found in 3:15. Here the "hand of the LORD" came upon Elisha, enabling him to prophesy to

(Please turn to page 92.)

Key Word: *Captivities of the Kingdom*

Second Kings records both the destruction and captivity of Israel by the Assyrians (2 Kings 17), as well as the destruction and captivity of Judah by the Babylonians (2 Kings 25).

The book was written selectively, not exhaustively, from a prophetic viewpoint to teach that the decline and collapse of the two kingdoms occurred because of failure on the part of the rulers and people to heed the warnings of God's messengers.

Key Verses: Second Kings 17:22–23; 23:27

Key Chapter: Second Kings 25

The last chapter of 2 Kings records the utter destruction of the city of Jerusalem and its glorious temple. Hope is still alive, however, with the remnant in the Babylonian captivity as Evil-Merodach frees Jehoiachin from prison and treats him kindly.

• • • and rebellion toward God can result in removal.

Introducing
2 KINGS

Author. Second Kings was originally the second half of one book which included 1 and 2 Kings (see "Content" below). This work must have been compiled some time after the capture of Judah by the Babylonians in 586 B.C. (see ch. 25). It seems to have been the product of one author, who was an eyewitness to the fall of Jerusalem. Though the authorship cannot be known with certainty, several suggestions have been made. Some have nominated Ezra as the compiler, while others point to Isaiah as the editor. Compare 18:19–20 with Isaiah 36—39. A number of scholars say that the writer of 2 Kings was an unknown prophet or some Jewish captive in Babylon at about 550 B.C. Because Josephus (a prominent Jewish historian of the first century A.D.) ascribes Kings to "the prophets," many have abandoned the search for a specific author. However, the most probable position is that the prophet Jeremiah was author of 1 and 2 Kings. Early Jewish tradition of the Talmud states that Jeremiah wrote Kings. This famous prophet preached in Jerusalem before and after its fall, and chapters 24 and 25 appear in Jeremiah 39—42; 52. The contents of all but the last appendix (25:27–30) could have been written by Jeremiah, and the final verses added by one of Jeremiah's disciples.

Date. Though the precise date for the composition of 1 and 2 Kings is uncertain, it is believed to have come into its final compilation sometime in the late sixth century B.C. The last event recorded in 2 Kings is the release of King Jehoiachin of Judah from imprisonment in Babylon. Since Jehoiachin was imprisoned in 597 B.C. (see 24:8–17) and released thirty-seven years later (see 25:27), then Kings must have been written after 560 B.C. to include this information. It is almost certain that the writer of Kings would have mentioned something as significant as the fall of Babylon to Persia in 538 B.C. had he known of these events. Since there is no mention of this prominent event in Kings, it is then concluded that 1 and 2 Kings probably was written before 538 B.C. Therefore the date of 1 and 2 Kings is fixed between 560 and 538 B.C., though some of the events recorded in these books occurred many years earlier.

Background. The events covered in 2 Kings span a period of almost three hundred years. Second Kings records the turbulent experiences of God's people from the reign of Ahaziah (the ninth king in the northern kingdom of Israel) around 853 B.C., through the fall of Israel to Assyria in 722 B.C., through the fall of Jerusalem and the deportation of Judah to Babylon in 586 B.C., and ends with the release of King Jehoiachin in 560 B.C. This was a difficult period in the history of God's people, a time of great change and upheaval. There was struggle from within and pressure from without. The result was a dark moment in the history of God's people: the collapse and eventual captivity of both nations.

Occasion and Purpose. Contemplating the horror of the exile of God's people, the author compiles 1 and 2 Kings to answer the looming question of why both the northern kingdom of Israel and the southern kingdom of Judah had been taken captive. He writes with a prophetic message, showing that this punishment by captivity to foreign pagan nations was the inevitable consequence of the persistent violation of God's covenant with them. Kings was written to cause the exiles to reflect on their history and return to the Lord. Perhaps this prophetic perspective is one reason why it was included in the "earlier prophets" in the Hebrew Bible.

Content. First and 2 Kings were originally one unbroken book, which formed a sequel to 1 and 2 Samuel. The composers of the Greek Old Testament (the Septuagint, or LXX) divided the work into "3 and 4 Kingdoms" (1 and 2 Sam. were "1 and 2 Kingdoms"). The title "Kings" is derived from Jerome's Latin translation (the Vulgate) and is appropriate because of the emphasis of these books on the kings who reigned during these centuries.

The Book of 2 Kings takes up recording the historical events of God's people where the Book of 1 Kings leaves off. However, 2 Kings is more than just a compilation of the politically important or socially significant happenings in Israel and Judah. In fact, it is not as detailed a history as might be expected (three hundred years in only twenty-five chapters). Instead, 2 Kings is a selective history, one with a theological purpose. Therefore, the author selects and emphasizes the people and events that are morally and religiously significant. Second Kings presents God as the Lord of history. From history, this book establishes God's providential working in and through the lives of His people for His redemptive purpose. It demonstrates the necessity of obedience to God's covenant and the painful consequence of disobedience. Therefore, the Book of 2 Kings is not to be viewed as mere history, but as theology and lessons from history.

Second Kings picks up the tragic history of the "divided kingdom" with Ahaziah on the throne of Israel, while Jehoshaphat is ruling in Judah. As with 1 Kings, the narrative is difficult to follow. The author switches back and forth between the northern kingdom of Israel and the southern kingdom of Judah, tracing their histories simultaneously. There were nineteen regents in Israel, all of them bad. In Judah, there were twenty rulers, only eight of them good. Second Kings records the last ten kings in Israel, and the last sixteen rulers in Judah. Some of these twenty-six regents are only mentioned in a few verses, while whole chapters are devoted to others. Major attention is directed to those who either serve as a model of uprightness, or to those who illustrate why these nations eventually collapsed.

Personal Application. The message of 2 Kings is as relevant today as when it was written. God still controls human affairs. The nation, leader, or person who responds to and obeys the Lord will enjoy the benefits of their relationship with Him. Those who refuse and rebel will experience God's discipline. Though people are sinful, God is the author of redemption, and He graciously forgives those who will repent and return to Him.

Power Key continued from page 90

King Jehoshaphat. The formula "hand of the LORD" referred to divine inspiration for prophets (see Ezek. 1:3), which, as noted above, is the Spirit of God. Such prophecy is a manifestation of the Holy Spirit, as confirmed in 1 Corinthians 12:7–11.

For more on the Holy Spirit in the kingdom period, read Keys to 1 Kings: Power Key and Keys to 2 Chronicles: Power Key.

Surveying
2 KINGS

I. THE DIVIDED KINGDOM 1:1—17:41.

A. The reign of Ahaziah in Israel (1:1–18). Ahaziah, king after Ahab, has injured himself in a fall. The messengers he sends to Philistia to inquire of Baal-Zebub are intercepted by Elijah and sent back. The angry prophet announces Ahaziah's doom, and when he dies, his brother Jehoram takes the throne. (See ch. 55 of this Handbook, §2.3.)

B. The reign of Jehoram in Israel (2:1— 8:15). Elijah taken up (2:1–18). Elijah is taken directly into heaven by the Lord, in a chariot of fire that appears as a whirlwind.

Elisha asks for a "double portion" of Elijah's spirit. This is a request to be Elijah's successor, for the heir and oldest son in a family is traditionally given a double portion of the family wealth as his inheritance. The request is granted (2:10–12).

Two miracles (2:19–25). Elisha's first two miracles set the tone of his ministry. When the people of Jericho appeal to him, Elisha purifies their waters. This is Elisha's ministry of mercy. But when a number of youths jeer at him and thus at God, challenging him to "go up" into heaven as Elijah had done, Elisha curses them. Two bears appear and maul forty-two of the scoffers. This is Elisha's ministry of standing up for God's honor and in

judgment of sin (see map, page 184).

Moab revolts (3:1–27; see ch. 55, §2.3).

Ministries of mercy (4:1—6:7). A number of wonders performed by Elisha are now reported. The mercy miracles are: saving a widow from her creditors (4:1–7), restoring a Shunammite woman's son to life (4:8–37), saving a company of prophets from poisoned food (4:38–41), multiplying food to feed the hungry (4:42–44), healing an enemy general of leprosy (5:1–27), and recovering a borrowed ax-head (6:1–7).

"Now when she came to the man of God at the hill, she caught him by the feet" (4:18–37). Distressed over her son's death, the Shunammite woman proceeds undeterred to Elisha to entreat the Lord for a miracle of healing. Since Elisha had previously spoken a miraculous life-giving promise to the barren couple (vv. 16–17), her faith persuaded her that God's prophet could again speak life into death. She went past Gehazi on the way (25–26), and refused to follow him back to Shunem (29–30). She would entrust herself only to Elisha, who was proven a worthy instrument of God's healing power, and she was not disappointed (36–37). Desperate circumstances engender determined faith—faith that presses through to lay hold of God's miracle answer.

> **"Go and wash in the Jordan seven times and your flesh shall be restored"**
> (5:9—14). Elisha's healing directive to leprous Naaman is not well received. Its indirect manner confronts Naaman's proud and presumptuous ways (v. 11), and he turns away in rage (12). Yet by yielding to wise counsel (13), he submits and obeys, opening the pathway to healing: Naaman's flesh is restored to childlike wholeness (14). God's ways of healing are not unreasonable; they move us beyond proud reason to the humble simplicity of receiving His great love with yielded heart and open hand.(See Healing, Divine.)

Ministries of national import (6:8—8:15). In the period of conflict with Aramaea, Elisha plays a vital role (see Spiritual Warfare). He often warns the king of Israel of Ben-Hadad's plans (6:9–10). Finally Ben-Hadad sends a raiding party to take Elisha. Instead the party is blinded and led to Samaria.

Later Samaria is besieged by Ben-Hadad, and its people begin to starve. The king of Israel sees this disaster as God's work (6:33) and determines to kill Elisha in revenge (6:31)! But Elisha promises that the next day God will lift the siege and flood the city with food.

That night the enemy army is stricken with terror. The men flee mindlessly, leaving food, riches, horses, and mules behind. The prophet's words have come true.

C. The reign of Jehoram in Judah (8:16–24). Jehoram reigns for eight years. He has married Jezebel's equally wicked daughter, Athaliah. Now Jehoram follows their religious and moral example. Judah loses authority over her vassal states during Jehoram's reign.

D. The reign of Ahaziah in Judah (8:25—9:29). Jehoram's only remaining son rules just one year. He follows his father's example, encouraged in "doing wrong" by his mother Athaliah. He is killed while visiting Joram of Israel.

Jehu's call by God (9:1–13). Elisha sends a prophet to anoint Jehu, a military commander, as king of Israel. Jehu is told to destroy Ahab's family in vengeance for all the followers of the Lord that Jezebel has murdered. Jehu responds immediately and leads his troops against Joram.

E. The reign of Jehu in Israel (9:30—10:36). All members of Ahab's royal house are killed, including forty-two members of

Judah's royal family, who were also Ahab's descendants through intermarriage.

Priests of Baal destroyed (10:18–28). Jezebel and Ahab have established the cult of Baal in Israel. Jehu assembles all its priests and leaders to the principal temple of Baal for sacrifice. There he has the cult leaders killed, and then destroys its idols and worship centers throughout Israel.

But Jehu keeps the false religious system established by Jeroboam I (1 Kings 12). As a result God begins to "reduce the size of Israel" (10:32). During the twenty-eight years of Jehu's rule neither the king nor the people know peace.

F. The reign of Queen Athaliah in Judah (11:1–16). When her son King Ahaziah is killed, Athaliah acts immediately to kill her grandchildren and seize power for herself! For six years she holds the throne for herself.

G. The reign of Joash in Judah (11:17—12:21). Athaliah has not destroyed all her grandchildren. One, Joash, is snatched up and hidden in the Jerusalem temple. He is hidden there until he reaches the age of seven. Then the high priest, Jehoiada, plans with the Levites and the military to restore this rightful descendant of David to the throne of Judah.

Athaliah hears them rejoicing and comes to investigate. She is killed there, just outside the temple, executed at last for her crimes.

Jehoiada the priest is the young king's chief advisor. During this period the great Jerusalem temple is restored and repaired (see Altar), financed by contributions from the people.

Joash is assassinated in bed by several of his servants.

H. The reign of Jehoahaz in Israel (13:1–9). Jehoahaz succeeds his father Jehu on Israel's throne. He continues in the religious policies established by Jeroboam (1 Kings 12), but he does turn to God for relief from the neighboring Aramaeans.

I. The reign of Jehoash in Israel (13:10–25). Jehoash follows the religious pattern of all the kings of Israel. Elisha suffers his final illness in the days of Jehoash. The king is honestly concerned about the prophet's coming death, for Jehoash views Elisha as his kingdom's greatest resource (14). Toward the end of his reign, Jehoash defeats the Aramaeans. Hazael dies, and this triggers a number of Israelite military victories.

J. The reign of Amaziah in Judah (14:1–22). Amaziah begins well. He obeys the written word and the messages of the prophets, and wins a victory over the

Edomites. But then he turns to idolatry. Judah is defeated by Israel, and the king taken captive. It's likely that Amaziah is kept in Samaria as captive for some years, for his son Uzziah (Azariah) becomes co-regent about the time of the defeat.

K. The reign of Jeroboam II in Israel (14:23-29).
Only a few verses in the Old Testament are devoted to Jeroboam II, yet his forty-one year rule is remarkable. Israel began a resurgence under Jehoash. Her power keeps on growing under Jeroboam, until Israel becomes the leading eastern Mediterranean state.

The time of Jeroboam II is a time of great prosperity. The wealth, and the luxury of the rich, as well as the lack of concern of that society for the poor, are graphically portrayed in the book of the prophet Amos. But the king and the people continue to do evil, nor will they turn away from the false religious system instituted by the first Jeroboam (1 Kings 12).

L. The reign of Azariah in Judah (15:1-7).
Uzziah, here called Azariah, rules for some fifty-two years in Jerusalem. He is a contemporary of Jeroboam II, and his reign is a time of great prosperity in Judah.

Uzziah is a godly king. At the end of his life, the king is struck with leprosy and lives in isolation until his death.

M. The reigns of Zechariah, Shallum, Menahem, Pekahiah, and Pekah in Israel (15:8-31).

N. The reign of Jotham in Judah (15:32-38).
It is difficult to sort out the dates of this king of Judah. While he is still co-regent with his father Uzziah, he makes his own son Ahaz his co-regent. Thus Judah has three overlapping kings living at the same time. Jotham is one of Judah's godly kings.

O. The reign of Ahaz in Judah (16:1-20).
When Ahaz becomes sole ruler on the death of his godly father, he turns his back on the Lord. He follows the most detestable of the pagan religious practices. God acts in quick judgment, and Judah becomes a vassal state of Assyria.

P. The reign of Hoshea in Israel (17:1-5).

Q. The captivity of Israel to Assyria (17:6-41).
When Tiglath-pileser of Assyria dies, Hoshea rebels against his son. A treaty is made with Egypt, and tribute to Assyria is withheld. This is foolish, for Egypt is in a particularly weakened state.

Shalmaneser V (727-722 B.C.) does not hesitate, and comes with his armies. Hoshea crumbles. He rushes to meet the Assyrian with his tribute money, but he is taken captive and

Israel is invaded. It takes three years (724-722), but Samaria finally falls, and the history of Israel ends.

II. THE KINGDOM OF JUDAH ALONE 18:1—25:30.

A. The reign of Hezekiah (18:1—20:21).
Hezekiah is co-regent with his father Ahaz when the northern kingdom falls to Assyria. He assumes full control some four years before his father's death.

Hezekiah proves to be one of Judah's most godly kings. He reopens the temple, reinstitutes the festivals ordained in the Law, and purges the land of its places for idol worship.

Unlike his father, Hezekiah is anti-Assyrian, but he wisely holds back from open hostilities until after the death of Sargon II in 705 B.C. However, his successor invades Judah in 701. When the fortified city of Lachish is taken by Sennacherib, Hezekiah submits. But the Assyrians seem determined to destroy Jerusalem. When a delegation jeers at the land and its *God, Hezekiah brings the matter to the Lord with great faith. Jerusalem is spared (2 Kin. 19:20-37; see ch. 55 of this Handbook, §3.7.d).

A number of events in Hezekiah's times are reported in detail in 2 Kings and 2 Chronicles, and in chapters 37 through 39 of Isaiah.

> "Now therefore, O LORD our God, I pray, save us from his hand, that all the kingdoms of the earth may know that You are the LORD God, You alone" (19:19-36). Hezekiah's faith-filled prayer for the Lord's salvation (v. 19; see Spiritual Warfare) bases its appeal not on personal need but on God's reputation—it is the living God the enemy had reproached (16). In times of threatening crisis, when either our enemy or our circumstances attempt to frustrate God's purposes, we may appeal to the Lord similarly. We may seek more than just our personal needs and seek His glory in every circumstance, so all may acknowledge "You alone."

Hezekiah's illness (20:1-11). Near death, Hezekiah prays emotionally for healing (see Healing, Divine). Isaiah announces God's reprieve. Hezekiah's thoughts and feelings at this time are recorded in Isaiah 38.

Envoys from Babylon (20:12-21). The king of Babylon sends Hezekiah congratulations on his recovery. At this time Babylon is a distant and insignificant power. Foolishly Hezekiah shows the envoys all his wealth and his armory. Isaiah angrily rebukes him: the day is coming when the Babylonians will carry away the wealth Hezekiah has displayed, and Judah's people as well.

B. The reign of Manasseh (21:1–18). Manasseh succeeds his father, Hezekiah, and rules for fifty-five years. The first eleven are as co-regent with his father. He is one of Israel's most evil kings. He practices sorcery and witchcraft, burns his sons in idol worship, and brings idols within the Jerusalem temple itself. It is probable that Isaiah is one of the prophets killed at his order.

The whole people's eager plunge into evil brings judgment. All of Judah will soon be led captive, as was Israel.

C. The reign of Amon (21:19–26). Amon is not touched by his father's experience. He does evil and is assassinated by his own officials in his second year.

D. The reign of Josiah (22:1–23:30). Josiah is the last good king of Judah. He is crowned when he is only eight, and rules in Jerusalem for thirty-one years. His reign is a time of peace.

Book of the Law found (22:3–20). Lost copies of the Mosaic Law are located when the temple is repaired. The first reading reveals how far short of obedience Judah has fallen, and that God is committed by His Word to punish Judah's wickedness (see Deuteronomy 28). Josiah sends to Huldah the prophetess, to inquire about what God will do (see Women). The response is encouraging. Judgment must come, but because Josiah has been responsive to God, the destruction will be delayed until after his death.

Total dedication (23:1–28). Guided by the Scriptures, Josiah sets about his reformation with fresh zeal.

Josiah's death (23:29–30).

E. The reign of Jehoahaz (23:31–34). Jehoahaz rules in Jerusalem for only three months. He is taken by Pharaoh Necho to Egypt, where he dies in captivity.

F. The reign of Jehoiakim (23:35—24:7). Jehoiakim is also a son of Josiah. Like his deposed brother, Jehoahaz, he is evil. Jehoiakim is the king who tears up the first draft of Jeremiah's written prophecies (Jer. 36:23). It is during his reign that Daniel and his friends are deported to Babylon. And it is from this first invasion and deportation that the seventy years of the Babylonian captivity will be numbered.

G. The reign of Jehoiachin (24:8–16). Just three months after Jehoiachin becomes king in Jerusalem, the city is besieged and Jehoiachin is taken captive to Babylon.

H. The reign of Zedekiah (24:17–20). Zedekiah has been placed on his throne by Nebuchadnezzar and given his name by that conqueror. He is the third son of Josiah to rule. Like his brothers, the new king refuses to follow God's guidance or to honor the Lord.

I. The fall of Jerusalem (25:1–7). Early in 588 B.C. Nebuchadnezzar marches west. After an interrupted siege, Jerusalem is taken. (See ch. 55, §3.7.d.)

J. The captivity of Judah (25:8–26). Zedekiah's children are killed and he is blinded. The remaining treasures of the temple are sacked, and the city and temple burned. Now most of the remaining population are taken captive to join their brothers in Babylon.

The era of the kingdom has ended as did the era of the judges—in sin, misery, and defeat.

K. The release of Jehoiachin (25:27–30).

TRUTH-IN-ACTION through 2 KINGS

Truth 2 Kings Teaches	**Action** 2 Kings Invites
1 Steps to Holiness Holiness among God's people brings Him honor. Unholiness dishonors Him. Holiness has two equally important dimensions. We are set apart to God and separated from the world. Just as God cannot be glorified by those who are not fully His, neither can He be glorified by those who are of the world. Therefore, we must live in the world, but we must not live as being	**5:19–27** Do not covet the world's reward for your ministry. Be wary lest it become an occasion for sin and judgment for you. **11:18** Know that true repentance involves rooting out anything that distracts from your worship of God. Eliminate any vestige of idolatry from your own life. **17:7–15** Understand that God judges His people severely when they persist in the world's ways and standards rather than His. Reject any areas where world-mindedness has taken root in you. **21:6** Do not practice abortion! Reject and flee from the occult! (continued)

Truth 2 Kings Teaches	**Action** 2 Kings Invites
1 Steps to Holiness *(continued)* of the world. Be careful that a negative focus on external behavior does not blind us to the true nature of unholiness and allow us to be seduced by the world.	
2 Steps to Dynamic Devotion Hear again the recurring theme of how God wants our hearts to be fully devoted to Him. Even zeal with an undevoted heart does not please Him.	**10:28–31** *Be zealous* for God with your whole heart. *Dedicate* your life to Him and to His purposes.
3 Key Lessons in Faith Faith is, in essence, taking God at His Word and His Word at face value. God has limitless supply of resources for all who trust in and obey Him. Fearing that we will not have enough in times of need insults the God who has revealed Himself as Yahweh-Yireh, The-Lord-Our-Provider.	**4:1–7** *Believe* that God is able to supply your needs, even when you have no idea how. *Know* that God promises to keep His people alive in famine. This applies spiritually, too: God's spiritual resources for you are limitless, even during times of spiritual drought. **4:43, 44** *Choose to believe* that you will always have enough resources to do the will of God.
4 Keys to Wise Living The God who is our wisdom and gives freely of His wisdom to those who trust in Him is careful to teach us His ways. He who is wise will never turn from the clear counsel of wisdom in God's Word.	**4:39–41** *Know the source* of any teaching you receive or pass on to others. *Always judge teachings* according to God's Word. **18:5–7** *Follow the Lord*, and He will grant you spiritual success.
5 Keys to Relating to Authority Relating properly to God's delegated authority is a key to spiritual prosperity.	**2:1–15** *Be loyal* to those to whom the Lord assigns you. *Understand* that the Lord will reward such loyalty. **2:23–25** *Avoid mocking or criticizing* those God anoints for leadership and ministry. *Understand* that God watches over them to protect them.
6 Lessons for Leaders God places great value upon the leaders He places among His people and wants them to be effective and fruitful in their ministry. Effective leadership flows out of God's anointing. This is also true for those who serve with you under your care. Those in leadership must be careful not to take credit for something that has resulted from God's working in their ministry.	**2:9** Leaders, *believe* that God has a greater anointing for your ministry. *Do not settle* for mediocre effectiveness in your ministry. **12:13–16** Leaders, *trust* the Holy Spirit's working in those who serve with you. **18:4** Leaders, *reject praise and honor God* for works He accomplishes through your ministry. *Teach* those you serve to do the same.

KEYS TO 1 CHRONICLES
God's Sovereign Grace

Kingdom Key: God's Purpose in View
Central to understanding the reign of David, as related in 1 Chronicles, is to grasp the development of Israel's worship of the Lord under his leadership. David tapped the heart of God in a way no person before or after him seems to have.

Under God's sovereign grace, during David's reign Israel's boundaries expanded to their broadest extent, and worship rose to greater heights than ever. A companion truth should also be clear: David's *heart* of worship and *hand* in warfare are not divided. Many of his psalms combine themes of worship and praise with invocations of divine aid in battle and declarations of triumph over Israel's enemies (Pss. 66, 68, 70; *see* also 25:2; 92:4; 60:12 and many others). Kingdom worship and warfare are to be joined. The former releases the grace of victory through the latter. Also, through worship, compassion toward humankind is maintained despite the violence of war.

David's understanding of God's sovereign grace, within the context of His laws and commandments, is the foundation of his forth-

> **God is a promise-maker and a promise-keeper, worthy to be trusted.**

right praise and worship of God. Perhaps the most dramatic evidence of his hunger for God's presence and his understanding of God's grace is seen in David's determination to bring the ark of the covenant to Jerusalem (chs. 13—16). A point often overlooked is that David erected a tent of his own to house the ark. In contrast to the common term "tabernacle of Moses," this tent is called the "tabernacle David erected" (16:1) or "tabernacle of David" (Is. 16:5; Amos 9:11; Acts 15:16).

David's sense of God's grace is seen in his insights about worship. Note: (1) David's perception of a future *New Covenant,* and how God's ultimate objective was to consummate the sacrificial system (Ps. 51:16–17); (2) his introduction of singers and musicians—*new offices*—which greatly
(Please turn to page 98.)

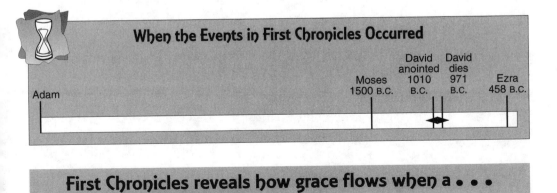

When the Events in First Chronicles Occurred

Adam

Moses
1500 B.C.

David
anointed
1010
B.C.

David
dies
971
B.C.

Ezra
458 B.C.

First Chronicles reveals how grace flows when a • • •

Kingdom Key *continued from page 97*

expand the exercise, tenor, and tone of worship (15:16–22; 25:1–31); and (3) his approach into God's presence—a *new intimacy*—"sealed" before the ark and permitted *within* the tabernacle (17:16; 2 Sam. 7:18), a place earlier tradition disallowed.

First Chronicles reveals how *grace* flows when a *worshiper's* heart comes to know *God's* heart, and when praiseful song broadens boundaries of life in God's will.

Master Key: God's Son Revealed

Christ is foreshadowed in 1 Chronicles in much the same way as in 1 Kings (*see* Keys to 1 Kings: Master Key). In 1 Chronicles, however, many find an allusion to Christ in reference to the temple. First Chronicles 21 (also 2 Samuel 24) explains that as a consequence of sin, a death plague had broken out against Israel. David buys a piece of property from Ornan on which to make a sacrifice to stop the plague. This site on Mount Moriah was the very place where Solomon would build the temple (2 Chr. 3:1). It is possible that this was the very mountain where Abraham was asked to sacrifice his son Isaac (Gen. 22:2). In the New Testament, Paul refers three times to believers as the "temple of God" (1 Cor. 3:16–17; 6:19; Eph. 2:19–22). It is Christ who has purchased the ground for this spiritual temple. His sacrifice has delivered us from death (Rom. 5:12–18; 7:24–25; 1 John 3:14).

> **Key Word:** *Priestly View of David's Reign*
>
> **Key Verses:** First Chronicles 17:11–14; 29:11
>
> **Key Chapter:** First Chronicles 17
>
> **P**ivotal for the Book of First Chronicles as well as for the rest of the Scriptures is the Davidic Covenant recorded in Second Samuel 7 and First Chronicles 17. God promises David that He will "establish him [David's ultimate offspring, Jesus Christ] in My house and in My kingdom forever; and his throne shall be established forever" (1 Chr. 17:14).

Power Key: God's Spirit at Work

Two clear references to the Holy Spirit appear in 1 Chronicles. The first is in 12:18, where "the Spirit" came upon or clothed Amasai and enabled him to give an inspired utterance. (*See* Keys to 1 and 2 Kings: Power Key, which describe the Holy Spirit's inspiring others to prophesy during the kingdom period.) The second reference is in 28:12, which explains that "the Spirit" revealed the plans of the temple to David.

Introducing
1 CHRONICLES

Author. First and 2 Chronicles were originally one book (*see* "Content" below). Since the identity of the author of this work is not stated in either 1 or 2 Chronicles, many have opted to refer to this unknown author simply as "the chronicler." However, Ezra is the most likely candidate for the authorship of Chronicles. The early Jewish tradition of the Talmud affirms that Ezra wrote 1 and 2 Chronicles. Also, the closing verses of 2 Chronicles (2 Chr. 36:22–23) are repeated as the opening verses of Ezra (*see* Ezra 1:1–3). Not only does this add to the case for Ezra's authorship of 1 Chronicles, it also may be an indication that 1 and 2 Chronicles and Ezra were once a consecutive work. In addition, 1 and 2 Chronicles and Ezra have similar style, vocabulary, and contents. Ezra was a scribe as well as a priest, and played a significant role in the community of exiles who returned to Jerusalem. Though we cannot be certain, it is reasonable to assume that "the chronicler" was Ezra.

Date. Though the precise date for 1 and 2 Chronicles cannot be established, it probably came into its final form sometime toward the end of the fifth century B.C. The last event recorded in the closing verses of 2 Chronicles is the decree of the Persian king Cyrus to allow the Jews to return to Judah. This is dated at 538 B.C. and gives the impression that Chronicles would have been composed shortly after this time. However, the latest person mentioned in 1 and 2 Chronicles is actually Anani of the eighth generation of King Jehoiachin (*see* 1 Chr. 3:24). Jehoiachin was deported to Babylon in 597 B.C. Depending on how these generations are measured (approximately twenty-five years), Anani's birth would have been sometime between 425 and 400 B.C. Therefore, the date for 1 and 2 Chronicles is between 425 and 400 B.C.

Background. The Book of 1 Chronicles covers the period from Adam to the death of David around 971 B.C. This is a remarkable scope of time, since it embraces the same period covered in the first ten books of the Old Testament, Genesis through 2 Samuel. Without the genealogies in 1 Chronicles 1—9, 1 and 2 Chronicles cover roughly the same time period as 1 and 2 Kings. However, the specific background of 1 and 2 Chronicles is the period after the Exile. During this time, the ancient world was under the control of the powerful Persian Empire. All that remained of the glorious kingdom of David and Solomon was the tiny province of Judah. The Persians had replaced the monarchy with a provincial governor. Though God's people had been allowed to return to Jerusalem and rebuild the temple, their situation was far removed from the golden days of David and Solomon.

Occasion and Purpose. The return of the exiles from Babylon necessitated the recording of the history of God's people, especially Judah. First Chronicles was written for the dual purpose of providing encouragement and exhortation to those who had returned to Jerusalem. The remnant that was left needed encouragement to keep their faith alive in the midst of difficulty, and they needed hope for the future. The emphasis of Chronicles on their spiritual heritage of David, Solomon, the temple, and the priesthood was a refreshing reminder that God was faithful and He would not forget His promises to David and to His people. Yet 1 Chronicles also served as a strong exhortation to motivate God's people to adhere to the Mosaic covenant and ritual, so that the tragedy of the past would not be repeated.

Comparison with Kings. One may question the need for the books of 1 and 2 Chronicles, since the material has already been covered in 1 and 2 Kings and other Old Testament books. However, though the books are similar, they are by no means identical. In the same way that there are four accounts of the life of Christ in Matthew, Mark, Luke, and John, there are two accounts of the history of God's people. Though 1 and 2 Kings and 1 and 2 Chronicles are alike in content, they offer two different historical perspectives. While the Books of Kings were written to those in exile, the Books of Chronicles address the postexilic community. They were written for two different purposes. Compare the "Occasion and Purpose" section of this introduction with the same sections in the introductions to 1 and 2 Kings. Also, Kings and Chronicles have different political perspectives. While Kings embraces both kingdoms, Israel and Judah, Chronicles focuses only on Judah. Finally, Kings and Chronicles differ in their theological perspectives. Kings presents a prophetic outlook, while Chronicles operates from a priestly vantage point. However, Chronicles is like Kings in that it is not mere history, but rather theology in the form of a historical narrative. *See* Introductions to 1 and 2 Kings: Content.

Content. In the original Hebrew Scriptures, 1 and 2 Chronicles formed one book, entitled "Events of the Days." It was divided and renamed "Things Passed Over" by the translators of the Greek Old Testament (the Septuagint, or LXX). The title "Chronicles" derives from Jerome. It is not a continuation of the history of God's people, but a duplication of and a supplement to 1 and 2 Samuel and 1 and 2 Kings.

The united work of 1 and 2 Chronicles can be divided into four main sections. First Chronicles gives genealogies (chs. 1—9) and outlines the reign of David (chs. 10—29). Second Chronicles sets forth the reign of Solomon (chs. 1—9) and traces the reigns of the twenty rulers of Judah (chs. 10—36).

The Book of 1 Chronicles has two main divisions. The first section is nine chapters of genealogies. The genealogies begin with Adam and proceed all the way through the Exile to those who returned to Jerusalem. This section is often passed over as unimportant. However, like the Gospels of Matthew and Luke, the genealogies form a foundation for the account that will follow. First Chronicles is weighted with genealogies to underscore the need for Judah's racial and religious purity. The genealogies are selectively compiled to highlight the line of David and the tribe of Levi.

The second part of 1 Chronicles (chs. 10—29) records the events and accomplishments in the life of King David. Chapter 10 serves as a prologue to summarize the reign and death of King Saul. In chapters 11 and 12 David becomes king and secures Jerusalem. The rest of the account of David focuses on the three significant aspects of his reign, namely the bringing of the ark of the covenant to Jerusalem (chs. 13—17), his military exploits (chs. 18—20), and the preparations for the building of the temple (chs. 21—27). The closing two chapters of 1 Chronicles record David's last days.

Personal Application. While 1 and 2 Kings draw out the fact of human responsibility, showing that sin leads to defeat, 1 Chronicles accentuates the sovereign deliverance of God. The twin themes of encouragement and exhortation still ring true today. God has been faithful throughout all of history to deliver those who cry out to Him. Chronicles skillfully tells the story of how God was true to His word and kept the promises He had made to His people. This is a great source of encouragement for believers of all ages. God is a promise-making and promise-keeping God who is worthy to be trusted. He is still a God of hope, and His purposes will prevail in the lives of His people. However, 1 Chronicles also exhorts us to learn from the failure of God's people in the past, in order that we might not make the same mistakes (1 Cor. 10:11; Heb. 4:11).

Surveying
1 CHRONICLES

I. THE ROOTS OF GOD'S PEOPLE 1:1—9:44. The writer of the Chronicles takes great care to provide genealogical information.

A. The heritage of the sons of Jacob (1:1—2:2).

B. The heritage of David's line in Judah (2:3—3:24).

C. The heritage of the Twelve Tribes (4:1—8:40).

D. The heritage of the remnant (9:1–34).

E. The heritage of King Saul in Benjamin (9:35–44). This section ends with the divine evaluation of Saul. His death is blamed on his unfaithfulness to the Lord (10:13). With his death, God turns the kingdom over to David (14).

II. THE REIGN OF KING DAVID 10:1—29:30.

A. David's affirmation as king (10:1—12:40). David crowned (11:1–3). It is 1003 B.C. when David is finally acknowledged as king of a united Israel.

David takes Jerusalem (11:4–9).

David's military organization (11:10—12:40). The six hundred men who joined David in his fugitive years form the core of his military forces. It is clear that leadership in the army is based in large part on personal merit and prowess in battle.

> **"Then the Spirit [of the Lord] came upon Amasai"** (12:18). Literally, "The Spirit clothed Himself" with Amasai. Amasai's inspired utterance, which spoke of his allegiance to David, and the assurance that God was David's helper (v. 18), helped unify and strengthen David's kingdom. Similarly, the Holy Spirit speaks prophetically through men and women today, edifying, exhorting, and comforting the church (see 1 Cor. 14:3).

B. David's acquisition of the ark (13:1—17:27). The ark is brought to Jerusalem (13:1–14; 15:1–18). David brings the ark to Jerusalem. Israel's capital will also be its worship center. David assembles priests and Levites (see Minister), and joyfully brings the ark to Jerusalem.

David defeats the Philistines (14:8–17).

David leads in worship (15:19—16:6). As David brings the ark into Jerusalem, he is caught up in worship. Dressed as the other worshipers, without robes of royalty or warrior's armor, David dances and praises God in the streets (1 Chr. 15:27–29).

David's psalm of praise (16:7–43).

"Oh, give thanks to the LORD, for He is good!"
(16:7–43). This psalm of David was presented to the choir leader on the day the ark—signifying God's presence—was placed in the tabernacle at Jerusalem (15:1; 16:1). The people are exhorted to *thank the Lord for His powerful works on their behalf and His personal covenant with them—which His presence affords (vv. 8–13; 15–22). Spirit-filled believers not only give joyful thanks for God's indwelling presence, which secures personal relationship (*see* 1 Cor. 3:16; Rom. 8:11; 2 Cor. 1:22), but they also greet in earnest the continuing fullness of His presence, whereby we experience His saving power through both our words and works (*see* Acts 1:8; 4:31, 33).

God's covenant with David (1 Chr. 17:1–27). David determines to build God a temple. When he inquires, the prophet Nathan is enthusiastic. But that night God gives Nathan a message for David. David is not to build God a house; instead God will build David's "house." The right to Israel's throne will pass from generation to generation of David's descendants, forever. David's prayer of response is in 1 Chronicles 17:16–27.

C. David's military advances (18:1—20:8).
David's military victories (18:1–13).

David's civil government (18:14–17). It was a monumental task to impose structure on a people unused to any kind of government control, and all in a single generation. The fact that David is able to design and build such a system is a testimony to the many gifts of this warrior, worshiper, and unmatched administrator.

Victory over the Ammonites (19:1—20:3).

Philistine wars reviewed (20:4–8).

D. David's arrangements for the temple (21:1—27:34).
David counts his people (21:1–30).

David prepares for building the temple (22:1—27:34). David is not permitted to build the temple himself (*see* 2 Samuel 7; 1 Chronicles 17), but he spends his later years preparing for this culminating expression of his love for God. David designs the structure, prepares building materials, and assembles millions of dollars worth of gold and silver. In addition he begins to organize and train the priests for work at the temple (ch. 23; *see* Praise). This is necessary because tasks assigned the Levites in the Law relate to transportation of a portable worship center. Now, with a central worship structure being built, the ministry of the Levites must be rethought. Roles for singers (ch. 25), gatekeepers, and treasurers (26), and others are created and their job descriptions developed.

E. David's last announcements (28:1—29:30).

"Now bless the LORD your God"
(29:20). Leading the way through his own lavish gifts, David's appeal for the people to give toward the temple building fund results in a willing outpouring of gifts, accompanied by great rejoicing (vv. 1–9). Before all the people, David blessed the Lord, acknowledging that He had made this possible (10–15; *see* Kingdom of God; Majesty); and after praying for the people, he instructed them to bless the Lord as well (20). Giving is an act of worship. We cheerfully offer to the Lord what our heart has purposed (2 Cor. 9:7), as the Holy Spirit inspires our giving and gives us joy as we give.

TRUTH-IN-ACTION through 1 CHRONICLES

Truth 1 Chronicles Teaches	**Action** 1 Chronicles Invites
1 Guidelines for Growing in Godliness Godliness means being faithful to God in all that we do. Faithfulness involves letting God and His Word be our exclusive resource of any knowledge we have about Him, His ways, or spiritual reality. The godly person avoids any contact with the occult.	**9:1** *Be warned* that unfaithfulness to God may result in our hearts and minds being taken captive by the world system. **10:13** *Do not seek out* spiritual information or insight from any spiritual source other than the Holy Spirit or Christ-centered counselors. *Be warned* that doing so can result in serious judgment, even death.
2 Steps to Dynamic Devotion We must never allow anything to become more important to us than our pursuit of God. Even learn to guard against letting the things of God become more important than knowing God Himself.	**22:19** *Understand* that God gives you times of peace and rest so that you can devote your heart and soul to seeking Him. **28:7–10** *Be diligent* in the things God gives you to do. *Serve God* with unswerving devotion. *Understand* that the Lord honors those who honor His Word and seek Him with all their heart.
3 Keys to Wise Living Wisdom counsels us that God's ways are higher than our ways and His thoughts than our thoughts. He knows the best way to do His work.	**13:7–10; 15:11–15** *Do not undertake* to do God's work in your own way. *Be warned* that employing human wisdom to accomplish God's work can result in frightening consequences.
4 A Key to Generous Living Knowing the extent of divine resource frees us to greater generosity.	**29:14** *Understand* that all we possess comes from the hand of the Lord.
5 Key to Relating to Authority God instructs us in how to relate to Him by instructing us in how to relate properly to those He sends.	**16:22** *Know* that God has sworn to protect those He sends to proclaim His Word. *Be careful* how you speak about and treat God's servants.
6 Lessons for Leaders God calls His leaders to realize that the work to which they are called is His and He will see to its completion.	**28:20** Leaders, *take courage* in the fact that the Lord pledges to be with those He calls until that to which He calls them has been completed.

KEYS TO 2 CHRONICLES
God's Sovereign Glory

Kingdom Key: God's Purpose in View

Second Chronicles begins with the construction of Solomon's temple and ends with its destruction. It begins with the appearance of God's glory (7:1–2) and ends with its withdrawal (Hab. 2:16). Since God's purpose in Christ is to display His glory in and through the church (John 17:22; Eph. 3:21), we look for (1) that which allows the release of God's glory among His people, and (2) that which causes its removal. Solomon's early leadership invites God's glory:

1. He seeks wisdom and knowledge in order to faithfully and effectively serve his people (1:7–12).

2. He strives to build "for the name of the LORD," indicating his objective to glorify God, rather than to exalt mankind (2:1).

3. He discerns between what is common and what is holy, and commits to keep the two separate (8:11).

4. He worships sacrificially, in the spirit of the timeless truth of God's Word as revealed by His prophets (8:12–16).

5. He prays humbly (6:12–13), acknowledging God's transcendence (He's bigger than *my* work!—6:18), yet believing in and inviting His personal presence and power (He'll work where I am!—6:19–20).

At the dedication of the temple, Solomon acknowledged that God's glory

> **God is faithful to deliver those who cry out to Him.**

abides only when His people remain faithful (6:22–42). Judah did not, and much of the rest of 2 Chronicles records their gradual slide away from God, resulting in the removal of His glory. Accounts of certain kings of Judah illustrate how this happened:

1. Ahaziah followed evil counsel from those whose wisdom is born of the spirit of the world (22:1–4).

2. Joash forgot that earlier blessings were born of obedience, not achievement; his heart hardened to resist God's Word (24:15–22).

3. Uzziah usurped an office not appointed by God, presuming authority not invested in him (26:16–23).

4. Manasseh supplanted the pure worship of God with efforts to manipulate people (33:9). His end was a *(Please turn to page 104.)*

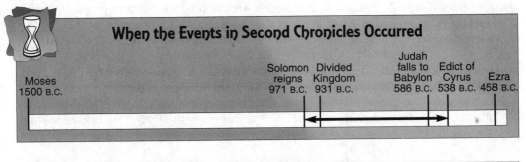

When the Events in Second Chronicles Occurred

Moses 1500 B.C.	Solomon reigns 971 B.C.	Divided Kingdom 931 B.C.	Judah falls to Babylon 586 B.C.	Edict of Cyrus 538 B.C.	Ezra 458 B.C.

2 Chronicles: God's glory will never abide on • • •

Kingdom Key *continued from page 103*

corrupt, demonic confusion (33:1–9).

5. Summarily, these kings disregarded God's Word until "there was no remedy" (36:16).

As the Sovereign Lord, God will never allow His glory to abide on anything or anyone who compromises the founding principles of His rule (Is. 42:8).

Master Key: God's Son Revealed

Christ is foreshadowed in 2 Chronicles in much the same way as in 2 Kings (*see* Keys to 2 Kings: Master Key). However, in 2 Chronicles, many see an allusion to Christ in reference to the temple. First Chronicles 21 (*see* also 2 Samuel 24) explains that as a consequence of sin, a death plague strikes Israel. David buys a piece of property from Ornan on which to make a sacrifice to stop the plague. This site on Mount Moriah was the very place where Solomon would build the temple (3:1). It is also possible that this was the mountain where Abraham was asked to sacrifice his son Isaac (Gen. 22:2). In the New Testament, Paul refers three times to believers as the "temple of God" (1 Cor. 3:16–17; 6:19; Eph. 2:19–22). Christ purchased the ground for this spiritual temple. It is His sacrifice that delivers us from death (Rom. 5:12–18; 7:24–25; 1 John 3:14).

Power Key: God's Spirit at Work

Three clear references to the Holy Spirit are found in 2 Chronicles. He is referred to as the "Spirit of God" (15:1; 24:20) and the "Spirit of the LORD" (20:14). In these references, the Holy Spirit gives inspired utterances through Azariah (15:1), Jahaziel (20:14), and Zechariah (24:20). Such inspiration by the Spirit to prophesy is cited also in 1 and 2 Samuel and 1 and 2 Kings. *See* Keys to 1 and 2 Kings: Power Key.

Many also see the Holy Spirit present at the dedication of the temple (2 Chr. 5:13–14; compare also 1 Kin. 8:10–11). This temple, built on a place that was purchased—a place where sacrifice was made for sin—is now filled with God's presence. In the New Testament, Paul explains that believers are the temple of God, the dwelling place of the Holy Spirit (1 Cor. 3:16; 6:19).

Finally, a possible reference to the Holy Spirit appears in 18:23. This reference parallels 1 Kings 22:24. (*See* note on 1 Kings 22:24.)

Key Word: *Priestly View of Judah*

The Book of Second Chronicles provides topical histories of the end of the united kingdom (Solomon) and the kingdom of Judah. More than historical annals, Chronicles is a divine editorial on the spiritual characteristics of the Davidic dynasty.

Key Verses: Second Chronicles 7:14; 16:9

Key Chapter: Second Chronicles 34

Second Chronicles records the reforms and revivals under such kings as Asa, Jehosphaphat, Joash, Hezekiah, and Josiah.

• • • anyone who compromises His principles.

Introducing
2 CHRONICLES

Author. Since 1 and 2 Chronicles were originally one book (*see* "Content" below), they are to be considered together in the matter of authorship. The fact that the identity of the author of this united work is not stated in either 1 or 2 Chronicles has led many to refer to this unknown author simply as "the chronicler." However, Ezra is the most likely candidate for the authorship of 1 and 2 Chronicles. The early Jewish tradition of the Talmud affirms that Ezra wrote 1 and 2 Chronicles. Also, the closing verses of Chronicles (2 Chr. 36:22–23) are repeated as the opening verses of Ezra (*see* Ezra 1:1–3). Not only does this add to the case for Ezra's authorship of 1 and 2 Chronicles, it also may be an indication that 1 and 2 Chronicles and Ezra were once a consecutive work. In addition, 1 and 2 Chronicles and Ezra have similar style, vocabulary, and contents. Ezra was a scribe as well as a priest, and played a significant role in the community of exiles who returned to Jerusalem. Though we cannot be certain, it is reasonable to assume that "the chronicler" was Ezra.

Date. Though the precise date of 1 and 2 Chronicles cannot be established, this unified work probably came into its final form sometime toward the end of the fifth century B.C. The last event recorded in the closing verses of 2 Chronicles is the decree of the Persian king Cyrus to allow the Jews to return to Judah. This is dated at 538 B.C. and gives the impression that 1 and 2 Chronicles would have been composed shortly after this time. However, the latest person mentioned in 1 and 2 Chronicles is actually Anani of the eighth generation of King Jehoiachin (*see* 1 Chr. 3:24). Jehoiachin was deported to Babylon in 597 B.C. Depending on how these generations are measured (approximately twenty-five years), Anani's birth would have been sometime between 425 and 400 B.C. Therefore, the date for 1 and 2 Chronicles is between 425 and 400 B.C.

Background. The Book of 2 Chronicles covers the period from the beginning of the reign of Solomon in 971 B.C. to the end of the Exile around 538 B.C. However, the specific background of 1 and 2 Chronicles is the period after the Exile. During this time, the ancient world was under the control of the powerful Persian Empire. All that remained of the glorious kingdom of David and Solomon was the tiny province of Judah. The Persians had replaced the monarchy with a provincial governor. Though God's people had been allowed to return to Jerusalem and rebuild the temple, their situation was far removed from the golden days of David and Solomon.

Occasion and Purpose. The return of the exiles from Babylon necessitated the recording of the history of God's people, especially Judah. Second Chronicles was written for the dual purpose of providing encouragement and exhortation to those who had returned to Jerusalem. The remnant that was left needed encouragement to keep their faith alive in the midst of difficulty, and they needed hope for the future. The emphasis of 2 Chronicles on their spiritual heritage of David, Solomon, the temple, and the priesthood was a refreshing reminder that God was faithful and He would not forget His promises to David and to His people. Yet Chronicles also served as a strong exhortation to motivate God's people to adhere to the Mosaic covenant and ritual, so that the tragedy of the past would not be repeated.

Comparison with Kings. One may question the need for the books of 1 and 2 Chronicles, since the material has already been covered in 1 and 2 Kings and other Old Testament books. However, though the books are similar, they are by no means identical. In the same way that there are four accounts of the life of Christ in Matthew, Mark, Luke, and John, there are two accounts of the history of God's people. Though 1 and 2 Kings and 1 and 2 Chronicles are alike in content, they offer two different historical perspectives. While the Books of Kings were written to those in exile, the Books of Chronicles address the postexilic community. They were written for two different purposes. Compare the Introductions to 1 and 2 Kings and 2 Chronicles: Occasion and Purpose. Also, Kings and Chronicles have different political perspectives. While Kings embraces both kingdoms, Israel and Judah, Chronicles focuses only on Judah. Finally, Kings and Chronicles differ in their theological perspectives. Kings presents a prophetic outlook, while Chronicles operates from a priestly vantage point. However, Chronicles is like Kings in that it is not mere history, but rather theology in the form of a historical narrative. *See* Introductions to 1 and 2 Kings: Content.

Content. In the original Hebrew Scriptures, 1 and 2 Chronicles formed one book, entitled "Events of the Days." It was divided and renamed "Things Passed Over" by the translators of the Greek Old Testament (the Septuagint, or LXX). The title "Chronicles" derives from Jerome. It is not a continuation of the history of God's people, but a duplication of and a supplement to 1 and 2 Samuel and 1 and 2 Kings.

Second Chronicles can be divided into two main sections. The first part of 2 Chronicles (chs. 1—9) outlines the reign of King Solomon. The account accents the construction of the temple (chs. 2—7), and the wealth and wisdom of this extraordinary king (chs. 8; 9). However, the narrative ends abruptly and makes no mention of Solomon's failure as is recorded in 1 Kings 11.

The second section of 2 Chronicles consists of chapters 10—36. After the division of the kingdom, 2 Chronicles concentrates almost exclusively on the southern kingdom of Judah and treats the history of the northern kingdom of Israel as incidental. Second Chronicles traces the reigns of Judah's twenty rulers down to Babylon's captivity of Judah in 586 B.C. The book concludes with Cyrus's decree for Judah's release and return (36:22–23).

Personal Application. While 1 and 2 Kings draw out the fact of human responsibility,

showing that sin leads to defeat, 2 Chronicles accentuates the sovereign deliverance of God. The twin themes of encouragement and exhortation still ring true today. God has been faithful throughout all of history to deliver those who cry out to Him. Second Chronicles skillfully tells the story of how God was true to His word and kept the promises He had made to His people. This is a great source of encouragement for believers of all ages. God is a promise-making and promise-keeping God who is worthy to be trusted. He is still a God of hope, and His purposes will prevail in the lives of His people. However, 2 Chronicles also exhorts us to learn from the failure of God's people in the past, in order that we might not make the same mistakes (1 Cor. 10:11; Heb. 4:11).

Surveying
2 CHRONICLES

I. THE REIGN OF KING SOLOMON 1:1—9:31.

A. The accession of Solomon as king (1:1-17).
Solomon quickly establishes his kingdom. He strengthens his relations with other states and marries a daughter of Pharaoh as part of an alliance with Egypt. Solomon also shows his love for God. God then appears to Solomon and instructs him to request whatever he wishes. Solomon asks only that God's promise to David be kept, and that Solomon be given the wisdom and knowledge needed to "judge this great people of Yours," and to distinguish between right and wrong (1 Kin. 3:9). This request pleases God. Solomon is promised wisdom and also is granted riches and honor.

Solomon's rule is a time of security for the people of Israel. During his reign, trade brings great wealth into Jerusalem and supports Solomon's growing court. (See ch. 55 of this Handbook, §3.3.)

B. The achievement of building the temple (2:1—7:22).
The great achievement of Solomon's reign is construction of the temple of Jerusalem. These chapters tell of its construction and the massive effort required. The temple is twice the size of the portable tabernacle: ninety feet long and thirty feet wide. Its design and furnishings are the same, reproducing the divinely ordained plan that carries so much spiritual meaning.

The ark brought to the temple (5:1–14). With the ark in place in the temple, God's glory visibly fills the new temple as it did the tabernacle in the wilderness. (See Praise.)

Solomon's sermon (6:1–11; see Faith's Confession).

Solomon's prayer of dedication (6:12–42).

Two weeks of worship (7:1–10). The *prayer of Solomon is accepted. The whole congregation sees fire fall from heaven to kindle the altar of sacrifice. (See Joyful; Prayer.)

God's response to Solomon's prayer (7:11–22). This is the second time God appears to Solomon. God has consecrated the temple by His very presence. God warns that if His people fail to observe the Law, and turn aside to worship other gods, they will be stripped of their glory and become objects of ridicule, scattered throughout the world.

> **"I will hear from heaven, and will forgive their sin and heal their land"**
> (7:14). This tremendous promise of national healing and blessing spoken to Solomon at the temple dedication is conditioned upon very specific stipulations. It is a cause and effect statement. God's people must *recognize* that which inhibits His blessing (v. 13); and they must *respond,* by (1) humbling themselves, including confessing and turning from sin; and by (2) seeking His face, recommitting themselves to knowing and doing His will. *Then* He will hear, forgive, and heal. God desires to bless all who earnestly seek Him!

C. The affluence of Solomon (8:1—9:31).

Solomon's many projects (8:1–18). Solomon starts ambitious building projects, keeps the annual festivals, and reaches out in varied trading ventures. Solomon also puts the descendants of the Canaanites who are left in the land to slave labor.

The Queen of Sheba (9:1–12).

Solomon's splendor (9:13–28). A summary is given of the wealth that flows into Israel from Solomon's various ventures.

Solomon's death (9:29–31). After his forty years as king, the book is closed on Solomon's reign. He is buried in Jerusalem, the city of his father, David.

II. THE REIGNS OF THE KINGS OF JUDAH 10:1—36:16.

A. The reign of Rehoboam (10:1—12:16). On Solomon's death, the northern tribes demand that taxes be lightened. When Rehoboam threatens to make the load even heavier, Israel immediately rebels.

Rehoboam's nation grows stronger, as those who are faithful to the Law migrate to the tribal areas of Judah and Benjamin to escape Jeroboam's apostasy in Israel. Rehoboam does not remain faithful (2 Chr. 12:1). Still, when Judah is threatened by Egypt, Rehoboam and his officials repent and turn to God. Judah is not occupied but becomes a vassal state.

Rehoboam fortifies a number of Judah's cities (2 Chr. 11:5–12). These are located in the south, suggesting that his major enemies were the Philistines and Egyptians rather than Israel.

B. The reign of Abijah (13:1–22). Abijah's brief reign is marked by a significant victory over an invasion force from Israel. Abijah's oration to Jeroboam in 2 Chronicles 13:4–12 identifies the basic distinction between Judah and Israel throughout their joint history.

C. The reign of Asa (14:1—16:14). Asa's attitude of humble dependence on God is shown in his prayer recorded in 2 Chronicles 14:11–12. After a victory against Egypt, an encouraging message from the prophet Azariah motivates Asa to purge the land of idolatrous worship centers and repair the temple altar at Jerusalem. He then leads a great revival worship service (2 Chr. 15:10–15) which causes additional thousands to move to Judah from Israel for freedom to worship God according to His Law.

Asa's forty-year reign does not end as well as it begins. War threatens with Israel and he fails to trust the Lord, relying instead on a pagan nation (16:7–10).

D. The reign of Jehoshaphat (17:1— 20:37). Jehoshaphat is the second good king of Judah. He battles the penetration of Baal worship in Judah and sends Levites on itinerant preaching missions to communicate God's Law to all. His own faith is shown when Judah is invaded by enemies.

His primary errors are to make alliances with Israel and to marry his son Jehoram to one of Ahab's daughters, who is as evil as her mother Jezebel.

> **"*Believe in the LORD your God, and you shall be established; believe His prophets, and you shall prosper"** (20:20–34). When Jehoshaphat and the people faced the enemy's threat, they beseeched the Lord on the basis of His word (vv. 1–12); and as they stood confidently focused on Him alone (13), the Lord spoke the answer to the crisis through His prophet (14–17; *see* Praise). In the midst of trial, faith urges us to rest in God's character, receive His direction, and respond obediently to see the reward of faith—His overcoming victory.

E. The reign of Jehoram (21:1–20). Jehoram's eight-year reign is short and brutal. He has married Jezebel's daughter, Athaliah. Now Jehoram follows their religious and moral example. He kills his six brothers to be rid of potential rivals, Edom and Libnah successfully rebel against Judah's authority, and the Philistines attack Judah and capture the king's family. When Jehoram dies there is relief in Judah; no one mourns.

F. The reign of Ahaziah (22:1–9). Jehoram's only remaining son rules just one year. He is killed while visiting Joram of Israel.

G. The reign of Queen Athaliah (22:10— 23:15). Athaliah shows herself to truly be the daughter of the cruel and vindictive Jezebel. When her son King Ahaziah is killed, she acts immediately to kill her grandchildren and seize power for herself! No one seems able to withstand the queen mother, and for some six years she holds the throne for herself.

H. The reign of Joash (23:16—24:27). Joash is snatched up and hidden from Athaliah in the Jerusalem temple until he reaches the age of seven. Then the high priest, Jehoiada, plans with the Levites and the military to restore this rightful descendant of David to the throne of Judah.

Athaliah hears them rejoicing and comes to investigate. There, just outside the temple, she is killed. Jehoiada leads in a service of covenant renewal, in which all the people again promise to be the Lord's. Immediately the crowds destroy the altars and worship centers of Baal, with great rejoicing.

During Jehoiada's life, Joash follows the Lord and restores the Jerusalem temple. But Jehoiada's death brings a change in Joash. He turns from God to worship idols.

God permits the Aramaeans under Hazael to overcome Judah's superior forces. Joash is wounded, and then is assassinated in bed by those who oppose the apostasy of their king.

I. The reign of Amaziah (25:1–28). Amaziah begins well (*see* Faith, Seed), but then turns to idolatry. His turn toward sin produces defeat for Judah. Judah is defeated by Israel, and the king taken captive. The treasures are taken from Jerusalem, and one wall of the city is torn down.

J. The reign of Uzziah (26:1–23). Uzziah rules for some fifty-two years in Jerusalem. For the first twenty-four he is co-regent with his father, Amaziah. During this time Judah knows a great resurgence of prosperity. Uzziah reorganizes his army, extends his territory, and after the death of Jeroboam II, surpasses Israel in influence.

Uzziah is a godly king, but his successes bring character change. "When he was strong his heart was lifted up [in pride], to his destruction" (2 Chr. 26:16). The king is struck with leprosy and lives in isolation until his death.

K. The reign of Jotham (27:1–9). Jotham is one of Judah's good kings. During his reign, religious reforms continued as well as building programs and military victories. Second Chronicles 27:6 says that Jotham "became mighty, because he prepared his ways before the LORD his God."

L. The reign of Ahaz (28:1–27). Ahaz turns his back on the Lord upon the death of his father. He follows the most detestable of the pagan religious practices. God acts in quick judgment. Judah is defeated on every side, and many of her people are taken captive. Ahaz is desperate and appeals to Assyria, thus surrendering any claim to independence, and Judah becomes a vassal state.

M. The reign of Hezekiah (29:1—32:33). Details are given of Hezekiah's steps toward religious revival. He gathers the Levites and reassigns them to the duties first planned by David (29:25). They cleanse and purify the temple, and once again make offerings there. Hezekiah sends couriers to all Judah and Israel, inviting them to come and keep the Passover.

> **"May the good LORD provide atonement for everyone who prepares his heart to seek God . . . and the LORD listened . . . and healed the people"** (30:18–20). Hezekiah reinstates the Passover nationwide in his reform effort following Ahaz's wicked reign. Although many Israelites receiving Passover had not prepared themselves properly according to sanctuary purification rites, Hezekiah's prayer entreats the Lord for His atonement on behalf of all who sought Him with pure hearts. Despite their failure to observe proper order in worship, the Lord was pleased with the attitude of their hearts, and He heard and healed. Reconciliation with God is the greatest healing miracle of all. God desires to mend the broken and estranged relationship with His people.

In Hezekiah's fourteenth year, Sennacherib of Assyria comes to Jerusalem, ridiculing Hezekiah's god, and demanding surrender and deportation. Hezekiah immediately seeks the Lord's counsel.

God's answer (32:20–23). Isaiah brings God's word to Hezekiah. The Lord has heard his prayer. Judah will survive.

That night 185,000 men in the Assyrian army die! Sennacherib returns to his capital of Nineveh, where he is assassinated by two of his sons. (*See* Angel; Vision.)

> **"King Hezekiah and the prophet Isaiah . . . prayed and cried out to heaven"** (32:20–23). Sennacherib's ominous threat provoked no panic or fearful reaction on the part of faith-filled Hezekiah. By partnering in prayer with the prophet Isaiah, he presented the enemy's threat at the throne room. In 2 Kings 19:14–19 we read that Hezekiah took Sennacherib's threatening letter and "spread it before the LORD" (v. 14), recognizing that the Assyrian reproached the living God (16). When facing crisis, faith inspires us to take our requests unto God and to agree in faith with fellow believers and the Lord. We thus resist the enemy's schemes and present ourselves in cooperation with the fulfillment of God's purposes.

N. The reign of Manasseh (33:1–20). Manasseh succeeds his father, Hezekiah, and rules for fifty-five years. He is one of Judah's most evil kings, leading his people into practices more evil than the Canaanites that God's people replaced! During his reign, he is taken captive by the Assyrians. Manasseh repents while in captivity, and is released, returning to Judah. There he spends the final four or five years of his rule attempting to recall Judah to serve the Lord (vv. 15–17). But he cannot undo the impact of forty-five years of evil example.

O. The reign of Amon (33:21–25). Amon is not touched by his father's experience. He does evil and is assassinated by his own officials in his second year.

P. The reign of Josiah (34:1—35:27). Josiah is the last good king of Judah. He is crowned when he is only eight, and rules in Jerusalem for thirty-one years. He destroys many pagan idols and worship centers, leads in the Passover, and brings the Levites back to temple service.

Q. The reign of Jehoahaz (36:1–3). Jehoahaz rules in Jerusalem for only three months. He is taken by Pharaoh Neco to Egypt and dies in captivity.

R. The reign of Jehoiakim (36:4–8). Jehoiakim is also a son of Josiah, and like his brother, Jehoahaz, he is evil. He is being politically pressed between Egypt and Babylon.

The issue is settled when Egypt and Babylon meet at Carchemish in 605 B.C. The Babylonian victory assures her king, Nebuchadnezzar, of unquestioned world dominance.

Judah is soon invaded. Jehoiakim submits and Judah becomes a vassal state.

S. The reign of Jehoiachin (36:9–10). After just three months as king in Jerusalem, the city is besieged and Jehoiachin taken captive to Babylon. At this time a much larger group of captives is deported, along with all the treasures left in the temple and royal treasury.

T. The reign of Zedekiah (36:11–16). Despite the desperate political situation, this king too is committed to evil. He is particularly set against the messages of God through Jeremiah.

III. JUDAH'S CAPTIVITY AND RETURN 36:17–23.

A. Babylon takes Judah captive (36:17–21). In 588 B.C. Nebuchadnezzar marches west. The Babylonians have little difficulty in disposing of Egypt and taking Jerusalem. Zedekiah and most of the remaining population are taken captive to Babylon.

B. The decree by Cyrus for Judah's return (36:22–23).

TRUTH-IN-ACTION through 2 CHRONICLES

Truth 2 Chronicles Teaches	**Action** 2 Chronicles Invites
1 Steps to Holiness Holiness requires that we guard our associations. We must be careful not only to shun unrighteousness and worldliness ourselves, but not to support or participate with others who promote it.	**19:2** *Be careful* not to promote the ungodly or to support those whose ways contradict the Scriptures and thus displease the Lord. **28:23** *Avoid* the evil ethic of expediency. *Do not employ* procedures or practices you suspect of being unethical or ungodly, even if they promise success.
2 Steps to Dynamic Devotion Scripture maintains a consistent testimony that those whose hearts are fully devoted to God are blessed by Him. Partial devotion to God—lukewarmness—inevitably results in spiritual mediocrity and sporadic communion with the Lord.	**1:10–12** *Be confident* that God honors those who depend upon His wisdom to carry out the work He has assigned them. **15:2–4** *Be confident* that if you seek God with all your heart and soul, He will surely be found by you. **16:9** *Maintain* a heart that is fully committed to the Lord. *Know* that the Lord seeks out such to strengthen them and prosper their works.
3 Steps in Developing Humility The humble person sees himself in the light of his relationship with Almighty God. A truly humble individual regards others more highly than himself because this self-assessment puts others in a better perspective. Also, the humble	**2:6** *Understand* that God fills the universe. *Know* that nothing we build can contain Him; the best we can do is reflect His glory. **7:14** *Identify* with the sins of your nation, confessing them as your own. *Repent* and *humble yourself. Seek God's face* to restore His blessing, and *believe* with all your heart that He will. *(continued)*

Truth 2 Chronicles Teaches	**Action** 2 Chronicles Invites
3 Steps in Developing Humility (continued) person is grateful for what he has received from the Lord and not lifted up in pride as a result of success or prosperity.	**26:16; 32:25** *Beware* the test of prosperity. *Guard against* pride when you have experienced success. *Be certain*, pride will lead to your downfall. *Repent* if pride is found in you.
4 Key Lessons in Faith Faith is rooted in a trust in God's witness in Scripture as illuminated by His Holy Spirit. Consequently, to grow in faith one must continually choose to receive and believe the witness of Scripture and become loyal to it.	**20:20** *Develop* spiritual 20/20 vision: *Choose* to believe the Bible as the absolute Word of God. *Rely upon* its witness to God's nature, character, and promises. *Believe* the words of those who proclaim God's Word. *Trust* prophetic "words" brought by godly men and women. **20:22** *Employ* and *believe* in praise as a mighty, effectual spiritual weapon.
5 Guidelines to Gaining Victory Exodus 17's revelation of God as "The-Lord-Our-Banner" (that is, "our victory" or "our miracle") forever secures victory for God's people. Victory in spiritual battles comes as we rely upon the Lord to fight on our behalf. This is what it means to trust the Lord in battle and stand still to see His deliverance.	**13:18** *Rely on* the Lord's wisdom, strength and abilities when confronting spiritual opposition. *Be assured* that this is the quickest way to victory. **14:11; 32:7, 8** *Rely upon* the Lord when the ungodly oppose or persecute you. *Be assured* that man, who is finite, cannot prevail against God. **20:15-25** *Covet* the presence of the Lord. *Depend* upon His presence when confronting any opposition. *Know* that the battle is not yours, but His. *Trust* the Lord to do your fighting for you.
6 A Key to Contentment Contentment results from knowing that the Lord is a ready resource for those who trust in Him.	**25:9** *Never allow* finances to determine obedience. *Know* that God will supply all you need to do His will. *Confess* poor stewardship and *accept* God's forgiveness; then *obey*.
7 Lessons for Leaders The spiritual leader praised in the Scriptures is faithful to instruct God's people in God's Word, making sure they know it thoroughly and are careful to obey it. God consistently honors those who speak only the message He has put in their mouths.	**14:4** Leaders, *teach* your people to seek the Lord and put His Word into practice. *Trust* that the Lord will cause them to prosper if they do. **17:9** Leaders, *make sure* that your people are thoroughly taught and well-read in the Scriptures. **18:7-27** Leaders, *be steadfast* in speaking only what God has given you to say. *Pursue* the reputation of being someone in whose mouth is the Word of the Lord.

KEYS TO EZRA
Restoration and Kingdom Worship

Kingdom Key: God's Purpose in View
The postexilic period graphically pictures what people encounter when they seek to recover what has been lost. Practical lessons abound in Ezra's narrative concerning the restoration of worship. No subject is more fundamental to kingdom life among believers, whether at the personal or congregational level.

In view of the widespread erosion of vitality in church worship today, the pathway to its restoration commands our attention. Three principles are essential, each illustrated by how worship was restored by Judah's returning exiles.

Principle 1: Worship recovery should begin at the Cross.

The offering of sacrifices upon the brazen altar began even *before* the temple foundation was laid (3:6). That ancient altar, where the sin offering was presented, clearly foreshadowed Calvary. The text suggests that revival of worship will flourish best where the Lamb of God is worshiped and His death for us is celebrated. Worship renewal involves a twofold emphasis: It must be rooted in redemption's work, and it must focus on Christ's person. The most vibrant praises of God's people spring from a warm, living gratitude to Jesus for His salvation.

> **Renewal and revival begin with anointed preaching.**

Principle 2: Worship recovery will always be resisted.

Ezra 4 and 5 detail the political struggle that arose when God's people sought to reinstate the worship of the Lord in Jerusalem. The rebuilding of the temple is a clear picture of any congregation's efforts to renew their assembly as a center of praise. Inevitably, resistance will come in some form, human or spiritual. In Ezra, such resistance arises in (1) attempts to discourage (4:4), (2) accusations of opposers (4:12, 15), and (3) complaints that the new isn't as good as the old (3:12).

At the same time, it is important to recognize that Ezra's "worship renewal" was not simply "new." "Old" implements of worship were respectfully restored (1:7–11). Any restoration of worship recommends the incorporation of traditional things or practices along with the new.

(Please turn to page 112.)

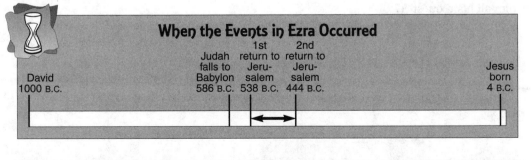

When the Events in Ezra Occurred

David 1000 B.C.	Judah falls to Babylon 586 B.C.	1st return to Jeru- salem 538 B.C.	2nd return to Jeru- salem 444 B.C.	Jesus born 4 B.C.

Ezra reminds us how easily God's people • • •

....

Kingdom Key *continued from page 111*

Principle 3: Worship recovery is released through prophecy.

Renewal and revival in worship are begotten by anointed preaching. Jeremiah, Haggai, and Zechariah played pivotal roles in the renewal of worship in Israel (1:1–5; 5:1–2). A parallel is found in teaching and preaching today which *draws* (not *drives*) the flock of God to find refreshment in God's presence.

Master Key: God's Son Revealed

Ezra himself foreshadowed Christ by the life he lived and the roles he fulfilled.

(1) As one who "had prepared his heart to seek the Law of the LORD, and to do it" (7:10), Ezra reminds us of Christ's description of Himself as the One who ardently obeys the Father (John 5:19).

(2) As "the priest" (7:11), Ezra foreshadowed Christ's role as the "great High Priest" (Heb. 4:14).

(3) As the great spiritual reformer who called Israel to repentance (ch. 10), Ezra typified Christ's messianic role by reshaping Israel's spiritual perspectives, calling her away from dead traditionalism and moral impurity (Matt. 11:20–24; 23).

Power Key: God's Spirit at Work

In Ezra the Holy Spirit is clearly seen as moving to fulfill God's promises. The phrase "the hand of the LORD" occurs six times.

By His Spirit "the LORD stirred up the spirit of Cyrus" (1:1) and "turned the heart of the king of Assyria" (6:22). It was also by the Holy Spirit that "Haggai and Zechariah . . . prophesied to the Jews" (5:1).

Key Word: *Temple*

The basic theme of Ezra is the restoration of the temple and the spiritual, moral, and social restoration of the returned remnant in Jerusalem under the leadership of Zerubbabel and Ezra.

Key Verses: Ezra 1:3; 7:10

Key Chapter: Ezra 6

Ezra 6 records the completion and dedication of the temple, which stimulates the obedience of the remnant to keep the Passover and separate themselves.

The Holy Spirit also worked in Ezra's personal life, both working in him, "Ezra had prepared his heart to seek the Law of the LORD" (7:10), and on his behalf, "the king granted him all his request" (7:6).

• • • can lose heart and their distinctives.

Introducing

EZRA

Author. The Book of Ezra, whose name likely means "The Lord Has Helped," derives its title from the chief character of chapters 7—10. We cannot be totally sure whether Ezra himself compiled the book or it was compiled by an unknown editor. The generally accepted conservative view is that Ezra compiled or wrote this book, along with 1 and 2 Chronicles and Nehemiah. The Hebrew Bible recognized Ezra-Nehemiah as a single book.

Ezra himself was a "priest, [a] scribe, expert in the words of the commandments of the LORD" (7:11). He led the second of three groups returning to Jerusalem from Babylon. A devout man, he firmly established the Law (the Pentateuch) as the basis of faith (7:10).

Occasion and Date. The events in Ezra cover slightly more than eighty years and fall into two distinct segments. The first segment (chs. 1—6) covers some twenty-three years, dealing with the first postexilic return under Zerubbabel and the reconstruction of the temple.

Following over sixty years in Babylonian captivity, God moves the heart of the ruler of Babylon, King Cyrus of Persia, to issue an edict stating that willing Jews can return to Jerusalem to rebuild the temple and city. A faithful group responds and departs in 538 B.C. under Zerubbabel. Temple construction is begun, but opposition from the non-Jewish inhabitants discourages the people and they cease their work. God then raises up the prophetic ministries of Haggai and Zechariah who call the people to complete the task. Though far less splendid than the previous temple of Solomon, the new temple is completed and dedicated in 515 B.C.

Nearly sixty years later (458 B.C.), another group of exiles returns to Jerusalem under the leadership of Ezra (chs. 7—10). They are sent by the then reigning Persian king, Artaxerxes, with additional monies and valuables to enhance the temple worship. Ezra is also commissioned to appoint leaders in Jerusalem to oversee the people. (*See* map on page 116.)

Once in Jerusalem, Ezra assumes the ministry of spiritual reformer for what was probably only one year. After that he likely lived as an influential private citizen into the time of Nehemiah. (*See* timeline on page 127 relating the events of Ezra, Esther, and

Nehemiah.) A devout priest, he finds an Israel which has adopted many of the pagan inhabitants' practices; he calls Israel to repentance and to a renewed submission to the Law, even to the point of divorcing their pagan wives.

Content. Two major messages emerge from Ezra: God's *faithfulness* and man's *unfaithfulness.*

God had promised through Jeremiah (25:12) that the Babylonian captivity would be limited in duration. In His ordained time, He faithfully keeps this promise and stirs the spirit of King Cyrus of Persia to issue an edict for the exiles to return (1:1–4). He then faithfully provides leadership (Zerubbabel and Ezra), and the exiles are sent off with booty, including items that had been taken from Solomon's temple (1:5–10).

When the people become discouraged because of the enemies' mockings, God faithfully raises up Haggai and Zechariah to encourage the people to complete the task. Their encouragement proves successful (5:1–2).

Finally, when the people stray from the truths of God's word, He faithfully sends a devout priest who artfully instructs the people in the truth, calling them to confession of sin and repentance from their evil ways (chs. 9; 10).

God's faithfulness is contrasted with the people's unfaithfulness. In spite of their return and divine promises, they allow their enemies to discourage them and they temporarily give up (4:24). Then, having completed their task so they can worship in their own temple (6:16–18), the people become faithless to the commandments of God; an entire generation is raised up whose "iniquities have risen higher than our heads" (9:6). However, as noted above, God's faithfulness triumphs in each situation.

Personal Application. The messages of Ezra are a constant reminder of how easily God's people can lose heart and their distinctives. God is fulfilling His promises. In spite of this, covenant people easily forget His promises and the moral distinctives that are to characterize "a royal priesthood, a holy nation, His own special people" (1 Pet. 2:9). When this happens God's plans are delayed. Erring saints cannot totally thwart God's sovereign plans, but they can delay or frustrate them. God is greater than we, and He does have ways of transcending our shortcomings. However, He wants us to walk in obedience so that His plans can be fulfilled as originally revealed.

Surveying

EZRA

I. THE RETURN UNDER ZERUBBABEL
1:1—2:70. In response to the decree of Cyrus, some fifty thousand people of Israel prepare to return to Jerusalem from Babylonian exile under the leadership of Zerubbabel. This return will span a time period of about twenty-three years, during which the reconstruction of the temple occurs. An important part of the success of the return is tied to the willingness of the people to give sacrificially.

A. Cyrus proclaims Israel's return (1:1–4). While the free will of man is never violated, the ultimate fulfillment of divine purposes is God's responsibility. Such interventions often appear to be the actions of men, but a closer look will generally evidence God's influence (2). When evil seems to race forward unchecked, divine control has a stabilizing effect.

B. The people prepare to return (1:5–11). The heads of households along with the priests and Levites modeled a readiness of spirit in leading the people. "All that was willingly offered" (6) indicates the spirit of the people in anticipation of their move.

C. The first returnees are named and numbered (2:1–67). A possible explanation for the discrepancy in the adding up of the names listed (64) may be the inclusion of those from other tribes beside Judah. Israel is mentioned in 10:25 with others who apparently were included, thus the references to "all Israel" (2:70; 6:17; 8:35).

D. The returnees give freely (2:68–70). Additional evidence of the spirit of the people is the action indicated here (68–69). They "offered freely" and "according to their ability," both of which mind-sets release the power of the Spirit in the kingdom. God never requires us to give what we don't have, yet He does desire that we be willing to give of everything that He has given to us.

II. THE TEMPLE RECONSTRUCTION
PROCESS 3:1—6:22. With worship having been re-established, the work on the temple begins. Almost immediately the people are faced with opposition in varying degrees. Strong leadership manifested in Jeshua and Zerubbabel encourages the people to continue until the temple is completed. The temple is dedicated with rejoicing as the people celebrate once again the Feast of Passover.

A. The altar is built and sacrifices begun (3:1–7). For the Jewish sacrificial system to be re-established, the altar must be rebuilt first. For a nation whose very identity was inseparable from their relationship with God, there was no other choice. The Feast of Tabernacles was the occasion for the presentation of their free-will offerings.

B. The foundation is laid, amid great praise and sorrow (3:8–13). Building materials were ordered from Lebanon, in an obvious attempt to follow the pattern of the building of the first temple, although little progress was made beyond the laying of the foundations. The completion of the foundations was marked by the bittersweet response of both rejoicing and weeping—rejoicing by the younger generation who were inspired at the prospect of re-establishing temple worship, and weeping by the older generation who had seen the former glory of Solomon's temple.

> **"Then all the people shouted with a great *shout"**
> (3:10–13). This action on the part of God's people is consistent with a kind of worship which is acceptable to the Lord. Periodically, every believer needs to confront in himself anything that would tend toward passivity regarding his worship of God. In verses 12 and 13, the volume of the shouting was more than cultural. Something was being established in the spirit as they moved ahead in boldness and were heard "afar off."

C. Enemies discourage the temple project (4:1–5). The Samaritans (as they are known in the New Testament) offered to assist in the building of the temple. This would have been a compromise for the returning captives because the Samaritans had compromised the worship of God by joining themselves to idolatrous people in marriage and in religious practice. Thus the offer is rejected.

D. Bishlam and his associates complain to King Artaxerxes (4:6–16). This is indicative of the kind of opposition they encountered repeatedly. It emphasizes the fact that the entire project faced difficulty all along the way.

E. Artaxerxes orders the work to cease (4:17–24). The adversity faced by the people of God continued to the point of temporary discontinuance.

F. Tattenai attempts to stop the temple project (5:1–17). The ministry of Haggai and Zechariah is introduced and becomes pivotal in the people's being encouraged to resume construction.

G. Darius assures Tattenai the project is legal (6:1–12). Darius demonstrates his importance in God's sovereign scheme by issuing a decree that insures the completion of the project.

H. The temple is completed and dedicated (6:13–18). Encouraged by the support of the king, the temple is completed in four years and dedicated.

I. The Passover is celebrated (6:19–22). Remembrance of God's delivering power is celebrated once again at Passover after the temple is completed.

III. THE RETURN UNDER EZRA 7:1—8:36. Another contingent of Jews return under the leadership of Ezra. His focus was on the restoration of worship and the teaching of the Law of God.

A. Ezra and more exiles depart from Babylon (7:1–10). Ezra had purpose as he led this next group of Jews from Persia. He had prepared his heart to teach the Law of the Lord to those in Israel.

B. Artaxerxes writes a letter of support to Ezra (7:11–28). Ezra recognizes the hand of the Lord upon him (28) through the instrument of the king. Ezra's perception indicates his certainty about his mission.

C. The second group of returnees are named and numbered (8:1–20). Those who traveled with Ezra are named.

D. The exiles return to Jerusalem (8:21–36). Given the precious lives and the valued possessions that would make the journey, Ezra calls for a fast to seek guidance from the Lord.

> **"Then I proclaimed a fast."** (8:21). Ezra models a dependence upon God which releases Him to work on the people's behalf. Fasting is affirmed by Jesus as an accepted—if not expected— practice in the life of every believer (Matt. 9:14–15). The fast, when understood as an expression of humble dependence, exerts significant force in spiritual warfare, leading to the fulfillment of the purposes of God. (*See* Spiritual Warfare.)

IV. EZRA'S REFORM 9:1—10:44. Upon arrival in Jerusalem, Ezra discovers the people have intermarried with the idolatrous people who lived there. Ezra intercedes and repents on behalf of the people and then takes action as God's appointed leader.

A. Ezra confesses Israel's transgressions (9:1–15). Ezra identifies himself with the people's sin and cries out in repentance for God to show mercy.

> **"I fell on my knees and spread out my hands to the LORD my God"** (9:5). This example of intercession inspires confidence for believers who live in the midst of compromising circumstances today. Remembering that to intercede is to come before God on behalf of someone else, we can effect changes in physical situations and in the spiritual realm. When we believe that God hears and answers the prayers of His church, we will exercise this kingdom privilege more often and more effectively.

B. Israel's leaders consent to reform (10:1–44). Revival begins with the leaders who understand the seriousness of their sin. Ezra leads the reformation.

TRUTH-IN-ACTION through EZRA

Truth Ezra Teaches	**Action** Ezra Invites
1 Knowing God Knowing God is knowing that He honors His Word, even above His name.	**1:1** *Be assured* God makes certain that His Word will be fulfilled.
2 A Guideline for Godly Living Godly living is standing up for what you believe even in the face of hostile opposition.	**3:3** *Be faithful* to God, and be bold in your faith in Him despite the possible hostility of the world around you. *Remember* that the Lord will honor those who honor Him.
3 Steps to Holiness The holy life is separated from the world and set apart to God.	**4:4, 5** *Be advised* that the world seeks to discourage and frustrate the purposes of God's people. *Seek counsel* from God, and *shun* the advice of the ungodly.

Truth Ezra Teaches	**Action** Ezra Invites
4 Steps to Dealing with Sin We must be careful lest we forget the cost of forgiveness. Sin is serious, and we must deal with it seriously! Sin sent God's only Son to the Cross. Let us not forget that God's conditions for forgiveness include our repentance, confession of, and forsaking of our sin.	**9:3, 4** *Avoid* becoming calloused to sin. *Let sin disturb you* and bring appropriate remorse. To mourn over sin is to be humbled when recognizing it. **10:1–17** Take sin seriously, and *deal* with it thoroughly. *Follow through* with repentance: *Take steps* to right the wrongs sin has brought about. *Do not pervert* forgiveness by continuing in sin.
5 Keys to Relating to Authority The righteous can manifest submission even when facing hostile civil authority. Our faith that God is sovereign beyond all authority allows the spirit of submission to prevail, knowing God can work beyond all authority to accomplish His will.	**6:1–12** *Submit* to all authority, knowing that it comes from God. *Trust* God to work through any authority to which you must respond. **7:11–28** *Believe* that God is able to work blessing for His people through civil authority, even when it may be hostile. *Trust* His ability to work His will, even beyond civil government.
6 Lessons for Leaders The biblical model for leaders is that of the "servant leader." The servant leader does not boss, dominate, or dictate to God's people. He "goes before" them. To lead as a servant is to "do it first," avoiding the way of the Pharisees who instructed people to do things they themselves would not do. The servant leader asks God's people to do what he himself has established in his own life. This should first be evident in the way he deals with sin and be manifest in his spirit of repentance.	**8:15–20** Leaders, *ask* the Lord to send others to help you in your assigned place of ministry. *Do not* try to accomplish the job alone. **8:21–23** Leaders, *employ* corporate fasting when you undertake a major project or enter a significant season in your church's life. *Be assured* that God regards the self-humbling that accompanies prayer and fasting. **8:28–33** Leaders, *pursue excellence* in your stewardship of material things. *Keep* all financial dealings "in the light"! **9:5–15** Leaders, *choose to intercede* for God's people rather than become upset with them. *Identify* with their sin, and *confess* it as your own. Leaders, *learn to lead* in the confession of sin as a model for your people.

Route of the Jews' Return from Exile

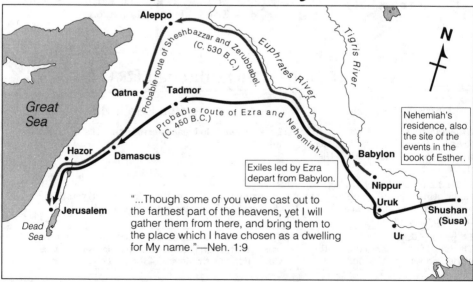

"...Though some of you were cast out to the farthest part of the heavens, yet I will gather them from there, and bring them to the place which I have chosen as a dwelling for My name."—Neh. 1:9

KEYS TO NEHEMIAH
Restoration and Kingdom Wholeness

Kingdom Key: God's Purpose in View

Salvation provides for a complete renewal of the person. God does not simply "forgive" or "save" and then fail to advance His ongoing purpose in people. What He begins through the work of salvation in Christ, He furthers through the workings of the Holy Spirit. Nehemiah's leadership in the massive task of rebuilding Jerusalem's walls, devastated over a century before, is a graphic picture of God at work in full kingdom-life restoration. Nehemiah's leadership models and represents something for which we must contend today.

Because Nehemiah's name means "comfort of Jehovah," many students and scholars consider his ministry and leadership as a foreshadowing of the role the *Holy Spirit* plays in leading believers unto wholeness. *Wholeness* bespeaks a complete recovery of the human being, from (a) the regeneration of the spirit (Titus 3:5), to (b) the renewal of the mind (Rom. 12:1–2), to (c) the mending of emotions (Luke 4:18), to (d) the restoring of physical health (Matt. 14:35–36).

Just as the rebuilding of the walls was a demanding project, many facets of human recovery can take a long time. While the instantaneous work of the Holy Spirit in "new birth" and "justification" secures the believer's *position* in Christ at once, the progressive work of renewing, healing, and bringing spirit,

> Nothing is ruined beyond God's ability to restore.

soul, and body into God's fuller intent is a *process* (1 Thess. 5:23–24). The Book of Nehemiah is a great source for discovering "kingdom life" principles of full human restoration through the gracious work of the Holy Spirit. (A thorough study of how this is illustrated in Nehemiah can be found in the book, *"Rebuilding the Real You,"* by J. W. Hayford, Regal Books, 1986.)

Nehemiah is also a rich source for examining the dynamic of yet another "kingdom key"—the role of *leadership* in restoration. The character and conduct of Nehemiah points the way for all who would help others find the restoration of their lives, homes, or dreams. Nehemiah is (1) self-sacrificing (5:14–18), (2) compassionate (1:1–4), (3) a faith-filled, prayerful,

(Please turn to page 120.)

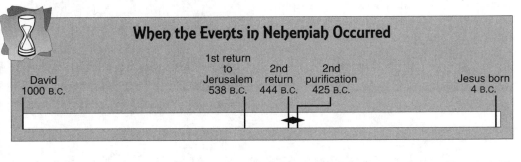

When the Events in Nehemiah Occurred

| David 1000 B.C. | 1st return to Jerusalem 538 B.C. | 2nd return 444 B.C. | 2nd purification 425 B.C. | Jesus born 4 B.C. |

Nehemiah: the Holy Spirit can use people • • •

Master Key: God's Son Revealed

Nehemiah, with his associate Ezra, called on the people of God to remember the Law. Doing so, he became part of the chain of inspired writers of Holy Scripture who put the people in the hands of the "tutor" (Gal. 3:23–24) to guard them until Christ should arrive.

While Christ is not directly referred to in Nehemiah, Nehemiah typifies Him by the life he modeled. He was a courageous leader, defying the odds and encouraging the people to do Yahweh's work (2:18), even as Christ defied the people's opposition and encouraged His disciples to endure (John 15:18–27). He was ardent in prayer (2:1–20; 6:9–14), even as Christ was (Luke 6:12). He was dedicated to God's Law (8:9–10), an important element in Christ's life as well (Matt. 5:17).

Power Key: God's Spirit at Work

Since creation, the Holy Spirit has been the hand of God on earth. Elihu spoke the truth when he said to Job, "The Spirit of God has made me" (Job 33:4). The pattern is consistent in that it is the Spirit of God who works to make us all that God desires us to be. Nehemiah 2:18 states, "And I told them of the hand of my God which had been good upon me." Ezekiel, a captive in Babylon before the liberation of God's people and their return to Jerusalem, wrote: "I will give you a new heart and put a new spirit within you; I will take the heart of stone out of your flesh and give you a heart of flesh. I will put My Spirit within you and cause you to walk in My statutes, and you will keep My judgments and do them. Then you shall dwell in the land that I gave to your fathers; you shall be My people, and I will be your God" (Ezek. 36:26–28).

Nehemiah, whose name means "Yahweh Comforts," was clearly an instrument of the Holy Spirit. Under the power of God's Spirit, he certainly modeled the Holy Spirit's workings and became one of the early fulfillments of this remarkable prophecy.

Key Word: *Walls*

While Ezra deals with the religious restoration of Judah, Nehemiah is primarily concerned with Judah's political and geographical restoration. The first seven chapters are devoted to the rebuilding of Jerusalem's walls, because Jerusalem was the spiritual and political center of Judah. Without walls, Jerusalem could hardly be considered a city at all.

Key Verses: Nehemiah 6:15–16; 8:8

Key Chapter: Nehemiah 9

The key to the Old Testament is the covenant, which is its theme and unifying factor. Israel's history can be divided according to the nation's obedience or disobedience to God's conditional covenant: blessings from obedience and destruction from disobedience. Nehemiah 9 records that upon completion of the Jerusalem wall the nation reaffirmed its loyalty to the covenant.

. . . in restoring lives, homes, and dreams.

Introducing

NEHEMIAH

Author: The book derives its present title from the main character whose name appears in 1:1. (*See* "Occasion and Date" below.) Our first glimpse of Nehemiah is in his role as cupbearer at the court of Artaxerxes. A cupbearer had a position of great trust as advisor to the king and had the responsibility of keeping the king from being poisoned. While Nehemiah no doubt enjoyed the luxury of the palace, his heart was in Jerusalem, a little city on the far frontier of the empire.

Nehemiah's prayer and fasting, qualities of leadership, powerful eloquence, inspirational organizational skills, confidence in God's purpose, and quick, decisive response to problems qualify him as a great leader and man of God. Most importantly, he shows us a self-sacrificing spirit whose only interest is summed up in his repeated prayer, "Remember me, O my God, for good."

Occasion and Date. In the Hebrew Scriptures Nehemiah was originally included with Ezra. Many scholars consider Ezra as the compiler/author of Ezra-Nehemiah, as well as 1 and 2 Chronicles. Though we cannot be sure, it does seem that Nehemiah contributed some of the material in the book bearing his name (chs. 1—7; 11—13).

Jerome, who translated the Bible into Latin, honored Nehemiah by naming the book after him as its main character. Nehemiah means "Yahweh Comforts." The story begins in the Book of Ezra and is completed in Nehemiah. Nehemiah, who twice served as governor of Judea, leaves Persia on his first mission in the twentieth year of Artaxerxes I of Persia, who reigned from 465 until 424 B.C. (2:1). He returns to Persia in the king's thirty-second year (13:6), but soon leaves again for Jerusalem. (*See* map, page 116.)

The contents of the book dictate that the work could not have been written until some time after Nehemiah's return from Persia to Jerusalem. Perhaps it was written in its completed form before the death of Artaxerxes I in 424 B.C.; otherwise the death of such a gracious monarch would probably have been mentioned in Nehemiah.

The historical period covered by the books of Ezra and Nehemiah is about 110 years. (*See* timelines on page 127.) The period of rebuilding the temple under Zerubbabel, inspired by the preaching of Zechariah and Haggai, was twenty-one years. Sixty years later Ezra brought a revival and proper teaching on temple worship. After thirteen years Nehemiah came to work on the walls. Malachi may also have prophesied during this time. If so, Nehemiah and Malachi worked together to eradicate the evil of the worship of many gods, and they attacked the evil of compromise with the peoples who had been forcibly resettled in the land by the Assyrians approximately two hundred years earlier. They succeeded so well that, during the intertestamental period, the people of God did not return to idolatry. Thus, when the Messiah came, people such as Zacharias and Elizabeth, Mary and Joseph, Simeon, Anna, the shepherds, and others were godly people with whom God would communicate.

Content. Nehemiah expresses the practical, everyday side of our faith in God. Ezra had led a spiritual renewal, while Nehemiah was the James of the Old Testament, challenging the people to show their faith by their works.

The first section of the book (chs. 1—7) deals with the wall. Protection from those outside the city was necessary for Judah and Benjamin to remain a people. In the wall-building period, the committed believers under this dynamic leader overcame laziness (4:6), mockery (2:20), conspiracy (4:9), and threats of physical attack (4:17).

The second section of the book (chs. 8—10) addresses the people inside the walls. The covenant was renewed, and the enemies inside the wall were exposed and dealt with very firmly. To lead His people God chose a man whose heart was right and who had a clear perspective on the issues, placed him in the right place at the right time, equipped him with His Spirit, and sent him forth to do works.

In the last section (chs. 11—13), the people are restored to obedience to God's Word, as Nehemiah the layman works with Ezra the priest. As governor during this period, Nehemiah used the influence of his office to support Ezra and to lead spiritually. Here is a man who wisely thinks things through in advance of his action ("after serious thought") and a man filled with boldness ("I contended with the nobles").

Personal Application. Four lasting principles stand out in Nehemiah. First, compassion is often the springboard of obedience to God's will. Second, cooperation with others is required to carry out God's will. Third, confidence results from fervent prayer and the exposition of the Word of God, which reveals God's will. Fourth, courage will manifest itself as sanctified tenacity in refusing to compromise on the conviction that one is doing God's will.

Kingdom Key *continued from page 117*

discerning intercessor (1:5–11), (4) a careful and practical planner (2:4–16), (5) quick to identify with those he leads (2:17), (6) bold to confront hateful resistance (2:19–20), (7) strategically wise in encouragement (4:10–23),

(8) undeterred by distractions (6:1–4), (9) Word-centered and positive (8:1–12), and (10) sensitive to discern and correct confusion (13:4–31).

Surveying

NEHEMIAH

I. NEHEMIAH GOES FROM EXILE TO REBUILD THE WALLS OF JERUSALEM 1:1—7:73.

A. Authority from Artaxerxes I to rebuild the wall (1:1—2:8). As a trusted official to the king, Nehemiah approaches Artaxerxes to request permission to return to Jerusalem for the purpose of rebuilding the city. Permission is granted. (*See* Redeemed.)

B. Planning the work, motivating and organizing the workers (2:9—3:32). Under the cover of darkness Nehemiah secretly inspects the walls. Immediately, he urges the leaders to accept the challenge to rebuild.

"You have no heritage or right or memorial in Jerusalem"
(2:20). This phrase demonstrates a significant principle for the individual engaged in spiritual warfare. As it was in the physical realm, so it is spiritually. The powers of darkness who would oppose God's rebuilding program have no legal right, present or future, within God's kingdom (*see* Col. 2:13–15). Declaring this in prayer becomes a powerful instrument against the Adversary.

C. Opposition and defense (4:1–23). Three methods of opposition are used against the workers: ridicule, anger, and discouragement. Each point of opposition was met with prayer, intercession, faith, and hard work.

D. Extortion and usury resisted by Nehemiah's godly example (5:1–19). Within the community there arises a spirit of greed and selfishness. Nehemiah is quick to address the situation.

E. Walls completed in spite of evil plots (6:1—7:3). With a determination born out of his commitment to the call of God, Nehemiah

successfully leads the workers to the miraculous completion of the wall in fifty-two days.

"They thought to do me harm. . . . They sent me this message four times. . . . They all were trying to make us afraid. . . . Now therefore, O God, strengthen my hands"
(6:2, 4, 9). These verses set forth the craftiness of satanic forces in their attempt to derail God's purpose and plan by attacking the leader. When engaged in spiritual warfare, we should recognize that man is not the enemy. Nehemiah recognized this fact and chose not to become embroiled in the battle with flesh and blood. Rather, he appealed to the Lord to strengthen his hands. Trusting in the Lord to do the fighting for him, Nehemiah could concentrate on the task at hand.

"This work was done by our God"
(6:15–16). Nehemiah and the others who built the wall demonstrate the effectiveness of a united effort of faith. Though a cursory reading of the previous chapters verifies the number of people and the amount of work required, nevertheless God is the One who does the work. Faith is an action of belief which puts a person in a position to trust God to accomplish His work.

F. Reestablishment of Jerusalem's citizens (7:4–73). Intent on establishing their national life, Nehemiah organizes the people and registers them. Included in this census was the clarifying of genealogies as well as describing the various gifts that had been given for the work.

II. EZRA AND NEHEMIAH WORK TOGETHER TO ESTABLISH THE PEOPLE 8:1—10:39.

A. Reading the Bible (8:1–12). The reading of the Law required some explanation and interpretation for the people (*see* Understand).

Ezra was assisted in this task by thirteen Levites.

B. Celebration of Feast of Tabernacles (8:13–18). In direct obedience to what had been read and explained to the people, they kept the Feast of Tabernacles. The enthusiasm demonstrated by the people bespeaks a revival beginning among them.

C. Confession of personal and corporate sin (9:1–37). The evidence that a revival is in process is demonstrated by the continued reading of the Law (*see* Statutes). The result is confession of sin and genuine worship.

> **"Then those of Israelite lineage separated themselves from all foreigners"**
> (9:2). Here we see an important kingdom principle as the people "separated themselves." Confession of sin generally will be substantiated by some kind of corresponding action. In this instance, one of their sins was in mingling with other peoples. Once they began to experience the impact of God's Word in their lives, they understood clearly and proceeded to take appropriate action. Paul later admonished the Corinthian Christians on this aspect of holiness (2 Cor. 6:14–18).

D. Commitment to keep the law and support the temple (9:38—10:39). The covenant that was made was twofold: to support God's house and to walk in God's Law. The strength of their commitment is demon-strated in that they allowed their names to be recorded.

> **"To bring the firstfruits . . . and to bring the tithes"**
> (10:37). A reliable sign that a person is growing in understanding and commitment is seen in his or her obedience in the area of finances. In the kingdom of God, a spiritual release is connected to our giving patterns (Mal. 3:8–11).

III. TRUE REPENTANCE RESULTS IN RIGHTEOUSNESS 11:1—13:31.

A. Census of Jerusalem and surrounding villages (11:1—12:26). To help reestablish Jerusalem, the people decided that one in every ten would come to live within the city walls. Therefore lots were cast to decide who would live there. A census of the Levites is taken in the interest of preserving the people's worship of the Lord.

B. Dedication of the walls and provision for the finances of the temple (12:27—13:3). With the walls completed there is now cause for great celebration. The dedication of the walls is followed by the willingness of the people to give with joy to the support of the temple personnel. (*See* ch. 55 of this Handbook, §3.7.d.)

C. Nehemiah's second term as governor, including further reforms and a final prayer (13:4–31). The people grow lax about keeping true to their covenant. Nehemiah reminds them about this and makes the necessary corrections.

TRUTH-IN-ACTION through **NEHEMIAH**

Truth Nehemiah Teaches	**Action** Nehemiah Invites
◻ Guidelines for Growing in Godliness Living God's way means making God's priorities our priorities, realizing that they often are different from ours. God still accomplishes all things through His Word. Therefore, the Scriptures are a guide for ordering our lives according to God's will. Understanding and obeying them brings joy. They also teach us to acknowledge God's hand in all of our success.	**1:4–11** *Make* the welfare of God's people a higher priority than your own welfare. *Understand* that a general sin of God's people is yours to confess, too. **8:1–6** *Give place* to the public reading of Scripture as a source of understanding and encouragement. **8:10** *Cultivate* and *promote* the joy of the Lord among God's people as a powerful source of spiritual strength. **12:27–43** *Observe* the regular celebration of holy success and spiritual progress. *Dedicate* your works to the Lord, knowing it is He who gives all success and progress.

Truth Nehemiah Teaches	**Action** Nehemiah Invites
2 Steps to Holiness True holiness is active and dynamic, not passive and static. We must actively remove the ways of the world from our lives.	**13:4–9** *Be willing to root out* worldly ways where they have become established in the life of the church. *Reject* carnal compromises. **13:23–27** *Refuse* evil alliances. *Do not marry* an unbeliever.
3 Keys to Wise Living Wisdom knows that the Lord is the source of any spiritual advancement. It is also aware that no such progress will go unopposed, but will incur spiritual opposition, sometimes expressed through human agency. Therefore, act with discernment. The wise will discern the true origin of many verbal attacks as an assault motivated by our spiritual adversary.	**1:11** *Understand* and *believe* that success and favor with men comes from the Lord. **2:12–16** *Understand* that wisdom involves searching out a matter before making any decisions or decrees. *Postpone* informing others until you have ascertained the mind of the Lord. **2:19** *Expect* and *do not be surprised or dismayed* at hostility when you undertake to do the will of God. **2:10** *Be aware* that any favor shown to God's people will anger our spiritual adversary. *Discern* that much human enmity is spiritually motivated. **6:12** *Discern* and *reject* negative prophecy from malignant sources.
4 Key Lessons in Faith Faith takes God at His word. Do not question His promises. Through faith, we can speak confidently, praising Him for promises that will bring success.	**2:4–6** *Pray* that your responses in demanding situations will be from the Lord. *Do not answer* impetuously or presumptuously. **2:8** *Express* gratitude for all success and favor.
5 Steps to Dealing with Sin Much sin is corporate. We must deal with such sin together and believe that God is faithful to forgive corporate sins.	**9:1–38** *Allow for* the public, corporate confession of sin when necessary. **9:17** *Teach* and *believe* that God is gracious and forgiving when confessing and repenting of sin.
6 Lessons for Leaders Leaders must insure the welfare of the church. They must lead the way so that everyone carries a fair share of the work and no one puts his own interests above those of others. Leaders are servants, providing examples of obedience and diligence to God's people. Only those who live this way should be entrusted with leadership responsibility.	**3:5** Leaders, *note* and *reprove* those who, due to their position or privilege, will not serve. **5:1–13** Leaders, *reprove* those who ignore the welfare of others, pursuing instead personal gain. *Champion* the cause of the poor and needy. **5:15, 16** Leaders, *do not lord it over* others. Rather, *devote yourself* to working diligently. **7:2** Leaders, *honor* men of integrity who fear the Lord. *Entrust* such with leadership responsibility. **9:29** Leaders, *understand* and *teach* that righteous living is obedient to the will of God as revealed in the Scriptures.
7 Keys to Generous Living We must be generous toward God's work first, making the care of His servants a high priority.	**13:10–13** *Insure* that God's servants are adequately cared for. *Avoid* any tendency to neglect the work of God in favor of personal concerns or selfish ambitions.
8 Guidelines to Gaining Victory Spiritual victory comes through faith that God fights for us. We can ignore the insults of those opposed to us and trust God for victory.	**4:1–6** *Ignore* the reproaches and insults of those who oppose your pursuit of God's will. *Trust* God's justice and faithfulness. **4:17–23** *Realize* that all spiritual ministry involves spiritual warfare. *Be prepared* for battle, *quick to aid* those who are under spiritual attack.

KEYS TO ESTHER
Restoration and Kingdom Intercession

Kingdom Key: God's Purpose in View

The historic facts and crucial significance of Esther's actions, at a time when the life of her people and nation was in doubt, underlines the significant place to which God has invited each citizen of His kingdom. It is no stretch to see in this story a prophetic picture of the place the ultimate King—Jesus the Messiah—has offered His bride. Although the relationship between Christ and His own is not strained by the imperialistic or chauvinistic traits that colored Ahasuerus's rule of ancient Persia, the lessons found here are fully applicable today.

Esther is a useful example today, as the Holy Spirit constantly works to reform and reshape the church to fill its destined role. This book can assist us to grasp the believer's potential in intercessory prayer. It illustrates our privilege of effecting the rescue of individuals, circumstances, and even nations through prayer. Consider the following as a picture of the church today, with each person, one by one, learning to take his or her place as an intercessor.

1. As Esther prepared for her appearance before her king (2:12), so the righteousness of God has been given to us in Christ to clothe and enhance our freedom of approach to His throne (2 Cor. 2:14–15; 5:20–21).

2. As Haman hatefully conspired to destroy the Jews (3:1–15), so the Bible reveals Satan's hateful efforts to oppose

> Timely interces-sion can neutralize evil plans.

God's purposes for humankind (John 10:10; Rev. 12:12).

3. As Mordecai caught Esther's attention, prompting her full sensitivity to (a) the gravity of the situation and (b) her possibilities as a redemptive instrument (4:13–14), so the Holy Spirit seeks to awaken today's believer to his or her potential as an intercessor. (*See* Eph. 6:10–20, noting the international implications of the prayer potential to which Paul refers.)

4. As Esther "loved not her life" (compare Rev. 12:11 with Esth. 4:16) but gave herself to fasting and bold intercessory entry before the king, so we are called today to break the power of evil through fasting and prayer. (*See* Matt. 9:15; Mark 9:29; Acts 14:23—note the latter text accompanies a prayer for power to (Please turn to page 124.)

When the Events in Esther Occurred

| David 1000 B.C. | Judah falls to Babylon 586 B.C. | 1st return to Jerusalem 538 B.C. | 2nd return to Jerusalem 444 B.C. | Jesus born 4 B.C. |

Esther shows the believer's potential for spiritually • • •

Kingdom Key *continued from page 123*

change nations.)

    5. As Esther was invited to "touch the scepter" (5:2), so each believer is invited to "reign" *in Christ*—above every principality and power (Rom. 5:17; Eph. 1:18–23; 2:6).

Master Key: God's Son Revealed

Queen Esther is similar to Jesus in several ways. She lived in submission, dependence, and obedience to her God-given authorities Mordecai and King Ahasuerus, even as the Lord Jesus during His earthly ministry lived in total submission, dependence, and obedience to His Father God.

    Esther also fully identified herself with her people and fasted for three days as she interceded to God on their behalf (4:16). Hebrews 2:17 tells us that "in all things He [Jesus] had to be made like His brethren, that He might be a merciful and faithful High Priest." As such, He both fasted and prayed for His own (Matt. 4:2; John 17:20).

    Third, Esther gave up her right to live in order to save the nation from certain death. For this she was exalted by the king. In like fashion Jesus gave up His life that a world of sinners might be saved from eternal death, and He was highly exalted by God (Phil. 2:5–11).

Power Key: God's Spirit at Work

Although the Holy Spirit is not mentioned directly, it is His work that produced in both Esther and Mordecai the deep level of humility, leading to their mutual love and loyalty (*see* Rom. 5:5).

    The Holy Spirit also directed and energized Esther to fast for her nation and to call her people to do the same (*see* Rom. 8:26–27).

Key Word: *Providence*

The Book of Esther was written to show how the Jewish people were protected and preserved by the gracious hand of God from the threat of annihilation. Although God disciplines His covenant people, He never abandons them.

Key Verses: Esther 4:14; 8:17

Key Chapter: Esther 8

According to the Book of Esther, the salvation of the Jews is accomplished through the second decree of King Ahasuerus, allowing the Jews to defend themselves against their enemies. Chapter 8 records this pivotal event with the accompanying result that "many of the people of the land became Jews" (8:17).

    • • • **effective actions to save people and change history.**

Introducing
ESTHER

Author. While the name of the author is unknown, the book was written by a Jew who was familiar with Persian customs and words. Mordecai or Ezra may have been the writer.

Background and Date. The Book of Esther is a graphic narrative, which relates how God's people were preserved from ruin during the fifth century B.C. (*See* timelines on page 127.)

The book takes its name from the beautiful, orphaned Jewess who became the queen of the Persian king Ahasuerus. He is generally believed to have been King Xerxes I who succeeded Darius I in 485 B.C. and ruled for twenty years over 127 provinces from India to Ethiopia. He lived in the Persian capital of Shushan. At this time a number of Jews were still in Babylon under Persian rule, even though they had been free to return to Jerusalem (Ezra 1, 2) for over fifty years. The story takes place over a period of four years, starting in the third year of Xerxes' reign.

Content. Esther is a study in the survival of God's people amidst hostility. Haman, the king's second in command, wants the Jews destroyed. He manipulates the king to call for their execution. Esther is brought on the scene and is used by God to save her people. Haman is hanged; and Mordecai, a leader to the Jews in the Persian Empire, becomes prime minister. The Feast of Purim is then instituted to mark their deliverance.

A unique feature of Esther is that the name of God is not mentioned. However, the imprint of God and His ways are obvious throughout, especially in the lives of Esther and Mordecai. From a human perspective, Esther and Mordecai were two of the most unlikely people to be chosen to play major roles in shaping a nation. He was a Jewish Benjamite exile; she was his adopted, orphaned cousin (2:7). Esther's spiritual maturity is seen in her knowing to wait for God's timing to make her request to save her people and to denounce Haman (5:6–8; 7:3–6). Mordecai also demonstrates a maturity to seek God for timing and direction. As a result, he knew the right time for Esther to disclose her identity as a Jew (2:10). These obviously divinely controlled restraints proved to be crucial (6:1–14; 7:9–10) and testify to the book's spiritual base.

Finally, both Esther and Mordecai feared God, not men. Regardless of the consequences, Mordecai refused to pay homage to Haman. Esther risked her life for the sake of her people by going to the king without being summoned. Their mission was always to save the life that the enemy planned to destroy (2:21–23; 4:1–17; 7:1–6; 8:3–6). As a result, they led a nation into freedom, were honored by the king, and received greater authority, privileges, and responsibilities.

Personal Application. One of the main purposes of the Book of Esther is to show us from the lives of Esther and Mordecai a classic example of successful teamwork. Their relationship vividly portrays the unity that the Lord Jesus prayed for His disciples to experience (John 17). The success of their individual roles, even their very survival, depended entirely upon their unity. Esther also shows how God destroys those who try to harm His people. From this we are reminded that He is faithful to destroy Satan and that His sovereign purposes ultimately prevail.

Surveying
ESTHER

I. A NEW QUEEN CHOSEN 1:1—2:18.

A. King Ahasuerus displays his power and holds a feast (1:1–8). Not uncommon to the ancient monarchies, kings would often make a show of their wealth and position. In this instance it was related to the strength of Persia as she went to battle against the Greeks (480 B.C.).

B. Queen Vashti is deposed (1:9–22). Ahasuerus removes Vashti as his queen because of her refusal to obey his command to appear before those attending his feast.

C. Esther is chosen to be queen (2:1–18). Esther is the adopted daughter of Mordecai, one of the captives of Israel, who also is her cousin. After a long period of preparation, she is brought before the king and consequently is selected to be his queen.

II. THE KING'S LIFE SAVED 2:19–23.
This is the beginning of the king's favor on Esther and Mordecai.

A. Mordecai uncovers a conspiracy (2:19–21).

B. Esther informs the king (2:22–23). The sovereign hand of God begins to become noticeable in that Esther alerts the king and gives the credit to Mordecai.

III. A PLOT AGAINST THE JEWS FORMED 3:1—4:17. A self-important court official (Haman) is infuriated when Mordecai

fails to show him the respect he feels he should receive. An order to destroy the Jews is the result; Esther intervenes with the king.

A. Haman plots to destroy the Jews (3:1–15). Because of his faith, Mordecai refuses to bow down to Haman. Haman in turn presents a plot to the king, claiming that the Jews are a disloyal and subversive group within the kingdom who should be destroyed. The king gives the signet ring to Haman to move ahead with his plan.

B. Mordecai persuades Esther to intervene (4:1–14). Drawing upon the argument that as a Jewess she would not escape, Mordecai convinces Esther that she should appeal on behalf of her people before the king. (*See* Women.)

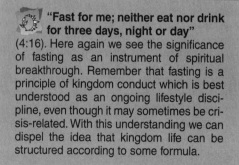
"Yet who knows whether you have come to the kingdom for such a time as this?"
(4:14). This oft-repeated question can be understood in relationship to a believer's life today. The Scripture suggests that God can use anyone at any point in time to accomplish His purpose (Acts 8:26). It is a partnership effort, however. God will not violate our will in order to use us. When we are willing and recognize the opportunity we have, we can experience the joy of being His instruments.

C. Esther solicits Mordecai's help (4:15–17). The appeal is made for spiritual help as Esther calls on "all the Jews" who were present in Shushan to fast for her before she goes unannounced into the king's presence—an action punishable by death if he did not extend the scepter to her.

"Fast for me; neither eat nor drink for three days, night or day"
(4:16). Here again we see the significance of fasting as an instrument of spiritual breakthrough. Remember that fasting is a principle of kingdom conduct which is best understood as an ongoing lifestyle discipline, even though it may sometimes be crisis-related. With this understanding we can dispel the idea that kingdom life can be structured according to some formula.

IV. MORDECAI EXALTED 5:1—6:14. The king receives Esther and grants her request.

A. Esther plans a banquet (5:1–8). With confidence at having been welcomed by the king, Esther plans a preliminary banquet during which she invites the king and Haman to another banquet to be held the next day.

B. Haman plots to destroy Mordecai (5:9–14). Driven by his hatred for Mordecai, Haman proceeds to build a gallows in order to execute him.

C. Haman is forced to honor Mordecai (6:1–14). This chapter displays the occasion where Haman is made to serve and honor Mordecai.

V. HAMAN HANGED 7:1–10. Divine justice is demonstrated in these verses.

A. Esther discloses her identity and exposes Haman (7:1–6). At the appointed time all the facts are revealed to the king.

B. Haman is hanged on gallows prepared for Mordecai (7:7–10). Esther is unmoved by Haman's appeal for mercy. He is hanged on his own gallows.

(7:10). This verse reminds us of the promise of God that "No weapon formed against you shall prosper" (Is. 54:17). God works to turn the very intent of the enemy around and use it against him for his destruction. Even the most serious threats against us can be used by God for our benefit and His glory.

VI. THE JEWS SAVED 8:1—9:17.

A. Esther brings her request to the king (8:1–6). Realizing that things related to the decree against the Jews are still pending, Esther makes her final request of the king.

B. The king issues a decree on behalf of the Jews (8:7–17). Mordecai actually writes the decree on behalf of the king and seals it with his signet ring. Thus the Jews were allowed to defend themselves from their attackers.

C. The Jews defeat their enemies (9:1–17). This defeat throughout the provinces was culminated with the hanging of the ten sons of Haman.

VII. THE FEAST OF PURIM ESTABLISHED 9:18—10:3.

A. The Jews celebrate the first Purim (9:18–32; *see* Generation).

B. The king advances Mordecai (10:1–3). Mordecai's reputation and influence extend throughout all the provinces.

TRUTH-IN-ACTION through ESTHER

Truth Esther Teaches	**Action** Esther Invites
1 Steps to Holiness Holy living realizes that inordinate honor or fawning and flattering to gain favor can be a form of idolatry. But wisdom also teaches that not showing such deference may incur the anger of those who expect it.	**3:2** *Be careful* that you worship no one but the Lord. *Understand* that showing undue honor or currying favor can be a form of worship. **3:8–15** *Be aware* that pursuing holiness and not living like others around you may incur the hatred and hostility of unbelievers.
2 Keys to Wise Living The wise man seeks to "discern the seasons and know what men ought to do." He uses God's favor, not as an opportunity to further selfish ambition, but as an occasion to serve His purpose.	**8:17** *Know* that God grants seasons of favor for His people in order to extend His kingdom. *Do not employ* such seasons for personal benefit. **4:12–14; 10:3** *Realize* that God places people in high positions to advance His purposes. *Always employ* any advantaged position for the welfare of God's people.
3 A Key Lesson in Faith The man of faith will not seek recognition because he knows that God sees and rewards.	**6:1–11** *Know* that God will not forget your acts of righteousness. *Believe* that He will reward them openly in His time.
4 A Lesson for Leaders The astute leader knows that his life is the most powerful sermon he will ever preach.	**1:17, 18** Leaders, *live* what you speak.

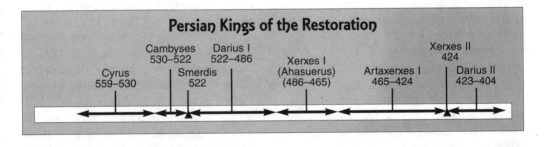

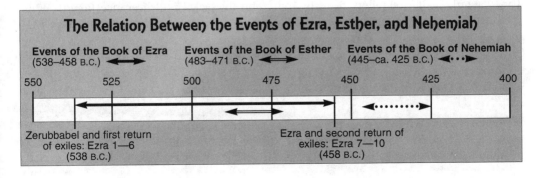

CHAPTER

18

KEYS TO JOB
Human Frailty and the Kingdom

Kingdom Key: God's Purpose in View

No book in the Bible has given rise to more unbiblical philosophy than Job, and no book more gloriously attests to God's faithfulness. That God permitted Satan to afflict Job is often taught as a normative experience, rather than as an instructive example. It is understandable how confusion arises. A common but incorrect supposition is that God always deals with people this way. Rather than being an example of God doling out suffering to mankind, Job's trial is a lesson about two more essential themes. This story provides divine revelation about (a) the mood and manner of Satan's hatefulness and readiness to attack humankind, and (b) the tendency of people to misinterpret those attacks. While many conclude that Job is written to describe God as intending suffering, it is more accurate to see in Job a revelation of Satan's efforts in extending it (1:6–12; 2:1–7).

The key to understanding God's kingdom rule and His divine ways as one reads Job is to carefully distinguish certain essential concepts. Sensitive discernment will allow us to learn from Job's suffering without sacrificing the message of Christ's healing grace. Even in life's darkest trials, when deliverance *through* suffering rather than deliverance *from* it may be our portion, we are best served to attempt the following:

1. Distinguish the place of suffering and human frailty. Human philosophizing, often passing for "theology" (as though to disclose truth about God), too often distorts the message of Job. Frequently, this book is

> ## God's sovereign might is never the enemy of His own.

interpreted to suggest that all suffering is a calculated part of God's divine destiny for humankind, thereby (a) to be endured as the will of God, and thus (b) somehow sanctified by Him. This view confuses human frailty and vulnerability with God's intent for human destiny. God has not destined us to suffer, nor does He approve it. Suffering is not in God's original purpose for humankind. Though we are not promised exemption from it, neither should we presume suffering to be God's will.

It *is* God's will that we turn to Him amid our suffering, that we may (a) receive His grace *within* it, and (b) seek His deliverance *from* it. While

(Please turn to page 131.)

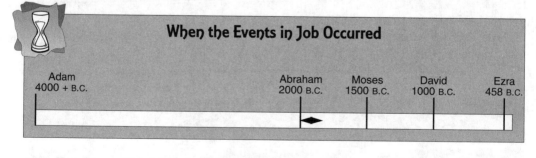

When the Events in Job Occurred

Adam 4000 + B.C.		Abraham 2000 B.C.	Moses 1500 B.C.	David 1000 B.C.	Ezra 458 B.C.

Job reveals hell's hatefulness in seeking

Master Key: God's Son Revealed

There is no direct reference to Christ in the Book of Job; however, Job may be seen as a type of Christ. Job suffered greatly and was humbled and stripped of all he had, but in the end he was restored and became the intercessor for his friends. Christ emptied Himself, taking on human form. He suffered, was persecuted for a time by men and demons, seemed forsaken by God, and became an intercessor. A significant difference between Christ and Job is that Christ *chose* to empty Himself, whereas Job's abasement came about through circumstances beyond his control.

The Book of James shows us the patience and endurance of Job. James states that, as God's intention toward Job was good, so our Lord's intention toward us is good (5:11).

Power Key: God's Spirit at Work

Elihu, in his debate with Job, makes three significant statements about the role of the Holy Spirit in His relationship to the people of God. In 32:8 he declares that a person's understanding is not due to his age or station in life, but rather it is a result of the operation of the Spirit of God. The Spirit then is the Author of wisdom, endowing one with the capacity to know and making sense out of life for him. Thus knowledge and wisdom are the Spirit's gift to humankind.

The Spirit of God is also the Source of life itself (33:4). Apart from the direct influence of the Spirit, humanity as we know it would not have come into existence. From the original creation it was so and continues to be so. Elihu states that his own existence witnesses to the life-giving power of the Spirit. The Spirit of God is the Spirit of life.

Key Word: *Sovereignty*

The basic question of the book is, "Why do the righteous suffer if God is loving and all-powerful?" Suffering itself is not the central theme; rather, the focus is on what Job learns from his suffering—the sovereignty of God over all creation.

Key Verses: Job 13:15; 37:23–24

Key Chapter: Job 42

Upon Job's full recognition of the utter majesty and sovereignty of the Lord, he repents and no longer demands an answer as to the "why" of his plight.

Because the Spirit gives life and wisdom, He is also essential to the very continuation of the human race. If God should turn His attention elsewhere, if He should withdraw His life-giving Spirit from this world, then human history would end (34:14–15). Elihu's point is that God is neither capricious nor selfish. Because He cares for us, He constantly sustains us by the abundant flow of His Spirit. Thus the Holy Spirit in the Book of Job is the Creator and Sustainer of life, and He gives meaning and rationality to life.

to defeat God's purpose in our lives.

Introducing

JOB

Author. The authorship of Job is uncertain. Some scholars attribute this book to Moses. Others attribute it to one of the ancient wise men whose works can be found in Proverbs and Ecclesiastes, perhaps even to Solomon himself.

Date. The manners, customs, and general lifestyle of Job are from the patriarchal period (about 2000–1800 B.C.). Scholars differ, however, regarding when it was compiled, as its writing was an obvious recording of a long-standing oral tradition. Those who attribute it to Moses opt for a fifteenth century B.C. date. Others opt for as late as the second century B.C. Most conservatives assign it to the Solomonic era, the mid-tenth century B.C.

Background. Scripture itself attests that Job was a real person. He is referred to in Ezekiel 14:14 and James 5:11. Job was a Gentile, is thought to have been a descendant of Nahor, Abraham's brother, and knew God by the name of "Shaddai"—the Almighty. (There are thirty references to Shaddai in the Book of Job.) Job was a wealthy man living a seminomadic lifestyle.

Content. The Book of Job has been called "a dramatic poem framed in an epic story" (J. Sidlow Baxter). Chapters 1 and 2 are a prologue, which give the setting of the story. Satan presents himself, with the sons of God, and challenges the piety of Job, stating, "Does Job fear God for nothing?" (1:9). He goes on to suggest that were everything to be taken away, Job would curse God. God gives Satan permission to try Job's faith by stripping him of his wealth, his family, and finally, his health. Yet, "Job did not sin with his lips" (2:10). Job is then visited by three friends—Eliphaz the Temanite, Bildad the Shuhite, and Zophar the Naamathite, who are so overwhelmed by Job's deplorable condition that they sit in silence with Job for seven days.

The bulk of the book is taken up with three dialogues between Job and Eliphaz, Job and Bildad, and Job and Zophar, followed by Elihu's challenge to Job. The four men seek to answer the question, "Why does Job suffer?" Eliphaz, basing his answer on experience, states that Job suffers because he has sinned. He argues that those who sin are punished. Since Job is suffering, obviously he has sinned. Bildad, resting his authority on tradition, suggests that Job is a hypocrite. He, too, takes the inferential approach and says that since trouble has come, Job must have

sinned. "If you were pure and upright, surely now He would awake for you" (8:6). Zophar condemns Job for verbosity, presumption, and sinfulness, concluding that Job is getting less than what he deserves: "Know therefore that God exacts from you less than your iniquity deserves" (11:6).

The three men come to the same basic conclusion: suffering is the direct outcome of sin, and wickedness is always punished. They argue that one can ascertain God's favor or disfavor toward a person by looking at his material prosperity or adversity. They falsely make the assumption that people can comprehend the ways of God without taking into account that divine retribution and blessing may extend beyond this present life.

In his replies to his friends, Job maintains his innocence, stating that experience proves that both the godly and ungodly suffer and both enjoy prosperity. He laments his deplorable condition and tremendous losses, venting his anger at them for accusing him rather than bringing him comfort.

After the three friends have concluded, a younger man named Elihu confronts Job, who chooses not to respond to his accusations. Elihu's argument is: God is greater than any human being; therefore, a person has no right or authority to require an explanation of Him. He argues that some things that God does are humanly incomprehensible. At the same time, Elihu suggests that God will speak if we will listen. His emphasis is on the attitude of the sufferer—that is, an attitude of humility allows God to intervene. This is the core of his message: instead of learning from his suffering, Job has the same attitude toward God as do the ungodly, and this is why judgment still afflicts him. Elihu's appeal to Job is: (1) to have faith in God Himself rather than to demand an explanation and (2) to change his attitude to one of humility.

It should not be concluded that all the objections of Job's friends represent other than the view of God contemporary to their times. As the revelation of God's nature has unfolded through history and the Scriptures, we find that some of their views have been shown as incomplete. This, of course, does not make the text less than inspired, but gives us a Holy Spirit-inspired report of the incidents as they occurred.

When the four have concluded, God answers Job out of a whirlwind. His response does not attempt to explain Job's sufferings, but by a series of interrogations, He seeks to humble Job. As we review the whirlwind address, we come to three conclusions regarding Job's suffering: (1) Job was not meant to know the explanation of his sufferings. Some things about human suffering God cannot possibly explain to us at the time without destroying the very purpose they were designed to fulfill. (2) God is involved in human affairs; Job and his grief meant enough to God to cause Him to speak. (3) God's purpose also was to bring Job to the end of his own self-righteousness, self-vindication, and self-wisdom, so he could find his all in God.

Personal Application. The Book of Job teaches several lessons: (1) God is sovereign. We cannot understand His workings by rational thinking alone; faith must rest in God's love and our knowledge of Him. Sovereignty means that God is all-powerful; He knows all, He is everywhere present, and His decision is final (Jer. 10:10; Dan. 4:17). God is the author of all the power of the universe. (2) We understand ourselves and our lives in direct relationship to our understanding of the character and workings of God. When we understand that

God's will toward us is good (John 10:10), that God cares and communicates His caring to His children—as He did to Job—this changes everything. Faith must have a resting place. When deep suffering threatens the foundations of faith, as was the case with Job, an assault on our faith can destroy us unless we are firmly rooted in these truths. (3) In times of tragedy we face the temptation of making God our adversary instead of our advocate. Like Job, we can focus on declaring our innocence and questioning the justice of God, or we can bow in humility and wait for God to reveal Himself and His purposes to us. (4) The struggle of faith is a personal one. We each enter the crucible of life alone; we must test the mettle of our faith in God against uncontrollable forces and win our individual victories. There will be times when family and friends may be taken from us and we must stand alone.

Kingdom Key *continued from page 128*

our individual human response to pain, difficulty, or tribulation may cause it to become a sanctifying force in our lives, still God has not sanctified suffering.

Jesus' ministry was filled with demonstrations of God removing suffering and releasing people from its agonies. In Christ's ministry we see God's heart: although suffering is a fact, it was not intended as a part of God's order for humanity.

Some of Job's responses do show righteous insights from which we all may draw in times of trial (e.g., 19:25–27; 23:10; 42:1–6). Beyond that, never mistake the truth: Job's trial is called a *"captivity"* (*see* 42:10—as the KJV best translates the Hebrew *shawbaw*), not a situation distilling from mere circumstance but from satanic contrivance. Further, his recovery was a deliverance from the devil's ploys, not simply a providential survival beyond normal "to-be-expected" human difficulty.

2. Distinguish the Creator of life from the cause of suffering. We must always remember that the Fall broke God's original order. Our present frailty and human vulnerability to suffering is a part of the Fall's aftermath. While Adam's sin brought upon us the curse of death and separation from God, it is also true that the awful *dimensions* of suffering are not solely the fruit of that Fall. Sin opened the door to the possibility of suffering, but its *proliferation* is advanced by the works of darkness. Thus, we see Job as a handbook of wis-

dom which, among other truths, discloses the stark reality that suffering is often the direct result of satanic attack and bondage. To overlook this is to miss a major truth of this book.

Job does not say that *all* suffering is satanic in origin, nor that *any* person is necessarily sick, afflicted, or pained as a direct result of his or her sin. Rather, Job balances the fact of human *frailty* with the fact of satanic *ferocity*, and in the end the true nature of God is revealed.

The climax of this book shows God (a) as mankind's Sustainer in trial, (b) as the Restorer of loss due to trial, and (c) as the Multiplier of blessings beyond trial (42:10–17).

3. Differentiate between the report and the revelation in Job. To read Job with discernment is to note the difference between human opinion and divine revelation. The true *report*, divinely inspired in its faithful record here, is an accurate statement of what the people said and felt. Their feelings and words, however, are not always true from God's perspective but the "truth" as they perceived it. For example, Eliphaz clearly misinterprets the presence and lies of a spirit of fear as being a word from God. A careful analysis of 4:12–21 reveals his confusion—and the subtle distortion of God's character argued by a lying spirit.

Another case of a faithful *record* that was not a divine revelation of truth may be seen in 13:24–27. Sorely tormented by pain, Job concludes that God has made him His enemy and

(Please turn to page 132.)

Kingdom Key *continued from page 131*

has calculated "bitter things" against him. This is not God's way or nature; it is only the cry of a sufferer. To fail to discern between such *reports*, and to conclude they *reveal* God's character in dealing with mankind, is to mistake the message of this book.

The kingdom key to Job is to avoid surrendering *either* (a) to the supposition that God ordains suffering, or (b) to the notion that the faithful are ever beyond its reach. To hold a balance that notes the fact of suffering without making God its source or minister is essential in order to join Job to the whole of the revelation of God through Christ and to avoid problematic reasonings. It is also essential to keep clearly focused the role of the Evil One in applying and advancing much of human pain and agony. Jesus did this (John 10:10; Acts 10:38), and as we do this we will approach Job more biblically than philosophically. Such discernment is essential to *gain* heaven's truth from Job, without *giving credence* to tales human imagination may spin from his dilemma.

Surveying

JOB

I. INTRODUCTION 1:1—2:13.

A. Job has both wealth and piety (1:1-5).

B. Satan challenges Job's character (1:6-12).
In God's own words, Job is "a blameless and upright man, one who fears God and shuns evil" (1:8).

But the main characters in these two chapters are the Lord and *Satan. The two enter into a contest, with Job as the battleground. Satan insists he will be able to move Job to "curse [God]" to His face if only the Lord removes the protection He maintains around Job. The Lord does so, and permits Satan to test Job. In a series of disasters whose timing and nature label them as supernatural, Job's wealth is stripped away, his children killed, and his body covered with agonizing boils.

C. Satan destroys Job's property and children (1:13-22).
In spite of his suffering, Job does not curse God.

D. Satan attacks Job's health (2:1-8).

E. Job's wife responds (2:9-10).
The test ends at 2:10 with this summary: "In all this, Job did not sin with his lips." Satan failed to accomplish what he said he would achieve.

F. Job's friends visit (2:11-13).
The first chapter refers to angels as "sons of God." This is a common Old Testament phrase, indicating direct creation or causation by God. The fact that all angels, good and evil, were required to present themselves at God's command shows that even those who have rebelled against God cannot deny His ultimate authority.

II. DIALOGUES BETWEEN JOB AND HIS THREE FRIENDS 3:1—26:14.

A. Job's outcry of despair (3:1-26).
Three of Job's friends hear of his tragedy and come to offer comfort. Stunned by his misery, they sit with him in silence for a week. This section of the book is a report of the dialogue which follows as the four men struggle to understand Job's suffering. In the dialogue Job's fears, frustration, and his suppressed resentment are expressed.

Job breaks the silence to complain. He might better have died at birth than live to experience such anguish.

B. First dialogue (4:1—14:22).
Eliphaz gently reminds Job that the innocent individual does not suffer (*see* Mortal). It is sinners whom God punishes. Since God is punishing Job, Job ought to turn to God quickly, for when he does God will restore him (*see* Trouble).

Job shares his terror (6:1—7:21). Job protests that he cannot be undergoing punishment, for he has done nothing wrong. He then expresses the terror his unexplained suffering is causing. Job simply cannot understand why God is letting this happen.

Bildad rebukes Job (8:1-22). Bildad is upset by Job's protestations of innocence. Is Job actually suggesting that God is unjust? So Bildad reminds Job of all the fathers have said about God. The Lord simply does not punish the upright person.

Job cries to God (9:1—10:22). Job cannot defend himself against this attack, for he too believes what Bildad says is true. But how can Job answer? Job is sure he has done nothing wrong! Looking up, Job addresses God and cries out his innocence. If Job is wrong, let God speak up and prove it (*see* Preserved).

Zophar challenges Job's "pride" (11:1-20). Job now is frightening his friends. So Zophar attacks Job, condemns his boasting, and insists that there must be some secret sin that God knows even if Job's friends do not. Zophar concludes with an appeal. If Job will only get his heart right with God, God will accept Job.

Job insists on his innocence (12:1—14:22). Now Job expressly states what he has before implied: he knows as much about God as his friends. Job knows God's attributes. But Job also knows that he is right! So his friends are being unfair to side with God!

Again Job appeals to God. He insists his treatment is unfair, protests his frailty, and weeps over his loss of hope.

> **"Yet will I trust Him"**
> (13:15). When everything else seems to fail, confidence in God's character is the bottom line. Job was so convinced of the redemptive nature of God (19:25), that he would trust in God even in the face of death. The issue of faith rests in God's ability to perform, while the action of faith rests in one's ability to believe. The ability to believe is given to every person (Rom. 12:3); how one uses this ability will determine the kind of relationship one will have with the God for whom nothing is impossible.

C. Second dialogue (15:1—21:34). Eliphaz' response (15:1—35). Job's self-defense has forced his friends into a difficult position. He has challenged their whole concept of God and their basis for understanding God's actions. Eliphaz now attacks Job, reminding him of truths they both accept: it is the wicked who suffer; it is the proud whom God brings low. The implication is clear. To suffer as Job has, he simply must be wicked!

Job's position hardens (16:1—17:16). Job bitterly complains about the "comfort" offered by his friends. He again states the facts as he knows them: God is against him; it is not because of any fault of Job's. Job's only hope is to die.

Bildad applies more pressure (18:1–21). Now Bildad takes up the attack. It's futile for Job to try to justify himself. The friends know it is the wicked who know calamity. They are the ones who see their families die. The wicked dash toward death in terror.

Job cries out (19:1–29). The pressure on Job is unbearable. Crushed by God, with relatives and friends turning against him, Job begs for pity. And he accuses his friends of fearing to take his side (*see* Flesh).

Zophar condemns Job (20:1–29). The appeal for pity falls on deaf ears. Zophar sternly tells Job to stop defending himself. He falls back on common knowledge about God and notes that while the wicked may prosper for a time, they suffer in the end. Again Zophar illustrates by naming events that have happened to Job. Zophar's accusation is clear. All the years that prosperity seemed to indicate God's blessing, there must have been some hidden wickedness in Job. Now the depth of Job's suffering has revealed to all the extent of the hidden wickedness!

Up to this point Job has agreed with the basic premise of the argument his friends have used against him (21:1–34). But now Job openly attacks the view of God which all have held. Job points to evidence that doesn't fit the accepted picture. Some people who are known to be wicked do prosper. Some who appear good do suffer. Faith may insist they will be punished or rewarded in the end. But when? Job charges that the case the friends have built, based on their idea of God and how He acts in the world, is a shroud of lies!

D. Third dialogue (22:1—26:14). Eliphaz continues his attack (22:1–30). If Job is so righteous, why does God reprove him? Eliphaz insists that deep in Job's heart sin must always have been hidden. Perhaps men could not see Job's wickedness, but God saw! Eliphaz ends with an appeal: turn and be saved. Hidden sins too can be forgiven.

Job refuses to bend (23:1—24:25). Job wishes aloud that he could talk with God, who would be forced to agree that Job is innocent. Job categorically denies doing wrong, and he again challenges God's ways. Sin does exist in the world, and God does not immediately punish those who murder, steal, commit adultery, or cause the poor to suffer.

Bildad affirms "faith" (25:1–6). Bildad will not respond to Job's argument nor join him in his questioning. Instead Bildad simply insists that God must be right, and that man has no right to question.

Job restates his position (26:1–14). The argument has gone around and around, with nothing resolved. Job sarcastically thanks his friends for their "comfort." And he insists that he will not lie, even to protect God's honor! Job has not sinned, and God is treating him unfairly.

III. JOB'S FINAL ADDRESS TO HIS FRIENDS 27:1—31:40. Zophar presents his final argument (27:13—28:28). [Note: Zophar's name is not in the text, but the speech picks up and continues his argument from 20:29. Thus most scholars suppose either that Zophar's name was omitted from the text, or that Job parodies his position. That position is the same as that of the other friends.] God is God, and He does judge the wicked.

The final statement is made by Job (29:1—31:40). He has not done wrong; he is clean and blameless. Thus Job has nothing more to say.

IV. ELIHU'S CHALLENGE TO JOB 32:1—37:24. Job and his friends are frustrated because they see no way out of their dilemma. All four are bound by the circular logic of their understanding of God. God brings suffering only on the wicked. Job is undergoing suffering caused by God. Thus Job is wicked. But then a young observer named Elihu breaks the grip of the logic that has trapped Job and his friends.

> **"But there is a spirit in man, and the breath of the Almighty gives him understanding"**
> (32:7–9). Wisdom frequently is equated with gray hair simply because older people have had a lifetime of experience in which to accumulate a reservoir of wisdom (12:12). But God can bestow His wisdom on a man as a pure gift if He so desires. Such is the word of wisdom, a pure gift from God which cannot be accessed by human effort.

Elihu changes the focus by pointing out that God may use suffering to instruct as well as to punish (33:19–30)! As soon as this new reason for suffering is suggested, the bondage of false logic is broken, and each of the four is free to confess that he does not *know* why God has permitted Job to undergo this experience. It is now possible to accept Job's testimony and still honor God as One who does right! Elihu does rebuke Job. Calling God unfair is hardly a valid solution to the problem of suf-

fering (34:10)! Twin themes dominate Elihu's discourse. The physical universe demonstrates that God's wisdom and understanding far surpasses man's. Why then should we expect to understand His ways of working in human lives? Since we are confident that God's character is marked by an abundant righteousness (*see* 37:23), when we cannot understand His actions we are simply to trust Him. This is perhaps the most significant message in the book.

V. GOD'S ADDRESS FROM THE WHIRLWIND 38:1—41:34. Now God speaks to Job, but He does not explain His servant's suffering! Instead God first reveals His omnipotence and wisdom, demonstrated in the creation (chs. 38, 39). When Job is invited to present his case, the awed sufferer simply covers his mouth. (*See* Restoration.) Then God emphasizes human frailty. Man is impotent even before the creatures that populate the earth. How then can any man expect to stand before the Creator of these awesome beasts (40:15—41:34)? The Lord is God; Job is merely a man.

VI. JOB'S RESPONSE 42:1–6. God's revelation of Himself seems inadequate to those who demand to know the reason for all things. But it is enough for Job. The sufferer now accepts his position as a creature and bows before the Creator. Having seen the Lord, Job makes no claim to righteousness, but simply submits to the Lord.

VII. CLOSING HISTORICAL SECTION 42:7–17. Job is told to pray (*see* Prayed) for his three friends, who have not spoken rightly about God, as Job has (7). Job's health is restored, his wealth is doubled, and his household blessed with many more children. (*See* Healing, Divine.)

TRUTH-IN-ACTION through JOB

Truth Job Teaches	**Action** Job Invites
❶ **Steps to Knowing God and His Ways** Knowing that God has sovereign control as Creator and Sustainer of both the physical and spiritual universe must govern the way we think. God is intimately involved with our lives in a way that eludes our grasp. Any wisdom that leads to truth comes from Him. The only way any man can know and understand God is by specific revelation. Understanding God's	**1:6–12** *Choose to trust* God's absolute sovereignty in any adversity. **2:3–6** *Understand* that while God may allow us to be tested, He sets strict limits on the tests. **7:17, 18** *Believe* that the Lord examines all your ways. **9:10–12** *Know* that God's works are often unfathomable by the human mind. **9:33–35; 16:19–22** *Understand* that Christ is our Advocate with the Father (see 1 John 2:1). *Know* our case is hopeless without Him. **31:15** *Understand* that God is the Creator of all men. *(continued)*

Truth Job Teaches	**Action** Job Invites
1 Steps to Knowing God and His Ways (continued) true nature will lead us to a hope in redemption and eternal life. [NOTE: See occasional foreshadowings of Christ in the discourses of Job and his friends.]	**34:10–12** *Understand* that God is totally righteous in what He renders to man and totally free from wrongdoing. **38:1—39:30** *Know* and *Understand* God as Creator and Sustainer of the Universe. *Learn* that He, not you, determines what is right.
2 Guidelines for Growing in Godliness Godliness will result from a true knowledge of God. Godly living rejects evil attitudes and looks for God in every circumstance.	**5:2** *Avoid* resentment, unforgiveness, and envy. *Believe* that they are self-destructive attitudes. **5:17** *Embrace* the Lord's correction. *Consider* it a blessing. *Know* that it evidences the Lord's love for you.
3 Steps in Developing Humility The true knowledge of God leads to humility. Humility is not the self-deprecation with which many of us are often acquainted. Rather, it is the refusal to trust oneself for fulfillment of needs, looking instead to the Lord.	**4:17; 9:2; 15:14; 25:4** *Understand* that man's own righteousness is a vain hope. *Believe* that only Christ's imputed righteousness can allow us to stand before God. **2:1; 42:4–6** *Diligently avoid* any form of self-righteousness. *Understand* that it makes one unteachable and unshapable in God's hand. **40:4, 5** *Humble* yourself regularly in the presence of the Lord. *Do not be hasty* to reply against God.
4 Keys to Wise Living The wise person lives in view of what he knows to be true about God, the world, and himself. His approach to God is humble and self-effacing. refusing to accuse God of any wrongdoing in adversities. Therefore, the wise man is able to patiently embrace and endure suffering, knowing that God's loving hand will prevail beyond it. Also, the wise man knows that although we are to seek to live righteously, our righteousness cannot earn God's favor: grace is a gift, not a debt.	**1:22** *Understand* that to accuse God of any wrongdoing is the sin of blasphemy. *Refuse* to question any of God's workings. **5:7** *Do not be surprised* at trouble. *Know* and *accept* that it is part of human life, which faith overcomes. **12:12** *Recognize* the value of the wisdom of those older than you. **12:14** *Resolve* yourself to the fact that God is the final word in all matters. **14:1, 2** *Understand* the transitory and trouble-filled nature of human life. **23:10** *Understand* that adversity is a fire by which God is seeking to purify your life. **36:8–12** *Discern* whether present adversity, opposition, or restraint is part of the Lord's discipline. *Agree* quickly with His correction and repent.
5 Key Lessons in Faith Fear is the converse of faith: it is believing what God says is not true. God commands us not to be afraid. Faith is able to trust God and not act out of fear.	**3:25** *Know* and *understand* that fear shows lack of faith in God and His promises. **5:21** *Rely* on the Lord's protection against verbal attacks and *do not fear* them. **13:15** *Believe* that God honors faith that is stronger than death.
6 Keys to Moral Purity Impurity may result from a failure to make a commitment to moral purity.	**31:1–40** *Commit* yourself to moral purity. *Keep* your eyes, hands, and body pure from sin.

KEYS TO PSALMS
Human Dignity and the Kingdom

Kingdom Key: God's Purpose in View

The Book of Psalms reveals the priority and power of worship as its central theme, because praise and worship are worthy of the Lord solely because of His majesty. But within the psalms, God reveals a companion purpose—that which we gain from worship and praise. The psalms reveal praise as an essential means by which redeemed humankind realizes fullest dignity and destiny. With worship, praise is a God-ordained capacity to apply the authority to which our regeneration as sons and daughters of God has restored us. Praise is a means of exercising redeemed humanity's reinstatement to partnership with God in exercising the power of His throne over earth's affairs (Eph. 2:6).

Psalm 8:3–5 expresses utter awe over God's intent and care for humans (8:4). Psalm 115:16 answers the question "What is man?" by showing how in God's will the earth was given to be our *domain,* an area over which we are charged to rule and to care for it. The present problem is that sin's corruption has removed our dignity (relationship with God) and therewith our ability to serve our destiny (rulership under God). Through redemption's provision (51:1–19) and grace's restoration (40:1–5), our partnership with God in kingdom dominion may now be recovered. Worship-filled praise is both the means for and the atmosphere in which this intent for human dignity may realize its destiny.

Psalmic Worship Is Founded on the Rule of God (Psalm 95):

Praise is the path- way to joyous living.

1. The earth is the Lord's by reason of His claim as Creator (24:1–2), and His overarching *rule* claims ultimate control (22:26; 103:19). While His intent is to share that rule with us as we abide in submission to Him, the final dominion remains God's and God's alone. Praise and worship extol this glory that belongs solely to Him.

2. Notwithstanding God's sovereign might, by reason of human sin, fierce enemies now contend for and gain temporal control of earth's affairs. This fact often wearies and mystifies the worshiper and occupies his song (37, 59, 74, 79, 94, and others). In such passages, praise *beyond* circumstance is modeled, sung forth in the confidence that God's ultimate rule can and will

(Please turn to page 140.)

When the Events in Psalms Occurred

			1st return from
Moses	David anointed	Death of Solomon	Babylon	Ezra
1500 B.C.	1010 B.C.	931 B.C.	538 B.C.	458 B.C.

(Ps. 90)

(Ps. 137)

Psalms underscores the priority and the

Master Key: God's Son Revealed

Approximately half of the Old Testament references to the Messiah quoted by New Testament writers are from the Book of Psalms. The apostles saw prophetic reference in this book to Christ's birth (Acts 13:33), His lineage (Matt. 22:42–45), His zeal (John 2:17), His teaching by parables (Matt. 13:35), His rejection (Matt. 21:42), His priesthood (Heb. 5:6), His betrayal by Judas (John 13:18), His vicarious suffering (Rom. 15:3), His triumphant Resurrection (Acts 2:25–28), Ascension (Acts 2:34), and reign (1 Cor. 15:27), as well as many other aspects of His ministry.

Some of the prophetic references to Christ are typical, that is, symbolic shadows of future realities. Other references are direct prophetic statements. Either way, the interpretation of these psalms as messianic is verified by Jesus' own words in Luke 24:44, where He declared that the Psalms spoke concerning Him.

Power Key: God's Spirit at Work

The Book of Psalms, and the principles of worship they reflect, minister to the soul of humankind and to the heart of God because they are the product of the work of the Holy Spirit. David, the major contributor to the Book of Psalms, was anointed by the Holy Spirit (1 Sam. 16:13). Not only was this anointing for kingship, but it was for the office of a prophet (Acts 2:30); the prophetic statements he recorded were by the power of the Holy Spirit (Luke 24:44; Acts 1:16). In fact, the lyrics of his songs were composed by the inspiration of the Spirit (2 Sam. 23:1–2), as were his plans for appointing chief musicians and choirs with their accompanying orchestras (1 Chr. 28:12–13).

Thus the Psalms are unique and vastly different from the works of secular composers. Both may reflect the depths of agony experienced by the tormented human spirit, with all its pathos, and express the rapturous joy of the freed soul, yet the Psalms move to a higher plane by the creative anointing of the Holy Spirit.

Specific statements show that the Holy Spirit is at work in creating life (104:30); that He faithfully accompanies the believer (139:7); that He guides and instructs (143:10); that He sustains the penitent (51:11–12); and that He interacts with the rebellious (106:33).

> ### Key Word: *Worship*
>
> The central theme of the Book of Psalms is worship—God is worthy of all praise because of who He is, what He has done, and what He will do. His goodness extends through all time and eternity.
>
> ### Key Verses: Psalm 19:14; 145:21
>
> ### Key Chapter: Psalm 100
>
> So many of the favorite chapters of the Bible are contained in the Book of Psalms that it is difficult to select the key chapter among such psalms as Psalms 1; 22; 23; 24; 37; 72; 100; 101; 119; 121; and 150. The two central themes of worship and praise are beautifully wed in Psalm 100.

power of worship and praise in all of life.

Introducing
PSALMS

Author. The Book of Psalms is a compilation of several ancient collections of Hebrew songs and poetry for use in congregational worship as well as in private devotion. In some collections the ancient compilers gathered together mostly David's superb songs—he wrote seventy-three of them. In others they drew from a variety of authors such as Moses, the Levitical singing clans of Asaph and Korah, Solomon, Ethan, Heman, and Jeduthun. Forty-nine are from unnamed sources. Jewish scholars called these "orphan psalms."

Date. The individual psalms may have been written at dates extending from the Exodus to the restoration after the Babylonian exile. But the small collections seem to have been gathered at specific periods in Israel's history: the reign of King David (1 Chr. 23:5), the rule of Hezekiah (2 Chr. 29:30), and during the leadership of Ezra and Nehemiah (Neh. 12:24, 26). This collection process helps explain the duplication of some psalms. For example, Psalm 14 is similar to Psalm 53.

The Book of Psalms was edited in its present form with several variations by the time the Greek Septuagint was translated from the Hebrew, a few centuries before Christ's advent.

The Ugaritic texts, when contrasted with the more recent Dead Sea Scrolls, show that the imagery, style, and parallelisms of some of the psalms reflect a very ancient Canaanite style and vocabulary. The Book of Psalms, then, reflects the worship, devotional life, and religious sentiment of approximately one thousand years of Israel's history.

Content. The Hebrew title of this book, *Sepher Tehillim*, means "Book of Praises." The Greek titles, *Psalmoi* or *Psalterion*, denote a poem that is to be accompanied by a stringed instrument. However, the Psalter contains more than temple songs and hymns of praise. It includes elegies, laments, personal and national prayers, petitions, meditations, instructions, historical anthems, and acrostic tributes to noble themes.

Psalms is the second of three Old Testament books designated as poetical: Job, Psalms, and Proverbs. These three were also called "books of truth."

In its final form in our canon of Scripture, the Book of Psalms is subdivided into five smaller books. Each book is a compilation of several ancient collections of songs and poems. A fitting doxology has been placed at the end of each book by its editors. In Book One (Pss. 1—41) most of the songs are attributed to David. Compiled before his death, the collection is largely personal psalms which reflect David's own experiences. Book Two (Pss. 42—72), probably added in the days of Solomon, is a collection of songs by, of, or for the sons of Korah, Asaph, David, and Solomon, with four anonymously written. Book Three (Pss. 73—89) is marked by a large collection of Asaph's songs. He was King David's choirmaster (1 Chr. 16:4-7). Although most psalms in Book Four (Pss. 90—106) are without given authors, Moses, David, and Solomon are contributors. These were collected in the days of the Exile. More of David's songs are found in Book Five (Pss. 107—150). The final book is strongly liturgical and probably was organized around the time of Ezra the scribe after the return from Babylonian captivity, although many psalms likely were used by the Hebrew people before their official compilation in these books. The series of songs called the Egyptian Hallel (Pss. 111—118) is found here as well. The final songs (Pss. 146—150) in Book Five are known as the "Great Hallel" series. Each song begins and ends with the Hebrew exclamation of praise, "Hallelujah!"

Informative subheadings are found at the beginning of many of the psalms. The Hebrew preposition used in many of the subheadings can be translated three ways: "to," "for," and "of"—that is, "dedicated to," "for the use of," and "belonging to." Those subheadings describing the historical occasion of the psalm all deal with the life of David. Psalms 7, 34, 52, 54, 56, 57, 59, and 142 refer to events during David's troublesome relationship with Saul; and Psalms 3, 18, 51, 60, and 63 cover the period when David reigned over both Judah and Israel.

Other subheadings preceding psalms refer to the musical instruments that are to accompany them; to the appropriate tune or melody; to the part of the choir which is to lead (for example, soprano, tenor, bass); or to what type of psalm it is (for example, meditation, prayer). Some of the meanings of these liturgical and musical notations are unknown to us today. The exact purpose of the term *Selah*, which occurs seventy-one times within the body of thirty-nine different psalms, simply is not known. The word means "to lift up" and is probably some kind of pause mark or musical signal.

A number of repeated themes have been noted in the psalms, and some psalms may be classified by their content. Types of psalms that have been identified are:

(1) Praise psalms, which focus on the person of God and praise Him by describing His

nature and qualities. Illustrations are 33, 103, 139.

(2) Historical psalms, which review God's dealings with His people. Illustrations are 68, 78, 105, 106.

(3) Relational psalms, which explore the personal relationship between God and the believer. Illustrations are 8, 16, 20, 23, 55.

(4) Imprecatory psalms, which call on God to overthrow the wicked. Illustrations are 35, 69, 109, 137.

(5) Penitential psalms, in which the psalmist expresses sorrow over his own failures. Illustrations are 6, 32, 51, 102, 130, 143.

(6) Messianic psalms, which refer in some sense to the Savior who will come from David's line. A number of such psalms can be identified by New Testament references to them. Psalms identified as messianic in the New Testament are: 2, 8, 16, 22, 40, 45, 69, 72, 89, 102, 109, 110, 132. Others also have messianic elements.

(7) Liturgical psalms, which were used at specific times of the year or on specific occasions. Most psalms had some public use. Special liturgical psalms may be illustrated by 30, 92, 120, 134.

Hebrew Poetry. English poetry relies on rhyme and rhythm for its impact. Thus it is difficult to translate into another language. But Hebrew poetry can be easily translated, for its major feature is not rhyme but parallelism. The balance of thought is vital to Hebrew poetry, not the balance of sounds or rhythm.

The basic unit of Hebrew poetry is the verse, in which the first line states a theme, and one or more following lines in some way develop that thought. This is what is meant by "parallelism": the balancing of thoughts by following lines. Among the various types of parallelism three are basic:

(1) Synonymous parallelism repeats the thought of the first line.

"Then our mouth was filled with laughter,
And our tongue with singing"
(Ps. 126:2).

(2) Antithetical parallelism emphasizes the thought of the first line by contrasting it with an opposite.

"The merciful man does good
for his own soul,
but he who is cruel
troubles his own flesh"
(Prov. 11:17).

(3) Synthetic parallelism uses the second line to fill in or complete the thought of the first.

"I will both lie down in peace, and sleep;

For You alone, O LORD,
make me dwell in safety" (Ps. 4:8).

A few parallelisms are causal, revealing the justification for the first line (31:21). Sometimes parallelism involves three lines (1:1), four lines (33:2–3), or more.

It is important to keep this parallelism in mind when reading or trying to interpret the Psalms and other Old Testament poetry.

Personal Application. The New Testament apostles frequently used references from the Book of Psalms as texts for teaching Christian doctrine. The forgiveness of sins by grace, the faithfulness of God, the sinfulness of all humanity (Jew and Gentile), the inclusion of Gentiles in the church, the existence of angels, and the appropriate conduct of saints all were reinforced by quotations from the Psalms.

Also, throughout the centuries the Psalms have been a source of personal inspiration and spiritual strength. In the course of dealing with the adversities of life, people are often frustrated by not being able to express adequately their emotional pain or mental anguish. The Psalms release us from that frustration. With emotionally drenched complaints, humble confessions, desperate pleas, penitent prayers, or screams of pain, the writers of the Psalms skillfully expose and express the yearnings of our deepest thoughts. This use of the Psalms is often the first step toward our own deliverance. By song and Spirit they comfort the lonely, strengthen the weary, bind the brokenhearted, and turn the eyes of the downcast up toward their Creator. Hope returns, faith is renewed, and life again becomes bearable.

As a whole the psalter is intended to help each of us see how to praise God and pray to Him. Of particular note are the ways the inner life and emotions of the psalmists are shared freely and completely with God. Thus Psalms is one of the most intimate and relational books of the Bible. And for each emotional need expressed by the worshiper, Psalms points us to an attribute of the Lord. He is an anchor when we are buffeted, a comfort when we feel abandoned, and an encouragement when support is desperately required.

The Psalms also have a rich history of liturgical and congregational use. King David organized choirs and orchestras, and appointed skilled conductors and composers to lead the worship (1 Chronicles 25). He not only composed many psalms himself, but he invented musical instruments (1 Chr. 23:5). Fifty-five psalms are specifically addressed to the "Chief Musician," or worship leader.

This orchestrated worship was continued in Solomon's temple, although at different periods of Israel's history the worship passed through seasons of misuse and abuse. (See 2 Chr. 7:6; 29:25–30; Amos 5:23.) With the destruction of the second temple in A.D. 70 and the cessation of animal sacrifices, the singing of psalms along with Scripture reading took a place of increasing importance in synagogue worship services.

The first Christian churches were comprised mainly of Jewish people, so it was natural that they incorporated the singing of psalms, hymns, and spiritual songs into their worship (Col. 3:16). Throughout the centuries, in most of the major Christian denominations, hymnbooks composed mostly of psalms set to cultural music patterns have been used in congregational singing. In modern times, churches continue to draw from the Book of Psalms for songs of worship. The worship the Christian church has adopted incorporates not only the lyrics and instruments of the psalms, but involves clapping (47:1), lifting up hands (141:2), bowing (95:6), standing (134:1), shouting (47:1), and dancing (149:3).

Kingdom Key *continued from page 136*

prevail.

Psalmic Worship Shows Praise as the Role of Humanity (Psalm 150):

1. Praise is revealed as the *means* by which God's rule is invited into dire circumstance (22:3). Such "kingdom-type" worship "enthrones" God. This is not to say God has no throne without our acknowledgement or praise. But human acknowledgement of God's rule (as of His salvation) opens the way for His effective, over-ruling entry. Praise and worship, in the face of "un-ruly" situations, invite God to establish His rule amid earthly turmoil or corrupt government. Praise bids God's entry (Psalm 140), that the divine order already secured in the heavens (119:89) might be realized here and now on earth. At these points we exalt Him above every other power.

2. Psalm 18 reveals the age-old struggle between God's ordained King (Messiah) and "the kings of the earth" (subjects of Satan). God's King intercedes (2:7–9) through His people's prayers and praise (Rom. 8:26–27), which (a) reflect Calvary's triumph (47:1–4), and (b) are sung with spiritual understanding (47:5–7). Such praise brings victory to the present moment (47:8–9; 60:12). It also proclaims the King's eventual global rule at the consummation of His kingdom (2:4–6; 132:13–18).

Surveying
PSALMS

I. BOOK ONE 1:1—41:13.

A. Introductory songs (1:1—2:12).

Psalm 1. The godly person is likened to a well-watered tree, while the ungodly are like dry chaff, blown away by winds (*see* Meditates).

> **"A tree planted by the rivers of water, that brings forth its fruit"**
> (1:3). The psalmist had learned to drink deeply of spiritual wisdom (v. 2), and that fruit would be ripe when needed. Likewise we come to the Fountainhead of wisdom and refreshment—the Living Word—who invited us, "Come to Me and drink," so that "out of his heart will flow rivers of living water" (John 7:37–38). He spoke of the

Holy Spirit, who releases Jesus' life in us and through us—like a flowing river. The Spirit-filled life is one of continuous refreshment in the Spirit *and* the Word together.

Psalm 2. This messianic psalm shows the futility of rebellion against God (vv. 1–6), and affirms the certainty of God's ultimate rule, to be established by His coming Son (7–12; *see* Evangelism).

B. Songs of David (3:1—41:12).

*Psalm 3. David experiences abandonment when he flees during Absalom's rebellion (1–2; *see* 2 Samuel 15; 16), his hope is restored by praise for God's protection and faithfulness (vv. 3–4), and he knows a peace which frees him to rest (5–8).

Psalm 4. David's experience when crushed by troubles (1–2) shows that prayer brings confidence (3), restored faith (4–5), and a present experience of peace (6–8).

Psalm 5. This prayer asks blessings for the godly (1–3, 7–8, 11–12), alternating with calls for judgment on the guilty (4–6, 9–10; *see*

Evil; Spiritual Warfare).

Psalm 6. A prayer for mercy, uttered while in deep distress.

Psalm 7. A psalm on the theme of righteousness. David reminds God he has lived righteously and calls for deliverance from wicked and violent enemies. (*See* Praise.)

Psalm 8. How awesome God is, whose greatness (*see* Honor) is shown in creation, and who stoops to care for individual persons! (*See* Human Worth.)

Psalm 9. In this praise psalm David honors God for His intervention in history on behalf of the righteous, and calls on Him to continue to judge wicked nations.

"I will praise You"
(9:1–2). A relationship with God cannot exist without praise. No one can express praise to *Yahweh* in an impersonal way. Praise results from a close relationship with God and must always be expressed or proclaimed. But praise is first an act of the will. Four times in these verses the psalmist declares, "I will." Our praise, like everything else we enjoy with God, is a result of His invitation, as He summons us into His presence.

Psalm 10. A prayer in a time of trouble, this psalm explores the ways and motives of the wicked (2–11) and calls on God the King to arise and defend the oppressed (12–18).

Psalm 11. This very personal expression of confidence in God comes when life's "foundations are [being] destroyed" (3)

Psalm 12. We can be confident in God's commitment to protect the righteous from those who lie about them and malign them.

Psalm 13. A brief prayer when feeling alone and abandoned.

Psalm 14. Here is a description of the "fool" (morally deficient individual) who denies God's existence as well as the depravity which follows rejection of the Lord. The psalm is quoted in Romans 3:10–12.

Psalm 15. A brief outline of the character of the man who lives in close relationship with the Lord. (*See* Brotherly Love.)

Psalm 16. This beautiful psalm expresses satisfaction with personal relationship to God. God alone is the source of all good (1–4), the One who assigns our place in life (5–6), and the One who guides us by His presence (7–8). The final verses (9–11) express David's expectation of resurrection, and are also messianic references to Christ (*see* Acts 2:25–28, 31; 13:35–37; Messianic Promises).

Psalm 17. An expression of devotion to God and confidence in Him.

Psalm 18. Shout out joy and love! David expresses his feelings when delivered from Saul and his other enemies. In graphic language David portrays God's coming to aid His trusting servant (*see* Exalted; Praise).

Psalm 19. Here is a measured statement of God's revelation of Himself in nature (1–6) and in the written Word (7–14; *see* Faith's Confession; Word of God).

Psalm 20. A public prayer for Israel's leader (1–5), expressing trust in the Lord rather than military power (6–9).

Psalm 21. Rejoicing in the Lord and in His strength.

Psalm 22. This messianic psalm focuses on the sufferings of Christ (1–18) and the exaltation that follows (19–31). Many New Testament passages quote or refer to this psalm, which prefigures the crucifixion of Jesus (*see* Matt. 27:35–46; John 19:23–25; Heb. 2:12; Kingdom of God; Messianic Promises; Praise).

Psalm 23. This famous Shepherd Psalm likens God to a good shepherd, who guides and supports (*see* Comfort) the believer through his life.

Psalm 24. The writer affirms God's sovereignty and expresses joy in His rule as King of Glory.

Psalm 25. This appeal for help is also an expression of trust (*see* Truth). David asks God to show him the Lord's ways (7), confident that one who follows the Lord will find release (8–15). This prayer is offered despite David's present loneliness and anguish (16–22).

Psalm 26. David appeals for vindication by God, deserved because of his trusting, obedient heart.

Psalm 27. A prayer of confidence in God, on whose person David's whole being is concentrated.

Psalm 28. God is appealed to as rock, strength, and shield, who will deliver us from the fate deserved by the wicked.

Psalm 29. Here is a psalm of pure praise, exalting in God's power over nature.

Psalm 30. Praise (*see* Joy) is given for answered prayer, after being healed.

"To the end that my glory may sing praise to You and not be silent"
(30:12). Biblical worship can be a fairly noisy affair (*see* note at 100:1–2)! Praise is part of the package of biblical worship. It springs joyously from the loving, creative spirits of men and women who understand the essence of true reverence for God because they have been set free by the grace of Jesus Christ.

Psalm 31. In a psalm of commitment

David leads the believer to surrender his situation to God and rely completely on Him. Verse 5 of this *great psalm of commitment was quoted by Christ on the Cross.

Psalm 32. Confession of sin, and God's subsequent forgiveness, brings joy. David shares his inner anguish at unconfessed sin (3–5) and the great release which comes when transgressions are brought to the Lord (6–11; *see* Teach).

Psalm 33. This public call to praise God (1–5) reminds us of the many benefits of a close relationship with the Lord (6–22).

Psalm 34. Protection granted at a time when David acted unwisely stimulated this teaching psalm on the benefits of relationship with God (*see* Taste).

> **"His praise shall continually be in my mouth"**
>
> (34:1–3). David's promise to give praise without ceasing suggests his relationship with *Yahweh* was extraordinary. His commitment to "bless the LORD at all times," even in the most discouraging circumstances, reminds us of the apostle Paul's admonition to the Philippian church to "rejoice in the Lord always" (Phil. 4:4). Living in the power of the Holy Spirit enables one to be continuous in both the attitude and action of praise. Such response will encourage others around us to join in, as David suggested in verse 3.

Psalm 35. An imprecation on David's enemies, who are malicious and evil. The tone of this psalm is one of wounded suffering rather than anger.

Psalm 36. The wicked (1–4) are held up and contrasted with God's loving faithfulness (5–12).

Psalm 37. David exhorts patience and trust (*see* Heart) when pressures come. The theme "wait on the LORD" is repeated, with warnings against hasty action. This is an important psalm for anyone wronged by others.

Psalm 38. David appeals to God when he feels crushed and deserted under divine discipline.

Psalm 39. An expression of the feelings of an individual under discipline.

Psalm 40. Remembrance of salvation (1–5) leads to willing commitment to God (6–10) and an appeal to God for support (11–17; *see* Poor).

Psalm 41. Sums up David's lifelong experience with God and praises the Lord for His mercy and faithfulness. (*See* Messianic Promises.)

> **"You will sustain him on his sickbed"**
>
> (41:1–3). The psalmist's confidence is fixed in the character of Yahweh. A careful study of the word "poor" in verse 1 establishes the context of the passage and the resulting action of the Lord on David's behalf. The connection of this word with the "poor" of Matthew 5:3 invites the entry of the kingdom and its dynamic of healing as the definitive work of Yahweh being proclaimed in verse three. Note the positive parallel of David's words "You will" and Christ's words "theirs is the kingdom."

C. Doxology (41:13).

TRUTH-IN-ACTION through PSALMS (Book One: Psalms 1—41)

Truth Psalms Teaches	**Action** Psalms Invites
1 A Step to Knowing God Knowing and believing that God is omniscient will keep us from trying to hide from Him.	**10:11–15** *Understand* that God sees and knows all things. *Believe* that nothing you do is hidden from Him.
2 Guidelines for Growing in Godliness Godly living is radically different from the way we learned to live while in the world. It offends our fleshly, sinful nature. Therefore, because godliness is unnatural to us, we must have the supernatural assistance of the Holy Spirit. Godly	**2:12** *Honor* the Lord Jesus Christ in your speech and conduct. **4:4** *Refuse* to respond out of anger. *Sleep on it* and *give time* for righteous reflection. **10:4** *Let God fill* your thoughts and thus *avoid* wickedness. **15:4** *Honor* commitments and your word even when it is costly to do so. **19:14** *Speak* and *think* only in ways that you know please the Lord. *(continued)*

Truth Psalms Teaches	**Action** Psalms Invites
2 Guidelines for Growing in Godliness *(continued)* living requires radical change in our speech, conduct, and thinking.	**36:4** *Understand* that righteousness actively rejects wrong-doing.
3 Steps to Holiness Holy people not only live in a manner distinct from the world, but also disallow the world's value system to have control in their lives. If we give place to the world, we will receive the results that ungodly living anticipates.	**1:1** *Do not conduct your life* as the world does, *do not participate* in questionable activities, and *do not be cynical. Live distinctly* from the world as God's own people. **7:14** *Understand* that allowing evil to develop in your heart will result in disillusionment and bring unnecessary trouble into your life.
4 Steps to Dynamic Devotion Consistently spending time with God effects permanent change in our lives. Insincere attempts at this result in half-hearted devotion. Those who make their devotion to God their highest priority are those whose lives know true, heart-felt devotion.	**1:2** *Practice* regular Bible meditation. *Delight* in the Scriptures and *let them* be your guide. **5:3** *Seek* the Lord in the morning. *Wait* on Him expectantly to speak to your heart and spirit. **5:7** *Prioritize* private and corporate worship. **19:7–11** *Thank* God daily that He has revealed Himself, His will and His promises to you in His Word. **27:4** *Make* time with God and His people your high priority and your delight. **29:1, 2** *Testify* regularly to God's goodness in your life. **40:6–8** *Choose* to live a life of disciplined obedience as God's servant.
5 Key Lessons in Faith God's people must actively, consciously trust that God's Word is true and that He always acts in accordance with it. Every situation we encounter is an opportunity to choose to trust God rather than our own inclinations. Faith involves an element of risk, but always yields the richest dividends.	**9:10** *Choose to believe* that the Lord will never forsake you when you trust Him. **12:6** *Know* that the Word of God has been proven to be absolutely trustworthy. **23:1–6** *Expect* Jesus' shepherding care. *Know* that He will keep you from want, protect you, and restore your life. **26:1** *Believe* the Lord for your vindication, not seeking it yourself. **37:5** *Consciously commit* all your plans to the Lord daily. *Do not presume* His help if it is uninvited.
6 Steps to Dealing with Sin Dealing properly with sin involves the courage to allow the Word of God and the Spirit of God to examine your heart and mind. Covering up sin and trying to hide it results in distress and usually greater sin. Agree with God about sinful behavior, turn from it, and God's gracious forgiveness will cover it.	**19:12, 13** *Receive* examination and correction from the Word of God. *Understand* that doing so will keep you from sin. **25:7** *Confess* and *turn from* sin and rebellion. *Receive* God's forgiveness. *Understand* God forgets as well. **32:1–5** *Acknowledge* and *confess* sin. *Understand* that God desires to forgive and restore you, but *do not* take God's forgiveness lightly.
7 How to Tame the Tongue Few sins exist that do not somehow involve the tongue. Righteous speech results from discipline and choice. Too easily do we speak too much, too hastily, and too freely. Choosing to speak much less and more carefully will result in less sinning.	**17:3** *Choose* to speak only that which is righteous. *Commit* yourself to godly conversation. **18:6** *Do not* grumble and complain when in distress or trouble. *Cry* out to God. *Trust* that He will hear and answer. **34:12–14** *Guard carefully* your speech. *Know* that righteous speech carries with it the promise of long life.

II. BOOK TWO 42:1—72:20.

A. Songs of the sons of Korah (42:1—49:20).

Psalm 42. Here is a psalm of encouragement for times of spiritual depression when God seems very far away.

Psalm 43. This plea for vindication is uttered, like Psalm 42, at a time of great discouragement.

Psalm 44. After a historical review of the principles of God's dealings with Israel under the Mosaic covenant, this psalm calls on God to restore His people and redeem them.

Psalm 45. This messianic psalm (*see* Heb. 1:8–9) dwells on the noble theme of God's rule (1–9) and pictures those who share the glory as the King's bride (10–17; *see* Virgins).

Psalm 46. God is His people's mighty fortress!

> **"Therefore we will not fear"**
> (46). Fear may be the most debilitating tool the enemy uses to challenge a believer's faith. If faith is believing what God has said to be true, then fear is *not* believing what God has said to be true. The psalmist opens with a declaration of truth accompanied by the facts of real living. Notice that he matches "God is" with the fact that real life involves "trouble" (v. 1). Then he makes his determination about how to live, even when apparently unchangeable things around us change (2–3). Real faith is clear-eyed and focused on God, not on circumstance. At least six times he returns to the fact of God's existence.

Psalm 47. A praise psalm, exalting God as Ruler of the nations (*see* Clap; Praise).

Psalm 48. God is great (1–7), and life in His land is satisfying (8–14).

Psalm 49. Peace comes when our hearts trust in God, not in riches.

B. Song of Asaph (50:1–23).

Psalm 50. All gather to hear God speak (1–6). He encourages His people to honor Him, which is more important to Him than sacrifice (7–15), and He warns the wicked (16–23; *see* Praise).

C. Songs of David (51:1—71:24).

Psalm 51. David's great penitential psalm was written after his adultery with Bathsheba (2 Samuel 11—12). Confession of his sin (1–6) brings forgiveness and cleansing (7–9), renewing David's ability to once again serve the Lord (10–19; *see* Prayer).

> **"Renew a steadfast spirit within me. . . . and do not take Your Holy Spirit from me"**
> (51:10–12). During repentance, David recognizes the restoration necessary for effective kingship—(1) a renewed constancy in his own spirit for service (v. 10), (2) a continued anointing of the Spirit for empowerment (v. 11), and (3) an overflowing joy from the Spirit for salvation life (v. 12). Remembering how Saul's disobedience led to the Spirit's departure (1 Sam. 15:26; 16:14), David pleads that God not remove his qualification for office—the Holy Spirit. Likewise, we honor our gifts and calling from the Lord, attending to our own spirit's framework, and praying for the Spirit's fullness—careful to always make His presence our passion.

Psalm 52. Disturbed by a great evil (1 Samuel 21—22), David reminds himself of the fate of the wicked (vv. 1–7) and destiny of the godly (8–9).

Psalm 53. Another psalm like 14 which describes the "fool" (morally lacking individual) who denies God.

Psalm 54. Here is a cry for help uttered when those David aided turned against him (1 Samuel 23).

Psalm 55. This is a deeply emotional expression of David's fear and anguish, magnified by the pain of his betrayal by those who were longtime friends (*see* Sustain). The situation described in the psalm fits the time of Absalom's rebellion (2 Samuel 15—17).

Psalm 56. Another psalm affirming trust in days of fear.

Psalm 57. David is confident in God's faithfulness, even when he is forced to hide from King Saul (1 Samuel 24).

Psalm 58. A call for judgment on unjust judges and rulers.

Psalm 59. This deliverance psalm likens the wicked who persecute God's people to snarling dogs that prowl the city at night.

Psalm 60. Praise is given to God, who has led the forces of David to victory over foreign enemies.

Psalm 61. David takes refuge in God and relies on the Lord's promises to support his throne.

Psalm 62. Rest can be ours in God, for He is strong and loving.

Psalm 63. Close personal relationship with God brings the believer to the place of *praise and joy.

"I will lift up my hands in Your name"
(63:4). Human hands represent what we do. They are instruments whereby we accomplish things. In this passage they represent one way we bless God. By lifting them in praise, we acknowledge that without God's presence in our lives we can accomplish nothing of lasting value. It is also a way of pointing to the Lord or reaching up to Him. In this way we acknowledge our weakness and express our need. Raised hands are an admission that we are not able to manage our own lives. We raise our hands in surrender to His power.

Psalm 64. A prayer for protection from conspiracy.

Psalm 65. God is honored for His rich provision in nature.

Psalm 66. An exalting expression of praise for God's works on behalf of His people.

Psalm 67. This simple expression of praise looks forward to a time when all peoples will know and praise the Lord.

"Let all the peoples praise You"
(67:3). The psalmist passes from a prayer for blessings upon Israel (v. 1) to a prayer for the nations. He prays that they might receive revelation (v. 2), praise God (v. 3), and submit to His rule (v. 4). We should be just as impassioned when we pray, "Your kingdom come" (*see* Matt. 6:10). God wants all peoples and nations to know Him (*see* Matt. 28:19) and to praise Him.

Psalm 68. This long psalm of praise extols God as *Father and Savior, and looks forward to a time when all the earth will gather to worship the Lord at His sanctuary (*see* Company; Family Life).

Psalm 69. This messianic psalm is quoted in Acts 1:16–20. It is a quiet sharing of David's personal distress and disappointments, mixed with frequent expressions of trust in God.

Psalm 70. An urgent prayer for speedy deliverance (*see* Needy).

Psalm 71. A stately confession of faith in God as sovereign Lord. (*See* Praise.)

Psalm 72. This strong messianic psalm looks forward to the day Messiah will rule over the whole earth. Like the prophets, this psalm emphasizes His endless, universal rule and portrays a time of justice for the oppressed and needy and prosperity for all.

D. Song of Solomon (72:1–17).

E. Doxology (72:18–19).

F. Concluding verse (72:20).

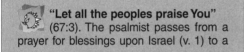

TRUTH-IN-ACTION through PSALMS (Book Two: Psalms 42—72)

Truth Psalms Teaches	**Action** Psalms Invites
1 Guidelines for Growing in Godliness Those who choose to live godly lives will not go unrewarded and will look for opportunities to share with others what God is doing in and through them.	**62:12** *Understand* and *know* that God will reward everyone according to his deeds. **64:1; 69:9** *Voice* any complaints to God alone. *Be zealous* that the purposes of God be fulfilled in and through the church. **45:17** *Be faithful* to bear witness to Jesus Christ as Lord and Savior.
2 Steps to Dynamic Devotion Worship and its biblically prescribed forms are an important part of our devotion to God. Unwisely, we often neglect certain unfamiliar elements of worship. God is remarkably present with those who worship Him as He asks. Also, in prayer we often forget to spend as much time listening as we do speaking to God. This is all the more amazing when we remember with whom we are communing when we pray.	**42:1, 2; 63:1, 2** *Cultivate* a conscious hunger and thirst for God. *Anticipate* that this will result in more time with Him. **59:16, 17** *Sing* to God in your times alone with Him. **47:1–7** *Practice* joyful and vocal worship. *Do not despise* hearty applause directed toward the Father. **46:10** *Understand* that knowing God involves experiencing regular times of silent waiting and expectant quietude. **44:22** *Offer* your life to God daily as a living sacrifice. *Consider* yourself dead to personal ambition.

Truth Psalms Teaches	**Action** Psalms Invites
3 Keys to Wise Living Wise individuals reject man's testimony about himself. Much confusion has been generated among God's people because they have accepted a mere humanistic belief in man's intrinsic goodness. As a result, many have stumbled because they trusted only in man and not in God.	**53:3** *Accept* God's testimony about man's basic nature. *Understand* the impact of sin on every human being. **44:3–8** *Understand* that it is not the hand, mind, or strength of the flesh that brings spiritual victory. *Be assured* that victory comes from the Lord alone.
4 Key Lessons in Faith Faith is a conscious choice to act on what God says is true, not some passive response of the Christian to his circumstances. Like everything else, faith requires practice to grow and become strong. Faith comes from God's Word illumined by the Holy Spirit and is released through acts of obedience. Faith requires a singleness of commitment that draws us from doubt and wavering.	**56:3, 4, 10, 11** When you are tempted to be afraid, *choose to trust* the Lord as an act of your will, not as a response to your emotions. *Practice* a determined, praise-filled refusal to be afraid. **55:22** *Quickly release* concerns and worries to the Father who wants to carry them for you. **51:10** *Beseech* the Lord to work in you a singleness of purpose in heart. *Ask* Him for a spirit that endures and stands fast on the truth you know. **43:3** *Expect* God's Spirit illuminating the Scriptures to give you clear guidance every day.
5 Necessity of Humility The unbroken, proud, and arrogant spirit is not pleasing to God. In order to commune with God, we must be humbled, acknowledging our sin and our need for cleansing by Him.	**51:1–19** *Understand* that the spirit of humility opens the pathway to fullness of joy.
6 Steps to Dealing with Sin Dealing with sin begins by understanding that sin originates in the heart.	**66:18** *Avoid* nullifying your prayers by planning, harboring, or entertaining sin or wickedness in your heart.

III. BOOK THREE 73:1—89:52.

A. Songs of Asaph (73:1—83:18).

Psalm 73. This unique psalm traces the experience of the poet, who feels envy at the prosperity of the wicked (1–12) and frustration at his own lot (13–16). He finds release by comparing the end of the wicked (18–20) with the blessings of his present and future fellowship with God (21–28).

Psalm 74. In exile, God's people call on Him to note the desecration of the sanctuary and to remember His covenant promises.

Psalm 75. Praise to God as righteous Judge.

Psalm 76. Exaltation of God as majestic.

Psalm 77. This deeply introspective psalm shares feelings and thoughts while in distress, and explains how hope was restored by recalling God's miracle works for His people.

Psalm 78. This teaching psalm, directed to future generations (1–8), recalls Israel's history and relationship with God (9–64; *see* Tempted) up to the time of David (65–72).

Psalm 79. A call for God to act and deliver shamed Israel, which has been carried into captivity and has seen Jerusalem in ruins.

Psalm 80. The exiles' prayer for restoration to the land.

Psalm 81. A divine promise of restoration for Israel—when God's people put away their idols and submit to Him.

Psalm 82. A psalm directed to rulers, reminding them that they exercise authority as God's representatives (which is the meaning of the phrase "gods" here).

Psalm 83. The psalmist calls on God to overthrow national enemies who seek to destroy Israel.

B. Songs of the sons of Korah (84:1—85:13).

Psalm 84. The blessings of worship and nearness to God are expressed in this psalm about service in God's temple.

Psalm 85. A prayer for revival and restoration.

C. Song of David (86:1–17).

Psalm 86. God's abounding love meets David's deepest needs (1–10) as he chooses to commit himself fully to God's truth (11–17; *see* Brotherly Love; Sign).

D. Songs of the sons of Korah (87:1— 88:18).

Psalm 87. The glories of the Holy City are extolled.

Psalm 88. This anguished cry for help to God, who does not seem to hear, mirrors the experience of many believers.

E. Song of Ethan (89:1–51).

Psalm 89. This praise psalm magnifies God's faithfulness (1–8), His rule (9–13), and His righteousness (14–18), each of which is expressed in the Davidic covenant (19–37). Based on God's character and covenant, the psalmist calls for Israel's restoration (38–51). This messianic psalm is quoted in Acts 13:22.

F. Doxology (89:52).

TRUTH-IN-ACTION through PSALMS (Book Three: Psalms 73—89)

Truth Psalms Teaches	**Action** Psalms Invites
1 A Step to Knowing God's Ways We must know that God honors His name and will see to it that it is exalted.	**79:9** *Understand* that God saves and blesses His people because of His name, that is, His honor, and not because of their works of righteousness.
2 Guidelines for Growing in Godliness Godliness adopts God's concerns for the widow, the orphan, the alien, the poor, and the needy because these are foremost in His heart as is care and training of our children. Also, the godly person resorts to God when troubled, rather than to the arm of the flesh.	**82:3, 4** *Understand* that God prioritizes ministry to the destitute, poor, and needy. *Do not fail* to help them when it is in your power to do so. **78:4–8** *Do not fail* to teach your children and train them up in the way of the Lord. **73:21, 22** *Avoid* letting a grieved heart become an embittered spirit. **73:16, 17** When bewildered, *spend time* in God's presence to gain proper understanding and perspective.
3 Steps to Dynamic Devotion God desires the hearts of all of us to be fully and singly devoted to Him. It takes commitment to develop such a devotion: One must continue to choose God above all else.	**86:11** *Seek God* continually for an undivided heart and the fear of the Lord. **76:11** *Understand* that vows are an acceptable and biblical means to making spiritual advances in difficult areas.
4 Keys to Wise Living Growing in wisdom means learning to discern the times by applying the principles of God's Word. It also means refusing to seek for the honor that can only come from God.	**75:6, 7** *Know* that all promotion or exaltation comes from the Lord. **74:9** *Understand* that when we reject God's way, the blessing and guidance of His Spirit may be withdrawn, leaving us in spiritual drought.
5 Steps in Developing Humility The humble person, acknowledging his need for continual growth, never develops an unteachable spirit.	**84:5** *Set your heart* on pilgrimage: *Humble yourself* and *accept* that you will "never arrive," that is, never stop needing to learn and grow.
6 A Key Lesson in Faith Never underestimate the power of personal testimony in persuading men to take bolder steps in faith.	**77:10–20** *Think about* and *testify to* God's mighty workings among His people in order to encourage them and build their faith.
7 Guidelines to Gaining Victory We can be our own worst enemies in the fight for spiritual victory. Even stronger than any external opposition we face may be negative influences in our own lives.	**81:13–16** *Pray for release* from disobedient and stubborn attitudes that hinder God's hand in granting you spiritual victory.

IV. BOOK FOUR 90:1—106:48.

A. Song of Moses (90:1-17).

Psalm 90. The only psalm attributed to Moses, this meditates on human frailty (1–12) and on dependency on the Lord (13–17; see Stewardship).

B. Anonymous songs (91:1—92:15).

Psalm 91. Security is found in the shadow of the *Almighty. (See Angels; Healing, Divine.)

> ### "Surely He shall deliver you from the snare of the fowler"
> (91:3). Most of the verses which follow this one deal with the demonic realm, a real world that impacts every person. Therefore, God mercifully states through the psalmist His intent: He *will* deliver! Successful spiritual warfare engages the supernatural on supernatural terms. It should come as no surprise, then, to hear Paul state in 2 Corinthians 10:4 that the weapons of our warfare "are not carnal but mighty in God for pulling down strongholds." Put on the weapons He has provided (Eph. 6:10–18)! Prepare for the battle in His power! And when the snare is set by the enemy, the Lord will deliver us.

Psalm 92. A psalm for liturgical use on the Sabbath, it proclaims that "it is good to give thanks to the LORD."

> ### "And to sing praises to Your name, O Most High"
> (92:1–4). The concept of singing praise to God can be challenging to many believers. However, the importance of praise for the purposes of spiritual breakthrough in the life of a kingdom person cannot be underestimated. In days of increasing warfare, we must sing praise to God more than ever before. To be willing to abandon one's self to songs of praise is to be available for use by the Holy Spirit as an instrument of great spiritual power (see 2 Chr. 20:1–22).

C. "The Lord Reigns" songs (93:1—100:5).

Psalm 93. God reigns. (See Kingdom of God.)

Psalm 94. God is praised as Avenger of evil, who sees all and who judges the wicked while supporting those who take refuge in Him.

Psalm 95. A call to rejoice (see Thanksgiving), worship, and hear God's voice.

Psalm 96. How to worship God, ascribing glory to His name.

> ### "Declare His glory among the nations"
> (96). This is a missionary psalm, calling upon God's people to declare the Good News of salvation daily among all people (vv. 1–3). This may be lived out in the lives of some believers by actually traveling to foreign lands to share the gospel. But Christ commanded *every* believer to take the gospel wherever he or she goes, to make disciples, to baptize them with water, and teach them all things that He has commanded (see Matt. 28:19–20). As we do, we have the promise of our Savior Himself: "I am with you always."

Psalm 97. God reigns, idols are empty, and those who worship the Lord are guarded from the wicked (see Love).

Psalm 98. This song of salvation is a jubilant shout of joy!

> ### "For He is coming"
> (98:8–9). What the psalmist saw in the triumph of *Yahweh* is doubtless prophetic of the Son of God who will come again to rule in righteousness. All believers are encouraged to the same expectation as well as the same kind of expressions of joy. Though the Second Coming will be a time of judgment, it will also be a cause for great joy and praise as all the earth and all the nations glory in His presence.

Psalm 99. Exalt the Lord (see Worship).

Psalm 100. A brief psalm of *praise.

> ### "*Serve the LORD with gladness"
> (100:1–5). The *attitude* of worship is as important as the *act* of worship. This psalm points out several reasons for the exhortation to praise God. The thoughtful worshiper will give the necessary time to meditate on the greatness and goodness of God before he begins his verbal, outward praise and thanksgiving. Both are necessary, but the Spirit-filled person can miss much by failing to maintain the loving attitude of heart-worship and giving place only to the outward expression of worship.

D. Songs of David (101:1-8; 103:1-22).

Psalm 101. God's love and justice find

reflection in the worshiper's relationship with others.

Psalm 103. Praise is offered to God for the gracious way He relates to David, and for God's great love for all who fear Him.

> **"Who *forgives all your iniquities, Who heals all your diseases"** (103:1–5). David makes an obvious connection between forgiven sin and the healing of sickness (*see* Healing, Divine). The essence of sin is to be separated from God, and the essence of the healing of sin is to seek a relationship with God. If sin exposes us to its results, then the healing of sin will bring a healing of the effects of sin, such as sickness. Exodus 15:26 declares God's promise of healing and the instruction for receiving it. Coupled with the wisdom of Proverbs 3:7–8, this gives believers a clear pathway for receiving healing from sickness. (*See* Angels.)

E. Anonymous songs (102:1–28; 104:1—106:47).

Psalm 102. This messianic psalm is quoted in Hebrews 1:10–12. The psalm records the prayer of an unnamed person who is greatly afflicted and pours out his heart to the Lord.

Psalm 104. All nature displays the glory of God.

Psalm 105. History calls to mind God's strength and all He has done for His people. Praise the Lord!

Psalm 106. Again the history of the Exodus period is retold as the basis for confidence that God will deliver again (*see* Gentiles).

F. Doxology (106:48).

TRUTH-IN-ACTION through PSALMS (Book Four: Psalms 90—106)

Truth Psalms Teaches	**Action** Psalms Invites
1 A Guideline for Godliness Fervent intercession for the church is a mark of a godly person.	**106:23** *Intercede* for God's people to bring repentance and avert judgment.
2 Showing Respect for God Humble postures in worship should reflect a humble attitude of heart.	**95:6–11** *Humble yourself* before the Lord through bowing and kneeling in worship. *Open your heart* to Him and to His will.
3 Keys to Wise Living The wise person gratefully receives God's teaching and discipline. He also turns away from procrastination and other time-wasters.	**94:12–15** *Expect* and *be grateful* for the Lord's discipline. *Know* it is His instruction, leading to patience and righteousness. **90:12** *Use time wisely. Understand* that squandering time is throwing away a part of your life.
4 Key Lessons in Faith Faith is a forward focus on God, His Word, and His promises. But faith also looks back at the blessings of God to gain strength. Faith allows us to flee confidently to God when in trouble and to abide in Him for protection.	**103:2–5** *Rehearse* periodically all of God's blessings as a source of encouragement and faith. **94:19** *Look* to the Lord for consolation when you have anxiety about anything. **91:9–13** *Abide* in Christ, *set your affection* on Him, and *acknowledge* Him in all you do. *Rest* in His protection and salvation.
5 Steps to Holiness As holy people it is better not to stare at or meditate on things that are inappropriate to a life separated to the Lord and His purposes.	**101:3** *Guard* your eyes zealously. Your inner life is affected by the things you focus on. **104:34** *Dwell* only on things that are pleasing to the Lord.

V. BOOK FIVE 107:1—150:6.

A. Thanksgiving song (107:1–43).

Psalm 107. A psalm of redemption—from wandering (4–9), prison (10–16), rebelliousness (17–22; *see* Healing, Divine), and distress (23–32).

B. Songs of David (108:1—110:7).

Psalm 108. Praise to God, who has made Israel His own.

Psalm 109. This messianic psalm describes Judas (*see* Acts 1:16–20). David's description of his own anguish (vv. 22–29) reflects Jesus' feelings at the time of the Crucifixion.

Psalm 110. This messianic psalm speaks of Jesus' exaltation and His present priesthood (*see* Matt. 22:43–45; Acts 2:33–35; Heb. 1:13; 5:6–10; 6:20; 7:21).

C. Egyptian Hallel (111:1—118:29).

Psalm 111. Praise is due God for the steadfastness of His works.

Psalm 112. The blessings (*see* Delights) of those who trust God are proclaimed.

Psalm 113. God is praised as an exalted Person who yet stoops to lift up the poor and seat them with princes.

> ### "Praise the LORD! . . . The LORD is high above all nations"
>
> (113:1–9). This psalm begins and ends with the Hebrew word, "Hallelujah!" It is a command to the congregation of God to praise Him. The transcendent nature of worship and praise are introduced with the fact of God's greatness and position above all else. In other words, by the spirit of praise and worship we may be ushered into the very presence of the Lord. Thus the psalmist sounds forth the imperative "Hallelujah!"

Psalm 114. This brief historical psalm praises God as earth-shaker.

Psalm 115. A call to Israel to trust God.

Psalm 116. Deliverance from death stimulates praise and personal commitment to the Lord.

Psalm 117. A two-verse psalm of praise.

Psalm 118. Here is a great affirmation of God as He whose "mercy endures forever."

D. Alphabetic song on the Law (119:1–176).

Psalm 119. The longest of the psalms, this is an acrostic poem, in which the first letter of each verse in each section begins with a different letter of the Hebrew alphabet. The impact of the *Word of God in the life of the believer is the subject of this great work of poetry. (*See* Ancients; Commandments; Companion; Precepts.)

E. Songs of ascents (120:1—134:3).

Psalms 120 through 134 are liturgical psalms, probably sung by the people of Israel as they journeyed to Jerusalem for the three annual feasts which the Law established as national festivals.

Psalm 120. God saves the godly in their distress.

Psalm 121. Our help is in the Lord, who neither slumbers nor sleeps.

Psalm 122. Prayer (*see* Pray; Prophecy) for the peace of Jerusalem.

Psalm 123. A plea for mercy.

Psalm 124. The Lord's help has won Israel's victories.

Psalm 125. Those who trust God are truly secure.

Psalm 126. God's deliverance from captivity filled His people with laughter and joy. (*See* Spiritual Warfare.)

Psalm 127. Joy can be found in God's gift of family (*see* Family Life).

Psalm 128. A right relationship with God brings blessings.

Psalm 129. God has freed the oppressed and will bless them.

Psalm 130. Praise for forgiveness and redemption (*see* Iniquities).

Psalm 131. Humility and trust bring hope.

Psalm 132. This messianic psalm (*see* Acts 2:30) rejoices in the Lord's choice of David and God's promises to him.

Psalm 133. Unity (*see* Brethren) is a great blessing.

Psalm 134. Praise from those who minister in God's sanctuary.

F. Anonymous songs (135:1—137:9).

Psalm 135. The greatness of God, and His superiority to all idols, is shown by His mighty acts in history.

> ### "Sing praises to His name, for it is pleasant"
>
> (135:1–4). One of the greatest joys for any believer is to discover the *pleasure* of a life filled with praise. The disturbing affairs of daily living often become the instruments by which the Adversary attempts to wear down the saints. Once the truth of praise and its power grip the soul, the resisting efforts of one's flesh and the world must give way to the beauty of praise and worship. Hear and heed the advice of David when he says, "Oh, taste and see that the LORD is good" (34:8).

Psalm 136. This great praise psalm repeats "His mercy endures *forever" as a response by worshipers to statements about God.

Psalm 137. Weeping marks the life of the exiles in Babylon, for they are cut off from the land promised to Israel by the Lord.

G. Songs of David (138:1—145:21).

Psalm 138. David praises God for His love and faithfulness (*see* Perfect).

Psalm 139. God is exalted as One who is omniscient (1–12) and who has known the psalmist intimately from before his birth (13–24).

Psalm 140. A cry for rescue from the wicked and from oppressors.

Psalm 141. The psalmist needs protection against hasty choices which might lead him into sin.

Psalm 142. Praise for the freedom to express needs to God.

Psalm 143. A cry for deliverance and guidance.

Psalm 144. A joyful call to God, who is strong to deliver, with praise for expected blessings that will follow God's answer.

Psalm 145. Pure praise, offered to God for His many wonderful attributes and qualities (*see* Bless; Praise).

H. "Praise the Lord" songs (146:1—149:9).

Psalm 146. We trust ourselves to God, not other people.

> **"Praise the Lord, O my soul!"**
> (146:1–10). Throughout the Psalms praise is seen as an activity which incorporates the entire being. The admonition of the psalmist necessitates an understanding of the "soul," if our soul is to be instructed to praise the Lord. Briefly, the soul is best understood as referring to the mind, emotions, and will. Paul refers to the *whole of a person* when he discusses the "spirit, soul, and body" in 1 Thessalonians 5:23. It is this totality—the spirit, mind, emotions, will, and body—that the psalmist has in mind when he cries, "Praise the Lord, O my soul!"

Psalm 147. Praise to God, who "takes pleasure in those who fear Him."

Psalm 148. Praise to God offered by the entire universe.

Psalm 149. Praise (*see* Sing Praises) to God offered by His saints.

I. Doxology (150:1–6).

Psalm 150. *Praise to God offered by everything that has *breath!

> **"Praise God in His sanctuary; Praise Him in His mighty firmament!"**
> (150:1–6). In this concluding psalm we find animated praise of the highest order. Nothing is left out in this final admonition to praise the Lord. One lesson it teaches is the thrill that comes to the one who understands the partnership in praise between heaven and earth. The joining together of mankind with the hosts of heaven is almost more than can be conceived. When we grasp it, however, we discover the ecstasy of realizing that we are not alone. If heavenly hosts exist to join with us in praise, then they also exist to join with us in spiritual warfare and triumph! Hallelujah!

TRUTH-IN-ACTION through PSALMS (Book Five: Psalms 107—150)

Truth Psalms Teaches	**Action** Psalms Invites
1 Guidelines for Growing in Godliness By living your life according to the Scriptures and its instructions you will grow in godliness.	**133:1** *Strive* for the unity of the church in all you do. **126:5, 6** *Sow* to righteousness through deeds of righteous obedience for a rich harvest. **119:56** *Practice* obedience to God's Word. *Understand* that it's the key to further understanding. **119:9** *Order* all your life according to God's Word as the key to purity. **111:10; 112:2** *Seek God* and *cultivate* the fear of the Lord; doing so leads to wisdom and results in great blessing.
2 Steps to Holiness Holiness involves trusting the Lord and not the world, most often requiring that we make a choice for the former and against the latter. The line between the two is drawn finer and closer to the Lord the longer we walk with Him.	**115:2–8** *Do not put your trust* in things you have built for security. *Know* that God calls this idolatry. **119: 105, 130** *Seek* illumination from God's eternal Word and not from man's finite wisdom. **119:36** *Set* your affections on doing God's word rather than on personal gain. **127: 1, 2** *Know* that employing your skills for the Lord is futile without His presence and anointing upon them.
3 Steps to Dynamic Devotion God wants our hearts, not just our verbal allegiance, and He desires that our affections be wholly His. Developing the disciplined practices that lead to this kind of life must be a high priority. This requires that we reorder our priorities accordingly.	**139:23** *Daily ask* the Lord to search and know your heart. **131:2** *Give yourself* to secluded times of quiet and stillness as a regular part of your devotion to God. **119:23, 24** *Regularly meditate* on the Scriptures in order to plumb their depths. **119:11** *Diligently practice* Scripture memorization, training your heart to avoid sin. **107:22** *Employ* praise songs as a vehicle of personal gratitude.
4 Keys to Wise Living Only the life lived in the light of God's Word is lived wisely. For this reason, our study of the Bible must be constantly accompanied with the petition that God will give us wisdom and understanding through our study so that we can learn to live in a way that pleases Him.	**143:10** *Ask* the Lord to teach you and lead you in the performing of His will. **119:128** *Take your stand* on the rightness of God's Word. *Understand* that evil is that which disregards God's instruction. **119:27** *Seek knowledge* but, most of all, *gain understanding.* *Know* that practical understanding is more important than mere knowledge. **119:18** *Daily ask* God to open your heart and mind through the ministry of the Holy Spirit to the message of the Scriptures.
5 Key Lessons in Faith God wants us to take Him at His Word and to take His Word at its face value. The truth therein is available through no other source. We must receive and believe them to benefit from them.	**139:7** *Be consoled* in the truth that God is always and everywhere present. **138:8** *Be assured* that if you continue in Him, the Lord will most certainly fulfill His purpose for you.
6 God Is True to His Word God is consistent and unchanging. His nature is reflected in His law.	**119:71** Even in your afflictions, *recognize* that God is true to His Word. You can *depend* on Him.

TRUTH-IN-ACTION through PSALMS (A Summary)

Editorial Note: In addition to the truths covered in each of the five book divisions of Psalms, a number of other directives are frequently repeated. This brief summary focuses on some of them.

Truth Psalms Teaches	**Action** Psalms Invites
Worship the Lord Worship means to ascribe worth to something or someone through speech and conduct. Worship addresses God directly, expressing reverence for His nature, character attributes, and power, and grateful praise for all He is and does.	a. *Worship* the Lord with all your heart and mind. *Rehearse* His attributes consciously. *Recount* how who God is affects you and is changing you. *Avoid worshiping* mindlessly or by rote or becoming passive in worship. *Give yourself* wholeheartedly to it. b. *Employ* singing, both with the spirit and with the understanding, using speaking, bowing, kneeling, dancing, corporate applause, and instrumental music to enhance expression of worship.
Praise the Lord To praise the Lord means to speak well of God with exuberance and enthusiasm to others and/or to Him because of what He has done. "Praise the Lord!" (Hebrew Hallelujah!) is a command to extol God's virtues and exalt Him because of His mighty acts. A praise gathering is a celebration of God's mighty power and purpose.	a. *Praise God* with a loud and enthusiastic voice. *Clap* your hands and *shout joyfully* to the Lord. *Participate* in processions of praise. *Speak* and *sing praise* to God. *Involve* such physical expressions as raising hands, dancing, applause, and kneeling. b. *Discipline* yourself to praise God for every benefit He provides. *Be disciplined* in corporate praise. *Be careful* to submit to leadership in praise services, not letting praise degenerate into fleshly enthusiasm.
Trust in the Lord Trust is the belief in and reliance on the integrity, strength, ability, surety of a person or thing. To trust in the Lord is to believe Him, (that is, to take Him at His word) and to believe absolutely that what He says is true.	a. *Trust* in the Lord and not in yourself. b. *Trust* in the Lord and not your wealth for financial security. c. *Trust* in the Lord and not in your physical strength or your nation's military prowess for protection. d. *Trust* in the Lord and not in political power or connections. e. *Trust* in the Lord and not in things you have built.
Thanksgiving The psalmists call for constant verbal expression of heartfelt gratitude to God for all of His benefits and gifts to man.	a. *Give thanks* to God, first of all, for who He is. b. *Give thanks* to God for all that He has given you. c. *Give thanks* to God for His loving kindness and mercy. d. *Give thanks* to God for His protection. e. *Give thanks* to God for His guidance. f. *Give thanks* to God for all His mighty acts. g. *Give thanks* to God that His purposes will prevail.
Proclaim As one of their major themes, the psalmists call God's people to declare openly His goodness, loving kindness, and mercy to them and to the nations.	a. *Proclaim* God's love, mercy, and forgiveness to all of Israel. b. *Proclaim* God's truth and justice to all the nations. c. *Proclaim* His righteousness. d. *Proclaim* His mighty acts. e. *Proclaim* all that He has done. f. *Proclaim* His salvation, day after day!
Rely upon God's Protection The psalmists encourage the people to turn to God and rely upon Him rather than on themselves, and their own strength in times of trouble.	a. *Rely upon God* when confronted by any enemy. b. *Rely upon God* whenever you are in any kind of distress. c. *Rely upon God* in times of natural calamity. d. *Rely upon God* in times of political crisis. e. *Rely upon God* when confronted with sickness or physical weakness.

KEYS TO PROVERBS
Human Responsibility and the Kingdom

Kingdom Key: God's Purpose in View

The awesome truth of God's sovereignty throughout the universe and His rule over all human affairs is absolute and undeniable. Yet equally true is the awesome fact of man's responsibility in all of his own affairs, as well as his determinative role in the affairs of earth. The Proverbs accentuate this decisive—indeed, ruling—role that each human being has in the issues of life. No one can hide from personal responsibility by suggesting that any failure is God's doing and therefore beyond human accountability.

In light of Revelation 1:5–6 and 5:10, which apply the role of "kings" to all who are redeemed, it becomes clear that the speech and actions of believers will effect a "rule" more often than we realize (or may even wish). As our words require close scrutiny and practical caution, our need for *wisdom* (the key word in Proverbs) becomes obvious. In view of this, the price of *foolishness* (Proverbs' term to contrast with wisdom) is seen as destructive.

Over twenty-five references to "the king" are present in Proverbs. These may be studied objectively and analyzed merely as interesting thoughts about how monarchs behave. New Testament kingdom understanding, however, recommends a subjective, personal, and self-examining application of such references. Thoughtful believers should study Proverbs with a heart to

> **True wisdom is in knowing God first.**

receive wisdom for "ruling in life." Attention to texts relating to the three following pairings will help: one pair serve as companions and the other two are antagonists.

1. Two Companion Steps— The Pathway to Wisdom

Examine the occurrence of the words *knowledge, instruction,* and *wisdom* in the Proverbs. They are not synonyms. Each one is part of the *process* toward effective living and successful relationships. Note two steps in the process. The first is to see how knowledge (information acquired) and instruction (the explanation or meaning of acquired information) must be *received*. For this, a teachable, childlike heart is needed (2:1–5; 4:1–4). Second, we must see how we are to *act* with wisdom, for wisdom is neither information (knowledge) nor explanation (understanding). Wisdom is

(Please turn to page 157.)

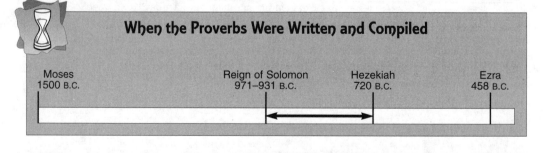

When the Proverbs Were Written and Compiled

Moses 1500 B.C.	Reign of Solomon 971–931 B.C.	Hezekiah 720 B.C.	Ezra 458 B.C.

Proverbs shows the way to values which will

Master Key: God's Son Revealed

No direct references to Christ, prophetic or typological, are conspicuous in the Book of Proverbs. In fact, the personification of wisdom is normally feminine throughout. Nevertheless some passages (such as 8:23–31) seem an unmistakable description of Jesus Christ, who was "in the beginning with God" (John 1:2), is "the wisdom of God" (1 Cor. 1:24), and "became for us wisdom" (1 Cor. 1:30).

Certainly the book performs a powerful service in whetting the human appetite for wisdom and understanding, a hunger that can only be fully satisfied in Christ.

Proverbs, much like the Mosaic Law, describes an ideal, an aspiration, a longing for perfection. Yet even Solomon himself was not perfectly wise, or he would not have so flagrantly disobeyed and thus displeased God (1 Kin. 11:9–11). Only later, in Jesus Christ, came the full example of all that Proverbs extols, the One "in whom are hidden all the treasures of wisdom" (Col. 2:3).

Point by point, the qualities of wisdom are the qualities of the Christ. Obedience to God, right behavior, patience, reliability, humility, diligence, the perception of things as they really are—all these, plus love, are perfectly illustrated in the Savior.

Power Key: God's Spirit at Work

The Holy Spirit is not mentioned directly in the Book of Proverbs. But Wisdom refers to her spirit (1:23), which of course is the Spirit of God. In fact, a main point of the book is that wisdom apart from God is impossible, so in that sense His Spirit is prominent throughout. However, the dominant word translated "spirit" in the book is almost always with the meaning of "attitude" or "demeanor" rather than a personality.

In our era, which is a time of a special work of the Holy Spirit, it is the Spirit who helps us mine the riches of the Proverbs, rather than Proverbs helping us understand the Spirit. It has been said of the Old and New Testaments, "The New is in the Old concealed; the Old is in the New revealed."

Key Word: *Wisdom*

Proverbs is one of the few biblical books that clearly spells out its purpose. The words "wisdom and instruction" in 1:2 complement each other because wisdom (hokhmah) *means "skill" and* instruction (musar) *means "discipline." No skill is perfected without discipline, and a person with skill has the freedom to create something beautiful. Proverbs deals with the most fundamental skill of all: practical righteousness before God in every area of life.*

Key Verses: Proverbs 1:5–7; 3:5–6

Key Chapter: Proverbs 31

The last chapter of Proverbs is unique in ancient literature, as it reveals a very high and noble view of women.

achieve character, wholeness, and satisfaction.

Introducing
PROVERBS

Author. Solomon, king of Israel, was the son of David and Bathsheba. He reigned for forty years, from 971 to 931 B.C., taking the throne at about twenty years of age.

No doubt influenced by the psalm-writing of his father, Solomon has left us more books than any other Old Testament writer except Moses. It seems probable that his Song of Solomon was written when he was a young romantic, his Proverbs when he was mature and at the height of his powers, and his Ecclesiastes when he had become more aged, more inclined to philosophical conclusions and perhaps more cynical. His strengths were not on the battlefield but in the realm of the mind: meditation, planning, negotiation, and organization.

Solomon's reputation for wisdom springs not only from its practical results, as in the case of the dispute over a baby (1 Kin. 3:16–27), but also from the direct statements of Scripture. In 1 Kings 3:12 God says, "There has not been anyone like you before you, nor shall any like you arise after you." In 1 Kings 4:31 he is called "wiser than all men," with names of other wise men cited in specific comparison.

Of Agur and King Lemuel (Prov. 30:1; 31:1) we know nothing except that, by their names, they were not Israelites. Wisdom is universal, not national.

Date. Since the Book of Proverbs is a compilation, its writing was spread over a period of years, with the main work probably centered about 950 B.C. Chapters 25 through 29 are identified as copied by "the men of Hezekiah," which places the copying at about 720 B.C., though the material itself was by Solomon, perhaps in a separate document found in Hezekiah's time.

Background. Under Solomon's leadership Israel reached its greatest geographical extent and enjoyed the least violence of the entire kingdom period. "Peaceful," the meaning of his name, describes Solomon's reign. And peace, with wisdom, brought unprecedented prosperity to the nation, which became a cause of wonder and admiration to the queen of Sheba (1 Kin. 10:6–9) and to the other rulers of the time. Wise sayings, like music or other art forms, tend to blossom in such a time, then endure through succeeding generations.

Content. The Book of Proverbs is not just a collection of sayings, but a collection of collections. Its unifying thought or theme is, "The fear of the LORD is the beginning of wisdom" (9:10), appearing in another form as, "The fear of the LORD is the beginning [or principal part] of knowledge" (1:7). Coming through the diversity of examples time and again are such truths as these:

1. Wisdom (the ability to judge and act according to God's directives) is the most valuable of assets.

2. Wisdom is available to anyone, but the price is high.

3. Wisdom originates in God, not self, and comes by attention to instruction.

4. Wisdom and righteousness go together. It is good to be wise, and it is wise to be good.

5. Evil men suffer the consequences of their evil deeds.

6. The simple, the fool, the lazy, the ignorant, the proud, the profligate, and the sinful are never to be admired.

Many powerful contrasts are found again and again. Antithesis helps to clarify the meaning of key words. Among the ideas set in vivid contrast with each other are:

Wisdom versus Folly
Righteousness versus Wickedness
Good versus Evil
Life versus Death
Prosperity versus Poverty
Honor versus Dishonor
Permanence versus Transience
Truth versus Falsehood
Industry versus Indolence
Friend versus Enemy
Prudence versus Rashness
Fidelity versus Adultery
Peace versus Violence
Goodwill versus Anger
God versus Humanity

Personal Application. The wisdom contained in the Book of Proverbs is as meaningful today as when it was written. Yet it is neither a prosperity pamphlet nor a "how to succeed" handbook in the worldly sense. Rather, it tells how to order one's values, which leads to character, which leads to wholeness, which leads to satisfaction. It warns of the pitfalls along the way and declares the folly of *not* developing the fear of the Lord. Because the thirty-one-chapter book contains so much that is worth daily meditation and is relevant for every era, many Bible readers have found it desirable to read a chapter a day, thus covering the entire book every month.

Unique Features. The book is different from all others in the Bible in these respects:

1. It gives clear internal evidence of multiple authorship. This is deduced or implied in some other Bible books, but never revealed so plainly as in Proverbs.

2. It also shows clear internal evidence of having been put together over the amazing span of about 250 years, since Hezekiah, mentioned in 25:1, lived about that long after King Solomon. Other books (Genesis, for example) may cover long *historical* spans of time, but none of them so clearly indicate the span of their *composition.*

Kingdom Key *continued from page 154*

actuation—the proper application of what has been received. Wisdom also manifests itself in a way of action as well as in the act; wisdom acts in humility and righteousness, sensitivity and discretion.

2. Two Opposite Women—The Contrast between Wisdom and Folly

The adulteress warned against in Proverbs (*see* 6:20—7:27; 9:13–18) is discussed not simply to give moralistic advice. This matter is more than an indulgence in biological adultery, as wrong as that is. Inherent here is a warning against spending the seed of life God has put within us in unfaithful, squandering, or destructive ways (5:15–18). Here is a call to turn from a pointless exercise of our words, ways, or works to *wisdom,* personified as a woman whom we embrace and to whom we make a commitment (8:1–36; 9:1–6). She is the fountain of happiness, joy, and righteous fruitfulness.

3. Two Opposite Men—The Righteous and the Wicked

More than a dozen traits of "the righteous" are declared, with certain blessings attending to each ("mouth," 10:11; "desire," 10:24; "hope," 10:28; "posterity," 11:21, and so forth). The righteous is "wise," but the wicked is "a fool." The fool in Proverbs is not necessarily without knowledge, so this term is not intended as an insult. Rather, the fool is without reverence for God or His ways, and thus demonstrates emptiness of wisdom.

Surveying
PROVERBS

I. INTRODUCTION 1:1–7.

A. Title, purpose, and introduction (1:1–6). Solomon has written proverbs (*see* Proverb) and begun this collection to help the reader acquire a disciplined and prudent life, doing what is right and just and fair.

B. Theme or motto (1:7).

II. A FATHER'S WARNINGS AND WISDOM'S ADMONITIONS 1:8—8:36.

A. A father's warnings, part one (1:8–19).

B. Wisdom's admonitions, part one (1:20–33). Warnings and exhortations describe the dangers of rejecting the wisdom offered and tell the benefits of accepting it. Solomon promises that the reader who hears and applies this wisdom will prolong his life and win a good name with God and man. He need only pay close attention and not swerve to the right or left of the righteous path the proverbs mark out. Relationship with God is crucial, for God is to be trusted when we make life's choices, not our own understanding. As God is acknowledged, and His ways are followed, He will make your paths straight.

C. A father's warnings, part two (2:1—7:27). Solomon warns against adultery and other folly (5:1—7:27). The danger of choices motivated by lust is treated extensively in these chapters. Also stressed are the dangers of laziness (6:6–11) and the characteristics of the villain (6:12–19). (*See* Direct; Instruction; Spiritual Warfare.)

D. Wisdom's admonitions, part two (8:1–36). Solomon praises wisdom. Much debate has developed over verses 12–31, which picture wisdom as a woman and speak as if she has separate identity as a person. To some this is merely a literary device. Others argue that there is a relationship between "wisdom" and the New Testament *Logos,* or Word, of John 1. There "Word" is a title for Christ. However, no New Testament passage refers to Christ as "wisdom," or refers to this proverb, so it is best to take Solomon's language as a picturesque way of dramatizing the way of wisdom to which Solomon calls his people.

III. THE WAY OF WISDOM VERSUS THE WAY OF FOLLY 9:1–18. The two ways of life are contrasted, with both Wisdom and Folly personified as women.

IV. SOLOMON'S PROVERBS AND SAYINGS OF THE WISE 10:1—29:27. The Old Testament tells us that Solomon wrote more than three thousand proverbs (1 Kin. 4:32; cf.

2 Chron. 9:1–24). The text indicates these are a few of the wise sayings he recorded. The sayings are couplets, using the literary device of contrast. These proverbs range over many topics, without special organization.

A. Solomon's proverbs—first collection (10:1—22:16; See ch. 55 in this Handbook, §3.4.b).

> **"And he who wins souls is wise"** (11:30). (See Dan. 12:3; James 5:19–20; Soul; Wicked.) The righteous are as trees of life that bear fruit (Prov. 11:30). Their fruit includes their reverence and love for God (see Matt. 22:37), their godly example to others (see Matt. 5:15), their mentoring of young believers in the ways of the Lord (see 1 Cor. 4:16–17), and their prayerfulness (see Eph. 6:18; Phil. 4:6). God wants us to be wise soul winners, knowing how to deal with the unconverted so that we might bring them to Christ (see 1 Cor. 9:19–22; 2 Tim. 2:15; 1 Pet. 3:15; Commit; Faith's Confession; Family Life; Friend; Refuge).

B. Sayings of the wise—first collection (22:17—24:22). No author of these "sayings of the wise" is indicated. These are longer sayings than the ones preceding them and tend to use synonymous parallelism. Like Solomon's short sayings, these describe wise and foolish conduct. (See Evangelism; Sorrow.)

C. Sayings of the wise—second collection (24:23–34). A brief addition to the "sayings of the wise."

D. Solomon's proverbs—second collection (by Hezekiah's men) (25:1—29:27). In the days of Hezekiah's revival, his scribes apparently worked from written sources which contained many of Solomon's sayings. The scribes edited them and included a number in an addition to the Old Testament scroll which contained the Proverbs. (See ch. 55, §3.4.b.)

These proverbs are also couplets, like Solomon's first collection (Proverbs 10—22). They tend to teach by synonym rather than contrast. (See Faithful.)

V. AGUR'S PROVERBS 30:1–33.

A. The life of God-fearing moderation (30:1–14). Agur and the others mentioned in verse 1 are unknown. The first section is personal, sharing the writer's awe of God and his own sense of inadequacy. (See Word of God.)

B. The observed wonders of life on earth (30:15–31). The rest of Proverbs 30 contains wise sayings that focus on nature rather than moral instruction.

C. The foolishness of pride and anger (30:32–33).

VI. KING LEMUEL'S PROVERBS 31:1–31.

A. A mother's standards for a noble son (31:1–9). Like Agur, Lemuel cannot be identified. The first section (1–9) contains his mother's advice to him, warning against strong drink.

B. An acrostic poem on the perfect wife (31:10–31). The second section is an acrostic, in which each verse begins with a different Hebrew letter. This famous poem contains the Old Testament's description of a wife who earns praise (see Blessed) for her noble character.

TRUTH-IN-ACTION through PROVERBS

EDITOR'S NOTE: Most books in the Bible are historical narrative, didactic discourse, apocalyptic prose, or poetic prayers or reflections. The Book of Proverbs, on the other hand, is largely loosely related aphorisms, each calling for meditation and requiring faithful application. One can understand most often how to put each into action with minimal reflection. In the following, we describe the five most dominant themes of the wisdom of Proverbs. Next we present a digest of the most often repeated imperatives of the book. The selected texts are just a small sampling of the wealth of wisdom you will find in these chapters.

Truth Proverbs Teaches	**Action** Proverbs Invites
1 Attaining Wisdom and Gaining Understanding "Wisdom is the principal thing; Therefore get wisdom. And in all your getting, get understanding" (4:7) exhorts Solomon. Wisdom is knowing the	**4:5–9** *Prioritize* wisdom. *Seek after* and *cherish* understanding. *Accept* that knowledge without wisdom and understanding is futile. **9:10** *Pursue* the fear of the Lord, reproofs, instruction, advice and humility. *Know* that from these come wisdom and understanding. *(continued)*

Truth Proverbs Teaches	**Action** Proverbs Invites
1 Attaining Wisdom and Gaining Understanding (continued) truth and how to apply it to any given situation: understanding is knowledge seasoned and modified by wisdom and insight. The words "wisdom" or "wise" and "understanding" occur over 140 times in Proverbs.	**2:1–6** *Apply* your heart, *pay attention* and *turn* your ear to wisdom and understanding. *Understand* that you must embrace them both, not just know about them. **3:13–18, 21–26; 8:12–21** *Embrace* wisdom and *follow after* understanding. *Know* that patience, discernment, favor, prosperity, safety, and other benefits will result.
2 Acquiring Knowledge The knowledge of Prov. consists of more than information. facts, and sense data. It is knowledge that begins with the fear of the Lord and is therefore godly knowledge that always includes Him as the primary factor. Because of its divine source, it comes with understanding implicit in it.	**2:4–6; 24:13, 14** *Seek out* knowledge. *Cherish* it as a valued possession when you have found it. **3:5, 6; 22:17–21** *Study* God's Word and *listen* to the Holy Spirit. *Believe* God's prophets. *Understand* that these are the true sources of godly knowledge. **14:3; 15:23; 20:15** *Be prudent* in how you give out knowledge. *Do not stray* from the words of knowledge. *Share* your knowledge with restraint, and do not let it become a source of pride.
3 Loving Instruction and Heeding Reproof Discipline involves both instruction and exercise designed to train in proper conduct or action. Punishment may also be inflicted as a means of correction.	**9:7–9; 17:10** *Embrace* the discipline of instruction and heed reproofs gladly. *Realize* that man is inclined to turn away from both. **10:8; 13:18** *Follow* instruction diligently. *Accept* the correction of reproof. *Value* their lessons. *Seek* after both instruction and reproof.
4 The Wise vs. the Fool Prov. presents two categories of people: the wise or prudent and the fool, scoffer, or mocker. The former seeks wisdom and loves instruction; the latter neglects discipline and spurns reproof. Also, each can be characterized by his response to parental and other authority, the former bringing joy and delight, the latter bringing shame, disgrace, and sadness. Prov. exhorts its reader to become wise and despise the foolish and his folly.	**10:14; 16:24; 17:27, 28** *Be careful* in what you say. *Measure* every word. *Do not speak* unless it is important that you do so. *Speak* only in order to build up and strengthen. *Be diligent* in all your work. **6:6–11** *Avoid* any form of laziness. *Serve* those to whom your lot assigns you with gladness. *Seek* to please those under or for whom you work. **3:9, 27, 28; 10:4, 5; 17:18; 23:1–3, 19–21, 26–28, 29–35** *Be frugal* in your handling of money. *Practice* good stewardship. *Avoid being* either a spendthrift or a miser. *Learn* the proper investment of time and substance. *Do not consume* unnecessarily. *Use, do not abuse* the things God gives you. *Avoid* drunkenness, excessiveness, and immoral sexual conduct.
5 The Proper Discipline of Children Perhaps biblical wisdom most significantly challenges our modern philosophies and practices of childrearing.	**22:6** *Train* children to honor authority, obey, and follow instruction. *Discourage* rebellion, stubbornness, and disobedience. **13:24; 19:18** *Practice* consistent discipline and corporal correction in rearing children. *Recognize* that children are trained to obedience by these.

KEYS TO ECCLESIASTES
Human Vanity and the Kingdom

CHAPTER 21

Kingdom Key: God's Purpose in View

Ecclesiastes is Solomon's "bully pulpit," his sermon that summarizes his explorations in and musings about life, with the conclusion that "Everything is emptiness [vanity]!" From God's viewpoint, as expressed through the Lord Jesus Christ, it might be said that Ecclesiastes verifies and, by contrast, illustrates three New Testament "life principles."

1. Life is fulfilling only when it is given away.

In direct contrast to Solomon's avowed pursuit of all that people think will satisfy, Jesus' call to His disciples is centered in a commitment to lay down one's life for others. Ecclesiastes complains, "I sought everything and found nothing." In contrast, Jesus says, "If you lose your life for my sake, you will find it" (Eccl. 2:10–11; Matt. 10:39; John 12:24–26).

2. Life in pursuit of excellence without sacrifice will ultimately disappoint.

In the same vein as the above, but significantly distinctive, is the warning of Ecclesiastes against searching for transient glory. However noble, neither the search for knowledge and wisdom (1:16–18) nor the erecting of man-made monuments or works of art (2:4–6) can bring contentment. Even such dignified pursuits as these,

> ## Only a life "poured out" brings content-ment.

which are higher in motive than questing after pleasure (2:1–3, 10) or searching for fame (2:17–20), still prove to be an illusion. Only the New Testament kingdom pathway of "pouring out" one's life (Phil. 2:17) can bring contentment (Phil. 4:11) and a sense of true achievement (Phil. 4:13).

3. Life that is lived solely on the earth-plane breeds cynicism.

The recurrent phrase "under the sun" (1:14; 2:18–20, 22) contrasts sharply with one's position in Christ, "seated in the heavenlies" (Eph. 2:6). Life seen from the spiritual viewpoint gives perspective to all things—goals, possessions, enjoyment, and knowledge. Without the "heavenly" perspective, even life's finest attainments become lackluster; life turns in on itself, and the short-lived nature even of earth's most durable things reveals their lack of substance.

Praise God that we can be born into a

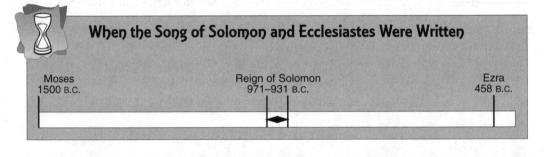

When the Song of Solomon and Ecclesiastes Were Written

Moses 1500 B.C.	Reign of Solomon 971–931 B.C.	Ezra 458 B.C.

Ecclesiastes unmasks self-centeredness in goals,

kingdom that transcends earth's limits (John 3:3, 5), a kingdom that increases in its joys and fulfillment (Is. 3:6–7), and a kingdom that shall never fade away (Luke 1:32–33).

Master Key: God's Son Revealed

Although the Book of Ecclesiastes contains no direct or typological prophecies of Jesus Christ, it anticipates a number of teachings of Him who was the fulfillment of the Law and the Prophets (Matt. 5:17). While Jesus said little about wisdom, Paul had much to say about the wisdom given by God (Rom. 11:33) contrasted to the wisdom of this world with its human limitations (1 Cor. 1:17; 3:19; 2 Cor. 1:12).

In Matthew 6:19–21 Jesus warned against seeking wealth in this life, urging instead an investment in eternal values, a perspective that echoes the Preacher's indictment of materialism in 2:1–11, 18–26; 4:4–6; 5:8–14. The stress Jesus laid on heaven likewise mirrors the Preacher's despair of finding true value "under the sun" (in this life). The conclusion to which the Preacher is driven—that true value lies only in reverence and obedience to God (12:13)—mirrors Jesus' teachings that one's values should be first determined by a proper attitude toward God (Matt. 22:37, quoting Deut. 6:5) and then a proper attitude toward one's fellow human beings (Matt. 22:39, quoting Lev. 19:18).

Power Key: God's Spirit at Work

All references to "spirit" in Ecclesiastes are to the life-force that animates the human or the animal (*see* 3:18–21). The book nevertheless anticipates some of the problems faced by the apostle Paul in the implementation of spiritual gifts in 1 Corinthians 12—14. People who believe that God speaks to them through the Holy Spirit in dreams and visions (Joel 2:28–32; Acts 2:17–21) would do well to heed the wise

Key Word: *Vanity*

The word vanity *appears thirty-seven times to express the many things that cannot be understood about life. All earthly goals and ambitions lead to dissatisfaction and frustration when pursued as ends in themselves apart from God.*

Key Verses: Ecclesiastes 2:24; 12:13–14

Key Chapter: Ecclesiastes 12

Only when the Preacher views his life from God's perspective "above the sun" does it take on meaning as a precious gift "from the hand of God" (2:24). Chapter 12 resolves the book's extensive inquiry into the meaning of life with the single conclusion, "Fear God and keep His commandments, for this is the whole duty of man" (12:13, NIV).

advice of the Preacher that not every dream is the voice of God (5:3). Paul seems to have a caution like this in mind for the revelatory gifts of tongues and prophecy in 1 Corinthians 14:29, when he advises an orderly manifestation followed by a judgment on the utterance by the assembly. Likewise, the Preacher's stress on reverence and obedience to God parallels Paul's concern for the edification of the church (1 Cor. 14:5). True spiritual gifts—genuine manifestations of miraculous utterance or deed—will be used in a spirit of reverence for the glory of God through Christ and for the edification of the believers.

possessions, enjoyment, and knowledge.

Introducing

ECCLESIASTES

Author and Date. The name *Ecclesiastes* is derived from the Greek word *ekklesia* ("assembly") and means "One Who Addresses an Assembly." The Hebrew word so represented is *qoheleth*, which means "One Who Convenes an Assembly," thus often being rendered "Teacher" or "Preacher" in English versions.

Ecclesiastes is generally credited to Solomon (about 971 to 931 B.C.), written in his old age. The rather pessimistic tone that pervades the book would be in keeping with Solomon's spiritual state at the time (*see* 1 Kings 11). Although not mentioned in 1 Kings, Solomon must have come to his senses before his death, repented, and turned back to God. Ecclesiastes 1:1, "The words of the Preacher, the son of David, king in Jerusalem," seems to point to Solomon. Scattered throughout the book are allusions to Solomon's wisdom (1:16), wealth (2:8), servants (2:7), pleasures (2:3), and building activities (2:4–6).

Because of the problems posed by an apostate Solomon writing Holy Scripture and because some of the language in Ecclesiastes belongs to a period much later in Israel's history, some scholars believe the book may have had its origin in the time of Ezra (about 450 B.C.).

Background. The book evinces a time when traditional solutions to life's great questions, particularly the meaning of life, have lost their relevance for the author. Rather than respond to such questions with citations from Scripture, the Preacher introduces a methodology that is predicated on observation and induction. Wisdom, when found in the other wisdom literature of the Bible (Job, Proverbs, and certain psalms), is a synonym for virtue and piety; its antithesis, folly, thus becomes "wickedness." In the Book of Ecclesiastes, the word "wisdom" is sometimes used in this manner when dealing with the conventional Israelite interpretation of wisdom (as in 7:1—8:9; 10:1—11:6). But in the opening chapter (1:12–18) the author deals with wisdom that is a process of pure thought, more like Greek philosophy, the enduring worth of which he questions. While never disputing the existence of God who has given meaning to His creation, the Preacher nevertheless determines to seek out that meaning through his own experience and observation so that he may personally verify it and pass it down to his disciples.

Content. The Book of Ecclesiastes gives every evidence of being a carefully composed literary essay that must be grasped as a totality before it can be understood in part. The content of the book is defined by nearly identical verses (1:2; 12:8), which circumscribe the book by anticipating and by summarizing the conclusions of the author. The theme is set forth in 1:3: "What profit has a man from all his labor in which he toils under the sun [that is, in this life]?" Or, can true wisdom be found by a human being apart from revelation from God?

The Preacher's quest is for some sort of fixed, unchanging value ("profit") that can be found in this life ("under the sun") that can serve as a basis for proper living. The Hebrew word translated "profit" is *yitron* (1:3), and may also be translated "gain, value." "Vanity" is a key word in the book, translating the Hebrew *hebel* (literally, "breath"), thus indicating what is mortal, transitory, and of no permanence. As he tries each of the avenues proposed by humanity to achieve the value being sought, he finds them elusive ("grasping for the wind") and fleeting, transitory ("vanity").

The "wisdom" of 1:12–18 is found bankrupt of real value. Neither is the answer to be found in pleasure, in wealth, in great accomplishments (2:1–11), in a doctrine of retribution (2:12–17), or in materialism (2:18–26).

If neither accomplishments nor things are *yitron*, what then should be one's attitude toward them, seeing they have no permanent value? The answer introduces the secondary theme of the book: one should enjoy both life and the things with which God has blessed him (3:11–12; 5:18–20; 9:7–10), remembering that in the end God will judge him for the way this is done (11:7–10).

Even human life itself, in any secular, humanistic sense, cannot be the *yitron* the Preacher seeks. The interplay of death and life is also a subordinate theme for the book.

But returning to the Preacher's grand quest: is it destined to conclude (12:8), as it began (1:2), on a note of despair? The Preacher's constant probing of all existence for meaning shows him to be an optimist, not a pessimist, and his failure to discover any absolute, abiding value in this life ("under the sun") does not mean his quest is a failure. Instead, he finds himself compelled (by his observation that God placed order in the universe at the time of its creation, 3:1–14) to seek the value he seeks in the world to come (not "under the sun" but "above the sun," so to speak). Although he does not specifically state it as such, the logic that undergirds his entire quest compels him to find the only real *yitron* in the fear (reverence) and obedience of God (11:7—12:7). This is affirmed in the epilogue: Reverence for God and keeping His commandments are the whole duty of mankind (12:13). This duty must be carried out in full knowledge that, while there is no real justice to be had in this life, God will eventually judge all that is and set it right (11:9; 12:14). On this profound note the book concludes.

Personal Application. Too often Christians in the modern church find themselves passive intellectually, accepting almost anything they are taught or simply challenging a doctrine on the basis of how it feels instead of looking to see whether it has a biblical foundation. The Preacher's challenge finds a parallel in the apostle Paul's words to the Ephesian Christians not to be "tossed to and fro and carried about with every wind of doctrine" (Eph. 4:14). With the privilege of interpreting the Scrip-

tures for oneself, clearly established by Luther and the Reformers, comes the obligation to "search the Scriptures" (John 5:39) and see what they really say.

The determination of the Preacher to find what is of real value in this life should be a challenge for any true believer in Jesus Christ, "the way, the truth, and the life" (John 14:6). The Preacher's failure to find real value in earthly things and comfortable lifestyles challenges the Christian who lives in this age of greed and materialism to concentrate on the things that are above (Col. 3:1) and not to glorify greed and possessions.

Surveying
ECCLESIASTES

I. PROLOGUE 1:1-2.

A. Identification of the book (1:1).

B. Summary of the Preacher's investigations (1:2). Solomon boldly states the theme he will demonstrate.

II. STATEMENT OF THE PROBLEM 1:3-11.

A. Statement of the problem: Can true value be found in this life? (1:3).

B. Exposition of the problem: A refutation of humanistic solutions (1:4-11). In a series of brief discourses, Solomon shares the reasoning by which he arrived at the conclusion that life is meaningless.

III. ATTEMPTS AT SOLUTIONS TO THE PROBLEM 1:12-2:26.

A. The refutation of pure reason: Human wisdom alone is useless (1:12-18). Knowledge disappoints. Solomon's own experience proves to him that knowledge and learning bring only grief. A less intelligent person might not have realized how meaningless life is!

B. The failure of hedonism: Pleasure in itself is meaningless (2:1-11). Pleasures are empty. Solomon's position made it possible for him to deny himself nothing. He finds that all is meaningless.

C. The failure of retribution: The wise and the fool face a common end (2:12-17). Contrasts are irrelevant. While ultimate meaning escapes us, isn't it possible that one person's life might be more meaningful than another's? No, for even distinctions between the wise and

the foolish are irrelevant, as death overtakes both.

D. The failure of materialism (2:18-26). Solomon's great accomplishments cannot give his life meaning. The good things of life can be accepted and enjoyed but will not give meaning to one's existence.

IV. DEVELOPING THE THEME 3:1—6:12.

A. Uselessness in man's efforts to change the created order (3:1-15). Life is organized in a pattern of repeated cycles. Yet observation of the cycles does not lead to an understanding of beginnings or endings. Only a grasp of origins or destiny might reveal life's meaning. (*See* Laugh.)

B. Uselessness in an equal end for unequal creatures (3:16-22). Injustice demonstrates meaninglessness. The existence of injustice is a demonstrable fact of life. There may be judgment after death. But from all that man can observe, a human being dies just like an animal. There is no evidence that the spirit of one rises up to God, and the other dissipates into dust.

C. Uselessness in an oppressed life (4:1-3).

D. Uselessness of envy (4:4-6). Oppression, toil, and friendlessness, human suffering, and ambition also give evidence of meaninglessness.

E. Uselessness in being alone (4:7-12).

F. Uselessness in a hereditary monarchy (4:13-16).

G. Uselessness in pretense in formal religion (5:1-7). The existence of God is evident to Solomon from the creation. But beyond that, little can be said by those limited to earth of a God who is in heaven (v. 2).

H. Uselessness in materialistic values systems (5:8-14). Riches are meaningless. However rich a person may be, he never seems to have enough, even though one can only consume a little.

I. Uselessness in leaving the products of one's labor behind at death (5:15–20). Possessions cannot make life meaningful.

J. Uselessness in the futility of a deprived life (6:1–9). Whatever the future holds for a newborn infant, its days will be without meaning.

K. Uselessness in the determinism of nature (6:10–12).

V. PRACTICAL WISDOM AND ITS USES 7:1—8:9. Solomon has demonstrated that no meaning or purpose to human life can be discerned by an examination of human experience. Still, Solomon concludes that some ways are better than others. He proceeds from his discoveries to suggest rules for the best life possible to us under the circumstances.

A. Moralizing proverbs about life and death, good and evil (7:1–10).

B. Wisdom and its applications (7:11–22). A fatalistic attitude is to be adopted, and extremes are to be avoided.

C. Miscellaneous wise observations (7:23—8:1). Wisdom is preferable to folly. (*See* Manhood.)

D. Wisdom in the king's court (8:2–9). One must submit to authorities.

VI. A RETURN TO THE THEME 8:10—9:18.

A. Uselessness in the failure of retribution (again) (8:10—9:12). Enjoy life's good things, even though they cannot make your life meaningful. Death awaits all, so enjoy life while you can.

B. Uselessness in the fickle nature of man (again) (9:13–18).

VII. MORE ON WISDOM AND ITS USES 10:1—11:6. Prepare for the future, though you cannot control it. (*See* Prosper.)

VIII. THE ONLY VALUE IS TO FEAR GOD AND OBEY HIM 11:7—12:7.

A. THE FIRST SUMMARY OF THE CONCLUSIONS DRAWN (11:7–10). Enjoy your youth.

B. The second summary: The allegory of old age and death (12:1–7).

IX. EPILOGUE: CONFIRMATION OF THE CONCLUSION 12:8–14.

A. Summary of the Preacher's conclusions (12:8).

B. Summary of the Preacher's conclusions by a disciple (12:9–14). Solomon looks back over the wasted years of his life, during which he turned from God's commandments. His final words point back to his youth, and invite us to fear God and obey His commandments.

TRUTH-IN-ACTION through ECCLESIASTES

Truth Ecclesiastes Teaches	**Action** Ecclesiastes Invites
1 Knowing God and His Ways We are to revere God as the Creator who works everything perfectly after the counsel of His own will.	**3:14** *Believe* that everything God does is perfect. **12:1** *Establish* your relationship with God while you are young, before the evils of life harden your heart.
2 Guidelines for Growing in Godliness The "Preacher" counsels his readers toward godly living. We are to live with a view to the futility and vanity of a life spent without reference to God. Much of the energy we spend trying to accomplish various tasks ends up "sowing to the wind." The life lived in fidelity and integrity is the only one that has any real meaning.	**2:24–26** *Seek to please God* in all you do. **3:22** *Endeavor* to find enjoyment in your work and daily life. **7:8, 9** *Avoid* rashness or hastiness. *Know* that God is never in a hurry. *Make no important decisions* with an agitated spirit. **8:5, 6** *Determine* to obey those who have the rule over you. *Believe* that you will know how and when to accomplish the assigned task. **9:7–10** *Conduct* a Spirit-filled life. *Honor* marital fidelity. *Serve* the Lord with all your might. **12:12–14** *Do not attempt* to substitute scholarship for obedience. *Cultivate* the fear of the Lord.
3 Keys to Wise Living The "Preacher" says that if you know God and seek to live your life before Him in a way that pleases Him, you will be living wisely. Wise living involves learning to assess the	**2:1–11** *Understand* that the pursuit of pleasure for its own sake is a vain pursuit. **2:12–16** *Understand* that a life lived strictly for the sake of wisdom is futile. **2:17–23** *Recognize* that dedication to work as its own reward is a vain pursuit. *(continued)*

Truth Ecclesiastes Teaches	**Action** Ecclesiastes Invites
3 Guidelines for Growing in Godliness *(continued)* relative value of choices one might make. The wise individual chooses those things that have lasting value. Often the wisest choices will not be those that are apparently best by the world's standards.	**5:18–20** *Get into work* you really enjoy and for which you can be grateful. *Understand* that to toil without enjoyment is vain and meaningless. **6:1, 2** *Understand* that to work so hard that you cannot enjoy the fruit of your labors is foolishness. *Beware* workaholism! **7:15–18** *Avoid* taking extreme positions unnecessarily.
4 Steps in Developing Humility One message in Ecclesiastes comes through loud and clear: Walk gently and humbly before the Lord. "God is in heaven, and you on earth." The more we know about God, the more humble we will be. The humble person recognizes his own limitations and accepts them.	**1:10, 11** *Accept* and *recognize* that human understanding of history is partial and distorted. *Know* that the facts mankind has forgotten could change your perspective entirely. **3:11** *Accept* your limitations. *Know* that you cannot comprehend eternity. *Learn to accept* God's perfect timing. **4:13–16** *Understand* that the pursuit of personal ambition is vain and futile. **7:1–4** *Be mindful* of your mortality. *Let bereavement bring* you times of sober self-assessment.
5 Keys to Handling Money Being a righteous steward of worldly wealth flows out of a godly perspective with regard to money. Money is a servant to utilize, not a god to serve. One's motives in acquiring and using money are the determining factors.	**5:10** *Consider* and *understand* that wealth is intrinsically elusive. **5:11** *Understand* that wealth is by its very nature deceptive. **5:19** *Know* the difference between wealth that has been sought and wealth that has come from the hand of God. *Understand* that the latter has no curse associated with it.
6 Steps to Dealing with Sin The wise person understands that to willfully practice sin is to become its slave, and to delay in dealing with sin appropriately is to promote it.	**8:8** *Understand* that you are the slave of any wickedness that you practice (see Rom. 6:16). **8:11** *Carry out* any discipline you determine is necessary without delay, because delay may foster wrongdoing.
7 How to Tame the Tongue When we speak, we must be aware that the Lord hears every word we say. Presumptuous speech displeases the Lord and can bring discipline.	**5:1–3** *Be quick* to listen and *slow* to speak. *Cultivate* humility and *learn* to walk softly before the Lord. **5:4–7** *Do not speak presumptuously* of spiritual commitment or endeavor. *Cultivate* reverence for the Lord.

KEYS TO SONG OF SOLOMON
Human Intimacy and the Kingdom

Kingdom Key: God's Purpose in View

The Song of Solomon is interpreted many ways—from an ancient poem celebrating romance, to a personal disclosure of Solomon's affection for his favorite wife, to an allegory of the relationship between Jesus Christ and His bride, the church. Whatever else may be said, this book categorically closes the door on any pietistic notions about human sexuality, married love-making, and sensual delights.

The beauty of this poem is in its tasteful yet candid setting forth of the fact that a married couple can rejoice in the emotional and physical interchange their relationship properly allows. Prudishness is not a requirement of spirituality.

The Song of Solomon is a forthright and graphic Holy Spirit-inspired disclosure of God's delight in a married couple's delight in one another, both in their romantic feelings and in their sexual relationship. No other passage in the Bible is so clear about this, though there is supporting evidence in the New Testament. For example, Paul's instructions to married couples in Corinth clearly states that a cool or prudish sexual withholding of oneself from a spouse is not consistent with God's intended order (1 Cor. 7:3–6). That he does not issue this as a "commandment" does not reduce its place as a divinely

True love is founded upon God's covenants.

ordained policy. Paul makes it clear that affectionate exchange and sexual responsiveness within a marriage cannot be commandeered. It can be achieved only through shared tenderness, communication, care, and respect.

The writer of Hebrews also confirms the worthiness and divine approval of the joys of the marriage bed (Heb. 13:4–5). However, the grammar in that text does not, as some suppose, say "Anything goes!" There are decadent practices, fostered by a perverted world, that are born of "covetousness" (Gk. *pleonexia*—"insatiable lusts"). The Hebrews text not only refuses to endorse a licentious marriage bed, it specifically issues an imperative* calling couples to defend their love-making against pollution. The simple purity, joyfulness, and pleasure-filled ecstasies of married love can and must be differentiated

When the Song of Solomon and Ecclesiastes Were Written

Moses 1500 B.C.	Reign of Solomon 971–931 B.C.	Ezra 458 B.C.

The Song of Solomon celebrates the joys

from any deadening, perverted practices of a world whose evil inventions are begotten in an atmosphere where the warmth of love has been lost or has never been known. The pure fires of passion are to be allowed, and hellish fires of perversion refused, in the kingdom couple's relationship.

* Footnote: A. T. Robertson notes that the grammatical structure of Hebrews 13:4 requires the understanding of an implicit imperative—"Let the bed be kept honorable" (*Word Pictures in the New Testament*, 444).

Master Key: God's Son
Revealed

In the Song of Solomon, as in other parts of the Bible, the Garden of Eden, the Promised Land, the tabernacle with its ark of the covenant, the temple of Solomon, and the new heavens and the new earth are all related to Jesus Christ, so it is not a matter of merely choosing a few verses that prophesy of Christ. The very essence of covenant history and covenant love is reproduced in Him (Luke 24:27; 2 Cor. 1:20).

Power Key: God's Spirit at Work

According to Romans 5:5, "the love of God has been poured out in our hearts by the Holy Spirit." On the basis of Jesus Christ, the Holy Spirit is the bond and the binding power of love. The joyous oneness revealed in the Song is inconceivable apart from the Holy Spirit. The very form of the book as song and symbol is especially adapted to the Spirit, for He Himself uses dreams, picture-language, and singing (Acts 2:17; Eph. 5:18–19). A subtle wordplay based on the divine "breathing" of the breath of life (the Holy Spirit, Ps. 104:29–30) in Genesis 2:7 seems to surface in the Song. It shows up in the "break" or breathing of the day (2:17; 4:6), in the "blowing" of the wind on the Shulamite's garden (4:16), and surprisingly in the fragrant scent and fruit of the apple tree (7:8).

Key Word: *Love in Marriage*

The purpose of this book depends on the viewpoint taken as to its primary thrust:

Fictional: To portray Solomon's attraction and marriage to a poor but beautiful girl from the country.

Allegorical: To present God's love for His bride Israel or Christ's love for His church.

Historical: To record Solomon's actual romance with a Shulamite woman. The various scenes in the book exalt the joys of love in courtship and marriage and offer a proper perspective of human love.

Key Verses: Song of Solomon 7:10; 8:7

of marriage in the light of divine order.

Introducing

SONG OF SOLOMON

Author. Solomon's authorship is disputed, but the glory of Solomonic symbolism is essential to the Song. Jesus referred twice to Solomon's glory and wisdom (Matt. 6:29; 12:42). As David's royal son, Solomon had a unique place in covenant history (2 Sam. 7:12–13). His two birth names, which symbolize peace (Solomon) and love (Jedidiah), readily apply to the Song (2 Sam. 12:24–25; 1 Chr. 22:9). Solomon's glorious kingdom was like a restoration of the Garden of Eden (1 Kin. 4:20–34), and the temple and palace he built embody the truths of the tabernacle and the conquest of the Promised Land (1 Kings 6—7). Solomon is perfectly cast as the personified blessings of covenant love since he appears in the Song with all of his regal perfection (1:2–4; 5:10–16).

Occasion and Date. Though the Song does not supply precise background information, Solomon reigned over Israel from 971 to 931 B.C. Similar language and ideals are also found in David's temple prayer for Solomon and for the people at Solomon's enthronement (1 Chronicles 29).

Purpose. "Love" is the key word in the Song. This love, presenting the passionate desire between a man and a woman, King Solomon and the Shulamite, celebrates the joyous potential of marriage in light of sworn covenant principles. The basis for all human love should be covenant love, the master metaphor of the Bible. This covenant love is also the basis of the relationship between God and man; therefore, the Song applies properly to both marriage and to covenant history. The Shulamite, therefore, personifies the wife in an ideal marriage and the covenant people and their history in the Promised Land under the blessings of royal Solomonic love.

Characteristics. The Song is the best of all songs, a literary work of art and a theological masterpiece. In the second century one of the greatest Jewish rabbis, Akiba ben Joseph, said, "In the entire world there is nothing to equal the day on which the Song of Songs was given to Israel." The Song itself is like its favorite fruit, pomegranates, alive with color and full of seeds. Quite unlike any other biblical book, it merits special consideration as a biblical archetype which presents anew the basic realities of man's relationships. The Song employs symbolic language to express timeless truths, much like the Book of Revelation.

Content. The Song contains portraits of the Shulamite woman along with a full array of her garden products. These should be taken both as poetic parallels of marital love and as covenant blessings of the people in their land.

Clear directions are given in the discovery of covenant blessings, "Follow in the footsteps of the flock" (1:8). Footsteps here is literally "heelprints," and may be an allusion to Jacob, the national father whose name connotes "a heel." Jacob's shepherd role and his lifelong struggle for the blessing of God and man are cited as the biblical norm for God's people (Hos. 12:3–6, 12–13). He was born grasping his brother's heel, a congenital manipulator. He was "disjointed" with deception at the core of his being as illustrated by his limp at Mahanaim (Genesis 32). He was forced to live outside the land under the threat of an angry brother. He returned to the land after twenty years with a faulty family foundation. Deception, lack of love, jealousy, anger, and love for hire (for mandrakes) went into the shaky substructure. The very names of the Twelve Tribes show the need for a new family history.

The Shulamite relives and rewrites that history. She does the memorial dance to Mahanaim (6:13; see Gen. 32:2). When she finds the one she loves she holds him and will not let him go (3:4; see Gen. 32:26). Fragrant mandrakes grow in her fields (7:11–13; see Gen. 30:14). When the daughters see her, they call her blessed or happy (6:9; see Gen. 30:13). In the Shulamite the corrupt family tree of Israel bears "pleasant fruits," the very best (7:13; see Deut. 33:13–17). The covenant blessings that had gone awry are redeemed.

These same incidents can be seen as portraits of marital love as well. In this respect it is her husband whom she holds and will not let go (3:4). It is her husband who praises her beauty (6:4–10), and it is a royal wedding procession and the bride and groom's rejoicing in one another that are portrayed in 3:6—5:1.

Personal Application. The Song is a constant goad to drifting marriages with its challenge to seek for openness, growth, and joyous relationship. It also makes an excellent premarital manual. As a biblical archetype, it can bring healing to the core of our being with its hope of covenant love as it reshapes our marriages. Its portrayal of the covenant love relationship also has application to the covenant love relationship enjoyed by God's church. In this regard, the Song can be rich in symbolism but should not be read as an arbitrary allegory with mysterious meanings supplied by the whim of the reader; rather, any such personal application of one's love relationship with Christ should be interpreted with solid application, using *obvious* biblical parallels.

Surveying
SONG OF SOLOMON

I. OPENING SCENES 1:1—2:7. The bride longs for her bridegroom. They meet and praise each other.

A. Remembering the love of the king with the good name (1:1–4).

B. The dark but lovely vineyard keeper (1:5–6).

C. Finding love in the footsteps of the flock (1:7–8).

D. Removing the marks of slavery (1:9–11).

E. The language of love (1:12–17).

F. The thorn and the tree (2:1–6).

G. The first sworn charge (2:7).

II. THE QUEST FOR OPENNESS 2:8—3:5. As their love grows, the bride praises the groom using figures from nature.

A. Beginning the quest (2:8–15).

B. The joy of love in the cool of the day (2:16–17).

C. The determined search for the primal goal (3:1–4).

D. The second sworn charge (3:5).

III. THE QUEST FOR MUTUALITY 3:6—5:8.

A. The royal wedding carriage of covenant love (3:6–11).

B. Getting acquainted with the Shulamite (4:1–7). The lover comes and praises the bride.

C. A view of the land from the top of Mount Hermon (4:8).

D. Intimate union life in a shared garden banquet (4:9—5:1).

E. The fall of the Shulamite (5:2–7). The lover has gone away, and the bride expresses her longing for him.

F. The third sworn charge (5:8).

IV. THE QUEST FOR ONENESS 5:9—8:4.

A. Getting acquainted with Solomon (5:9—6:3).

B. The Shulamite's triumphant glory (6:4–10).

C. The Shulamite's noble people (6:11–12).

D. The memorial dance to Mahanaim (6:13—7:9). The lover returns, the marriage is consummated, and the happiness of the couple is celebrated.

E. The initiation of a new love as equals (7:9—8:3).

F. The fourth sworn charge (8:4).

V. CLOSING SCENES WITH SUMMARY ACHIEVEMENTS 8:5–14.

A. Achieving the primal goal (8:5).

B. Achieving authentic love (8:6–7).

C. Achieving motherhood and peace (8:8–10).

D. Achieving a vineyard equal to Solomon's (8:11–12).

E. Achieving the inheritance (8:13–14).

TRUTH-IN-ACTION through SONG OF SOLOMON

EDITOR'S NOTE: The Song of Solomon is often interpreted as an allegory of the love of Yahweh for Israel or of Jesus for His bride, the church. However, the grammatical-historical approach to exegesis interprets the Song simply as one of the finest examples of ancient, Oriental love poetry. The Hebrew culture celebrated the sexual relationship experienced between a man and a woman within the sanctity of marriage as an exquisitely beautiful gift from our Creator.

Minimal research into Oriental and Semitic symbology will yield rich dividends and help bring this book alive for the reader.

Truth the Song Teaches	**Action** the Song Invites
1 Keys to Moral Purity Maintaining sexual purity until marriage is a key to establishing a strong Christian marriage. In view of the prevailing social acceptance of sexually immoral behavior, it is of great importance that God's holy people renounce impurity and make a renewed effort to rebuild commitment to moral purity in the church.	**1:2–4** *Understand* that physical desires for your spouse are entirely appropriate. **2:7** *Refuse* any sexual involvement before marriage. . . . *Knowing* it diminishes sexual fulfillment within marriage. **3:5** . . . *Knowing* it compromises necessary objectivity in important premarital evaluations and decisions. **8:4** . . . *Knowing* it seriously weakens a couple's ability to make necessary sexual adjustments within marriage. **8:8, 9** Christian families: *Get involved* in the development of your children's sexual morality. *Encourage* and *support* their sexual purity and virginity. *Build defenses* against attempts to seduce them away from sexual righteousness. **8:10–12** *Value* virginity very highly! *Do not ever discredit* the inestimable value of being able to present to your new spouse your body and soul, wholly undefiled and kept pure for him/her.
2 Advice to Dating Couples Using courtship to maximum advantage minimizes difficulties in marriage. Many couples enter marriage unprepared to deal with the things they will face. Though brief and indirect, the advice given by Solomon and the Shulamite should be heeded by those preparing for marriage.	**1:7** *Understand* that it is of the utmost importance that we learn to know and accept our intended spouse as he/she is. *Accept* as wrong thinking any hidden plans to change that person. **1:8** *Know* it is better not to follow through with plans for marriage than to marry one you cannot accept as he/she is. **2:14, 15** *Take time* to identify and resolve potential problems to your marriage. *Face* them honestly and candidly. **8:6, 7** *Determine* to build a strong, unbreakable commitment to each other in your marriage.
3 Keys to an Enduring Marriage Successful marriages result from the disciplined practices that have been proven through the centuries by countless couples whose love and commitment grew stronger and more passionate. Today when the cultural environment wars against the Christian marriage—seeking to redefine, dilute, and delude our understanding of God's institution—recovering these dynamic principles is essential. God's Word is, of course, the place to start looking. And where better than God's love song?	**4:1–7** Marriage partners: *Learn* the lost art of verbal lovemaking. *Learn* to speak words of love that caress your mate's soul. **5:1** *Understand* and *believe* that the Lord continues to view the sexual relationship within the sanctity of marriage as "very good" and to bless it. **6:4–9** Throughout marriage *extol* your spouse's virtues above those of others. **7:10–13** *Set aside* regular, periodic times away with your spouse to *refresh* and *renew* the romance in your marriage.

KEYS TO ISAIAH
The Kingdom and Certain Hope

Kingdom Key: God's Purpose in View

The major prophets stand like monoliths of certainty amid the uncertainties of the transient kingdoms in which they ministered. With the world swirling around them as nations and empires toppled one after another, the ultimate kingdom was boldly announced from their lips and in their writings. Isaiah's message was one of ultimate hope.

The message of the kingdom of God not only *contains* the certainty of ultimate hope, but the ministry of the kingdom *constrains* its bearers to declare that hope with conviction, whatever the present climate or circumstance. Such hope is anchored in rock-solid reality.

Identifying Isaiah's grounds for *certain hope* provides a place for all kingdom proclamation to find its "reason for hope" (1 Pet. 3:15). Note Isaiah's message of:

1. Hope for a Righteous King

The opening verse of Isaiah describes the political environment of his ministry. Of the four kings he knew, only one consistently lived and served in the ways of the Lord. Uzziah fell because of pride and presumption (2 Chr. 26:19); Jotham, though faithful, was unable to restrain corruption or lead in a way which reversed the habits of his people (2 Chr. 27:2); and Ahaz was committed to evil ways (2 Chr. 28:1–4). Only Hezekiah proved

A

messianic

hope is a

rock-solid

reality.

steadfast for God in his leadership (2 Chronicles 29—32). Isaiah's proclamation of a faithful, just, and righteous king-to-come lifted believing hearts, especially in the midst of the sixteen-year wicked reign of Ahaz. The same message will achieve the same result today, whatever the surrounding failure or confusion of man or society. Proclaim the truth of Isaiah 9:6–7 and 11:1–2. There *is* a certain hope of a glorious King, who will begin His reign within us *now*, through us for a *lifetime*, and with us *forever!*

2. Hope for an Atoning Savior

Redemption and recovery are God's antidote to human brokenness and loss. Whoever a kingdom messenger faces today, one thing will be certain: honest souls need, and most long for, the confidence of an adequate savior. Examine Isaiah's declarations of forgiveness and salvation from sin and guilt: (a) 1:18—total cleansing; (b) 43:25—failures forgiven

(Please turn to page 174.)

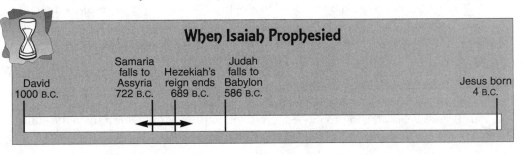

When Isaiah Prophesied

David	Samaria falls to Assyria	Hezekiah's reign ends	Judah falls to Babylon	Jesus born
1000 B.C.	722 B.C.	689 B.C.	586 B.C.	4 B.C.

Isaiah heralds God's future Redeemer-King as • • •

Master Key: God's Son Revealed

After His resurrection Jesus walked with two of His disciples and "expounded to them in all the Scriptures the things concerning Himself" (Luke 24:27). To do so He must have drawn heavily from the Book of Isaiah, because seventeen chapters of Isaiah contain prophetic references to Christ.

Christ is spoken of as the "LORD," "Branch of the LORD," "Immanuel," "Wonderful, Counselor," "Mighty God," "Everlasting Father," "Prince of Peace," "Rod of Jesse," "Cornerstone," "King," "Shepherd," "Servant of Yahweh," "Elect One," "Lamb of God," "Leader and Commander," "Redeemer," and "Anointed One."

Chapter 53 is the greatest single Old Testament chapter prophesying the Messiah's atoning work. No other chapter in either Testament more completely sets forth the purpose of Christ's vicarious death on the Cross. It is quoted many times by New Testament writers: 52:15 (Rom. 15:21); 53:1 (John 12:38; Rom. 10:16); 53:4 (Matt. 8:17); 53:5 (Rom. 4:25; 1 Pet. 2:24); 53:7–8 (Acts 8:32–33); 53:9 (1 Pet. 2:22); 53:10 (2 Cor. 5:21); 53:12 (Luke 22:37). There are also many New Testament fulfillments of details in chapter 53.

Key Word: *Salvation Is of the Lord*

The basic theme of this book, sometimes called "the fifth gospel," is found in Isaiah's name: "Salvation Is of the Lord." Humanity has great need for salvation, and only God's great provision will suffice.

Key Verses: Isaiah 9:6–7; 53:6

Key Chapter: Isaiah 53

Along with Psalm 22, Isaiah 53 lists the most remarkable and specific prophecies of the atonement of the Messiah.

Power Key: God's Spirit at Work

The Holy Spirit is mentioned specifically fifteen times in the Book of Isaiah, not counting references to the Spirit's power, effect, or influence apart from the mention of His name. There are three general categories under which the work of the Holy Spirit may be described:

1. The Spirit's anointing upon the Messiah to empower Him for His rule and administration as King on the throne of David (11:1–12); as the suffering Servant of the Lord who will heal, liberate, enlighten, and bring justice to the nations (42:1–9); as the Anointed One (Messiah) in both His advents (61:1–3; Luke 4:17–21).

2. The Spirit's outpouring upon Israel to give them success in their rehabilitation after the pattern of the Exodus (44:1–5; 63:1–5); to protect them from their enemies (59:19); and to preserve Israel in covenant relationship with Yahweh (59:21). However, Israel must be careful not to rebel and grieve the Holy Spirit (63:10; Eph. 4:30).

3. The Spirit's operation at creation and in the preservation of nature (40:13; *see* also 48:16).

The Lord Jesus, whose earthly ministry was carried out in the power and anointing of the Holy Spirit, as Isaiah had prophesied, promised to pour out His Spirit upon the church to empower it for its ministry in fulfilling the Great Commission.

. . . the antidote to human brokenness and loss.

Introducing

ISAIAH

Author. The first verse of this book names its author as Isaiah, the son of Amoz. The name "Isaiah" means "Yahweh Is Salvation." The vision and prophecy are claimed four times by Isaiah; his name is mentioned an additional twelve times in the book. His name also occurs twelve times in 2 Kings and four times in 2 Chronicles.

The Book of Isaiah is directly quoted twenty-one times in the New Testament and attributed in each case to the prophet Isaiah. Some scholars who have difficulty with detailed prophetic prediction of future events have denied to Isaiah the authorship of chapters 40—66. They term this section Second Isaiah and insist that since these chapters deal with events that took place long after Isaiah's day, such as the Babylonian captivity of Judah, the return from exile, and the rise of Cyrus, the Persian ruler who mandated the return from exile (45:1), they were written later and attached to Isaiah.

If divine inspiration of Scripture and the possibility of the supernatural are accepted, however, one should have no difficulty with the unity of authorship of Isaiah. After all, Isaiah and other prophets of his time prophesied events in the life of Jesus that happened seven hundred years later. Furthermore, critics overlook the fact that Isaiah had access to the Book of Deuteronomy, which predicted both a captivity and a return from exile (Deuteronomy 29; 30). If the mention of Cyrus (44:28; 45:1) is a stumbling block, what about Bethlehem, Jesus' birthplace, named and predicted by Micah, a contemporary of Isaiah (Mic. 5:2)?

Other arguments favor single authorship: (1) key words and phrases are equally distributed throughout Isaiah; (2) references to landscape and local coloring are also uniform. The greater beauty in style of Hebrew poetry in the latter chapters of Isaiah can be explained by the change in subject matter from judgment and entreaty to comfort and assurance. In any case, as clearly likely as it is that Isaiah was written via one penman, contending for this position is not intended to impugn the sincerity of any with contrary opinion.

Date. The prophet states that he prophesied during the reigns of "Uzziah, Jotham, Ahaz, and Hezekiah, kings of Judah" (1:1). Some accept his call to the prophetic office as being in the year that King Uzziah died, which was about 740 B.C. (6:1, 8). It is likely, however, he began during the last decade of Uzziah's reign. Since Isaiah mentions the death of the Assyr-ian king, Sennacherib, who died about 680 B.C. (37:37–38), he must have outlived Hezekiah by a few years. Tradition has it that Isaiah was martyred during the reign of Manasseh, Hezekiah's son. Many believe that the clause "sawn in two" in Hebrews 11:37 is a reference to Isaiah's death. The first part of the book may have been written in Isaiah's earlier years, the latter chapters after his retirement from public life.

If Isaiah began prophesying about 750 B.C., his ministry may have briefly overlapped those of Amos and Hosea in Israel, as well as that of Micah in Judah. (See map, page 184.)

Background. Isaiah prophesied at the most crucial period in the history of Judah and Israel. Both the southern and northern kingdoms had experienced nearly a half-century of increasing prosperity and power. Israel, ruled by Jeroboam and six other minor kings, had succumbed to pagan worship; Judah, under Uzziah, Jotham, and Hezekiah, had maintained an outward conformity to orthodoxy, but had gradually fallen into serious moral and spiritual decline (3:8–26). Secret places of pagan worship were tolerated; the wealthy oppressed the poor; the women neglected their families in the quest of carnal pleasure; many of the priests and prophets became drunken men-pleasers (5:7–12, 18–23; 22:12–14). While there would come one more revival in Judah under King Josiah (640–609 B.C.), it was clear to Isaiah that the covenant recorded by Moses in Deuteronomy 30:11–20 had been so completely violated that judgment and captivity were inevitable for Judah, even as it was for Israel.

Isaiah entered his ministry at about the time of the founding of Rome and the first Olympic games of the Greeks. European powers were not quite ready for wide conquest, but several Asian powers were looking beyond their borders. Assyria particularly was poised for conquest to the south and to the west. The prophet, who was a student of world affairs, could see the conflict that was imminent. Assyria took Samaria in 722 B.C.

Purpose. One of Isaiah's purposes was to declare God's displeasure with and judgment upon sin in Judah, Israel, and the surrounding nations. Almost all the Hebrew words for sin are employed by the prophet. A parallel purpose was to endeavor to turn God's people away from disobedience in order to avert disaster, a purpose that was only partially successful. Perhaps the greatest purpose, however, was to lay a foundation of hope and promise for the faithful remnant of God's people. Thus the book is full of promises of restoration and redemption, of the certain advent of the Messiah, of salvation for all the nations, and of the triumph of God's purposes in spite of intervals of suffering.

Personal Application. No Old Testament book, with the possible exception of the Psalms, speaks more powerfully and appropriately to the modern-day church than the Book of Isaiah. Isaiah has been called both the "messianic prophet" and the "evangelical prophet." He prophesied for all future ages, predicting both the First and Second Advents of Christ. His very name means "Salvation," a salvation not only for those of his day, but also a salvation of the peoples of the nations for all time. This salvation issues from a Savior or Redeemer who has provided a ransom; it is always a vicarious salvation by grace. The prophetic time frame of Isaiah will not close until the Son of David rules over His kingdom of peace (2:1–5; 11:1–10; 42:1–4; 61:1–11; 65:17–25; 66:22–23).

Isaiah speaks as powerfully to our day as he did to the society of his day. He focused a spotlight of holiness upon the sordid sins of Israel; he summoned his contemporaries to cease from their social injustice, their quest for carnal indulgence, their trust in the arm of flesh, and their hypocritical pretense of orthodox religion. He also warned of the consequences of judgment if sin continued.

Kingdom Key *continued from page 171*

and forgotten; (c) 44:22—sin's record eradicated; and (d) 52:13—53:12—an adequate sacrifice promised, bringing a full provision for all human need.

3. Hope for a Universal Deliverer

Beyond the narrowness of his society's provincialism, Isaiah sees God's day of deliverance for all mankind. He sees a multi-ethnic unity in worship, as peoples "flow together" to seek the Lord (2:1–4). Over 750 years before Christ, he prophesied the breaking of the barricade between Jew and Gentile (9:1–2), declaring God's intent to bring together "one body" (Eph. 2:14–18). Finally, he reveals the spirit and style of this Deliverer of all peoples (42:1–4): (a) He is not self-promotional (v. 2); (b) He is tender and restoring (v. 3); and (c) He is unrelenting until He completes His objectives of deliverance (v. 4).

Surveying

ISAIAH

I. PROPHECY OF DENUNCIATION AND INVITATION (PART ONE) 1:1—35:10. Covering just over one half of the entire book, these first chapters are written in a contemporary style. They are prophecies given from the standpoint of Isaiah's day.

A. Messages of judgment and promise (1:1—6:13).

1. An indictment of rebellion, call to repent (1:1–31). Judah and Jerusalem are introduced as being the subjects of this prophecy. The twofold accusation is very clear as it is presented. Incorporating the figure of a diseased body (vv. 5–6), Isaiah indicts the nation because of their ingratitude and their rebellious apostasy. The mention of a remnant establishes the fact that God is showing Himself merciful toward them. The emptiness of their worship comes under the scrutiny of the Lord, and on that basis He announces His rejection of their religious show (11–15; *see* Blood, The). Only genuine repentance and ongoing obedience will save the people. The Lord appeals to them to come and reason together with Him in order that they might understand His mercy and His justice.

2. Future glory, punishment for perversion (2:1—4:1). In this section both Jerusalem and Judah are informed of a forthcoming time of judgment, identified as "the day of the Lord." Such judgment is for sinners and is preparatory for establishing the kingdom as it is described (vv. 1–5). It is a judgment that can cleanse and equip the nation for the kingdom mission. The type of sin that defines the current state of things is seen in detail (3:16—4:1). These sins, which were contemporary to the prophet, require the judgment of the day of the Lord if any national blessing is to be forthcoming.

> **"The righteous . . . shall eat the fruit of their doings"**
> (3:10). While specifying sin-induced consequences for Judah's rebellion, the prophet proclaims a promise to the righteous remnant. By doing right, the righteous plant the seed for a harvest of righteousness to come. In the New Testament the apostle

Paul wrote, "He who sows to his flesh will . . . reap corruption, but he who sows to the Spirit will . . . reap everlasting life" (Gal. 6:8). Abundant life in the Spirit requires sowing to the Spirit—and a harvest is promised!

3. Branch of the Lord (4:2–6). This is Isaiah's first messianic reference. Other prophets use the same figure of a "Branch" to refer to the future Messiah. Isaiah pays additional attention to this idea (11:1–3; *see* Restoration).

4. Song of the vineyard, and assorted woes (5:1–30). The nation of Israel is represented as the vineyard of the Lord. In spite of all the tender care given the vineyard—fertile soil, careful cultivation, a selected vine, etc.—the vineyard fails to produce the desired fruit. Instead, wild grapes of injustice and oppression are the product. A comparative study is found in Matthew 21:33–45, when Jesus pronounces judgment on Israel and announces that the kingdom of God will be given to another nation who will bear righteous fruit.

5. The prophet, his vision, and call (6:1–13). The features of Isaiah's call include seeing God, hearing His voice, and seeing himself as undone and needy. There comes a cleansing and a commissioning of the prophet, followed by the revelation of the extent to which Israel would deteriorate and the news that a remnant would survive and return to the land.

> **"I saw the Lord sitting on a throne, high and lifted up, and the train of His robe filled the temple"**
> (6:1). The one who is called of God carries a responsibility beyond vocational identity. The person who would be God's servant must have a working understanding of who God is. The prophet gained this insight from having seen the Lord. Our worship of God is the best means for gaining such a perspective on our call and leadership. Once we have experienced the glory of the Lord and the sinfulness of self, nothing else matters; He has our focus. (*See* Angels; Seraphim.)

> **"Here am I! Send me"**
> (6:8). Changed in the Lord's presence, Isaiah overhears God's voice calling for a messenger, and he responds. His personal encounter prepares him to discern

God's call to witness: he perceives God clearly (vv. 1–3), understands his own unrighteousness (v. 5), and receives God's forgiveness with humbled heart (vv. 6–7). Becoming a channel of God's grace requires this personal experience of grace. As the Spirit of God purges our hearts in the penetrating light of His presence, we can offer a pure testimony from first-hand experience of His redeeming work (*see* Leadership, Spiritual).

B. Messages concerning Immanuel (7:1— 12:6). After King Ahaz of Judah is threatened by Syria and the northern kingdom of Israel, Ahaz unwisely appeals to Assyria for help despite Isaiah's warning against it.

1. Invasion against Ahaz, Yahweh's sign: a Child's birth (7:1–25). Ahaz and the people are hard-pressed and must decide where to turn for help. Isaiah brings an encouraging word to Ahaz about Judah's not being conquered, but Ahaz turns to Assyria for help instead. Ahaz's unbelief prompts Isaiah to reveal God's sign to all of mankind: a virgin would conceive and bear a Child, who would be Immanuel (God with us, 7:14; *see* Messianic Promises).

> **"If you will not believe, surely you shall not be established"**
> (7:9). Jesus spoke this same principle (John 12:36) at a time when the people around Him had just heard the Father speak from heaven. The issue for kingdom people is to believe and be established! Signs and wonders will appear because Jesus said they would. Time and again, however, He declared the importance of simply believing in Him, regardless of what we see around us. If we would advance the kingdom of God, it must be on the basis of what we believe rather than what we see (Rom. 4:17). Take care to strengthen your kingdom influence through a believing lifestyle.

2. Assyria, the Lord's instrument (8:1–22). The imagery of three children is used to tell of the fall of Damascus and Samaria. Note the prophetic emphasis of each of the names of the children: (a) Shear-Jashub, 7:3 ("a remnant shall return"); (b) Maher-Shalal-Hash-Baz, 8:1–4 ("quick to plunder, swift to the spoil"); and (c) Immanuel, 7:13–14 ("God with us"). Ahaz and the people chose Assyria as their source of help rather than God (*see*

Fear). This unwise action would be met with a flood of Assyrians who would overwhelm Judah. However, because of Immanuel, the nation would not be obliterated by the "flood."

> **"Seek those who are mediums and wizards, who whisper and mutter"**
> (8:19). These words hold a frightening potential if they are ever followed. The source of the "whisper" and the "mutter" is directly linked to the demonic. These utterances will only destroy the person who seeks them. If there is anything of the occult in your background, follow wholeheartedly the example of the believers at Ephesus (Acts 19:19–20), so that the word of the Lord will grow and prevail mightily in you!

3. A great light, God's wonderful Child (9:1–7). Isaiah introduces the Messiah as one who is the Light in the midst of the darkness of judgment. The hope of His coming and presence would ensure liberation for the nation from all of its oppressors. Messiah's humanity and divinity are set forth in the terminology of this passage.

> **"And the government will be upon His shoulder"**
> (9:6). The entitlement to rule that was given to Jesus Christ the Messiah (*see* Messianic Promises) has been transmitted to His body, the church (Matt. 16:18; 28:18–19). As citizens of the kingdom we have been authorized and anointed to move forward, advancing His kingdom under His authority. (*See* Kingdom of God).

4. God's judgment upon Israel and Assyria (9:8—10:19). Verse 9 introduces pride as the reason for God's judgment to be meted out against Israel through Assyrian and Philistine invasions. Whereas Assyria had been an instrument of God to chasten His people, God will not withhold His judgment from them as well.

5. The remnant of Jacob, Branch of Jesse (10:20—11:16). "In that day" depicts the time when the faithful remnant would return, at the day of the Lord. Historically there was a fulfillment of this, but what Isaiah is seeing also has a future fulfillment, which will occur in Palestine. The righteous rule of Messiah and of the kingdom He establishes are the conclusion of this section.

> **"The Spirit of the LORD shall rest upon Him"**
> (11:1–3). The coming Davidic ruler, whose name is Immanuel (7:14), will judge the people with righteousness and fairness (11:3–5), by bearing the effectual qualities of the Spirit's work in His ministry—*wisdom, understanding, counsel, might, knowledge, and the fear of the Lord (v. 2). All these expressions of the Spirit were present within Jesus' life for anointed ministry (Luke 4:14), for "God was with Him" (*see* Acts 10:38). When we receive the Spirit's fullness, Jesus' life becomes alive in us—God is with us—and His ruling authority flows through us in multiplied ministries and gifts (1 Cor. 12:4–11).

6. Songs of praise to the Lord (12:1–6). "In that day," the day of the Lord (*see* YAH), there shall be sung a united song of redemption as the people together recognize Him for who He is.

> **"And in that day you will say: 'Praise the LORD' "**
> (12:4–6). This entire chapter demonstrates the kind of worship and praise that accentuates the life of kingdom people. Singing and shouting are shown to be instruments of spiritual warfare. And special attention is paid to the focus of worship: "the Holy One of Israel [is] in your midst!"

C. Messages of judgment upon the nations (13:1—24:23). The central message of this section is that God's sovereignty is unmistakable and His people should understand that the world was His at creation and continues to be His now and forever.

> **"How you are fallen from heaven, O Lucifer, son of the morning!"**
> (14:12). This familiar verse opens a section that has a dual application. One is a historical reference to Babylon, and the other is a type of Satan. Two things are important to see: "Lucifer" was the devil's name when he was a part of God's heaven (*see* Angels); it is a regal name of splendor, but he is no longer worthy of the name. He is now Satan, and in our dealing with him we should never give him the dignity of the heavenly name. Second, Scripture informs us that it was Satan who weakened the nations. When we engage in spiritual war-

fare, these verses clarify the nature of our Adversary.

"In that day . . . the LORD will punish on high the host of exalted ones"
(24:21). The spiritual war is brought to the forefront in these verses. The prophetic significance perhaps is best seen through the pen of Paul in 2 Corinthians 10:5. The day Isaiah is speaking of prophetically is "today," when all hell appears to be breaking loose around us. At these times, warfare requires a confronting and casting down of the enemy when it exalts itself against the Most High God. Our boldness will come from realizing that God Himself will punish the enemy.

D. Messages of judgment, praise, promise (25:1—27:13).

1. The Lord's deliverance, the kingdom age (25:1–12). The end of the tyranny is declared with particular reference to the conclusion of death and pride. Additionally, the reference to "wonderful" and "counsel" in verse 1 should be compared to the Immanuel prophecy of chapter 9.

2. The Rock of Ages and the resurrection (26:1–21). Whereas the overthrow of the Godless faction was discussed in the previous chapter, we now come to the description of the peace that comes to those who remain faithful. This is signified in the metaphorical description of a well-secured city.

"In that day this song will be sung"
(26:1–4). Isaiah is speaking futuristically about the restoration of Israel as well as the "day of the Lord." The "day of the Lord" holds great portent for every believer in Christ. As ones who have experienced the entry of the kingdom in part, we are the ones who then can sing this song. The passage goes on to talk about walls of salvation and open gates (of praise, *see* 60:18). The song of the Lord is a song of praise based on the salvation He has provided. As ones who enjoy the fruits of salvation, let us enter into His presence through the open gates of praise.

---

3. Doom of oppressors, Israel restored

(27:1–13). No longer is God's wrath against His vineyard (cf. 5:6). God is always more interested in restoring than destroying, as demonstrated in His disposition toward Israel.

"He shall cause to take root . . . and fill the face of the world with fruit"
(27:6). The promise of restoration wipes away the earlier disappointment of an unfruitful vineyard (*see* 5:1–7). Now the Lord is planting anew, watering daily (v. 3), clearing briars (v. 4), and promising expansive fruitfulness (v. 6). The picture is that of the Messiah, the true Vine (John 15:1–8), extending His disciples as fruit-bearing branches to the world. The fruit is the Lord's doing, yet He asks participants to come and be willing to be planted. Believers who are pliable before the Spirit—yielded to His direction and dynamic, willing to be stretched and sent forth—will bear much fruit.

E. Woes to unbelievers and immoral in Israel (28:1—33:24).

1. Woe to drunkards and scoffers (28:1–29). Once again the sins of Israel in Isaiah's day reveal how vulnerable the nation is to the hand of Assyria waiting to overtake them. The leaders come under special attack (7); they have misled rather than faithfully led the people.

(28:11–12). The apostle Paul adapts this passage in 1 Corinthians 14:21 and refers to it as a statement from the Law. He challenges the Corinthian believers to recognize that the Old Testament context from which he takes his quote served as a judgment against those who would not hear the message of the prophet. In the New Testament context, the application is much the same, directed at the hardheartedness of believers. (*See* Holy Spirit Gifts; Rest.)

---

2. Woe to hypocrites in Zion (29:1–24). "Ariel" stands for Mt. Zion/Jerusalem. It will be attacked and crushed, but those who do it themselves will be destroyed, because they only pay Him lip-service. But there is coming a day when the ones who have been deaf and blind to His message will hear and see and once again obey and fear Him.

3. *Woes to those who trust in Egypt (30:1—31:9).* Judah has entered a pact with Egypt and thinks that she is secure against Assyria. Isaiah has warned against this kind of thing. And when it comes to the time of living up to her side of the pact, Egypt does nothing while Assyria invades Judah (chs. 36—37). Note the grace of God in that the very one they would not trust is the One who calls them one more time to come back to Him (31:6).

4. *About the coming King and His reign of peace, mingled with assorted woes (32:1—33:24).* Looking far into the future, Isaiah sees a time (*see* Times) of lasting peace, justice, and righteousness as a result of an outpouring of the Spirit of God on His people (*see* Man). But before the King comes, the existing evil must be done away with and the people shaken out of their complacency.

> **"The Spirit is poured upon us . . . and the wilderness becomes a fruitful field"**
> (32:15–18). The rule of the messianic King is linked to the ministry of the Spirit, whose outpouring turns barren wasteland into fruitful forest. As water penetrates and permeates dry ground, so the Spirit indwells and fills thirsting hearts—and fruitfulness replaces fallowness. The Holy Spirit establishes Christ's rule by saturating our lives with His presence (*see* Dwellings) and power. Thus Jesus becomes real to us, and all that He is and does can impact our lives. This includes such graces as justice and righteousness (v. 16), peace, quietness, and assurance (v. 17)—evidences of the King's establishing His order and rule.

F. Summary (34:1—35:10).

1. *Judgments upon ungodly nations (34:1-17).* This passage is apocalyptic, suggestive (through symbolic language) of the Battle of Armageddon and the ultimate destruction of the Gentile world power. It concludes with a divine promise that Israel will possess and inhabit the land (16–17).

2. *Joy and blessing to God's people (35:1-10).* This chapter brings to conclusion the various "woes" that began in chapter 28. The restoration is a complete one impacting the geography, climate, and people of Israel. Verse 10 is the capstone of this passage, reflecting the ultimate expression of joy for the redeemed.

> **"Behold, your God will come with vengeance, with the recompense of God"**
> (35:3–5). The coming of the Lord will be purposeful, bringing to an end the destructive works of darkness and meting out His justice in the interest of His children. One of the clear indicators of the certainty and imminence of His return is the presence of the kinds of things described in the succeeding verses: when the kingdom is ministered with power and understanding, and blind eyes and deaf ears begin to be opened, we can enthusiastically declare the Second Coming of Jesus.

II. GOD'S DEALING WITH HEZEKIAH 36:1—39:8.

A. God's deliverance of Judah (36:1—37:38). With unsurprising arrogance the Assyrian army challenges the Lord and demands from Hezekiah the surrender of Judah. (*See* Prayer.)

B. God's healing of Hezekiah (38:1–22). With Isaiah's announcement of impending death, Hezekiah turns to God and pleads for God to remember him. The prayer is heard and God's promise to Hezekiah is for an additional fifteen years of life, during which he would see deliverance from the Assyrians.

> **"I have heard your prayer . . . I will add to your days fifteen years"**
> (38:5). According to 2 Kings 20:3, Hezekiah walked faithfully before Yahweh with a loyal heart. Evidently, his terminal condition was not the result of sin in his life. His appeal, made on this basis, was considered by Yahweh, and fifteen additional years were granted to him. Believers praying about sickness and disease should consider the possibility of the reversal of things that have been declared terminal. All things are possible to him who believes.

C. God's censure of Hezekiah (39:1-8). Hezekiah falls victim to his own foolishness and pride when he displays his wealth and power to visitors from Babylon. Isaiah rebukes him, and he in turn responds positively to the rebuke.

III. PROPHECY OF COMFORT AND PEACE (PART TWO) 40:1—66:24.

These twenty-seven chapters comprise what could be referred to as a long messianic poem. Recurrent throughout the poem is the subject of the coming Christ, the restoration of Israel, and the ultimate consummation in the form of the kingdom.

A. The assurances of comfort and peace (40:1—48:22).

1. The greatness of Yahweh the Comforter (40:1–31). The comforting revelation given here is that God's dealing with Jerusalem has justly changed from judgment to grace. This suggests that through repentance and an open receptivity there would come the removal of obstacles that would otherwise hinder full access to God's glory (*see* Evangelism). Compared to God, nations are like weightless dust on scales; regardless of the amount of sacrifice, nothing in creation adds to His glory. It should be clear that from the creation of the universe God is transcendent, and rulers of nations are insignificant and powerless under His judgment. Weary and faint persons can face the difficulties of life when they live in God, for they are renewed in their strength by the Creator's limitless strength (*see* Feed).

2. His challenge to the nations and Israel (41:1–29). God invites the whole world to amass their strength for a dispute with Him. God's case is that He is the sovereign Lord of human events, and the evidence is that of history when He raised up Cyrus in military victories. The only evidence the world can produce outside of God is a humanistic effort toward good. As unworthy but chosen servants, God's people are encouraged that they will be transformed into those who overcome every difficult situation in order for God to be glorified. God challenges the idols and finally provides proof of His absolute deity.

3. Yahweh's servants: Christ and Israel (42:1–25). Through divine enabling God's beloved servant will overcome all. God, as the creative source of all life, will be seen through the servant who brings truth and freedom to all nations. Both heaven and earth are exhorted to praise God. Contrary to God's will (*see* Law), Israel's rebellion led to divine judgment, which left them like a people who had been robbed and placed in prison.

"I have put My Spirit upon Him" (42:1). This first song of Isaiah develops the servant motif by uniting two broader identifications—the servant as national Israel (41:8–13) and as spiritual Judah (44:1–3)—into one Person. Upon Him the Spirit rests for kingdom purpose: to establish a righteous order of justice throughout the earth (vv. 1, 4), a ministry

---

that establishes a standard for truth according to God's principles. When God puts His same Spirit upon us, we are enabled to partner with the King in His charismatic ministry.

"I will . . . give You as a covenant to the people, as a light to the Gentiles" (42:6–7). Isaiah underscores the Messiah's mission, which is the church's mandate. To those who "sit in darkness" in "the prison house" of sin's darkening captivity (v. 7), the Servant-Redeemer offers (1) light—opening of eyes to perceive His great grace, unfolding the pathway to freedom, and (2) covenant—contractual release from prison's punishment, securing the potential of responsible relationship. Our witness announces this glorious liberty, available through the Savior, Jesus Christ. He is the Prison-Opener, who holds "the keys of Hades and of Death" (Rev. 1:18) for all who need freedom, and who offers "the keys of the kingdom of heaven" (Matt. 16:19) to all who would proclaim His freedom.

"Sing to the LORD a new song" (42:10–12). This prophetic exhortation reflects the many times David included this activity in his own devotional walk. The value of singing new songs (that is, songs in the Spirit or in your spoken language that are not of previous composition) has tremendous devotional impact for the believer. "New songs" born of the Spirit of God can help break through spiritual barriers when nothing else seems to be working.

---

4. Yahweh's gracious redemption (43:1—44:5). The people of God need not fear that life's trials will destroy them (*see* Waters). God will deliver them from Babylon as He did in the Exodus. So they should not live in the past; rather, they should look for the present life of God.

"You are my witnesses . . . and My servant whom I have chosen" (43:9–10). The Lord holds His people
continued on next page

continued from preceding page

accountable as His servants and responsible as His witness to the nations. In a courtroom scene, the nations can offer no truthful witness to their deities (v. 9); yet God's people cannot plead ignorance—they were chosen to know Him, believe in Him, and understand who He is (v. 10). Besides Him, "there is no savior" (v. 11). Thus it is incumbent upon us to articulate with intelligent faith the uniqueness of our saving Lord, proclaiming that He alone is God, who offers salvation to all who believe and receive Him.

"I will pour My Spirit on your descendants"

(44:3). God assures Jacob's descendants of the Spirit's outpouring—His blessing—upon those who thirst. The vivid picture of a flood saturating dry, parched ground portrays the expansive and satisfying dimension of the Spirit's blessing. The simple qualification for reception is *desire*—recognizing our need for refreshing, and responding by earnestly seeking His presence. His blessing—the blessing of Abraham (*see* Gen. 12:1–3; Gal. 3:2–9)—is extended beyond Jacob's offspring to those adopted into His family (v. 5). As the Spirit's refreshment is seen in and through us, others are drawn to the fountain of His living water.

5. *Yahweh's indictment of idolatry (44:6–23).* Nothing will explain reality and bring a rock-like stability to human life except God. Thus we should fearlessly witness to the truth He has revealed. Idolatry is irrational and utterly futile. No barriers exist between God and His people since God took care of the sin question through redemption. This is cause for heaven and earth to rejoice.

6. *Yahweh's using Cyrus as a deliverer (44:24—45:25).* God reveals Himself as the sole Creator of heaven and earth and the One who alone gives the meaning of history through His Word; He shapes the future by raising up Cyrus to end the Babylonian captivity and bring restoration to Jerusalem and the temple. Cyrus is oblivious of this divine destiny.

The ultimate consequences of history will fully satisfy Israel's God; foreigners will willingly be brought to God, idolatry will be discredited, and Israel will be saved. Because of the inadequacies of idolatry (*see* In Vain) and the adequacy of God, those who remain are left without a case. Thus all should turn to the Lord and fulfill His redemptive purposes.

"Ask Me of things to come"

(45:11). In the Gospel of John (16:13) Jesus discusses the coming of the Holy Spirit of promise. He assures us that we, kingdom people, can expect to hear from the Lord. In fact, God speaks to us far more than we tend to listen! The issue is not whether God speaks to us but whether we are hearing Him.

"Look to Me, and be saved, all you ends of the earth!"

(45:22–23). God extends His revelation to those who seek Him (v. 19), even to the idolater who has strayed from truth (v. 20). God consistently extends the invitation to know Him (v. 21) if the individual will only turn toward Him. Our witness is the Lord's commission to "the ends of the earth," announcing the righteousness of God available in Christ and inviting all to the personal relationship that righteousness affords. For this purpose the Spirit empowers us, that we might be His "witnesses . . . to the end of the earth" (Acts 1:8).

7. *Yahweh and idols contrasted (46:1–13).* Unlike Babylonian deities which break down in real life, there is continuity between the promise of God and His performance. By comparison with God, idolatry is a costly, lifeless burden with no ability to save humanity.

8. *Yahweh's judgment upon Babylon (47:1–15).* The humiliating fall of Babylon is symbolized by the picture of a delicate lady being degraded to the place of a slave girl. The main moral cause for Babylon's fall is her gross inhumanity to God's people, along with pride. Regardless of her rationalizing, Babylon's judgment is certain. The astrologers were not able to save themselves or the city from judgment.

9. *Yahweh's rebuke to Israel followed by promise (48:1–22).* Before Israel can experience the present joy of the new creation that God has revealed, she must put away her arrogant attitude and give up her rebellion. God's judgment is based in His character, but it is accompanied by mercy. Israel is encouraged to pay attention to God (*see* Teaches) much in

the same manner as creation responds to Him. If she does she will experience an abundance of peace, righteousness, fruitfulness, and immortality.

B. The Lord's Servant, the Author of comfort and peace (49:1—57:21). This section presents us with a sequence of portraits of the Servant and His mission. Add to this presentation of His mission the message He brings to His people. "Servant" is used in a dual manner: on the one hand it represents the nation of Israel, while on the other it can refer to the One who was to come as the true representative of Israel.

1. The Servant's restoration of Israel and light to the nations (49:1–26). In spite of what appears to be fruitlessness, the Servant informs the entire world that he has faith in the mission he has been prepared for from birth. Through God's strength and faithfulness, the despised Servant is encouraged as he embraces the task of bringing a globally impacting salvation to Jew and Gentile. As an agent of salvation, the Servant will usher in the inheritance of God's people, much like the Exodus took Israel from bondage to joy-filled freedom. Zion is assured that restoration will come because of the unfailing love of God.

> **"I will also give You as a light to the Gentiles, that You should be My salvation to the ends of the earth"**
> (49:5–6). The ministry of the Servant-Redeemer reaches beyond the restoration of receptive Jews and offers life–giving light to the Gentiles as well—a Savior for all peoples. This light came on for faithful Simeon, who applied this text to Christ as he witnessed and proclaimed the universal salvation now present (Luke 2:25–32). This light was carried forth by Paul and Barnabas, who applied this text to their ministry, turning from Jew to Gentile in their gospel proclamation (Acts 13:46–47). Our ministry of witness is that of light-bearers—beacons of Christ's light to nations afar and neighbors next door.

2. The disobedience of Israel and the obedience of the Servant (50:1–11). Charging Israel with desertion, God declares His innocence from having failed the nation in any way. It would be inconsistent with His character to do so. The Servant is unjustly sentenced and severely brutalized, but he is certain that he will triumph through God's help. Thus he submits to God's Word like a dedicated student in order to give answer to the dilemma of human despair.

3. Yahweh's remnant encouraged to listen (51:1—52:12). God encourages the people to look back and draw comfort from their history, and to look forward to the greatest exodus which is yet to come. Fear of others who are mere mortals must not be the norm for God's people, because they are the object of eternal salvation. It is time to shake off the grief and lethargy. There is good news, because it is God who pleads the cause of His people, and He is about to escort His people home.

> **"How beautiful . . . are the feet of him who brings good news"**
> (52:7–10). Isaiah's imaginative picture of the messenger speeding across the hills toward Jerusalem, announcing the coming salvation (*see* Redeemed), captures the passion and excitement of gospel proclamation. There is the determination of the messenger—the one who carries Good News of the kingdom, hurrying to pronounce his message, "Your God reigns" (v. 7); and there is the delight of the watchman who receives it (v. 8)—those who hear His salvation break into songs of joy (v. 9). Such is the discipline and desire of our witness, as Paul applies these verses to gospel evangelism (Rom. 10:15). We are the ones who herald the freeing truth of God's Word to all who are ready to receive it.

4. The Servant's triumph through vicarious suffering (52:13—53:12). The transformation of the lowly Servant whose humanity has been effaced to a position of great exaltation is a startling revelation to the nations. This lonely figure is of one who has paid a price. He has borne the whole burden of sin and sickness of others. His silent submission in the midst of an unjust trial leads to his violent death and unusual burial. The spiritual spoils for the Servant as well as through him to others are because his sin-bearing death was the divine plan, bringing release to God's people. (*See* Messianic Promises.)

> **"And by His stripes we are healed"**
> (53:4–5). Jesus began to fulfill these prophetic words when He started His healing ministry (Matt. 8:16–17, citing Is. 53:4; *see* Healing, Divine). Luke defines the
> *continued on next page*

continued from preceding page
Lord's works by telling what He "began" to do and teach (Acts 1:1–2). The obvious reason for this emphasis is because Jesus went on to do the same kinds of works in and through the early church (1 Cor. 12:6; Gal. 3:5). And He continues to do them. Isaiah's words allow for an understanding that the continuing ministry of Messiah includes healing as well as forgiveness for sin.

5. The resulting restoration of Israel (54:1–17). The exhortation calls for Zion, who was like a barren woman, to break forth into singing because the restoration is going to enable her to bear offspring. Her shame will be removed because God is her husband. Her reconciliation is guaranteed because it is grounded in the unchanging covenant love of God (*see* Family Life).

6. God's grace and peace toward repentant sinners (55:1—56:8). The new condition of salvation by grace through faith is illustrated by God portrayed as a market vendor, freely giving the best in life to any who will come to Him. There is a call to repentance based on the urgency of the opportunity, the abundance of divine grace, and the otherwise awful distance between God and man. The lasting memorial that God establishes is His people who move from bondage into authentic existence with Him, accompanied by an inner life of joy and peace. (*See* Word of God.)

7. The rebuke of false leaders and idolatrous backsliders (56:9—57:21). The national leaders are condemned, for they are like insensitive, selfish shepherds. The result of their sin is separation from God. Idolatry, the national addiction, has surfaced once again. The unthinkable act of child sacrifice to demon gods is the unfortunate hallmark of their worship. In spite of all this, the way back to God is open.

"I have seen his ways and will heal him"

(57:18–19). In the Old Testament, Yahweh is always the answer to sin and its devastation in the lives of people. Repentance and returning to submission to Yahweh result in the eradication of both corporate and individual sin. Droughts end, armies are victorious, plagues cease, and individual iniquity and disease are healed. Even when judgment fails to break the addiction to sin, Yahweh remains merciful to heal.

C. The realization of comfort and peace (58:1—66:24).

These final scenes of sin and failure are mixed with scenes of future glory.

1. False and true worship compared (58:1–14). An exposé of the people's sins answers the question of why their religious acts of fasting had accomplished nothing. Their fasts were not acceptable because they were done solely for their own ends even at the expense of others. To be acceptable, fasting must issue from a heart of submission to the Lord and result in practical, loving deeds that center on service to others.

"Is this not the fast that I have chosen?"

(58:6). The power of the fast is directly related to God's involvement. We certainly can decide to fast as we wish; however, the result may be that we simply go without food. When we respond to the "call of the Lord to fast" there is no telling what He has in mind to accomplish! Scripture teaches us that the power of the fast breaks bondage in individuals and weakens the oppression of the enemy. We can be certain that if we respond obediently He will accomplish great and mighty things as a result of our partnering with Him in His fast (*see* Restoration).

2. Israel's sin and God's Redeemer (59:1–21). The real reason for man's separation from God is sin. It breeds deadly destruction. When allowed to go unchecked, sin is a form of death that separates man from God. However, because of a covenant guarantee of God's Spirit and His Word to all generations, redemption is available to all who will repent.

"My Spirit . . . is upon you, and My words . . . shall not depart from your mouth"

(59:21). Spiritual victory is assured as the Lord marches fully armed against His enemies (vv. 17–18), offering redemptive relationship to those accepting His victory (v. 20). Even when the enemy's resistance carries the force of mighty waters, the Spirit raises the battle standard—Christ's victory on the Cross—rallying the righteous sons of Zion (v. 19), those who will stand with Messiah to rule with Him. Through the new covenant we can have God's empowering Spirit upon us, equipping us for spiritual warfare (Eph. 6:10–18)—and the charismatic word gifts become a continuous flow of prophetic victory proclamation (1 Cor. 12:7–11).

3. The well-being and peace of the redeemed of the Lord (60:1–22). Standing in the gap between the shameful Israel and her *glory is the redeeming, avenging God who loves. Here the new city is described. Its light will be God Himself. There will be no more darkness or mourning. The people of the new city will be righteous and fruitful—products of God Himself.

4. The Spirit-anointed Redeemer who brings the kingdom of peace (61:1—62:12). The Lord's anointed Messenger describes the blessings of His liberating mission, which is like a proclamation (*see* Mention) of Jubilee. The once-ruined land is restored, and the people are able to be full-time priests to God. There is coming a universal spiritual fame for the people of God which is the result of a covenant based on the justice of God. The joys of reconciliation are symbolized by the intimate affections of a marriage between Zion and God.

"Because the Lord has anointed Me"
(61:1–3). This messianic prophecy, fulfilled in Jesus, is loaded with implications for Spirit-filled believers. Messiah's ministry as outlined in these verses describes the kind of ministry to which Jesus calls New Testament believers. "Anointed" believers today have the opportunity to continue the works of Christ to the extent described in John 14:12.

"The garment of praise for the spirit of heaviness"
(61:2–3). Common to every believer are those times when discouragement, despair, and depression seem to overwhelm. This passage gives a clear identification of a "spirit of heaviness" which can be dealt with in *praise. The metaphor is one of a garment to be put on. The ultimate victory, however, is contextually linked to the "vengeance of our God." He is the one who overthrows the enemy, while the role of the believer is to put on the garment of praise.

"Surely your salvation is coming; ...and you shall be called Sought Out, A City Not Forsaken."
(62:11–12). The ancient prophet foresees the coming of Christ a second time and identifies those who are with Him. The identification of the sought-out city is none other than the church of Jesus, the New Jerusalem (Heb. 12:22). In his revelation of Jesus, John also identifies the New Jerusalem as the church in Revelation 3:12, and specifically as coming down from heaven (Rev. 21:2, 10). In this light, the living church has reason for a joy-filled existence and a Spirit-filled impetus for mission.

5. God's vengeance and Israel's prayer for deliverance (63:1—64:12). A conversation with an approaching blood-stained conqueror shows that the way to redemption for Zion is through judgment on Edom. It is a work that God Himself must do because there is no one who can help. From the human side, Israel's rebellion is a reminder that the Holy Spirit's redemptive purpose in the Exodus under Moses has not been fully realized. Prayer for another unique Exodus-like revelation is offered. (*See* Rejoices.)

6. God's answer to prayer and Israel's future hope (65:1—66:24). Since God is a sovereign Spirit, He must be worshiped in spirit and in truth. Mosaic sacrifices and offerings are no better than murder and idolatry if they are accompanied by disobedience. Zion will bear her new sons free of labor pains and with no danger of abortion because it will be a divine deliverance. The prosperity and motherly comfort found in Jerusalem (the kingdom of God) will vindicate the servants of the Lord. All nations will see the sign of God's glory as survivors escape a universal judgment. In the new creation, the people of God will be permanent, continual worship will be universal, and the triumph over evil will be complete as the rebels are forever tormented.

"For behold, the LORD will come with fire.... For by fire and by His sword the LORD will judge all flesh"
(66:15–16). This passage looks ahead to the ultimate fulfillment when Jesus returns the second time. Spirit-filled believers should understand that the Father desires to burn away anything of flesh in us today.

continued on next page

continued from preceding page
The presence of the Holy Spirit (in the familiar form of fire) and the Word (in the familiar form of a sword) assure us that

God's Word under the touch of His Spirit will be all that is required to ready His church for that concluding moment.

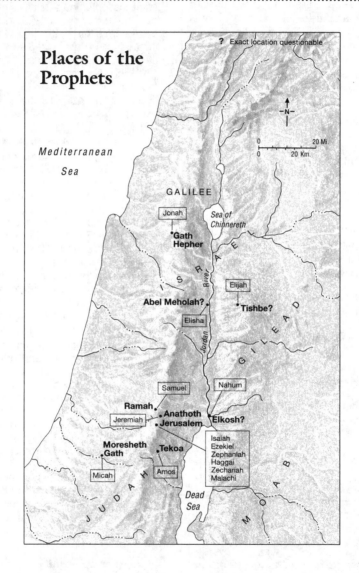

Places of the Prophets

? Exact location questionable

–N–

0   20 Mi.
0   20 Km.

Mediterranean

Sea

GALILEE

Jonah

Sea of Chinnereth

•**Gath Hepher**

I S R A E L

Jordan River

Elijah

Abel Meholah?

•**Tishbe?**

Elisha

G I L E A D

Nahum

Samuel

Ramah

Jeremiah

•**Anathoth**
•**Jerusalem**   **Elkosh?**

Isaiah
Ezekiel
Zephaniah
Haggai
Zechariah
Malachi

Moresheth Gath   •**Tekoa**

M O A B

Micah   Amos

J U D A H

Dead Sea

TRUTH-IN-ACTION through ISAIAH

Truth Isaiah Teaches	**Action** Isaiah Invites
1 Steps to Holiness God's people have often gotten in trouble by employing unholy means toward holy ends and thinking about holy things in an unholy way. The ends do not justify the means. Unholy methodology leads to unholy alliances that can become our undoing.	**8:19, 20** *Reject* spiritual counsel from anyone who does not speak according to the Word of God. *Avoid* any form of the occult or spiritism. **30:1, 2** *Be wary* of plans or relationships God has not ordained and, therefore, will not bless. *Seek the Lord* for wisdom in making plans and entering covenantal relationships. **31:1–3** *Employ* only God's methods to do God's work.
2 Steps in Developing Humility Humility is essential to righteous, Christ-like behavior. Humility and meekness are Spirit-engendered characteristics in the mature believer. Their opposites, pride and arrogance. have a diabolical source. Humility refuses to promote its own interests. but looks out, rather, for the interests of others.	**6:5–7** *Humble* yourself in the presence of the Lord. *Understand* this is the only way to be cleansed and gain a clear perspective on your call to ministry. **14:12–21** *Beware of* selfish ambition that sets itself above God and pride that takes glory from God. *Understand* that they are the hallmarks of Satan's rebellion through which he became God's enemy.
3 Steps to Dynamic Devotion God wants His people to be fully devoted to Him. We cannot feign devotion: God knows our hearts and knows whether what we say has integrity. This is the best reason to pursue worship with a whole heart. We are to seek God's face continually, expressing our wholehearted devotion to Him.	**29:13, 14** *Realize* that God only honors worship that is accompanied by genuine obedience and heartfelt adoration. *Know* that insincere worship can result in diminished wisdom and understanding. **55:1–5** *Hunger* and *thirst* after the knowledge of the Lord (see Phil. 3:10–13) and not after the perishable things this world offers. **62:1–5** *Continually pray* for a fresh moving of the Holy Spirit and revival.
4 Key Lessons in Faith Faith takes God at His word when circumstances seem to deny the truth of His promises. Our ability to endure to the end will depend upon our allowing the Holy Spirit to train us in this kind of faith.	**8:12–15** *Believe* that the Lord is your refuge, and *overcome* worldly fear that threatens in times of major crisis. **40:29–31** *Understand* that spiritual strength comes from waiting upon the Lord. **42:23—43:7** *Trust* that God knows how to protect His righteous ones from the judgment and wrath He pours out upon others. **55:10, 11** *Choose to believe* that God's Word is the most powerful force in the universe and *act* accordingly.
5 Steps to Dealing with Sin We may believe that if we sin, we will be immediately aware of it: but sin is subtle, and our hearts may not perceive or acknowledge our guilt. So those most in need of repentance and cleansing may have no awareness of their spiritual state. Therefore, we must continually examine ourselves before the Lord, asking Him to enlighten our hearts to any unacknowledged sin and to cleanse us of all unrighteousness.	**1:16, 17** *Understand* that when we disagree with God's agenda, we must repent and change our way of thinking. **1:18–20** *Understand* that repentance and obedience are reasonable to a willing and obedient heart, but folly to one with a resistant and rebellious attitude. **5:12** *Celebrate* the Lord's goodness ahead of turning to amusement and entertainment. *Judge* any such tendencies in yourself and repent. **53:4–12** *Believe* that your sins and iniquities were placed on Jesus, the sinless Lamb of God. *Choose* to forgive others' sins against you. **59:1–15** *Know* that God often does not answer our prayers because our own sin and iniquity prevents it. *Allow* unanswered prayer to become an occasion for soul-searching and possible repentance.

KEYS TO JEREMIAH
The Kingdom Beyond Loss

Kingdom Key: God's Purpose in View

Jeremiah's ministry is often characterized by the "jeremiad"—the prophecy of woe or doom. This view, however, does not capture Jeremiah's total message. Though he announced the certainty of Jerusalem's fall—due to its backslidings and socio-spiritual decay—beyond this loss he declared God's promise of a divinely provided possibility for recovery.

1. Personal recovery is available *now*. The message of God's kingdom offers every individual the present possibility of change. Though every circumstance surrounding a person may be collapsing, personal transformation is possible. In 3:11, 14, and 22, an appeal is made to turn from "backslidings": "If you will . . . return to Me . . . you shall not be moved" (4:1). The pathway of return is shown in 6:16–17: (a) refuse novelty, by committing to God's changeless truth (v. 16); and (b) listen to the alarm call of the Holy Spirit (v. 17).

2. Practical living while reaping sin's harvest. As Judah reaped its bitter harvest of judgment for having sown the seed of sin, Jeremiah's instructions to those who would be taken to Babylon offer practical counsel today (ch. 29). Though people coming to Christ are forgiven as instantly as they are spiritually reborn, quite often a long history of having

....

When nations fall, God is still present.

....

sown to the flesh leaves an unpleasant harvest of pain. Marital discord, economic deterioration, physical problems due to addictions or dissipation—such conditions are not resolved overnight, even though a person has been saved. For such a season, Jeremiah offers words of practical wisdom: We are to (a) "settle in"—that is, commit to the long run, not the short sprint (v. 5); (b) seek to minister to others while we recover, rather than focus only on our own needs (v. 7); and (c) receive the confidence of God's secured destiny for our future (v. 11).

Note: Jeremiah is also the key to keeping modern day Israel's destiny in clear biblical focus. The message of the *presence* of God's kingdom, as Jesus preached it for us today, has prompted some to neglect or deny the *promises* of the kingdom that God has made for national Israel's future. Some hold the idea that

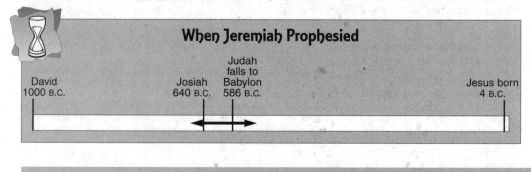

When Jeremiah Prophesied

David		Josiah	Judah falls to Babylon		Jesus born
1000 B.C.		640 B.C.	586 B.C.		4 B.C.

Jeremiah: a model of a believer who remains

Jeremiah 11:3, 10–17 consummated the covenant God had made with Israel as a people, and that since they broke that covenant they no longer have a special place today in God's prophetic purpose. But Jeremiah 32:37–41 and 33:19–26 show differently. God still has a distinct covenant with and role for Israel. It is this great fact—the promise of a "kingdom beyond loss"—that gives rise to Paul's exegesis of Israel's future destiny as a people and as a nation. (*See* Romans 9—11; also Ezekiel 36—48.)

Master Key: God's Son Revealed

Through his action and attitude Jeremiah portrays a lifestyle similar to that of Jesus, and for this reason he may be called a type of Christ in the Old Testament. He showed great compassion for his people and wept over them. He suffered much at their hands, but he forgave them. Jeremiah is one of the most Christlike personalities in the Old Testament.

Several passages from Jeremiah are alluded to by Jesus: "Has this house, which is called by My name, become a den of thieves in your eyes?" (7:11; Matt. 21:13); "Who have eyes and see not, and who have ears and hear not" (5:21; Mark 8:18); "Then you will find rest for your souls" (6:16; Matt. 11:29); "My people have been lost sheep" (50:6; Matt. 10:6).

Power Key: God's Spirit at Work

A symbol of the Holy Spirit is fire. God assured Jeremiah, "I will make My words in your mouth fire" (5:14). At one point Jeremiah wanted to stop mentioning God, but "His word was in my heart like a burning fire shut up in my bones; I was weary of holding it back, and I could not" (20:9). Today we would call this the work of the Holy Spirit in Jeremiah.

> **Key Word: *Judah's Last Hour***
>
> *In Jeremiah, God is seen as patient and holy: He delays judgment and appeals to His people to repent before it is too late. Judah's time for repentance will soon pass.*
>
> **Key Verses:** Jeremiah 7:23–24; 8:11–12
>
> **Key Chapter:** Jeremiah 31
>
> *Amid all the judgment and condemnation by Jeremiah are the wonderful promises of Jeremiah 31. Even though Judah has broken the covenants of her great King, God will make a new covenant and write it on their hearts.*

Apart from the normal work of inspiring the prophet and revealing God's message to him, the Holy Spirit is the one to carry out the promise of a new covenant that will put God's law in the minds of His people and write it on their hearts. The external commands of the old covenant will now be internalized, and the believer will have the power to conform in every respect to the moral law of God. The knowledge of God will be universal, and other peoples will be included in God's blessing. Under the old covenant forgiveness was promised, but now forgiveness comes with the promise that God will remember their sin no more.

a constant witness in the face of opposition.

Introducing
JEREMIAH

Author. Jeremiah, son of Hilkiah, was a prophet from the priestly town of Anathoth (*see* map, page 184) and perhaps was descended from Abiathar. The meaning of his name is uncertain, but "Yahweh Exalts" and "Yahweh Throws" are possibilities. More is known about the personal life of this prophet than any other in the Old Testament because he has given us so many glimpses into his thinking, concerns, and frustrations.

Jeremiah was commanded not to marry or have children to illustrate his message that judgment was pending and that the next generation would be swept away. His closest friend and associate was his scribe Baruch. Other than this he had few friends. Only Ahikam, Ahikam's son Gedaliah, and Ebed-Melech seem to qualify. Partly, this was because of the message of doom proclaimed by Jeremiah, a message contrary to the hope of the people and one that included a suggestion of surrender to the Babylonians. In spite of his message of doom, his scathing rebuke of the leaders, and contempt for idolatry, his heart ached for his people because he knew that Israel's salvation could not be divorced from faith in God and a right covenantal relationship expressed by obedience.

Date. Jeremiah prophesied to Judah during the reigns of Josiah, Jehoiakim, Jehoiachin, and Zedekiah. His call is dated at 626 B.C., and his ministry continued until a short time after the fall of Jerusalem in 586 B.C. The prophet Zephaniah preceded Jeremiah slightly, and Nahum, Habakkuk, and Obadiah were contemporaries. Ezekiel was a younger contemporary who prophesied in Babylon from 593 to 571 B.C.

Background. Jeremiah began his ministry in the reign of Josiah, a good king who temporarily delayed God's judgment promised because of the frightful rule of Manasseh. Events were changing rapidly in the Near East. Josiah had begun a reform, which included destruction of pagan high places throughout Judah and Samaria. The reform, however, had little lasting effect on the people. Ashurbanipal, the last great Assyrian king, died in 627 B.C. Assyria was weakening, Josiah was expanding his territory to the north, and Babylon under Nabopolassar, and Egypt under Necho, were trying to assert their authority over Judah.

In 609 B.C., Josiah was killed at Megiddo when he attempted to prevent Pharaoh Necho from going to the aid of the Assyrian remnant.

Three sons of Josiah (Jehoahaz, Jehoiakim, and Zedekiah) and a grandson (Jehoiachin) followed him on the throne. Jeremiah saw the folly of the political policy of these kings and warned them of God's plan for Judah, but none of them heeded the warning. Jehoiakim was openly hostile to Jeremiah and destroyed one scroll sent by Jeremiah by cutting off a few columns at a time and throwing them into the fire. Zedekiah was a weak and vacillating ruler, at times seeking Jeremiah's advice, but at other times allowing Jeremiah's enemies to mistreat and imprison him.

Content. The book consists mainly of a short introduction (1:1–3), a collection of oracles against Judah and Jerusalem which Jeremiah dictated to his scribe Baruch (1:4—25:14), oracles against foreign nations (25:15–38; chs. 46—51), events written about Jeremiah in the third person, probably by Baruch (chs. 26—45), and a historical appendix (ch. 52), which is almost identical to 2 Kings 24 and 25. The prophecies in the book are not in chronological order.

Jeremiah had a compassionate heart for his people and prayed for them even when the Lord told him not to do so. Yet he condemned the rulers, the priests, and false prophets for leading the people astray. He also attacked the people for their idolatry and proclaimed severe judgment unless the people repented. Because he knew God's intentions, he advocated surrender to the Babylonians and wrote to those already in exile to settle down and live normal lives. For his preaching he was branded a traitor by many. Jeremiah, however, had their best interest at heart. He knew that unless God's covenant was honored, the nation would be destroyed. God was also interested in individuals and their relationship to Him. Like Ezekiel, he stressed individual responsibility.

Jeremiah was just a youth when he was called to carry a severe message of doom to his people. He attempted to avoid this task but was unable to remain silent. The people had become so corrupt under Manasseh that God must bring an end to the nation. Defeated and taken into exile, they would reflect on what had happened to them and why. Then, after proper chastisement and repentance, God would bring a remnant back to Judah, punish the nations who had punished them, and fulfill His old covenants with Israel, David, and the Levites. And He would give them a new covenant and write His law on their hearts. David's throne would again be established, and faithful priests would serve them.

The oracles against foreign nations illustrate the sovereignty of God over the whole world. All nations belong to Him and all must answer to Him for their conduct.

Literary Features. Jeremiah uses many literary

styles and devices. His book is the longest in the Bible, and while some chapters are written in prose, most are poetic in form. His poetry is as beautiful and lyrical as any in Scripture. He effectively makes use of repetition, such as the phrase "by the sword, by the famine, and by the pestilence" (14:12 and note), the threefold "earth, earth, earth" (22:29) and "the temple of the LORD" (7:4), and words such as "a hissing" (18:16). Symbolism occurs in the use of the linen sash (13:1), the potter's earthen flask (19:1), and the bonds and yokes (27:2). Cryptograms are used in 25:26 and 51:1, 41. Jeremiah is a keen observer of plants and animals (2:21, 23). He has given us many beautiful phrases (2:13; 7:11; 8:20, 22; 31:29, 33).

Personal Application. Jeremiah saw that religion was essentially a moral and spiritual relationship with God, a relationship that required the devotion of each individual. Each person is

responsible for his or her own sin. The new covenant (31:27–40) is the spiritual bond between God and the individual. This is a new and unconditional covenant that involves God's writing the Law on human hearts, the forgiving of iniquity, and the remembering of sin no more. All this was fulfilled in the Incarnation of Christ and in the gospel He preached.

Much of the message of Jeremiah is relevant because it is timeless. Sin always must be punished, but true repentance brings restoration. Our idolatry, which consists of such things as wealth, talent, or position, is called by new names, but the sin is the same, and the remedy is the same. God calls for obedience to His commands in a pure covenantal relationship. Sin requires repentance and restoration; obedience leads to blessing and joy.

Surveying
JEREMIAH

I. CALL OF JEREMIAH 1:1–19. Jeremiah is a young man when God calls him to prophesy to a hardened Judah. God Himself has designed Jeremiah's ministry and affirms to Jeremiah that: he has been set apart from before birth to become a prophet to the nations (v. 5), he is to speak what God commands (6–10), and he is to prepare himself to face opposition (17–19).

Jeremiah is given two visions at this time. One is of an almond branch, the first of the trees to bud in the spring. Jeremiah's messages will blossom to an early fulfillment (11–12; see Ready). The other vision is of a boiling cauldron, symbolizing disasters to be poured out on Judah from the north (13–16).

II. COLLECTION OF DISCOURSES 2:1— 33:26.

A. Earliest oracles (2:1—6:30). First love forsaken (2:1–13). Jeremiah begins with an indictment. Israel loved God when He brought her into the land (2:1–4). Now Israel has abandoned the source of living water (see John 4:10–14; Rev. 21:6) and carved idols that, like a cracked cistern, will never hold the waters that can meet their spiritual needs (2:12–13).

God is rejected (2:14–30). Judah's present depressed condition is a direct result of aban-

doning God (14–19). Her rejection was conscious and willful.

Punishment assured (2:31—3:5). God cannot simply welcome back His adulterous "wife," Israel, after she has prostituted herself with a host of lovers (idols). Her past actions show the falseness of her present cajoling pleas for mercy (3:1–5).

Faithless Israel (3:6—4:19). Though Judah has seen Israel's destruction, she has not heeded the warning. She has continued to give herself to idolatry. Still, God calls out to individuals to return to Him. The remnant of believing individuals who do turn will be regathered and restored, but it is too late for the corrupt society to respond as a whole (3:14—4:4; see Understanding). Jeremiah's vision of a ruined land moves him to weep in anguish (4:18–19; see also ch. 6). But the future is fixed: the Lord has pronounced a sentence of devastation.

None righteous (5:1–31). Jeremiah searches desperately through the streets of Jerusalem for one righteous person (cf. Gen. 18:16–33), but there is none to be found (see Backsliding). Judgment on such a nation and people is a moral necessity (1–9)! Jeremiah hoped that the fire of his prophetic message would purge the impurities from Judah, as a refiner's fire purges metal ore. Instead, it has only demonstrated conclusively that the people of Judah are totally corrupt (26–29).

B. Temple sermon and cultic abuses (7:1— 8:3). Jeremiah is sent by God to the temple gates to announce the certain approach of ruin and exile (7:1–29). In this message he confronts their blind superstition which argues that because God has chosen Zion (1 Kin. 9:3), He is bound to protect it. The result is a shallow, cultic faith, which emphasizes ritual and ignores the moral aspect of covenant relationship with God. Jeremiah admonishes the people that true religion requires walking in God's ways. Certain destruction will be the result if they do not repent.

C. Miscellaneous materials (8:4—10:25). The reasons why judgment must strike God's people are carefully explained. (*See* Correct; Restoration; Slightly.) The punishment is fixed: wailing and death will soon fill this land (9:17–25).

Jeremiah condemns their idolatry (Is. 44:6–20). Judah has turned from the Maker of the heavens and earth to bow down to images no more powerful than a scarecrow in a melon patch (10:1–16)!

D. Events in Jeremiah's life (11:1—13:27). Jeremiah is sent through Judah to teach that obedience to law is vital to the covenant relationship of each generation with the Lord (11:1–17). His message rouses such hatred that his life is threatened (11:18–23). The plot against Jeremiah's life has shaken him. He turns to God, questioning God's justice in permitting the wicked to prosper even temporarily (12:1–4).

God's answer (12:5–17). Judgment will come swiftly. The people will be uprooted, but the enemy will be uprooted in his turn, so that a remnant can return to relationship with God (14–17).

Five warnings (13:1–27; *see* Humble).

E. Drought and other catastrophes (14:1—15:21).
Drought (14:1–12). When a drought strikes Judah (1–6), the people beg God to send water, but ignore their sins (7–9). Jeremiah is told not to pray for this people (10–12). This theme, that Judah's sins have at last brought her beyond the help of prayer, is sounded often in Jeremiah (cf. 7:16; 11:14).

False prophets (14:13—15:2). False prophets, whom God has not sent, tell lies in the Lord's name. Jeremiah is told to announce to them a disaster so sure that even if Moses and Samuel should pray for Judah, God would not listen.

Four destroyers (15:3–21). Graphically, the prophet now exposes the fate that awaits his people.

F. Warnings and promises (16:1—17:18). To communicate the grim reality of the approaching disaster, Jeremiah is told not to marry and have children. Children born in his day will only die (1–4). Also, the prophet is not to mourn the death of friends, nor is he to take part in any feasting (5–9). Instead, Jeremiah is told to speak words that condemn and to hold up the sin and faithlessness of God's people (10–13; *see* Strength).

Psalms of trust (17:5–18). The wickedness of humanity's incurable heart problem can be healed only by trust in God (5–10). This beautiful psalm concludes with an appeal by Jeremiah for vindication (14–18). He has not run from his heartbreaking and lonely task. He has served as God's shepherd to a wayward people.

> **"Heal me, O LORD, and I shall be healed"**
> (17:14). Sometimes a person needs healing in his or her emotions. Such is the case with Jeremiah. In the circumstances to which he was called, emotional support and healing were necessary. Additionally, being rejected by those to whom he was called to preach further bruised his soul. Declaring the Lord to be his praise implies Jeremiah's understanding of how he would receive the healing for which he prayed. When we face sicknesses of the soul, we are wise to recognize the resource of praise as an instrument of the Lord's healing (30:17; *see* Save).

G. Keep the Sabbath day holy (17:19–27). Despite the personal anguish Jeremiah feels, he faithfully obeys when God sets him at the gates of Jerusalem on the Sabbath to confront those who break the Sabbath law and work on the holy day.

H. Lessons from the potter (18:1—20:18). Jeremiah's next series of messages is stimulated when he is sent to watch a potter at work. As he worked, occasionally a defect would appear and the clay could not be worked properly. Then the potter squeezed the clay into a lump and began again. God will deal with His people as the potter deals with unmanageable clay (1–6); they will be crushed so He can begin again to shape them toward the holiness His nature requires Him to demand.

In the message that follows, God reveals an important biblical principle. When He announces judgment on any nation, that judgment is conditional. If its people repent and change their ways, judgment will be withheld. In the same way, national blessing is contingent on moral behavior (7–10).

Jeremiah is told to gather some priests

and elders and bring them, with a clay jar, to the Valley of the Son of Hinnom (19:1–9). As the leaders watch, Jeremiah breaks the jar. This is what the Lord will do to their nation and city.

Again Jeremiah stands in the temple court and preaches disaster. This time, however, Jeremiah is beaten and placed in stocks. He is released the next morning. But the strain of his lonely ministry tells on the prophet, and the constant stream of derision throws him into deep depression (20:7–18).

"Sing to the Lord! Praise the Lord! For He has delivered" (20:13). The connection between praise and the idea of deliverance is obvious when "deliverance" is understood in its broadest application. The greatest deliverance for any believer is Christ on the Cross at Calvary. Our salvation is the beginning of a lifetime of deliverances that in turn will issue into a lifetime of praise for perceptive believers.

I. Oracles against kings, prophets, and people (21:1—24:10). As Nebuchadnezzar mounts an attack against Judah's fortified border cities, Zedekiah sends representatives to Jeremiah. Jeremiah only repeats his message of doom. The God who once fought for His people will now fight against them (3–7).

Jeremiah stands in the king's palace to deliver a word of condemnation. The same themes are repeated: Do justice. Keep the covenant, or the palace will become a ruin.

The Branch (23:1–8). Jeremiah warns those who are Israel's shepherds (a term that applies to both political and spiritual leaders), that they will be punished for their evil. In the future God himself will provide a "righteous branch" to rule Israel wisely. (See Fill.)

Delusion (23:25–40). The prophets who fill Jerusalem with lies and lead the people astray live in a world of delusion (25–32).

After the second deportation, in 597 B.C., Jeremiah passes the temple and sees two baskets of figs. One is ripe and succulent, the other shriveled and spoiled (24:1–2). God tells Jeremiah that the good figs represent the exiles. God will watch over His people in Babylon, give them a heart to know Him, and bring them back to the land. But Zedekiah and those in Jerusalem will be treated like rotted fruit. They will be rejected and destroyed.

J. The Babylonian Exile (25:1—29:32).

Babylon is identified as the agent of God's judgment (25:1–10).

Seventy-year captivity (25:11–14). The prophet also reveals the length of time the Hebrew people will be held captive in Babylon: seventy years.

The cup of wrath (25:15–38). This symbolic cup is now held out to Judah and the nations of the world, as Jeremiah looks beyond the captivity to a day when all evildoers will be punished.

Jeremiah stands in the court of the temple and passionately announces his prophecy of desolation (26:1–6). Furious priests and prophets demand that Jeremiah be put to death for the unpatriotic message (7–9). Jeremiah survives (10–19), but the danger is real; another prophet has already been executed (20–23).

Jeremiah sends a word from the Lord to surrounding nations, to the king, and to the populace. Those who submit to Nebuchadnezzar will survive. Those who resist will be crushed and taken into exile (27:1–17; see Intercession).

Jeremiah again acts out his prophecies. He appears at the temple wearing a yoke (27:1–2), to symbolize submission to Babylon. Hananiah confronts Jeremiah and announces in God's name that Babylon's yoke will be broken. He claims the captives taken by Nebuchadnezzar will be returned, with all the temple booty.

Hananiah then takes the wooden yoke Jeremiah wears and breaks it (28:1–10). Shortly afterward, God sends Jeremiah to Hananiah. This man is persuading God's people to trust lies! Hananiah will soon die and God will forge an unbreakable yoke of iron to fit the shoulders of his sinning people. Within two months Hananiah is dead (11–17).

Jeremiah sends a letter to those who survived the long trek to Babylon. They must adjust to their captivity, for seventy years will pass before anyone returns (29:4–14; see Spiritual Warfare). Jerusalem and the homeland will be destroyed (15–23).

K. The book of consolation (30:1—33:26). Among Jeremiah's grim warnings of disaster are three chapters that contain one of the Old Testament's most significant revelations of hope for all mankind.

The restoration of Israel (30:1—31:22). The repeated phrase "that day" (30:7–8) immediately indicates that the restoration of which the prophet now speaks takes place at history's end (see Isaiah 2–4). Then the promised Davidic ruler, the Messiah, will save God's people (30:2–10; see Man).

> ### "Sing . . . shout . . . proclaim, give praise"
>
> (31:7). The directives of this verse are familiar territory for Spirit-filled believers! The Lord specifies that this type of praise is related to testifying to onlookers about the purposes of God and His relationship to His people. When we express our praise with singing, shouting, and proclamation, we should remember that through these means God is being represented in His greatness to those who would wonder about Him and what His relationship to mankind is really all about.

Righteousness within (31:23–40). After the return described in these chapters, the land of Judah will again be addressed as a "righteous dwelling" (23). The Lord announces He will "make a new covenant with the house of Israel." The new covenant will write God's law on hearts, not stone tablets.

The prophet purchases a field (32:1–44). Jerusalem is now surrounded by the Babylonian army. In the midst of this grim situation, a relative appears and asks Jeremiah to buy a plot of land in occupied territory. Jeremiah makes the purchase and seals the deeds in a jar, where they will be protected for decades. Years from now the deed will be good, for the lands of Judah again will be bought and sold (1–15). The purchase is a sign of trust in God's faithfulness. As Jeremiah's words of judgment have come true, so will the prophet's promises of restoration.

Restoration reaffirmed (33:1–26). Still in confinement (32:1–2), Jeremiah is told by God of a restored Judah to stand where there is now only death and desolation (1–13; see Call; Spiritual Warfare).

III. HISTORICAL APPENDIX 34:1—35:19.

A. Warning to Zedekiah (34:1–7). Jeremiah tells Zedekiah that while he will be taken captive, he will not die by the sword, but peacefully in Babylon (1–7). This promise may have been made by God in response to a movement to free Jews who were enslaved by their fellow Hebrews. The Law provided that servitude should last only six years and then freedom be granted. The king led the people to return to this practice and to make a solemn covenant of blood in the temple itself, before the Lord.

B. Manumission of slaves revoked (34:8–22). But the people changed their minds and forced their fellow countrymen back into service (8–16)! Judah violated this covenant just as they violated their covenant

relationship with God and will be delivered up to those who seek their lives.

C. The symbol of the Rechabites (35:1–19). Jeremiah invites to the temple a family which remained faithful to the command of a distant ancestor. God commends the Rechabites and promises to bless them for their faithfulness. What a contrast they make to the people of Judah, who have ignored and disobeyed the word of the living God!

IV. TRIALS AND SUFFERINGS OF JEREMIAH 36:1—45:5.

A. Jehoiakim and the scrolls (36:1–32). Jeremiah is restricted and not allowed to go to the temple. God commands him to record all the prophecies he has spoken concerning Judah, then sends the secretary, Baruch, out to read the prophetic words Jeremiah cannot deliver (1–7). The words are reported to the king. When he hears them, the furious Jehoiakim cuts the scroll apart and burns it (8–26). He orders the arrest of both Jeremiah and Baruch. But the words of the first scroll are quickly rewritten, and "many similar words are added."

B. Siege and fall of Jerusalem (37:1—40:6). As the grip of the Babylonians around Jerusalem tightens, terror heightens the tensions within its walls. A clique of officials determined to resist Babylon have effectively taken over authority. King Zedekiah, who wavers fearfully between resistance and surrender, is too frightened to exercise his supposed authority. In this deteriorating situation, Jeremiah's life is in great danger.

Jeremiah imprisoned (37:1–21). Jeremiah's continual urgings to surrender to the Babylonians made him very unpopular. When the siege is temporarily lifted and Jeremiah attempts to go out, he is arrested and accused of deserting to the enemy. He is beaten and locked in a cell controlled by one of the most vicious of his enemies. Zedekiah intervenes, and Jeremiah is moved to a cell where his life will not be in danger.

Jeremiah placed in an empty cistern (38:1–13). The resistance leaders demand that Jeremiah be killed, for his messages discourage the soldiers and the people of Jerusalem. The cowardly Zedekiah fears opposing them, and Jeremiah is turned over. The aged prophet is lowered into a now-empty cistern, where water had been stored for the siege. Now he sinks into the muck at its dark bottom and is left to die.

Another official of the king, Ebed-Melech, gets permission from Zedekiah to take a troop of men and rescue Jeremiah. His quick action saves the prophet's life, and Jeremiah is returned to confinement in the courtyard of the royal guard.

    Questioned by Zedekiah (38:14–28). Jeremiah is questioned by the crumbling king and repeats the familiar words that God has given him. Jeremiah remains confined until the city falls.

    Jerusalem falls (39:1–18). After a long siege Jerusalem's wall is breeched and resistance crumbles. Zedekiah flees but is captured near Jericho. Jeremiah is found in his prison by the Babylonians. When he is recognized, he is treated with respect (*see* Free).

C. Gedaliah and his assassination (40:7—41:18). After Jerusalem is destroyed, only a few of the poor are left in Palestine. They are given land to farm, and Gedaliah is appointed governor of this last remnant. Jeremiah elects to remain.

    Gedaliah assassinated (40:7—41:15). Gedaliah reassures the few who remain that they will be safe under Babylonian rule. But almost immediately Gedaliah is assassinated! The killers escape.

D. The flight to Egypt (42:1—43:7). The Jews who remain are terrified of the Babylonian's response to this new act of rebellion. They beg Jeremiah to pray to God for direction and promise to obey His word. (*See* Dwell.)

E. Jeremiah in Egypt (43:8—44:30). When the prophet tells them to remain in Israel, and not to fear—and especially warns them against a flight to Egypt—Jeremiah is accused of lying! Again God's word is directly disobeyed and the frightened company heads south.

    When Jeremiah speaks out to condemn the idolatry the survivors practice, and to threaten further disaster (44:1–14), the whole assembly tells Jeremiah openly that they plan to continue their worship of idols! They will listen to no more words from God (15–18). A final word of judgment is announced. These people will perish in Egypt and never return to the land. The pharaoh with whom they think they have found shelter will be destroyed by Nebuchadnezzar, just as Zedekiah was destroyed (19–30).

F. Oracle to Baruch (45:1–5). Jeremiah's secretary is told not to expect any reward, but is promised that his life will be spared.

V.   ORACLES AGAINST FOREIGN NATIONS 46:1—51:64. Jeremiah records a series of prophecies against Judah's enemies. God's people have undergone discipline. Surely pagan nations will not escape.

A. Against Egypt (46:1–28).

B. Against the Philistines (47:1–7).

C. Against Moab (48:1–47).

D. Against the Ammonites (49:1–6).

E. Against Edom (49:7–22).

F. Against Damascus (49:23–27).

G. Against Kedar and Hazor (49:28–33).

H. Against Elam (49:34–39).

I. Against Babylon (50:1—51:64). This extended oracle looks toward the time when Babylon will be destroyed in her turn. Of special note are the promise of a true revival to take place among the captives (50:4–5) and the description of Babylon's destiny (50:39–40; *see* World).

VI. HISTORICAL APPENDIX 52:1–34. In an appendix, the Book of Jeremiah provides another description of the fall of Jerusalem and the razing of the temple. The words the great prophet uttered about Jerusalem have passed from the realm of vision into history. The historic record of Jerusalem's fall stands before us today as a testimony to the trustworthiness of the prophetic word.

A. Zedekiah's reign (52:1–3).

B. Siege and fall of Jerusalem (52:4–27).

C. Summary of three deportations (52:28–30).

D. Release of Jehoiachin from prison (52:31–34).

TRUTH-IN-ACTION through JEREMIAH

Truth Jeremiah Teaches	**Action** Jeremiah Invites
1 Guidelines for Growing in Godliness The godly person learns to perceive his life from God's standpoint. He is teachable and adjusts his way as the Lord instructs. He is careful to avoid presumption in all he says and does.	**1:6–8** *Seek to understand* that the Lord's calling on your life is based on His power and not simply on your natural abilities. *Believe* that God will empower you to do all that He demands. **5:3** *Learn* that responsiveness to the Lord's correction or discipline keeps the heart soft and helps you to hear God's voice clearly. **14:14–16** *Be absolutely certain* God has spoken before saying "the Lord told me," and *do not speak* presumptuously in His name.
2 Keys to Wise Living The wise individual accepts God's testimony about human inclination to sin. He judges himself by the Word of God, rather than by the flattering words of those around him.	**5:31** *Be cautioned* at how people naturally incline to follow carnal leadership due to shortsightedness. **6:10** *Open* your ears to God's Word, even when it is not pleasant to you. **7:28** *Realize* that receiving correction results in the ability to discern the truth of a matter.
3 Steps to Dynamic Devotion The goal of single-minded devotion is to know God. Remember that the final judgment will be measured ultimately by how much we have come to know the Lord and allowed Him to live through us.	**9:23, 24** *Define* your life and service by your desire to know God. **31:34** *Understand* that the focus of the New Covenant is a people who know their God. *See* how God defines eternal life in terms of the substance of your relationship with Him.
4 Key Lessons in Faith A person of faith takes God at His Word and realizes that God is committed to His Word. He knows that God honors His Word above His name and has settled in his heart that God intends to bring His Word to fulfillment. He remains confident in God's promises and takes His warnings seriously.	**1:9, 10** *Believe* that God's Word is sovereign over the nations and all of history. **1:11, 12** *Rest* in the confidence that God is always working to fulfill His Word. **6:16** *Evaluate* any "new" teaching, and *stay close* to the plain meaning of God's Word. *Be assured* that you cannot improve on the Bible. **29:10–20** *Remember* that God intends good for His people to give them hope.
5 Lessons for Leaders Those God calls to leadership among His people must be willing servants of His Word. God creates, builds faith, and governs through His Word. But the Bible tells us that we must have our minds renewed. Without this transformation, we "follow the devices and desires of our own hearts." Leaders must face this fact and remain faithful, not being too concerned about how popular they are.	**1:17–19** Leaders, *believe* that the Lord is the strong defense of all those He commissions and sends to proclaim His Word. *Have courage* when facing opposition for preaching the truth of God's Word. **37:16** Leaders, *bear in mind* that God's servants have often been persecuted for faithfully proclaiming God's Word without compromise. **43:2–7; 15:19–21** Leaders, *do not compromise* the truth due to disfavor or *alter* God's Word to appease men. *Trust* that the Lord protects those He sends to speak His word. **23:25–27** Teachers, *know* that the Lord will not hold anyone guiltless who speaks his own opinions in the Lord's name. **48:10–12** Leaders, *stand fast* in faithfully preaching the full counsel of God.

KEYS TO LAMENTATIONS

The Kingdom Beyond Grief

Kingdom Key: God's Purpose in View

Jerusalem's devastation by Nebuchadnezzar's troops, coupled with the massive relocation of thousands of Judeans to Babylon, presented as distressing and destructive a scene as one might imagine. In the rubble after the warfare, Jeremiah lifts his lament for sin's just deserts; but as with his prophecy in the book by his name, even in the Book of Lamentations there is a strain of divine mercy and hope.

The message of God's kingdom *never* leaves a devastated scene or person without some prospect of hope. Even when a tumultuous circumstance is the direct result of an individual's ignorance, rebellion, or failure, the word of the kingdom brings a ray of promise.

Notice in chapter 1 some experiences that still bring despair today:

1. Loneliness resulting from a death or separation (1–2).

2. Pain or agony due to affliction (3).

3. Sorrow resulting from lost or displaced children (5).

4. Shame or loss due to one's having sinned gravely (8).

Into such human devastation two themes must be declared—the first with compassion, the second with expectancy.

(a.) With compassion, declare the justice of God's judgment. The kingdom messenger should always affirm that God's jus-

> **Amidst grief and loss, mercy still abides.**

tice is sure, however gracious His ways. Sin breeds confusion, gives place to evil, invites destruction, and produces death. There is nothing vindictive about God's judgment. His essential need to deal retributively and correctively with humanity should never be declared in a harangue. Instead, Jeremiah *weeps* as he explains the cause of judgment: "The LORD is righteous" (1:18). Note with what detail he explains the ways God has executed judgment (2:1–2, 5, 7–8).

(b.) With expectancy, declare the mercies and call of God. When judgment comes, the proper question should never be, "Why this?" but rather, "Why not more?" In 3:22, the answer is given: God's mercies have left us *alive*, with hope for a future. Further, even though He must deal justly with violations of the divine Law, He still is halting—"He does not afflict willingly" (3:33).

(Please turn to page 196.)

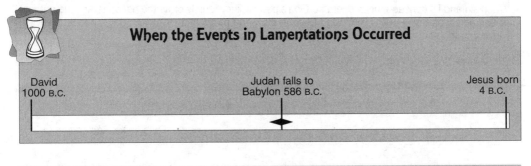

When the Events in Lamentations Occurred

David 1000 B.C.	Judah falls to Babylon 586 B.C.	Jesus born 4 B.C.

Lamentations holds forth the contrast between • • •

Kingdom Key *continued from page 195*

Jeremiah reveals that (1) God's compassions are unfailing (3:22–23), (2) God is good (3:25), and (3) God's judgment is not a permanent disposition of His will toward anyone— He "will not cast off forever" (3:31). Even in the worst of circumstances, when judgment is deserved and delivered, the message of the kingdom is that there is still mercy beyond grief.

Master Key: God's Son Revealed

This book shows how weak people are under the Law, and how unable they are to serve God in their own strength. This drives them to Christ (Rom. 8:3). Even in these poems, however, glimpses of Christ shine through. He is our hope (3:21, 24, 29). He is the manifestation of God's mercy and compassion (3:22–23, 32). He is our redemption and vindication (3:58–59).

Power Key: God's Spirit at Work

Divine grief over the sins of Israel (2:1–6) reminds us that the Holy Spirit was, and still is, often grieved by our behavior (Is. 63:10). Repentance is also an indication of the work of the Holy Spirit among God's people (3:40–42; John 16:7–11).

Key Word: *Lamentations*

Three themes run through the five laments of Jeremiah. The most prominent is the theme of mourning, but with confession of sin and an acknowledgment of God's righteous judgment comes a note of hope in God's future restoration of His people.

Key Verses: Lamentations 2:5–6; 3:22–23

Key Chapter: Lamentations 3

Lamentations 3:22–25 expresses a magnificent faith in the mercy of God—especially when placed against the dark backdrop of chapters 1, 2, 4, and 5.

The Road to Renewal

When sin and its consequences overtake God's people, individually or as the nation Israel, the author of Lamentations holds onto a profound hope in God and prays that He will lead His people back to Him along the path of sorrow and repentance to restored faith.

Sin ——▶Suffering (1:8)

          Sorrow ——▶Repentance (1:20)

                    Prayer——▶ Hope (3:19-24)

                              Faith——▶ Restoration (5:21)

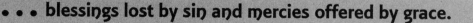

• • • blessings lost by sin and mercies offered by grace.

Introducing
LAMENTATIONS

Name of the Book. As was their custom, the Jews used the first word of the book as its title, and it originally became known as *'ekah,* "How!" This word was commonly used to mean something like "Alas!" Compare its use in 2:1; 4:1; and Isaiah 1:21. Some also referred to the book as *qinot* or "lamentations," however, and this is how we arrived at the English title.

Author. The author is not named, but traditions long before Christ claim that Jeremiah wrote it. Some scholars have doubted this and point to a number of differences between the use of poetic style, words, and expressions in this book and those used in the Book of Jeremiah, as well as to certain differences in emphasis. However, the prophet was known to compose laments (2 Chr. 35:25), and there is an even more impressive array of similarities, as we shall see when we examine the text. The differences, therefore, could simply be due to the different circumstances under which Lamentations was written.

Historical Background. The Judahites had been able to think of themselves only as God's chosen race. As such, they felt that they would always experience good things. God had made covenants of blessing with them, but these were conditional. Blatant disobedience would mean that the pleasurable aspects of blessing would be replaced by punishment. The fulfillment of the promises of blessing could always skip a few generations of disobedient Israelites.

The books of 2 Kings and 2 Chronicles describe the moral decline of the kingdom of Judah (in spite of prophetic warnings) that would lead to its defeat and captivity (*see* 2:17). When King Zedekiah rebelled against the Babylonians, to whom Judah was subject, Nebuchadnezzar came against Jerusalem (2 Kin. 24:20). While he was besieging it, the people inside were starving. When he breached the wall, Zedekiah and the soldiers managed to escape (2 Kin. 25:4). But they were soon taken captive. Nebuzaradan, Nebuchadnezzar's official, destroyed most of Jerusalem, burned the temple, and carried all but the poorest people into exile (2 Kin. 25:8–12).

The poems of this book seem to have been composed during and after the time in which all this was happening. These poems are especially heartrending when they contrast the former blessings and strengths of Judah with the chaos and suffering their sin had brought on them (*see* note on 1:7). The chosen, favored people had lost everything and were in a hopeless position. Everything of significance had been destroyed. But the poems also describe the ministry of Jeremiah, sent again as a prophet to speak about the changed circumstances of God's people. He helped them to give the necessary expression to their grief and to comfort them in it. He also encouraged them to think about the hand of God on them in punishment and helped them to submit penitently to the judgment they deserved until it had passed (3:28–33). Only after the people were completely humbled would they be able to think of restoration.

Structure. Laments were typically composed as poetry in the ancient world. Jeremiah had already written some (*see* Jer. 7:29; 9:10, 19), and so had other prophets. (*See* Ezek. 19:1–14; Amos 5:1–3.) But this book contains the longest and best known of such poems. There are five poems. The first four are acrostics, or poems in which each stanza begins with a successive letter of the Hebrew alphabet. These were probably acknowledged as special artistic achievements in those days. A number of the psalms are acrostics. (*See* Pss. 25, 34, 37, and 119.) This device may have assisted memorization, but it also seems to indicate here that the poet was expressing all his feelings from *Aleph* to *Tau,* or as we would say, from *A* to *Z.* He was working through every grief, hurt, and fear, and was opening up completely to both humanity and God.

The fifth poem is not an acrostic, probably because it is a personal prayer, which could have made the material unsuitable for the acrostic form.

There is little systematic arrangement of subject matter throughout the book as a whole, except for a possible climax in chapter 3 and a progressive conclusion in the final two chapters. But this is, after all, the nature of grief. It waxes and wanes, goes away, and returns again unexpectedly.

Themes. Lamentations features six major themes, all linked with the concept of suffering:

1. Their Suffering Was the Result of Their Sin. This strong theme is acknowledged in each chapter (as in 1:5; 2:14; 3:42; 4:13; 5:16). By the time the poems were written, this was obviously fully accepted. Even the Babylonians acknowledged the fact (Jer. 40:3). They knew that their suffering had not come upon them by chance. It was due to the wrath of God provoked by their sin (2:1). He was dealing with their spiritual condition, and they were supposed to take it personally.

2. Their Suffering Was Seen as Coming from God Rather Than from Men. The Babylonians were no more than an instrument in His hands. The fact that He was the ultimate cause is brought out throughout the book. No

less than forty-four verses refer to this fact—an average of 1 out of every 3.5 verses. A few examples are 1:13, 15; 2:1, 4; 3:1, 37–38.

3. Their Suffering Could Direct Them Toward God. The prophet is constantly conscious of God, of His purposes, and of His dealings with His people. There is no indication here of suffering resulting in a total abandonment of God or an eradication of His principles from their minds.

4. Suffering, Tears, and Prayer Belong Together. They were encouraged to pour out their hearts to God, to weep before Him, and to tell Him all the details of their pain, grief, and frustration. Each chapter, except chapter 4, ends with a prayer. But then the whole of chapter 5 is a prayer, as though making up for this lack. The prayers are both detailed (2:20–21; 5:1–10) and emotional (1:20–21; 3:48–51). They contain the language of grief and repentance (1:20; 3:40–42), and are an indication that it is entirely appropriate to pray like this when the occasion demands it.

5. Prayer Should Always Look for Some Ray of Hope. It should never be completely given over to sorrow. After the detailed descriptions of suffering and sorrow in the first two and one-half chapters, a new understanding seems to surface in 3:21–24. Here the poet speaks about hope, and about God's mercies, compassion, and faithfulness. It was a realization that a manifestation of God's discipline did not mean that His love had ceased. When the discipline had accomplished His purpose, the circumstances would change (3:31–32). God may have been using Babylon, but that did not mean that they were His elect or that He favored their cruel methods (3:34–36). The future held a vindication of Israel over their enemies (3:58–66).

6. Their Responsibility Was to Submit to Their Sufferings Patiently. Their sorrow had to be accepted in patience, with the realization that it would end when God's will had been accomplished (3:26–32).

Personal Application. This book has a great deal to say to us today:

1. The best way to survive grief is to express it. It needs to be shared with others and with God. There is a therapeutic value in working through each aspect of sorrow.

2. The destruction of Jerusalem and the lessons God taught His people were so significant that the Jews started reading this book at an annual service to commemorate the destruction of Jerusalem. They did not want the painful experience to be forgotten. Defeats as well as victories need to be remembered. If the church would commemorate some of its failures, for which God has had to discipline it, these failures would be less likely to be repeated.

3. When Christians have received much blessing and enlightenment from God, and then turn their backs on Him, it is an extremely serious matter. Privileges do not protect us either from responsibility or from discipline. They increase our responsibility and our culpability, and deserve more serious discipline. This is particularly true of church leaders.

4. To what extent does God punish His people for their sins today? Christ's death for us and His Resurrection have certainly redeemed us. We do not bear retributive punishment for any sin we commit, since Christ has suffered in our place. We are living under a different covenant than did the Jews of 586 B.C. Even unbelievers are not normally punished for their sins until the next life (2 Pet. 2:4–10). But both believers and unbelievers sometimes have to suffer the consequences of past sins, such as drug addiction, drunkenness, and murder. And God often allows suffering in our lives to discipline us (Heb. 12:3–17). Through it we learn to obey Him and become stronger Christians (vv. 9, 12–13).

Another consideration is church discipline. Christians who turn their backs on God should undergo some discipline in their home church. God sometimes disciplines people Himself by allowing suffering (1 Cor. 5:1–6) and even death (Acts 5:1–11). The main purpose of discipline, however, is restoration (2 Cor. 2:5–8). Even though we are not retributively punished for our sins, God will sometimes allow us to suffer when we have sinned in order to restore us to fellowship with Him. We need to submit to what God is doing and attempt to learn from the experience. If it is God's discipline, it will last as long as is necessary. There is no quick-fix solution to some of these problems and no easy way out. Discipline will direct us to God, drive us to prayer, and bring us into submission. We need it.

5. Of course, not all suffering is the result of God's discipline. Satan, too, can bring suffering on us (Job 2:7; Luke 13:16), but the suffering he brings is destructive rather than restorative.

Surveying
LAMENTATIONS

I. THE FIRST POEM: THE MISERY, SIN, AND PRAYER OF JERUSALEM 1:1–22.

A. The defeat, humiliation, sorrow, and sin of Jerusalem (1:1–11). Deserted Jerusalem is slumped in ruins, like a widow who has lost all her children (1–7). Her sins have been exposed, and she is despised by all (8–11).

B. Telling the uncaring world about her punishment (1:12–19). Though she stretches out her hands piteously, no one comes near to comfort her, and her enemies delight in the torment the Lord has brought upon her (12–22; *see* Righteous).

C. A prayer for vindication in great suffering (1:20–22).

II. THE SECOND POEM: GOD'S DESTRUCTION AND THE PROPHET'S REACTION 2:1–22.

A. How God Himself has destroyed Israel (2:1–10). The fierce anger of the Lord has caused the ruin of Jerusalem (1–9).

B. The prophet's sorrow, hopelessness, and exhortation to prayer (2:11–19). Jerusalem's condemned people faint, caught in the grip of famine (11–13). All the lying visions of the false prophets, who promised perpetual security, are now seen to be illusions. The Lord has done what He has planned (14–17)!

C. Judah's anguished prayer (2:20–22). In deep anguish the poet weeps for those who once peopled Jerusalem.

III. THE THIRD POEM: GOD'S SEVERITY AND MERCY; HUMANITY'S SUBMISSIVENESS AND PRAYER 3:1–66.

A. The severity of punishment leads to thoughts of mercy (3:1–24).

B. Submissiveness and humility bring mercy (3:25–39). Hope is found in God's past faithfulness to Israel and in the very fact that the exiles have survived the destruction of Judah with their lives (*see* Wait).

C. Their repentance comes too late (3:40–47).

D. Prophet and people trust God for eventual vindication (3:48–66). All the tears and terrors now experienced are a consequence of the people's sins (48–54). But Jerusalem's outcasts can call on the Lord to redeem them and to punish their enemies (55–66).

IV. THE FOURTH POEM: DEVASTATION, THE RESULT OF DISOBEDIENCE 4:1–22.

A. The devastation of the people and their leaders (4:1–11). Fondly the poet recalls the past, as picture after picture of better days is cast against the raw horror of Jerusalem's destruction.

B. Disobedience and its results (4:12–20). The poet confesses that all this has come about because of sin, particularly the sins of the priests and the prophets who were charged by God with the care of His flock.

C. Edom to be punished and Israel to be relieved (4:21–22).

V. THE FIFTH POEM: A PRAYER RECORDING JERUSALEM'S SUFFERING AND FINAL PLEA 5:1–22.

A. A reminder of their pitiful state (5:1–10). The collection of dirges ends with a poem in which the writer expresses the exiles' cry to the Lord for mercy.

B. No one exempt from suffering (5:11–14). Sin has worked its sure consequences and the joy has left the people's hearts.

C. All joy and pride gone (5:15–18).

D. The final, desperate plea (5:19–22). At last a true cry of repentance is expressed, as the poet expresses the prayer of the people. "Turn us back to You, O LORD, and we will be restored" (v. 21; *see* Remain).

TRUTH-IN-ACTION through LAMENTATIONS

Truth Lamentations Teaches	**Action** Lamentations Invites
1 Steps to Knowing God and His Ways Lamentations calls attention to God's faithfulness and righteousness in judgment. No judgment, chastisement, or reproof ever comes as the result of divine caprice. It is always God's righteous response to sin and rebellion. God loves us and allows calamity only as a last resort to restore us to righteousness.	**1:18** *Remember* that the Lord is always righteous in His judgment. *Know* that judgment is the fruit of sin and rebellion. **3:22–32** *Acknowledge* that the Lord is faithful to His Word. *Wait* on the Lord and *expect* daily expressions of His mercy to you. **3:31–33** *Be confident* that judgment will often be followed by compassion and restoration because of God's love. *Understand* that God does not relish judgment as a disciplinary means. even though it is sometimes necessary. **3:58–66** *Entrust* yourself completely to the care of the Lord, who is completely just in all His dealings.
2 Guidelines for Growing in Godliness The godly person responds to judgment with intercession and prayer, recognizing that only the repentance of his people can effect the healing of their land (see 2 Chr. 7:14).	**2:19** *Let* impending judgment call you to seasons of intercession for God's people. *Implore* God to pour out a spirit of repentance and to show mercy. **3:25, 26** *Seek the Lord, expecting* that He will bring good things to pass for you. *Wait* quietly for Him to show you His salvation in any distress.
3 A Key Step to Dynamic Devotion All too often God's people wait too long to develop good devotional habits. It is vitally important that we train our youth to seek God earnestly.	**3:27** *Realize* that it is never too early to begin spiritual development. *Encourage* young people to become earnest and fruitful in their pursuit of God. *Challenge* and *inspire* those who would otherwise postpone godliness until later in life.
4 Keys to Wise Living The wise person does not complain about adversity knowing that it can contribute to godliness. Response with dependence on God's Word and repentance, when needed, will bring restoration.	**3:39–42** *Do not complain* about adversity in your life. *Accept* God's discipline as an expression of His love to turn us from rebellion or disobedience.
5 Lessons for Leaders All of the major prophets put a great deal of responsibility for Israel's and Judah's sins squarely on the shoulders of their leaders: their priests, their prophets, and their kings. This should become a strong admonition for those who lead God's church today. When God's people are judged due to the sins of their leaders, God's people tend to lose all respect even for legitimate leadership and faithful leaders thus often lose righteous influence.	**1:14** Leaders, *be reminded* that when God's leaders fail to deal with sin, He holds them responsible for the judgment, which inevitably follows. **4:12–16** Leaders, *walk obediently, remembering* that your sins can cause the downfall of God's people, bringing judgment to whole churches or fellowships of churches.

KEYS TO EZEKIEL
Accountability and the Kingdom

Kingdom Key: God's Purpose in View

Anyone in Adam's race may try to escape responsibility for unwise or inappropriate actions, negligence, or unbecoming behavior. Since the Fall, when Adam avoided personal responsibility and pointed to Eve's actions as his excuse for sin, the squirming quest to escape accountability seems to be a genetically implanted bad habit. As with Ezekiel, we are called to minister the word of God's kingdom to a society that rejects moral absolutes, thereby supposing to escape moral and spiritual responsibility. Ezekiel makes two assertions against this disposition:

1. We are responsible for our attitudes. More than twenty times, the prophet declares God's assessment: "This is a rebellious house/people/nation" (2:3, 5–6, 8). The root of disobedience and sin is identified as a fundamental attitude of *bitterness* (Hebrew *mawraw,* translated "to rebel"). Commonly today, as it was six hundred years before Christ, people try to explain their actions by blaming those who made them unhappy, uncomfortable, inconvenienced, or who corrected them. Thus, the proposition argues, the bitterness of resentment that ignited the rebellious action is presumed to be the right of the rebel, and thereby the fault lies with the object of the resentment. Ezekiel's diagnosis instead is, "They are impudent and stubborn" (2:4).

2. We are responsible for our sin. The

> ### Each person is account-able to God's law.

prophet confronts a proverb of his time, "The fathers have eaten sour grapes and the children's teeth are set on edge" (18:2). The quote was an effort of some to deny their own responsibility. They did not recognize that every human being must answer for himself or herself. These supposed that the second commandment, which explains how the sins of parents have a long-term impact on their offspring (Ex. 20:4–6), gives them an excuse for their sin: "I couldn't help it. I got it from my parents!" But those seeking to hide behind this excuse forgot that *every* commandment begins with at least an implied *"You."* There are no second-hand commandments. Thus Ezekiel dismantles the argument with a direct charge from God: "The soul who sins shall die" (18:4), and if

(Please turn to page 203.)

When Ezekiel Prophesied

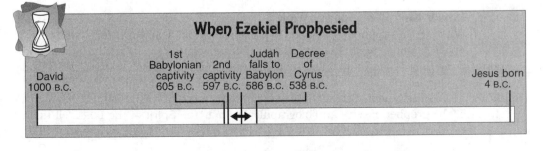

| David 1000 B.C. | 1st Babylonian captivity 605 B.C. | 2nd captivity 597 B.C. | Judah falls to Babylon 586 B.C. | Decree of Cyrus 538 B.C. | Jesus born 4 B.C. |

Ezekiel: individuals who neglect their • • •

Master Key: God's Son Revealed

In Ezekiel, Christology and the Person and work of the Holy Spirit are inextricably bound together. Although a messianic figure is not clearly discernible in Ezekiel's final vision, several messianic titles and functions in the book indicate that a Messiah is part of his eschatological vision.

The title "Son of Man" occurs some ninety times in Ezekiel. While the title is applied to Ezekiel himself, it was appropriated by Jesus as His favorite self-designation. Therefore, Ezekiel may be regarded as a type of Christ. As such, Ezekiel was empowered as a prophetic voice of the messianic age when "the Spirit of the LORD fell" upon him (11:5). The descent of the Holy Spirit upon Jesus at Jordan empowered Him to articulate the advent of the messianic kingdom (Luke 4:18–19).

Another messianic title is reflected in the vision of the Lord God as the divine Shepherd who gathers again His scattered flock (34:11–16). The figure evokes images of Jesus as the Good Shepherd (John 10:11–16).

Ezekiel further develops the fundamental idea of Israel as "a kingdom of priests and a holy nation," which was rooted in the covenant of Sinai (Ex. 19:6). A restored sanctuary in the midst of a regathered people whose head is the King-priest, the Davidic Messiah (37:22–28), foreshadows the restored tabernacle of David, the church (Amos 9:11; Acts 15:16).

A final messianic prophecy of Christ employs the figure of a sprig of cedar planted by the Lord Himself on a lofty mountain, which becomes a lofty cedar providing fruit and nests for birds. This nature metaphor, like "the Root of Jesse" (Is. 11:1, 10; Rom. 15:12), serves to represent the future Messiah. Birds and trees represent Gentile nations to show Christ's universal reign.

> **Key Word:** *The Future Restoration of Israel*
>
> *The broad purpose of Ezekiel is to remind the generation born during the Babylonian exile of the cause of Israel's current destruction, of the coming judgment on the Gentile nations, and of the coming national restoration of Israel.*
>
> **Key Verses:** Ezekiel 36:24–26; 36:33–35
>
> **Key Chapter:** Ezekiel 37
>
> *Central to the hope of the restoration of Israel is the vision of the valley of the dry bones. Ezekiel 37 outlines with clear steps Israel's future.*

Power Key: God's Spirit at Work

Whether the prophetic revelation is presented symbolically in visions, signs, parabolic actions, or in human speech, Ezekiel claims for them the power and authority of the Holy Spirit. In addition, there are numerous references to the Spirit of God in the book. One might almost characterize the Book of Ezekiel as the "Acts of the Holy Spirit" in the Old Testament. Several of these references merit special notice.

In 11:5, the prophet asserts autobiographically that "the Spirit of the LORD fell upon

(Please turn to page 204.)

• • • responsibility for their souls must pay a price.

Introducing

EZEKIEL

Author. The author, whose name means "God Strengthens," is identified as "Ezekiel the priest, the son of Buzi" (1:3). Although this identification has been challenged, there seems to be no valid reason for doubting it. He was probably a member of the Zadokite priestly family that came into prominence during the reforms of Josiah (621 B.C.). He was trained in the priesthood during the reign of Jehoiakim, was deported to Babylon (1:1; 33:21; 40:1) in 597 B.C., and settled in Tel Abib on the Chebar Canal near Nippur (1:1). His ministry briefly overlapped Jeremiah's.

Date. Ezekiel's call came to him in 593 B.C., the fifth year of Jehoiachin's reign. The latest date given for an oracle (29:17) is probably 571 B.C., making his ministry about twenty years long. The death of his wife occurred about the time of the destruction of Jerusalem in 586 B.C. (24:1, 15–17). Exiled in the second siege of Jerusalem, he wrote to those yet in Jerusalem about its imminent and total destruction, including the departure of God's presence. Parts were also apparently written after Jerusalem's overthrow. (*See* map, page 184.)

Content. Ezekiel's personality reflects a mystical strain. The immediacy of his contact with the Spirit, his visions, and the frequency with which the word of the Lord came to him provide a connection between the older ecstatic prophets and the classical writing prophets. His spiritual experiences also anticipated the activity of the Holy Spirit in the New Testament. To him rightly belongs the title "charismatic."

Ezekiel's message was addressed to a demoralized remnant of Judah exiled in Babylon. The moral responsibility of the individual is a primary theme in his message. Corporate responsibility no longer shields the individual.

Each individual must accept personal responsibility for the national calamity. Each individual is responsible for his or her individual sin (18:2–4). It is the weight of the cumulative sin of each individual that contributed to the breaking of God's covenant with Israel, and each bears a share of the blame for the judgment that resulted in the exile to Babylon.

The book is easily divided into three sections: Judah's judgment (chs. 4—24), the heathen nations' judgment (chs. 25—32), and future blessings for God's covenant people (chs. 33—48).

Two theological themes act as a counterpoise in the prophet's thought. In Ezekiel's doctrine of man, he placed the emphasis on personal responsibility (18:4, "the soul who sins shall die"). On the other hand, he emphasized the divine grace in the rebirth of the nation. The repentance of the faithful remnant among the exiles would result in the re-creation of Israel from the dry bones (37:11–14). The divine Spirit would quicken them to a new life. By this emphasis on the Holy Spirit in regeneration Ezekiel anticipated the New Testament doctrine of the Holy Spirit, especially in the Gospel of John.

Personal Application. Three very important personal, relevant lessons can be learned in Ezekiel. First is the importance of individual moral responsibility. Although it is true that God still blesses and corrects entire local churches (Revelation 2; 3), His primary dealings are with individuals. As such, one cannot appeal to the righteousness of others as his righteousness nor need he fear personal correction for the sins of another (18:20).

Second, Ezekiel teaches that though God is reluctant to discipline His people severely, He must. He is a righteous and jealous God as much as He is merciful and forgiving (12:1–16).

Third, Ezekiel assures us that God will ultimately triumph in history. His enemies may be winning battles now, but future judgment will totally destroy them (35:1–15).

Kingdom Key *continued from page 201*

"he is just; he shall surely live" (18:9).

All the wonders of divine forgiveness, mercy, and grace, as well as the blessing of knowing the joy and privilege of restored

dominion through Christ, become the portion of those who say, "God, be merciful to me a sinner" (Luke 18:13; *see* also 1 John 1:6–10).

Power Key *continued from page 202*

me, and said to me." The oracle that follows is thus God's Word in Ezekiel's words, inspired by the Holy Spirit. The same chapter (11:24) presents the Spirit as active in a vision: "Then the Spirit took me up and brought me in a vision by the Spirit of God into Chaldea, to those in captivity."

Perhaps the best-known instance of the Spirit's activity is in chapter 37, the vision of the valley of dry bones: "The hand of the LORD came upon me and brought me out in the Spirit of the LORD, and set me down in the midst of the valley; and it was full of bones" (v.

1). The subsequent vision relates the spiritual rebirth of the remnant then in exile.

A final aspect of the Spirit's action in the life of the prophet is found in 36:26, "I will give you a new heart and put a new spirit within you." It is not solely an external act of the Spirit "falling upon" someone, but the prophesied subjective experience of the Spirit's presence within, such as Ezekiel uniquely experienced when "the Spirit entered" him (2:2). Ezekiel anticipated the new covenant's "new birth" experience, which would be done by the Spirit.

Surveying
EZEKIEL

I. THE OPENING VISION AND CALL OF EZEKIEL 1:1—3:21.

A. Introductory visions (1:1–28). Ezekiel has been in exile in Babylon since the second deportation, settled with his fellow countrymen in a district along one of the great irrigation canals (the "Chebar River") that make the land around the capital city so fertile (vv. 1–2).

In his stunning vision, Ezekiel realizes that he sees the glory of the Lord and falls face down before Him. The figure of God is glimpsed by Ezekiel, so radiant He cannot be described, but bearing human form. This is far more than others have seen!

B. The prophet's commission (2:1–3:21). Ezekiel is told to stand and is given his commission. God sends him as a prophet to the rebellious people of Israel.

> **"Then the Spirit entered me when He spoke to me, and set me on my feet"**
> (2:1–2). Under the Spirit's charge, Ezekiel is assigned a prophetic ministry to the remnant of Judah exiled in Babylon. Ezekiel would first have to *digest*—eating the scroll spread before him as the message was incorporated into his soul (2:9—3:2), and then *declare*—speaking His Word boldly despite the resistance announced beforehand (3:4–9). The Spirit through His indwelling first embodies God's Word in our hearts, and then through His filling empowers us to proclaim it (Acts 4:31).

Ezekiel is called "son of man" some ninety times in this book. Later the phrase will have messianic implications, as when Jesus applies it to Himself (e.g., Matt. 8:20; 12:8). Here the phrase simply emphasizes Ezekiel's humanity.

Ezekiel's mission (3:1–27). Ezekiel eats a scroll on which God's words to rebellious Israel are written, symbolizing his full acceptance of the message and mission (1–3).

> **"And go, get to the captives, to the children of your people, and speak to them . . . whether they hear, or whether they refuse"**
> (3:10–11). Ezekiel's prophetic call as a watchman (v. 17), who warned the people concerning Jerusalem's imminent destruction and their moral responsibility, illustrates a key principle of proclaiming God's truth: the command is to go and speak, whether the message is received or not. The variables of receptivity and resistance function as guideposts in our proclamation, but they do not garrison the message. What we receive into our heart and hear with our ears of the Lord's Word (v. 10) we speak unashamedly and boldly, allowing the Spirit to quicken, convict, and draw hearts to the place of receptivity and response.

Ezekiel has been appointed a watchman to warn the wicked. The title "watchman" is often applied to true prophets (Is. 62:6; Jer. 6:17). Their responsibility is to be sensitive to the word of God, to communicate it accurately, and thus to warn God's people of danger.

II. PROPHECIES AND VISIONS OF JERUSALEM'S DESTRUCTION 3:22—24:27.

A. Oracles of judgment (3:22–7:27). Ezekiel begins his prophetic ministry to the exiles by acting out four oracles that concern the fate of Jerusalem.

Ezekiel builds model siege works (4:1–3) against a clay tablet that represents Jerusalem. This is a sign to the exiles of that city's coming fate.

The prophet is told to lie on his side a fixed number of days, to represent the years of Israel's and Judah's rebelliousness (4:4–8).

During this time he eats a daily ration of about eight ounces of food and a pint of water (4:9–17)! His own diet reflects the desperate straits of Jerusalem under siege.

At the end of the enacted siege, Ezekiel shaves his beard and his head with a sword (5:1). The hair is divided into three parts, to show the fate of Jerusalem's inhabitants when the city falls.

Ezekiel announces to the mountains of Israel that destruction is about to visit them. God's anger is unleashed now! The long promised doom bursts upon Judah. (See High Places.)

B. Visions of idolatry in the temple (8:1— 11:25). In September of 592 B.C., while the elders of the community in exile are gathered at Ezekiel's house, the prophet is carried in a vision to Jerusalem (8:1–3).

Idolatry in the temple (8:1–18). Ezekiel first notices the glory of God in the temple; then many desecrations are pointed out. God must act and purge His people from such detestable sins.

"The Spirit lifted me up . . . and brought me in visions of God"
(8:3–4). One way a prophet receives his message is in a vision, and Ezekiel's experience is a case in point. Sometimes a prophecy will be delivered as the prophet describes a picture he is seeing in his mind. This method can be seen in both Old Testament and New Testament prophets and is the fulfillment of Joel 2:28.

Marked out for life (9:1–11). The glory of the Lord now moves away from its resting place to the temple door. Ezekiel hears instructions given. Every individual in Jerusalem who is grieved by these sins is to be marked, and when the city falls his or her life is to be preserved.

God's glory departs (10:1–22). The fires of judgment will supplant the radiant presence of God, for the glory leaves the temple.

The prophet looks toward a future regathering (11:16–17) when a new heart will be given to God's people (18–21), and they will be purified. But now, the glory of the Lord mounts up and moves away from the city, coming to rest above the distant mountains.

C. Judah's exile and captivity (12:1— 24:27).

1. Messages of judgment against Judah (12:1— 19:14). Ezekiel now prophesies repeated messages of judgment against Judah. He condemns the prophets who have lied and promised peace (13:9–10). He denounces the idolatrous practices of those who have set up "idols in their hearts" (14:3). God announces that anyone guilty of this inner idolatry who dares inquire of a prophet of the Lord will be immediately judged (7–11).

Beautifully and emotionally, God speaks an allegory about His long relationship with His people. At birth, they were thrown out in a field to die. God rescued and cared for them (16:4–6). Later He entered into a marriage contract with them. But like a faithless wife who turned into a prostitute, she even offered the gifts God gave her to her lovers (idols) (16:15). Although God's people are faithless (see Ashamed), God remains faithful to His commitments and to His word (see Heb. 6:13–20).

Ezekiel further warns against Judah's unfaithfulness in another allegory about two eagles, representing Babylon and Egypt. A vine represents Judah, now under the domination (and protection) of Babylon. But the vine turns from the eagle that sustains it to bend toward the second eagle (17:1–10). Judah's King Zedekiah is secretly breaking his oath of allegiance to Nebuchadnezzar and has sent envoys to Egypt. God will punish this oath-breaking (11–21), but eventually He will plant and nurture a fruitful tree on the mountain heights of Israel.

"I will plant it; and it will . . . bear fruit"
(17:22–24). Ezekiel addresses the people's resistance to judgment. Refusing to acknowledge God's disciplinary instrument, Babylon, they look to Egypt for assistance. Judgment falls, yet hope is promised; a Davidic ruler would arise from humble beginnings, growing fruitful and majestic. As members of His kingdom— enjoined as branches—we grow fruitful by His Spirit working in us (1 Cor. 6:17). The Lord produces growth and fruitfulness as we remain in union with Him even in times of discipline.

The people of Judah exhibited a fatalistic attitude. They blamed their misfortunes on the sins of their ancestors and shrugged. What could they do about the past? Both Jeremiah (31:29) and Ezekiel speak against this irresponsible attitude. Judgment never comes solely because of others' actions. Judah willfully participates now in the sins of the fathers, and her judgment is just (18:1–4).

The principle is illustrated (18:5–20). Three examples are provided by the prophet. A righteous man who does right will live (5–9). A violent and wicked son of a righteous man will die for his own sins (10–13). The righteous son of a wicked father will live (14–18). Each individual will be judged on the basis of his own response to God and to God's laws.

No individual's fate is determined by his parent's behavior. Even his own sins (see Transgressions) need not bind him! A wicked man can save his life by turning from his sin to righteousness. Thus the message of personal responsibility brings with it a message of hope. God will not reject anyone who turns to Him (18:21–32).

This section culminates in a dirge poem lamenting the fate of Judah's kings.

2. Oracles before the fall of Jerusalem (20:1–24:27). Now without using allegory (cf. chs. 16; 23), Ezekiel reviews (see Preach) Israel's history and its witness to Israel's endless rebellion.

Ezekiel turns to face south where Judah lies (20:45–49). Babylon is identified as God's sword, to be used now against the Lord's own people.

The sins of Jerusalem are chronicled in three oracles in chapter 22 (see Gap; Prayer; Spiritual Warfare).

Chapter 23 features the two sisters, a famous allegory portraying the twin nations of Israel and Judah. They are adulterous sisters. Despite seeing the fate of Israel, Judah, the other "sister," continues to sin.

Judgment begins (24:1–14). In a poetic allegory, Jerusalem is pictured as a cooking pot, and her inhabitants are the meat stewed in it by the fires of judgment (3–12).

Death of Ezekiel's wife (24:15–27). A few days later Ezekiel is warned that his wife, "the desire of your eyes," will die suddenly. The prophet is not to mourn or weep (15–18). Ezekiel explains his reaction to the wondering exiles. Their relatives in Judah will soon be cut off as well, and they too will sit crushed, wasting away as a result of their sin.

III. ORACLES OF DOOM AGAINST FOREIGN NATIONS 25:1—32:32.

A. Against Ammon (25:1–7).

B. Against Moab (25:8–11).

C. Against Edom (25:12–14).

D. Against Philistia (25:15–17).

Short prophecies are uttered against Israel's near neighbors in a sequence beginning to the northeast of Israel and swinging southward around to Philistia in the southwest.

E. Against Tyre (26:1—28:19). Tyre's destruction is coming (26:1–21). A month after the news of Jerusalem's fall reaches the exiles, God turns the prophet's words against Tyre. She too will fall to Nebuchadnezzar.

The shipwreck of Tyre (27:1–36). The city is pictured allegorically as one of her own wealthy trading vessels.

Downfall of the prince of Tyre (28:1–10). Ezekiel now drops the use of allegory and speaks clearly of the contemporary prince of Tyre who claimed deity.

Lament over the king of Tyre (28:11–19). The shift in terms from "prince" to "king" as this passage begins, as well as the description of an original perfection (see Beauty), have led some to believe the description is of Satan before his fall and before man's creation.

F. Against Sidon (28:20–26). Judgments are announced against Sidon, a neighboring city long associated as a trading partner of Tyre.

G. Against Egypt (29:1—32:32). The sins of Egypt (29:1–16), pride and failure to support Israel from its days of servitude, are condemned. Egypt will fall.

Egypt's loot is promised to Nebuchadnezzar (29:17–21). The land of Egypt and its wealth are reserved as a reward for Babylon's king.

The great tree fallen (31:1–18). An allegory portrays Egypt as a noble cedar tree.

Lament for Pharaoh (32:1–32).

IV. PROPHECIES OF RESTORATION 33:1—48:35.

A. Ezekiel as watchman (33:1–33). The prophet's duty (1–9). It is the duty of a watchman to sound warnings in time of danger. This is the prophet's mission as well.

"If the watchman sees the sword coming and does not blow the trumpet . . . blood I will require at the watchman's hand"
(33:6–11). Although Ezekiel's prophetic assignment and the severity of failure to proclaim are unique to his call, all of us share the burden to witness. "Am I my brother's keeper?" is a question each should ask seriously concerning those we

have opportunity to influence. Likewise all believers serve as watchmen to a dying world, warning of sin's destruction, inviting all to redemption's freedom. We hold the message of Good News, and we are both responsible and accountable to proclaim it.

God's invitation to repent, given by the prophets, lays the responsibility for response squarely on the shoulders of each individual (33:10–20).

Jerusalem's fall is explained (21–33). Israel's failure to respond to prophetic words of warning (31) is the reason why the crushing judgment has fallen on this generation.

B. God as Shepherd (34:1–31). The rulers of Israel were to guard her people against oppression. God will therefore take upon Himself the role of Shepherd of His people (*see* Good; Restoration).

C. Judgment against Edom (35:1–15). When Jerusalem fell, the neighboring Edomites turned fugitives over to the Babylonians to be killed, and searched for loot in Judah's ruined towns. Because of this evil, God will make desolate their land.

D. Restoration of Israel (36:1—37:28). The mountains of Israel have witnessed her spiritual adultery, and now they are assured by the prophet that the future holds a complete renewal. Ezekiel reveals God's motives for the coming restoration. The Lord's holiness will be demonstrated to all the nations. Only God is able to take such sinners and transform them, so they at last respond to His Spirit and desire to keep His laws (22–27).

> **"I will put My Spirit within you and cause you to walk in My statutes"**
> (36:26–27). While challenging the Jewish exiles concerning their need for spiritual renewal (36:16—37:14), Ezekiel extends this hope-filled promise of a Spirit-inspired transformation. A threefold process is indicated: (1) a spiritual cleansing from idolatry's filth (v. 25), (2) a heart change from hardness to pliability (v. 26), and (3) an inward deposit of God's own Spirit (v. 27). The result would be a renewed willingness to walk in God's ways. We can receive a fresh consecration to obedient living through such a transforming work of the Holy Spirit, taking us from repentance to renewal, and then to refreshment—the dynamic result of yielding to the Spirit's presence.

New life for the nation (37:1–14). Ezekiel sees a valley full of dry bones—remains of the long dead. He is told to prophesy to them. As he does, the bones come together, become covered with flesh, but still lie dead on the valley floor. The prophet is then told to speak to "the breath." This word in Hebrew means "breath, wind, or spirit." The appeal is to the Spirit to come and breathe life into the dead. As the prophet speaks, the dead come to life (1–10).

The vision is interpreted in verses 11 through 14. This is not a vision of individual resurrection. It is a vision of the regathering and spiritual restoration of the nation of Israel.

> **"I will put My Spirit in you, and you shall live"**
> (37:14). As the Lord breathes His Spirit's freshness into our souls, a valley of dry bones (vv. 1–2) becomes a mighty army (v. 10); the dryness that characterizes spiritual death gives way to the dynamic of His life, and health replaces hopelessness. The breath of God's Spirit in our midst is the key to spiritual renewal—it reunites people and rekindles purpose.

A united people (37:15–28). Two sticks represent the northern and southern kingdoms. Gripping them in one hand, the prophet announces that God will again unite His people into one kingdom.

E. Judgment against Gog (38:1—39:29). These chapters contain an apocalyptic vision of a great battle in the far future "last days." The events described fit the picture given by other prophets of a final great battle between the evil forces of the north and God's people (*see* Jer. 4:5—6:26; Joel 2:28–32; Zeph. 1:14–18; Is. 29:5–8; Zech. 12:1–9; 14:1–15). While details are difficult to interpret with confidence, the main thrust of the prophecy is stated boldly and clearly.

The chapters include seven oracles, each of which is introduced by "Thus says the Lord GOD."

The armies gather (38:3–9).

Gog's intent (38:10–13). Greed and a desire for plunder motivate this attack on an unsuspecting, peace-loving people.

Invasion! (38:14–16). The great horde advances against Israel.

Massacre of Gog's army (38:17–23). A great natural disaster strikes the invaders. The timing and focus of the disaster unmistakably mark it as a direct intervention by God.

Destruction of the invaders (39:1–16).

Feast of the beasts (39:17–24). As the beasts gather to gorge on the bodies of the slain, Israel will realize that the Lord is still their God (22), while the nations of the world learn that a holy God punishes evil—in His own people and in others (23–24).

God's goal for Israel (39:25–29). A purified people, regathered in their own land and in a true relationship with God, will know the full blessing of His Spirit in their lives.

> **"I will not hide My face from them ... for I shall have poured out My Spirit on the house of Israel"**
> (39:29). Ezekiel's final prophetic message of restoration for God's people (vv. 21–29) promises a witness of God's glory going forth (v. 21). The Lord is revealed to His people by (1) the assurance of His presence—the Lord will no longer hide His face, and (2) the authentication of His presence—His Spirit will be poured out. Thus

> God's Spirit-presence seals His covenant relationship with His people and serves as a continuing sign of His promised blessing (37:26–28).

F. Restoration of the temple (40:1—46:24). Detailed measurements are taken as Ezekiel is shown the restoration of Jerusalem's temple and the service of the priests. A most significant element of the vision involves the return of the glory of the Lord (43:1–12).

G. Restoration of the land (47:1—48:35). A great river full of life springs from the temple, flowing away in four branches. References to this river are made throughout Scripture (see Joel 3:18; Zech. 14:8; Rev. 22:1) and may also prefigure the Holy Spirit's work in New Testament believers (John 7:37–38).

Ezekiel closes with a new division of the land among the twelve tribes of Israel. Jerusalem will lie in the center of the regathered tribes, and it will have a new name: THE LORD IS THERE!

Ezekiel's Temple

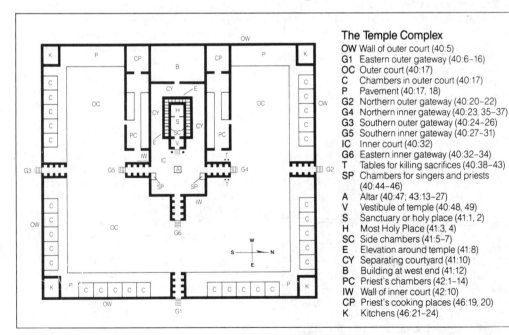

The Temple Complex

OW Wall of outer court (40:5)
G1 Eastern outer gateway (40:6–16)
OC Outer court (40:17)
C   Chambers in outer court (40:17)
P   Pavement (40:17, 18)
G2 Northern outer gateway (40:20–22)
G4 Northern inner gateway (40:23, 35–37)
G3 Southern outer gateway (40:24–26)
G5 Southern inner gateway (40:27–31)
IC Inner court (40:32)
G6 Eastern inner gateway (40:32–34)
T   Tables for killing sacrifices (40:38–43)
SP Chambers for singers and priests (40:44–46)
A   Altar (40:47; 43:13–27)
V   Vestibule of temple (40:48, 49)
S   Sanctuary or holy place (41:1, 2)
H   Most Holy Place (41:3, 4)
SC Side chambers (41:5–7)
E   Elevation around temple (41:8)
CY Separating courtyard (41:10)
B   Building at west end (41:12)
PC Priest's chambers (42:1–14)
IW Wall of inner court (42:10)
CP Priest's cooking places (46:19, 20)
K   Kitchens (46:21–24)

TRUTH-IN-ACTION through EZEKIEL

Truth Ezekiel Teaches	**Action** Ezekiel Invites
1 Steps to Knowing God and His Ways God's Word reveals that He was silent as a judgment against His people, neither answering their prayers nor speaking through prophets. God rejects false teachers and prophets who speak out of their own imaginations.	**7:26, 27** *Understand* lack of prophetic leadership and vision comes to any people who refuse to obey God's revealed will. **13:8–23** *Remember* that God says that teaching or prophesying falsehood is "lying."
2 Guidelines for Growing in Godliness Godliness is not inherited. Each individual must seek out God and establish a personal relationship with Him. Godliness comes by divine transformation of our hardened or rebellious hearts, not by self-effort.	**14:15–20** *Be assured* that you will not be saved by another's righteousness or be judged for another's sin. **36:26, 27** *Understand* that God will bring about true transformation among His people by renewing their minds and hearts and filling them with His Spirit. *Welcome* the exchange of heart and spirit God offers to you. *Yield* to God's Spirit and *receive* His law of life in your heart to be truly transformed.
3 Keys to Wise Living The wise person knows that his flesh is at war with his spiritual desires. The carnal nature attempts to reject the Word of God and its renewing work, and to defend the fortress of self-will (see 2 Cor. 10:4–6).	**3:7–9** *Understand* that the carnal ear is rebellious and stubborn against God's Word. **12:1, 2** *Remember* that the evidence of rebellion is spiritual blindness and deafness. **13:1–12** *Be assured* that God is against those who speak falsely in His name. *Know* that He has set Himself against those who speak things He has not said and who teach His Word falsely. **13:19** *Understand* that the false teacher, whose motive is gain, causes injustice and iniquity among God's people.
4 Steps to Dealing with Sin The prophet laments that God's people and their leaders "heal their sins lightly." Only paying lip service to sin and its devastation, they fail to confront or deal thoroughly with sin.	**14:7** *Be advised* that God will not answer the unrepentant prayers of an idolater or one who continually entertains sin in his heart, although he may be of God's people. **18:30–32** *Repent* in sincerity. *Seek* God for a new heart and a renewed spirit. *Understand* that true spiritual transformation involves repentance.
5 Lessons for Leaders Ezek. focuses on the common failure of God's servants. This results from their gauging their success by man's approval rather than by God's standards. Ezek. is rich with insight into the hearts of God's people. Though ostensibly desiring God's will and way, some seek their own benefit and personal gain. God warns the prophets not to presume the outward devotion of people is genuine unless sacrificial and transformed living is manifest.	**2:3–8** Leaders, *do not use* "success" alone to gauge how well people seem to receive you. **3:16–27; 33:1–9** Leaders, *remember* the principle of your responsibility as God's spokesman or watchman: *Accept* your tasks to teach and correct, whether people listen or not. **33:30–33** Leaders, *remember* that popularity is no final measure of righteousness or your true effectiveness. *Beware* of people's tendency to view preaching as a form of entertainment. **34:1–10** Leaders, *be warned* that God sets Himself against pastors who take care of themselves and not the welfare of His people.
6 A Key Lesson in Faith God will ultimately supply the final answer to mankind's most perplexing problems through the outflow of the Holy Spirit.	**47:1–12** *Rejoice* that the prophesied outflow of God's Spirit will produce healing and restoration. *Welcome* this grace in your life and circumstance.

KEYS TO DANIEL
Personal Passion for the Kingdom

Kingdom Key: God's Purpose in View

Daniel has the unique distinction of being listed by another prophet as one of three distinguished Old Testament saints noted for remarkable righteousness (Ezek. 14:14, 20). This quality in Daniel's walk with God is not merely in a purity he maintains, but also in the passion with which he pursues God's will. Kingdom living is not just a matter of holiness; *it involves a* whole-heartedness *as well. True Holy Spirit-filled living is marked by a zeal for God's kingdom purposes, and not only by an obedient submission to them. Daniel and his companions demonstrate such a surrender to God's rule in their lives.*

1. They will not be shaped by the world's tastes or values (ch. 1). Captured, exiled, and thrust into another kingdom, when promised a privileged place if they will conform to it's culture, they refuse. The fact of their refusal, and their bold offer to demonstrate the superiority of their values, results in their retaining their own standards and still gaining an opportunity to impact the culture to which they have come.

2. They demonstrate the practicality of living in the resources of the gifts of God's Spirit (ch. 2). The king's call for an interpreter of dreams requires more than the usual: the interpreter must reveal the dream too! Daniel and his companions are possessed with a passion that seeks beyond the ordinary to the realm of the supernatural. Kingdom people learn that such a quest transcends a search for the sensational. Spiritual gifts are to be sought for the sake of kingdom *ministry,* not for entertainment. (*See* also ch. 5.)

....

Faithful-ness to God unlocks true power.

....

3. They are unbending before assault (chs. 3 and 6). In separate episodes, Daniel and his three companions are tested by calculated efforts to discredit and destroy them. Literal fires of opposition and the jaws of lions are set before them, threats intended to produce either compromise or death. Few words in the Bible more poignantly declare the pure passion of those committed to God's rule than Nebuchadnezzar's commendation of Shadrach, Meshach, and Abed-Nego: "Blessed be [their God] who . . . delivered His servants

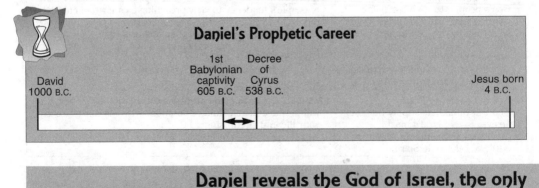

Daniel's Prophetic Career

| David 1000 B.C. | 1st Babylonian captivity 605 B.C. | Decree of Cyrus 538 B.C. | Jesus born 4 B.C. |

Daniel reveals the God of Israel, the only

who trusted in Him, and they have frustrated the king's word, and yielded their bodies, that they should not serve or worship any god except their own God!" (3:28).

Note also that Daniel's passion in intercessory prayer was motivated by his heartfelt belief in the truth of the prophetic word of God (9:2). It was also manifest in his desire to fast and pray in the midst of spiritual pursuit and warfare (9:3; 10:2–3), thus realizing a spiritual breakthrough (10:12–13) and receiving spiritual insight (9:20–27; 10:14).

Master Key: God's Son Revealed

Christ is first seen as the "fourth man" standing with Shadrach, Meshach, and Abed-Nego in the fiery furnace (3:25). The three had remained faithful to their God; now God stands faithful with them in the fire of their judgment, delivering them even from the "smell of fire" (3:27).

Another reference to Christ is found in Daniel's night vision (7:13). He describes "One like the Son of Man, coming with the clouds of heaven," a reference to the Second Advent of Jesus Christ.

A further vision of Christ is found in 10:5–6, where the description of Jesus is almost identical to John's in Revelation 1:13–16.

Power Key: God's Spirit at Work

The Holy Spirit never announces His presence in Daniel, but He is clearly at work. The ability of Daniel and the other Hebrews to interpret dreams was through the power of the Holy Spirit. The predictive prophecies, both with local and future applications, indicate the supernatural insights given to Daniel by the Holy Spirit.

Key Word: *God's Program for Israel*

Daniel was written to encourage the exiled Jews by revealing God's sovereign program for Israel during and after the period of Gentile domination. The "Times of the Gentiles" began with the Babylonian captivity, and Israel would suffer under Gentile powers for many years. But this period is not permanent, and a time will come when God will establish the messianic kingdom which will last forever.

Key Verses: Daniel 2:20–22; 2:44

Key Chapter: Daniel 9

Daniel's prophecy of the seventy weeks (9:24–27) provides the chronological frame for messianic prediction from the time of Daniel to the establishment of the kingdom on earth.

God, as the ruler over the destiny of nations.

Introducing
DANIEL

Author. Daniel was deported as a teenager in 605 B.C. to Babylon where he lived over sixty years. He was likely from an upper-class family in Jerusalem. The deportation of the royal descendants into Babylon had been prophesied by Isaiah to Hezekiah (Is. 39:7). Daniel initially served as a trainee in Nebuchadnezzar's court; he was later an advisor to foreign kings.

His importance as a prophet was confirmed by Jesus in Matthew 24:15.

Daniel means "God Is My Judge." His unshakable consecration to Yahweh and his loyalty to God's people strongly affirmed that truth in his life.

Date. Although the siege and carrying away of captives into Babylon lasted several years, the mighty men of valor, the skilled, and the educated were taken from Jerusalem early in the war (2 Kin. 24:14). The date usually given for Daniel's captivity is 605 B.C. His prophecy covers the time span of his life.

Background. Along with thousands of captives from Judah who were taken into Babylonian exile between 605 B.C. and 582 B.C., the treasures of Solomon's palace and the temple were also transported. The Babylonians had subdued all the provinces ruled by Assyria and had consolidated their empire into an area that covered much of the Middle East.

To govern such a diversified kingdom over such an expanse of space required a skillful administrative bureaucracy. Slaves who were educated or possessed needed skills became the manpower for the government. Because of their wisdom, knowledge, and handsome appearance, four young Hebrews were selected for the training program (1:4). The outstanding character of Daniel, Hananiah, Mishael, and Azariah secured positions for them in the king's palace; and it was Daniel who rose to excel over all the wise men of that vast empire (6:1-3).

Purpose. The purpose is to show that the God of Israel, the only God, is in control of the destiny of all nations.

Content. Daniel has three main sections: Introduction to the person of Daniel (ch. 1), Daniel's key tests of character and the development of his prophetic interpretation skills (chs. 2—7), and his series of visions about future kingdoms and events (chs. 8—12). In this final section, Daniel emerges as a key prophetic book for understanding much of the Bible. Many insights into end-times prophe-

cies are dependent upon an understanding of this book. Jesus' comments in the Olivet Discourse (Matthew 24; 25) and many of the revelations given to the apostle Paul find harmony and cohesion in Daniel (see Romans 11; 2 Thessalonians 2). Likewise, it becomes a necessary study companion to the Book of Revelation.

Although the interpretation of Daniel, like Revelation, is subject to great diversity, for many the dispensational approach has become quite popular. It is an interpretive approach that sees in Daniel keys to help unlock the mysteries of such subjects as the Antichrist, the Great Tribulation, the Second Coming of Christ, the Times of the Gentiles, future resurrections, and judgments. This approach also sees most unfulfilled prophecy as revolving around two major focal points: (1) the future destiny of the city of Jerusalem and (2) the future destiny of Daniel's people, national Jews (9:24). (See Prophecy, especially section 10.)

Daniel's writing covers the reign of two kingdoms, Babylon and Medo-Persia, and four kings: Nebuchadnezzar (2:11—4:37); Belshazzar (5:1-31); Darius (6:1-28); and Cyrus (10:1—11:1).

Personal Application. One of the beautiful themes of this book is the emphasis on separation to God, with Daniel as the ultimate example. From their decision not to eat the king's food to the refusal to bow to the image of the king, Daniel and his three friends (now named Shadrach, Meshach, and Abed-Nego) displayed such an uncompromising spirit that spectacular opportunities were opened for God to display His power on their behalf. Their courageous commitment presents a timeless challenge to believers not to compromise their testimony of Jesus Christ. Even though it may mean a fiery-furnace testing, the Lord's protection and deliverance will be there.

Another theme of Daniel is the absolute superiority of God over occult attempts to reveal or interpret spiritual mysteries. Try as they did, all the magicians, soothsayers, wise men, and astrologers of the king's court could not arrive at the truth (5:8). This is an enduring encouragement to believers. Spiritual counterfeiters can never stand before the wisdom and power of the Holy Spirit (2 Cor. 10:3-6).

The prophetic section not only gives future understanding to a believer's future, but serves to reassure us that God has history under His sovereign control.

Prophetic Key. According to many interpreters, Daniel 9 contains a pivotal prophecy. It has come to be known as "Daniel's Seventy Weeks of Years." An understanding of these weeks is crucial to one school of interpretation of latter-day prophetic events. Understandably, the interpretation of this section is diverse among equally dedicated, committed Christians. These notes reflect the frequently accepted dispensational approach. However, additional comments at the end of this section will address the more historic classical, conservative view. Both are valid considerations for dedicated students to examine, and the exercise occasions the healthy reminder that prophetic Scripture interpretation is not a place for committed Christians to part company, although differences exist.

As Daniel sought the Lord to find out how long the Babylonian captivity would last, God showed him that the original prophecy of Jeremiah, indicating that the captivity would last seventy years, would be extended to "seventy sevens," or 490 years (Jeremiah 29). This revelation, in fact, covers the history of Jerusalem and the Jews from the time that Artaxerxes decreed they should rebuild the city of Jerusalem (Neh. 2:1–10) to the time of the Great Tribulation (Matt. 24:15–31).

This whole period is called "the Times of the Gentiles" because Gentile political authority will be the major force until the final destruction of all Israel's enemies at the end of the Great Tribulation. This will culminate in the Battle of Armageddon and the Second Advent of the Messiah. He will at that time destroy all the armies that have come against Jerusalem.

The "seventy sevens" are divided into three sections: seven weeks, sixty-two weeks, and one week. Each week represents seven years. The decree of Artaxerxes was in 446–445 B.C. (Neh. 2:1). The first two sections of weeks total 69 weeks or 483 years. This period ended in A.D. 32 when the Messiah was "cut off" (9:26), or when Jesus was crucified on Calvary.

The Abomination of Desolation, which Daniel prophesied would be part of the Seventieth Week, was clearly dated by Jesus as being part of the Great Tribulation or end-time period (Matt. 24:15). Nearly two thousand years have passed and the Seventieth Week has not happened. We are still living in the parenthetical time called the Times of the Gentiles, which precedes that culminative prophetic "week."

From this interpretive perspective, the Book of Daniel unveils a march of events in God's relationship, not only with His people, but with the world political system. Basic facts distilled from this book seem to illuminate other difficult passages, presenting these apparent forthcoming events:

1. The Messiah will return before the millennial period (2:31–37; 44–45; 7:13–14).

2. God's kingdom will literally be established on the earth with the Messiah-King as ruler (2:44–45; 7:26–27).

3. The four metals of Nebuchadnezzar's dream image symbolize four empires: Babylonian, Medo-Persian, Macedonian-Greek, and Roman (2:37–40).

4. The fourth kingdom, Rome, will enjoy a last-day revival in the form of a united confederacy in Europe. Out of this system the Antichrist will emerge (7:8, 20–21; 8:23).

5. The False Prophet and the Antichrist are persons, not merely a system (7:7–8, 20–26; 9:27; 11:36–45).

6. God will continue to deal with the nation of Israel (9:20–27).

7. National Israel is the prophetic time clock for last-day events (9:24).

8. The False Prophet and the Antichrist will dominate the last portion of the last week of Daniel's Seventy Weeks of Years. At the end of the "week," after the Great Tribulation, Jesus the Messiah will return to establish the kingdom of God, which will resolve all prophecies of Daniel (9:24, 27).

CLASSICAL INTERPRETATION: In contrast to the dispensational hermeneutical approach, many evangelicals interpret Daniel using classical (Covenant) hermeneutical principles. Classical interpreters do so, realizing that biblical prophecy may have multiple levels of fulfillment.

The classical view sees the initial fulfillment of Daniel's prophetic sections in past historical events, such as the second-century B.C. invasion of Jerusalem by Antiochus Epiphanes and the events of the fall of Jerusalem in A.D. 70. Classical interpreters do, however, also see ultimate fulfillment of many of the prophecies at the end of this age. For an example, see the note on 9:26–27.

Furthermore, the classical approach does not always press for strict literalness, especially when the New Testament itself makes nonliteral application. For example, see James's quote of Amos 9:11–12 in Acts 15:16–17.

Surveying
DANIEL

I. THE RELIGIOUS CONVICTIONS OF DANIEL 1:1–21.

A. Judah's exile (1:1–2). Nebuchadnezzar is one of the ancient world's most effective rulers. Among his practices is the selection of promising youths from subject nations for training as administrators of the empire.

B. Daniel's decision to maintain his separation (1:3–21). Daniel, with three friends, all members of noble families brought from Judah in 605 B.C., is selected for such training (1:3–7).

Daniel immediately rejects the diet provided for the students by the king, which apparently violates Jewish dietary laws. He asks for ten days to prove the restricted diet is healthy. They pass and are permitted to eat as they choose. After three years of training, when the graduates are questioned by Nebuchadnezzar himself, Daniel and his friends surpass the rest (8–21).

II. NEBUCHADNEZZAR'S FIRST DREAM 2:1–49.

A. The dream forgotten (2:1–28). When Nebuchadnezzar has a strange dream, he calls his advisors to interpret it. The king demands the group not only interpret the dream but first prove their interpretation is valid by relating the dream itself! When the astrologers confess they cannot, the furious ruler orders all the "wise men" of Babylon executed (2:1–12).

Daniel and his friends are among the class of wise men and so are also condemned! Daniel promises that God will tell the dream and its meaning.

> ### "I thank You and praise You, . . . You have given me"
> (2:20–23). Daniel is fully aware of God's sovereign power, yet he is not hesitant to acknowledge the partnership he has been given with Him. When we discover the awesome truth that God's intent is to work in tandem with His people, our life of praise becomes radically impacted. Given our place of utter dependence upon God as His children, to understand that we are called into a partnership with the Almighty is a humbling truth to which we can only respond with full-hearted praise to God.

B. Daniel's revelation and interpretation (2:29–45). Daniel tells Nebuchadnezzar his dream. The king has seen a great statue, with a gold head, silver chest and arms, a bronze belly and thighs, legs of iron, and feet of mixed iron and clay. A rock, not cut out with human hands, shatters the statue, grinds it into dust, and then grows to fill the whole earth.

God tells Daniel that this statue represents succeeding kingdoms, each inferior to the previous one. The rock represents a kingdom that God will set up and that will never be destroyed (39–45). These prophecies so clearly match the events of world history in the centuries following that many have denied the Book of Daniel could have been written in the Babylonian era. (*See* map, page 217.)

C. Daniel honored by promotion (2:46–49).

III. DELIVERANCE FROM THE FIERY FURNACE 3:1–30.

A. Call to worship the golden image (3:1–7). Daniel is the unquestioned leader of the small group of Hebrews in the Babylonian administration, but the other three prove their faith is just as committed.

B. Refusal of the three Hebrews to bow to the image (3:8–25). Nebuchadnezzar sets up a gold statue. At its dedication he commands all his officials to worship it. When the three refuse, the furious monarch orders them thrown into a blazing furnace. But then Nebuchadnezzar leaps to his feet in amazement! The three are not consumed and a fourth figure appears with them, walking in the white-hot center of the flames. To Nebuchadnezzar this fourth figure looks like a "son of the gods" (that is, a deity). Many believe this is a preincarnate appearance of Jesus.

> ### "Our God whom we serve is able to deliver us"
> (3:1–27). The three Hebrew children demonstrate remarkable faith in the face of a vicious attack of their adversaries. To understand their faith we must make the connection between their commitment and their conduct. That connection allows the entry of the presence of the Holy Spirit. His presence serves to strengthen and protect in the midst of the trial; however, it often goes unnoticed until you are in the middle of the fire. Therein lies the challenge of faith.

C. The king's confession of the true God (3:26–30).

IV. NEBUCHADNEZZAR'S SECOND DREAM 4:1–37.

A. Nebuchadnezzar's dream (4:1–18). Near the end of his forty-three-year reign, Nebuchadnezzar has a second prophetic dream. He sees a great tree, which a heavenly messenger commands be cut down. The stump, bound with iron, remains in the field.

B. Daniel's interpretation (4:19–27). Nebuchadnezzar is the tree, and the messenger is an angel from God. The Lord has decreed that Nebuchadnezzar will be driven from human society, to live with the animals and eat grass like cattle until he acknowledges the rule of God. Then his kingdom will be returned and he will recover.

C. Fulfillment of the dream (4:28–33). A year after the dream, Nebuchadnezzar is suddenly filled with pride at all his accomplishments. Immediately the king is struck with madness and rushes from the city into the fields, until such time as he acknowledges God's sovereignty (v. 34). The chapter closes with Nebuchadnezzar's praise and acknowledgment of God's sovereign rule over all earthly kingdoms.

D. Nebuchadnezzar's prayer and restoration (4:34–37).

V.   BELSHAZZAR'S   BLASPHEMOUS FEAST 5:1–31.

A. The handwriting on the wall (5:1–9). At a great banquet held in Babylon, a hand appears and writes unknown words on the wall.

B. Daniel's interpretation of the writing on the wall (5:10–31). Daniel is called. He interprets the writing, announcing God's judgment on the ruler, who has been weighed and found wanting (22–29). That very night Belshazzar is killed and the kingdom passes into the hands of Cyrus the Persian.

VI. DANIEL IN THE LIONS' DEN 6:1–28.

A. Plot against Daniel (6:1–9). In the reorganized Persian kingdom, the empire is divided into 120 districts, overseen by a council of three on which Daniel serves. Daniel is resented by some of his subordinates, but he is so honest and efficient they can find nothing with which to charge him. At last they influence Darius to issue a written decree. No one can make a request to any god or person other than the king for thirty days. But Daniel continues to pray openly at the window in his home, facing Jerusalem. (*See* Manhood.)

B. Daniel cast into the lions' den (6:10–28). He is charged and the frustrated ruler has no choice but to condemn Daniel to the lions' den. There Daniel is protected by angels. The next morning the agitated Darius, who has not wanted to carry out his binding decree, takes Daniel from the den alive.

> **"Your God, whom you serve continually, He will deliver you"** (6:1–23). There is a kind of faith which can create faith in those around you. Darius the king had grown close to Daniel as he served in the king's court. The consistency of character he observed in Daniel impressed Darius enough to be able to make a faith statement of his own when faced with a crisis.

VII. DANIEL'S FIRST VISION 7:1–28.

A. Daniel's dream of four beasts (7:1–14). In 553 B.C. Daniel is given a vision. He sees four beasts, one after the other. As one "horn" of the last beast uproots its other horns, God Himself appears. ("Horn" in the Old Testament is a symbol of a ruler or ruling power.) The final power is destroyed when one "like a son of man" is given authority over the earth and establishes a kingdom which will never be destroyed.

B. Daniel's interpretation (7:15–28). The vision is explained to Daniel by an angel. The beasts are identified as world kingdoms. The "horn" from the last beast is a ruler who will directly oppose God and oppress His saints (v. 25). But then God's everlasting kingdom (*see* Kingdom of God) will be established.

VIII. DANIEL'S SECOND VISION 8:1–27.

A. Daniel's dream of a ram, a goat, and the horns (8:1–14). In 551 B.C. Daniel has another vision concerning these kingdoms. He sees a ram that overpowers the world. It is defeated by a goat with one great horn. At the height of its power the great horn is broken off, to be replaced by four horns. From one of these comes another horn, which sets itself up as "prince of the host" and desolates God's own sanctuary, causing sacrifices to cease.

B. Gabriel's interpretation (8:15–27). The focus of the vision is "the appointed time of the end." The two-horned ram is specifically identified as Medo-Persia (20), and the goat as "the king of Greece" (21; *see* map, page 217). Just as Daniel foretold, this king, Alexander, did die suddenly and was replaced by four hellenic kingdoms. Following that, a "stern-faced king" will emerge from one of these four empires and devastate God's people.

IX. PROPHECY OF THE SEVENTY WEEKS 9:1–27.

A. Daniel's prayer (9:1–19). Daniel discovers Jeremiah's promise that the captivity will last seventy years (Jer. 25:11–14). Now, in 538

B.C., the appointed years are almost complete. So Daniel pleads with God to act.

B. Daniel's vision (9:20–27). The angel Gabriel appears as Daniel is praying, to give God's answer (*see* Messiah). This is a unique prophecy in that, rather than being indefinite about time, the whole prophecy focuses on time and announces in advance a prophetic time framework. (For more detail see notes *on* Daniel 9 in the *Spirit-Filled Life Bible.*)

X. DANIEL'S FINAL VISION 10:1—12:13.

A. Daniel's vision of a glorious being (10:1–9). Daniel's final vision comes after he has fasted and prayed for three weeks.

B. Angelic visitation (10:10–21). An angel messenger appears to Daniel to "make you understand what will happen to your people in the latter days" (14).

This chapter provides a special insight into the realm of angels. Both good and evil angels seem to be organized in ranks and active in national events as well as with individuals. The angel (*see* Angels) overseeing Satan's affairs in the Persian kingdom blocked the passage of God's messenger to Daniel (12–13). It was not until an angel of even higher rank came to open the way that God's messenger was able to proceed.

"O Daniel, man greatly beloved" (10:11). The context of this passage points out the intercessory role Daniel had during this time. In his intercession, he was warring against great spiritual forces. With faithful response to his task, Daniel was finally able to realize the answer to his prayer. However, it did not come without struggle in the heavenlies. Because he persisted, Daniel is addressed by the angel as one who is loved by God. We, too, are called to remain faithful to what God has called us, and in doing so, we know that God has great love for us as well.

C. Wars of kings of north and south (11:1–45). The same pattern seen previously of history moving toward the time of the end is seen in the information given Daniel by the angel messenger.

D. The time of trouble (12:1–13). With destruction of God's enemies there comes a new beginning! Daniel's book closes with a return to its most unique element: a prophetic treatment of specific periods of time (*see* 9:20–27). The three-and-one-half-year period spoken of immediately calls to mind the seven-year period of Daniel 9:27, to begin sometime after the cutting off of Christ.

TRUTH-IN-ACTION through DANIEL

Truth Daniel Teaches	**Action** Daniel Invites
1 Steps to Knowing God We must know that God will judge and that everyone will give an account to God for his/her conduct.	**5:22–24** *Understand* that God judges as idolatry and blasphemy the arrogance of all who refuse to honor Him. **5:25–28** *Recognize* that God measures, judges, or rewards us according to our conduct.
2 Guidelines for Growing in Godliness Godly living requires that we exhibit faith during times of adversity and want, as well as during times of prosperity and peace. Compromising our faith when threatened with persecution forfeits the most powerful opportunities for God to manifest His glory.	**1:8–16** *Stand fast* for your righteous standards, despite pressure to sin. *Believe* that God will give you a means of escape. *Trust* that He will show you favor and give you wisdom through "creative alternatives." **3:12** *Reject compromise* of your godly convictions, and *refuse* to "run with the multitude" to do evil and worship false gods. **6:4–9** *Live in such a way* that no charge (except your commitment to your faith) can be found against you. **6:10–16** *Continue to practice righteousness* even when it may be socially frowned upon or politically prohibited. **6:21, 22** *Maintain* a clear conscience by living a blameless life.
3 Steps to Dynamic Devotion The individual devoted to God affirms that the Lord is sovereign and seeks to glorify His name.	**2:20–23** *Recognize* and *speak open praise* to God for His sovereignty over all circumstances, even those strongly adverse to you. *Believe* that He will equip you to prevail in adversity.

(continued)

Truth Daniel Teaches	**Action** Daniel Invites
❸ Steps to Dynamic Devotion *(continued)*	**9:4–19** *Intercede* before God, identifying with the sins of those for whom you pray. *Base* all petitions on the desire to *glorify* God's name.
❹ Keys to Wise Living Wisdom is necessary to achieving one's full spiritual potential. The spiritually wise man knows when and when not to speak of things he has seen and heard and knows when and when not to pursue certain spiritual experiences.	**7:28** *Be wise* and *understand* that certain of God's secrets and visions are not to be shared but to be kept in your heart. *Be assured* that if you share God's secrets unwisely, He may not entrust them to you again. **8:27; 10:8, 9, 15–17** *Understand* that experiencing the spiritual reality of visions and other divine encounters may have physiological consequences. Pursue them neither frivolously nor lightly.
❺ Key Lessons in Faith Daniel and his friends provide the model for a faithful testimony under the threat of torture and death. Although relatively few believers are required to face this ultimate test, those who do are consistently given the highest honor in the heavenly rolls (see Heb. 11:33, 34).	**2:14** *Trust* God to give you wise and tactful words. When speaking to antagonists, *seek to speak* words that are entreating and not full of threats. **2: 17, 18** When facing threatening circumstances, *turn quickly* to the Lord for help. **2:27, 28** *Bear testimony* that God enables you to overcome otherwise impossible circumstances. *Believe* that God is still in the miracle-working business. **3:16–18** *Believe* that God is able to deliver you from the most difficult circumstances. *Be willing to endure* death rather than deny your faith in God's power to deliver you.

Alexander's Greek Empire
(Daniel 2, 7, 8, 11)

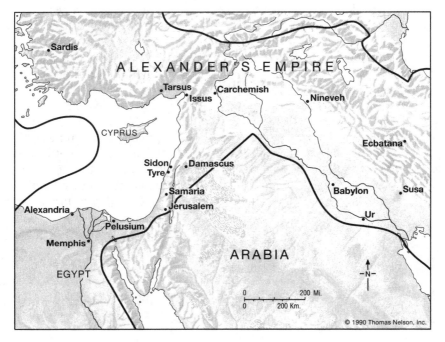

KEYS TO HOSEA, JOEL AND AMOS

A Trilogy on the King's Love, Power, and Authority

Kingdom Key: God's Purpose in View

Each of the minor prophets contains an attribute of God that is declared in the Old Testament and is manifest in the person of Jesus the King in the New Testament.

Hosea: Prophet of the King's Relentless Love

The prophet's call to acquire a bride who had violated God's standards (3:1), and at his own expense (3:2), prefigures heaven's Ultimate Lover—Jesus our Savior. As the kingdom's King, He has not taken rule by means of His power so much as by the overwhelming glory of His love. He has *bought* (1 Pet. 1:18–19) and *brought* a bride for Himself (Eph. 5:25–27, 32), bringing her from shame (Rev. 3:18) unto virginal purity, beauty, and acceptability (1 Cor. 6:9–11; 2 Cor. 11:2). God's divine love in Christ is illustrated in advance by the way God rejects Israel's sin (1:6–9) and then declares that His love will abide until they return (2:23). This prophesy is adopted by Peter and applied to the redeemed in Christ

> Though sinful man may resist, God's love persists.

(1 Pet. 2:9–10). What majestic love!

Joel: Prophet of the King's Promise of Power

Never were a people more stripped of strength or ruined of resource than those to whom Joel prophesied (1:1–20). Their helpless, drained, and burned out condition is addressed with God's word about a day when restoration and refreshment will revitalize and empower (2:18–27). This promise defines the Holy Spirit's fullness of power, which is not so much an endowment of might as an enduement of grace. New wine (2:24—refreshing) and new rain (2:23—bringing harvest) are promised—a promise that was fulfilled by the outpouring of the King's wine and rain at Pentecost (Acts 2:12–18). What the Father foretold in the *(Please turn to page 221.)*

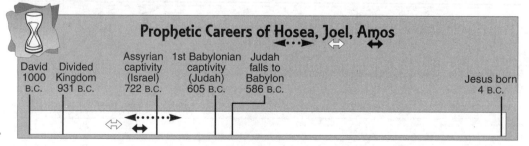

Prophetic Careers of Hosea, Joel, Amos

David 1000 B.C.	Divided Kingdom 931 B.C.	Assyrian captivity (Israel) 722 B.C.	1st Babylonian captivity (Judah) 605 B.C.	Judah falls to Babylon 586 B.C.	Jesus born 4 B.C.

These prophets unfold God's everlasting love,

Master Key: God's Soŋ Revealed
Hosea

The New Testament writers draw upon Hosea for teaching about Christ's life and ministry. Matthew sees 11:1 as a prophecy that was fulfilled when Jesus as a baby was taken into and brought out of Egypt, parallel to Israel's long stay in Egypt and the Exodus (Matt. 2:15). The writer of Hebrews sees Jesus as the One who enables believers to offer acceptable sacrifices of praise (14:2; Heb. 13:15). For Peter, Jesus provides the basis by which individuals outside the family of God are admitted into a relationship with Him (1:6, 9; 1 Pet. 2:10). To Paul, Jesus fulfills Hosea's promise of One who would break the power of death and the grave and so bring resurrection victory (13:14; 1 Cor. 15:55). Paul's teaching on Christ as the Groom and the church as the bride corresponds to the marriage ceremony and vows whereby God entered into a permanent relationship with Israel (2:19–20; Eph. 5:25–32).

Jesus also, in at least two of His sermons to the Pharisees, takes His text from Hosea. When questioned about spending His time in the homes of tax collectors and sinners, Jesus quotes Hosea to show that God desires not just empty words or heartless rituals but a genuine care and concern for people (6:6; Matt. 9:13). And when the Pharisees accuse Jesus' disciples of Sabbath-breaking, Jesus defends them with the same reminder, that God places concern for human need above religious form (Matt. 12:7).

Joel

Joel looked forward to a time when the Lord would bring judgment to the enemies of God and of Israel, when the nations would be called to give account for their actions. He also saw a day of great plenty flowing from the righteous reign of the Lord in Zion. The instrument through which these great events would come was the Messiah. Jesus

---

Key Word: *The Loyal Love of God for Israel*

The themes of chapters 1—3 echo throughout the rest of the Book of Hosea. The adultery of Gomer (chap. 1) illustrates the sin of Israel (chaps. 4—7); the degradation of Gomer (chap. 2) represents the judgment of Israel (chaps. 8—10); and Hosea's redemption of Gomer (chap. 3) pictures the restoration of Israel (chaps. 11—14). More than any other Old Testament prophet, Hosea's personal experiences illustrate his prophetic message.

Key Verses: Hosea 4:1; 11:7–9

Key Chapter: Hosea 4

The nation of Israel has left the knowledge of the truth and followed the idolatrous ways of their pagan neighbors. Central to the book is Hosea 4:6.

Key Word: *The Great and Terrible Day of the Lord*

The key theme of Joel is the day of the Lord in retrospect and prospect.
(continued oŋ next page.)

---

irresistible power, aŋd iŋterŋatioŋal authority.

is the One who will bring this age to a close, defeating His enemies, rewarding His church, and setting up His final kingdom of righteousness.

Furthermore, it is Jesus who promises the coming of the Spirit in response to His finished work of redemption and return to the Father (John 14:15–18; 16:5–24). In the coming of the Spirit at Pentecost we have the spiritual return of Christ to indwell His people and direct His body, the church. His literal and physical return is foretold here in Joel.

Amos

There are no direct references to Christ in Amos. No typology is present either. There does seem to be an allusion, however, to Amos 1:9–10 in Jesus' statement in Matthew 11:21–22. Amos speaks of the judgment to come upon Tyre. Jesus says that if the mighty works performed in Chorazin and Bethsaida "had been done in Tyre and Sidon, they would have repented long ago in sackcloth and ashes." One other concept from Amos is picked up by John in Revelation. Amos speaks of God's prophets as servants and says that God does nothing without revealing His plan to His servants the prophets (Amos 3:7). John speaks about the sounding of the seventh trumpet when the "mystery of God would be finished, as He declared to His servants the prophets" (Rev. 10:7).

Power Key: God's Spirit at Work
Hosea

The Book of Hosea teaches two outstanding lessons concerning the Holy Spirit: (1) It is important to depend on the presence of the Spirit, and (2) negative things happen when the Holy Spirit is missing from one's life. Twice Hosea uses the phrase "the spirit of harlotry" (4:12; 5:4), and reveals the consequences of being filled with an unholy spirit. Like Paul in Ephesians, Hosea connects such a spirit with wine, which enslaves the heart. This spirit of harlotry also causes people to stray into false ways and false worship, in contrast to the Holy Spirit who guides

---

continued from preceding page

Joel uses the terrible locust plague that has recently occurred in Judah to illustrate the coming day of judgment.

Key Verses: Joel 2:11, 28–29

Key Chapter: Joel 2

The prophet calls for Judah's repentance and promises God's repentance (2:13–14) from His planned judgment upon Judah if they do indeed turn to Him.

Key Word: *The Judgment of Israel*

The basic theme of Amos is the coming judgment of Israel because of the holiness of God and the sinfulness of His covenant people.

Key Verses: Amos 3:1–2; 8:11–12

Key Chapter: Amos 9

Set in the midst of the harsh judgments of Amos are some of the greatest prophecies of restoration of Israel anywhere in Scripture. Within the scope of just five verses the future of Israel becomes clear, as the Abrahamic, Davidic, and Palestinian covenants are focused on their climactic fulfillment in the return of the Messiah.

us in true ways and true worship (4:11–13; Eph. 5:17–21). John records the words of Jesus concerning the ministry of the Holy Spirit, who will witness to Christ; on the other hand, the spirit of harlotry keeps people from knowing God (5:4; John 15:26).

The love of Hosea for his wayward wife reminds us that the preeminent fruit of the Spirit is love (Gal. 5:22). "The love of God has been poured out in our hearts by the Holy Spirit who was given to us" (Rom. 5:5).

Joel

Joel is remarkable in his references to the Holy Spirit. It is obviously the Holy Spirit who has inspired the prophet to see God's hand in all that is taking place and to be able to leap forward to the terrible day of the Lord.

But the most astounding passage in Joel is 2:28–32. Here the prophet sees a time in the future, "afterward," when the Spirit of God will be poured out "on all flesh." Young and old alike, both women and men, will experience this outpouring. This section of Scripture hangs suspended for nearly eight hundred years. Though the Spirit had come upon prophets and priests, never had there been such a general outpouring of the Spirit. Then, on the Day of Pentecost, the Spirit came with such power and force that it captured the attention of the masses gathered in Jerusalem for the festival. Peter takes hold of this prophetic section and declares, "But this is what was spoken by the prophet Joel" (Acts 2:16). A new age is born, the church is empowered, and now "whoever calls on the name of the LORD shall be saved."

Amos

The work of the Holy Spirit is not mentioned specifically in Amos. The process of inspiring the prophet and revealing God's message is usually attributed by other prophets to the Spirit (see Is. 48:16; Ezek. 3:24; Mic. 3:8). As is the case in most of the prophets, it is almost impossible to draw a distinction between the Lord and His Spirit. Amos does not happen to mention the Spirit in his work, but those activities ascribed to the Spirit by other prophets are present in Amos.

Kingdom Key *continued from page 218*

Old Testament, His Son, King Jesus, fulfilled in the New Testament.

Amos: Prophet of the King's Global Authority

Yahweh, the Lord God of Israel, may have been viewed by some of the contemporaries of Amos and the ancient Jews as a regional or provincial, tribal deity. But Amos thundered to the contrary: "The LORD God of hosts, He who touches the earth and it melts . . . the LORD is His name!" (9:5–6). That advances the prophet's earlier claims in Amos 2—4, where the nations surrounding Israel are confronted by the authority of Yahweh's throne. Unsurprisingly, then, the coming of Yahweh's Son— the King of the Eternal Kingdom—is announced as having authoritative implications for the whole earth (Luke 2:12–14): (1) He has come to provide salvation for all humankind (John 3:16); (2) He is the appointed judge over the whole world (Acts 17:30–31); and, ultimately, (3) before Him every earthly being shall bow (Phil. 2:9–10).

Introducing
HOSEA

Author. Hosea, whose name means "Salvation" or "Deliverance," was chosen by God to live out his message to his people by marrying a woman who would be unfaithful to him. His sensitivity toward the sinful condition of his countrymen and his sensitivity toward the loving heart of God fitted him for this difficult ministry.

Background and Date. Hosea gives the historical setting for his ministry by naming the kings of the southern kingdom of Judah (Uzziah, Jotham, Ahaz, and Hezekiah) and the king of the northern kingdom of Israel (Jeroboam II) who ruled during the period of his prophecy (1:1). This sets the dates from 755 B.C. to 715 B.C. Though all the gauges of outward success seemed positive for Israel, underneath disaster was lurking. The people of this period enjoyed peace, plenty, and prosperity; but anarchy was brewing, and it would bring the political collapse of the nation in a few short years. Hosea describes the characteristic social conditions of his day: corrupt leaders, unstable family life, widespread immorality, class hatred, and poverty. Though people continued a form of worship, idolatry was more and more accepted and the priests were failing to guide the people into ways of righteousness. In spite of the darkness of these days, Hosea holds out hope to inspire his people to turn back to God.

Content. The Book of Hosea is about a people who needed to hear the love of God, a God who wanted to tell them, and the unique way God chose to demonstrate His love to His people. The people thought that love could be bought ("Ephraim has hired lovers," 8:9), that love was the pursuit of self-gratification ("I will go after my lovers who give me," 2:5), and that loving unworthy objects could bring positive benefits ("They became an abomination like the thing they loved," 9:10). God wanted Israel to know His love, which reached out for unlikely and unworthy objects ("When Israel was a child, I loved him," 11:1), which guided with gentle discipline ("bands of love," 11:4), and which persisted in spite of the peoples' running and resisting ("How can I give you up?" 11:8).

The problem was how to get this message of God's love to a people not inclined to listen, and not likely to understand if they did listen. God's solution was to let the prophet be his own sermon. Hosea would marry an impure woman ("wife of harlotry," 1:2), love her fully and have children by her (1:3), and go after her and bring her back when she strays ("Go again, love," 3:1). In sum, Hosea was to show by his own love for Gomer the kind of love God had for Israel.

Personal Application. These lessons stand out clearly from the Book of Hosea:

1. If the people around us do not see the love of God in us, they will not find it anywhere. Like Hosea, all believers are called to demonstrate to their neighbors by their attitudes and by their actions God's love in Christ to a world blindly groping for indications of authentic love.

2. We cannot separate our witness and our ministries from our lives. Hosea's strongest sermon was his relationship with his wife. The source of his power for preaching was his home and his family.

3. The only perfect example of love is found in God Himself. When God enters into marriage with His people, He recites vows that promise permanence, a right relationship, fair treatment, love unfailing, tenderness, security, and continuing self-revelation (2:19–20). Our love must drink from this spring, then draw for others, offering to them, not the best form of human love we can give, but the pure, undiluted love of God in Christ.

Surveying
HOSEA

I. HOSEA AND GOMER 1:1—3:5. Hosea is told to "take to yourself an adulterous wife."

A. Hosea's marriage to Gomer (1:1–9).

1. *The setting (1:1).*

2. *The marriage (1:2–3).*

3. *The children (1:3–9).* The prophet and Gomer have three children. Each is named to communicate a message to Israel. The first is called Jezreel, name of the city where Jehu took the throne by massacring his predecessor's family. The other children, "Unloved" and "Not My People," symbolize God's forced rejection of Israel.

B. Yahweh's marriage to Israel (1:10—2:23).

1. *Israel as God's people (1:10—2:1).* God's commitment to His people is unchanged, even though Israel is unfaithful. In the end He will reunite the divided kingdoms and bless them under the promised messianic King.

2. Israel's unfaithfulness (2:2–8). Hosea's words about Israel help us to understand his feelings about his relationship with Gomer, even as his family tragedy helps us to understand the Lord's emotions as He watches His idolatrous people (*see* Baal) run from relationship with Him.

3. Israel's punishment for unfaithfulness (2:9–13). Using the metaphor of adultery, God, through the prophet, shares the anguish and the anger He feels at Israel's spiritual adultery.

4. God's love for Israel (2:14–23; see Family Life; Hope; Mercy*).*

C. Hosea's taking back of Gomer (3:1–5).

1. Gomer bought out of slavery (3:1–3). After the birth of their children, Hosea's wife deserted him. She lived with other men and apparently was at last forced to sell herself as a bondservant (1–2). Now God sends Hosea to her. Hosea purchases Gomer from her master and brings her home. There she is forced to live a continent life "for many days."

2. Israel's return to God (3:4–5). This disciplinary experience mirrors the years that Israel will be forced to live under foreign powers, without political independence (5; *see* Fear). But then there is a full restoration of the relationship between Hosea and Gomer, just as there will be a full restoration of Israel.

II. YAHWEH AND ISRAEL 4:1—14:9.

A. Sin and judgment (4:1—10:15).

Each Old Testament prophet pointed out sins that warped relationship with God and called for judgment. No one could complain that God failed to make His ways plain to His people or to express His horror at unrighteousness. Hosea too denounces, and thus defines, the actions that make Israel guilty before God.

1. Israel's sinful state (4:1–19). Charges against Israel: cursing, lying, murder, stealing, and adultery have replaced faithfulness and love in Israel (1–2). Israel has ignored God's Law to the point of practicing ritual prostitution at the sites where they commit idolatry (4–14).

2. Announcement of judgment (5:1—6:11). A day of wrath is coming (8–12). Even when Israel recognizes her vulnerability, she turns not to God but to Assyria! God must wait until at last misery will drive His people to *seek Him.

Israel's heart is revealed by her actions rather than her words. Despite verbal expressions of repentance (6:1–3), she consistently turns back to her sins.

> ### "Come, and let us return to the LORD"
>
> **(6:1–3).** The key to revival is not penance but repentance; not wallowing in sin but awakening to the Lord—we return to Him, and He restores us completely, every part made whole! Returning means *pursuing with passion* an intimate relationship with Jesus, who assuredly responds to persistent seeking. Returning holds out a *promise of pouring;* the Spirit is given in immeasurable fullness to all who thirst after Him. The cry of revival is *let it rain*—Holy Spirit, come!

God does not seek words from Israel, or ritual sacrifices, but faithfulness to a covenant law that prohibits the murders and other shameful crimes that God witnesses in Ephraim (6:4–11).

3. Israel's sins listed (7:1—8:14). Deceit fills the land, tainting every class, from the common thieves who break into others' houses (7:1–2) to those who surround the throne with drunkenness and intrigue (7:3–7). Israel's actions are a daily testimony to their rebellion against God and to the fact that they have not repented (7:8–16).

The whirlwind of judgment (8:1–14). God's judgment will roar down like a tornado (*see* Trumpet) upon this land of broken covenants. The religious and political evils that are practiced in Israel (2–6) have sold the people to devastating punishment. Now they must experience it in full.

4. Forms of judgment specified (9:1—10:15). Israel's doom is announced (*see* Watchman). Judgment comes because of "all their wickedness" (9:15). God must now reject this generation which has rejected Him and refused to respond. Israel's population will become wanderers among the nations. The people who rejected God as king will be taken to Assyria (10:6). They have planted (*see* Sow) wickedness; they will reap evil. All that is about to happen comes "because of your great wickedness" (10:15).

B. Love and restoration (11:1—14:9).

1. God's father love for Israel (11:1–12). God affirms His love for Israel. Hosea keeps the intimacy of the family context (*see* Family Life) but changes the image. He now reveals God's love focused on Israel as if the nation were a precious child (3).

✎ "But they did not know that I healed them"

✎ "But they did not know that I healed them"
(11:3–4). God's healing sometimes occurs without our recognizing it. This is frequently the case when it comes to the health one receives from the nourishment of being nurtured. Hosea describes this kind of health and healing using the metaphor of a parent with their child. Beyond the obvious practical application for parents, this message emphasizes that God always has His children in His heart, and He is constantly about the business of bringing them to health and wholeness.

God looks ahead. He sees the suffering that will come because His child rejects the ties of love with which He seeks to bind her and is determined to turn away (5–7). We can sense the anguish the Lord feels as He cries out, "How can I give you up, Ephraim?" The discipline must come, but God will not surrender His people. Instead God will bring His people back and "let them dwell in their houses" (11).

2. God in Israel's history (12:1—13:6). The themes emphasized throughout Hosea are found in this bold sermon of the prophet, who again confronts Israel with her sins. Twisting away from her relationship with God, Israel has turned from the Lord to make treaties with Assyria and Egypt (12:1–6). Her prosperous people love to defraud and show only contempt for the prophets God sends them (12:7–14). Israel has now thrown herself into frenzied pursuit of spiritual wickedness, even offering human sacrifice and kneeling to kiss the calf-idols (13:1–3).

3. God in Israel's future (13:7–16). The great

reality that Israel has forgotten will soon confront her. "I am the LORD your God," the prophet relays. The One who cared for Israel as she wandered on the burning sands of the wilderness can and will destroy her, and this without compassion (*see* Grave). Now the people of Samaria must bear their guilt. They have rebelled against the only One who can redeem.

4. God's promise of restoration (14:1–9). This generation will experience judgment as a result of their sins. But this does not mean God has rejected His people! The prophet calls on the exiles to "take words with you, and return to the LORD" (2). When the people appeal for forgiveness, God will heal their waywardness and love them freely (2–3). Then people and land will flourish again, and Ephraim will have nothing more to do with idolatry. God's grace will be revealed in the forgiven, healed, and holy land.

✎ "Your fruit is found in Me"
(14:4–8). The Lord promises to love His people unconditionally, healing their waywardness (v. 4), growing them into mature expressions of Himself—that His beauty and fragrance might be evident (vv. 5–6)—and extending them everywhere (v. 7). But growth requires response. When the rhetorical question, "What have I to do anymore with idols?" (v. 8) is answered by affirmative action, fruitfulness comes from the Lord. His growth agent, the Spirit, expresses through us the fruit of Christ's character and life. As idolatrous images are put away, the Spirit always erects the image of the Son in their place.

TRUTH-IN-ACTION through HOSEA

Truth Hosea Teaches	**Action** Hosea Invites
1 Steps to Knowing God Hosea, perhaps more than any other prophet, reveals the loving heart of God. God desires to bless, not to chastise His people. The Lord puts a premium value on His relationship with us.	**6:1–3** *Recognize* that God's heart is for the full restoration of His people. *Understand* that He calls us to press on to know Him so that He can bring rich blessings to us. **6:6** *Be assured* God values our relationship with Him more than He desires our service.
2 Guidelines for Growing in Godliness Paul caught the essence of godliness when he wrote, "Therefore be imitators of God as	**1:2, 3** *Recognize* that a person's life is the most powerful sermon he or she can preach. *Understand* that God calls us to act out His Word in our lives.

(continued)

Truth Hosea Teaches	**Action** Hosea Invites
2 Guidelines for Growing in Godliness (continued) dear children" (Eph. 5:1). Just as God called Hosea to live out His undying, eternal love for His people by instructing him to marry an unfaithful woman, He calls us to illustrate His Word and His very character in the way we live.	**3:1-5** *Know* that Hosea acted out God's loving forgiveness for His people. *Emulate* God's forgiveness for His people in the way you continually forgive others. **8:4** *Inquire* of the Lord and *invoke* His hand in any selection of leadership in the church. **14:9** *Be prudent, wise,* and *righteous. Choose* to walk in the way of the Lord.
3 Steps to Holiness Holiness demands rather than requests our total dependence on God and His provision.	**10:13** *Depend* wholly on the Lord. *Reject* the deceptive fruit of wickedness, the lie of self-sufficient strength and wisdom.
4 Keys to Wise Living The pursuit of spiritual knowledge and understanding should be high on our list of priorities.	**4:6, 7** *Recognize* that "what you do not know *can* hurt you. *Pursue* and value true spiritual knowledge. *Do not neglect* God's Word. **4:14** *Pursue* and value spiritual understanding. *Seek* to lay hold of it. *Recognize* that understanding keeps you from ruin.
5 Steps to Dealing with Sin Give sin no place to develop in your life. A fallow heart is excellent soil in which to cultivate sin. Deal with sin quickly and ruthlessly whenever it is found. Do not be lulled to sleep by those who claim God does not care about obedience. He looks for those who obey His Word and honor it by their behavior.	**5:15** *Recognize* that God often allows misery into the lives of His people to cause them to seek him earnestly. *Be quick* to admit your guilt of sin. *Do not deny* that you are a sinner. *Confess, repent,* and *be restored* to God. **9:17** *Settle it* in your heart: God *does reject* those who continue to disobey him. **10:12** *Beware* of any hardness of heart. *Seek* radical remedy for a fallow spiritual life. *Believe* that the Lord will honor and visit those who seek Him with their whole heart.

Introducing

JOEL

Author. The name "Joel" means literally, "Yahweh Is God." This is a very common name in Israel, and Joel the prophet is specified as the son of Pethuel. Nothing is known about him or his life circumstances. It is likely that he lived in Judah and prophesied in Jerusalem.

Date. There is no way to date the book with absolute certainty, and scholars vary in their opinions. There are references in both Amos and Isaiah which are also in Joel. (Compare Amos 1:2 with Joel 3:16 and Is. 13:6 with Joel 1:15.) It is the opinion of most conservatives that Amos and Isaiah borrowed from Joel, making him one of the very earliest of the minor prophets.

Furthermore, the worship of God, which the high priest Jehoiada restored during the reign of Joash (2 Kings 11; 2 Chr. 23:16), is assumed by Joel. Therefore, many hold that Joel prophesied during the first thirty years of the reign of Joash (835–796 B.C.) when Jehoiada was the king's adviser. This would place Joel's ministry around 835–805 B.C.

Background. Joel prophesied at a time of great devastation to the entire land of Judah. An enormous plague of locusts had denuded the countryside of all vegetation, destroyed the pastures of both the sheep and the cattle, even stripped the bark off the fig trees. In only a few hours what was once a beautiful, verdant land had become a place of desolation and destruction. Contemporary descriptions of the destructive power of swarms of locusts corroborate Joel's picture of the plague in his time.

The plague of locusts Joel wrote about was greater than anyone had ever seen. All crops were lost and the seed crops for the next planting were destroyed. A famine and drought had seized the entire land. Both people and animals were dying. It was so profound and disastrous that Joel saw only one explanation: it was the judgment of God.

Content. The Book of Joel is naturally divided into two sections. The first (1:1—2:27) deals with the present judgment of God, a call to repentance, and a promise of restoration.

In Moses' sermon to Israel (Deut. 28:38–46) he warned that, if the nation was disobedient, "Locusts shall consume all your trees and the produce of your land." The prophet sees that just such a day has come. He graphically describes the horrible armies of locusts in prophetic and poetic language. Four waves of these armylike creatures have consumed everything. Drinkers have no wine. The priests have nothing to offer in sacrifice to God. Farmers and vinedressers have nothing to care for. There is no part of Judah's life that has not been dramatically and tragically affected.

The second section (2:28—3:21) explains that this plague, horrible as it may be, is nothing compared to the judgment of God that is coming. This will be a time when not only Judah, but all the nations of the world, will be called before God. It will be a time when the sounds of locusts will be muted as "the LORD also will roar from Zion, and utter His voice from Jerusalem; the heavens and earth will shake" (3:16).

Terrifying heavenly portents will take place. "The sun shall be turned into darkness and the moon into blood" (2:31). This will be none other than "the great and awesome day of the LORD" (2:31).

However, we must not overlook the most remarkable section of this short prophecy. Through the anointing of the Holy Spirit, Joel looks hundreds of years ahead to a time when God will pour out His Spirit "on all flesh" (2:28). This will be a prelude to the devastation and judgment of the day of the Lord. It will be a time when all believers will experience the indwelling of the Spirit of God and will form a prophetic community on earth. It will be a time when prophecy will come from young and old alike, when both men and women will prophesy. Salvation will not just be the unique blessing on Judah. It will be a time when "whoever calls on the name of the LORD shall be saved" (2:32).

Personal Application. Joel prophesies the inauguration of the age of the church—a time when all people everywhere can call on the name of the Lord, be saved from their sins, and become participants in the kingdom of God. Through the indwelling of the Holy Spirit, the church becomes the body of Christ in the world. The redemptive purposes of God are therefore extended and made available through every Spirit-filled believer.

This is the time in which we now live. Ours is the wonderful privilege of not only experiencing salvation ourselves, but also of being those who bring the Good News to all who will listen. What Joel was to ravaged Judah, the church is to a ravaged world—namely, a prophetic voice, bringing God's viewpoint into clear focus, calling for repentance, and extending the hope of salvation from the final and terrible day of the Lord.

The message of Joel is concise and clear: "If you think the plague of locusts is bad, wait until you see the final judgment of the Lord." But, as every true prophet of God, Joel does not stop with the prediction of doomsday. He clearly announces the day of God's grace.

Surveying
JOEL

I. THE LORD'S HAND IN THE PRESENT 1:1—2:27.

A. The destruction by the locusts (1:2—2:11).
The worst swarm of locusts in memory sweeps into Judah (1:2–4), stripping not only the leaves but even the bark from the trees (5–7). Despair (see Mourn) grips the people as the crops they depend on for life are destroyed (8–12).

Joel calls on the priests to declare a fast and gather the people to God's house to cry out to the Lord (1:13–20).

> "For the day of the LORD is at hand"

(1:15). The historical fulfillment of this passage symbolically represents Christ's introduction of His kingdom. He did so with the announcement that "the kingdom of heaven is at hand" (Matt. 4:17). This proclamation from the Lord announced the beginning of the end for the powers of darkness. The gospel of the kingdom could be described as the forward advance of the power of the life of Jesus, unseating principalities and powers as it proceeds. God's hand of destruction is ready to execute His vengeance on spiritual darkness wherever He is invited to do so.

Joel powerfully announces that the locusts are a divine judgment—a contemporary expression of that final "day of the Lord," known to be "a day of darkness and gloominess, a day of clouds and thick darkness" (2:2). The cloud of insects pours down the mountainside like a great army; the whirring of their wings sounds like the crackling of a consuming fire (2:5). The modern world is just as helpless before locust swarms as was the ancient world: the army of judgment which the Lord Himself leads against Judah (2:11) is invincible.

B. The repentance of Judah (2:12–17). Jeremiah 18:7–10 teaches that God's announcements of judgment on a nation are conditional. If a nation or person turns from the sins which made judgment a necessity, God will relent. As the locusts swarm over the land, Joel declares that even now it is not too late for Judah. "Turn to Me with all your heart," God pleads through the prophet, that He may "turn and relent" (12, 14). Priests and citizens of Judah join in a sacred assembly, begging the Lord to spare His people (15–17).

C. The restoration of the Lord (2:18–27). God responds by driving the locusts from the land. Most swarms of locusts do not approach Israel from the north, although some have been so recorded. The direction is significant. It is from the north that all Bible prophecy sees the enemy approach for the great battle at history's end.

The answer to Joel's generation is an affirmation of fruitfulness and a promise that Zion's people will yet rejoice in their God (21–24). Then God will restore the years the locusts have devoured, and Joel's generation will know that there is a God in Israel. Those who are His people will never be put to shame (25–27).

> **"And praise the name of the LORD your God, Who has dealt wondrously with you"**
> (2:23–27). This exhortation to praise is nestled into a passage with particular implications for the Spirit-filled believer. The outpouring of the Holy Spirit is part of the wondrous way in which God has dealt with His people. Not only is there additional reason for offering praise to God, but, by virtue of the presence of the Holy Spirit within, there are additional methods or expressions by which praise may be offered. The purpose for our praise can be found in the Lord's provisional aspect. He is the One who has given latter rain, full threshing floors, and overflowing vats, all of which speak of the renewing feature of His Spirit.

II. THE LORD'S DAY IN THE FUTURE 2:28—3:21. The plague of locusts corresponds in several ways to a great battle to be fought at history's end. Many prophets speak of this battle (cf. Ezekiel 38, 39). The invaders swarm from the north in irresistible force, bringing devastation. God acts supernaturally to destroy the enemy and, in a great turning to God, His people are given the Lord's Spirit. The parallels between the judgment and following blessing experienced in Joel's own day and in the "day of the Lord" launch Joel into what may be the first of the Old Testament's extended written apocalyptic visions.

A. The grace of the Lord (2:28–32). Joel begins with the great promise of the Spirit of God. The Spirit will be poured out on all people in the day of final wonders, when "everyone who calls on the name of the Lord will be saved." God's intention, even in the final cataclysmic judgment, is not to destroy but to heal (see Restoration).

This passage is quoted by Peter on the Day of Pentecost. He explains the strange behavior of the disciples and their speaking with other tongues as due to that pouring out of the Spirit of which Joel speaks.

> **"And it shall come to pass afterward that I will pour out My Spirit on all flesh"**
> (2:28–29). The prophet Joel announces the future outpouring of God's Spirit, which commenced on the Day of Pentecost, inaugurating the church era. On that day in Jerusalem the disciples "were all filled with the Holy Spirit and began to speak with other tongues" (Acts 2:1–4)—thus explained by the apostle Peter as he quotes from the Joel passage (vv. 17–21). He identifies Joel's "afterward" as "the last days" (compare Joel 2:28 and Acts 2:17), suggesting that the Spirit's outpouring is not a one-time event but a continuous period of the Spirit's effusion, available to all who would receive it. (See Dreams.)

B. The judgment of the Lord (3:1–17). The blessings are preceded by terrors. God will call all nations to the "Valley of Jehoshaphat [the Lord is Judge]" (3:2). The people who oppressed Judah, and who even then gather against her, will be crushed.

The gathering together of the nations to war against Judah is an indication that the day of the Lord is near (3:9–14). There are other indications—cataclysmic changes in the heavens and the earth (3:15–17; see Roar).

C. The blessing of the Lord (3:18–21). Then God will act to establish His authority. A for- given Israel will live peacefully in her land forever (17–21).

TRUTH-IN-ACTION through JOEL	
Truth Joel Teaches	**Action** Joel Invites
1 **Steps to Knowing God and His Ways** The knowledge of God is to be passed from generation to generation by instructing our children in the nature, character, and ways of God. Thus trained, a deeper understanding of God's current move, whether in judgment or revival, is possible. This understanding avoids reliance on fleshly or demonic sources of guidance, and allows the alignment of our priorities with God's purpose.	**1:3** *Train up* your children in the nurture and admonition of the Lord. *Be an example* your children can follow to know the ways of the Lord and walk in them. **2:28, 29** *Gratefully receive* the Holy Spirit, by whom God accomplishes His purposes on the Earth. *Be renewed* by the outpouring of the Holy Spirit. **2:30, 31** *Believe* that signs, wonders, and miracles are part of God's unchanging nature and working.
2 **Steps to Receiving God's Grace** Receiving the grace of God is neither complex nor difficult, It requires only the decision that God is both able and willing to save, and the act of humbly calling on His name. He is ready to be our Deliverer. The choice is ours.	**2:32** *Choose to call* on the name of Jesus for salvation and deliverance. *Recognize* that "calling on His name" relates to inviting His saving and delivering action in all facets of your life, not only your initial experience of New Birth.
3 **Steps to Dealing with Corporate Sin** Joel's prophecies explain how a people must deal with corporate sin. His prophetic warnings and exhortations are addressed primarily to the spiritual leaders. He calls them first to lead in wholehearted repentance and then to confront the people's sin. Corporate fasts and solemn assemblies to cry out to the Lord are some of the practices Joel recommends to deal with corporate sin.	**1:13** *Understand* that the sin of God's people is serious and calls for serious repentance and mourning on the part of spiritual leaders. **2:1** *Warn God's people* of the consequences of sin. **1:14** *Teach the church* to repent corporately for corporate sin. *Declare* a time for corporate fasting and solemn assemblies to identify sin and pray for restoration in the body. **2:12–14** *Repent quickly* with mourning when sin is discovered in you. *Confess* your sin and *let God work* in your heart. *Continually turn* to God and set your affections on His will and His ways. **2:15–17** *Call for revival. Enjoin* the elders to lead in fasting and prayer. **3:21** *Be assured* that there is no sin for which Jesus' blood cannot atone.

Introducing
AMOS

Author. Amos, whose name means "Burden-Bearer," was a native of the small town of Tekoa in the Judean hills, about sixteen kilometers (ten miles) south of Jerusalem (*see* map, page 184). He is the first of the so-called "writing prophets" of the eighth century B.C. The others include Hosea to Israel, and Micah and Isaiah to Judah. Amos disclaimed training as a professional prophet, admitting he was a shepherd and one who tended sycamore-fig trees. In spite of his background, Amos was called to deliver God's message to the northern kingdom of Israel.

Date. Amos prophesied during the reigns of Uzziah of Judah (792–740 B.C.) and Jeroboam II of Israel (793–753 B.C.). His ministry was between 760 and 750 B.C. and seems to have occupied less than two years.

Background. The middle of the eighth century

B.C. was a time of great prosperity for both Israel and Judah. Under Jeroboam, Israel had again gained control of the international trade routes—the King's Highway through Transjordan, and the Way of the Sea through the Jezreel Valley and along the coastal plain. According to 2 Kings 14:25, he restored the borders of Israel from Lebo Hamath (in the north) to the Sea of the Arabah (the Dead Sea in the south). Judah, under Uzziah, regained Elath (the seaport on the Gulf of Aqaba), and expanded to the southwest at the expense of the Philistines. Israel and Judah had reached new political and military heights, but the religious situation was at an all-time low. Idolatry was rampant; the rich were living in luxury while the poor were oppressed; there was widespread immorality; and the judicial system was corrupt. The people interpreted their prosperity as a sign of God's blessing on them. Amos's task was to deliver the message that God was displeased with the nation. His patience was exhausted. Punishment was inevitable. The nation would be destroyed unless there was a change of heart—a change that would "let justice run down like water, and righteousness like a mighty stream" (5:24).

Content. The Book of Amos is basically a message of judgment: judgment on the nations, oracles and visions of divine judgment on Israel. The central theme of the book is that the people of Israel have broken their covenant with God. As a result, God's punishment of their sin will be severe. Amos begins with a series of indictments against the seven neighbors of Israel, including Judah, and then he indicts Israel, too (1:3—2:16). Each foreign nation is to be punished for specific offenses either against Israel or some other nation. This judgment on the nations teaches us that God is a universal monarch. All nations are under His control. They must answer to Him for their mistreatment of other nations and peoples. Israel and Judah, however, will be punished because they have broken their covenant with God. The next section (3:1—6:14) is a series of three oracles or sermons directed against Israel. These include the threat of exile. A third section (7:1—9:10) is a series of five visions of judgment, in two of which God withdraws. Finally, Amos promises restoration for Israel (9:11–15).

Literary Features. Even though Amos downplays his professional training, his style suggests a well-educated person. He skillfully uses puns or wordplays. In 8:1–2, for example, the Hebrew word for "summer fruit" sounds similar to the word for "end." Like summer fruit, Israel is ripe for harvest. The geographical-psychological approach in the judgment of the nations (1:3—2:16) is another indication of literary craftsmanship. Beginning with the nations on the four corners (Damascus, Gaza, Tyre and Edom), Amos crosses the land twice and draws the circle ever tighter with Ammon, Moab, and Judah. He uses a literary method known as graduated numbers or numerical parallelism: "For three transgressions . . . and for four" (see, for example, 1:3, 6, 9). This numerical system suggests the meaning, "For enough transgressions . . . for more than enough." Similar uses of graduated numerals are found in Proverbs 6:16; 30:15, 18, 21, 29; Micah 5:5.

Amos uses the messenger style of speech, indicating he is speaking in the name of another: "Thus says the LORD" (1:3, 6) or "Hear this word" (3:1; 4:1; 5:1). Amos sings a funeral dirge for Israel in anticipation of her demise (5:1–2). He uses many metaphors from the country life he knew as a shepherd and farmer (1:3; 2:13; 3:12; 4:1; 9:9). Amos has the ability to develop a series of sayings into a powerful climax: the oracles against the nations (1:3—2:16), the recitation of calamities leading to God's visitation (4:6–12), and the visions that move from God's forbearance to His judgment (7:1–17; 8:1–3).

Personal Application. Amos stresses that righteousness and justice are essential to a healthy society. Religion is more than observing feast days and holding sacred assemblies; true religion demands righteous living. The way a man treats his neighbor reveals his relationship with God. Jesus said the greatest commandment is to love God. The second is to love our neighbor as ourselves. This is the message of Amos. This is the message needed today. We also are living in a prosperous, materialistic society. Because we are prosperous, we may also deceive ourselves into believing that we have God's blessing on us. The tendency to give God material goods and believe we have satisfied Him is ever with us. Material prosperity often leads to religious and moral corruption. Observation of external rites is not enough. God demands our obedience— a heartfelt attitude that issues in action to meet the needs of our fellow human beings.

Surveying
AMOS

I. INTRODUCTION 1:1–2.

II. JUDGMENT ON THE NATIONS 1:3–2:16.

Amos's mission is to identify sins that call for judgment and to announce the doom about to fall on the transgressors. He begins his sermon by looking first at the nations around Israel. Loudly he pinpoints their offenses and then announces the punishment God will bring on them.

But after a look at the sins of the sister kingdom, Judah, Amos turns on Israel. Brutally, with a list of concrete examples, the prophet exposes the practices God must judge.

A. Damascus (1:3–5).

B. Gaza (1:6–8).

C. Tyre (1:9–10).

D. Edom (1:11–12).

E. Ammon (1:13–15).

....

Judgment Against Eight Nations

The phrase "For three transgressions . . . and for four" is a literary device to communicate "fullness (three) to overflowing (four)." The judgment spirals out from Judah and Israel to the surrounding nations.

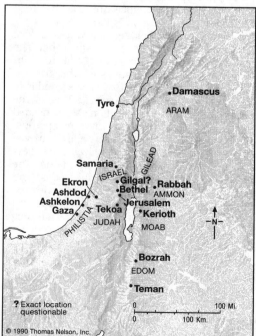

? Exact location questionable

0   100 Mi.
0   100 Km.

© 1990 Thomas Nelson, Inc.

F. Moab (2:1–3).

G. Judah (2:4–5; see Despised).

H. Israel (2:6–16). The detailed list of evils provided by Amos focuses on the sins of the wealthy and on a justice system that is bribe-hungry and corrupt.

III. ORACLES AGAINST ISRAEL 3:1–6:14.

A. Judgment on God's chosen people (3:1–15). First Sermon: Judgment plan is revealed.

1. Punishment announced (3:1–2).

2. Punishment deserved (3:3–10). In this sermon Amos reminds his listeners that God *reveals His plan through the prophets (7). Now Amos himself stands to speak out against the family that God brought up from Egypt.

It is because God chose Israel that He will judge her (2). The fact of privilege makes punishment for sin certain. This is illustrated by a series of cause-and-effect statements; Israel's sin (cause) must be followed by judgment (effect; 3–6).

3. Punishment described (3:11–15).

B. Judgment on God's unresponsive people (4:1–13). Second Sermon: Israel refuses to turn to God.

1. The oppressive women of Samaria (4:1–3). Amos addresses the first words of this sermon to the wives of the wealthy. These women, who urge their husbands to keep on providing luxuries, are also guilty of oppressing the poor (1).

2. Sacrificial transgression (4:4–5). Amos then reviews God's dealings with Israel.

3. Failure of Israel to respond to calamities (4:6–11). Time and again disciplinary judgments struck Israel. They knew drought, disease, and military defeats. But the people remained unresponsive and would not turn to the Lord. (See Satisfied.)

4. Punishment on hardened people (4:12–13). Amos closes with a grim and final warning, "Prepare to meet your God, O Israel." The One to whom Israel might have turned for healing will overtake them—to judge.

C. Judgment on God's unrepentant people (5:1–6:14). Third Sermon: Call to seek God.

1. A funeral dirge for Israel (5:1–3). This sermon begins with a lament for the fallen nation and what is about to happen. But Amos moves quickly to invitation; the people are urged to "seek God and live!"

2. A call to repentance (5:4–9). It must be God Himself they seek, not a religion of ritual.

3. Enumeration of evil acts (5:10–13). These are people who trample on the poor, who hate truth, who love their luxuries, and take bribes to deprive the oppressed of justice.

4. *A second call to repentance (5:14–15).* For them to find God they must learn to seek good and not evil.

5. *Judgment will bring wailing and mourning (5:16–17).*

6. *The Day of the Lord (5:18–20).* Passionately, Amos announces the coming day of the Lord; a "day of darkness, and not light."

7. *Need for justice instead of festivals (5:21–27).* God, who loves justice, utterly hates the religious facade that masks oppression and inner idolatry with a thin coating of religion (*see* Restoration).

8. *Woe to those who are complacent (6:1–7).*

9. *Judgment on unrepentant people (6:8–14).* The pride of this people, so abhorrent to the Lord God, will be smashed along with the kingdom when God stirs up a foreign land against them. In that day, God promises His sinning people, His nation of oppressors, that the enemy whom God calls against them "will oppress you all the way."

VI. VISIONS OF JUDGMENT 7:1—9:10. These chapters relate five visions of judgment seen by the prophet. They also report the response of the men of Israel who heard the Lord's words—and expelled His prophet from the kingdom!

A. Relented visions (7:1–6).

1. *Locusts swarms (7:1–3).* God shows Amos that He is preparing swarms of locusts to strip the land of its crops. At Amos's intercession the Lord relents. The judgment is averted.

2. *Consuming fire (7:4–6).* God now shows Amos preparations He is making for a great fire to sweep Israel and devour the land. Again the prophet begs God to stop, and again God relents. But the judgment will not always be put off.

B. Unrelented visions (7:7—9:10).

1. *The plumb line (7:7–17).*

The vision (7:7–9). Amos sees God standing beside a wall. He is holding a weight, tied to a line. This instrument is used by builders to tell if their walls are upright. God tells Amos that the time has come to go among His people and measure them. Israel is not upright, and God will spare her no longer.

Opposition of Amaziah (7:10–17). Amos is a citizen of the southern kingdom, Judah. His mission to neighboring Israel is not appreciated! His announcements of judgment and promises that "Israel will surely go into exile" are viewed as an attempt to stimulate a conspiracy against Jeroboam! Amaziah, the priest in charge of the Bethel worship center, demands that Amos go home and stop prophesying against Israel.

"I was a sheepbreeder . . . then the LORD took me as I followed the flock" (7:14–15). A call to be the Lord's mouthpiece does not depend upon prior experience. Amos was "no prophet" nor the "son of a prophet" (v. 14)—just a herdsmen and gardener—yet the Lord called him (v. 15). Amaziah opposed Amos's message (vv. 10–13), but Amos refuted him on the basis of the Lord's assignment—he was in Bethel because God had commanded him. Our witness to the Lord's truth is authenticated neither on our past achievement nor present ability. Our basis is His authority—for the Spirit empowers our witness and confirms our message as we go (*see* Acts 1:8; 1 Cor. 2:1–4).

Now the prophet turns on Amaziah. This man who has tried to silence the word of the Lord will die in a pagan country, his family will be killed, and his wife will become a prostitute in the city.

2. *The basket of summer fruit (8:1–14).*

The vision (8:1–3). The Lord shows Amos a basket of ripe fruit, which represents Israel. The time is now ripe for judgment. God will no longer spare (1–3).

The exposition (8:4–14).

3. *The Lord beside the altar (9:1–10).*

The vision (9:1–4). Now God calls to Amos to witness a vision of judgment executed. The buildings shake, the leaders are dragged into exile, and the commoners are killed by the sword (1). Although the people flee in terror and scramble to find hiding places, they are hunted down. God's own eye is "fixed on them for evil and not for good" (2–3).

The exposition (9:5–10). The Lord's piercing gaze is fixed "on the sinful kingdom" and he will "destroy it from the face of the earth" (5–8). Even in this vision of judgment there is a glimpse of grace. The destruction will not be total. There will be survivors. Although the sinners of Israel will die, the good, like kernels of grain, will be shaken out and distributed among the nations. In time they will be gathered and returned (*see* Layers).

V. RESTORATION OF ISRAEL 9:11–15.

A. Tabernacle of David raised up (9:11–12). Most of the prophets' messages conclude with a promise of Israel's ultimate blessing. Amos is no exception. The severe judgment of God on a sinning generation is neither complete rejection of the whole people nor withdrawal of God's commitment to Abraham's children. Thus Amos closes with a vision of hope.

A day is coming when a ruler from David's line will be placed on David's throne (11). In that day many nations will bear the name of the Lord (12).

B. The land and people restored and blessed (9:13–15). The earth will know unmatched prosperity (13). Then a regathered Israel will dwell in the promised land (14), never to be uprooted again (15).

TRUTH-IN-ACTION through AMOS

Truth Amos Teaches	**Action** Amos Invites
❶ Steps to Knowing God and His Ways God's judgments should never be a complete surprise because we already know what His standards are. His Word (both the Scriptures and also as incarnate in the Lord Jesus Christ) will announce beforehand any judgment to give His people ample opportunity to repent and turn from their sin (see 2 Chr. 7:14).	**3:6** *Understand* that God sent calamity to turn the people back to Him. **3:7** *Understand* that God never does anything He has not announced beforehand through His prophets. *Develop* an ear to hear what the Spirit is saying (through the prophets) to the churches. **7:7–9** *Know* that God judges everyone equally by the standards of His Word and by the life of Jesus Christ.
❷ Guidelines for Growing in Godliness The rebellious and disobedient among God's people tend to actively discourage godly and righteous behavior on the part of others. God says He will bring severe judgment against these. God wants us to do all we can to encourage His people to seek Him and obey His Word.	**2:4** *Understand* that ignorance of God's Word leads to believing lies. *Know* that empty traditions tend to transmit deception. **2:11, 12** *Do not discourage* godliness, *nor put* roadblocks in the way of those who pursue godliness and truth. **7:16, 17** *Allow* the full expression of the prophetic ministry so that God's people can be warned. *Encourage* the straightforward preaching of God's Word. **8:11, 12** *Hunger* and *thirst* for the Word of God while it is available.
❸ Keys to Wise Living The wise person does not depend on past achievement of spiritual experience to guarantee success in the future. Nor is he idle and self-indulgent today. God rejects both complacency and self-indulgence.	**6:1** *Be zealous* for the things of God. *Reject* any attitude of spiritual elitism. **6:3–8** *Exercise control* in your appetites. *Practice temperance* in all things. *Be unselfish. Let* Christ's zeal and selfless love characterize your life.

KEYS TO OBADIAH, JONAH, AND MICAH
A Trilogy on the King's Global Standards of Mercy and Justice

Kingdom Key: God's Purpose in View

Obadiah, Jonah, and Micah add to the declarations of God's attributes that are manifested in the Old Testament by His Word and revealed and incarnated in the New Testament through His Son.

Obadiah: Prophet of the King's Global Standards

God's moral standards as to what individuals and nations *ought* to be and to do is affirmed in the prophet's repeated phrase, "You should not have . . . nor should you have. . . ." (1:12–14). Philosophical relativism and cultural anthropology argue for elastic or removable lines of moral duty, denying ethical absolutes and pointing to widely varying taboos among earth's peoples. But Obadiah declares, "The kingdom shall be the LORD's!" (1:21). So, at His coming, Christ shall (1) banish evil (Matt. 13:36–43); (2) call every man or woman to an accounting (Rev. 20:11–15); (3) execute judicial authority (Acts 17:30–31); (4) according to the Father's standards of justice (Rom. 2:3–11); and then (5) deliver all things into the Father's hand (1 Cor. 15:24–28).

> **God calls every person to live justly.**

Jonah: Prophet of the King's Global Mercy

To understand the central problem addressed in Jonah we must grasp the separatist, nationalistic mindset of his people. God, to their thinking, was *their* God. Though He was God *above* all the earth (1:9), they hardly saw Him as God *for* all peoples. That is why Jonah complains when God displays mercy when the Ninevites repent (3:10— 4:3). Jonah seems to express gratitude for his hope in God's mercy, as he cries out for his own deliverance (2:7–9). But when the king of Nineveh calls his people to seek the same mercy, and then receives it (3:7–9), Jonah grows resentful. God then concludes instructing Jonah about His mercy, lessons which the New Testament reveals are incarnated in King Jesus: His

(Please turn to page 236.)

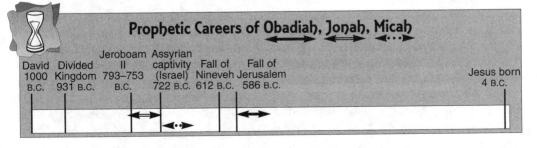

Prophetic Careers of Obadiah, Jonah, Micah

David 1000 B.C.	Divided Kingdom 931 B.C.	Jeroboam II 793–753 B.C.	Assyrian captivity (Israel) 722 B.C.	Fall of Nineveh 612 B.C.	Fall of Jerusalem 586 B.C.	Jesus born 4 B.C.

These prophets proclaim God's absolutes, • • •

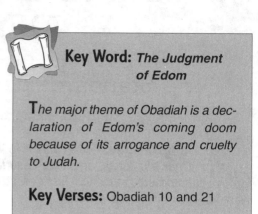

Master Key: God's Son Revealed
Obadiah

The final verse of Obadiah makes reference to "saviors" through whom God would exercise His dominion over the mountains of Esau. They would function as "judges" or "deliverers" from their center at Mount Zion or Jerusalem. Hebrew judges were "saviors" for the people. They liberated them from the oppression of foreigners, provided help for the widows and orphans, and executed justice in disputes. These saviors foreshadow God's ultimate Deliverer, Jesus Christ Himself, the Messiah who comes as the final Judge, both to be and to bring God's most glorious Word concerning the kingdom. Through Jesus, God offers His lordship and dominion to all humankind. He carries the message of deliverance especially to the downtrodden and oppressed (*see* Luke 4:16–21).

Key Word: *The Judgment of Edom*

The major theme of Obadiah is a declaration of Edom's coming doom because of its arrogance and cruelty to Judah.

Key Verses: Obadiah 10 and 21

The "day of the LORD" (v. 15) and the kingdom of God (v. 21) proclaimed by Obadiah anticipate Jesus Christ's entry into the world. The prophet's announcement that "the kingdom shall be the LORD's" (v. 21) is a theme that occupied much of Jesus' teaching. Time and again He spoke of the "kingdom of God" (*see* Luke 6:20; 9:27; 13:18–21) or the "kingdom of heaven" (*see* Matt. 5:3; 13:1–52). The nature of that kingdom and the manner of its coming are different from the image of Obadiah. Jesus ushers in a quiet kingdom of peace, a spiritual kingdom entered by faith in Him. But truly, the "day of the LORD" and the coming of His kingdom are inseparable from Jesus Christ. The Second Coming of Jesus will conform more closely to the picture painted in the prophecy of Obadiah than did His first coming.

Jonah

God's words to Jonah in 4:10–11 are paralleled by Jesus' words in John 3:16. God is concerned for all the earth's inhabitants. It is true that Christ has a special relationship with members of His body, the church, but His love for the world was dramatically demonstrated when He died on the Cross for the sins of all. John the Baptist acknowledged the universality of this love when he cried, "Behold! The Lamb of God who takes away the sin of the world!" (John 1:29). God's love for all, as taught to Jonah, was demonstrated ultimately in Jesus Christ, who declared a coming day when the elect will be gathered

Key Word: *The Revival in Nineveh*

God's loving concern for the Gentiles is not a truth disclosed only in the New Testament. More than seven centuries before Christ, God commissioned the Hebrew prophet Jonah to proclaim a message of repentance to the Assyrians.

Key Verses: Jonah 2:8–9; 4:2

continued on next page

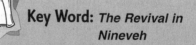

• • • His mercy, and His justice for all humankind.

from the north, east, south, and west (Matt. 24:31).

Micah

Prophecies about Christ make Micah's book glow with hope and encouragement. The book opens with a magnificent display of Yahweh's coming (1:3–5). Later prophecies will assert aspects of His arrival in historical time, but the disposition of God to come down and interact is established at the outset.

The first messianic prophecy occurs in a shepherding scene. After their homeland had been defiled and destroyed, a remnant of the captives would be rounded up like sheep and enclosed in a fold. Then one would break open the enclosure and lead them out into freedom (2:12–13). This one is their "king" and "LORD." This episode accords beautifully with Jesus' announcement of liberty to captives (Luke 4:18), while setting both physical and spiritual captives free.

Micah 5:2 is one of the most famous of all Old Testament prophecies. It authenticates biblical prophecy as "the word of the LORD" (1:1; 2:7; 4:2). The term Yahweh's "word" (4:2) is a title applicable to Christ (John 1:1; Rev. 19:13). The Micah 5:2 prophecy is explicitly messianic ("Ruler in Israel") and specifies His birthplace as Bethlehem at a time when Bethlehem was hardly known. Micah's words were given centuries before the event; he had no local cues to draw on. Another feature of this prophecy is that it cannot refer just to any leader who might originate from Bethlehem. Christ is the only one to whom it could refer, because it equates the Ruler with the eternal One: "Whose goings forth are from of old, from everlasting." This prophecy sublimely asserts both the humanity and deity of the Messiah.

Micah 5:4–5 asserts the Messiah's shepherdhood ("feed His flock"), His anointing ("in the strength of the LORD"), His deity ("in the majesty of the name of the LORD") and humanity ("His God"), His universal

continued from preceding page

Key Chapter: Jonah 3

The third chapter of Jonah records perhaps the greatest revival of all time as the entire city of Nineveh "[believes] God, and [proclaims] a fast," and cries out to God.

Key Word: *The Judgment and Restoration of Judah*

Micah exposes the injustice of Judah and the righteousness and justice of God. About one-third of the book indicts Israel and Judah for specific sins. Another third of Micah predicts the judgment that will come as a result of those sins. The remaining third of the book is a message of hope and consolation. God's justice will triumph and the divine Deliverer will come.

Key Verses: Micah 6:8; 7:18

Key Chapters: Micah 6; 7

The closing section of Micah describes a courtroom scene. God has a controversy against His people, and He calls the mountains and hills together to form the jury as He sets forth His case. There can only be one verdict: guilty.
Nevertheless, the book closes on a note of hope. The same God who executes judgment also delights to extend mercy (7:18–20).

dominion ("He shall be great to the ends of the earth"), and His leadership of a peaceful kingdom ("this One shall be peace").

The climax of the prophecy (7:18–19), plus the final verse (7:20), while not including the name of the Messiah, definitely refers to Him. In the expression of divine mercy and compassion, He is the One who "will subdue our iniquities," dropping them into the ocean depths that God might pardon sins and replace sin with truth.

Power Key: God's Spirit at Work
Obadiah

Nowhere in Obadiah is there specific reference to the Holy Spirit or the Spirit of God. His working, however, must be assumed. He is Obadiah's source of inspiration, the One who imparts the "vision" (v. 1) that comprises Obadiah's message. In addition, although not specifically identified as such, He functions as the One who instigates the judgment of Edom, calling forth the nations to rise up against the enemy of God's people. Though God uses human agents to carry out His justice, behind it all is the working of His Spirit, pushing, prompting, and punishing according to the plan of God.

Jonah

God's Spirit inspired Jonah to prophesy that land and position would be recovered by Israel. This happened under the leadership of Jeroboam II (2 Kin. 14:25). When the Spirit directed Jonah to go to Nineveh and prophesy against the people there, the prophet refused to follow the Lord's guidance. The Spirit of God did not cease His work, but continued to intervene in Jonah's life and induce him to do God's will. When Jonah relented, the Spirit worked godly sorrow in the hearts of the people and they responded to the message of judgment. When Jonah refused to accept this divine work, the Holy Spirit showed him the contrast between his concern for a gourd and God's concern for the inhabitants of Nineveh.

Micah

One outstanding reference to the Spirit of God occurs in Micah's contrast of the authority behind his ministry with that of the counterfeit prophets of his day. While other men were made bold by intoxicants to fabricate tales in the format of prophecies, the true power, might, and justice behind Micah's message came from his anointing "by the Spirit of the LORD" (3:8).

Kingdom Key *continued from page 233*

mercy in healing (Luke 18:39), His mercy in delivering from demonic bondage (Matt. 17:15–18), and His endlessly available mercy to each of us today (Heb. 4:16).

Micah: Prophet of the King's Global Justice

God's justice is how He makes *right* what has been *wrong*. This is why the attributes justice and righteousness are synonymous. His justice is not merely an attitude that disdains wrong or injustice or unrighteousness; it constrains Him to rectify wrong and restore right, for the blessing of the victimized. This first essence of God's way as Judge is seen in Micah 7:9, which declares that God judges righteously in order to bring deliverance. God expects His creatures to deal justly too, undoing the pain and problem of evil, and showing mercy and humility in all life's relationships (Micah 6:8).

The New Testament reveals this quality of righteousness and justice in Jesus' ministry as "delivering, not condemning." Matthew 12:20 describes Jesus sending forth "justice to victory"; that is, the Savior takes the burnt ("smoking flax") and the broken ("bruised reed") and brings them to wholeness. The Messiah's grand ability to execute *judgment that frees* is the fulfillment of the spirit of Micah's prophecy, as well as Isaiah's, whom Matthew quotes in the above reference.

Introducing

OBADIAH

Background. Relations between Israel and Edom were marked by animosity throughout the Old Testament period. The bitterness began when the twin brothers Esau and Jacob parted company in dispute (*see* Genesis 27; 32; 33). Esau's descendants eventually settled in the area called Edom, south of the Dead Sea, while Jacob's descendants continued the promised line, inhabited Canaan, and grew into the people of Israel. Over the years, numerous conflicts between the Edomites and Israelites developed. The events recorded in Numbers 20:14–21 are an example of this hostility.

This bitter rivalry forms the background to Obadiah's prophecy. Over a period of some twenty years (605–586 B.C.), the Babylonians invaded the land of Israel and made repeated attacks on the sacred city of Jerusalem, which was finally devastated in 586 B.C. The Edomites saw these incursions as an opportunity to quench their bitter thirst against Israel. So the Edomites joined with the Babylonians against their distant relatives and helped to desecrate the land of Israel. Psalm 137:7, Lamentations 4:21–22, and Ezekiel 25:12–14 decry the participation of the Edomites in the destruction of Jerusalem.

Date. The background of Jerusalem's destruction places the date of Obadiah's prophecy shortly after 586 B.C., the year in which the sacred city fell to the Babylonians. The message likely was given during the period of Judah's exile, as Obadiah warns Edom of God's impending vengeance and assures Judah of the Lord's continued concern.

Author. The prophet through whom the denunciation comes is known only as Obadiah, "Servant/Worshiper of Yahweh." No additional information is available about him. More than ten men bear the name *Obadiah* in the Old Testament. (*See* 1 Kin. 18:3–16; 1 Chr. 3:21; 7:3; 8:38; 9:16; 12:9.) One tradition connects the author of the prophecy with the Obadiah identified as King Ahab's steward. (*See* 1 Kin. 18:3–16.) But Ahab reigned in the northern kingdom from 874 through 853 B.C., a period that likely does not coincide with the dating of the prophecy of Obadiah.

Purpose. Obadiah's prophecy speaks to people mourning over the ruin of their beloved city of Jerusalem and the deaths of family, friends, and relatives. The inhabitants of Judah who had not been carried off into captivity were few in number and confined to a fragment of the territory they once had claimed as their country. They subsisted on a virtual rubbish heap that once had been their sacred city. The Book of Lamentations rehearses the grief experienced by the people of Judah.

Into this setting, Obadiah brings his message of assurance that God has neither forgotten His people nor overlooked the wickedness of the Edomites. He will intervene to redress the situation, to punish Edom, and to restore His people. His message confronts Edom as a severe word of condemnation, but comforts the people of Judah with the promise of God's continued care, His victory, and their eventual restoration.

Content. Obadiah is the shortest book in the Old Testament. It begins with a heading identifying the prophecy as "the vision of Obadiah" and attributing the pronouncement to the Lord God (v. 1).

The body of the book divides into two major sections. The first (vv. 1–14) is addressed to Edom and announces her inevitable fall. From her position of pride and false security, God will bring her down (vv. 2–4). The land and the people will be pillaged and plundered, the destruction complete and final (vv. 5–9). Why? Because of the violence Edom undertook against his brother Jacob (v. 10), because Edom rejoiced over the suffering of Israel and joined with her attackers to rob and rape Jerusalem in the day of her calamity (vv. 11–13), and because the Edomites prevented the escape of the people of Judah and handed them over to the invaders (v. 14).

The second major section of the prophecy contemplates the day of the Lord (vv. 15–21). This Day will be a time of retribution, of reaping what has been sown. For Edom, this is a pronouncement of doom (vv. 15–16), but for Judah, a proclamation of deliverance (vv. 17–20). Edom will be judged severely, but the people of God will experience blessing and glorious restoration to their land. Mount Zion will rule the mountains of Esau, and the kingdom will belong to the Lord (v. 21).

Personal Application. Obadiah forcefully addresses the matter of relationships. How easy it is for those we know best to become the objects of our most bitter resentment. Logically, Edom should have sided with Judah against Babylonia, but years of hatred caused emotions to override good sense. Such fractured relationships almost inevitably result from personal pride, pride that prevents our seeing the error of our own ways, pride that builds barriers to block the way to reconciliation. The Book of Obadiah calls us to confront the incredible cost of pride, and to realize that the importance of preserving our pride fades into oblivion when we must stand face-to-face with an angry God and try to justify our arrogance. The book calls us to repent of our pride, to seek reconciliation in broken relationships, and to model a lifestyle of forgiveness and acceptance (*see* Matt. 5:21–26).

The prevailing theme of Obadiah is well stated by Paul in Galatians 6:7: "Do not be deceived, God is not mocked; for whatever a man sows, that he will also reap." Or, in the words of Obadiah himself, "As you have done, it shall be done to you" (v. 15). Retribution is a reality. God is just, and He will punish injustices perpetrated against other people, both individuals and nations. The Lord takes very seriously the covenant promises He makes. In Genesis 12:1–3 He had promised to bless those who bless His people and curse those who curse them. The Lord so closely identifies Himself with His people, that to curse His people is to curse Him, to reject them is to reject Him. Edom's end then foreshadows the fate of all who abuse the people of God. The Lord is determined to keep faith with His people, even when His people are faithless and disobedient.

And He will keep faith—in spite of appearances. The desecration of Jerusalem and the people of Judah sent a message to the world of Obadiah's day: The God of Israel had been defeated by the gods of Babylon, Edom, and the other oppressing nations. But that was a false message, because appearances can be deceiving. In His sovereignty God uses circumstances to accomplish His purposes, to purify and protect His people. As Lord of all the earth He was already masterminding Edom's doom, announcing victory in the face of smoldering defeat, and controlling the course of the future in order to accomplish His plan. The Lord who did all that for Israel is the Lord who still works for His people today.

Surveying

OBADIAH

I. TITLE 1.
II. THE DECREE OF THE LORD 1–14.

A. Edom's condemnation (1–4). The major city of Edom was Petra. This impregnable city is carved into solid rock and set deep in a canyon which can only be entered through a single, narrow, easily defended gap. God condemns their pride and false security.

B. Edom's collapse (5–9).

C. Edom's crimes (10–14). The disaster comes because of a promise made in God's covenant with Abraham (*see* Gen. 12:3). It is this very covenant (the "birthright" Esau despised) that now becomes the basis for his descendant's doom (Gen. 25:27–34).

III. THE DAY OF THE LORD 15–21.

A. Day of divine retribution (15–16). As with so many other prophets, the focus of Obadiah's *prophecy is the distant future. He looks forward to "the day of the Lord" as a time of vindication.

B. Day of divine restitution (17–20). Some prophets stress the judgments that will fall on Israel when "that day" arrives (*see* Isaiah 2—4). Others stress judgments that will fall on the pagan nations that are Israel's enemies (*see* Ezekiel 38—39). In this passage judgment is focused on Edom. Then this people will find their deeds returning on their own heads.

C. Day of divine rule (21). As a result of God's intervention, the lands of Israel's enemies will be occupied by God's people.

TRUTH-IN-ACTION through OBADIAH

Truth Obadiah Teaches	**Action** Obadiah Invites
1 Steps to Knowing God and His Ways God hates pride, It is pride to believe we are invulnerable and to place our trust in any other than God. He will humble those who exalt themselves in this way.	**v. 4** *Exalt* God. *Glorify* Him for the security and success you experience. **v. 15** *Refuse to judge* others, knowing that any judgment or criticism you pass may return to you. *Do not rejoice* in judgment on others.
2 Guidelines for Growing in Godliness The godly person does not rejoice in the destruction of	**v. 3** *Ask God to reveal* any areas in which your heart is deceived because of pride. *(continued)*

Truth Obadiah Teaches	**Action** Obadiah Invites
☑ **Guidelines for Growing in Godliness** *(continued)* God's people, but, like God, he seeks their reconciliation to God and their restoration to holiness and blessing. He avoids pride and the deception it produces within human hearts.	**v. 12** *Receive* the reconciliation and restoration that come through repentance.

Introducing

JONAH

Background. The pagan Assyrians, long-standing enemies of Israel, were a dominant force among the ancients from about 885 to 665 B.C. Old Testament accounts describe their forays against Israel and Judah in which they ravaged the countryside and carried away captives. Assyrian power was weaker during Jonah's time, and Jeroboam II was able to reclaim areas of Palestine from Hamath southward to the Dead Sea, as had been prophesied by Jonah (2 Kin. 14:25).

Author and Date. The matters of author and date of Jonah are closely related. If Jonah wrote the book, then it would obviously date during the reign of Jeroboam II in the early eighth century, approximately 793–753 B.C. If a narrator wrote the book, it could have been written any time after the incident described therein.

Of those who hold to an author other than Jonah (usually referred to as a narrator), some date the book in the late eighth century or early seventh, based on the dates for the preexilic reign of Jeroboam II. Others prefer a postexilic date after the destruction of Nineveh in 612 B.C., some as late as the third century B.C. This contention is based upon 3:3, which says that Nineveh *was* a great city. Those who support the preexilic dating explain that this could be merely a literary form used in telling the story, or that Nineveh was in existence, but not a great city.

Jonah. As indicated in 2 Kings 14:25, Jonah was the son of Amittai and a native of Gath Hepher, a village three miles northeast of Nazareth, within the tribal borders of Zebulun (*see* map, page 184). Prophesying during the reign of Jeroboam II and immediately before Amos, he was a strong nationalist who was fully aware of the havoc the Assyrians had wrought in Israel over the years. Jonah found it difficult to accept the fact that God would offer mercy to Nineveh of Assyria when its inhabitants deserved severe judgment.

He was the only prophet sent to preach to the Gentiles. Elijah was sent to Zarephath to live for a season (1 Kin. 17:8–10) and Elisha journeyed to Damascus (2 Kin. 8:7), but only Jonah was given a message of repentance and mercy to preach directly to a Gentile city. His reluctance to preach at Nineveh was based upon a desire to see their decline culminate in a complete loss of power. Also he feared that God would show mercy, thus extending the Assyrians' opportunity to harass Israel.

Jonah's name means "Dove" or "Pigeon." Dispositionally, he is represented as strong-willed, fretful, pouting, hasty, and clannish. Politically, it is obvious that he was a loyal lover of Israel and a committed patriot. Religiously, he professed a fear of the Lord as God of heaven, the Creator of the sea and land. But his initial willful disobedience, his later reluctant obedience, and his anger over the extension of mercy to the Ninevites reveal obvious inconsistencies in the application of his faith. The story ends without indicating how Jonah responded to God's object lesson and exhortation.

Purpose. The book was written to emphasize that God loves all people and desires to show them mercy based upon repentance. It has been called the outstanding missionary book of the Old Testament. God declared that all nations of the earth would be blessed through the Abrahamic covenant (Gen. 12:3). The Scriptures reveal that Israel became very nationalistic and exclusivistic and refused to fulfill that mission. Jonah had a strong commitment to this same viewpoint. The love of God for all was dramatically revealed to Jonah when He answered the prayers of the Gentile sailors and responded to the repentance of the pagan Ninevites. The message was further amplified by the lesson of the plant, the worm, and the east wind.

Content. The Book of Jonah, though placed among the prophets in the canon, is different from other prophetical books in that it has no prophecy that contains a message; the story is the message. That story recalls one of the most profound theological concepts found in the Old Testament. God loves all people and desires to share His forgiveness and mercy with them. Israel had been charged with revealing that message but somehow did not grasp the importance of it. This failure eventually led to extreme religious pride. In Jonah can be found the seedbed of New Testament Pharisaism.

Jonah the prophet is asked by God to arise and go eight hundred miles east to Nineveh, a city of the dreaded and hated Assyrians. His message is to be a call to repentance and a promise of mercy if they respond affirmatively. Jonah knows that if God spares Nineveh, then that city will be free to plunder and pillage Israel again. This nationalistic patriotism and his disdain that mercy will be offered to noncovenant people prompt Jonah to decide to leave Israel and the "presence of the LORD." No doubt he hopes that the Spirit of prophecy will not follow. Jonah is displeased and somehow convinces himself that a trip to Tarshish will relieve him of the responsibility God has placed upon him.

The trip to Tarshish soon provides evidence that Yahweh's presence and influence are not confined to Palestine. God sends a storm to buffet the ship and causes circumstances that bring Jonah face-to-face with his missionary call. After determining that Jonah and his God are responsible for the storm, and after exhausting all alternatives, the sailors throw Jonah overboard. No doubt the sailors and Jonah assume this will end Jonah's earthly existence; but God has prepared a great fish to swallow Jonah and, after three days and nights, the fish deposits him upon land.

Again God instructs Jonah to arise and go to Nineveh to deliver the message of deliverance. This time the prophet reluctantly agrees to make the journey and declare God's message. To his dismay the Ninevites, from the common people to the king, respond and indicate their repentance by ceremonial fasting, sackcloth, and ashes. Even the animals are forced to participate in this humbling behavior.

Jonah's heart is still unchanged and he reacts with anger and confusion. Why would God have mercy on people who had abused the nation of Israel? Perhaps hoping that the repentance is not genuine, or that God will choose another strategy, Jonah builds a shelter on a hill overlooking the city from the east. There he waits for the appointed day of judgment.

God uses this waiting time to teach a valuable lesson to Jonah. He prepares a plant to grow overnight in a location that shaded Jonah's head. The prophet rejoices in his good fortune. Then God prepares a worm to cut the stem of the plant and cause it to wither. He further intensifies Jonah's uncomfortable situation by preparing a hot east wind to dry Jonah's parched body. Jonah laments the death of the vine and expresses his displeasure to God. God responds by showing the inconsistency of being concerned for a gourd, but being totally unconcerned about the fate of the inhabitants of Nineveh whom God loved.

Personal Application. Jonah's story has much to say about the heart of God and the mission of God's people. God desires to show His mercy and offer forgiveness to all peoples of the earth. He has committed this ministry of reconciliation and the message of reconciliation (2 Cor. 5:18–19) to the church. Just as Israel was commissioned to reveal God to the world (Gen. 12:3), so the church has been commissioned to go into all the world and preach the gospel (Matt. 28:18–20). When the church has the attitude of exclusiveness exhibited by Jonah and Israel, it fails to accomplish its task. But, when the church takes seriously the command of God to arise and go to the nations of the world, those people who hear the Word and respond in faith experience the mercy and forgiveness of God in life-changing, culture-impacting measure.

Surveying
JONAH

I. DETERMINED RETREAT 1:1–3.

A. "Arise, go to Nineveh" (1:1–2). Called to go to Nineveh and preach against it (2), Jonah flees.

> "Now the word of the LORD came to Jonah . . . arise, go to Nineveh" (1:1–2). When the Lord gives direction to His chosen messenger, His assignment is neither optional nor open to debate— immediate obedience is required. Refusal to respond carries with it unavoidable repercussions; as with Jonah, the Lord often hems us in until we see His way. Promptings in our heart to share God's Word with a friend or neighbor must be heeded. Most likely the Spirit has prepared a receptive heart to receive the truth we bring, placing that person on our heart at the point of divine timing, just as Nineveh was ready to respond city-wide to Jonah's message.

B. Jonah flees to Tarshish (1:3). He takes a ship from Joppa bound for Tarshish, a port on the Spanish coast as far from Nineveh as the prophet can go.

II. PROVIDENTIAL RETURN 1:4—2:10.

A. The Lord sends a storm (1:4–9). At sea a violent storm threatens to break up the ship. When the mariners cast lots to see if the storm may be caused by some sin, the lot falls to Jonah.

B. The sailors throw him overboard (1:10–16). Jonah tells them the only way the storm can be stopped is for them to throw him overboard. The unwilling sailors struggle to reach shore. Finally, as the sea grows even wilder, they do as the prophet has instructed. The raging waters calm. The men on board the ship recognize God's hand and worship Him— but Jonah is gone.

C. The Lord provides a great fish (1:17). God has "prepared a great fish to swallow Jonah." For three days and nights the prophet is in the belly of the fish.

D. Jonah prays (2:1–10). This poetic section reveals Jonah's inner struggle and submission. In great danger, the prophet finally turns to the Lord. "Look toward Your holy temple." This phrase, repeated in verses 4 and 7, is significant. Solomon had asked at the dedication of the temple: "When a prayer or plea is made

by any of your people Israel—each one aware of his afflictions and pains, and spreading out his hands toward the temple—then hear from heaven, your dwelling place. Forgive, and deal with each man according to all he does" (2 Chr. 6:29–30 NIV). The Lord does as He has promised. Jonah is forgiven and will be restored to his place of service.

E. He is deposited on land (2:10).

III. SUCCESSFUL REVIVAL 3:1–10.

A. A second chance is given to "arise and go" (3:1–3). God repeats Jonah's commission. This time Jonah obeys, traveling to this "very large city." It takes three days for Jonah to cover all its districts.

B. Jonah preaches (3:4). He stands on its street corners to deliver his message: "Yet forty days, and Nineveh shall be overthrown!"

> "Go to Nineveh, that great city, and preach to it the message that I tell you" (3:1–5). The Lord's commission to share His word begins with the compelling instruction, "Go" (see Matt. 28:19). Consternation over the form and facts of our communication must not inhibit us; He will inform us of the message to share. *We go* to be His mouthpiece, and *He gives* us the message we need.

C. The population repents (3:5–9). Amazingly, the king and nobles lead the whole population in confession and repentance. The people turn from evil practices and humble themselves before the Lord (see Fast).

D. God relents (3:10). Judgment does not come.

IV. NEGATIVE REACTION 4:1–11.

A. Jonah is angry (4:1–5). Jonah is angry that his preaching has stimulated repentance. He complains to God, revealing his motive for fleeing in the first place. Jonah knows God is merciful (2), but he does not want mercy shown to this enemy of his people! Jonah wants Nineveh destroyed.

As a patriot, Jonah loved his own people and rightly feared the enemy who would one day devastate his homeland. But the Lord is God of the whole earth. His compassion reaches beyond Israel and Judah, to encompass all peoples. Yes, God will act to judge sins. But God would far rather be gracious.

B. God teaches a lesson (4:6–11). The disgruntled prophet finds a hillside east of the city and settles down to see what will happen. When the Lord makes a vine grow to shade the prophet from the sun, Jonah is very happy. But the next morning the plant dies. Now, as the day grows unusually hot and windy, the bitter prophet grows angry at the Lord.

God then speaks to Jonah. The prophet cared passionately about the vine. But he had closed his heart to the people who would have been destroyed with Nineveh. Jonah did not care about these people. But God did care! How good to see here the love and grace of God extended to all mankind and to know that in the Old Testament as well as the New Testament our God is shown to be full of compassion.

TRUTH-IN-ACTION through JONAH

Truth Jonah Teaches	**Action** Jonah Invites
1 Knowing God and His Ways God's prevailing self-revelation is His love, graciousness, forgiveness, and mercy. We must allow this knowledge of God's nature to shape our character accordingly.	**4:1–11** *Never underestimate* the Lord's mercy and His willingness to forgive. *Never discourage* repentance, *nor be grieved* when an enemy decides to repent and escape the judgment you may feel he deserves.
2 A Guideline for Godliness A godly person displays instant, willing obedience to God's bidding. Godly people are not stubborn people.	**1:1–3** *Promptly do* what the Lord directs you to do. *Remember* that your stubbornness causes trouble—for you!
3 A Key to Wise Living The wise person understands that God responds to disobedience by making circumstances oppose us. He knows what is required to cause a change in our hearts and behavior. The path by which we flee from God will become the highway to repentance because of His intervention.	**1:17; 2:7; 3:3** *Recognize* God's opposition to your disobedience. *Repent* and *obey. Change your heart* as well as your behavior.
4 Understanding Sin God cannot allow known sin to remain unconfronted in the lives of any who love and serve Him. Because sin cannot stand in the presence of God's holiness, prayer is vain and useless until confession of sin removes the spiritual barrier we have constructed between ourselves and Him.	**1:4–15** *Confront sin* in your life. *Readily confess* any wrongdoing. *Remember* that you cannot hide from God.

Introducing
MICAH

Author. Micah was contemporary with Isaiah in the eighth century before Christ. Both concentrated their ministry in the southern kingdom, Judah, yet included Samaria (Israel) and "the nations" within the scope of their prophecies. For a few years in his early career Micah also was contemporary with Hosea, a prophet located in the northern kingdom. Micah lived in a town about twenty miles southwest of Jerusalem and prophesied mostly in that region (*see* map, page 184).

Micah's name predicates a likeness to the Lord: "He Who Is Like Yahweh." Micah was so completely and sincerely committed that he was even willing to go stripped naked on occasion to get his message across (1:8). Micah's prophecy had an impact that extended far beyond his local ministry. A century later his prophecy was remembered and quoted (Jer. 26:17–19), and events seven centuries later attest to the authenticity of Micah's prophecy (Matt. 2:1–6; John 7:41–43).

Date. Micah prophesied according to his own statement (1:1) during the reigns of the southern kings Jotham (740–731 B.C.), Ahaz (731–716 B.C.), and Hezekiah (716–686 B.C.). Since he died during the administration of Hezekiah and before Manasseh's partly overlapping era (696–642 B.C.), a date between 704 and 696 B.C. seems likely.

Background. In the period between the beginning of the divided Solomonic kingdom (Israel to the north, and Judah to the south) and the destruction of the temple, many "high places" had been introduced in Judah through the influence of Samaria. This placed Canaanite idolatry in competition with the true temple worship of the Lord (1:5). Micah shows how this spiritual declension will inevitably lead to judgment on the whole land. And, although King Hezekiah had won a notable victory over Sennacherib and the Assyrian army, Judah was bound to fall unless the nation turned back to God in wholehearted repentance.

Style. Micah's introductory statement (1:1) is in prose form, but the entire compilation of prophecies after that is poetry. The advantage of poetry to his contemporaries was that the rhythmic message would be easier to remember. The disadvantage to us is that poetry is more difficult to translate into another language without loss. Micah depends on shortened units of thought (with the nonessential words implied), plentiful parallelisms and nameplays (since name meanings were important to Hebrews), and poetic prepositions. He also uses an abundance of word pictures. For instance, instead of abstractly saying the Lord will conceal or otherwise make invisible our sins, he declares: "You will cast all our sins into the depths of the sea" (7:19). He cannot avoid the abstract word "sins," but he concretely depicts for us their burial like weights into the ocean depths, never to be recoverable again.

Content. Micah is a prophecy about the Lord, who has no rivals in pardoning sins and having compassion on sinners. His compassionate faithfulness keeps covenant with Abraham and his descendants. "The majesty of the name of the LORD" (5:4; *see* also 4:5; 6:9) is featured, as well as the Lord's face (3:4), His glory (2:9), His ways (4:2), His thoughts (4:12), His strength (5:4), His righteousness (6:5; 7:9), and His consequent indignation (7:9) and anger (5:15; 7:18) against all forms of moral rebellion.

In the opening vision, the Lord comes from His holy sanctuary in heaven to witness against the people (1:2). The most remarkable factor in the Lord's handling of His case is how far down He has come to make His complaint (6:2), even being willing to sit at the defendant's table and let His people bring any grievances with the way God has treated them (6:3). Moreover, one who truly repents will have the Lord as his defense lawyer (7:9)!

While Babylon was not yet a world power that could stand independently of Assyria, the Babylonian captivity (over a century later) was clearly predicted as the judgment of God for rebellion against Him (1:16; 2:3, 10; 4:10; 7:13). But as with Isaiah, Micah's colleague, hope was held out for a remnant to be restored, whether from this captivity or from a spiritually restored people (the church) in the days of the Messiah (2:12–13; 4:6–7; 5:3, 7–8; 7:18). The Lord would deliver the remnant (2:12–13; 4:3–8, 10; 5:9; 7:7).

Micah had to censure the leadership of the nation for consuming the flock with which they were entrusted. Nevertheless, God's great compassion colors His every attitude and action toward His people, portrayed as an errant daughter (1:13; 4:8, 10, 13), for His compassion that once redeemed Israel from Egypt (6:4) will also redeem Judah from Babylon (4:10). His compassionate faithfulness to Abraham and the patriarchs (7:20) is updated with each new generation. This message is focused on the one central question for the entire prophecy: "Who is a God like You, pardoning iniquity and passing over the transgression of the remnant of His heritage?" (7:18). Yahweh's compassion (7:18–19) is the precious attribute no false deity can match. Compassion and covenant faithfulness are unique with God. The people's hope to live under God's full blessing was bound up with the coming of the Messiah. God in His love, foreseeing the glories of His grace to be manifested in Jesus, kept declaring that future Day and kingdom as the event in which the faithful should place their hopes.

Personal Application. Micah has much to contribute to the knowledge of one's ongoing relationship with the Lord Jesus Christ. Relief from the foremost moral and religious sins of greed and idolatry in that ancient day can be had today by following Jesus into the kingdom of God. Micah's prophecy should make everyone stand in awe of the incomparable Yahweh who revealed Himself in the humanity of Jesus as the compassion and truth of God personified.

Micah's generation was overrun by mercenary activities of faithless rulers, priests, and prophets (3:11). Contrast these with that greatest of all "Shepherd of the sheep" (Heb. 13:20), whose compassion caused Him to give Himself for the sheep, even to pouring out His blood. Likewise, Micah, a true prophet of God, was willing to pay any personal price to perform his ministry.

Surveying
MICAH

I. THE LORD'S DRAMATIC COMING IN JUDGMENT 1:1—2:13.

A. On the capital cities of Samaria and Jerusalem (1:1–9). The prophet describes God's awesome descent to the earth to judge Israel and Judah for their idolatry.

B. On the towns southwest of Jerusalem (1:10–16). Graphically the prophet describes the shame and weeping that judgment brings.

C. On the crimes that bring foreign occupation (2:1–11). Micah contrasts human plans and God's. The people of Judah and Israel lie awake nights, plotting how to defraud others of their homes. As soon as morning comes, they rush to carry out their evil designs (1–2). But God is planning too. His plan is for disaster to strike all those who walk so proudly now.

Then Micah turns on those who try to silence his voice (6–7). These people do not want to hear the truth. They are eager for liars and deceivers to come and tell them what they want to hear (8–11).

D. On all but a remnant delivered by Yahweh (2:12–13). The chapter's closing verses relate the only good news that Micah can honestly share. Though there is no hope for this present civilization, a "remnant of Israel" will be brought together by God.

II. THE LORD'S CONDEMNATION OF THE LEADERSHIP 3:1–12.

A. On leaders who consume the people

Geographical Puns in Micah 1:10–14

The prophet employs a series of clever word plays in announcing God's coming judgment on Judah by means of the invading Assyrian army. James Moffatt's *The Bible: A New Translation* translates the Hebrew word plays into English quite successfully:

Weep tears at Teartown (Bochim),
grovel in the dust at Dustown (Beth Aphrah),
fare forth stripped, O Fairtown (Saphir)!
Stirtown (Zaanan) dare not stir,
    Beth-esel. . . .
and Maroth hopes in vain;
for doom descends from the Eternal
to the very gates of Jerusalem.
To horse and drive away, O Horse town
    (Lachish),
O Source of Sion's sin, where the crimes of
    Israel centre!
O maiden Sion, you must part with
    Moresheth of Gath;
and Israel's kings are ever balked at
    Balkton (Achzib).

© 1990 Thomas Nelson, Inc.

(3:1–4). The political leaders of Israel should have protected the innocent, but they "have forgotten justice" and they ravage the flock they are charged to care for.

B. On the prophets, excepting Micah (3:5–8). The prophets "who lead My people astray" with their promises of continued blessing are also condemned (5–12). How different Micah's approach to ministry is from those who "tell fortunes for money." It is because of them and their sins that Jerusalem will soon be nothing but a heap of rubble and brush will grow on the temple hill. But Micah remains true to his calling. He does have an impact on his generation (8). If only all were as true to their calling!

"But truly I am full of power by the Spirit of the LORD, and of justice and might"
(3:8). Micah indicates that God's Spirit had empowered him to boldly speak God's word against the people's sinful waywardness. Previously he told them God's Spirit was unrestricted in speaking through His prophet, even when denouncing wicked schemes (2:6–7). Now as he challenges the social and societal evils of the nation (vv. 9–12), Micah contrasts himself with those prophets only speaking peace (vv. 6–7). His qualification was the Spirit, who filled and equipped him with power, might, and justice. Likewise, the Spirit's filling will equip us with strength and courage for all ministry tasks.

C. On officials: rulers, priests, prophets (3:9–12).

III. THE LORD'S COMING UNIVERSAL KINGDOM 4:1—5:15.

A. Attraction of all nations to Yahweh's name (4:1–5). Micah looks beyond the coming disaster and sees a new temple erected on its old site. It is a place of glory, and all peoples stream to it. The scene described is one of universal peace under the rule of God's Law, when "no one will make them afraid" (4; *see* Ever).

B. Compassion on His outcast, dependent people (4:6–13). God's ultimate plan is for an age of endless blessing (6–8). Judah will first writhe in agony, and her people will be carried away to Babylon (10). But after the judgment, the glory days will surely come. (*See* Lord.)

C. Messiah's birthplace and administration (5:1–6). The glory days are linked to the appearance of the promised Davidic king (*see* Messianic Promises). Micah 5:2 is quoted in the New Testament as a prophecy of Jesus' birth.

Israel will be abandoned until this time (3–4). But after the exile among the nations (5–9), the promised ruler will lead Israel to triumph.

D. Restoration of a remnant in an idol-free zone (5:7–15). All that is unholy in Israel will be destroyed, and vengeance will be taken on pagan nations.

IV. THE LORD'S PRESENTATION OF HIS CASE 6:1—7:6.

A. His redemptive care in their history (6:1–5). Micah uses a familiar prophetic device. He pictures a courtroom and God presenting His case. God has serious accusations to make against this people whom He has cared for and loved.

B. His expectations for a proper response (6:6–8). He has not asked for their multiplied sacrifices and ritual, but "has shown you, O man, what is good; And what does the LORD require of you"? Micah goes on to ask. "To do justly, to love *mercy, and to walk humbly with your God" (6:8).

C. His basis for judgment of the wicked (6:9—7:6). Guilty Israel, a nation of dishonest merchants, of violence, and of deceit, will be given over to ruin (9–16).

Micah shares the misery that God feels as he observes the wickedness of his people. The godly have been swept from the land, rulers demand gifts, and judges accept bribes. The only skill left to the hands of his people is a talent for doing evil! No neighbor can be relied on; no friend can be trusted. Even the family is shattered, as its members turn against one another (7:1–6). Such a nation must fall.

V. THE LORD'S SALVATION AS THE NATION'S HOPE 7:7-20.

A. In spite of the temporary judgment (7:7–9; *see* Wait).

B. In spite of the nation's enemies (7:10–17). The people will bow under God's wrath until a day comes when He will lead them into the light (8–13). Then at last God will have His inheritance in His people, and they will praise Him for His faithfulness to His promises to Abraham and for the forgiveness they enjoy.

C. Because of His incomparable compassion (7:18–20). The Lord will "hurl all our iniquities into the depths of the sea"—a beautiful picture of complete forgiveness. As His redeemed, our sins too are forgiven—and gone.

TRUTH-IN-ACTION through MICAH

Truth Micah Teaches	**Action** Micah Invites
1 Understanding Godliness In its simplest definition, godliness means for us to be overflowing with the fruit of the Spirit.	**6:8** *Adopt* the four consummate virtues of Christian living: justice, mercy, humility, and faithfulness.
2 A Step to Holiness Holiness is relying totally upon God's ways and resources and turning from your own.	**5:10–15** *Understand* that God will eventually root out any dependence we show upon things that He has not established or way He has not directed.
3 Key Lessons in Faith Faith is simpler than it seems. It is a choice rather than an ability. Many of God's promises are so astounding that we are not able to comprehend them, let alone fully "believe" them. But we can always choose to believe, or to commit to His Word, regardless of the magnitude of the challenge.	**2:7** *Remember* that God's Word always accomplishes the good for which it is intended. **4:13** *Believe* that God will eventually funnel the world's wealth to those who will serve His kingdom's concerns and interests. **7:8, 9** *Understand* that only God can judge His people. *Trust* that He will also restore them.
4 Keys to Wise Living Wisdom teaches us to accept God's assessment of man, as difficult as it may be due to our humanistic milieu.	**2:11** *Be warned* that only listening to what we want to hear will breed disobedience and ungodliness.
5 Lessons for Leaders Spiritual leadership is a sacred trust. Though often coveted by the spiritual neophyte, it is a costly role for anyone who serves in it. Leaders are asked to speak forth boldly and must not use their positions to secure financial position or undue power for themselves.	**2:6, 7** *Never discourage* leaders from speaking the whole counsel of God. *Do not reprove* teachers and preachers for speaking correction or warning. *Refuse* to listen to God's Word selectively. *Receive* the corrective as well as the affirmative. **3:5–7** Leaders, *believe* that God will stop speaking in revelation to leaders who become mercenary in their ministries. **3:11** Leaders, *be warned: never, never set a price* on your ministry. *Never deceitfully seduce* people to become your financial support by using psychological or spiritual manipulation.

KEYS TO NAHUM, HABAKKUK, AND ZEPHANIAH
A Trilogy on the King's Judgment, Triumph, and Purifying Pathways

Kingdom Key: God's Purpose in View

Nahum: Prophet of the King's Inescapable Judgment

While Micah so beautifully proclaims a "judgment which brings *release*," where human responsiveness and repentance are evident, Nahum declares God's judgment which brings *retribution*, even though His hand has been long-stayed in patience. Nahum notes that though God "reserves wrath" and is "slow to anger," He still ultimately "avenges and is furious" (1:2–3). His message addresses the same city Jonah warned—Nineveh—which at that time repented but later returned to wickedness. Nahum's prophecy against Nineveh is a timeless reminder that God's mercy is not a plaything. God's Son reveals this same divine attribute of limited patience with human presumption. Even amid His habitual show of mercy and gentleness, Jesus displayed anger at unrepentant, persistent, and arrogant sinfulness

....

God's mercy is never to be taken lightly.

....

(Mark 3:5; 11:15–17). He is capable of anger and wrath when human pride presses its limits. At His Second Coming, His consuming wrath shall destroy the arch-representative of evil himself (2 Thess. 2:8). The Lamb is indeed our merciful Savior and Redeemer, but He is also capable of righteous wrath (Rev. 6:10)—an expression of His perfect nature, not a venting of mere humanistic emotion.

Habakkuk: Prophet of the King's Irrepressible Triumph

Habakkuk's candor in his complaining inquiry to the Lord is received and responded to by God. The prophet is puzzled that evil and violence seem to prevail (1:3) and that wickedness and perverted justice continue (1:4). God not only affirms that He will do a work in Habakkuk's lifetime (1:5), but that ultimately His triumph shall bring a worldwide relief from such anguish caused
(Please turn to page 251.)

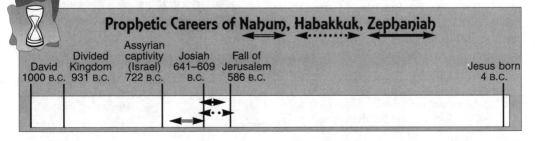

Prophetic Careers of Nahum, Habakkuk, Zephaniah

David 1000 B.C.	Divided Kingdom 931 B.C.	Assyrian captivity (Israel) 722 B.C.	Josiah 641–609 B.C.	Fall of Jerusalem 586 B.C.	Jesus born 4 B.C.

This trilogy offers God's promises of retribution, • • •

Master Key: God's Son Revealed
Nahum

The Book of Nahum pronounces God's judgment on sin and evil, as personified in the wickedness of the Assyrians. Nineveh was indeed destroyed, but that partial and temporary defeat of evil awaited the complete and permanent conquest that would come only through Jesus Christ. Nahum's prophecy proclaims that God cannot look upon evil and that sin must be cut off from the earth. At Christ's crucifixion, God drove the final nail into sin's coffin by cutting off His own Son (*see* Matt. 27:46; 2 Cor. 5:21). God's final judgment on wickedness and evil took place at the Cross.

But the counterpart, God's greatest demonstration of His goodness, is also revealed in Jesus Christ. Nahum proclaims that God is good, but His goodness was brought to its climax only in Christ (Rom. 5:6–11). God's goodness was made manifest in Jesus, a living declaration of the good tidings of peace. Now humanity has a way to return to its God-appointed tasks and calling (Nah. 1:15). The wicked lioness (Nah. 2:11–12) has been defeated and replaced by the righteous Lion of the tribe of Judah (Rev. 5:5). God's vengeance against sin has been satisfied through His Son's sacrifice.

Key Word: *The Judgment of Nineveh*

If ever a city deserved the title "Here to Stay," Nineveh was that city. But Nahum declares that Nineveh will fall.

Key Verses: Nahum 1:7–8; 3:5–7

Key Chapter: Nahum 1

Nahum 1:2–8 portrays the patience, power, holiness, and justice of the living God. He is slow to wrath, but God settles His accounts in full. This book concerns the downfall of Assyria, but it is written for the benefit of the surviving kingdom of Judah.

Habakkuk

The terms used by Habakkuk in 3:13 join the idea of salvation with the Lord's Anointed. The Hebrew roots of these words reflect the two names of our Lord: Jesus, meaning "Salvation," and Christ, meaning "the Anointed One." The context here is God's great power manifested in behalf of His people through a Davidic King to bring them deliverance from their enemies. The Messiah came in the fullness of time (2:3; Gal. 4:4), was given the name "Jesus" as a prenatal prophecy of His ministry (Matt. 1:21), and was born "in the city of David a Savior, who is Christ the Lord" (Luke 2:11).

As Habakkuk waits for the answer to his

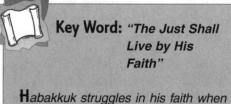

Key Word: *"The Just Shall Live by His Faith"*

Habakkuk struggles in his faith when he sees men flagrantly violate God's law and distort justice on every level, without fear of divine intervention. He wants to know why God allows this growing iniquity to go unpunished. God's answer satisfies Habakkuk that he can trust Him even in the worst of

continued on next page

• • • relief, and restoration for His people.

questions, God gives him a truth that satisfies his unspoken longings as well as provides the solution to his present situation: "The just shall live by his faith" (2:4). The apostle Paul sees this statement of Habakkuk as the foundation stone of the gospel of Christ (Rom. 1:16–17). Christ is the answer to human needs, including cleansing from sin, relationship with God, and hope for the future.

Zephaniah

The meaning of Zephaniah's name ("The LORD Has Hidden") conveys the ministry of Jesus Christ. The truth of the Passover in Egypt, where those hidden behind blood-marked doors were protected from the angel of death, is repeated in the promise of 2:3, where those meek of the earth who have upheld God's justice will be hidden in the day of the Lord's anger. Colossians 3:2–3 spells out this aspect of Christ's ministry: "Set your mind on things above, not on things on the earth. For you died, and your life is hidden with Christ in God."

The rejoicing over a saved remnant (3:16–17) is connected with the work of Jesus, the Savior. Jesus spoke, "I say to you that likewise there will be more joy in heaven over one sinner who repents than over ninety-nine just persons who need no repentance" (Luke 15:7). The picture of a joyful Redeemer who waits to receive His own is again depicted in Hebrews 12:2, "Looking unto Jesus, the author and finisher of our faith, who for the joy that was set before Him endured the cross, despising the shame, and has sat down at the right hand of the throne of God."

Power Key: God's Spirit at Work
Nahum

No specific references to the Holy Spirit occur in the Book of Nahum. However, the Spirit's work in prophecy and in the direction of the events depicted in the book must be assumed.

The heading of the book describes it as

continued from preceding page

circumstances because of His matchless wisdom, goodness, and power.

Key Verses: Habakkuk 2:4; 3:17–19
Key Chapter: Habakkuk 3

The Book of Habakkuk builds to a triumphant climax reached in the last three verses (3:17–19). The beginning of the book and the ending stand in stark contrast: mystery to certainty, questioning to affirming, and complaint to confidence.

Key Word: The Day of the Lord

God is holy and must vindicate His righteousness by calling all the nations of the world into account before Him. The sovereign God will judge not only His own people but also the whole world. Wrath and mercy, severity and kindness, cannot be separated in the character of God.

Key Verses: Zephaniah 1:14–15; 2:3
Key Chapter: Zephaniah 3

The last chapter of Zephaniah records the two distinct parts of the day of the Lord: judgment and restoration. Following the conversion of the nation, Israel finally is fully restored. Under the righteous rule of God, Israel fully inherits the blessings contained in the biblical covenants.

"the vision of Nahum" (1:1). The Holy Spirit functions here as the Revealer, the One who opens to Nahum the message from the Lord that he is commissioned to deliver.

The Holy Spirit must also function as the Great Instigator in the downfall of Nineveh. Enemies, among them the Babylonians, Medes, and Scythians, gather forces against the Assyrians and sack the city. God uses human agents to carry out His judgment, but behind it all is the working of His Spirit, prompting, pushing, and punishing according to the will of God. By the work of the Spirit, the Lord mustered His troops and led them into victorious battle.

Habakkuk

Though no direct references to the Holy Spirit are found in Habakkuk, there are intimations of His life working in the prophet. As Habakkuk surveys the ruin brought about by the invading armies, he nevertheless expresses an abiding joy that even a disaster on so large a scale cannot steal from him, reminding us that "the fruit of the Spirit is . . . joy" (Gal. 5:22).

Also, in Galatians, Paul links the most famous verse from Habakkuk with the reception of the promised Holy Spirit through faith (2:4; Gal. 3:11–14). The righteous person lives by his faith in all aspects of his life, including entering into the life of the Spirit.

Zephaniah

Jesus said that one work of the Holy Spirit would be to convict the world of judgment because the ruler of the world is judged (John 16:8–11). Since His coming, the Holy Spirit has been crying out to the world as Zephaniah did: "Gather yourselves . . . before the decree is issued, or the day passes like chaff, before the LORD's fierce anger comes upon you, before the day of the LORD's anger comes upon you!" (2:1–2).

Now, as then, to refuse the warning is to reject the Holy Spirit. In the address that sealed his martyrdom, Stephen declared to the council, "You stiff-necked and uncircumcised in heart and ears! You always resist the Holy Spirit; as your fathers did, so do you" (Acts 7:51).

A more joyous work of the Holy Spirit is found in the promise that God will restore a pure language to the peoples that they may serve Him with one accord (3:9). The curse of Babel was the confusion of languages, which prevented people from working in unity to achieve their evil goals (Gen. 11:1–9). The outpouring of the Spirit promised in Joel 2:28–32 came to pass on the Day of Pentecost (Acts 2:1–11) to begin God's process of messianic restoration. In light of Zephaniah's prophecy, it is interesting to note that Pentecost included the dimension of languages, allowing all to hear the gospel.

Furthermore, the gift of tongues was used to bring believing Gentiles and astonished Jews together in unity of faith and purpose during Peter's reluctant visit to the home of Cornelius (Acts 10:44–48). This gift of tongues also has served to merge believers of widely divergent theological persuasions into the modern charismatic movement. They have been enabled to transcend boundaries of tradition and nationality to serve the Lord together in the unity of the Spirit. These may be partial fulfillments of 3:9.

Kingdom Key *continued from page 247*

by evil men (2:14–20). This prompts the prophet's hymn of confidence (3:17–18). Habakkuk's song is doubtless much like the consumate song of God's victory which the King now sings with His redeemed (Heb. 2:10–12) and will sing in the future (Rev. 15:2–4). This is because Christ's ultimate triumph has already been established through His Cross (Col. 2:14–15) and is progressively being realized by His own as they move under the banner of His grace (2 Cor. 2:14).

Zephaniah: Prophet of the King's Purifying Pathways

Zephaniah was God's instrument, partnered beside the faithful young King Josiah (1:1), at a time Judah desperately needed a purifying revival. Second Kings 21 and 2 Chronicles 33:1–9 describe the extent of spiritual decay and national corruption into which God commits Himself to "bring His justice to light" (3:5). He says, "Then I will restore to the peoples a pure language, that they all may call upon the name of the LORD, to serve Him with one accord" (3:9). What Isaiah experienced personally (Is. 6:4–7), and what Zephaniah prophesied would spread among mankind (3:8–9), Christ the King has come to begin and perfect in the worship of those He has saved. Whatever our past pollution of speech or habit, from redeemed lips He creates the pure fruit of praise as a new, pure sacrifice offered to God (Heb. 13:15–16; Is. 57:19).

Introducing
NAHUM

Author. Nahum, whose name means "Comforter" or "Full of Comfort," is unknown except for the caption that opens his prophecy. His identification as an "Elkoshite" does not help greatly, since the location of Elkosh is uncertain (*see* map, page 184). Capernaum, the city in Galilee so prominent in the ministry of Jesus, means "Village of Nahum," and some have speculated, but without solid proof, that its name derives from the prophet. He prophesied to Judah during the reigns of Manasseh, Amon, and Josiah. His contemporaries were Zephaniah, Habakkuk, and Jeremiah.

Date. In Nahum 3:8–10, the prophet recounts the fate of the Egyptian city of Thebes, which was destroyed in 663 B.C. Nineveh's fall, around which the entire book revolves, occurred in 612 B.C. Nahum's prophecy must date between these two events, since he looks backward to one and forward to the other. Most likely, his message was delivered shortly before the destruction of Nineveh, perhaps as Assyria's enemies were marshalling their forces for the final attack.

Background. The kingdom of the Assyrians, with their capital at Nineveh, had been a thriving nation for centuries by the time the prophet Nahum appeared on the scene. Their territory, which changed over the years with the conquests and defeats of various rulers, lay north of Babylonia, between and beyond the Tigris and Euphrates rivers. Ancient documents attest the cruelty of the Assyrians against other nations. Assyrian kings boast of their savagery, celebrating the abuse and torture they inflicted on conquered peoples.

In 722 B.C., the Assyrians conquered the northern kingdom of Israel. At that time they also severely threatened Judah, the southern kingdom. Only divine intervention prevented the desecration of Jerusalem a few years later in 701 B.C. (*see* 1 Kin. 17—19). Now, over a century later, the empire whose atrocities made the world tremble and who acted as God's instrument against a sinful Israel, teetered on the verge of divine destruction.

The fall of the Assyrian Empire, climaxed by the destruction of the capital city of Nineveh in 612 B.C., is the subject of the prophecy of Nahum. The doom about to descend upon the world's great oppressor is the single occasion for Nahum's pronouncement. Consequently, the prophecy is judicial in style, incorporating ancient "judgment oracles." The language is poetic, forceful, and figurative, underscoring the intensity of the topic with which Nahum wrestles.

While the judgment of Assyria is the overwhelming theme of Nahum, the book is primarily a message of comfort to the people of Judah. News of the destruction of the world's great tyrant would come as welcome relief to people shuddering with apprehension and anxiety. Political bondage was always a theological problem for the people of Israel, because this was one of the curses God had promised for disobedience (Deut. 28:33, 36–37, 49–52). Release from the terror of Assyrian domination would bring with it a renewed sense of God's good favor. Nahum's two-pronged proclamation of condemnation and comfort is well summarized in 1:7–9. Unfortunately, Judah failed to heed the warning seen in Assyria's fall and the subsequent rise to power of Babylon. She continued in moral rebellion, which would result in her fall to Babylon in 586 B.C.

Content. The Book of Nahum focuses on a single concern: the fall of the city of Nineveh. Three major sections, corresponding to the three chapters, comprise the prophecy. The first describes God's great power and how that power works itself out in the form of protection for the righteous but judgment for the wicked. Though God is never quick to judge, His patience cannot forever be taken for granted. All the earth is under His control; and when He appears in power, even nature shrinks before Him (1:1–8). In her state of distress and affliction (1:12), Judah could easily doubt God's goodness and even question His power. But the Lord promises to restore peace (1:15), to defeat the enemies of His people (1:13–15), and to remove the threat of renewed affliction (1:9). The prediction of Nineveh's doom forms a message of consolation to Judah (1:15).

The second major section of the prophecy describes the coming destruction of Nineveh (2:1–13). Attempts to defend the city against her attackers will be in vain because the Lord has decreed the fall of Nineveh and the rise of Judah (2:1–7). Floods will inundate the city, sweeping away all the mighty, man-made structures (2:6). Nineveh's citizens will be carried away captive (2:7); others will flee in terror (2:8). Precious treasures will be plundered (2:9); all strength and self-confidence will melt away (2:10). The mighty lion's den will be reduced to desolation, because " 'I am against you,' says the LORD of hosts" (2:11–13).

The third chapter forms the final section of the book. God's judgment may seem overly harsh, but He is justified in His condemnation. Nineveh was a "bloody city" (3:1), a city guilty of shedding the innocent blood of other people. She was a city known for deceit, falsehood, theft, and debauchery (3:1, 4). Such vice was an offense to God, so His verdict of judgment was inevitable (3:2–3, 5–7). Like No Amon, an Egyptian city that fell despite numerous allies and strong defenses, Nineveh cannot escape divine judgment (3:8–13). All efforts to survive prove futile (3:14–15). Troops scatter, leaders perish, and the people run for the hills (3:16–18). God's judgment has fallen, and the peoples Assyria once victimized so mercilessly rejoice and celebrate in response to the news (3:19).

Personal Application. Nahum graphically portrays the seriousness of sin in the sight of God. Though His mercy and patience may cause Him to withhold judgment for a season, God will ultimately announce a day of reckoning. When His righteous judgment is unleashed, no human or superhuman power can withstand its force. His dominion extends over all that exists, and He sits on the bench as Judge over both individuals and nations.

Nahum calls us to serious self-examination and warns against the subtle sin of believing that life can be lived apart from the will and the ways of God. He chides us for becoming overly smug and secure in our faith, for Assyria, once used as God's instrument (Is. 10:5–6), now becomes the object of His wrath. The most frightening words anyone could ever experience are those directed toward Nineveh by the Lord: "Behold, I am against you" (2:13). With such prospects in view, serious self-examination should lead us into wholehearted repentance.

Misuse and abuse of other people is sin in God's sight. Assyria built an empire by raping and plundering others, but national or personal kingdoms founded on deceit and tyranny also are displeasing to the Lord and will be judged by Him. A life of wickedness eventually will lead to isolation, not only from other people, but also from God. Others will withdraw from you, and God will finally be forced to judge (3:19).

Graciously, His judgment against the sinful is offset by His mercy toward the faithful. To the proud, the arrogant, and the rebellious He comes with condemnation. To the humble, the devoted, and the faithful He comes with comfort.

Assyria's long-awaited doom teaches that God's goodness and justice will prevail, though circumstances may seem contradictory. His concern for His people is unceasing, though He may sometimes seem slow to act or far removed. The antidote for discouragement among believers is a revitalized vision of the person and power of God. It is a renewed understanding that vengeance is the work of God, not of ourselves. True faith leaves judgment in the hands of God.

The truth of God's judgment upon sin and the sinner should prompt believers to a renewed evangelistic mission. Those we fail to reach with the saving message of the gospel will indeed suffer the wrath of God.

Surveying
NAHUM

I. TITLE 1:1. Nahum's words are intended to comfort the people of Judah who suffer as subjects of Assyria. But Nahum announces the destruction of the great capital city of the enemy.

The author is identified as Nahum, a man from the village of Elkosh. We do know more about the prophet's time. From Nahum's statements we know he writes after the fall of Thebes to the Assyrians (663 B.C.) and that Nineveh is still standing as capital of an unchallenged world empire. The picture of Judah's oppression by Nineveh (*see* 1:13; 2:2) fits the reign of Manasseh. Thus Nahum probably spoke his message between 663 and 655 B.C.

II. THE VERDICT OF GOD 1:2–15. The theme is God's judgment on Assyria. This is not unique to Nahum. Isaiah especially speaks of Assyria's judgment (*see* Is. 10:5–19; 14:24–27; 17:12–14; 18:4–6; 30:27–33; 31:5–9; 37:21–35).

A. The jealousy of God (1:2–6). The prophet begins with a vision of God. God is "jealous and the LORD avenges." Although slow to anger, the Lord will not leave the guilty unpunished. It is always important to link the fact of guilt with the concept of God's wrath. This Nahum does and goes on to describe the earth trembling as God comes burning with indig-nation, His wrath pouring out like fire before Him (1–6).

B. The gentleness of God (1:7). Nahum balances his picture of an angry God with an affirmation that "the LORD is good, /A stronghold in the day of trouble."

C. The judgment of Nineveh (1:8–14). It is only those who plot against the Lord and plan evil that He will cut down (9–11).

D. The joy of Judah (1:15). Though Judah has suffered, God is about to turn against her oppressor. He will destroy Nineveh, filling Judah with joy (12–15; *see* Peace).

III. THE VENGEANCE OF GOD 2:1–13.

A. The destruction of Nineveh (2:1–12). Nahum warns the city of Nineveh. An enemy advances against her—dashing against the city wall and throwing open the river gates. Looking ahead, Nahum sees the great palace of the king crumble and collapse. Nineveh's endless supply of gold and silver is stripped by her conquerors (1–10). This once fearsome den of lions will soon be torn down.

B. The declaration of the Lord (2:13). " 'I am against you,' says the LORD of hosts."

IV. THE VICTORY OF THE LORD 3:1–19.

A. The sins of Nineveh (3:1–4). In a final exalted poem, Nahum revisits his vision and describes Nineveh's fall. He sees the corpses of the people piled in the streets and fires that blacken the skies.

B. The siege of Nineveh (3:5–18). Nothing can stay the stroke or heal the deadly wound that God will give to this city of blood.

C. The celebration over Nineveh (3:19). All will rejoice over the fall of this wicked city.

TRUTH-IN-ACTION through NAHUM

Truth Nahum Teaches	**Action** Nahum Invites
🛑 Key Lessons in Faith A key test of faith for God's people comes when God judges the nations around them. For Christians, this can mean that God may judge the nation in which they live. He is able to protect and spare His people from judgments that fall even on their neighbors.	**1:7** *Trust* that: (a) God is good! (b) He is a place of safety for us when we are in trouble. (c) He is faithful to care for those who trust Him to do so. **1:12, 13** *Believe* that God is willing and able to deliver us from any bondage. *Know* that He will eventually stop any attack upon us. **1:15** *Hear* and *believe* the good news of deliverance from our soul's enemy through Jesus Christ. See Rom. 16:20.

Introducing
HABAKKUK

Author. The name "Habakkuk" means "Embrace," either signifying that he was "embraced by God" and thus strengthened by Him for his difficult task, or "embracing others" and so encouraging them in time of national crisis. The musical notation in 3:19 may indicate that Habakkuk was qualified to lead in temple worship as a member of the Levitical family. The prophet is imbued with a sense of justice, which will not let him ignore the rampant unrighteousness around him. He has also learned the necessity of bringing the major questions of life to the One who created and redeems life.

Background and Date. Habakkuk lived during one of Judah's most critical periods. His country had fallen from the heights of Josiah's reforms to the depths of violent treatment of its citizens, oppressive measures against the poor, and collapse of the legal system. The world around Judah was at war, with Babylonia rising to ascendancy over Assyria and Egypt. The threat of invasion from the north added to Judah's internal turmoil. Habakkuk probably wrote during the interval between the fall of Nineveh in 612 B.C. and the fall of Jerusalem in 586 B.C.

Content. The Book of Habakkuk gives the account of a spiritual journey, telling of one man's pilgrimage from doubt to worship. The difference between the beginning of the book (1:1–4) and the end of the book (3:17–19) is striking.

In the first four verses Habakkuk is overwhelmed by the circumstances all about him. He can think of nothing except the iniquity and violence he sees among his people. Although Habakkuk addresses God (1:2), he believes God has removed Himself from the earthly scene: His words are forgotten; His hand is not manifest; God is nowhere to be found. Men are in control, and evil men at that. And they act just as one would expect men to act without God's restraint. These words and phrases describe the scene: "iniquity . . . trouble . . . plundering . . . violence . . . strife . . . contention . . . law is powerless . . . justice never goes forth . . . wicked surround the righteous . . . perverse judgment proceeds."

How different is the scene in the last three verses of the book (3:17–19)! All has changed. The prophet is no longer controlled by or even anxious over his circumstances, for his sights have been raised. Temporal affairs no longer fill his thoughts, but his thoughts are on things above. Instead of being ruled by worldly considerations, Habakkuk has fixed his hopes on God, for he realizes that God does take an interest in His creatures. He is the Source of the prophet's strength and joy. Habakkuk has discovered that he is made for higher ground: "He will make me walk on my high hills" (3:19). The words in the last paragraph contrast sharply with those in the first: "rejoice in the LORD . . . joy in the God of my salvation . . . God is my strength . . . feet like deer's feet . . . walk on my high hills" (3:18–19). So Habakkuk has gone from complaining to confidence, from doubt to trust, from man to God, from the valley to the high hills.

If the heart of the gospel is change and transformation, the Book of Habakkuk demonstrates evangelical renewal. At the center of the change and at the center of the book stands this clear credo of faith: "The just shall live by his faith" (2:4). For the prophet, the promise is for physical protection in time of great upheaval and war. When the predicted invasion by foreign armies becomes a reality, that righteous remnant whose God is the Lord, whose trust and dependence is in Him, will be delivered and they will live. For New Testament writers, such as Paul and the author of Hebrews, this statement of confident faith becomes a demonstration of the power of the gospel to give assurance of eternal salvation. For Martin Luther, Habakkuk's theme becomes the watchword of the Reformation.

Personal Application. Habakkuk reminds us that the question "Why?" can, should, and must be asked. His circumstances demanded that he ask God about the apparent reign of unrighteousness around him. Because he believed in God, he believed that God had an answer to his problem. His questions demonstrated the presence of faith, not the lack of it. For an atheist the question "Why?" has no meaning; for a believer the question "Why?" finds its ultimate answer in God.

Paul the apostle takes the statement of Habakkuk 2:4 and makes it the heart of the gospel. The righteousness of God is attained only through faith, so that the right way to live is to trust. Habakkuk calls all believers in all times to trust God, to be faithful to Him, and so to find life as God means it to be lived.

The final verses of this prophecy teach that it is possible to rise above circumstances, and even to rejoice in them, by focusing on God who stands above all. Habakkuk does not deny his problems, nor does he treat them lightly; instead, he finds God sufficient in the midst of his troubles.

Surveying
HABAKKUK

I. HABAKKUK'S QUESTIONS 1:1–17.

Habakkuk alternates poetic laments with prophecy. The first chapter contains two laments. Each expresses a question that troubles Habakkuk deeply.

A. A question about God's concern (1:1–11).

1. The question stated: "Why doesn't God do something?" (1:1–5).

2. The answer given: "I will use the Chaldeans" (1:6–11). God does answer and makes clear to the prophet that He is not tolerating Judah's injustice but beginning to raise up judgment.

B. A question about God's methods: "Why does God use wicked men?" (1:12–17).

Habakkuk cries to God because of the injustice that pollutes his society. God has been silent, and to Habakkuk, that silence implies tolerance of wrong! Habakkuk can no longer stand the doubt and anguish this situation creates. He must have an answer from God.

The answer at first satisfies Habakkuk (12). But Habakkuk is again troubled. Jealous for the glory of God, Habakkuk wonders how God can remain silent while some treat others like fish to net and feast on. Won't their successes lead men away from God, to worship their own power?

II. GOD'S ANSWER 2:1–20.

A. The prophet waiting (2:1).

B. The Lord responding (2:2–20).

1. The significance of the reply (2:2–3). God explains the hidden processes of judgment that are at work in the lives of the wicked. All of their successes eventually turn back on their own heads.

2. The central truth for believers (2:4; see Shall Live*).*

3. The consequences of the truth for unbelievers (2:5–20).

Woe to the greedy (2:5–8). They are never satisfied (5). Success does not bring the wicked person rest or satisfaction. Instead, his gains make him desire more. Mistreatment of others creates enemies, who will turn on the wicked when they can (6–8).

Woe to the complacent (2:9–11). They have a false security. The wicked use their gains to build a "nest on high." But no matter how they try to protect themselves from disaster, they will never escape.

Woe to the violent (2:12–14). The future holds no lasting hope for the wicked.

Woe to the shameless (2:15–17). The wicked exult in the shame of others. But they themselves will be exposed to disgrace.

Woe to the idolaters (2:18–20). That which the wicked worship, whether idols or their own power (1:11, 16), has no ability to guide them or to deliver.

III. HABAKKUK'S PRAYER 3:1–19.

Habakkuk is intellectually satisfied. But now, in a prayer later set to music, Habakkuk examines his own fears and struggles to come to a triumphant faith.

A. The Lord's power (3:1–16).

1. A call for mercy (3:1–2). Habakkuk's first reaction is an eager cry for God to bring on the purifying judgment.

2. Power in nature (3:3–11). God gives His prophet a vision of what judgment involves.

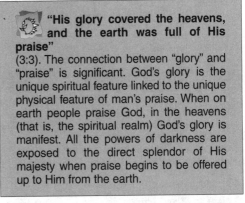

"His glory covered the heavens, and the earth was full of His praise" (3:3). The connection between "glory" and "praise" is significant. God's glory is the unique spiritual feature linked to the unique physical feature of man's praise. When on earth people praise God, in the heavens (that is, the spiritual realm) God's glory is manifest. All the powers of darkness are exposed to the direct splendor of His majesty when praise begins to be offered up to Him from the earth.

3. Power over nations (3:12–16). Habakkuk looks back across sacred history. Now Habakkuk must struggle to remember that judgment is ultimately intended "to save your people." Stunned, the prophet slumps, his legs trembling, crushed by the terror of his vision. He must wait patiently for the day of calamity, knowing now the misery it will bring.

B. The prophet's faith (3:17–19).

1. Confidence in spite of circumstances (3:17–18). With all the material things in which men take *joy gone, Habakkuk knows, "I will rejoice in the LORD, I will joy in the God of my salvation" (18).

2. Confidence because of God (3:19).

"I will rejoice in the LORD" (3:17–19). Habakkuk always listened to God's revelation of His righteousness, His majesty, and His inscrutable ways. Habakkuk believed God. God's answer to the prophet gave him a deep consciousness of God's answer to the meaning of life. This discovery will magnify faith in anyone's life.

TRUTH-IN-ACTION through HABAKKUK

Truth Habakkuk Teaches	**Action** Habakkuk Invites
1 Steps to Dynamic Devotion God requires that we make our relationship with Him our highest priority, that we bring our deepest questions and turmoils before Him, expecting His answers and guidance.	**2:1** *Set aside* a regular time and place that is holy to the Lord. *Spend time listening* for His word as you read, study, and meditate on Scripture. *Be faithful* in daily prayer. **2:2, 3** *Document* those things the Lord speaks to you or quickens to your heart. *Record* biblical promises He makes alive to you, and *hold fast to them*, knowing they will come to pass.
2 The Life of Faith When all the circumstances of our life present a negative picture—in failure and loss or when the natural reaction would be grief or complaint—this is the time to put faith in God and in His Word. Thus we can see through God's eyes to the final glorious outcome. This brings worship and praise even before our circumstances have changed.	**2:4; 3:16–19** *Determine to praise* and worship and thank God for His faithfulness, no matter how devastating the circumstances. *Look with the eye of faith* at God's plan for the future.
3 A Step to Holiness Though some only think of idols as material images, what truly defines an idol is the place it occupies in a person's life. Any person, thing, or desire that stands in the way of an immediate, wholehearted "Yes, Lord!" to anything He asks of us is an idol and must be eliminated.	**2:18–20** *Examine yourself!* Ask the question, "Is there anything in my life that hinders my obedience to God?" *Take down* any idol in your life by humbling yourself before God and by refusing other interests to rule your heart.
4 Keys to Wise Living The worldly theory of success that centers on personal power and the amassing of financial riches is a highly deceptive trap. The wise person defines success in the light of God's plan for his life. Living in a manner that honors God and relies on His promises, brings success.	**2:9** *Know* that success by the world's measure is a vain pursuit. *Build* your house—your life and vocation—on the rock of God's Word. **2:12–14** *Plan your life* by the wisdom of God. *Be a success in Him.*

Introducing
ZEPHANIAH

Author. Zephaniah ("The LORD Has Hidden") was a prophet to Judah. He identified himself better than any other of the minor prophets, tracing his ancestry back four generations to Hezekiah, a good king who had led the people back to God during the prophet Isaiah's time. King Josiah, whose reform brought about a period of renewal in Jerusalem, was not only a contemporary of Zephaniah, but a distant relative. Thus the men could have been friends and equally zealous for a return to the pure worship of God.

The intimacy of emotion as well as the familiarity of place when Zephaniah writes about Jerusalem (1:10–11) indicate that he had grown up there and was deeply troubled by prophesying the city's destruction. According to the arrangement of Hebrew Scriptures, Zephaniah was the last of the prophets to write before the captivity. His prophecy was the swan song of the southern kingdom of Judah. (*See* map, page 184.)

Date. Zephaniah gives the general time of his writing as being "in the days of Josiah, the son of Amon, king of Judah" (1:1), about 641 to 609 B.C. The height of Josiah's reform was in the 620s. Since the fall of Nineveh in 612 B.C.

had not yet taken place (2:13–15), most scholars set the date of writing between 630 and 627 B.C. His contemporaries included Jeremiah and Nahum.

Background. About one hundred years before this prophecy, the northern kingdom (the ten tribes of Israel) had fallen to Assyria. The people had been carried away by their captors, and the land had been resettled by foreigners. Under King Manasseh and King Amon, King Josiah's father, tribute had been paid to keep Assyria from invading the southern kingdom.

The alliance with Assyria not only affected Judah politically, but also Assyria's religious, social, and fashion practices set the trend in Judah. Official protection was given in Judah to the magical arts of diviners and enchanters. Astral religion became so popular that Judah's King Manasseh erected altars for the worship of the sun, moon, stars, zodiac signs, and all the host of heaven, on the roof of the temple (2 Kin. 23:11). The worship of the mother-goddess of Assyria became a practice that involved all members of Judean families (Jer. 7:18). However, as the young Josiah took over the reins of government, the Assyrian threat was diminishing. The final blow to their power came with a Babylonian uprising that eventually resulted in the destruction of Nineveh.

After a long silence, true prophetic voices were once again heard in Judah. Along with Zephaniah, Jeremiah was encouraging the revival led by King Josiah. The Book of the Law had been found in the temple. As a consequence, the land was purged of idolatrous practices and priests, the temple was cleansed, and thousands of sacrifices were offered when Passover was once again observed (2 Chronicles 34; 35).

In retrospect the reform was one of externals, since the hearts of the people had not been changed. Even so, there was a sense that everything was right with God and the world, for they were living in momentary peace and prosperity. Into this complacent atmosphere the devastating message of Zephaniah comes like a searing blast.

Content. Zephaniah viewed the political development of Israel (the northern kingdom), Judah (the southern kingdom), and all the surrounding nations from the perspective that the people should learn that God was involved in all the affairs of history. Speaking as an oracle of God, he understands that God uses foreign governments to bring about judgment upon His rebellious chosen people. Zephaniah is appalled that, after the catastrophe of the northern tribes, the people of Judah still maintain the preposterous notion that God is helpless to do good or evil (1:12).

As is true in most of the prophets, Zephaniah's writings have three components: (1) the pronouncement of specific and often universal judgment for sin; (2) an appeal for repentance because God is righteous and willing to forgive; and (3) a promise that the remnant who have made God their refuge will be saved.

Few biblical writers describe the wrath of God or the joy of God as vividly as does Zephaniah. God is seen searching the streets of Jerusalem with lamps to find the wicked He will punish (1:12); the prophecy describing the day of the Lord in 1:14–18 is a terrible chant of doom. A call to repentance appropriately follows these passages. The first two and a half chapters prophesy judgment so complete that even nature will be consumed (1:2–3) and "all the earth shall be devoured with the fire of My jealousy" (3:8).

Because of the repeated use of the term "the day of the LORD," the Book of Zephaniah has meaning for end times. The day of the Lord is either the period of time or the actual day when God will bring His purposes to culmination for mankind and for the earth. The righteous will be rewarded with eternal blessing, and the wicked will be consigned to eternal damnation.

Amos was probably the first to use the term "the day of the LORD" (Amos 5:18–20). Isaiah, Jeremiah, Obadiah, and Joel all speak of it as a time of final judgment. In the New Testament "the day of Jesus Christ" (Phil. 1:6) carries the same meaning.

While the message of Zephaniah has future significance, Judah and the surrounding nations expected an immediate and local fulfillment of the prophecies. Beginning with Assyria, the judgments were fulfilled in a few years when the temple was utterly destroyed and the Jews were carried into Babylonian captivity.

Though the prophets were called by God to convey a dreadful message, they were also aware that wrath and judgment expressed only one side of God's nature. Habakkuk eloquently reminded the Holy One "in wrath [to] remember mercy" (Hab. 3:2). In the Book of Zephaniah, God does remember, for He promises that He will purify and restore the faithful remnant (3:9). He assures this humbled people that no one will make them afraid again, for He has cast out their enemy (3:13, 15).

Then He bids them to sing, to shout, to rejoice with all their hearts. And God joins in the celebration like a victorious general returning with the comrades he has rescued.

In jubilation God sings and dances and shouts for joy as He tells them of His love (3:14–17).

Zephaniah ends with God's tender promise that He will gather all those who have been driven out and will give them fame and praise among all the people of the earth (3:20).

Personal Application. Four timeless lessons for both believers and unbelievers are found in Zephaniah:

1. God is perfect justice as well as perfect love (3:5). If the call to repentance is continually ignored, God's judgment must consequently fall.

2. Punishment is not God's choice, for "God so loved the world that He gave His only begotten Son that whoever believes in Him should not perish but have everlasting life" (John 3:16).

3. To settle into the complacency of financial prosperity (1:10–13) and to participate in the ritual of a well-structured religious life without obeying God's voice, receiving correction, or drawing near to Him (3:2) is an ever-present possibility. Even more tragic is to have no awareness of such spiritual emptiness.

4. Even to the rebellious, God offers last-minute reprieve (2:1–3). The remnant who humble themselves and seek righteousness will be hidden in the day of the Lord's anger (2:3). They will be gathered to Him and healed (3:18), for God dwells in their midst (3:17). This abiding promise to God's people is the essence of the gospel.

Surveying
ZEPHANIAH

I. INTRODUCTION 1:1. Habakkuk looked deep within the personality of the wicked and saw processes of judgment at work. Zephaniah, a contemporary, looks ahead. There Zephaniah sees a day when God will act dramatically and history will prove that He is Judge of all.

A. Identification of author (1:1). Zephaniah is a descendant of the godly King Hezekiah. He lives and prophesies during the reign of Josiah.

B. Time of writing (1:1). Because the picture Zephaniah sketches of widespread idolatry in Judah fits best before the great religious revival, which Josiah led in 621 B.C., his book is usually dated in Josiah's earlier years.

II. THE DAY OF JUDGMENT AGAINST JUDAH 1:2–13.

A. Judgment on all creation (1:2–3). Zephaniah begins with two warnings of universal judgment. Everything will be swept away when the judgment comes.

B. Judgment against religious leaders (1:4–7; see Day).

C. Judgment against political leaders (1:8–9).

D. Judgment against business leaders (1:10–11).

E. Judgment against unbelievers (1:12–13). Those in Judah who think, "The LORD will not do good, nor will He do evil," will be jolted from complacency when the day of wrath comes (1:13).

III. THE DAY OF THE LORD 1:14–18. Zephaniah speaks of a "great day of the Lord." Like other prophets, his primary focus is on the final judgment which is to sweep the whole earth just before history's end. But Zephaniah, like others, also sees divine punishments that fall on a nation as a contemporary expression of that day.

A. Near and coming quickly (1:14). Now Zephaniah sees a day of judgment that is "near and hastens quickly."

B. A day of wrath (1:15–16). This day "of trouble and distress, . . . of darkness and gloominess, . . . of clouds and thick darkness" will bring distress to all the people of Judah.

C. The whole land to be devoured (1:17–18).

IV. A CALL TO REPENTANCE 2:1–3.

A. A call to gather (2:1–2).

B. A call to seek the Lord (2:3). Because judgment is imminent, Zephaniah urges individuals who are responsive to God to "seek righteousness, seek humility." They will not escape the troubles that come when their nation falls, but "it may be that you will be hidden in the day of the LORD's anger."

V. THE DAY OF JUDGMENT AGAINST SURROUNDING NATIONS 2:4–15. Now the prophet seems to lift his eyes and look beyond the borders of Judah.

A. To the west—Philistines (2:4–7). Turning full circle from west to north, Zephaniah predicts judgment to strike Philistia.

B. To the east—Moab and Ammon (2:8–11).

C. To the south—Ethiopia (2:12). Ethiopia is also known as Cush.

D. To the north—Assyria (2:13–15).

VI. THE DAY OF JUDGMENT AGAINST JERUSALEM 3:1–7.

A. Against the leaders (3:1–4). The immediate future holds only woes for this city of rebels and oppressors.

B. The Lord an unfailing witness in her midst (3:5). These unresponsive and faithless people will be punished by a God who is righteous and who does no wrong.

C. Jerusalem has not changed (3:6–7).

VII. A FAITHFUL REMNANT 3:8–20.

A. To speak with purity and honesty

(3:8–13). At history's end another fate awaits the city. Then, when the whole world is bathed in the fire of God's anger, Jerusalem's people will be purified. "I will leave in your midst," God promises, "a meek and humble people." The survivors of the final judgment will be those who *trust in the name of the Lord.

B. Judgments to be taken away and their enemy cast out (3:14–15). Then Jerusalem will sing!

C. God Himself celebrating (3:16–17). Then God will be with the city and her people.

D. The people restored (3:18–20). He will at last give the oppressed praise and honor among all the peoples of the earth.

TRUTH-IN-ACTION through ZEPHANIAH

Truth Zephaniah Teaches	**Action** Zephaniah Invites
1 Growing in Godliness The sin of pride is most often revealed by the words that we speak. Language becomes unclean with repeated expressions of self-will, or the profane use of God's name.	**3:9–13** *Purify your heart* and your speech will be pure also, *Allow* God to purify your lips and language.
2 Steps to Dynamic Devotion The key to knowing God is to continually seek Him. The chief danger in this quest is the temptation to be satisfied with past encounters so that no fresh pursuits are made. Complacency is the enemy of spiritual growth.	**1:6** *Persevere* in following the Lord. *Do not turn back. Find your answer* in God, **1:12** *Remain zealous. Refuse* complacency. **3:5** *Seek God faithfully* every day. Trust that the Lord behaves justly. *Keep your appointments* with the Father.
3 A Step to Holiness Avoid letting attitudes and character be shaped by the worldliness that surrounds. We are citizens of another kingdom.	**1:8** *Reject* anything foreign to God's kingdom rule in your life.
4 Lessons for Leaders The wise leader accepts the Scripture's testimony about man and rejects the prevailing, humanistic doctrine that teaches man's intrinsic goodness. An unteachable attitude is the tip of the iceberg of ungodliness. This wisdom should influence one's self-view. causing all of us to guard ourselves from insincerity and pride in any of its manifestations.	**3:2** Leaders, *understand* that the clearest evidence that someone does not trust the Lord or seek Him diligently is a rebellious, disobedient, and unteachable nature. **3:3** Leaders, *avoid* being among those who speak loudly, who promise great things, but produce nothing that lasts or bears fruit in the long run. **3:4** Leaders, *avoid diligently* any form of arrogance or pride in your ministry. *Do not profane* the ministry by mishandling God's Word in any way. *Never teach* your own opinions as God's Word.

KEYS TO HAGGAI, ZECHARIAH, AND MALACHI
Messages of Promise and Assurance

Kingdom Key: God's Purpose in View

Haggai: Prophet of the King's Promise of Glory

What Jeremiah prophesied took place through Daniel's prayers (compare Jer. 29:10 with Dan. 9:2–3). The return of Judah's exiled families prompts their efforts to rebuild the temple. When opposition rises, Haggai and Zechariah's preaching rallies the people's faith and action (*see* Ezra 4 and Hos. 2:1–9). Some of the returning group had seen Solomon's temple before its destruction and they speak demeaningly of the efforts to rebuild (2:3). Then the prophet asserts: "The glory of this latter temple shall be greater than the former" (2:9). This was truer than anyone could have imagined, for it was into this building Jesus Himself entered centuries later! Though it was an expanded structure, embellished by Herod's enterprise, God's glory incarnate, "full of grace and truth" arrived in fullest splendor as

> **Partner-ship with God's purposes brings fruitful-ness.**

prophesied (John 1:4–18; 2:13–22). He still enters humble settings today, to bring glory to His church!

Zechariah: Prophet of the King's Promise to Build

Teamed with the older prophet Haggai, the young man Zechariah prophesied at a decisive time, when faith was seeking to find roots again in Jerusalem. The returned exiles, blocked by political ploys of opponents, are discouraged. The prophet is stirred by God to go to Zerubbabel, their leader, and declare: "[Your] hands have laid the foundation . . . [your] hands shall also finish it" (4:9). He gives God's assurance that this shall be achieved, "Not by might or by power, but by My Spirit!" (4:6–7).

God's King arrives—Jesus the Messiah—and announces *His* intent to build another "temple"—"I will build My church" (Matt. 16:18–19). Even (Please turn to page 263.)

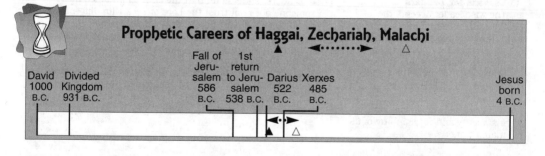

Prophetic Careers of Haggai, Zechariah, Malachi

| David 1000 B.C. | Divided Kingdom 931 B.C. | Fall of Jerusalem 586 B.C. | 1st return to Jerusalem 538 B.C. | Darius 522 B.C. | Xerxes 485 B.C. | Jesus born 4 B.C. |

After the Exile, three voices encourage God's

Master Key: God's Son Revealed
Haggai

Two references to Christ in the Book of Haggai are highlighted. The first is 2:6–9, which reveals that what God will do in the new temple will one day gain international attention. After an upheaval among the peoples of the earth, the nations will be drawn to the temple to discover what they had been looking for: the One whom all the nations have desired will be revealed in splendor in the temple. The presence of this One will make the memory of Solomon's glorious temple fade, so that only Christ's glory remains. Along with the glory of Christ's presence will come great peace, since the resplendent Prince of Peace Himself will be there.

The second reference to the coming Messiah is 2:23. The book closes with a mention of Zerubbabel, which ties this book, near the end of the Old Testament, with the first book in the New Testament. Zerubbabel is one of the people listed in the genealogies of Jesus. Two things make Zerubbabel significant and link him to Christ:

1. Zerubbabel is a *sign* of a man chosen by God, through whose yielded nature God brings life, leadership, and ministry. What Zerubbabel did in part, Jesus did in full as the Servant of the Lord.

2. Zerubbabel is also in the *line* of the Messiah. The lists of Jesus' ancestors in Matthew and Luke include the name of Zerubbabel, the son of Shealtiel, whose own personal significance was surpassed by his role as one who pointed ahead to the coming Savior of the world.

Key Word: *The Reconstruction of the Temple*

Haggai's basic theme is clear: the remnant must reorder its priorities and complete the temple before it can expect the blessing of God upon its efforts.

Key Verses: Haggai 1:7–8; 2:7–9

Key Chapter: Haggai 2

Verses 6–9 record some of the most startling prophecies in Scripture: "I will shake heaven and earth, the sea and dry land" (the Tribulation) and "they shall come to the Desire of All Nations" and "in this place I will give peace" (the Second Coming of the Messiah).

Zechariah

Zechariah is sometimes referred to as the most messianic of all the Old Testament books. Chapters 9—14 are the most quoted section of the Prophets in the passion narratives of the Gospels. In the Book of Revelation Zechariah is quoted more than any prophet except Ezekiel.

Zechariah prophesies that the Messiah will come as the Lord's Servant the Branch

Key Word: *Prepare for the Messiah*

The first eight chapters frequently allude to the temple and encourage the people to complete their great

continued on next page

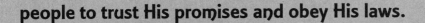

people to trust His promises and obey His laws.

(3:8), as the Man the Branch (6:12), as both King and Priest (6:13), and as the True Shepherd (11:4–11). He bears eloquent testimony to Christ's betrayal for thirty pieces of silver (11:12–13), His Crucifixion (12:10), His sufferings (13:7), and His Second Advent (14:4).

Two references to Christ are of profound significance. Jesus' Triumphal Entry into Jerusalem is described in detail in 9:9, four hundred years before the event (*see* Matt. 21:5; Mark 11:7–10). One of the most dramatic verses of prophetic Scriptures is found in 12:10 when, in the majority of manuscripts, the first person is used: "Then they will look on Me whom they pierced." Jesus Christ personally prophesied His eventual acknowledgement by the house of David.

Malachi

In this last book of the Old Testament we find clear prophetic utterances regarding the sudden appearance of Christ—the Messenger of the (new) covenant (3:1). That day is a time of judgment. "Who can stand when He appears?" (3:2). No one can in his own strength, but for those who fear the Lord, "the Sun of Righteousness ['the Messenger of the covenant,' Jesus (3:1)] shall arise with healing in His wings," that is, in victorious triumph (4:2).

Power Key: God's Spirit at Work
Haggai

A brief but beautiful reference to the Holy Spirit is found in 2:5. The previous verses show that the people of God are discouraged because they have been comparing the temple they are building with the glorious temple of Solomon, which the new temple is to replace. The word of the Lord to them is: "Be strong . . . and work." The motivation is: "For I am with you" (v. 4).

Haggai 2:5 then explains how the Spirit of God is meant to interact with the spirit of the people in order to get the work accomplished. Verse 5 includes these significant points:

1. The Holy Spirit is a vital part of God's

---

continued from preceding page

work on the new sanctuary. As they build the temple, they are building their future, because that very structure will be used by the Messiah when He comes to bring salvation.

Key Verses: Zechariah 8:3; 9:9

Key Chapter: Zechariah 14

Zechariah builds to a tremendous climax in the fourteenth chapter, where he discloses the last siege of Jerusalem and the ultimate holiness of Jerusalem and her people.

Key Word: *An Appeal to Backsliders*

The divine dialogue in Malachi's prophecy is designed as an appeal to break through the barrier of Israel's disbelief, disappointment, and discouragement. God reveals His continuing love in spite of Israel's lethargy. His appeal in this oracle is for the people and priests to stop and realize that their lack of blessing is not caused by God's lack of concern, but by their disobedience of the covenant law.

Key Verses: Malachi 2:17—3:1;
4:5–6

Key Chapter: Malachi 3

The last book of the Old Testament concludes with a dramatic prophecy of the coming of the Messiah and John the Baptist: "I send My messenger, and he will prepare the way before Me" (3:1).

covenant with His people, "according to the word that I covenanted with you."

2. The Holy Spirit is an abiding gift to the people of God: "My Spirit remains among you."

3. The presence of the Holy Spirit removes fear from the hearts of God's people. Therefore, "Do not fear!"

These principles remain the same for God's people today. At the heart of God's covenant with His people is the constant operation of the Holy Spirit, working to release them from fear, so that they may move boldly in fulfilling the divine commission.

Zechariah

The most quoted Old Testament verse in reference to the work of the Holy Spirit is 4:6. Zerubbabel is comforted in the assurances (1) that rebuilding the temple will not be done by military might or human prowess alone but by the ministry of the Spirit of God, and (2) that the Holy Spirit will remove every obstacle that stands against the completion of God's temple.

A sad commentary in 7:12 reminds the people of their rebellion against the words of the Lord delivered by the prophets. These words were transmitted by His Spirit.

Although the reference to *ruach* (spirit/Spirit) in 12:10 is translated by some as God's disposition rather than as the Holy Spirit, others translate it as the Holy Spirit. As such it is one of the most beautiful titles for the Holy Spirit found in Scripture. God's promise is to pour on the house of David and Jerusalem "the Spirit of grace and supplication." This immediately precedes their reception and mourning over the One they had pierced. The preparation of the heart by the Holy Spirit is always antecedent to conversion.

Malachi

The working of the Holy Spirit in Malachi is evident in his personal life and prophetic ministry. His writings show him to have been a dedicated prophet—a person clearly in tune with the Holy Spirit. As such, he could be used effectively to warn people about their sinful behavior and to urge them to conform to the Law of the Lord. The Holy Spirit also granted him the privilege of bringing the line of faithful, dedicated writing prophets to a close, allowing him to proclaim with clarity and fervency his telescopic vision of Christ's coming.

Kingdom Key continued from page 260

today powers seek to resist its upbuilding, but He still sends His Spirit to bring breakthroughs (see numerous cases in Acts), and He provides apostolic and prophetic truth and preaching to strengthen its footings (Eph. 2:19–22). Jesus' appearance to John on Patmos is a dramatic statement of the way in which His presence and power may enter any setting where His leaders are temporarily blocked. He is "in the midst" of the churches (Rev. 1:1–13, 20) and powerful to break hellish opposition (Rev. 1:17–18).

Malachi: Prophet of the King's Nearness to Hear

The criticizing and complaining people who questioned Malachi about God's presence, goodness, and faithfulness (1:2, 12; 2:17) reveal a temptation present among some believers today. Malachi affirms God's nearness (1) to *hear* the cry of those who revere His Name (2:5; 3:16–17) and (2) to *abound* to the need of those who worship with their tithes and offerings (3:8–12). Similar circumstances among any of the Lord's people will bring the King who was prophesied to draw near (James 4:8). The "Sun of Righteousness" of whom Malachi prophesied (4:2) will rise—Christ, the "Day Star" from on high (2 Pet. 1:19), and He is ready to hear and answer His people, to reveal God's might, miracles, and manifest graces!

Introducing

HAGGAI

Author. Haggai, whose name means "Festive," was one of the postexilic prophets, a contemporary of Zechariah. Haggai had the qualities of a good pastor. An encourager whose word was in tune with the hearts of the people and the mind of God, he was the Lord's messenger with the Lord's message, bringing to his discouraged band the assurance of God's presence.

Date. Haggai's ministry covered a period of slightly less than four months during the second year of the reign of King Darius, who ruled Persia from 522 to 486 B.C. This fixes Haggai in history at 520 B.C. (*See* map, page 184.)

Background. As Haggai came to his task in 520 B.C., he joined the exiles who had returned to their homeland in 538 B.C. to rebuild the temple of the Lord. They had started well, building an altar and offering sacrifices, then laying the foundation for the Lord's house the following year. Construction had ceased, however, as enemies mocked the builders' efforts. But the ministry of Haggai and Zechariah caused the people to rally and complete the task within five years. The rebuilt temple was dedicated in 515 B.C.

Content. The Book of Haggai addresses three problems common to all people of all times, and gives three inspired solutions to those problems. The first problem is *disinterest* (1:1–15). The people had returned from exile for the stated purpose of rebuilding the temple in Jerusalem (Ezra 1:2–4) and had made a start on their assigned task, but opposition had appeared and the work had stopped. The people had become more concerned with building beautiful houses for themselves, perhaps in an attempt to blot out the memory of their exile in a strange land (1:4). To wake them from their apathetic attitude, God speaks twice to the people. They first need to realize that they are fruitless (1:5–6) because they have turned from God's house to their own houses (1:7–9). All their efforts at building their own kingdom can never produce lasting results. After seeing their problem, the people then need to understand that God will accept what they do, that He will be glorified if they will only yield to Him what they have (1:8).

The second problem is *discouragement* (2:1–9). Some of the older people in the band of returned exiles had seen Solomon's temple when they were children, so that no building, however beautiful, could compare with the glory of that former temple (2:3). The discouragement of the older people had quickly influenced the younger ones until, less than a month after the rebuilding began, work on the temple had ceased. But again Haggai brings a message designed to deal decisively with discouragement.

The solution has two parts: one to deal with the immediate problem, the other to bring a long-range resolution. For the present it is enough for the people to "be strong . . . be strong . . . be strong . . . and work" (2:4). The other key to overcoming discouragement is for the builders to know that they are building for the day when God will so fill this house with glory that it will surpass the glory of Solomon's temple (2:9).

The final issue that Haggai has to face is the problem of *dissatisfaction* (2:10–23). Now that the people are working, they expect an immediate reversal of all their years of inactivity. So the prophet comes with a question for the priests (2:12–13) about clean and unclean things and their influence on one another. The response of the priests is that uncleanness is infectious while holiness is not. The application is obvious: Do not expect the work of three months to undo the neglect of sixteen years.

The Lord's next word to the people is a surprise: "But from this day I will bless you" (2:19). The people needed to understand that God's blessings cannot be earned, but come as gracious gifts from a giving God. God has chosen Zerubbabel to be a sign (2:23), that is, to represent the servant nature to be fulfilled ultimately in Zerubbabel's greatest Son, Jesus. Note Zerubbabel's name in both the genealogical lists in the Gospels (Matthew 1; Luke 3), indicating that God's final, highest blessing is a Person, His Son Jesus Christ.

Personal Application. Haggai issues a clear call to his own people and to us that we should set ourselves to the task assigned to us by God. We should not allow difficulties, enemies, or selfish pursuits to turn us aside from our divinely given responsibilities. The noble nature of our calling and the promised presence of God and His Holy Spirit encourage us to fulfill our commission.

By emphasizing the cooperative roles of prophet, priest, prince, and people, Haggai also demonstrates the necessity for teamwork in carrying out God's purposes on earth.

Surveying
HAGGAI

I. THE LORD'S FIRST MESSAGE: CONSIDER YOUR WAYS 1:1-15.

A. Consider what you have done: neglected God's house (1:1-6).

B. Consider what you should do: build God's house (1:7-11). Haggai calls for the rebuilding of the temple. He conveys the Lord's message that blessing has been withheld because the people have failed to put God first.

C. Results of considering your ways (1:12-15). The leaders and the people recognize the voice of God in Haggai's words, and they obey. God stirs up (see Stirred) enthusiasm for the project, and the whole community comes together to begin work.

II. THE LORD'S SECOND MESSAGE: BE STRONG AND WORK 2:1-9.

A. Comparison of the new temple with Solomon's temple (2:1-3).

B. Call to be strong (2:4-5). Under the Mosaic Law (see v. 5), God committed Himself to be with each generation that obeys Him. These people have obeyed. Thus God announces through Haggai that He will keep His word (4).

C. Coming glory of the new temple (2:6-9).

But how can a people on the bare edge of poverty rebuild the temple? God announces through Haggai that He is owner of all the gold and silver of the world (see Stewardship). God will meet the need, and "the glory of this present house will be greater than the glory of the former" (i.e., Solomon's temple).

III. THE LORD'S THIRD MESSAGE: I WILL BLESS YOU 2:10-23.

A. A question for the priests (2:10-19). Haggai is sent to make a public inquiry of the priests concerning a point of Mosaic Law. Under the Law an object or person that is ceremonially unclean makes unclean whatever it touches. Under the Law nothing that is holy can make any defiled thing clean. Haggai applies the principle. This people is not to think that the presence of the *temple makes them holy. They are defiled by sin. But God operates among them in grace.

B. A promise for Zerubbabel (2:20-23). The same day Haggai receives a message from God to give to Zerubbabel. This individual is of the royal family. He is not king, for Judah is under the domination of Persia. But the words of Haggai look forward to a time when God will shake the nations. Then Zerubbabel (that is, the family of David), will again be established.

Thus Haggai's final words are a reaffirmation to Judah and to future generations of the great covenant of God with David. The time is coming when God will fulfill His promises. The future envisioned by all the prophets will become a reality.

TRUTH-IN-ACTION through HAGGAI

Truth Haggai Teaches	**Action** Haggai Invites
◆ **Key Lessons in Faith** The challenge to faith is the same in every generation: seek first the things of God and trust Him to provide the daily necessities of life. The glorification of any work we pursue comes by the presence of God in it. God calls us to commit what we are, what we have, and all that we do to Him.	**1:1-4** *Make the work of God a priority,* both with your time and with your money. **2:6-9** *Understand* that it is the presence of Jesus that produces glory. See 2 Cor. 3:18, **2:15-19** *Choose to believe* and *reckon as true* that when we turn from selfish ambition and personal agenda to focus on advancing God's kingdom, He will bless us toward that end.

Introducing
ZECHARIAH

Author. Zechariah, whose name means "Yahweh Remembers," was one of the postexilic prophets, a contemporary of Haggai. With Haggai, he was called to arouse the returned Jews to complete the task of reconstructing the temple (see Ezra 6:14). As the son of Berechiah and grandson of Iddo, he came from one of the priestly families of the tribe of Levi. He is one of the most messianic of all the Old Testament prophets, giving distinct, verifiable references to the coming Messiah.

Date. Zechariah's prophetic ministry began in 520 B.C., two months after Haggai had completed his prophecy. The vision of the early chapters was apparently given while the prophet was still a young man (*see* 2:4). Chapters 7 and 8 occur two years later in 518 B.C. The reference to Greece in 9:13 may indicate that chapters 9–14 were written after 480 B.C., when Greece replaced Persia as the great world power. The prophecies comprising the Book of Zechariah were reduced to writing between 520 and 475 B.C.

Background. The exiles who returned to their homeland in 538 B.C. under the edict of Cyrus were among the poorer of the Jewish captives. Some fifty thousand people returned to Jerusalem under the leadership of Zerubbabel and Joshua. (*See* map, page 116.) Quickly they rebuilt the altar and began construction on the temple. Soon, however, apathy set in as they were beset with opposition from the neighboring Samaritans who eventually were able to get an order from the Persian government to halt construction. For about twelve years construction had been choked by discouragement and preoccupation with other pursuits. Zechariah and Haggai urged the people to return to the Lord and His purpose to restore the ruined temple. Zechariah pointed God's people to a day when the Messiah would rule from a restored temple in a restored city.

Content. The Book of Zechariah begins with the impassioned word of the Lord for the people to repent and turn again to their God. The book is replete with Zechariah's references to the word of the Lord. The prophet does not deliver his own message, but he faithfully transmits the message given to him by God. The people are called on to repent of their lethargy and complete the unfinished task.

God then assures His people of His love and care for them through a series of eight visions. The vision of the man and the horses reminds the people of God's watchful care. The vision of the four horns and four craftsmen recalls God's judgment, first on Judah and then on her enemies. In the vision of the man with the measuring line there is an apocalyptic glimpse of God's beautiful, peaceful city. Joshua, the high priest, portrays cleansing from sin. The magnificent vision of the lampstand among the olive trees assures Zerubbabel that God's purposes will be accomplished only by His Spirit. The flying scroll emits God's

pronouncement against stealing and lying. The vision of the woman in a basket signifies the holiness of God and the removal of sin. The vision of the four chariots depicts God's sovereign control over the earth.

The visions are followed by a coronation scene in which Joshua is crowned as both king and priest. This is powerfully symbolic of the coming Messiah.

In chapters 7 and 8 God takes the occasion of a question concerning fasting to reinforce His mandate for justice and righteousness to supersede religious formalities.

Chapters 9—14 contain much eschatology (the study of the last things). Zion is restored and radiates the glory of her ruling King. Two prophetic messages emerge. The first prophecy, or "burden," is in chapters 9—11. God will deliver His people (ch. 9), there will be a restoration of prosperity for the people of God (ch. 10), and the Shepherd of Israel will initially be rejected, bringing great desolation (ch. 11). The second prophecy is in chapters 12—14. Again God delivers His people, and they mourn for the One they have pierced (ch. 12). A fountain is then opened to cleanse from sin and uncleanness (ch. 13). Then the Lord will reign from a restored Zion as King over all nations (ch. 14).

Personal Application. Zechariah challenges his contemporaries and he challenges us to complete the task God has given us. This entails repentance for neglecting the building up of the house of God. Under the New Covenant, we are to give ourselves to the restoration and cleansing of the temple of God individually and corporately in the church. The glory of God emanating from a restored Zion is not the result of human ingenuity but rather the renewing ministry of the Holy Spirit.

Many Bible students believe the promises of a restored Zion are to apply primarily to a cleansed, invigorated church. A fountain of cleansing is opened to all who repent and look to the One who was pierced for them. William Cowper received the inspiration for the hymn "There Is a Fountain" from this beautiful truth in 13:1.

As we live in harmony with God's purpose to restore what has lain desolate, we rest in the assurance that God sovereignly governs the affairs of earth. The smitten Shepherd will be worshiped as King, and Israel will receive her Messiah. The task of world evangelization will be accomplished. Jesus shall reign.

Surveying
ZECHARIAH

I. THE CALL TO REPENTANCE 1:1–6. The covenant promises are still in force, so Zechariah urges a wholehearted response to God, not a superficial response like the ones made by Judah during revivals before the Exile.

II. THE EIGHT VISIONS 1:7—6:8. Zechariah is shown eight visions. In them he is not a passive observer. He is actively involved and free to question the angel God has provided as a guide. The meaning of most of these visions is explained in their context.

A. The man and horses: God's mercy (1:7–17). In the first vision Zechariah sees four horsemen whom an angel identifies as watchers who patrol the whole earth (10). The four report to the Angel of the Lord that the world is at rest and peace. This is not good news for Judea. Haggai proclaimed just a few months before that the nations must be shaken before Messiah comes and Jerusalem's peace is assured. But God reassures the prophet. God does care deeply for Jerusalem and Judah, and He is angry with the nations that have been their persecutors. God will return to Jerusalem with mercy, and goodness will overflow. (See Built.)

B. The four horns and four craftsmen: God's judgment (1:18–21). Zechariah sees four horns (representing the world powers that will hold political domination over Jerusalem). Zechariah also sees four smiths or craftsmen. These are workmen, bearing heavy hammers or chisels, whose function it is to throw down the "horns of the nations" that have acted against Jerusalem.

C. The man with the measuring line: God's city (2:1–13). Now Zechariah sees a man with a measuring line. He is about to survey the city of Jerusalem. But Zechariah's angel guide sends another angel to hurry after this man with good news. Jerusalem will overflow beyond her walls. Walls will be unnecessary, for God Himself will "be a wall of fire all around her," and "I will be the glory in her midst" (5). When at last God dwells among His people, "many nations shall be joined to the Lord in that day and they shall become My people" (11; see Inheritance).

D. The high priest: God's cleansing (3:1–10). Zechariah sees the high priest, Joshua, dressed in filthy clothing, standing before the Angel of the Lord (3). As Zechariah watches, the filthy clothing is removed and the high priest, Joshua, is dressed in rich gar-

ments (1–5). Symbolically cleansed of sin and clothed by God with righteousness (4), Joshua is charged to "walk in My ways" (the moral law) and "keep My command" (a term used in the Old Testament of ritual duties of the priesthood). If Joshua does so, he will exercise sole religious authority and have access to God (6–7; see Wondrous Sign).

E. The lampstand and olive trees: God's Spirit (4:1–14). It is clear from the chapter that many in Judah doubted that the temple, whose foundation was now laid, could be finished. They must also have doubted that this tiny community would one day reshape the world. But God promises that the temple will be finished by Zerubbabel (9), for the true resources to accomplish any work set by God are spiritual and do not rest on human abilities.

> "Not by *might nor by power, but by My Spirit, says the LORD of hosts" (4:6). Zechariah encourages Zerubbabel, the civil governor of postexilic Judah, that the temple rebuilding is not insignificant. The lampstand with its seven lamps (v. 2) portrays the glowing presence of God upon His chosen people—they are to be a light to the nations. The temple's completion is crucial for this testimony. Therefore, Zerubbabel is not to despise "the day of small things" (v. 10), but to recognize the Spirit's power enabling beyond human ability. As priests in the church—God's present temple—we also are dependent upon the provision of the Spirit's anointing for effective ministry.

F. The flying scroll: God's pronouncement (5:1–4). This vision features an open scroll, some ten yards by five. On it are written two of the commandments, representing the Mosaic Law's teaching of duty to God and to neighbor. These words are called a "curse," for God has promised to punish all who refuse to obey.

G. The woman in a basket: God's holiness (5:5–11). Zechariah sees wickedness personified, locked in a large container used to measure out grain. Powerless, wickedness is carried away to Babylon by two angels.

Earlier God's people had been carried captive to Babylon because of their wickedness. In the future God will separate His people from evil, and evil will be taken captive and sent far away from Jerusalem into exile.

H. The four chariots: God's sovereignty (6:1–8). The angelic patrols that cover the earth (see 1:7–17) are mounted in war chariots and sent out to sweep over the earth. In

Bible prophecy the north represents the nations and power of evil (cf. Joel 2:20; Ezekiel 38—39).

III. THE CROWNING OF THE HIGH PRIEST 6:9-15.
Zechariah is to take gold and silver and shape a royal crown. The Hebrew word for "crown" is always used of a royal crown, never of a priest's headdress.

According to Zechariah 3:8, Joshua stands symbolically in these visions "for things to come," and especially for the promised Branch (Messiah). The picture is one of a union between the office of priest and that of king in a single individual. When He comes to "be a priest on His throne," the final and true temple of the Lord will be erected (11–13; see Counsel).

IV. RELIGIOUS RITUAL OR REAL REPENTANCE? 7:1-14.
The Hebrew text of verse 2 is difficult. It is best understood as telling of a royal officer (a *regum meleck*) named Sharezer (cf. Jer. 39:3), who leads a delegation from the large Hebrew community that still remains in the land of captivity. He comes to inquire of the priests and prophets. His question: Now that the temple is nearly rebuilt, should they continue to keep the holy days set aside by the exiles for fasting and mourning the events associated with the fall of Jerusalem?

A word from God comes to Zechariah "to all the people of the land and to the priests" (5). What is the purpose of their fasting? Is it really for the Lord? Fasting must not be motivated by self-interest but by concern for the glory of God (4–7). God's real concern is that His people "execute true justice; show mercy and compassion everyone to his brother." The issue is not fasts, but the willingness of this people to commit to a life that pleases God.

> **"Refusing to hear"**
> (7:12). This verse implies two important truths related to the gift of prophecy. First, God does speak by prophecy, and second, humankind can refuse to heed what God says. When people choose not to hear what God has said, even through a prophet, they still will have to deal with the consequences of their action, since God is the one who is being rejected, not the prophet.

V. THE RESTORATION OF ZION 8:1-23.
A series of sayings of the Lord assures His people that they are the objects of His love (8:1–8; see Zealous).

Zechariah now looks ahead and twice contrasts the future with the unhappy past.

The people are encouraged to finish the temple with the promise that the poverty they have known will be turned to prosperity (9–13).

> **"For the seed shall be prosperous, the vine shall give its fruit . . . and the heavens shall give their dew"**
> (8:3–15). These verses depict what the present experience of the church should be, based on this prophetic promise. The *seed*, which is God's Word, shall be prosperous; the *vine*, which is the church, will give fruit; and the blessing of the Holy Spirit, depicted as the *dew of heaven*, will be given. No wonder the prophet twice says "Let your hands be strong" (9, 13).

The answer (8:18–19). God looks ahead and promises a day when the fasts they find burdensome now will become "joy and gladness and cheerful feasts." Zechariah looks forward to the day when all nations will seek the Lord and come to Jerusalem to find Him. In those days God's presence will be plain among His people.

> **"The inhabitants of one city shall go to another, saying, 'Let us continue to go and pray before the LORD, and seek the LORD of hosts' "**
> (8:20–23). As encouragement to the exiles in their rebuilding project, the Lord speaks a promise of restoration through His prophet Zechariah—the Lord will again "do good to Jerusalem" (v. 15). The renewed celebration of God's grace (v. 19) will rekindle a passion for the Lord, attracting peoples from afar (v. 20) and inspiring enthusiastic expressions of recommitment between whole communities (v. 21). Our witness goes forth in the excitement that accompanies a personal experience of His grace, compelling us to share the Good News of salvation, calling others to the rewarding place of relationship with Christ.

VI. THE TRIUMPH OF THE KINGDOM OF GOD 9:1—14:21.
Chapters 9 through 14 contain two groups of apocalyptic oracles. The prophet describes events associated with the end times. His particular focus is on how God will intervene in history to bring about the time of blessing, which all the Old Testament prophets foresee.

A. The first prophecy: The Messiah rejected (9:1—11:17).
The marauding forces of the peoples who have oppressed Jerusalem

will be crushed, and God will keep personal watch over His own (9:1–8). Shouts of joy greet the promised King (*see* Messianic Promises) as He enters Jerusalem on a donkey, bringing salvation (9).

> **"His *dominion shall be from sea to sea"**
> (9:10). The authority and rule of Jesus will only increase and not decrease. Because the days are numbered for Satan, it stands to reason that dominion over him will increase worldwide as the kingdom continues advancing. While the kingdom's advance remains a divine mystery, the obedience of believers in proclaiming and demonstrating the gospel in word and deed makes the kingdom's advance visible.

God arrives to keep His blood covenant with His people. This marks the beginning of blessings (9:11—10:1).

God rebukes deceitful leaders (10:2–3).

The time of restoration is marked by God's own intervention. God promises to redeem, restore, and return His scattered people (10:6).

In a difficult allegory God speaks to a person yet unnamed (11:4) and tells him to pasture the flock "marked for slaughter." They are so marked by their own leaders, who think only of the profit they can gain by selling out their people (11:4–6).

But when the Good Shepherd comes to care for the flock, He is rejected! The only pay they offer is "thirty pieces of silver." Strikingly, this price is the amount set in Old Testament Law as compensation to be paid for a dead slave (Ex. 21:32)! And the price of the Good Shepherd is thrown "into the house of the LORD for the potter" (11:13).

The Gospels present this passage as a prophecy about Jesus (Matt. 26:14–16; 27:1–10; John 10:11–18).

B. The second prophecy: The Messiah reigns (12:1—14:21). The second block of apocalyptic teaching continues from the first

and is linked with it. Now, however, the emphasis is on the suffering associated with the final intervention as the Lord acts to establish Himself King of all.

Jubilation in Jerusalem (12:1–9). God pictures a time when all the nations gather against Jerusalem and Judea. It is then that God will act and her enemies will be consumed.

Mourning for the One pierced (12:10—13:1). Zechariah pictures a day of national conversion (*see* Grace). This comes when they "look on Me whom they pierced" (cf. John 19:34–37).

Rejection of deceitful leaders (13:2–6). In that day all false prophets and deceitful leaders will be rejected.

The Shepherd slaughtered (13:7–9). Again the prophet returns to the death of the Shepherd. But this time the focus is on what happens to the sheep after His death. They are to be scattered, with two-thirds struck down and only a third to live (*see* Refine).

Cataclysm in Jerusalem (14:1–15). Again the prophet returns to the final battle. All nations are gathered against God's people. But God Himself intervenes and fights for them, His "feet . . . on the Mount of Olives" (4). The picture of the split mountain and of the streams of living waters that flow from Jerusalem matches the picture of the New Jerusalem drawn in Ezekiel 40—48.

> **"In that day . . . living waters shall flow from Jerusalem. . . . And the LORD shall be King over all the earth"**
> (14:3–9). The symbolism of these verses reveals that the fullness of the Holy Spirit will be overflowing the church of Jesus at the time of His return. The proclamation of Jesus as King will be the recurring declaration from lips filled with this living water of the Spirit.

The Lord King over all (14:16–20). In the end all nations will go up to worship God in Jerusalem, and the city will be holy to the Lord.

TRUTH-IN-ACTION through ZECHARIAH

Truth Zechariah Teaches	**Action** Zechariah Invites
1 Steps to Knowing God and His Ways Anything that God has said He will do, He will do. He does not	**1:2–6** *Understand* that God does not issue threats of judgment in vain, and He always keeps His word. *(continued)*

Truth Zechariah Teaches	**Action** Zechariah Invites
1 Steps to Knowing God and His Ways (continued) make empty promises or vain threats. We must not interpret His patience and longsuffering toward disobedience as a failure to execute judgment. Rather, He desires our repentance and return. If we will return to Him, He will complete the work of perfecting He has promised.	**1:16, 17** *Believe* and *understand* that God fully intends to bring His people to the maturity and prosperity He has always promised. **3:3–5** *Believe* and *accept* that God forgives the sins of all who repent and turn to Him. *Be clothed* with His righteousness.
2 Guidelines for Growing in Godliness Godliness involves godly practices from a godly heart. God rebukes those who fast or practice other religious acts to serve their own ends. The godly person keeps an open ear for God's Word, even when it is not pleasant or calls for change.	**7:4–7** *Make sure* that when you fast your motives are unselfish. *Accompany* your fastings with attitudes and actions of righteousness and obedience. **7:11, 12** *Open your ears* to prophetic or solemn warnings. *Know* that not to do so can result in calamity.
3 Steps to Holiness Holiness is a commitment to live exclusively for God in the way He has instructed.	**4:1–6** *Depend on* the Holy Spirit to accomplish the things God has called you to do. **8:16, 17** *Practice* honesty, truth, integrity, and justice in all interpersonal dealings. *Examine* your heart, and *avoid* any form of insincerity or hypocrisy.
4 Keys to Wise Living We must learn how to interpret circumstances from God's standpoint.	**4:7–10** *Do not* allow yourself to be discouraged by "small things." *Understand* that God does not give the importance we do to the size of things. *Be assured* that what God has begun, He will complete in triumph. **13:9** *Understand* that God's refining works are to purify His people and to train them in righteousness.
5 A Lesson in Faith The work of establishing and completing the ultimate temple (His body) is assigned to Jesus, but He wants our participation through obedience to His voice. Our gift becomes a memorial, but the glory is all His.	**6:10–15** *Understand* that Jesus Christ has committed Himself to building His church and to completing it as a manifestation of His glory. *Remember* that your gift (v. 10) is important to the task and that your privilege is to *render all glory* to Him (v. 11).
6 A Lesson for Leaders Remember that God's Word is always true! Teach God's Word faithfully so that the long-term result will be fruitfulness and well being.	**10:2** Leaders, *understand* that false prophecies, teaching that is erroneous or diluted, and personal opinion taught as truth all result in a church that lacks power, stability, and security.

Introducing
MALACHI

Author. Though some attribute Malachi to an anonymous writer, thought by some to have been Ezra, using the pseudonym *Mal'aki* ("My Messenger"), it is best to see the book as written by the named prophet himself. Malachi is not mentioned anywhere else in the Bible, but from his writing we learn he had a great love for the people of Judah and the temple ceremonies. He was likely a contemporary of Nehemiah.

Date. The lack of the mention of any kings or identifiable historical incidents makes dating the book somewhat difficult. The use of various Persian words in the text and the reference to a rebuilt temple (1:10) make a post-exilic date concurrent with Nehemiah the most likely (about 450 B.C.). Malachi wrote as the last of the twelve Minor Prophets, the final inspired writer of Scripture until the New Testament. (*See* map, page 184.)

Background. As noted, Malachi is the last of a number of divinely inspired men who, over a period of a thousand years, foretold the coming of the Just One. Not only did they prophesy about the coming Messiah, but they clearly spelled out to the people their sins and warned them of God's righteous judgment.

Following their return from exile, the people of Israel lived as a restored community in the land of Palestine. Instead of learning from their past negative experiences and returning to the worship and service of the God of their ancestors, Abraham, Isaac, and Jacob, they became immoral and careless. The ritual and political reforms initiated by the postcaptivity leaders, Nehemiah and Ezra, had not prevented a serious spiritual decline among the Israelite population. This grave situation caused Malachi to be burdened heavily with the spiritual problems of his people. With divine fervency he addressed their common disregard for their loving Lord.

Content. In his opening statement Malachi points out God's unchanging love for His people, due to His mercy that endures forever. This is the background for the following rebukes and exhortations. First, the prophet addresses the arrogant, open contempt of the priests for the Law and their negative influence upon the people. He points out to them that they cause many to stumble in sin. Therefore he warns them that the Lord will not be an idle spectator but, unless they repent, will severely punish them.

Next he addresses, in no uncertain terms, the treachery of priests and laymen in divorcing faithful wives and marrying heathen women who practice idol worship. This is followed by an earnest plea to guard their passions and be faithful to the wives of their youth, given to them by the Lord.

The prophet furthermore rebukes the irreligious practices of the people, their denial of God's justice, and their defrauding the Lord by withholding the required tithes and offerings.

In glowing and fervent language Malachi continues to describe the original type of priesthood. He prophesies of the Sun of Righteousness, the Messenger of the covenant, and the great and terrible day of divine judgment in which the righteous will be rewarded and the wicked punished.

Finally, Malachi exhorts the people to observe the laws given to Israel through Moses and promises a coming Messiah and His forerunner Elijah (John the Baptist). This statement concludes the Old Testament and ties it to the Good News of God's provision in the Sun of Righteousness described in the New Testament.

Personal Application. Malachi's criticism of abuses and religious indifference is still valid today. God's people always need to confess their inadequate response to divine love. Initial devotion to God and enthusiasm may diminish. Genuine worship frequently turns into mechanical observance of religious practices. Delinquent tithing, divorce of faithful spouses, and intermarriage between God's covenant people and nonbelievers often create havoc in families. Selfish desires, combined with proud and arrogant attitudes, lead to serious problems for which God is blamed. Instead of acknowledging our neglect and changing our lives by the power of the Holy Spirit, we ask the question, "Where is the God of justice?" (2:17). However, true repentance still prepares the way for necessary reforms and Holy Spirit-inspired revivals.

Surveying
MALACHI

I. THE TITLE 1:1.

II. THE LORD'S LOVE FOR ISRAEL 1:2–5.
The book begins with an affirmation by God of love for His people, immediately establishing the basis on which God seeks to relate to believers. But God's affirmation of love draws an incredulous response: "How have You loved us?"

The next verses return to the covenant God gave to Abraham, Isaac, Jacob, and their descendants. Looking back to the patriarchs, God reminds His people, "Jacob I have loved, but Esau I have hated" (2–3). "Love" here is used in an elective sense: God has chosen to transmit the covenant promises through Jacob. Current history demonstrates the continuation of that elective love. The presence of this people in their land, with the temple standing on its old site, is living proof of God's love.

III. FAILURE OF THE PRIESTS 1:6—2:9.
The love God has for His people is stable (see Gracious), but their love has cooled. This is shown by a pattern of neglect of God. Cooling love is clearly shown by priest and people who bring blind or crippled animals for sacrifice

(1:6–14). They would never offer such an animal to their governor!

When people find it a burden to worship and offer God only what they do not want themselves, then clearly their love for Him has drained away. God is a great King, and He deserves our very best!

Cooling love by the priests is shown in their neglect of their ministry and by drifting in their private lives (2:1–9). These men not only fail to instruct others (see Knowledge); they also neglect to keep the Law themselves!

IV. UNFAITHFULNESS OF THE PEOPLE 2:10–16.
God's faithfulness to His covenant promises is a clear indication of His love. But Judah has broken covenant, and this unfaithfulness indicates her loss of love. Intermarriage with pagans from the surrounding nations and the easy divorces some obtain as their wives grow older (14; see Family Life) are both expressions of unfaithfulness to covenant relationship with God. When a people become unfaithful in their relationship to God, breakdown of relationships with one another will inevitably follow.

V. THE DAY OF JUDGMENT 2:17—3:5.
Another indication of a drift from God is expressed in a cynical query the prophet picks up from the attitude of his countrymen. "Where is the God of justice?" Because God's hand is not seen in dramatic intervention in human affairs, the people begin to doubt His presence.

VI. BLESSING IN GIVING 3:6–12.
God urges this generation to return to Him, but again they ask incredulously, "How are we to return?" They are unable to see that they have turned away!

The failure of the people to bring ordained tithes to the temple for the support of the priests and temple sacrifices proves that they doubt the significance of God in their lives (see Faith, Seed; Room Enough).

VII. THE DESTINY OF THE RIGHTEOUS AND THE WICKED 3:13—4:3.
In Malachi's day, as in every other, there are individuals who are spiritually sensitive (see Healing). They respond to Malachi's message, while the community as a whole remains dull to God's word (3:16–18).

VIII. EXHORTATION AND PROMISE 4:4–6.
The book closes with an exhortation to remember the Law of God while they wait for the promise of His coming.

"The Sun of Righteousness shall arise with healing in His wings" (4:2–3). One of the hallmarks of the return of Jesus will be the presence of His healing work. Care must be taken not to limit the range of healing to only the physical realm. The salvation brought to humanity is complete in every way. Mighty deliverances from spiritual bondage, restoration for those emotionally bruised, as well as healing of the physical body are acceptable norms in the life of the Spirit-filled believer.

The Coming of Christ

Malachi's Prophecy	Confirmed in the New Testament
As Messenger of the covenant, Christ comes to His temple (3:1) and purifies His people (3:3).	Christ cleanses the temple (John 2:14–17) and sanctifies His people (Heb. 13:12).
His coming brings judgment (4:1).	Those whose names are not in the Book of Life are cast into the lake of fire (Rev. 20:11–15).
As the Sun of Righteousness, Christ heals His people (4:2).	Christ heals the multitudes; ultimately all sickness will pass away (Matt. 12:15; Rev. 21:4).
His forerunner prepares for the coming of the Lord (3:1; 4:5).	John the Baptist announces Christ (Matt. 11:10–14).

TRUTH-IN-ACTION through **MALACHI**

Truth Malachi Teaches	**Action** Malachi Invites
1 Steps to Knowing God and His Ways God sees and rewards, not according to our timetable, but by His. We must not think that either good or evil conduct goes unrecognized or unjudged. God will honor the faithful.	**2:17** *Be assured* that God never honors evil conduct. *Do not speak against* the justice of God. **3:17, 18** *Believe* that God differentiates between good and evil behavior.
2 Steps to Covenant Life The covenant relationship of marriage is highly esteemed by the Spirit of God. He instructs believers to seek a believing partner to insure holiness in the marriage. He also requires just and faithful behavior within the marriage bonds. God hates the hard-hearted attitudes that destroy this sacred covenant and produce divorce.	**2:11–16** *Obey* God; *marry only in the Lord. Be loving* and *faithful* to your marriage partner. *Reject divorce* as an answer to marital problems. *Honor* your covenant with God. *Trust* Him to recover the hope in a seemingly "hopeless" marriage. *Be willing* to relearn love, understanding, and forgiveness.
3 Keys to Personal Purity Christ comes as the purifier and refiner of His people, that they, being clean, may offer service and worship acceptable to God. To offer the Lord less than our best is unworthy of His holy name.	**1:12, 13** *Give* the best that you have to the Lord. **3:2–5** *Submit* to the work of the Lord as refiner and purifier. *Worship* God from a purified heart, and *serve* Him from clean motives. *Commit* to true worship, and *avoid* mere formalism.
4 Lessons for Leaders The personal conduct of God's chosen leaders and the example of their ministry causes God to be received or rejected by the world. If leadership rejects the law of God, the people will not be taught justice, and so cannot live in peace.	**2:1–9** Leaders, *make sure* that your conduct and your ministry cause people to *give the Lord honor and glory.*
5 Keys to Generous Living Tithing, though included in the Law, was part of the Abrahamic life of faith and is part of faithful living. Tithing obediently expresses faith that God is our true source. To fail to tithe is to dishonor and rob God.	**3:8–10** *Practice tithing! Understand* that the tenth already belongs to God (Lev. 27:30). *Expect* financial well-being to follow when you tithe. *Realize* that tithing is not only a part of the Mosaic Law. It is a timeless covenant of privilege to exercise in joyous faith—not as a grudging legal requirement (2 Cor. 9:7).

The "Kingdom" in the New Testament

The chart below summarizes a panoramic view of the kingdom of God as it unfolds in the New Testament, revealing two phases: the lighting up and the living out of the kingdom.

First, the historical narratives of the Gospels and Acts show the ignition of the kingdom; how "the Light of the World" had now come, and "brought life and immortality to light through the gospel" (2 Tim. 1:10). We see how Jesus, who unveils the kingdom in preaching and in practice, soon transmits His mission, manner, and mightiness to His church. He who came to make possible the revelation of God's Word made flesh in the world now pours out the Holy Spirit to continue that incarnation. God's kingdom purposes, incarnate in the Person of Jesus, become incarnate in the body of His church, thus making possible the realization of God's Word of life, light, and love throughout the world.

Secondly, the Epistles and Revelation show the cognition of the kingdom—how the early church learned to understand and apply the rule of God in practical, Spirit-directed living. Personal, individual lessons in "realizing" the kingdom are seen in the human case studies encountered in these books, as lives are shaped by the rule of God working in every kind of life-circumstance. Also, the corporate, congregational "realizing" of the kingdom is seen in the situations addressed by the apostles, as they write to churches and leaders who are learning how the rule of God is intended to shape the new community of faith.

	The Books	The Light	The Gospel	The Word
1	Gospels and Acts	Ignition— "lighting up"	Revelation, demonstrated with power	Incarnate in Christ, then in the church
2	Epistles and Revelation	Cognition— "living out"	Realization, applied in practice	Incarnate in circumstance and in congregations

KEYS TO MATTHEW
The Introduction of "Kingdom Come"

Kingdom Key: God's Purpose in View

The Incarnate King introduced "kingdom come," because where the King is personally, the kingdom is presently. From the inception of His ministry, Jesus announces: "Repent, for the kingdom of heaven is at hand" (4:17—"has drawn near," Greek engidzo*). He declares the "gospel of the kingdom"—the Good News that God's rule is present in power to forgive sin, heal sickness, break demonic bonds, and release from oppression (4:23–25; 8:14–17; 9:35–38). He pointedly states that His dominion over demons proves that the kingdom is present (12:29) and that the Holy Spirit is also present, empowering Him to do the works of the kingdom (12:32; see also His argument in verses 22–30). Wonders and miracles follow.*

Beyond unveiling the kingdom's dominion over darkness, including its dynamic to heal and deliver, the King also introduces the personal implications of *life* in the kingdom. It calls people to character (5:1–12), to credible service and witness (5:13–16), to obedience to God's laws (5:17–20), to renunciation of anger (5:21–26), to physical and mental purity (5:27–30), to marital commitment (5:31–32), to control of the tongue (5:33–37), to a non-retaliatory spirit (5:38–42), and to a love for all humankind (5:43–48). Jesus' "Kingdom Manifesto" (the Sermon on the Mount, chs. 5—7) points away from the empty traditions of humanly generated religion (6:1–8, 16–18) and toward vital, faith-filled prayer (6:9–15; 7:7–12).

> When the King is present, God's kingdom has come.

The kingdom lifestyle is power-filled but not power-hungry. Unselfish (6:19–24) and non-judgmental living (7:1–6), free from slavery to material concerns (6:25–34), will characterize true kingdom people (7:13–14, 24–29), in contrast to kingdom pretenders (7:15–23). The former walk in obedience, while the latter's claims to prophecy and power are contradicted by a lack of kingdom character.

The King introduces kingdom truth through stories the crowds understand, thereby calling them to responsibility (13:1–23): "If you have ears, *hear*" (receive this seed of truth and allow it to grow by your right response). Many of these parables begin, "the kingdom of (Please turn to page 279.)

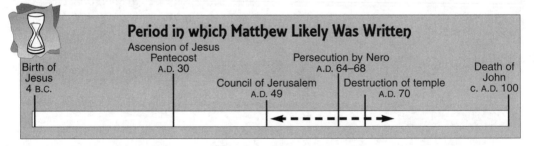

Period in which Matthew Likely Was Written

Birth of Jesus 4 B.C.	Ascension of Jesus Pentecost A.D. 30	Council of Jerusalem A.D. 49	Persecution by Nero A.D. 64–68	Destruction of temple A.D. 70	Death of John c. A.D. 100

Matthew announces that the coming of God's Messiah

Master Key: God's Son Revealed

This Gospel presents Jesus as the fulfillment of all messianic hopes and expectations. Matthew carefully structures his narrative to reveal that Jesus fulfilled specific prophecies. He saturates his Gospel with quotations from and allusions to the Old Testament, introducing many of them with the formula "that it might be fulfilled."

In Matthew's Gospel, Jesus often refers to Himself as the Son of Man, a veiled reference to His messiahship (*see* Dan. 7:13–14). Not only did the term allow Jesus to avoid common misunderstandings stemming from popular messianic titles, but it enabled Him to interpret both His redemptive mission (as in 17:12, 22; 20:28; 26:24) and His return in glory (as in 13:41; 16:27; 19:28; 24:30, 44; 26:64).

Matthew's use of the title "Son of God" clearly underscores Jesus' deity (*see* 1:23; 2:15; 3:17; 16:16). As the Son, Jesus has a direct and unmediated relationship with the Father.

Matthew presents Jesus as Lord and Teacher of the church, the new community, which is called to live out the new ethic of the kingdom of heaven. Jesus declares "the church" as His select instrument for fulfilling the purposes of God on earth (16:18; 18:15–20). Matthew's Gospel may have served as a teaching manual for the early church, including the amazing world-oriented Great Commission (28:12–20), with its guarantee of Jesus' living presence.

Power Key: God's Spirit at Work

The activity of the Holy Spirit is evident in every phase of Jesus' life and ministry. By the power of the Spirit, Jesus was conceived in Mary's womb (1:18, 20). Before Jesus began His public ministry, He was filled with the Spirit of God (3:16), and followed the Spirit's leading into the wilderness to be tempted by the devil as further preparation for His messianic role (4:1). The power of the Spirit enabled Jesus to heal (12:15–21) and to cast out demons (12:28).

Key Word: *Jesus the King*

By quoting repeatedly from the Old Testament, Matthew validates Christ's claim that He is, in fact, the prophesied Messiah (the Anointed One) of Israel.

Key Verses: Matthew 16:16–19; 28:18–20

Key Chapter: Matthew 12

The turning point of Matthew comes in the twelfth chapter when the Pharisees, acting as the leadership of the nation of Israel, formally reject Jesus Christ as the Messiah. Christ's ministry changes immediately with His new teaching of parables, increased attention given to His disciples, and His repeated statement that His death is now near.

Just as John immersed his followers in water, Jesus will immerse His followers in the Holy Spirit (3:11). In 7:21–23 we find a warning directed against false charismatics, those in the church who prophesy, cast out demons, and do wonders, but who do not do the will of the Father. Presumably, the same Holy Spirit who inspires charismatic activities must also empower the people of the church to do the will of God (7:21).

(Please turn to page 279.)

has opened a new era in human possibilities.

Introducing
MATTHEW

Author. Although this Gospel does not identify its author, early church tradition attributes it to Matthew, the apostle and former tax collector. Other than his name and occupation, little is known about him. Tradition says that for fifteen years following the Resurrection of Jesus he preached in Palestine and then conducted missionary campaigns in other nations.

Date. The external evidence, such as quotations in Christian literature of the first century, testifies to the early existence and use of Matthew. Church leaders of the second and third centuries generally agreed that Matthew was the first Gospel to be written, and various statements in their writings indicate a date between A.D. 50 and 65. However, many modern scholars feel that both Matthew and Luke relied heavily on Mark in writing their Gospels, and accordingly date Matthew later. The ongoing tension between Jew and Gentile that is reflected in the Gospel suggests a period when Judaism and Christianity still overlapped.

Purpose. Matthew's aim is to present Jesus, not only as the Messiah, but as the Son of David, and to elaborate this truth in such a way that it would aid the Christians in their controversies with the Jews. He shows how Jesus fulfilled Old Testament prophecy, and how the Law is filled with new meaning and supplemented in the Person, words, and work of Christ. Matthew also points out how Israel's rejection of Christ is in accordance with prophecy, and how that rejection caused the transference of the divine privileges of the chosen people from the Jewish to the Christian community. "The kingdom of God will be taken from you [Israel] and given to a nation bearing the fruits of it" (21:43).

Content. The purpose of Matthew is evident in the structure of his book, which groups the teachings and deeds of Jesus into five divisions. The fivefold structure, common in Judaism, may reveal Matthew's purpose of showing Jesus as the fulfillment of the Law. Each division concludes with the formula, "And when Jesus had ended these sayings" (7:28; 11:1; 13:53; 19:1; 26:1).

In the prologue (1:1—2:23), Matthew shows that Jesus is the Messiah by linking Him with promises made to Abraham and David. The birth of Jesus highlights the fulfillment theme, portrays Jesus' royalty, and underscores the significance of Jesus for the Gentiles. The first division (chs. 3—7) contains the Sermon on the Mount, in which Jesus describes how people should live under God's reign.

The second division (8:1—11:1) features the instructions of Jesus to His disciples when He sent them out on their missionary journey.

The third division (11:2—13:52) records several controversies in which Jesus was involved and seven parables describing some aspect of the kingdom of heaven, coupled with the necessary human response.

The major discourse in the fourth division (13:53—18:35) concerns the conduct of believers within the Christian fellowship (ch. 18).

Matthew's fifth division (19:1—25:46) narrates the final journey of Jesus to Jerusalem and reveals His climactic conflict with Judaism. Chapters 24 and 25 contain the teaching of Jesus relating to the last things. The remainder of the book (26:1—28:20) details events and teachings pertaining to the Crucifixion, the Resurrection, and the Lord's commission to the church. Except at the beginning and at the end of the Gospel, Matthew's arrangement is not chronological and not strictly biographical, but is designed to show that in Jesus Judaism finds the fulfillment of its hopes.

Personal Application. Matthew's emphasis on Jesus as the fulfillment of prophecy (forty-one Old Testament quotes) shows that Jesus' life and ministry were part of the single plan of God throughout the history of Israel, and not an act of desperation. The entire Gospel stresses that Jesus is Immanuel—God-With-Us.

Jesus' teachings in Matthew's Gospel call for obedience and continue to expose sham and hypocrisy in personal and corporate life.

The book also gives to the church a clarion call to mission, the proclamation of the Good News to all peoples. Christian disciples must learn to live within the tension of two ages, the present age of fulfillment in the Person of Jesus (in His words and works through His church by the Spirit's power) and the age to come, that is, the consummation of all things. In the interim, Christians are called to be humble, patient, genuine, faithful, watchful, and responsible—assured of the risen Jesus' presence as they are expectant of His return when faith will give way to sight.

Kingdom Key *continued from page 276*

heaven is like this" (13:24–52; 18:21–35; 20:1–16; 22:1–14; 25:1–46. Note that Matthew uses "kingdom of heaven" and "kingdom of God" as synonyms; *see* 19:23–24).

To spread the kingdom message to the needy multitudes (9:35–38), the King begins to equip disciples and then to commission them to go with the same message He preaches, to expect the same wonders He works, and to face the same opposition He has faced (10:1–26). This strategy, designed to propagate the gospel of the kingdom, reaches its pivotpoint when the King announces His plan to "build My church" (16:18). He reveals that this church consists of a people (the Greek *ekklesia* means "called out ones"), a new commu-

nity (a) founded upon a clear confession of who He is—the Christ, the Son of God (16:13–17); (b) established with the authority and dominion over the dark powers, which "the keys of the kingdom" grant to His followers; and (c) grounded in a clear understanding that His Cross is the fountainhead of kingdom life and power (16:20–27; 26:52–54).

Matthew repeatedly quotes Old Testament prophets to verify that in the person of Jesus the promised Messiah—God's King—has come, and that His arrival has opened a new era in human possibility—bringing forgiveness, life, and power over the oppressive rule of the flesh and Satan.

Power Key *continued from page 277*

Jesus declared that His works were done in the power of the Holy Spirit, giving evidence that the kingdom of God had come and that the power of Satan was being overthrown. Therefore, to ascribe the power of the Spirit to the devil was to commit an unpardonable sin (12:28–32).

In 12:28 the Holy Spirit is connected to Jesus' exorcisms and the present reality of the kingdom of God, not solely by the fact of exorcism per se, for the Pharisees' sons (disciples) also practiced exorcism (12:27). Rather, the Holy Spirit is with the Messiah effecting a new

event—"the kingdom of God has come upon you" (v. 28).

Finally, the Holy Spirit is found in the Great Commission (28:16–20). The disciples are commanded to go and make disciples of all nations, "baptizing them in the name of the Father and of the Son and of the Holy Spirit" (v. 19). That is, they are to baptize them "unto/with reference to" the name, or authority, of the triune God. In their obedience to this commission, Jesus' disciples are assured of His ongoing presence with them.

Surveying
MATTHEW

I. PROLOGUE: GENEALOGY AND INFANCY NARRATIVES 1:1—2:23.

A. The genealogy of Jesus (1:1–17). The first thing Jewish believers would demand is proof that Jesus has a right to the messianic throne. Thus Matthew provides proof: Jesus is a descendant of Abraham and of David.

The reference to Joseph deserves special mention. Only he is not said to be the "father of" the next individual in line, but instead is identified as "husband of Mary, of whom was born Jesus." Jesus inherits a legal right to Israel's throne through his foster father. But he is the Son of God, not of Joseph.

B. Jesus' Birth (1:18–25). Matthew emphasizes the unique aspect of Jesus' birth. The

Holy Spirit of God quickened Mary for the birth of the child, thus fulfilling the prediction of Isaiah some seven hundred years before that a virgin would have a child. Joseph was also told to name the child Jesus, which means "savior" or "deliverer." (*See* Just.)

C. Worship of the wise men (2:1–12). Some months after Jesus is born, travelers from the east come to Jerusalem asking about the newborn king of the Jews (*see* Prophet). The travelers are Magi, a class of wise men long associated with government in Persia.

This appearance terrifies Herod, who has already killed several of his own sons to protect his throne from imagined threats. The crafty Herod sends the Magi on to Bethlehem to search for the child, first making them promise to report to him, "so I too may go and worship him."

The Magi are guided to the house where the family now lives (11). They find the young child with Mary and bow down to worship

Him. They also give gifts that characteristically are presented to royalty. The Magi do not return to Herod. Warned away in a dream, they return home by a different route.

D. The flight into Egypt, the slaughter of the infants, and the return to Israel (2:13–23). Joseph is warned in a dream to take the family to Egypt. Joseph does not wait. That very night he rouses Mary and Jesus and leaves for Egypt (14). The family remains in Egypt until the death of Herod the Great.

When the Magi do not return, Herod orders every male child two years old and younger in and around Bethlehem killed! Many die by Herod's cruel decree—but Jesus is safe.

Joseph is informed of Herod's death by another dream. He brings his family back but fears to settle in Judea, where one of Herod's sons rules. Again he is given divine direction and turns aside to settle in Nazareth of Galilee. Matthew links each step of these travels to Old Testament passages. He shows that, in detail after detail, the early life of Jesus fulfills prophetic visions of the Messiah.

II. PROCLAMATION OF THE KINGDOM OF HEAVEN 3:1—7:29.

A. Narrative: Beginning of Jesus' ministry (3:1—4:25). Like the prophets of old, John the Baptist boldly strikes out against the sins of God's people (cf. Luke 3:10–13). He calls for repentance (*see* Repent), warning that the kingdom of heaven is almost upon them! John explains that he is the forerunner of another who will "baptize with the Holy Spirit and with fire." This is powerful imagery to listeners familiar with Old Testament prophecy. They know the promised kingdom (*see* Kingdom of God) is associated with dire judgments and heart-purification, both accomplished by a pouring out of God's Spirit when Messiah arrives (Is. 32:15; Ezek. 11:19; 36:26–27; Joel 2:28–29).

> **"He will baptize you with the Holy Spirit and fire"**
> (3:11). John's baptism of repentance (3:6) brought the cleansing of forgiveness as sinners were baptized in water. Jesus' baptism, however, is with the Holy Spirit (John 1:33), whose presence in believers' lives demonstrates their saving relationship with God (Rom. 8:9–11). The figure of fire relates to the purifying and empowering of believers in their lives and ministries.

Jesus baptized (3:13–17). Jesus travels from Galilee to be baptized by John. As Jesus comes up out of the waters, the Spirit of God visibly descends on Jesus, and God's voice of commendation is heard.

The temptation of Jesus (4:1–11). The Spirit leads Jesus into a desolate desert between Jericho and Jerusalem. After a forty-day fast, when Jesus is physically weakened, Satan comes to tempt him.

Jesus' primary resource is Scripture. He does not quote it as some magical saying to ward off evil; He quotes a principle which then guides His decisions. When we permit God's *Word to determine our choices, we too will experience victory.

The temptations completed, and Satan defeated, *angels come and attend Jesus (11).

> **"You shall worship the Lord your God"**
> (4:1–11). The ultimate point of all demonic assault is to draw worship away from God. In Satan's rebellion against God, described in Isaiah 14:12–14 and Ezekiel 28:2, the issue is taking God's place. Worship acknowledges the true sovereignty of God. Here, Satan's endeavor to secure Jesus' worship was a brazen attempt to stop God's Son before His mission could begin.

Jesus' preaching mission (4:12–25). Jesus begins His preaching in the province of Galilee. On this tour He calls four fishermen to be His disciples (18–22). His ministry also involves healing (23–25), and great crowds gather from all over to hear Him. (*See* Kingdom of God.)

> **"They brought to Him all sick people who were afflicted with various diseases and torments, and those who were demon-possessed, epileptics, and paralytics; and He healed them"**
> (4:23–24). Jesus is the Healer (*see* Healing, Divine). Note that here Jesus heals "diseases" (physical), "torments" (pains, even psychosomatic problems—mental), and "demon possession" (spiritual). Verse 23 assures us that Jesus healed *all* kinds of sicknesses and diseases. Our Redeemer has come to save our souls and heal our bodies.

B. Discourse: Sermon on the Mount (5:1—7:29; *see* Kingdom of God).

The Beatitudes (5:1–12). Jesus introduces a new set of values by which His followers are to live. The values run counter to the values found in human societies and cultures. It only makes sense to try to live by these values if we truly believe that God rules in our lives and that He governs our circumstances. (*See* Blessed; Merciful; Pure.)

Values expressed in action (5:13–16). Any true value will find some expression in behavior. Jesus is not presenting a morality to which we can give lip service. He is teaching a morality that is to shape our lives!

"To fulfill the Law" (5:17–48). It is the ambition of every rabbi (teacher) to give the true and full interpretation of God's Word, something the first century rabbis call fulfilling it. Jesus promises this revelation!

Jesus now moves on to give illustrations. The Law focuses on behavior (*see* Judgment). The Law says, "Do not murder," but God's deeper concern is with human motives and intent. Thus anger, which leads to the harming of a brother, is also God's concern!

Each case Jesus cites follows this pattern. Law regulates acts of adultery; God is concerned with lust (27–30). Law permits divorce; God is concerned with lifelong faithfulness (31–32). The Pharisees' traditions demanded binding oaths; God wants a people so honest that their word is their bond (33–37). The Law permits revenge; God seeks a people who will act lovingly (*see* Brotherly Love) even to those who are enemies (38–48; *see* Compels).

The kind of lifestyle Jesus describes is impossible for mere men. But those who have a personal relationship with God as Father (48) will find His kingdom power at work within them.

The kingdom misplaced (6:1—7:23). Jesus warns His listeners against pathways that appear to lead to God but that in fact lead a person further and further from personal experience of the kingdom's presence in our lives.

(1) *The path of visible piety (6:1–18).* Jesus warns that outward religion (*see* Hypocrites) is not the issue. An inner sensitivity to God, and a desire to please Him, is the secret to life in Jesus' present kingdom. The "Lord's Prayer" guides Jesus' disciples to an understanding of the relationship between *prayer (see also* Pray) and the coming of the kingdom with power.

(2) *The pathway of material success (6:19–34).* In Jesus' day the people believe that wealth is a sign of God's blessing. Jesus warns against focusing on wealth as an evidence of spiritual prosperity. God, a loving Father, meets the daily needs of His children (6:25–31; *see* Worry).

(3) *The pathway of authority over others (7:1–14).* This warning is for those who see the kingdom of God as an opportunity to exalt themselves over others. (*See* Ask.)

Understanding these pathways helps us to recognize false leaders (7:15–23). They may speak in Jesus' name (21–23), but their character unmasks them.

"Therefore by their fruits you will know them"

(7:16–20). Beware of false prophets: while their outward appearance may suggest propriety, their inward motives can be impure (v. 15). We can discern these imitators on the basis of their fruit—their lifestyle, character, and teaching. False prophets are energized by spirits of error, their bad fruit the work of darkness; true teachers and prophets are energized by the Holy Spirit, their good fruit the product of the Spirit of truth (vv. 17–18). True Spirit-filled leaders will be Christlike in character, and integrity will be the watchword of their ministry. Behavior is as important as belief.

The kingdom discovered (7:24–27). What then is the way to find God's kingdom? We are to look to the King and follow His words. The wise man, whose life is built on solid rock, "hears these words of mine and puts them into practice."

III. JESUS' MINISTRY IN GALILEE 8:1— 11:1.

Jesus has claimed the knowledge needed to explain the inner meaning of God's law, and the wisdom to direct each individual's life by His words. Now, in a series of miracles, Jesus proves His right to royal command.

A. Narrative: Ten miracle stories (8:1— 9:34). A leper asks Jesus to heal him, "if you are *willing" (2). Christ touches the man and cures the disease. The King is willing to use His authority in our lives!

Then Jesus is approached by a Roman military officer. The man expresses belief in Jesus' ability to cure a sick servant who is miles away! Jesus speaks the word and the servant is healed. No distance can limit our Lord's power to act for those who have faith in Him.

"I have not found such great faith, not even in Israel!"

(8:10). The centurion's faith in Jesus did not
continued on next page

continued from preceding page
require a touch or a visit—only a word, and he received the miracle for his servant. The centurion's understanding of submission to true (spiritual) authority enabled him to trust in Jesus and believe His word.

Matthew now crowds together reports of a number of events that demonstrate Jesus' authority over forces that hold humanity in bondage.

"He Himself took our infirmities and bore our sicknesses"
(8:15–17). The Gospel writer quotes Isaiah 53 here and directly applies it to Jesus' ministry of healing (*see* Healing, Divine). The relationship between the dual roles of Messiah who "was wounded for our transgressions . . . and by his stripes we are healed" (Is. 53:5) makes Jesus active in our deliverance both from sin and its effects in sickness (Gen. 3:19). Our salvation from sin was purchased on the Cross of Calvary; so was our healing.

Jesus exercises authority over nature (He calms the storm, 8:23–27; *see* Little Faith), over demons (who are cast into a herd of pigs, 8:28–34), over disease (He heals a paralytic, 9:1–8), over the grip of sin in a person's life (He calls Matthew the tax collector to a new life, 9:9–13), and authority over death (a dead girl is raised, 9:18–26).

"What have we to do with You, Jesus, You Son of God?"
(8:28–33). Demonic power recognizes the presence of Jesus Christ (29) and yields to the authority of His spoken word (32). The issue of demonic possession was no controversy for Jesus; demons are real, and in the New Testament He is found casting them out of people wherever they are encountered.

"When Jesus saw their faith"
(9:2). The faith of those who carried the paralytic brought them to the feet of Jesus. Whenever human need is brought to the Savior, more is received than could ever be anticipated. Here, the man is healed, but more important, he is forgiven by our loving Lord.

"According to your faith let it be to you"
(9:29–30). The two blind men confessed their faith in Christ's ability to heal them based on their knowledge of His miracle power (9:26). However, they made an important decision as they announced Jesus as "Son of David," a distinctly important messianic title that proclaimed their faith in Him.

B. Discourse: Mission and martyrdom (9:35—11:1). Jesus has used His royal authority to serve people trapped in bondage to sin, to demons, and to sickness. His motive is one of compassion (9:36).

"He was moved with compassion for them, because they were weary and scattered, like sheep having no shepherd"
(9:35–36). Jesus' motive in ministry and His desire toward people flow out of His compassion for the helpless state of human domination by sin and sickness. Jesus loves people and heals them. In chapter 10, to multiply His caring ministry, Jesus gives His twelve disciples authority to heal the sick and free people from demonic bondage. Jesus' instructions to the disciples describe a lifestyle appropriate for all of His followers.

When Jesus shares His authority with the Twelve, He does not lift them above others. Instead, spiritual authority makes them the servants of others. Disciples are called to a humble life of service.

"He gave them power over unclean spirits, to cast them out, and to heal all kinds of sickness and all kinds of disease"
(10:1). The authority to heal was given to the *disciples along with their assignment to preach "The kingdom of heaven is at hand" (v. 7). Part of their mission was to heal and deliver the people, thus demonstrating the power of their message and

administering the compassion of God's love.

"For it will be given to you in that hour what you should speak"

(10:18–20). This passage shows one aspect of Christian witness as it relates to persecution. The witnessing appears as the effect rather than the cause when presented in this light by Jesus. It would be a mistake to use this text to support non-preparation for the witnessing life. Second Timothy 4:2 indicates the need to be prepared when dealing with the Word of God. Whether by study or by example, witnessing must be attended to. However, when the pressure is on and it is not of one's own doing, there is great security in knowing that the Spirit of God will supply all that the situation requires.

IV. CONTROVERSY STORIES AND PARABLES 11:2—13:52.

A. Narrative: Controversy which escalates (11:2—12:50).

Jesus has now proven His power. But He does not use it to set up a national kingdom (see Kingdom of God)! Instead Jesus has used His power to heal the hurts of humanity. He does not claim royal glory but acts as a humble servant of all who seek His help. Even John the Baptist is confused (see Offended) and sends messengers to ask Jesus if He really is the Messiah. Jesus points to His actions (11:5). To John, the echoes of Isaiah's description of the Messiah will be clear (cf. Is. 29:18; 33:24; 35:4–6; 61:1). As John's disciples leave, Jesus identifies him as that "Elijah" who is to prepare Israel for the Messiah (7–10; see Easy; Manhood).

Lawbreaker! (12:1–21). Jesus' disciples pluck some grain on the way to the synagogue and eat it as they walk. By the Pharisees' interpretation, this is "harvesting" and against the Sabbath law! Jesus shows that the Pharisees are the true lawbreakers, for they condemn the innocent without mercy (1–8).

In the synagogue they point out to Jesus a man with a withered hand and ask if it is "lawful" to heal (i.e., work) on the Sabbath. Jesus' answer stuns them. Any one of them would lift one of his sheep out of danger on the Sabbath. A man is far more important than a sheep. Thus "it is lawful to do good on the Sabbath."

Inspired by Satan (12:22–37). To counter speculation that Jesus might be the Messiah, the angry Pharisees attack Jesus openly, accusing Him of being in league with the prince of demons (24).

"The blind and mute man both spoke and saw"

(12:22). The Pharisees insisted that Jesus' miracle with this man came from demonic power exercised by our Lord. The rejection of the miracle power of God by the self-righteous is nothing new. Wherever the presence of God manifests itself in signs and wonders there will be plenty of scoffers, including theologians and religionists, who will reject it as unworthy, excessive, emotional, or demonic. But the Lord continues to heal (see Healed) today because people are in need, and the Word of God is to be confirmed as we proclaim the message of Christ.

Here Jesus introduces the much debated "unforgivable sin" (31). It is best to understand the unforgivable sin in the context of the unique blasphemy the Pharisees committed that day. The Pharisees recognize the supernatural nature of Jesus' power, but they harden their hearts to Jesus' explanation and to all the evidence. Committing themselves to oppose God, they even label the Spirit's works as the work of Satan! By their own decision they have passed beyond the possibility of repentance (cf. Matt. 11:20–24).

"For a tree is known by its fruit"

(12:33). Jesus identified the Pharisees' slandering of the Holy Spirit as more than an impulsive remark—their speech betrayed hearts set against the truth concerning Jesus. Speech expresses and exposes the depths of the heart (v. 34). Just as a tree is known by its fruit (v. 33), so also a man is known by his speech and actions which spring from the reservoir of his heart (v. 35). When hearts are yielded to the Spirit's influence and the abundance of treasure He offers, wholesome speech comes forth as a Spirit-produced grace, evincing the good fruit of Christlike character (see Eccl. 10:12; Gal. 5:22–23; Col. 4:6; Justified).

No more proofs (12:38–50). Jesus now refuses to give more signs, "except the sign of the prophet Jonah." His Resurrection, after a three-day burial, will be conclusive proof of His claims! (*See* Will.)

B. Discourse: Parables of the kingdom (13:1–52). Now Jesus uses a unique kind of parable, which both reveals and conceals. The subject of these parables is truth not revealed in the Old Testament (13:35). Before the time arrives for the earthly kingdom of the Messiah that the Old Testament promises, the kingdom of heaven (*see* Kingdom of God) will take an unexpected form.

Jesus' explanations of the parables, with the information that the subject matter is the "secrets of the kingdom of heaven" (13:11), gives us the principles and keys needed to understand the other parables as well. (*See* Desired; Evangelism; Good.)

V. NARRATIVE, CONTROVERSY, AND DISCOURSE 13:53—18:35.

A. Narrative: Various episodes preceding Jesus' final journey to Jerusalem (13:53—17:27). The next events recorded by Matthew show continuing resistance to Jesus and an increasing emphasis by the Lord on faith. Jesus' Nazareth neighbors are offended at the pretensions of this "carpenter's son" (13:53–58). John the Baptist is beheaded (14:1–12). A few recognize Jesus. Among them is a Canaanite woman (*see* Compassion). But the disciples seem amazed when Jesus walks on the waters; even Peter pauses and doubts (14:22–34). When Jesus strikes out against the Pharisees, the disciples fail to grasp His teaching (15:1–20; *see* Faith's Confession; Fornications).

" 'O woman, great is your faith! Let it be to you as you desire.' And her daughter was healed from that very hour"
(15:22–31). The relationship between faith and healing is emphasized throughout the New Testament. Without the woman's faith in Jesus Christ as the Healer, her daughter would never have received healing.

Jesus' continuing miracles win praise for God (15:31). But the active opposition of the Pharisees and general spiritual dullness combine to withhold the commitment of the nation to the Servant King. (*See* Fill.)

Chapters 16—17. Matthew now introduces the theological turning point in his Gospel. Before these chapters, Jesus' preaching has emphasized the kingdom and its ethics. After these chapters the emphasis shifts to discipleship and to the Cross.

Pharisees and Sadducees (16:1–12). These hostile sects have now joined to combat Jesus. Jesus refuses to speak with these leaders who cannot read the signs of the times and warns His disciples against their approach to religion.

The Christ (16:13–20). Peter's confession of faith correctly identifies our Lord (16; *see* Leadership, Spiritual).

Simon is given the name "Peter," which means "stone." Jesus goes on to say, "Upon this rock I will build My church." Even the Roman Catholic fathers disagree about the rock on which the church is to be built. "Stone" (*petros*) and "rock" (*petra*) are different words in Greek. In fact, the foundation is the reality that Peter affirms: Jesus truly is "the Christ, the Son of the living God!"

The next verse speaks of "keys of the kingdom" (19), and the power of binding and loosing on earth and in heaven.

Crucifixion ahead (16:21–28). The theological turning point is found in verse 21: "From that time Jesus began to show to His disciples that He must . . . be killed, and be raised the third day." The nation has rejected its King (*see* Offense); now the Cross becomes the focus of Jesus' teaching.

The disciples too are taught (24–26). They must deny themselves, take up their cross, and follow Jesus. The cross speaks here of God's will. Just as Jesus turns toward the Cross because it is God's will for Him, so each disciple must daily commit himself to whatever God's will may be for him.

"The Son of Man will come in the glory of His Father with His angels"
(16:27–28). Three things can be understood by Jesus' words in these verses: (1) He will return in His glory, (2) judgment will occur, and (3) the kingdom will be established. Little controversy surrounds the first two—however, the issue of the coming of the kingdom is complicated in verse 28 by the phrase "some . . . shall not taste death till they see the Son of Man coming in His kingdom." Many understand this as referring to the Transfiguration (17:1–4), others to the fall of Jerusalem or other sociopolitical developments of the first century. However, the kingdom of God is being revealed in part through Christ's earthly ministry and only completely in His return. Mark 1:14 and Luke 17:21 affirm the presence of the kingdom now, without denying its future fulfillment.

Transfigured (17:1–13).

Faith, not natural relationships (17:14–27). Jesus explains that faith is the key to accomplishment in the hidden kingdom.

> **"Jesus rebuked the demon"**
> (17:14–18). The disciples' failed attempt to cast out this demon led to Jesus' rebuke of their "unbelief" (v. 20). However, the Lord does suggest in this passage that some demonic strongholds in people's lives are stronger than others. His counsel concerning prayer with fasting reveals a deeper level of bondage or a stronger order of demonic power involved in this situation. Jesus here addresses the demon, which has been manifested in the person's life in a form of epilepsy (v. 15), and casts out the spirit. We should not conclude from this passage that all epilepsy is demonically inspired.

> **"If you have faith as a mustard seed"**
> (17:20). This is the kind of faith that begins small and grows (*see* Faith, Seed); it is the kind of faith that places the presence and power of the kingdom above any physical or spiritual obstacle. The disciples could not cast out the demon because of their lack of faith. Verse 21 encourages them to pray and fast for the authority to deal with a kind of situation that was beyond their experience, for which their faith needed to grow.

B. Discourse: Teaching on the church (18:1–35).

Greatness introduced (18:1–9). The disciples ask Jesus who is greatest in His kingdom. He does not answer but calls a small child over to Him. To be great, the disciple must "become as little children" and "humble himself as this little child" (3–4; *see* Humbles; Kingdom of God).

Three illustrations (18:10–35). The relational key to life as God's little ones is found in the attitude believers take toward each other (*see* Agree). Jesus gives three illustrations that show His disciples that every effort is to be made toward reconciliation and forgiveness (*see* Kingdom of God).

VI. JESUS IN JUDEA AND JERUSALEM 19:1–25:46.

A. Narrative: Jesus' final journey and the mounting conflict (19:1–23:39). Matthew now reports events that explore three detours

religious people sometimes take in search of greatness.

Careful observance of Law (19:1–15). The Pharisees took pride in observing the Law more carefully than others. Now these men come to Jesus and ask a legal question: "Is it lawful for a man to divorce his wife?" Jesus points out God's ideal at creation of a permanent union (*see* Family Life). Sin warps and twists the ideal. But this means that law is not God's highest standard at all! Law actually is a lower standard than the ideal.

Doing good (19:16–30). The rich young ruler represents honest humanitarianism. His response to Jesus shows that, for all his goodness, he puts his money before his God. Service to others will flow from relationship with God. But humanitarian effort apart from God is no pathway to kingdom greatness (*see* Kingdom of God; Possible).

Harder work (20:1–16). A parable illustrates the third detour. A landowner hires workers at different times during the day. But all are given a full day's pay! When those who worked all day complain, the owner explains that he is generous. God does not evaluate by how long or hard we work, but is generous in rewarding whatever task (or time!) He calls us to.

Servanthood (20:17–34). James and John enlist their mother to beg for high places in Jesus' coming kingdom. The anger of the other ten when they hear leads to a clear statement of how to achieve greatness. Like Jesus, His disciples must give their lives for others! (*See* Ransom.)

Triumphal entry (21:1–17). Jesus enters the city to the cheers of the crowd and fulfills Zechariah's prophecy (9:9; *see* Lowly). Going to the temple, Jesus drives out of the great temple court the businessmen who buy and sell sacrificial animals. Angrily He says the temple is to be a house of prayer, not a den for thieves!

> **"Out of the mouths of babes and nursing infants You have perfected praise"**
> (21:15–16). Jesus forcibly asserts that childlikeness is demanded of all who would enter the kingdom of heaven (Matt. 18:3). The simplicity of *praise from a child without an agenda—without doctrinal, liturgical, or traditional taboos against unbridled praise—opens the way for genuine appreciation for the presence and power of God. Here Jesus contrasts the chief priests and scribes who have withheld praise of Him with the children who receive Him gladly.

Against the Pharisees (21:18—22:14). The religious leaders challenge Jesus to cite His authority for the acts of yesterday (21:23–27). Jesus turns the question against them. "Was John's authority from God or men?" Knowing the common people hold John to be a prophet, and aware that if they say "from God" Jesus will ask why they rejected his message, the frustrated "leaders" are still. (See Baptism.)

> **"If you have faith and do not doubt"**
> (21:21–22). The authority to speak in the name of Jesus is based on our faith. Our faith is a function of our relationship to Christ and obedience to His Word. Our confidence is in knowing God; our faith cannot be wracked with doubt because we know whom we have believed (2 Tim. 1:12).

Jesus then tells a series of stories. The furious chief priests and Pharisees realize Jesus is talking about them. But they are afraid to arrest Him because of the people.

Traps set for Jesus (22:15–46). Desperate now, the leaders try to trap Jesus into some admission that will turn the crowds against Him. In a rare display of tact, diplomacy, and confrontation, Jesus answers and turns their questions back on themselves (see Render).

Judgment announced against leaders (23:1–37). The leaders have slunk away, and Jesus turns to His disciples. They are to permit no hierarchy to develop among them. "You have only one Master," Jesus explains. Titles such as "father" and "teacher" draw attention away from God the Father and Christ the Teacher. Human leaders are to find their greatness in servanthood (23:1–12).

Seven woes are now pronounced against the Pharisees and teachers of the Law.

B. Discourse: Jesus' eschatological teaching (24:1–25:46). The disciples' attention to the beauty of the temple buildings stimulates a series of questions about the future. "When will the temple be thrown down? What will be the sign of Your coming? And, what will be the sign of the end of the age?" The questions are answered in reverse order.

The sign of the end of the age (24:4–26). The years that stretch out toward the future will be marked by tension, disasters, wars, growing wickedness, and persecution for Jesus' followers (see Endures). But these common disasters are only a foreshadowing of what is known in the Old Testament as the "day of the Lord," which Jesus describes here as a time of "great tribulation, such as has not been since the beginning of the world until this time" (24:21).

> **"And this gospel of the kingdom will be preached in all the world as a witness"**
> (24:14). Jesus cites the Good News of the kingdom as evidence presented before the world. Earlier He had pointed to it when responding to the inquirers sent from John the Baptist (11:4–5). Witnessing, from a biblical point of view, must not be separated from the expectation of something happening that will serve as evidence for the case (see Evangelism). The gospel of the kingdom is very inclusive and broad in its application, as should be the believer's witness.

The sign of Jesus' coming (24:27–35). Jesus identifies no special sign to mark His coming, except to note that it will be "after the tribulation of those days" (24:29). That return will be visible to the whole earth, for He will come "with power and great glory."

Jesus does not tell His disciples the answer to the first question they asked (24:3), about the destruction of the Jerusalem temple, but history answers that question for us. In A.D. 70 Roman armies under Titus crushed a Jewish revolt, destroyed the city, and tore down the temple, just as Jesus had foretold.

Exhortations to watch (24:36—25:46). Jesus does not dwell on the prophetic details. Instead, He turns the thoughts of His disciples to the life they are to live until He returns (see Abundance [Have]; Faith, Seed; Human Worth; Messianic Promises; Trimmed). "Watch," Jesus exhorts, "for you do not know what hour your Lord is coming" (24:42).

> **"As the days of Noah were"**
> (24:37). The deplorable moral condition of the world at the return of Christ can only be compared to the lawless wickedness of Noah's times. God's disgust then was so great that He "was sorry that He had made man . . . and He was grieved in His heart" (Gen. 6:6). We cannot know the *time* of Christ's return (vv. 43–44), but we can discern the *times* and prepare ourselves in purity of heart and a faithful witness to our world.

> **"These will go away into everlasting punishment, but the righteous**

into eternal life"
(25:41–46). Jesus is excruciatingly plain here: good works reflect a transformed character (Eph. 2:10). Our position in Christ is based on our faith in Him alone. However, the witness of Christ's work in believers is based on character (Gal. 5:22–25) and good works (vv. 41–46).

VII. THE PASSION NARRATIVE 26:1—27:66.

Now events move swiftly. Unable to touch Jesus openly, the chief priests plot to arrest and kill him (26:4). Judas agrees to betray Him for thirty pieces of silver (cf. Zech. 11:12)!

Jesus shares a final meal with His disciples and reveals that the promised New Covenant is about to be written in His own blood (26:17–30; *see* Blood, The; Flesh). Jesus predicts Peter's denial and desertion by the others and then goes aside to pray. It is here that a crowd of armed rabble, led by Judas, comes to arrest the Lord (26:47–56; *see* Leadership, Spiritual).

The trial is swift and illegal. Jesus is taken at night before the Sanhedrin, Israel's court and governing body. In the meantime Peter, who is outside in the courtyard, denies that he knows Jesus (26:69–75). Judas, remorseful now, flings his blood money on the temple floor and wanders away to commit suicide (27:1–10).

"You will see the Son of Man sitting at the right hand of the Power, and coming on the clouds of heaven"
(26:64). At Christ's return, Jesus will not have to prove Himself to men as expected here, in this sham of a trial. The irrefutable proof of His claims as Messiah and Savior will be demonstrated in the fulfilling of Daniel 7:13, and the witness of heaven will be complete in Him when He returns.

The Jewish court has no power to sentence a person to death. So Jesus is taken to Pilate, the Roman governor. He admits to being King of the Jews and refuses to defend Himself. Pilate is convinced of Jesus' innocence, yet yields to pressure and pronounces the death sentence (27:11–26; *see* Judgment Seat). Jesus is whipped, mocked (27:27–31), and led away to be crucified. (*See* Human Worth.)

The death of Jesus is one of the focal points of Old Testament prophecy. Matthew is careful to show how the events that lead up to the Cross, and what happens there, are predicted in the Old Testament. Jesus' body is taken down and laid in a nearby garden tomb. His apparently victorious enemies set a guard on the tomb. They want none of the disciples to steal the body of this pretender who prophesied His own resurrection (27:57–66)!

VIII. THE RESURRECTION NARRATIVE 28:1–20.

Jesus' body lies in the tomb for three days. Then, on the first day of the week, an angel comes and rolls away the stone that blocks the door. The purpose is not to release the resurrected Lord, but to permit the disciples to see the place where the body lay!

The Gospel of Matthew ends now, with Jesus' appearance to his eleven disciples, and with what has come to be called the "Great Commission" (Matt. 28:16–20). Trusting in the power of the risen Lord, the Eleven—and all other followers of Jesus—are commissioned to "go . . . and make disciples of all the nations . . . teaching them to observe all things that I have commanded you" (28:16–20).

His promise supports us to this very day. "I am with you always, even to the end of the *age."

"All authority has been given to Me. . . . Go therefore . . . I am with you"
(28:18–20). For the follower of Jesus, the mandate is clear. We are to go and make disciples (*see* Evangelism) with the confidence of His presence attending us as we do. Great strength and comfort are found in knowing that the One who made disciples out of us is the One who will make disciples through us. By His authority it will be done; His presence will secure each disciple. Our faithful decision to obey will lead to the Master's commission being fulfilled.

See Truth-in-Action, page 310.

KEYS TO MARK
The Passion for the Kingdom

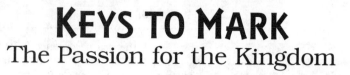

Kingdom Key: God's Purpose in View

Throughout the Gospels one finds elements of the multi-dimensional traits of the life Jesus introduced—that life potential when one enters and learns to live in the "kingdom of God." These traits of blessing and triumph are the first wave of heaven overflowing earth to restore to its inhabitants those elements of the original order that sin and death have marred.

God's strategy is revealed: (1) He sends Jesus as the Savior who will live, die, and rise again, to break the curse of death by the merit of His sinless life; (2) during His ministry Jesus will model methods to spread the message of the kingdom following His Resurrection; (3) Jesus will commission His followers to go to all the world with that word; (4) He will confirm that "word" as it was confirmed during His own ministry; thus, (5) in breaking the powers of the curse, loosing the chains of demonic works, and verifying His claim as Risen Lord, the King will summon those who hear the message to repentance and to life in Him—and through them the cycle repeats itself.

Mark's Gospel reveals the personal *passion* that is essential for such a strategy. Two instructive keys are offered, calling each believer beyond a mere academic acknowledgment of the kingdom to live it out and

Spiritual passion leads to spiritual break-through.

see it multiplied. Both require passion—a heartfelt desire to partner with Christ in the ministry of His kingdom today.

1. The Kingdom and Spiritual Warfare

Jesus continually confronted and cast out demons (Mark 1:21–28, 34, 39; 5:1–20; 9:14–29). He sent His disciples to do the same (6:7–13), then he said that this confrontation would continue through all who believed and followed Him—into the future, until today (16:17). When the invading power of God's kingdom expelled demons, challenges arose. People were unaccustomed to this ministry (1:25–27). Religious leaders bitterly criticized Him, even accusing Him of being demonically motivated (3:20–30).

The price of passionately pursuing kingdom ministry in this regard has not changed. The call to prepare the soul (9:29) and to obey the Lord (6:7; 16:17) extends to us, *(Please turn to page 291.)*

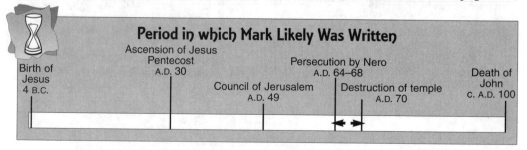

Period in which Mark Likely Was Written

| Birth of Jesus 4 B.C. | Ascension of Jesus Pentecost A.D. 30 | Council of Jerusalem A.D. 49 | Persecution by Nero A.D. 64–68 | Destruction of temple A.D. 70 | Death of John c. A.D. 100 |

Mark reveals Christ's power ministry, devoid

Master Key: God's Son Revealed

This book is not a biography but a concise history of redemption accomplished through the atoning work of Christ. Mark substantiates the messianic claims of Jesus by emphasizing His authority as a Teacher (1:22) and His authority over Satan and unclean spirits (1:27; 3:19–30), sin (2:1–12), the Sabbath (2:27–28; 3:1–6), nature (4:35–41; 6:45–52), disease (5:21–34), death (5:35–43), legalistic tradiions (7:1–13, 14–20), and the temple (11:15–18).

The opening title of Mark's work, "The beginning of the gospel of Jesus Christ, the Son of God" (1:1), provides his central thesis concerning the identity of Jesus as the Son of God. Both the Baptism and the Transfiguration testify to His sonship (1:11; 9:7). On two occasions evil spirits confess Him to be the Son of God (3:11; 5:7; *see also* 1:24, 34). The parable of the wicked vinedressers alludes to Jesus' divine sonship (12:6). Finally, the narrative of the Crucifixion concludes with the centurion's confession, "Truly this Man was the Son of God!" (15:39).

The title that Jesus uses most frequently for Himself, fourteen times in Mark, is "Son of Man." As a designation for the Messiah, this term (*see* Dan. 7:13) was not as popular among the Jews as the highly nationalistic title "Son of David." Jesus chose the title "Son of Man" both to reveal and to conceal His messiahship and to relate Himself to both God and man.

Mark, with his eye upon discipleship, suggests that Jesus' followers must possess a penetrating insight into the mystery of His identity. Even though many people understand His person and mission, and while demons confess His divine sonship, Jesus' disciples must see through to His mission, take up their crosses, and follow Him. The Second Coming of the vindicated Son of Man will fully unveil His power and glory.

> ## Key Word: *Jesus the Servant*
>
> **M**ark's theme is captured well in 10:45 because Jesus is portrayed in this book as a Servant and as the Redeemer of humanity (cf. Phil. 2:5–11). Mark shows his Gentile readers how the Son of God—rejected by His own people—achieved ultimate victory through apparent defeat.
>
> ## Key Verses: Mark 10:43–45; 8:34–37
> ## Key Chapter: Mark 8
>
> **M**ark 8 is a pivotal chapter showing the change of emphasis in Jesus' ministry after Peter's confession, "You are the Christ." After this point Jesus begins to fortify His men for His forthcoming suffering and death.

Power Key: God's Spirit at Work

Along with the other Gospel writers, Mark records the prophecy of John the Baptist that Jesus "will baptize you with the Holy Spirit" (1:8). Believers would be just as thoroughly immersed in the Spirit as John's candidates were in the waters of the Jordan River.

The Holy Spirit descended upon Jesus at His Baptism (1:10), empowering Him for His

(Please turn to page 291.)

of pride, power-seeking, and possessiveness.

Introducing
MARK

Author. Even though the Gospel of Mark is anonymous, early tradition is unanimous that the author of this Gospel was John Mark, a close associate of Peter (*see* 1 Pet. 5:13) and a companion of Paul and Barnabas on their first missionary journey. The earliest witness to Markan authorship stems from Papias, bishop of the church at Hierapolis (about A.D. 135–140), a witness that is preserved in Eusebius's *Ecclesiastical History.* Papias describes Mark as "the interpreter of Peter." Although the early church was careful to maintain direct apostolic authorship for the Gospels, the church fathers consistently attributed this Gospel to Mark, who was not an apostle. This fact furnishes indirect confirmation of Mark's authorship.

Date. The church fathers state that the Gospel of Mark was written after Peter's death, which occurred during the persecutions by the Emperor Nero in about A.D. 67. The Gospel itself, particularly chapter 13, indicates that it was written before the destruction of the temple in A.D. 70. The bulk of the evidence supports a date between A.D. 65 and 70.

Background. In A.D. 64 Nero accused the Christian community of setting the city of Rome on fire, and thereupon instigated a fearful persecution in which Paul and Peter perished. In the milieu of a persecuted church, living constantly under the threat of death, the evangelist Mark writes his "good news." Clearly he wants his readers to draw encouragement and strength from the life and example of Jesus. What was true for Jesus was to be true for the apostles and disciples of all ages.

At the heart of the Gospel is the explicit pronouncement "that the Son of Man must suffer many things, and be rejected by the elders and chief priests and scribes, and be killed, and after three days rise again" (8:31). This pronouncement of suffering and death not only is repeated (9:31; 10:32–34), but becomes the norm for committed discipleship: "Whoever desires to come after Me, let him deny himself, and take up his cross, and follow Me" (8:34). Mark leads his readers to the Cross of Jesus, where they can discover meaning and hope in their suffering.

Content. Mark structures his Gospel around various geographical movements of Jesus, which are climaxed by His death and subsequent Resurrection. After the introduction (1:1–13), Mark narrates the public ministry of Jesus in Galilee (1:14—9:50) and Judea (chs. 10—13), culminating in the Passion and Resurrection (chs. 14—16). The Gospel may be viewed as two halves joined together by the hinge of Peter's confession of Jesus as the Messiah (8:27–30) and Jesus' first announcement of His crucifixion (8:31).

Mark is the shortest of the Gospels, containing no genealogy and no account of the birth and early Judean ministry of Jesus. It is the Gospel of action, moving rapidly from one scene to another. John's Gospel is a studied portrait of the Lord; Matthew and Luke present what might be described as a series of colored slides, while Mark's Gospel is like a motion picture of the life of Jesus. Mark accents the activity he records by the use of the Greek word *eutheos*, usually translated "immediately." The word occurs forty-two times in Mark, more than in all the rest of the New Testament. Mark's frequent use of the Greek imperfect tense, denoting continuous action, also moves the narrative at a rapid pace.

Mark is also the Gospel of vividness. Graphic, striking phrases occur frequently to allow the reader to form a mental picture of the scene described. The looks and gestures of Jesus receive unusual attention. There are many Latinisms in the Gospel (*see* 4:21; 12:14; 6:27; 15:39). Mark places little emphasis on Jewish law and customs, always interpreting them for the reader when he does mention them. This feature tends to support the tradition that Mark wrote for a Gentile, Roman audience.

In many ways, Mark emphasizes the Passion of Jesus so that it becomes the gauge by which the whole of Jesus' ministry and the ministry of His disciples may be measured: "For even the Son of Man did not come to be served, but to serve, and to give His life a ransom for many" (10:45). Jesus' entire ministry (miracles, table fellowship with sinners, choice of disciples, teaching on the kingdom of God, etc.) is set within the context of the self-giving love of the Son of God, climaxed in the Cross and Resurrection.

Personal Application. Mark's Gospel teaches that the life of discipleship means following Jesus along the same path of misunderstanding and rejection that He encountered. For followers of Jesus in all ages the warning and promise are sure: "Whoever desires to come after Me, let him deny himself, and take up his cross, and follow Me. For whoever desires to save his life will lose it, but whoever loses his life for My sake and the gospel's will save it" (8:34–35).

Mark underscores the need for faith in the person, message, and power of Jesus to help those in need (*see* 1:15; 2:5; 4:40; 5:34, 36;

6:6; 9:19; 11:22–24). The opposite of such faith can be seen in the motif of hard hearts (*see* 3:5; 7:14–23; 8:17). The incarnate Christ that Mark describes is One who is willing and able to help those in extreme need.

Finally, Mark's Gospel assures Christian workers of all generations that the same attesting miracles that accredited the ministries of the apostles will continue as characteristic features of God's people under the New Covenant (16:17–18).

Kingdom Key *continued from page 288*

for human bondage continues as hellish minions still oppress multitudes. By remaining open to our Savior's passion for human liberation and wholeness, and by remaining humble and unshrinking before criticism, we can assure that the spiritual breakthrough which is needed in individuals, families, cities, and nations today will be realized.

2. The Kingdom and Personal Transformation

Jesus recognized that entrusting kingdom power to humans could be continuously granted only if radical change occurs in those endowed with heaven's authority. While a new *birth* begins life in the kingdom (John 3:3), a dramatic *growth* is essential on passionate terms. Jesus uses two figures which should call forth another type of passion from that which appropriately pursues His intent for our power-ministry over sickness and demons. In Mark 10:13–16 and 23–25, two ideas emerge as Jesus twice speaks of "entering" the kingdom (that is, entering into the mode of life that it affords us, in grace and power). He indicates the cost—a price paid in humilty and submission to the spirit of Jesus. He calls His followers to (a) a receptivity to childlikeness and (b) a rejection of acquisitiveness. As you read the two passages, note how Jesus calls us to something beyond simply receiving children and renouncing wealth. Jesus is saying that those who would function in kingdom power will be protected from headiness and pride only if they are stripped of adult pride (unto a simple, childlike heart) and are fully freed of preoccupation with the wealth or benefits such ministry might yield.

These two kingdom keys balance Christ's call to a power-ministry because they help keep us from being caught in the traps of power-seeking, pride, or possessiveness.

Power Key *continued from page 289*

messianic work in fulfillment of Isaiah's prophecy (Is. 42:1; 48:16; 61:1–2). The account of Jesus' subsequent ministry bears witness that His miracles and teaching resulted from the anointing of the Holy Spirit.

Mark graphically states that "the Spirit drove Him into the wilderness" (1:12) to be tempted. This suggests the urgency of meeting and defeating Satan's attempts to defile Him before He embarked on a mission of breaking the enemy's power in others.

The sin against the Holy Spirit is set in contrast to "all sins" (3:28), for these sins and blasphemies can be forgiven. The context defines the meaning of this frightening truth. The scribes blasphemed against the Holy Spirit in that they attributed Jesus' Holy Spirit-effected exorcisms to Satan (3:22). Their prejudiced vision made them incapable of true discernment. Mark's explanation confims this as the reason Jesus makes such a severe pronouncement (3:30).

Jesus also refers to the Holy Spirit's inspiration of the Old Testament (12:36). Of particular encouragement to Christians facing the hostility of unjust authorities is the Lord's assurance that the Holy Spirit will speak through believers when they testify of Christ (13:11).

In addition to explicit references to the Holy Spirit, Mark employs words associated with the gift of the Spirit, such as power, authority, prophet, healing, laying on of hands, Messiah, and kingdom.

Surveying
MARK

I. INTRODUCTION 1:1–13.

A. Summary statement (1:1; see Gospel).

B. Fulfillment of Old Testament prophecy (1:2–3).

C. John the Baptist's ministry (1:4–8).

> **"I indeed baptized you with water, but He will baptize you with the Holy Spirit"**
> (1:7–8). John the Baptist clearly refuses any claim to being the Messiah. While he does not hesitate to identify himself as the one who administers baptism in water as an outward symbol of purification, neither does he confuse who it is that will pour forth the inward reality. Jesus is the Baptizer with the Holy Spirit.

D. Jesus' baptism (1:9–11). Jesus' release to ministry is directly related to baptism and the descent of the Spirit upon Him. The heavenly voice heard by all signals the perfection of God's Son and the readiness for His revelation to the world.

E. Jesus' temptation (1:12–13). Following the Spirit's outpouring on Christ, He is immediately challenged by the devil, who attempts to stop His mission before it can be started.

II. JESUS' GALILEAN MINISTRY 1:14—9:50.

Mark plunges into describing a round of activities that show Jesus as a man of action and a man with authority. This man Jesus is committed to His mission; He does not pause to rest, but gives Himself totally to His work.

A. Beginnings: initial success and conflict (1:14—3:6). Jesus' announcement of the kingdom is highly significant here. The power of hell is about to be overthrown by the coming of the *kingdom of God. For all those who refused to believe that God was interested in delivering His people it was now time to "repent, and believe in the gospel" (v. 15). Mark describes a series of wide-ranging events in which Jesus acts decisively.

Jesus speaks to several successful fishermen, and they leave their business to follow Him (1:16–20; see Left). He not only "teaches as one who had authority," but also acts with authority. He speaks sternly to evil spirits, who are forced to obey His orders (1:21–28).

> **"For with authority He commands even the unclean spirits"**
> (1:23–28). Jesus has the spiritual authority and the right as the Creator to liberate people from demonic power (Luke 4:18). Repeatedly in Scripture the demons recognize Jesus' authority even when people in the crowds do not. Jesus silences the demons and casts them out with the word of His authority.

He works late into the night healing those with various diseases (1:29–34). Before the next morning dawns, Jesus is up ahead of His disciples, praying in a solitary place (1:35–37).

This Man, with His amazing stamina, is also sensitive. He feels a rush of compassion at the misery of a leper and reaches out to touch and cure (1:40–45; see Healing, Divine). He announces forgiveness of a paralytic's sin.

Mark does not give extended accounts of what Jesus says as He travels. But he does focus on incidents that show Jesus speaking with compelling authority.

> **" 'But that you may know that the Son of Man has power on earth to forgive sins'—He said to the paralytic, 'I say to you, arise, take up your bed, and go to your house.' "**
> (2:3–12). Jesus identifies Himself as "Son of Man"—and in declaring forgiveness to the man He asserts His own divinity (Mic. 7:18). The proof of His power to forgive is demonstrated in His rulership over the paralysis of the man. The healing confirms Jesus' right to forgive sin.

B. Later stages: heightened popularity and opposition (3:7—6:13). The crowds respond to this man who cannot be cowed, and the press of those begging to be healed becomes so great that Jesus has to teach from a small boat, floating just off shore (3:7–12).

> **"That He might send them out to preach . . . and to cast out demons"**
> (3:10–15). Jesus' ministry of casting out demons is a consistent part of His serving the physical, emotional, and spiritual needs of the multitudes. His teaching times are punctuated with healings and exorcisms (vv. 10–11). In His commissioning of the Twelve to ministry He includes the *power to cast out demons (v. 15). This privilege to function in Christ's authority is based on their submission to Him, and through them

Jesus' ministry is being extended. Their authority and their commission both come from Christ.

The work is now so great that the Twelve He has called earlier are now appointed disciples and designated "apostles." They are to remain with Him and go out to preach where He sends them (3:13–19). But the press around Jesus continues. The pace is so frantic He has no time even to eat! Jesus has thrown Himself so completely into His ministry that His family worries He has gone "out of his mind," and His enemies call Him demon-possessed! They even suggest that His power over demons comes from the prince of demons himself (3:20–22)!

"By the ruler of the demons He casts out demons"

(3:20–27). The religious establishment frequently throughout history has been found resisting the work of deliverance from demonic power. Jesus is accused of being demon-possessed because He casts out spirits that destroy the people they torment. Jesus' answer concerning a divided kingdom must be seen in the context of the differences between the kingdom of light and the kingdom of darkness. 1 John 4:8 declares, "God is love." God's all-powerful love overrules the destructive power of Satan, bringing deliverance to the captives.

Jesus shows up the foolishness of their argument and warns them. Calling the works that He performs in the power of God's Spirit the work of demons is a sin that will not be forgiven (3:23–30)!

Mark now concludes with a report of several of Jesus' parables. He explains that these sayings are designed to hide truth from those without spiritual perception, and that they are carefully explained to the disciples (4:1–34; see Faith, Seed; Mystery). Mark reports only four of the parables, while Matthew gives fifteen and Luke nineteen. But in this Gospel of Christ in action, Mark finds room to report eighteen miracles!

Mark brings his vivid pictures of Jesus' authority to a climax with three extended stories. A furious squall strikes as Jesus and His disciples cross the water. Jesus sleeps on, until roused by the frantic disciples. He calmly commands the wind and waves to "Be still!" The wind dies and the waters become completely calm (4:35–41).

"How is it that you have no faith?"

(4:40). Jesus' incredulous response to the disciples was based on their ignorance of His authority over natural elements. Nothing is too hard for the Creator of everything! Faith for small things may seem easier than faith for big things, but Jesus is telling the disciples that it is all the same to Him.

On the other side of the lake a demon-possessed man, whom no one is strong enough to subdue, falls on his knees before Jesus. The demons, tortured by the very presence of One they recognize as "the Son of the Most High God," are sent into a herd of pigs, which then hurtles off a cliff to destruction (5:1–20).

"When he saw Jesus from afar, he ran and worshiped Him"

(5:1–16). Despite his demon-controlled behavior which is bizarre and socially deplorable, this man, by an act of his will, comes to Jesus. Though Jesus is able to speak only to the demons rather than the man himself, the Lord casts a "legion" of demons (v. 9) from him with the word of His power and the man is completely restored (v. 15; see Mind). The destruction of the pigs (v. 13) has been questioned on occasion, but the value of a human soul far outweighs any economic consideration or relative value of an animal.

Back on the Jewish side of the lake, Jesus heals an incurable illness while on His way to help a sick child. When He arrives at her house, the girl is already dead. Ignoring the wailing and words of ridicule, Jesus takes the girl by the hand. To the astonishment of His disciples and the parents, the girl responds and her life is restored (5:21–43). Jesus controls the awesome powers of nature, demons, and even death itself.

"Daughter, your faith has made you well. Go in peace, and be healed of your affliction"

(5:25–34). The word used for "healed" (see Healing, Divine) comes from the Greek root word sodzo, which is also translated elsewhere as "saved." Once again Jesus emphasizes faith as the pathway to healing. It is faith that "saves" us, spirit, soul, and body.

It might appear that life would hold no challenges to a man with Jesus' powers. Mark goes on to show the many conflicts and tensions that placed great demands on the character of the Lord.

Jesus is rejected by His relatives and His old neighbors at Nazareth (6:1–6). When He sends out disciples two by two, some towns welcome them but others turn them away (6:7–13).

> **"They cast out many demons, and anointed with oil many who were sick, and healed them"**
> (6:13). The preaching of repentance and the demonstration of the presence of God's kingdom power (Mark 1:14–15) are recurrent themes throughout the synoptic Gospels. The presence of the kingdom of God assures acceptance of the repentant, hope for the sick, and freedom for the demon-possessed. Here, the disciples minister with the power of their Lord.

C. Ministry outside of Galilee (6:14—8:26). John the Baptist, Jesus' cousin and also a prophet, is beheaded by Herod (6:14–29). When the crowds do come out, the press is so great that Jesus has no time even to eat. Jesus tries to lead the Twelve to a quiet place where they can rest, but they are followed. Despite His own hunger and exhaustion, Jesus performs a miracle and feeds some five thousand people (6:30–44). At night Jesus, in an attempt to be alone, sends the disciples across the lake in a small boat. When a storm comes up and the men strain at the oars because the wind is against them, Jesus comes to them, walking on the water. Again the sea calms. At the shore crowds of sick persons beg for healing (6:45–56).

The pressures on Jesus include open opposition. Pharisees and other religious leaders come to criticize and are boldly rebuked. Jesus corrects the distortions of God's word that the traditions of these men have caused, but even His own disciples fail to grasp His point (7:1–23; *see* Pride)!

> **"He sighed, and said to him, 'Ephphatha,' that is, 'Be opened.' Immediately his ears were opened, and the impediment of his tongue was loosed."**
> (7:32–37). Jesus' practice of healing with the deaf man was unorthodox—fingers in ears, spitting, touching his tongue (v. 33). However, the issue is not the methodology

of healing but the fact that Jesus is the Healer. Bringing the man to Jesus was the pathway for healing, as it still is today.

Again the Pharisees harry Jesus. When the Lord warns the Twelve against their teachings, they misunderstand. Frustrated, Jesus twice cries out, "Do you still not understand?" (8:11–21; *see* Hardened).

Mark, in this series of sharp sketches, has shown us the pressures under which Jesus lived. Yet, in spite of these discouragements and the constant pressure, Jesus never falters. He continues to press on in His ministry of teaching and healing, demonstrating over and over again that He has not come "to be served, but to serve, and to give His life a ransom for many" (Mark 10:45).

D. Ministry on the way to Judea (8:27—9:50). The series of frustrations culminates when, after another healing (8:22–26), Jesus asks who people say He is. The disciples report that He is considered a great prophet! But He is not accepted as the Son of God (8:27–28).

The crowds do not recognize Jesus, but the disciples do. "You are the Christ," Peter affirms for them all (8:27–30). For Mark, as well as Matthew, this is the turning point. Immediately Jesus "began to teach them that the Son of Man must suffer many things," be rejected, killed, and rise again the third day (8:31–33). Now the rapidly unfolding events are for the instruction of the Twelve.

The healing of an epileptic boy in the grip of an evil spirit leads to private instruction on faith (9:14–32).

> **"Lord, help my unbelief"**
> (9:23–24). The desperate cry of a father seeking deliverance for his son brings him to the feet of Jesus. Jesus' statement concerning faith is not a theological cudgel to break the spirit of the man; it is intended to summon the man's attention on Jesus' sufficiency in the midst of his need. The boy is healed (*see* Healing, Divine) because his father brought him to Jesus, and that is faith in action.

When rivalry develops, Jesus teaches the Twelve about servanthood (9:33–37). He also teaches the Twelve not to reject others who believe, but who are "not one of us" (9:38–41). He warns of the seriousness of causing any who believe in Him to sin (9:42–50).

III. JESUS' JUDEAN MINISTRY 10:1— 16:20.

A. Ministry in the Transjordan (10:1-52).

When the Pharisees raise questions of law, Jesus shows that in some points even the Law of Moses dips below God's ideal. Later, privately, Jesus shows His disciples that they must go back to basic principles for guidance (10:1-12; see Joined). The next day the disciples are reproved for keeping young children away. "Of such is the kingdom of God," Jesus tells them (10:13-16). The rich youth who appears next illustrates Jesus' point. He asks what he can do to "inherit eternal life." The young man is moral and honest. But when Jesus tells him to give away his wealth and follow the Lord, he turns away. How unlike a trusting child (10:17-22)!

Later Jesus and the Twelve discuss the incident, and Jesus points out the difficulty of the rich in abandoning trust in their wealth to trust in God. The disciples again misunderstand and Jesus reassures them. Salvation, impossible for man, is possible with God (10:23-31). As they move on together toward Jerusalem, Jesus speaks again of His coming death (10:32-34).

But the Twelve still do not seem to understand. They maneuver to gain preferred places in Jesus' coming kingdom. Again Jesus stresses the importance of servanthood for His disciples. Jesus' followers will serve others, not rule them (10:35-45)!

As if to illustrate, Mark concludes this section with the report of one last incident. In Jericho, on the way to Jerusalem, a blind man cries out to Jesus. The crowd hushes him, but Jesus stops. "What do you want Me to do for you?" The blind man begs for, and receives, his sight. And the disciples have a vivid demonstration of what it means to set aside one's own great burden, to give everything in service to others (10:46-52).

> **"Your faith has made you well"**
> (10:52). Bartimaeus, in a state of total blindness, does two important things: (1) He calls out to Jesus, "Son of David," the Messiah, and (2) he walks to Christ as he is commanded in the midst of his blindness. Faith seeks the Lord first, making no excuse for its inability. Faith boldly comes to Christ, who is completely able.

B. Ministry in Jerusalem (11:1—13:37).

Jesus begins His journey to the Cross. Mark has brought us to the last week of Jesus' life.

He now relates the events that bring Jesus closer and closer to His death.

The week begins with a triumphal entry into Jerusalem, the air filled with the shouts of the crowd (11:1-11). When Jesus drives the sellers of animals and the money changers out of the temple, the enraged chief priests plot to kill Him (11:12-19).

Jesus has cursed a figless tree, demonstrating the power of prayer (11:20-25) and the reality of an authority which the leaders of Israel challenge the next time He enters the city. As at other times, Jesus easily silences them (11:20-26; see Spiritual Warfare).

> **"Have faith in God"**
> (11:22-24). *Faith is not a feeling about what is to occur; nor is it a flood of positive mental energy. "Faith is the substance of things hoped for, the evidence of things not seen" (Heb. 11:1). Our faith is in the living God, who is able and willing to answer us according to His Word in order to meet our need (see Faith, Seed; Faith's Confession).

A series of confrontations with the authorities follows. Jesus likens them to tenants whose landlord has sent his son to collect the fruit due at harvest. Wickedly they plot to kill the son (12:1-12). When the leaders try to "catch Jesus in words," He easily avoids their traps (12:13-34; see Matthew 22; Mind). Then Jesus puts a question to them which they cannot answer except by admitting that Jesus must be God's Son as well as the descendant of King David (12:35-37).

Publicly Jesus warns against teachers of the law whose religion masks pride and greed. "These will receive greater condemnation," He says, to the delight of the crowd (12:38-40). Privately Jesus points out a poor widow to His disciples. She slips in to put her last two coins in the temple treasury. Jesus tells the Twelve that this gift from poverty means more than all the gold given by the rich (12:41-44).

Leaving the temple that day, Jesus describes the future that awaits the world. Wars and disasters will continue; Jesus' followers will suffer persecution (13:1-13). But finally the time of the end foretold by the prophets will arrive, marked by the desecration of a Jerusalem temple predicted by Daniel (9:25-27). After the dreadful sufferings of the end time Jesus will return, visible to all, "with great power and glory." But when this will be is not known. Until the day comes, Jesus' followers are to watch and to be busy about the task assigned each by God (13:32–36).

> ### "Take heed, watch and pray"
> (13:1–37). Jesus' simple instructions to His church endure for all time (*see* Reader)—in anticipation of the end of time, be prepared! The breakdown of culture (v. 9) and the nuclear family (v. 12), along with the presence of spiritual deception (vv. 21–22), all mark the signs of Christ's return. Jesus' words produce no panic when His people pray and attend to their mission (v. 10).

C. The Passion (14:1—15:47). Chapter 14 describes Thursday of Passion Week. In Bethany an unidentified woman pours expensive perfume on Jesus' head. Some are indignant. Why wasn't the perfume sold and the money given to the poor? Jesus tells them to leave her alone. She has done a beautiful thing, preparing Him beforehand for burial. As Jesus speaks, Judas slips away to the chief priests and bargains to betray Him (1–11).

In Jerusalem that evening, Jesus and the Twelve share a Passover meal (12–26). There Christ prophesies His betrayal and explains that His broken body and shed blood will institute the long-promised New *Covenant. After the meal Jesus listens to Peter's declaration that, whatever others do, he will never desert his Lord. Jesus tells Peter that he will disown Him that very night (28–31).

The little company continues on in the darkness to an olive grove called Gethsemane. As the disciples doze, Jesus, "overwhelmed with sorrow to the point of death," prays (32–41). They are there together when Judas arrives with an armed mob. Jesus is taken and dragged to the home of the high priest, while His disciples all desert Him and flee. Nighttime trials are illegal in Israel, but the whole Sanhedrin, the court of the Jewish people, is waiting.

When false testimony will not stand up, the high priest asks Jesus bluntly if He is the Son of God. Jesus answers clearly: "I am." To these men who reject and hate Jesus this is a clear case of blasphemy, and "all condemn him as worthy of death" (53–65).

Outside, Peter crouches in the courtyard and when questioned curses, swearing he doesn't even know that man, Jesus (66–72).

Christ's Trial and Crucifixion

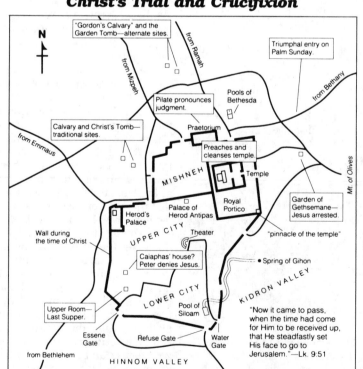

Thursday is over. The next dawn will bring the day of Jesus' execution.

Chapter 15 is Friday. Very early in the morning Jesus is brought to the Roman governor, Pilate. The Sanhedrin cannot execute; only Rome has that authority.

Pilate questions Jesus, who admits being the King of the Jews but will not answer the other accusations of the chief priests. Pilate realizes that Jesus is innocent and recognizes the envy that has turned the leaders against Him. But when the leaders and the crowd cry out, "Crucify him," Pilate turns Jesus over for execution (1–15).

The Roman soldiers in charge of the execution detail, as normal preparation for crucifixion, whip Jesus brutally and mock Him. Then they lead Him off to be crucified (16–20).

The execution ground is outside the city. Weakened by loss of blood from the beatings, Jesus is unable to carry the crossbeam of His cross. A watching visitor who has come to Jerusalem to keep Passover is pressed into service.

As Jesus' enemies mock Him, and the disinterested soldiers gamble for the right to sell His clothing, Jesus hangs suspended between two robbers. Even one of these two joins the bystanders in heaping insults on the suffering Savior (21–32).

A sudden midday darkness shrouds the scene, hiding the figure on the Cross. Those nearby hear a loud cry! Jesus has breathed His last (33–41).

At sunset one of Israel's holiest days will begin. Jesus' body is taken down from the Cross in the late afternoon, carefully wrapped, and laid in a tomb carved into rock. A stone is rolled against the entrance (42–47). No matter how admirable this Man may have been, His story seems to be ended.

D. The Resurrection (16:1–20). But Jesus' story is not ended at all! The first verse in Mark's Gospel had announced "the beginning of the gospel about Jesus Christ, the Son of God." Now we realize that the gospel story will never end!

Mark simply tells the story. The women creep up to the tomb the first day of the new week, carrying spices to anoint the body that is no longer there. They find the stone rolled away, and angels point to the empty shelf carved in the rock where the body had been

placed. "He is not here," they tell the women. "He is risen!"

Trembling and bewildered, and more than a little afraid, the women go away. They do not realize it yet, but they have entered a world made forever new by the Resurrection of the Son of God.

"Go into all the world and preach the gospel"

(16:15–16). Mark includes a different side of the witnessing life (*see* Evangelism). His emphasis has Jesus stressing the preaching of the gospel, while Matthew underscores the making of disciples (Matt. 28:19). When the gospel is preached and a person believes, then he will be saved; it is important to rest on this fact. Proclaiming the gospel will establish a witness of Jesus like nothing else. The question is not which witnessing form is better than the other—rather, which style or form is the Holy Spirit directing?

"These signs will follow those who believe"

(16:17–18). The confirmation (*see* Confirming) of the preaching of the gospel is seen through signs in salvation (v. 15), breaking demonic bondage (v. 17), speaking with new tongues (v. 17), divine protection (v. 18), and healing (v. 18). The strong affirmation of Jesus' words here leaves no doubt; the people of faith *will* have these signs accompanying their ministry.

MARK'S ENDINGS

Early copies of Mark differ in the way the Gospel ends. While the ending represented by verses 9–20 in our English versions is one of the oldest, the most reliable Greek manuscripts do not include it. Many New Testament scholars believe that these verses were not written by Mark; however, the verses do reflect adequately the ongoing miracle flow of ministry experienced by the church. The authenticity of the verses may be challenged by scholars. Their truth, however, has been experienced by multitudes of believers from the first century to today.

See Truth-in-Action, page 310.

KEYS TO LUKE
The Anointing of the Kingdom

Kingdom Key: God's Purpose in View

A perceptive study of Luke's writings reveals the depth of his concern that the source of kingdom life and power should be clearly seen: the Holy Spirit's ministry! Luke is more occupied with this issue than the other Gospel writers. Perhaps his scientific mind and skills as a researcher—especially one who had not experienced Jesus' ministry as the others did—motivated him to "find the secret" to the glory behind it all. Luke makes three times as many references to the Spirit of God as any of the other three evangelists, and he interweaves a variety of expressions to describe the work of the Spirit.

It is Luke who captures the foundational kingdom expression *anointed*. In Luke 4:16–22, Jesus reveals that His own ministry fulfills Isaiah's classic prophecy of the Messiah's ministry (compare Is. 49:8–9; 61:1–2). The significance of Jesus' use of this text is its specific relationship to the meaning of "Messiah"—*the anointed one*. In claiming that "anointing," Jesus was announcing Himself as the Messiah (for an angry reaction to this, *see* 4:23–30). Such "anointing" refers to a heaven-sent flow of the Holy Spirit's power, symbolized in the oil that was poured over the heads of Israel's kings (1 Sam. 10:1; 16:13). Jesus declares the "anointing" is present because He is God's King, and that where the King is, the authority of His kingdom is present—"at hand"—waiting to be manifest in grace and power.

> ....
> **Kingdom advance follows anointing by God's Spirit.**
> ....

In Luke 4:18 we have an outline which characterizes all "anointed" ministry of the gospel of the kingdom. (1) The "poor" (needy, impoverished, disenfranchised, oppressed) hear the Good News of salvation and deliverance. (2) The "broken-hearted" (grieved, disappointed, lonely, and those with shattered relationships) receive healing. (3) The "captives" (the socially ensnared or incarcerated, or the demonically tormented or bound) hear of possible deliverance. (4) The "blind" (physically impaired, prejudicially insensitive, or those bereft of hope or vision) may have recovery of sight. (5) The "oppressed" (bruised by societal pressures, beaten down by circumstance, wounded from destructive encounters) can be set at liberty.

(Please turn to page 301.)

Period in which Luke Likely Was Written

Birth of Jesus 4 B.C.	Ascension of Jesus Pentecost A.D. 30	Council of Jerusalem A.D. 49	Persecution by Nero A.D. 64–68	Destruction of temple A.D. 70	Death of John C. A.D. 100

← – – – →

Luke shows the Holy Spirit's power

Master Key: God's Son Revealed

In addition to presenting Jesus as the Savior of the world, Luke gives the following witness of Him:

1. Jesus is the Prophet whose role becomes equated with Servant and Messiah (*see* 4:24; 7:16, 39; 9:19; 24:19).

2. Jesus is the ideal Man, the perfect Savior of imperfect humanity. The title "Son of Man" is found twenty-six times in the Gospel. The term not only emphasizes the humanity of Christ in contrast to the expression "Son of God," which stresses His deity, but it also describes Jesus as the perfect, ideal Man, the true representative of the entire human race.

3. Jesus is Messiah. Not only does Luke affirm Jesus' messianic identity, but he defines the nature of His messiahship. Jesus is preeminently the Servant who steadfastly sets His face to go to Jerusalem to fulfill His role (9:31, 51). Jesus is the Son of David (20:41–44), the Son of Man (5:24), and the Suffering Servant (4:17–19) who was numbered with transgressors (22:37).

4. Jesus is the exalted Lord. Luke refers to Jesus as "Lord" eighteen times in his Gospel (fifty times in Acts). Even though the title takes on new significance after the Resurrection (*see* Acts 2:36), it denotes the divine Person of Jesus even during His earthly ministry.

5. Jesus is the friend of lowly outcasts. He is consistently gracious to society's rejected ones—publicly acknowledged sinners, Samaritans, Gentiles, and the poor. His attitude toward women in a patriarchal age is likewise affirming and sensitive. Luke includes much material that underscores Jesus' positive ministry of kindness and sympathy toward these groups.

Key Word: *Jesus the Son of Man*

*L*uke portrays Christ in His fullest humanity by devoting more of his writing to Christ's feelings and humanity than any other gospel.

Key Verses: Luke 1:3–4; 19:10

Key Chapter: Luke 15

*C*aptured in the three parables of the Lost Sheep, Lost Coin, and Lost Son is the crux of this gospel: that God through Christ has come to seek and to save that which was lost.

Power Key: God's Spirit at Work

Luke refers explicitly to the Holy Spirit seventeen times, stressing His activity in the life of Jesus and previewing His activity in the continuing ministry of Jesus through the church. Four kinds of action are especially significant:

First, the Holy Spirit's action is seen in the lives of various faithful people connected with the births of John the Baptist and Jesus (1:35, 41, 67; 2:25–27), as well as in the fact that John fulfilled his ministry under the anointing of the Holy Spirit (1:15).

Second, the Holy Spirit anoints and empowers Jesus to fulfill His unique ministry as Messiah. In chapters 3 and 4, the five explicit references to the Spirit progress in their force: (1) the Spirit *comes upon* Jesus in bodily form like a dove (3:22); (2) He *leads* Jesus into

(Please turn to page 301.)

at the heartbeat of Jesus' ministry.

Introducing
LUKE

Author. Both style and language offer convincing evidence that the same person wrote Luke and Acts. "The former account" of Acts 1:1 then is likely a reference to the third Gospel as the first of a two-volume series, and the fact that the writer dedicates both books to Theophilus also strongly argues for common authorship. Since church tradition unanimously attributes these two works to Luke the physician, a close associate of Paul (Col. 4:14; 2 Tim. 4:11; Philem. 24), and since the internal evidence supports this view, there is no reason to dispute the Lukan authorship.

Date. Scholars who assume that Luke used Mark's Gospel as a source in writing his own account date the third Gospel in the A.D. seventies. Others, however, point out that Luke wrote his Gospel prior to Acts, which he wrote during Paul's first Roman imprisonment, about A.D. 63. Since Luke was in Caesarea during Paul's two-year incarceration there (Acts 27:1), he would have had ample opportunity during that time to conduct the investigation he mentions in 1:1–4. If this is the case, then Luke's Gospel may be dated around A.D. 59–60, but possibly as late as A.D. 75.

Purpose. Luke clearly states that his purpose in writing this Gospel is to present "an orderly account" (1:3) "of all that Jesus began both to do and teach" (Acts 1:1), so that Theophilus may have historical evidence of the teachings he had received (1:4). While the Gospel is specifically addressed to one individual, apparently a high official, its intent is to give all believers the assurance that Christianity is not one of many speculative systems searching for theological or ethical values, but a movement bound up with an event in history. Luke substantiates the certainty and accuracy of his work with four reasons: (1) his concern with early origins, with priority given to eyewitnesses (v. 2); (2) his aim to be comprehensive, "all things"; (3) chronological, "an orderly account"; and (4) accurate, "the certainty" (v. 4).

In achieving his purpose, Luke traces in his two volumes the Christian movement from its beginnings with Jesus of Nazareth to its development into a worldwide fellowship transcending the limits of Jewish nationality and embracing Jews and Gentiles impartially. Luke presents Jesus not as a mere Jewish Messiah, but as a world Savior.

Content. A distinguishing feature of Luke's Gospel is its emphasis on the universality of the Christian message. From Simeon's song praising Jesus as "a light . . . to the Gentiles" (2:32) to the risen Lord's commission to preach "to all nations" (24:47), Luke stresses the fact that Jesus is not merely the Jewish Deliverer, but the Savior of the entire world.

In order to support this theme, Luke omits much material that is strictly Jewish in character. For example, he does not include Jesus' pronouncement of condemnation upon the scribes and Pharisees (Matthew 23), nor the discussion about Jewish tradition (Matt. 15:1–20; Mark 7:1–23). Luke also excludes the teachings of Jesus in the Sermon on the Mount that deal directly with His relation to the Jewish Law (*see* Matt. 5:21–48; 6:1–8, 16–18). Luke also omits the instructions of Jesus to the Twelve to refrain from ministering to the Gentiles and Samaritans (Matt. 10:5).

On the other hand, Luke includes many features that demonstrate universality. He sets the birth of Jesus in a Roman context (2:1–2; 3:1), showing that what he records has meaning for all people. While Matthew traces Jesus' ancestry from Abraham, Luke follows it back to Adam, connecting the Lord to the entire human race.

However, Luke also emphasizes the Jewish roots of Jesus. Of all the Gospel writers, he alone records the circumcision and dedication of Jesus (2:21–24), as well as His temple visit as a boy of twelve (2:41–52). Luke alone relates the birth and infancy of Jesus in the context of pious Jews such as Simeon, Anna, Zacharias, and Elizabeth, who were among the faithful remnant "waiting for the Consolation of Israel" (2:25). Throughout his Gospel, Luke makes it clear that Jesus is the fulfillment of Old Testament expectations concerning salvation.

A key verse in Luke's Gospel is 19:10, which states that Jesus "has come to seek and to save that which was lost." In presenting Jesus as the Savior of all sorts of people, Luke includes material not found in the other Gospels, such as the account of the Pharisee and the sinful woman (7:36–50); the parables of the lost sheep, coin, and son (15:1–32); the parable of the Pharisee and the tax collector (18:9–14); the story of Zacchaeus (19:1–10); and the pardon of the thief on the cross (23:39–43).

Luke highlights Jesus' warnings about the danger of riches and His sympathy for the poor (*see* 1:53; 4:18; 6:20–21, 24–25; 12:13–21; 14:13; 16:19–31; 19:1–10).

This Gospel has more references to prayer than do the other Gospels. Luke especially emphasizes the prayer life of Jesus, recording seven occasions on which Jesus prayed that are not found elsewhere (*see* 3:21; 5:16; 6:12; 9:18, 29; 11:1; 23:34, 46). Luke alone has the Lord's lessons on prayer taught in the parables of the persistent friend (11:5–10), the persistent widow (18:1–8), and the Pharisee and the tax collector (18:9–14). In addition, the Gospel abounds in notes of praise and thanksgiving (see 1:28, 46–56, 68–79; 2:14, 20, 29–32; 5:25–26; 7:16; 13:13; 17:15; 18:43).

Personal Application. No one who reads this book should feel beyond the reach of the gospel of salvation. Throughout the book, Luke presents Jesus as the Savior of the whole world. This is true from Simeon's song about Jesus being "a light . . . to the Gentiles" (2:32) to the final instructions of the risen Lord to His disciples, in which He told them that "repentance and remission of sins should be preached in His name to all nations" (24:47).

Luke emphasizes the fact that the gospel is not only for Jews, but for all peoples— Greeks, Romans, Samaritans, and all others without regard to race or condition. It is not only for males, but also for females, including widows and prostitutes as well as the socially prominent. It is not only for freemen, but also for slaves and all others rejected by society— the lowly poor, the helplessly weak, the crucified thief, the outcast sinner, the despised tax collector.

Kingdom Key continued from page 298

In the expression, "the acceptable year of the Lord" (4:19), Jesus quotes Isaiah's reference to the ancient "Year of Jubilee" (Leviticus 25). The primary benevolent actions of that celebration—debts are cancelled, property is restored, slaves are freed—have broad ramifications and application to present human need. Jesus penetrates to the core of human pain and problems and declares that the glorious gospel of the kingdom brings "all of the above," including forgiveness, restoration, and liberation.

In his varied terminology for the Holy Spirit's ministry, Luke uses "virtue" (Greek *dunamis*) to describe the grace flowing from Jesus (6:19 and 8:46; see also 5:17 as "the *power* of the Lord"). Luke shows that the kingdom comes because the King has been *anointed* (4:1, 14). Small wonder, then, that he concludes with the Messiah's command to His own (24:44). Here Jesus commands His disciples to be "endued with power from on high." Thereby the advance of the kingdom will be assured where the anointing of the kingdom is received and ministered.

Power Key continued from page 299

the wilderness to be tempted (4:1); (3) following His victory over temptation, Jesus returns to Galilee *empowered by* the same Spirit (4:14); (4) in the Nazareth synagogue Jesus reads the messianic passage, "The Spirit of the LORD is upon Me" (4:18; Is. 61:1–2), *claiming its fulfillment* in Him (4:21); then, (5) He ministers with *abundant charismatic power and compassion* (4:31–44), continuing throughout the whole of His ministry.

Third, the Holy Spirit, through petitionary prayer, implements the messianic ministry. At critical junctures in that ministry, Jesus prays before, during, or after the crucial event (3:21; 6:12; 9:18, 28; 10:21). The same Holy Spirit that was effective through Jesus' prayers will empower the disciples' prayers (18:1–8) and will link His ministry to theirs (see 24:48–49).

Fourth, the Holy Spirit spreads joy, both to Jesus and to the new community. Words denoting joy or exultation are used twice as often in Luke as they are in Matthew or Mark. Examples of such joyfulness include these occasions: When the disciples returned with joy from their mission (10:17) and "Jesus rejoiced in the Spirit" (10:21); and when they waited for the promised Spirit (24:49), and "they worshiped Him, and returned to Jerusalem with great joy, and were continually in the temple, praising and blessing God" (24:52–53).

Surveying
LUKE

I. PROLOGUE 1:1–4.

II. THE INFANCY NARRATIVE 1:5—2:52.

A. Announcement of John the Baptist's birth (1:5–25).

The forerunner (1:5–25). The angel Gabriel appears to a priest named Zechariah, to announce that his wife Elizabeth will bear a son (1:17). This reference to a prediction in Malachi 4:5 is evidence that the Messiah is about to appear. The child will be John the Baptist.

> **"Filled with the Holy Spirit, even from his mother's womb"**
> (1:15). John the Baptist's anointing and message were to come from the presence of the Holy Spirit, enabling him "to turn many of the children of Israel to the Lord their God" and announce the coming of Messiah. John the Baptist, as the last of the Old Testament-style prophets, is specially anointed for the task from birth (Jer. 1:5; see Service).

B. Announcement of Jesus' birth (1:26–38).
Six months after John is conceived, Gabriel visits a young virgin named Mary. The angel announces that Mary is the chosen one. His message is clear. Conception will come by the "power of the Most High" (v. 35). The child will be both "the Son of God" and the one fulfilling the prophet's promise of a king of David's family line. Like the other Gospel writers, Luke establishes the fact that the person of whom he writes is God in the flesh (cf. Matt. 1:23; Mark 1:1; John 1:14; see Women).

C. Visit of the two mothers (1:39–56).
Mary hurries to visit an older relative, Elizabeth, who is the wife of Zechariah.

> **"The babe leaped in her womb; and Elizabeth was filled with the Holy Spirit . . . his father Zacharias was filled with the Holy Spirit"**
> (1:41, 67). The godly character of Elizabeth and Zacharias should be understood as unique to them. Their experiences do not fully explain why John was able to be an effective prophet. Though godly heritage is desirable, godly children do not necessarily follow godly parents. Spirituality is not genetic; it must be developed on the basis

of a personal experience with the Lord Himself, who is the Baptizer with the Holy Spirit.

> **"My soul magnifies the Lord, and my spirit has rejoiced in God my Savior"**
> (1:46–47). Mary's beautiful words follow Elizabeth's prophetic reception of the young girl who is carrying Jesus in her womb. She had nothing to do with the begetting of the child, and her praise declares her thanksgiving and wonder for God's work within her.

D. John the Baptist's birth (1:57–80).
At John's birth Zacharias is moved by the Holy Spirit to prophesy. This and other events surrounding John's birth fill the neighbors with awe.

> **"Zacharias was filled with the Holy Spirit"**
> (1:67). Like Elizabeth in 1:41, Zacharias is experiencing the temporary inspiration of the Holy Spirit, which results in prophecy concerning his own son, John the Baptist, and his mission to herald the coming of Messiah. At this moment, Zacharias is healed from being mute, an affliction which resulted from his doubting God's promise (1:20). This miracle reinforces the uniqueness of John's mission and adds further witness to the coming of Messiah. (See Peace.)

E. Jesus' birth (2:1–40).
Mary and Joseph travel to Bethlehem to be taxed, for Joseph is from David's line and this is his home. The birth takes place in a warm cave, such as are commonly used for stables in that area (vv. 1–7).

The shepherds' report of the angels' visitation is something for Mary to "treasure up" and "ponder in her heart" (vv. 8–20).

> **"Glory to God in the highest, and on earth peace, goodwill toward men!"**
> (2:14). This angelic proclamation points to the redemptive nature of God's coming to earth. Jesus' incarnation was a blessing to every person. The limits of human wisdom and ingenuity would now be superseded by the Prince of Peace, who will one day bring

the peace of His kingdom to every part of our world.

"The shepherds returned, glorifying and praising God for all the things that they had heard and seen, as it was told them"
(2:20). These men were hardened realists, not given to visions and supernatural encounters. But when they heard and saw the angels they were convinced of God's powerful entry into their world, summoning highest praises from their lips.

Jesus' presentation at the temple (2:21–40). Each firstborn son of a Jewish family belongs to the Lord and must be redeemed (cf. Exodus 13—16). At the temple the family is approached by two devout persons, Simeon and Anna. Each is moved by the Spirit to recognize Jesus as the promised Redeemer.

The fact that only two pigeons were offered in sacrifice (2:24) shows the family was poor. If able, they would have offered a lamb (cf. Lev. 5:7). (*See* Thoughts; Women.)

F. The boy Jesus in the temple (2:41–52). A final sketch shows Jesus at the temple on His first Passover trip to Jerusalem. He sits listening to the teachers of the law and asking questions, amazing all with His grasp of spiritual truth (*see* Understanding). Luke's last words about Jesus' childhood tell of His return to Nazareth with His parents, to live as an obedient son in the carpenter's family.

Luke has carefully blended two apparently contradictory themes: (1) Everything about Jesus' birth is unique beginning with His virgin birth. (2) Everything about Jesus' birth is also commonplace. He is born into a poor family, in a stable behind a Bethlehem inn. Jesus is just another Jewish child who is born, grows up, and lives quietly in a small town. For over thirty years Jesus lives this hidden and normal life as a pious, hard-working Jew. His mother has only memories of amazing events to ponder as she watches Him grow to manhood.

III. PREPARATION FOR PUBIC MINISTRY 3:1—4:13.

A. John the Baptist's ministry (3:1–20). John preaches that the Messiah will come soon, promises that "one more powerful than I" will soon appear (*see* Leadership, Spiritual). This person will also baptize, but with the Holy Spirit and fire rather than water.

"He will baptize you with the Holy Spirit and fire"
(3:16). Fire in Scripture represents two vital dimensions of the work of God, both present in the ministry of Christ. First, fire represents power for ministry, as seen in Acts 2. The second is judgment and purification, even of the works of believers (1 Cor. 3:12–15). Both truths are at work in this passage. Jesus will empower His church, and at His Second Coming He will judge all things with fire.

B. Jesus' baptism (3:21–22). Jesus comes to be baptized by His cousin and is identified by the Spirit as God's Son.

C. Jesus' genealogy (3:23–38). This genealogy differs from the one given by Matthew in two ways. Luke's purpose is to show the full humanity of Jesus; Matthew's is to show the right of Jesus to the Davidic throne. Several names differ, for Luke traces the lineage through Mary, and Matthew through Joseph.

D. The temptation (4:1–13). Luke gives a different sequence of the temptations than Matthew (4:1–11). Matthew's theme is Jesus as the promised King. Thus to him the offer of all the world's kingdoms is the culminating test. Luke emphasizes Jesus' humanity, and the culminating temptation is the suggestion to prove God's presence by leaping from the temple (9–12; *see* ch. 55, §6).

"Then Jesus, being filled with the Holy Spirit"
(4:1). Too often the infilling with the Holy Spirit is viewed as a kind of apex to the Christian life. In Jesus, the evidence is that it was actually the launching of His ministry. This concept is supported later at the birth of the church when Luke cites in Acts 2:4, "They were filled . . . and began." The qualifying nature of the infilling with the Holy Spirit is such that it prepares a person for moving into areas of spiritual warfare and conquest. After Jesus was filled, He was led into the wilderness for the confrontation with Satan.

"When the devil had ended every temptation, he departed from Him until an opportune time"
(4:13). The temptation of Jesus was com-
continued on next page

continued from preceding page

plete in both the substance of the temptation and the power that attended it (Heb. 4:15). Jesus was tempted physically, emotionally, and spiritually. His victory is a monumental triumph in the history of the redemption of God's people. However, notice that the devil withdrew from Him "until an opportune time." The devil's plan is to seek out times of weakness, discouragement, exhaustion, or diminished capacity to wage his most furious assaults on the people of God.

IV. THE GALILEAN MINISTRY 4:14—9:50.

A. At Nazareth and Capernaum (4:14–44).

Jesus is rejected at Nazareth (4:16–30). In His home synagogue Jesus reads an Old Testament passage about the Messiah and applies it to Himself! This stimulates a furious reaction (*see* Wrath).

Israel suffered for centuries under the rule of Gentiles. They want the Savior to appear, but not to save them from their own sins. They want Him to come and punish the foreigners they hate! Ultimately, they will reject God's Son and His message of forgiveness (*see* Kingdom of God).

Jesus' ministries (4:31–44). The Old Testament prophets speak of Messiah's mission as one of saving and of judging. When Jesus reads from Isaiah 61 in the synagogue (4:17–20) He emphasizes release and stops just before reading these words: "and the day of vengeance of our God" (61:2). Now Luke demonstrates Jesus' mission to the oppressed.

> **"What a word this is!"**
> (4:33–36). The proof of Jesus' power is in the authority of His Word. Now His authority has been given to the church (Eph. 1:20–23), and His people are privileged to speak His Word with power. John 12:49 underscores the principle by which the word of authority works—"I have not spoken on My own authority; but the Father." Understanding the heart of the Father and His will for a particular situation provides the key to the believer functioning in this authority.

B. From the call of Peter to the call of the Twelve (5:1—6:16).

Jesus' command to the professional fishermen who became His first disciples leads to a great catch of fish, so

astonishing that Peter falls down before Jesus and begs Him to leave! "Don't be afraid," Jesus says, and promises "from now on you will catch men" (v. 10). Jesus not only deals with sin but enables the sinner to serve God (*see* Faith, Seed).

The leper healed (5:12–16). Three Gospels tell this story emphasizing Jesus' willingness to deal with *and touch* this man, whose disease made him an outcast.

Now the religious leaders come to observe this new preacher and healer. As they watch, a paralytic is brought to Jesus for healing (vv. 17–26; *see* Healing, Divine). Seeing the faith of the man and those who carry him, Jesus announces, "Friend, your sins are forgiven" (20). The teachers of the law see this as blasphemy. Only God can forgive sin, and they will not recognize Jesus as God's Son. So Christ shows His authority to forgive by healing the man. (*See* Perceived.)

Jesus calls Levi, a man we know better as Matthew, author of the first Gospel (27–32).

Jesus and new wineskins (5:33–39). Jesus intends to initiate a new era. The new will not fit in the container for the old; new ways of life will come that fit the new revelation Jesus brings.

Jesus is Lord of the Sabbath (6:1–11). The Sabbath is set apart in the Old Testament as a day of rest, patterned on God's own rest after creation (Genesis 1). The Pharisees belong to a religious sect that places supreme value on keeping the details of Mosaic Law. Now Jesus shows up the hard-heartedness of these men, whose religion fails to reflect God's values. Immediately He acts to heal a man with a shriveled hand, while the Pharisees and teachers of the law watch closely, hoping to accuse Him. Boldly Jesus announces that it is "lawful to do good" on the Sabbath.

C. Sermon on the Plain (6:17–49).

> **"A great multitude . . . came to hear Him and be healed of their diseases, as well as those who were tormented with unclean spirits. And they were healed. And the whole multitude sought to touch Him, for power went out from Him and healed them all."**
> (6:17–19). Jesus' healing ministry is not restricted to a particular type of need or a particular type of person. The compassion of the Savior and the needs of people converge as the multitude comes to Christ.

The Beatitudes (vv. 20–26) show that Jesus values persons for themselves alone.

Following Jesus means learning a new value system which puts disciples in conflict with society and often will lead to rejection. Social acceptability has never been a sign of spiritual achievement!

"Love your enemies" (vv. 27–36) reveals that our human interpersonal relationships (see Brotherly Love) are to model our relationships on God, who is merciful (see Bless) and "kind to the ungrateful and wicked."

Relationships with others are to be free of judging, filled with forgiveness (v. 37; see Faith, Seed).

> **"For every tree is known by its own fruit"**
> (6:43–44). A healthy tree does not bear decayed fruit, nor does a sickly tree produce good fruit (v. 43). Here Jesus explains the relationship between heart and action—life lived by Law tends toward hypocrisy, condemning others to cover up inconsistency (vv. 41–42), but life lived righteously proceeds from the heart's good treasure, with good character producing right conduct (v. 45). Since the tree "is known by its own fruit" (v. 44), when believers pursuing Christlike behavior allow the Holy Spirit to infuse the fullness of Christ's life into their hearts, the good fruit of Christlike actions proceeds from their lives (see Gal. 5:16, 18, 22–25).

D. Narrative and dialogue (7:1—9:50).

The centurion (7:1–10). The prime model of faith in Jesus is not a Jew but a Roman army officer. He asks Jesus simply to say the word, and the servant will be healed. The officer explains that he is a man "under authority." That is, others obey him because ultimately all the power of Rome stands behind his orders. To see Jesus too as one "under authority" is to recognize that all of God's power stands behind what He says and does!

Jesus raises the widow's son (7:11–17).

John the Baptist is shaken when Jesus does not set up the expected kingdom immediately (v. 20). John's messengers are sent back with a report of miracles of healing. Messiah is to care for the oppressed as well as to judge.

Jesus is anointed by a sinful woman (vv. 36–50).

> **"Your faith has *saved you"**
> (7:50). We receive forgiveness through faith in Christ. Jesus certifies the

woman's act of devotion—in washing His feet and tearfully anointing them—as faith. The woman's consciousness of her sins (v. 47) and her hopeless debt bring a repentance, humility, and devotion that lead to salvation.

Training the disciples (chs. 8—9). The crowds following Jesus are large (see Women). But this parable of the sower points out that only a few will respond to Jesus' words.

Jesus now performs four miracles, most witnessed primarily by the Twelve (vv. 22–56). This series of miracles shows the full scope of Jesus' power: over nature, over the demonic, over disease, and over death (see Healing, Divine).

> **"Your faith has made you well"**
> (8:48). Without Jesus' knowledge the woman touched the hem of His garment and she was healed. Jesus is very clear that her faith—not His—healed her. She believed that God would heal her if she could get close enough to Jesus. Healing was the reward of her faith. Though there is no absolute one-to-one correlation between the exercise of faith and the miracle of healing, the absence of faith certainly causes many to miss God's healing and blessing.

Jesus now sends out the Twelve with authority to heal and preach (9:1–9).

> **"He sent them to preach the kingdom of God and to heal the sick"**
> (9:1–6). Healing in the New Testament is provided for three distinct reasons. (1) Healing comes from the compassionate heart of God for people in pain and disease. (2) Healing comes as a result of the presence of God's kingdom (see Kingdom of God) overthrowing the works of hell and taking back the things lost to sin and resulting sickness. (3) Healing comes to confirm the gospel preached and to witness to the Person and power of Christ. The disciples are given the ministry of both proclamation and healing as part of their function in God's kingdom.

Feeding the five thousand (9:10–17). When Jesus feeds the crowds, it is the disciples who know the full scope of the miracle. All these experiences strengthen the disciples' faith for the confession that now comes (cf. 8:25 with 9:20).

Peter's confession of faith (9:18–27). The crowds identify Jesus with one of the great prophets of long ago. But the disciples are now ready to affirm Him as "the Christ of God" (v. 20).

The Transfiguration (9:28–36). Jesus' Transfiguration gives three of the Twelve a glimpse of the glory about which Jesus has spoken (see Majesty).

Following Jesus (9:46–56). The disciples have realized who Jesus is but are still far from sharing His attitudes and values. This is shown as the disciples fall to bickering over which of them will be greatest. (See Destroy.)

V. THE TRAVEL NARRATIVE (ON THE WAY TO JERUSALEM) 9:51—19:27.

When some Samaritans refuse to welcome Jesus and His followers into their village, James and John want to call down fire from heaven to destroy them. The disciples must still learn that belief in Jesus is simply a beginning. Progress along the way requires a transformation of attitudes and values, until the follower reflects his Lord.

The necessity of choice (9:57–62). This chapter concludes with three brief sketches of people who want to follow Christ. To each there is a single message: unconditional commitment to Jesus is a requirement of discipleship.

Seventy-two missionaries sent out (10:1–24). Earlier Jesus sent out the Twelve. Now seventy-two are sent out in pairs to preach and heal.

> **"Heal the sick there, and say to them, 'The kingdom of God has come near to you' "**
> (10:9). The confrontation between "the ruler of this world," Satan (John 14:30), and the kingdom of God is seen clearly in the ministry of healing (see Healing, Divine). Not all sickness is related to the activity of demons, but wherever the kingdom of God is proclaimed, healing of the sick and casting out of demons occur, both in the ministry of Christ and His disciples. The kingdom of God brings health and freedom.

> **"Rejoice because your names are written in heaven"**
> (10:17–19). Jesus puts the deliverance ministry of the disciples in perspective by directing their attention to the most remarkable of miracles: their salvation. This does not negate the miracle of exorcism or relegate it to insignificance. However, the human preoccupation with power (v. 17) must always be balanced with the priority of the person.

The story of the Good Samaritan (vv. 25–37; see Human Worth).

In the home of some of His followers, two sisters respond differently to Jesus (vv. 38–42; see Women). One is distracted by work; the other sits at Jesus' feet and listens. Mary, the listener, has "chosen what is better."

Jesus on prayer (11:1–13). The "disciples' prayer" (v. 2) begins with confidence in the unique relationship we have with God in Christ. He is "Father" as well as Sovereign Lord (see Kingdom of God)!

Jesus' illustration of the man who knocks at a friend's door to ask for bread involves teaching by contrast. One who needs to borrow from a neighbor may get what he wants simply by making so much noise the bread is given to be rid of him! But God is our Father, and all who come to God as Father in prayer will receive.

Opposition develops (11:14–53). Jesus' growing popularity alarms the religious leaders, who feel their place and authority threatened. Jesus answers their charges, but refuses to give them more signs except the "sign of Jonah"; as Jonah was in the whale, so Jesus will lie for three days in the grave.

> **"Surely the kingdom of God has come upon you"**
> (11:20). The *kingdom of God brings the rulership of the King to every situation where it is invited. Jesus' deliverance ministry demonstrates the power of the kingdom of God overruling the lesser kingdom of darkness. The proclamation of Luke 4:18 places exorcism within the appropriate scope of Jesus' ministry. And all believers are privileged to function in the power of this kingdom (Luke 17:21).

It is while dining at a Pharisee's house, not before the crowds, that Jesus scathingly exposes the spiritual *darkness He has just spoken of symbolically (vv. 35–54). Rather than respond with repentance, the Pharisees and teachers of the law "assail Him vehemently."

Jesus on materialism: on guard (12:1–12). The disciples of Jesus are to be on guard against the ways of the Pharisees.

The rich fool (12:13–21) reflects the materialistic attitude common to the Pharisees.

Do not worry (12:22–32)! God cares for the flowers and the birds. We, "much more valuable" to God than these, need not worry about "what you will eat or drink." Without the pressure of worry about future needs, we are able to give freely to others.

> ### "O you of little faith"
> (12:28). The human propensity to fret over the most mundane of needs belies God's commitment to provide for His children (Ps. 37:25). Our call to faith is in seeking the advancement of the kingdom of God (v. 31). The Father will provide all we need to accomplish His purpose.

Jesus does not promise an easy life, for His own life is filled with stress and tension. And discernment is needed for both the times and the people that can cause this tension (12:49–59).

Call for repentance (13:1–35). Jesus warns His hearers that they must repent or they too will perish (1–5; see Sinners). God has given Israel its last opportunity to produce fruit (6–9).

A woman comes to a synagogue while Jesus is teaching. He heals her—and is again criticized for "working" on the Sabbath (10–17)!

> ### "'Woman, you are loosed from your infirmity.' And He laid His hands on her, and immediately she was made straight, and glorified God"
> (13:10–17). This healing prompted the indignant response of the synagogue ruler. Jesus broke the legalistic notion that people were created to observe religious ritual; He insisted that God created His Law to help and serve people. Healing on the Sabbath was not a crime, but a sensitive response to the crippling effects of sickness. Jesus' answer elevates people, not the Law, to the focus of God's heart and passion.

Two parables (vv. 18–21) suggest that God's kingdom begins with the small and grows gradually, becoming all pervasive.

The narrow door (vv. 22–30) Jesus refers to is repentance and willingness to associate oneself with the small and apparently insignificant. (See Cures.)

At a Pharisee's house (14:1–14). The same old conflicts between Jesus and the religious people of His time again emerge (1–6).

The parable of the banquet (14:15–24). The sullen unresponsiveness of the religious leaders causes Jesus to tell a story about a great banquet and the guests who are invited to come. One after another they hang back until, angry at all the excuses, the homeowner sends his servants out to fill the hall with the outcasts of society.

Jesus' disciples may not be "socially acceptable," but they are those who respond to God's invitation to come!

The cost of discipleship (14:25–35). Each listener is invited to consider the cost before making his or her commitment.

Parables of God's love (ch. 15). The parable of the lost sheep (15:1–7) and the parable of the lost coin (15:8–10) show that God does welcome sinners—and rejoices when even one turns to Him.

The two earlier stories have prepared the way for what we know as the story of the two sons. The young son is given the freedom he demands by his father, but the choices he makes lead to personal disaster as he becomes "the prodigal." Finally this son comes to his senses. He returns to his father, ready to confess his sin and hoping to be accepted as a hired man. The father welcomes him back with joy and orders a feast prepared for him.

The second (older) son is angry that the father is so forgiving. Like the Pharisees, the older son will neither see his own attitude as sin nor take any joy in the rescue of his brother from sin's bondage.

Use of possessions (ch. 16). The shrewd manager (16:1–18). A business manager about to be fired (see Put Out) goes to his employer's creditors and has them falsify their debts. The employer later commends the manager, not for his dishonesty, but because he looked ahead and tried to use possessions in his care to prepare for his future!

The money-loving Pharisees who hear the story sneer (14–15), but Jesus is speaking of them. Love of money means devotion to one of this world's idols (13) and conflicts with love of God. Like the dishonest manager, Jesus' hearers should at least look ahead and prepare for the eternity that awaits them (see Kingdom of God; Word of God).

The rich man and Lazarus (16:19–31). The story Jesus now tells underlines the importance of preparing for eternity and receiving the testimony of Scripture. (See Angels.)

The coming kingdom (ch. 17). Jesus tells His disciples that they are to extend unlimited forgiveness to each other (1–4).

> **"The apostles said to the Lord, 'Increase our faith.'"**
> (17:5–6). These had witnessed the most awesome of miracles, and now they asked for an increase of faith. They believed—but Jesus now changes the paradigm on their understanding of their mission. Forgiveness—seven times in one day, the same person for the same offense (v. 4)—requires faith that goes beyond miracles. It demands the transformation of our lives and the softening of our hearts toward the failings of others. This is faith in the midst of the most unfair of situations, and in spite of repeated evidence of wrong. This faith replaces our self-preservation instinct with trust in the Lord, who will protect and keep us.

When ten lepers are healed, only one turns back to thank Jesus (vv. 11–19).

> **"Were there not ten cleansed? But where are the nine? Were there not any found who returned to give glory to God except this foreigner?"**
> (17:12–19). Healing glorifies God (*see* Healing, Divine). Jesus conveys a deeper meaning to the one returning leper when He says, "Your faith has *made you well*" (v. 19). This indicates a complete healing that transcends his deliverance from leprosy. The others were cured by a gracious act of Christ; this one was saved by faith.

Jesus explains to the Pharisees that the kingdom is "among you" (v. 21; *see* Kingdom of God), and in this He means that the kingdom is now present in the person of the King. Later Jesus talks with His disciples. The time will come when Jesus is no longer with them. Then His return will be visible, sudden—and unexpected by the people who live on the earth (28–37).

> **"As the lightning that flashes . . . , so also the Son of Man will be in His day"**
> (17:22–37). Lightning is unmistakable in the evening sky, and lightning occurs in an instant of time. Believers will not have to guess about Jesus' return—it will be bright as lightning—but neither will they have time to prepare; His coming will be instantaneous. All believers should be in a permanent state of readiness for Christ's return.

Various incidents (18:1—19:27). It is nearly time for Jesus to enter Jerusalem for His last week. Luke groups several incidents that are not closely related.

The persistent widow (18:1–8).

The Pharisee and tax collector (18:9–14).

A wealthy ruler (18:15–30) asks Jesus what he can "do to inherit eternal life." To reveal to this "good" man his own need, Jesus tells him to sell his possessions and give all to the poor. This is not a general command for all believers, but a specific command to a specific individual, designed to show him that, for all his "goodness," he values his money more than his God (22–23).

Jesus again tells His disciples of His rapidly approaching death (vv. 31–34; *see* Insulted), and heals a blind man (35–43).

> **"He received his sight, and followed Him, glorifying God. And all the people, when they saw it, gave praise to God"**
> (18:43). Praise is the only reasonable response to the working of a miracle—by both the blind man and the onlookers. The shout of praise, the uplifted hands of praise, and exuberance are all natural responses to a work of God in this magnitude. They reflect no liturgical practice or trained response. They are the overflow of hearts touched by the presence of God's compassion and power.

Zacchaeus's conversion (19:1–10; *see* Salvation) and response to Jesus are witnessed by a change in his values.

Several servants of a nobleman are given sums of money to put to work for their master. Those who use the money wisely are rewarded, but the servant who does not put his resources to work loses what he has (vv. 11–27). In Jesus' story those who serve are each given the same praise and proportionate rewards.

VI. THE JERUSALEM MINISTRY 19:28—21:38.

A. Events at Jesus' entry (19:28–48). Jesus enters Jerusalem early Sunday morning. The crowds shout praises, but onlooking Pharisees insist Jesus rebuke His followers!

> **"I tell you that if these should keep silent, the stones would immediately cry out"** (19:40). Jesus' triumphal entry into Jerusalem marks the coming of the Son of God who is about to fulfill His mission—to die for the sins of the world. The multitude is ignorant of the significance of Christ's coming, but the long-sought-for redemption of humanity's sin is about to be accomplished. All people were created to praise the Lord, and at this pinnacle moment the very creation would have cried out at the presence of Jesus the King had the crowd failed to respond.

Jesus enters the temple and drives out the merchants. This further arouses the chief priests.

B. Controversy stories (20:1—21:4).
Jesus' authority questioned (20:1–19). Jesus refuses to respond when the chief priests and elders demand to know the source of His authority.

Traps avoided (20:20–40). Some of the leaders try to trick Jesus into open conflict, but He easily avoids the traps.

Hypocrisy and faith (20:41—21:4). Jesus now turns on His questioners. He demands that they explain how the Christ can be both David's descendant and David's Lord. The only possible answer is that the Christ is both God and man. But the "leaders" remain silent.

C. Eschatological discourse (21:5–38).
Each of the synoptic Gospels contains Jesus' teachings to His disciples about what will take place after His death and resurrection. (See Souls.)

VII. THE PASSION AND GLORIFICATION OF JESUS 22:1—24:53.

A. The Passover meal (22:1–38).
Betrayal! (22:1–6). Judas, one of the Twelve, has gone to the chief priests and arranged to betray Jesus for money.

The Last Supper (22:7–38; see ch. 55, §6.1). Jesus announces that His body and blood will institute the long-promised new covenant (17–23). Jesus again must emphasize servanthood as His disciples argue over which of them is greatest (24–30). Peter's denial is predicted (31–38; see Lack).

B. The passion, death, and burial of Jesus (22:39—23:56).

The long night (22:39–71). The supper ends, and Jesus is launched on a final night on earth. He is arrested while praying (39–53). Peter follows the mob, but in a courtyard outside the building where Jesus is being tried, Peter denies Jesus three times (54–62). Mocked and beaten by the temple guard, Jesus admits openly what He has often taught: He is the Son of God (63–71).

Before Pilate (23:1–25). The leaders of the council bring Jesus to Pilate and charge Him with "subverting the nation" by claiming to be king. Neither Pilate nor Herod will condemn Jesus. Pilate announces that he will punish then release Jesus. But the leaders loudly shout their demand: "Crucify him!" Pilate finally bows to the pressure and turns Jesus over to be executed.

The Crucifixion (23:26–43). Crucifixion is an especially painful form of death. Jesus is hung on a cross between two criminals and jeered at by those who stand and watch.

Jesus' death and burial (23:44–56). Jesus' life was not torn from him. He did not die under protest, struggling against the inevitable. After several hours on the Cross, as a curtain of darkness is drawn over the scene, Jesus commits Himself to His Father and dies.

Jesus' death comes long before the normal two to three days expected for crucifixion. One of the council of elders, who did not agree with the verdict against Jesus, boldly goes to Pilate and asks permission to bury the body. Because the next day is the first day of the festival of Passover, the body must be buried without preparation. Jesus' body is laid in a tomb cut into the rock near Calvary, and His sorrowful followers leave to observe the days of rest.

C. The Resurrection and the Ascension (24:1–53).
On the Sunday following the Crucifixion several women go out to the tomb. They find the stone rolled away and are told by angels not to "look for the living among the dead"! Just as Jesus promised, He has been raised (vv. 1–12).

The blindness of the disciples is linked to a common blindness (vv. 13–35) to one Old Testament truth: that the promised King would also be a suffering Savior (Is. 52:13—53:12). When two of Jesus' followers walk home that afternoon to a village called Emmaus, the Lord joins them, unrecognized. The two share their dashed hopes and tell of resurrection rumors, which they do not believe (cf. 24:17). Jesus then traces through the Old Testament those passages that tell of Messiah's suffering. Finally, together in the Emmaus home, the disciples' eyes are opened and they recognize Jesus! He disappears, but they do not hesitate. They rush back to Jerusalem to join the Eleven, who have also at last realized, "It's true!"

Luke carefully reports other post-Resurrection appearances of Jesus. But most important to Luke, Jesus now opens their minds so they can understand the Scriptures. The Resurrection puts the whole Old Testament in a new perspective. (*See* Troubled.)

Jesus is with them for only a short time. When the appointed days pass, Jesus returns to the Father. But He leaves His followers with a great promise. He will send them the Spirit, and soon each one will be "clothed with power from on high."

"Repentance and remission of sins should be preached"
(24:47–48). The witness that comes through preaching will call for an action on the part of the listener (*see* Evangelism).

Jesus states clearly what those actions are to be. Additionally, He includes actions to be evidenced in the life of the preachers (24:48). As effective witnesses to Jesus, our lives will carry the greatest impact in sharing the Good News when we *flesh out* the things we are preaching.

"Tarry in the city of Jerusalem until you are endued with power from on high"
(24:49). Jesus had received such power at His baptism and now insists at His ascension that His disciples receive it themselves. This promise of the Holy Spirit also was declared in Isaiah 44:3 and Joel 2:28. As Luke continues his New Testament record in Acts 1:8 we are reminded again of this promise, which is fulfilled in Acts 2:1–4.

TRUTH-IN-ACTION through THE SYNOPTIC GOSPELS

EDITORIAL NOTE: Scholars refer to Matthew, Mark, and Luke as the synoptic Gospels because they are parallel accounts of the life and ministry of Jesus of Nazareth. To offer maximum insight into a faithful application of the teaching of Jesus recounted in the synoptic Gospels and to avoid unnecessary repetition, we are presenting this summary of the first three Gospels. In this chart, each "Action" will reference, as appropriate, from one to three of the Synoptics.

Truth the Synoptics Teach	**Action** the Synoptics Invite
1 Guidelines for Growing in Godliness With the Gospels, as with the whole NT godliness (or godly living) takes on a new dimension. Jesus has come and demonstrated the desirability of personal godliness, and given the Holy Spirit to live this life through us. As a result, we have the hope of experiencing the very life of God. Jesus' life and teaching gave us instruction in how to live a godly life. Though godliness never earns access to heaven from Earth, through godly living we discover the blessing of heaven on Earth.	**Matt. 5:17–20** *Understand* that Jesus' ministry fulfilled the Law; it did not abolish it. *Be warned* that those who teach lawlessness will not be great in the kingdom. **Matt. 5:31, 32; 19:4–6; Mark 10:6–12; Luke 16:18** *Understand* that divorce must never be employed as an expedient. *Recognize* that divorce upsets the intended created order and is, therefore, sin. **Matt. 10:32, 33; Luke 12:8, 9** *Boldly confess* Jesus before others; *believe* He will acknowledge you before the Father. **Matt. 15:1–9; Mark 7:1–13** *Beware* the danger of religious tradition. *Recognize* and *guard against* the tendency of men to teach religious tradition as a substitute for God's Word. **Luke 12:47, 48** *Know* that those who have the greatest knowledge of truth will be held accountable for the greatest fruitfulness.
2 Steps to Holiness Under the Old Covenant, holiness called Israel to live distinctly from the nations, primarily in the external matters of the Law. However, Jesus calls His people to a holiness that proceeds from the heart. Holiness is now the outcome	**Matt. 5:13–16; Mark 9:50; Luke 11:33; 14:34, 35** *Recognize* that your life has either a positive or negative effect. *Live* responsibly to bring glory to God. **Matt. 6:24; Luke 16:13** *Be loyal* to God. *Forsake* any ambition that compromises your commitment to God. **Matt. 10:28; Luke 12:4, 5** *Acknowledge* that only God has power over death and hell. *Have reverence* for Him. *(continued)*

Truth the Synoptics Teach	**Action** the Synoptics Invite
2 Steps to Holiness *(continued)* of personal loyalty to God and the realization of the fulfilling fruitfulness originally intended for mankind.	**Matt. 22:15–22; Mark 12:13–17; Luke 20:20–26** *Discern* between "Caesar's" claims and those of God. *Honor* the Lord as the highest authority.
3 Steps to Dynamic Devotion Whereas the Old Covenant focused on the external practices of devotion, Jesus presents devotion as a matter of the heart. He contrasts sincere, heartfelt devotion with the external. hypocritical, pretentious practices of piety among the Pharisees. He warns His disciples against allowing even genuine, good works to distract from whole-hearted devotion to Him. Devotion is a matter of developing an intimate relationship with the living God, learning the warmth of a life that draws near to His Father-heart.	**Matt. 6:5–8** *Always pray* in an honest and sincere manner. *Experience* times of private prayer. *Forsake* any display of religion that is done only for man's approval. **Matt. 6:9–13; Luke 11:2–4** *Employ* "The Lord's Prayer" daily as an outline for personal worship, intercession, petition, warfare, and praise. **Luke 10:38–42** *Avoid* setting the Lord's work as a priority over the Lord's Presence. *Prefer* "Mary's place," learning at the feet of Jesus Himself, but *serve* like Martha whom He commended. **Luke 18:1–8** *Practice* patient, persistent, persevering prayer. **Matt. 22:34–40; Mark 12:28–34; Luke 10:25–28** *Know* that only total love for God can empower you to *love rightly* yourself and your neighbor. **Matt. 26:26–29; Mark 14:22–25; Luke 22:15–20** *Celebrate* the Lord's Supper often. *Approach* it with faith, receiving the life and healing it provides.
4 Steps to Faithful Obedience Obeying the Father was supremely important to Jesus. Obedience is the response of faith to any instruction from God. Jesus taught that true faith will always be manifested in obedience to God's revealed will. Successful Christian living results from seeking and knowing God's will and then doing it in faith.	**Luke 1:38** *Adopt* Mary's attitude. *Submit* your plans and future to God's will. **Matt. 6:22, 23; Luke 11:34–36** *Be full* of the light of life so that there is no darkness in you. Have a "good" eye. *Develop* a personal commitment to the Lord and His will. **Matt. 13:1–23; Mark 4:1–20; Luke 8:4–15** *Be aware* that the fruitfulness of the Word of God in your life is determined by your receptivity and teachability. *Determine* to obey God's Word. **Matt. 26:39; Mark 14:36; Luke 22:42** *Prefer* God's will to your own.
5 Steps in Developing Humility Jesus has a great deal to say about humility. And no wonder, since it was pride that first caused man's downfall. As the New Adam, Jesus exemplified this aspect of righteous living. Man fell because he presumed his own way above God's, but restored godliness requires that man do the opposite and humble himself before God's will and way. Then true God-given exaltation and recognition will come to those who least expect it and who least seek it.	**Matt. 5:38–42; Luke 6:29, 30** *Renounce* any form of retaliation. *Leave* all vengeance to God. **Matt. 5:43–48; Luke 6:27, 28, 32–36** *Love* by choice, not by circumstance. *Let* mistreatment by others remind you to *overcome their evil* through love. **Matt. 18:21–35; Luke 17:3, 4** *Forgive* daily those who have sinned against you. *Allow* God's forgiving nature to guide you in forgiving others. **Luke 14:7–11** *Humble* yourself. *Be wary* of the serious danger of pride and arrogance. *Avoid striving* for public recognition and *promoting* yourself or your ministry. **Luke 18:9–14** *Recognize* and *confess* before God any sin in your life. *Do not seek to justify yourself* by comparing yourself with other sinners.
6 Keys to Godly Relationships A major emphasis of Jesus' teaching is how to build and maintain right relationships with God and man. He views these relationships as neither unimportant nor extraneous, but as the essence of which life is made. Knowing God is our highest priority, but this pursuit should not replace or diminish our interpersonal relationships with	**Matt. 5:21, 22** *Know* that Jesus equates anger with murder. *Be very careful* how you speak to others lest hateful words bring you into God's judgment. **Matt. 5:24, 25; Luke 12:57, 58** *Practice* instant reconciliation. *Understand* that conflicts cause much greater damage to relationships when left unresolved. **Matt. 6:14; Mark 11:25** *Understand* that God forgives us our sins as we forgive others who have sinned against us. *Adopt* the forgiveness of others into your prayer life as a daily discipline.

(continued)

Truth the Synoptics Teach	**Action** the Synoptics Invite
6 Keys to Godly Relationships (continued) others. Rather, our personal interaction with God should produce within us the qualities of character that build and sustain all our relationships.	**Matt. 7:1–5; Luke 6:37, 38, 41, 42** *Correct* your faults and solve your own problems before attempting to correct faults or problems in others. *Let* any judgmental attitude in yourself signal the need to *examine yourself* for things that bother you about others.
7 How to Develop Dynamic Discipleship With Jesus, righteousness no longer consists in observance of an external legal code. Jesus defines it as an apprenticeship to Himself as Master Teacher through the Holy Spirit. Righteousness is now defined by the Person of Jesus and not by the Law. However, this Person who is righteousness requires our loyalty: true discipleship requires total commitment without distraction or compromise.	**Matt. 10:17–20** *Understand* that legalistic religion is a ferocious enemy of the loving "life" quality of the kingdom of God. *Trust* that Jesus will give you the wisdom and words to overcome such opposition. **Matt. 10:37–39; Luke 14:26, 27** *Know for certain* that Jesus requires a loyalty to Himself greater than loyalty to any other human being. *Understand* that discipleship means submitting your own interests in favor of God's. **Matt. 10:34–36; Luke 12:51–53** *Recognize* and *anticipate* that personal discipleship and commitment to Jesus can even result in division and rejection. **Matt. 16:24–26; Mark 8:34–36; Luke 9:23–25** *Understand* and *accept* that discipleship means forsaking all selfish personal ambition. *Know for certain* that every true disciple must take up his cross. **Matt. 28:18–20** *Recognize* that Jesus calls His disciples to go to people of all nations and *teach* them how to know Him and live for Him. *Teach* others that Christ must be the center of all their life. **Matt. 8:18–22; Luke 9:57–62** *Remember* that the demands of discipleship are costly. *Know* that God will test all of your relationships to prove that following Jesus is your highest priority.
8 Keys to Understanding God's Kingdom The dominant theme of Jesus' teaching is the kingdom of God. Jesus presents numerous word-pictures of what this supernatural realm "is like." But the kingdom is not merely to be understood with the mind. Rather, it is spiritual and is to be comprehended and entered into by spiritual means and in practical living. Let us meditate daily on Jesus' words in order to receive the keys of the kingdom.	**Matt. 11:12–14; Luke 16:16** *Enter* the kingdom of God by "violent" determination. *Be aggressive* about serving Christ. **Luke 17:20, 21** *Understand* that the kingdom is an internal rulership unobservable by the natural eye. **Matt. 13:44–52** *Recognize* that the kingdom of God requires your highest commitment. *Understand* that the kingdom is worth more than any other pursuit. *Be ready* to forsake any personal goal that hinders your entering into it. **Matt. 18:1–5; Mark 9:33–37; Luke 9:46–48** *Recognize* that kingdom people are childlike (not childish) in their faith, trust, and blamelessness. *Pursue* childlikeness in all your interpersonal dealings.
9 Keys to Wise Living Jesus motivates His disciples to live righteously by emphasizing that such living comes from the heart with love and in trust, more than through observance of an external code of ethics. Conse-quently, NT wisdom reveals the differences between a correct behavior, based only on the Law, and righteous actions that proceed from the heart of a new life reborn in Christ.	**Matt. 7:13, 14; Luke 13:23, 24** *Suspect* things that are popular or favored by the world-minded majority. **Matt. 15:10–20; Mark 7:14–23** *Understand* that evil originates in the heart. **Matt. 7:15–20; Luke 6:43–45** *Understand* that the results of an individual's life and work are better indications of personal motives than are appearance or claims. **Matt. 7:21–23; Luke 6:46; 13:24–30** *Be warned* that what you practice demonstrates your relationship with Jesus. *Never undervalue* obedience. *Know* that many who expect divine approval will receive censure or even judgment instead. **Luke 16:14, 15** *Beware* of judging yourself and your success by human standards. *Remember* that popularity and human approval do not necessarily indicate God's approval of a situation. *(continued)*

Truth the Synoptics Teach	**Action** the Synoptics Invite
9 Keys to Wise Living (continued)	**Matt. 20:20–28; Mark 10:35–37; Luke 22:24–27** *Understand* that God's kingdom authority and the world's systems of authority are often opposites.
10 Learning the Righteous Use of Money Although in the Bible wealth is shown as an aspect of God's blessing and approval. the NT brings the added emphasis of the possession and use of wealth or money in connection with heart attitude and internal motivation. A righteous heart does not serve money. Mammon is closely associated with money—perhaps even naming the demonic principality dominating the world's economy. Jesus equates love for money with the service of mammon. Money must be handled carefully and used wisely lest desire for it seduce us from true devotion to God.	**Matt. 6:19–24; Luke 12:33, 34** *Remember* your heart follows your treasures. *Put your treasures* where you want your life to be. *Avoid* misplacing your affections and loyalty because of personal possessions. *Sell* unnecessary or distracting possessions and give the money to the poor or to the Lord's work. **Luke 12:13–15** *Practice* generosity toward God! *Stop* any form of hoarding (fear-motivated clamoring for "things") or laying up treasures on Earth. **Luke 16:1–13** *Employ* material wealth for the kingdom, not for personal selfish ambition. *Remember* that such a use of your financial resources has eternal results. **Matt. 19:21–26; Mark 10:21–27; Luke 18:22–27** *Free* your heart of your possessions. *Do not seek* your security in financial holdings or material possessions.
11 Miscellaneous Instructions Here are several important instructions found in the synoptic Gospels, but which are not included in the above categories.	**Matt. 3:11, 12; Mark 1:8; Luke 3:16, 17** *Expect* and *welcome* the refining work of the *Holy Spirit* as the result of His indwelling and continual infilling. **Matt. 5:27–30** *Develop* a godly hatred for all immorality and sexual sin. *Know* that sexual sin begins with a lustful thought, glance, or inappropriate touch. **Matt. 6:25–34; Luke 12:22–34** *Name worry* as sin. *Discipline* yourself to turn from any anxiety, and *choose to trust* the Lord. **Matt. 9:16, 17; Mark 2:21, 22; Luke 5:36–39** *Avoid* imposing past traditional structures on present renewals. *Understand* that yesterday's structures and forms are often incapable of handling today's dynamic of spiritual renewal. **Matt. 12:43–45; Luke 11:24–26** *Be warned* that returning to a past bondage from which you were once delivered results in deeper bondage. **Matt. 13:31, 32; Mark 4:30–32; Luke 13:18, 19** *Recognize* that faith is decision and obedience rather than ability. *Understand* that obedient faith releases Holy Spirit power to accomplish the task.

New Testament Women

Luke is notable for his focus on women, beginning with Elizabeth (Luke 1:5, 13) and Mary, the mother of Jesus (Luke 1:26-56). Other notable women of the New Testament include:

Anna (Luke 2:36-38)	Drusilla (Acts 24:24)	Mary Magdalene (Matt. 27:56-61; Mark 16:9)
Bernice (Acts 25:13)	Eunice (2 Tim. 1:5)	
Candace (Acts 8:27)	Herodias (Matt. 14:3-10)	Phoebe (Rom. 16:1-2)
Chloe (1 Cor. 1:11)	Joanna (Luke 8:3)	Priscilla (Acts 18:2, 18-19)
Claudia (2 Tim. 4:21)	Lois (2 Tim. 1:5)	Salome (Matt. 20:20-24)
Damaris (Acts 17:34)	Lydia (Acts 16:14)	Sapphira (Acts 5:1)
Dorcas (Tabitha; Acts 9:36–41)	Martha and Mary (Luke 10:38-42)	Susanna (Luke 8:3)

KEYS TO JOHN
The Kingdom and the Cosmos

Kingdom Key: God's Purpose in View

John's Gospel provides insight into Jesus' own perception of His mission as the Lamb of God, taking away the sin of the world. Seeing the world-order as He saw it, and the redemptive work He was here to achieve, helps us in our understanding of kingdom truth.

First, the word "world" must be defined and discerned in its usage. The Greek *kosmos* occurs over seventy-five times in John and is clearly a theme being developed by the writer. John relates the Lord's view of this world as being under the temporary rule of Satan, whom Jesus refers to as "the ruler of this world" (12:31; 14:30; 16:11). It is essential to grasp the meaning of *kosmos,* as distinguished from the words for (1) the physical earth (*ge*), (2) the era of man (*aiown*, age) and (3) the whole universe (*panta*, "all things," 1:3).

Kosmos refers to this world in terms of its "order of things," that is, the social, political, and spiritual structures governing the way life is. It refers essentially to all of *humankind*—that is, not to the geophysical or biological world so much as to the anthropological and the forces which govern humanity. Thus, Jesus does not concede that the *planet* is in Satan's hands but that

....
God's incarnate Word embodies light, life, and love.
....

mankind on earth has come under his sway. (This is consistent with the way Jesus spoke to Satan in the wilderness temptation. When the Adversary offered "all the kingdoms of the world and their glory" [Matt. 4:8], Jesus did not question his right to make the offer; He simply rejected it.) The Savior saw the Fall as not only separating humankind from God but also bringing the race under the dominance of Satan's influence and his controlling enterprise. (Paul notes this—Eph. 2:1–2; 1 Cor. 2:12; 2 Cor. 4:3–4; as does John elsewhere—1 John 4:3–4; 5:19; Rev. 12:9.)

These observations underscore the truth that when Jesus says, "God so loved the world that He gave His only begotten Son" (John 3:16), He is addressing a broader dimension of redemption in His Cross than is commonly thought. Jesus came to die and rise again not only to save humankind from *(Please turn to page 316.)*

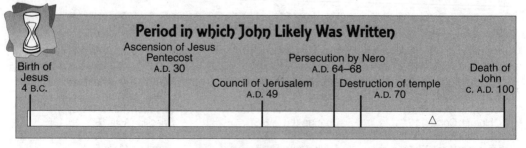

Period in which John Likely Was Written

| Birth of Jesus 4 B.C. | Ascension of Jesus Pentecost A.D. 30 | Council of Jerusalem A.D. 49 | Persecution by Nero A.D. 64–68 | Destruction of temple A.D. 70 | Death of John C. A.D. 100 |

John displays Jesus as God's Son, verified by signs

Master Key: God's Son Revealed

The book presents Jesus as the only begotten Son of God who became flesh. For John, Jesus' humanity meant essentially a twofold mission: (1) as the "Lamb of God" (1:29), He procured the redemption of mankind; (2) through His life and ministry He revealed the Father. Christ consistently pointed beyond Himself to the Father who had sent Him and whom He sought to glorify. In fact, the miracles Jesus performed, which John characterized as "signs," bore testimony to the divine mission of the Son of God. As the Son glorified the Father in ministry and passion, so the Father glorified the Son. But, as John shows, the Son's glorification came at the Crucifixion (12:32–33), not only in the post-resurrection exaltation. By believing that Jesus is the Christ, the readers of John's Gospel become participants in the life Jesus brought out of death (20:31).

Power Key: God's Spirit at Work

Unique to John is the designation of the Holy Spirit as "Comforter" or "Helper" (14:16), literally "one called alongside." He is "another Helper," namely, one of the same kind as Jesus, thereby extending the ministry of Jesus to the end of this age. It would be a grave error, however, to understand the Spirit's purpose merely in terms of one needed in predicaments. On the contrary, John demonstrates that the Spirit's role encompasses every facet of life. In regard to the world outside of Christ, He works as the agent who convicts of sin, righteousness, and judgment (16:8–11). The experience of being "born of the Spirit" is descriptive of New Birth (3:6). Because God in essense is Spirit, those who worship Him must do so spiritually—that is, as directed and motivated by the Holy Spirit (4:24). Further, in anticipation of Pentecost, the Spirit becomes the divine enabler for authoritative ministry (20:21–23).

The Holy Spirit also fulfills a definite function in relation to Christ. While the Father sent the Spirit in the name of Christ, the Spirit never draws attention to Himself, nor does He speak in His own authority. Instead, His mission is to glorify Jesus and to declare Christ's teaching to the disciples (16:14).

John reveals the function of the Holy Spirit in continuing the work of Jesus, leading

(Please turn to page 316.)

Key Word: *Believe*

The fourth gospel has the clearest statement of purpose in the Bible: "But these are written that you may believe that Jesus is the Christ, the Son of God, and that believing you may have life in His name" (20:31). John selected the signs he used for the specific purpose of creating intellectual ("that you may believe") and spiritual ("that believing you may have life") conviction about the Son of God.

Key Verses: John 1:11–13;
                              20:30–31
Key Chapter: John 3

John 3:16 is without doubt the most quoted and preached verse in all of Scripture. Captured in it is the gospel in its clearest and simplest form: that salvation is a gift of God and is obtainable only through belief.

that point to faith, commitment, and service.

Introducing

JOHN

Author. Early church tradition attributes the fourth Gospel to John "the beloved disciple" (13:23; 19:26; 20:2; 21:7, 20), who belonged to the "inner circle" of Jesus' followers (*see* Matt. 17:1; Mark 13:3). According to Christian writers of the second century, John moved to Ephesus, probably during the Jewish War of A.D. 66–70, where he continued his ministry. For instance, Irenaeus, the bishop of Lyons in the latter part of the second century, stated that "John, the disciple of the Lord, who also leaned upon His breast, did himself publish a Gospel during his residence in Ephesus in Asia" (*Against Heresies* 3.1.1).

Some scholars suggest that John 19:35 and 21:24 may reflect another author who faithfully collected the apostle's eyewitness account and testimonials. However, the bulk of the evidence, both internal and external, supports John the apostle as the author.

Date. The same tradition that locates John in Ephesus suggests that he wrote his Gospel in the latter part of the first century. In the absence of substantial evidence to the contrary, most scholars accept this tradition.

Purpose. In a broad sense, John wrote to provide the Christians of the province of Asia (now in part of modern Turkey) with a fuller understanding of the life and ministry of Jesus Christ. More specifically, he wrote to lead his readers to a settled faith on the basis of the words and works of Jesus, with the result that they "may have life in His name" (20:31).

John and the Synoptic Gospels. While John most likely knew of the other three Gospel accounts, he chose not to follow their chronological sequence of events as much as a topical order. In this case they may have used common oral and/or literary traditions. The broad outline is the same, and some particular events in Jesus' ministry are common to all four books. Some of the distinctive differences are: (1) instead of the familiar parables, John has lengthy discourses; (2) in place of the many miracles and healings in the Synoptics, John uses seven carefully picked miracles, which serve as "signs"; (3) the ministry of Jesus revolves around three Passover Feasts, instead of the one cited in the Synoptics; (4) the "I am" sayings are uniquely Johannine.

Content. John divides the ministry of Jesus into two distinct parts: chapters 2—12 give insight into His public ministry, while chapters 13—21 relate His private ministry to His disciples. In 1:1–18, called the "Prologue," John deals with the theological implications of the first coming of Jesus. He shows Jesus' preexistent state with God, His deity and essence, as well as His incarnation.

Personal Application. In seeking to fulfil his purpose as stated in 20:20, 31, John confronts his readers with claims of Jesus that demand a personal response. A positive response of faith in "Jesus . . . the Christ, the Son of God" results in "life in His name." John records Jesus' assertion that He came "that they might have life and that they might have it more abundantly" (10:10), and he makes it clear that life is not an independent quality unrelated to God or to Christ. The knowledge of "the only true God and Jesus Christ" (17:3), which implies fellowship as well as intellectual understanding, is the key to the meaning of eternal life.

Kingdom Key continued from page 314

sin and death but to break Satan's control over the world's order of things. He says He is here to "judge" the prince of this world (12:30–31; 16:11).

Jesus came to overthrow the hellish powers that control societies and shape cultures, which not only resist God, but inevitably self-destruct. However, because of His Cross, no one need "perish, but may have everlasting life"(3:16)! Through His salvation, Christ has provided not only forgiveness and the promise of heaven, but He also has released us (1) from hell's dominion, (2) from the present order of society's futility, and (3) unto restored partnership with our Creator. Thus, "life" has been given a new definition. (The Kingdom Key article for John's Epistles deals with this.)

Power Key continued from page 315

believers to understand the meanings, implications, and imperatives of the gospel, and enabling them to do "greater works" than those done by Jesus (14:12). Present-day believers in Christ may thus view Him as their contemporary, not merely as a figure from the distant past.

Surveying

JOHN

I. PROLOGUE: THE WORD BECOMES FLESH 1:1–18.

John launches us back before Creation to introduce Jesus. Jesus is "the Word": God Himself, who existed before the beginning (1:1). The title focuses our attention on Jesus as the One through whom God has always expressed Himself (cf. Luke 10:22; John 14:9). In the past Jesus revealed God in the Creation itself (1:3; cf. Ps. 19:1–4), in the unique gift of life (1:4) that transformed the barren universe, and in "light" (1:5). In John, "light" and "darkness" are moral terms (*see* Comprehend). The very fact that human beings have moral awareness is a powerful testimony to the existence of God (cf. Rom. 2:15).

> **"This man came for a witness, to bear witness of the Light"**
> (1:7). The fact that John the Baptist was a prophet of God did not preclude him from functioning in another arena of gifting. The notion that individuals are limited only to one particular gift is erroneous. All are called upon to bear evidence of the gospel of Christ in their lives, regardless of how the Holy Spirit might choose to use them otherwise.

The one who lived as Jesus of Nazareth is the eternal Son of God. Through incarnation He communicates God's glory in an entirely new way. The God who spoke in creation, in life itself, in moral awareness, and through human intermediaries in the written Word (1:17) has now come in person, communicating a glorious message of grace and truth (1:17).

II. JESUS' PUBLIC MINISTRY 1:19—12:50.

John begins testimony about Jesus and boldly presents Jesus as God incarnate. Now he reports several testimonies to that identity.

A. Preparation (1:19–51). John the Baptist is recognized as a prophet, and many come to hear him. Those who do repent are baptized by John as a visible confession. When John is questioned about his identity, he tells his listeners that he is the one foretold in Isaiah who prepares the way for the coming of the Lord (1:23; Is. 40:3). As a prophet, John's testimony can be trusted.

God has told John that one who is the Son of God will be revealed to him when the Holy Spirit, in the form of a dove, comes from heaven and rests on Him. When Jesus is baptized, John sees the Spirit come. "I have seen," John says, "and testified that this is the Son of God" (1:29–34; *see* Sin).

> **"Upon whom you see the Spirit descending, and remaining on Him, this is He who baptizes with the Holy Spirit"**
> (1:32–33). Jesus contrasts John's baptism in water with the baptism with the Holy Spirit (Acts 1:5). Jesus Himself is the baptizer, and He ushers us into the realm of Holy Spirit fullness. This is not accomplished by human institution or sacramental practice. It is a personal work of God in the life of the individual.

B. Wedding at Cana (2:1–12). Jesus' first miracle, turning water to wine, is one of many that "revealed his glory."

C. Ministry in Jerusalem (2:13—3:36). In Jerusalem a furious Jesus drives those who conduct business out of the temple court at Passover. His zeal for God's house reflects a prophetic statement in Psalm 69:9.

When Nicodemus comes at night to Jesus (3:1–21), he makes a startling revelation. He admits that the ruling council and the Pharisees "know you are a teacher who has come from God." The fact that Nicodemus comes by night suggests that opposition is already strong and he does not want to be seen. Jesus goes immediately to the heart of the issue and proclaims the need for a new birth. Startled, Nicodemus asks, "How can this be?"

Jesus explains two births: flesh can only give birth to flesh. The Spirit must give birth to spirit. Nicodemus, as one of Israel's teachers (v. 10), should have understood, for the Old Testament prophets foretold a new inner life for mankind (cf. Jer. 31:33). Jesus, coming from heaven, speaks with authority about this reality: God will give new and eternal life to "everyone who believes" in Jesus, His Son.

"Whoever" (v. 16) simply trusts himself to the Son of God will be given eternal life. Now only one issue remains: "He who believes in Him is not condemned; but he who does not believe is condemned already" (18). There are only two destinies: the destiny of death and the destiny of life. Faith in Jesus Christ releases us from death and brings us life (*see* Been Done; Faith, Seed; Kingdom of God; Loved).

D. Jesus and the Samaritan woman (4:1–42). Samaria lay between Jerusalem and Galilee, on the west side of the Jordan. The district was populated by a mixed people, brought into the land by the Assyrians when the old northern kingdom of Israel fell in 722 B.C. Their claim to be worshipers of Yahweh was sharply rejected by the Jews, and a deep hostility between the two peoples existed. Jews often crossed the Jordan River and traveled many extra miles to avoid "contamination" in this land of a people whom they felt mongrelized their faith.

Now Jesus not only leads His disciples into Samaria, but He even stops near the town of Sychar! Jesus rests beside a well dug nearly two millennia before by the patriarch Jacob, and there He speaks with a woman.

"But He needed to go through Samaria"

(4:4). The Holy Spirit's leadership is absolutely essential to one's being an effective witness. Certainly Jesus could have remained in Judea, where He could have witnessed to many people. But the *Lord of the harvest,* who is the Holy Spirit, knows just when, where, and to whom we should share our faith. One should not make the mistake, however, of waiting for direction alone. The Bible directs each believer to be ready for witness whenever asked and as a matter of Christian duty (2 Tim. 4:2; 1 Pet. 3:15). Effective witnessing is the result of prayerful obedience to the Word and sensitive response to the Holy Spirit.

Jesus speaks of a water that will forever satisfy the woman's thirst. He lets her know that He is aware of her sins but is not repelled by her (15–18). When she introduces one of the theological differences between the Jews and Samaritans, He affirms the accuracy of the Old Testament revelation but quickly moves on. Even now God is seeking "true worshipers [who] will worship the Father in spirit and *truth" (21–24). Then Jesus identifies Himself as the promised Messiah, expected by the Samaritans as well as the Jews. (*See* Prayer.)

The Samaritan woman hurries to her village and tells of her encounter with the Lord. A new community of faith is born as many affirm, "We know that this man really is the *Savior of the world."

E. Healing the nobleman's son (4:43–54).
Jesus' challenge to the gathering crowd concerns their faith based on "signs." His compassion, however, is demonstrated in the healing of the boy.

"He went to Him and implored Him to come down and heal his son"

(4:46–53). Jesus heals the boy with a word and nothing else, even though the boy is in another town. But Jesus challenges the people concerning the need for "signs and wonders" as the basis of their faith in Him. Signs and wonders are a witness to the truth of who Jesus is, but our faith is in Him—His person, His Word—and nothing else.

F. Sabbath healing at the pool of Bethesda (5:1–15).
Jesus finds a man who has been paralyzed for thirty-eight years and asks the critical question for healing, "Do you want to be made well?"

"See, you have been made well. Sin no more, lest a worse thing come upon you"

(5:5–15). Earlier, Jesus asks the man, "Do you want to be made well?" (v. 6). Not all people who seek healing want to be made well, and Jesus' words at the conclusion of the man's healing indicate a deeper need than being paralyzed from birth. Sin brings devastation that cripples all of us to some extent. Only the forgiveness of God and our obedience to Him protect our lives. (*See* Withdrawn.)

G. Honoring the Father and the Son (5:16–29).
Jesus makes a series of claims:
• Jesus and the Father are one in Jesus' miracles. The Jews may criticize His Sabbath healings, but when they do they criticize God!
• Jesus and the Father give one judgment. The critics implicitly claim the right to judge Jesus. But God has given Jesus the right to judge them!
• Jesus and the Father are one source of life. By the Father's choice, Jesus is the source of all life. The life Jesus gives others will be fully expressed at the Resurrection.

H. Witnesses to the Son (5:30–47).
The truth of what Jesus says is witnessed by John and by Jesus' own miracles (36). But God Himself is the strongest witness. Those who are responsive to God will recognize Jesus as the One spoken of in the Old Testament (*see* Scriptures). Those who refuse to believe show that they "do not have the love of God" in their hearts.

I. Ministry in Galilee (6:1–71). When Jesus feeds five thousand persons on the shore of the Sea of Galilee (6:1–14; *see* Thanks) with just a few loaves of bread and two small fish, the excited crowds intend to "come and take Him by force to make Him king" (15; *see* Immediately).

Jesus openly tells the crowds they have followed because He fed them—not because they believe in Him. They suggest that Jesus should provide a sign, specifying "bread from heaven" as appropriate, because Moses provided manna during Israel's wilderness years (25–31). This provided the background for Jesus' discourse on Himself as the bread of eternal life (cf. Exodus 16). Jesus Himself is God's supernatural provision both of eternal life and of all that is needed to sustain that life up to the very time of our resurrection (vv. 40, 53; *see* Blood, The).

Many grumble about the difficulty of this teaching. Jesus explains that He does not expect a literal eating of His flesh and drinking of His blood but a spiritual appropriation of the life He offers (61–65; *see* Lord).

J. Conflict in Jerusalem (7:1—9:41). Jesus is now the focus of speculation. He has been endorsed by John the Baptist and has performed many miracles. But many will not believe. Their reaction is a hostility so great that the leaders are already determined to see Jesus killed (7:1, 20, 25; *see* Unrighteousness). Unbelief by Jesus' own brothers (v. 5) produces accusations and ridicule.

Jesus begins to teach openly, claiming that His message is from God, who gave the Law through Moses. The crowds accuse Jesus of being demon-possessed (7:20)! Yet none of them have kept the Law, and even now they plot to kill Jesus in violation of the Law.

Many are moved to believe as Jesus teaches. Hearing the whispers that identify Jesus as the Christ, the chief priests and Pharisees are furious but fear confronting Him openly. Instead they send temple guards to arrest Him. But the guards are so awed that they will not carry out their orders (7:30, 44). When Nicodemus objects to condemning Jesus before He is given a full hearing, the other leaders strike out at him (7:52).

In chapter 8 Jesus claims deity. John continues his report of events at the Feast of Tabernacles (7:2) and shares what is called Jesus' "Temple Discourse"! Now John focuses on a sharp conflict in which Jesus makes a clear claim to deity and explains the nature of truth.

> **"For the Holy Spirit was not yet given, because Jesus was not yet glorified"**
> (7:37–39). These verses reveal Jesus' strategy for His followers. His plan was to so fill them with His life and powerful love that their overflow would affect those around them. But this was not to happen until Pentecost. John interprets Jesus' words to have a future point of application. At the appointed time, the river would begin to flow. History shows that this flow of the river of the Spirit has continued to the present.

In the attempt to trap Jesus, the Pharisees catch a woman "in the act" of *adultery (8:1–11). The Pharisees bring only the woman and release the man. They care only about using her against Jesus. When the accusers slink away, Jesus refuses to condemn her. He releases the woman to live a new life, freed from her past sins.

Jesus is challenged by the Pharisees (8:13). They refer to a dictum of Old Testament law: any fact must be established by at least two witnesses. Jesus' claims are unsupported and thus must be rejected (23). But Jesus is supported by the active testimony of God the Father! One day that testimony will be open and visible to all (27–28). Now the testimony is within the hearts of those who hear Jesus' words and believe (30).

Biblically, "truth" involves knowing and experiencing reality. Jesus promises His disciples that they will come to *know the truth by personal experience when they keep His words—and thus will find freedom (8:31–32).

When Jesus claims to be the I AM known by Abraham millennia ago, the crowds grasps for stones to kill Him for blasphemy. "I AM" is the revealed name of God in the Old Testament, and Jesus' statement is a bold and unequivocable claim to deity (8:48–59; *see* Healing, Divine; Taste).

A blind man is healed (9:1–12).

> **"A Man called Jesus made clay and anointed my eyes and said to me, 'Go to the pool of Siloam and wash.' So I went and washed, and I received sight."**
> (9:1–12). The disciples were interested in knowing the reason for the man's blindness. Was it the sin of the man or his
> *continued on next page*

continued from preceding page
parents? Jesus rejects the notion that sin is the cause. He wants them to focus instead on the miraculous healing of the man as a point of witness to God's work (see Works). Healing may simply be for the glorification of God by the people.

The Pharisees' reaction (9:13–34) of frustration cannot deny the miracle. At last they give up interrogating the blind man and simply insist, "We know this man [Jesus] is a sinner." Others fear to contradict them (22). But the now-sighted man openly confronts the Pharisees' hypocrisy. The leaders are so furious at this new evidence that they willfully shut their eyes to the truth.

Later, as the blind man kneels in worship before Jesus, the Lord observes that the nearby Pharisees—who claim that they are able to see—are blind to the only release humanity will ever have from the guilt of sin (vv. 35–41).

K. Jesus the Good Shepherd (10:1–42). The Old Testament uses the image of a *shepherd to represent both political and religious leaders of God's people (Is. 56:11; Jeremiah 25; Ezekiel 34). One of the great messianic promises in the Old Testament is that the Lord, whom David knew as "my shepherd" (Psalm 23), will come to personally care for His people (Is. 40:11; Ezek. 34:23; 37:24). Now Jesus announces that He is the promised Good Shepherd.

Shepherd recognized (10:1–6). Those who belong to God will recognize and follow Jesus.

Thieves and robbers (10:7–10). The leaders of the Jews are like thieves and robbers because they harm and use the sheep (see Abundantly; Faith, Seed; Human Worth; Restoration).

Good Shepherd gives life (10:11–13). The true shepherd is recognized by his willingness to give his life to preserve the sheep from danger.

Jesus willingly gives His life (10:14–21). Life will not be torn from Jesus as an unwilling victim. Jesus' life will be given, that people from every nation may become God's "one flock."

Unbelief (10:22–42). Jesus again plainly tells the Jews (e.g., the leaders) that He is the Christ. When He claims oneness with the Father the Jews attempt to stone Him, "because You, being a Man, make Yourself God" (v. 33; see Sanctified).

L. Ministry at Bethany (11:1—12:11). Jesus is in Galilee when He receives word that

a beloved follower (see Friend) named Lazarus is desperately ill. He waits two days and then heads for Bethany, in Judea. The disciples view returning to Judea as so dangerous to Jesus that they will "die with" him. But Jesus goes to raise the dead, "so that God's Son may be glorified" and "so that you may believe" (11:4, 15).

Jesus arrives and comforts the two sisters. Each affirms faith in Jesus as the Son of God. Each is sure that if Jesus "had been here, my brother would not have died" (21, 32). But they have not yet grasped what it means for Jesus to be "the resurrection and the life" (24). When Jesus orders the stone blocking the tomb of Lazarus moved, Martha objects. After four days "there [will be] a bad odor." But they obey. Jesus calls, and the dead man comes out, alive again. (See Groaning.)

The raising of Lazarus stimulates faith in some. But the chief priests and Pharisees, who admit He is "performing many miraculous signs," still will not believe (11:47–48). The high priest announces that Jesus must die (49–53). Hatred has hardened into a determined plot to destroy Jesus.

Jesus is anointed (12:3). At a dinner in Lazarus's home, Mary anoints Jesus with expensive perfumes. Jesus says this speaks of "the day of My burial." The last Passover is near, and the hatred of the leaders is so great they even plan to murder Lazarus!

M. Triumphal entry to Jerusalem (12:12–19). With the recent raising of Lazarus, Jesus' popularity (see Name) is at its peak. When He enters Jerusalem, Jesus is lauded as the promised Messiah and King of the Jews.

N. Final rejection: unbelief (12:20–50). Jesus again predicts His coming death, but promises it will produce a harvest of life for all who trust and follow Him (20–26; see Brotherly Love).

Again Jesus presents Himself as the object of faith and warns that God, who has sent Jesus, will judge those who reject Him (12:44–50; see Darkness). But even those who do believe are now afraid to confess their faith openly.

III. JESUS' MINISTRY TO THE DISCIPLES 13:1—17:26.
John now moves to the last night of Jesus' life on earth and tells of an intimate supper Jesus shares with His disciples.

A. Modeling servanthood (13:1–20). The relationship between a disciple and his teacher was well established in Judaism. The disciple actively served his master. Now, at the beginning of the evening meal, Jesus puts aside His outer clothing and stoops to wash His disciples' feet! This is a shocking reversal of roles! The emotional impact of the act is so great that Peter at first refuses (8). Only by this dramatic act is Christ at last able to convey to His disciples that He really intends His followers to *serve* one another (13–17; *see* Leadership, Spiritual).

B. Pronouncements of betrayal and denial (13:21–38). Now, before the teaching, Jesus predicts His betrayal. John reports that it is now night (30). Only when the Resurrection is an accomplished fact will John report that a new day dawns (20:1).

Warning His disciples that He will soon leave them, Jesus introduces what He calls His "new commandment" (13:34; *see* Human Worth; Restoration). When He is gone, the new community that will be established is to be marked by love for one another, a love modeled on Jesus' love for His own.

This instruction is followed immediately by Peter's honest affirmation that he will "lay down his life" for Jesus (*see* Follow). But Jesus knows human weaknesses and predicts Peter will disown Him that very night.

C. Preparation for Jesus' departure (14:1–31). Many topics are covered by Jesus in this significant passage, which touches on vital aspects of the new relationship of believers with Jesus (*see* Messianic Promises). Jesus is the only way by which individuals can approach the Father (14:6). Jesus emphasizes His unity with the Father and promises that He will continue to work in answer to His disciples' prayers (14:7–14).

"Greater works than these he will do" (14:12). Those who believe in Christ will do "greater works" than Jesus, because He will send the Holy Spirit (vv. 16–18; *see* Another; Holy Spirit Gifts). "Greater works" refer to miracles, signs, wonders, preaching, and ministry to the world—in both number and magnitude. Obviously, Jesus is not referring to His ultimate work of the Cross and redemption; those can only be accomplished by God Himself. The works of Holy Spirit-filled believers are to be supernatural signs of the God they serve and His unlimited power to address human need. Love for Jesus will move His followers to obey the Lord (vv. 15–24; *see* Manifest; Word of God). Jesus will leave, but He will not desert His followers. He will send

the Holy Spirit to be with them, and He Himself will come again (25–31).

D. Fruitfulness by abiding (15:1–17). The picture of a vine shows the nature of our relationship with Jesus. As the vine, Jesus supplies each branch with the nourishment needed to bear fruit. Apart from an intimate and close relationship, expressed in the word *abiding* ("keeping close"), we can do nothing (1–5).

Jesus' reference to branches that wither and are burned is not a reference to hell. Jesus is speaking about fruitfulness, not salvation. God's desire is that we do not live a worthless, barren life, but "bear much fruit." (*See* Brotherly Love.)

E. Dealing with rejection (15:18—16:4). The hatred men have felt for Jesus will also be directed against Jesus' disciples.

"And you also will bear witness, because you have been with Me" (15:26–27). To be considered as a witness in court, a person must have some kind of testimony that will serve as evidence for the case. Jesus is stressing that His followers will be sufficient evidence for His case and His gospel on the basis of abiding with Him. The best witness we can have with people around us is the witness we never speak—a persuasive witness because of the overflow of Jesus in our lives. (*See* Helper.)

F. Understanding Jesus' departure (16:5–33). Jesus is the one in whom the Bible's teachings about sin, righteousness, and judgment all come together. It is the Holy Spirit who deals with these issues, presenting Christ to the world and convicting those who will not believe. The Spirit also is at work for believers. He is the living voice of Jesus to us, who guides us into an experience of God's truth (16:5–16).

The first reaction of the disciples when Jesus is gone will be heartbreak. But after mourning, grief will be transformed into joy. Then the implications of relationship with the resurrected Jesus and the power of prayer will be known (16:17–24; *see* Take).

Whatever happens in the next hours, Jesus will not be alone. "My Father is with me," and to the Father Jesus will return (16:25–33; *see* Tribulation).

G. Jesus' prayer for His disciples (17:1–26). This is often called Jesus' "high priestly" prayer, because it is primarily a prayer of intercession for His followers.

Coming return to glory (17:1–5). The time has come for Jesus to be glorified. This word, when applied to God, usually speaks of the splendor of the deity's disclosure. Jesus had glory with the Father when He existed before the world's creation. At His Second Coming He will also be seen in "power and great glory" (Mark 13:26). On earth Jesus' glory was both hidden and revealed in the Incarnation. The great splendor of God's overwhelming presence was masked by Jesus' human flesh. But Jesus has shown a new aspect of God's glory—a glory known only through servanthood and by "completing the work" God the Father gave Him to do.

Jesus prays for His disciples (17:6–19). Jesus asks that His followers might be kept safe and receive "My joy fulfilled in themselves" (13).

Jesus prays for all believers (17:20–26). He makes it clear that He includes all who will ever "believe in me through their word" in this great prayer for His disciples (20). Looking into the future the focus of Jesus' prayer is "that they may be made perfect in one" (23).

IV. JESUS' PASSION AND RESURRECTION 18:1—21:23.

John now reports the all-too-familiar story told in each Gospel. The sequence of events is the same, but John adds special insights.

A. Jesus' arrest (18:1–14). A mob led by Judas arrests Jesus. Jesus allows Himself to be taken, first negotiating the release of His disciples (8–9). John tells us that Peter boldly strikes out to protect his master but succeeds only in cutting off the right ear of a servant of the high priest. Jesus rebukes Peter. What happens now is the will of the Father.

B. Trial before the high priest (18:15–27). Jesus is taken at night to the residences of various Jewish leaders. Peter trails behind and in a courtyard fulfills Jesus' prediction: he denies any relationship with Jesus.

C. Trial before Pilate (18:28—19:16). Jesus stands before Pilate (18:28–40). Jesus has several confrontations with Pilate, the Roman governor of Judea. Only Pilate has the authority to pass the death sentence (see Judge). The Jews thus must bring Jesus before him, but after careful examination he announces to the Jews that there is no basis for their charges against Jesus! (See Kingdom of God; World.)

The angry Jews shout their demands for crucifixion, finally revealing that the real reason they want Jesus killed is that He claims to be the Son of God. This revelation frightens Pilate, who questions Jesus again and then tries to set Him free. But the Jews threaten Pilate, and he capitulates, turning Jesus over to them for crucifixion (19:1–16).

D. Crucifixion and burial (19:17–42). Pilate orders a notice identifying Jesus as king of the Jews attached to the cross. As Jesus hangs in anguish from the torment of this cruel method of execution, He commits His mother to the care of the John who writes this Gospel.

Jesus' death corresponds to Old Testament prophecies found in Exodus 12:46, Numbers 9:12, Psalm 34:20, and Zechariah 12:10. The flow of blood and water is characteristic of one who dies in this way (19:34; see Testimony). Jesus is laid in a new tomb in a garden near the public execution grounds.

E. Resurrection and appearances (20:1—21:23). The empty tomb (20:1–9). John is with Peter when the two run to the garden tomb after Mary of Magdala reports the stone has been rolled away. John tells how Peter goes into the tomb and sees laying there the empty linens in which Jesus was wrapped.

Jesus' post-Resurrection appearances (20:10–31). Christ has now performed the ultimate miracle. To prove it He appears to Mary of Magdala (10–18; see Saw), to the disciples with Thomas absent (19–23; see Evangelism; Sent), and to the disciples with Thomas present (24–31). Thomas has sworn not to believe unless he touches Jesus' nail-pierced hands and puts his hand in the gash torn in Jesus' side by the Roman soldier's spear (19:34). But when Jesus appears, Thomas drops to his knees in worship, acknowledging Jesus as "my Lord and my God" (20:28). Many millions who have not seen what Thomas saw that evening have believed on Jesus since.

Jesus and the great catch of fish (21:1–14). After these events Jesus meets seven disciples who have gone fishing. On His directions they throw their net on the other side of the boat, and the nets are filled. On shore Jesus shares a meal with His followers.

Peter had denied Jesus three times. Now Jesus asks Peter three times if he loves Him. Three times Peter affirms his *love for the Lord. And three times Peter is reassured. His denial of Jesus in a moment of weakness has not disqualified him from service. Peter will shepherd and care for many of Jesus' lambs (21:15–25).

Jesus then speaks of Peter's death (18–19). Tradition tells us that Peter was later crucified in Rome, upside down, after a long life of loving service to Jesus' flock.

John also reports that Peter asked Jesus about the future of another disciple. Jesus rebukes him: "What is that to you? You follow Me" (22). What a truth for each of us to remember! The resurrected Jesus is Lord. Each disciple is committed to follow Jesus and to give others the freedom to be personally responsible to our risen Lord (cf. Rom. 14:1–4).

V. EPILOGUE 21:24–25.

John records the astounding truth that there is much, much more to Jesus' ministry that has not been recorded—"the world itself could not contain the books that would be written!"

The "I AM" Statements

Our Lord's meaningful "I AM" (Greek, *ego eimi*) is found twenty-three times in John's Gospel (4:26; 6:20, 35, 41, 48, 51; 8:12, 18, 24, 28, 58; 10:7, 9, 11, 14; 11:25; 13:19; 14:6; 15:1, 5; 18:5, 6, 8). In several of these He joins His "I AM" with seven metaphors which are expressive of His saving relationship toward the world.

"I AM the *bread* of life" (6:35, 41, 48, 51)
"I AM the *light* of the world" (8:12)
"I AM the *door* of the sheep" (10:7, 9)
"I AM the *good shepherd*" (10:11, 14)
"I AM the *resurrection* and the *life*" (11:25)
"I AM the *way,* the *truth,* and the *life*" (14:6)
"I AM the true *vine*" (15:1, 5)

Titles of Christ

The two most popular titles or names Christians use in speaking of our Lord are *Jesus,* a translation of the Hebrew word *Joshua.* which means "YAHWEH Is Salvation," and *Christ,* a transliteration of the Greek term *Christos,* meaning "Anointed One" or "Messiah." Other significant names or titles are used in the New Testament, each expressing a distinct truth about Him.

Adam, Last Adam (1 Cor. 15:45)	Lamb of God (John 1:29)
Alpha and Omega (Rev. 21:6)	Light of the World (John 9:5)
Bread of Life (John 6:35)	Lord of Glory (1 Cor. 2:8)
Chief Cornerstone (Eph. 2:20)	Mediator between God and Men
Chief Shepherd (1 Pet. 5:4)	(1 Tim. 2:5)
Firstborn from the Dead (Col. 1:18)	Only Begotten of the Father (John 1:14)
Good Shepherd (John 10:11)	Prophet (Acts 3:22)
Great Shepherd of the Sheep (Heb. 13:20)	Savior (Luke 1:47)
High Priest (Heb. 3:1)	Seed of Abraham (Gal. 3:16)
Holy One of God (Mark 1:24)	Son of Man (Matt. 18:11)
Immanuel (God With Us; Matt. 1:23)	The Word (John 1:1)
King of kings, Lord of lords (Rev. 19:16)	

TRUTH-IN-ACTION through JOHN

Truth John Teaches	**Action** John Invites
1 Guidelines for Growing in Godliness To the NT disciple, godly living is living in, through, and for Jesus. Godliness can be summarized in three words: love, obedience, and unity. By living godly lives, we learn to see things as God does and adopt His Word as our only standard.	**7:24** *Judge* spiritual things by spiritual standards, not by appearance. **12:32** *Exalt* Jesus in your life and service to draw men to Him. **15:9–14** *Recognize* that love obeys Jesus and lays down its life for others. **17:20–23** *Commit yourself* to bringing about the unity of the church. **18:36** *Practice* Christian citizenship, but *do not depend on* political means to bring about spiritual ends.
2 Steps to Dynamic Devotion John's Gospel introduces the Holy Spirit as the key to a truly dynamic devotion to God. It anticipates the outpouring of the Holy Spirit who will become the very energy of the believer's devotional life. The Holy Spirit will maximize prayer and worship, minister through the Lord's Supper, and enable the believer to continually draw his life from Jesus Christ Himself.	**4:21–24** *Worship* God frequently, employing your spiritual language as well as your understanding. **6:53–58** *Draw on* Jesus' life and healing while partaking of His body and blood in the Lord's Supper. **12:2–8** *Do not allow* your ministry for Jesus to distract you from your more important ministry to Him. **15:1–8** *Reject* independence from God. *Nurture* an increasingly deepened relationship with Jesus Christ.
3 Steps to Faithful Obedience Obeying Jesus is the primary evidence that we love Him and are His disciples. Our decision to obey is the key to understanding the spiritual reality of the Scriptures and frees the Holy Spirit to teach us.	**2:5** Follow this advice: *Practice* instant obedience to whatever Jesus tells you to do. **5:16–23** *Do only* what you see Jesus doing just as He did only what He saw the Father doing. **7:17** *Determine* to obey the Lord. *Align your will* with His will and *receive* understanding of His Word. **12:47–50** *Speak* as the Lord commands. *Know* you will be judged by the words of Jesus. **14:15–24** *Know* that you show your love for Jesus by obeying Him. Diligently *keep* God's Word so that His presence will steadfastly abide with you.
4 Guidelines for Growth in the Spirit John's Gospel introduces the Holy Spirit's role in spiritual growth. The New Birth and the baptism with the Holy Spirit endow the believer with the life and gifts of the Holy Spirit, including the ability to pray in Spirit power. The Holy Spirit is our Teacher, Helper, Advocate, and Guide. He is our source of true spiritual understanding. He lifts up Jesus and builds up believers, enabling them to live the Christian life.	**3:3** *Understand* that perceiving the kingdom of God and entering it are impossible without spiritual rebirth. **14:25, 26** *Understand* that the Holy Spirit enables God's people to understand and live by the truth. **16:8–11** *Ask* the Holy Spirit to bring conviction to men's hearts. *Understand* that is one of His primary ministries. **16:12–15** *Understand* that knowing the truth of God's Word is made possible by the Holy Spirit.
5 Key Lessons in Faith The key word in John's Gospel is "believe." Faith unlocks our understanding of Scripture and releases the Spirit's activity in our lives. Faith, like love, evidences itself in obedience. Finally, faith approaches God boldly to receive from Him the things it needs.	**10:37, 38** *Believe* in the miracles of Jesus. **11:40** *Understand* that the glory of God is revealed to those who believe. **13:17** *Recognize* that it is what you practice of God's Word that brings blessing to yourself and others. **14:6, 7** *Recognize* that Jesus is the only way to God. *Know* Jesus to know God. **14:12–14** *Pray for* and *expect* the "greater things" ministry of the church. **16:24** *Do not neglect* to ask the Father for those things you need to live and do His work.

KEYS TO ACTS
The Church's Kingdom Message

Kingdom Key: God's Purpose in View

A primary truth in the Book of Acts is that the message Jesus preached—the gospel of the kingdom—was continued and carried forth as the theme and thrust of the church's ministry. Believers empowered and anointed by the Holy Spirit became the continuing vehicle (literally, the physical body) through which the message of redemption and restoration travelled. In other words, what began as God's role—incarnated and extended in Jesus Christ—now was being transmitted through His church, "His body, the fullness of Him who fills all in all" (Eph. 1:23).

Acts testifies that in "all that Jesus began both to do and teach" (1:1) He commissioned His followers to continue. This book contains the evidence that they did exactly that, further confirming His message that "the kingdom has come." Now, with His death, Resurrection, and Ascension securing humanity's reinstatement to favor and functional partnership with God, Jesus promises power to minister God's overruling grace and power to break Satan's strongholds and set people free.

There are eight direct references to "the kingdom of God" in Acts. These combine to verify that this message is to be the timeless theme of the church's proclamation.

1. Acts 1:3 reveals that Jesus' last days with the apostles—following the Resurrection but prior to the Ascension—are devoted to deepening and reviewing the message of "the kingdom" with them. They especially need this practical instruction now, since all they have been taught before is taking on new meaning in the light of His accomplished work of redemption. The truth of the gospel and their mission to spread it is becoming clearer than ever.

2. Acts 1:6 clarifies the church's mission to *minister* rather than to speculate. This text contains an exchange which resolves the perpetual questions that often preoccupy prophecy-minded Bible students: "When will the kingdom come?" (This refers to the ultimate manifestation of the millenial rule of the

> **Believers ignited by the Spirit overcome the strong-holds of hell.**

(Please turn to page 327.)

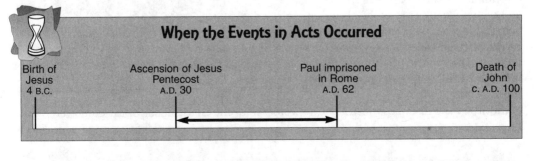

When the Events in Acts Occurred

| Birth of Jesus 4 B.C. | Ascension of Jesus Pentecost A.D. 30 | Paul imprisoned in Rome A.D. 62 | Death of John C. A.D. 100 |

Acts shows Jesus as still at work through • • •

Master Key: God's Son Revealed

The Book of Acts records a consistent pattern in the early apostolic proclamation of the gospel of Jesus Christ. First, Jesus is presented as a historical figure, a man empowered to perform signs and wonders (2:22; 10:38). Next, the death of Jesus is attributed equally to the wickedness of men and to the purpose of God. On the one hand, the Jews had "crucified" Him "by lawless hands" (2:23; *see* 3:13–15; 4:10; 5:30; 7:52; 10:39; 13:28). On the other hand, Jesus had been "delivered by the determined purpose and foreknowledge of God" (2:23; *see* 17:3). Then the Resurrection of Jesus is emphasized, particularly as the fulfillment of Old Testament prophecy and as God's reversal of men's verdict on Jesus (1:3; 2:24–32; 4:10; 5:30; 10:40–41; 13:30–37; 17:31). The apostles declared that Jesus had been exalted to a position of unique and universal dominion (2:33–36; 3:21; 5:31). From that place of supreme honor and executive power Jesus had poured out the promised Holy Spirit (2:33), who bears witness to Him (5:32) and empowers believers (1:8). Jesus has been "ordained by God to be Judge of the living and the dead" (10:42), and He will return in triumph at the end of the age (1:11). Meanwhile, those who believe in Him will receive forgiveness of sins (2:21; 3:19; 4:12; 5:31; 10:43; 13:38–39) and "the gift of the Holy Spirit" (2:38). Those who do not believe in Him have a terrible destiny (3:23).

Power Key: God's Spirit at Work

The power of the Holy Spirit through the church is the most striking feature in Acts. The book has even been called *The Acts of the Holy Spirit*. The work of the Spirit in Acts, however, cannot be understood without seeing the relationship between Acts and the Gospels, which demonstrates an essential continuity. Both the public ministry of Jesus in the Gospels and the public ministry of the church in Acts begin with a lifechanging encounter with the Spirit; both are essential accounts of the results of those encounters.

> ### Key Word: *Empowered for Witness*
>
> **B**ecause of Luke's strong emphasis on the ministry of the Holy Spirit, this book could be regarded as "The Acts of the Spirit of Christ working in and through the Apostles."
>
> ### Key Verses: Acts 1:8; 2:42–47
>
> ### Key Chapter: Acts 2
>
> **C**hapter 2 records the earth-changing events of the Day of Pentecost when the Holy Spirit comes, fulfilling Christ's command to wait until the Holy Spirit arrives to empower and direct the witness. The Spirit transforms a small group of fearful men and women into a thriving, worldwide church that is ever moving forward and fulfilling the Great Commission.

The power of the Spirit in Jesus' life authorized Him to preach the kingdom of God and to demonstrate kingdom power by healing the sick, casting out demons, and setting the captives free (Luke 4:14–19; Matt. 4:23). The same Spirit power in Acts 2 gave the same authority to the disciples. Jesus is the prototype of the Spirit-filled, Spirit-empowered life

(Please turn to page 328.)

• • • His church by the Holy Spirit's power.

Introducing
ACTS

Author. The Book of Acts does not specifically mention its author, but many indicators point to Luke, "the beloved physician" (Col. 4:14). The author was the same person as the one who wrote the third Gospel (1:1–2). He was a close associate of Paul, as indicated in the "we" sections of the book. The writer was a man of culture, as indicated by his literary style; he had a universal outlook; and he revealed an interest in medical matters. In addition, church tradition uniformly declares that Luke was the author of Acts. Therefore, the bulk of the evidence, both external and internal, supports Luke as the author.

Date. Luke tells the story of the early church within the framework of geographical, political, and historical details that could only fit in the first century. For example, Luke's use of regional Roman governmental titles, which only someone living at the time could know precisely, suggests that the book was probably written within its actual time frame. Furthermore, there is no mention of the fall of Jerusalem in A.D. 70, and Nero's persecution of the Christians, which began about A.D. 64. Therefore, because of these facts, and because the book does not record the death of Paul but leaves him a prisoner in Rome, it is logical to date the writing of Acts near the end of the apostle's imprisonment there in about A.D. 62.

Content. Acts is a sequel to the life of Christ in the Gospels, and it records the spread of Christianity from Jerusalem to Rome. It is the initiation of Jesus' Great Commission to make disciples of all nations (Matt. 28:18–20; Luke 24:46–49).

Acts 1:8 is the key to the book. Not only does this verse predict the outpouring of the Spirit and its powerful witness, but the geographical references present a simple outline of the narrative. In general, Acts relates the step-by-step expansion of Christianity westward from Palestine to Italy. The book thus begins in Jerusalem (chs. 1—7), with Peter assuming the major role and Jews as the recipients of the gospel.

Following the death of Stephen (7:60—8:1), widespread persecution broke out against the church, and believers scattered, sowing the seed of the gospel in Samaria and among the Gentiles (chs. 8—12). During this period of history the conversion of Saul occurred (ch. 9), an event of such importance that Luke includes three long descriptions of the incident (chs. 9; 22; 26).

The longest section of Acts focuses on the development and expansion of the Gentile ministry directed by Paul and his associates (chs. 13—28). It concludes with Paul's arrival in Rome, capital of the empire and representative of "the end of the earth." The book ends rather abruptly, probably because Luke had brought the matter up to date, and there was no more to write.

Purpose. The key to the purpose of Acts is in the first verse, where Luke implies that the book is a continuation of the Gospel of Luke. The Gospel told what "Jesus began both to do and teach," and Acts tells what the risen Lord continues to do and teach through the Holy Spirit.

Personal Application. Acts is a record of *practicing* Christianity under the power of the Holy Spirit. It teaches believers how to live together in meaningful Christian fellowship, sharing freely with one another (2:42; 4:32–35).

Conversely, Acts also shows that Christians inevitably will have disagreements (6:1; 11:1–3; 15:2, 7, 36–39), but that God gives wisdom and grace to settle differences (15:12–22). Even though the early church had its share of strong personalities, there was still a willingness to listen and to submit to one another (15:6–14).

Probably the most prominent characteristic of the early Christians was their spiritual power. They fasted and prayed fervently (2:42; 6:4; 13:3), and their faith released the miracle-working power of God (3:16). Acts is about ordinary people doing extraordinary things. Signs followed those who believed!! (*See* Mark 16:17–18.)

....

Kingdom Key continued from page 325

Messiah, including Israel's full restoration to God's intentions for her). Without criticizing their interest in this significant but secondary issue, Jesus puts them on the *primary* track of their call and mission. His answer essentially is: "Don't worry about *that* feature of 'the kingdom,' but *remain open to the Holy Spirit*. He will enable you to do 'kingdom business' until I come again" (1:6–8; *see* Luke 19:11–13)!

3. Acts 8:12 describes Phillip's evangelistic ministry in Samaria as he "preached the things concerning the kingdom of God." The context defines such preaching as: (a) being grounded in God's Word (8:4), (b) glorifying Christ (8:5), and (c) ministering in the authority of His name (8:12).

4. Acts 14:22 reveals how the message of
continued on next page

continued from preceding page

"the kingdom of God" is never so triumphalistic that it is unrealistic; that is, its positive note of victory is not violated by the presence of trials, nor is it insensitive to the temporary struggle they introduce. Paul and Barnabas were wise and patient to teach that even while the rule of God is entering our midst, its presence is not without seasons of travail and trial. It is spread through human vessels who often are opposed by hostile circumstances.

5. Acts 19:8 and 20:25 disclose the style of Paul's extended ministry in Ephesus and his final intimate exchange with the elders there. The combined texts define his preaching and teaching ministry, which is summarized with the double appearance of the phrase *"kingdom of God."* "(He) spoke boldly . . . reasoning and persuading concerning the things of the kingdom of God"; and, "I have gone preaching the kingdom of God." The context

reports the evidences of such ministry: (1) miracles of healing and deliverance (19:11–12); (2) resistance of spiritual opposition (19:9; 21–41); (3) God's Word prevailing as it is propagated (19:18–20); and (4) large numbers of believers added (19:26).

6. Acts concludes with two final references to the way the continuing testimony of Christ extended to and throughout the capital of the empire itself. Paul's ministry in Rome is again described by the message inherent in the words "kingdom of God" (28:23, 30–31). Thus the Book of Acts, which models the early church at work in the power of the Holy Spirit, (a) denotes our assigned message theme, (b) defines its content, and (c) describes the results we can expect to follow its proclamation: "The King has come, and His kingdom grace and power are here for you today!"

Power Key *continued from page 326*

(10:38). *The Book of Acts is the story of the disciples receiving what Jesus received in order to do what Jesus did.*

Luke's terminology in describing people's experience with the Holy Spirit in Acts is fluid. He is more interested in conveying a relational dynamic than in delineating a precisely worded theology. He notes that people were "filled with the Holy Spirit" (2:4; 9:17), that "they received the Holy Spirit" (8:17), that "the Holy Spirit fell upon [them]" (10:44), that "the Holy Spirit had been poured out on [them]" (10:45), and that "the Holy Spirit came upon them" (Acts 19:6). These are all essential equivalents of Jesus' promise that the church

would "be baptized with the Holy Spirit" (1:5; see especially its immediate fulfillment in 2:4, which Luke describes as a filling).

Three of these five instances record specific special manifestations of the Spirit in which the people themselves participated. Those on the Day of Pentecost and the Gentiles of Cornelius's house spoke with other tongues (2:4; 10:46); the Ephesians "spoke with tongues and prophesied" (19:6). Although it is not specified, it is generally agreed that there was also some type of manifestation in which the Samaritans participated because Luke says that "when Simon *saw* that . . . the Holy Spirit was given" (8:18).

Surveying
ACTS

I. PROLOGUE 1:1–14.

Preface (1:1–3). Acts takes up the gospel story, moving from what "Jesus began both to do and teach," to report on Jesus' post-Resurrection ministry through his disciples.

The promise of the Holy Spirit (1:4–8). Luke immediately picks up one of his major themes: the Holy Spirit. The disciples are to wait in Jerusalem for His "baptism." At first the church contained only Jewish believers, who continued to worship at the Jerusalem

temple and to live according to Old Testament Law. They were distinct only because they worshiped Jesus as God and recognized Him as the one who fulfilled the Old Testament messianic promises (*see* Kingdom of God).

Here, Jesus declares the source of power for the ministry, the Holy Spirit (1:6–8). And according to Luke 24:49, they are to continue to wait in Jerusalem for the Spirit's coming.

> "But you shall receive power when the Holy Spirit has come upon you; and you shall be witnesses to Me in Jerusalem, and in all Judea and Samaria, and to the end of the earth"

(1:8). The power for effective witness (*see* Evangelism) that shakes the world comes from the Pentecostal outpouring of the Spirit in Acts 2. Jesus would never have assigned the church a task it could not do; and it is impossible to convert a pagan world with human energy, strategy, and power. Evangelism by a Holy Spirit-filled church involved in local, regional, and global mission is God's plan to reach the world. (*See* Times.)

The Ascension of Christ (1:9–11). As if to punctuate the importance of the promise of the Holy Spirit, Jesus' Ascension adds miracle confirmation to His words.

"Jesus . . . will so come in like manner as you saw Him go into heaven"
(1:11). The Ascension (Luke 24:50–53) created an indelible impression of the opening of heaven and Jesus being "carried up into heaven." The same supernatural action that took Jesus to heaven will attend His return. The promise of His return is certain, and the manner of that return will be marked with the same splendor and supernatural witness (*see* Messianic Promises) as that of the Ascension.

The Upper Room prayer meeting (1:12–14). Here the stage is set for the launching of the ministry of this timid band of believers, who will soon spread the Good News through their world. (*See* Leadership, Spiritual.)

II. PETER AND THE MINISTRY OF THE JEWISH CHURCH IN JERUSALEM 1:15—12:24.

A. The selection of Matthias as the twelfth apostle (1:15–26). A man named Matthias is chosen to take the place of Judas. The term "apostle" now replaces the familiar "disciple" of the Gospels to identify the small group of men who followed Jesus. "Disciple" means "learner." "Apostle" means "one sent on a mission." (*See* Transgression.)

B. The Pentecostal outpouring of the Holy Spirit (2:1–47). Pentecost is the Old Testament harvest festival known as the "Feast of Weeks" (Ex. 34:22; Deut. 16:9–12). It is one of three religious festivals all Jews are to attend in Jerusalem, during which an offering is to be returned to God, according to His blessing of His people. In Jesus' surrender of His life on Calvary the ultimate blessing has been given. Now it is time for God to receive the first of a great harvest of believers, to be His own special people.

1. *The outpouring of the Spirit (2:1–4).* The promised coming of the Spirit (cf. 1:5) is marked by three unmistakable signs. There is a sudden roaring sound (2:2), visible tongues of fire rest on each of the 120 gathered for prayer (2:3, cf. 1:15), and all begin to speak in tongues as a supernatural display from the Holy Spirit (2:4; *see* Holy Spirit Gifts). This miracle manifestation resulted in an irresistible witness being born by the disciples to pilgrims who had come from all over the Mediterranean region for the feast.

"They were all filled with the Holy Spirit and began to speak with other tongues, as the Spirit gave them utterance"
(2:4–13). The miracle of Pentecost resulted in the infant church being filled with the Spirit. The manifestation of tongues took place as each person began to speak in a language they had not learned as a result of their being filled with the Spirit. Foreigners visiting Jerusalem recognized some of these languages spoken by the 120 who were filled, and they were amazed at hearing the testimony of "the wonderful works of God" in their native tongue.(*See* Accord.)

2. *The crowd's confused response (2:5–13).* Crowds of these visitors now stand stunned as "each one" hears Jesus' Galilean followers "speaking in our own tongues" (2:8, 11; *see* Works). Only to those who did not understand the foreign tongues did the speaking seem like drunken babbling (vv. 5–13).

3. *Peter's explanatory sermon (2:14–39).* Peter's explanation (2:14–39; *see* Leadership, Spiritual) quotes a long passage from Joel to explain the phenomenon. Before the day of the Lord comes God promised that the Spirit would be poured out on all peoples (2:14–18), and that in those days "whoever calls on the name of the LORD shall be saved" (2:21). What all see is evidence that the Spirit has at last come! Peter moves on immediately to tell his hearers that they can be saved by calling on the name of Jesus as Lord. The message concludes with a call to repentance and obedience, followed by reception of "the gift of the Holy Spirit" (v. 38).

> **"This Jesus God has raised up, of which we are all witnesses"**
> (2:32). Peter's witness is of Christ's resurrection (v. 31) and the fulfillment of His role as the crucified Son of God. We too share in that witness because the same resurrection power that was at work in Christ has been at work in the life of every believer (Rom. 6:4–5). Using the testimony of our changed lives, the Holy Spirit makes our witness of Christ's work in us real to people around us, drawing them to faith in Christ.

> **"Repent, and let every one of you be baptized in the name of Jesus Christ for the remission of sins; and you shall receive the gift of the Holy Spirit"**
> (2:38). Peter clearly describes the experience available to all people who are willing to follow Christ. Repentance and water baptism in the name of Jesus Christ establishes a person in the body of Christ. And as a part of Christ's body the supernatural gift of the Holy Spirit is available to all who will receive it, just as they have witnessed it on this Pentecost Day.

4. *The new church after Pentecost (2:40–47).* Peter's preaching leads to the conversion of some three thousand people! These form a devoted company, so committed to loving one another (*see* Fellowship; cf. John 13:33–34) that they are willing to sell their possessions to meet one another's needs.

> **"They ate their food with gladness and simplicity of heart, praising God and having favor with all the people"**
> (2:45–47). Praise was a way of life in the early church. They were experiencing rapid growth after Pentecost, and the daily gathering of converts focused on instruction in the Bible and praising God according to the patterns given in the Psalms. Speaking praise, clapping and lifting of hands, shouting, kneeling, singing, dancing, and more are all biblical expressions of praise used by the people of God. (*See* Manhood.)

C. The healing of the lame man (3:1— 4:31).

1. *The healing miracle (3:1–10).* One "miraculous sign" performed by the apostles is the healing of a cripple who begged at one of the temple gates. At the time of afternoon prayers, there are a host of witnesses to the healing performed in Jesus' name.

> **"Silver and gold I do not have, but what I do have I give you: In the name of Jesus Christ of Nazareth, rise up and walk"**
> (3:1–10). This is the first recorded healing after Pentecost. The disciples who were instructed to heal when Jesus was with them are now empowered to heal in His absence, as they have received the power of the Holy Spirit. This miracle-working power, present throughout the whole of the Book of Acts, is present in the church today. Peter clearly states that he has no power except that which is in the name of Jesus (3:16; *see* Faith's Confession).

2. *Peter's explanatory sermon (3:11–26).* Peter's message after this healing (*see* Healing, Divine) is the same as his Pentecost sermon (2:22–41). Israel has turned the Messiah (Christ) over to execution. But God has raised Him from the dead (14–15). It is Jesus' power that has been exercised to make "this man strong, whom you see and know." Each listener has the opportunity through Jesus to "be converted, that your sins may be blotted out" (19; *see* Restoration).

> **"His name, through faith in His name, has made this man strong"**
> (3:16). The name of Jesus is linked with His character, power, and Person. As we declare "in Jesus name," it is not on our own authority or privilege that we speak, but His. Acts 19:13–16 illustrates the folly of merely speaking the name Jesus without accompanying faith in that name. His name is not a chant or mantra, but, when spoken in living faith based on a personal relationship with Christ, it is the key to the release of heaven's power.

3. *The arrest of Peter and John (4:1–4).* The Sanhedrin was responsible for forcing the crucifixion of Jesus. Understandably, they are "greatly disturbed" at the miracles and the announcement of Jesus' resurrection and the five thousand new believers.

4. *Peter's defense before the Sanhedrin (4:5–12).* When Peter is asked about the source of the miracle, he proclaims not only the

source of healing, but the way of salvation in Christ.

> ### "Then Peter, filled with the Holy Spirit"
>
> (4:8). This text does not suggest that Peter was "refilled" with the Holy Spirit in the sense that he ceased to live in Spirit fullness. It refers to the ongoing development of Spirit fullness in Peter's life and the unique sense of the operation of the Holy Spirit at this moment of deep need as Peter speaks to the Sanhedrin concerning the healing of the man in Acts 3. (*See* Evangelism; Other.)

5. *The Sanhedrin's response (4:13–22).* The leaders are determined to stop the movement from spreading beyond Jerusalem (16).

Peter and John boldly confront the leaders of their people. Fearlessly they announce, "Nor is there salvation in any other." Although the leaders threaten Peter and John, the two openly announce that they will do what is right in God's sight.

> ### "We cannot but speak the things which we have seen and heard"
>
> (4:20). Peter and John are answering the charges of hostile spiritual leaders in Jerusalem, who are disturbed by the growing number of converts. The testimony of the early church consisted of their witness of Jesus Christ as the Messiah and Son of God, and their words were confirmed by miracle demonstrations of the Holy Spirit's power (3:2–10). This pattern of witness is irresistible to human systems and reason, and it is fatal to the works of darkness attempting to thwart world evangelism.

6. *Thanksgiving for the apostle's release (4:23–31).* Peter and John report these threats to the believing community and all turn together to God in *prayer. All the rage of the leaders and their plot against Jesus has been in vain. God's will has been accomplished, through their hatred! Now the believers ask God as Sovereign Lord not for protection, but for boldness and power to speak out in the name of Jesus.

> ### "When they had prayed, the place where they were assembled together was shaken; and they were all filled with the Holy Spirit, and they

spoke the word with *boldness"

(4:31). The relationship between prayer and the release of dynamic Holy Spirit-energized action is clear (*see* Spiritual Warfare). As the disciples prayed there was physical and spiritual demonstration of the Holy Spirit's presence and power which was experienced by "all." Some were filled for the first time with the Holy Spirit, while others experienced a fresh energizing of the Spirit's power to boldly proclaim and witness about Jesus.

D. Apostolic authority in the early church (4:32—5:42).

1. *Oversight of charitable gifts (4:32–37).* This first threat of persecution caused the early church to draw even closer together. It stimulated not only prayer but also the willingness of each to help meet the needs of others (34; *see* Stewardship). The description here and in 2:44–45 is not of some "Christian communism." It is instead a demonstration of Jesus' kind of selfless love for others (cf. John 13:33–34).

> ### "With great power the apostles gave witness to the resurrection of the Lord Jesus"
>
> (4:33). This great *power was first seen in Acts 2 with the conversion of three thousand on the Day of Pentecost. Now, the leaders of the infant church have just experienced a bona fide prayer meeting, complete with an earthquake (v. 31) and the release of Holy Spirit power which accompanies their witness. This serves as a pattern to be observed today. Our hope in reaching the world is not in marketing the gospel. Our hope is in sensitized, Holy Spirit-orchestrated witness, anointed with supernatural power, which comes only as the church seeks the Lord in prayer. (*See* Faith's Confession.)

2. *Judgment of sin: Ananias and Sapphira (5:1–11).* Seeing the honor in which those who gave all for their brothers and sisters were held, one couple sells land and agrees together to lie about the amount when they present part to the apostles for the church. This hypocrisy and dishonesty is a serious threat to the unity of prayer and love that exists (4:23–37). God acts and judges Ananias and Sapphira immediately. The awe inspired by the sudden deaths (5:11) deepens the aware-

ness of the church and the community that God is among this people.

> ### "Ananias, why has Satan filled your heart?"
>
> (5:3–5). "A certain man" (v. 1) signifies that Ananias was known to the disciples as one who had followed their teachings and ministry. The presumption here is that Ananias had a choice in the matter of filling his heart with Satan. There is no specific mention concerning Ananias' spiritual condition before his deception; however, his presence within the church and the harsh judgment upon him and his wife suggests that he is responsible for the consequence of his actions. Ecclesiastes 9:3 describes the destruction of a human heart that has refused the way of God.

3. Healings and miracles (5:12–16). The crowds continue to gather to hear the apostles and be healed. (*See* Esteemed.)

> ### "They brought the sick out into the streets and laid them on beds and couches, that at least the shadow of Peter passing by might fall on some of them"
>
> (5:15–16). This amazing account goes beyond the healings recorded in the Gospels. Verse 16 insists that "they were all healed." The same power that Jesus possessed in healing the sick was present in the Book of Acts. Our boldness to continue in the ministry of healing is based on the promise of His Word and the work of the Holy Spirit.

4. Powerlessness of the opposition (5:17–42).

Supernatural release from prison (5:17–21). This rouses jealousy and the apostles are arrested and brought before the Sanhedrin.

The boldness of the apostles (5:22–32). Peter and the others boldly present Christ and His offer of forgiveness of sins (5:31–32). But there is no repentance from the leaders who murdered the Lord.

> ### "We are His witnesses to these things, and so also is the Holy Spirit whom God has given to those who obey Him"
>
> (5:32). A profound conviction of the Holy Spirit was felt by all who heard Peter's

words in the Jerusalem council. It is a scene repeated whenever Christ is witnessed to by His children. Jesus promised the coming of the "Helper" (John 15:26): "He will testify of Me." Whenever any believer begins to speak of Jesus Christ, the Holy Spirit not only assists the witness, but confirms and personalizes it to each hearer in such a way that the Truth cannot be ignored.

The counsel of Gamaliel to release the apostles (5:33–42). Gamaliel persuades the Sanhedrin not to press for execution. This most influential rabbi, the teacher of the apostle Paul before his conversion (Acts 22:3), argues that if the movement is not of God, it will fail. If the Christian movement is from God, the leaders will not be able to stop it. Temporarily persuaded, the court settles for beating the apostles.

E. The ministry of Stephen (6:1—7:60).

1. His selection as one of the seven deacons (6:1–7). Another serious internal problem develops when some Greek-speaking Jewish Christians complain that their widows are not given a fair share in the daily food distribution. The apostles ask the whole community to choose seven "known to be full of the Spirit and wisdom" to oversee this ministry. The twelve will be free to devote themselves to prayer and teaching.

> ### "Seek out from among you seven men of good reputation, full of the Holy Spirit and wisdom"
>
> (6:3). In the selection of leaders to assist the Twelve in serving the needs of the multitudes of new converts, three sets of qualities were essential. First, they sought men of "good reputation"—with character and confirmed, consistent lifestyles. Second, they wanted men committed to supernatural living in the power of the Holy Spirit (*see* Spiritual Warfare). Third, they desired people who were wise—not novices, but people who had experienced enough of life to be able to make discerning decisions in ministry.

> ### "A man full of faith and the Holy Spirit"
>
> (6:5). This passage highlights two dramati-

cally different aspects of the work of the Holy Spirit in the life of a person. First, there is character transformation based on the fruit of the Spirit and having "crucified the flesh" (Gal. 5:22–24). Second, there is the power of Holy Spirit baptism at work in and through us as we receive, through faith, Spirit fullness for the working of miracle power and gifts of the Holy Spirit. Both are necessary for those who will be set apart for leadership in the church (v. 3).

2. His power, ministry, and arrest (6:8–15). Stephen's witness to Jesus is so powerful that his frustrated opponents seize him and bring him before the Sanhedrin. They have arranged for perjured testimony to be given against him. (*See* Blasphemous.)

> **"Stephen, full of faith and power, did great wonders and signs among the people"**
> (6:8). Miracles in the post-Pentecost church were not restricted to apostolic activity. The promise from Jesus was that those who believe will do "greater works" than those witnessed in His own ministry (John 14:12). God's desire to confirm the Word and to meet human need makes any person of faith—like Stephen—a candidate for Holy Spirit miracle power. (*See* Wisdom.)

3. His defense before the Sanhedrin (7:1–53). Stephen recites the history of Israel's relationship with God (*see* Promised). He demonstrates from the Old Testament that the Hebrew people have always resisted the Lord. And he applies this truth pointedly. They killed the prophets; now this generation has betrayed and murdered their Messiah. (*See* Holy.)

4. His martyrdom (7:54–60). When Stephen announces that he sees Jesus now, standing at God's right hand in heaven, the yelling crowd drags him out of the city. They stone Stephen to death. There has been no trial, no verdict, and the Sanhedrin lacks authority to condemn anyone to death. Stephen has been murdered by a mob.

> **"But he (Stephen) being full of the Holy Spirit, gazed into heaven and saw the glory of God"**
> (7:55). At Stephen's martyrdom, the obvious presence of the Holy Spirit sustaining

the witness of this man of God is impressive to all. Stephen draws on the supernatural presence of the Spirit in his life as he declares Christ to them. The irresistible truth, confirmed by the Holy Spirit in Stephen's words, inflames the crowd and results in his being received into glory by the Lord.

F. The first ministry to non-Jews (8:1–40). The persecution of believers which follows the murder of Stephen scatters Christians across Judea and Samaria. One of the chief persecutors is a man we will come to know well: Saul, who became the apostle Paul.

1. To the Samaritans (Philip and Peter) (8:1–25). Luke traces the ministry of Philip, one of the seven of Acts 6:5, to illustrate the witness of the scattered believers. Philip proclaims Christ in a Samaritan city and there is a great response (8:7, 12). (*See* Church.)

> **"Those who were scattered went everywhere preaching the word"**
> (8:4). The witness in preaching included "those who were scattered"—specifically referring to some who were not apostles (v. 1). Some today consider the proclamation of Christ prohibitive to those who are not educated, spiritual, or holy enough. The call to preach is not complicated—it is the call to tell people about Jesus and what He has done in a believer's life. The growth of the early church is directly related to the scattering of the witness by "ordinary" church members who accepted Jesus' challenge in Acts 1:8 to "be witnesses to Me."

> **"Unclean spirits, crying with a loud voice, came out of many who were possessed; and many who were paralyzed and lame were healed"**
> (8:6–7). The incidence of demon possession was verified by Luke the physician, who meticulously distinguishes between physical, emotional, and spiritual problems in Luke and Acts. Philip casts out the demons and heals the lame as the presence of the kingdom of God manifests itself. Note that Philip is not one of the Twelve, just a man "full of the Holy Spirit and wisdom" (Acts 6:3–6).

Report of the revival brings Peter and John from Jerusalem. In this instance the

Holy Spirit is given by the laying on of the apostles' hands (8:15–17).

This chapter also tells of a sorcerer, Simon, who had convinced the Samaritans he has some great power. Stunned by the real miracles of Peter and Philip, he professes faith and follows them, to learn the secret of their power. But his old motivations are strong and he tries to buy power from Peter. Simon may have been a believer, but he was not able to share in the ministry, for his motives and character were still in the grip of sin (20–23). Salvation is for all who believe. Ministry is for those whose faith brings them significant inner transformation.

"Then they laid hands on them, and they received the Holy Spirit" (8:14–17). The Samaritans believed in Christ and had been baptized by Philip (8:12). When Peter and John arrived from Jerusalem to examine this revival they discovered that they had yet to "receive the Holy Spirit." Both Peter and John laid hands on these converts, who "received" the Holy Spirit. This is consistent with the pattern given by Peter in Acts 2:38. It is obvious that some supernatural activity occurred when hands were laid on the converts, because when Simon the sorcerer saw what happened he offered to buy from the apostles the power to receive the Holy Spirit (8:18–19).

2. To the Ethiopian (Philip) (8:26–40). Philip is led away (*see* Angels) from the revival in Samaria by God to witness to an individual. The man is an official (*see* Authority) in the court of the Ethiopian queen—a Jew or Jewish convert who had come to Jerusalem to worship. Philip interprets the passage he is reading in Isaiah 53 and leads him to faith in Jesus. The conversion is sincere, and at the Ethiopian's urging, Philip baptizes him along the roadside.

"Then Philip opened his mouth, and beginning at this Scripture, preached Jesus to him" (8:26–40). It is a proven fact that evangelism one-on-one is the most effective form of witness. Philip and the Ethiopian eunuch are experiencing a Holy Spirit-orchestrated moment where the hunger of the eunuch's heart and the presence of Philip result in his conversion. The single greatest joy for any believer is to be used to tell a person about Jesus and watch the Holy Spirit expand and deepen the testimony of Christ until a decision is made and faith in Christ declared. Many Christians have never led another person to faith because they have not been sensitive to the open door of ministry or bold enough to enter through that door. People are hungering for the reality of God in their life. Jesus is our message and their answer.

G. The conversion of Saul (9:1–31). The high priest has legal authority from Rome to arrest those Jews who break the Jewish religious law. Saul obtains letters of authority from him and heads toward Damascus intending to arrest "any who were of the Way" (9:2).

On the way, Christ appears to Saul in blazing light. Blinded, Saul must be led to Damascus. There the Lord sends a believer to restore his sight. Three great convictions which will rule Saul's life are born in this experience: Saul now knows for certain that (1) Jesus is Lord, (2) Jesus must be preached, and (3) Saul is God's chosen instrument to carry the name of Jesus to the Gentiles.

"Jesus, who appeared to you on the road as you came, has sent me that you may receive your sight and be filled with the Holy Spirit" (9:17). Saul's Damascus road experience with Jesus has resulted in a dramatic conversion to Christ. Ananias then is instructed to lay hands on Saul for the restoration of his sight and so that Saul may be filled with the Holy Spirit. In this case Spirit fullness precedes baptism in water. Though there is no mention of a miracle manifestation, clearly the apostle Paul later functions in the gifts of the Holy Spirit and enthusiastically speaks in tongues (1 Cor. 14:18).

At once Saul begins to preach (*see* Preached) in the synagogues of Damascus, boldly showing that Jesus is the Son of God. As Saul learns, his preaching becomes more powerful and compelling. Soon the life of the zealous convert is threatened and he barely escapes the city (9:29).

He returns to Jerusalem, but the Christians there fear a trick and will have nothing to do with him. Finally Barnabas, who later will be his first missionary companion, accepts the risk and brings him to the apostles. Within weeks Paul's bold and fearless preaching seems about to arouse a fresh wave of persecution! The brothers "brought him down to Caesarea and sent him out to Tarsus" (v. 30; *see* Comfort.)

H. Aeneas and Dorcas healed through Peter's ministry (9:32–43). Peter travels about the country, teaching and healing as he visits the saints. The profound miracles attending his ministry are reminiscent of Jesus' power in the raising of the dead. His ministry brings him to Joppa, where he stays with a tanner named Simon.

I. The story of Cornelius (10:1—11:18).

1. Cornelius and his house come to Christ (10:1–48). Cornelius is a Roman army officer. The term "God-fearing" is a technical term for a person who believes in God and worships Him, but who has not been circumcised or converted to Judaism. This man now has a vision in which he is told to send to Joppa and summon Peter.

Peter's vision (10:9–23). "Uncleanness" is a religious concept from the Old Testament. One who is ritually unclean is unable to participate in worship or other religious practices until he or she has been cleansed. The Jews avoided anything which could cause them to become unclean, and especially avoided unclean foods. Gentiles were considered to be unclean by the Jews of the first century, and a pious Jew would not enter a Gentile home or eat with him.

As the messengers of Cornelius travel to Joppa, Peter falls into a trance on the roof of Simon's home. He sees a great canvas sheet let down from heaven, filled with unclean animals. A voice from heaven commands Peter to kill and eat. Shocked, Peter refuses. Three times this experience is repeated, with the voice telling Peter, "What God has cleansed you must not call common" (15). As Peter ponders the meaning of the vision, the Holy Spirit tells him of Cornelius' messengers and says specifically, "Go down and go with them, doubting nothing; for I have sent them" (20). God is about to announce that He has made clean a people the Jews have considered impure!

At Cornelius' house (10:23–48). Peter tells Cornelius how God has "shown me that I should not call any man common or unclean" (28) and asks why he has been sent for. Cornelius tells of his vision and, for the first time, Peter preaches Jesus to a Gentile audience (34–43; *see* Partiality).

As Peter is speaking, the Holy Spirit comes on these new believers and they speak in other languages in praise of God (44–46; cf. Acts 2:1–4; *see* Holy Spirit Gifts). Peter recognizes that this is compelling evidence that

these Gentiles are to be accepted as full participants with them in the new community of faith! Peter accepts this evidence and baptizes the new believers in the name of Jesus Christ.

"The Holy Spirit fell upon all those who heard the word"
(10:44). As Peter preached to Cornelius's household, where Gentiles had gathered to hear about Christ, there was a Holy Spirit outbreak among the listeners. They spoke in tongues and magnified God (v. 46). The Jews witnessing the event declared that these Gentiles had obviously received the Holy Spirit and should therefore be baptized. Here the evidence of the Spirit's reception was the presence of tongues, just as it occurred in Acts 2. Clearly, the outbreak of the Spirit was directly related to faith in Christ by the listeners, who had just heard Peter declare that "whoever believes in Him will receive remission of sins" (v. 43).

2. Peter defends his witness to the Gentiles (11:1–18). Even though Peter is an apostle, his visit to Cornelius stimulates strong criticism. Peter's defense lays a new basis for acceptance of other believers and leads toward the realization that relationship with Jesus and not the Mosaic Law provides the foundation for fellowship in the universal church.

Peter simply reports what has happened (11:4–18). He emphasizes five historic facts. (1) Through a vision God taught him not to think of other persons as "unclean." (2) The Holy Spirit directed him to go to Cornelius' house. (3) An angel was sent by God to Cornelius. (4) The angel promised that Peter would share the message of salvation. And (5), there was outward evidence that the Holy Spirit baptized these Gentiles.

"And as I began to speak, the Holy Spirit fell upon them, as upon us at the beginning"
(11:15–17). In recounting the experience with Cornelius's household, Peter relates Jesus' promise of Holy Spirit baptism to his experience in Caesarea (10:44). The proof that the Gentiles received the "same gift" (v. 17) as those at Pentecost was tongues. The Jewish church in Jerusalem concludes from this that the Gentiles have been included by God in the plan of salvation (v. 18).

J. The witness of the early church (11:19—12:24).

1. Paul and Barnabas at Antioch (11:19–30). When Gentiles in the Greek city of Antioch turn to Christ in great numbers, the Jerusalem believers accept the movement as a work of God (11:19–26). Barnabas is sent to Antioch. He recognizes God's hand, brings Saul from Tarsus to help, and the two stay to teach and minister in this first Gentile congregation.

The Gentile church demonstrates its sense of oneness with the Jewish church of the holy land when prophets foretell a famine. The years of famine fall between A.D. 43 and 47. It is only a little over a decade since the crucifixion of Jesus, and already the first colony of God's people has been established in the Gentile world.

"Agabus, stood up and showed by the Spirit that there was going to be a great famine throughout all the world"
(11:27–28). Agabus prophesied through one of the gifts of the Holy Spirit as recorded in 1 Corinthians 12:7–11 (*see* Prophecy). The purpose of the gift was not simply to tell the future, but to prepare the infant church for a ministry opportunity and allow the people of God time to prepare for the great need that would arise during the famine.

2. Peter's miraculous escape from Herod's prison (12:1–24). The Herod who initiates the third persecution of the believers is the grandson of Herod the Great, and nephew of that Herod who beheaded John the Baptist. His harassment, begun to please the Jewish leaders, led to the death of John's brother, James. Now Herod seizes Peter as well.

In 12:5–19, an angel frees Peter from his prison the night before his trial is scheduled. Peter joins a group gathered at the home of Mark's mother to pray for him (*see* Prayer).

Shortly after Peter's release, Herod dies suddenly (v. 23). The date, fixed from secular sources, is A.D. 44. This ends the third wave of persecution in Jerusalem, which probably began about A.D. 41 when Herod began his rule.

III. PAUL AND THE INTERNATIONAL OUTREACH OF THE CHURCH AT ANTIOCH 12:25—28:31.

A. Paul's first missionary journey (12:25—14:28).

1. Paul's apostolic commission (12:25—13:3).

Set aside by God (13:1–3). Barnabas and Saul return from Jerusalem, to which they have delivered relief funds (12:25). Now they are called by God to a special work (*see* Ministered). Their commission from the Holy Spirit is affirmed by the church (13:3; *see* Leadership, Spiritual; Prayer), and they set off together on their first missionary journey.

2. Exorcism on Cyprus (13:4–12). Cyprus has been an important trading center from the 19th century B.C. It has had a large Jewish population for at least two hundred years. Paul proclaims the Word in the Jewish synagogues and travels the whole island preaching the gospel. On these travels he meets the Roman governor of the province, a proconsul named Sergius Paulus. At Paul's word, the Lord strikes a false prophet who advises Paulus—with blindness. The governor, amazed at the message of Jesus, becomes a believer.

"Then Saul, who also is called Paul, filled with the Holy Spirit, looked intently at him"
(13:9). Saul was "filled with the Holy Spirit" in 9:17. However, this passage vibrates with the passion of a moment in ministry when the presence of the gospel in an entire nation (Cyprus) is being challenged by demonic forces focused in Elymas. The drama is highlighted by Paul's pronouncement against this enemy of God and the salvation of the proconsul (v. 12).

3. Preaching and revival at Antioch in Pisidia (13:13–50). This inland city was included in the Roman province of Galatia. It had a large Jewish and Roman population.

On the Sabbath the missionaries attend the synagogue and, as is the custom, are invited to share a "word of exhortation for the people" (15). The message which Paul preaches clearly parallels the early preaching of Peter and Stephen.

The response of the hearers will be duplicated over and over again across the years of missionary endeavor. The Jews debate the message among themselves; the Gentiles respond enthusiastically. When "almost the whole city" gathers to hear the Word of the Lord the next Sabbath, the Jews grow jealous and angry. Jealousy shuts their hearts to the gospel, and they stir up persecution against the missionaries. (*See* Leadership, Spiritual; Promise; Strangers.)

4. Signs and wonders at Iconium (13:51—14:5).

> ### "And the disciples were filled with joy and with the Holy Spirit"
>
> (13:52). Even though Paul and Barnabas were persecuted and driven out of Antioch, the Holy Spirit imbued their hearts with an abundance of joy (vv. 42–44; 51–52). Jesus told His disciples that great blessing and reward await those who can rejoice in trial (Matt. 5:10–12). Whether put down for our faith or discredited in our testimony, the Spirit is ready to permeate our souls with "joy inexpressible" (1 Pet. 1:8), a Christlike fruit of those who walk in the Spirit (Gal. 5:22). During times of crisis, He releases His great joy within us, inspiring courage and perseverance as we surrender to the Spirit's impression upon our hearts.

Barnabas and Paul continue on to several key cities in Asia, preaching the gospel and establishing new churches.

The ancient settlement of Iconium (14:1–5) is the principal city of Lycaonia. The missionaries stay in the city for some time, until its population is deeply divided and their enemies plot to kill them.

5. *Healing and stoning at Lystra (14:6–20).* Lystra is a small rural mountain town, well off the major trade routes. There is a tradition that it was once visited by the gods in human form. When Paul and Barnabas heal a cripple there, the two are believed to be gods themselves.

> ### "Paul, observing him intently and seeing that he had faith to be healed"
>
> (14:8–10). The miracle healing of the crippled man demonstrates a healing gift. However, it also illustrates the role of discerning the understanding and readiness of a person to receive the miracle work of God. The presence of the man's faith was crucial to the reception of the gift of healing.

The apostles stop the crowd from sacrificing to them and preach the gospel. Soon some Jews from Antioch and Iconium turn the people against them. Paul is stoned and left for dead outside the town. (*See* Useless.)

6. *Follow-up ministry and return to Antioch (14:21–28).* After two years on mission, the team returns to the Antioch church which sent them out. They report how the door to faith is wide open to the Gentiles. (*See* Kingdom of God.)

Leaders appointed. Verse 23 speaks of Paul and Barnabas "appointing" elders when they revisit the newly established churches. The word in Greek does not require hierarchical interpretation. Instead it probably suggests official recognition or ordination of those whom God has put forward and the people have recognized as their leaders.

B. The council at Jerusalem to discuss law and grace (15:1–35). Some converted Pharisees (cf. 15:1 with 15:5) come to the Gentile churches and try to impose the Mosaic Law on the Gentile church (15:5). This teaching stimulates a serious debate.

Paul and Barnabas are appointed, with others, as a delegation to go to Jerusalem and discuss the issue with the apostles and elders.

Peter points out that God has accepted the Gentiles as they are and given them the Holy Spirit just as He has given the Spirit to Jewish believers.

> ### "So God, who knows the heart, acknowledged them by giving them the Holy Spirit, just as He did to us"
>
> (15:8). Peter's statement to the council of Jerusalem reaffirms the place of the Gentiles in the body of Christ. The miracle demonstration of tongues in 10:46 forever answers the question concerning God's intention about the inclusion of Gentiles in the church by "giving them the Holy Spirit."

Then Barnabas and Paul add their testimony of God's work among the Gentiles, reporting the miraculous signs (*see* Wonders) that authenticate the movement as a work of God (12).

Finally James, who has emerged as the leader of the Jerusalem church, speaks up. He quotes God's words from Amos 9:11–12 showing that God predicted the salvation of Gentiles *as Gentiles.* The Jewish church then should also accept their Gentile brothers as they are (13–18; *see* Restoration), without insisting they adopt Judaism.

James sums up the sense of the council (vv. 13–21). They should not "trouble" the Gentiles who are turning to God. He suggests only that four guidelines be passed on to the Gentile churches. They should abstain from all association with idol worship, reject sexual immorality, give up unbutchered meat (a prohibition which may be related to Lev. 17:10–12), and abstain "from blood."

The official letter (15:22–35) sent out by the apostles and elders is no authoritative command. Instead it simply tells the Gentile churches that any who came from Jerusalem "and troubled you" did so without authorization of the leaders. Led by the Spirit, the Jerusalem congregation has been led not to "burden" the Gentiles with anything other than the four issues James suggested.

The Jerusalem council has dealt wisely with a basic issue, an issue Paul recognized and writes of in Galatians. Not only is the unity of the church on the sole basis of faith in Christ reaffirmed, but the Mosaic Law is beginning to be seen by believers in a new perspective.

> **"Judas and Silas, themselves being prophets also, exhorted and strengthened the brethren with many words"**
> (15:32). Ephesians 4:11 teaches that Jesus Himself has given gifts to His church. The office gift of prophet is one of these gifts, acknowledged in this passage. Those called to be prophets regularly functioned in the gift of prophecy as a matter of their call to ministry. Though all believers who have received the baptism with the Holy Spirit are privileged to prophesy, and are encouraged to do so (1 Cor. 14:1), it is not necessarily a regular function in their personal ministry.

C. Paul's second missionary journey (15:36—18:22).

1. Paul and Barnabas divide over Mark (15:36–41). A sharp disagreement breaks up the missionary team of Paul and Barnabas. The tragic dispute shows that even the great apostle is fallible.

2. Follow-up ministry with Timothy (16:1–5). Paul forms a new team and sets out on another journey. He first visits Gentile churches, sharing the conclusion of the Jerusalem council. At this point Luke joins the missionary team. From Acts 16:10 on he reports the journeys in Acts as something which "we" undertook.

3. The vision to evangelize Greece (16:6–10). Paul and his team are led by God into Europe. (*See* Leadership, Spiritual.)

4. Baptism of Lydia at Philippi (16:11–15). There are too few Jews in Philippi to establish a synagogue, but Paul finds a few worshipers of the Lord gathered by a river on the Sabbath. The first European convert is a woman named Lydia.

5. Imprisonment at Philippi (16:16–40). When Paul casts a demon out of a slave girl used as a fortune-teller, her furious owners charge that the missionaries "exceedingly trouble our city."

> **"I command you in the name of Jesus Christ"**
> (16:16–18). Paul's ministry to the young woman bound by the spirit of "python" (v. 16, Greek) is done in the name of Jesus Christ. Paul does not presume to minister in his own authority (John 12:49). It is interesting that it takes "many days" (v. 18) for Paul to either discern her bondage or take action on it; it is not until the distraction she makes becomes annoying that Paul casts the demon out.

A crowd joins in the attack, and the city magistrates have Paul and Silas beaten and thrown into prison. When an earthquake opens the prison doors, the jailer intends suicide. But no prisoners are gone, and the jailer, who has apparently heard the missionaries' preaching, asks Paul how to be saved. (*See* Charge; Praise.)

> **" 'Sirs, what must I do to be saved?' So they said, 'Believe on the Lord Jesus Christ, and you will be saved, you and your household.' "**
> (16:29–32). The Philippian jailer's world has crashed around him. The earthquake has destroyed his jail, and the fear of a prison escape has brought him to the point of suicide. Now he is ready to receive Christ. A heart softened to receive the gospel at a critical moment in life shows the work of God bringing that individual to Christ. As life becomes drained of superficiality, and the reality of human finiteness grips a soul, there is a place for sensitive, Holy Spirit-filled, loving witness.

The next day the missionaries are discovered to be Roman citizens! Their beating without trial was illegal. Humbly the city magistrates come and apologetically request that Paul and Silas leave.

6. Riot at Thessalonica (17:1–9). The pattern seen earlier is now repeated in this, the largest and most important city in Macedonia. The team of missionaries goes first to the synagogue. Gentiles respond enthusiastically. (*See* Suffer.)

7. Openness to the Word in Berea (17:10–15). Berea is a small city some sixty miles from Thessalonica. The Jews there listen for three Sabbaths to Paul teach from the Old Testament. Many of these Jews are convinced and, with prominent Greek men and women, become Christians. All goes well until the Jews of Thessalonica send agitators to stir up trouble.

8. Philosophizing in Athens (17:16–34). Paul's stay in Athens is brief—but important to our understanding of missions. Here his preaching is appropriate to an audience which is very different from the Jews and God-fearing Gentiles whom Paul usually approaches first.

Athens is the ancient home of Plato and Aristotle and still the center of philosophical speculation in the ancient world (*see* Babbler). So Paul begins his talk with reference to an altar to an "unknown God" that he has observed among their many objects of worship (22–23).

Paul has done what many missionaries today argue should be done in our outreach efforts. He has contextualized the gospel. He has not changed the message of Jesus and resurrection. But he has put the message in a form suited to the thought patterns of his listeners. (*See* Human Worth.)

9. One and a half years in Corinth (18:1–17). Corinth is a bustling port city, the capital of Achaia. It is very prosperous and is a center for worship of the love goddess, Aphrodite. Corinth is well known for its easy immorality and extravagances. Paul comes to this city shortly after the emperor Claudius has expelled the Jews from Rome (18:2, A.D. 49) and while Gallio, who is the brother of the philosopher Seneca, is proconsul (18:12, c. A.D. 51). Paul is to stay in Corinth for at least eighteen months.

> **"Do not be afraid, but speak, and do not keep silent; for I am with you and no one will attack you to hurt you; for I have many people in this city"** (18:9–10). Jesus' words underscore two important principles in evangelism: (1) "speak, do not keep silent," and (2) God has people prepared to respond whenever witness is given. The devil will use any means to discourage or intimidate believers to silence in their witness—don't let him silence you! The results belong to the Lord, but we are commanded to witness in obedience to His leading. The Lord has many people in your city; allow Him to use you to reach them.

10. Return to Antioch (18:18–22). After an extended ministry in Corinth, Paul sets sail for Ephesus, taking his fellow tentmakers Priscilla and Aquilla with him. Promising to return to Ephesus for a longer stay later, Paul soon moves on to his "home base" in Antioch.

D. Paul's third missionary journey (18:23—21:14).

1. Ministry, miracles, and rioting in Ephesus (18:23—19:41). Ephesus is known as the gateway to Asia. It is situated on a great harbor and it is the terminus of a major highway between the coast and central Asia Minor. The city also contains one of the seven wonders of the ancient world: the great temple of Artemis. This is the religious center of all Asia, and metalworkers make a rich living from the sale of shrines and miniature silver images of the goddess.

Apollos is a learned Jew who has heard only the message of John the Baptist. He vigorously preaches that the Messiah is coming. When Apollos comes to Ephesus and gives his message in a local synagogue, Priscilla and Aquila from Corinth hear him and invite him to their home. There in private they "explained to him the way of God more accurately."

When the Bible refers to the couple who shared Christ with Apollos it is the wife, Priscilla, who usually is listed first. She is evidently recognized as one of the leaders of the early church (cf. Rom. 16:3; 1 Cor. 16:19; 2 Tim. 4:19).

Upon Paul's return to Ephesus, he finds others who know of John the Baptist's ministry but have not yet heard of Jesus (cf. 18:24–26; *see* Fervent). They believe and are filled with the Holy Spirit—evidence that Jesus truly is the one whom John foretold (19:1–7; *see* Holy Spirit Gifts).

> **"Did you receive the Holy Spirit when you believed?"** (19:1–7). Paul rebaptizes the Ephesians since they did not have full knowledge of the Holy Spirit's work, having received only the baptism of John the Baptist (18:24–28). After Paul baptized them "in the name of the Lord Jesus," he laid hands on them and "they spoke with tongues and prophesied." This pattern of hands being laid on a person for reception of the Holy Spirit is seen in Acts 8:17 and 9:17, but it is absent in Acts 2:4 and 10:46.

Many respond to the missionary team. This passage shows the dramatic impact of the gospel on the life of a typical pagan city

(13–20), and also reveals more of Paul's missionary strategy. By choosing capital cities and trade centers for their preaching, the missionary team makes sure that converts will carry the word through their own provinces. Within two years of the concentrated effort in Ephesus, the gospel has been spread throughout the province of Asia (cf. 19:10).

"Even handkerchiefs or aprons were brought from his body to the sick, and the diseases left them and the evil spirits went out of them"
(19:11–12). Paul's healing ministry was "unusual" even by Book of Acts standards (v. 11). The mode of healing was through blessed pieces of cloth which Paul had touched. There is no pattern to be established on how to minister healing, only the fact that God is creative and uses any means that will help people to exercise faith in Jesus for healing.

"Jesus I know, and Paul I know; but who are you?"
(19:13–20). The terrifying words of the demon preceded a vicious physical assault that left the seven sons of Sceva "naked and wounded" (v. 16). Their presumption to cast out demons on the authority of Paul, without a personal relationship with Christ, was folly of the first order. The demon in this passage was capable of recognizing the level of spiritual relationship the men had with Christ and determined they had no authority for exorcism. (*See* Word.)

Riot in Ephesus (19:21–41). Paul has decided to travel to Jerusalem and then on to Rome. Before he leaves Ephesus there is a riot, led by a silversmith whose idol-making business is being ruined by the mass conversion of the population (23–28)! The magistrates finally quiet the crowds, insisting that if anyone has a grievance it should be handled through the courts or in a legal assembly (35–41). The response of the city officials shows the great value of Roman authority to the early church. Rome controls the western world, and Rome insists on legal due process (cf. 19:39).

2. Journeys in Greece (20:1–6).
Through Macedonia (20:1–2). Paul revisits the churches he has established in Macedonia and Greece.

3. Paul's all-night sermon in Troas (20:7–12). His sense of urgency to impart all he can to these young believers is illustrated by his all-night teaching at Troas.

4. From Troas to Miletus and Paul's farewell address to the Ephesian elders (20:13–38). Luke shows us more clearly the sense of urgency that now drives Paul. He is unwilling to take time to revisit Ephesus and sends messengers to have the elders of that city meet him as he passes by. Paul reviews his ministry with them (17–21; *see* Humility) and shares that he is "bound in the spirit" to go to Jerusalem, aware that danger, imprisonment, and hardships await (22–31).

"I kept back nothing that was helpful, but proclaimed it to you, and taught you publicly and from house to house, testifying to Jews, and also to Greeks, repentance toward God and faith toward our Lord Jesus Christ"
(20:20–21). Paul's proclamation is complete as he presents the need to turn from our sin and accept Christ's invitation of salvation. The gospel is Good News and must be presented that way. Good News is that we no longer need to be held captive by our sin and failure; Good News is that the Father has been waiting patiently for us to turn to Him. Let our witness be touched with the same Holy Spirit love and directness that has transformed us since the moment we placed our faith in Christ. (*See* Give.)

5. Paul is warned about Jerusalem in Tyre and by Agabus in Caesarea (21:1–14). The trip to Jerusalem is marked by other warnings of the dangers facing Paul (1–11; *see* Women). But Paul is firm. Though the tears of his brothers and sisters break his heart, Paul will die for Jesus' name if this is God's will (12–14).

"Thus says the Holy Spirit, 'So shall the Jews at Jerusalem bind the man who owns this belt, and deliver him into the hands of the Gentiles'"
(21:9–12). Agabus the prophet offers Paul the word of the Lord concerning his decision to return to Jerusalem. This *prophecy confirmed to Paul's heart the necessity of his decision to continue on to Jerusalem. The presence of such prophecy is to be confirming in the life of a person rather than directive. The ministry of the Holy Spirit is

consistent in substance and direction, reinforcing a person's understanding of God's purpose for their life.

E. Paul's journey to Rome through Jerusalem (21:15—28:31).

1. Paul returns to Jerusalem (21:15—23:35).

Paul's return and arrest (21:15-36). In the holy city Paul is welcomed and told of thousands of Jews who now believe in Jesus. These Christian Jews also are zealous adherents of the Law of Moses. Because Paul is a Jew, the leaders suggest Paul show his piety by joining several brothers who have made a vow in the old way (*see* Offering). He will thus show "that you yourself are living in obedience to the law" (24). Paul does as they advise.

Paul's defense before the Jerusalem mob (21:37—22:29). Paul is recognized in the temple, and his companions are taken to be Gentile converts! For Gentiles to enter the temple area where only Jews are permitted was a great desecration. Paul is dragged out of the courtyard and barely rescued by Roman troops that rush down from the nearby fortress Antonia to break up the riot.

Paul's defense before the Sanhedrin (22:30—23:10). Paul receives permission from the Roman officer to speak to the crowd. He identifies himself and tells of his background (22:3-5; *see* Zealous). He reveals his conversion to Jesus (6-13). But when Paul reports a vision in which God commands him to go with the gospel to the hated Gentiles, the riot explodes again (14-22; cf. Luke 4:27-30).

Paul, the Roman citizen (22:23-29). The military commander orders Paul beaten to discover what he has done to set off the riot. Paul appeals to his Roman citizenship. The commander immediately sends away the examiners. Under the empire, no Roman citizen could be so examined until legally convicted in a court of law.

The Roman military commander of Jerusalem orders the Sanhedrin to gather and brings Paul to the assembly. He is determined to find out the cause of the rioting. That night an angel announces that Paul has fulfilled his mission to the Jews (cf. 9:15). Now he must testify in Rome itself. (*See* Resurrection.)

The plot to kill Paul (23:11-35). Paul's nephew, hearing of a conspiracy by over forty men to murder Paul, warns the apostle. When the plot is reported to the military governor, he acts immediately and sends Paul with a guard of several hundred troops to the Roman governor in the port city of Caesarea.

2. Paul's defense before Felix (24:1-27). Secular sources tell us much about Felix, who was procurator of Judea from A.D. 52 to 59. This childhood friend of the emperor Claudius apparently felt safe because of that relationship and was extremely corrupt. In five days Paul is arraigned for trial before this man, charged by the high priest and some of the Sadducee party who have come down from Jerusalem (1-4; *see* Courtesy). Several charges are brought against Paul.

Paul defends himself skillfully. He caused no uprising. He has only been in Jerusalem for about two weeks, for the purpose of worship.

As governor of this religion-mad province, Felix has "more accurate knowledge of the Way," as Christianity is known locally. Felix refuses to make an immediate decision. Later he confers with his Jewish wife, Drusilla, and listens with some terror as Paul talks with him about faith in Jesus and coming judgment.

Felix keeps Paul confined in Caesarea for some two years, hoping to be offered a bribe by the apostle.

3. Paul's defense before Festus and Agrippa (25:1—26:32). In A.D. 59 Felix was replaced in Judea by Porcius Festus. Festus no sooner arrives in Judea than the chief priests bring up the case of Paul and demand it be settled. In Caesarea the Jews bring a number of false, but serious, charges against Paul. When Festus asks Paul if he is willing to go to Jerusalem for trial, Paul recognizes the danger of another conspiracy (*see* Acts 23:20-21) and officially appeals to Caesar. The right of legal appeal to Caesar is an important perquisite of Roman citizenship, resting on some five centuries of legal precedent. By the act of appeal, Paul takes himself out of the jurisdiction both of the Jewish court and of Festus as well. (*See* Done No Wrong.)

A few days later Herod Agrippa II, son of the Herod mentioned in Acts 12:23 and a high Roman administrator in Judea, visits the new procurator. When Agrippa and his sister Bernice arrive, the frustrated Festus asks for advice about the unfamiliar Jewish customs and beliefs which complicate the case of this Roman citizen, Paul. Festus is also confused about Paul's strange statements concerning "a certain Jesus, who had died, whom Paul affirmed to be alive" (19).

The next day all the important people in Caesarea assemble with the Roman administrators to witness the interrogation. Agrippa and Bernice enter with great pomp. Festus introduces Paul's case and the apostle is then invited to speak out for himself. Agrippa puts Paul off, but both Festus and Agrippa agree, whatever Paul's beliefs, there is nothing in them that deserves death or imprisonment under Roman law. If Paul had not appealed to Caesar he could have been set free.

> **"Having obtained help from God, to this day I stand, witnessing both to small and great, saying no other things than those which the prophets and Moses said would come"**
> (26:16–27). Paul's witness to King Agrippa is poignantly highlighted by his personal testimony (*see* Witnessing) of his Damascus road experience with Jesus, and the living testimony of God through the Old Testament. The Bible is one of the key ways the Holy Spirit is able to convince and inspire faith in the hearts of unbelievers. The Bible, coupled with the winsome testimony of God's personal grace in the life of the believer, gives the Holy Spirit all that He needs to bring people to faith in Christ. (*See* Leadership, Spiritual.)

4. The voyage to Rome (27:1—28:31).

Shipwreck (27:1–44). Luke's graphic description of travel on the Mediterranean in the time of Christ has been studied carefully. Every detail matches—and adds to—the understanding of ancient sea trade and travel gained from other sources.

Most important to us is the picture Luke gives of Paul. He is being taken under guard to Rome, yet clearly this prisoner is the dominant personality, to whom all look for support and encouragement. His unshakable faith in God gives him a confidence which causes the others to trust him even in the most dangerous situations (*see* Disaster).

> **"I believe God that it will be just as it was told me"**
> (27:25). Paul's certainty concerning the desperate circumstance of the ship is based on an angelic encounter with a message from God (vv. 23–24). This confidence is based on the operation of spiritual discernment (1 Cor. 12:10) as a gift from God,

and the maturity of walking with God for years. "Angels of light" (demons, 2 Cor. 11:14) can mislead unbelievers and neophytes in the faith. Angelic messages can only be certified through (1) consistency with the Bible, (2) confirmation of personal witness already present in the believer, (3) discernment given by the Holy Spirit, and (4) confirmation of elders in the body of Christ. Extrabiblical revelation, bizarre behavior outside of God's pattern of dealing with a person, and messages unsubstantiated by mature leadership who "judge" (1 Cor. 14:29) are to be rejected by the people of God.

The shipwreck survivors winter on Malta, a small island some seventeen miles long, about sixty miles south of Sicily. When Paul survives the bite of a poisonous snake and cures many who are ill, the whole company is made welcome (28:1–10; *see* Kindness).

> **"Paul went in to him and prayed, and he laid his hands on him and healed him. So when this was done, the rest of those on the island who had diseases also came and were healed."**
> (28:8–9). The Bible teaches that healing is normative for the people of God (*see* Healing, Divine). It is not exceptional, but rather to be expected. No doubt the expectation of healing and simplicity of faith exercised by those who ministered healing and by those who were sick were dynamic keys to the continual flow of miracles.

When the company arrives in Rome (28:16), the missionaries are met by Christians living there. Paul is allowed to rent his own quarters and to live there with a military guard.

For two years Paul waits for his case to be heard. He welcomes visitors to his home and shares the gospel with both Jews and Gentiles "with all confidence, no one forbidding him," preaching the kingdom of God and teaching about the Lord Jesus Christ (*see* Salvation).

TRUTH-IN-ACTION through Acts

Truth Acts Teaches	**Action** Acts Invites
1 How to Insure Complete Conversion In Acts we find the historical record of the first conversions to faith in Jesus Christ. Here in detail is the message of the apostles and the response of the people. Here, also, is found the promise of the gift of the Holy Spirit to all who believe, an experience of empowering that was normative in the early church. Our message today should be the same as this, regarding the gift of the Holy Spirit and the life He produces.	**2:38–41** *Repent, be baptized,* and *receive* the gift of the Holy Spirit. *Be saved.* **3:19, 20** *Receive* your sins forgiven and forgotten by *being converted. Enjoy* the refreshing that comes from God's presence. **4:12** *Know* that only the name of Jesus Christ provides salvation. **10:47, 48** *Insure* that everyone you lead to Jesus is water baptized. *Remember* that water baptism was an integral part of the preaching of the apostles. **22:16** *Recognize* that the act of water baptism pictures the exchange of guilt and "sin consciousness" for the knowledge of cleansing from sin by the death of Christ and a new consciousness of God's presence.
2 In the OT only those uniquely called or anointed of God received the Holy Spirit. But under the New Covenant every believer is offered the Promise of the Father (Luke 24:49), the active presence of the Holy Spirit. It is by this activity of the Spirit's fullness in the life of every believer that the ministry of Christ in His church continues.	**1:8** *Believe* that the power of God comes only by the Holy Spirit. *Do not attempt* ministry without the Holy Spirit. **2:4; 4:8; 13:9** *Seek* and *receive* the baptism in the Holy Spirit. Continually be refilled with the Spirit to regularly renew your life and ministry. *Exercise* your prayer language as a part of the Spirit's flow in your life. **4:13** *Expect* your Spirit-filled relationship with Jesus to help you speak boldly, with courage and spiritual understanding. **10:44, 45** *Share* Jesus boldly. *Ask* the Holy Spirit to confirm your testimony.
3 Lessons for Leaders Acts is indispensable material for those who wish to learn the power principles of Christian leadership. The leadership in Acts is some of the most spiritually powerful the church has ever known. Whenever Christian leadership has forgotten the models shown in Acts, they have lost most of their power. Applying the lessons for leaders given in Acts will help give today's Christian leader a ministry of increased power and effectiveness.	**2:42–47** Leaders, *incorporate* these four elements into your congregation's life. *Believe* evangelism will result from a church living in obedience to Jesus' invitations. **4:24–31** Leaders, *frequently pray* this fervent prayer in your congregational worship. **6:1–6** Leaders, *share* your ministry. *Do not* weaken your life and ministry by doing work others should do. **12:5** Leaders, *give* prayer a central place in your church life. **13:1–3** Leaders, *submit* to the Spirit's guidance when confronting decisions. *Call* leadership to prayer and fasting in such times. *Release* ministry freely when asked to do so by the Holy Spirit. **14:14–18** Leaders, *do not receive* inordinate praise from people. *Dispel* unrighteous adulation by admirers. **16:1–5** Leaders, *personally train* young men who are called to ministry. **20:28–32** Leaders, *guard against* disloyalty. *Insure* that no one makes disciples for himself. *Assume* the responsibility of guarding the flock of God from "savage wolves." **20:27** Leaders, *make certain* that you teach "the whole counsel of God." *Live* in obedience to the gospel, and see the results in evangelism and spiritual growth.
4 Key Lessons in Faith Acts summons us to a bold faith, which may be unfamiliar to many of us. It is refreshing to read about men and women who believed in our great God to do great things in a great way. Let us have the courage to do the same. These accounts invite us to the kinds of risks associated with this bold faith.	**3:21** *Believe steadfastly* that God will fulfill everything he has promised in His Word. **14:3** *Humbly call* to the Lord to perform signs, wonders, and miracles to confirm with power the gospel message of His Son.

KEYS TO ROMANS
The Kingdom and Personal Triumph

Kingdom Key: God's Purpose in View

The kingdom concept, which teaches that a life of dominion and victory is available in Christ, is biblical and obtainable. Jesus has indeed come to reinstate in the redeemed the Father's original intent for His creatures: "Be fruitful, multiply . . . have dominion" (Gen. 1:28). This is not a glib offer, nor is it grounded in human resources. The "triumphant life" is one that is (a) grounded in God's Word, (b) learned through Christ's Cross, and (c) developed through test, travail, and warfare.

The Book of Romans concludes: "The God of peace will crush Satan under your feet shortly!" (16:20). This promise is true, but it is rooted in truth that calls us to understand the foundations for personal triumph. They are elaborated in Romans 8, though the entire epistle lays out the groundwork for settled faith on solid footings.

Triumph is gained and sustained:

1. By having the curse of condemnation broken from the soul, once and for all. Romans 8:1–4 asserts a *law of life*—that is, "in Christ Jesus" there is no longer in God's presence a record assigning sin to those who have received Him as Savior (3:24–26). Therefore, peace of heart and mind may be constantly experienced (5:1–11).

2. By allowing the Holy Spirit to fill,

> **God's gift of righteousness is provided in Christ.**

lead, and lift us above the drive in our flesh to master our body and soul, to sustain patterns of sin in our lives (8:5–17). Walking in the fullness of the Spirit will release the power of Jesus' resurrection life in us—power that will break the death-dealing force of sin and unworthy habits (8:11; 6:1–14).

3. By remembering that God has never promised trouble-free living, yet that He has guaranteed the certainty of our triumph through and beyond every trial (8:18–22). Remember (a) to confront every stressful circumstance with Holy Spirit-begotten hope (8:23–25), and (b) to enter into Holy Spirit-assisted intercession (8:26–27). Do this in the confidence that these means will secure God's purpose for your life (8:28).

(Please turn to page 346.)

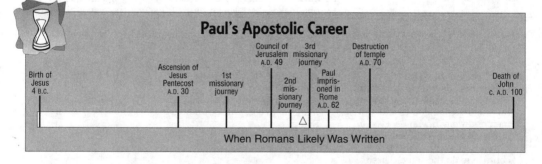

Paul's Apostolic Career

| | | | Council of Jerusalem A.D. 49 | 3rd missionary journey | | Destruction of temple A.D. 70 | | |
| Birth of Jesus 4 B.C. | Ascension of Jesus Pentecost A.D. 30 | 1st missionary journey | | 2nd missionary journey | Paul imprisoned in Rome A.D. 62 | | | Death of John c. A.D. 100 |

When Romans Likely Was Written

Romans outlines the whole gospel, from the futility

Master Key: God's Son Revealed

The whole epistle is the story of God's plan of redemption in Christ: the need for it (1:18—3:20), the detailed description of Christ's work and its implications for Christians (3:21—11:36), and the application of the gospel of Christ to everyday life (12:1—16:27).

More specifically, Jesus Christ is our Savior, who obeyed God perfectly as our representative (5:18–19), and who died as our substitute sacrifice (3:25; 5:6–8). He is the One in whom we must have faith for salvation (1:16–17; 3:22; 10:9–10). Through Christ we have many blessings: reconciliation to God (5:11); righteousness and eternal life (5:18–21); identification with Him in His death, burial, and resurrection (6:3–5); being alive to God (6:11); freedom from condemnation (8:1); eternal inheritance (8:17); suffering with Him (8:17); being glorified with Him (8:17); being made like Him (8:29); and the fact that He even now prays for us (8:34). Indeed, all of the Christian life seems to be lived through Him: prayer (1:8), rejoicing (5:11), exhortation (15:30), glorifying God (16:27), and, in general, living to God and obeying Him (6:11; 13:14).

Power Key: God's Spirit at Work

The Holy Spirit gives power in preaching the gospel and in working miracles (15:19), dwells in all who belong to Christ (8:9–11), and gives us life (8:11). He also makes us progressively more holy in daily life, empowering us to obey God and overcome sin (2:29; 7:6; 8:2, 13; 15:13, 16), giving us a pattern of holiness to follow (8:4), guiding us in it (8:14), and purifying our consciences to bear true witness (9:1). The Holy Spirit pours God's love into our hearts (5:5; 15:30), along with joy, peace, and hope by His power (14:17; 15:13). He enables us to pray rightly (8:26) and to call God our Father, thereby giving inward spiritual assurance that we are God's children (8:16). We are to set our minds on the things of the Spirit if we wish to be pleasing to God (8:5–6). Though Paul discusses spiritual gifts briefly in Romans (12:3–8), he makes no explicit mention of the Holy Spirit in connection with these gifts, except to refer to them as "spiritual" (or "of the Spirit") in 1:11. The present work of the Holy Spirit in us is only a foretaste of His future heavenly work in us (8:23).

Key Word: *The Righteousness of God*

The theme of Romans is found in 1:16, 17: God offers the gift of His righteousness to everyone who comes to Christ by faith.

Key Verses: Romans 1:16–17; 3:21–25

Key Chapters: Romans 6—8

Foundational to all teaching on the spiritual life is the central passage of Romans 6—8. The answers to the questions of how to be delivered from sin, how to live a balanced life under grace, and how to live the victorious Christian life through the power of the Holy Spirit are all contained here.

---

of the sinner to the fullness of the justified.

Introducing
ROMANS

Background. When Paul wrote Romans about A.D. 56, he had not yet been to Rome, but he had been preaching the gospel since his conversion in A.D. 35. During the previous ten years he had founded churches throughout the Mediterranean world. Now he was nearing the end of his third missionary journey. This epistle is therefore a mature statement of his understanding of the gospel. The church at Rome had been founded by other Christians (unknown to us, but see "visitors from Rome" in Acts 2:10); and Paul, through his travels, knew many of the believers there (16:3-15).

Occasion and Date. Paul most likely wrote Romans while he was in Corinth in A.D. 56, taking a collection to help the needy Christians in Jerusalem (15:25-28, 31; 2 Corinthians 8-9). He planned to go to Jerusalem with this collection, then visit the church in Rome (1:10-11; 15:22-24). After being refreshed and supported by the Christians in Rome, he planned to travel to Spain to preach the gospel (15:24). He wrote to tell the Romans of his impending visit. The letter was likely delivered by Phoebe (16:1-2).

Purpose. In view of his personal plans, Paul wrote to introduce himself to a church he had never visited. At the same time he set forth a full and orderly statement of the great principles of the gospel that he preached.

Characteristics. Romans is commonly considered the greatest exposition of Christian doctrine anywhere in Scripture. It contains an orderly, logical development of profound theological truths. It is filled with the great themes of redemption: the guilt of all mankind, our inability to earn favor with God, the redeeming death of Christ, and the free gift of salvation to be received by faith alone. Since Paul had not visited Rome, the epistle does not address specific local problems, but contains general teaching applicable to all Christians for all time. Throughout the history of the church, expositions of Romans have sparked many revivals as people have become aware of the magnificence of God and His grace toward us.

Content. The overall doctrinal theme that Paul seeks to demonstrate is that God is righteous. In spite of all that happens in this world—even though all people are sinful (1:18—3:20); even though God does not punish but forgives repentant sinners (3:21—5:21); even though believers may not fully live in a way consistent with God's righteousness (6:1—8:17); even though believers suffer and final redemption is delayed (8:18-39); even though many Jews do not believe (9:1—11:36)—still God is perfectly righteous, and by His grace has forgiven us. Because of this great mercy from an all-righteous God, we should live a pattern of life consistent with God's own righteousness (12:1—16:27).

Personal Application. Romans teaches us that we should not trust in ourselves for salvation, but in Christ (chs. 1—5); that we should imitate the faith of Abraham (ch. 4); be patient in times of trouble (5:1-11); rejoice in our representation by Christ (5:12-21); grow in daily death to sin (6:1—7:25); walk according to the Spirit each moment (8:1-17); hope in future glory and trust that God will bring good out of present sufferings (8:18-39); pray for and proclaim the gospel to the lost, especially the Jews (9:1—11:32); and praise God for His great wisdom in the plan of salvation (11:33-36). Especially in chapters 12—15 the letter gives many specific applications to life, showing how the gospel works out in practice both in the church and in the world. Finally, we can even learn to imitate Paul's deeply personal care for many individual believers (ch. 16).

....

Kingdom Key *continued from page 344*

4. By rejoicing in the absolute commitment God has made to us to ensure our victory with Him through grace (8:29-32), and by answering any circumstance or lie of our Adversary (8:33-34) with this grand, biblical hymn about certainty of conquering: Romans 8:35-39!

Surveying
ROMANS

INTRODUCTION 1:1-17.

A. Paul's identification (1:1-7). Paul's greeting declares him to be a slave for Christ and an apostle to the church (v. 1).

B. Paul's desire to visit Rome (1:8-15). Paul expresses his longing to visit the believers at Rome for whom he prays (8-10). Such a visit would be an opportunity for mutual ministry; each will strengthen the other's faith.

> **"I long to see you, that I may *impart to you some spiritual gift, so that you may be established"**
> (1:11). Paul is confident that his ministry will result in the strengthening of the church and the deposit of a "spiritual gift." The specific nature of the gift is not important, although the sum of Paul's experience, understanding, and Spirit-filled ministry constitutes a gift from God that surely will benefit the congregation.

C. Summary of the gospel (1:16-17). Paul has experienced the power of the gospel at work in himself and in others. He shares it, then, with full confidence, sure he will never be embarrassed (16). The phrase "first for the Jew, then for the Gentile" is historical; Paul's missionary strategy followed this pattern.

In this gospel about Jesus, a unique righteousness is revealed—a righteousness that "is by faith from first to last." Righteousness that comes to us through Jesus, and is appropriated by faith, is the theme of Paul's letter to the Romans.

I. ALL HAVE SINNED 1:18—3:20. The Jewish people assumed that righteousness was theirs, for they possessed the Law of God and thus knew God through revelation.

A. Gentiles know of God but reject Him (1:18-32; See Stewardship). The pagan peoples around them simply stumbled after God in darkness. First, then, Paul must show that no one lives without some knowledge of God. In point of fact it is the way that Jew and Gentile both have responded to God that demonstrates so clearly the need of all mankind for a righteousness that can come only through faith.

Paul makes a bold statement. God's righteousness is revealed in His deep-seated anger against humankind, for people wickedly suppress the truth about Him (1:18). God can be known, for He communicates Himself in the creation (cf. Ps. 19:1-4) and directly to the human conscience.

Their response to God (1:21-22) demonstrates so clearly humanity's need for righteousness. Rather than turn toward God, or thank Him, people turn away. With their ability to reason darkened (see Futility), they even stoop to the worship of idols shaped like mortal man or animals.

Society demonstrates the impact of this rejection of God. Sexual perversion (23-27) and every kind of wickedness is expressed in interpersonal relationships (28-31).

B. Jews have God's laws but are not righteous (2:1-29). Paul has just shown that the Gentiles do have truth about God but have turned away from Him. He will now show that, while the Jews have more extensive knowledge about God, they have responded no better than the pagans they scorn!

Great knowledge of God should have produced humility and repentance (2:4). It is not immorality but "your stubbornness and unrepentant heart" which shows the Jewish people have responded no differently to God than have the Gentiles! God will judge all persons, not by what they know, but by what they do (vv. 6-13)!

God made human beings moral "by nature" (2:14). This does not mean all know the specific moral standards revealed in Scripture. But it does mean that every society recognizes the same general "moral issues" and sets moral standards. Paul's point is that no human being lives up to even his own standards, much less God's. God is even willing to judge persons by their own standard and not the Lord's. Even with lowered standards, every individual's conscience testifies that he or she has fallen short.

To have the Law of God does mean having a superior standard of morality. In fact, Israel violates the very law it teaches (2:17-29)!

Paul then mentions circumcision (25-29). Many Jews counted on this physical relationship as a basis for relationship with God (cf. John 8:33-47). Paul argues that circumcision guarantees nothing. Those who are circumcised and fail to keep the law stand condemned by the law. It is not a physical and outward sign of relationship God seeks, but a heart that is responsive to His Spirit.

C. God is just to judge all persons (3:1-20). The fact that both Gentile and Jew need righteousness does not imply that Jews have no advantages. They do—in their possession of God's very words in Scripture (3:2; see True).

What then does the Old Testament say about righteousness? Paul has earlier pointed to empirical evidence of mankind's need. Now he proves his thesis by quoting from the very Old Testament Law in which the Jews mistakenly hoped: "There is none righteous, no, not one" (3:10).

This teaching is stunning to the Jew of New Testament times, who thinks of law as God's way of salvation. If the law is not God's way to make men holy, what then is its purpose? To Paul the answer is clear. Law reveals God's standards of right and wrong behavior in order to make people *conscious of sin!*

II. JUSTIFICATION IS BY FAITH ALONE 3:21—5:21.

A. God's righteousness preserved through Christ's death for us (3:21–26). The notion that righteousness comes through faith is not new. Christ brings this righteousness into sharp focus, for His death reveals how God can be "just" in His offer of a salvation by faith to those who have sinned (21–24).

Righteousness is now available to Jew and Gentile alike through faith. Thus it is clear that justification is a matter for faith and something totally apart from "observing the law." (*See* Blood, The; Evangelism; Redemption.)

B. Justification is by faith alone (3:27–31). Paul adds one more thought for the stunned Jew who might read his argument. Faith does not make law irrelevant. Instead it "upholds the law," by giving it the role God always intended for it, as a revelation to humanity of each person's need for a righteousness that can only be found through faith (cf. 3:19–20).

C. Abraham justified by faith, not works (4:1–25). Paul goes back now to the Old Testament to show that the faith principle has always operated in the same way. Abraham's faith was credited (*see* Accounted) to him for righteousness, according to Genesis 15:6 (4:1–5). And in Psalm 32:1–2 David speaks of the same truth (4:6–8). As for circumcision, Abraham was justified by faith before the rite was given (Gen. 17:3–14). Thus Abraham's justification by faith sets the pattern for both Jews and Gentiles (4:9–12). Paul goes on to show that God's covenant promise was received by faith and thus is not related to law either (4:13–17). It is clear then from this analysis that justification by faith is boldly affirmed in the Old Testament!

> **"He did not waver at the promise of God through unbelief"**
> (4:19–21). Abraham was promised a son by God (Gen. 12:2). Though Abraham and Sarah moved beyond the physical limits of child bearing, and though the promise was delayed for many decades, God had spo-

ken, and Abraham obediently waited for that of which he was absolutely certain (Heb. 11:12). His faith was in God's promise.

D. Once justified by faith, we triumph even in sufferings (5:1–11). Faith awakens a sense of rejoicing confidence in our acceptance by God, and our inner experience is confirmed by objective evidence. God "demonstrates His own love toward us, in that while we were still sinners, Christ died for us" (5:6–9; *see* Blood, The). Now that we have been brought into harmonious relationship with God (reconciled), we are sure that God will complete the saving work He has begun and preserve us from all that is destructive.

> **"Now hope does not disappoint, because the *love of God has been poured out in our hearts by the Holy Spirit who was given to us"**
> (5:5). God's work of love in the human heart is a gift. Disappointing things happen to believers, but we cannot be disappointed. With lives centered in Christ and maintained by His love, we know that ultimately our hopes are all found in Him.

E. We gained death through Adam's sin, but eternal life through Christ's obedience (5:12–21). This passage is one that theologians puzzle over in an attempt to understand the origin of sin and spiritual death. The basic point of Paul's analogy is clear: All human beings have been affected by Adam's first act of sin, which brought spiritual death to all. Now all humanity is affected by Christ's act of obedience, which makes it possible for God to justify sinful individuals. Adam is the first member of a lost race, bringing mankind under condemnation. Jesus is the first member of a saved race, bringing forgiveness and release from the judgment merited by each person's sins.

Paul is saying that the sins every individual commits document the reign of death and the grip of death on humanity. Now, as individuals respond in faith and accept the gift of life offered by Christ, the quality of righteousness will be expressed in their actions and will document the transforming grace of God.

III. PRACTICING RIGHTEOUSNESS IN THE CHRISTIAN LIFE 6:1—8:39. It is only natural that Paul's reinterpretation of law would frighten many of his readers. Law is an expression of the holiness of God. In setting

aside the law is the apostle also setting aside the need for holy living?

A. Overcoming sin in the Christian life (6:1–23). Freedom from law does not mean freedom to sin. Paul points to the baptizing work of the Spirit of God and teaches that He unites us with Jesus in a real, though mystical, way. A believer who is united by faith with Jesus becomes one with Him, so that he is considered to have participated in Christ's death and in His resurrection.

Sin rendered powerless (6:5–10). The old pull of sin will still make itself felt within us. There will be temptations to sin. But our mystical union with Jesus in His death and resurrection has a freeing impact in our daily life. The "old self," with its package of warped and sinful responses, is "rendered powerless." Passions may swirl within us, but the spiritual death that once held us in an unbreakable grip is no longer master!

New life lived by faith (6:11–14). Paul carefully shows us how to experience the freedom he promises. We are to count ourselves dead to the pull of sin when we sense it within (11). And we are not to let sin rule but rather offer ourselves to God to do His will (12–13).

The believer becomes a slave to righteousness (6:15–23). Who would want to choose righteousness if law did not force him or her to do so? Paul answers this question, which he expects to be in the minds of his readers. Man, Paul says, has only two choices he can make. He can lend his heart and mind and body to serve sin—or he can surrender all these capacities to serve righteousness (*see* Obeyed). Sin may seem attractive, but to choose it means to go on living in the empty realm where death reigns.

B. We are dead to the powerless system called "law" (7:1–6). Paul uses marriage as an illustration. Under law a married couple become one, bound together until one of them dies. But the death of one partner frees both from the law of marriage—and the survivor can remarry! We who are in union with Christ (Rom. 6:1–4) died with Him, and law has no authority over a dead man. Thus Christ's death legally releases us from the authority of God's law.

Paul now returns to what he has said earlier about the purpose of law (3:19–20; 5:20). Law not only reveals sin, but it also "arouses the sinful passions" (7:5). The do's and don'ts of law simply charge the old nature with energy and lead to acts of sin. (*See* Spirit.)

C. The law cannot empower us to obey (7:7–25). There is nothing wrong with law. As an expression of God's character, law is "holy, and the commandment holy and just and good." What is wrong is human nature. Law acts on the old nature to produce in the individual "all manner of evil desire," so that sin "revived" and shouts for domination. Paul shares his own struggle as a believer trying to keep the law.

D. We fulfill God's righteousness by living in the power of the Spirit and according to the Spirit (8:1–17). Romans 8 affirms our release from condemnation. Our new life, energized by the Spirit (the "law of the Spirit") overcomes the principles of sin and death (1–2; *see* Free; Holy Spirit Gifts).

Paul describes the difference in relational terms. Through Christ's death sin has been condemned and the Holy Spirit given. He is now within to guide us (3–4). When we live in harmony with His promptings (5) we find that He controls the sin nature within (6–7).

> **"To be carnally minded is death, but to be spiritually minded is life and peace"**
> (8:6). In contrast to the person in darkened understanding, the one before Christ (Eph. 4:18–20) is instructed to "put off . . . the old man." Crucifying the old man and the former ways is the first step in being liberated from the deadly nature of our carnal past. Ephesians 4 also insists that we "put on the new man." This man is renewed in his mind by the Spirit of God (Eph. 4:23), and "created according to God, in true righteousness and holiness" (v. 24), bringing peace and life to the believer on God's terms.

The Spirit of God within us, who raised Jesus from the dead, is able to lift us up too, to a new and righteous kind of living (vv. 9–11).

E. Longing for complete redemption (8:18–25). The promise of righteousness is for now—and for eternity. What now seems a struggle will become full liberation when Jesus returns, when the fact of our sonship is made plain to all. Then even the creation will share in a great purification, as every trace of sin is removed. In the meantime we have the assurance that the Spirit "helps in our weaknesses."

F. Help and assurance in hardship (8:26–39; *see* Purpose).

>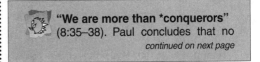
> **"We are more than *conquerors"**
> (8:35–38). Paul concludes that no
> *continued on next page*

continued from preceding page
social, cultural, physical, or spiritual circumstance is severe enough to separate believers from God's love. Our salvation is secure in Christ. The specific mention of "angels," "principalities," and "powers" affirms that even hell's furies cannot snatch the believer out of God's hand.

IV. GOD AND ISRAEL 9:1—11:36.

A. Though Israel is unfaithful, God is righteous (9:1-33). Paul is a Jew, proud of his race and heritage. He is deeply aware of the gifts God has given Israel. The present rejection of his people is a great sorrow to Paul. But it does not cast any doubt on the faithfulness of God or suggest His Word has failed.

Paul's argument from history can be summed up in brief statements. Physical descent from Abraham never guaranteed an individual a right to God's grace (9:7-8). God retains the right to choose and the freedom to be merciful to whomever He chooses (9:15; *see* Mercy). Scripture reveals that God chose long ago to bring salvation to Gentiles (9:17). The Jewish nation has lost its place because of its failure to seek righteousness through faith (9:32). On no count, then, can God be charged with unfairness in the way He has dealt with Israel. Every principle of action that He has taken in Christ is clearly laid down in the Old Testament. The sacred history vindicates God.

B. Israel has willingly rejected the gospel (10:1-21). Paul again expresses his deep desire for the salvation of his own people and restates the reason for Israel's rejection: "They . . . have not submitted to the righteousness of God" (10:3). Because Israel is unwilling to approach God on the basis of faith and insists on misusing the law, rejection has come—and is deserved (10:1-4)! Paul again states the gospel. Christ has come down from heaven, has died, and is risen again. All that is left for any person to do is to *believe (see* Faith's Confession). Jew and Gentile must relate to God through faith, knowing He will bless all who call on Him (10:5-11; *see* Evangelism).

C. A remnant now remains, and someday full salvation will come to Israel (11:1-32). Israel has not been completely rejected. Paul himself is a Jew, and yet he is a believer. For its first decade the early church was a Hebrew church. There are thousands upon thousands of Jewish Christians when Paul writes his letter to the Romans. As always in history, there is a remnant that has been chosen by grace.

Paul reveals in this passage that Israel's rejection is also temporary (9:24; *see* Blindness). God has opened the door of faith to the whole world, but He has not rejected the people who were the original branches, growing from that tree of faith which has its historic roots in God's first great acts of self-revelation. The day is coming when Israel will be grafted back into that original vine.

Paul promises that "all Israel will be saved" when "the full number of Gentiles has come in." His quotes from Isaiah 59 and 27 make it clear that Paul believes the promises of the Old Testament prophets to Israel will be literally fulfilled (9:26-27; *see* Prophecy).

D. Praise for God's infinite wisdom (11:33-36). Paul concludes this section with a doxology that links the words of Isaiah 40:13 and Job 41:11. God's plan is great and complex. Its very complexity shows us the depth of the riches of His wisdom and knowledge.

V. PRACTICAL APPLICATIONS 12:1—15:13.

A. Present yourselves as sacrifices to God (12:1-2). When we offer ourselves to live for the Lord (cf. 6:15-23), we begin a process of inner transformation that will lead to an entirely new outlook on life (*see* Conformed).

"**Present your bodies a living sacrifice, holy, acceptable to God, which is your reasonable service**" (12:1). The Greek word for *service* can also be translated *worship*. Worship is our most urgent service to God. The presentation of our bodies in worship is not simply a matter of "showing up" for church services. It is an active, conscious presentation of all of our being to God (*see* Stewardship). David declared the power of our physical involvement in worship: "The lifting up of my hands as the evening sacrifice" (Ps. 141:2). Only human pride and ignorance deny the patterns of forthright physical, biblical exercise of praise for the pattern of worship in the church today.

B. Use of spiritual gifts (12:3-8). The world's way is competitive, with each individual seeking to be superior to others. In Christ's body a new way is made possible; each person is valued (*see* Human Worth), for each has a spiritual gift that enables him or her to contribute to others.

"Having then gifts differing according to the grace that is given to us"
(12:6–8). These gifts come from God the Father (v. 3). Commonly referred to as "motivational gifts," they are present in each person's life, helping determine the substance and focus of a person's ministry (see Cheerfulness). They are not to be confused with gifts of the Holy Spirit in 1 Corinthians 12 (see Holy Spirit Gifts), available to any Spirit-baptized believer, and the office gifts of Christ to the church in Ephesians 4.

C. Relating to Christians (12:9–13). The climate of the new community is to be marked by a sincere love for one another. It is this climate that makes possible maximum growth in righteousness.

D. Relating to unbelievers (12:14–21). The exhortation toward peaceful living with all (v. 18) and the overcoming of evil with blessing shapes this new community in its reach to the world.

E. Relating to government (13:1–7). Submission to secular authorities introduces God's purpose for the institution of human government as a restraining influence on sin and has permitted it the use of force (cf. Gen. 9:6; see Manhood).

F. The law of love (13:8–14). At the same time, God is concerned with far more than good citizenship! God is building a new community. This community is not marked off by its ideals or even by its rules and high standards; it is marked off by a deep love for one another which makes rules irrelevant, for "love does no harm to a neighbor; therefore love is the fulfillment of the law" (10; see Provision.)

G. Toleration and love in minor things (14:1–23). Paul insists we abandon judgmental attitudes and neither condemn nor look down on brothers or sisters whose convictions or practices differ from our own. Christ, the Master of each of us, is able to bring each of us to obedience and to maturity.

"For the kingdom of God is not eating and drinking, but righteousness and peace and joy in the Holy Spirit"
(14:17). The fruit of the Spirit in a person's life is produced by living consistently as a person ruled by Christ. Those who live under the protection of and in keeping with the laws of the kingdom of God can expect the benefits of the Holy Spirit.

H. Caring for each other (15:1–13). The freedom of others to engage in "eating and drinking" practices with a clear conscience may lead such people either to judgmentalism or to follow practices that are against their own conscience. While Paul firmly upholds the principle of freedom and teaches that we have no right to judge one another, he balances this truth with another: "We then who are strong ought to bear with the scruples of the weak, and not to please ourselves" (15:1).

The accepting attitude underlying the teaching of this section reveals the fact that Jesus has accepted us, imperfect as we are.

"Praise the LORD, all you Gentiles! Laud Him, all you peoples!"
(15:5–11). Quoting from Psalm 117, the apostle Paul instructs his readers to praise God for the full measure of salvation which has been extended to all people of the earth. The Pentecost revival has swept beyond the limits of Israel and, to the surprise and joy of the infant church, the Gentiles have been welcomed by God. This praise to be offered to God is the same for Jew and Gentile alike; the most gracious God has made a way for all sinners to be forgiven! Praise the Lord! (See Family Life.)

VI. PAUL'S OWN SITUATION 15:14–33.

A. His ministry (15:14–22). Paul closes by sharing several revealing personal matters. He expresses his confidence in the believers in Rome. (See Goodness.)

B. His plans (15:23–33). Paul also shares his desire to travel to Spain, to pioneer there as a missionary. Paul asks the prayers of these believers about dangers he may soon face in Judea (cf. Acts 19:21—28:31), and tells his plans to visit them in Rome on his way to Spain.

"In mighty signs and wonders, by the power of the Spirit of God"
(15:19). Signs and wonders occurred as Paul "fully preached the gospel of Christ" (v. 19). This confirmation of the gospel can and should be expected today as God's people declare truth and the Holy Spirit moves in miracle power.

"I beg you, brethren, through the Lord Jesus Christ, and through the love of the Spirit, that you strive together with me in prayers to God for me" (15:30). Paul identifies love as a universal motivation of all those who have come to experience new life in Christ and the presence of the Holy Spirit in their life. Bearing each others' burdens (Gal. 6:2) fulfills the law of Christ and is a practical demonstration of concern and care for others in the body of Christ. Paul's appeal for prayer should remind us to spiritually care for those around us.

VII. PERSONAL GREETINGS 16:1-24. Paul includes a word of warning against those who would cause divisions or would contradict the principles of Christian experience which the Romans have been taught (16:17–18; cf. 2 Peter and Jude; *see* Crush; Women).

VIII. BENEDICTION 16:25-27. Paul's last words commit the dear brothers and sisters at Rome to the care of God, who alone "is able to establish you according to my gospel and the preaching of Jesus Christ."

TRUTH-IN-ACTION through ROMANS

Truth Romans Teaches	**Action** Romans Invites
1 Key Lessons in Faith Faith is choosing boldly and unswervingly to believe what God has said. Twentieth-century faith must learn again to believe totally the testimony of Scripture! Among the keys to faithful living is the truth of our conversion. Faith frees us to live as never before for the good of others.	**1:16** *Proclaim* the gospel boldly. **4:17, 18** *Release* the creative power of God's Word by believing it in the face of challenging circumstances. **4:20–25** *Stand* when tempted by unbelief, knowing that God can do what He promises. **6:1–10** *Understand* that through baptism, you have been crucified with Christ. *Choose to believe* that you were also united with Jesus in His death, burial, and resurrection. **15:1–3** *Live* in a manner that strengthens the weak in faith. *Commit* to the upbuilding of your neighbor.
2 Steps to Dynamic Devotion The Word of God illuminated by the Holy Spirit is the only true means for transforming the human heart. Salvation by faith is a specific occasion, while the renewing of the mind by the Word is a continuing process. The disciple devotes himself to God's Word to be transformed into a holy person, radiantly Christ-like and radically different from the world. Spiritual disciples devour God's Word because in it is the key to a more dynamic relationship with their living Lord and a greater availability to the Holy Spirit.	**10:17** *Be constant* in your reading and study of God's Word. *Recognize* that your faith will grow only as much as you feed on God's Word. **12:1, 2** *Let* God's Word and His Holy Spirit radically transform your way of thinking. *Renew your mind* to know and do the will of God, giving your body a living sacrifice. **15:4** *Recognize* that the OT was written through the Spirit for the church. *Incorporate* the OT into your daily Bible study.
3 Keys to Wise Living The believer's two natures often baffle and confuse him or her. The wisdom found in Rom. will help in managing this conflict by identifying which aspects of behavior result from the Holy Spirit's life and which result from the fleshly nature's activity. Thus, we can navigate our new life with Spirit-engendered wisdom and understanding.	**1:18–23** *Understand* that judgment is self-induced. *Know* that men choose to reject God. **2:24** *Be sensitive* to the fact that how you live can bring honor and glory to God, or it can bring reproach and blasphemy against His name. **8:7, 8** *Be clear* that any hostile or disobedient tendency toward God's Word comes out of your fleshly nature. **13:8–10** *Recognize* that love is binding and obligatory on believers. *Understand* that any lack of love is lawlessness and rebellion.

Truth Romans Teaches	**Action** Romans Invites
4 Steps to Dealing with Sin Rom. reveals a new, victorious method for our dealing with sin. Living free of sin's rule is now possible because we are no longer slaves of sin, but have become slaves of God, able to choose righteousness rather than being bound to the old nature. Obedience to the Word of God gains a new nature of holiness.	**6:11–14** *Say "No!" to sin* whenever it confronts you. *Recognize* that you are really free from its demands. **6:16–23** *Obey Christ*, your new Master, not sin, your old master. **7:17, 20** *Believe with conviction* that it is your old, sinful nature, not your new nature in Christ that manifests itself in acts of sin.
5 Guidelines for Growth in the Spirit Through the indwelling presence of the Holy Spirit, the very life of Jesus Christ is brought into effect in our mortal bodies. As we yield ourselves to Him, Jesus becomes in and through us the very fulfillment of the Law and Word of God.	**8:1–11** *Recognize* that the Law is fulfilled by the Holy Spirit in us. *Know* that His presence in you is the very life of Jesus Christ. **8:13–17** *Choose* to live by the Spirit. *Put to death* fleshly attitudes and actions. *Acknowledge* your adoption as a child of God, calling Him "Father."

The City of Rome

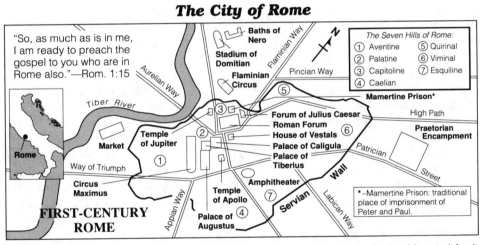

"So, as much as is in me, I am ready to preach the gospel to you who are in Rome also."—Rom. 1:15

The Seven Hills of Rome:
① Aventine   ⑤ Quirinal
② Palatine   ⑥ Viminal
③ Capitoline ⑦ Esquiline
④ Caelian

*–Mamertine Prison: traditional place of imprisonment of Peter and Paul.

FIRST-CENTURY ROME

Founded in 753 B.C., by the first century Rome was the greatest city in the world, noted for its magnificent buildings. It had more than one million inhabitants, but the majority of them were slaves. The church in Rome was well known (Rom. 1:8) and had been established for several years when Paul wrote his letter to them. The many believers evidently met in several places (16:1–16). The Roman historian Tacitus reports that "an immense multitude" of Christians were persecuted under Nero in A.D. 64.

KEYS TO 1 CORINTHIANS
The Kingdom and Personal Dynamics

Kingdom Key: God's Purpose in View

The remarkable thing about the Corinthian church is not that this vital congregation had problems; it is that there were not more problems! Carved by the Holy Spirit from the most corrupt city in the Roman Empire, the Corinthians were a composite of people from virtually every point on the spectrum of human sin and depravity (6:9–11). Their Christian zeal was born of an overwhelming joy in having tasted the firstfruits of God's deliverance, and at times their zeal outran their wisdom.

Despite his need to instruct and sharply correct, Paul expresses gratitude to God for their spiritual vibrancy and their readiness to move into vital, Spirit-gifted kingdom ministry (1:4–7). Unlike some today who decry the Corinthians' failures and so neglect to explore their supernatural giftings, Paul patiently addresses and resolves confusion. He even expresses his own delight in exercising himself "more than all" of them in his use of tongues (14:18). One might think the Corinthians' unwise use of this gift would have prompted him to omit any affirmation of it in his own life. But Paul is not only a towering theologian (as evident in Romans). He is a pragmatic minister who knows that truth without passion and power—academics without the King's anointing—will not impact the darkness and advance God's kingdom through Christ's church.

Balance passion and zeal with discipline and wisdom.

Central to Paul's pastoral concern is that the church be "edified"—that is, built up, growing, and advancing (8:1; 10:23; 14:5, 12, 17, 19, 26). He elaborates on two primary dynamics which, if they work together, are certain to produce edification: (a) that believers grow *out* in evangelism and (b) believers grow *up* in maturity and character. The Holy Spirit's power is shown as the source of these two essential dynamics, which occur only as an individual member of the body invites Him to work in him or her personally. These two dynamics are the Spirit's *gifts* and *love:* He enables the former and engenders the latter.

The gifts of the Holy Spirit are

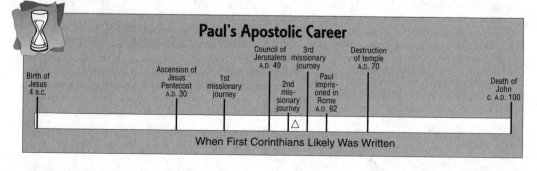

Paul's Apostolic Career

| Birth of Jesus 4 B.C. | Ascension of Jesus Pentecost A.D. 30 | 1st missionary journey | Council of Jerusalem A.D. 49 | 3rd missionary journey | 2nd missionary journey | Paul imprisoned in Rome A.D. 62 | Destruction of temple A.D. 70 | Death of John c. A.D. 100 |

When First Corinthians Likely Was Written

First Corinthians calls believers to be open to the

"kingdom" manifestations because of the anointing attending His presence and work (12:7). As the "anointer/enabler," His supernatural operations—gifts transcending human abilities—can make the local church truly effective (12:8–12). The gifts of the Holy Spirit (as differentiated from Christ's office gifts in Eph. 4:7–11 and the Father's motivational giftings in Rom. 12:3–8) involve such supernatural promptings and workings that human dispositions sometimes get in the way. On the one hand, some believers are reticent to exercise them because the call to yield to such supernatural graces (*charismata*—12:4) seems "beyond" them. On the other hand, some are tempted to pride, pushiness, or elitist attitudes, as though a *gift* from God indicated advanced faith, maturity, or achievement. This is why the gifts of the Holy Spirit must be companioned to *love*.

First Corinthians 13 is the Holy Spirit's masterstroke. It is not only the loveliest and most dignified hymn on "love" ever written. It is His way of saying, "I want the gifts which I desire to distribute (12:11) to manifest the loving heart of the God who gives them!" Kingdom-minded people will see in 1 Corinthians our call to an openness to *both* (a) the gifts of the Spirit, and (b) the spirit of the gifts—*love*. Together, these bring abundance in ministry which will result in an abounding church.

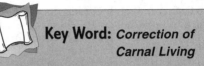

Key Word: *Correction of Carnal Living*

The cross of Christ is a message that is designed to transform the lives of believers and make them different as people and as a corporate body from the surrounding world. However, the Corinthians are destroying their Christian testimony because of immorality and disunity.

Key Verses: First Corinthians 6:19–20; 10:12–13
Key Chapter: First Corinthians 13

This chapter has won the hearts of people across the world as the best definition of "love" ever penned.

Master Key: God's Son Revealed
The letter contains an unmatched revelation of the Cross of Christ as a counter to all human boasting (chs. 1—4). Paul cites Christ as our example in all behavior (11:1) and describes the church as His body (ch. 12). Especially important are the powerful consequences of Christ's resurrection for the whole of creation (ch. 15).

Power Key: God's Spirit at Work
The manifestations or gifts of the Spirit make up the best known passages about the Holy Spirit (chs. 12—14). But we should not overlook the role of the Holy Spirit in revealing the things of God to the human spirit in a way that prevents all grounds for pride (2:1–13). Perhaps most illuminating amid current debate in the church at large is the way the apostle leads the Corinthians into a balanced employment of speaking with tongues, affirming this practice and refusing any the right to prohibit it (ch. 14).

gifts of the Spirit and to the Spirit of the gifts.

Introducing

1 CORINTHIANS

Author. The authenticity of 1 Corinthians has never seriously been challenged. In style, language, and theology, the letter belongs to Paul.

Occasion and Date. Paul established the church at Corinth about A.D. 50–51, when he spent eighteen months there on his second missionary journey (Acts 18:1–17). He continued to carry on correspondence and exercise care for the church after his departure (see 1 Cor. 5:9; 2 Cor. 12:14). During his three-year ministry in Ephesus, on his third missionary journey (Acts 19), he had received disturbing reports concerning moral laxity among believers in Corinth. To remedy the situation, he sent the church a letter (1 Cor. 5:9–11), which has since been lost. Shortly afterward, a delegation sent by Chloe, a member of the church in Corinth, reported to Paul concerning the existence of divisive factions in the church. Before he could write a corrective letter, another delegation from Corinth arrived with a letter asking him certain questions (1 Cor. 7:1; 16:17). Paul immediately sent Timothy to Corinth to help correct conditions there (1 Cor. 4:17). He then wrote the letter that we know as 1 Corinthians, expecting it to reach Corinth before Timothy (16:10). Since Paul apparently wrote the letter near the end of his Ephesian ministry (16:8), it may be dated about A.D. 55.

Purpose. First Corinthians is a pastoral letter, written to resolve doctrinal and practical problems within the local church. Paul's authorship gives the letter apostolic application to all "the churches of God" (11:16).

Background. The letter reveals some of the typical Greek cultural problems of Paul's day, including the gross sexual immorality of the city of Corinth. The Greeks were known for their idolatry, divisive philosophies, spirit of litigation, and rejection of a bodily resurrection. Corinth was one of the most important commercial cities of the day and controlled much of the shipping between the East and the West. It was located on the narrow neck of land which served as a landbridge between the mainland of Greece and the Peloponnesian peninsula. Corinth was infamous for its sensuality and sacred prostitution. Even its name became a notorious proverb: "to Corinthianize" meant to practice prostitution. The city's chief deity was Aphrodite (Venus), the goddess of licentious love, and a thousand professional prostitutes served in the temple dedicated to her worship. The spirit of the city showed up in the church and explains the kind of problems the people faced.

It also reveals some of the problems the former pagans had in not transferring previous religious experiences to the ministry experience of the Holy Spirit. They may have associated some of the frenzied antics of paganism with the exercise of spiritual gifts (see 12:2).

Content. The letter consists of Paul's response to ten separate problems: a sectarian spirit, incest, lawsuits, fornication, marriage and divorce, eating food offered to idols, wearing of the veil, the Lord's Supper, spiritual gifts, and the resurrection of the body.

Personal Application. No epistle in the New Testament gives a clearer insight into the life of the first-century church than 1 Corinthians. In it Paul provides straightforward instructions for such moral and theological problems as sectarianism, spiritual immaturity, church discipline, ethical differences, the role of the sexes, and the proper use of spiritual gifts. Where these same problems exist in the modern church, the remedies are the same.

Those from non-Pentecostal or non-charismatic churches may receive a fresh challenge from the vitality and spiritual gifts evident in the Corinthian church, and may lay aside traditional prejudices against such things. Those from charismatic and Pentecostal churches, where worship is less structured and spiritual gifts are prominent, may reexamine their own practices in the light of Paul's guidelines for congregational services.

Surveying

1 CORINTHIANS

INTRODUCTION WITH GREETINGS AND THANKSGIVING 1:1–9. Paul founded this church during his second missionary journey (Acts 18:1–17). The apostle's encouragement of the Corinthians as "sanctified" and "saints"

is a remarkable insight into the heart of a shepherd who is about to deal with devastating moral problems in the congregation. "That you may be blameless in the day of our Lord" (1:8) is the purpose of his writing.

> "So that you come short in no *gift, eagerly waiting for the revelation of our Lord Jesus Christ" (1:7). Paul is referring here to a complete

measure of every "gift of grace" (*charismata*) available to the Corinthians (12:31ff). Paul's passion for the growth and maturity of the church is matched by his desire for the effective spiritual exercise of ministry by the church.

I. THE PROBLEM OF A SECTARIAN SPIRIT THAT AROSE FROM A PREFERENCE FOR RELIGIOUS LEADERS BECAUSE OF THEIR SUPPOSED SUPERIOR WISDOM 1:10—4:21.

The factionalism in the church has brought about a challenge to Paul's apostolic authority. Here, Paul lays out the groundwork for the entire epistle—the "demonstration of the Spirit and of power" (2:4) and the coming of the kingdom of God "in power" (4:20) are all the proof necessary of Paul's authority and wisdom which comes from heaven.

A. The contrast between human and divine wisdom over the Cross shows the fallacy of a sectarian spirit that stems from human wisdom (1:10—3:4).

Paul's disappointment with the division of the church leads him to the question, "Is Christ divided?" (1:13). The ludicrous nature of the inquiry highlights the confusion within the young church. Paul made no disciples in his own name; all are to be disciples of Jesus.

Next, Paul addresses the Cross of Christ as the ultimate contradiction. Its power is universal, unstoppable, and eternal. Yet, to the world it is incomprehensible. The wisdom of the Cross is rejected by the world as "foolishness" (1:18). Paul continues to say that even the spiritual "rulers of this age" (2:6, 8) did not comprehend the power and wisdom of the Cross or "they would not have crucified the Lord of glory" (2:8).

Paul corrects the Corinthians in 3:1–3 as still being spiritual "babes" and "carnal." They are not ready for a mature diet (*see* Word of God) if they cannot move beyond their divisiveness.

> **"Jesus Christ and Him crucified"**
> (2:2). Paul's rejection of any other message is a change from the well-reasoned discourse he presented to the philosophers in Athens. Immediately before coming to Corinth, Paul preached the brilliant sermon in Acts 17 which addresses current pop-theology in the culture (v. 28) and uses culturally relevant religious notions to introduce Christ to them (v. 23). His discourse as recorded by Luke contains no specific reference to the Cross of Christ. The definitive statement in 1 Corinthians 2:2 marks a transformation in Paul's understanding on communicating Christ to any culture.

B. The role of religious leaders shows they are important but should never be the cause for boasting (3:5—4:5).

Paul demonstrates that there should be no jealousy among the leaders in the church (3:9), emphasizing the unique gifts each brings to the body of Christ. However, the foundation for every believer is Christ (3:10), and as the person of God "builds" their life the quality of the materials selected to work with will be determined by whether that person can withstand the "fire"—both of God's inspection and of the "fiery trial" of life (1 Pet. 4:12). This is not a matter of salvation. It is secure. At stake here is the substance of our life's work. (*See* Craftiness.)

> **"Judge nothing before the time, until the Lord comes"**
> (4:5). All will be judged at the coming of the Lord (2 Cor. 5:10). Harsh criticism of believers within the body of Christ is unnecessary. God is judge; God is just; and God will reward according to the scales of eternity, not according to the balances of humanity.

C. An open rebuke by ironic comparison of the Corinthian's pride with Paul's foolishness (4:6–21).

Paul's introduction of the Corinthians' being "wise" and "strong" places them directly in the category of the worldly in chapter 1. Paul appeals for them to "imitate me" (4:16) rather than to continue in their confused ways.

II. THE PROBLEM OF INTERNAL CHURCH DISCIPLINE BROUGHT ON BY A CASE OF INCEST 5:1–13.

Living in the midst of a promiscuous culture, the Corinthian church has adopted some of the same moral indifference toward sin in the congregation. Incest is occurring, which is so abhorrent that this "is not even named among the Gentiles—that a man has his father's wife!" (5:1). Paul reminds them of a previous letter where he instructed them "not to keep company with sexually immoral people" (5:9). Now Paul extends the ban on fellowship to all those in the congregation who are determined to live lives of compromise with impunity (5:10–11; *see* Sincerity).

> ### "Deliver such a one to Satan for the destruction of the flesh."
>
> (5:5). The ultimate potential of this action is to bring a response that may result in salvation for the individual "in the day of the Lord." (*See also* 1 Tim. 1:20.) Paul's instruction in the matter is important. This discipline is to be done "when you are gathered together" (1 Cor. 5:4). This is not a private matter for the leadership, but a matter of congregation-wide understanding and unity. Paul describes the attitude of such discipline not in anger or frustration, but in mourning (1 Cor. 5:2).

III. THE PROBLEM OF LAWSUITS BETWEEN CHRISTIANS BEFORE PUBLIC COURTS 6:1–11.

The integrity of relationships within the congregation should require that differences among brothers be settled within the church. It is a "shame" to the Corinthians that they choose to sue each other in public pagan courts rather than agree to simply give up their claim (*see* Covetousness). Paul insists that believers will one day "judge angels" (*see* Kingdom of God). Why not settle a simple matter like this in the congregation with godly wisdom and counselors?

IV. THE PROBLEM OF SEXUAL MISUSE OF THE BODY FROM A MISAPPLICATION OF PAUL'S ETHICAL TEACHING 6:12–20.

Paul preaches liberty in Christ—yet the Corinthians have taken liberty to extremes Paul never intended (*see* Stewardship). Paul's freedom to eat foods offered to idols (8:4) cannot be compared to the Corinthians' attitude toward sex. Corinth was known for its profligate lifestyle and sexual indulgence, with over one thousand temple prostitutes at work in the city. Paul insists that "he who is joined to a harlot is one body with her" (vv. 16–17). The human personality cannot be separated (as some Corinthians are teaching) into spirit and body which have no connection to each other. Sexual immorality is a sin against: (1) the believer's own body and (2) the temple where the Holy Spirit dwells.

V. THE PROBLEM OF THE RELATIONSHIP BETWEEN THE SECULAR SPHERE AND THE BELIEVER'S SPIRITUAL LIFE, ESPECIALLY IN THE AREAS OF SEX, MARRIAGE, AND SLAVERY 7:1–40.

Paul is about to answer a series of difficult questions put to him by the Corinthians in a letter to him. (*See* Family Life; Reconciled.)

Single people should remain single to better serve the Lord (7:32). However, "each one has his own gift from God," and this may not include a gift of celibacy. In that case it is better for a person "to marry than to burn with passion" (7:9).

Paul's next subject deals with the married person—if you are married, stay married, even if your spouse is an unbeliever. If you have been abandoned by an unbelieving mate, then "a brother or a sister is not under bondage in such cases" (7:15). Paul acknowledges the possibility for dissolution of a marriage on grounds which are broader than those specifically mentioned in Matthew 19:9.

Some teaching in Corinth forbade believers to marry. (*See also* 1 Tim. 4:3.) Paul asserts that "if you do marry, you have not sinned" (v. 28). Even for the widow, Paul directly affirms the right to remarry (v. 39).

VI. THE PROBLEM OF ETHICAL DIFFERENCES BETWEEN BRETHREN CAUSED BY THE EATING OF FOOD OFFERED TO IDOLS 8:1—11:1.

In exiting a pagan society, many of the Corinthian converts had questions about how to relate to things out of their past. Paul affirms our freedom in the Lord; while asserting our responsibility to serve people at the point of their need, not according to our preference in privilege.

A. The basic principle of love versus knowledge (8:1–13). Paul's instruction on food offered to idols has a universal point of wisdom that must dominate the thinking of the church in all situations. If our liberty becomes a "stumbling block to those who are weak" (v. 9), then the law of love demands that we not exercise our freedom.

B. Paul's personal example in forgoing his rights (9:1–27). Paul illustrates his freedom to receive payment from the Corinthians for his work in the gospel. The pattern is for those who work in the gospel to receive maintenance in their work; however, Paul has chosen not to give his enemies cause to criticize him. Therefore, he does not accept material substance so that he "may not abuse my authority in the gospel" (v. 18; *see* Partaker; Void).

C. The application of the principle in attitude and action (10:1—11:1). Paul warns the church to "flee from idolatry" and to not "have fellowship with demons" (10:14, 20). There is no way in our Christian freedom (*see* Liberty) to have a continued relationship with the past: "You cannot drink the cup of the Lord and the cup of demons" (10:21; *see* Blood, The).

VII. THE PROBLEM OF THE ROLE OF THE SEXES IN LIGHT OF THE REMOVAL OF THE VEIL 11:2–16.

Paul now turns his

attention to the conduct of public worship services. The first issue concerns women in the church and their proper relationship to authority (v. 10). In that culture, it was a custom for a woman to cover her head in order to honor her husband and show submissiveness to his authority in the home (*see* Family Life; Manhood). Conversely, the unveiled woman was shockingly inappropriate, undignified, and suggestive of deficient character. Paul uses this cultural symbol to affirm the spiritual issue of submission to authority, which is necessary for the proper exercise of spiritual gifts in the congregation.

VIII. THE PROBLEM OF DESECRATING THE LORD'S SUPPER 11:17–34. The Corinthians also misunderstood the purpose of the Lord's Table. The indulgence of the love feast had led to drunkenness and selfishness, completely contrary to the concept of Christ's sacrifice. Therefore, Paul offers a pattern for their partaking of the Lord's Supper. (*See* Faith's Confession; Recognized.)

"Let a man examine himself"
(11:28). This passage has been misapplied in much of the church. The purpose is not to deny participation, but to assess the spiritual needs of the believer in order to receive the dynamic release, potential for healing, and spiritual renewal available through partaking at the table. It is not a matter of the Lord's visitation of wrath upon an unworthy individual, but that those who are "not discerning the Lord's body" (v. 29) do not receive the intended benefits. As a result there is weakness, sickness, and even death.

IX. THE PROBLEM OF SPIRITUAL MANIFESTATIONS WHICH AROSE FROM A MISUSE OF THE GIFT OF TONGUES 12:1—14:40. The next three chapters open the extended discussion of spiritual gifts and their operation in the church. Paul is anxious that the Corinthians understand not only the operation of the gifts of the Spirit but, (1) the purpose of spiritual gifts, (2) the motive that energizes the believer in their operation, and (3) the administration of the gifts.

A. The need for variety (12:1–31). Paul's opening contrast is between the operation of the Holy Spirit and the conduct of those "carried away with dumb idols" (*see* Accursed). The Lord's people are submitted to Him and are never out of control (14:32, 40). Paul explains that "the manifestation of the Spirit is given to each one for the profit of all" (v. 7). The

purpose is ministry, not acquisition or demonstration.

"Now concerning spiritual gifts, brethren, I do not want you to be ignorant"
(12:1–31). In verse 1, "spiritual gifts" is literally translated "spirituals" (*pneumatikon*), which is later defined as "gifts" (v. 4), "ministries" (v. 5), and "activities" (v. 6). The gifts of the Spirit (vv. 6–10; *see* Holy Spirit Gifts) are given to each member of the body as directed by the Spirit. However, the gifts of the Father (Romans 12) and the gifts of Christ (Ephesians 4) also are found in this chapter (vv. 28–30). These in no way constitute an exhaustive list of the things the Godhead does to resource the church for ministry, but they create categories of ministries and gifts that are used to further the witness of the gospel to the world and the release of ministry to each member of the church.

"*The word of wisdom*" (12:8) is a supernatural utterance that reveals God's purpose or perspective to a specific circumstance.

"*The word of knowledge*" is supernatural revelation of information concerning a specific situation, event, or person.

"*Faith*" (12:9) goes beyond saving faith, but is specifically related to God's activity in a particular matter.

"*Healings*" is the miraculous manifestation of healings of diseases beyond the scope of natural or human intervention (*see* Healing, Divine).

"*Working of miracles*" (12:10) is the superseding of natural law and process for the accomplishing of God's purpose in a situation.

"*Prophecy*" is the work of the Spirit that discloses truth, bringing edification, exhortation, and comfort to God's people.

"*Discerning of spirits*" means the supernatural recognition of demonic activity in a situation or in the motives of people.

"*Different kinds of tongues*" is the supernatural utterance of a language not known to the speaker. This is used both for witness (Acts 2:8–13) and for personal communication with God for the purpose of edification in prayer and worship (1 Cor. 14:2).

"*Interpretation of tongues*" is the public interpretation of a message in tongues for the benefit of the congregation.

Paul does not suggest that the gifts are

the possession of the individual or to be ranked in terms of their importance. The function of the gifts is like the individual placement of people in the body of Christ. Each person has a place, and each person is resourced with the Holy Spirit in such a way as to benefit the whole body (12:19; see Apostles; Human Worth; Leadership, Spiritual).

B. The need for love (13:1–13). Paul's "more excellent way" (12:31) contrasts with the way the Corinthians have exercised spiritual gifts (see Holy Spirit Gifts). Love is the motive for the gifts and the method by which they are to be conveyed. "Love never fails" (v. 8).

"(Love) . . . believes all things" (13:7). Since God is our loving Father and His Word is absolutely true, our faith is secure in Him. Love that believes all things seeks out the best in other people, looks for the redemption of Christ in every situation, and makes room for God's miracle power in the bleakest of circumstance.

"Prophecies . . . will fail; tongues . . . will cease; knowledge . . . will vanish away" (13:8). The ceasing of the gifts of the Holy Spirit will take place at a specific time "when that which is perfect has come" (v. 10). Historically, Bible scholars have agreed that this means the return of Jesus Christ. Some have interpreted it to mean the completion of the canon of Scripture by inserting this completely foreign thought into the passage. The gifts of the Holy Spirit are not simply for the founding of the church in the first century; they are for the ministry of the church until Jesus comes again.

C. The need for control (14:1–40). Paul teaches the place of both tongues and *prophecy in the local congregation (see Desire). In verse 5 he equates prophecy with tongues that are interpreted for the congregation; both benefit the congregation and can be understood by visitors. He reinforces the supernatural benefits of the exercise of these gifts in public (see Holy Spirit Gifts), especially in the presence of unbelievers (v. 25).

"Since you are zealous for spiritual gifts, let it be for the edification of the church" (14:1–40). Paul affirms the desirability and practical reasons of (1) personal edification and (2) public witness in the use of tongues (vv. 2, 4–5, 15, 22, 39). At the same time he asserts the primacy of prophecy as the congregation gathers for public worship (vv. 1, 3–5, 24–25, 31, 39). The key to the chapter is in verse 40, "Let all things be done decently and in order" (see Subject). Paul concludes this chapter with an exhortation about the encouragement of prophecies as the believers gather: "Do not forbid to speak with tongues."

X. THE PROBLEM OF THE RESURRECTION OF THE DEAD 15:1–58. The witness to the resurrection of Christ is certain! The vital importance of this issue is highlighted in verses 14 and 17. The resurrection is the verification that the Cross of Christ is efficacious in the life of the believer. If Christ is risen, so will all believers be resurrected (v. 22).

"Those who are Christ's at His coming" (15:23). "In Christ all shall be made alive" (v. 22) refers to the resurrection of the dead. Jesus led the way in resurrection for all of His who will follow. Those who have received Christ as their Savior and placed their faith in Him will be part of the resurrection which will occur at His *coming again (see Moment).

XI. CONCLUDING PERSONAL REMARKS 16:1–24. Paul instructs the church concerning the offering for the believers in Jerusalem for the relief of their suffering in a way that maximizes its potential and minimizes possible inconvenience of it. Paul discusses the coming of Timothy and the future visit of Apollos.

Paul's conclusion to the letter is positive and uplifting. The last strokes of his pen reiterate the fact that his passion and concern for them are the motivation for such a confrontational letter. "My love be with you all in Christ Jesus, Amen."

TRUTH-IN-ACTION through 1 CORINTHIANS

Truth 1 Corinthians Teaches	**Action** 1 Corinthians Invites
1 Guidelines for Growing in Godliness Godliness is transparent, selfless, replete in integrity and excellent character. The godly person views personal relationships as one of life's highest priorities and sees failure in this area as most serious. In order to maintain peace within the church, the godly will refuse to enter legal action against a fellow believer. The godly person seeks reconciliation and healing in the family rather than divorce. He honors and supports those God has set in authority in the church. The godly person accepts any loss in order to secure or maintain right relationships in the family or the church and commits them to God for His restoration and reparation.	**3:17** *Recognize* that your body is God's temple. *Refuse to defile* this house of God. **6:1–11** *Never* go to the law against a fellow believer. *Commit* yourself to keeping you marriage healthy and intact. **7:10–16** *Do not divorce* an unbelieving spouse if he/she wants to stay with you or restrain him/her if he/she wishes to dissolve marriage bonds. (This does not mean that a believer must accept brutal neglect, abuse, or immoral treatment.) **9:11–14** *Recognize* and *honor* the devoted minister's right to support from those he serves. **13:1–8** *Discipline yourself* in the practice of agape love in every attitude, thought, word, and deed.
2 Steps to Holiness Holy living calls for us to rely totally on God for spiritual wisdom, rejecting the wisdom of the world. Holiness devotes time and energy to knowing the Lord, choosing to associate with other believers rather than be unduly influenced by the world's values.	**1:25–29** *Acknowledge* that there is no spiritual dynamic in mere human abilities. *Understand* that God uses that which without His presence is ineffectual. **2:13–16** *Recognize* that the natural mind cannot understand or receive from the Holy Spirit. *Know* that only the spiritually alive can discern spiritual wisdom. **7:29–31** *Remember* that earthly values are transient, and *embrace* the eternal. **15:33** *Recognize* that evil associations influence your conduct toward evil.
3 Steps to Dynamic Devotion Devotion makes full use of the key resources God has made available for that purpose: the Scriptures and spiritual gifts. Both the OT and NT are important for the believer. Employing spiritual language (tongues) as a private devotional discipline results in a holy self-edification. The devoted disciple knows that the Lord's Table is an important means to nurture spiritual life and growth.	**10:6–12** *Recognize* that the OT is an example for the church. *Submit yourself* to the wisdom of the OT. *Read, study,* and *apply* the OT. **11:20–29** *Celebrate* the Lord's Supper frequently. *Receive* Jesus' life from it through faith. *Approach* Communion humbled and cleansed through confession of sin. **14:13–22** *Employ* both spiritual and natural language in worship and devotion. *Desire* prophetic utterance. *Differentiate* between prophetic utterances and the prophetic office.
4 Vital Keys to Dynamic Church Life The body life of the church, not the independent believer, is the key to understanding God's dealings in the NT. We should not presume that the apostles thought with a predisposition toward rugged individualism. God deals with the church as a body and with individuals as parts or members. Individual members ought to put the body's or congregation's concerns above their own. This will	**1:10** *Know* that believers are to be unified in their devotion to the gospel of Christ. *Acknowledge* where you fall short, and *repent.* **3:1–4** *Recognize* that division in the church is sin. **5:1–8** *Do not neglect* church discipline. *Understand* that such neglect emboldens unrestrained and undisciplined living. **12:12–27** *Promote* unity within the body of Christ. *Believe* that God places every member in the body as will best serve His purposes. **14:26–40** *Maintain* order in church gatherings. *Allow* no "tongue" to go uninterpreted. *Allow* no prophetic utterance to go unjudged. *(continued)*

Truth 1 Corinthians Teaches	Action 1 Corinthians Invites
4 Vital Keys to Dynamic Church Life *(continued)* open our understanding to dynamic truth God has intended for the church.	
5 Guidelines for Growth in the Spirit Learning how to employ the spiritual gifts is vital, because they are the means God has given us to nurture growth. This occurs in the congregation through edification and beyond it through evangelism.	**12:4–11** *Understand* that God works through spiritual gifts to reproduce the ministry of the Lord Jesus Christ in His church. *Recognize* the importance of these gifts for dynamic ministry. **14:1–5** *Accept* the importance of tongues for holy self-edification.
6 Key Lessons in Faith Faith believes and focuses on proclaiming God's Word without reservation.	**4:20** *Recognize* that kingdom ministry involves signs, wonders, and miracles that demonstrate the power of God. *Humbly call* for God to restore the miraculous dimension to the church. **15:58** *Never give up! Continue steadfastly* in faith and abound in service to God. *Know* that nothing done in Jesus' name is in vain.

New Testament Lists of Spiritual Gifts

The New Testament provides several lists of spiritual gifts. No one list is exhaustive, and the contents of each list depend on the specific purpose of the author. For a full discussion of spiritual gifts, see the entry "Holy Spirit Gifts and Power" in the Encyclopedic Dictionary.

Romans 12:6-8	1 Cor. 12:8–10	1 Cor. 12:28–30	Eph. 4:11	1 Pet. 4:9–11

Prophecy
Serving
Teaching
Exhortation
Giving
Leading
Showing Mercy
	Word of
	  Wisdom
	Word of
	  Knowledge
	Faith
	Healings
	Miracles
	Prophecy
	Discerning of
	  Spirits
	Tongues
	Interpretation of
	  Tongues
		Apostleship
		Prophecy
		Teaching
		Miracles
		Healing
		Helping
		Administrating
		Tongues
		Interpretation of
		  Tongues
			Apostleship
			Prophecy
			Evangelism
			Pastor/Teacher
				Speaking
				Serving

KEYS TO 2 CORINTHIANS
The Kingdom and Personal Struggles

Kingdom Key: God's Purpose in View

From Jesus' ministry we have seen that extending the kingdom of God in word and works evokes conflict—personal struggles with both men and demons. Perhaps the most demanding is learning to discern the latter. In Paul's correspondence with the Corinthians, he identifies cases of such confrontations that too frequently are simply passed off today as ordinary situations of human problems alone. It requires discernment to identify the devil at work without falling prey to either of two tendencies: (1) irresponsibility, blaming Satan for problems which attention to duty might have preempted, and (2) superstition, assigning a demonic presence to anything that annoys or troubles a person.

It is helpful to note where Paul identifies the Adversary at work, since Paul clearly saw his role as an agent of God's kingdom, invading darkness with Christ's light and reclaiming lost souls from hell's dominion (2 Cor. 4:1–6; Acts 26:16–18; Col. 1:12; 2 Tim. 2:24–26). Understandably, then, he expected either frontal assault from the Enemy (Eph. 6:10–12) or retaliatory attacks (2 Cor. 10:3–6).

He is unabashed about describing his struggle with a prolonged physical affliction resulting from a demonic enterprise. The meaningless ongoing debate over the "what" of Paul's thorn in the flesh ought to recommend a more significant inquiry: "Who did it come from?" The apostle answers this

Mere human vessels may bear heaven's richest treasure.

himself. It is "a messenger of Satan" (2 Cor. 12:7), undoubtedly a "fiery dart of the wicked one" (Eph. 6:16).

Paul also warns the Corinthians of Satan's subtle efforts to produce unforgiveness among members of a local church (2:10–11). Such an insight provides a stern caution to leaders and laity alike. The health and unity of the congregation requires wisdom in dealing with confusion or conflict. A similar precautionary directive is found in the apostle's warning against false teachers whose apparent "light" (insights, revelations, ministries) are born of hell, not heaven (11:13–15).

It is not superstitious to *(Please turn to page 366.)*

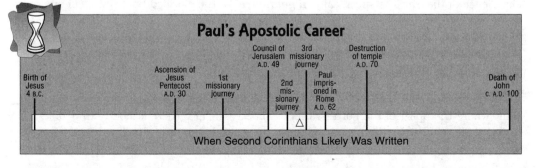

Paul's Apostolic Career

				Council of Jerusalem A.D. 49	3rd missionary journey		Destruction of temple A.D. 70		
Birth of Jesus 4 B.C.		Ascension of Jesus Pentecost A.D. 30	1st missionary journey		2nd missionary journey	Paul imprisoned in Rome A.D. 62			Death of John C. A.D. 100

When Second Corinthians Likely Was Written

Second Corinthians: human frailty can overcome • • •

Master Key: God's Son Revealed

Jesus Christ is the focus of our relationship with God. All God's promises to us are Yes in Jesus, and we say "Amen" to God's promises in Jesus (1:19–20). Jesus is God's Yes to us and our Yes to God. Only in Christ do we see the glory of God, and only in Him are we transformed by that glory (3:14, 18), for Christ is the very image of God (4:4–6). God came to us in Christ, reconciling the world to Himself (5:19). Thus, it is "in Christ" that we have become new creatures (5:17). This change was accomplished through the marvelous act of God's grace in which Christ, "who knew no sin," became "sin for us, that we might become the righteousness of God in Him" (5:21).

Jesus is also the focus of our service to God. We proclaim Jesus as Lord and ourselves as servants for His sake (4:5). We willingly share not only Christ's life and glory but also His dying (4:10–12), His willingness to be weak so that others might experience the power of God (13:3–4, 9), and His willingness to be impoverished so that others might be enriched (8:9). We experience His weakness but also His strength as we seek to bring "every thought into captivity to the obedience of Christ" (10:5).

Jesus is the focus of our present life in this world, where we simultaneously experience in our mortal bodies both "the dying of the Lord Jesus" and His life (4:10–11).

Jesus is the focus of our future life, for we will be raised up with Jesus (4:14), who is the "betrothed . . . husband" of the church (11:2) and the judge of all people (5:10).

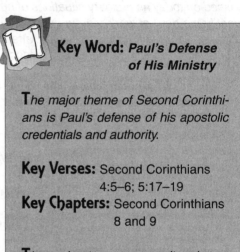

Key Word: *Paul's Defense of His Ministry*

The major theme of Second Corinthians is Paul's defense of his apostolic credentials and authority.

Key Verses: Second Corinthians 4:5–6; 5:17–19

Key Chapters: Second Corinthians 8 and 9

These chapters are one unit and comprise the most complete revelation of God's plan for giving found anywhere in the Scriptures.

Power Key: God's Spirit at Work

The Holy Spirit is the power of the New Covenant (3:6), because He makes real to us the present and future provisions of our salvation in Christ. By the gift of "the Spirit in our hearts as a guarantee," we are assured that all God's promises are Yes in Christ, and that we are anointed and "sealed" as belonging to Him (1:20–22). The present experience of the Spirit is specifically "a guarantee" of the glorified bodies we will one day receive (5:1–5).

We do not merely read about the will of God in the "letter" of Scripture, for "the letter [alone] kills." The Spirit who gives life (3:6) changes our way of living by opening our eyes to the living reality of what we read. Thus, we progressively experience and embody the will of God, and we ourselves become epistles of Christ, "known and read by all men" (3:2).

When we submit ourselves to the work of the Spirit, we experience a miracle. We find that "where the Spirit of the Lord is, there is liberty" (3:17). There is liberty to behold the unveiled glory of the Lord and to be changed more and more into the likeness of what we

(Please turn to page 366.)

• • • weakness and trial through God's presence and grace.

Introducing

2 CORINTHIANS

Background and Date. In various ways 2 Corinthians reflects Paul's dealings with the church in Corinth during the period from the founding of the church in about A.D. 50 until the writing of this letter in A.D. 55 or 56. The various episodes in the interactions between Paul and the Corinthians can be summarized as follows:

1. The *founding visit* to Corinth lasted about eighteen months (*see* Acts 18).

2. Paul wrote an *earlier letter* than 1 Corinthians (*see* 1 Cor. 5:9).

3. Paul wrote *1 Corinthians* from Ephesus, about A.D. 55.

4. A brief but *painful visit* to Corinth caused "sorrow" for Paul and the church (*see* 2 Cor. 2:1; 13:2).

5. Following the painful visit, Paul wrote a *severe letter,* delivered by Titus (*see* 2 Cor. 2:4; 7:6–8).

6. Paul wrote *2 Corinthians* from Macedonia, while on his way to Corinth again, in A.D. 55 or 56.

7. Paul's *final visit* to Corinth (Acts 20) was probably when he wrote Romans, just before returning to Jerusalem. The *painful visit,* which Acts does not record, and the *severe letter* provide immediate background for the writing of 2 Corinthians.

We do not possess the *severe letter,* although some scholars have suggested that 2 Corinthians 10—13 may have been part of that epistle. There is no manuscript evidence to support this view, however.

Occasion and Purpose. First Corinthians was not as effective as Paul had hoped in settling the crisis at Corinth. The party opposing Paul gained strength, and its leader was particularly obnoxious to him (2:5–11; 10:7–12). Paul hurriedly traveled to Corinth from Ephesus in an attempt to meet the situation. Although this visit is not mentioned in Acts, it is implied in 2 Corinthians 12:14. Paul failed to achieve his desired objective (2:1; 12:14, 21; 13:1–2), and experienced open hostility from the leader of the opposition (2:5–8; 7:12).

Paul then returned to Ephesus, where he wrote a severe letter to the Corinthians, putting into it the full weight of his apostolic authority. He sent the letter by Titus, and then made his way to Macedonia, where Titus met him with an encouraging report (2:12–13;

7:6–16). The majority had been won back to Paul and had taken disciplinary action against the offender (2:5–11). However, there was still a rebellious minority (chs. 10—13). Paul wrote to express a message of conciliation to the loyal majority and to rebuke the rebellious minority. He also gave instructions concerning the offering he was collecting for the impoverished church in Jerusalem.

Characteristics. Second Corinthians is the most autobiographical of Paul's letters, containing numerous references to the hardships he endured in the course of his ministry (*see* 11:23–33). Paul mentioned these to establish the legitimacy of his ministry and to illustrate the nature of true spirituality.

In defending his ministry, Paul opens his heart, showing his deep emotion. He reveals his strong love for the Corinthians, his ardent zeal for the glory of God, his uncompromising loyalty to the truth of the gospel, and his stern indignation in confronting those who disrupt the fellowship of the church. His life was bound up in the life of his converts, and he was not coldly professional in his ministry (*see* 1:6; 5:13; 7:3–7; 11:2; 12:14–15).

Content. Second Corinthians consists of three main parts. The first seven chapters contain Paul's defense of his conduct and his ministry. He explains the change in his plans to visit Corinth and responds to a charge of fickleness. In discussing the Christian ministry, he expounds on its nature, its problems, its motivating principles, and its responsibilities.

The second unit, chapters 8 and 9, deals with the offering being raised by Paul for the poor saints in Judea. Paul urged the Corinthians to be liberal and cheerful in giving so that God might bless them in every way.

Chapters 10 through 13 form the third segment of the letter and contain a message of rebuke to the remaining detractors in the church. Paul responds to the jibes and slanders of his critics and fully vindicates his authority as an apostle.

Personal Application. Second Corinthians is a valuable guide in examining our own motives for serving the Lord, whether as lay people or as ordained pastors and evangelists. As an instrument of the Holy Spirit, this letter can refine our motives until we reflect the kind of selfless giving best exemplified in Christ, but also found in His servant Paul. The instructions concerning the collection for Jerusalem (chs. 8 and 9) emphasize generosity in the area of financial resources, just as Paul emphasized generosity in self-giving throughout the book.

Kingdom Key *continued from page 363*

expect satanic attack and counter-measures as God's kingdom advances in our lives, in our homes, or in our congregations. Part of our call to service in the kingdom of God is to dis-

cern evil spirits at work, and then—through the armor of God and effective prayer warfare—to discharge them (Eph. 6:12–18).

Power Key *continued from page 364*

behold. The Holy Spirit gives us freedom to see and freedom to be what God wants us to be (3:16–18).

The work of the Holy Spirit is evident in daily inward renewal (4:16), spiritual warfare (10:3–5), and the "signs and wonders and mighty deeds" of Paul's ministry in Corinth

(12:12). Paul ended his letter with a blessing, which included "the communion [fellowship] of the Holy Spirit" (13:14). This could indicate a sense of the Spirit's presence or, more likely, an enjoyment of the fellowship the Spirit gives us with Christ and with all people who love Christ.

Surveying
2 CORINTHIANS

I. GREETING 1:1–2. Paul is consumed with concern for the response of the Corinthians to the strong rebuke by letter and his last unscheduled visit to them, that caused great pain in the church.

II. EXPLANATION OF PAUL'S MINISTRY 1:3—7:16. Paul goes into a lengthy explanation of past events.

A. Comfort and suffering (1:3–11). Suffering (vv. 6–7) will allow the consolation of God's comfort to fill their lives as they submit to the working of grace among them (v. 5).

B. Changes in plans (1:12–2:4). Some in the church have suggested that Paul's change in plans in not visiting the church reflected instability and untrustworthiness. Rather, Paul's change in plans is due to the fact that he did not want another hostile or difficult encounter with the church, feeling it would produce only frustration for him and for the church. (*See* Abundantly; Guarantee.)

C. Forgiving the offender (2:5–11). "The offender" appears to refer to the person who has severely challenged Paul's authority and occasioned Paul's harsh response. In responding to Paul's confrontation of the situation, the church had disciplined the man (7:6–13). Paul now counsels restoration, suggesting that an overly harsh response opens the door to satanic deception and loss of the person.

D. Distraction in Troas (2:12–13). Paul could not be comfortable in Troas because Titus had not yet returned with word from

Corinth about the church's reaction to his last letter.

E. Nature of Christian ministry (2:14—7:4). Paul explains the differing response of people to his ministry and teaches that God's people are to be "ambassadors for Christ" (5:20), extending to the world the ministry of reconciliation.

1. Life and death issues (2:14–17). Paul is not "peddling" Christ as some of the false teachers are. He is consumed with his message for the sake of those who need to hear it.

2. Living letters of commendation (3:1–3). Paul does not need letters to commend himself or his message to them. The transformed lives of the Corinthians are eloquent proof of the sufficiency of their ministry.

3. Sufficiency from God (3:4–6). The contrast between the letters of stone, which symbolize the Old Covenant, and the ministry of the Spirit in the New Covenant is obvious. With respect to the Law, "the letter kills, but the Spirit gives life" (v. 6). The promise of this New Covenant is not unique to Paul but is a fulfillment of what Old Testament prophets saw (Jer. 31:33; *see* Word of God).

4. Unveiled in the New Covenant (3:7–18). The glory of the Old Covenant is undisputed; however, the New Covenant is "much more glorious" (v. 11). Some have been veiled from the truth, yet Paul declares that when the veil is taken away we all will see the glory of God in us, as we are being changed into the likeness of the Lord (v. 18).

5. Integrity and openness (4:1–6). Paul's preaching is marked by "manifestation of the truth" in changed lives and demonstration of miracles, differentiating him from those who are "handling the word of God deceitfully."

"The god of this age"

(4:4). The New Testament uses a number of terms to describe the spiritual forces opposed to the advance of the ministry of Christ's kingdom (*see* John 12:31; 1 Cor. 2:8; Eph. 2:1). The overthrowing of these demonic forces takes place as God's people extend the rulership of King Jesus through prayer, witness, and spiritual warfare. In 2 Corinthians 10:4 Paul describes the key to successful conduct of this spiritual warfare.

6. *Dying and living with Jesus (4:7–15).* The role of believers is to declare the message of Christ, which at times is very costly, "hardpressed . . . perplexed . . . persecuted." However, the Lord is faithful in preserving His people. (*See* Excellence.)

7. *Eternal perspective (4:16—5:11).* Paul acknowledges the present struggle, but is motivated by "the things which are unseen." The physical life will one day give way to an eternal one. Therefore, Paul cautions the Corinthians to be "pleasing to the Lord," since we will all be judged by God.

"We must all appear before the judgment seat of Christ"

(5:10). These words were meant to remind all believers to maximize their lives in Christ. The judgment of believers appears elsewhere (Matt. 25:14–46; Luke 19:12–27; John 5:25–27; Acts 10:42), and the faithful believer who has taken seriously the charge to "bear much fruit" (John 15:7–8) will be appropriately rewarded at this judgment.

8. *Reconciled and reconciling (5:12—6:2).* At times it may appear to the Corinthians that Paul is out of his mind, as his critics suggest (5:13). Yet, the apostle is unrelenting because of the hope of the new creation and the weight of the eternal consequence of our life. (*See* Compels.)

"If anyone is in Christ, he is a new creation"

(5:17). This action of God's Spirit begins the moment a person places faith in Jesus Christ. The *new creation brings a person into an eternal relationship with God, who becomes our Father when we are "born again" (John 3:3, 16).

9. *Paying the price to minister (6:3–10).* Paul's ministry has been marked by blessings, hardships, and persecution. It also has been verified in character, spiritual commitment, and self-sacrifice.

10. *Heartfelt appeal for holiness (6:11—7:4).* The apostle asks the church to demonstrate and return love for him by living obediently to the words he has written. The warnings against unholy alliances are profound as Paul challenges, "What communion has light with darkness?" (6:14).

"Do not be unequally yoke."

(6:14). This verse alludes to Deuteronomy 22:10 regarding the yoking of an ox and a donkey for the purpose of plowing a field. Deuteronomy also refers to the mixing of seed in the vineyard and the mixing of fabric in a garment. The idea is clear: God's people are to be pure and holy. They must invest their lives in relationships that bring glory to God and offer the potential of furthering His kingdom. When applied to marriage it is particularly significant that God's people raise families to the glory of God, for the Lord "seeks godly offspring" (Mal. 2:15).

F. Rejoicing over the report from Corinth (7:5–16). Paul's relief is complete as Titus brings the good report of the mended relationship with the church. Paul acknowledges the sorrow caused by his letter (*see* Downcast), and yet he has joy. This is not joy in being right, but that their godly sorrow produced both Paul's vindication and their own deliverance (7:11).

"Godly sorrow produces repentance leading to salvation"

(7:10). "The sorrow of the world" leads to depression and defeat. Godly sorrow, however, affects the life of the believer in a way that advances God's purpose. Sorrow, in God's purpose, motivates change— "repentance"

III. GENEROSITY IN GIVING 8:1—9:15. This passage offers the most complete view of the matter of giving as a Christian duty. In terms of the theology, the administration, and the blessing of giving, Paul presents a powerful picture of the benefits of obedience, generosity, and joy for the people of God. In this regard, Paul is collecting money for the hardpressed church in Jerusalem. The gifts of the churches in Asia and Macedonia will be greatly used to ameliorate suffering there.

A. Macedonians and Jesus as examples (8:1–9). The other churches in Macedonia have been generous in their giving despite "their deep poverty" (8:2). Paul identifies a pattern in their giving that needs to be repeated by all people of faith (8:5). They were not merely manipulated to give; they were deliberate in their commitment to Christ, and then gave with a sense of divine mission.

This is the pattern that Jesus demonstrated with His own life (8:9; *see* Poor). As Jesus gave Himself sacrificially, so ought God's people to give.

B. Fulfilling good intentions (8:10–12). Paul asks the Corinthians to fulfill their pledge. He reminds them that it is the willingness to give that makes the gift acceptable, regardless of its size (Luke 21:1–4).

C. Sharing resources (8:13–15). Paul's appeal is based on the blessing of the abundance present in the church and the city. The time to give is now.

D. A trustworthy delegation (8:16–24). The wisdom of the approach to the offering shows that the temptation for abuse of money is universal. Both Titus and a compatriot will receive what is collected.

E. Timely preparation of the gift (9:1–5). The church is instructed to prepare the offering in advance so that the gifts could be processed efficiently and so that all would have ample time to make a generous offering.

F. Blessing of giving (9:6–15). The spiritual principle works as surely as the physical one: little sowing, little harvest—bountiful sowing, bountiful harvest (*see* Faith, Seed). God's grace flows with sufficiency for the purpose of providing for "every good work" (v. 8; *see* Cheerful).

IV. DEFENSE AND USE OF APOSTOLIC AUTHORITY 10:1—13:10. The discussion of spiritual authority in chapter 10 emphasizes the difference between authority based in human boasting and authority that "the Lord commends."

Paul describes his ministry in terms that contrast with other self-proclaimed authorities (11:13).

Finally, Paul confirms his intent to visit them for a third time and trusts he will find them committed to the truth so that he will have no need to bring correction again (13:10).

A. Rebuke of superficial assessment (10:1–11). While Paul is weak and gentle in nature, he recognizes that the true arena of conflict is spiritual and not human; therefore, the weapons of warfare for the people of God are spiritual (10:4–5). Paul refuses to fight in the flesh but is quite willing to address the central issues of conflict in spirit. (*See* Obedience.)

B. Rebuke of foolish comparisons (10:12–18). The ultimate measuring rod of Paul's effectiveness will not be found in comparing him with others, but "as your faith is increased, we shall be enlarged by you in our sphere" (10:15; *see* Evangelism).

C. Godly jealousy for the church (11:1–4). Embarrassed, Paul continues in his discussion of himself and "boasts" in order to refute the boasting of others. He will continue in his boasting so that they will not be deceived. (*See* Jealousy.)

D. Comparison with false apostles (11:5–15). Although untrained, and unpolished by some standards, Paul's teaching has been clear and life-transforming. However, he advances the controversy one step further by declaring self-appointed apostles to be deceivers (11:14).

"Satan himself transforms himself into an angel of light" (11:12–15). Satan is the ultimate deceiver (Rev. 20:10) and the "father of lies" (John 8:44). Human reason and logic offer no match to the power of Satan and his workers to deceive. The defense for God's people against such deception is twofold: (1) a clear understanding of the Bible, with an absolute surrender to its authority in a believer's life, and (2) the discerning of spirits as taught in 1 Corinthians 12:10.

E. The Corinthians' misguided tolerance (11:16–21). They have submitted themselves to bondage by following false teachers. Their absence of discernment is a great issue with Paul.

F. Paul's reluctant boasting (11:22—12:13). The personal history of Paul in ministry far outweighs any of those of his detractors.

"A messenger of Satan" (12:7–10). Paul's assault of either physical or spiritual torment—"thorn in the flesh"—was orchestrated by Satan to wear down Paul's resolve with discouragement, impair his judgment with frustration, or prevent him from pursuing his apostolic work.

It is clear, however, that the *grace of God is more than able to carry a believer through such seasons of assault (vv. 9–10).

G. Announcement of a third visit (12:14—13:10). The first visit founded the church; the second is referred to in 2:1 and 7:12. With some apprehension and damaged feelings, Paul is coming to them again (12:15).

1. Integrity of Paul's motives (12:14–19). The only intention of their mission has been to edify the church in Christ.

2. Warning to remaining rebels (12:20—13:4). In this visit Paul will not tolerate the sinful and contentious persons in the congregation. (*See* Mighty.)

3. Call to self-examination (13:5–10). The call to examine their lives, motives, and actions has a twofold purpose: (1) "that you may be made *complete" (v. 9) and (2) so that Paul need not give further correction (v. 10).

V. CONCLUDING GREETINGS 13:11–14. Paul exhorts them toward unity and peace, surrendering them to the grace of God and the communion of the Holy Spirit.

TRUTH-IN-ACTION through 2 CORINTHIANS

Truth 2 Corinthians Teaches	**Action** 2 Corinthians Invites
1 Guidelines for Growing in Godliness Godly living may result in disfavor with others because it warns of judgment for the ungodly. Godly individuals live by the ethic of love, selflessly asking, "How can I live for the benefit of others?" They are not lawless or sloppy in the way they live; rather, they seek to do right in everything.	**2:14–17** *Conduct* yourself with a clear conscience so that you will not be easily shaken by people's reactions. *Realize* that righteousness also sometimes triggers negative reactions. **5:10** *Know* and *understand* that you will give an account to Jesus as Judge for every thought, word, and deed. *Let this influence* your conduct. **5:15–17** *Appropriate* the fact that God has called you to live for Him. *Avoid* any selfishness or personal ambition, **8:21** *Practice* diligence in everything. Do what is right. *Make sure* your ethics reflect Jesus Christ in all your conduct.
2 Steps to Holiness Holiness requires that we live according to God's standard, not that of the world. Holiness recognizes the serious nature of partnerships and will not enter into them with those who are not believers. Planning a marriage to an unbeliever will produce an unequal alliance that is to be avoided. To experience a happy union, the believer should align with one whose ideals and visions center in Jesus Christ.	**1:12** *Conduct* yourself in the sincerity and holiness that come by God's grace. *Turn from* any worldly wisdom toward which you may naturally incline. **6:14–18** *Refuse to enter* any covenant or partnership with unbelievers. *Live* as a holy person. **2:9** *Know* and *observe* the necessity of obedience in Christian living.
3 Key Lessons in the Faith Faith chooses to believe God's word above the evidence of the senses, knowing natural circumstances are to be kept subject to the Word of God. Faith is not in denying the circumstances; rather, it is in believing God's testimony and living in agreement with it.	**4:16–18** *Focus* on the unseen and eternal. *Consider* and *dwell upon* the glory that follows this life. *Know* the inward man is being renewed. **5:7** *Live* according to the truth of God's Word and the testimony of His Spirit. **11:3, 4** *Identify as evil* any who would pervert the Word of God. *Do not accept* distortions of the gospel's truth.
4 Steps in Developing Humility Humility looks to God for what it needs. Humility is not shocked to discover its own weaknesses, having learned to trust God's strength. Nor do the humble take faith for granted, always drawing near to	**10:17, 18** *Give God the glory*, and let any commendation be from Him. **12:7–10** *Allow* Jesus' strength to be exhibited and exalted through your weakness. *Know* that His grace is large enough to meet you in your problems. **13:5, 6** *Practice* regular, diligent self-examination.

(continued)

Truth 2 Corinthians Teaches	**Action** 2 Corinthians Invites
4 Steps in Developing Humility *(continued)* God, distrusting self.	
5 Guidelines for Growth in the Spirit We must be determined to grow spiritually. Such growth is painful because one undergoes stretching, molding, and refining by the Holy Spirit. Spiritual people deal ruthlessly with any carnal thoughts in their own minds.	**3:2, 3** *Be shaped* by the Holy Spirit so that people can come to know Jesus through what they see. **3:17, 18** *Spend time* in "God's presence." *Expect* the Spirit to transform you into the image of His glorious Son. **10:3-5** *Recognize* the spiritual war in your mind. *Take captive* every thought that is hostile to God. *Memorize* Scripture and meditate as a "military discipline."
6 Lessons for Leaders God's leaders depend entirely on Him for their direction and empowering in the ministry. They never exalt or glorify themselves, acknowledging their lack of power and ability to fulfill any mission alone.	**3:5, 6** Leaders, *depend* on the Spirit as your only true source of ability. *Beware* building your ministry on mere human training or ability alone. **4:1-6** Leaders, *handle* God's Word diligently and with great care. *Be careful* not to read your own ideas into God's Word. *Ask* God to enlighten His Word. **4:7-15** Leaders, *never lose sight* of your weakness. *Give room* for the power of Jesus' dying to work in you so that His life-power can result in others.

The Agora of Corinth

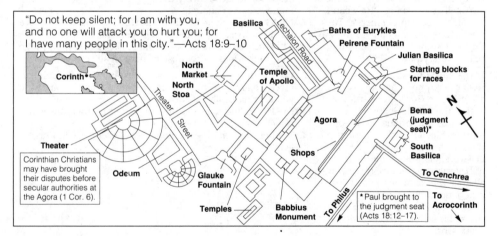

"Do not keep silent; for I am with you, and no one will attack you to hurt you; for I have many people in this city."—Acts 18:9–10

Corinth

Corinthian Christians may have brought their disputes before secular authorities at the Agora (1 Cor. 6).

Basilica
Baths of Eurykles
Peirene Fountain
Julian Basilica
Lechaion Road
North Market
Temple of Apollo
Starting blocks for races
North Stoa
Theater Street
Agora
Bema (judgment seat)*
Theater
Shops
South Basilica
Odeum
Glauke Fountain
To Cenchrea
Temples
Babbius Monument
To Philus
*Paul brought to the judgment seat (Acts 18:12–17).
To Acrocorinth

KEYS TO GALATIANS
The Spirit and the Kingdom

Kingdom Key: God's Purpose in View

This epistle reveals a tension in kingdom truth between Paul's message of grace and his opponent's insistence on the Law. The first is the true message that all salvation is the result of Christ's work, not man's. The other erroneously insists that for salvation believers must observe Old Testament Law in addition to faith in Christ's work. To show the true way, Paul uses Old Testament evidence to affirm that salvation has always been by faith alone. He also shows that the "seed of promise"—those who have "received the Spirit" (3:2)—are the true people of God.

Underscoring this observation are Paul's words (3:3) which establish another key kingdom concept: "Having begun in the Spirit, are you now being made perfect by the flesh?" This question still challenges believers today to examine every aspect of their life and ministry. Besides the great truth that salvation cannot be attained or improved upon by human effort, the apostle calls the kingdom-minded to remember that in *any part* of believing life we may depend upon human efforts in believing and serving God. This involves much more than merely being tempted to overt carnality. Even in attempting good things we may pursue their achievement through human (fleshly) energy—*our* will and *our*

> **Having begun in the Spirit's power, don't retreat to less.**

work—rather than by the Spirit's power.

The Galatians were "bewitched" by vain suppositions. They believed that their religious efforts were essential for salvation. We may not believe this particular error, but we may fall prey to other false notions about the efficacy of self-efforts. How easily we may "begin in the Spirit"—that is, in full dependence upon God's power—and then digress into leaning on human wisdom and ability. Even well-intentioned believers may be drawn subtly to depend on educational achievement, economic advance, material security, personal skills, or even spiritual insights rather than God's power. Once the flesh (Please turn to page 373.)

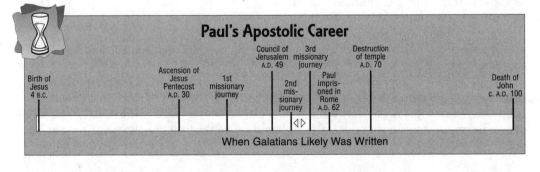

Paul's Apostolic Career

		Council of Jerusalem A.D. 49	3rd missionary journey		Destruction of temple A.D. 70	
Birth of Jesus 4 B.C.	Ascension of Jesus Pentecost A.D. 30	1st missionary journey	2nd missionary journey	Paul imprisoned in Rome A.D. 62		Death of John c. A.D. 100

When Galatians Likely Was Written

Galatians reaffirms salvation by grace alone, and • • •

Master Key: God's Son Revealed

Paul teaches that Jesus places those who have faith in Him (2:16; 3:26) in a position of liberty (2:4; 5:1), freeing them from bondage to legalism and to license. The apostle's main emphasis is on the Crucifixion of Christ as the basis for the believer's deliverance from the curse of sin (1:4; 6:14), self (2:20; *see* 5:24), and law (3:12; 4:5). Paul also describes a dynamic faithunion with Christ (2:20), visibly portrayed in baptism (3:27), which relates all believers to each other as brothers and sisters (3:28). Concerning the Person of Christ, Paul declares both His deity (1:1, 3, 16) and His humanity (3:16; 4:4). Jesus is the substance of the gospel (1:7), which He Himself revealed to Paul (1:12).

Power Key: God's Spirit at Work

The Judaizers were as wrong about the means of sanctification as they were about the way of justification. A key passage is 3:2–3, in which Paul asks the Galatians, who would readily admit that they had begun their Christian life by the Spirit, why they were seeking spiritual maturity by performing works of the Law. The implication is that the same Spirit who alone regenerated them alone causes their new life to grow.

In 3:5 Paul asks a similar question concerning the Holy Spirit. The language he uses indicates an experience of the Spirit that extended beyond the Galatians' initial reception. The verb "supplies" suggests a continual supplying in bountiful measure, while "works" indicates that God was continuing to perform miracles in their midst through Spirit-filled believers who had not slipped into legalism. The word "miracles" refers to the charismatic manifestations of the Spirit evidenced by outward signs, such as those described in 1 Corinthians 12—14.

Key Word: *Freedom from the Law*

This epistle shows that the believer is no longer under the law but is saved by faith alone. Galatians is the Christian's Declaration of Independence.

Key Verses: Galatians 2:20–21; 5:1

Key Chapter: Galatians 5

The impact of the truth concerning freedom is staggering: freedom must not be used "as an opportunity for the flesh, but through love serve one another" (5:13). This chapter records the power, "Walk in the Spirit" (5:16), and the results, "the fruit of the Spirit" (5:22), of that freedom.

The phrase "the promise of the Spirit" in 3:14 also was used by Peter to explain the outpouring of the Holy Spirit at Pentecost (Acts 2:33).

These verses teach that we receive the Spirit by faith alone and that the Spirit continues to manifest Himself in power as we walk in faith.

In 5:16–25 Paul graphically describes a fierce and constant conflict between the flesh— our lower nature prone to sin—and the indwelling Spirit. Only the Holy Spirit, when we submit to His control and actively walk in Him, can enable us to die to the flesh (vv. 16–17), deliver us from the tyranny of the law (v. 18), and cause the fruit of holiness to grow in our

(Please turn to page 374.)

• • • that saving faith is to be expressed as living faith.

Introducing
GALATIANS

Destination. Galatians is the only letter Paul specifically addressed to a group of churches. Galatia was not a city, but a region of Asia Minor, which included many towns. Its name originated in the third century B.C. when a tribe of people from Gaul migrated to the area. In the first century A.D. the term "Galatia" was used geographically to denote the north-central region of Asia Minor, where the Gauls had settled, and politically to designate the Roman province in southcentral Asia Minor. Paul sent this letter to churches in the province of Galatia, an area that included the towns of Antioch, Iconium, Lystra, and Derbe.

Date. The question of the date of Galatians hinges mainly on the correlation of 2:1–10 with Paul's visits to Jerusalem recorded in Acts. Although chapter 2 may be identified with the famine visit of Acts 11:30, fewer difficulties are encountered by identifying it with the events of Acts 15. Paul probably wrote the letter about A.D. 55 or 56, when he was in Macedonia or Corinth on his third missionary journey.

Occasion and Purpose. Legalists in the church, called Judaizers, taught that certain Old Testament laws were still binding upon Christians. They reasoned that God's promises extended only to Jews, and that Gentiles must be circumcised before they could fully experience salvation. The Judaizers did not deny that faith in Jesus was necessary, but insisted that it was inadequate. One must add to faith observance of the Law.

This doctrine was in direct contradiction to Paul's insistence that salvation was by grace through faith, so the Judaizers sought to discredit his teachings by challenging his authority. They charged that he was a second-hand apostle, inferior to Peter and James. Furthermore, they argued, he was a compromiser who made the gospel more attractive to Gentiles by removing its valid legal demands.

Paul vehemently reacted to the evil propaganda of the Judaizers by asserting his apostolic authority and explaining the gospel of grace through faith.

Content. Galatians contains biographical, doctrinal, and practical divisions of two chapters each. In the first section (chs. 1 and 2), Paul defends his apostolic independence, not in a spirit of personal indignation, but to establish the divine origin of his gospel. In the doctrinal section (chs. 3 and 4), Paul presents a series of masterful arguments and illustrations to prove the inferiority of the Law to the gospel and to establish the true purpose of the Law. In the practical application of his doctrine (chs. 5 and 6), Paul exhorts the Galatians to use their Christian liberty properly. Rather than giving license to sin, the gospel provides the enabling means to attain the righteousness that the Law demands.

Personal Application. The same perversion of the gospel that Paul combats in this letter keeps appearing in various forms. Legalism, which teaches that justification or sanctification depends upon a person's own efforts, thus denying the sufficiency of the Cross, is the most persistent enemy of the gospel of grace. Circumcision and other requirements of the Mosaic Law may no longer be issues pertaining to salvation, but oftentimes the observance of certain rules, regulations, or religious rites is made coordinate with faith in Christ as the condition of Christian maturity. Galatians clearly declares the perils of legalism and establishes the essential truth of salvation by faith alone. This epistle was the battle cry of the Protestant Reformation and is the *Magna Charta* of spiritual liberty for all time.

Kingdom Key *continued from page 371*

owns our capacity for action, it is easy for a believer to depend upon human ability, instead of a primary dependence upon the Holy Spirit.

The kingdom key to Galatians is found not only in the reminder of the life-versus-death contrast between the harvest of the Spirit and the flesh (6:8). Two other vital lessons are underscored:

1. Watch for signs of the flesh's energy to manifest in your efforts. Are personal frustrations answered with "outbursts of wrath" or "contentions" (5:19–21), or are they attended by the Spirit's fruit of "longsuffering" and "self-

control" (5:22–23)?

2. People who are spiritual, i.e., "walking in" and "led by" the Holy Spirit (5:16–18), will be gracious, gentle, and restoring to those who are weak or fallen. They will not be judgmental or attacking.

Life in the kingdom and "walking in the Spirit" are one and the same thing. To know the Spirit's fullness in prayer is to maintain intimacy with the Father (4:6).

Furthermore, to abide in the Spirit requires continual vigilance over our walk. There may even be critics who oppose the

(Please turn to page 374.)

Kingdom Key *continued from page 373*

believer's commitment to a pursuit of Holy Spirit-filled living (4:29–31).

Galatians is not only a timeless call to dependence upon faith and grace alone unto salvation. It also shows how to discern between a life of kingdom service—energized, motivated, and enabled by the Holy Spirit of God—and a life that advances through human zeal, tradition, or self-effort.

Power Key *continued from page 372*

lives (vv. 22–23).

This section (5:16–25) is a part of Paul's exhortation concerning the proper use of Christian liberty. Apart from the controlling, sanctifying work of the Holy Spirit, liberty is certain to degenerate into license.

Surveying
GALATIANS

I. INTRODUCTION 1:1–10. Paul's claim to authority as an apostle comes directly from Acts 9:5 and his personal revelation of Jesus Christ. He is writing to the churches in the central Asia region of Galatia, founded during Paul's first missionary journey (Acts 13—14).

A. Salutation (1:1–5). Paul moves directly to the conflict that occasions the letter. "Deliver us from the present evil age" (v. 4) is not a simple reference to the condition of the world outside of Christ, but a response to the heresy that is attempting to lead people away from Christ.

B. Defection of Galatians (1:6–7). Local preachers mislead the believers in the area with "another gospel," which is the central issue of the epistle. Paul describes it as a "perversion." (*See* Called.)

> **"The gospel of Christ"**
> (1:7). Jesus Christ has come into the world—"Immanuel . . . God with us" (Matt. 1:23). This Jesus who was born of a virgin is both God and man together. He has come for only one purpose: "to save His people from their sins" (Matt. 1:21). Jesus lived a sinless life and offered His life on the Cross "for many for the remission of sins" (Matt. 26:28). He was resurrected to life three days later by the power of God (Matt.28:1–7). John 3:16 completes the gospel of Christ by proclaiming that whoever "believes in Him should not perish but have everlasting life." This is the unchangeable gospel of Christ of which Paul writes.

C. Denunciation of the Judaizers (1:8–9). The "other gospel" Paul acknowledges mixes both faith in Christ and Jewish tradition as being necessary for salvation. Paul's repudiation is complete; if someone preaches this false gospel, "let him be accursed."

D. Statement of Paul's integrity (1:10). Paul is writing in a way that he knows will not necessarily be popular to all, but his commitment to serve Christ prevails.

II. BIOGRAPHICAL: PAUL DEFENDS HIS AUTHORITY 1:11—2:21. Paul gives a brief personal history that lends perspective on the dimension of his understanding of the problems with the false gospel.

A. Source of his authority (1:11–24). The encounter on the Damascus road transformed Saul of Tarsus—persecutor of the church (1:13). His defense of Judaism had reached a radical point that exceeded that of any of his contemporaries (v. 14).

B. Recognition of his authority (2:1–10). James, Cephas, and John all approved of Paul and Barnabas's apostolic mission (2:9).

C. Manifestation of his authority (2:11–21). Paul even rebuked Peter for the way he changed his habits around the Gentile believers based on who happened to be watching him (*see* Hypocrite). In much of the church Gentile believers were forced to accept Jewish custom in order to be accepted in the community of faith. Paul rejects this on the basis of being "justified by faith in Christ and not by the works of the law" (v. 16; *see* Eager).

III. DOCTRINAL: PAUL DEFENDS HIS GOSPEL 3:1—4:31. Paul's attention to detail in outlining the terms of the gospel can leave no doubt in the mind of the reader that Paul's analysis of the issue is correct: Faith is the issue essential to salvation, not the traditions of the Law.

A. By argument (3:1—4:11). Paul recites to

the Galatians the facts of their life in Christ and concludes that faith is the issue of ultimate importance, offering a bleak picture of the past contrasted with the bright reality of life in Christ through faith.

1. Experience of the Galatians (3:1–5). The validation of experience in Christ has been the receiving of the Spirit.

> **"He who *supplies the Spirit to you and works miracles among you, does He do it by the works of the law, or by the hearing of faith?"**
> (3:5). Jesus is the baptizer with the Holy Spirit in response to our faith. And the release of every gift of the Spirit and each operation of miracle power is given by the Holy Spirit in response to our obedient exercise of faith. God seeks partners in reaching the world who will exercise faith for the release of His power.

2. Teaching of the Old Testament (3:6–14). Paul cites Genesis 15:6, where Abraham was justified by faith. Paul's doctrine is the same doctrine that has always been taught throughout the Bible; faith is the issue. The works of humanity are inadequate to please God or merit His grace.

3. Character of the covenant with Abraham (3:15–18). Paul argues that the promise to Abraham came 430 years before Moses received the commandments. However, the coming of the commandments did not negate the promise, whose fulfillment is in Christ.

4. Purpose of the Law (3:19–24). This crucial portion of the epistle outlines the purpose of the Law and its differentiation from faith in order to secure righteousness. The Law was given to point out the need for grace in the midst of humanity's inability to keep God's Law, thus becoming "our tutor" in order to instruct us about our need for faith in the justification and forgiveness of sin (v. 24; *see* Mediator).

5. Status of those in Christ (3:25—4:7). The believer's sonship comes through faith in Christ Jesus (3:26). Paul's imagery here relates the picture of God's people being submitted to a tutor—like a child submitted to an instructor. The Law served this purpose until "the fullness of time" (4:4) brought Jesus, and as a result we have been adopted as sons (4:5, 7).

6. Folly of those reverting to legalism (4:8–11). Paul is incredulous that they could return to the "beggarly elements"—doctrines that cannot bring righteousness.

B. By appeal (4:12–20). Paul reminds the Galatians of their gratefulness when they first received the gospel. In contrast, the promoters of the "new gospel" have mixed motives for tempting the Galatians to turn from faith. (*See* Formed.)

1. Based on their affection for Paul (4:12–18). The discovery of faith for the Galatians has brought a deep love between the apostle and them.

2. Based on Paul's affection for them (4:19–20). Paul is still laboring on their behalf, "until Christ is formed in you" (v. 19).

C. By allegory (4:21–31). Paul appeals to another portion of the account of Abraham's life, comparing the son of the free woman and the son of the slave to our choice of liberty or bondage. The promise of inheritance belongs to those who are born free. But slavery is the lot of those who revert to the bondage of slavery to past doctrines.

IV. PRACTICAL: PAUL EXHORTS THE GALATIANS 5:1—6:10. Paul is certain of the Galatians' response (5:10). However, his anger in 5:12 toward the Judaizers suggests that they should not stop with circumcision of themselves but go on to complete castration!

A. To use properly their Christian liberty (5:1–15). The believer cannot return to the past to find freedom. If someone attempts to live by the law they have "fallen from grace" (5:4) and will be judged according to the Law, which only brought bondage to their lives.

B. To walk by the Spirit (5:16–26). Paul's appeal to liberty is twofold. First, the Law never controlled the evil impulses of people that bound them in sin. Second, do not use your Christian freedom to fulfill the lusts of the flesh, because the lusts of the flesh are completely at odds with the work of the Spirit. Since the Spirit brings liberty, the flesh can only return the believer to bondage.

> **"The fruit of the Spirit is love, joy, peace, long-suffering, *kindness, goodness, faithfulness, gentleness, self-control"**
> (5:22–23). Each of these attributes is found in the general population. However, without the energizing of Holy Spirit power (*see* Holy Spirit Gifts) they are limited to the extent of human tolerance, compassion, and maturity. When they are activated by
> *continued on next page*

continued from preceding page
the Spirit, there is an endless supply of this fruit as we surrender to the Spirit's work in our lives and allow the shaping of our character by God's grace. (*See* Manhood.)

C. To bear one another's burdens (6:1–10). Paul offers an interesting dual message here (vv. 2, 5). Our responsibilities have to do with the things we can do—each one is accountable. Our burdens have to do with the things we cannot handle alone—our sin and failure. The apostle pleads for gentleness toward the fallen, while offering a profound insight "lest you also be tempted" (v. 1; *see* Evangelism; Faith, Seed).

V. CONCLUSION 6:11–18. The new creation

is all that matters to Paul. Circumcision and uncircumcision are immaterial in Christ Jesus (v. 15).

A. Warning against legalists (6:11–13). Paul is writing in big letters to emphasize the importance of his message.

B. Centrality of the Cross (6:14–16). The only merits of a believer's life can be found in the Cross of Christ. Everything else is superfluous and worldly.

C. Marks of an apostle (6:17). Paul has experienced rejection and persecution for the sake of this gospel, while others are seeking to escape it (v. 12).

D. Benediction (6:18). The words "grace" and "spirit" are familiar to the entire book and serve as a reminder for Paul's purpose in writing.

TRUTH-IN-ACTION through GALATIANS

Truth Galatians Teaches	**Action** Galatians Invites
1 Guidelines for Growing in Godliness Godliness results from Jesus Christ living through you by the Holy Spirit. It is not achieved by observing some external code. Any attempt to achieve righteousness through a list of external dos and don'ts is fruitless. God calls us to love others and serve others just as Jesus did, by the power of the same Holy Spirit and in the same gracious freedom.	**3:26–29** *Think* as if you have put on the life of Jesus Christ like clothing. *Let Christ* live freely through you. **4:19, 20** *Concern yourself* with God's Word becoming incarnate in you. *Consider* yourself as being "under construction" with Christ's likeness the objective. **5:1–3** *Walk* in the freedom that Christ purchased. *Do not submit* your soul to legalist rules regardless of how right arguments in their favor may seem. **5:4–6** *Cherish* the grace of God. *Do not attempt* to earn what can only be received as a gift. *Love others freely* as an act of obedient faith. **6:7–9** *Remember* the "law of sowing and reaping" applies to everyone. *Sow* only those things you desire to reap. God guarantees that harvest will come. **6:10** *Do "good"* to others when you have opportunity. *Be especially responsive* to your brothers and sisters in Christ.
2 Key Lessons in Faith Faith accepts God's testimony in a trusting, childlike manner, and salvation as a free gift. The Law was given to lead us to Christ: thus any use of the Law as a means of earning our salvation is a distortion. By nature mankind presumes to seek salvation by works. It seems an offense to the flesh to believe we cannot. But God's Word says it is an offense to Him to believe we can.	**1:6–9** *Do not* change, amend, distort, or add to the gospel. *Know* that severe judgment awaits those who do. **2:16** *Understand* that justification through observing laws or codes is impossible. *Receive* God's gift of justification through faith. **2:19–21** *Understand* that you died with Christ so that Christ can live through you. **3:1–11** *Understand* that it is just as impossible to maintain your relationship with God through works as it was to earn it in the first place. **3:23–29** *Understand* that God intended the Law to lead His people to Christ. **6:9** *Continue walking* in faith ceaselessly. *Recognize* and *believe* in the certainty of victory for those who "endure to the end."
3 Guidelines for Growth in the Spirit The Holy Spirit is the key to living under God's grace. Only	**3:14** *Understand* that you receive "the promise of the Spirit" (Acts 2:38, 39) the same way you receive salvation through Christ. *(continued)*

Truth Galatians Teaches	**Action** Galatians Invites
3 Guidelines for Growth in the Spirit *(continued)* the indwelling Holy Spirit can fulfill the Law through us as the life of Christ and truly free us from the Law.	**5:16–26** *Live* under the Holy Spirit's control. *Obey* every leading of the Holy Spirit. *Know* that this will defeat any fleshly or carnal inclination you may have. *Believe* that this will result in Jesus' life being reproduced in you.
4 Steps to Dealing with Sin We must not allow our freedom from the Law to become an occasion for fleshly activity. Also, we are accountable for one another and need to keep watch for one another as well as for ourselves.	**5:13** *Be free* from the controlling influence of sin. *Do not use* the liberty you have in Christ to sin against your brother or sister in Christ. *Recognize* that the outcome of liberty should be loving service to others. **6:1, 2** *Do not allow* others to remain captive to sin. *Be ready* to do what is needed to restore the brother who is in sin. *Behave gently*, without haughtiness, *being aware* that you, too, can be tempted.
5 One Step in Developing Humility If we believe we are too spiritually mature to fall, we should beware! The Bible portrays the sins of past spiritual leaders as a warning to us to remain humble and open to correction. We each need to reassess our personal walk with God in honesty before Him. Each of us will be held responsible for our actions and attitudes.	**6:3–5** *Be sober* in your self-assessment. *Employ only* Jesus' life and teachings as your standard for judgment, not the performance of others.

Law and Grace in Galatians

The Function		The Effect	
Of Law	*Of Grace*	*Of Law*	*Of Grace*
Based on works (3:10)	Based on faith (3:11–12)	Works put us under a curse (3:10)	Justifies us by faith (3:3, 24)
Our guardian (3:23; 4:2)	Centered in Christ (3:24)	Keeps us for faith (3:23)	Christ lives in us (2:20)
Our tutor (3:24)	Our certificate of freedom (4:30–31)	Brings us to Christ (3:24)	Adopts us as sons and heirs (4:7)

As our tutor, the law functions to (1) declare our guilt, (2) drive us to Christ, and (3) direct us in a life of obedience. However, the law is powerless to save us.

KEYS TO EPHESIANS
The Kingdom and the Heavenly Places

Kingdom Key: God's Purpose in View

No New Testament letter more clearly describes the church's mission and her privileged position "in Christ" than Ephesians. As noted elsewhere (see Colossians "Key"), the words "in Christ" and the believer's place "in the kingdom" are synonymous. The emphasis in Ephesians on the believer's position as "accepted in the Beloved" (1:6) establishes the believer's adequacy to function "in the heavenly places" (2:6; 6:12).

The term "heavenly places" translates the Greek *epouranios*. This striking word describes the realm of the invisible—the real world of spiritual encounter and conflicts. The "heavenly places" are not some location in the distant heavens, such as John sees (Revelation 4—5). Rather, these are realms of invisible spiritual conflict on earth, where demon powers try to sustain control of humankind and world affairs (2:2–3).

"The heavenly places" introduces us to the church's place of intended dominion and dynamic operation. It focuses on Jesus' assertion, "My kingdom is not of this world" (John 18:36), and reminds us that our arena of action is spiritual, not political. Anytime in church history that God's people have forgotten this, the church has fallen into sore confusion.

> **Our wealth in Christ enables our walk and our warfare.**

Ephesians shows that the church is to *shape* the affairs of this world. It is to do so by its effectiveness "in heavenly places"—that is, by making the advance of God's kingdom known and felt through confrontation with and mastery over dark powers. This is achieved by a ministry of prayer warfare (6:10–20) and by the spread of the gospel (2 Cor. 4:1–6).

Ephesians refers to "the heavenly places" five times, shedding light on the church's qualifications for dynamic kingdom advance.

1. We are qualified for effective ministry through our being "blessed . . . in the heavenly places" (1:3). This blessing is decidedly *(Please turn to page 381.)*

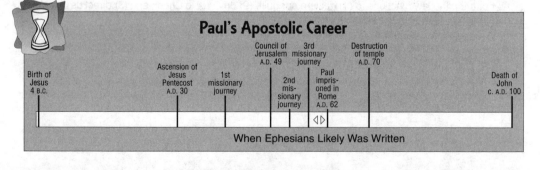

Paul's Apostolic Career

			Council of Jerusalem A.D. 49	3rd missionary journey	Destruction of temple A.D. 70	
Birth of Jesus 4 B.C.	Ascension of Jesus Pentecost A.D. 30	1st missionary journey	2nd mis- sionary journey	Paul impris- oned in Rome A.D. 62		Death of John c. A.D. 100

When Ephesians Likely Was Written

Ephesians details the resources and means

Master Key: God's Son Revealed

Ephesians has been called "the Alps of the New Testament," "the Grand Canyon of Scripture," and "the Royal Capstone of the Epistles," not only because of its grand theme, but because Christ's majesty is revealed here. In chapter 1, He is the Redeemer (1:7), the One in whom and by whom history will ultimately be consummated (1:10); and He is the resurrected Lord who not only has risen over death and hell but reigns as King. He pours out His life through His body, the church—the present expression of Himself on earth (1:15–23). In chapter 2, He is the Peacemaker who has reconciled humanity to God and who makes reconciliation among people possible as well (2:11–18); and He is the Chief Cornerstone of the new temple, His own people indwelt by God Himself (2:19–22). In chapter 3, He is the Treasure in whom life's unsearchable riches are found (3:8); and He is the Indweller of human hearts, securing us in God's love (3:17–19). In chapter 4, Jesus is the Giver of ministrygifts to His church (4:7–11); and He is the Victor who has broken hell's ability to keep humankind captive (4:8–10). In chapter 5, He is the Model Husband, unselfishly giving Himself to enhance His bride—His church (5:25–27, 32). In chapter 6, He is the Lord, mighty in battle, the resource of strength for His own as they arm themselves for spiritual warfare (6:10).

Power Key: God's Spirit at Work

As with Christ, the Holy Spirit is revealed in widely varied ministry to and through the believer. In 1:13 the Holy Spirit is the Sealer, authorizing the believer to represent Christ; in 1:17 and 3:5 He is the Revealer, enlightening the heart to perceive

---

Key Word: *Building the Body of Christ*

Ephesians focuses on the believer's responsibility to walk in accordance with his heavenly calling in Christ Jesus and encouraging the body of Christ to maturity in Him.

Key Verses: Ephesians 2:8–10; 4:1–3

Key Chapter: Ephesians 6

Even though the Christian is blessed "with every spiritual blessing in the heavenly places in Christ" (1:3), spiritual warfare is still the daily experience of the Christian while in the world.

God's purpose; in 3:16 He is the Empowerer whom Christ gives to strengthen believers within; in 4:3–4 He is the Spirit of Unity desiring to sustain the bond of peace in the body of Christ; in 4:30 He is the Spirit of Holiness who is grieved by insistence on carnal pursuits; in 5:18 He is the Fountain from which all believers are to be continuously filled; in 6:17, 18 He is the Giver of the Word as a sword for battle and the heavenly Assistant given to aid us in prayer and intercession until victory is won.

by which Christ's church fulfills her call.

Introducing
EPHESIANS

Background. Ephesus was a principal port on the west coast of Asia Minor, situated near present-day Izmir. It was one of the seven churches to whom Jesus addressed His letters in Revelation 2 and 3, a relevant fact for studying this epistle since it was originally circulated to approximately the same group of churches.

Although Paul had been to Ephesus earlier (Acts 18:21), he first came there to minister in the winter of A.D. 55. He ministered there for over two full years (Acts 19:8–10), developing so deep a relationship with the Ephesians that his farewell message to them is one of the Bible's most moving passages (Acts 20:17–38).

Occasion and Date. While imprisoned in Rome, Paul wrote Ephesians, Philippians, Colossians, and Philemon. Confined and awaiting trial (3:1; 4:1; 6:20), the apostle writes this encyclical letter—one to be read by several congregations. Ephesians is probably the same letter referred to in Colossians 4:16 as being circulated from Laodicea.

It appears that after writing Colossians, Paul was deeply stirred by an expanding revelation about the church. Now seeing the church as Christ's body and as God's instrument to confound and overthrow evil powers, he writes an elaboration of these themes.

Purpose. Ephesians unveils the "mystery" of the church as no other epistle. God's "secret" intention is revealed: (1) to form a body to express Christ's fullness on earth (1:15–23); (2) to do this by uniting one people—both Jew and Gentile, among whom God Himself dwells (2:11—3:7); and (3) to equip, empower, and mature this people to the end that they extend Christ's victory over evil (3:10–20; 6:12–20).

Content. The throbbing message of Ephesians is "to the praise of His [God's] glory" (1:6, 12, 14). The word "glory" occurs eight times and refers to the exceeding excellence of God's love, His wisdom, and His power. The magnificent goal is in Jesus' announced commitment to build a glorious, mature, and ministering church, "not having spot or wrinkle" (5:27).

Ephesians unfolds the process by which God is bringing the church to its destined purpose in Christ. Basic maturing steps are taken toward the church's battle with dark powers: (1) before the church is called to *war,* she is taught to *walk;* and (2) before being called to *walk,* the church is taught where she *stands.*

The epistle divides into two sections: (1) the believer's position, chapters 1—3, and (2) the believer's practice, chapters 4—6. In chapter 1, the recurrent term "in Christ" sums up the Christian's position, as having been given "every spiritual blessing." Several of these blessings are enumerated: chosen, blameless (1:4), adopted, accepted (1:5–6), forgiven, predestined, and sealed (1:7, 11, 13).

With sweeping strokes, Paul moves to a bold, new assertion in the first of two prayers in this letter. He prays that each Christian may perceive God's grand purpose in raising Christ to triumph—that now the church may know Christ's victorious fullness as we resist evil and face life's trials (1:15—2:10).

Chapter 2 describes how God's grace has formed a united people among whom He can dwell in His fullness and glory. Through this people His high purpose is to be unveiled. Grasping the message of Ephesians requires understanding two words from chapter 3— "dispensation" and "mystery" (vv. 2–3). The apostle declared that God's "secret" in planning the church is hidden no longer (3:3–4— *now* the "mystery" is *known*). He has designed the church to administer ("to dispense") Christ's fullness everywhere (3:2, 9), ministering as a living body, spreading over the earth and penetrating "the heavenlies." God's "manifold wisdom" now demonstrates His glory in the church (3:10–11), a manifestation that eventually will issue in the believer's strengthening (3:14–20), maturing (4:15), confrontation, and victory (6:10–20). However, the church cannot approach this without a practical understanding of how this present glory of God's grace and presence is to affect everyday living.

The great call to "walk worthy of the calling" introduces this letter's second section (chs. 4—6). Systematically, Paul presents the ethical and moral implications of Spirit-filled living (4:1—6:9). The maturing process of the believer's "equipping" (4:11–16) and the appeal to help each other forward ("speaking the truth in love") will bring growth in the disciplines essential to the triumphant spiritual warrior's life (6:10–20).

Personal Application. In short, Ephesians discloses awesome blessings of grace ("accepted in the Beloved," 1:6) and awesome dimensions of spiritual authority over evil ("according to the power that works in us," 3:20). But this awaits the believer's first accepting the disciplines of unity (4:1–16), purity (4:17–31), forgiveness (4:32), and walking in the fullness of the Holy Spirit (5:1–21). With this, relationships at every point must be in order (5:22—6:9), the idea being firmly established that true spiritual power flows from true obedience to the divine order in relationships and personal conduct.

Kingdom Key *continued from page 378*

spiritual (*pneumatika*, here, is also used for the gifts of the Holy Spirit in 1 Cor. 12:1). The place of Holy Spirit gifts in overthrowing the works of hell are hereby noted.

2. We are secured in Christ in a "seat" of triumph and dominion over all dark powers (1:19–23; 2:6). The combination of these two texts not only reveals the present place of our Lord's dominion over the devil; it also declares our present partnership with Him in exercising that dominion.

3. We are shown God's great delight in how His "wisdom" takes ordinary creatures, now redeemed and restored through His Son,

and uses them—the church—to make His awesome power known (3:9–10). Here is a humbling truth: God's joy is to confound the Adversary by displaying His glorious power through those He has rescued from hopelessness (2:12) and restored to kingdom partnership in Christ (2:6).

4. In this light we are assigned to take action. The ministry of prayer, intercession, and spiritual warfare is the pathway to expanded conquest over hell's hold on the people and affairs of this planet. Girded in God's armor, we are to engage the warfare with confidence (6:10–20).

Surveying
EPHESIANS

OPENING GREETING 1:1–2. Acts 19 describes Paul's colorful and extremely fruitful ministry in Ephesus. In writing to the church, Paul offers no personal greetings, which are common in many of his letters, no doubt because this letter was to be circulated in a number of churches. Paul is in prison at this time and is concerned to see that the work in Asia continues as both Jews and Gentiles are forming the rapidly growing church.

I. THE BELIEVER'S POSITION IN CHRIST 1:3–14. Some of the most meaningful and reassuring truths in all the Bible are found here about God's eternal interest in His people and His absolute commitment to bring His will to pass in their lives.

A. The blessings of full redemption (1:3–8). We have been chosen, predestined, adopted, redeemed, and forgiven! What more can be said about the unsearchable richness of God's love for us in Jesus Christ?

> "To the praise of the glory of His grace, by which He has made us accepted in the Beloved"
> (1:3–6). This passage offers the most beautiful and complete statement of our acceptance in Christ and the lavish love of Father God for His children. "From before the foundation of the world" we were chosen in Christ as His children, and our predestination is found in the infinite knowledge of the Lord toward us. Our *praise is for the God

> who knew us before we knew Him, who loved us before we could love back, and who has accepted us in Christ even when our sin is so abhorrent that we cannot accept ourselves.

B. Partnership in God's purpose (1:9–14). God's purpose for His people will come to pass; the inheritance of the saints is assured. The salvation of the saints is certain, as they have been "sealed with the Holy Spirit of promise" (v. 14).

II. THE APOSTLE'S PRAYER FOR INSIGHT 1:15–23. Paul prays for wisdom and knowledge for the church so that they may know: (1) "the hope of his calling," related to the eternal nature of their promise in Christ, and (2) the "greatness of His power," which is available to the church as the body of Christ in the world.

A. For hearts that see with hope (1:15–18). The enlightenment of God's people regarding their privilege in Christ can only come through a supernatural vision assisted by the Spirit of God (*see* Prophecy). The human heart and mind are incapable of grasping the dimension of Christ's purpose for His people.

B. For experience that shares Christ's victory (1:19–21). The complete vanquishing of the powers of darkness by Christ as described in Colossians 2:15 and 1 Corinthians 2:8 has established His preeminent place in heaven.

C. The church: Christ's body (1:22–23). All things have been placed under Christ's feet. Now, it remains for the church to walk in the same authority given to it as Christ's body here on earth.

III. THE BELIEVER'S PAST, PRESENT, AND FUTURE 2:1–22. The work of grace is described as being personally significant and corporately significant in creating a completely new order of relationship in the church.

A. The past order of the living dead (2:1–3). Unbelievers are the "children of wrath" (v. 3), who are dominated by the spiritual powers of darkness. They are "dead" in sin, but by the power of Christ are made alive as they come to faith.

B. The new order of God's loving life (2:4–10). Salvation is a matter of faith—which is a gift from God (2:8). In this new relationship we are seated together with Christ "in heavenly places" (1:20; 2:6).

> **"We are His workmanship, created in Christ Jesus for good works"**
> (2:10). A believer's good works have nothing to do with his or her salvation (Is. 64:6). "Good works" result from the "*workmanship" of Christ in the life of the person by the Holy Spirit. Paul's message is that faith saves the individual and good works flow from the life of a person growing in God's grace.

C. The past separation and hopelessness (2:11–12). Paul is addressing Gentiles who were "strangers from the covenants of promise." The cultural and religious separation between Jews and Gentiles was pronounced in the first century. The miracle of Christ's new life in the believer is also moving toward a new community.

D. The new union and present peace (2:13–18). In Christ, Jews and Gentiles are "one new man from the two" (v. 15), both having "access by one Spirit to the Father" (v. 18; *see* Blood, The).

E. The church: Christ's building (2:19–22). Paul continues with the imagery of a building that has a foundation of the apostles and prophets, but Jesus is the "chief cornerstone." Jews and Gentiles (*see* Foreigner) *together* are being "built together for a dwelling place of God in the Spirit" (v. 22). This radical new concept is socially inconceivable, yet happening.

> **"Together for a dwelling place of God in the Spirit"**
> (2:22). The transformation of Jesus Christ in the lives of individuals brings them from death to life, and the same is true within the culture of the church. Racial hatred, social separation, and cultural division in the body

of Christ are completely unacceptable. Divisions among people are assailed throughout the New Testament. Jew and Gentile, male and female, master and slave are meaningless terms from God's perspective on the individual (Gal. 3:28). "Together" the church is the dwelling place of God; separated the church ceases to be the instrument of redemption God intended it to be in the world.

IV. THE APOSTLE'S MINISTRY AND MESSAGE 3:1–13. Paul elaborates his mission as the apostle to the Gentiles and encourages them in the midst of his current personal struggle in prison.

A. The stewardship Paul has been given (3:1–7). The God-appointed mission of the apostle is to bring the Gentiles into the church as "fellow heirs" and "partakers of His promise" (v. 6).

B. The stewardship each believer is given (3:8–13). We are privileged to have instant access to the Father through faith. (*See* Manifold.)

V. THE APOSTLE'S PRAYER FOR POWER 3:14–21. Paul's prayer is for the church to know the full measure of a personal relationship with Christ that reveals His love and power, bringing about the fullness of Christ in their lives.

A. For strength by the Holy Spirit (3:14–16). Paul prays that the inner man be changed and encouraged by grace. (*See* Family Life; Prayer.)

B. For faith and love by Christ's indwelling (3:17–19). "Filled with all the *fullness of God" (v. 19) is the ultimate heart cry of the apostle for all those in his care.

> **"That Christ may dwell in your hearts through faith; that you, being rooted and grounded in love"**
> (3:17). First John 3:8 categorically identifies the presence of love for other people as the sign of a life transformed by the Spirit of God. Our faith in Christ opens the way for the Spirit of God to make true *agape* (God's love) a reality in our lives, making us candidates for "the fullness of God" (v. 19) to be at work within us. Only then can a person function in the selfless, servant-like spirit that the Bible commands.

C. The church and God's glory (3:20–21).

"The power that works in us" (v. 20) is God's power by the Holy Spirit. All of the requests for knowledge, fullness, love, and faith come as the result of our personal participation with God in allowing the Holy Spirit access to the hidden parts of our lives.

VI. THE BELIEVER'S CALL TO RESPONSIBILITY 4:1–16.

Here is the turning point in the epistle. The doctrinal and theological treatment of our place in Christ now shifts to the character, lifestyle, and relationships of the people of God.

A. To pursue unity with diligence (4:1–6).

Unity is not an option for the ecumenical-minded in the body of Christ—it is commanded: "Keep the unity of the Spirit in the bond of peace" (v. 3).

B. To accept grace and gifts humbly (4:7–11).

The Lord Jesus Himself gives gifts to His church for the purpose of furthering ministry (see Holy Spirit Gifts). These gifts are in the form of leaders who will lead, train, equip, and release the people of God in service to the world.

C. To grow in ministry as part of the body (4:12–16).

Every part of the Lord's body must be edified and matured so that each can take his or her place in ministry to the world.

> ### "*Equipping the saints for the work of ministry"
>
> (4:12). Offices in the church have only one purpose in Scripture: preparing the people of God for their mission in the world. The tradition of trained clergy being the "ministers" of the congregation has bankrupted the church of its vitality and purpose. If the Great Commission in Matthew 28 were addressed merely to the disciples, the church would be a single-generation phenomenon. The responsibility for disciple-making belongs to the whole church. Each person has a unique sphere of influence, but it is the job of the church leadership to equip the people of God for this work.

VII. THE BELIEVER'S CALL TO PURITY 4:17—5:14.

Believers must cooperate with the work of God's Spirit in the process of having personal transformation take place in attitude, action, and lifestyle.

A. To refuse worldly mindedness (4:17–19).

The new convert needs "reprogramming" in terms of thinking and feelings. Life in Christ is a radical reorientation to a world of ignorance, blindness, and lewdness which can no longer be allowed to dominate the believer.

B. To put off the old and put on the new (4:20–32).

Symbolically done at baptism, the Holy Spirit supplies both the power and the opportunity for the old man to be challenged and done away with by the believer. The consequence of such action allows the new man to be put on (see Manhood). The holiness and "true righteousness" of this new man are related to the work of God's grace referred to in 2:10.

C. To progress in untainted love (5:1–7).

"Be imitators of God . . . walk in love." Paul exhorts the church to act on its life in Christ. Describing the awful consequences of a worldly lifestyle—"the wrath of God"—Paul cautions, "do not be partakers with them [the world]."

D. To shine as undimmed light bearers (5:8–14).

The people of the light live in the light, and they have no fellowship with the "unfruitful works of darkness" (v. 11). These believers carry the responsibility to beam the light of God's love and righteousness in their own lives and in the culture around them. The church is not on a self-righteous mission but a redemptive one in the light of God's love.

VIII. THE BELIEVER'S CALL TO SPIRIT-FILLED LIVING 5:15—6:9.

The Christian's personal walk with God and all relationships are affected by the commitment to be God's person. Nothing is the same when Christ takes over a life.

A. To pursue God's will and wisdom (5:15–17).

Walking "circumspectly" means to be aware of what is happening around you and how you relate to it. The wise believer is not ignorant of the devil's devices to deceive and destroy. Neither is the believer to be ignorant of the carnal nature of one's own desire, which can become a snare. (See Stewardship.)

B. To maintain the fullness of the Holy Spirit through worship and humility (5:18–21).

Spirit fullness is contrasted with the drunkenness that comes from too much wine. The world's wine brings "dissipation"; the Spirit fullness that accompanies the worship life of the believer (see Praise) builds the person of God.

> ### "Do not be drunk with wine in which is dissipation; but be filled with the Spirit"
>
> (5:18). The Holy Spirit outpouring in Acts 2:15 appeared to some to be drunkenness, but Holy Spirit power never diminishes a person's capacity for reason, sound-
>
> continued on next page

continued from preceding page

minded action, or sensitivity to other people. Paul exhorts all believers to live consciously in the ever-flowing stream of the fullness of the Holy Spirit.

"Speaking to one another in psalms and hymns and spiritual songs, singing and making melody in your heart to the Lord"

(5:19–20). This joyful song is to result in the giving of thanks to the Lord (v. 20). The people of God are to live with the melody of Christ in their hearts, with the overflow of song being one evidence. Songs focused on Jesus and God's Word can lift the heart and strengthen the people of God in their daily walk with the Lord.

C. To conduct all relationships according to God's order (5:22—6:9). All believers are to submit to each other "in the fear of God" (v. 21). Wives are to submit to their husbands; husbands submit to loving their wives as Jesus loved the church (*see* Manhood). Children are to obey; fathers are to nurture their children in a way that brings respect rather than provocation (*see* Family Life). Slaves are to be obedient; masters must rule with the understanding that they themselves have a master, God Himself. Paul offers a clear picture of the rights and the responsibilities each of us have in the various relationships of our life.

IX. THE BELIEVER'S CALL TO *SPIRITUAL WARFARE 6:10–20. The spiritual world is real, and it makes an impact on more than is obvious to most believers. Paul offers insight and direction for not being taken unaware in the midst of the invisible battle around us (*see* Withstand).

A. The reality of the invisible conflict (6:10–12). Our principal warfare is not against our circumstances or opposition from people who seem to stand in the way of progress. Our true enemies must be identified and then assaulted with the spiritual weapons at the disposal of the Christian.

B. Armor for the warrior (6:13–17). Believers must be protected from the spiritual con-

flict that surrounds them. The purpose of the armor of God is to "withstand in the evil day" (v. 13).

C. The action involved in warfare (6:18–20). Prayer and God's Word are the two weapons of the people of God who are engaged in spiritual combat. The Word of God offers the terms of God's purpose on the issues being "wrestled" over, and prayer is the spiritual exercise that ultimately brings the victory of God to our struggles. Jesus said, "Ask anything" in John 14:14; He also informs us that the agreement of the saints in prayer brings the action of God (Matt. 18:19).

"We do not wrestle against flesh and blood"

(6:10–18). The warfare of the believer is not against human resistance but against spiritual powers. Our demonic Adversary divides sincere brethren, causes stress in families, misdirects a believer's attention, and tempts people to sin and eventual bondage. The Word of God (v. 17) and prayer (v. 18) are effective weapons for overcoming spiritual powers (v. 12) that cause havoc in our world. However, in the midst of battle Paul instructs us on the "whole armor of God" to protect us in the battle.

"That I may open my mouth boldly to make known the mystery of the gospel, for which I am an *ambassador in chains"

(6:19). Paul solicits prayer from the Ephesians so that he might be a bold witness. To us this seems ridiculous; Paul is the very definition of boldness. However, we learn elsewhere that Paul's witness as a prisoner is shaking the emperor's palace in Rome (Phil. 4:22). Pray for God to anoint you with boldness to share the testimony of Christ with the people who need it most.

CONCLUDING REMARKS 6:21–24. Paul is sending the letter with Tychicus, who will "make all things known to you" as he continues and elaborates the ministry intended by the letter.

TRUTH-IN-ACTION through EPHESIANS

Truth Ephesians Teaches	**Action** Ephesians Invites
1 Guidelines for Growing in Godliness Simply put, godliness is living the way God wants us to. Few books speak as clearly and succinctly to this subject as does Eph. Here godliness is exhorted in terms of behavior, motivating dynamic, and example. Godly behavior is modeled after God Himself, especially as He has revealed Himself in His fullness in Jesus Christ.	**4:1** *Understand* that your conduct is the most effective sermon you will ever preach. *Live* a life that will give consistent, undeniable evidence of the truth of the gospel. **5:1, 2** *Model* your life after Jesus, imitating Him rather than others. *Understand* that He is the perfect example of the love God requires. **5:18–20** *Be continually filled* with the Holy Spirit. *Overflow* with a continual song of praise and thanksgiving to maintain a Spirit-filled flow in your life. **6:18–20** *Give yourself* to constant, faithful prayer. *Let God change* your prayer life to a life of prayer.
2 Steps to Holiness A major facet of holiness is living a life separated from the world. Jesus stressed this by saying that although we live in the world, we are not to be of the world.	**4:17** *Be careful* to avoid and reject the world's way of thinking. *Realize* that thinking as the world does will unavoidably lead to sensuality and impurity.
3 Keys to Godly Relationships Eph. has much to say about building godly relationships. This is one of the major themes of the NT. Our relationships are to be loving, truthful, selfless, and submissive. Simply put, Eph. exhorts that we relate to others as Jesus relates to the Father and to us.	**4:25–27** *Diligently practice* honesty and truthfulness in all your relationships. *Deal with anger* quickly, not allowing it to influence your treatment of others. **5:21—6:4** *Maintain* a selflessly submissive attitude in all your family relationships. *Understand* that this will provide evidence that Christ rules your home. **6:5–8** *Do not be* merely a people-pleaser at work! *Serve the Lord* in all you do. *Recognize* that it is He who has assigned you to that post of responsibility.
4 How to Tame the Tongue Proper speech is crucial to effective Christian living. Proverbs points out that life and death are in the power of the tongue. How important it is for us to realize that our speech can be spiritually motivated.	**4:29** *Be careful* how you speak and what you say. *Reject* evil attitudes; and *develop* compassionate, forgiving attitudes toward others. **5:3–7** *Avoid* and *reject* any impure or immoral speech or behavior. *Be certain* that it contradicts your profession of faith in Christ.
5 Guidelines to Gaining Victory Eph. gives us insight into the nature of the spiritual warfare we face daily. Our combat is against spiritual forces, not men. Great is the protection and resources God has provided us to meet this enemy.	**6:10–13** *Stand in readiness* for spiritual combat. *Recognize* that your demonic enemies are behind much of what comes against you to harm you. **6:14–17** Each day, consciously *put on* the spiritual armor God supplies. *Learn* and *understand* the nature of this divine protection.
6 Keys to Wise Living Perhaps wisdom is what is most necessary in governing our use of time.	**5:15** *Use* time wisely, and *do not squander* it. *Be certain* that you will give an account of how you use God's gift of time.
7 Keys to Generous Living Selflessness is most concretely expressed in generosity.	**4:28** *Think* of how you can give rather than how you can get.

KEYS TO PHILIPPIANS
The Kingdom and the Mind

Kingdom Key: God's Purpose in View
The call to kingdom life is a call to live with a new mindset. More than any New Testament book, Philippians focuses on the renewed mind as a key to harmony in relationships and victory in daily living. The "mind" is shown in a way that distinguishes mere "intellectual achievement" from (a) intelligent living, (b) sensible caring, and (c) clear-thinking humility.

1. The spiritually enlightened mind begins with a believer who has "the mind of Christ" (2:5). This is a mindset ruled by (a) the non-self-seeking way of Jesus (2:6), (b) the servant-spirit of Jesus (2:7), and (c) the self-sacrificing humility of Jesus (2:8).

2. Such a renewal of the mind brings an agreeable spirit to human relationships (4:2). This does not preclude conflicts among believers, but a mutual commitment to the mindset of Christ produces a mood and manner conducive to resolving conflict through the love of Christ.

3. The kingdom mindset learns to unite in purpose and objective with others who are serving Christ (2:1–4). This does not demand programmed "mind control" or losing the diversity of varied viewpoints. It does call us to willingly, sensitively, and sensibly move together with

> **Certainty of triumph brings a constancy of rejoicing.**

others to prize the advance of God's kingdom above our private agendas or opinions. (Note, for example, Paul's attitudes toward those who opposed him, even though they were preaching Christ—1:15–18.)

4. Mental discipline is called for if the mind is to be kept tuned to kingdom values. Such discipline begins by disallowing any preoccupation with things unworthy in the redeemed person's thoughts (4:8–9). This does not mean unworthy thoughts will never assail or find a momentary harbor in a believer's mind, but these will not be allowed serious consideration or an abiding presence.

5. Finally, a kingdom mindset cultivates *confidence in living.* This quality differentiates kingdom-thinking from cultish, mind-controlled thinking. The Spirit of God does not pro-

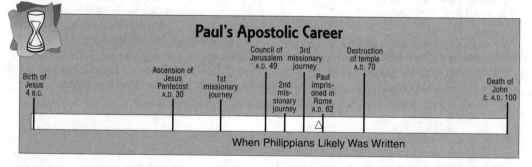

Paul's Apostolic Career

Birth of Jesus 4 B.C.

Ascension of Jesus Pentecost A.D. 30

1st missionary journey

Council of Jerusalem A.D. 49

2nd missionary journey

3rd missionary journey

Paul imprisoned in Rome A.D. 62

Destruction of temple A.D. 70

Death of John c. A.D. 100

When Philippians Likely Was Written

Philippians: the renewed mind is a key to harmony

duce religious robots, but confident, free, and gracious people who know how to think like Jesus Christ—and better yet, to live in His power: (a) with confidence for the future (1:6); (b) with confidence of God's purpose, notwithstanding present trial (1:12–18); (c) with a joyful confidence born of certainty of God's enabling Spirit (3:3–4); and (d) with confidence of God's sufficiency whatever the present need (4:11–13, 19).

Master Key: God's Son Revealed

For Paul, Christ is the sum and substance of life. To preach Christ was his consuming passion; to know Him was his highest aspiration; to suffer for Him was a privilege. Paul's chief desire for his readers was that they might have the mind of Christ. To support his exhortation for self-forgetting humility, the apostle describes the attitude of Christ that moved Him to set aside the glory of heaven and suffer and die for our salvation (2:5–11). In doing so, he presents the most concise New Testament statement concerning the preexistence, the incarnation, and the exaltation of Christ. Both the deity and the humanity of Christ are stressed.

Power Key: God's Spirit at Work

The Spirit's work in three areas is mentioned in the letter. First, Paul declares that the Spirit of Jesus Christ will direct the accomplishment of God's purpose in His own experience (1:19). The Holy Spirit also promotes unity and fellowship in the body of Christ (2:1). Common participation in Him breeds singleness of purpose and maintains a community of love. Then, in contrast to the lifeless ritual observance of formalists, the Holy Spirit inspires and directs the worship of true believers (3:3).

Key Word: *To Live Is Christ*

Central to Philippians is the concept of "For to me, to live is Christ, and to die is gain" (1:21).

Key Verses: Philippians 1:21; 4:12

Key Chapter: Philippians 2

The grandeur of the truth of the New Testament seldom exceeds the revelation of the humility of Jesus Christ when He left heaven to become a servant of humanity.

Seeking and Finding

Seek:	Find:
Christ above all (Phil. 1:21; 3:7–8)	Righteousness in Christ and the power of His resurrection (3:9–11)
Christlike humility (2:4–7)	God's will in the believer (2:12–13)
A divinely appointed goal (3:14)	The prize of eternal salvation (3:14)
All things that are true, noble, just, pure, lovely, virtuous, and praiseworthy (4:8)	The presence of the God of peace (4:9)

in relationships and to victory in daily living.

Introducing

PHILIPPIANS

Background. Acts 16:12–40 records the founding of the Philippian church. Paul established the church during his second missionary journey, about A.D. 51. From its inception, the church displayed a strong missionary zeal and was consistent in its support of Paul's ministry (4:15–16; see 2 Cor. 11:8–9). Paul enjoyed a closer friendship with the Philippians than with any other church.

Occasion and Date. Paul most likely wrote his letter to the Philippians during his first Roman imprisonment, about A.D. 61, to thank them for the contribution he had received from them. He also warmly commended Epaphroditus, who had brought the gift from Philippi and whom Paul was sending back.

Purpose. While his primary reason for writing the letter was to acknowledge the gift sent by the Philippians, Paul also appealed for a spirit of unity and steadfastness among them. In addition, he warned against dangerous heresies that were threatening them, probably Judaism and Gnosticism.

Characteristics. In many respects, this is the most beautiful of Paul's letters, full of tenderness, warmth, and affection. His style is spontaneous, personal, and informal, presenting us with an intimate diary of Paul's own spiritual experiences.

The dominant note throughout the letter is that of triumphant joy. Paul, though a prisoner, was exultantly happy, and called upon his readers to rejoice in Christ always. It is an ethical and practical letter in its emphasis and centers on Jesus Christ. To Paul, Christ was more than an example; He was the apostle's very life.

Content. The abiding message of Philippians concerns the nature and grounds of Christian joy. For Paul, true joy is not a surface emotion that depends on favorable circumstances of the moment. Christian joy is independent of outward conditions, and is possible even in the midst of adverse circumstances, such as suffering and persecution.

Joy ultimately arises from fellowship with the risen, glorified Christ. Throughout the letter, Paul speaks of joy in the Lord, emphasizing that through Christ alone is Christian joy realized, as are all other Christian graces. Essential to this joy is the confident conviction of the lordship of Christ, based on experience of the power of His resurrection. Because of this conviction, life for Paul attained meaning. Even death became a friend, because it would bring him into a fuller experience of the presence of Christ (1:21–23).

The joy presented in Philippians involves eager expectation of the near return of the Lord. That this expectation was dominant in Paul's thinking is seen in his five references to Christ's return. In the context of each reference is a note of joy (1:6, 10; 2:16; 3:20; 4:5).

Paul further describes a joy that springs from fellowship in the spreading of the gospel. He begins the letter by thanking the Philippians for their partnership in spreading the gospel through their monetary gifts. The gifts, however, are only an expression of their spirit of fellowship, or as he puts it in 4:17, "the fruit that abounds to your account." So Christian joy is an outgrowth of being in the active fellowship of the body of Christ.

Personal Application. This letter reveals the timeless message that true joy is to be found only in a dynamic personal relationship with Jesus Christ and in the assurance that God is able to turn adverse circumstances to our good and His glory. Because he was united to Christ by a living faith, Paul could claim contentment in all circumstances. His unadorned testimony was "I rejoice . . . and will rejoice" (1:18), and his unqualified command was, "Rejoice . . . again I will say, rejoice!" (4:4).

Surveying

PHILIPPIANS

INTRODUCTION 1:1–11. "I long for you all with the affection of Jesus Christ" (v. 8), Paul writes to friends. Acts 16 describes the miraculous beginning of this first church in Europe.

A. Salutation (1:1–2). Paul confers "sainthood" upon them, not because of what they have done, but to observe what Christ has done for all who place faith in Him.

B. Thanksgiving (1:3–8). They have shared the gospel mission with Paul (v. 5), and they have supported him in the midst of the imprisonment (4:14). They truly are "partakers" with him of the grace of God. This is no feigned show of thanks or polite obligation; Paul knows this church has suffered and has sustained him in his time of need. (See Good.)

C. Prayer (1:9–11). Paul's passion is for their growth in love, which brings knowledge and discernment and, of course, "the fruits of righteousness" (v. 11).

I. CIRCUMSTANCES OF PAUL'S IMPRISONMENT 1:12–26.

Paul is not complaining about his circumstance, but rather is rejoicing (v. 18) because his jailing is winning souls of influential people in Rome!

A. Had advanced the gospel (1:12–18). Some of Paul's enemies have gloated over his misfortune. Yet, Paul refuses to condemn them as they "preach Christ even from envy and strife . . . from *selfish ambition" (vv. 15–16). For the apostle, the most important thing is that Christ be preached!

B. Had brought assurance of blessing (1:19–21). Paul had the unconquerable attitude of a giant in the faith. Paul is certain of his deliverance—because the Philippians prayed, and because of the presence of God's Spirit with him. Even if he is executed, his mission will be completed and Christ will be magnified!

C. Had created dilemma for Paul (1:22–26). Paul's surrender to the purpose of God is complete—life or death, it does not matter. The furtherance of the gospel and the strengthening of the church is Paul's sole concern.

II. EXHORTATIONS 1:27—2:18.

Paul's appeal is to servant-heartedness and Christ-mindedness; in our humility comes the release of great spiritual authority (2:9–11).

A. Live worthy of the gospel (1:27—2:4).

Throughout the epistle Paul appeals for them to be of "one mind" (1:27; 2:2, 5; 3:16; 4:2). This can only be accomplished by allowing the Spirit of Christ and His servant perspective to enter our lives. Selfish ambition, conceit, and indifference to the needs of others will damage the church and restrict the cause of Christ.

B. Reproduce the mind of Christ (2:5–11). Paul describes in majestic terms the three-step process of Jesus' humbling of Himself in verse 7: He (1) emptied Himself, (2) became a servant, and (3) became a man. His obedience unto death made possible eternal life for all who place their trust in Him. In this has come His exaltation above all of the seen and unseen creation. (*See* Manhood.)

> **"God also has highly *exalted Him"**
> (2:9). The pathway to exaltation and final spiritual authority for Christ led Him from heaven to earth, from master to servant, from life to death. That is also the pathway for spiritual growth and power for the people of God (*see* Faith's Confession). Jesus' words in Mark 8:35 reflect the same principle: Life in God can only be discovered through our willing surrender of ourselves to live in Him.

C. Cultivate the spiritual life (2:12–13). The highest commendation imaginable: "My

---

The Mind of Christ

Philippians 2 vividly contrasts the mind of Christ, the second Adam, with that of the first Adam (Genesis 1—3).

Adam	Christ
Made in the divine image.	Is the form and very essense of God.
Thought it a prize to be grasped at to be as God.	Thought it not a prize to be grasped at to be as God.
Aspired to a reputation.	Made Himself of no reputation.
Spurned the role of God's servant.	Took upon Himself the form of a bondservant (slave).
Seeking to be like God,	Coming in the likeness of men,
And being made a man (of dust, now doomed),	And being found in appearance as a man,
He exalted himself,	He humbled Himself,
And became disobedient unto death.	And became obedient to the point of death.
He was condemned and disgraced.	God highly exalted Him and gave Him the name and position of Lord.

beloved, as you have always obeyed, not as in my presence only, but now much more in my absence." God will achieve His purpose in them because of such faithfulness.

D. Leave off murmurings and questionings (2:14–18). Beware of the human tendency to focus on differences or shortcomings. Our unity in Christ is a witness to the world.

III. COMMENDATION OF AND PLANS FOR PAUL'S COMPANIONS 2:19–30. Paul is a cautious pastor in not allowing ministry to the flock that is unproven or without sufficient character. Gifting alone cannot advance God's purpose among God's people. Those who teach and lead must be "like-minded" (v. 20) and of "proven character" (v. 22).

A. Timothy (2:19–24). Timothy is trusted, not just as Paul's son in the faith, but as a pastor who is passionate for the Lord's people and surrendered to the Holy Spirit's work in his life.

B. Epaphroditus (2:25–30). This brother had been the messenger who conveyed the love and gifts of the Philippians to Paul in his need. There he served Paul with great vigor and at substantial personal cost (v. 30). Now he returns with the letter and the responsibility to serve the flock. Paul's request: Hold him in esteem.

IV. WARNINGS AGAINST ERROR 3:1–21. Spiritual leadership must be evaluated by submission to the Word of the Lord and by a consistent lifestyle, and there is a rising problem in Philippi with teachers of error. Paul, the ever-wary sentinel, cries out, "Beware of dogs!" There are those who want to drag the Philippians to unproductive former spiritual systems which can only frustrate their freedom in Christ and the fruitfulness of their life in Christ.

A. Against the Judaizers (3:1–16). Paul rises to his full apostolic stature as he declares that his own Jewish heritage is more esteemed than that of those who are misleading the people. Paul asserts that the things he might take pride in from his past are "rubbish." Paul has set aside everything in his past so that he "may gain Christ" (v. 8). And he is still advancing in the things of the Lord. Genuine spiritu-

ality acknowledges that, no matter where a believer has progressed in Christ, we must all "press toward the goal for the prize of the upward call of God in Christ" (v. 14). Any teacher who insists on his or her own perfection of understanding or person, contrary to Paul's teaching, is disqualified.

B. Against sensualism (3:17–21). Paul weeps pastoral tears, declaring that those "whose god is their belly" are enemies of the Cross. They walk disobediently to the way of God, and their rejection of Christian morality is a surrender to the world. But Paul reminds the flock that their citizenship is in heaven.

"Our citizenship is in heaven" (3:20–21). Our Savior is in heaven, preparing a place for us (John 14:3); our ultimate destination is to be with Him. Therefore, believers will never be completely at peace with the world, because they do not belong there (Eph. 2:19). When Jesus comes for His people they will discover the ultimate place and purpose of their heavenly citizenship.

CONCLUSION 4:1–23. Paul is thankful for the generous partnership and loving care he has received from the Philippians. As a result he blesses the flock with this promise: Just as they have supplied his need, so also "my God shall supply all your need according to His riches in glory by Christ Jesus" (v. 19).

A. Final appeals (4:1–9). Stop the petty fighting. Focus on eternal things that are "true . . . noble . . . just . . . pure . . . lovely . . . of good *report . . . virtue . . . praiseworthy" (v. 8).

B. Acknowledgment of the Philippians' gift (4:10–20). Paul refers to their generosity when no other church would help. And he declares that their gift to him was "a sweet smelling aroma, an acceptable sacrifice, well pleasing to God."

C. Greetings (4:21–22). The greetings from Rome include those from converts within the palace in Rome itself.

D. Benediction (4:23; *see Jesus).

TRUTH-IN-ACTION through PHILIPPIANS

Truth Philippians Teaches	**Action** Philippians Invites
1 Guidelines for Growing in Godliness Those who observe a godly life see what God is like. This is one of the church's primary functions. Godliness avoids anything that brings disunity or division in the church. It lives unselfishly, making others the primary focus of its concerns.	**1:27** *Conduct your life* as a gospel sermon for observers of your life. *Develop* the heart attitude of unity. **2:3, 4** *Live unselfishly! Turn away from* any selfish ambition or conceited attitudes. *Esteem* others as being more important and more worthy than you are.
2 How to Develop Dynamic Discipleship Discipleship is apprenticeship to the life of Jesus, focusing on Christ as Mentor and Model. Jesus chose to lay aside His divine form and adopt the lowly form of man. Even as a Man He did not choose wealth, power, or worldly position, but came as a servant, and died the death of a criminal. In everything He humbled Himself, trusting God to exalt and establish His name. Discipleship may call the Christian to choose to lay aside rights much valued in our culture, and to accept the life-role assigned by God. This role may not appear to be a place of acknowledgment, but trust God to choose how to establish and promote you.	**2:2** *Seek to maintain* unity with other believers in your thoughts, attitudes, love, spirit, and purpose. *Recognize* that a separatist "right to one's own opinion" is not a biblical teaching. *Repent* and *surrender* such arrogance for the sake of unity in the body of Christ. **2:5–11** *Adopt* Christ's attitude of *unselfishness, servanthood, humility,* and *obedience.* **2:12, 13** *Commit yourself* to obedience. *Allow* God's work of salvation to have its full work in you. *Recognize* that your whole Christian life, from being willing to doing it is all God's work. **2:20, 21** *Understand* that being concerned for the interests of Jesus Christ means being concerned selflessly for the welfare of others. **4:8, 9** *Determine* your own thought life. *Do not let* others do it for you. *Cause your mind to dwell* on those things that bring peace to you and glory to God. *Follow* holy leadership as a pattern for life and faith.
3 Key Lessons in Faith Our inheritance as believers can only be received fully by taking a stand on what God has said in the face of contradicting circumstances, sometimes even suffering and death. The stance of faith eliminates fear and worry and brings the freedom to "rejoice evermore." True faith never says, "I cannot!" Such an utterance betrays unbelief.	**1:6** *Believe* that God always finishes what he starts, including His work in you! **1:21–24** *Do not fear death. Remember* that dying in God's timing and will is only victory for a believer. **1:29** *Recognize* and *accept* that true faith in Jesus Christ will involve suffering for His sake. **4:4–7** *Rejoice* as a constant discipline! *Refuse* to worry about things. *Understand* that Jesus gives peace to those who trust Him and ask for His help. **4:11** *Choose* to be contented in all circumstances. **4:13** *Know* and *believe* that Jesus Christ will enable you to do anything He asks of you. Nothing is impossible for him who believes!
4 Steps to Dynamic Devotion Devotion focuses on the pursuit of intimacy with God. It is "devoting oneself" to knowing Jesus Christ. One measure of maturity is the degree to which this pursuit becomes our consuming focus and desire. Nowhere is the disciple of Jesus more challenged to become a man or woman "after God's own heart" than here.	**3:7–9** *Understand* that no personal achievements earn spiritual position. *Do not be afraid* to lose everything in your quest to know Christ. *Make* "knowing" Christ your main goal in life. *Know* that this quest always involves sacrifice and unselfish living. **3:12–14** *Aim* to achieve the goal God has set for you. *Spare no cost* in this quest. *Spare no effort* in your pressing toward the mark of knowing Christ, **3:15** *Recognize* that a single-eyed pursuit of God is the hallmark of true spiritual maturity. **3:17–19** *Know* that those who offer cheap alternatives to knowing Christ become His enemies.

KEYS TO COLOSSIANS
The Kingdom and the Cross

Kingdom Key: God's Purpose in View

Nothing is more fundamental to the message of the kingdom of God than the finished work of Jesus Christ on the Cross. His sinless atonement, His justifying action, and His perfect accomplishment of full redemption are the foundation for everything offered to us who have been delivered "from the power of darkness" and conveyed "into the kingdom of the Son of His love" (l:13).

This "new kingdom" position is solely and completely made possible through Christ's redeeming work and the forgiveness provided through "His blood" (1:14). Any understanding of the authority, dominion, restored partnership, and God-ordained privileges that "kingdom living" provides, if it fails to acknowledge its source and foundation in the Cross, misses the heart of God's redemption plan. Just as Jesus Christ is the *giver* of life in the kingdom, and just as God's Holy Spirit fills us with the *glory* of that life, so the Cross is the *grounds* of that life.

Colossians shows that our acceptance before God, and thereby our authority under Him, result from our finding both pardon and position in Christ. "In Christ" is the grand New Testament expression that declares both (1) our place of secure refuge and (2) our platform of confident authority. To be "in Christ" is to be placed "in the Anointed One," the Messiah established as the King of God's kingdom. "In Christ," each believer has been invited to be a "joint-heir" with Christ (Rom. 8:16–17), possibly the most amazing proposition in the whole of redemption's provisions. It is a grand thing to be completely forgiven and acquitted of all past sin. It is also a grand thing to be promised the marvels of eternal life in the presence of God. But between these two miracles, in the meantime of our present life, consider how miraculous it is that He would invite us to share equally with Jesus today in the abounding resources of His life, power, and dominion!

From our position "in Christ" we are given the promise of victory and authority over hell's powers today. Yet wisdom always remembers:

> ### Jesus Christ is Lord of all—in all and above all.

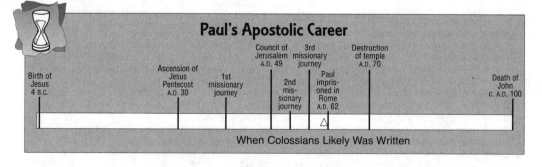

Paul's Apostolic Career

				Council of Jerusalem A.D. 49	3rd missionary journey		Destruction of temple A.D. 70		
Birth of Jesus 4 B.C.		Ascension of Jesus Pentecost A.D. 30	1st missionary journey		2nd missionary journey	Paul imprisoned in Rome A.D. 62			Death of John c. A.D. 100

When Colossians Likely Was Written

Colossians sets forth the universal lordship of

1. Christ's dominion throughout the universe, which is His by right of His role as Creator and Sustainer of all things (1:15–17), can be shared with humankind only through what He did on the Cross (1:18–20). The Cross was the price of this restored dominion.

2. Christ's dominion over all the works of darkness ("principalities and powers") is ours to claim for one reason alone: Jesus broke their power and gained the victory, which He invites us to share—*all through the blood of His Cross.*

Colossians reveals how the health and continuing life of the church is found as we glory in the Cross (2:8–10; 3:1–4)

Master Key: God's Son Revealed

Paul lifts up Christ as the center and circumference of all that exists. The incarnate Son of God, He is the exact revelation and representation of the Father (1:15), as well as the embodiment of full deity (1:19; 2:9). He who is Lord in creation (1:16), in the church (1:18), and in salvation (3:11) indwells believers and is their "hope of glory" (1:27). The supreme Creator and Sustainer of all things (1:16–17) is also a sufficient Savior for His people (2:10).

Power Key: God's Spirit at Work

Colossians has a single explicit reference to the Holy Spirit, and it is found in association with love (1:8). Some scholars also understand "wisdom and spiritual understanding" in 1:9 in terms of gifts of the Spirit. For Paul, the lordship of Christ in the believer's life is the most crucial and clearest evidence of the Spirit's presence.

Key Word: *The Preeminence of Christ*

The resounding theme in Colossians is the preeminence and sufficiency of Christ in all things. The believer is complete in Him alone and lacks nothing because "in Him dwells all the fullness of the Godhead bodily" (2:9).

Key Verses: Colossians 2:9–10; 3:1–2

Key Chapter: Colossians 3

Chapter 3 links the three themes of Colossians together showing their cause and effect relationship: Because the believer is risen with Christ (3:1–4), he is to put off the old man and put on the new (3:5–17), which will result in holiness in all relationships (3:18–25).

The Preeminence of Christ in Colossians

- **In universal government**—the visible image of God (1:15); the agent of creation (1:16); the Sustainer (1:17); the Head of the church (1:18).
- **In reconciliation**—pleases the Father (1:19-20); reconciles us through His death (1:21-22); lives in us as our hope of glory (1:27).
- **In wisdom and knowledge**—the source of all the treasures (2:2-3); worldly philosophy does not conform to Him (2:8).
- **In personal observance**—we are alive in Him (2:11-13); no need for legalism and ritualism (2:16-23).
- **In Christian living**—He is our life (3:3); we can avoid immorality and can bless others (3:5-14).

Christ in creation, in the church, and in salvation.

Introducing
COLOSSIANS

Background. Paul had never visited Colosse, a small town in the province of Asia, about one hundred miles east of Ephesus. The Colossian church was an outgrowth of his three-year ministry in Ephesus about A.D. 52–55 (*see* Acts 19:10; 20:31). Epaphras, a native of the town, and probably a convert of the apostle, was likely the church's founder and leader (1:7–8; 4:12–13). The church apparently met in Philemon's home (Philem. 2).

Conservative scholars believe Paul wrote this letter during his first Roman imprisonment, around A.D. 61. Tychicus delivered the letters to the Colossians, to Philemon, and to the Ephesians.

Occasion and Purpose. Sometime during Paul's imprisonment, Epaphras solicited his help in dealing with false teaching which threatened the church at Colosse (2:8–9). This heresy apparently was a blend of pagan-occultism, Jewish legalism, and Christianity. The error resembles an early form of Gnosticism, which taught that Jesus was not fully God and fully man, but merely one of the semidivine beings that bridged the chasm between God and the world. He, therefore, was said to be lacking in authority and ability to meet the needs of the Colossians. Enlightened believers could, however, achieve spiritual fullness through special knowledge and rigorous self-discipline.

With an urgency heightened by the return of the runaway slave, Onesimus, to his master at Colosse, Paul wrote this epistle with a fourfold purpose: (1) to expose and rebut the heresy; (2) to instruct the Colossians in the truth and alert them to the danger of returning to pagan vices; (3) to express personal interest in the believers; and (4) to inspire them to promote mutual love and harmony.

Characteristics. No other book of the New Testament sets forth more fully or defends more thoroughly the universal lordship of Christ. Combative in tone and abrupt in style, Colossians bears a close resemblance to Ephesians in language and subject matter. More than seventy of the 155 verses in Ephesians contain expressions echoed in Colossians. On the other hand, Colossians has twenty-eight words found nowhere else in Paul's writings and thirty-four found nowhere else in the New Testament.

Content. The false teachers at Colosse had undercut the major doctrines of Christianity, not the least of which was the deity, absolute lordship, and sufficiency of Christ. Colossians sets forth Christ as supreme Lord in whose sufficiency the believers find completeness (1:15–20). The first two chapters present and defend this truth; the latter two unfold practical implications.

Jesus Christ's supremacy hinges upon His uniqueness as God's eternal, beloved Son and Heir (1:13, 15). In Him dwells the totality of divine attributes, essence, and power (1:19; 2:9). He is the exact revelation and representation of the Father, and has priority in time and primacy in rank over all creation (1:15). His sufficiency depends upon His superiority. The conviction of Christ's absolute sovereignty gave impulse to Paul's missionary activity (1:27–29).

Paul declares Christ's lordship in three primary ways, at the same time proclaiming His adequacy. First, Christ is Lord over all creation. His creative authority encompasses the whole material and spiritual universe (1:16). Since this includes the angels and planets (1:16; 2:10), Christ deserves to be worshiped instead of the angels (2:18). Further, there is no reason to fear demonic spirit-powers or to seek superstitiously for protection from them, because Christ has neutralized their power at the Cross (2:15), and the Colossians shared His triumphant resurrection power (2:20). As sovereign and sufficient Potentate, Christ is not only Creator of the universe but also its Sustainer (1:17), its Uniting Principle, and its Goal (1:16).

Second, Jesus Christ is preeminent in the church as its Creator and Savior (1:18). He is its Life and Leader, and to Him alone may the church submit. The Colossians must remain rooted in Him (2:6–7) rather than become enchanted with empty speculation and traditions (2:8, 16–18).

Third, Jesus Christ is supreme in salvation (3:11). In Him all man-made distinctions fade and barriers fall. He has made all Christians into one family in which all members are equal in forgiveness and adoption; and He is all that matters. Therefore, contrary to the heresy, there are no special qualifications or requirements for experiencing God's favor (2:8–20).

Chapters 3 and 4 deal with the practical implications of Christ in the Colossians' daily life. Paul's use of the word "Lord" nine times in 3:1—4:18 indicates that Christ's supremacy impinges upon every aspect of their relationships and activities.

Personal Application. Because this is an age of religious pluralism and syncretism (that is, a diluting of truth for the sake of unity), Christ's lordship is deemed irrelevant by many religious groups that believe one religion is as good as the other. His preeminence is denied by others that place the Christian stamp upon a fusion of beliefs from several religions. Usually hailed as an advance beyond apostolic Christianity, this blend promises self-fulfillment and freedom without surrender to Christ.

"Jesus is Lord" is the church's earliest confession. It remains the abiding test of authentic Christianity. Neither the church nor the individual believer can afford to compromise Christ's deity. In His sovereignty lies His sufficiency. He will be Lord of everything or not Lord at all.

Surveying
COLOSSIANS

I. INTRODUCTION 1:1–14.
Paul writes to a church he has never visited (2:1). The church has been infiltrated with mystical notions that life in Christ can supply more "fullness" through "vain philosophy" (2:8), religious ritual (2:11), or "worship of angels" (2:18). Paul declares that "in Him dwells all the fullness of the Godhead bodily; and you are complete in Him" (2:9–10).

A. Salutation (1:1–2). Paul affirms the "faithful brethren" who are sincere in their pursuit of God and their commitment to Christ.

B. Prayer of praise for the Colossians' faith (1:3–8). The church was formed during the time of Paul's ministry in nearby Ephesus. Epaphras and Philemon are both from Colosse and have informed the apostle of the faith and the challenge found in that church.

> **"The truth of the gospel, which has come to you, as it has also in all the world, and is bringing forth fruit"** (1:5–8). The truth of God and the work of the Holy Spirit in a life demand growth and "fruit." John 15 states clearly that a Christian is to be fruit-bearing in his or her life in Christ. There is no exception or substitute: "By this my Father is glorified, that you bear much fruit; so you will be My disciples" (John 15:8). This fruit-bearing, however, is a function of simply staying closely attached to the vine; it is not born of human effort, but of a faithful relationship with Christ, the true vine (John 15:4–5).

C. Prayer of petition for their growth in Christ (1:9–14). Paul's prayer is substantial for the needs of the church: "You may be filled . . . walk worthy . . . be *strengthened." They have been delivered from the power of darkness (v. 13) by the work of Christ on the Cross; now they will live for Him alone (see Kingdom of God).

II. CHRIST'S SUPREMACY DISPLAYED 1:15—2:7.
There is no need for additional revelation, knowledge, or human systems to improve on what Christ has done.

A. In creation (1:15–17). Christ is the acknowledged creator and sustainer (v. 17) of the whole world (see Creation), including spiritual powers and forces (see Angels).

B. In the church (1:18). Christ is the ultimate authority, the preeminent One who alone is worthy to be worshiped.

C. In reconciliation (1:19–23). Christ alone has "reconciled all things" (v. 19; see Blood, The), and He has reconciled all believers (v. 21). There is no need for intermediaries or complicated human systems.

D. In Paul's ministry (1:24—2:7). Paul contrasts the "mystery" of Christ (which he openly declares [1:26] and which will "perfect" every believer through faith) with those who would "deceive you with persuasive words . . . cheat you through philosophy" (2:4, 8) taught by some in the church. (See Kingdom of God; Working.)

III. CHRIST'S SUPREMACY AND SUFFICIENCY DEFENDED 2:8–23.
The believer's salvation in Christ is absolute; it cannot be improved upon.

A. Against false philosophy (2:8–15). Pagan philosophy introduced to the church identifies "the basic principles of the world" (v. 8) as a force to be reckoned with in the spiritual realm—Paul declares that Christ supersedes it all. Jewish believers have incorporated the idea that observance of the rites of circumcision will improve the believer's spiritual standing, but Paul cites water baptism as the Christian's "circumcision of the flesh" (vv. 12–13).

> **"Buried with Him in baptism"** (2:12–13). Jesus' command to be baptized in water (Mark 16:16) is in part a matter of obedience and public acknowledgment of faith in Christ. But here Paul declares it to be the spiritual equivalent of circumcision. The miracle of baptism opens the way to our sharing in the death and
> continued on next page

continued from preceding page
resurrection of our Lord. We are buried because the old man was "dead in trespasses," and now we have been "made alive together with Him." Victory over the flesh of the "old man" becomes possible after baptism, as the new man is "made alive." (*See* Kingdom of God; Wiped Out).

B. Against legalism (2:16–17). Ascetic observance does not enhance our standing before God.

C. Against angel-worship (2:18–19). Paul warns the Colossians about the dreadfully serious state of confusion that allows for the worship of angels—"not holding fast to the Head" (v. 19). Our salvation depends on staying related to the Head of the church—Jesus Christ alone. Without that the whole body becomes malnourished and disconnected.

> **"Worship of angels"**
> (2:18). The Colossian church represents a hunger for personal spiritual reality and power. The "cheating" that comes from angel worship is not from the absence of spiritual experience but the deceiving nature of it. Our preoccupation must be with Jesus Christ and God's Word. Our appeal is to the Holy Spirit, who makes available every gift necessary for our lives and for the liberating work of Christ in the world. The pursuit of angels or demons or spiritual powers leads to deception and spiritual bondage.

D. Against asceticism (2:20–23). Paul calls it "self-imposed religion . . . of no value against the indulgence of the flesh" (v. 23).

IV. CHRIST'S SUPREMACY DEMANDED IN CHRISTIAN LIVING 3:1—4:6. Belonging to Christ means that we "put to death" (3:5) the things that compromise our life in Christ and "put on the new man" (3:10).

A. In relation to Christ (3:1–8). This occurs when you "seek" and "set your mind on things above." The new life requires a new way to think and a Christ-centered focus of our attention. (*See* Appears.)

B. In relation to the local church (3:9–17). A transformed nature is demonstrated in the crucible of human relationships. (*See* Forgiving.)

> **"Let the word of Christ dwell in you richly in all wisdom, teaching and admonishing one another in psalms and hymns and spiritual songs, singing with grace in your hearts to the Lord"**
> (3:16–17). Our praise and worship must be in "spirit" and "truth" (John 4:23). Songs can be used to help in the memorization of Scripture and the fixing of doctrinal truth in the believer's heart and mind. However, Jesus taught us about the "spirit" of worship as well. Our worship is not simply the statement of propositional truth, but the passionate expression of love, trust, obedience, and joy between people and their Creator.

C. In relation to the family (3:18–21). The balance of the epistle points to both the proper order of the Christian family (*see* Family Life) and the necessary sensitivity of each member to make the family work.

D. In relation to work (3:22—4:1). The first-century culture included slavery (*see* Family Life), but Paul points toward: (1) a new relationship between masters and slaves—equality in Christ (3:11; *see* Partiality) and (2) a higher call to both servant and master in their ultimate obligation to please God in their responsibilities.

E. In relation to non-Christian society (4:2–6). Our witness to the world is to be received through our "speech . . . seasoned with salt." (*See* Time.)

V. CONCLUSION 4:7–18. Paul's desire is for the epistle to circulate among the churches of the region, specifically in Laodicea. Heresy is like cancer and must be addressed before it gains a foothold in the church and cannot be eliminated.

A. Paul's companions (4:7–9). One of the Colossians, Onesimus, will deliver the letter personally with Tychicus.

B. Final greetings (4:10–15). Of particular interest in verse 14 is Demas, acknowledged again in 2 Timothy 4:9 as having "forsaken" the apostle.

C. Final exhortations and benediction (4:16–18). Paul asks for prayer in the midst of his own personal need.

TRUTH-IN-ACTION through COLOSSIANS

Truth Colossians Teaches	**Action** Colossians Invites
1 A Definition of Godliness This passage defines NT godliness concisely and completely.	**1:10, 11** *Believe* that a "walk worthy of the Lord," 1) pleases the Lord, 2) is fruitful in good works, 3) grows in knowing God, and 4) is strengthened by God's power.
2 Steps to Holiness Under the old covenant the Law's system only allowed limited access to God. The new covenant no longer poses rules for cleansing, but calls to faith and acceptance of the completed work of Jesus. We are not to allow anything other than the Word of God to control or judge us. We are neither judged holy nor unholy by external regulations, but by the condition of our heart.	**2:16–23** *Reject* rules that aim to cleanse the spirit by means of humanly contrived regulations. *Realize* that in Christ you are no longer subject to human wisdom or works, but to God. **3:1–11** *Set* your thinking and affections on Jesus Christ, and *build* your relationship with Him. *Do not allow* worldly pursuits to waste your mental or emotional energy.
3 Lessons for Leaders Wise leaders focus their ministries on Jesus Christ and avoid presumptuous and transient teachings. Let us prioritize believers' maturity, stressing the finished work of Christ.	**1:28, 29** Leaders, *concentrate* on the spiritual maturity of your people. *Lessen* your emphasis on any programs that do not foster maturity. **2:2, 3** Leaders, *focus* on Jesus Christ. *Build* your congregation's unity and understanding on Him. **2:11–14** Leaders, *teach* your people to base their whole life on the work done in them through Christ's death and resurrection.
4 Keys to Wise Living Many believers are slowed in their spiritual growth for lack of wisdom. Sometimes teaching that stymies spiritual growth is enthusiastically endorsed because believers do not know the Scriptures. We should heed Paul's warning against listening to people who pander to the flesh, rather than edifying in the truth.	**2:8** *Be aware* that human philosophy and erroneous religious tradition are contrary to Christ. *Do not be deceived.* **2:18–23** *Hold fast* to Christ and *honor Him* to please the Father. *Be wise* in evaluating "spiritual experiences," knowing that they are not to produce pride or elitism. *Know* the importance of commitment to a local church and of submission to righteous spiritual authority. **3:18–22** *Submit* to God's ordained order in the home, church, and workplace.
5 Steps to Dynamic Devotion Always in the NT, the call to wholehearted discipleship is accompanied by the call to a life of devotion. To devote is "to concentrate on a particular pursuit or purpose." A life of devotion to Christ pursues His purpose—His being reproduced in us.	**1:25–29** *Understand* that all hope of real "glory" is in discovering Christ's very life in you. **3:16, 17** *Be diligent* in Bible study and *practice* Scripture memorization and meditation. *Let the Word* in you *produce* praise to God and edification of others. *Serve* Jesus' purposes in every thought, word, and deed. **4:2–6** *Become* a person of prayer. *Repent* of any prayerlessness in your life. *Recognize* God's gift of time and use it wisely. *Speak with grace and wisdom* in answer to all.
6 Keys to Godly Relationships Human relationships were designed to be fueled and filled by righteousness. To the degree we give in to the urging of our flesh nature, we will fail to experience righteous or fulfilling relationships. To the degree we practice those things God commands, our relationships will become a sampling of heaven on Earth.	**3:5–11** *Reject, turn from,* and *refuse to practice* any form of relational unrighteousness or sin: wrong sexual activity, angry exchanges, jealous or envious attitudes, greedy desire for things, gossip, or coarse humor. **3:12–14** *Adopt* and *practice diligently* every form of relational righteousness: love, compassion, humble attitudes, self-giving behavior, freely flowing forgiveness, and patience with others. **3:15** *Choose peace* to govern all of your relationships.

KEYS TO
1 AND 2 THESSALONIANS
The Kingdom and Christ's Return

Kingdom Key: God's Purpose in View

The promise of the Second Coming of Jesus Christ is established by our Savior's own words: "I will come again and receive you to myself" (John 14:3). By both parable and precept, Jesus made clear that the kingdom of God would have both a present and a future expression. He taught that what began *with His ministry would* expand *through His church and would* consummate *at His return.*

The two Thessalonian epistles are laden with balancing insights concerning the coming of the Lord. These kingdom truths, well-studied and applied, provide a means for every believer to keep the delicate tension needed between two great facts:

(1) Jesus *has* come. In introducing the kingdom of God He has ushered in its possibilities at a viable, dynamic point of *beginning,* a beginning He manifested in ministry, and then delegated to be continued through His church until He comes again (Acts 1:1–2; Luke 19:13).

(2) Jesus *will* come. In consummating the purposes of the kingdom of God He will usher in the *ultimate* expression of God's rule, a manifesting of all the prophecies that

Beyond all else, Jesus Christ is coming again!

focus on His eventual global rule, as well as His final restoration of national Israel.

All eight chapters of the Thessalonian letters contribute to understanding the Second Coming and other climactic expressions about the kingdom of God as it relates to earth and humankind.

- These truths help awaken men and women to the urgency of deciding for Christ and prepare people to avoid the wrath of eventual judgment (1 Thess. 1:9–10).

- These truths stir the hearts of spiritual leaders, who serve and teach their flocks in order to present them with joy to Christ at His coming (1 Thess. 2:19–20).

(Please turn to page 400.)

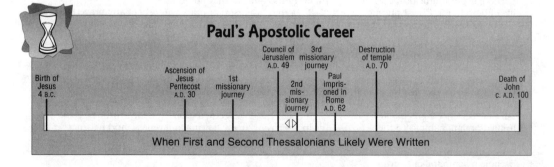

Paul's Apostolic Career

| Birth of Jesus 4 B.C. | | Ascension of Jesus Pentecost A.D. 30 | 1st missionary journey | Council of Jerusalem A.D. 49 | 3rd missionary journey | Destruction of temple A.D. 70 | | Death of John c. A.D. 100 |

2nd missionary journey
Paul imprisoned in Rome A.D. 62

When First and Second Thessalonians Likely Were Written

The Thessalonian epistles balance the truths that kingdom

Master Key: God's Son Revealed
1 Thessalonians

Jesus is the Son of God (1:10), whose death and resurrection (1:10; 2:14–15) provide an example to believers who suffer now (1:6; 2:14–15) but who, as He was, will be raised in the future (1:10; 4:14, 16). Believers then and now have a mystical spiritual position "in the Lord" (1:1, 3; 4:1; 5:18), which, nevertheless, is practical enough to be the ground of respect for ruling elders (5:12). From Christ comes grace (5:28).

But above all in 1 Thessalonians, Christ emerges as the coming King, the conqueror of death, whose awaited return from heaven (1:10) gives comfort to the bereaved (4:17–18; 5:11) and joy to his expectant subjects (2:19–20). This will be His day, the "day of the Lord" (5:2; *see* 2 Thess. 2:2, "day of Christ").

2 Thessalonians

The coequality of Christ with God receives particular attention in 2 Thessalonians. Father and Son together are the source of grace and peace (1:2, 12; 3:16, 18), comfort and stability (2:16–17), love and patience (3:5). Though the church is located geographically in Thessalonica, its spiritual position lies "in God our Father and the Lord Jesus Christ" (1:1; 3:12). As in 1 Thessalonians, the Lord Jesus will come again (1:7, 10; 2:1), and "with the breath of His mouth" (2:8) He will subdue the Man of Sin at the moment of His return (2:8) and take vengeance on those who have no knowledge of God (1:8).

Power Key: God's Spirit at Work
1 Thessalonians

All Christians can affirm that it is God who has "given us His Holy Spirit" (4:8). The Spirit inspires joy even amid affliction (1:6). When the gospel arrived in Thessa-

---

Key Word: *Holiness in Light of Christ's Return*

Throughout this letter is an unmistakable emphasis upon steadfastness in the Lord and a continuing growth in faith and love in view of the return of Christ.

Key Verses: First Thessalonians 3:12–13; 4:16–18

Key Chapter: First Thessalonians 4

Chapter 4 includes the central passage of the epistles on the coming of the Lord when the dead in Christ shall rise first, and those who remain are caught up together with them in the clouds.

Key Word: *Understanding the Day of the Lord*

The theme of this epistle is an understanding of the day of the Lord and the resulting lifestyle changes.

Key Verses: Second Thessalonians 2:2–3; 3:5–6

Key Chapter: Second Thessalonians 2

The second chapter is written to
(Please turn to page 400.)

---

graces are present now, but kingdom glory is yet to come.

lonica, it came not only in word "but also in power and in the Holy Spirit and in much assurance" (1:5), suggesting a balanced mix of intellectual argument, the Spirit's power (probably with "signs and wonders"), and deep personal response. First Thessalonians 5:19–21 reveals a lively charismatic character to the worship at Thessalonica—

Key Word *continued from page 399*

correct the fallacious teaching that the day of the Lord has already come upon the Thessalonian church.

prophetic activity, which some were inclined to subdue, but for which Paul asks tested acceptance: his words were to be read "to all the holy brethren" (5:27).

2 Thessalonians

In the single direct reference to the Holy Spirit in 2 Thessalonians, Paul gives thanks to God for the Thessalonians, whose selection for salvation by God "from the beginning" the apostle describes comprehensively as "through sanctification by the Spirit and belief in the truth" (2:13). The Spirit's sanctifying work is one way to see God's intent for saving His people. Prophetic utterance from the Spirit, or that alleged to be so (2:2), must always be tested (1 Thess. 5:20–21; 1 Cor. 14:29).

Kingdom Key *continued from page 398*

- Balanced truth informs us that "tribulation" is not avoided *by* faith but traversed in victory *through* faith; that "increase," "abounding," and "establishing" likewise are advanced through faith, and help prepare us for Jesus' coming (1:3; 4:11–13).
- These truths comfort believers bereaved of dying Christian friends or loved ones because of the assurance that they shall be reunited at Christ's return (4:13–18).
- These truths assure us that we shall be delivered from the era of "God's wrath" on the earth and that His Spirit will preserve us unto Jesus' Coming (5:9–10, 23).
- These truths clarify that Christ's Second

Coming shall be attended by judgment upon the disobedient of the earth (2 Thess. 1:6–10).
- These truths advise of a special season in the future when the *general* prevailing spirit of antichrist (1 John 2:18, 22) will find a *personal* expression through a human being called the Man of Sin—one who shall be the epitome of wickedness, and who shall be destroyed with the coming of Christ (2 Thess. 2:1–10).
- These truths call us to wait in patience and to remain unwearied in service as we anticipate Jesus' return (3:5, 13).

Introducing
1 THESSALONIANS

Origin of the Church at Thessalonica. The gospel first reached Europe around A.D. 49. That occurred when, on his second mission tour, Paul and his party responded to the night vision of the Macedonian man by sailing from Troas (site of the ancient city of Troy), via the Aegean island of Samothrace, to Neapolis—the port city for Philippi (Acts 16:8–12). Here the apostle met the businesswoman Lydia, cast a spirit of divination out of a young female slave, and was publicly beaten and wrongfully arrested as a result. On learning that Paul and Silas were Roman citizens, the imperial authorities gingerly apologized, freed the apostles, and urged them to leave town. They did (Acts 16:13–40).

Traveling ninety miles southwesterly, Paul and Silas came to Thessalonica. "As his custom was," Luke reports, Paul went to the synagogue there and over several weeks preached by arguing that Jesus, the carpenter's son from Nazareth, was in fact God's Anointed One—the Messiah—long promised in the Jewish Scriptures (Acts 17:1–3). Here Paul established the second major church on the European continent.

Among those who accepted the message were not only Jews like Aristarchus (Col. 4:10–11) but also "devout Greeks"—Gentiles who attended the synagogue services but never became full converts to Judaism by taking circumcision. In addition, a considerable number of prominent women in the city responded to Paul's message (Acts 17:4). The faith of Christian believers at Thessalonica became widely known (1 Thess. 1:7–8). Twice, at least, the Philippian church sent financial support to Paul while he was at Thessalonica, where he stayed for several weeks (Phil. 4:16).

While Acts emphasizes the Jewish origins of the church at Thessalonica, Paul's letters to them make it clear that many of them had "turned to God from idols" (1 Thess. 1:9). Since worship of idols in New Testament times was a Gentile and not a Jewish practice, ethnic variety marked the church of the Thessalonians.

Late in the fourth century B.C., a Macedonian king named the city of Thessalonica for his sister. The capital of its district of the Roman province of Macedonia, Thessalonica had a fine natural harbor. It was located on the famed Via Egnatia, a major Roman military highway that stretched from the western Balkan coast to present-day Istanbul, and was ruled by *politarchs*—a class of officials peculiar to the region. Luke shows his usual historical sensitivity by using this rare term (Acts 17:6, "rulers of the city," NKJV).

As earlier in Philippi and afterward in Berea, Paul's ministry in Thessalonica caught the attention both of Roman officials and Jewish opponents. Jewish leaders were not pleased with the redirected loyalties of the synagogue adherents. They brought charges that Paul and his band had "turned the world upside down"—a highly serious charge, much closer to civil rebellion than to tolerable public mischief suggested by long use of familiar words. To call Jesus "Lord" was to employ a title otherwise applied to the emperor: "these are all acting contrary to the decrees of Caesar, saying there is another king—Jesus" (Acts 17:7). Quite possibly, the very Roman authorities who reviewed the case included husbands of the "prominent women" persuaded by Paul. Their ire may have been added to the Jewish hostilities.

When Paul could not be found, his host Jason was arrested and made to pay bail. Under cover of night, Paul and Silas left for Berea—sixty miles to the southwest. "But when the Jews from Thessalonica learned that the word of God was preached by Paul at Berea, they came there also and stirred up the crowds" (Acts 17:13). Thus, from three cities in succession—Philippi, Thessalonica, and Berea—Paul and his team left amid civil unrest and with their work cut short. Such was the initial reception of the gospel on the European continent.

Occasion and Date. During his brief ministry in Athens, Paul was deeply concerned with the state of affairs within the infant church at Thessalonica. He had tried to return twice before, but Satan hindered (2:18). So when he could no longer endure the uncertainty nor conclusively plan a visit, he sent Timothy back to the church to investigate its progress (3:1–2).

Timothy brought back a good report. The Thessalonians were thriving in their faith and were equally concerned for Paul. News of their faith amid trouble had spread widely through Macedonia and Achaia, the province to the south. Both Paul and the Thessalonians longed to be reunited.

But there was more ministry for Paul in Corinth, about fifty miles west of Athens. From Corinth, it appears, refreshed by the good news from Thessalonica, he wrote the letter today called 1 Thessalonians.

From calculations based on the Gallio inscription—a public copy of a letter from the Roman emperor to the proconsul of Achaia—it can be affirmed that 1 Thessalonians was written in A.D. 50 or 51. The letter (with the possible exception of Galatians) is therefore the earliest preserved letter of Paul and, in fact, the first book of the New Testament to have been written. (The four Gospels, though they describe earlier events, were published in their final form somewhat later.)

Character and Content. Written primarily in a mood of relief and gratitude, 1 Thessalonians is marked by thankfulness over the growth of the church in Paul's forced absence. The letter contains no elaborate theology like Romans, no rebuke of a threatening heresy like Galatians, no extensive pastoral counsel like 1 Corinthians.

The usual pattern in Paul's letter—theological teaching followed by practical application—is slightly modified in 1 Thessalonians. First Thessalonians 1—3 rehearse Paul's remembrances of his ministry among them, his concern for the state of their faith, his commission of Timothy to return to the church, and his conspicuous delight upon learning of their steadfast faith. First Thessalonians 4 and 5 contain the characteristic exhortations toward such matters as sexual purity (4:1–8; 5:23), responsible love (4:9–12), esteem and support for leaders (5:12–13), patience and helpfulness toward the varieties of human need (5:14–15).

It is clear that Paul here only repeats what he had taught them earlier when he was with them. The Thessalonians already follow his counsel but should do so "more and more" (4:1), "just as you also are doing" (5:11). From the carefully balanced phrases in 1:3 and the repetition of the terms in 5:8, it is likewise clear that Paul and probably other early Christian missionaries repeatedly spoke of faith, hope, and love as a favorite trio of Christian virtues.

One doctrinal and practical concern, probably brought back by Timothy to Paul, led to the major theological emphasis of 1 Thessalonians. They had clearly understood his teaching that Jesus, brought back from the dead by God, would come again in triumph. Since Paul had left Thessalonica, however, several of the Thessalonian believers had died. What would become of them, the Thessalonians wondered, since Christ had not yet returned?

Paul's response offered hope and therefore comfort to those who grieved the loss of loved ones. The dead in Christ, in fact, would be the first to be resurrected. Then living Christians would join them and all would be caught up to meet the Lord in the air and forever be with Him. Comfort indeed!

Paul's language describing the Coming of Jesus is far removed from today's vocabulary of urban technology. First-century Mediterranean people were quite accustomed to the splendorous, joyful, and anticipated arrival ("coming") of a visiting royal figure. On the appointed day, citizens would go outside the city to meet the royal visitor—who came with a vast cortege. Shouts of welcome and acclaim would rise as he passed by, and those who lined the road would then join the monarch as he was borne to an appointed place. Here, special recognitions and awards would be made (2:19). There was joy and awe at the king's arrival. So shall it be when the living and the dead go up, not out, to meet the King who comes from heaven.

The theme of Christ's return, though concentrated in 4:13–18, spills over into 5:1–11 as well. Indeed, the Coming of Christ occurs from one end of the letter (1:10) to the other (5:23; see also 2:19; 3:13). Every chapter in 1 Thessalonians refers to this decisive future event.

Personal Application. Christians of all ages, like Paul ("we who are alive," 4:15), have confidently awaited the return of Christ in their own time. Throughout the history of the church, there have been those who deprived the return of Christ of its intended force by setting dates or specifying limits. Those of any age who do so are claiming to know more than Jesus Himself: "But of that day and hour no one knows, not even the angels in heaven, nor the Son, but only the Father" (Mark 13:32).

Immediately following the prediction of Christ's return (4:13–18), Paul makes the point (5:1–11) that the suddenness of the coming of Jesus will not surprise prepared Christians who have donned the appropriate armor (5:8), which works in all dimensions of time: faith (past), hope (future), and love (present).

Two things are certain: (1) the return of Christ is an assured future event, and (2) that event is closer than it has ever been before. But to specify a date for the Second Coming, or to specify a time by which the Lord must surely return, or to focus solely on detailed prophetic systems that attempt to sequence precisely various final events described in Scripture—such efforts dilute the force of Christ's return as revealed in 1 Thessalonians. Paul's bottom line—twice affirmed (4:18; 5:11: the Greek text uses exactly the same words)— is comfort in the face of death. Such a message also encourages contemporary believers who mourn "those who sleep in Jesus." This does not discourage expectancy (5:1–10), but neither does it provide encouragement to presumptuous systems of dating Jesus' return.

Scripture presents both signs and suddenness as descriptions of the Lord's return.

That may seem contradictory. But alert Christians observe the signs and know that the "mystery of lawlessness" is perennial. They avoid date-setting, leaving the times and the seasons in the hands of the Lord of history (1 Thess. 5:1). Yet they live expectantly, knowing that whether they live or die they are the Lord's (Rom. 14:8; 1 Thess. 5:10).

Before novel teachings that originated with charismatic prophecy are adopted, they should be tested (1 Thess. 5:19–20). One such test is surely consistency with the generally accepted beliefs—"traditions"—of the historic church and especially alignment with apostolic beliefs. It is sobering to learn that even the Man of Sin, the Antichrist, will possess miraculous powers. Miracles, surprisingly, are never a sufficient ground for faith (Matt. 7:21–23; John 2:23–25): they can be imitated. But the enduring love of God, which is poured out in the hearts of believers by the Holy Spirit (Rom. 5:5), continues into eternity even after charismatic gifts have passed (1 Cor. 13:8–13). Love, then, is the way believers experience eternity within time.

Father God Revealed. God the Father (1:1, 3; 3:11, 13) is the source of wrath and displeasure (2:15–16) to those who oppose Him, but for those who serve Him He is the recipient of thanks (1:2; 2:13; 3:9) and the origin of salvation (5:9), courage (2:2), peace (5:23), and approval (2:4). God raised Jesus and will raise the dead who trusted Him (1:10; 4:14). He is the living and genuine God (1:9), the opposite of idols (1:9), the incontestable witness (2:5). God's will relates to moral purity (4:3, 7), as well as to continual thanksgiving (5:18). His word, "the gospel of God" (2:2, 8–9: compare "gospel of Christ," 3:2), remarkably, comes through human words (2:13; 4:8). In 1 Thessalonians, as elsewhere in the Bible, God is the source and end of all that relates to both natural and spiritual life.

Surveying
1 THESSALONIANS

I. TYPICAL LETTER OPENING 1:1.

A. Authors. These are familiar names to the Thessalonians. Paul and Silvanus (Silas) evangelized the city only weeks before, and Timothy had just come to Paul from Thessalonica.

B. Addressees. The Thessalonians had responded enthusiastically to the gospel, causing much controversy in their city (Acts 17:5–10).

C. Greeting. The Thessalonians needed God's grace. They were a young church with much to learn.

II. PAUL'S MINISTRY RECALLED 1:2—3:13.
The infancy of the faith of this church stirs Paul with pastoral worry. His ministry had been power-packed (1:5), personal (2:8), and very brief (2:17) in the city.

"Our gospel did not come to you in word only, but also in power, and in the Holy Spirit"
(1:5). A powerless gospel can be ignored. As the Holy Spirit confirms our witness, signs and wonders follow (Mark 16:17–18). As we declare the Good News of Christ, the demonstration of a believer's changed life testifies to the mighty work of God's Spirit.

A. Thanks for Thessalonian faith, hope, love (1:2–10). Paul certainly refers to more than a mere acceptance of the gospel message, but an active Holy Spirit-powered walk in Christ (v.5; *see* Hope).

"You became followers of us and of the Lord, having received the word in much affliction, with joy of the Holy Spirit"
(1:6). The fruit of joy in a person's life is not the result of happy or pleasing circumstances. It is not transitory or subject to temporary emotions. Joy is the deep-seated knowledge of God's love for you, God's never-ending process of redemption at work within you, and the ultimate triumph of His love and grace that make you His child.

"Jesus who delivers us from the wrath to come"
(1:10). Believers will not suffer God's wrath when judgment comes to earth at the end of time. The patient expectation of His coming and the faithful pursuit of ministry
continued on next page

continued from preceding page
by His people focus the attention of the church on its Savior and mission. This is the essence of being prepared for the Second Coming.

B. How Paul ministered there (2:1–12). Paul and Silas had developed a deep affection for the people, and their ministry was out of parental concern for them (v. 11).

1. Like a nurse: gentle (2:1–8). Paul's description of pastoral care uses the metaphor of a nursing mother with her children (v. 7). The passionate words of the apostle insist that it was not only the gospel "but also our own lives" that they received.

2. Like a father: concerned (2:9–12). Once again, the imagery is convincingly personal.

C. Thanks for Thessalonian endurance (2:13–16). They are, once again, "imitating" older brothers and sisters in the Lord in that they are enduring suffering with faith (v. 14; *see* Effectively).

D. Paul's anxiety over the Thessalonians (2:17–20). Paul's almost desperate pastoral concern recounts that "Satan hindered us" in coming to finish the job of establishing the church.

E. Timothy's mission and Paul's relief (3:1–10). Following Timothy's report of the ministry and news of the conduct of their faith, Paul is comforted (v. 7).

> **"We were comforted concerning you by your faith"**
> (3:7). Paul's pastoral concern reveals his deep commitment to those he has brought to Christ and the confidence of knowing that a genuine work of the Holy Spirit results in abiding faith.

F. Paul's continued hope to see the Thessalonians (3:11–13). Paul's passion is to see all the flock established and ready for Christ's return (v. 13; *see* Holiness).

III. CHRIST'S RETURN AWAITED 4:1—5:11. This passage is the most extensive teaching in the Bible on the rapture of the church. Paul's perspective is clear: The resurrection of Christ assures us that we too will be resurrected. Since there is no way to know the time, we must be ever vigilant and ready for the "Day" (5:4).

A. For the present: lifestyle qualities (4:1–12). Paul wants them to "abound more and more" (v. 1); this is a result of walking in a way that pleases God.

1. Marital fidelity (4:1–8). Sexual immorality defrauds others and demonstrates our rejection of God (4:8). Lust is not an option for God's people (v. 6).

2. Brotherly love (4:9–10). The challenges endured by this young church have solidified this attribute among them. Paul encourages them to "increase more and more."

3. Personal responsibility (4:10–12). Be busy about your own business and live for the Lord. This is a powerful witness to unbelievers.

B. For the future: the return of Christ (4:13—5:11). The infant church has no answer for the plaguing questions about what happens when one dies. The Greek converts and the new Jewish converts are frightened for the loss of their loved ones.

1. The coming of the King: comfort for the bereaved (4:13–18). The Lord Jesus will come for us personally! He will rescue the living and the dead and will provide for a triumphant reunion in the air!

> **"We who are alive and remain shall be *caught up together with them in the cloud to meet the Lord in the air"**
> (4:15—5:3). The rapture of the church is found in these verses. The sparing of the church from God's outpouring of wrath and the joyous reunion with Christ in the air open the way for the permanent establishment of Christ's kingdom on earth (*see* Messianic Promises).

2. The coming of the King: no surprise for the prepared (5:1–11). This is another place in the New Testament where the church is warned to be ready at all times. No one knows when Christ will return for His church.

> **"Comfort one another with these words"**
> (4:18). The paranoia over the return of Christ is fueled by two basic fears: (1) Will I be ready when Jesus comes? and (2) How can I be sure? First, the Lord is seeking His children and will come for them; His intention is to save all those "who have loved His appearing" (2 Tim. 4:8). Second, "God did not appoint us to wrath, but to obtain salvation" (1 Thess. 5:9). Let's live for Jesus with a passion, knowing that His coming may be today.

IV. CLOSING COUNSELS 5:12–28. Paul outlines a practical and helpful set of commands for believers to follow.

A. Respect for leaders (5:12–13). A recurrent theme in the epistles (1 Tim. 5:17; Heb. 13:17).

B. Peace in the community (5:13). Our love for each other must supersede our differences.

C. Help for the needy (5:14). Here is a warning to the "unruly"—literally, idle persons. Believers also are encouraged to live generously toward others (Eph. 4:32).

D. Christian universals (5:15–22). This kind of wisdom integrates everything related to our lives as the people of God—"spirit, soul, and body" (v. 23; *see* Prophecies).

1. Benevolence toward all (5:15).

2. Joy at all times (5:16). Joy is not a superficial happiness based on circumstance, but an abiding confidence in knowing that the God of the universe is the Lord of our life.

3. Pray always (5:17).

4. Thanksgiving everywhere (5:18).

5. Charismatic affirmation (5:19–22). The hope of the church is to stay sensitive to the Holy Spirit and live with a vibrancy that anxiously waits to respond to the Spirit's promptings and acts upon them in faith.

E. Closing challenges (5:23–28).

TRUTH-IN-ACTION through **1 THESSALONIANS**

Truth 1 Thessalonians Teaches	**Action** 1 Thessalonians Invites
1 Guidelines For Growing in Godliness Godly believers live unto God and for God. They seek to honor and reflect God in everything they think, say, or do. Godliness lives quietly, is absorbed in doing good for others and works productively. Godliness has a good reputation with unbelievers. Godliness is knowing the commands of Scripture and doing them.	**1:3** *Understand* that successful Christian living consists of 1) work that flows from faith, 2) labor that flows from love, and 3) patient endurance that is born of living hope. *Insure* that your life is thus characterized. **3:10** *Be faithful to intercede* for other believers and other congregations. **4:1** *Live your life* in order to please God, not yourself. **4:11, 12** *Live* a quiet, peaceful life. *Never gossip. Be diligent* in whatever work you have chosen to do. *Earn* a good reputation with unbelievers. **5:6** *Conduct your life*, being alert and self-controlled. **5:16–22** *Practice* the commands of Scripture.
2 Key Lessons in Faith The person of faith prays that God will demonstrate His power in the church today. Faith is able to receive God's Word through human beings, believing God's ability to use human vessels. And faith looks forward to the promise that the Lord will appear a second time for salvation's consummation.	**1:5** *Pray* that your preaching of the gospel will be attended by the power of signs, wonders, and miracles. **2:13** *Receive* the preaching and teaching as God's Word! *Refuse* to receive the Scripture as merely human opinion, and *avoid* negating its authority or nullifying its effectiveness for growth in your life. **4:17** *Encourage* brothers and sisters in Christ often, giving hope through expecting Jesus Christ's return.
3 Lessons for Leaders Although righteous spiritual leaders speak the truth of God boldly, they do so gently. They are unmoved by flattery or praise from humankind. They only seek praise from God. They are diligent workers who never take advantage of those they serve.	**2:5, 6** Leaders, *seek to please* God, rather than cater to humans. *Never employ* flattery; rather, *speak* the truth *forthrightly. Look* only to God for praise. **2:7** Leaders, *practice gentleness* in your ministry. **2:9** Leaders, *understand* that ministry means hard work and long hours.
4 Keys to Moral Purity The church must sustain a biblical commitment to sexual purity. The worldly attitude that produces sexually immoral behavior rejects God and His ways.	**4:3–6** *Recognize* that sanctification includes sexual purity and moral self-control. *Never defraud* others; that is, *do not cheat* brothers through wrongful sexual liaisons. **4:7, 8** *Understand* that living in sexual impurity is a rejection of God as well as His Word.

Truth 1 Thessalonians Teaches	**Action** 1 Thessalonians Invites
5 **Keys to Relating to Authority** Pastoral leadership is a gift from God. We must treat God's appointed leaders and teachers with appropriate respect.	**5:12, 13** *Honor* church leadership. *Recognize* that their Bible-based instruction comes with Jesus' own authority.

Introducing
2 THESSALONIANS

Occasion and Date. First and 2 Thessalonians are very similar in language, suggesting that Paul wrote 2 Thessalonians within a few weeks of 1 Thessalonians. The return of the Lord is of central importance in both letters. First Thessalonians reveals that some Thessalonians were perplexed over the death of loved ones and whether these might miss the Lord's return. In 2 Thessalonians, a different problem surfaces—one still related to the Second Coming of the Lord.

Both in 1 Thessalonians (1:6; 2:14; 3:3–5) and in 2 Thessalonians (1:4–7), it is clear that believers there suffered certain persecutions and hardships—just as Paul and Silas themselves did, leading to their departure by night from the city (Acts 17:5–10; 1 Thess. 2:2). Paul's concern for the spiritual stability of the Thessalonian church had led him to send Timothy and to express, in writing 1 Thessalonians, joyful relief upon learning of their spiritual health (1 Thess. 2:17—3:10). The steadfastness of the Thessalonians, their persistence and patience amid adversity, drew the frequent praise and gratitude of the apostle (1 Thess. 1:3; 2 Thess. 1:4). Still, there were clear concerns over imbalanced attitudes related to Christ's Second Coming.

"We hear," said the apostle (3:11), "that there are some who walk among you in a disorderly manner, not working at all." Work stoppage, it seems, was prompted by an erroneous teaching that someone, unnamed, had brought to Thessalonica—a doctrine that announced that "the day of Christ had come" (2:2). Such a teaching may have falsely claimed a charismatic origin ("by spirit," 2:2). Or it may have surfaced in a letter falsely attributed to Paul.

Whatever the source of the erroneous teaching, Paul quickly wrote 2 Thessalonians to round out the proper way to understand the return of the Lord. That day, he clarifies, will not occur until certain events take place. First,

there will be a falling away and more importantly, the Man of Sin will be revealed—the "son of perdition" (2:3). This figure, called the Antichrist in the letters of John (1 John 2:18; 4:3; 2 John 7), will blasphemously call himself God (2:4). He will deceive many, for he will possess charismatic powers, including the ability to perform miracles (2:9). The spirit of such a figure, the "mystery of lawlessness" (2:7) was already at work in Paul's day. But a restraining power—not clearly identified by the apostle—controls the Man of Sin to keep him from interfering with God's consummation of the course of human events through the return of Christ at the Second Coming.

Twice in 2 Thessalonians (2:15; 3:6), the apostle appeals to the "tradition"—fixed beliefs within the churches—as a check upon charismatic but novel teaching. Frequently in the Thessalonian letters he reminds his readers to continue in the things he taught earlier (1 Thess. 2:11–12; 3:4; 4:2; 2 Thess. 2:5, 15; 3:4, 6, 10, 14). Already in these letters, probably the earliest of New Testament books to be written, a body of fixed Christian beliefs is developing.

Second Thessalonians, if written only a few weeks after 1 Thessalonians, would also have been written about A.D. 50.

Personal Application. Scripture presents both signs and suddenness as descriptions of the Lord's return. That may seem contradictory, but alert Christians observe the signs and know that the "mystery of lawlessness" is perennial. They avoid date-setting, leaving the times and the seasons in the hands of the Lord of history (1 Thess. 5:1). Yet they live expectantly, knowing that whether they live or die they are the Lord's (Rom. 14:8; 1 Thess. 5:10).

Father God Revealed. As elsewhere in the New Testament, God is seen as the Father (1:1; 2:16), the source of grace (1:12) and love (3:5), and the object of thanks (1:3; 2:13). He has chosen (2:13) those in His kingdom (1:5) and makes them worthy of His saving call (1:11), but He also repays evildoers (1:6) and allows delusion to those who despise the truth (2:11) and who do not know Him (1:8). The churches are His (1:4); they rest in Him (1:1).

Surveying
2 THESSALONIANS

I. TYPICAL LETTER OPENING 1:1–4.

A. Authors (1:1).

B. Addressees (1:1).

C. Greetings (1:2). Whenever blessing is conferred by spiritual authority, the Holy Spirit conveys a measure of "grace" otherwise not present.

D. Thanksgiving (1:3–4). Paul again affirms the faith and works of this young church.

> **"Your faith grows exceedingly"**
> (1:3). Faith development among the Thessalonians is simply put in verse 4: "You endure." The late 20th-century focus of the western church on miracles, health, and wealth as evidences of faith pales in the face of the relentless persecutions that awaited believers in Thessalonica. Unwavering commitment to Christ at the price of their lives (*see* Endure) is proof of their faith.

II. DOCTRINE 1:5—2:12.
The Thessalonians are concerned that the rapture of the church has occurred and the Tribulation begun. The first verse of chapter 2 implies that a letter bearing the apostle's name has been circulated and is the cause of their confusion and fear.

A. Consequences of the coming (1:5–12). God will "repay" (v. 6) those who "do not know God" and have caused tribulation of the faithful with "everlasting destruction" (v. 9). The righteous will receive "rest" (v. 7).

1. To the righteous: established worthiness (1:5, 10–12). The commitment of the righteous makes them "worthy of the kingdom," and with Jesus they will share "His goodness and the work of faith with power" (v. 11).

2. To the unjust: declared banishment (1:6–9). The punishment never ends and is related to banishment from the presence of the Lord.

B. Indicators of the coming (2:1–12). There are signs for the coming Day: (1) the falling away and the end-time rebellion against God and (2) the revelation of the Man of Sin (v. 3).

1. The falling away (2:1–3). This general reference to a great "falling away" is unclear regarding a specific group, but is likely related to the Antichrist (1 John 2:18, 22; 4:3; Rev. 13:14).

> **"That Day will not come unless the falling away comes first"**
> (1:7—2:8). The announcement of the Second Coming will be heralded with trumpets, lightning, and the coming of the Lord in the clouds. Before that happens there will be a massive apostasy (Matt. 24:11; 1 Tim. 4:1–3) marked by satanic deception represented in one who will exalt himself above the one true God (2 Thess. 2:4). The apostle's warning brings us to the wisdom and simplicity of loving Jesus first and only.

2. The Man of Sin (2:3–5). This is the great deceiver, who will demonstrate unusual powers and solicit the worship of those who betray the Lord Jesus Christ.

3. The restrainer (2:6). This is the restraining influence of the Holy Spirit through those who will not follow, but rather resist this power of evil.

4. The lying wonders (2:7–12). Miraculous powers are only a partial proof of legitimate spiritual authority. The final issue is determined by our worship. Those who worship someone other than the living God will be thoroughly deceived and condemned (vv. 11–12).

III. EXHORTATION 2:13—3:16.
Confusion and potential fear are unnecessary for those who live in Christ (3:3).

A. To steadfastness (2:13–17). Paul's instructions are simple: "Stand fast and hold the traditions" and the Lord will "establish you in every good word and work."

B. To prayer (3:1–5; *see* Confidence).

C. Against idleness (3:6–13). Some have concluded that if the world is coming to an end they should not work (v. 10). Work is a moral obligation for the believer (1 Thess. 4:11).

D. To discipline (3:14–15). Paul exercises apostolic authority by instructing the church to reject those who reject the teaching of the epistle.

E. To peace (3:16). They have been greatly disturbed—with pastoral grace Paul declares an end to the turmoil.

IV. CONCLUDING COMMENTS 3:17–18.
Given the apparent confusion in 2:1, Paul wants to assure them of the authenticity of the letter.

A. An accrediting signature (3:17).

B. A wish for grace (3:18).

TRUTH-IN-ACTION through 2 THESSALONIANS

Truth 2 Thessalonians Teaches	**Action** 2 Thessalonians Invites
1 Guidelines For Growing in Godliness Three faces of godliness in believers are 1) enduring trials through faith and hope, 2) faithfulness in intercession for other believers, and 3) faithfully confronting those who are out of order, exhorting to repent.	**1:4** *Recognize* the value of perseverance and faith maintained in the face of persecutions and tribulations. **1:11** *Pray* for other believers and for churches, for the fulfillment of God's purpose for them. **3:6–15** *Work diligently*, and *pay* your bills. *Do not encourage* idleness by supporting those who will not work.
2 Key Lessons in Faith Faith is unmoving in the face of tribulation and recognizes that it has a role to play in the effectiveness of other ministries through prayer partnership with them.	**2:15** *Stand fast* and *hold firmly* to the truth of God's Word. **3:1, 2** *Pray* for church leaders that their evangelistic ministries will be fruitful and that they will be kept safe from those who oppose them.
3 A Key to Wise Living The wise believer correctly discerns between deceptive satanic signs and wonders and the true gifts of the Holy Spirit.	**2:9, 10** *Understand* and *beware* of the counterfeit nature of satanic signs and wonders. *Know* that they will deceive those who reject the truth.
4 A Step to Holiness We must realize that practical holiness is not a possession, but it is a process that calls for continual submission to the Spirit's work and continued steadfastness in faith.	**2:13** *Recognize* and *embrace* the continuing work of God's grace that involves 1) the sanctifying work of God's Holy Spirit and 2) our continuing to advance through believing the truth.
5 A Step to Faithful Obedience We must practice discriminating sensitivity in our fellowshipping.	**3:14** *Recognize* the importance of obeying God's Word. *Notice* that restoration is the object of rejecting fellowship with careless disciples.

KEYS TO 1 AND 2 TIMOTHY
The Kingdom and Daily Church Life

Kingdom Key: God's Purpose in View

The word "doctrine" appears more frequently in these two epistles than in any combination of two or three other New Testament books. Didaskalia *is the word that signals this vital pastoral concern. "Sound doctrine" refers not only to right believing, but to right behavior. (1) It teaches that God has come in the flesh to redeem humankind (1 Tim. 3:16), and that "life" (now) and "immortality" (forever) have been brought to light through the gospel (2 Tim. 1:10). (2) Therefore, the living church should manifest this in the responsible daily behavior of its members.*

This is the biblical context in which "doctrine" ought always be seen and studied. First Timothy 1:9–11 shows "doctrine" to do more with behavior, attitude, and conduct than it does with a creed or system of beliefs. This does not deny the practical value or biblical validity of ordering or studying biblical truth. But it is essential to know that the revelation of Scripture is not intended merely to be a cerebral pursuit or to create an elite group of experts in theology. Instead, God's Word is meant to be incarnate in the lives of those who allow its truth to set them free from carnal, self-centered living by the power of the Holy Spirit. It is intended for our understanding, that we might see how we are called to love one another, to serve in the Spirit of Christ, and to reach the lost with grace as well as with truth.

Thus Paul emphasizes that "godly edification" and "love from a pure heart" is the essence of pure doctrine. He contests the claims of those whose bookish concerns with spiritual perceptions blind them to the practical and ethical demands of vital faith in Christ (1 Tim. 1:3–7).

> ## Guard the gospel; pass it on faithfully.

Notice that 1 Timothy 3 focuses more on the character and conduct of spiritual leaders than it does on their intellectual or academic attainment. Clearly, teachers and elders should be qualified in the Word (1 Tim. 4:1–8). But the qualification for bishops and deacons (as well as Paul's appeal to "Pastor Timothy" regarding his own lifestyle) emphasize attitude, character, and responsibility in relationships even *(Please turn to page 411.)*

(Please turn to page 411.)

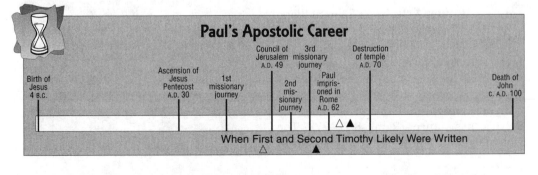

Paul's Apostolic Career

			Council of Jerusalem A.D. 49	3rd missionary journey		Destruction of temple A.D. 70		
Birth of Jesus 4 B.C.		Ascension of Jesus Pentecost A.D. 30	1st missionary journey		2nd missionary journey	Paul imprisoned in Rome A.D. 62		Death of John c. A.D. 100

When First and Second Timothy Likely Were Written

Paul's letters to Timothy mark the path of practical, • • •

Master Key: God's Son Revealed
1 Timothy

The deity of Jesus is apparent because Paul equates Him with God the Father (1:1–2; 3:16) and proclaims His universal sovereignty and eternal nature (6:15–16). Jesus is the source of grace, mercy, and peace (1:2, 14) who commanded Paul's apostleship (1:1) and enabled him for service (1:12). Christ is both Lord (1:2, 12, 14; 5:21; 6:3, 14–15) and Savior (1:1, 15) "who gave Himself a ransom for all" (2:6). By virtue of His redemptive work He is the "one Mediator between God and men" (2:5), the way of access to God. He who became incarnate has ascended (3:16). Meanwhile, He is our hope (1:1), and the promise of His return is an incentive to fidelity in service and to purity in life (6:14).

2 Timothy

For Paul, the gospel is more than statements and propositions; it is Christ (see 2 Tim. 1:8). Spiritual blessings, such as grace, mercy, peace, and even life itself, reside in Him and are derived from Him (2 Tim. 1:1–2, 9–10, 13, 16, 18; 2:1). Jesus came to earth as a man (2:8) to be our Savior (1:10; 2:10; 3:15) and was resurrected (2:8). He is faithful to those who follow Him (2 Tim. 1:12; 2:11–12; 4:17–18, 22) and consistent in His purposes (2:12–13). He also grants spiritual understanding (2:7). Christ will appear at His Second Coming as the righteous judge (4:1, 8; see 1:18; 4:14, 16).

Power Key: God's Spirit at Work
1 Timothy

Direct references to the Holy Spirit in 1 Timothy are rare, but He was at work from the inception of the church at Ephesus (see Acts 19:1–7). The "intercessions" (2:1) are prayers that involve the Holy Spirit's assistance (Rom. 8:26–27). The statement that "the Spirit expressly says"

Key Word: *Leadership Manual*

The theme of this epistle is Timothy's organization and oversight of the Asian churches as a faithful minister of God. Paul writes so that Timothy will have effective guidelines for his work during Paul's absence in Macedonia (3:14, 15).

Key Verses: First Timothy 3:15–16; 6:11–12

Key Chapter: First Timothy 3

Listed in chapter 3 are the qualifications for the leaders of God's church, the elders and deacons. Notably absent are qualities of worldly success or position. Instead, Paul enumerates character qualities demonstrating that true leadership emanates from our walk with God rather than from achievements or vocational success.

Key Word: *Endurance in the Pastoral Ministry*

Paul commissions Timothy to endure faithfully and carry on the work that the condemned apostle must now relinquish, using the Word of God constantly in order to overcome growing obstacles to the spread of the gospel.

• • • obedient behavior, especially for church leaders.

(4:1) underscores the continuing activity of the Holy Spirit and Paul's sensitivity to His promptings. In 4:14 Paul reminds Timothy of "the gift" that was given to him "by prophecy," a special ability for ministry given as a *charisma* of the Spirit when hands were laid on him. Furthermore, "a good testimony" (3:7) would also include a leader's being "full of the Holy Spirit" as with the first appointment of leaders (Acts 6:3).

2 Timothy

The Holy Spirit had given Timothy a gift and Paul exhorted him to use it actively (2 Tim. 1:6). Furthermore, the Holy Spirit grants power, love, and a sound mind (1:7). The indwelling Holy Spirit enables us to be faithful to the gospel and to safeguard its purity (1:13–14).

Key Verses: Second Timothy
2:3–4; 3:14–17
Key Chapter: Second Timothy 2

The second chapter of Second Timothy ought to be required daily reading for every pastor and full-time Christian worker. Paul lists the keys to an enduring ministry: a reproducing ministry (vv. 1, 2), an enduring successful ministry (vv. 3–13), a studying ministry (vv. 14–18), and a holy ministry (vv. 19–26).

Kingdom Key *continued from page 409*

ahead of a leader's grasp of the Word (1 Tim. 3:1–13; 4:12–13).

Note also how 2 Timothy emphasizes the practical path of faith.

1. Clear guidance is given for such basic ministries as (a) care for those without earthly means of support (1 Tim. 5:3–15), and (b) counsel for those seeking freedom from impure practices or spiritual defilement (2 Tim. 2:19–26).

2. Warnings are found in negative examples of people who claim truth but who oppose it by their sinful behavior (2 Tim. 1:15; 2:17; 4:10, 14). In contrast, the solid terrain of the inspired Word of God is pointed to as grounds for durable living and for edifying, life-enriching teaching (2 Tim. 3:14—4:5).

3. A clear-headed focus is maintained toward sound living in a fickle world, while a clear-eyed vision is kept toward the ultimate kingdom, the fullest manifestation of which is yet to come, at which time all who belong to the King will want to be found faithful (2 Tim. 4:1, 18).

Words from a Mentor
(2 Timothy)

Timothy must . . .	Because . . .
Share in suffering for the gospel (1:8; 2:3)	Through such sharing others will be saved (2:10)
Continue in sound doctrine (1:13; 2:15)	False doctrine spreads and leads to ungodliness (2:16–17)
Flee youthful lusts (2:22)	He must be cleansed and set apart for the Master's use (2:21)
Avoid contentiousness (2:23–25)	He must gently lead others to the truth (2:24–26)
Militantly preach the gospel (4:2)	Great apostasy is coming (4:3–4)

Introducing
1 TIMOTHY

Background. On their first missionary journey Paul and Barnabas preached in Lystra, a city of Lycaonia, and experienced success amid persecution. It is likely that a Jewess named Lois and her daughter Eunice were converted to Christ during that ministry. Eunice was married to a Gentile, by whom she had Timothy, probably an only child. Timothy evidently had been instructed in the Jewish religion, but his father refused to allow his son to be circumcised. From the beginning a close relationship developed between Paul and Timothy.

When Paul returned to Lystra on his second journey, he found Timothy to be a member of the local church and highly recommended by the leaders there and at Iconium. Under the prompting of the Holy Spirit Paul added Timothy to his apostolic party. Since they were going to be ministering among the Jews, Paul admonished Timothy to be circumcised, not for righteousness' sake, but to avoid offending the Jews since his mother was Jewish.

Author. All the Pastoral Epistles (1 Timothy, 2 Timothy, Titus) name the apostle Paul as their author. In addition, early tradition unanimously insists that Paul wrote them. Many scholars question this claim, however. They point out that the Pastoral Epistles include words that do not appear in Paul's uncontested letters. Moreover, the Pastorals record certain events that are difficult to harmonize with the account of Paul's journeys in Acts. For example, Paul has conducted a mission in Crete (Titus 1:5), plans to spend the winter in Nicopolis (Titus 3:12), and has made visits to Ephesus (1 Tim. 1:3), to Miletus (2 Tim. 4:20), and to Troas (2 Tim. 4:13). Furthermore, some scholars feel that these letters describe a church organization too far advanced for Paul's time.

So far as vocabulary is concerned, we may conclude that the subject matter of the Pastorals is so different from that of Paul's other letters that he would necessarily use some words he had not previously employed. It would be foolish to restrict an educated man like Paul to a limited vocabulary. The fact that he was writing to close associates is also a consideration.

The obvious answer to the problem of harmonizing the accounts of Paul's journeys in the Pastorals with those in Acts is that Paul was released from the Roman imprisonment described in Acts and continued his ministry for several more years. There is solid evidence from the writings of early Christian leaders that this was the case. During this period of continued activity, Paul wrote 1 Timothy and Titus. Later he was arrested again and wrote 2 Timothy during his second Roman imprisonment.

The mention of elders, bishops, and deacons in the Pastorals does not imply a monarchical episcopacy that demands a date later than Paul's time. Paul appointed elders in the churches on his first missionary journey (Acts 14:23) and greeted bishops and deacons in his Philippian letter. Furthermore, Paul used the terms "bishop" and "elder" interchangeably (see Titus 1:5–7).

The preponderance of evidence supports Paul as the author of the Pastoral Epistles.

Date. Paul visited Ephesus in about A.D. 63, following his release from his first Roman imprisonment. Soon thereafter, he left, placing Timothy in charge of the church there. He probably wrote the first letter in about A.D. 64.

Purpose. The primary purpose of the first epistle was to encourage Timothy in his difficult task of dealing with doctrinal errors and practical problems in the church at Ephesus, and to give him instructions concerning pastoral responsibilities and the qualifications and duties of church leadership.

Content. The work to which Paul assigned Timothy involved serious difficulties, and he felt it necessary to write instruction to his young associate as he faced the problems. In Paul's first letter he told Timothy how to combat false teachers, how to order the church's worship, how to choose church leaders, and how to deal prudently with different classes in the church. All the while Timothy was to teach the apostolic faith and lead an exemplary life.

Personal Application. First Timothy not only guided Timothy in fulfilling his responsibilities as a church leader, but it has been a handbook for pastors throughout the whole church age. A clear lesson gleaned from Paul's instructions is that the church must have a well-trained, deeply devoted, and highly consecrated ministry. Furthermore, ministers must stay in constant touch with God through prayer and study of the Bible (see 2:1, 8; 4:6, 12–16). The pastor must first nourish his own soul in the words of faith and good doctrine (4:6) and then teach the people the essentials of the faith (4:11). Practicing godliness in his own conduct, he must bring his congregation to do the same (4:16).

Surveying
1 TIMOTHY

INTRODUCTION 1:1–20. Paul comforts and encourages Timothy, his son in the faith, in the midst of severe challenges.

A. Salutation (1:1–2). More than simply one of Paul's converts, Timothy mirrors the spiritual commitment and ministry that make him a son in the faith.

B. Charge to Timothy (1:3–11). Lead with boldness that puts an end to error and pointless fascination with things of no eternal consequence (v. 4; *see* Idle Talk).

C. Thanksgiving (1:12–17). Paul's perspective on his entire life is revealed here—that others might see God's eternal and patient love for him and believe in Jesus Christ for their own salvation.

D. Restatement of the charge (1:18–20). In the midst of the battle Timothy has been called and commissioned with prophetic instruction to wage spiritual warfare.

> **"Prophecies previously made concerning you"**
> (1:18). Prophecies made over Timothy are related to his commissioning to ministry (4:14). The power of the "laying on of hands" endures and is to be remembered in the midst of trial. Paul refers to this again in 2 Timothy 1:6. The call to service in the kingdom is accompanied by awesome spiritual authority that Timothy has not yet fully recognized.

I. INSTRUCTIONS CONCERNING THE CHURCH 2:1—3:16. In the congregation and its leadership, Paul calls for a life that radiates faith, prayer, propriety, and reverence for God, which translate into a productive life and healthy relationships.

A. Its worship (2:1–15). Prayer is the first order of our Christian commitment, along with properly ordered relationships within the body of Christ.

> **"I exhort first of all"**
> (2:1–2). Paul is writing to Timothy in the midst of a hostile and pagan culture. Paul's exhortation is not related to the acceptance of the spiritual, social, or political agenda of their leaders. Paul insists that the authority of the church to change things in the world is irresistible as we pray.

> **"I do not permit a woman"**
> (2:12). The context here is the conduct of the public worship service (*see also* 1 Cor. 11:5). Some offer a cultural explanation for these words, but Paul's reference to the creative order makes this a spiritual issue. The question remains as to what role it is permissible for a woman to have in the church. Answer: servant/deacon (such as Phoebe, Rom. 16:1), prophetess (Acts 2:17; 21:9; 1 Cor. 11:5), "labored with me in the gospel" (Phil. 4:3). Priscilla and Aquila are acknowledged together as having the church meet in their home (1 Cor. 16:19). Clearly, women are permitted ministry and are allowed to speak. Paul's concern here is to prevent having a disorderly congregation and to maintain an appropriate response to authority in the church.

B. Its officers (3:1–13). Here and in Titus are listed general requirements for all spiritual leaders (*see* Leadership, Spiritual). There is a differentiation in qualifications of "bishops" and "deacons" with the apparent emphasis on the ability of the "bishop" being "able to teach" (v. 2; *see* Gentle) and that he is "not a novice" (v. 6; *see* Reverent).

C. Its function in relation to the truth (3:14–16). Paul's appeal to doctrine and conduct is based on the church being the "pillar and ground of the truth" to the world.

II. INSTRUCTIONS CONCERNING PASTORAL DUTIES 4:1—6:10. Paul's exhortation to Timothy includes the phrase "command and teach" (4:11). Exercising pastoral authority, Timothy is to preach doctrine, cut off error in teaching and practice, and instruct the congregation in practical matters of personal relationships.

A. Toward the church as a whole (4:1–16). The call to asceticism and legalism threatens the church with "doctrines of demons" which cause people to "depart from the faith."

> **"Do not neglect the gift that is in you, which was given to you by prophecy with the laying on of the hands of the *eldership"**
> (4:14). The laying on of hands conveys healing (Mark 16:18) and, here, it conveys spiritual gifts consistent with Timothy's call to leadership in the church. Some believe this refers to Timothy's ordination to ministry (by Paul, 2 Tim. 1:6) and the prophetic witness to God's purpose for his life. It is certain that this event was significant to young Timothy, marking a distinct change in his life.

B. Toward various classes in the church (5:1—6:10). Practical wisdom of the older and wiser apostle offers guidance to the young pastor. The instruction concerning widows highlights the regard for marriage and fidelity. Paul offers perspective on spiritual leaders: They are "worthy of double honor."

III. CONCLUDING EXHORTATIONS 6:11–21. Paul warns the "man of God" to flee the pursuit of money. Instead, one should continue in the battle for souls awaiting the return of Christ.

A. To keep the faith and fight the fight (6:11–16). "Lay hold of eternal life"; keep your priorities clear; remain blameless before God. (*See* Gentleness; Power.)

"Keep this commandment" (6:14–15). Paul commands Timothy to "fight the good fight of faith, lay hold on eternal life" (v. 12). Earlier in the chapter there is a warning about doctrinal error and the love of money. Coupled with the injunction in 2 Timothy 2:22, "flee youthful lusts," there is a dramatic contrast between the things that help believers prepare for Christ's coming and those things that deceive and mislead the people of God.

B. To present the claims of Christ to the rich (6:17–19). Paul directs that particular emphasis be placed on instructing the rich in the stewardship of their wealth and the potential for arrogance in plenty.

C. To guard the truth (6:20–21). Paul closes as he begins: Be vigilant about the truth God has committed to you!

TRUTH-IN-ACTION through 1 TIMOTHY

Truth 1 Timothy Teaches	**Action** 1 Timothy Invites
1 Guidelines for Growing in Godliness God's Word instructs in godly conduct, which must issue from godly attitudes in life and worship. If the heart is tuned to God, modesty and acceptable worship will be the result. God has defined godliness in the example of the Lord Jesus Christ. Believers are to conform to Christ as an act of faithful obedience.	**2:9, 10** *Dress* with appropriate modesty. *Stress* internal beauty. **3:14–16** Let all those in the church *conform* to the high standards to be observed by leaders. *Acknowledge* the order Christ has set in the church. **4:7, 8** *Recognize* that godliness is necessary to this life and to life eternal. *Be disciplined* in body, soul, and spirit. **4:12** *Conduct yourself* in an exemplary manner in every detail of your life.
2 Steps to Holiness Holiness does not reject that which God has created for man's benefit, nor does it condemn those who rightly use what God has called good. The source of holiness is a personal relationship with Jesus, not a system of works. The stomach does not defile man, but the heart can.	**4:3–5** *Reject* teaching that bases holiness on works. *Receive thankfully* the natural blessings from God. *Sanctify* by prayer what you so receive.
3 Keys to Wise Living The wise believer sees the trap of theological debate and avoids it. Realizing that truth is more practice than theory, he judges all teaching by what it produces, not by how it sounds. Therefore, he avoids the deception of demonically inspired teachings that sound good, but bring destruction and death in the end.	**1:3–7** *Teach* only sound, thoroughly biblical doctrine. *Do not attempt to teach* what you do not fully understand. *Operate* from a motive of love, faith, and good conscience in all you do. **4:1, 2** *Be warned* that some will abandon faith in Jesus Christ for demonically inspired teaching. *Understand* that hypocrisy is an open door to deceiving spirits. Liars will believe "the lie." **1:8–11** *Recognize* that the law is to instruct and judge the ungodly, not to induce condemnation in the righteous. **6:20, 21** *Guard carefully* the truth you have been taught! *Reject* human knowledge that denies the faith.

Truth 1 Timothy Teaches	**Action** 1 Timothy Invites
4 Key Lessons in Faith Prophetic "words" can be the basis for much hope and faith for many. We should never despise or reject such ministry. These utterances can encourage us to endure ferocious and demanding battles as we carry out the Lord's will.	**1:18** *Heed* confirmed, prophetic utterances. *Recognize* their value in spiritual warfare and maintaining strong, positive faith. *Know* that faith and a good conscience keep you from spiritual disaster. **6:12** *Recognize* that excellence in Christian ministry often involves long and arduous struggles. *Do not give up; stand firm. Endure* in your struggle for righteousness regardless of the cost.
5 Lessons for Leaders Christian leadership should conform to the scriptural requirements given here, being stable in the basics of life and grounded in the faith. All leadership must be established on the motivation of service, and is to maintain faithful order in the church. All God's people are to pray constantly for those who have authority over the church as well as throughout society.	**2:1–6** Leaders, *lead* in regular, fervent prayer for civil authority. *Pray* that the gospel will spread and God's people will be protected. **3:1–7** Leaders, *open* leadership roles to those who are qualified. *Refuse* leadership responsibility to anyone who is unqualified spiritually. **3:8–13** Leaders, *recognize* and *honor* those who help in practical service to the church. *Insist* on a time of testing before they are recognized. **4:11** Leaders, *recognize* the imperative nature of biblical truth. *Know* that to teach and not cultivate obedience dilutes scriptural intent and misrepresents divine authority. **4:13** Leaders, *focus* ministry around the public reading of Scripture. **5:3–16** Leaders, *establish* a benevolence fund for widows and others who are in genuine need. *Be faithful* to help those who have no other means of legitimate family support. **5:19** Leaders, *do not welcome* or *consider* unwarranted criticism against fellow leadership. **5:22** Leaders, *do not involve* others in roles of responsible leadership too quickly. **6:3–5** Leaders, *avoid* the love of money. *Reprove* any covetousness among God's people. *Reject* teaching motivated by greed. *Rebuke* greedy teachers. **6:17–19** Leaders, *urge* and *persuade* any wealthy in your congregation to give liberally to God's work. *Teach* against the selfish use of personal wealth.

Introducing
2 TIMOTHY

Background. As far as we can determine, Paul was released from Roman imprisonment shortly after Acts was written and engaged in additional missionary travels, journeying as far as Spain. During the era of persecutions initiated by Nero in A.D. 64, Paul was arrested again, probably in Troas (4:13), and taken to Rome. The circumstances of his second Roman imprisonment were quite different from those of his first. Previously, he was in his own hired dwelling and was able to receive visitors freely, but now he was confined in a dungeon and friends could only see him with difficulty. Formerly he had expected to be released, but now he looked forward to death (4:6–8). At the writing of this letter, only Luke was with Paul (4:11), all others having left for various reasons.

Occasion and Date. The letter was occasioned by Paul's concern for Timothy's needs as well as for his own. He reminded Timothy of his responsibilities and admonished him to give himself wholeheartedly to his task. As for himself, Paul needed certain personal effects (4:13) and in his loneliness desired to see Timothy and Mark (4:9–11). There is little question that Paul wrote this letter shortly before his death. Therefore, since he was probably executed before Nero's death in A.D. 68, the letter may be dated around 66–67.

Purpose. Paul's immediate purpose in the letter was to issue an affectionate appeal to Timothy to come to him (4:9, 11, 13, 21). Paul's continuing concern, however, was the welfare of the church, and he gave Timothy instructions for perfecting its organization and safeguarding the gospel. With the realization that his death was imminent, and that Timothy might not reach him in time for a final visit, Paul injected into this letter solemn words of admonition. His preoccupation was with the gospel, and he expressed to Timothy his concern that his young coworker would faithfully transmit the gospel after the old warrior's death. The letter urges Timothy to be faithful in the face of hardships, desertions, and error.

Characteristics. Although Paul is terse and to the point, he is also tender, warm, and affectionate. Second Timothy reveals Paul's emo-

tions more than his intellect, because his heart was speaking. Consequently, the letter is not an orderly, well-planned literary production, but a personal note containing the apostle's last will and testament.

Personal Application. This epistle is a handbook for young ministers of the gospel. The church needs more Timothys who are determined to guard the gospel as a sacred deposit committed to them, who are faithful to proclaim it, who are ready to suffer for it, and who will pass it on to faithful followers.

Surveying
2 TIMOTHY

I. INTRODUCTION 1:1–5. This is Paul's final letter as he awaits execution in Rome. Rearrested, Paul has been betrayed by "traitors" (3:4) in Asia who "resist the truth" (3:8). Paul displays a tenderness toward Timothy, a faithfulness in his witness for Christ, an ominous warning to those who recant their faith, and a heavenly perspective on the course of Timothy's life.

A. Salutation (1:1–2). "The promise of life" is a particularly poignant phrase, as Paul knows that he will not escape execution in Rome this time.

B. Thanksgiving (1:3–5). In the discomfort of prison and the disappointment of betrayal, Paul's prayers are for Timothy. There is no self-pity here.

II. FIDELITY IN THE FACE OF HARDSHIP 1:6–14. The temptation toward fear or compromise can only be addressed by an exercise of faith and by reminding ourselves of the gifts of God (v. 6) and of the Spirit of God (v. 7), which belong to the people of faith at these times.

A. Because of the nature of Christian experience (1:6–8). Because of Timothy's godly heritage, and his having a supernatural measure of God's blessing, he is able to stand in the face of withering assault and the sufferings experienced by the beloved apostle.

> **"Stir up the gift of God which is in you through the laying on of my hands"** (1:6). Timothy can either use the gifts of

God present in his life or allow them to remain useless. Spiritual ministry demands the use of spiritual gifts, and Timothy is encouraged to move beyond the realm of the convenient, familiar, and earthly as he performs his ministry. (*See* Mind.)

B. Because of the greatness of the gospel (1:9–11). This gospel transcends the temporary trials and defeats in life. The abolition of death and immortality are ours in Christ.

C. Because of the example of Paul (1:12–14). Paul is prepared for eternity and confident that the message he has invested his life in guarantees his future. Paul's counsel; "Hold fast . . . keep by the Holy Spirit who dwells in us" (vv. 13–14).

III. FIDELITY IN THE FACE OF DESERTIONS 1:15—2:13. Paul describes "traitors" (3:4), "evil men and impostors" (3:13) who have "turned away" (1:15), "forsaken me" (4:9, 16), "did me much harm" (4:14). The obvious torment of those who once were part of the fruit of Paul's ministry is a bitter disappointment. Yet, Paul manifests a true pastor's heart toward them in his desire for their repentance and deliverance from the work of the devil (2:25–26).

A. The example of Onesiphorus (1:15–18). The ministry of this man has lightened the burden of Paul's chains. (*See* Mercy.)

B. The character of Timothy's work (2:1–7). A soldier in battle, an athlete in competition, a farmer during harvest—each demands dedication to the final goal. Timothy, as a faithful pastor, is to discipline himself and to pay the price for the final reward.

> **"Commit these to faithful men"** (2:2). The future of the church

depends on the discipleship of young leaders to a place of ministry in their generation. The Great Commission of Matthew 28:19–20 was to "make disciples." Here Paul offers insight into the process: Teach men to teach others. The training of people with character, passion for Jesus Christ, and an ability to transmit their faith and lifestyle to others in the power of the Holy Spirit is a must for the expansion of the church in the world.

C. The redemptive work of Christ (2:8–13). The Lord is faithful to us, even though we may not be faithful to Him. He promises that we shall "reign" (v. 12) if we will endure the current suffering.

> **"Jesus Christ, of the seed of David, was raised from the dead according to my gospel"**
> (2:8). The Good News that Paul proclaims is the news that has changed his own life. It must become the gospel of every believer—our testimony must be of what God has done in us. This is no strange doctrine, but the personal commitment and ownership of the Good News that Paul shares with the world.

IV. FIDELITY IN THE FACE OF ERROR 2:14—4:18. Timothy must make himself well versed in the Word of God (2:15). Paul declares that Scripture is "given by inspiration of God"—literally, God-breathed (3:16). Therefore the authority to teach and lead God's people is directly related to the declaration of truth.

A. Doctrinal error (2:14–26). Doctrinal error is never simply mental; it always leads to dramatic compromise in lifestyle—increased ungodliness (v. 16) that leads believers into

the "snare of the devil" (v. 26). (*See* Lusts; Stewardship; Word of God.)

B. Practical error (3:1—4:8). Paul is concerned for the church's preparedness to resist error. The "*perilous times" of 3:1 are linked to the willful, deliberate, and cunning attempts of some to lead the people of God astray (3:7, 13; *see* Word of God).

V. CONCLUSION 4:9–22. This final farewell exhorts Timothy to come soon (v. 21). Paul offers greetings to the faithful and information on those who have injured him in their defection.

> **"The crown of righteousness"**
> (4:8). The righteous have nothing to fear on the day of Christ's return. The reward for our service and faithfulness to our mission in Christ will come from Jesus, our Judge. Our salvation is free. However, for enduring temptation, there is the crown of life (James 1:12); for those who shepherd the people of God faithfully, there is a crown of glory (1 Pet. 5:14); and for our hard work for Christ, there is a reward in heaven (1 Cor. 3:14).

A. Instruction (4:9–13). Paul needs a coat, some books and papers, and Mark, who is to accompany Timothy. Note the change in Paul's attitude toward the young man who had previously frustrated him (Acts 15:37–39).

B. Warning (4:14–15). Alexander is still capable of doing more damage to the church in Ephesus.

C. Explanation (4:16–18). Paul describes the faithfulness of God which has "delivered [him] out of the mouth of the lion."

D. Greetings (4:19–21). The love of the pastor for his flock.

E. Benediction (4:22). Paul's final affirmation that we are never alone. (*See* Christ.)

TRUTH-IN-ACTION through 2 TIMOTHY

Truth 2 Timothy Teaches	**Action** 2 Timothy Invites
1 Guidelines for Growing in Godliness Being like God is living like He has told us to live; this involves studying and applying the Scriptures. Those who do so will become living reproof to those who do not and thus will often encounter persecution.	**1:3** *Strictly maintain* a clear conscience before God and man. **2:15** *Devote yourself to* responsible Bible study. *Become* a sensible interpreter of Scripture. **3:12** *Recognize* that godly living always encounters persecution. *Expect* this because a godly life testifies against godlessness in others.
2 Key Lessons in Faith Faith believes absolutely in the divine inspiration of the Scriptures. Therefore, the man of faith has a very high view of the Bible, and is able courageously to face opposition unmoved.	**3:16** *Revere* God's Word very highly. *Recognize* its fully divine source of inspiration. *Submit* to it absolutely. **4:5** *Do not be frustrated* by opposition. *Continue* to stand strong. *Be tirelessly faithful* in those things God has commissioned you to do.
3 Guidelines for Growth in the Spirit Spiritual growth is learning to depend upon the Holy Spirit's life in you through His indwelling presence and the spiritual gifts He has given you.	**1:6** *Faithfully exercise* charismatic gifts that have been imparted to you. *Discipline yourself* continually to employ them in boldness and in love. **2:1** *Be strong* in grace; *draw deeply* on God's enabling power and energy to accomplish His purpose through you. **2:22** *Strictly avoid* any fleshly indulgence, and *do not succumb to* fleshly desires. *Devote yourself* to Spirit-filled living, bearing the fruit of the Spirit.
4 Keys to Wise Living One with spiritual wisdom possesses spiritual perception and a wise value system. He realizes that any theological quarreling is unproductive and refuses to be drawn into it. Rather, he learns gently to persuade others to godliness, not being easily deceived by feigned godly behavior. He also recognizes the human tendency to avoid the demands of truth and to listen, rather, to what they want to hear.	**2:14** *Be warned* that theological quarreling is ruinous and almost never helpful. **2:24–26** *Avoid* being drawn into arguments or quarrels. *Learn* how to persuade others to believe and practice truth, but *do so* gently and kindly. **3:5** *Do not be deceived* by jargon or religiosity. *Look for* true spiritual power and godliness in others.
5 Getting Motivated for Ministry Ministry is service, and a "minister" of the gospel is primarily a servant of God's Word, boldly and courageously sharing its message. He treasures the Word of God and defends it tirelessly, being careful to communicate its truth with absolute accuracy. This is no easy task because the Word of God faces violent opposition. Thus the "minister" of God's Word learns that patience, endurance. and hard work are necessary for success in his calling.	**1:8** *Preach the gospel* boldly, without fear! **1:13, 14** *Recognize* that the Word of God is a treasure of inestimable value. *Guard* it diligently. *Hold firmly* to the truth you have received. *Do not let* the Enemy *corrupt* it. **2:2** *Communicate* truth exactly and accurately. *Train* others to do the same. *Make sure* that none of it is ever distorted, diluted, or deleted. **2:3–7** *Learn from* the "ministry" examples of 1) the soldier enduring hardship, 2) the athlete in strict training, and 3) the hardworking, patient farmer, what ministry really means. **4:2** *Become* a committed servant of God's Word. *Be prepared* at any time, whether convenient or inconvenient, *to proclaim* it and to *patiently instruct* those who do not understand or accept it.

KEYS TO TITUS AND PHILEMON
The Kingdom and Personal Relationships

Kingdom Key: God's Purpose in View

Just as the letters to Timothy point toward the practical priorities of faith, rather than to philosophical debate over theology, Titus and Philemon characterize the practical path of healthy relationships. Both letters show qualities of personal relationships in the kingdom that stand in contrast to the world. They reveal how Jesus Christ has brought God's grace not only to redeem us but to restore a quality of life between people—"His own special people" (Titus 2:14).

Titus: Pastoral Care for Kingdom Citizens

- Note the warm intimacy of new-found relationship in Paul's description of Titus, whom he calls "a true son" (1:4). Today, as then, broken people need access to a redemptive power that not only restores them to God, but also redeems broken relationships.

- The phrases "husband of one wife" (1:6) and "women to love their husbands" (2:4) indicate the New Testament church's view of marriage. God's intent to restore humankind to His creative purpose is seen in this call to a monogamous married

> **Vital faith relates with love, generosity, and winsomeness.**

relationship filled with mutual affection and devotion.

- Here is a typical New Testament call to every follower of Christ. Each believer is to live with a practical sense of duty regarding relationships within their vocational endeavors. Each age group is called to display on the job a spirit which will "adorn the doctrine of God our Savior in all things" (Titus 2:6-10). This call is made all the more demanding by its implications upon every person—especially those in a free society—in that even believing slaves are called to a submitted spirit of godly

(Please turn to page 421.)

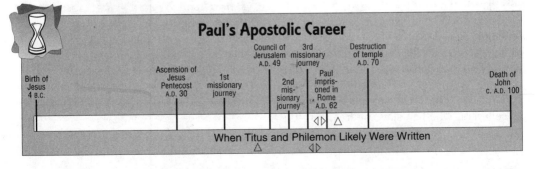

Paul's Apostolic Career

Birth of Jesus 4 B.C. — Ascension of Jesus Pentecost A.D. 30 — 1st missionary journey — Council of Jerusalem A.D. 49 — 2nd missionary journey — 3rd missionary journey — Paul imprisoned in Rome A.D. 62 — Destruction of temple A.D. 70 — Death of John c. A.D. 100

When Titus and Philemon Likely Were Written

Titus and Philemon characterize practical, • • •

Master Key: God's Son Revealed
Titus

Underlying the instructions of Paul to Titus is the theme that Christ is building His church, carefully choosing the stones that make up this habitation for God. Paul also emphasizes Christ as our Redeemer (2:14; 3:4–7) and presents His Second Coming as an incentive to holy living (2:12–13).

Philemon

The epistle to Philemon powerfully applies the message of the gospel. Once an estranged slave, Onesimus is now "a beloved brother" in Christ as well (v. 16). Philemon is challenged to show to Onesimus the same unconditional pardon that he received through the grace and love of Jesus. Paul's offer to pay a debt that was not his, on behalf of a repentant slave, is a clear picture of the spirit of Calvary. Paul's intercession is also analogous to Christ's ongoing intercession with the Father on our behalf.

Power Key: God's Spirit at Work
Titus

The ministry of the Holy Spirit is understood throughout the entire epistle to Titus. The people of Crete cannot change themselves (1:12–13), and regeneration can only be the work of the Holy Spirit (3:5). The one who experiences a new birth receives the Holy Spirit in order to maintain a victorious lifestyle patterned after that of Christ (3:6–8).

Philemon

While not specifically mentioned in Philemon, the Holy Spirit was definitely active in Paul's ministry and in the life of the church. It is the Holy Spirit who baptizes all believers, whether slave or free, into the

(Please turn to page 421.)

Key Word: *Conduct Manual for Church Living*

This brief letter focuses on Titus's role and responsibility in the organization and supervision of the churches in Crete. It is written to strengthen and exhort Titus to firmly exercise his authority as an apostolic representative to churches that need to be put in order.

Key Verses: Titus 1:5; 3:8

Key Chapter: Titus 2

Summarized in Titus 2 are the key commands to be obeyed which insure godly relationships within the church.

Key Word: *Forgiveness from Slavery*

Philemon develops the transition from bondage to brotherhood that is brought about by Christian love and forgiveness. Just as Philemon was shown mercy through the grace of Christ, so he must graciously forgive his repentant runaway who has returned as a brother in Christ.

Key Verses: Philemon 16, 17

• • • **healthy relationships among the faithful.**

Introducing
TITUS

Background. It is strange that a person whose name is listed among the books of the New Testament is so little known. Even though Titus was a companion and valuable coworker of Paul, there is no mention of him in the Acts of the Apostles.

Titus was a Greek and evidently a convert of Paul. The fact that Titus was not circumcised (Gal. 2:3) indicates that he had not been raised in Judaism or become a proselyte. Paul highly esteemed Titus, and the apostle was restless when there was little or no news of the young man's whereabouts and activities.

Occasion and Date. Although the New Testament does not record a ministry of Paul in Crete, such passages as Titus 1:5 clearly indicate that he and Titus had conducted a mission there. This campaign probably took place sometime during A.D. 63–64, after Paul's release from his first imprisonment in Rome. Since his time was short, Paul left Titus on Crete to care for the new churches. Then the apostle departed to other fields of labor. Somewhere enroute to Nicopolis of Greece (3:12), he wrote to Titus. The letter gives evidence of having been written during the fall of the year, probably around A.D. 64 (see 3:12).

Purpose. Paul gave to Titus, a relatively young preacher of the gospel, the difficult assignment of directing the work in Crete. Later he wrote this letter to give Titus more detailed instructions concerning the performance of his pastoral duties.

Content. The letter to Titus has an affinity with 1 Timothy. Both epistles are addressed to young men who had been assigned positions of responsible leadership in their respective churches during Paul's absence. Both epistles are occupied with the qualifications of those who are to lead and teach the churches. The worldly corruptions that face the new churches are the same.

Titus has three great themes—church organization, sound doctrine, and holy living. Titus was to ordain elders in every city where the nucleus of a congregation existed. They must be men of high moral character, and must be adamant on questions of principle, maintaining the true apostolic doctrine and able to refute objectors.

Personal Application. Difficulties in the church are compounded when there are problems with the leadership. The letter to Titus teaches that the supreme aim of church government is the preservation of revealed truth and the safeguarding of ethical standards. Therefore, church leaders must be exemplary in lifestyle and sound in doctrine. This letter also stresses the close connection between sound doctrine and morals. Truth is always intended to determine life and to promote godliness.

Kingdom Key *continued from page 419*

behavior in serving their tasks.
- Perhaps the most explicit and demanding call is that believers remember the "relational" responsibilities they have toward those who are in government. A right attitude is mandated first (3:1). Then an extended passage (3:2–8) calls the believer above petty or judgmental criticism of rulers, however evil they may be. This appeal is made in the light of remembering that "we ourselves were once also foolish, disobedient," and so forth (3:3).

Philemon: Relationships within the Kingdom

The letter to Philemon provides us with one of the most touching and instructive insights in the New Testament. Here is an appeal to a person who has been sorely violated by another, and who now is called not only to forgive that person but also to suffer financial loss in doing so. Paul's personal relational style shines here: he neither manipulates Philemon nor mandates anything of him. He relates so magnificently in the Spirit of Christ that Philemon is coaxed toward the finest action—loving action decided on his own rather than commanded by another (v. 9–14).

Life for the growing kingdom-person calls for the love of God to shine in all human relationships, showing how salvation and true spirituality are neither privatistic nor merely religious. True believing life is generous, loving, patient, understanding, and winsome in every dimension.

Power Key *continued from page 420*

body of Christ (1 Cor. 12:13). Paul applies this truth to the lives of Philemon and Onesimus. Love, a fruit of the Spirit, is evident throughout the letter.

Surveying
TITUS

I. INTRODUCTION 1:1–5. Paul writes to encourage the development of a church in Crete that is challenged at the point of faith and character.

A. Statement of Paul's office, hope, and functions (1:1–3). Paul affirms his apostolic authority in his selfless service (v. 1), and in the miracles which accompany his preaching (v. 3).

B. Salutation (1:4). Titus is experiencing great dissention in the church where Paul left him during his fourth missionary journey.

C. Charge to Titus (1:5). Although a young man, Titus is encouraged to exercise the God-given authority entrusted to him for "setting things in order" and for appointing church leadership approved in faith and lifestyle. He is to do this "with all authority" (2:15), without regard for his age or the potential resistance before him.

II. INSTRUCTIONS CONCERNING ELDERS 1:6–16. The characteristics of godly leaders are outlined here on the basis of sound faith, healthy family life, and established productive living skills. Church leaders must integrate spirituality with lifestyle and interpersonal relationships.

A. Their qualifications (1:6–9). In the midst of a culture of confusion, church leaders must have one wife and children who reflect in their behavior the order that Jesus brings to families alive and growing in Him. Leaders also must reflect the temperance and self-control that demonstrate the lordship of Christ in their lives.

B. The need for proper administration (1:10–16). Paul's emphasis on truth and sound doctrine directly addresses the "deceivers" (v. 10; see Idle Talk), "liars" (v. 12), "men who turn from the truth" (v. 14), and those who "deny Him" (v. 16). The authentication of a life transformed by God can only be measured in obedience to His Word.

III. INSTRUCTIONS CONCERNING CHRISTIAN CONDUCT 2:1—3:7. Titus is to teach the people of Crete how to live for God. The priorities are clearly stated to "older men," "older women," "young women," "husbands," "young men," "bondservants," and "masters" about the way they talk and how they treat each other. The integrity with which they live points toward the reality that "we should

become heirs according to the hope of eternal life" (3:7).

A. Among themselves (2:1–15). Paul clearly outlines the purpose of Titus's teachings to the church: "Denying ungodliness and worldly lusts, we should live *soberly" (v. 12) as we await the "blessed hope" (v. 13) of the return of Christ.

> **"The blessed hope"**
> (2:13) The people of God are to be excited about Christ's return. The prophecies of trauma on the earth and the increasingly godless society before Jesus returns can bring an awful sense of foreboding. However, before Jesus returns the world will be fully evangelized with the greatest revival in history (Rev. 7:9) and the presence of grace abounding on the earth (Rom. 5:20–21). Our "blessed hope" will appear when the hour is darkest and the work of the church most fruitful. Praise God, He is coming for a church fully equipped, fully engaged, fully prepared for Him!

B. Toward the outside world (3:1–7). Our conduct outside the church must reflect the "washing of regeneration and *renewing of the Holy Spirit" (v. 5). Paul is not suggesting that lifestyle changes and healthy relationships are a product of human effort. New birth in Christ throws open the door to a new way of living as the Holy Spirit transforms the believer.

IV. CONCLUDING INSTRUCTIONS 3:8–11. Paul's directives overflow with practicality and loving-kindness. "Maintain good works" (v. 8), things that are a blessing to others. And "Reject a divisive man" (v. 10). Here the voice of experience shouts wise counsel for all generations.

A. To teach spiritual truths (3:8–11). Some things build people and relationships; others demean and destroy. Titus's charge is to "affirm constantly" (v. 8) these practical truths. Lives change slowly; patience and diligence are required in the teaching process.

B. To avoid dissension (3:9–11). There is no place in the church for people who strive constantly to divide the body. Paul pronounces them "warped and sinning, being self-condemned" (v. 11).

V. DIRECTIONS AND GREETINGS 3:12–15. Paul's parting words sound the continual theme of the epistle, for the people to grow in good works so that there will be much fruit in their lives.

TRUTH-IN-ACTION through TITUS

Truth Titus Teaches	**Action** Titus Invites
1 Guidelines for Growing in Godliness Depending on God's grace (godliness is impossible any other way), the godly person exemplifies self-control. Say "No!" to ungodly and worldly attitudes and behavior and say "Yes!" to righteous and godly living. This involves submissive obedience to governing authorities. A key part of godly living is an eager readiness to do good works! Godly speech is humble, peaceable, and never slanderous or argumentative.	**2:11-15** *Stand strongly* in grace. *Say "No!"* to ungodliness and worldliness. *Be self-controlled* in your practice of godly behavior. *Be eager* to do what is good! **3:1** *Be subject* and *obedient* to authority—civil, family, church, and employers. **3:2** *Never slander* anyone. *Humbly be at peace* with all men and be considerate of them. **3:8** *Devote yourself* to doing good works! **3:9-11** *Warn* those who are divisive and shun them if they do not heed a second warning.
2 Lessons for Leaders Christian leaders are not called to lead alone. Rather they are to involve other faithful, qualified persons to help them oversee the people of God. The primary role of the Christian leader is teaching. He is to instruct others in godly living, regardless of his station in life. Also, he is to guard God's church from false teachers and deceivers who take advantage of the people of God. The godly leader's teaching is to be first through the life that he lives: people should be able to look at the Christian leader and say, "That is how I am supposed to live." Also. he needs to be an able communicator of truth.	**1:5-9** Leaders, *appoint* qualified elders (overseers) to share ministry with you. *Make sure* they practice truth and are able to communicate it effectively. **1:10-16** Leaders, *silence* the rebellious! *Identify* and *rebuke sharply* those whose lives are only talk and who seek to deceive others. *Aggressively prevent* the ruination of homes and churches by disallowing such to teach false doctrine. **2:1-10** Leaders, *take an active role* in teaching others how to live self-controlled, exemplary, and fruitful lives. **2:7, 8** Leaders, *teach* both by precept and example. *Exemplify* excellent character and self-control. *Do not allow* your words to provide an occasion for accusation. **2:9, 10** Leaders, *teach* your people to be excellent employees, not stealing, not rebelling against their employer's author-ity—always being loyal and never injuring their employer's reputation.

Introducing

PHILEMON

Background. Philemon is Paul's personal appeal to a wealthy Christian slaveowner. It appears that Philemon had been converted under Paul's ministry (v. 19), that he resided in Colosse, and that the Colossian church met in his house (v. 2). Onesimus, one of his slaves, had fled to Rome, apparently after damaging or stealing his master's property (vv. 11, 18). In Rome, Onesimus came in contact with the imprisoned Paul, who led him to Christ (v. 10).

Paul eventually wrote to the church in Colosse and evidently included this letter on Onesimus's behalf. Tychicus and Onesimus apparently delivered both letters. (See Col. 4:7-9; Philem. 12.) The close relationship between Paul and Philemon is evidenced by their mutual prayers (vv. 4, 22) and an "open door" hospitality (v. 22). Love, trust, and respect characterized their friendship (vv. 1, 14, 21).

Slavery was an accepted economic and social reality in the Roman world. A slave was his master's property, without rights. Under Roman law, runaway slaves could be severely punished and even condemned to death. Slave uprisings in the first century resulted in fearful and suspicious owners. While the early Christian church did not directly attack the institution of slavery, it reordered the relationship between master and slave. Both were equal before God (Gal. 3:28), and both were accountable for their behavior (Eph. 6:5-9).

Occasion and Date. Paul wrote Philemon during his first Roman imprisonment about A.D. 61. He desired a genuine Christian reconciliation between a wronged slaveowner and a forgiven slave. Paul tactfully, yet urgently, interceded for Onesimus and expressed complete confidence that Philemon's faith and love would result in restoration (vv. 5, 21).

Purpose. Paul's primary goal in writing Philemon was to see his friend freely embrace the fugitive Onesimus as a brother in Christ. He also expressed joy in Philemon's ministry and encouraged him to continue (vv. 4–7). The apostle made clear his desire for Onesimus to stay with him, but insisted on reconciliation first (vv. 13–14).

Content. While the shortest of Paul's epistles, Philemon is a deep revelation of Christ at work in the lives of Paul and those around him. The tone is one of warm, personal friendship rather than apostolic authority. It reveals how Paul politely yet firmly addressed a central issue of the Christian life, namely love through forgiveness, in a very sensitive situation. It presents Paul's persuasion in action.

The epistle is a hallmark expression of true Christian relationships. After personally greeting Philemon and his fellow believers, Paul expresses thanksgiving for their love and faith toward Christ and their fellow believers.

Brotherly love often requires practical grace and mercy, and Paul soon comes to this point. He explains the conversion of Onesimus and the slave's new value in the ministry and family of Jesus Christ (vv. 12–16). This transformation, along with Paul's deep friendship with both men, is the basis for a new beginning.

This is no shallow appeal by Paul, for he writes a "blank check" on behalf of Onesimus for any outstanding debts (vv. 17–19). He brings the petition to a close knowing that Philemon's love and character will prevail. As he concludes, one can sense the unity of the Spirit among all the saints involved.

Personal Application. Philemon presents the incredible power of Christ to bring healing to broken lives. It includes the personal reunion between Jesus Christ and the runaway sinner, as well as the wonderful restoration of two believers who were formerly separated. Only with Christ's example of forgiveness through the Cross are we able to overcome our hurts and mistakes and be reconciled to our brothers and sisters in Christ.

Surveying
PHILEMON

I. SALUTATION VV. 1–3. Philemon was converted to Christ by Paul, and here Paul affirms their relationship with respect and affection.

II. THANKSGIVING CONCERNING PHILEMON VV. 4–7. Philemon has demonstrated the characteristics of an effective leader. His reputation delights Paul.

A. Personal praise (v. 4). Paul's devotion as a servant and shepherd can only be lived out in prayer while he is imprisoned.

B. Praiseworthy characteristics (vv. 5–7). Philemon's ministry in Colosse embraces the saints with genuine love and refreshes the weary.

III. PAUL'S PETITION FOR ONESIMUS VV. 8–21. The problem with Onesimus, Philemon's slave, is the reason for Paul's letter. Paul appeals to his friend for consideration. Onesimus's stealing should be considered in the light of his conversion. Onesimus is now more than a servant; he is a brother in Christ.

"More than a slave—a beloved brother"

(16). The New Testament simply acknowledges the presence of slavery in the culture of the first century. Whenever mentioned, slave masters are commanded to treat slaves with dignity, for God is the ultimate Master of all, slave and free (Eph. 6:9). The new relationship between those who have come to know Christ is to supersede every other human relationship (Gal. 3:28). The gospel of Jesus Christ has done more to bring equality and liberty to all people in all cultures than has any other social force in human history.

A. A plea for acceptance (vv. 8–16). Paul's plea is unrelated to the obvious justice of the situation. Onesimus was wrong, and by the legal principle of the day he should be punished. However, Paul is suggesting that the events of the past may have occurred "for this purpose" (v. 15), that Philemon's slave might return to him as a brother (*see* Receive).

B. A pledge to repay (vv. 17–19). Paul accepts any responsibility for restitution that Philemon might insist upon. However, the apostle reminds Philemon that he owes a debt to Paul.

C. A confidence in obedience (vv. 20–21). Paul trusts the depth of Philemon's maturity in Christ. The slave will be restored, and the kingdom of God will profit.

IV. PERSONAL CONCERNS VV. 22–25. Paul looks forward to returning to Colosse. In the meantime, he is sending this letter with Tychicus and Onesimus as well as letters for the churches in Colosse and Laodicea (Col. 4:16).

A. Hope for release (v. 22). Paul prays for his release from prison to continue his apostolic work.

B. Greetings (vv. 23–24). Paul shares greetings from others who work with him.

C. Benediction (v. 25). Paul encourages the building of their spirit in God's grace.

TRUTH-IN-ACTION through PHILEMON

Truth Philemon Teaches	**Action** Philemon Invites
◨ Guidelines for Growing in Godliness Sharing Jesus with others gives us a deeper insight into our inheritance in Christ. The godly person is immediately available for restored relationships. Sharing your home, food, and possessions with strangers is a greater blessing to you who show hospitality than it is to the one who receives it.	**v. 6** *Understand* that by sharing your faith in Jesus, you gain a fuller understanding of your inheritance in Christ. **vv. 8–16** *Practice instant forgiveness* of those who have offended you. *Make room* for the restoration of broken relationships. **v. 22** *Practice hospitality.* Provide lodging for traveling servants of God.

How Love Works
(Philemon)

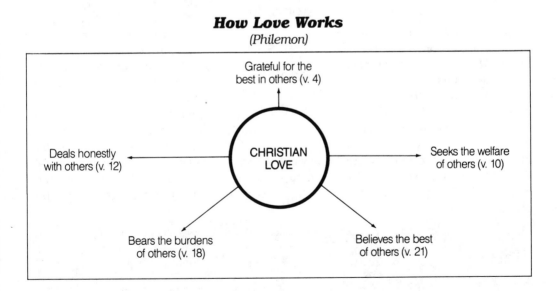

KEYS TO HEBREWS
The Kingdom and Human Destiny

Kingdom Key: God's Purpose in View

The book of Hebrews expands on the theme of Christ's majesty as the superior, ultimate, and complete instrument of human redemption. An especially difficult theme in the book is the magnification of God's intention for human destiny and Christ's achievement of its realization.

The difficulty is not because the presentation is unclear, but because too often people take on a piety that hesitates to make as much of man as God has. God has a "high" destiny for man. Religious pretensions presume that a "lowness" is necessary to humilty. Some teachers seem to avoid spelling out God's revealed intent for human beings, lest the grandeur of the truth would elevate man too highly and risk tempting the redeemed believer to pride. On the contrary, a clear view of the incredible love and purpose of God for His redeemed ones should only produce a deeper humility, for the grander the dimensions of grace, the greater the worship of those who grasp even a part of the wonder.

God's will for human destiny is captured in chapter 2. After introducing the concept of "so great a salvation," the writer proceeds to "the world to come" (v. 5). This phrase refers to the ulti-

....

Christ's blood and Cross— our only source of redemption.

....

mate kingdom—*the world as it will be*—and it describes the high place intended for redeemed humans in that new order (2:8). The "son of man" (here refering to human beings as the objects of Christ's salvation), though frail and temporarily of an order lower than angels (2:6–7), is destined for grander things (2:7). Indeed, we were created for this, and though fallen, are being redeemed to be placed over "all things" (2:7–8). In these phrases, the issue of human destiny is simply and directly declared. Only one problem obstructs God's will for us: our fallenness.

With this problem in view, the writer develops a theme throughout the epistle: Christ is the superior and ultimate way to human redemption and restoration. Man isn't "there" yet, but Christ is bringing us toward God's goal. Paraphrasing verses 8–9, we may read: "Even though all things have been put

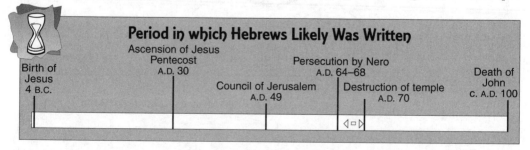

Period in which Hebrews Likely Was Written

| Birth of Jesus 4 B.C. | Ascension of Jesus Pentecost A.D. 30 | Council of Jerusalem A.D. 49 | Persecution by Nero A.D. 64–68 | Destruction of temple A.D. 70 | Death of John c. A.D. 100 |

Hebrews: Christ is God's only—and therefore superior

under humankind, we don't see that occurring as yet. But there is one thing we do see: *We see JESUS!*"

The message is clear: Jesus the Savior, who became man to save mankind, has risen to the place of dominion intended for humans. As a human, His sinless life and sacrificial death have done more than bridge the chasm between God and man. Jesus has also (1) broken the power of death to block God's high purpose for humankind (2:14–15) and (2) paved the way to "bring many sons to glory"—that is, to fulfill the glorious original intention of God for mankind!

Hebrews discloses the magnificent way in which Jesus fulfilled in His priestly ministry and sacrificial work to make the full payment for human redemption. That redemption involves both *reconciliation* with God, through the perfect blood atonement for our sins, and *restoration* unto God's purpose, through Christ's bringing us to the Mount of God as participants in "a kingdom that cannot be shaken" (12:22–28).

The kingdom key to Hebrews is its disclosure of human destiny. But the most moving message in this book is its revelation of how this "key" turns: Through the blood of the everlasting covenant, God is committed to work in you "what is well pleasing in His sight, through Jesus Christ, to whom be glory forever and ever. Amen" (13:20–21).

Master Key: God's Son Revealed

To speak of Christ in Hebrews is to describe the entire book. In striving to keep his readers from apostasy, the writer emphasizes the superiority of Christ to all that has gone before in Old Testament times. Like no other book in the Bible, Hebrews points out the importance and the ministry of the preincarnate Christ.

Key Word: *The Superiority of Christ*

*T*he basic theme of Hebrews is found in the word better, *describing the superiority of Christ in His person and work (1:4; 6:9; 7:7, 19, 22; 8:6; 9:23; 10:34; 11:16, 35, 40; 12:24). The words* perfect *and* heavenly *are also prominent. He offers a better revelation, position, priesthood, covenant, sacrifice, and power.*

Key Verses: Hebrews 4:14–16; 12:1–2

Key Chapter: Hebrews 11

*T*he hall of fame of the Scriptures is *located in Hebrews 11 and records those who willingly took God at His word even when there was nothing to cling to but His promise.*

Power Key: God's Spirit at Work

The ministry of the Holy Spirit is seen in a variety of ways, applying to both the Old and New Testament periods: gifts of the Holy Spirit for ministry (2:4); witness to the inspiration of the Old Testament (3:7; 10:15); descriptive of the experience of believers (6:4); interpreting spiritual truth (9:8); assisting in the ministry of Jesus (9:14); insulted by apostasy (10:29).

and ultimate—instrument of eternal salvation.

Introducing

HEBREWS

Author. Hebrews does not name its author, and there is no unanimity of tradition concerning his identity. Some scholars point out certain internal evidences that may indicate a Pauline authorship, while others suggest that one of Paul's associates, such as Barnabas or Apollos, may have written the book. Speculation has proved fruitless, and the best conclusion may be that of Origen in the third century, who stated that only God knows for certain who wrote Hebrews.

Date and Location. The content of Hebrews indicates that it was written before the destruction of the temple in A.D. 70 (10:11; 13:11). The only evidence concerning the site of the book's writing is the greeting sent by "those from Italy" (13:24), perhaps indicating that the author was either in Rome or was writing to Christians in Rome.

Background and Purpose. The majority of early Christians were Jewish. Apparently they expected Christ to return soon, but the delay in His coming and the persecutions against them (10:32–34) caused them to wonder if they had made the right choice in becoming Christians. Consequently, they were in danger of returning to Judaism.

This epistle was written to wavering Jewish believers, encouraging them to stand fast in their faith. The writer points out the overwhelming superiority of Christ over all that they had experienced under the Law. Because what is offered to them through Christ is so much better, they should never consider turning back. The author dwells on the incomparable glory of the Person and work of Christ, showing His supremacy over prophets (1:1–3), angels (1:4—2:18), Moses (3:1–19), Joshua (4:1–13), Aaron (4:14—7:18), and the whole ritual of Judaism (7:19—10:39).

Content. A key word of the epistle is "better," used to describe Christ and the benefits of the gospel (1:4; 7:19, 22; 8:6; 9:23; 10:34; 11:16, 35, 40).

Most of the blessings of Judaism had to do with earthly things: an earthly tabernacle or temple, earthly priests, earthly sacrifices, a covenant that promised earthly prosperity. In contrast, Christ is "at the right hand of the Majesty on high" (l:3), where He dispenses heavenly blessings (3:1; 6:4; 8:5; 11:16; 12:22–23).

The high point of the epistle is the presentation of the high priestly ministry of the Lord. Christ is High Priest after the order of Melchizedek, who had no predecessors and no successors in the priesthood. Thus, Melchizedek was a perfect type of Christ, who received the office of high priest by the direct call of God, not by inheritance (5:5–6). Whereas the Aaronic priest had to offer sacrifices continually for his own sins as well as for the sins of the people, Christ once and for all offered Himself as the perfect sacrifice. In His flesh He experienced the testing that all believers know, and thus He is able to intercede compassionately on their behalf.

Chapter 11 lists some of the great heroes of faith of the Old Testament. Verses 4–35 record marvelous blessings and outstanding victories achieved through faith, while verses 36–38 record those who through faith endured great trial, suffering, and persecution. Significantly, there is no mention of the sins and shortcomings of those listed. The obvious reason is that the blood of Jesus Christ had blotted out the sins and failures, so that their iniquities are remembered against them no more.

Personal Application. Although Hebrews is specifically addressed to Jewish Christians, its teachings and practical admonitions are equally applicable to Gentile believers. In Christ there is no distinction between Jew and Gentile (Col. 3:11). The church today needs the teaching provided in the Old Testament laws of worship, which this book so beautifully relates to Christ and the gospel of eternal salvation. Christianity is not something added on to Judaism. It is something new, but a fuller understanding of the Old Covenant gives a richer and more marvelous appreciation of the New Covenant of God's grace through our Lord Jesus Christ.

While the epistle is primarily doctrinal in its content, it is also intensely practical. After each doctrinal passage the writer inserts a section in which he gives some very pointed and powerful admonitions based on the teachings presented. At least fifteen times he uses the expression "let" or "let us" (4:1, 11, 14, 16; 6:1; 10:22–24; 12:1–2, 28; 13:1, 5, 13, 15, 17).

Surveying
HEBREWS

I. THE SUPERIORITY OF CHRIST JESUS' PERSON 1:1—4:13.

The Jewish Christians to whom this book is written knew that God had spoken to their fathers through Moses and the prophets. The Old Testament was unquestionably the Word of God. Thus, the writer begins his closely reasoned appeal for full commitment to Christianity by pointing out that Jesus is the ultimate expression of God's Word, for He is Himself God.

A. Jesus better than the prophets (1:1-3).
The Old Testament revelation came in a progressive and fragmentary way (v. 1). But now a final, authoritative message has been given, which draws the whole of God's purposes together, and has in fact been spoken to us by the Son of God.

B. Jesus better than the angels (1:4—2:18).
A series of quotes from the Old Testament now demonstrate that it too recognizes the superiority of the Son to the supernatural messengers (*see* Angels; Ministers) the Jews so deeply respected.

First warning: against neglect (2:1-4). There are four warning sections in the Book of Hebrews. This first warning focuses on the importance of heeding the salvation message brought by Jesus. The first verse contains two nautical terms, and means, "We must eagerly anchor ourselves to the truths we've been taught, or we are likely to drift away from our moorings" (*see* 2:1). Turning back to Judaism means abandoning a great salvation which can be found only in Jesus.

The "world to come" in rabbinic thought is the age when Messiah will rule from David's throne. The writer points out that God intends to subject that world to men, not angels.

The suffering of Jesus was always hard for the Jews to accept. Now the writer argues that His suffering was appropriate. Thus Jesus chose to share fully in our human condition. The implications here are stunning. Jesus stooped to share all that we are, identifying Himself fully with us, so that He might then lift us up to share all that He is!

Finally, the writer points out that, through sharing in our humanity and dying as a human being, Jesus destroyed the hold of Satan over mankind. The fear of death and the one who wielded it no longer holds us enslaved, for Jesus has nullified Satan's power (14–16; *see* Praise).

C. Jesus better than Moses (3:1-19).
Moses was honored above all men by the Jews. He was viewed by the rabbis as even greater than the angels, because of his role as giver of God's Law. Jesus is superior to Moses, just as the person who plans, designs, builds and pays for a house is greater than a butler who serves in it (4–5).

There is another reason for the comparison with Moses. The law code that bears Moses' name patterned all of life for the Jewish people. It should follow then, since Jesus has come with His superior message, that He will also introduce a superior way of life! The writer now develops this thought as he urges believers to listen for Jesus' living voice which speaks "today."

The writer cites an incident from Moses' time to demonstrate the urgency of responding to each fresh word from God. The children of Israel had been poised on the borders of the Promised Land when God called on them to enter, but they refused to listen. Rebelliously, they hardened their hearts. As a result they were unable to enter the land of rest but were turned away to wander and die in the wilderness (7–11). Today a fresh word from God has come through Jesus. Today, too, it is vital to guard against an unbelieving heart. A return to the lifestyle of Judaism would be a rebellion against God's contemporary voice. Such a return would place the present generation in a position of forfeiting God's promised rest (15–19; *see* Partakers).

D. Jesus better than Joshua (4:1-13).
Second warning: against unbelief (4:1-3, 11-13). This complicated passage is based on the repeated affirmation that God always speaks in the "today" of His people (1, 7–8).

"Rest" is used in three senses in Hebrews 3 and 4. First, it is used to describe life in the Promised Land, free of bondage. Second, the word is used in relation to God's rest, which He entered on completing creation. The third use of "rest" is an application of these first two to Christian experience. Our effort to "enter that rest" (v. 11) does not mean struggle against circumstances but instead constant attention to our hearts, lest we become like unresponsive Israel and refuse to listen to God's voice.

The writer now describes God's Word as alive and active today (4:12–13; *see* Powerful). God's voice moves deep within us, penetrating to our inmost thoughts and attitudes. God, who knows all, is present within to guide us daily by His living and active contemporary voice (*see* Faith's Confession).

II. THE SUPERIORITY OF CHRIST JESUS' MINISTRY 4:14—10:18.

A. Jesus better than Aaron (4:14—6:20).
1. Understanding and compassionate (4:14—5:4). Even though our high *priest is "Jesus

the Son of God" (4:14), He is able to "sympathize with our weaknesses." This is because Jesus has been put to the same tests we are, yet never sinned. This point is important. We never know the full power of the temptation unless we resist it. Jesus experienced the full impact of every temptation that can be known by humanity, but He never surrendered to them (4:15). We can be sure that He will extend us mercy when we fail and will provide help to meet our need when we require strength to overcome as He did.

Jesus' priestly ministry (5:1–10) is explained on the foundation of what these Jewish Christians already know about a high priest. He is chosen from the human family, to represent mankind to God (v. 1). He is to have a controlled sympathy for sinners, but he deals with sins by sacrifice rather than overlooking them (2–3). The honor of the high priesthood goes only to one selected by God, as was Aaron (4).

2. After the order of Melchizedek (5:5–10). Now the writer explains that Jesus has already functioned as a high priest. He offered up what was, to the rabbis, the most significant kind of prayers ("with tears"). And His resurrection proves that God heard Him (7)! The note that He "learned obedience" and was "made perfect" (8–9) speaks of Jesus' full personal experience of the cost of obedience when His suffering was involved. He was "made perfect" in the sense that He retained His integrity under every assault and thus fully established His qualifications for sympathetic priesthood. Then, as the culminating ministry of a high priest, He offered a sacrifice which made Him the "source of eternal salvation for all who obey him" (9–10).

Third warning: against lack of maturity (5:11—6:20). The writer first expresses frustration. These people, so knowledgeable about the Old Testament priesthood, seem unable to grasp the meaning of Christ's priesthood (5:11). The warning, then, is against continuing in immaturity.

"Leaving" the elementary teachings does not mean to abandon them, but to view them as a beginning. Christians are to build on elementary truths as a foundation, taking them as givens rather than constantly and doubtfully returning to them (6:1–3).

There are four interpretations of this difficult passage. One: the writer speaks of Jews who have stopped just short of faith in Christ. Two: he speaks of believers who have fallen into sin and will lose their reward. Three: he refers to believers whose unbelief means loss of salvation. Four: he gives a hypothetical

illustration, to show how foolish it is to think of a return to Judaism.

The writer turns again to maturity and its products. God is concerned that a useful crop grow from the land He waters (cf. Is. 5:1–7). Thorns and thistles on cropland are worthless and must be burned off so the land can be productive (6:7–9).

As though he senses this warning might shake his readers, the writer expresses confidence in them. He is persuaded that the better things which are always associated with salvation (9) do and will mark their lives as well (10; *see* Patience).

God's promise is sure (6:13–20). The writer concludes by affirming the security of the Christian's foundational truths. God has spoken and given His oath.

B. The Melchizedek priesthood, thus Jesus Christ's, better than Aaron's (7:1—8:5). In Hebrews 5:6 the writer noted that Christ's priesthood is "after the order of Melchizedek." Now he explains some vital implications:

1. Abraham paid tithes to Melchizedek (7:1–10). The argument of this passage has deep roots in rabbinic interpretation of the Old Testament. The person named appears only briefly, in Genesis 14:18. He is identified as both a king and priest. No genealogy is given; no birth or death are recorded. He simply stands there for a timeless instant, his greatness demonstrated by the fact that Abraham paid him a tithe and that Melchizedek blessed Abraham.

2. Aaronic priests made nothing perfect (7:11–22). The writer now points out to these Hebrew Christians so eager to return to the Aaronic priesthood of Judaism that if that priesthood could have brought perfection there would have been no Old Testament promise of a priesthood "in the order of Melchizedek" (11–17). Jesus has come and now has been raised to "an indestructible life." Thus Jesus is qualified for the long-promised new priesthood! Jesus' superior and endless priesthood means the coming of a superior covenant. Under the new covenant, the superior priest, Jesus, is "able to save completely.

3. Aaronic priests died (7:23–28). In four ways then Jesus' priesthood is superior to the Old Testament priesthood which so attracts these converted Jews. One: Jesus is qualified by His Resurrection to endless life for an eternal priesthood. Two: Jesus' priesthood is guaranteed by God's oath. Three: Jesus is a permanent priest who "always lives to make *intercession" for us (23–25). Four: the priests of the Old Testament were themselves weak and sinful men, for whom sacrifices must be made.

4. Aaronic priests served only shadows (8:1–5). Because every element of the Law was linked, a change in priesthood implies a corresponding change in the whole and in every other element (cf. 7:12). The writer now argues that, since Jesus' priesthood is superior, it follows that His whole new covenant will be superior!

The Old Testament sanctuary in which the priests ministered was constructed on a pattern delivered by God. That pattern symbolically represented heavenly realities (8:3–5). Because the covenant that Jesus administers is founded on reality and not shadow, it is vastly superior and promises much more to mankind (6).

C. Jesus mediates a better Covenant (8:6—10:18).

1. The better Covenant (8:6–13). The Old Testament is itself the source of the term "new covenant" (Jer. 31:31–34). The very name "new" marks the old Mosaic code as something which was temporary. The author's quote shows two vital areas in which the new replaces and is superior to the old. Old Testament Law stood outside man, pointing out what men must do and condemning when men failed. But the living Word of the New Covenant is written within the believer's very personality, freeing us to spontaneously do the good and the moral. The second great difference is that under the New Covenant there is complete forgiveness for sinning humanity.

2. The Old Covenant's sanctuary and sacrifices (9:1–10). The Old Testament *tabernacle, and the *temple which followed, were the setting for an annual drama, which took place each Day of Atonement. On that day the high priest entered the curtained inner chamber to present a blood offering to God, for his own sins and for the sins of the people (1–7; *see* Mercy Seat). This atonement drama was also symbolic (9). Old Testament sacrifices covered over sins but were not able to clear the consciences of the worshipers. The fact that a thick curtain continually blocked off the inner sanctuary showed that "the way into the Holiest of All was not yet made manifest" (8).

The writer does not mention it here, but the Gospel of Luke reports that at the moment of Jesus' death "the curtain of the temple was torn in two" (Luke 23:45). With the sacrifice of Jesus on Calvary, the "time of reformation" (Heb. 9:10) had finally come!

3. The New Covenant's sanctuary and sacrifices (9:11—10:18). The next verses develop striking contrasts. (*See* Blood, The; Remission.)

"He will appear a second time" (9:28). Our forgiveness was complete on the Cross—"It is finished" (John 19:30; *see* Offered). However, our salvation will be completed when Christ returns. The removal of sin from the world, the establishment of Christ's kingdom on earth, and the setting in order of the eternal purpose of God for His people without the limitations of a planet in rebellion against Him will be finalized, and with it our salvation.

In chapter 10 the writer continues his explanation of the superiority of Christ's sacrifice of his own life for our sins.

Verses 10:5–10 quote an Old Testament passage which shows God could never be satisfied with the sacrifices the Law required. Christ's coming revealed what God had determined from the first to be necessary to deal with sin. By Jesus' one sacrifice, He has set apart and made holy all who believe in Him.

The effectiveness of Jesus' sacrifice is demonstrated in three ways. First, Jesus "sat down" at God's right hand. Second, Jesus "made us perfect." This phrase means that He completed what God intended for us; His act has a present and continuing impact on us. Third, God has forgiven our "sins and iniquities." We stand before Him in Christ and are pronounced holy (14, 17–18)!

III. THE SUPERIORITY OF THE WALK OF FAITH 10:19—13:25.

A. A call to full assurance of faith (10:19—11:40).

1. A call to steadfastness of faith (10:19–39). The writer calls on Hebrew Christians to live together in light of all Jesus has done as high priest and as a sacrifice (*see* Endurance).

The writer strongly warns Hebrew believers who have given up "meeting together" (10:24) and who are even now turning back to Judaism. His argument takes a common rabbinic form, reasoning from the lesser to the greater.

Fourth warning: against turning back (10:26–39).

Persevere! (10:32–39). He now begs them not to "throw away" their confidence. Only after a person has done the will of God can he expect to receive the promise (35–36). Jesus will come, and then all that God has promised will be received. Until then we must live by faith (37).

2. A description of faith (11:1–3). The validity of "faith" does not rest on the sincerity of the believer but on the reliability of what is believed (*see* Framed).

3. Heroes of faith (11:4–40). Without the confidence that God exists and wants a relationship with man (v. 6), no one can be pleasing to Him. We may not see the object of our faith, but we do have evidence. Faith has a visible impact on human experience. Over and over again, those who have trusted God have demonstrated by their lives the validity of their faith (*see* Faith's Confession; Heirs; Looked; Manhood). Here then is a great hall of fame.

> 🖊️ **"By faith"**
> (11:29–35). The Old Testament figures of faith acted in hope, performed miracles, received strength in battle, and endured tribulation. "All these, having obtained a good testimony through faith, did not receive the promise" (v. 39). All this took place before Christ! Their faith was based on something they believed God would do in the future. And now, *Christ has come*—the hope answered, the prophecies fulfilled, the promise received!

B. The endurance of faith (12:1–29).

1. Jesus' endurance (12:1–4). The saints who across the ages have lived by faith are a great crowd of witnesses who give a common testimony. In view of their evidence (ch. 11; *see* Looking), we are to "run with endurance the race that is set before us" (1). Jesus' example of committed obedience should encourage and strengthen us.

2. The value of chastening (12:5–24). The Jewish Christians to whom this is written had become discouraged and lost heart. Christians need to understand opposition and difficulties as training provided by God. The writer points out several things concerning God's discipline.

God's discipline is always loving (v. 6).

God's discipline is a family matter (12:7–8). A father only accepts responsibility for the training of legitimate children!

God's discipline is purposeful (10). God never acts on impulse. He always looks ahead and has our benefit in view.

God's discipline is effective (11). God's training may bring a temporary pain, but it will produce righteousness and peace.

> 🖊️ **"Now no chastening seems to be joyful for the present, but painful; nevertheless, afterward it yields the peaceable fruit of righteousness"**
> (12:11). The development of spiritual fruit in

a person's life is not simply a by-product of our new birth in Christ; it is related to our growth in the grace of God. This process of maturation is superintended by God's Spirit, often accompanied by seasons of correction. Submission to the process and cooperation with the Holy Spirit will bring about an increased harvest of the "peaceable fruit of righteousness" in every area of our lives.

Fifth warning: against refusing God (12:12–29). One last warning is now included. The writer begins by pointing out three dangers. The interpersonal danger (14) is that we will fail to live in peace with our brothers and sisters. The inner danger (15) is that we will not see God's grace in what happens to us and become bitter. The outward danger (16–17) is that we will choose immorality and other sensual pleasures instead of our spiritual birthright. (*See* Restoration.)

C. Admonitions to love (13:1–17). The writer closes with a series of brief exhortations.

1. Love in the social realm (13:1–6). Hospitality and visiting those who are in prison or suffering are examples of "*brotherly love."

Be holy (13:4–6). Personal holiness involves forsaking sexual immorality and love of money. (*See* Helper.)

2. Love in the religious realm (13:7–17). Be responsive to leaders. The lives and the faith of leaders are to be observed and imitated. "Strange teachings" are to be rejected.

Bear the disgrace (13:11–14). Jesus suffered a death which was considered shameful by Israelites. He was even taken outside Jerusalem so His execution would not contaminate that holy place. The writer urges them instead to bear the disgrace of exclusion from the Old Testament community. In doing so, they will be going out to join Jesus.

Offer praise (13:15–16). The rabbis taught that in the messianic age the only required sacrifices would be thank offerings. The writer mentions this belief when he points out that all believers can now offer God *praise and sacrifice of their own dedication to "doing good."

> 🖊️ **"Let us continually offer the sacrifice of praise to God, that is, the fruit of our lips, giving thanks to His name"**
> (13:15). Throughout the Old Testament the sacrifice of praise is commanded of God's people for the purpose of giving thanks.

Thankful people not only recognize the blessing of God in their life but continually live in the flow of that blessing. It is the thankless who are in danger of rejecting God's merciful goodness and wasting themselves in the fruitless pursuit of the creation rather than the Creator (Rom. 1:21).

D. Conclusion (13:18–25). The writer, as the apostle Paul often does, closes with a request that the recipients of the letter pray for him. And he commends them to God (20–21).

The reference to brother Timothy suggests that Timothy was imprisoned some time after Paul's execution in A.D. 67 or 68, but won his release.

TRUTH-IN-ACTION through **HEBREWS**

Truth Hebrews Teaches	**Action** Hebrews Invites
1 Key Lessons in Faith Faith accepts the Bible's record of who Jesus is and what He has accomplished on our behalf. It also draws near to God and clings to Him tenaciously. The believer accepts the benefits of Jesus' sacrifice and enters God's presence with confidence. Faith believes the Bible implicitly, knowing it is God's living self-expression and so submits to its judgment. Finally, faith is willing to suffer with Christ, knowing it will receive a good reward.	**2:14–18** *Recognize* that Jesus has destroyed the fear of death for you by overcoming the Devil. **3:6** *Consciously hold onto* the courage and hope that is implied by your confession of faith. **4:12, 13** *Allow* the Word of God to judge the intents and thoughts of your heart. **4:14** *Be tenacious* in holding onto God's promises. *Aggressively pursue* God, *study* His Word, and *build up* your faith. **4:16** *Draw near to* God with confidence when in need. *Believe* He understands your suffering. **10:23** *Hold on to* hope! *Develop* a sense of high destiny. **13:11–13** *Recognize* that following Jesus brings reproach. *Do not fear* human mockery, rejection, and scorn.
2 Steps to Dynamic Devotion Devotion is concentration on a particular pursuit, purpose, or cause. He who is devoted to Jesus recognizes his fleshly tendency to become lackadaisical and studies to avoid it. The Scriptures shape his thinking, and he devotes time to prayer, to waiting upon the Lord, and to praise and thanksgiving.	**2:1–4** *Give your full attention* to God's Word and your relationship with Jesus. **3:1** *Let* Jesus and His Word be the foundation and sustainer of your thinking. **9:11–15** *Celebrate daily* that you have gained access to God through the shed blood of Jesus Christ. **10:22** *Continually draw near* to God with a blameless heart and faith. **10:25** *Gather often* with God's people to encourage and urge them on in righteousness. **11:6** *Seek God* diligently. *Believe* that He will reward you for it. **13:15** *Practice* persistent and patient praise.
3 Steps to Faithful Obedience Faith believes what God says and acts in line with His Word. Faith allows the believer to enter the rest into which God has called all His people. It acknowledges the completed work of salvation, while faithfully obeying every instruction from God.	**4:1–10** *Enter* the rest promised by God. *Mix* your faith with God's Word. *Do not allow* rebellion to harden your heart. **4:8–11** *Devote your whole heart* to obeying God and His Word. *Trust* Him to do the things He says He will do. **5:8–10** *Study* Jesus' life as your model for suffering and obedience. **12:25** *Never reject* a message because it makes you uncomfortable. *Accept* correction from God's Word. **13:17, 18** *Obey* church leadership. *Recognize* and *cooperate* with leadership to make their job easier. *Pray* for them continuously and faithfully.
4 How to Develop Dynamic Discipleship The disciple is an apprentice to Jesus, learning to live as He did. God disciplines His children, correcting and training them to live in His kingdom.	**5:12–14** *Recognize* that it is only through a sustained daily effort to apply God's Word to your life that you will become mature. **6:11, 12** *Turn* from laziness and *patiently endure*, sustaining diligence in your pursuit of Christlikeness. *(continued)*

Truth Hebrews Teaches	**Action** Hebrews Invites
4 How to Develop Dynamic Discipleship *(continued)* Correction, if received with the right attitude of heart, produces the fruit of righteousness. The Father's object is to bring His children to maturity.	**12:1–3** *Discard* any attitude or practice that hinders your walk with Christ. *Model* your life after Jesus. *Give careful thought and study* to the life of Jesus for encouragement in your struggle with sin. **12:4–10** *Embrace* God's discipline. *Know* that it is evidence that He is training you as His child. **12:11** *Accept* God's correction as necessary for spiritual growth. **13:7** *Honor, consider,* and *imitate* those God has put over you to lead you.

The Furniture of the Tabernacle
(Heb. 9:1-10)

Ark of the Covenant
(Ex. 25:10–22)
The ark was most sacred of all the furniture in the tabernacle. Here the Hebrews kept a copy of the Ten Commandments, which summarized the whole covenant.

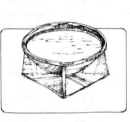

Bronze Laver
(Ex. 30:17–21)
It was to the laver of bronze that the priests would come for cleansing. They must be pure to enter the presence of God.

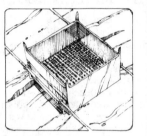

Altar of Burnt Offering
(Ex. 27:1–8)
Animal sacrifices were offered on this altar, located in the court in front of the tabernacle. The blood of the sacrifice was sprinkled on the four horns of the altar.

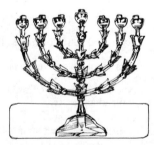

Golden Lampstand
(Ex. 25:31–40)
The gold lampstand stood in the holy place, opposite the table of showbread. It held seven lamps, flat bowls in which a wick lay with one end in the oil of the bowl and the lighted end hanging out.

Table of Showbread
(Ex. 25:23–30)
The table of showbread was a stand on which the offerings were placed. Always in God's presence on the table were the 12 loaves of bread representing the 12 tribes.

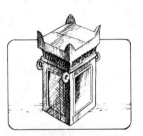

Altar of Incense
(Ex. 30:1–10)
The altar of incense inside the tabernacle was much smaller than the altar of burnt offering outside. The incense burned on the altar was a perfume of a sweet-smelling aroma.

KEYS TO JAMES
The Kingdom and the Law

Kingdom Key: God's Purpose in View

By showing the believer's place in God's kingdom, James addresses the believer's responsibility before God's law. James's blunt and forthright manner is a powerful tempering agent for those who may see God's grace as an excuse for carnal indulgence or sin.

James describes the law in the light of the New Testament. It is the "perfect law of liberty!" (2:12). Jesus said He came to fulfill the law (Matt. 5:17–20). The New Covenant does not bypass the law; it enables believers to *live it!* Just as Paul describes the possibility of a life of obedience to the law by the power of the Holy Spirit (Rom. 8:1–4), so James spells out just what such obedience will entail. He identifies clear points of accountability to the law.

1. Accountability to God's Word (1:21–25). Living in God's kingdom means heeding His laws. The objective of such obedience is not a quest for self-acquired righteousness, which the flesh never can attain. We are simply to allow the power of God's Word to reveal areas of disobedience and lead us into self-correction and obedience to Him.

2. Accountability to active works (2:14–26). In James's structure of values, "works" are not humanistic exer-

> **Grace and law meet in obedient belief and behavior.**

cises. They are spiritual acts. (*See* 2:26, where his parallelism demonstrates that the "spirit" of the law is shown in our works.) James distinguishes between the obedience of spiritless legalism ("What am I required to do?") and the obedience of benevolent and obedient actions ("What can I do to show God's love?"). (*See also* the parable of the two sons, Matt. 21:28–32.)

3. Accountability for one's words (3:1–18). How a person talks shows to which kingdom he or she truly belongs. No punches are pulled: "hell" (3:6) and "demonic" (3:15) are words James uses to describe the source of people's speech if their words do not align with God's law.

4. Accountability to transforming worship (4:7-10). Central to the fourth chapter is the call: "Submit to God. . . . Draw near to God. . . . Humble yourselves [before God]." This is true kingdom worship, *(Please turn to page 437.)*

Period in which James Likely Was Written

Birth of Jesus 4 B.C.	Ascension of Jesus Pentecost A.D. 30	Council of Jerusalem A.D. 49	Persecution by Nero A.D. 64–68	Destruction of temple A.D. 70	Death of John c. A.D. 100

James shows the believer's duty before God, the • • •

Master Key: God's Son Revealed

Beginning in the first verse and throughout the letter, James recognizes Jesus' lordship over him, referring to himself as the Lord's "bondservant" or slave. That term applies to all Christians who acknowledge Jesus' sovereignty over their lives and willingly commit themselves to His service. Christ is the object of our faith (2:1), the One in whose name and by whose power we minister (5:14–15). He is the rewarder of those who are steadfast in the midst of trials (1:12) and the Coming One for whom we patiently wait (5:7–9). James identifies Christ as the "glory" (2:1), referring to the Shekinah, the glorious manifestation of God's presence among His people. He is also the divine Glory, the presence of God on earth (*see* Luke 2:30–32; John 1:14; Heb. 1:3).

Of considerable interest is the close parallel between the content of this letter and the teachings of Jesus, particularly the Sermon on the Mount. Although James does not quote any statement of Jesus exactly, there are more reminiscences of the Lord's teachings in this letter than in all the other New Testament epistles combined. These allusions indicate a close association between James and Jesus and a strong influence of the Lord in the author's life.

Power Key: God's Spirit at Work

The letter specifically mentions the Holy Spirit only in 4:5, which states the indwelling Spirit's strong desire for our undivided loyalty, jealously brooking no rivals.

The activity of the Holy Spirit may be seen in the ministry to the sick described in 5:14–16. In light of other biblical terminology connecting anointing with the Spirit (*see* Is. 61:1; Luke 4:18; 1 John 2:20–27), anointing with oil is best understood as symbolic of the Holy Spirit. Furthermore, the definite article used in the Greek with the word for "faith" in 5:15 suggests that James is referring to the manifestation of the gift of faith (1 Cor. 12:9).

Key Word: *Faith That Works*

James develops the theme of the characteristics of true faith, using them as a series of tests to help his readers evaluate the quality of their relationship to Christ.

Key Verses: James 1:19–22; 2:14–17

Key Chapter: James 1

One of the most difficult areas of the Christian life is that of testings and temptations. James reveals our correct response to both: to testings, count them all joy; to temptations, realize God is not the source.

Introducing
JAMES

Author. The author of this letter identifies himself simply as James. The name was quite common, and the New Testament lists at least five men named James, two of whom were Jesus' disciples and one of whom was His brother. Tradition has ascribed the book to the Lord's brother, and there is no reason to question this view. Evidently the writer was well known, and James the brother of Jesus became the leader of the church in Jerusalem at an early date (Acts 12:17; 15:13–21; 21:18; Gal. 1:19; 2:9, 12). The language of the epistle is similar to James's speech in Acts 15. James apparently was an unbeliever during the ministry of Jesus (John 7:3–5). A post-Resurrection appearance of Christ to him (1 Cor. 15:7) probably led to his conversion, for he is numbered with the believers in Acts 1:14.

Date. The Jewish historian Josephus indicates that James was stoned to death in the year A.D. 62, so if he is the author the letter was evidently written before that date. The contents of the book suggest that it may have been written as early as shortly before the church council of Acts 15, which convened about A.D. 49. We can only conclude that the letter likely was written between A.D. 48 and 62.

Purpose. James is primarily practical and ethical, emphasizing duty rather than doctrine. The author wrote to rebuke the shameful neglect of certain Christian duties. In doing so, he analyzed the nature of genuine faith and urged his readers to demonstrate the validity of their experience with Christ. His supreme concern was reality in religion, and he set forth the practical claims of the gospel.

Content. Rather than speculating or debating on religious theories, James directs his readers toward godly living. From beginning to end the mood of his letter is imperative. In 108 verses, fifty-four clear commands are given, and seven times James calls attention to his statements by using imperative terms. This "bondservant of God" (1:1) writes as one supervising other slaves. The result is a statement of Christian ethics which stands on a par with any such teaching in the New Testament.

Personal Application. The book's call for ethical living based on the gospel makes it perennially relevant. James gives a practical exposition of "pure and undefiled religion" (1:27). His two fundamental emphases are personal growth in the spiritual life and sensitivity in social relationships. Any faith that does not deal with both personal and social issues, he contends, is a dead faith. The message of James speaks especially to those who are inclined to talk rather than walk their way to heaven.

Kingdom Key *continued from page 435*

not merely an excitable or flippant approach made in a moment amid a crowd. Such private brokenness before God will be expressed in purity (4:1–6), generosity (4:11–12), humility (4:13–17), equity in one's dealings (5:1–6) and patience with perseverance rather than wilting before test or trial (5:7–12).

5. Accountability for the weak (5:13–20). The hallmark of a true kingdom person is his or her mercy and compassion. The assignment to pray for the sick (5:14–15), minister forgive-

ness to the sinful or failing (5:13, 16), and reach out to those falling away (5:19–20) is buttressed with the assurance that God's power is available to fulfill such kingdom assignments (5:16–18).

James points a practical way toward spiritual power. This is not an outline for cold duty; it is a promise that God will warm the heart and produce godly behavior and service in those who receive His law in all its life-liberating power.

Surveying
JAMES

I. SALUTATION 1:1. James, the half-brother of Jesus (Gal. 1:19) and leader of the church in Jerusalem (Acts 15:13), writes to the Jews of the Diaspora. The church spread beyond Jerusalem on the Day of Pentecost, when Jews gathered from all over the world witnessed the outpouring of the Holy Spirit (Acts 2:5).

II. PRACTICAL RELIGION AND TRIALS 1:2–18. Trials-faith-patience (vv. 2–3)—this is the universal formula for maturing for the people of God.

A. Outward adversities (1:2–12). Trial comes to every believer. It is not a matter of "if" but "when" (v. 2). James sees the benefit possible from such difficulty as we learn to believe God "with no doubting" (v. 6; *see* Manhood;

Reproach). Our faith must be related to our relationship with God, not on the limitations or advantages of the temporary circumstances of our life (vv. 9–11).

B. Inward enticements (1:13–18). James conclusively addresses the subject of temptation—*God does not tempt us.* Our carnal desires tempt us, and sin results when temptation "gives birth" (v. 15).

> **"God cannot be tempted by evil, nor does He Himself tempt anyone"**
> (1:13). God has no malicious intent toward man—ever. In fact 1 Corinthians 10:13 assures us that in the midst of temptation "God is faithful." Paul says unequivocally that when temptation is about to overwhelm the believer, God makes a way of escape. The responsibility for fleeing temptation belongs with the individual, but God delivers us.

III. PRACTICAL RELIGION AND GOD'S WORD 1:19–27. Our speech and our actions must be consistent with what we believe and know to be true in God's Word.

A. Hear the Word (1:19–20). Our wisdom is to listen carefully, speak after much thought, and resist the human tendency to act out of anger.

B. Receive the Word (1:21). Our reception of "the implanted word . . . is able to save your souls."

C. Obey the Word (1:22–27). Our obedience to the Word (*see* Word of God) demonstrates that we have truly "heard." "The perfect law of liberty" (v. 25) refers to the commandments of believing life. This is to be contrasted with the Law of Moses, which has been a harsh master. The Jewish converts are to act upon the law that frees them. The emphasis James places on response relates to moral purity and charity to the truly needy—"widows and orphans."

IV. PRACTICAL RELIGION AND HUMAN RELATIONSHIPS 2:1–26. Showing respect for all people and living out our faith by serving and demonstrating care and compassion for others—this is the cry of James's heart. The passion and purpose of the entire epistle are found here: "Faith by itself, if it does not have works, is dead" (v. 17). Genuine faith stirs faith-filled actions. "As the body without the spirit is dead, so faith without works is dead also" (v. 26).

A. Negative partiality (2:1–13). The "royal law" is "You shall love your neighbor as yourself" (v. 8; also Mark 12:31). The forbidding of *partiality toward the rich or influential is well known to Judaism (Lev. 19:15). In the freedom we experience in Christ, we are bound ever more closely to the heart of God and to love for people (*see* Human Worth).

B. Positive compassion (2:14–26).
Faith acts! People of faith serve others. If faith does not act, then it is not true faith. James boldly asserts that the people of faith in the Old Testament had their faith "made perfect" by their works (v. 22; *see* Working Together).

V. PRACTICAL RELIGION AND SPEECH 3:1–18. The epistle now turns attention to two areas: a believer's speech and a believer's motives. Our speech can bring either a blessing or a curse (v. 9); it can offer bitter or fresh water. The tongue can also create a "world of iniquity" (v. 6). Also, the motives of believers must be kept in perspective—envy and self-seeking are "earthly, *sensual, demonic." (*See* Leadership, Spiritual; Perfect.)

> **"The tongue is a fire"**
> (3:6). Proverbs 18:21 declares that death and life are in the power of the tongue. The tongue will either (1) be set ablaze by the Holy Spirit in the beauty of spiritual language and be graced with the authority to prophesy, praise, bless, and give life, or (2) be set ablaze by hell and unleash corruption, destruction, cursing, and death. The authority of a believer to declare the promise of the Lord in ministry situations is directly related to the careful and conscious use of one's tongue for God's purpose. Faith talk is not simply repeating God's promises; it is being linked to God's heart and God's Word in such a way that all speech is always redemptive.

> **"The wisdom that is from above is first pure, then peaceable, gentle, willing to yield, full of mercy and good fruits, without partiality and without hypocrisy"**
> (3:17–18). This is also true of the people who have allowed the Holy Spirit to perform these works of grace in their lives. We become like the One we worship. As we serve the Lord and welcome the Holy Spirit's transformation in us, we are completely and irreversibly changed to be like Jesus.

VI. PRACTICAL RELIGION AND WORLDLINESS 4:1–12.
"Resist the devil and he will flee from you" (v. 7). Make friends with God, not the world. Humble yourself before the Lord and experience His grace toward you. Speak kindly to the brethren. In other words, live for the Lord and love people.

> **"Resist the devil and he will flee from you"**
> (4:7). Protecting God's people from the work of the devil is based on two important factors. The first is our submission to God in both word and spirit. The Bible offers complete resources for establishing righteousness in a person's walk with the Lord, leaving no room for a satanic foothold. However, our submission to the Holy Spirit applies God's instruction to our circumstance and relationships. The second is our forceful resistance to demonic intrusion (v. 7). The "violence" of the kingdom of heaven (Matt. 11:12) is not passive action; "pressing into" the kingdom of God (Luke 16:16) is aggressive and bold. Through prayer, fasting, and unrelenting witness our spiritual warfare (2 Cor. 10:4) is victorious (*see* Life Up).

VII. PRACTICAL RELIGION AND BUSINESS AFFAIRS 4:13—5:6.
The Lord holds tomorrow in His hand; our responsibility is to seek His will today and not delay to do good. James rebukes the rich who oppress the poor. "Miseries . . . are coming upon you!" (5:1).

VIII. FINAL APPEALS 5:7–20.
The writer mentions three concluding concerns: the return of Christ, ministry to the sick, and witness to the sinful.

A. For patience (5:7–11). As believers prepare for Christ's return—"Establish your hearts" (v. 8), being careful to live in right relationships with other believers.

B. For pure speech (5:12). The apostle insists on clear, direct speech, with a believer's claim to authority based on his or her own character rather than some oath.

C. For prayer (5:13–18). Finally, James's concern turns to the sick. He instructs the elders to anoint with oil, pray with faith, and receive confession of sin—"And the prayer of faith will save the sick . . . and if he has committed sins, he will be forgiven" (v. 15; *see* Faith, Seed).

> **"Is anyone among you sick?"**
> (5:13–16). It is the responsibility of the sick to seek out eldership to pray. The anointing with oil in 5:14 is not done for medicinal purposes. Rather, it symbolizes the presence of the Holy Spirit. In some traditions, anointing with oil is performed only when death is imminent. Nothing could be more remote to the meaning of this text. Prayer and anointing will bring healing. Oil in the Bible is a symbol for the Holy Spirit. Thus in verse 15 anointing with oil becomes part of the means by which our faith is communicated in the healing process (*see* Healing, Divine). And in verse 16 the connection between sickness and sin is made. Confession of sin can be a crucial part of the release of physical healing (*see* Spiritual Warfare). Jesus came to save us—spirit, soul, and body (1 Thess. 5:23).

D. For compassion (5:19–20). The final two verses reveal the heart of a shepherd who deeply loves his flock. His desire is to reach any in the flock who have wandered from the faith. "Save a soul from death and cover a multitude of sins" (v. 20) by turning a *sinner away from destruction and back to the Lord.

TRUTH-IN-ACTION through JAMES

Truth James Teaches	**Action** James Invites
1 How to Have Patience in Trials The testing of faith produces patience (the ability to endure), which is the hallmark of the mature believer. Only under the pressure of trials can the believer test the true depth of his faith in God. The established heart will not waver, but will rejoice in the knowledge of the goodness of God.	**1:2** *Rejoice* when trials come to test your faith. **1:3** *Know* that patience results when your faith is tested by trials. **1:4** *Endure* so that God has enough time to bring about the Christlikeness He intends through trial (see Rom. 8:28, 29). **1:5** *Ask* God for wisdom! When a trial comes, if you do not know what to do, He does. And He wants to help you through your trials. **5:7, 8** *Develop patience:* To receive the harvest and the crown of life that you desire, you must persevere.
2 Being a Doer of the Word Obedience to the Word of God brings about the work of God. We are to hear the Word and do the work. To hear and to do nothing is one sign of a deceived heart. Faith acts. To believe is to do!	**1:22–25** *Evaluate!* In what areas do you claim faith, while your actions declare unbelief? *Acknowledge* those areas. *Decide* to act on the faith you have! *Practice today* what you proclaim.
3 Learning to Avoid Partiality Some may argue that preferring the rich and famous is only human, but the Bible rejects partiality. God is not an exalter of persons: neither should His children be.	**2:1–8** *Be uninfluenced* by a person's social station. *Show love* to all without partiality. **2:9** *Differentiate* between sinful partiality and "due honor" (Rom. 13:7).
4 How to Tame the Tongue Nothing can cause more damage than the tongue. Keeping our speech under closer control is a discipline believers must develop.	**3:1** *Avoid presumptuousness!* Do not take the position of being a teacher until God has placed you there. You increase your liability for judgment if you do. **3:2** *Bridle your tongue!* Monitoring every word we speak may seem cumbersome at first, but it will serve to advance righteousness. **3:9–12** *Speak well of others.* Criticism, slander, backbiting, and gossip are "bitter waters," which issue out of demonic, worldly wisdom.
5 Steps in Developing Humility True faith is humble. And humility is the opposite of the proud selfishness and self-centered ambition that characterizes this present evil age. Self-centeredness is the essence of worldliness. Therefore, to be a self-centered person is to be at enmity with God. James calls for believers to humble themselves.	**4:1, 2** *Renounce strife!* Refuse unnecessary argument and personal strife. Seek to be at peace with others, preferring them to yourself. **4:7** *Renounce rebellion!* Submit yourself to God. Renounce the Devil and reject all his suggestions. **4:8** *Be quick to confess sin!* Nothing more effectively humbles a man than to admit sincerely that he is a sinner. **4:11** *Renounce slander!* Rather, *speak highly* of others, even to your own discredit. **4:13–16** *Express* continued dependence upon God! An independent spirit wars against godly humility. **4:17** *Do the good you know to do,* regardless of the cost. Not to do so is sin!
6 The Dangers of Money The consistent scriptural witness is that money, though necessary and a blessing from God, can be a dangerous commodity. Things we think we own may really own us! God calls us to put material goods into proper perspective and to use them wisely under His direction.	**1:10** *Recognize* the fact that all material possessions will perish and have no eternal value. **5:1–6** *Avoid* unnecessary acquisition. Acquired wealth can bring unwelcomed problems to your life. *Embrace simplicity!* Simplicity and poverty are not the same. Simplicity is simply acting responsibly with what God gives you!

CHAPTER

49

KEYS TO 1 PETER
Submission and the Kingdom

Kingdom Key: God's Purpose in View

The full release of power and joy in kingdom living comes through the pathway of submission. First Peter mentions this theme frequently (2:13, 28; 3:1, 7; 5:5), finally focusing on the central issue: submitting to God (5:6). True submission is best explained by examining the Greek word hupotasso. *This word mean proper "arrangement" or "order," as with a military group strategically deployed for battle. In other words, God's divine order is not designed to humiliate through hierarchy but to advance through our acknowledgment of and response to His arrangement of things. Submission is also best understood as something that is invited or called for, not demanded or enforced.* Subjugation *(the reduction of a person or group though domination) and* submission *(the acknowledgment and acceptance of proper order) are two entirely different things.*

The call to kingdom dominion is a call to learn a life of submission to God's Word, order, and ways. Peter notes arenas of submission which, rightly responded to, release power in the believer's life because kingdom order is appropriately seen and served. There are at least four of these:

1. Submission to civil authority (2:13–14). Even if one experiences suffering (4:12–14), "submission" is the ultimate instrument of triumph. This runs against every human inclination, and it seems passive, if not cowardly. But this was Jesus' way, and clearly He won in the end (Phil. 2:6–11).

2. Submission of spouses to one

> **In trial or triumph, maintain patience and holiness.**

another (3:1–7). The "likewise" in verse 7 indicates that the measure of submission (each acknowledging his or her proper role) summoned from the wife is expected of the husband as well (*see* Eph. 5:22–33).

3. Submission of servants to masters (2:13). Peter seems almost indifferent to the possibility of exploitation of believing slaves by their owners. Ephesians 6:9 shows a matching duty to be accepted by believing masters. The essence of this is to believe that any degree of evil is conquerable through faith in God's ultimate justice, rather than through anger, retaliation, or rebellion (4:18–21).

(Please turn to page 442.)

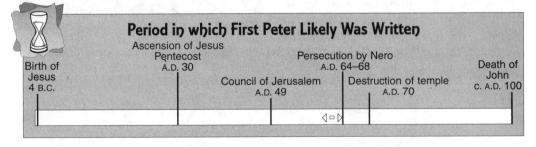

Period in which First Peter Likely Was Written

Birth of Jesus 4 B.C.	Ascension of Jesus Pentecost A.D. 30	Council of Jerusalem A.D. 49	Persecution by Nero A.D. 64–68	Destruction of temple A.D. 70	Death of John C. A.D. 100

First Peter: The pathway of submission leads • • •

Kingdom Key *continued from page 441.*

4. Submission to one another (5:5). This incorporates (a) acceptance of your spiritual leaders (1 Cor. 16:13–16); (b) their demonstration of godly, servant-spirited care for souls in their charge (5:1–4); and, (c) a commitment to loving care and mutual trust among all believers (3:8–12; 4:7–11).

None of the above issues are viable without the foundational issue of submission to God (5:6–11) being settled. The spirit of submission will characterize our obedience when we are convinced that God will honor such submission with the reward of fulfillment and true dominion in life. God has not called us to a "blind" submission, but to a faith that "sees" beyond the moment, to His kingdom's ultimate triumph.

Master Key: God's Son Revealed

In four separate passages Peter links Christ's sacrificial sufferings with the glory that followed His death (1:11; 3:18; 4:13; 5:1). The letter details the fruits of Christ's suffering and victory, including provision for a new life now and hope for the future (*see* 1:3, 18–19; 3:18). Anticipation of Christ's return in glory causes believers to rejoice (1:4–7). In other ways also Christ now makes a profound difference in the lives of Christians: they love Him (1:8); they come to Him (2:4); they offer "spiritual sacrifices" through Him (2:5); they are reproached because of Him (4:14); they should expect to be rewarded when He returns (5:4).

Power Key: God's Spirit at Work

The Holy Spirit is active in the entire process of salvation: the "Spirit of Christ" in the Old Testament prophets "testified beforehand" concerning the Cross and the subsequent glory (1:11); Christ was raised from the dead "by the Spirit" (3:18); evangelists preached the gospel by the Spirit; believers responded in obedience "through the Spirit" (1:2, 22); a foretaste of the coming glory is ours through the Spirit (compare 4:14 with v. 13 and 5:1).

Key Word: *Suffering for the Cause of Christ*

The basic theme of 1 Peter is the proper response to Christian suffering. Knowing that his readers will be facing more persecution than ever before, Peter writes to give a divine perspective so that they will be able to endure without wavering.

Key Verses: First Peter 1:10–12; 4:12–13
Key Chapter: First Peter 4

Central in the New Testament revelation concerning how to handle persecution and suffering caused by one's Christian testimony is 1 Peter 4. Christ's suffering is to be our model (4:1, 2), but we also are to rejoice in that we can share in His suffering (4:12–14).

• • • to the full realization of power and joy.

Introducing

1 PETER

Author. The letter claims to be from the apostle Peter, and there is no evidence that Petrine authorship was ever challenged in the early church. Silvanus, who accompanied Paul on his second missionary journey, was likely Peter's secretary in composing 1 Peter (5:12), which probably explains the polished Greek style of the letter.

There are linguistic and literary parallels between 1 Peter and Peter's speeches recorded in Acts. Peter's Pentecost address and 1 Peter have the following in common: Christ's sacrifice was "foreordained" (compare 1 Pet. 1:20 with Acts 2:23); Christ's resurrection and ascension glory are presented together (compare 1 Pet. 1:21 with Acts 2:32–35); baptism is related to forgiveness of sins (compare 1 Pet. 3:21 with Acts 2:38). Peter's speech at the Jerusalem council and 1 Peter yield the following: God's "choice" in salvation (compare 1 Pet. 1:2; 2:9 with Acts 15:7); purity of heart with response to the gospel (compare 1 Pet. 1:22 with Acts 15:9). Other examples could be noted.

Occasion and Date. Peter addresses Christians living in various parts of Asia Minor who are suffering rejection in the world because of their obedience to Christ (4:1–4, 12–16). He therefore reminds them that they have a heavenly inheritance (1:3–5).

Peter has learned of their trials and thus addresses them as "pilgrims of the Dispersion" (1:1), a phrase reminiscent of exiled Israel in the Old Testament, but also appropriate for these Christians (see 1:17; 2:11). They are mostly converted Gentiles. At one time they were "not a people" (2:10, hardly true of Jews). Their former life was one of lewdness, drunkenness, and idolatries (4:3), more descriptive of pagan Gentiles than of first-century Jews.

Their compatriots are surprised that they now live differently (4:4). Although suffering is a "fiery trial" (4:12), it apparently does not entail martyrdom as yet. Furthermore, persecution is often the exception (see 3:13–14; 4:16).

Ancient tradition suggests that Peter was martyred in Rome in conjunction with Nero's severe persecution of Christians after the burning of Rome in A.D. 64. This letter was likely written toward the end of Peter's life, but while he could still say, "Honor the king" (2:17). The early sixties are a good estimate for the composition of 1 Peter.

Content. In addition to giving several exhortations for faithful living in an ungodly society, Peter discusses the salvation promised in the gospel. The future salvation that awaits believers at the revelation of Christ is especially prominent at the outset of the letter (1:3–13). This is the "hope" of the Christian referred to in 1:3, 13, 21; 3:15. Even as Christ suffered and then was glorified, so Christians should anticipate the glory ahead, though they may be persecuted for their faith in this life (1:6–7; 4:12–13). Patience in the midst of unjust suffering is "commendable before God" (2:20).

Peter also addresses the importance of believers pointing others to God by their godly lifestyles. They thus proclaim the praises of God (2:9), influence pagans to glorify God (2:12), silence foolish people by doing good works (2:15), win spouses to Christ by their examples (3:1), shame their ungodly critics (3:15–16), and puzzle former companions (4:4). Christians are to be a redeeming force in the world, though they suffer.

Personal Application. Since all true Christians experience hostility from an ungodly world, the call to patience and holiness amid suffering is applicable to all. However, the message is most pertinent where the opposition is severe. In many areas of the world persecution of Christians is as great today as it was in the first century, and 1 Peter offers hope to those suffering for Christ's sake.

Surveying

1 PETER

INTRODUCTION 1:1–2. Peter, often referred to as the apostle to the Jews, is writing to the "pilgrims of the Dispersion"—Jews in Asia who had been converted to Christianity. Portions of the epistle appear to address Gentiles as well. The culture of central Asia, where this letter is destined, is pagan, and the believers are com-ing under stiff resistance in the beginning of a period of persecution.

A. Salutation (1:1). Peter, chief among the disciples of Jesus, is probably writing from Rome, where he will be executed during Nero's persecution, which began around A.D. 64.

B. Addressees (1:2). These are the "elect," familiar terminology to Paul in Romans 8:33 and Colossians 3:12. They have been a part of God's plan; their selection has been according to His "foreknowledge"—this is far removed from the concept of pre-selection by God.

I. THE BELIEVER'S FAITH AND HOPE IN

THE WORLD 1:3—2:10. Peter is writing to the church under severe trial. His pastoral encouragement is for them to know the promise of God's keeping power in the midst of persecution (1:5) and the refining purity that will take place as they are obedient to the way of Christ (1:22).

A. Rejoicing in the hope of Christ's return (1:3–12). As with every generation since the Resurrection, the faithful have anticipated Jesus' imminent return. "Abundant mercy . . . living hope . . . inheritance incorruptible and undefiled" all await the faithful who live in the power of God (see Kept) in these desperate times.

B. Righteous living because of the hope (1:13—2:3). Peter's instructions ring with practicality: Change the way you think—"gird up the loins of your mind" (1:13); walk in purity and obedience to the truth in the Spirit's power—"love one another fervently with a pure heart" (1:22); feed on God's Word— "desire the pure milk of the word" (2:2; see Blood, The; Human Worth; Sincere; Word of God).

C. Renewal for God's people (2:4–10). To the believer, Jesus is precious and the "chief cornerstone." Likewise all believers are "living stones"—a part of the spiritual house, "the church." Peter's reference in verse 10 is to Hosea 1, and here he acknowledges this new band of the faithful as fulfilling God's plan for spiritual Israel.

> **"You also, as living stones"**
> (2:5). Peter's words are well chosen and reminiscent of Jesus' words to him about being "the rock." Clearly, Peter does not understand Jesus' words as giving him a unique place of authority in the church. We are together the "living stones" God is using to build the church. The promise of authority in Matthew 16:19 can be claimed by all who are part of this living organism— the body of Christ.

> **"You are a *chosen generation, a royal priesthood, a holy nation, His own special people, that you may proclaim the praises of Him who called you out of darkness into His marvelous light"**
> (2:9). As those who have been "called out of darkness," our praises declare that we have been translated into another kingdom

(Col 1:13; see Kingdom of God). Jesus Christ is our King, and He has made us a royal priesthood, with His authority and His Spirit to serve the world around us. Our *praise focuses on His throne and dominion, from which we derive all our benefits as subjects of His kingdom.

II. THE BELIEVER'S CONDUCT IN EVERYDAY CIRCUMSTANCES 2:11— 5:11. If a believer is going to survive the times, his or her conduct must be as enduring as the gospel by which he or she is saved. In relation to civil authority, one must be blameless. Servants should submit to masters. As Jesus did, families must live in the divine pattern; the eternal patterns for successful living never change. The apostle then goes on to explain the place of suffering and the resource of rescue available for those who suffer.

A. Submission and respect toward others (2:11—3:12). As pilgrims in a strange land, we must have a radical lifestyle which is deemed "honorable among the Gentiles," as a brilliant witness to the lost (2:12). The issue here is our submission to the Lord in every part of our lives. Jesus offers the living pattern (see Example). Although we are free in Christ, this liberty compels us to live as "bondservants of God" (2:16) who accept their charge to serve in every arena of human relationship.

> **"Himself bore our sins in His own body on the tree, that we, having died to sins, might live for righteousness—by whose stripes you were healed"**
> (2:24). Matthew 8:17 places the application of the prophecy of Isaiah 53 (referred to here) in the realm of physical healing. James accepts the premise that healing is found in the atonement of Jesus Christ on the Cross. Healing is secured through Christ's sacrifice, just as our salvation is assured on the Cross. The imperfect human assimilation of healing will be corrected in eternity (1 Cor. 15:40–43), where the impact of sin on man will be completely overturned.

Particularly of interest in this passage is the word to wives and husbands (see Family Life): "Wives . . . be submissive to your own husbands" (3:1; see Women), "husbands . . . [give] honor to the wife . . . that your prayers may not be hindered" (3:7). The chaste and modest conduct of a woman of God who has the "beauty of a gentle and quiet spirit, which is very precious in the sight of God" (3:4) is powerful. Even if a husband is an unbeliever and inconsiderate of his wife, the godly behavior of a wife can win her husband's heart to the Lord over time (3:1). In the meantime the Lord knows and cares about the challenge of living in an unequal marriage. The Lord also places a challenge before the husband. Wives are to be treated with understanding of their needs; they are to be treated with honor and dignity; wives are joint heirs with their husbands of "the grace of life." These godly wives are daughters of the living God, and the Father will personally reject the prayers of any husband who violates the marriage relationship.

> **"Wives, likewise, be submissive to your own husbands, that even if some do not obey the word, they, without a word, may be won by the conduct of their wives"**
> (3:1). Family members who see us at our best and worst may be particularly difficult to witness to with words. Peter says here that the demonstration of a changed life may be the most effective witness tool as the Holy Spirit testifies to a loved one.

B. Suffering for Christ's sake (3:13—4:19). The subject now moves to suffering—"Christ also suffered once for sins, the just for the unjust" (3:18). The Lord offers a pattern for all believers—if our suffering is "for righteousness' sake" the believer is blessed (3:14; *see* Lewdness).

> **"He went and preached to the spirits in prison"**
> (3:19). This extremely difficult passage is interpreted a number of ways. The most common interpretation is that Jesus spoke to the disembodied "spirits" (2 Pet. 2:4; Jude 6). When coupled with Acts 2:31 and Ephesians 4:9, it is suggested that this was accomplished during the time between the Crucifixion and the Resurrection. One point of error concerning this possible interpretation asserts that Jesus' atonement was not complete on the Cross and that during this time Christ completed what was lacking. First Peter completely forbids any such interpretation—**"Christ also suffered once for sins."** Jesus' words on the Cross settle the matter—**"It is finished!"**

> **"As each one has received a gift, minister it to one another, as good *stewards of the manifold grace of God"***
> (4:10). Every believer has a gift, and 1 Corinthians 12 emphasizes the unique place each gift has in the body of Christ. Every Christian must take a place and exercise his or her gift in order for the church to be vital and healthy. It is a matter of stewardship of God's gifts that we must serve where we are called—and do so in the grace of God for the benefit of the whole body of Christ.

C. Serving humbly while suffering (5:1–11). Motives of those who lead the flock of God must be pure. Jesus, the Chief Shepherd, is the pattern. As the devil continues the relentless attack "like a roaring lion" against the people of God, we must resist—and this can only be done "in the faith" (v. 9).

> **"When the Chief Shepherd appears, you will receive the crown of glory"**
> (5:4). To all who lead the flock of God there is a reward for faithful service—"the crown of glory." These leaders are worthy of "double honor" (1 Tim. 5:17) by the people of God because of: (1) their qualifications in teaching; (2) their vulnerability to specific assault by the demonic powers (1 Tim. 3:2, 6); and (3) the "stricter judgment" that comes to those who teach (James 3:1; *See* Care.)

> **"The devil walks about like a roaring lion"**
> (5:8–9). The power, stealth, swiftness, and ferocious nature of the lion bring terror and death to its prey. Peter is not offering a poetic metaphor, but a stern warning concerning the physical and eternal consequences of falling prey to this lion. Our resistance to evil (v. 9) must be direct and aggressive (Matt. 12: 28–29; Luke 11:22) and based not on our own strength but on Christ's.

CONCLUSION 5:12–14. "Babylon" probably refers to Rome, the place where this letter was written. Mark, "my son," is with Peter. (Paul had asked Mark to come to Rome in 2 Tim. 4:11.)

A. Silvanus, co-author of this letter (5:12). This is Silas, who traveled with Paul in Acts 15:40.

B. Greetings (5:13). There is an obvious

affection between the apostle and Mark, the Gospel writer.

C. Final exhortation with benediction (5:14). Peace to all those who have come to know the "Prince of Peace"—Jesus the Lord.

TRUTH-IN-ACTION through 1 PETER

Truth 1 Peter Teaches	**Action** 1 Peter Invites
1 Guidelines for Growing in Godliness Godliness invites others to ask why we have so much hope. Godly living involves suffering. We know this because Jesus suffered as our example. The godly person returns good for evil. When insulted, he blesses: and when caused to suffer, he never threatens in return.	**2:12** *Live* so unbelievers will give God glory because your life is righteous. **2:21** *Recognize* that Jesus suffered as our example. *Know* that you must suffer also. **2:23** *Refuse* to retaliate against any who attack you. *Never threaten* those who cause you suffering. **3:9** *Always bless* those who insult you. **3:15** *Always be prepared* to explain the difference that Jesus has made in your life. **4:9** *Practice* hospitality.
2 Steps to Holiness Being holy is being set apart unto God and from the world. People committed to God's holiness say "No!" to fleshly demands and live for the will of God. The holy person is always alert. keeping his mind clear, fit for his walk with God.	**1:15** *Set your life apart* fully to God, and *be holy* as God has commanded. **1:17** *Live* as strangers in this world. **2:1** *Be honest, sincere,* and *pure* in all your relationships. **2:11** *Refuse* to succumb to any demands of the flesh. **4:2** *Do not live* solely for your own desires; *do* the will of God. **4:7, 8** *Pray* with dedication, knowing the time is short. *Love* one another fervently.
3 Steps to Faithful Obedience God calls His people to obedience. As Jesus was absolutely obedient to His Father's will, so His church is to be to His. Obedience is to characterize the lives of the saints. This means that they do God's will and deny the desires that formerly controlled them. Faithful obedience purifies God's people.	**1:2** *Understand* that we were chosen in God and set apart by the Holy Spirit in order to live obediently to Jesus Christ. **1:14** *Become* characteristically obedient! *Do not let* former desires continue to shape or direct your life. **1:22** *Let* obedient living purify your life!
4 Key Lessons in Faith Faith in the Person of Christ and in the completed work of the Cross allows a Christian to endure rejection by the world. This rejection may even lead to death. The faith-filled Christian glorifies God and can count it as a blessing to stand for his Lord. Such a stand for Christ is preceded by the denial of fleshly lust so that the Spirit is in control.	**1:6, 7** *Know* that the steadfastness of your faith brings glory to Jesus. *Value* your faith more than gold. **1:10–12** *Understand* that the OT can be fully understood in the light of the NT. **4:1, 2** *Live* according to the will of God by ceasing from sin. **4:12–16** *Count* as a blessing any reproach or suffering for the name of Christ.
5 Keys to Relating to Authority All rightful authority is derived from God; therefore, to submit to authority honors God. Submission is an act of faith, establishing God as the ultimate authority over the relationship, be it connected with government, church, employment,	**2:13–17** *Submit* to and *respect* all authority. *Do not use* your freedom in Christ as an excuse for sin. **2:18** *Obey* and *respect* your employer. **5:5–7** *Submit* yourself to the authority of those who govern the church. *Humble* yourself before God; *trust* Him to promote you as He wills.

Truth 1 Peter Teaches	**Action** 1 Peter Invites
5 Keys to Relating to Authority *(continued)* or home. The higher the authority, the greater the accountability to God.	
6 Keys to Godly Relationships God designed marriage to illustrate the relationship He intends to have with His people. The husband is to give his wife honor and understanding, protecting her and acknowledging that she is a fully partnered heir of God. The wife is to accept the care and authority of the husband, living in a manner that honors him. The beauty of character and gentleness of spirit of such a woman will be precious to God and to her husband.	**3:1–6** Wife, *place* yourself in submission to your husband. *Live* in a way that honors your husband and God. *Believe* that this godly conduct will win an unsaved husband to Christ. **3:7** Husband, *be kind* and *gentle* with your wife. *Honor* her as your very best friend. *Listen* to her and *spend time* with her. *Cherish* her and make her feel extremely important. *Recognize* that not doing so will hinder your prayer life and obstruct answers. **4:8** *Love* all believers fervently.

A Comparison of 1 and 2 Peter

1 Peter	2 Peter
Emphasis: Hope in the midst of suffering	Emphasis: The danger of false teaching and practices
Christology: The sufferings of Christ for our salvation and example at His incarnation	Christology: The glory of Christ and the consummation of history at His return
The day of salvation when Christ suffered, died, and rose from the dead	The day of the Lord when Christ returns in judgment
Redemptive title: Christ	Title of dominion: Lord
Be encouraged in your present trials	Be warned of eschatological judgment
We need hope to face our trials	We need full knowledge to face error
Numerous similarities to Paul (especially Ephesians and Colossians)	Almost identical similarities to Jude (compare 2 Peter 2 with Jude 4–18)

KEYS TO 2 PETER AND JUDE
The Kingdom and the Last Call

Kingdom Key: God's Purpose in View

Both Peter and Jude look at a world gone berserk with its proud mockery of God (2 Pet. 3:3; Jude 18). At the same time, they both observe a terrible decline of morality and faith among some religious leaders (2 Pet. 2:1–22; Jude 4–16). The parallel thrust of the two epistles indicates that the two authors shared similar concerns but addressed them to separate audiences.

The "last call" is an expression commonly used to describe the end times, as God's last invitation goes out to mankind. His patience and grace have been awesome in their availability to humanity (2 Pet. 3:8–9). Such compassion requires a similar grace from His people, that they always reach out to "save with fear" one last soul. Because people of Christ's kingdom are never told when the concluding call will be, we are instructed in a lifestyle that *guards* against ever-increasing sinfulness and that experiences *growth and gains* for the kingdom through ever-increasing faith (2 Pet. 1:1–11; Jude 1–3).

The kingdom-minded must never give place to cynicism or lovelessness when facing the deepening decadence of the world. Though there are corrupt people within the circle of faith (2 Peter 2, Jude 4–17) as well as out-

> **Stand firm in the faith first given to us.**

side, growing worse and worse (2 Peter 3, Jude 18–19), the believer is called to constancy.

- "Contend for the faith" (Jude 3). Stand your ground, with a firmness born of an assurance that the Living Christ is within you and no power of darkness can triumph over you (2 Pet. 1:8–11; 3:14–18; Jude 24–25).
- Constantly "remember" (2 Pet. 1:12–13, 15). Three times Peter expresses the need to be renewed through remembrance, a triple reminder that might possibly have been born of his own triple failure (Mark 14:30, 72).
- Keep "praying in the Spirit" (Jude 20). A constancy in prayer—energized and enabled by the Holy Spirit (*see* 1 Cor. 14:15; Rom. 8:26–27; Eph. 6:18)—is an effective means of (a) intercession for the

(Please turn to page 451.)

Period in which Second Peter and Jude Likely Were Written

	Ascension of Jesus Pentecost A.D. 30		Persecution by Nero A.D. 64–68		
Birth of Jesus 4 B.C.		Council of Jerusalem A.D. 49		Destruction of temple A.D. 70	Death of John c. A.D. 100

Second Peter and Jude: remain true; beware of

Master Key: God's Son Revealed
2 Peter

The deity of Christ is evident in the way that God and Christ are closely linked in 2 Peter 1:1–2. God knows Christ as His "Son" (1:17). Divine purpose and activity are centered in Jesus Christ as His grace and power are given to believers (1:2–3, 8; 2:9, 20; 3:18) who are to look for His Coming (1:16) and for the arrival of His eternal kingdom (1:11). It is the Scriptures that assure the believer of a destiny with Jesus Christ (1:16–21; *see also* 3:1–2).

Jude

The present activity of the living Christ is assumed in Jude's letter. Jude is His servant and He preserves His own (v. 1), though false teachers deny Him (v. 4). Believers await the future blessing of "the mercy of our Lord Jesus Christ unto eternal life" (v. 21).

Power Key: God's Spirit at Work
2 Peter

The only direct reference to the Holy Spirit is in 2 Peter 1:21, which describes the Spirit's work in "moving" the human authors of the prophetic Scriptures, which in turn disqualifies any "private interpretation" (*see* note on 1:20). However, the Spirit is obviously at work in providing the "divine power" for growth in the grace and knowledge of Jesus Christ (1:2–8; 3:18).

Jude

The Holy Spirit causes biblical teaching to come alive, so that the Christian community is built up in its "most holy faith," that is, in the apostolic teaching (*see* Jude 20). This is accomplished through "praying in the Holy Spirit" (v. 20). Accordingly, the Spirit is important as the One through whom God preserves His own from worldly error (*see*
(Please turn to page 450.)

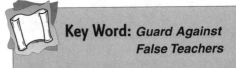

Key Word: *Guard Against False Teachers*

The basic theme that runs through 2 Peter is the contrast between the knowledge and practice of truth versus falsehood.

Key Verses: Second Peter 1:20–21; 3:9–11

Key Chapter: Second Peter 1

The Scripture clearest in defining the relationship between God and man on the issue of inspiration is contained in 1:19–21. Three distinct principles surface:

(1) that the interpretation of Scriptures is not limited to a favored elect but is open for all who "rightly [divide] the word of truth" (2 Tim. 2:15);

(2) that the divinely inspired prophet did not initiate the Scripture himself; and

(3) that the Holy Spirit (not the emotion or circumstances of the moment) moved holy men.

Key Word: *Contend for the Faith*

This epistle condemns the practices of heretical teachers in the church and counsels the readers to stand firm,
(Please turn to page 450.)

false or corrupt leaders dealing in half-truths.

Power Key *continued from page 449*

Jude 1, 24). In contrast, the false teachers are devoid of the Spirit (v. 19), despite whatever claims they may make.

Key Word *continued from page 449*

grow in their faith, and contend for the truth.

Key Verse: Jude 3

Introducing
2 PETER

Author and Date. Peter's letter gives instruction and exhortation from the apostle as he nears the end of his life (2 Pet. 1:1, 12–15). According to early church tradition, Peter was martyred in Rome during the reign of Nero. If the tradition is reliable, then his death occurred before A.D. 68, when Nero died.

Many New Testament scholars question Peter's authorship of this letter, primarily because it differs in style and thought from 1 Peter and because there is little evidence from the early church fathers supporting Peter as the author. Some scholars maintain that an author passed on apostolic teaching after Peter's martyrdom by writing in his name, suggesting that this was an accepted literary practice in the first century. However, conservative scholars usually hold that Peter wrote both epistles, explaining the differences by Peter's use of an amanuensis (stenographic reporter) other than Silvanus (1 Pet. 5:12), or by writing the letter himself, without scribal help.

Certain references in 2 Peter indicate Petrine authorship: The author identifies himself as Simon Peter, an apostle (1:1); he claims to have been with Christ on the Mount of Transfiguration (1:16–18); he had written a previous letter to the people to whom 2 Peter is addressed (3:1); and he uses many words and phrases similar to those found in 1 Peter. These factors point to 2 Peter as a genuine work of the apostle Peter.

Background. Whereas 1 Peter encourages Christians facing opposition from the world, 2 Peter warns Christians against false teachers within their fellowship who would lead them into apostasy. Fidelity to the apostolic teaching is the main concern (*see especially*

1:12–16; 3:1–2, 15–16). Heretical teachers will appear (2:1–2) and in fact are already on the scene (2:12–22). They deny the Lord, exhibit a sensuous life-style, and are destined for destruction. They ridicule the idea of the Lord's return. These characteristics fit the Gnostic heresy, which developed more fully in the second century, but whose roots were fixed in the first century.

The author evidently has a specific community in mind (3:15), and if that community is the same as that addressed in 1 Peter (*see* 3:1), then this letter was intended for Christians somewhere in Asia Minor.

Content. The answer to encroaching error is steadfastness through growing in the knowledge of the Lord. The letter opens and closes with the theme of cultivating Christian maturity (1:2–11; 3:14–18). "Knowledge" in 2 Peter is more than intellectual perception. It is an experience of God and Christ that results in moral transformation (1:2–3; 2:20). This is the true *gnosis* (knowledge), which combats heretical Gnostic influence. The basis for that knowledge is the Scriptures, called the "prophetic word" (1:19–21) and the apostolic teaching (3:1–2, 15–16).

Chapter 2 gives a lengthy description of and warning against the false teachers. Apparently they at one time had "escaped the pollutions of the world through the knowledge of the Lord and Savior Jesus Christ" (2:20).

The last chapter emphasizes the Second Coming, an object of attack by scoffers, and explains why this hope is yet unfulfilled. It also assures the fulfillment of the promise of the Lord's return and teaches that its expectation should motivate Christians to godly behavior.

Personal Application. The concerns of 2 Peter are also concerns of the contemporary church as it counteracts worldliness and humanistic philosophy. There are still false teachers who deal in half-truths regarding the Christian faith, and this letter provides a clear response to them.

Kingdom Key *continued from page 448*

lost, (b) warfare against dark powers, and (c) a God-ordained means of edification. To "build yourself up" is not to be "puffed up" with self-

ish concern; it is to erect spiritual walls of defense against evil, and to cultivate spiritual strength in your own soul (1 Cor. 14:1–4).

Surveying
2 PETER

I. GREETING 1:1–2. This general epistle to the church is not addressed to a specific group. Peter is the author, although there are questions about differing vocabulary and style from 1 Peter. However, those differences could be explained by a change in scribes between the two letters.

II. TRUE VERSUS FALSE TEACHING 1:3—2:3. Peter announces that his purpose in writing is so that his readers can be "partakers of the divine nature" (1:4). In personal character and faith, nothing will be withheld from the people of God "to make your call and election sure . . . so an entrance will be supplied to you abundantly into the everlasting kingdom of our Lord and Savior Jesus Christ" (1:10–11).

A. Pursuit of moral graces (1:3–11). "Divine power has given to us all things" (v. 3). Peter goes on to declare that "all things" are directly related to knowing the Lord, becoming like Him, and growing in character (vv. 5–7; *see* Brotherly Love; Virtue). We are then accountable to live within this "power" as His people, whom the Lord has "cleansed from his old sins" (1:9).

B. Peter's testament (1:12–15). Peter knows that he is going to die (John 21:18–19). Probably writing from Rome, Peter is "careful to ensure that you always have reminder of these things after my decease" (1:15). It is possible that there is some reference here to other "reminders." First Peter 5:13 informs us that "Mark my son" was with him; some have suggested that Peter's influence is prominent in Mark's Gospel.

C. Prophetic Scriptures versus false teachers (1:16—2:3). Peter contrasts his eyewitness experience with Jesus to the "cunningly devised fables" of false teachers. Peter witnessed the transfiguration of the Lord, heard the voice of God, and now declares that "we have the prophetic word confirmed" (1:19). This is the confirmation of *prophecy in the Scriptures so that the apostolic witness is irre-

sistible and irrefutable truth in the presence of "false prophets" and "false teachers" (2:1; *see* Heresies).

> **"No prophecy of Scripture is of any private interpretation"** (1:20). The Word of God is not to be handled arbitrarily and is not subject to the novel interpretation of those who would distort it for their own purposes. In the matter of Bible interpretation, the Holy Spirit has assisted the people of God in "rightly dividing the word of truth" for two thousand years. A bizarre or contradictory interpretation of Scripture is a sure sign of self-serving or heretical teachers.

III. EXPOSURE AND DOOM OF FALSE TEACHERS 2:4–22. "Like natural brute beasts made to be caught and destroyed" (v. 12). Peter describes false teachers as "carousing in their own deceptions while they feast with you" (2:13). These teachers are in the church, threatening the message of Christ.

A. Destruction of the false teachers (2:4–10). There is a certainty of judgment against those who mislead the flock. Like fallen angels, and those who rejected Noah's message, false teachers will not be spared.

B. Description of the false teachers (2:11–22). "Eyes full of adultery . . . enticing unstable souls," these false teachers announce that life in Christ is spiritual, and that therefore the sins of the body are immaterial to life in Christ. "They have forsaken the right way. . . . These are wells without water, clouds carried by a tempest, for whom is reserved the blackness of darkness forever" (vv. 15–17). In the proclamation of "liberty" these false teachers have caused some saints to return to the sins they rejected after coming to Christ. The tragic return to sin is described in the vilest terms: "A dog returns to his own vomit . . . a sow, having washed, [returning] to her wallowing in the mire" (v. 22).

IV. WARNING AGAINST END-TIME DECEIVERS 3:1–18. The apostle now turns to the return of Christ. Deceivers ask, "Where is the promise of His coming?" Peter's soul-searching response highlights God's ever-reaching love: "The Lord is . . . not willing that any should perish" (v. 9). God's patience in returning is based on His compassion to reach those who will respond.

A. Scoffers in the last days (3:1–7). These people reject the word of God. The world came into existence by the word of God, and is sustained in the same way. This same word guarantees both the return of the Lord and judgment of the unrighteous (*see* Pure).

B. Believers and the day of the Lord (3:8–18). Because believers are to look forward to a new heaven and a new earth, they must "be diligent to be found by Him in peace, without spot and blameless" (3:14). Reject the deceivers and "grow in the grace and knowledge of our Lord and Savior Jesus Christ."

> **"The day of the Lord will come as a thief in the night"**
> (3:8–14). This passage offers three promises. First is the *promise of salvation for all who respond in faith (v. 9); second, the melting, burning destruction of the entire earth (v. 10); third, the coming of new heavens and a new earth (v. 13). All this happens quickly, without warning—like a thief.

TRUTH-IN-ACTION through 2 PETER

Truth 2 Peter Teaches	**Action** 2 Peter Invites
1 Guidelines for Growing in Godliness People who are controlled by the lusts of the flesh have no respect for the life-style of the godly. Such people delight in enticing others into sin. However, God knows the godly and will deliver them, as He knows the ungodly and will judge them. It is His desire that every Christian be able to appear before Him in purity.	**2:9** *Persevere* in godliness. *Know* it is the safest place you can be. **2:19** *Diligently avoid* returning to practices from which you have been delivered. *Understand* that the resulting bondage will be even greater. **3:14–18** *Live* a blameless life. *Do not alter* your course toward Christlikeness. **3:16** *Be careful* how you handle the Bible. *Recognize* that the untaught distort the truth. *Be careful* what teaching you listen to. *Measure* everything by God's Word.
2 Steps to Fruitfulness Peter gives us a progressive list of Christian virtues that, when established in our lives, will cause us to be fruitful in the very knowledge of God. The life that comes from the knowledge of God can produce only good in its response to others. To fail to grow in Christ results in an inability to perceive the blessings received in initial salvation so that our identification with Jesus is forgotten or ignored.	**1:5–8** *Recognize* that an effective and productive life results by sanctification (character transformation) that begins with faith and results in love.
3 Steps to Dynamic Devotion Devotion to Jesus supplies what we need for godliness. Strong devotion results from an unyielding commitment to God's Word, which alone is the source for Christian thinking. Any other source will eventually corrupt the believer's mind.	**1:3, 4** *Understand* that God's power provides everything you need to live a godly life through your relationship with Jesus Christ. **3:1, 2** *Strengthen* your thinking by reading, rereading, and studying the Bible. *Understand* that wholesome thinking resuits from dwelling upon God's Word.
4 How to Identify the False Teacher The false teacher or false prophet is led by the flesh, seeking to obtain power or gain for himself from the	**2:1–3** *Reject* any teaching that denies the lordship of Jesus. *Know* that the false teacher brings about distrust of true ministers of God. *Judge* the words of every teaching. *Let God judge* the teacher. *(continued)*

Truth 2 Peter Teaches	**Action** 2 Peter Invites
4 How to Identify the False Teacher (continued) ministry. Initially, his message may not be false, but his motivation in ministry is fleshly, so he appeals to the fleshly in others, offering them some carnal or soulish satisfaction. He will ultimately introduce some doctrine that is contrary to the truth. Each of us must use the Word of God to measure the words any preacher speaks, and any variation or imbalance in what is taught must be questioned. We also need to be sensitive to the prompting of the Holy Spirit in this judgment. We are to judge only the teaching. God will judge the teacher.	**2:18–22** *Beware* teaching what sounds good but means nothing. *Be established* so that you cannot be lured back into sin by false doctrine.
5 Key Lessons in Faith Logic alone cannot lead us to effective Christian living: faith is needed. The Christian life is the result of hearing God's Word, trusting it, and applying it through faithful obedience. Faith may not yield immediate dividends: its ultimate return will be realized in eternity.	**1:4** *Understand* that God's promises result in our 1) sharing in God's very nature and 2) escaping moral and spiritual corruption. **1:16–21** *Recognize* the divine origin of the Scriptures. *Understand* that any personal understanding must be scrutinized in the light of God's Word. **3:11–13** *Understand* that the ultimate goal of the believer is not in this life. *Know* that our hope is in the new heaven and new earth. *Live* with a holy disregard for this world's values and all that controls it.

Introducing

JUDE

Author and Date. The author of Jude identifies himself as the "brother of James," likely the James who was the brother of our Lord and leader of the Jerusalem church (*see* Acts 15:13; 21:18; Gal. 1:19; 2:12). Mark 6:3 mentions Jude (Judas) as a brother of the Lord.

Considerations in establishing the date of Jude include whether this letter is dependent upon 2 Peter, or whether 2 Peter is dependent upon Jude, or whether both letters have drawn from a third document, which circulated as a warning against false teachers. Since most of Jude has parallels in 2 Peter, some kind of interdependence is obvious. If Jude was written before 2 Peter, it may have been as early as A.D. 65. If it was written after 2 Peter, as many scholars assume, it may have been as late as A.D. 80.

Background. Jude urgently warns an unknown community of Christians against false teachers. As in 2 Peter, these would-be leaders are sensual (vv. 4, 16, 18), they pervert the truth (v. 4), and they are destined for divine judgment (vv. 14–15). They are called "dreamers" in verse 8 (perhaps given to dreams or visions), they are "clouds without water" (v. 12), and they are exposed as "not having the Spirit" in verse 19. The last reference hints that the false teachers represented themselves as those who did have the Spirit (*see* Matt. 7:22–23). They may also be forerunners of Gnostic heretics in the second century who claimed spirituality.

Content. Jude begins and ends with an affirmation of God's gracious action on behalf of believers, stressing divine preservation (vv. 1, 24). However, Christians themselves are "to contend earnestly for the faith" (v. 3). *Their* responsibilities are further developed in verses 20–23 by a series of practical exhortations. The balance of the letter uses Old Testament analogies to expose false teachers secretly at work within the community. These evil workers seek to overthrow the faith of God's people.

Personal Application. Today, perpetrators of unbiblical ethical standards, who may even claim to have the Spirit, threaten the godly commitment of Christians. However, God's power is able to keep us from falling. *Our responsibility is to build ourselves up in the truth through praying in the Holy Spirit and to anticipate our final salvation.* The Scriptures are our resource. At the same time, we are to be alert and vocal in warning those who are being swayed by false, humanistic philosophies prevalent today.

Surveying
JUDE

GREETING VV. 1–2. Jude asserts apostolic authority and encourages the "called" and "sanctified" ones.

I. WARNING AGAINST FALSE TEACHERS WITHIN THE COMMUNITY VV. 3–19. Using images from Israel's past, Jude warns God's people against the teachers of deceptions, the sensually indulgent, and rebellious ones among them who pollute the purity of the church. The church is not to be surprised by the infiltration of the insincere and the spiritually defective, because Jesus warned of "mockers in the last time" (v. 18).

A. Reason for the warning (vv. 3–4). The persecution of the church by the Romans is far less serious than the threat of corruption from the infiltration of teachers who "turn the grace of our God into lewdness" (v. 4; *see* Lord).

B. Reminder of former ungodly persons (vv. 5–7). Referring to the wickedness of the Nephilim in Genesis 6:1–4 and the judgment of Sodom and Gomorrah, Jude warns the church of the consequence of immorality.

C. Character and judgment of false teachers (vv. 8–19). The murderous Cain, the greedy Balaam, and the rebellious Korah are the spiritual predecessors of these false teachers. They abrogate to themselves privilege that even the archangel Michael would not dare assume (*see* Angels). Their words betray the pride and manipulation of those who divide the body of Christ, and they are void of the Holy Spirit (*see* Error).

"The Lord rebuke you!"
(9). This pattern of rebuke is also found in Zechariah 3:2, where the high priest, standing in the presence of God, was unwilling to personally rebuke Satan. The awareness of devilish power should bring humility to all believers in dealing with the demonic. Believers have no authority to cast out spirits apart from their relationship with Jesus Christ (Acts 19:15–16)—only as His disciples are Christians privileged to exercise this power (Matt. 10:1). The place of unbelievers in God's judgment is dramatically declared as being "the blackness of darkness forever" (v. 13).

"The Lord comes with ten thousands of His saints"
(14–15). The judgment of the ungodly with eternal punishment will occur at the coming of Christ (2 Thess. 1:9). Christ will come with the angels (Matt. 24:31), as surely as He was attended by them at His incarnation in Bethlehem (Luke 2:13). This time they will assist in the judging process.

II. EXHORTATION FOR PERSEVERANCE VV. 20–23. The answer to the threat and confusion of the deceivers is the fullness of the Holy Spirit. "Praying in the Holy Spirit" edifies the believer (1 Cor. 14:4). The power to be sustained in the midst of such spiritual assault comes only from the Holy Spirit.

A. Maintaining the faith (vv. 20–21). Our ability to continue in relationship with Christ demands that we keep ourselves in God's love; it is an active choice we make daily. (*See* Holy Spirit Gifts.)

B. Rescuing those deceived (vv. 22–23). Deceivers deliberately destroy faith and are subject to God's wrath. The deceived are objects of compassion in need of rescue.

DOXOLOGY VV. 24–25. Our confidence is in the fact that God the Father will personally keep us eternally safe by His power (*see* Able).

TRUTH-IN-ACTION through **JUDE**

Truth Jude Teaches	**Action** Jude Invites
1 Be Warned; Be Wise There have always been those who attempt to divert God's people from their main purpose. Whether angels or men, God knows how to deal with the rebellious, but believers are warned not to participate with any such persons. The wicked appeals to the lusts of the eye, lusts of the flesh and to inordinate pride. They will pretend to love God, appear to do good works, but on close examination they are as fruitless as the fig tree that Jesus cursed. The wise will be able to identify those whose object is to be god, rather than to serve God. It will take a deeply spiritual heart to know how to reach any who are deep into evil without being contaminated—hating the sin but still loving the sinner.	**v. 3** *Contend strongly* for biblical faith. *Accept* no form of alteration. **v. 4** *Reject* anyone who teaches that grace is "God's permission to sin." *Understand* that such teaching is godlessness. **vv. 8-19** *Recognize* the marks of false teachers. *Rebuke* and *reject* any teacher who . . . (1) teaches things one cannot apply. (2) practices licentious behavior. (3) speaks disrespectfully of authority. (4) rejects established authority. (5) is more worried about money than the welfare of those to whom he ministers. (6) promises things he cannot and does not produce. (7) constantly changes his message; always teaches "some new thing." (8) shows no enduring fruit. (9) complains and criticizes others. (10) is motivated by personal gain. (11) is a self-promoter. (12) flatters others when it is to his advantage. **vv. 17, 18** *Decry* and *reject* any minister who 1) follows his own desires, 2) is divisive in any way, or 3) gives no evidence of Holy Spirit life and dynamic in his life. **vv. 20, 21** *Pray continuously* in the Spirit. *Know* that this promises a certain and holy self-edification, which is imperative if you want to build others up. *Persist* in loving attitudes and behavior through the Holy Spirit. **v. 23** *Warn, exhort,* and *save* others from error when possible. *Do not let others fall* when it is in your power to prevent it.
2 Key to Joyful Worship We fully acknowledge that only by the working and grace of God is anyone able to come joyfully into His presence in blameless worship. He is the lawful Ruler of every life. Our God is King of the Universe. How blessed we are to serve Him!	**vv. 24, 25** *Trust in the ability of God* to bring you blameless into His presence.

KEYS TO 1, 2 AND 3 JOHN
The Life of the Kingdom

Kingdom Key: God's Purpose in View

The opening two verses of 1 John rivet our attention upon "life." John earlier quoted Jesus as defining life in His own Person ("I am the life"—John 14:6). Now John testifies: "We have seen . . . looked upon . . . handled . . . life" (1:1). The New Testament writers—and especially John—use this word to mean that "in Christ" a completely new and different order of life has entered the human arena.

"Eternal life" (in some translations "everlasting," but all translating the same Greek word) is revealed as more than a *quantity* of life; it focuses on a *quality* of life. The adjective "eternal" clearly denotes unlimited duration of existence, but new birth has done more than bring the believer into an endless kingdom. God's salvation has introduced us into a new realm—a new creation (2 Cor. 5:17). Beyond mere human experience is a divine dimension of life with a new richness of quality, depth of meaning, and increase of purpose. A fallen creature (of a limited order of life) has been returned to the Creator's original order and intent. This requires that we speak of the "life" now available through Jesus Christ in some new ways.

John clearly wishes to convey this and is profoundly emphatic about the new dimensions of "life" in Christ's king-

> To live in His fellowship, walk in Christ's light.

dom. His emphasis is seen in the frequency and manner of his usage. For example, though John's writings occupy less than twenty percent of the chapters in the New Testament (50/260), his use of the word "life" (Greek: *zoe*) involves almost forty percent of its occurrences (68/186). Since John seldom uses the phrase "kingdom of God," it seems that his use of the word "life" intends the understanding of "kingdom-life"—life under another order; that is, the rule of the Creator.

Trench's *Synonyms of the New Testament* notes the striking distinction between two Greek words for "life." *Zoe*, which is consistently used in the New Testament to describe the life brought by Christ's redemption, refers to life *intensive*, while *bios* is life *extensive*. The first focuses on substance and meaning (or quality), the *(Please turn to page 458.)*

Period in which First, Second, and Third John Likely Were Written

Ascension of Jesus
Pentecost
A.D. 30

Persecution by Nero
A.D. 64–68

Birth of Jesus
4 B.C.

Council of Jerusalem
A.D. 49

Destruction of temple
A.D. 70

Death of John
C. A.D. 100

The Epistles of John: constancy of faith in Christ is

Master Key: God's Son Revealed
1 John

John emphasizes both the deity and the humanity of Jesus, declaring that in Him God fully entered human life. A test of Christianity is correct belief about the Incarnation (1 John 4:2, 15; 5:1). Jesus is our Advocate with the Father (2:1). Sin is incongruous in the life of a Christian; but if he does sin, Jesus pleads his case. Jesus is the propitiation for our sins (2:2; 4:10). Jesus is also Savior, sent by God to rescue us from sin (1:7; 3:5; 4:14). Only through Him can we have eternal life (5:11–12).

John presents the Second Coming of Jesus as an incentive for us to remain firm in the faith (1 John 2:28), and he gives assurance that our complete transformation into Christ's likeness will occur at His return.

2 John

In his second letter John presents both the deity of Christ (v. 3) and His humanity (v. 7). Anyone who denies the fundamental truth concerning the divine-human Person of Jesus Christ does not have God (v. 9). John views fellowship as a distinctive feature of the Christian life, but he leaves no doubt that biblical fellowship is impossible where the apostolic doctrine of the Person and work of Christ is denied or compromised.

3 John

In 3 John the apostle presents Jesus as the Truth in whom we should walk. Devotion to Him motivates genuine teachers in their itinerant service (v. 7). The lives of Gaius and Demetrius exactly harmonized with the teaching of Christ and gave strong witness to the power of His love. On the other hand, the attitude of Diotrephes shows a marked contrast to the true life in which Christ is to be first in everything.

(Please turn to page 458.)

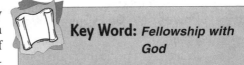

Key Word: *Fellowship with God*

The major theme of 1 John is fellowship with God. John wants his readers to have assurance of the indwelling God through their abiding relationship with Him (2:28; 5:13). Belief in Christ should be manifested in the practice of righteousness and love for the brethren, which in turn produces joy and confidence before God.

Key Verses: First John 1:3–4; 5:11–13

Key Chapter: First John 1

The two central passages for continued fellowship with God are John 15 and 1 John 1. John 15 relates the positive side of fellowship, that is, abiding in Christ. First John 1 unfolds the other side, pointing out that when Christians do not abide in Christ, they must seek forgiveness before fellowship can be restored.

Key Word: *Avoid Fellowship with False Teachers*

The basic theme of this brief letter is steadfastness in the practice and purity of the apostolic doctrine that the *(Please turn to page 458.)*

shown in brotherly love and in commitment to Him.

Power Key *continued from page 457*

Power Key: God's Spirit at Work
1 John

In his first epistle John describes a threefold ministry of the Holy Spirit. First, God's gift of the Spirit assures us of our relationship to Christ, both that He abides in us (1 John 3:24) and that we abide in Him (4:13). Second, the Holy Spirit testifies to the reality of the Incarnation of Christ (4:2; 5:6–8). Third, the Spirit leads true believers into a full realization of the truth concerning Jesus, that they may successfully oppose the heretics who deny that truth (2:20; 4:4).

2 John

Although the second epistle does not specifically mention the Holy Spirit, His ministry is evident, particularly in bearing witness to the truth concerning the Person of Christ. The Spirit enables the true believer to discern false teachings and to "abide in the doctrine of Christ."

Key Word *continued from page 457*

readers "have heard from the beginning" (v. 6).

Key Verses: Second John 9, 10

Key Word: *Enjoy Fellowship with the Brethren*

The basic theme of 3 John is to enjoy and continue to have fellowship (hospitality) with fellow believers, especially full-time Christian workers. This is contrasted between the truth and servanthood of Gaius and the error and selfishness of Diotrephes.

3 John

The third epistle also does not refer directly to the Holy Spirit, but again His ministry is apparent throughout its message, particularly in enabling believers to "walk in the truth" and empowering itinerant missionaries in their ministries. The fruit of the Spirit is evident in the lives of Gaius and Demetrius.

Kingdom Key *continued from page 456*

second only on existence and duration (or quantity). (*Psuche* also occurs on occasion, simply meaning "animate" life.)

These words emphasize a beautiful truth. "Eternal life" in "the kingdom" is born of another source (John 3:3, 5—"from above"), is nurtured by another supply ("I am the bread of life"—John 6:48), and has no equal or meaningful counterpart outside of Christ: "He who has the Son has life; he who does not have the Son of God does not have life" (1 John 5:12). Indeed, in the King, the Creator's original intent for life's meaning and substance has been once again restored: "This is the testimony: that God has given us eternal life, and this life is in His Son" (1 John 5:11).

Introducing
1 JOHN

Author and Recipients. Although the first epistle is anonymous, its style and vocabulary clearly indicate that it was written by the author of the Gospel of John. Internal evidence also points to John as the author, and ancient testimony unanimously ascribes the epistle to him.

The tone of 1 John is friendly and fatherly, reflecting the authority that age and apostleship bring. The style is informal and personal, revealing the apostle's intimate relationship with God and God's people. Lack of a special dedication and salutation indicates that the letter was circular, probably sent to the churches near Ephesus, where John spent his latter years.

Date. The weight of early and strong Christian tradition that John spent his latter years at Ephesus, together with the fact that the tone of the writings suggests that they are the product of a mature man who has enjoyed profound spiritual experience, points to a date near the end of the first century. In addition, the character of the heresy combated in the letter points to the same time, approximately A.D. 90.

Occasion and Purpose. John states that he wrote his first letter to give assurance of eternal life to those "who believe in the name of the Son of God" (1 John 5:13). The uncertainty of his readers about their spiritual status was caused by an unsettling conflict with the teachers of a false doctrine. John refers to the teachings as deceitful (2:26; 3:7) and to the teachers as "false prophets" (4:1), liars (2:22), and antichrists (2:18, 22; 4:3). They had once been within the church, but had withdrawn (2:19) and had "gone out into the world" (4:1) to propagate their dangerous heresy.

The heresy was a forerunner of second-century Gnosticism, which taught that matter is essentially evil and spirit is essentially good. This dualistic viewpoint caused the false teachers to deny the Incarnation of Christ and, hence, the Resurrection. The true God, they taught, could never indwell a material body of flesh and blood. Therefore, the human body that Jesus supposedly possessed was not real, but merely apparent. John wrote vigorously against this error (see 2:22–23; 4:3).

They also taught that since the evil human body was merely an envelope for the spirit within, and since nothing the body could do could affect the inner spirit, ethical distinctions ceased to be relevant. Hence, they had no sin. John answered this error with indignation (see 2:4, 6, 15–17; 3:3, 7, 9–10; 5:18).

"Gnosticism" is a word derived from the Greek *gnosis*, meaning "knowledge." Gnostics later taught salvation by mental enlightenment, which came only to elite spiritual initiates, not to ordinary Christians. Hence, they substituted intellectual pursuits for faith and exalted speculation above the basic tenets of the gospel. John reacted strenuously (see 2:20, 27), declaring that there is no private revelation reserved for a few intellectuals, and that the whole body of believers possesses the apostolic teaching. John's purpose in writing, then, was to expose the heresy of the false teachers and to confirm the faith of the true believers.

Content. First John stresses the themes of love, light, knowledge, and life in its warnings against heresy. These major elements are repeated throughout the letter, with love being the dominant note. Possessing love is clear evidence that one is a Christian, and lack of love indicates that one is in darkness (1 John 2:9–11; 3:10–23; 4:7–21).

John affirms that God is light, and fellowship with Him causes one to walk in the light in true fellowship with other believers. Fellowship with God and the brethren enables one to recognize, through the anointing of God, false doctrine and the spirit of the Antichrist.

Fellowship with God necessitates walking in the light and obeying the commandments of God (1:6–7; 2:3–5). The one "who practices righteousness is righteous, just as He is righteous" (3:7), while "whoever does not practice righteousness is not of God" (3:10). The love of the Father and the love of the world are totally incompatible (2:15–17), and no one born of God is in the habit of practicing sin (3:9; 5:18). Christ is the antithesis of sin, and He has appeared that He might take away all of our sins (3:5).

Chapter 4 continues the theme of understanding the rival spirits—the false prophets who have gone out into the world (v. 1). In order to test the spirits we must find whom they acknowledge as savior and lord. Every spirit that does not acknowledge that Jesus Christ is God in the flesh is not from God (v. 3).

The epistle ends with the testimony of Jesus the Son of God. Jesus is the One who came. The technical title of the Messiah is "He who comes" or "He who is to come" (Matt. 11:3; 1 John 5:6). John identifies Him as the One who came by water and by blood, the God who came and dwelt among us, the Word that was made flesh.

Personal Application. The positive note of Christian certainty is prominent in 1 John. Thirty-nine times the verb "know" occurs.

Christian truth is beyond the realm of speculation, because it is irrevocably moored to the historical event of Jesus Christ and the apostolic witness to that event. In addition, Christians possess the anointing and witness of the Holy Spirit to assure them of the truth about God, Christ, and their own spiritual standing.

Three tests prove the genuineness of Christianity: the test of belief (1 John 4:2), the test of obedience (2:3), and the test of love (4:20). The same affirmations are stated negatively. The one who professes to be a Christian, but who cannot pass the test of belief (2:22), the test of obedience (1:6), and the test of love (4:20), is a liar. John brings all three tests together in 5:1–5, where he indicates that a profession of Christianity is false unless it is characterized by correct belief, godly obedience, and brotherly love. The same tests are valid today.

Surveying
1 JOHN

I. THE INCARNATION 1:1–10. John is not writing a doctrinal treatise; he is declaring to his readers that he has "heard," "seen," and "handled" the Word of Life—Jesus. Jesus was not a phantom, an apparition of a spirit being; He was flesh and blood. This point is absolutely crucial in the late first century A.D., as the last of the twelve apostles affirms the physical existence of Jesus, the God/Man.

A. God became flesh in human form (1:1–4). This form is familiar to the first chapter of John's Gospel. The current theological ideas about Jesus want to exclude humanity from Jesus' nature. John is setting the record straight. If Jesus was not human, then His death on the Cross was make-believe. Jesus really lived, really died, and really paid for the redemption of Adam's lost race. John demands that the reception of this truth is the basis for fellowship in Christ (v. 3).

"Concerning the Word of life—the life was manifested, and we have seen, and bear witness, and declare to you that eternal life which was with the Father and was manifested to us" (1:1–2). In verse 1, John declares that "we" saw Jesus, touched Jesus, and now bear witness to Jesus. The testimony of all believers must convey that Jesus was a real person and at the same time was God in the flesh come to dwell among us (John 1:14). Because Jesus was really human, He could die for our sins. Because Jesus was really God, He could be sinless and offer a pure sacrifice to redeem us from our sins. Anything less in our witness of Christ is unacceptable.

B. God is light (1:5–10). The light has to do with the absence of the darkness of sin. John knows that the problem with all humanity is sin. We have been darkened by it, and only confession of our sin to God can bring forgiveness and cleansing (v. 9; *see* Blood). Denial of our involvement in sin only brings condemnation.

II. THE LIFE OF RIGHTEOUSNESS 2:1–29. This chapter gives four simple commands to "my little children" (v. 1): "Keep His commandments" (v. 3), "love the brethren" (v. 10), "do not love the world" (v. 15), and "abide in Him" (v. 28). A life of righteousness insists on obedience to the Word, wholesome relationships, avoidance of the pollution of the world, and staying close to Jesus.

A. Walking in the light (2:1–17). Keeping God's Word ensures our being "*perfected in love" (v. 5). Rejection of God's Word ultimately brings a person to violate either the walk with God the Father or a relationship with another person. Immorality, corruption, hatred, and separation from God result.

B. Warning against the spirit of Antichrist (2:18–29). The denial of the Son is the spirit of Antichrist. The denial in verse 19 came from a part of the church that rejected the Christ of the Bible and the Christ John himself knew and substituted a false christ—these people are "liars" (v. 22) and "they do not have the Father either" (v. 23; *see* Prophecy).

III. THE LIFE OF THE CHILDREN OF GOD 3:1—4:6. The children of God take on the character of their Father—"We shall be like Him" (3:2). Children live with their Father—"Whoever abides in Him does not sin" (3:6). Clearly, this is not a reference to the accomplished perfection of true children of God. The definitive statement in 2:1 declares that the apostle is writing so that his flock will not sin. However, "if anyone sins, we have an Advocate with the Father, Jesus Christ the righteous." The true children of God also act like their Father—"Let us not love in word or in tongue, but in deed and in truth" (3:18). Finally, children ask from their Father and receive what they need (3:22).

A. Righteousness (3:1–12). Our righteousness is from God, and it empowers us to live a life that is not habitually overrun with disobedience. We have the living seed of our Father, the righteous one, within us, and it will continue to grow in the climate of obedience (v. 9).

> **"When He is revealed, we shall be like Him"**
> (3:2). The revelation of Christ occurs at His return. The promise of our transformation into His likeness is not physical or intellectual; it is both moral and spiritual (*see* Pure). The sanctification of believers affects all aspects of their lives (1 Thess. 5:23). The result is Christ-likeness, His image stamped into us by the work of the Holy Spirit (2 Cor. 3:18).

> **"The Son of God was manifested, that He might destroy the works of the devil"**
> (3:8). The death, disease, and destruction which came to man in the Garden (Genesis 3) have been overcome by Jesus Christ in His victory at Calvary. Through sin, the devil has exploited the weakness of people and has been able to "work" the pain, cruelty, and evil of his kingdom on the human scene. Jesus' total triumph has completely undone the works of the devil (1 Cor. 2:6–8).

B. Love (3:13–24). Our love for each other in the body of Christ is proof of our being resurrected into new life (v. 14).

C. Belief (4:1–6). Our faith is in Jesus Christ who "has come in the flesh" (v. 2). This truth allows us to stand confident against the spirit of Antichrist. (*See* Prophecy.)

> **"He who is in you is greater than he who is in the world"**
> (4:4). These familiar words inspire great courage as they are applied in the spiritual confrontations with hellishness. Believers have the life of the living God within them. The Lord has triumphed over every demonic power at the Cross. The power of

this triumph is within every believer. Our confidence is not in ourselves, but in the King of all who is our Father.

IV. THE SOURCE OF LOVE 4:7–21. Since God loved us in Christ, we have no excuse not to love one another (vv. 10–11; *see* Propitiation). Love, according to John, is set in a relational context. It is not an abstract feeling. The verification of our relationship with the Father is that we live rightly related to others.

> **"Perfect love casts out *fear"**
> (4:18). The context of this well-worn phrase is not simply our love for the Father. It is living in the full range of relationships where the love of God is present. As we live in healthy relationships with others, we not only disallow the devil from having a place to attack us with fear, but we also have confidence with God as His obedient and faithful children.

V. THE TRIUMPH OF RIGHTEOUSNESS 5:1–5. Our victory over the world is our faith (v. 4)! However, John has set a broader context for our understanding of faith as the children of God—obedience to His commandments (v. 2).

VI. THE ASSURANCE OF ETERNAL LIFE 5:6–12. The baptized Jesus, the crucified Jesus, and the Holy Spirit all definitively testify of salvation in Christ. The announced Lamb of God at His baptism (John 1:29) fulfills His mission with His own blood on the Cross (John 19:30). There were some who insisted that the Holy Spirit abandoned Christ on the Cross—this is error. Now the Spirit of Christ reveals these truths to the hearts of those who will receive them—and give them eternal life.

VII. CHRISTIAN CERTAINTIES 5:13–21. Several truths confront the reader as John closes the letter. Once again John reminds us of the faithfulness of the Lord to answer *prayer (v. 15; also *see* John 14—16). John assures the flock that even though the whole world "lies under the sway of the wicked one" (v. 19), the child of God is safe—"the wicked one does not touch him" (v. 18). And we have the understanding that comes from God—we will not be deceived. With a final stroke of the pen, John declares, "Little children, keep yourselves from idols. Amen."

TRUTH-IN-ACTION through 1 JOHN

Truth 1 John Teaches	**Action** 1 John Invites
1 Steps to Sharing the Love of God God revealed Himself to us through Jesus Christ, thai we might have the light of life within by the presence of the Holy Spirit. Our mission is to let the light abide within us and shine forth to the glory of God. This produces light in the lives of others, extending the fellowship of God. Love for others is the sure sign that God lives in us and that we are in the fellowship of His love.	**1:3, 4** *Be full of joy. Have fellowship* with God and His people. **2:24, 25** Let God's word live in you, so that you can *live* in God. *Have eternal life!* **3:7–15** *Understand* that righteousness manifests itself in behavior. *Understand* that righteousness manifests itself in righteous behavior. *Practice* righteousness. *Love* your brother. **4:7–19** *Understand* that fear shows an absence of love. *Know* that Christ's presence always results in love.
2 Steps to Holiness Living in the world without partaking of the spirit of the world is the Christian's call. When the Spirit of God reveals to us the true spiritual poverty in which the world exists, it becomes easier to overcome the lures seeking to attract us back into that condition. When we understand the fullness of our inheritance in Christ, the world's offer seems poor indeed. When we truly set our affection on God, the lusts of the flesh are reduced as a problem. Unlike Lot's wife, who regretted the loss of the world, let us look ahead to the glorious hope of love, life, and light where God rules eternally.	**2:9–11** *Recognize* that hate for others means that you are in darkness. **2:15–17** *Do not* set your affections on, or live sacrificially on behalf of anything that 1) appeals to your fleshly appetites, 2) appeals to your covetousness or greed, or 3) fosters pride or arrogance. **5:21** *Do not allow* anything to lessen even slightly your worship, service, or devotion to God.
3 A Step to Faithful Obedience Faith realizes that there is no alternative to obedience for anyone who knows Christ and has been born by His Spirit.	**2:3–6** *Recognize* that only those who obey Jesus really know Him. *Understand* that obedience is the first evidence of love for God. *Know* and *believe* that only those who are learning to live like Jesus know and love Him.
4 Keys to Wise Living The wise take time to discern the spirit behind any teaching or word of ministry. Unless the literal incarnation of Jesus Christ, the Virgin-born Son of God, is professed, the spirit is not from God. The out-working of faith is obedience to God's commands, and the result of obeying God is love manifested to others.	**2:29** *Understand* that the best evidence for New Birth is in your conduct and behavior. **3:4–9** *Know* that continued, willful sinning in the life contradicts a genuine conversion. **3:11–15** *Know* that continued hatred 1) is impossible for those in Christ, and 2) will inevitably be leveled at believers by the world. **3:16–18** *Know* that love 1) denies its own interests on behalf of others, and 2) is expressed practically. **4:1–6** *Exercise* discernment when listening to any teaching. *Make sure* all teaching conforms to God's Word. **5:1–8** *Understand* that one who is born again 1) loves other believers, and 2) obeys the Word of God and the Holy Spirit. **5:16, 17** *Pray* for your brother who is in sin. *Know* that all lawlessness is sin.
5 Key Lessons in Faith Faith is based on knowledge of God's Word and His Character. The spirit of the world is in opposition to God. When we determine to stand	**3:1, 2** *Look forward* to seeing Christ at His Coming. *Know* you will *be transformed* into His likeness when He comes. **3:21–24** *Base* your confidence on the witness of the Holy Spirit and growing obedience in your life.

Truth 1 John Teaches	**Action** 1 John Invites
5 Key Lessons in Faith (continued) in faith, the world loses its controlling influence over us.	**4:4** *Be assured* that victory is already ours in Christ. **5:4** *Know* that those who are born again can never be conclusively defeated. **5:14, 15** *Practice* the principles of faith-filled prayer. *Know* that God 1) hears all prayers that are in accord with His will, and 2) says "Yes!" to every prayer He hears.
6 Vital Keys to Dynamic Church Life Unity is a vital key to power in the local church. The Enemy seeks to destroy this unity by placing deceiving decoys within congregations to cause division and strife. When Christians refuse to accuse and reject one another, choosing instead to forgive and to love, strife is replaced by unity, and the church receives the power of the Spirit.	**1:5–10** *Be open* and transparent in all you do. *Admit* your weakness to God. *Trust* Him to cleanse and forgive. **2:18, 19** *Recognize* that the Devil brings about all separation and division in the body of Christ.

Introducing

2 AND 3 JOHN

Author and Recipients. Although the early testimony concerning the authorship of 2 and 3 John is not as strong as that of 1 John, they are nevertheless linked with John by vocabulary and general subject matter. In both 2 and 3 John, the writer refers to himself as "the Elder," suggesting that he was older than the other Christians and that his personal knowledge of the faith went back much further than theirs.

John addresses his second epistle to "the elect lady and her children," indicating that the recipient was a hospitable Christian mother whose children persevere in the faith (v. 4). John even includes greetings from her nieces and nephews (v. 13). From the designation John gives her in verse 1 (Greek: *eklekte kyria*), many commentators have speculated concerning her personal name, suggesting titles such as "the elect Kyria," "the lady Electa," and "Electa Kyria."

Others suggest that the designation does not denote an individual at all, but is the personification of a local church. "Her children" are the members of that church, and "the children" of her "elect sister" are the members of the local church in the place from which John is writing. A definite conclusion seems unattainable; the question remains open.

Nothing is known about "the beloved Gaius" beyond the warm tribute John pays to

him in the address of the third letter. Gaius was a common name in the Roman world, and the New Testament mentions a Gaius in Corinth (Rom. 16:23; 1 Cor. 1:14), in Macedonia (Acts 19:29), and in Derbe (Acts 20:4). There is no evidence for associating the Gaius of 3 John with any of these men. Evidently he was a leader in some church of Asia.

Date. The weight of evidence that John wrote all three epistles bearing his name points to about A.D. 90, shortly after 1 John was written and near the end of his life.

Occasion and Purpose. Second John is concerned with the relation of Christian truth to hospitality extended to those teachers traveling from church to church. Such hospitality was often abused. False teachers, probably from the same group that is the subject of 1 John, were confusing the fellowship of believers. John therefore gave instructions concerning which itinerant teachers to welcome and which to refuse. Genuine Christians, who could be recognized by the orthodoxy of their message (v. 10), are worthy of aid; but heretical teachers, especially those who denied the Incarnation (v. 7), are to be rejected. John also commends "the elect lady" for walking in the truth.

Whereas in 2 John itinerant heretics were disturbing the faith of Christians, in 3 John genuine teachers of truth are making a circuit of the churches. Whereas in the previous letter John forbade hospitality toward the false teachers, here he encourages hospitality. However, Diotrephes, a domineering person in one of the churches, opposed the authority of John. In addition, he refused hospitality to the traveling missionaries and prohibited others from entertaining them, excommunicating them when they did. John wrote to encourage Gaius in his generosity and to rebuke Diotrephes for his uncharitable conduct.

Content. In 2 John the apostle encourages "the elect lady" to continue showing hospitality, but he also warns and guards against the abuse of Christian fellowship. Throughout the epistle he stresses truth as the basis and test of fellowship. In particular, he insists on a correct belief regarding the Incarnation of Christ, and charges that those who reject this reality have gone beyond the doctrine of Christ (2 John 9). He urges readers of the letter to keep close to Christ by abiding in the truth.

In fulfilling his purpose in the third epistle, John describes three personalities. The first is Gaius, who has demonstrated his Christian faith by his generous hospitality, even to strangers. The second is Diotrephes, whose selfish pride was disrupting the harmony of the fellowship. The third is Demetrius, whose life exemplified Christian fidelity and was worthy of imitation. These three men bear positive and negative witness to proper relationships among Christian brethren.

Personal Application. John's message in 2 John is timeless in that seductive teachings continue to threaten the doctrinal stability of the church. The epistle reminds us to receive Jesus as *the* Son of God, not as *a* son of God or as *a* powerful god. John warns about those who advance beyond the doctrine of Christ, accepting new teachings and leaving apostolic doctrine behind (v. 9). To receive such people is to be identified with their evil (v. 11) and to run the risk of losing the faith (v. 8).

Third John portrays the church as a family united by bonds of love, with its members extending gracious hospitality toward one another. Selfish ambition and factious jealousy imperil the church's fellowship, and its members must guard against such attitudes and strive to maintain a loving relationship with each other.

Surveying
2 AND 3 JOHN

INTRODUCTION 2 JOHN 1–3.

I. COMMENDATION FOR PAST LOYALTY V. 4. Walking in truth is related to the place of the Word in a Christian's behavior and of Christ in his or her life.

II. EXHORTATIONS VV. 5–11. Love within the church and doctrinal clarity on the Person of Christ are themes of this epistle.

A. To love one another (vv. 5–6). The young church cannot survive in a hostile world when factions divide the body and personal grievances go unattended.

B. To reject error (vv. 7–11). John insists that the error of denying the humanity of Christ is a matter of salvation (v. 9). This is a virulent lie that has divided churches and brought disaster in lives.

CONCLUSION VV. 12–13.

SALUTATION 3 JOHN 1.

I. MESSAGE TO GAIUS VV. 2–8. "Gaius" was a common name. He was likely a leader of a local congregation near Ephesus, where John served as the presiding elder.

A. Prayer for his health (v. 2). This prayer is most meaningful coming from the pen of the man who was present at Christ's crucifixion and is described as "the disciple whom He (Jesus) loved" (John 29:26).

B. Commendation for his adherence to the truth (vv. 3–4). Gaius's faithfulness to doctrine gives the church a trustworthy witness that will outlive the last of the original twelve (John) who were with Christ.

C. Commendation for his hospitality (vv. 5–8). Gaius is encouraged to treat itinerant preachers with hospitality, as he has already done. These preachers were no doubt sent out by John to solidify the churches during a time of false teaching circulating in the region.

II. CONDEMNATION OF THE HAUGHTINESS OF DIOTREPHES V. 12. Diotrephes' resistance to the letter regarding the itinerant preachers is obvious; he "loves to have preeminence among them" (v. 9). His pride has resulted in rejection of brethren and a schism among the local churches. By contrast, another local leader, Demetrius, is praised for his doctrine and testimony among believers.

CONCLUSION VV. 13–14.

TRUTH-IN-ACTION through 2 JOHN

Truth 2 John Teaches	**Action** 2 John Invites
▣ **Guidelines for Growing in Godliness** Truth is to he present and active in the life of every Christian. This requires a heart that can discern error and reject it. Study of the Word, prayer, meditation, and, most importantly, the Holy Spirit are the means by which a believer receives or rejects any doctrine. Guard your heart and mind with great care.	**v. 4** *Walk* in the truth of God's Word. *To know truth requires doing it.* **v. 5** *Love;* this pleases God. **v. 6** *Follow the commandments* of God in your behavior toward others. **vv. 7, 8** *Receive* your full reward from God. *Confirm the confession* of anyone who is received into fellowship. **v. 9** *Beware* of those who act presumptuously and do things God has not told them to do. *Understand* that this is as evil as doing things He has forbidden. **v. 10** *Do not fellowship* with those who teach error. *Do not give* false teachers *access* to God's people.

TRUTH-IN-ACTION through 3 JOHN

Truth 3 John Teaches	**Action** 3 John Invites
▣ **Guidelines for Growing in Godliness** The godly desire physical health, emotional stability, and prosperity to be established in the lives of others. Those who are so blessed should be eager to receive and support those ministers who are serving God.	**v. 2** *Prosper* in your soul. *Understand* that health and prosperity are affected by the spirit. **v. 4** *Be assured* that God rejoices over His children who put God's Word into practice daily, **vv. 5–8** *Be eager and faithful* to show hospitality to those who labor in the gospel. *Recognize* that this is how God wants us to treat His servants. **vv. 9–11** *Beware* of those who want pre-eminence in the church. *Reject* those who are malicious gossips. *Reprove* those who reject righteous ministry because of envy and jealousy.

KEYS TO REVELATION
Unto the Ultimate Kingdom

Kingdom Key: God's Purpose in View

There is a dynamic tension, best expressed in the words "Now, but not yet," which must be maintained in all present day proclamations of "the gospel of the kingdom." In other words, the power and presence of God's rule and working is mightily available today, just as He worked in Jesus' ministry (Heb. 13:8). As Jesus said, "The kingdom of God is within you!" (i.e. "in your midst," Luke 17:21), and "The kingdom of God is at hand" (i.e., "has drawn near," Matt. 4:24).

Nevertheless, although the blessing, power, and grace of God's rule is indeed *now* manifest through His Spirit's work in the church, there is also a *not yet* sense that we must recognize. Simply, the consummation has not yet come. The complete realization of everything inherent in the perfect and full reinstatement of God's will and purpose for humankind on earth will not be seen or fulfilled until Jesus Christ returns.

The Book of Revelation records the age-long processes that relentlessly move us toward the ultimate kingdom, and it describes the events that shall usher in that consummation. Even though the book gives some details about that final triumph, it also teaches that an interim struggle remains before the fulfillment of all things. Let us see how to stand faithfully,

> **Jesus Christ is alive and leading His church to victory.**

presently engaged as "kingdom warriors" until the final battle is won.

1. In 1:9, now exiled to Patmos "for the word of God and for the testimony of Jesus Christ," John describes himself in words each servant of the Lord should remember: "Your brother and companion in the tribulation and kingdom and patience of Jesus Christ." His use of the victory and authority word "kingdom" between two words denoting "stress" and "extended waiting" sets a balanced and healthy perspective. Though undergoing persecution and severe trial, John is not a defeatist. But neither can he be called a triumphalist (that is, a person who overlooks or denies that some kingdom victories only come through long struggle or even trials and sufferings.) We *are* "kingdom

(Please turn to page 469.)

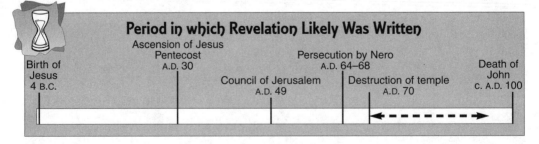

Period in which Revelation Likely Was Written

Birth of Jesus 4 B.C.	Ascension of Jesus Pentecost A.D. 30	Council of Jerusalem A.D. 49	Persecution by Nero A.D. 64–68	Destruction of temple A.D. 70	Death of John c. A.D. 100

Revelation discloses the age-long struggle between

Master Key: God's Son Revealed

Nearly every title employed elsewhere in the New Testament to describe the divine-human nature and the redemptive work of Jesus is mentioned at least once in Revelation. Together with numerous additional titles, Revelation provides the only multidimensional unveiling of the present position, continuing ministry, and ultimate victory of the exalted Christ.

Although Jesus' earthly ministry is telescoped between His Incarnation and Ascension in 12:5, Revelation asserts that the Son of God, as the Lamb, has completely finished His redemptive work (1:5–6). By His blood sinners have been forgiven, cleansed (5:6, 9; 7:14; 12:11), liberated (1:5), and made kings and priests (1:6; 5:10). All ensuing manifestations of His applied victory are based in His finished work on the Cross; hence, Satan has been defeated (12:7–12) and bound (20:1–3). Jesus, raised from the dead, is enthroned as absolute Sovereign over all Creation (1:5; 2:27). He *is* "King of kings and Lord of lords" (17:14; 19:16), and He is entitled to the same ascriptions of adoration as God the Creator (5:12–14).

The only One who is "worthy" to execute the eternal purpose of God is "the Lion of Judah," who is not a political Messiah but a sacrificed Lamb (5:5–6). "The Lamb" is His primary title, used twenty-eight times in Revelation. As the One who has conquered, He has the rightful authority and the power to control all the forces of evil and their consequences for His purposes of judgment and salvation (6:1—7:17). The Lamb is on the throne (4:1—5:14; 22:3).

The Lamb, as "One like the Son of Man," is always in the midst of His people (1:9—3:22; 14:1), whose names are recorded in His Book of Life (3:5; 21:27). He knows them intimately, and with immeasurable holy love He watches over, protects, disciplines, and challenges them. They share fully in His present and future victory (17:14; 19:11–16; 21:1—22:5), as well as in His present and future "marriage supper" (19:7–9; 21:2). He dwells *in* them (1:13), and they dwell *in* Him (21:22).

As "One like the Son of Man," He also is

(Please turn to page 469.)

Key Word: *The Revelation of the Coming of Christ*

The purposes for which Revelation was written depend to some extent on how the book as a whole is interpreted.

(1) The symbolic or idealist view *maintains that Revelation is not a predictive prophecy, but a symbolic portrait of the cosmic conflict of spiritual principles.*

(2) The preterist view *(the Latin word* praeter *means "past") maintains that it is a symbolic description of the Roman persecution of the church, emperor worship, and the divine judgment of Rome.*

(3) The historicist view *approaches Revelation as an allegorical panorama of the history of the (Western) church from the first century to the Second Advent.*

(4) The futurist view *acknowledges the obvious influence that the first-century conflict between Roman power and the church had upon the themes of this book. It also*

(Please turn to page 470.)

good and evil and guarantees Christ's final triumph.

Introducing
REVELATION

Author. Four times the author refers to himself as "John" (1:1, 4, 9; 22:8). He was so well known to his readers and his spiritual authority was so widely acknowledged that he did not need to establish his credentials. Early church tradition unanimously attributes this book to the apostle John.

Background and Date. Evidence within Revelation indicates that it was written during a period of extreme persecution of Christians, which possibly was that begun by Nero after the great fire that nearly destroyed Rome in July of A.D. 64 and continued until his suicide in June of A.D. 68. In this view, the book was written before the destruction of Jerusalem in September of A.D. 70 and is an authentic prophecy concerning the continuing suffering and persecution of Christians, which would become even more intense and severe in the years ahead. On the basis of isolated statements by the early church fathers, some interpreters date the book near the end of the reign of Domitian (A.D. 81–96), after John had fled to Ephesus.

Occasion and Purpose. John had no doubt been reflecting on the horrifying events occurring both in Rome and Jerusalem when the Holy Spirit gave him "the prophecy" of what was impending. The Spirit revealed to John the intensification of the spiritual warfare confronting the church (1:3), perpetrated by an anti-Christian state and numerous anti-Christian religions. This message provides pastoral encouragement to persecuted Christians by comforting, challenging, and proclaiming the sure and certain Christian hope. John also assures his readers that in Christ they are sharing in the sovereign God's method of totally overcoming the forces of evil in all its manifestations. Revelation is also an evangelistic appeal to those who are presently living in the kingdom of darkness to enter the kingdom of light (22:17).

Content. The central message of the Revelation is that "the Lord God Omnipotent reigns!" (19:6). This theme has been validated in history by the victory of the Lamb who is "Lord of lords and King of kings" (17:14).

Yet, those who follow the Lamb are involved in a continuing spiritual conflict, and Revelation provides deeper insight into the nature and tactics of the Enemy (Eph. 6:10–12). The dragon, frustrated by his defeat at the Cross and the consequent restraints placed upon his activity, and desperate to thwart the purposes of God before his inevitable doom, develops a counterfeit trinity "to make war" on the saints (12:17). The first "beast" or monster symbolizes anti-Christian government and political power (13:1–10, 13); and the second, anti-Christian religion, philosophy, and ideology (13:11–17). Together they produce the ultimately deceptive and seductive anti-Christian secular society, commerce, and culture, the harlot Babylon (chs. 17, 18), composed of those "who dwell on earth." These thus bear the "mark" of the monster, and their names are not registered in "the Lamb's Book of Life." The dragon continually delegates his restricted power and authority to the monsters and their followers in order to deceive and discourage anyone from God's creative-redemptive purpose.

NOTE: For additional insights into interpretive approaches to the Book of Revelation, see Kingdom Dynamics note No. 10 under Prophecy in the Encyclopedic Dictionary section of this volume.

Personal Application. God has created the orders of community, that is, marriage and the family, economic activity, government and the state (*see* Rom. 13:1–7; 1 Tim. 2:1–2). Satan, unable to create anything, tempts others to distort and misuse what God has created. Christians must discern whether a government is functioning *under* divine authority or *as* a divine authority. When the latter is the case, Christians must pray, courageously endure, and patiently accept the consequences of obeying the God whose image and seal they bear (*see* Mark 12:16–17; Acts 4:19). They must do so in the confidence that after their victorious sufferings they will reign with Him.

Behind the pomp and power of the world lies the absolute sovereignty of the Lord God who is the Lamb. He ensures the ultimate doom of sin and evil. God is utilizing all the forces of evil, all the consequences of sin, even the suffering of His saints, to accomplish His own purposes. Believers undergoing persecution need to know that their sufferings are not meaningless, and ultimately they will be vindicated. The mainspring of Christian hope and courage is the certainty that the Enemy has been defeated and is doomed. Followers of the Lamb are not fighting a losing cause. He has already overcome, and therefore they can and will be overcomers!

Literary Form. After a preface, Revelation begins (1:4–7) and ends (22:21) as a typical New Testament letter. Although containing seven letters to the seven churches, it is clear that every member is to "hear" the message to each of the churches (2:7, 11, 17, 29; 3:6, 13, 22), as well as the message of the entire book (1:3; 22:16), in order that they might obey it

(1:3; 22:9). Within this letter is "the prophecy" (1:3; 10:11; 19:10; 22:6–7, 10, 18–19). According to Paul, "he who prophesies speaks edification and exhortation [encouragement] and comfort to men" (1 Cor. 14:3). The prophet speaks God's Word as a call to obedience in the present and immediate future situation in the light of the ultimate future. This prophecy was not to be sealed up (22:10) because it is relevant to Christians in every generation.

Method of Communication. John received these prophecies through a series of vivid visions containing symbolic images and numbers that echo those found in the prophetic books of the Old Testament. John records these visions in the chronological order in which he received them, many of them pictures of the same events from different perspectives. He does not, however, provide a chronological order in which certain historical events are to occur. For example, Jesus is born in chapter 12, is exalted in chapter 5, and is walking in the midst of His churches in chapter 1. The beast who attacks the two witnesses in chapter 11 is not brought into existence until chapter 13. John records a series of successive visions, not a series of consecutive events.

The Revelation is a cosmic pageant—an elaborate, colorful series of tableaux, accompanied and interpreted by celestial speakers and singers. The spoken word is elevated prose, more poetic than our translations indicate. The music is similar to a cantata. Repeatedly, themes are introduced, later reintroduced, combined with other themes, and developed.

The entire message is "signified" (1:1). This is a key to the understanding of the visions, all of which contain figurative language pointing to the spiritual realities in and behind historical experience. Signs and symbols are essential because spiritual truth and unseen reality must always be communicated to human beings through their senses. Symbols point to what is ultimately indescribable. For example, the account of the demonic locusts from the abyss (9:1–12) creates a vivid, horrifying impression, even though the minute details are not intended to be interpreted.

Kingdom Key *continued from page 466*

people," holding to the promises of victory that we have in God's Word, but we also may have to endure trials as we proceed toward ultimate victory. These are not conflicting truths.

2. In 12:10 John provides the answer for beleagured servants of God. We must shout, "Now salvation, and strength, and the kingdom of our God . . . have come." This text does *not* reveal the final end of Satan, but it is a revelation of what became of him through Christ's triumph on the Cross (Col. 2:24–25). His end *will* come (Rev. 20:7–10), but at the present moment his rabid fury is fueled by his desperation (12:12). In this season we are promised this certainty: We shall overcome! Through God's Word (the promises of the kingdom) and the blood of the Cross (securing the authority of the kingdom), we are assured ongoing victory-unto-victory (as people of the kingdom) (12:11). Finally, the end shall come!

3. In Revelation 11:15 all heaven rises to declare the introduction of events that begin the final triumph, and chapters 19 and 20 describe that triumph's consummation on earth. The day is sure! All Old and New Testament prophecies about the ultimate rule of our God and His Christ will be fulfilled, and the kingdom of God shall have achieved its full purposes through Christ's redemption.

Until that day, the whole of God's Word teaches that the complete fulfillment of God's kingdom purposes in Jesus Christ will not be realized until Christ's Second Coming. On that day He will reveal the fullest display of (1) His rule over evil, expelling it completely, and (2) His throne over all the earth, unto the glory of the Father.

Master Key *continued from page 467*

the Lord of the final harvest (14:14–20). He pours out His wrath in judgment upon Satan (20:10), his allies (19:20; 20:14), and the spiritually "dead" (20:12, 15)—all those who have chosen to "dwell on the earth" (3:10).

The Lamb is the God who is coming (1:7–8; 11:17; 22:7, 20) to consummate His eternal plan, to complete the creation of the new community of His people in "a new heaven and a new earth" (21:1), and to restore the blessings of the Paradise of God (22:2–5). The Lamb is the goal of all history (22:13).

continued on next page

Power Key: God's Spirit at Work

The description of the Holy Spirit as "the seven Spirits of God" (1:4; 3:1; 4:5; 5:6) is distinct in the New Testament. The number seven is a symbolic, qualitative number conveying the idea of completeness and, when related to God, the idea of perfection. The Holy Spirit is thus denoted in terms of the perfection of His dynamic, manifold activity. The "seven lamps of fire" (4:5) suggest His illuminating, purifying, and energizing ministries. That the seven Spirits are before the throne (1:4; 4:5), and simultaneously are the seven eyes of the Lamb (5:6), signifies the essential triunity of God, who has revealed Himself as Father, Son, and Holy Spirit. This is a mutuality of Persons without having three Gods or dissolving the distinctions of essential being and function.

Each of the messages to the seven churches is from the exalted Lord, yet the individual members are urged to hear "what the Spirit says" (chs. 2; 3). The Spirit only says what the Lord Jesus says.

The Spirit is thus the Spirit of prophecy. Every genuine prophecy is inspired by the Holy Spirit and bears witness to Jesus (19:10). The prophetic visions are communicated to John only when he is "in the Spirit" (1:10; 4:2; 21:10). The content of these visions is nothing less than "The Revelation of Jesus Christ" (1:1).

"The Spirit and the bride say, 'Come!'" (22:17). All genuine prophecy demands a response. The Spirit is working continuously in and through the church to invite those who remain outside the City of God to enter. Only by the empowering of the Spirit is the bride enabled to witness and "patiently endure." The Spirit thus injects into the present experience of believers a foretaste of the kingdom's future fulfillment.

Key Word *continued from page 467*

accepts the bulk of Revelation (chaps. 4—22) as an inspired look into the time immediately preceding the Second Advent (the Tribulation, usually seen as seven years; chaps. 6—18), and extending from the return of Christ to the creation of the new cosmos (chaps. 19—22).

Advocates of all four interpretive approaches to Revelation agree that it was written to assure the recipients of the ultimate triumph of Christ over all who rise up against Him and His saints. The readers were facing dark times of persecution, and even worse times would follow. Therefore they needed to be encouraged to persevere by standing firm in Christ in view of God's plan for the righteous and the wicked.

Key Verses: Revelation 1:19; 19:11

Key Chapters: Revelation 19—22

When the end of history is fully understood, its impact radically affects the present. In Revelation 19—22 the plans of God for the last days and for all of eternity are recorded in explicit terms.

Surveying
REVELATION

PROLOGUE 1:1–8. This book is a revelation by and of Jesus (v. 1; *see* Angels). The phrase "must shortly take place" uses a word indicating rapid execution (but *see* 2 Pet. 3:8–9). The phrase in verse 3 tells us that Revelation was intended for public reading in congregations, a practice the early church adopted from the synagogue.

John intends this letter for the seven major centers of Christianity in Asia Minor. His greeting is a typical one, including a blessing and also a clue to the thrust of his letter (1:4–8; *see* Kingdom of God; Witness).

> **"Every eye will see Him"**
> (1:7). Jesus' return will not take place in a far corner of the world. When He comes, all will know Him, "even they who pierced Him" (v. 7). Those who have opposed God's people, joined with the spirit of Antichrist (1 John 2:18), and refused to repent will now cry for the rocks to cover them (Luke 23:30; Rev. 6:16). All will see Jesus Christ for who He is, Lord of All!

I. THE LETTERS TO THE SEVEN CHURCHES 1:9—3:22.

A. The setting: One like the Son of Man (1:9–20). John's vision came on the island of Patmos, a rocky and desolate speck in the Aegean Sea, used by the Roman government as a penal colony. John had been sentenced there because of "the word of God and for the testimony of Jesus Christ" (9).

> **"I, John, both your brother and companion in the tribulation and kingdom and patience of Jesus Christ, was on the island that is called Patmos for the word of God and for the testimony of Jesus Christ"**
> (1:9). John's witness cost him his freedom as he was banished to Patmos. This gospel John has declared has been resisted by Satan and sometimes rejected by men. Yet, even from exile John is about to testify to the final chapter of all human history and the ultimate victory of Christ. No matter the resistance today, God will have the final word with every person.

He speaks of his vision taking place on the Lord's Day. This phrase may mean Sun-day, or it may mean that John is transported in his vision to the eschatological "day of the Lord" to come at history's end (v. 10). John is told to write what he sees in his vision to seven churches in Asia Minor (11).

John turns to see from where the voice instructing him comes, and sees a scene full of reminders of the Old Testament worship center. As in the tabernacle and temple, there are lampstands (cf. Zech. 4:2) and among them a person in priestly clothing (cf. Ex. 28:4). The person himself is described in terms that reflect Old Testament visions of God (cf. Dan. 7:9), and John falls at His feet, stunned by His splendor. The figure identifies Himself as the glorified Jesus (1:17–20).

There is a constant repetition of "seven" in this chapter and throughout the book. It is generally agreed that seven indicates completeness or perfection. Thus the "seven Spirits" of verse 4 is taken to represent the Holy Spirit, and the "seven lampstands" to indicate heaven, the true worship center of which the Old Testament tabernacle was merely a copy (cf. Heb. 8:1–6). The selection of seven churches is taken to indicate that in some way they, or the messages to them, sum up what God has to say to all His people.

B. The letters (2:1—3:22). There is no doubt these churches did exist in John's day, in what is now Turkey. There were, however, many other churches in Asia Minor. Apparently these seven were selected because of conditions that existed in each congregation and because of the need created by those conditions for a special word from God. The letters deal with lovelessness (2:1–7), persecution (2:8–11; *see* Poverty; Tested), compromise (2:12–17), corruption (2:18–29; *see* Hearts), lifelessness (3:1–6), faithfulness (3:7–13), and apathy (3:14–22). (*See* chart, page 478.)

II. THE SEVEN SEALS 4:1—8:1.

A. The setting (4:1—5:14).

1. The throne of God (4:1–11). Now John is brought up into heaven itself, to be shown "what must take place after this" (v. 1; *see* Prophecy). (Observations regarding how various Christians have interpreted this verse appear in Kingdom Dynamic No. 10 under Prophecy in the Encyclopedic Dictionary.) The sight that draws John's eyes is a great throne (2), such as kings and judges use when making official pronouncements. A transparent crystal rainbow circles the throne, reflecting prismatic colors. Twenty-four smaller thrones circle the central one, each occupied by a crowned "elder" dressed in white. Thunder rumbles and lightning flashes from the central throne, while blazing lamps identified as the sevenfold Spirit of God obscure the dazzling person seated there (5–6).

Standing close to the throne, surrounding it, are four "living creatures." They have the same aspects as the creatures described in Ezekiel 1:10–28 (vv. 6–7). Each constantly worships the Lord (8). The twenty-four elders join in the praise, prostrating themselves before the one on the throne (*see* Worship).

2. *The Lamb and the scroll (5:1–14)*. John sees that the still indistinct figure on the throne holds a document in His right hand. It is covered with writing and sealed with seven seals (v. 1). The seals are stamped wax impressions, which authenticate a first-century document. Roman law directed that a will should be sealed by seven seals of seven witnesses.

No one is found who is worthy to open this document (vv. 2–4) until a voice announces the triumphant Lion of Judah, the Root of David. Each is an Old Testament designation of the Messiah, who is from the tribe of Judah and David's royal line (*see* Is. 11:1).

Now the Lamb appears. This particular word for "lamb" is used exclusively in the New Testament of the resurrected Jesus (6). Now too a new theme is introduced in the praise of the living creatures and elders. They earlier praised God as Creator (4:11). Now the Lamb is praised because "You were slain, and have redeemed us to God by Your blood" (v. 9).

> **"And they sang a new song, saying: 'You are worthy to take the scroll, and to open its seals; for You were slain, and have redeemed us to God by Your blood' "**
> (5:9–14). At the return of Christ and the revelation of the Lord of glory coming to establish His throne on earth, the heavens will sing a song of praise to the One who is worthy. That song will be picked up by all the hosts of heaven (v. 11), and then by every *creature on earth (13). Jesus is coming again. As we join our voices with the continual song of praise around His throne, we share in the final victory of our God over every power of sin and every remnant of resistance to His kingdom.

The hymn of praise is joined by myriads of angels, proclaiming the worthiness of the Lamb (vv. 11–12), and they in turn are joined by "every creature which is in heaven and on the earth and under the earth and such as are in the sea" offering God and the Lamb "blessing and honor and glory and power . . . forever and ever" (13).

B. The seals (6:1—8:1). As the *Lamb breaks the seals, great disasters strike the earth.

1. *First seal: white horse (6:1–2)*. This horseman goes forth to conquer.

2. *Second seal: red horse (6:3–4)*. Horseman is released to mount warfare (1–4).

3. *Third seal: black horse (6:5–6)*. This brings famine.

4. *Fourth seal: pale green horse (6:7–8)*. All sorts of devastating plagues destroy a quarter of the earth.

5. *Fifth seal: souls under the altar (6:9–11)*. John sees thousands "slain for the word of God" who call out to God to avenge them (9–10). They are "under the altar," the place where the blood of Old Testament sacrifices was poured out.

6. *Sixth seal: cosmic catastrophe (6:12–17)*. Nature itself is jolted, and the fabric of the universe begins to tear (12–14). The seven groups listed in verse 15 represent the seven classes (*see* Free) which made up first-century society, and thus show that all mankind is stricken by the judgments.

  a. First interlude: 144,000 sealed (7:1–8). On earth, judgment is held back until an angel can put a seal on the foreheads of the servants of God (vv. 1–3). The "seal" in the first century would speak of the tattoo worn by a slave or soldier or member of a guild. It was a mark of ownership, which here identifies the bearers as God's servants. There are 144,000 who are sealed. Their Jewish origin is emphasized in the text (4–8).

  b. Second interlude: a great multitude (7:9–17). Back in heaven, John sees an uncountable multitude "of all nations, tribes, peoples, and tongues" gathered before the throne to praise the Lamb (9–10).

> **"Crying out with a loud voice, saying, 'Salvation belongs to our God who sits on the throne, and to the Lamb!' "**
> (7:9–12). John describes multitudes from every nation under heaven proclaiming the salvation of their God, who is the Lamb slain on their behalf. This eternally grateful throng come out of the time of tribulation at the end of the world and now await the imminent entrance of Christ and His return to earth. Our blessed hope in Christ's return resounds throughout the millennia of church history; all Christians have looked expectantly to His coming: "Even so, come, Lord Jesus!" (Rev. 22:20).

Their worship is joined by the angels, the elders, and the living creatures (7:11–12). One of the elders tells John they are those "who [have] come out of the great tribulation" (13–15) and now possess great blessings (15–17).

7. *Seventh seal: silence in heaven (8:1).* The breaking of the seventh seal brings a hushed silence, an ominous pause that lasts for half an hour.

III. THE SEVEN TRUMPETS 8:2—11:18.

A. The setting: the golden altar (8:2–6). Then seven angels standing before the throne are given trumpets (v. 2).

Before the trumpets sound, however, another angel beside the altar offers incense and the prayers of the saints up to God. The prayers ascend and immediately the angel takes coals of fire from the altar and hurls them to the earth, accompanied by thunder, lightning and earthquakes (3–5).

B. The trumpets (8:7—11:18). Now the angels begin to sound their trumpets in sequence. As each sounds, a fresh judgment strikes the reeling earth.

1. *The first trumpet: earth (8:7).* A third of the land area is devastated by fire.

2. *Second trumpet: sea (8:8–9).* A third of the seas are polluted.

3. *Third trumpet: river (8:10–11).* A third of the fresh waters are made bitter, taking many lives.

4. *Fourth trumpet: sun (8:12).* The sun and moon and even the stars darken.

5. *Fifth trumpet: first woe—demonic locusts (8:13—9:12).* As John watches, a great vulture (not "eagle") drifts through the gloom-shrouded skies, crying out in a loud voice, "Woe, woe, woe to the inhabitants of the earth" (8:13).

The judgment of the two trumpets described in chapter nine are called woes. The first woe comes as the Abyss is opened (9:1–2). This "bottomless pit" was considered to be a prison for demons and disobedient spirits. The creatures released are described as locusts, which sting like scorpions, and are given power to torment men (3–6). The description seems to indicate they are more than insects (7–11).

6. *Sixth trumpet: second woe—cavalry (9:13–21).* A mounted cavalry is released to kill a third of mankind (9:13–16). The mounts are no natural animals, for they have leonine heads and breathe out sulfurous flames (17–19).

Despite these two awesome woes, the survivors of mankind refuse to turn to God, or to repent of their idolatry and immorality (20–21; *see* Sorceries).

a. First interlude: the little scroll (10:1–11). John sees a mighty angel coming down from heaven. He holds a small scroll which has been opened (vv. 1–2). Part of the angel's message is not to be shared (3–4). But John reports that the angel announces that now, at last, history is about to close (5–8). John eats the little scroll and stands ready to "prophesy again" (9–11).

b. Second interlude: two witnesses (11:1–14). Very specific time periods are specified. These correspond with time periods in Daniel 9 and 12. He sees Jerusalem trampled for forty-two months (vv. 1–2) and two unnamed witnesses prophesy for 1,260 days (3). They are divinely protected from their enemies and given power to bring drought and plagues (5–6).

When they have finished the work God set for them, "the beast that ascends out of the bottomless pit" attacks and kills them (7). The world rejoices as the witnesses lie dead in the streets of Jerusalem (8–10; *see* Spiritually). Then after three-and-a-half days, they are resurrected and called up to heaven in a cloud as their enemies look on (11–12). Their departure is marked by earthquakes and destruction, which so terrify the survivors that they acknowledge God's hand (13). This marks the passing of the second woe (14).

> ### "I will give power to my two witnesses"
>
> (11:3). In the final moments of human history, two witnesses will be raised up to testify of Jesus Christ, and then the end comes. This pictures the church in its most glorious moment, most heated battle, and most dangerous hour. Our Lord will come to judge the world of sin and reward His people. Our testimony of Christ embraces the hard reality that rejection of God brings with it judgment. He is "not willing that any should perish but that all should come to repentance" (2 Pet. 3:9). Therefore we must be faithful in our witness, for the consequences for all are eternal.

7. *Seventh trumpet: third woe—voices in heaven (11:15–18).* God is about to take His kingdom.

IV. THE SEVEN SIGNS 11:19—15:4.

A. The setting: the ark of the covenant (11:19).

B. The signs (12:1—15:4). Now John

reports a vision that appears in the heavens and is clearly identified as a "sign" (v. 1).

1. The woman, dragon, child, Michael (12:1–17). The vision is of a pregnant woman, about to give birth. A dragon (Satan) seeks to devour the child who "was to rule all nations with a rod of iron" (2–4). The child is snatched up to heaven and the woman hides in the desert. Again a 1,260-day period is specified (5–6).

John then observes a war in heaven, in which Satan and his *angels are hurled down to earth (7–9; *see* Spiritual Warfare).

Then a voice announces from heaven that "salvation, and strength, and the kingdom of our God . . . have come" (10; *see* Kingdom of God). Satan is overcome but furiously strikes out "because he knows that he has a short time" (11–12; *see* Blood, The; Faith's Confession).

The dragon seeks to destroy the woman who gave birth to the child, but she is safely hidden by God (13–16). The raging (*see* Enraged) dragon turns to make open war on those who "have the testimony of Jesus Christ" (12:17).

> **"They overcame him by the blood of the Lamb and by the word of their testimony"**
> (12:7–11). All victory for the people of God is found in Jesus' work on the Cross. The blood of Christ provides for forgiveness of sins and eternal life (Matt. 26:28–29); the sufferings of Christ bring healing (Matt. 8:16–17), thereby overcoming the destructive work of Satan. The testimony of God's people (Rom. 10:9–10) appropriates the work of the Cross through faith. The testimony of Christ is more precious than life itself (v. 11), and ultimately more powerful than the devil's ability to kill. God's resurrection power brings eternal life to all His children who have been victimized by Satan.

2. The beast from the sea (13:1–10). Now John watches as a horned beast emerges from the sea (v. 1). His shape reflects the form given Gentile world powers in Daniel 7. This beast is energized by Satan and followed by a worshiping world (2–4).

Again the forty-two-month period is specified. During it the beast holds power and makes war on the saints (5–10).

3. The beast from the earth (13:11–18). John then sees another beast, emerging this time from the earth. He resembles a lamb but

speaks like the dragon (11). He performs miracles to authenticate the claims of the first beast (12–14) and forces the people of the beast to worship his image (15–17). The "number" of this beast is given as 666.

4. The Lamb and the 144,000 (14:1–5). Next, John's sees the Lamb, returned to earth and standing on Mount Zion (v. 1). The 144,000 are with Him and are honored for their total commitment in following Him (2–5).

5. Four proclamations (14:6–13). At this point three angels are seen. The first announces to all humanity the Good News (gospel) (6–7; *see* Everlasting). The second announces the fall of Babylon the Great (8). The third announces the endless doom and torment of all who worship the beast and exhorts patient endurance on the part of the saints (9–13; *see* Rest). Then a voice from heaven is heard, pronouncing a blessing on the dead "who die in the Lord from now on" (13).

6. The final harvest (14:14–20). When John looks up, he sees a figure, crowned and seated on a cloud (14). Angels, equipped for harvest, cry out to Him. The gathering and the trampling out begin, and blood gushes from the city for a distance of some 180 miles!

7. The seven angels and the song of the Lamb (15:1–4). Again John peers into heaven and sees seven angels who will bear the "seven last plagues" that complete God's wrath (15:1). God is praised for His holiness and the vindication of His name that will come when at last all nations must prostrate themselves before Him (15:2–4).

V. THE SEVEN BOWLS 15:5—16:21.

A. The setting: the tent of witness (15:5—16:1). On command seven angels pour out the bowls of wrath on the earth (*see* Testimony).

B. Seven bowls (16:2–21).

1. First bowl: earth (16:2). Sores break out on the followers of the beast.

2. The second bowl: sea (16:3). All living things in the sea die.

3. Third bowl: rivers (16:4–7). All the fresh waters turn to blood.

4. Fourth bowl: sun (16:8–9). The sun flares and sears the earth.

5. Fifth bowl: throne of the beast (16:10–11). Darkness and anguish follow.

6. Sixth bowl: Euphrates (16:12). The river is dried up.

Interlude: three unclean spirits (16:13–16). Finally demons are loosed to move the leaders of all the nations to gather for battle against God (14; see Signs). The armies gather and assemble at a place called in Scripture Armageddon (15–16).

"I am coming as a thief"
(16:15). The warnings throughout the New Testament to be prepared for the Lord's return leave nothing to uncertainty. No one knows the time, so a constant state of preparedness for His coming must be maintained. "Watch . . . keep your garments" and the parable of the ten virgins reinforce this truth (Matt. 25:1–25). Luke 19:13 and Luke 23:36 give instruction for this time so that no one is unprepared.

---

7. *Seventh bowl: the cities of the nations (16:17–21).* The earthquakes and natural disasters destroy the cities.

VI. THE SEVEN SPECTACLES 17:1—20:3.

A. The setting: a wilderness (17:1–3). John is now shown the punishment of someone identified as the "great harlot" who commits adulteries (see Committed Fornication) with the kings of the earth (1–2).

B. The spectacles (17:3–20:3).

1. *The woman on a scarlet beast (17:3–5).*

2. *The mystery of the woman and the beast (17:6–18).* The woman is drunk "with the blood of the saints and with the blood of the martyrs of Jesus" (6). The angel explains the mystery, again identifying the beast as the Antichrist (7–8). Aspects of the beast with symbolic meaning are explained (9–15). The woman, identified as "that great city which reigns over the kings of the earth," will in time be destroyed by the beast, who wants sole possession of all power (16–18).

3. *Seven voices: Babylon fallen (18:1—19:10).* Now an angel with great authority shouts out his announcement. Babylon the Great has fallen (18:1–3). In counterpart, a voice from heaven calls on God's people to "come out of her," for she is doomed to be consumed by fire (4–8). The kings and merchants of the earth who profited from relationship with Babylon will *mourn (9–20). But Babylon will be overthrown with great violence (21–24). Of particular note is the repeated phrase "in one hour" (cf. vv. 10, 17, 19). The destruction of Babylon will be swift and complete.

The final sequence is about to be played out. John hears the massed, triumphant shout of heavenly multitudes (see Servants), praising God for His victory over the great prostitute (19:1–5; see Revelation 17). He then

hears a joyous announcement: God reigns, and the "marriage of the Lamb" has come at last (6–10; see Prophecy; Restoration).

"I heard a loud voice of a great multitude in heaven saying, 'Alleluia! Salvation and glory and honor and power belong to the Lord our God!' "
(19:1–6). With the final battle about to commence, and the absolute liberation of earth immediately before us, the song of victory and voice of the multitude can be heard. The themes are familiar: salvation belongs to Him, His judgments are righteous, and the awaited time of the bridegroom receiving His bride is here. This joyous conclusion to our world as we know it offers hope to every Christian in every nation. We rejoice and look to the great Day when all things are finished.

---

4. *King of kings and Lord of lords (19:11–16).* At this, heaven stands open and Christ appears as a rider on a white horse, with the armies of heaven following Him.

"He Himself treads the winepress of the fierceness and wrath of Almighty God"
(19:11–16). The ferocious wrath of God against sin is judging the source of every war among nations, the pathogen of every disease afflicting humanity, the wicked separation that brings about every divorce ruining homes and people, the fountainhead of every bondage that destroys individuals, and death itself. God Himself will destroy everything that has opposed Him and brought death and destruction to people, and finally He will establish His kingdom forever.

---

5. *The supper of the great God (19:17–18).* The birds are called to come, to feast on the flesh of the armies gathered to war against God.

6. *The war (19:19–21).* In the clash which follows the earthly armies are destroyed, and the beast and false prophet thrown "alive into the lake of fire burning with brimstone."

7. *Satan bound (20:1–3).* This chapter picks up and continues from chapter 19. Satan is said to be chained in the Abyss, captive there for a thousand years, and unable to deceive the nations anymore.

> ### "He cast him into the bottomless pit"
> (20:2–3). Satan will be bound for one thousand years by an angel assigned to the task. This future act will result in the establishing of Christ's kingdom on earth without interference and will begin at the time of His return.

VII. THE SEVEN SIGHTS OF THE CONSUMMATION 20:4—22:5.

A. The setting (20:4–10).

1. Living and reigning with Christ (20:4–6). Those who were martyred during the rule of the beast came to life and "reigned with Christ for a thousand years" in a "first resurrection" which is distinct from the final resurrection (*see* Judgment).

2. Satan released to deceive (20:7–10). After the thousand-year period has passed, Satan is released. He again succeeds in deceiving the nations which surround Jerusalem to war against God's people (7–9).

The last rebellion is as futile as the rest. Fire from heaven destroys the armies, and the devil is thrown into the lake of burning sulphur to be "tormented day and night forever and ever" (9–10).

> ### "The devil . . . was cast into the lake of fire"
> (20:7–10). The final destination of the devil and those who follow him, resisting God's plan on earth, is the lake of fire (vv. 10, 15). Their torment is eternal. God's decision to punish those who oppose Him is final. The rejection of Christ brings eternal damnation, but the grace of God available to all who would place their faith in Christ is indestructible.

B. The scenes (20:11—22:5).
The physical universe dissolves, and all the dead are called to stand before God.

1. The great white throne (20:11).

2. The last judgment (20:12–15). Those not written in the Book of Life are judged "according to their works, by the things which were written in the books." All whose names are not written in the Book of Life fall short, and are condemned to the lake of fire.

3. The new *heaven and new earth (21:1).

4. The New Jerusalem (21:2–8). A New Jerusalem, made of jewels and transparent gold, a foursquare some 1400 miles square, drifts in the sky over the refashioned earth. This is the inheritance of the children of God (*see* Prepared).

5. The bride of the Lamb (21:9–21). The bride is described in the terms of the heavenly city. (*See* Reward.)

6. The light of God's presence (21:22–27). The city contains no temple. None is needed, for the Lord God Almighty and the Lamb are there, and all mankind will walk in the light of their presence. Peopling this new universe are those whose names are written in the Lamb's Book of Life.

7. Paradise regained (22:1–5). A final vision of the new heavens and earth reveals a crystal river, flowing from God's throne. Its current carries it down the middle of the great street of the city, watering trees whose fruit and leaves mean healing for once-cursed humanity. The redeemed will walk in this city of God, serving Him, seeing His face. In the light shed by His presence they will rule with Him, forever and ever.

EPILOGUE 22:6–21.

A. Seven confirming witnesses (22:6–17).
John concludes his report, communicating both a warning and a promise. Jesus announces, "Behold, I am coming quickly!" The blessings of this book are carefully reserved for all who have washed their robes (in the blood of the Lamb).

> ### "I am coming quickly"
> (22:12). When eternity is the measure, "quick" is a relative term that may not carry the same meaning to time-bound humanity. Every generation since the time of Jesus has carried the same anticipation—Christ's imminent return. The Bible clearly declares the gospel will be preached to all nations (Luke 24:47) and disciples made among all people groups of the world (Matt. 28:19). As the church fulfills its mission, we can anticipate, with joy, Jesus coming again.

B. Final warning and assurance (22:18–20).
The last words of the book, which are the last words of our Bible, sum up the hope of Christians throughout the ages.

"Surely I am coming quickly," sounds the promise (*see* Messianic Promises; Quickly).

And all the saints gladly reply:

"Amen. Come, Lord Jesus!"

C. Benediction (22:21).

TRUTH-IN-ACTION through REVELATION

Truth Revelation Teaches	**Action** Revelation Invites
1 Steps to Holiness Jesus calls His people to be fully separated from the world's value system and to be totally committed to Him. They are to find the spiritual power source in their lives in Christ, not in occult practices. The believer is to gauge success by the measuring rod of God, rather than by the world's social and financial standard. When the Christian understands God's view from the eternal, the present comes into correct perspective.	**3:17** *Do not value* worldly success. *Do not trust* worldly wealth. *Repent* wherever you have done these things. *Recognize* that worldly assets have no spiritual or heavenly value! **3:18** *Return* to a spiritual value system wherever you have departed. **13:16** *Do not adopt* the world's way of thinking or its standards of behavior.
2 Key Lessons in Faith Faith is established in the knowledge of God, trusting Him for understanding and wisdom in the face of persecution. Faith's commitment to overcome, based on the shed blood of Jesus, does not fear even death.	**1:3** *Trust God for understanding* when you read Rev. **2:10, 11** *Be faithful to Jesus* when confronted with persecution and death. **2:13** *Never renounce* faith in Jesus. **13:10; 14:12** *Understand* that the Lord calls His people to faithfulness and patient endurance. *Never give up!*
3 Steps to Dynamic Devotion Jesus requires absolute devotion and rejects lackadaisical, half-hearted followers. Zeal for the Lord is not optional for His disciples. Devotion willingly submits to Jesus' discipline because it recognizes His love in it.	**2:4** *Give* your love for Jesus first place in your life. *Commit* yourself both emotionally and intellectually to Christ. **3:15** *Avoid* lukewarmness; *stir up* your zeal for the Lord. **3:19** *Repent quickly* whenever the Spirit convicts you of sin.
4 Keys to Wise Living The wise believer takes the time to listen with his spiritual hearing to what the Spirit is saying to the church. This is as needed today as it was in the first century. One who hears and follows the voice of the Holy Spirit does not need to fear the deception that leads to apostasy. Rather, he will walk where Jesus requires and will grow in the things of the Spirit of God, which produce healthy, vibrant, Spirit-filled churches capable of preaching Jesus to all the world.	**2:7, 11, 17, 29** *Develop* your spiritual ear. **3:6, 13, 22** *Listen* to what the Spirit is saying to the church. When forced to choose, *obey* God, not man! **2:9, 10** *Understand* that one may be rich in the Spirit but poor in the world's eyes. *Be faithful* and *receive* the crown of life.
5 Keys to Moral Purity The church is pictured as the bride of Christ; thus sexual impurity and apostasy are linked. Christians are required to be faithful to Christ, being sexually pure, worshiping no carnal idol.	**2:14, 20** *Reject* any teaching or practice that allows sexual immorality among God's people. **14:4, 5** *Maintain* sexual purity. *Practice* absolute obedience to Jesus. *Live* a blameless life.
6 Steps in Developing Humility The believer is constantly to strengthen the things of God that have become established in his life.	**3:1-5** *Do not be* lulled to sleep because of a good reputation. *Keep on pressing* into Jesus. *Make sure* you practice the teachings you have received. *Obey* God's word to you. *(continued)*

Truth Revelation Teaches	**Action** Revelation Invites
6 Steps in Developing Humility *(continued)* Being ready to repent for any failure, to make right any sin, will cause the believer to refine his walk in the Spirit. Outward works do not always indicate a right condition of heart, but a right condition of heart produces good works.	
7 Guidelines to Gaining Victory Spiritual victory is something we enter into. Jesus Christ has already won the victory through His death, burial, and resurrection.	**12:11** *Conduct spiritual warfare* on the basis of Jesus' shed blood and through the declaration that He died for your sins and rose again for your justification. *Love* Jesus more than life itself.

The Seven Churches of Revelation

	Commendation	Criticism	Instruction	Promise
Ephesus (2:1–7)	Rejects evil, perseveres, has patience	Love for Christ no longer fervent	Do the works you did at first	The tree of life
Smyrna (2:8–11)	Gracefully bears suffering	None	Be faithful until death	The crown of life
Pergamos (2:12–17)	Keeps the faith of Christ	Tolerates immorality, idolatry, and heresies	Repent	Hidden manna and a stone with a new name
Thyatira (2:18–29)	Love, service, faith, patience is greater than at first	Tolerates cult of idolatry and immorality	Judgment coming; keep the faith	Rule over nations and receive morning star
Sardis (3:1–6)	Some have kept the faith	A dead church	Repent; strengthen what remains	Faithful honored and clothed in white
Philadelphia (3:7–13)	Perseveres in the faith	None	Keep the faith	A place in God's presence, a new name, and the New Jerusalem
Laodicea (3:14–22)	None	Indifferent	Be zealous and repent	Share Christ's throne

SPECIAL
REFERENCE
FEATURES

VISUAL SURVEY
OF THE BIBLE

by
Kenneth D. Boa, Ph.D., D. Phil.
Mylan W. Lorenzen

Introduction

The Visual Survey gives you a complete overview of the Bible. Taking people, events, and themes of the Bible as focus points, this handy study tool unfolds for you the contents of Scripture. Quotations from the Bible are taken from the New King James Version.

Take a moment to familiarize yourself with the first chart, which compares the Old and New Testaments. Note particularly the timeline at the bottom of the page. This timeline divides the Old Testament into five periods and the New Testament into two. It is the key to the rest of the charts.

As you look through the following pages, notice that each chart has its own timeline containing both biblical and extrabiblical events. The maps portray the major movement of each period; the boxes present the key topics. The charts also summarize the themes of the Old Testament poetic and prophetic books, and the themes of the New Testament Epistles.

The ten life applications are an important part of this Survey. Based on the flow of each period, they crystallize the central spiritual truths of Scripture. Each principle leads into the next, and all of them relate to your own life.

(This edition of the Visual Survey has been adapted slightly for Hayford's Bible Handbook.*)*

VISUAL SURVEY...

OLD TESTAMENT

THE OLD TESTAMENT

Size	First ¾ths of the Bible
Years of History	Over 4000 years
Number of Books	39
Theme	Our relationship with and rulership under God—lost through our sin, restored through His plan of redemption.
Key Word (John 1:17)	Law: "The law was given through Moses . . ."
Jesus Christ Is seen in:	Over 300 prophecies
	The passover lamb
	The priesthood and sacrifices

Adam	Noah	Abraham	Moses	David	Ezra
Before 4000 B.C.	?	2000 B.C.	1500 B.C.	1000 B.C.	450 B.C.

History of the Early World		History of Israel			
Pre-Flood	After the Flood	The People	The Land	The Kingdom	The Remnant
11 Chapters (Gen. 1—11)		Over 38 Books (Gen. 12—Mal.)			

...OF THE BIBLE

THE NEW TESTAMENT

NEW TESTAMENT

ACTS

GOSPELS   EPISTLES

Last ¼th of the Bible	
About 100 years	
27	
Sacrificing Himself for us, Christ provides kingdom grace now, kingdom glory forever.	
Grace: ". . . grace and truth came through Jesus Christ."	
Flesh and blood (Matt.—John)	
The teachings of the Apostles (Acts—3 John)	
His coming return (Rev.)	

"Your word I have hidden in my heart, that I might not sin against You."
Psalm 119:11

Throughout this visual survey, the symbol above will focus on a key principle of life change that grows out of that section of the Bible survey.

Jesus		Peter	Paul	John

4 B.C.   A.D. 27–30   A.D. 100

History of the Messiah	History of the Early Church		
The Life of Christ	In all Jerusalem	In all Judea & Samaria	To all the Earth
(Matt.—John)	(Acts—Rev.)		

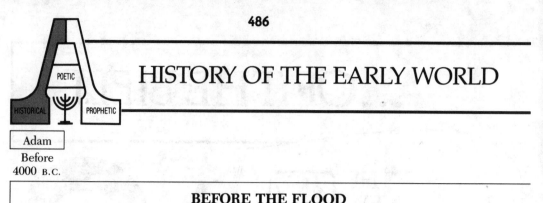

Adam

Before
4000 B.C.

BEFORE THE FLOOD

CREATION (Origin of humanity)	FALL (Origin of sin)	SPREAD OF SIN
Gen. 1; 2	Gen. 3	Gen. 4—9

THE CREATIVE WORK OF GOD

	Genesis 1	Genesis 2
Creation Accounts	God the creator Elohim God as powerful Creation of the universe Climaxes with humankind The six days of creation	God the covenant-keeper Yahweh God as personal Creation of humanity Climaxes with marriage The sixth day of creation
Genesis 1:2	"without form . . ."	". . . and void"
Six Days of Creation	In the first three days, God shaped the Creation Day 1: light Day 2: water, atmosphere Day 3: earth, vegetation	In the second three days, God populated the Creation Day 4: sun, moon, stars Day 5: sea creatures, birds Day 6: animals and humans

TEMPTATION: THE TWO ADAMS CONTRASTED

1 John 2:16	Genesis 3:6 (First Adam)	Luke 4:1–13 (Second Adam—Christ)
"the lust of the flesh"	"the tree was good for food"	"command this stone to become bread"
"the lust of the eyes"	"it was pleasant to the eyes"	"the devil . . . showed Him all the kingdoms"
"the pride of life"	"a tree desirable to make one wise"	"throw Yourself down from here"

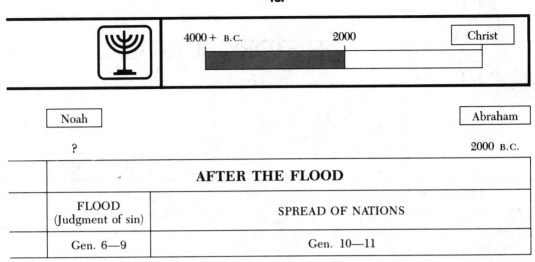

Noah			Abraham
?			2000 B.C.

AFTER THE FLOOD	
FLOOD (Judgment of sin)	SPREAD OF NATIONS
Gen. 6—9	Gen. 10—11

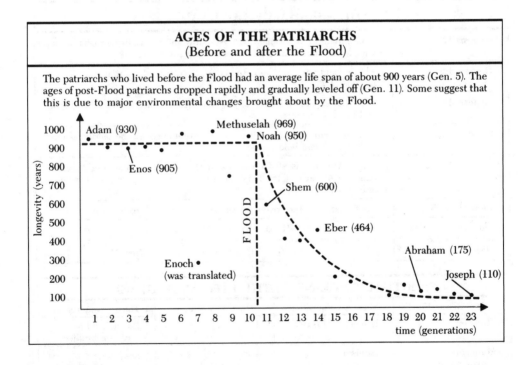

AGES OF THE PATRIARCHS
(Before and after the Flood)

The patriarchs who lived before the Flood had an average life span of about 900 years (Gen. 5). The ages of post-Flood patriarchs dropped rapidly and gradually leveled off (Gen. 11). Some suggest that this is due to major environmental changes brought about by the Flood.

Adam (930)
Methuselah (969)
Noah (950)
Enos (905)
Shem (600)
Eber (464)
Abraham (175)
Joseph (110)
Enoch •
(was translated)
FLOOD

longevity (years): 1000, 900, 800, 700, 600, 500, 400, 300, 200, 100

time (generations): 1 2 3 4 5 6 7 8 9 10 11 12 13 14 15 16 17 18 19 20 21 22 23

Principle: Righteousness is creative; sin is destructive (Gen. 2:17; Rom. 6:23).

Practice: Genesis 1—11, the prologue not only to Genesis, but to the entire Bible, begins with the ordered and life-giving activity of the holy Creator. The fall of mankind and the consequent spread of sin stand in stark contrast to the work of God and illustrate the disorder and death that always accompanies rebellion against the purposes of the Lord. God is not mocked; in a moral and spiritual universe, sin must be judged. What must we do, according to Romans 3:21–26, to escape the condemnation of our Creator?

HISTORY OF ISRAEL:

Abraham	Joseph
2000 B.C.	1975 B.C.

THE PEOPLE

THE PATRIARCHS	BONDAGE IN EGYPT

2135 Birth of Abraham	1991 Beginning of Egyptian Middle Kingdom	Jacob Enters Egypt with His Family	1790 Code of Hammurapi

THE ABRAHAMIC COVENANT	
Genesis 12:1–3	God initiated His covenant with Abram when he was living in Ur of the Chaldeans, promising a land, descendants, and blessing.
Genesis 12:4, 5	Abram went with his family to Haran, lived there for a time, and left at the age of 75.
Genesis 13:14–17	After Lot separated from Abram, God again promised the land to him and his descendants.
Genesis 15:1–21	This covenant was ratified when God passed between the sacrificial animals Abram laid before God.
Genesis 17:1–27	When Abram was 99 God renewed His covenant, changing Abram's name to Abraham ("the father of a multitude"). Sign of the covenant: circumcision.
Genesis 22:15–18	Confirmation of the covenant because of Abraham's obedience.
This covenant was foundational to other covenants.	Land: Palestinian covenant (Deut. 30). Descendants: Davidic covenant (2 Sam. 7). Blessing: "old" (Ex. 19) and "new" covenants (Jer. 31).

SPIRITUAL DECLINE IN THE PATRIARCHAL AGE			
First Generation	**Second Generation**	**Third Generation**	**Fourth Generation**
Abraham	Ishmael and Isaac	Esau and Jacob	Joseph and his eleven brothers
Abraham: man of faith believed God	Ishmael: not son of promise Isaac: called on God believed God	Esau: unspiritual little faith Jacob: at first compromised, later turned to the Lord	Joseph: man of God showed faith Brothers: treachery, immorality, lack of separation from Canaanites
Abraham: built altars to God (Gen. 12:7, 8; 13:4, 18; 22:9)	Isaac: built an altar to God (Gen. 26:25)	Jacob: built altars to God (Gen. 33:20; 35:1, 3, 7)	No altars were built to God in the fourth generation

THE PEOPLE	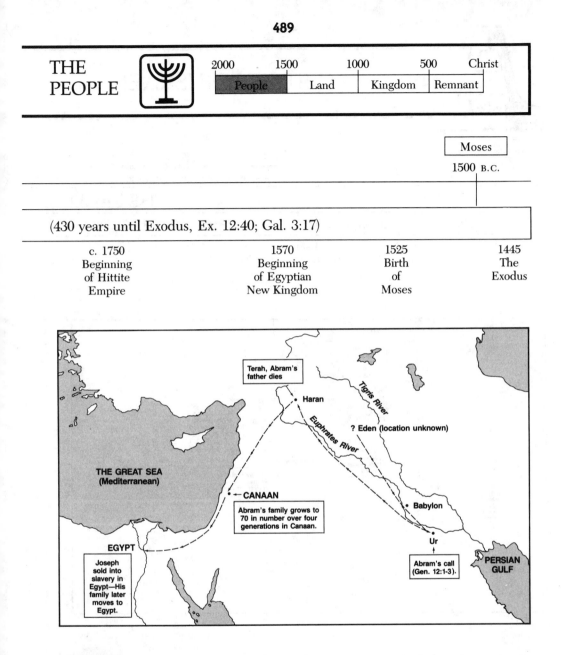	2000	1500	1000	500	Christ
			People	Land	Kingdom	Remnant

Moses

1500 B.C.

(430 years until Exodus, Ex. 12:40; Gal. 3:17)

c. 1750	1570	1525	1445
Beginning of Hittite Empire	Beginning of Egyptian New Kingdom	Birth of Moses	The Exodus

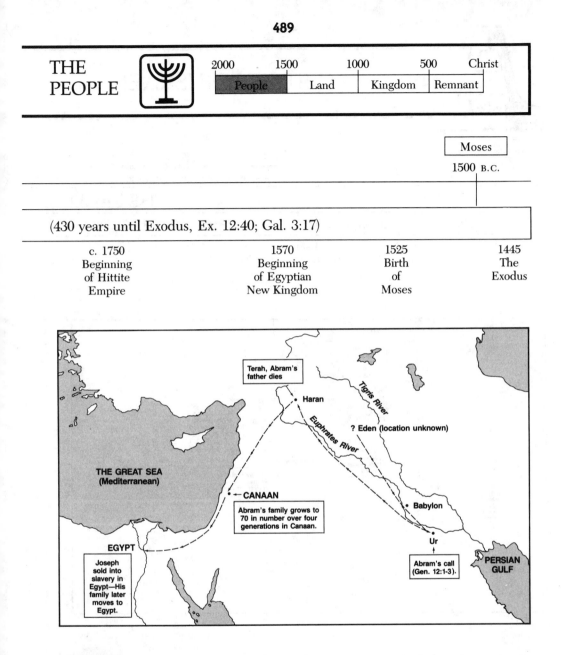

Terah, Abram's father dies · Haran

Tigris River

Euphrates River

? Eden (location unknown)

THE GREAT SEA (Mediterranean)

CANAAN — Abram's family grows to 70 in number over four generations in Canaan.

Babylon

Ur

EGYPT

Joseph sold into slavery in Egypt—His family later moves to Egypt.

Abram's call (Gen. 12:1-3).

PERSIAN GULF

Principle: The destructiveness of sin is overcome by a faith that takes God at His word in spite of appearances and circumstances to the contrary (Gen. 15:6; John 3:16; Heb. 11:8–22).

Practice: Beginning in Genesis 12, God called a man who would be the father of the people from whom and to whom the Messiah would come. Abraham became a friend of God through faith. In spite of appearances to the contrary, he went to a land he had not seen, believed God's promise of a son, and offered up that son at the same area where God's own Son would be crucified. Because he believed God, his faith was accounted to him for righteousness. In the same way, we can enter into a relationship with God by placing our trust in the person and work of His Son. Have you made that decision?

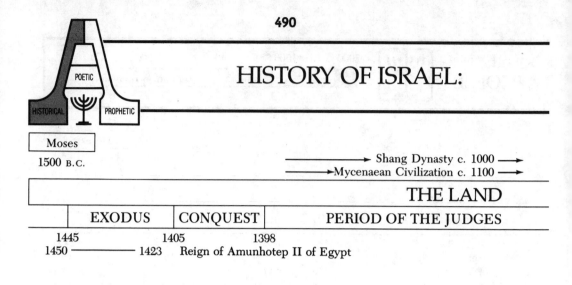

HISTORY OF ISRAEL:

POETIC

HISTORICAL

PROPHETIC

Moses

1500 B.C.

→ Shang Dynasty c. 1000 →
→ Mycenaean Civilization c. 1100 →

THE LAND

EXODUS	CONQUEST	PERIOD OF THE JUDGES

1445   1405   1398
1450 ———————— 1423   Reign of Amunhotep II of Egypt

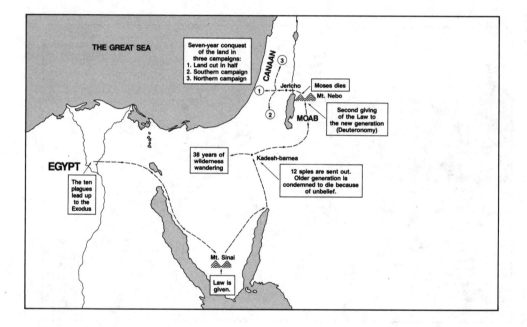

THE GREAT SEA

Seven-year conquest
of the land in
three campaigns:
1. Land cut in half
2. Southern campaign
3. Northern campaign

CANAAN

Jericho   Moses dies

Mt. Nebo

MOAB

Second giving
of the Law to
the new generation
(Deuteronomy)

38 years of
wilderness
wandering

Kadesh-barnea

12 spies are sent out.
Older generation is
condemned to die because
of unbelief.

EGYPT

The ten
plagues
lead up
to the
Exodus

Mt. Sinai

Law is
given.

Principle: Revelation demands obedience, and obedience brings blessing (Deut. 6:1–15; Josh. 1:8; John 15:12–17).

Practice: After redeeming His people from bondage, the Lord spoke to them in power and glory at Mt. Sinai. The revelation of the Mosaic law required a response of obedience. Their success as individuals and as a nation would depend on the degree of their conformity to God's moral, civil, and ceremonial law. Likewise, disobedience would lead to disaster (e.g., the wilderness wandering and servitude in the time of the Judges). As believers in Christ, our success is measured by the degree of our conformity to His character. Are you committed to growing with Christ as the Lord of your life?

THE LAND		2000	1500	1000	500	Christ
			People	Land	Kingdom	Remnant

	Samuel	David
	1105–1020	1000 B.C.

c. 1100 Greek Dark Ages ⟶

1191	1043
Gideon beats Midianites	Saul anointed King

THE LAW After their deliverance from Egyptian bondage, the children of Israel needed to learn to walk with their God. The Law was given to instruct the people about the person and the ways of their Redeemer so that they could be set apart to a life of holiness and obedience, not to save anyone but to reveal the people's need to trust in the Lord. As Paul told the Galatians, "Therefore the law was our tutor to bring us to Christ, that we might be justified by faith" (Gal. 3:24).

The Law combines poetry, salvation history, legislation, and exhortation. The three major divisions of the Law (Deut. 4:45) are the testimonies (moral duties), the statutes (ceremonial duties), and the judgments or ordinances (civil and social duties). The moral portion of the Law is summarized in the Ten Commandments (Ex. 20:1–17; Deut. 5:6–21):

THE TEN COMMANDMENTS (Moral Law)		
1–4	Duties to God	"You shall love the Lord your God" (Matt. 22:37).
5–10	Duties to humans	"You shall love your neighbor" (Matt. 22:39).

THE JUDGES: A CASE STUDY IN DISOBEDIENCE

Each of the seven cycles found in Judges 3:5—16:31 has four steps: sin, servitude, supplication, and salvation. The cycles connect as a descending spiral of sin (2:19), with Israel vacillating between obedience and apostasy.

Cycle	Oppressor	Years of Oppression	Judge/Deliverer	Years of Peace
1. (3:7–11)	Mesopotamians	8	Othniel	40
2. (3:12–30)	Moabites	18	Ehud	80
(3:31)	Philistines		Shamgar	
3. (4:1—5:31)	Canaanites	20	Deborah/Barak	40
4. (6:1—8:32)	Midianites	7	Gideon	40
5. (8:33—10:5)	Abimelech	3	Tola/Jair	45
6. (10:6—12:15)	Ammonites	18	Jephthah/Ibzan/Elon/Abdon	6/7/10/8
7. (13:1—16:31)	Philistines	40	Samson	20

HISTORY OF ISRAEL:

POETIC		
HISTORICAL	PROPHETIC	

David	Solomon		Elijah	Elisha		Homer (Iliad & Odyssey)
1000 B.C.			852			c. 800

THE KINGDOM

UNITED KINGDOM	DIVIDED KINGDOM
1043	931

Samuel anoints Saul			ISRAEL: 10 Tribes (North-Samaria)
SAUL	DAVID	SOLOMON	← Civil War Divides Kingdom
			JUDAH: 2 Tribes (South-Jerusalem)

THE LIFE OF DAVID: A Man after God's own heart

1041 B.C.				1011			971 B.C.
DAVID'S 70 YEARS							
David as Subject (30 Years)				David as King (40 Years)			
As a son to his father	As a servant to King Saul			King over the South	King over all 12 tribes		
	His rise over Saul	Rejected by Saul	Refuge with Philistines	Growing ⟋	⟍ Growing		
	17–18	19–26	27–31	Success			Crisis
Psalms	1 Samuel			2 Samuel			1 Kings
23	17	19:1–10	31	7	11 14–18	24	2:10

↑ David the Shepherd ↑ Kills Goliath ↑ Protected by Jonathan ↑ Saul and Jonathan killed at Gilboa ↑ Promise of Christ ↑ Sins with Bathsheba ↑ Absalom's Rebellion ↑ David's Census ↑ David Dies

---

Principle: Obedience grows out of a heart for God (Deut. 6:5; 1 Sam. 13:14; 1 Chr. 28:9; Acts 13:22).

Practice: Saul and David are a study in contrasts. The key to Saul's failure was his lack of a heart for God; the key to David's greatness was his obvious love for the Lord. David's relationship with God became the standard by which all the kings of Judah would be measured. To know God is to love Him, and to love Him is to desire to obey Him. Read Psalm 23 as a model of a man who was intimate with God. What are the things that could be hindering your growth in the knowledge of God?

THE KINGDOM

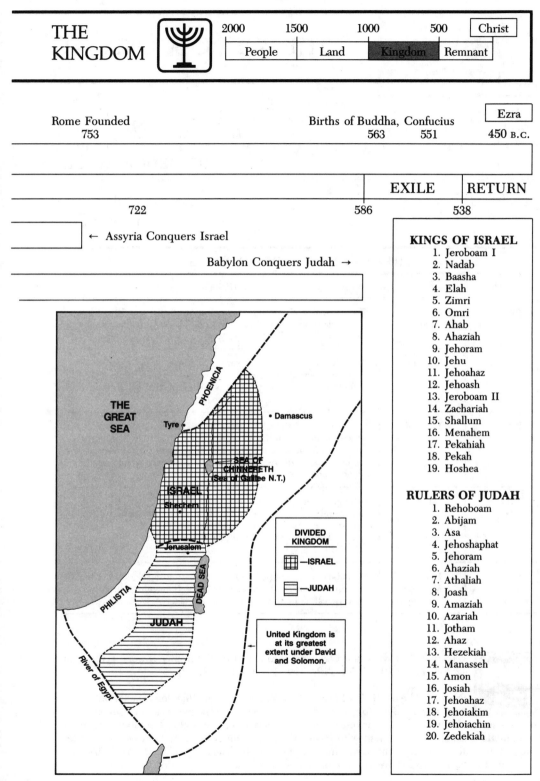

2000	1500	1000	500	Christ
People	Land	Kingdom	Remnant	

Rome Founded
753

Births of Buddha, Confucius
563   551

Ezra

450 B.C.

EXILE | **RETURN**

722   586   538

← Assyria Conquers Israel

Babylon Conquers Judah →

THE
GREAT
SEA

PHOENICIA

Tyre

• Damascus

SEA OF
CHINNERETH
(Sea of Galilee N.T.)

ISRAEL

Shechem

Jerusalem

DEAD SEA

PHILISTIA

JUDAH

River of Egypt

DIVIDED KINGDOM

⊞ —ISRAEL

⊟ —JUDAH

← United Kingdom is at its greatest extent under David and Solomon.

KINGS OF ISRAEL
1. Jeroboam I
2. Nadab
3. Baasha
4. Elah
5. Zimri
6. Omri
7. Ahab
8. Ahaziah
9. Jehoram
10. Jehu
11. Jehoahaz
12. Jehoash
13. Jeroboam II
14. Zachariah
15. Shallum
16. Menahem
17. Pekahiah
18. Pekah
19. Hoshea

RULERS OF JUDAH
1. Rehoboam
2. Abijam
3. Asa
4. Jehoshaphat
5. Jehoram
6. Ahaziah
7. Athaliah
8. Joash
9. Amaziah
10. Azariah
11. Jotham
12. Ahaz
13. Hezekiah
14. Manasseh
15. Amon
16. Josiah
17. Jehoahaz
18. Jehoiakim
19. Jehoiachin
20. Zedekiah

THE POETIC BOOKS:

HISTORICAL   POETIC   PROPHETIC

Abraham	Moses	David
2000 B.C.	1500 B.C.	1000 B.C.

HISTORY OF ISRAEL

JOB		SOLOMON
		ASAPH

THEMES OF THE POETIC BOOKS		
BOOK	**KEY WORD**	**THEME**
Job	Sovereignty	God revealed Himself in His majesty and power to Job. It became clear that the real issue was not Job's suffering (caused by Job's sin) but God's sovereignty.
Psalms	Worship	The five books of psalms span the centuries from Moses to the postexilic period, covering the full range of human emotions and experiences. Suited for service as the temple hymnal, they were set to music and focused on worship.
Proverbs	Wisdom	Proverbs was designed to equip the reader in practical wisdom, discernment, discipline, and discretion. The development of skills in all the details of life are stressed, so that beauty and righteousness will replace foolishness and evil through dependence upon God.
Ecclesiastes	Vanity	The Preacher applied his great mind and resources to the quest for meaning and purpose in life. He found that wisdom, wealth, works, pleasure, and power all led to futility and striving after wind. The only source of ultimate meaning and fulfillment is God Himself.
Song of Solomon	Love in Marriage	This beautiful song portrays the intimate love relationship between Solomon and his Shulamite bride. It magnifies the virtues of physical and emotional love in marriage.

Principle: To have a heart for God is to approach life from His perspective (Job 42:1–6; Ps. 1; 19; 63; 73; 119; Prov. 2:1–9; Rom. 12:1–3).

Practice: The poetic books record the struggles of men like Job, David, Solomon, Asaph, and others to gain a divine perspective on their lives and circumstances. As they learned to set their minds on the person, powers, and perfections of God, their wills and emotions came into alignment with His truth. True wisdom is seeing life from God's side, and this is rooted in setting our minds (meditating) on the things above (Col. 3:1–3). Try dipping into the Psalms and Proverbs on a daily basis and prayerfully ponder what you read.

THE HEART OF THE JEWS

Ezra	Christ
450 B.C.	4 B.C.

THE PATH TO TRUE SUCCESS

Question	Principle
1. What is wisdom?	Wisdom is the key to a life of beauty, fulfillment, and purpose (Prov. 3:15–18). Wisdom is the skill in the art of living life with every area under the dominion of God. It is the ability to use the best means at the best time to accomplish the best ends.
2. How do we pursue wisdom?	The treasure of wisdom rests in the hands of God. Since it comes from above (Prov. 2:6; cf. James 3:17), we cannot attain it apart from Him.
3. What are the conditions for attaining wisdom?	True wisdom can only be gained by cultivating the fear of the Lord (Job 28:28; Ps. 86:11; 111:10; Prov. 1:7; 9:10).
4. What is the fear of the Lord?	To fear God is to have an attitude of awe and humility before Him (Prov. 15:33). It is to recognize Him as our Creator and our complete dependence upon Him in every activity of our lives.
5. Why have so few people developed this fear of God?	The temporal value system of this world is based on what is seen, while the eternal value system of Scripture is based on what is unseen (2 Cor. 4:16–18; 5:7). The former exerts a powerful influence upon us, and we struggle with giving up the seen for the unseen.
6. What can enable us to choose the eternal value system?	This choice is based on faith (believing God in spite of appearances and circumstances), and faith is based on trust.
7. How do we grow in faith?	Our ability to trust God is directly proportional to our knowledge of God. The more we open to Him, the more we will trust Him.
8. How can we increase in our knowledge of God?	We become intimate with God as we talk with Him in prayer and listen to His voice in Scripture. The better we know God, the more we love Him and want to respond to His desires for our lives. Faith in God is simply trusting Him as a person, and trust is manifested in action.

THE PROPHETIC BOOKS:

David		Elijah	Elisha		Zerubbabel	Ezra	Nehemiah
1000 B.C.			852			538	

THE KINGDOM

UNITED KINGDOM	DIVIDED KINGDOM	EXILE	RETURN

	ISRAEL	← 722	70	3-stage return
UNITED KINGDOM	← 931		Years in	1st: Zerubbabel
		586 →	Babylon	2nd: Ezra
	JUDAH			3rd: Nehemiah

PROPHETS BEFORE THE EXILE		EXILE PROPHETS	PROPHETS AFTER THE EXILE
To Israel: Amos (760) Hosea (755) To Nineveh: Jonah (760) Nahum (620) To Edom:	To Judah: Isaiah (740) Micah (735) Zephaniah (630) Jeremiah (627) Habakkuk (607) Joel (600) Lamentations (586) Obadiah (580)	To Jews in Babylon: Daniel (605) Ezekiel (592)	To the Remnant after returning: Haggai (520) Zechariah (520) Malachi (450)

Principle: God's disciplines are designed to restore a heart for Himself (Jer. 17:5, 7; Joel 2:12, 13; Heb. 12:5–11).

Practice: God had to discipline His people because of their moral and spiritual rebellion and their refusal to heed the warnings of His prophets. Reproof is designed to bring repentance and repentance brings restoration. The same prophets who pronounced the condemnation of God also announced the consolation of God. Similarly, because God loves us, we will experience chastening when needed. Are you willing to respond with a teachable spirit at such times?

THE HOPE OF THE JEWS

	Christ
	4 B.C.

THE REMNANT

	400 YEARS UNTIL CHRIST

THEMES OF THE PROPHETIC BOOKS

The Major Prophets

BOOK	KEY PHRASE	THEME
Isaiah	Salvation Is of the Lord	Twofold message of condemnation (1–39) and consolation (40–66). God's judgment on the sins of Judah, the surrounding nations, and the world, followed by future salvation and restoration.
Jeremiah	Judah's Last Hour	Declaration of certain judgment of God against Judah. God promises to establish a new covenant with His people.
Lamenta-tions	Lamentations	This beautifully structured series of five lament poems is a funeral dirge for the fallen city of Jerusalem.
Ezekiel	Future Resto-ration	Ministry to the Jewish captives in Babylon before and after the fall of Jerusalem. The fate of Judah's foes and an apocalyptic vision of Judah's future.
Daniel	God's Program for Israel	Outlines God's plan for the gentile nations (2–7) and portrays Israel during the time of gentile domination (8–12).

The Minor Prophets

BOOK	KEY PHRASE	THEME
Hosea	God's Love for Israel	The story of Hosea and his faithless wife illustrates the loyal love of God and the spiritual adultery of Israel.
Joel	Day of the Lord	A recent locust plague illustrates the far more terrifying day of the Lord. God appeals to the people to repent in order to avert the coming disaster.
Amos	Judgment of Israel	In eight pronouncements of judgment, Amos spirals around the surrounding countries before landing on Israel. He lists the sins of Israel and calls for repentance.
Obadiah	Judgment of Edom	Condemns the nation of Edom (descended from Esau) for refusing to act as a brother toward Judah (descended from Jacob).
Jonah	Revival in Nineveh	The repentant response of the people of Nineveh to Jonah's one-line prophetic message caused the God of mercy to spare the city.
Micah	Judgment and Restoration of Judah	In spite of divine retribution against the corruption of Israel and Judah, God's covenant with them will be fulfilled in Messiah's future kingdom.
Nahum	Judgment of Nineveh	About 140 years after Nineveh repented under the preaching of Jonah, Micah predicted the destruction of the city because of its idolatry and brutality.
Habakkuk	Live by Faith	Troubled with God's plan to use the Babylonians as His rod of judgment on Judah, Habakkuk praises the Lord after gaining a better perspective on His power and purposes.
Zephaniah	Day of the Lord	The coming day of the Lord is a time of awesome judgment followed by great blessing. Judah stands condemned, but God will restore the fortunes of the remnant.
Haggai	Reconstruction of the Temple	After the Babylonian exile, Haggai urges the Jews to put God first and finish the Temple they had begun so that they can enjoy God's blessing.
Zechariah	Prepare for the Messiah	Like Haggai, Zechariah exhorts the Jews to complete the construction of the Temple. He relates it to the coming of Messiah in a series of visions and messianic prophecies.
Malachi	Appeal to Backsliders	The spiritual climate of the people had grown cold, and Malachi rebukes them for their religious and social compromise. If they return to God with sincere hearts, they will be blessed.

HISTORY OF ISRAEL: THE REMNANT

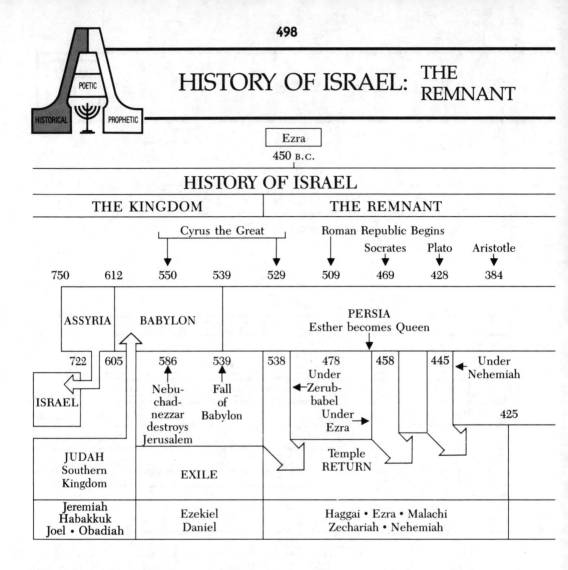

Ezra
450 B.C.

HISTORY OF ISRAEL

THE KINGDOM	THE REMNANT

Cyrus the Great

Roman Republic Begins

Socrates   Plato   Aristotle

750	612	550	539	529	509	469	428	384

ASSYRIA   BABYLON

PERSIA
Esther becomes Queen

722	605	586	539	538	478	458	445	Under Nehemiah

ISRAEL

Nebu-chad-nezzar destroys Jerusalem

Fall of Babylon

Under ←Zerub-babel

Under Ezra→

425

JUDAH
Southern
Kingdom

EXILE

Temple
RETURN

Jeremiah Habakkuk Joel • Obadiah	Ezekiel Daniel	Haggai • Ezra • Malachi Zechariah • Nehemiah

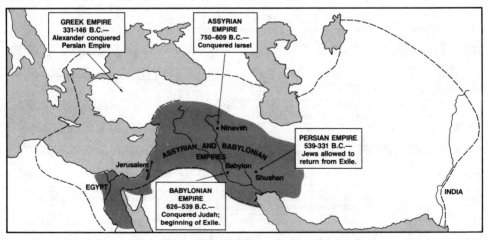

GREEK EMPIRE 331-146 B.C.— Alexander conquered Persian Empire

ASSYRIAN EMPIRE 750-609 B.C.— Conquered Israel

PERSIAN EMPIRE 539-331 B.C.— Jews allowed to return from Exile.

BABYLONIAN EMPIRE 626–539 B.C.— Conquered Judah; beginning of Exile.

Nineveh • Jerusalem • Babylon • Shushan • EGYPT • INDIA

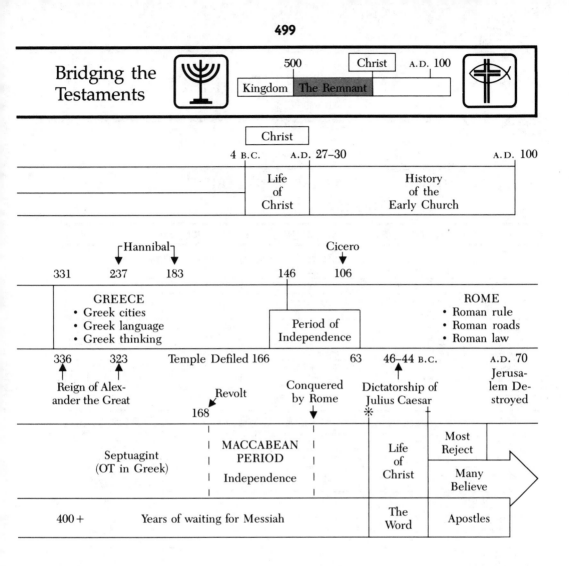

Bridging the Testaments

| | | | 500 | Christ | A.D. 100 |
| | | Kingdom | The Remnant | | |

Christ

4 B.C.   A.D. 27–30   A.D. 100

| Life of Christ | History of the Early Church |

┌Hannibal┐   Cicero

331   237   183   146   106

GREECE
- Greek cities
- Greek language
- Greek thinking

Period of Independence

ROME
- Roman rule
- Roman roads
- Roman law

336   323   Temple Defiled 166   63   46–44 B.C.   A.D. 70

Reign of Alexander the Great   Revolt   Conquered by Rome   Dictatorship of Julius Caesar   Jerusalem Destroyed

168

Septuagint (OT in Greek)   **MACCABEAN PERIOD**   Independence   Life of Christ   Most Reject / Many Believe

400+   Years of waiting for Messiah   The Word   Apostles

Principle: True restoration results from being molded by the Word within rather than the world without (Ezra 7:10; 9:10–15; Is. 46:3, 4; Acts 7:51–53).

Practice: Even after the chastening of the Exile, most of the returning Jews became enmeshed once again in the affairs of the world and neglected their relationship with God. For some, the problem was external religiosity without internal reality; for others, the problem was being more influenced by culture than Scripture. God has always had to work with a faithful minority who love Him enough to stand against the tide of the world system. Is your quality of life different from that of those who love the world more than the Lord?

THE LIFE OF CHRIST

4 B.C.   A.D. 9 (Temple Discussion)

EARLY CHILDHOOD	YEARS AT NAZARETH (Luke 2:51, 52)

Birth   Luke 2:41–50

THE GOSPELS COMPARED AND CONTRASTED

Topics	The Synoptic Gospels			John
	Matthew	Mark	Luke	
Probable Date	A.D. 58–68	A.D. 55–65	A.D. 60–68	A.D. 80–90
Place of Writing	Syria Antioch or Palestine	Rome	Rome/Greece	Ephesus
Original Audience	Jewish mind (Religious)	Roman mind (Pragmatic)	Greek mind (Idealistic)	Universal
Theme	Messiah-King	Servant-Redeemer	Perfect Man	Son of God
Traditional Picture of Christ (cf. Ezek. 1:10; Rev. 4:6–8)	The Lion (strength, authority)	The Bull (service, power)	The Man (wisdom, character)	The Eagle (deity, person)
Portrait of Christ	God-**man**			**God**-man
Perspective	Historical			Theological
Unique Material	Less unique (Matthew, 42%; Mark, 7%; Luke, 59%)			More unique (92%)
Chronology	Only one Passover mentioned			Three or four Passovers mentioned
Geography	Concentrates on Galilean ministry			Concentrates on Judean ministry
Discourse Material	More public			More private
Teaching Method	Parables			Signs
Teaching Emphasis	More on ethical, practical teachings			More on the person of Christ
Relationship to Other Gospels	Complementary			Supplementary

CHRIST'S PUBLIC MINISTRY

Masses drawn to His miracles and teachings

Popularity peaks
Leaders attribute His miracles

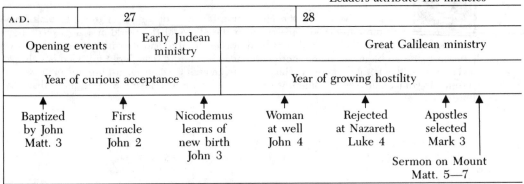

A.D.	27		28
Opening events	Early Judean ministry		Great Galilean ministry
Year of curious acceptance		Year of growing hostility	

Baptized
by John
Matt. 3

First
miracle
John 2

Nicodemus
learns of
new birth
John 3

Woman
at well
John 4

Rejected
at Nazareth
Luke 4

Apostles
selected
Mark 3

Sermon on Mount
Matt. 5—7

501

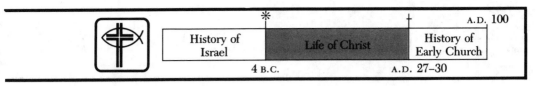

History of Israel	Life of Christ	History of Early Church

4 B.C.   A.D. 27–30   A.D. 100

A.D. 27   A.D. 30

PUBLIC MINISTRY

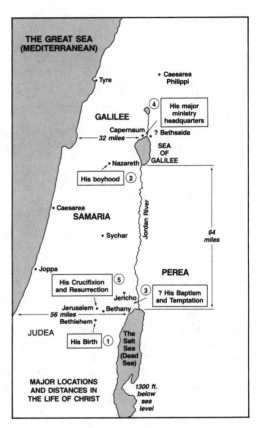

Principle: Jesus, the living Word, lives His life in and through us as we walk in dependence upon Him (John 1:11, 12; 10:10; 15:4, 5; Gal. 2:20).

Practice: In Christ, God personally revealed Himself in human flesh: to see Him is to see God (John 12:45; 14:9), to know Him is to know God (John 8:19), to receive Him is to receive God (Mark 9:37), to honor Him is to honor God (John 5:23), and to reject Him is to reject God (Luke 10:16). He is the vine, the source of life; we are the branches, the channels of life. It is only as we draw our life from Him that we bear lasting fruit. To what extent are you looking to Jesus as the true source of your security, significance, and fulfillment? In what ways are His kingdom graces and other evidences of the Holy Spirit's presence and power made manifest in your life, growth, and service?

THE GREAT SEA (MEDITERRANEAN)

MAJOR LOCATIONS AND DISTANCES IN THE LIFE OF CHRIST

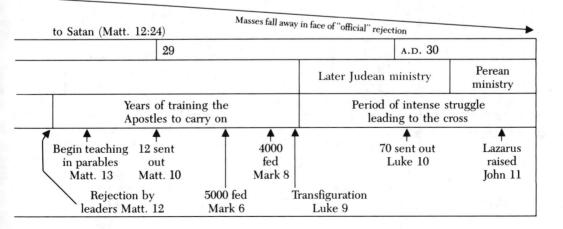

to Satan (Matt. 12:24)

Masses fall away in face of "official" rejection

29   A.D. 30

Later Judean ministry | Perean ministry

Years of training the Apostles to carry on

Period of intense struggle leading to the cross

Begin teaching in parables Matt. 13   12 sent out Matt. 10   4000 fed Mark 8   70 sent out Luke 10   Lazarus raised John 11

Rejection by leaders Matt. 12   5000 fed Mark 6   Transfiguration Luke 9

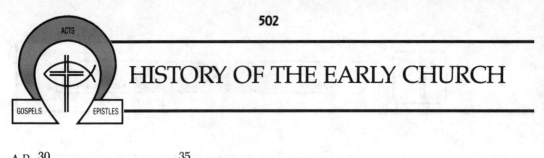

HISTORY OF THE EARLY CHURCH

A.D. 30   35

HISTORY OF THE EARLY CHURCH	
IN JERUSALEM	IN ALL JUDEA AND IN SAMARIA

Pentecost
Acts 2

Stephen
martyred
Acts 6

Philip brings
Samaritans to
Christ
Acts 8

Paul's
conversion
Acts 9

Peter brings
Gentiles to
Christ
Acts 10

THE BOOK OF ACTS IN OVERVIEW

"But you shall receive power when the Holy Spirit has come upon you; and you shall be witnesses to Me in Jerusalem, and in all Judea and Samaria, and to the end of the earth" (Acts 1:8).

Chapters	Acts 1–7	Acts 8–12	Acts 13–28
Spread of the Church	The church in Jerusalem	The church in all Judea and Samaria	The church to all the earth
The Gospel	Witnessing in the city	Witnessing in the provinces	Witnessing in the world
Theme	Power and progress of the church	Expansion of the church	Paul's three journeys and trials
People Addressed	Jews	Samaritans	Gentiles
Key Person	Peter	Philip	Paul
Time	2 years (A.D. 33–35)	13 years (A.D. 35–48)	14 years (A.D. 48–62)
Development	Triumph	Transition	Travels and trials

503

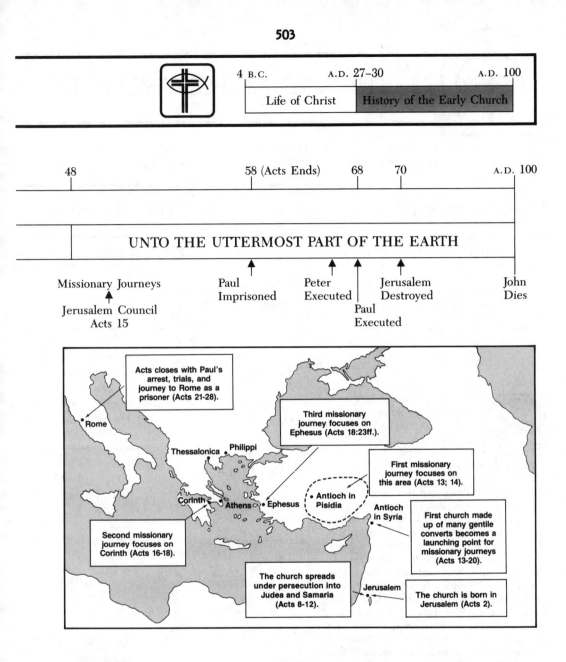

4 B.C.　　　　　　A.D. 27–30　　　　　　　A.D. 100

Life of Christ　　History of the Early Church

48　　　　　　　58 (Acts Ends)　　68　　70　　　　A.D. 100

UNTO THE UTTERMOST PART OF THE EARTH

Missionary Journeys　　　Paul　　　　Peter　　　Jerusalem　　　John
　　　　　　　　　　　　Imprisoned　　Executed　　Destroyed　　Dies
Jerusalem Council　　　　　　　　　　　　　　Paul
Acts 15　　　　　　　　　　　　　　　　　Executed

Acts closes with Paul's
arrest, trials, and
journey to Rome as a
prisoner (Acts 21-28).

Rome

Third missionary
journey focuses on
Ephesus (Acts 18:23ff.).

Thessalonica　Philippi

First missionary
journey focuses on
this area (Acts 13; 14).

Corinth　Athens　Ephesus　　Antioch in
　　　　　　　　　　　　　Pisidia　　　Antioch
　　　　　　　　　　　　　　　　　　in Syria

First church made
up of many gentile
converts becomes a
launching point for
missionary journeys
(Acts 13-20).

Second missionary
journey focuses on
Corinth (Acts 16-18).

The church spreads
under persecution into
Judea and Samaria
(Acts 8-12).

Jerusalem

The church is born in
Jerusalem (Acts 2).

Principle: Christ's life is reproduced in others when we take the initiative to witness in the power of the Holy Spirit (Matt. 28:18–20; Acts 1:8; Col. 4:2–6).

Practice: The Book of Acts records the spread of the gospel from the city of Jerusalem to the whole province of Judea and Samaria, and ultimately through the Roman Empire and beyond. These first-century Christians were sold out for the cause of Christ and transformed their world as their lives became living epistles of the Good News. God has called us to a life-style of evangelism in which we build relationships with non-Christians. These friendships in turn become natural bridges for communicating the gospel. Take a close look at Colossians 4:2–6 to learn how to become more effective as an instrument of the Holy Spirit to reproduce the life of Christ in others.

THE WRITINGS OF THE EARLY

Paul converted A.D. 34	Cornelius converted 40	1st Missionary Journey 48	Jerusalem Council 50

FOCUS ON PETER			FOCUS ON PAUL

PAUL THE LEARNER / PAUL THE MISSIONARY

Paul spends nearly 3 years at Damascus and 10 years in obscurity in Tarsus before he is ready for mission work.	1st Journey	The Jerusalem Council Acts 15	2nd Journey

A.D. 50

Galatians (49)

1 Thessalonians (51)

2 Thessalonians (51)

Principle: God wants us to grow in our understanding that Christ's life and destiny is our life and destiny (2 Cor. 4:16–18; Eph. 1:3, 17–19; 3:16–19; Phil. 1:21; 3:20, 21; 1 Pet. 1:3–9).

PAUL'S LETTERS

Practice: Paul, Peter, and the other apostles learned the secret of developing an eternal perspective in the midst of earthly problems. They were able to live above their circumstances and rejoice even while being persecuted because of their firm grasp on who they were in Christ and where they were going. In spite of his imprisonment, Paul could write, "For to me, to live is Christ, and to die is gain" (Phil. 1:21). Are you looking more at "the things which are seen" or at "the things which are not seen"? The former are temporary, but the latter are eternal (2 Cor. 4:18).

James (44, 45)

LETTERS BY OTHERS

GOSPELS & ACTS

Matthew (c. 40's)

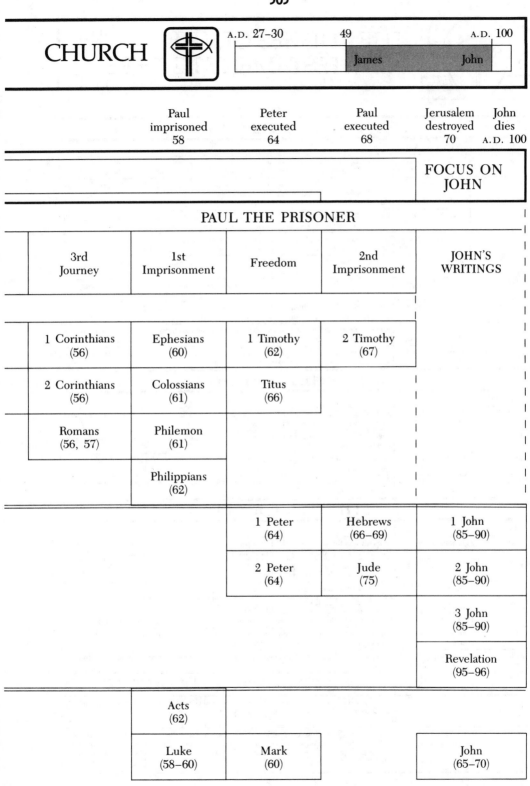

CHURCH		A.D. 27–30	49		A.D. 100
			James	John	

	Paul imprisoned 58	Peter executed 64	Paul executed 68	Jerusalem destroyed 70	John dies A.D. 100

FOCUS ON JOHN

PAUL THE PRISONER

3rd Journey	1st Imprisonment	Freedom	2nd Imprisonment	JOHN'S WRITINGS
1 Corinthians (56)	Ephesians (60)	1 Timothy (62)	2 Timothy (67)	
2 Corinthians (56)	Colossians (61)	Titus (66)		
Romans (56, 57)	Philemon (61)			
	Philippians (62)			
	1 Peter (64)	Hebrews (66–69)	1 John (85–90)
	2 Peter (64)	Jude (75)	2 John (85–90)
			3 John (85–90)
			Revelation (95–96)
	Acts (62)			
	Luke (58–60)	Mark (60)		John (65–70)

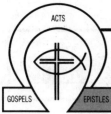

THE THEMES OF THE NEW TESTAMENT LETTERS

PAUL'S LETTERS TO CHURCHES

BOOK	KEY PHRASE	THEME
Romans	Righteousness of God	Portrays the gospel from condemnation to justification to sanctification to glorification (1–8). Presents God's program for Jews and Gentiles (9–11) and practical exhortations for believers (12–16).
1 Corinthians	Correction of Carnal Living	Corrects problems of factions, immorality, lawsuits, and abuse of the Lord's Supper (1–6). Replies to questions concerning marriage, meat offered to idols, public worship, and the Resurrection (7–16).
2 Corinthians	Paul Defends His Ministry	Defends Paul's apostolic character, call, and credentials. The majority had repented of their rebellion against Paul, but there was still an unrepentant minority.
Galatians	Freedom from the Law	Refutes the error of legalism that had ensnared the churches of Galatia. Demonstrates the superiority of grace over law, and magnifies the life of liberty over legalism and license.
Ephesians	Building the Body of Christ	Extols the believer's position in Christ (1–3), and exhorts the readers to maintain a spiritual walk that is based upon their spiritual wealth (4–6).
Philippians	To Live Is Christ	Paul speaks of the latest developments in his imprisonment and urges his readers to a life-style of unity, humility, and godliness.
Colossians	The Preeminence of Christ	Demonstrates the preeminence of Christ in creation, redemption, and the relationships of life. The Christian is complete in Christ and needs nothing else.
1 Thessalonians	Holiness in Light of Christ's Return	Paul commends the Thessalonians for their faith and reminds them of his motives and concerns on their behalf. He exhorts them to purity of life and teaches them about the coming of the Lord.
2 Thessalonians	Understanding the Day of the Lord	Paul corrects false conclusions about the day of the Lord, explains what must precede this awesome event, and exhorts his readers to remain diligent.

PAUL'S LETTERS TO PEOPLE

BOOK	KEY PHRASE	THEME
1 Timothy	Leadership Manual for Churches	Paul counsels Timothy on the problems of false teachers, public prayer, the role of women, and the requirements for elders and deacons.
2 Timothy	Endurance in Ministry	A combat manual designed to build up and encourage Timothy to boldness and steadfastness in view of the hardships of spiritual warfare.
Titus	Conduct Manual for Churches	Lists the requirements for elders and instructs Titus in his duties relative to the various groups in the churches.
Philemon	Forgiveness from Slavery	Paul appeals to Philemon to forgive Onesimus and to regard him no longer as a slave but as a brother in Christ.

LETTERS FROM OTHERS

BOOK	KEY PHRASE	THEME
Hebrews	Superiority of Christ	Demonstrates the superiority of Christ's person, priesthood, and power over all that preceded Him to encourage the readers to mature and to become stable in their faith.
James	Faith that Works	A practical catalog of the characteristics of true faith written to exhort James' Hebrew-Christian readers to examine the reality of their own faith.
1 Peter	Suffering for Christ	Comfort and counsel to those who were being maligned for their faith in Christ. They are encouraged to develop an attitude of submission in view of their suffering.
2 Peter	Guard Against False Prophets	Copes with internal opposition in the form of false teachers who were enticing believers into their errors of belief and conduct. Appeals for growth in the true knowledge of Christ.
1 John	Fellowship with God	Explores the dimensions of fellowship between redeemed people and God. Believers must walk in His light, manifest His love, and abide in His life.
2 John	Avoid Fellowship with False Teachers	John commends his readers for remaining steadfast in apostolic truth and reminds them to walk in love and avoid false teachers.
3 John	Enjoy Fellowship with the Brethren	John thanks Gaius for his support of traveling teachers of the truth, in contrast to Diotrephes, who rejected them and told others to do the same.
Jude	Contend for the Faith	This exposé of false teachers reveals their conduct and character and predicts their judgment. Jude encourages his readers to build themselves up in the truth and contend earnestly for the faith.
Revelation	Revelation of the Coming Christ	The glorified Christ gives seven messages to the church (1–3). Visions of unparalleled judgment upon rebellious mankind are followed by the Second Advent (4–19). The Apocalypse concludes with a description of the new heaven and new earth and the marvels of the new Jerusalem (20–22).

THE INTERTESTAMENTAL PERIOD

The reader of the New Testament quickly becomes aware of having entered a world quite different from that of Malachi. New religious and political parties have risen to prominence. A new world power is in control. Even Jewish popular perceptions regarding the Law and God's promised Messiah have changed.

No canonical records exist for the four-hundred-year period between the return from Babylon and the birth of Jesus, but an understanding of the historical and religious developments during this time is critical to our understanding of the New Testament world. Jesus' ministry and the development of the early church take place within this new context and are shaped, at least in part, by more recent events as well as by Israel's Exodus, kingdom, and the Exile.

One Period—Six Divisions

If the Book of Malachi was completed in about 450 B.C., then the period under consideration begins at that point and continues until the angel's announcement of the birth of John the Baptist (Luke 1:11–17). Six historical divisions are observable within this time span: The Persian Era, which actually dates to 536 B.C. but coincides with the Intertestamental Period from 450 to 336 B.C.; the Greek Era (336–323 B.C.); the Egyptian Era (323–198 B.C.); the Syrian Era (198–165 B.C.); the Maccabean Era (165–63 B.C.); and the Roman Era (63–4 B.C.). This study will look at these six divisions chronologically, giving attention to the historical situation and the religious developments within each segment.

The Persian Era (536–336 B.C.)

Historical Situation

The Persians were the dominating power in the Middle East as far back as 536 B.C. God had used the Persians to deliver Israel from the Babylonian captivity (Dan. 5:30–31).

Persia's attitude was tolerant toward the Jewish remnant in Palestine, until internal rivalry over the politically powerful office of high priest resulted in partial destruction of Jerusalem by the Persian governor. Otherwise the Jewish people were left undisturbed during this period.

Religious Developments

The Babylonian captivity was used by God to purge idolatry from His people. They turned to Jerusalem with a new reverence for the Scriptures, especially the Law of Moses. They also had a firm grasp on the theological concept of monotheism. These two influences carried over into the Intertestamental Period.

The rise of the synagogue as the local center of worship can be traced to this period. Scribes became important for the interpretation of the Scriptures in the synagogue services. By the time Jesus was born, the synagogue was well developed in organization and was spread throughout the Jewish communities of the world.

Another development that affected the

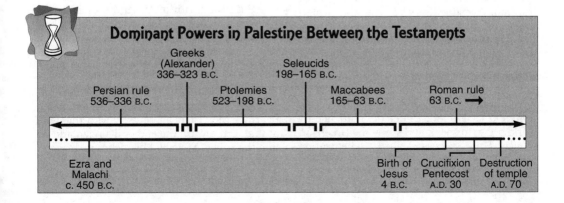

Dominant Powers in Palestine Between the Testaments

		Greeks (Alexander) 336–323 B.C.		Seleucids 198–165 B.C.		
Persian rule 536–336 B.C.		Ptolemies 523–198 B.C.		Maccabees 165–63 B.C.		Roman rule 63 B.C. →

Ezra and Malachi c. 450 B.C.

Birth of Jesus 4 B.C.

Crucifixion Pentecost A.D. 30

Destruction of temple A.D. 70

Ptolemaic Control of Palestine
(270 B.C.)

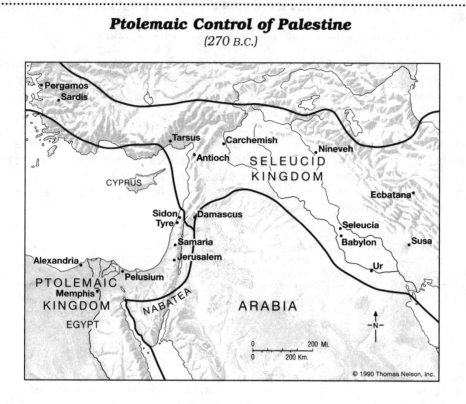

spread of the gospel during New Testament times had its origin toward the end of the Persian rule. A temple was founded in Samaria, establishing a form of worship that rivaled Judaism. That event encouraged the ultimate social and religious separation between Jew and Samaritan.

The Greek Era (336–323 B.C.)

Historical Situation

Alexander the Great was the central figure of this brief period. He conquered Persia, Babylon, Palestine, Syria, Egypt, and western India. Although he died at the age of thirty-three, having reigned over Greece only thirteen years, his influence lived long after him.

Religious Developments

Alexander's cherished desire was to found a worldwide empire united by language, custom, and civilization. Under his influence the world began to speak and study the Greek language. This process, called Hellenization, included the adoption of Greek culture and religion in all parts of the world. Hellenism became so popular that it persisted and was

encouraged by the Romans even into New Testament times.

A long and bitter struggle developed between the Jews and Hellenism's influence upon their culture and religion. Although the Greek language was sufficiently widespread by 270 B.C. to bring about a Greek translation of the Old Testament (the Septuagint), faithful Jews staunchly resisted pagan polytheism.

The Egyptian Era (323–198 B.C.)

Historical Situation

With the death of Alexander in 323 B.C., the Greek empire became divided among four generals: Ptolemy, Lysimachus, Cassander, and Selenus. These were Daniel's "four kingdoms" that took the place of the "large horn" (Dan. 8:21–22).

Ptolemy Soter, the first of the Ptolemaic dynasty, received Egypt and soon dominated nearby Israel. He dealt severely with the Jews at first, but toward the end of his reign and on into the rule of Ptolemy Philadelphus, his successor, the Jews were treated favorably. It was during this time that the Septuagint was authorized.

Seleucid Control of Palestine
(c. 190 B.C.)

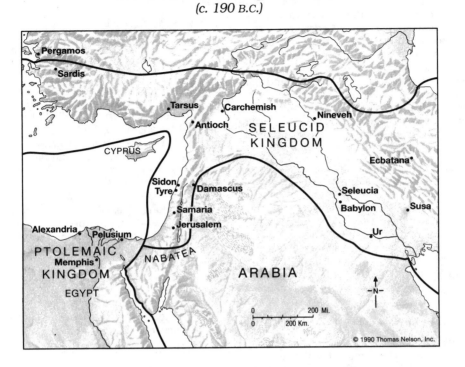

The Jews prospered until near the end of the Ptolemaic dynasty, when conflicts between Egypt and Syria escalated. Israel again was caught in the middle. When the Syrians defeated Egypt in the Battle of Panion in 198 B.C., Judea was annexed to Syria.

Religious Developments

The policy of toleration followed by the Ptolemies, by which Judaism and Hellenism coexisted peacefully, seriously undermined the Jewish faith. It brought a gradual infiltration of Greek influence and an almost unnoticed assimilation of the Greek way of life.

Hellenism's emphasis on beauty, shape, and movement encouraged Jews to neglect Jewish religious rites that were aesthetically unappealing. Thus worship was influenced to become more external than internal, a notion that had a lasting impact upon Judaism.

Two religious parties emerged: the Hellenizing party, which was pro-Syrian, and the orthodox Jews, in particular the Hasidim or "Pious Ones" (predecessors of the Pharisees). A struggle for power between these two groups resulted in a polarization of the Jews along political, cultural, and religious lines. This same conflict led to the attack of Antiochus Epiphanes in 168 B.C.

The Syrian Era (198–165 B.C.)

Historical Situation

Under the rule of Antiochus the Great and his successor Seleucus Philopater, the Jews, though treated harshly, were nonetheless allowed to maintain local rule under their high priest. All went well until the Hellenizing party decided to have their favorite, Jason, appointed to replace Onias III, the high priest favored by the orthodox Jews, and to bring this about by bribing Seleucus's successor, Antiochus Epiphanes. This set off a political conflict that finally brought Antiochus to Jerusalem in a fit of rage.

In 168 B.C. Antiochus set about destroying every distinctive characteristic of the Jewish faith. He forbade all sacrifices, outlawed the rite of circumcision, and cancelled observance of the Sabbath and feast days. The Scriptures were mutilated or destroyed. Jews were forced to eat pork and to sacrifice to idols. His final act of sacrilege, and the one that spelled his ultimate ruin, was to desecrate the Most Holy Place by building an altar and offering a sacrifice to the god Zeus. Many Jews died in the ensuing persecutions.

Perhaps a reminder of God's way of working with man is needed at this point. He creates or allows a desperate situation, then calls upon a special, faithful servant. However, man often attempts to rescue himself and may seem almost at the point of success before winding up in worse shape than before. This was about to happen in the life of God's people the Jews. God was simply setting the stage for the coming of the true Deliverer.

Religious Developments

The Jewish religion was strongly divided over the issue of Hellenism. The groundwork was laid for an orthodox party, generally led by the scribes and later called the Pharisees, and for what we may call a more pragmatic faction of the Jews that became more or less associated with the office of high priest. This latter group's pattern of thinking later fostered the rise of the Sadducees.

The Maccabean Era (165–63 B.C.)

Historical Situation

An elderly priest named Mattathias, of the house of Hasmon, lived with his five sons in the village of Modein, northwest of Jerusalem. When a Syrian official tried to enforce heathen sacrifice in Modein, Mattathias revolted, killed a renegade Jew who did offer sacrifice, slew the Syrian official, and fled to the mountains with his family. Thousands of faithful Jews joined him, and history records one of the most noble demonstrations of holy jealousy for the honor of God.

After the death of Mattathias three of his sons carried on the revolt in succession: Judas surnamed Maccabeaus (166–160 B.C.), Jonathan (160–142 B.C.), and Simon (143–134 B.C.). These men had such success that by December 25, 165 B.C., they had retaken Jerusalem, cleansed the temple, and restored worship. This event is commemorated today as the Feast of Hanukkah (Dedication).

Fighting continued in the outlying areas of Judea, with several futile attempts by Syria to defeat the Maccabeans. Finally, under the leadership of Simon, the Jews received their independence (142 B.C.). They experienced almost seventy years of independence under the Hasmonaean dynasty, the most notable leaders of which were John

Hyrcanus (134–104 B.C.) and Alexander Jannaeus (102–76 B.C.).

Religious Developments

The most significant religious development of this period resulted from a strong difference of opinion concerning the kingship and high priesthood of Judea. Over hundreds of years the position of high priest had taken on some obvious political overtones. Emphasis had not been upon the Aaronite line but upon political strength. Orthodox Jews resented and resisted this development. When John Hyrcanus became governor and high priest of Israel, he conquered Transjordan and Idumaea and destroyed the Samarian temple. His power and popularity led him to refer to himself as a king. This flew in the face of the Orthodox Jews, who by this time were called Pharisees. They recognized no king unless he was of the lineage of David, and the Hasmonaeans were not.

Those who opposed the Pharisees and supported the Hasmonaeans were called Sadducees. These names appeared for the first time during the reign of John Hyrcanus, who himself became a Sadducee.

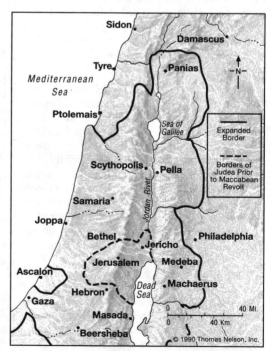

Expansion of Palestine Under the Maccabees
(165–63 B.C.)

The Roman Era (63–4 B.C.)

Historical Situation

The independence of the Jews ended in 63 B.C., when Pompey of Rome took Syria and entered Israel. Aristobulus II, claiming to be the king of Israel, locked Pompey out of Jerusalem. The Roman leader in anger took the city by force and reduced the size of Judea. Israel's attempt at freedom from oppression had paid off for a while, but now all hope seemed to be lost.

Antipater the Idumaean was appointed procurator of Judea by Julius Caesar in 47 B.C. Herod, the son of Antipater, eventually became the king of the Jews around 40 B.C.

Although Herod the Great, as he was called, planned and carried out the building of the new temple in Jerusalem, he was a devoted Hellenist and hated the Hasmonaean family. He killed every descendant of the Hasmonaeans, even his own wife Marianne, the granddaughter of John Hyrcanus. Then he proceeded to murder his own two sons by Marianne, Aristobulus and Alexander. This was the man on the throne when Jesus was born in Bethlehem.

Religious Developments

In addition to the Pharisees and Sadducees, two other parties joined the political mix of this time. The *Zealots* were even less tolerant of change than the Pharisees, and they added a strong nationalistic spirit to the Pharisee's devotion to the Law. The *Herodians* went a step further toward pragmatic politics than the Sadducees, openly supporting Herod's government and opposing any hint of rebellion. A fifth group, the *Essenes,* responded to cultural and political issues by withdrawing into a monastic lifestyle.

Despite their differences, all of these people shared a concern for the future of the Jews. And each group had its own expectations for the long-promised Messiah.

Conclusion

More than four hundred years after Malachi, the Intertestamental Period came to an end when God sent John the Baptist to announce the coming of His Son, the faithful Servant of the Lord, the Christ—God's ultimate revelation to man.

Roman Control of Palestine
(63 B.C.– beyond N.T. times)

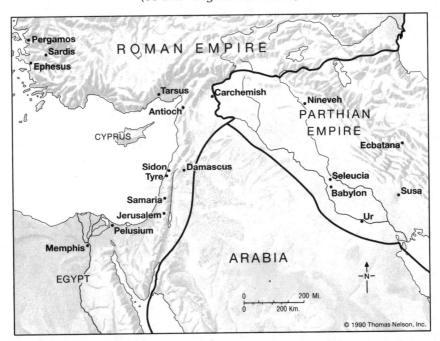

© 1990 Thomas Nelson, Inc.

IMPORTANT ARCHAEOLOGICAL DISCOVERIES AND THE BIBLE

§1. Definition and Importance of Biblical Archaeology. The last 150 years have witnessed the birth, growth, and phenomenal development of the science of biblical archaeology. This new science has performed many wonders in furnishing background material and in illustrating, illuminating, and in many cases authenticating the message and meaning of the Old and New Testament Scriptures.

Biblical archaeology may be defined as a study based on the excavation, decipherment, and critical evaluation of the records of the past as they affect the Bible. While the general field of archaeology is fascinating, much more so is the study of biblical archaeology, since it deals with the Holy Scriptures. This is the reason for the growing enthusiasm for biblical archaeology. The attraction lies in the supreme importance of the message and meaning of the Bible. The Scriptures, by virtue of their character as the inspired revelation of God to people, have naturally held a paramount place in the interest and affection of humankind. Biblical archaeology, illustrating the Bible in its historical background and contemporary life, attracts a measure of the interest that lies in the Bible itself. Accordingly, this science has a worthy ministry of expanding biblical horizons on the human plane. No field of research has offered greater challenge and promise than that of biblical archaeology.

Until the beginning of the 19th century very little was known of biblical times and biblical backgrounds, except what appeared on the pages of the Old Testament or what happened to be preserved in the writings of classical antiquity. This was considerable for the New Testament era but very little indeed for the Old Testament period. The reason for this is that Greek and Latin historians catalogued very little information before the fifth century B.C. As a result, the Old Testament period was very little known extrabiblically, and what was known was confined to what the Bible gave. This from the viewpoint of contemporary secular history was sparse. The result was that before the beginning of the science of modern archaeology there was practically nothing available to authenticate Old Testament history and literature. One can therefore imagine the fervor aroused among serious Bible students by illuminating discoveries in Bible lands, especially from about 1800 to the present. In fact, modern archaeology may be said to have had its beginning in 1798, when the rich antiquities of the Nile Valley were opened up to scientific study by Napoleon's Egyptian expedition.

§2. Foundational Discoveries of the 19th Century. Although the most notable discoveries affecting the Bible and particularly the Old Testament were not made until the 20th century, foundational discoveries were made in the 19th century and prepared the way for the modern era.

§2.1. The Rosetta Stone—Key to Egypt's Splendid Past. This very important monument was discovered in 1798 at Rosetta (Rashid), near the westernmost mouth of the Nile River, by an officer in Napoleon's expedition to Egypt. It was a slab of black basalt trilingually inscribed, which may be said to be the key that unlocked the door to knowledge of the language and literature of ancient Egypt and turned out to be the inscription that opened the modern era of scientific biblical archaeology.

The three languages in which this monument was found to be inscribed were the Greek of 200 B.C. and two forms of Egyptian writing—the older, more complicated hieroglyphic script and the later simplified and more popular demotic writing, which was the common language of the people. The Greek could at once be read and provided the clue to the decipherment of the other two ancient Egyptian scripts. Sylvester de Sacy of France and J. D. Akerblad of Sweden succeeded in unraveling the demotic Egyptian by identifying the Greek personal names it contained, namely Ptolemy, Arsinoe, and Berenike. Thomas Young of England then proceeded to identify the name of Ptolemy in the hieroglyphic portion, where groups of characters enclosed in oval frames, called cartouches, had already been surmised to be royal names. From this point on, the young Frenchman Jean François Champollion, 1790–1832, was able to decipher the hieroglyphics of the

Revised and updated by Dr. Charles R. Page, II, Academic Dean, Jerusalem Center for Biblical Studies. Many of the place names mentioned in this article can be located on one of the maps on pages 522 and 523.

monument, show the true nature of this script, make a dictionary, formulate a grammar, and translate numerous Egyptian texts, from the year 1818 to 1832.

Champollion's achievement formally opened up the science of Egyptology. Scholars from henceforth were able to read Egyptian monumental inscriptions and reliefs. From that time forth the literary treasures of the Nile Valley have been opened to scholarly study. Today many universities maintain chairs in the language and culture of ancient Egypt. These studies have opened up vistas of history hitherto unknown so that, from the beginning of Egypt about 2800 B.C. to 63 B.C. when Rome took over, the entire history of the land of the Nile can fairly well be traced.

All of this has tremendous bearing on the background of the Bible. Egypt figures largely in the patriarchal narratives and the Book of Exodus and all through the Pentateuch. As a result, the background of the story of Joseph and of the sojourn of the children of Israel in Egypt, their deliverance under Moses, and much of their sojourn in the desert and later history in Canaan can now be set in the general framework of Egyptian history. It can be said that the whole context of the Old Testament history, in its broad span from Abraham to Christ, is made immeasurably clearer because of the vast strides in our knowledge of Egypt. That great nation of antiquity interacted with the mighty Assyro-Babylonian empires on the Tigris-Euphrates and with the Hittite power on the Halys across the tiny bridge that was ancient Palestine.

§2.2. The Behistun Inscription— Gateway to Assyro-Babylonian Antiquity.
This famous monument was the key to the languages of Assyria and Babylonia. It consists of a large relief panel containing numerous columns of inscription, which was boldly carved on the face of a mountain about five hundred feet above the surrounding plain of Karmanshah on the old caravan route from Babylon to Ecbatana. Unlike the Rosetta Stone written in ancient Egyptian hieroglyphics, and later in popular demotic and in the Greek of the third century B.C., the Behistun Inscription was written in the wedge-shaped characters of ancient Assyria Babylonia. It contained about twelve hundred lines of inscription. The three languages in which it was inscribed were all written in cuneiform characters, consisting of Old Persian, Elamite, and Akkadian. The third language, the Akkadian, was the wedge-shaped language of ancient Assyria and Babylonia, in which

thousands upon thousands of clay tablets discovered in the Tigris-Euphrates region are inscribed.

Early excavations revealed a mass of material on which this curious wedge-shaped Babylonian-Akkadian writing appeared. But it was an unsolved riddle. Practically no progress was made until a young English officer in the Persian army, Henry C. Rawlinson, in 1835 and the following years made the dangerous climb to the Behistun Inscription and made copies and plaster of paris impressions of it. Rawlinson knew modern Persian and set to work to decipher the old Persian, the cuneiform part of the inscription. After a decade of labor, he finally succeeded in translating the five columns, nearly four hundred lines of the old Persian portion of the Behistun Inscription, and sent it to Europe in 1845. The text translation and commentary on it were published in 1847 in the Journal of the Royal Asiatic Society.

In conjunction with the literary part of the monument was a life-sized figure with numerous individuals bowing before it. This person turned out to be Darius the Great (522–486 B.C.), the Achemenid prince who saved the Persian Empire from a rebellion. The scene depicts the king, as Rawlinson's translation of the Persian portion of the inscription shows, receiving the submission of the rebels. The emperor is portrayed at the top of the relief accompanied by two attendants. His foot is placed upon the prostrate form of a leading rebel. The king's left hand holds a bow, while his right hand is lifted toward the winged disc symbolizing Ahura-Mazda, the spirit of good, whom Darius, an ardent follower of Zoroaster, worshiped. Behind the rebel stands a procession of rebel leaders, roped together by their necks. Beside and beneath the sculptured panel the numerous columns of the inscription appear, relating in three languages how Darius defended the throne and crushed the revolt.

Working on the supposition that the other inscriptions told the same story, scholars were soon enabled to read the second language, which was the Elamite or Susian. Then last, but most important, they could decipher the Akkadian or Assyro-Babylonian. This was a great discovery, for this wedge-shaped character of writing is recorded on numerous literary remains from the Tigris-Euphrates Valley. It opened up a vast new field of biblical background, so that today, as in the case of the Rosetta Stone opening up the science of Egyptology, the Behistun Inscription has given birth to the science of Assyriology. Moreover, both Egyptology and Assyriology offer great help in understanding biblical backgrounds and biblical history. No Bible dictionary, Bible handbook, or commentary that is up-to-date can ignore the great findings of these sciences.

The task of deciphering cuneiform is increasing with every decade. Numerous cuneiform libraries have been discovered from antiquity. Two unearthed at Nineveh contained thousands of clay tablets. The library of Ashurbanipal (669–625 B.C.) contained some twenty-two thousand tablets. Among the tablets unearthed in this collection and sent to the British Museum were Assyrian copies of the Babylonian creation and flood stories. The identification and decipherment of these particular tablets by George Smith in 1872 produced great excitement in the archeological world.

Not only in Babylonia but in many other places large bodies of cuneiform literature have been uncovered. For example, the famous *Amarna Letters* from Egypt were discovered in 1886 at Tell el-Amarna about two hundred miles south of modern Cairo. These Amarna Tablets proved to be diplomatic correspondence of petty princes of Palestine in the 14th century B.C. with the Egyptian court at Amarna. The *Amarna Letters* give an inside glance into conditions in Palestine just before the conquest by Joshua and the Israelites. Many scholars actually think that they describe aspects of that invasion. One of the documents from the governor of Jerusalem (Urusalim) tells Amenophis IV that the "Habiru" (perhaps the Hebrews) were overrunning many Palestine cities and could not be held back.

Other important bodies of cuneiform literature bearing upon the Bible have been retrieved from Boghaz-Keui and Kanish in Asia Minor. Others come from Susa and Elam, others from the city of Mari on the middle Euphrates, others from Ras Shamra (ancient Ugarit), mentioned in the *Amarna Letters* and located in North Syria. Others stem from various sites within and without Babylonia.

§2.3. The Moabite Stone—A Sensational Literary Find.

This important inscription, found in 1868, offers another example of the discoveries of the 19th century that prepared the way for the great finds of the 20th century. The inscription dates from about 850 B.C. It was erected by Mesha, king of Moab, and is often styled the *Mesha Stone*. It tells of the wars of Mesha of Moab with Omri, king of Israel, and Omri's successors. It also tells of Mesha's wars with the Edomites. The material recorded on the *Moabite Stone* parallels biblical history recorded in 2 Kings, chapters 1 and 3. Numerous places mentioned in the Old Testament occur on the stele (inscribed monument). Among them are Arnon (Num. 21:13; Deut. 2:24), Ataroth (Num. 32:34), Baal Meon or Beth Baal Meon (Josh. 13:17), Beth Bamoth or Bamoth Baal (Josh. 13:17), Beth Diblathaim (Jer. 48:22), Bezer (Josh. 20:8), Dibon (Num. 32:34), Jahaza (Josh. 13:18), Medeba (Josh. 13:9), and Nebo (Num. 32:38).

This inscribed monument or stele measures 3 feet 8½ inches in height, 2 feet 3½ inches in width, and 1 foot 1¾ inches in thickness. Its thirty-four lines constitute the longest single literary inscription yet recovered extrabiblically dealing with Palestine in the period 900–600 B.C. It records that Moab had been conquered by Omri and his son Ahab but was set free from the Israelite yoke by Mesha's god Chemosh. This deity is represented as commanding King Mesha to go to war against Israel, who, according to 2 Kings 3:27, offered up his eldest son as a burnt offering upon the wall to propitiate the god Chemosh and to secure his favor.

The *Moabite Stone* is written in the language of Moab, which was very similar to the Hebrew of the time of Omri and Ahab. This inscription, therefore, has great value in tracing the development of early Hebrew through the centuries. When it was discovered, the *Mesha Stone* was not only the longest and oldest Phoenician-Hebrew inscription then in existence, it was the only one. Now the *Gezer Calendar* is known and dates from c. 925 B.C. It is a school boy's exercise written in perfect classical Hebrew. This small limestone tablet, found at ancient Gezer, gives an incidental sidelight on Palestinian agriculture as well as on ancient Hebrew writing. Such discoveries as the *Gezer Calendar* and the *Mesha Stone* not only give glimpses into the background of the Bible but form important links in the culture and history of the people outside the pale of Israel.

§3. Great Discoveries of the 20th Century.

Although such discoveries as the Rosetta Stone, the *Behistun Inscription*, and the Moabite Stone are important for their time and laid the foundations of scientific archaeology in the 19th century, it remained for the 20th century to produce the most thrilling and outstanding archaeological finds. During this period biblical archaeology came to be a refined and precise science, adding to the frontiers of biblical knowledge on the human plane and making tremendous contributions to the background, historical and cultural, of the written Word of God.

§3.1. The Code of Hammurabi—Light on Mosaic Laws.

Hammurabi (actually named Hammurapi), the sixth king of the first dynasty of Babylon who ruled in Babylon from 1728 to 1676 B.C., was not always the great world power as we think of him today. Instead, according to the *Mari Documents* (*see* Mari Texts under a separate heading in this article), he was somewhat of a minor power when compared to other kings of his day in the early years of his reign. Yet, he is memorialized for eternity with the discovery of the Code of Hammurabi, discovered in 1901. The code, a copy of which was discovered by Jacques de Morgan at Susa in Elam, where it had been carried off by the Elamites from Babylon, is inscribed on a stele of black diorite over seven feet tall and approximately six feet wide. On the stele the code contains some 250 laws or stipulations. At the top of the stele is a bas-relief showing the king receiving the law code from the god Shamash, the god of justice and law.

The code, which is not actually a code per se, but more of a collection of laws, written near the end of Hammurabi's reign, is important in furnishing background material for comparison with other ancient bodies of law. It is natural that it should offer comparative data for the study of the law of the Torah or Pentateuch. This type of code contains a form of laws known as casuistic law or case law, based on specific cases of human conduct. The formula for this type of law is: "If someone does this to another human being (and the infraction is defined), then the penalty is (whatever is prescribed in the code)." James West, in his book *Introduction to the Old Testament* (Macmillan, 1981, page 180), states, "The social, civil, and criminal laws in the Pentateuch are cast in this form. The subjects covered include the various facets of a complex society, but, as compared with Hebrew laws, the extra-biblical codes exhibit a greater concern with property rights, a less rigorous attention to persons, and scarcely any regulation at all of religion and cult."

It is believed by some scholars that the Code of Hammurabi was not actually written to be used in the practice of law, but is more of an expression of philosophical, intellectual, or literary ideas and ideals to demonstrate the ethical and legal thinking of the day. Furthermore, the code was certainly not written by Hammurabi himself, but most likely by scribes in his employment who penned his name to the document.

For Jewish and Christian tradition the code has value because it enables us to better understand some of the legal writings found in the Pentateuch, such as the Covenant Code (from Exodus 21—23). But the law found in the Torah (Pentateuch) is also very different in places. For example, much of the law found in the Torah is known as apodictic law, which take the form of imperatives such as "You shall . . . , or You shall not . . . ." A good example of apodictic law is found in the Ten Commandments.

§3.2. *The Elephantine Papyri—Light on the Ezra-Nehemiah Era.*

Discovered in 1903 on the island of Elephantine at the First Cataract of the Nile in Egypt, these important documents give an interesting glimpse of one of the outlying regions of the Persian Empire in the latter part of the fifth century B.C. *The Elephantine Papyri* come from a Jewish military colony settled at that place. Inscribed in Aramaic, the language of diplomacy and trade throughout western Asia in the Persian period and that was gradually replacing Hebrew as the everyday tongue of the Jewish people, the contents are varied, ranging from the copy of the *Behistun Inscription* of Darius to such a document as a Jewish marriage contract. The letters tell us about the sacking of a Jewish temple at Elephantine in an anti-Jewish persecution about 411 B.C. The Jews at this far-off colony worshiped the Lord whom they referred to by the name of Yahu.

Other letters from Elephantine that have in recent years become known and have been published by the Brooklyn Museum demonstrate that the temple was rebuilt after its destruction. They contain mention of Yahu as "the god who dwells in Yeb, the fortress." Compare Psalm 31:3. These new papyri demonstrate that Egypt was still under the authority of Persia in the first years of Artaxerxes II (404–359 B.C.).

The Elephantine Papyri therefore illuminate the general background of the period of Ezra-Nehemiah and the earlier Persian period. They shed important light on the life of the Jewish dispersion in a remote frontier place such as Elephantine in Egypt. They also are invaluable in giving the scholar a knowledge of the Aramaic language of that period, and many of the customs and names that appear in the Bible are illustrated by these important literary finds.

§3.3. The Hittite Monuments from Boghaz-Keui—Mementos of an Imperial People.

In 1906 Professor Hugo Winkler of Berlin began excavations at Boghaz-Keui, a site that lies ninety miles east of Ankara in the great bend of the Halys River in Asia Minor. It was discovered that this was an ancient Hittite capital. Numerous clay tablets were dug up written in texts containing six different languages. A large number of these were inscribed in the cuneiform characters of the Hittite language. Eventually deciphered through the labors of three men and particularly of the Czech scholar Friedrich Hrozny, this language proved to be the key to a great deal of background of interest to the biblical student.

Before the Boghaz-Keui tablets revealed the Hittites to be an ancient people, the biblical references to them used to be regarded in critical circles as historically worthless. In the five books of Moses, references to the Hittites as inhabiting the land of Canaan and as among those whom the Israelites drove out occur in several places (Ex. 33:2; Deut. 7:1; 20:17; Josh. 3:10; 24:11). In the various lists the order varies, and there is not an inkling that one reference might be the name of a powerful imperial people and the other a small local tribe. Less than a century ago the "Hittites" meant little more to the reader of the Bible than the "Hivite" or the "Perizzite" still does.

It was commonly known from the biblical record that when Abraham settled in Hebron he had Hittites as neighbors. It was everyday knowledge that one of David's eminent soldiers was Uriah, a Hittite. But who would have expected that "Hittites" were more prominent than "Gadites" or "Beerothites"?

Now it is known that two great periods of Hittite power are to be noted. The first goes back to about 1800 B.C., and the second is dated from around 1400 to 1200 B.C. In this latter period of Hittite supremacy the powerful rulers reigned at Boghaz-Keui. One of these was named Suppiluliuma. This great conqueror extended his empire to the confines of Syria Palestine. The great Rameses II of Egypt, in the famous battle of Kadesh, collided with Hittite power. A Hittite treaty of peace with the pharaoh in the twenty-first year of the latter's reign was confirmed by a royal marriage.

About 1200 B.C. the great Hittite Empire collapsed, and the Hittite city of Boghaz-Keui fell. However, important centers of Hittite power remained at Carchemish, Sengirli, Hamath, and other places in north Syria. As a result of the excavation and decipherment of various Hittite monuments, the whole context of the ancient biblical world has been illuminated.

Because of this increased background knowledge, such allusions as those to the "kings of the Hittites" (1 Kin. 10:29; 2 Chr. 1:17) are much better understood. Also Ezekiel's reference to unfaithful Jerusalem as having an Amorite for a father and a Hittite for a mother (Ezek. 16:45) are now comprehensible. The manner in which archaeology has brought to light the ancient Hittites furnishes a good example of the way this important science is expanding biblical horizons.

§3.4. The Religious Texts from Ras Shamra (Ugarit)—Canaanite Cults Exposed.

One of the most important discoveries of the 20th century was the recovery of hundreds of clay tablets that had been housed in a library situated between two great temples, one dedicated to Baal and another dedicated to Dagon, in the city of *Ugarit*—modern *Ras Shamra* in north Syria. These clay tablets date from the 15th to early 14th centuries B.C. They are inscribed in the earliest-known alphabet written in wedge-shaped signs. Professor H. Bower of the University of Halle recognized this new writing as Semitic. Numbers of scholars such as E. Dhorme and Charles Virolleaud began working on the decipherment of this new Semitic language.

First intimations of the archaeological importance of the ancient city of Ugarit, which was unknown until 1928, came in the spring of that year when a Syrian peasant plowing in his field a little north of present-day Minet el-Beida suddenly came across some antiquities. On April 2, 1929, work began at Minet el-Beida under the direction of Claude F. Schaffer. After a month's work he changed to the nearby tell of Ras Shamra. Only a few days' work demonstrated the importance of the new location. On May 20 the first tablets were uncovered. Schaffer continued excavations from 1929 to 1937. Between 1929 and 1933, the bulk of significant religious texts were recovered in the royal library in the area. Many of these were inscribed in an early Canaanite dialect of the late Bronze and early Iron periods.

§3.4.a. The City of Ugarit.

This flourishing second-millennium city, which had been known by scholars from Egyptian inscriptions from the *Tell el-Amarna Letters* and Hittite documents, was located on the north Syrian coast opposite the island of

Cyprus, about eight miles north of Latakia and fifty miles southwest of Antioch. It was situated on a bay and had a port that could be used by seagoing trade ships. It was a harbor town known in Greek times as Leukos Limen, the white harbor. It is now called Ras Shamra, "hill of fennel," because fennel grows there.

The hill that comprises the ruin of the ancient city has the form of a trapezium with the long side about 670 yards north and south and the longer diagonal about 1,100 yards. The hill is about twenty-two yards high. The site was located on the important trade route along the coast from Egypt to Asia Minor, which was connected by a road with Aleppo, Mari on the Euphrates, and Babylon. The sea route from Ugarit to Alashiya—that is, Cyprus—was a short one.

Very early, Ugarit struck up a brisk trade with the Aegean Islands. It became an important harbor. One of the main exported articles was copper, which was used in the production of bronze. Copper was imported from Asia Minor and Cyprus. Bronze was produced in Ugarit. Being a Phoenician town, Ugarit, like its sister cities, delivered timber to Egypt. Not only cedars from the interior were exported but other kinds of wood as well. There were also blue dye factories. Great heaps of murex shells indicate this. These shells, abundantly found along the east Mediterranean coast, produced a famous dye of antiquity.

§3.4.b. Literary Importance of the Texts.

After preliminary work by many scholars, Cyrus Gordon worked out a *Ugaritic Grammar* and later put out an edition of the texts called *Ugaritic Literature*. The decipherment of the texts showed the important parallels between Ugaritic and Hebrew literary style and vocabulary. By 1936 H. L. Ginsberg had made some far-reaching observations with regard to common structural elements. Ginsberg's study showed that Canaanite poetry, like Hebrew, was basically accentual, that is, it consisted of numbers of feet, each of which was accented. Since the Ugaritic language is very closely connected with biblical Hebrew, much light has been shed upon Hebrew lexicography. Any recent lexicon of Hebrew must take into consideration the vocabulary used at Ugarit. Future Hebrew dictionaries will include many words hitherto misunderstood or only partially known.

For example, the word *beth-heber* (Prov. 21:9; 25:24) hitherto rendered "house" has been shown from Ugaritic and Assyrian to mean specifically "a storehouse." These verses could then be rendered "It is better to dwell in a corner of the housetop, than with a contentious woman and in a storehouse." It is of interest to note that the Egyptian proverbs of Amenemope, which have many parallels to the biblical Book of Proverbs, employs a word for "storehouse" in exactly the same sense.

§3.4.c. Religious Significance of the Ugaritic Inscriptions.

By far the most important contribution of the religious texts from Ras Shamra (Ugarit) is in giving the Bible student background material for the study of Old Testament religions. The epics set forth very clearly the Canaanite pantheon. We now know that this pantheon of the Canaanites was headed up by the god El, the supreme Canaanite deity. This is also a name by which God is known in the Old Testament (cf. Gen. 33:20). This name, El, often occurs in Old Testament poetry (Ps. 18:31, 32; Job 8:3). It occurs frequently also in prose in compound names, for example, *El Elyon*, the God Most High (Gen. 14:18); *El Shaddai*, Almighty God (Gen. 17:1); *El Hai*, the living God (Josh. 3:10). El is a common Semitic word for God.

§3.4.d. Later Excavations at Ugarit.

During World War II excavations at Ras Shamra were discontinued. They were resumed in 1948 and have been going on regularly. Work under the direction of C. F. Schaffer has been centered upon uncovering the great palace. The most important discoveries in connection with this structure were the royal archives. These archives, discovered in the palace, were of a historical nature in contrast to the mythological ritual texts of the early years, 1929–1937. The archives in the west wing of the building contained administrative documents to a large degree relating to the royal estates. Those in the east wing had documents relating to the capital city. Those in the central archive were mainly legal finds. Almost all documents were inscribed in the common language of these centuries, namely Akkadian. A few were written in Hurrian and Ugaritic. The names of twelve Ugaritic kings were found in the documents that date from the 18th to the 13th centuries B.C. The seals of the royal acts are remarkable as they all are identical in design at the top, without regard to the name of the reigning king. The motif is well known from Babylonian glyptic art and shows homage being paid to the deified king.

Numbers of fine objects have been recovered from the palace, especially pieces from the king's bedroom. Especially noteworthy was the large ivory foot panel of the royal bedstead, perhaps the largest single piece of ivory carving yet recovered in the Near East. Another remarkable piece found in the campaign of 1952–1953 is the ancient Ugaritic alphabet of thirty letters. This piece is now housed in the National Museum at Damascus.

§3.5. The Nuzi Tablets and the Biblical Horites.

From this city east of ancient Asshur and a short distance west of Arrapkha, which flourished in the middle centuries of the second millennium B.C., have come several thousand cuneiform texts. These texts have proved of immense value, illustrating the rise of the Hurrians and patriarchal customs. The present site of Nuzi is Yoghlan-Tepe. It is a mound 150 miles north of Baghdad near the foothills of southern Khurdistan. Nuzi was excavated in 1925–1931 by the American School of Oriental Research in Baghdad and Harvard University. The name "Nuzi" was used during its occupation by the Hurrians.

Before the time of the Hurrian settlement the site of Nuzi was occupied by a different ethnic group, called the Subarians. In this older period, the city bore the name of Gasur, and its earliest occupation goes back to prehistoric times. But the vital interest in the town stems from its occupation by the Hurrians and the cuneiform texts that have been excavated from it and from nearby Arrapkha, modern Kirkuk, some nine miles to the east.

§3.5.a. The Nuzi Tablets and the Hurrians.

Modern archaeology has not only resurrected the ancient Hittites, who were for centuries practically unknown except for sporadic references on the pages of the Bible, but also the enigmatic Horites. In the books of the Pentateuch there are numbers of references to a perplexing people called Horites. These people were defeated by Chedorlaomer and the invading Mesopotamian army (Gen. 14:6). They were governed by chiefs (Gen. 36:20–30). They are said to have been destroyed by Esau's descendants (Deut. 2:12, 22).

This unknown people used to be thought of as a very local, restricted group of cave dwellers. The name "Horite" was thought to be derived from the Hebrew *hor;* "hole" or "cave." Other than this etymological description the Horites remained completely obscure, not appearing outside the Pentateuch or in extrabiblical literature. Within the last thirty-five years, however, archaeology has performed a miracle in resurrecting the ancient Hurrians, the biblical Horites. They are known not to be a local, restricted group but to be a prominent people who took a preeminent place on the stage of ancient history. It is now known that they not only existed but played a far-reaching role in ancient Near Eastern cultural history. As a result of the discovery of the Hurrians, the popular etymology that connects them with "cave dwellers" has had to be abandoned.

The Hurrians or Horites were non-Semitic peoples who, before the beginning of the second millennium B.C., migrated into northeastern Mesopotamia. Their homeland was in the region south of the Caucasus. They appear first upon the horizon of history about 2400 B.C. in the Zagros Mountains east of the Tigris River. In the period around 2000 to 1400 B.C., the Hurrians were very common and widespread in Upper Mesopotamia.

§3.5.b. The Nuzi Tablets and the Patriarchs.

The main interest of the Nuzi tablets lies in the illumination of patriarchal times and customs. In the patriarchal narratives, many local practices have been quite obscure to the modern reader. Numerous clay tablets from Nuzi and nearby Arrapkha have in many cases illuminated these customs, so that now we see them as they existed in the general historical background of the time. Although the Nuzi tablets are to be dated in the 15th and 14th centuries B.C., sometime after the patriarchal period (c. 2000–1800 B.C.), nevertheless, they illustrate the times of the patriarchs. The reason is that when the patriarchs came out of Ur, they sojourned in Haran and mingled in west Hurrian society. But the same customs prevailed by extension among the west Hurrians as among the east Hurrians at Nuzi and Arrapkha. Hence, the results obtained at Nuzi are valid by extension for the west Hurrians, as well as for a period considerably later than the patriarchs.

In Genesis 15:2 Abraham laments his childless condition and the fact that his servant Eliezer was to be his heir. In the light of this situation, God assures the patriarch that he is to have a son of his own to inherit his property. The Nuzi tablets explain this difficult matter. They tell how a trusted servant, an apparent outsider, could be heir. At ancient Nuzi, it was customary in Hurrian society for a couple who did not have a child to adopt a son to take care of his foster parents as long as they lived, take over when they died, and then in return for his filial duty to become their heir. But it is important to note that if a natural son was born, this agreement was nullified, at least in part, and the natural son became heir. Eliezer was plainly Abraham's adopted son. But the miraculous birth of

Isaac, as the promised posterity, altered Eliezer's status as heir.

At Nuzi a marriage contract occasionally included the statement that a given slave girl is presented outright to a new bride, exactly as in the marriage of Leah (Gen. 29:24) and Rachel (29:29). Other marriage provisions specify that a wife of the upper classes who was childless was to furnish her husband with a slave girl as a concubine. In such a case, however, the wife was entitled to treat the concubine's offspring as her own. This last provision illuminates the difficult statement in Genesis 16:2 with its punning: "I shall obtain children by her," which means "I may be built up through her." It is interesting to note that the related law of Hammurabi, paragraph 144, offers no complete parallel. There the wife is a priestess and is not entitled to claim the children of the concubine for herself.

It is thus seen that in Nuzian law and society in which the patriarchs moved for a time, marriage was regarded primarily for bearing children and not mainly for companionship. In one way or another, it was considered necessary for the family to procreate. After Isaac's birth, Abraham's reluctance to comply with Sarah's demand that Hagar's child be driven out is illustrated by local practice at Nuzi. In the event the slave wife should have a son, that son must not be expelled. In Abraham's case, only a divine dispensation overruled human law and made the patriarch willing to comply.

Cases involving rights of the firstborn occurring in Genesis are also illustrated. In the Bible Esau sells his birthright to Jacob. In the Nuzi tablets one brother sells a grove that he has inherited for three sheep. Evidently this is quite comparable in value to the savory food for which Esau sold his right.

In Hurrian society birthright was not so much the matter of being the firstborn as of paternal decree. Such decrees were binding above all others when handed down in the form of a deathbed declaration introduced by the following formula: "Behold now, I am old." This situation helps to illuminate Genesis 27, the chapter that tells of Jacob stealing the family blessing.

The obscure *teraphim* are also explained in Nuzian law. We now know that the teraphim were small household deities. Possession of them implied headship of family. In the case of a married daughter, they assured her husband the right to her father's property. Laban had sons of his own when Jacob left for Canaan. They alone had the right to their father's gods. The theft of these important household idols by Rachel was a notorious offense (Gen. 31:19, 30, 35). She aimed at nothing less than to preserve for her husband the chief title to Laban's estate.

The texts from Arrapkha and Nuzi have at last supplied details for explaining these difficult customs. In special circumstances the property could pass to a daughter's husband, but only if the father had handed over his household gods to his son-in-law as a formal token that the arrangement had proper sanction.

Another custom illuminated is that found in Genesis 12:10–20; 20:2–6; 26:1–11, where the wife of a patriarch is introduced as his sister with no apparent worthy reason. The texts from Nuzi, however, show that among the Hurrians marriage bonds were most solemn, and the wife had legally, although not necessarily through ties of blood, the simultaneous status of sister, so that the terms "sister" and "wife" could be interchangeable in an official use under certain circumstances. Thus, in resorting to the wife-sister relationship, both Abraham and Isaac were availing themselves of the strongest safeguards the law, as it existed then, could afford them.

§3.5.c. Critical Value. Discoveries such as those at Nuzi and Arrapkha are forcing higher critics to abandon many radical and untenable theories. For example, not long ago it was customary for critics to view the patriarchal stories as retrojections from a much later period and not as authentic stories from the Mosaic age, namely, the 15th century B.C. But now the question rises, How could such authentic local color be retrojected from a later age? The Nuzi tablets have done a great service to students of early Bible history in not only attesting the influence of social customs in the patriarchal age and in the same portion of Mesopotamia from which the patriarchs come but also have demonstrated these narratives are authentic to their time. Such discoveries add greatly to our historical background and enable us in our modern day to reveal them in their genuine local color and historical setting.

§3.6. The Mari Letters—Light on the World of the Patriarchs. One of the most historically and archaeologically rewarding sites that has been discovered in Mesopotamia and Bible lands is the city of *Mari*, modern Tell el-Hariri on the Middle Euphrates, about seven miles northwest of Abu-Kemal, a small town on the Syrian side of the Syro-Iraq frontier.

The ancient city owed its importance to being a focal point on caravan routes crossing the Syrian desert and linking the city with Syria and the Mediterranean coast and with the civilizations of Assyria and Babylonia. This site was further identified by William Foxwell Albright in 1932.

Mari began to be excavated in 1933 by Andre Parrot under the auspices of the Musée du Louvre. The results were the digging up of an ancient imperial city of great importance and splendor. World War II interrupted excavations in 1939, after six highly successful campaigns had taken place. In 1951 this work was resumed. After four further campaigns it was broken off in 1956, as a result of the trouble over the Suez Canal.

Among the most important discoveries at Mari was the great *temple of Ishtar,* for the Babylonian goddess of propagation, and a temple-tower or ziggurat. The temple itself had courts of the Sumerian type, columns, and a cella. The ziggurat or temple-tower was similar to that at Ur and other Mesopotamian sites. Statuettes were uncovered to illustrate the popularity of the Ishtar fertility cult. One of the palace murals depicts the fact that the ruling monarch at Mari was believed to have received his staff and ring, the emblems of his authority, from Ishtar.

Another important discovery at Mari was the *royal palace.* A sprawling structure contemporary with the first dynasty of Babylon, it was built in the center of the mound and contained almost three hundred rooms. The throne room furnished some rare specimens of well preserved wall paintings. This huge building with its beautifully colored mural paintings, its royal apartments, administrative offices, and scribal school is considered one of the best preserved palaces of the Middle East. The structure was built by later Amorites, who worshiped the deities Adad and Dagon. In the postwar campaign the excavation centered mainly around the older strata going back to buildings of the pre-Sargonic period from the time of the dynasty of Akkad.

§3.6.a. The Royal Archives. The most interesting finds, however, were the so-called *Mari Letters,* some twenty thousand clay tablets dug up, which have revolutionized knowledge of the ancient biblical world. These documents were written in the dialect of Old Babylonian. They date from the era of Hammurabi, about 1700 B.C., the same monarch whose code was discovered in 1901 at Susa. These records constitute memoranda of the king and governors of the city-state of Mari

and belong to the time of the kings Yasmah-Adad, under whose reign the construction of the palace was begun, and Zimri-Lim, under whom it was completed. Some of the correspondence is that of King Yasmah-Adad with his father, the powerful empire builder King Shamshi-Adad I of Assyria, as well as with the representatives of the provinces of his realm. King Zimri-Lim's correspondence also figures in exchanges of diplomatic correspondence with King Hammurabi of Babylon, as well as with the king of Aleppo and other vassals. Two letters dispatched from Aleppo to Zimri-Lim deal with prophetic utterances delivered in the name of the god Adad of Aleppo. The subject and tenor of these remind one of biblical prophecies.

§3.6.b. Biblical Value of the Mari Texts. These records are of great value to biblical students because they stem from the region that was the home of the Hebrew patriarchs for a number of years before going on to Canaan. At the time of the third dynasty of Ur, Mari was ruled by the governors of the kings of Ur. Eventually, however, a prince of Mari, Ishbi-Irra, who had brought the city-state of Isin under his dominion about 2021 B.C., was instrumental in bringing about the downfall of the city of Ur.

Nahor, which figures prominently in the patriarchal narratives (Gen. 24:10), is mentioned quite often in the *Mari Letters.* One letter from Nahor is sent from a woman of that town to the king and runs as follows:

"To my lord say, Thus Inib-Sharrim, thy maid servant. How long must I remain in Nahor? Peace is established and the road is unobstructed. Let my lord write and let me be brought that I may see the face of my lord from whom I am separated. Further, let my lord send me an answer to my tablet."

The term "Habiru," very important since Abraham is the first individual in the Bible to be named a "Hebrew" (Gen. 14:13), is found frequently in the *Mari Letters,* as is also the case in the Nuzi tablets. In both instances the term apparently means "a wanderer," "one who crosses over," or "one who passes from one place to another." This explanation fits Abraham and the early patriarchs very well since they were nomadic travelers. When Abraham left Ur in southern Mesopotamia to migrate to Canaan, he no doubt passed through the magnificent city of Mari. There can be little doubt that he and Terah with their families put up in one of the caravansaries there. Perhaps they spent days or weeks in the famous city and went sightseeing in the

THE SETTLEMENT IN CANAAN

© 1995 by Thomas Nelson

THE ANCIENT NEAR EAST

© 1995 by Thomas Nelson

palace, traces of whose grandeur are still visible to the eye of the modern archaeologist.

§3.6.c. Historical Value of the Mari Letters. These documents establish that Shamshi Adad I of Assyria, who ruled about 1748–1716 B.C., and Hammurabi the Great of Babylon were contemporaries. With these facts and other details furnished by the Mari documents, the date of Hammurabi can be fixed at about 1728–1676 B.C. This and other evidence have forced scholars to give up identifying Hammurabi of Babylon with Amraphel (Gen. 14:1).

Hammurabi became a strong military leader and administrator. He was a member of the first dynasty of Babylon that reigned from 1830 to about 1550 B.C. The power of this dynasty reached its height under Hammurabi's rule. Hammurabi defeated Rim-Sin of Larsa and established himself over all the city-states of Lower Babylonia. His expanding military machine enabled him to destroy Mari. It was his code of laws, as we have seen, that was discovered at Susa in 1901. This famous codification has remained classic in illustrating and illuminating Israelite laws.

It was during the reign of Hammurabi that the Babylonian story of creation was composed. The poem glorified Marduk, the patron god of Babylon, whom Hammurabi established as the national god of Babylonia. In this period, the early Sumerian language became an antiquity and Semitic-Babylonian came into common usage.

§3.6.d. The Mari Letters and the Amorites. About 2000 B.C. the Semitic-nomadic peoples, who lived along the desert fringes of the Fertile Crescent, invaded the centers of established civilization. Known as "Westerners," they are preserved in the Old Testament as "Amorites." Amorite states came into existence all over the Mesopotamian area. Nahor, Haran, Mari, Qatna, and Ugarit all appear as Amorite cities with Amorite kings. Babylon itself became the capital of an Amorite state under Hammurabi. This important historical fact is clearly reflected in the *Mari Letters* and in the peoples known as "Amorites" or "Westerners." In such a manner archaeology is slowly but surely outlining the historical framework of the patriarchal age. Such discoveries as the *Mari Letters* prove of incalculable assistance to the historian of the ancient biblical world.

§3.7. The Lachish Ostraca—Jeremiah's Age Lives Again. In the excavations at Lachish, a southwestern Palestinian city, the most astonishing finds were some letters embedded in a layer of burnt charcoal and ashes. They were eighteen in number and were in Hebrew writing done in the ancient Phoenician script. Three more of these letters were discovered in later campaigns in 1938.

Almost all of the letters were written by someone named Hoshiah, who was stationed at some military outpost, to Jaosh, who was evidently a high-ranking officer in the garrison at Lachish. It was the era of the Babylonian overrunning of Palestine several years before the fall of Jerusalem in 586 B.C. The Babylonians had attacked and partly burned Lachish some ten years before in the reign of Jehoiakim. These particular letters were in the layer of ashes that represent the final destruction of the city. Accordingly, they are to be dated from 587 B.C., when Nebuchadnezzar was making the final siege of Jerusalem and also of Lachish and Azekah.

§3.7.a. Identification of Lachish. This large mound, one of the largest occupied in Palestine, is located thirty miles southwest of Jerusalem, twenty miles inland from the Mediterranean, and fifty miles west of Hebron. It is mentioned in the *Amarna Letters* and in earlier Egyptian sources. Its strategic importance is attested by its being on the main route from central Palestine to Egypt. It overlooked the rich Shephelah (terrain that descended to the coastal lowland). The fortress city was an ideal barrier between the Philistine plains and the elevated Judean country. It was one of the principal fortified cities of Judah and one of the bastions taken by the Israelites in their conquest of Palestine (Josh. 10:31–35). The site of Umm-Lakis was first thought to be Lachish. Then the location was sought at Tell el-Hesy by Sir Flinders Petrie, a pioneer archaeologist. William Foxwell Albright finally identified it correctly with the large mound of Tell el-Duweir.

Nebuchadnezzar captured Lachish in 588–586 B.C. (Jer. 34:7). Marks of a huge conflagration on the road leading up to the gate and on the adjacent wall display that the attackers relied largely upon fire, for which felled olive trees not yet harvested supplied the fuel.

§3.7.b. Excavations at Lachish. The Wellcome-Marston Archaeological Expedition in 1933 commenced work there, under the direction of J. L. Starkey. In 1938 Starkey was killed by Arab brigands, and the work was carried on by Lankester Harding and Charles H. Inge.

Besides evidences of earlier occupation, Lachish disclosed settlement by the Hyksos about 1720–1550 B.C. These people overran Egypt during this period. A typical Hyksos defense ditch or *fosse*, with a ramp of clay and lime that apparently provided an enclosure for their horses, was brought to light. In the fosse three Canaanite Egyptian temples built between 1450 and 1225 B.C. were excavated. A Persian temple of a much later period was also found. Cemeteries at Lachish yielded a great quantity of pottery, jewelry, scarabs, and skeletal evidence. A well, 200 feet deep, was located within the city, the remains of a tremendous engineering excavation for water storage, which was not completed. A shaft of about 85 feet terminates in a rectangle 80 x 70 feet cut to a depth of 80 feet. The aim was a water system that would have been much larger than that provided by Hezekiah for Jerusalem in the Siloam Tunnel and comparable to similar systems at Gezer and Megiddo.

A good quantity of inscribed material has been removed from the Lachish excavations. A bronze dagger from about 1700 B.C. contains four pictographic signs, samples of the early script. A bowl and a ewer contain specimens of the same early writing as that found at Serabit el-Khadem. The name "Gedaliah" was found on a jar handle and may be the official whom Nebuchadnezzar set over the land after the fall of Jerusalem (cf. Jer. 40—42).

§3.7.c. Contents of the Lachish Letters. But of all the epigraphic discoveries at Lachish, the most important are the *Lachish Letters*. These letters may be briefly described as follows: Letter 1 lists names, the majority of which are found in the Old Testament. Letters 2 and 5 consist largely of greetings. Letter 3, the longest, contains the most information. This concerns movements of Jewish troops and also makes an interesting note to an unnamed prophet and his word of warning. Letter 4 states that Hoshiah, though observing the signals of Lachish, cannot see those of Azekah. Azekah may well have fallen earlier, for this letter states, "We are watching for the signal station at Lachish according to all the signals you are giving, because we cannot see the signals of Azekah." Letter 6 contains the biblical expression, "to weaken the hands of the people." This recalls Jeremiah, who uses a similar expression (Jer. 38:4).

§3.7.d. Historical Importance of the Letters. The *Lachish Letters* give us an independent view of conditions in Judah in the last days before the fall of Jerusalem. As the Neo-Babylonian army advanced, the doom of Jerusalem was sealed, in contrast to its deliverance under the Assyrian, Sennacherib, as Isaiah had predicted (2 Kin. 19:20, 32–36). Relentlessly, Nebuchadnezzar advanced on the city after a terrible eighteen-month siege in 587–586 B.C. The walls of the city were broken down, the houses and the temple burned, and the people carried away to exile (2 Kin. 25:1–12).

Jeremiah conducted his difficult ministry in these agonizing times. His reference to Azekah and Lachish is most interesting. "When the king of Babylon's army fought against Jerusalem and all the cities of Judah that were left, against Lachish and Azekah; for only these fortified cities remained of the cities of Judah" (Jer. 34:7).

Tell Zakariya in the Shephelah region has been identified as Azekah. In 1898 it was excavated by Frederick K. Bliss of the Palestine Exploration Fund. It had a strong inner fortress buttressed with eight large towers.

The *Lachish Letters* concern the time just prior to the fall of the city and present the same conditions of turmoil and confusion that are revealed in the Book of Jeremiah. Numerous place names that occur in the Bible are found in the letters, as well as personal names. Hoshaiah appears in Jeremiah 42:1 and Nehemiah 12:32. God is referred to by the four-letters YHWH, which are the consonants of the name "Jehovah" or "Yahweh." It is also interesting to note that many of the men's names have Yahweh endings. A prophet like Jeremiah is referred to in the letters. But this is most probably not Jeremiah himself.

So complete was the destruction by the Babylonians that it took many centuries for Judah to recover. The returned remnant was tiny and weak. The small Jewish state stamped its coins with the name "Yehud," that is, Judah, but not until after 300 B.C. do substantial archaeological remains appear, and then they are not abundant. Certainly the Babylonians did a thorough job of destroying Jewish power for many centuries.

§3.7.e. The Paleographic Importance of the Letters. Being inscribed in biblical Hebrew, in which the Old Testament Scriptures were written, and with stylistic and vocabulary similarities to the Book of Jeremiah, these letters are of great paleographic importance. They help the scholar to trace the evolution of the Hebrew alphabet, noting the formation of the letters and their style. They also enable one to see how the Old

Testament Scriptures, which were then written, appeared.

Surely research of this type, that makes it possible for the scholar to look back, to resurrect the past, and to see how the language of the Old Testament developed, is fascinating. Great strides are being made in this field of enquiry. It is one truly bright spot in original biblical studies. This type of study is of immense value in expanding historical backgrounds and illuminating Holy Scripture on the human plane.

§4. The Dead Sea Scrolls. The middle of the 20th century saw the greatest manuscript discovery of modern times. In 1947 a young Bedouin shepherd stumbled upon a cave south of Jericho, containing many leather scrolls of Hebrew and Aramaic writing and about six hundred fragmentary inscriptions. Great excitement prevailed in the archaeological world. In 1952 new caves containing fragments of later scrolls in Hebrew, Greek, and Aramaic were found. These other startling manuscript discoveries have been followed by news of additional manuscripts found in other caves in the Dead Sea area.

§4.1. The Date of the Scrolls. After intensive study of the manuscripts from the Dead Sea area, scholars define three periods: 1. The Archaic Period, about 200–150 B.C.; 2. the Hasmonean Period, about 150–30 B.C.; and 3. the Herodian Period, about 30 B.C. to A.D. 70. The great majority originated in the second and third periods, especially the last half of the second period and last half of the third period.

Although attacks have been made against the antiquity and authenticity of these manuscripts, two lines of evidence substantiate their antiquity. The evidence of *radiocarbon count,* a scientific method of dating, places the linen in which the scrolls were wrapped in the general era of 175 B.C. to A.D. 225. Scholars relying on *paleographic evidence* date these documents by the form of the letters and the way they are written in comparison with other eras of writing. They are able to demonstrate that they come in the intermediate period between the script of the third century B.C. and of the middle of the first century A.D. W. F. Albright observes, "All competent students of writing conversant with the available material and with paleographic method date the scrolls in the 250 years before A.D. 70."

§4.2. The Contents of the Scrolls. Literally hundreds of scrolls and scroll fragments were found through the excavation at Qumran. A summary of these findings are as follows:

In Cave One there were seven major scrolls found. Among these were two copies of Isaiah, one complete and one partially complete; The *Manual of Discipline; Pesher on Habakkuk* (a commentary); *Thanksgiving Hymns; The War Scroll;* and *Genesis Apocryphon.* There were also additional fragments from other scrolls found here. In Cave Two there were thirty-three fragments discovered. From Cave Three fourteen fragments were reclaimed. Cave Four produced the largest collection of materials. Literally thousands of scroll fragments were found here, both biblical and sectarian. In Cave Five twenty-five fragments were found. Cave Six contained some thirty fragments. Cave Seven contained nineteen fragments written in Greek. This was unique because most of the other scrolls and scroll fragments were written in Hebrew or Aramaic. In Cave Eight there were five fragments. Cave Nine produced only one fragment. From Cave Ten the archaeologists recovered an inscribed piece of pottery. Finally, in Cave Eleven approximately eighteen fragments were discovered.

Copies of every book of the Hebrew Scriptures were found here with the exception of the Book of Esther. Sectarian books found here include the *Manual of Discipline, The War Between the Children of Light and Darkness, The Book of Jubilees,* and *The Copper Scroll.* From these sectarian scrolls and scroll fragments we have been able to learn much about first-century Palestinian Judaism and also about the Essene sect, the scribes who copied the Dead Sea Scrolls. The biblical books found are the earliest extant copies to date. Before the discovery of the Dead Sea Scrolls, the earliest manuscript of the Hebrew Scriptures dated to the ninth century A.D.

Most of the scrolls are written in either Hebrew or Aramaic, but we have some scroll fragments written in Greek. The scrolls are usually written in one of four types of script: archaic, Hasmonean, Herodian, or ornamental.

§4.3. Other Manuscript-Yielding Sites. In 1952 a cave was uncovered at Murabbaat in another part of the desert. This yielded manuscripts chiefly from the second century A.D. in Hebrew, Greek, and Aramaic, including a few texts of Genesis, Exodus, Deuteronomy, and Isaiah. Several Hebrew letters were discovered from the period of Simon ben Keseba, that is, Bar Kochba, who led the revolt in A.D. 132–135. A notable exception to the second century A.D. date of this material is an archaic Hebrew papyrus piece, a palimpsest, a list of names and numbers, dated in the sixth century B.C.

In the same general area, other caves have been found, one group in Khirbet Mird, northeast of the monastery of Mar Saba. These contain Arabic papyri, Greek and Christo-Palestinian-Syrian documents, with fragments of biblical codices, all late Byzantine and early Arabic. Another group of manuscripts date from the period of the bulk of the Murabbaat material. Among them is a version of the minor prophets in Greek and a corpus of Nabatean papyri, both of great biblical and historical importance.

§5. Excavations at Khirbet Qumran.

Khirbet Qumran was excavated between 1951 and 1954. This Essene community, with the nearby caves, proved to be the richest manuscript-yielding center. Members of this community copied these manuscripts and preserved them by hiding them in the caves. The Essenes at Khirbet Qumran, seven miles south of Jericho near the shores of the Dead Sea, were next to the Pharisees and Sadducees in importance in sectarian Judaism. This site has become one of the most publicized places in Palestine because of the phenomenal manuscript finds in the cave-dotted cliffs.

Excavations at Khirbet Qumran have fully authenticated this site as the center of Essenic Judaism. As the result of the recovery of coins, pottery, and architectural remains, the story of Qumran's occupation can now be told. Four periods in the later history of the site are traced.

§5.1. Period 1 extends from its founding about 110 B.C. under John Hyrcanus. Numerous coins of this ruler were dug up, as well as of other Hasmonean rulers including Antigonus, 40–37 B.C., the last ruler of this line, to the seventh year of Herod, 31 B.C. At this time an earthquake apparently leveled the site.

§5.2. Period 2 at Qumran dates from the rebuilding and enlargement about A.D. 1 until the Roman destruction in June, A.D. 68. During this era in the lifetime of Jesus, John the Baptist, and the early Christian apostles, Qumran flourished, influencing Judaism and the early Christian church. Coins have been found dating from the reign of Archelaus, 4 B.C. to A.D. 6, and from the time of the Roman procurators down to the second year of the first Jewish revolt in A.D. 66–70. The Roman army, which took Jericho in June, A.D. 68, evi-

dently likewise captured Qumran. One coin, marked with an X, belonged to the Tenth Legion. Iron arrowheads were found in a layer of burned ash in the excavation.

§5.3. Qumran fell to Roman occupation. Some coins describe Judaea Capta. These date from the reign of Titus, A.D. 79–81, and mark Period 3 as the Roman occupation after Jerusalem's destruction in A.D. 70. Evidence that Qumran structures were converted into army barracks indicates that a Roman garrison was stationed there from about A.D. 68 to A.D. 100. At this time the site apparently was abandoned.

§5.4. Period 4. Qumran is distinguished by reoccupation of the site during the second Jewish revolt, A.D. 132–135. Coins dating from this era indicate that here the Jews made their last stand to drive the Romans from their country. After that Qumran sank into obscurity.

§5.5. Architectural Remains at Qumran. The main edifice at Qumran is 100 feet by 120 feet and formed the communal center and hub of the complex. At the northwest corner was a massive defense tower with thick walls enforced by stone embankments. Some coins from the time of the second Jewish revolt (A.D. 132–135) attest its use as a fortress against Roman power.

Alongside the general meeting room is the largest hall of the main building. Here was located the scriptorium. Several inkwells of the Roman period, and even some dried ink, indicate that the manuscripts had been copied by the community's scribes.

Also in the complex were two cisterns (artificial reservoirs) carefully plastered. There were installations for ablutions and baptisms. Of the possibly forty cisterns and reservoirs, the bulk of them must have been used for storage of water in the very hot, dry climate.

Of great interest is the cemetery, containing about one thousand burial places. De Vaux excavated many of these tombs. They are noted for their lack of jewelry and any evidences of luxury.

§5.6. Khirbet Qumran and the Essenes. Not only do the excavations at Khirbet Qumran demonstrate that it was the headquarters of Essenic Judaism but three authorities who were contemporary witnesses attest the same fact, namely, Josephus, Philo, and Pliny. Pliny, for example, locates the Essenes at precisely the spot where Qumran is situated, namely, "on the west side of the Dead

Sea." He also designates the town of En Gedi as situated "below the Essenes."

Josephus relates their unselfish character, industry, and communal life. He extols their love for common toil, says they dressed in white, and describes their three-year probationary period before admission to the sect, and other phases of discipline. He also mentions their various lustrations and says that they numbered about four thousand. He comments on their celibacy, piety, convictions concerning immortality, and their belief in rewards for righteousness.

Philo gives a similar description of this group in Judaism. The library at Qumran attests their delight in the Bible and literature. This is reflected in information given by Philo and Josephus. The Essenes carefully copied Holy Scripture and took pains to preserve it.

§6. Recent Excavations in Jerusalem. The Ophel Garden. One of the most exciting excavations to take place in Jerusalem in the past three decades is also one of the most recent: the excavations to the south of the Temple Mount, known as the Ophel Garden. Here we find a collection of buildings and architectural styles representing various periods dating from the Turkish Period all the way back to the time of King Solomon. The stones found here were used in the construction of buildings from the Second Temple Period, from the temple of Herod the Great. These are the stones pushed from the temple walls by the Romans when they destroyed the temple in A.D. 70.

What makes this excavation so special? It reveals additional walls of the temple from the Second Temple Period (37 B.C. to A.D. 70). Up until the early 1980s, all we had of the Herodian temple was that small part of the outside wall known as the Western Wall or the "Wailing Wall." Now a new section of the wall to the west and the south has been opened for public viewing. This new section helps us to better see and understand just how magnificent the temple must have been. Some of the stones revealed here weigh an estimated eighty tons—some of the largest building stones ever found anywhere in the world! But there is also more.

The archaeologists who supervised most of the work are two very prominent Israeli scholars, Benjamin Mazar and Meir Ben-Dov. Much of their work has been published in an excellent work entitled *In the Shadow of the Temple* (Jerusalem: Keter Publishing, 1982). There is such a wealth of knowledge from their work that we cannot possibly do this excavation justice here. We can, however, lift up a few of their findings.

First, from their work we have learned of a long street that ran the entire length of the western wall of the temple, more than five hundred meters long. Along this wall, at its base, were shops, probably for the sale of religious articles used in the home (such as the menorah, mezzuzah, tefilin, or talit). In addition, deep in the ground beneath the southwestern corner a stone was found upon which was written the inscription "To the place of trumpeting." This must have fallen from the wall above during the Roman destruction. According to Jewish historical sources, the "place of trumpeting" was known as the "Pinnacle of the Temple," the place from which the shofar or ram's horn was blown to announce the beginning and ending of the Sabbath or Shabbat, daily temple worship, festivals, feast days, and holidays. It is this very place that is identified with one of the temptations of Jesus reported in the New Testament Gospels. Until this discovery it had been assumed that the pinnacle of the temple was located on the southeastern corner of the temple wall because it stood high overlooking the Kidron Valley. This, of course, would make no sense at all, since most of the people who needed to hear the trumpeting were living inside the wall in the lower city and near to the Temple Mount.

Second, Mazar and Ben-Dov found a collection of ancient, first-century miqvot or miqvah baths (Jewish ritual immersion baths) in the area of the southern steps that led into and out from the temple (these will be discussed in detail later). These miqvot would have been used by men entering the temple for worship and prayer, particularly priests, to satisfy ritual cleanliness for which religious Jewish men had a passion. Perhaps Jesus even used these baths when he entered the temple from the south.

Third, there are two sets of gates found here for entering and exiting the temple. Both sets are now sealed or closed. The eastern gate (known as the Eastern Huldah Gate, named for the prophetess Huldah) was for entrance into the Court of the Gentiles, the large court that surrounded the temple itself. The western gate (known as the Western Huldah Gate) was for exiting from the temple. However, there was a provision that stated that a person in mourning could enter through the exit and exit from the entrance. By this people would know that they were in mourning and could offer words of comfort.

Finally, here we find the remains of a massive staircase leading into the temple area. These steps were not only an entrance, but also a place where rabbis could teach privately, in a non-traditional way. When a rabbi would teach publicly he would teach inside the Court of the Gentiles, in a colonnade known as the "Royal Stoa." These teaching sessions were characterized with questions and answers, a common Jewish style of teaching, and open to anyone who wanted to listen or dialogue. This public teaching would take place on the Temple Mount. But if a rabbi wanted to teach more privately and in a manner not open to questions (in other words, if the teacher wanted to deliver a lecture), this would take place on the steps at the southern end of the Temple Mount. These steps were known colloquially as the "Teaching Steps." Perhaps it was here that Jesus spoke the words found recorded in Matthew 23.

All in all, this excavation has vastly increased our knowledge of these areas found outside of the Temple Mount to the south and southwest and has given us a clearer picture of the vastness of the temple.

§6.1. The Essene Quarter. Where was the place of the Last Supper? This has been a hotly debated question for centuries. At last we think we have an answer! For centuries, when Christian pilgrims would visit Jerusalem, they would be taken to an "Upper Room" at present-day Mount Zion; and here they would read or tell the story of the Last Supper. In fact, this is a traditional site that cannot be dated back any farther than the Crusader Period, and this room was used as a place of prayer by the Muslims during the Turkish Period. This is certainly not the place where Jesus shared the Passover meal with His disciples the night of His arrest. That place has been long since destroyed.

If, then, this is not the place of the Last Supper, where should we look? Our answer lies in two unrelated sources: the New Testament and the writings of Josephus Flavius, a first-century Jewish historian. According to Luke 22:10–13, we find " 'Behold, when you have entered the city, a man will meet you carrying a pitcher of water; follow him into the house which he enters. Then you shall say to the master of the house, "The Teacher says to you, 'Where is the guest room where I may eat the Passover with My disciples?' " Then he will show you a large, furnished upper room; there make ready.' So they went and found it just as He had said to them, and they prepared the Passover." For those who know a little of Jewish culture, there is something strange here. In the first century men did not usually carry water. This would have been considered as women's work. Why would a man be carrying water? Perhaps because he was an Essene monk.

Josephus tells us that there was a major earthquake in 31 B.C., and during this earthquake the Essene monastery of Qumran was destroyed. Herod the Great gave the Essenes a place in the Upper City of Jerusalem to establish a monastery there and they moved their headquarters to Jerusalem. This area was known as the Essene Quarter. Following the death of Herod the Great in 4 B.C., the Essenes moved back to the wilderness of Judea and rebuilt their monastery at Qumran. However, they left behind a small group of monks to maintain their monastery in Jerusalem. Perhaps it was here that Jesus shared the Last Supper, the Passover, with His disciples. There is no better explanation of why this man would be carrying water and why Jesus wanted His disciples to follow this man.

Where was this Essene monastery of Jerusalem located? Until the mid–1980s no one knew. At about that time, however, the remains of a gate was found not far from the traditional Upper Room, behind the Dormition Abbey on Mount Zion, with the inscription "The Essene Gate." We now know where the monastery was located and a new excavation is under way to recover this place where Jesus had the Last Supper with His disciples.

§6.2. Ebla. The modern Arabic name for this 140-acre mound in the Northwest corner of Syria is Tell Mardikh. Archaeologists of the University of Rome began digging this mound in 1964 and found an inscription in 1968 that identified this site as ancient Ebla. They uncovered portions of impressive buildings from the time of the biblical patriarchs (1900–1700 B.C.); and beneath these were palaces and temples of the Early Bronze Age (2400–2250 B.C.). This was the discovery of an early but advanced civilization that was previously unknown.

In 1974, 1975, and 1976, three rooms of one palace yielded almost seven thousand well-preserved clay tablets and about thirteen thousand fragments of other tablets with cuneiform writing on them. This archive of ancient Sumerian and Canaanite literature is very important. The tablets contain economic, political, and legal records of Ebla. (Understanding the cultures of Israel's neighbors aids biblical interpretation.) They show that Ebla was a merchant empire. Its rulers controlled trade routes that reached into the Mesopotamian Valley, into the mountains of modern-day Turkey, and to the edge of the Nile Valley.

But more importantly, some tablets are dictionaries—the earliest known—providing the meanings of words used in both the Sumerian and early Canaanite (Eblaite) languages. (Languages help archaeologists understand the cultures.) Many Canaanite words at Ugarit and Hebrew words in the Old Testament can be understood more accurately because they also occur on these early tablets.

Many place names occur in the Ebla records, including those familiar to readers of the Bible: Haran, Damascus, Hazor, Beth Shan, Shechem, Joppa, Eshkelon, Jerusalem, Dor—and some scholars believe also Sodom and Gomorrah. Since the Bible itself presents these as real places, the Ebla tablets help support its historical reliability.

About ten thousand names of people are found on the tablets. Among them are biblical names such as Adam, Eve, Noah, Jubal, Abram, Ishmael, Hagar, Keturah, Bilhah, Israel, Micah, Michael, Saul, David, Jehorum, and Jonah. Although these names do not refer to the biblical personages, they establish that the names in Scripture are authentic.

Sometimes, however, the tablets contain mythic and legendary stories that conflict with the Scriptures (e.g., different creation accounts). Such cases illumine the biblical authors' polemics against pagan worldviews.

The excavation project continues until the present and may be expected to cast more light on the Bible's meaning and reliability.

§7. The thrilling story of biblical archaeology is not yet completed. Other great discoveries as a result of continuous research in Bible lands promise even greater contributions to biblical studies in future years. For example, the recovery of thirteen Coptic codices from Nag Hammadi in Upper Egypt, since 1945, have almost rivaled the Dead Sea Scrolls in actual biblical importance. These even include the apocryphal "Gospel of Thomas" and are of inestimable value, especially from a critical standpoint in dating New Testament literature.

What new and exciting discovery affecting the Bible may we expect the archaeologist's spade to turn up next? The prospect should engender a love for the Scriptures and a desire to study them employing history, linguistics, and archaeology as the means under the Holy Spirit to a more accurate understanding of the Bible's message to humankind.

ENCYCLOPEDIC
DICTIONARY

Encyclopedic Dictionary

Over 1,000 items in this one A-to-Z resource help you gain deeper insight into the truths of God's Word for Spirit-filled living. The entries are of three kinds:

(1) Entries explaining important biblical and doctrinal terms. These are marked by the open Bible icon in the margin: .

(2) Word Wealth entries, word studies of key Greek and Hebrew words. These are marked by a sword icon: ⚔ . Each word study also gives the number for that word in *Strong's Exhaustive Concordance*. Word Wealth entries are indexed in the back of this volume both by the English term and by Scripture reference.

(3) Twenty-two mega-entries that bring together as complete articles the hundreds of "Kingdom Dynamics" features distributed throughout the *Spirit-Filled Life Bible.* These are marked by a dove icon: 🕊 . Indexes in the back of this volume identify these articles by title, including major topics, and listing in biblical sequence the major Scripture passages commented on.

ABBA [AB ah] *(father)*—an Aramaic word which corresponds to the English "Daddy" or "Papa." It occurs three times in the New Testament: in Jesus' prayer amid His struggle in the Garden of Gethsemane (Mark 14:36); and twice in Paul's words describing the believer's intimacy with God through the "Spirit of adoption" (Rom. 8:15; Gal. 4:6).

ABLE. (Num. 13:10) *yakol* (yah-*kole*); *Strong's* #3201: To be able, to have power; having the capacity to prevail or succeed. This verb is used two hundred times in the Old Testament. Generally it is translated by such English words as "can," "could," or "be able"; in a few references, "prevail" (1 Kin. 22:22, Esth. 6:13); sometimes, "to have power." In Esther 8:6, it is translated as "endure"; the compassionate queen asks, "How can I endure to see the evil that will come to my people?" Here in Numbers 13, Caleb uses the intensive repetition of *yakol*: "Let us go up . . . for we are well able to overcome it." *Also* (Jude 24) *dunamai* (*doo*-nam-ahee); *Strong's* #1410: To be able, have power. The word combines power and willingness, inherent strength, and action.

ABLUTION—the ceremonial washing of one's body, vessels, and clothing for the purpose of religious purification. The word is sometimes used to translate the Greek word *baptismos* (literally, "dipping"), which can be translated "washings" (Heb. 6:2; 9:10). Ablutions are not related to washing for sanitary or hygienic purposes. They were performed in order to remove ritual defilement. Some of the causes of ritual uncleanness in Bible times were bloodshed (Lev. 17), childbirth (Lev. 12), sexual intercourse (Lev. 18), leprosy (Lev. 12), menstruation (Lev. 15), and contact with dead bodies (Num. 19).

At Mount Sinai, the Israelites were told to wash (literally, "trample") their clothes in preparation for worship (Ex. 19:10, 14). Similarly, the Levites as well as Aaron and his sons were prepared for service by washing their clothes and their bodies (Ex. 40:12–13).

By New Testament times, ceremonial washings became almost an end in themselves. The Pharisees were preoccupied with ritual purifications (Matt. 15:2; Mark 7:4). Jesus exhorted the scribes and Pharisees to "cleanse the inside of the cup and dish"—that is, cleanse their hearts and spirits—and not just wash the outside by religious rituals. Moral filth cannot be washed away with physical cleansing agents (Jer. 2:22; Is. 1:16). Jesus Christ is to be praised, for He "loved us and washed us from our sins in His own blood" (Rev. 1:5; 7:14). Also see ch. 55, §5.5., 6., 6.1.

ABOMINATION—anything that offends the spiritual, religious, or moral sense of a person and causes extreme disgust, hatred, or loathing. Among the objects described as an "abomination" were the carved images of pagan gods (Deut. 7:25–26), the sacrifice to God of inferior blemished animals (Deut. 17:1), the practice of idolatry (Deut. 17:2–5), and the fashioning of a "carved or molded image" of a false god (Deut. 27:15; Is. 44:19).

Other abominations were sexual transgressions (Lev. 18), the adoption of the dress of the opposite sex (Deut. 22:5), and the practice of magic, witchcraft, and "spiritism" (Deut. 18:9–12). Most of the Hebrew words translated "abomination" have the meaning of "impure," "filthy," and "unclean"—that which is foul-smelling and objectionable to a holy God.

ABOMINATION OF DESOLATION—a despicable misuse of the temple of the Lord during a time of great trouble—an event foretold by the prophet Daniel.

The phrase is found in Matthew 24:15 and Mark 13:14 as a quotation from Daniel 11:31 and 12:11. Daniel prophesied that the temple would be used for an "abominable" purpose at some time in the future. As a result, God's faithful people would no longer worship there.

In the Gospels, a similar misuse of the temple is predicted. Jesus said this would show that a time of great trouble was coming on Judea. People should take warning and flee to the mountains (Matt. 24:16; Mark 13:14).

Some believe Daniel's prophecy was fulfilled about 165 B.C. when Antiochus IV (Epiphanes), Greek ruler of Syria, polluted the Jewish temple in Jerusalem by sacrificing a pig on the holy altar. This sacrificing of an *unclean pig was the worst kind of abomination that could have taken place. Others see

the prophecy in Matthew and Mark as being fulfilled when the Romans sacked the Jewish temple about A.D. 70. Still others insist that the abomination of desolation refers to the future, to an idolatrous image or the "Man of Sin" who will take over God's place in the temple and make people bow down and worship him (2 Thess. 2:3–4). According to this interpretation, this will be the final act of sacrilege that marks the beginning of the end time.

ABRAHAM—see ch. 55, §3.5.b., 3.6.b.

ABRAHAM'S BOSOM—a synonym for the life hereafter. According to the Old Testament, when a person died he went to "be with his fathers" (Gen. 15:15; 47:30; Deut. 31:16; Judg. 2:10). The patriarch Abraham was regarded as the "father" of the Jews (Luke 3:8; John 8:37–40.) At death, therefore, the Jewish believer went to his forefathers or, to "father Abraham."

The only Bible use of "Abraham's Bosom" is in Jesus' parable of the rich man and Lazarus (Luke 16:19–31).

ABSOLUTION—a release from sins pronounced by a priest as, for example, in the sacrament of penance (Roman Catholic Church). Absolution is an ecclesiastical term, not found in the Bible, which proclaims the atoning work of Christ as the only way a sinner may receive "absolution" or forgiveness (Luke 7:36–50; Col. 1:13–14).

ABSTINENCE—the voluntary, self-imposed, and deliberate denial of certain pleasures, such as food, drink, and sex. The noun abstinence is found only once in the NKJV (Acts 27:21), where the apostle Paul is described as having experienced "long abstinence." The verb abstain is found six times in the NKJV (Acts 15:20, 29; 1 Thess. 4:3; 5:22; 1 Tim. 4:3; 1 Pet. 2:11).

Abstinence is basically of two kinds: (1) a total abstinence involving an absolute renunciation of a forbidden thing, such as in a Nazirite vow; and (2) a temporary abstinence as, for example, the mutual consent of husband and wife to give up sexual relations for a time, in order to give themselves "to fasting and prayer" (1 Cor. 7:5).

The Israelites were commanded to abstain from eating flesh that contained blood (Gen. 9:4). They were to refrain from eating certain animals (Lev. 11). Priests could not drink wine while exercising their holy ministries (Lev. 10:9). Others abstained from drinking wine (Jer. 35:6).

The apostle Paul taught that the Christian lives by the laws of love and freedom—and that he should voluntarily abstain from food sacrificed to idols, lest it cause a weaker brother or sister in Christ to stumble (Rom. 14:13; 1 Cor. 8:13). The believer's body, said Paul, is the "temple of the Holy Spirit" (1 Cor. 6:19) and should not be polluted by unclean things.

Paul also exhorted the church of the Thessalonians to "abstain from sexual immorality" (1 Thess. 4:3); indeed, they were to "abstain from every form of evil" (1 Thess. 5:22).

The Christian is called to live a life of unselfish and sacrificial love. Abstinence should always seek to glorify God and build up fellow believers in the faith.

 ABUNDANCE (HAVE). (Matt. 25:29) *perisseuo* (per-is-*syoo*-oh); *Strong's #4052:* To superabound, have in excess, greatly surpass, excel. The word shows the generosity of God's grace, giving assurance that faithful use of one's talents and gifts sets the stage for one's own advancement.

ABUNDANTLY. (John 10:10) *perissos* (per-is-soss); *Strong's #4053:* Superabundance, excessive, overflowing, surplus, over and above, more than enough, profuse, extraordinary, above the ordinary, more than sufficient. *Also* (2 Cor. 2:4) *perissoteros* (per-is-sot-*er*-oce); *Strong's #4056:* The adverbial form of a comparative adjective, suggesting something done or possessed in a greater degree, excessively, with superfluity.

ACCEPT, ACCEPTANCE—to receive or treat with favor. In the Bible, a person is accepted by the grace, mercy, or covenant-love of God through faith and repentance.

When the Bible mentions individuals being accepted by God, offerings frequently are mentioned (Gen. 4:37; Job 42:8–9). In the Old Testament, offerings were acceptable to God when made as prescribed (Lev. 1:4; 22:27), but they were unacceptable when God's instructions were ignored (Lev. 7:18; 19:7; 22:23–25). However, they were flatly rejected when the attitude of one's heart was wayward or irreverent (Amos 5:22; Jer. 14:10; Mal. 1:8, 10).

In the primary New Testament passage on acceptance, the apostle Paul explains that God has fully accepted believers through the merits of Christ (Eph. 1:6). God will not reject them. He opens Himself to His own by welcoming them.

The apostle speaks also of a teaching "worthy of all acceptance," or deserving of universal, wholehearted welcome by Christians (1 Tim. 1:15; 4:9). Worship, prayers, the work of one's hands, spiritual sacrifices, and life's service can be favorably received by God (Ps. 19:14; 2 Cor. 5:9). God accepts us fully in Jesus Christ because of His offering and receives what we return to Him.

ACCORD (WITH ONE). (Acts 2:1) *homothumadon* (hom-oth-oo-mad-*on*); *Strong's #3661:* Being unanimous, having mutual consent, being in agreement, having group unity, having one mind and purpose. The disciples had an intellectual unanimity, an emotional rapport, and volitional agreement in the newly founded church. In each of its occurrences, *homothumadon* shows a harmony leading to action.

ACCOUNTED. (Gen. 15:6) *chashab* (kahshahv); *Strong's #2803:* To think, reckon, put together, calculate, imagine, impute, make account; to lay one's thoughts together, to form a judgment; to devise, to plan, to produce something in the mind, to invent. This verb is normally the equivalent of the English word "to think," but also contains a strong suggestion of "counting." *Chashab* is the consideration of a great number of elements, which results in a conclusion based on a wide overview. In this verse, God added up everything that Abraham's belief meant to Him, and computing it all together, determined that it was equal to righteousness. *Also* (Rom. 4:3) *logidzomai* (log-id-zom-ahee); *Strong's #3049:* Compare "logistic" and "logarithm." Numerically, to count, compute, calculate, sum up. Metaphorically, to consider, reckon, reason, deem, evaluate, value. *Logidzomai* finalizes thought, judges matters, draws logical conclusions, decides outcomes, and puts every action into a debit or credit position.

ACCURSED. (1 Cor. 12:3) *anathema* (an-*ath*-em-ah); *Strong's #331:* An animal to be slain as a sacrifice, devoted to destruction. Because of its association with sin, the word had an evil connotation and was synonymous with a curse. In the sacrificial scheme, *anathema* meant alienated from God without hope of being redeemed.

ADAD—see ch. 55, §3.6., 3.6.a.

ADJURATION—an earnest urging or advising; the action by which a person in authority imposes the obligations of an oath upon another. Some of those who adjured others were King Saul, King Ahab, and some itinerant Jewish exorcists (1 Sam 14:24; 1 Kin. 22:16; Mark 5:7; Acts 19:13).

Perhaps the most famous example of adjuration in the Bible is found in Matthew 26:63. The high priest said to Jesus, "I adjure You by the living God that You tell us if You are the Christ, the Son of God." The words "I adjure You" in this case mean, "I solemnly command that you testify on oath and tell the truth, the whole truth, and nothing but the truth." Jesus answered: "It is as you said"; that is, He was affirming He is the Christ, the Son of God!

 ADOPTION—the act of taking voluntarily a child of other parents as one's child; in a theological sense, the act of God's grace by which sinful people are brought into His redeemed family.

In the New Testament, the Greek word translated adoption literally means "placing as a son." It is a legal term that expresses the process by which a man brings another person into his family, endowing him with the status and privileges of a biological son or daughter.

In the Old Testament, adoption was never common among the Israelites. Adoption in the Old Testament was done by foreigners or by Jews influenced by foreign customs. Pharaoh's daughter adopted Moses (Ex. 2:10) and another pharaoh adopted Genubath (1 Kin. 11:20). Furthermore, there is no Hebrew word to describe the process of adoption. When the pharaoh's daughter adopted Moses, the Hebrew text says, "And he became her son" (Ex. 2:10).

By New Testament times, Roman customs exercised a great deal of influence on Jewish family life. One custom is particularly significant in relation to adoption. Roman law required that the adopter be a male and childless; the one to be adopted had to be an independent adult, able to agree to be adopted. In the eyes of the law, the adopted one became a new creature; he was regarded as being born again into the new family—an illustration of what happens to the believer at conversion.

The apostle Paul used this legal concept of adoption as an analogy to show the believer's relationship to God. Although similar ideas are found throughout the New Testament, the word adoption, used in a theological sense, is found only in the writings of Paul (Rom. 8:15, 23; 9:4).

In Ephesians, Paul's emphasis was that our adoption rests with God, who "predestined us to adoption as sons" (Eph. 1:5). In his letter to the Romans, Paul used the term to describe Israel's place of honor in God's plan (Rom. 9:4). However, Gentile believers have also been given the "Spirit of adoption," which allows them to cry, "Abba, Father" (Gal. 4:6).

God's adoption of the believer also has a future dimension, the assurance that the believer's body will be resurrected (Rom. 8:23).

 ADULTERY—willful sexual intercourse with someone other than one's husband or wife. Jesus expanded the meaning of adultery to include the cultivation of lust: "Whoever looks at a woman to lust for her has already committed adultery with her in his heart" (Matt. 5:28).

In the Ten Commandments God emphatically prohibited adultery when he said, "You shall not commit adultery" (Ex. 20:14). Under Mosaic Law, when a couple was caught in the act of adultery, both parties were to be killed (Deut. 22:22).

Adultery plays havoc with personal, domestic, and national happiness. A case in point is David's affair with Bathsheba. Their adultery led to a cover-up, which was followed by the murder of Bathsheba's husband (2 Samuel 11). Nathan the prophet later came to David, accusing him of his sin and declaring that because of it, violence would become commonplace in David's household (2 Sam. 12:10). One disaster after another struck his family, including rape, murder, and revolt (2 Samuel 13—15).

Adultery reached epidemic proportions in Jeremiah's time. The prophet repeatedly spoke out against this and other sins (Jer. 7:9; 23:10). The problem was so rampant that even the other prophets of Jerusalem were guilty of it (Jer. 23:14), and Jeremiah predicted God's judgment on them (Jer. 23:15).

Occasionally, the marriage covenant was used as an analogy to describe God's relationship to His people. When the people of Israel and Judah refused to obey Him, or when they practiced idolatry, the prophets accused them of spiritual adultery (Jer. 3:6–10).

The record of the woman taken in adultery—who, according to the Law of Moses, would have been stoned to death—reveals the wisdom and grace of Jesus (John 8:39). He knew that her accusers were not without sin, and, therefore, they were being self-righteous when they condemned her. When Jesus said to her, "Go and sin no more" (John 8:11), He did not excuse her sin; He forgave her of adultery but also commanded her not to continue in it.

The apostle Paul catalogued a series of sins that exclude a person from the kingdom of God. The sin of adultery was included in this list (1 Cor. 6:9).

ADULTERY. (John 8:3) *moicheia* (moy-*khi*-ah); *Strong's #3430:* Unlawful sexual intercourse, illicit connection with a married person, marital infidelity. *Moicheia* is incompatible with the harmonious laws of family life in God's kingdom; and since it violates God's original purpose in marriage, it is under God's judgment.

ADVERSARY—one who opposes or hinders another. In the Bible, this word is often used of

*Satan, the adversary of God and His plan of righteousness and redemption in the world. Since his fall, Satan has opposed God's plan to establish His kingdom on earth. He deceived Eve (Gen. 3:1–15) in order to use man to establish his kingdom rather than God's. Satan later opposed Jesus by questioning His identity as the Messiah and by tempting Him to misuse His powers as God's Son (Matt. 4:1–11).

Satan and his host oppose the knowledge of God (2 Cor. 10:3–5) and is still the Christian's adversary (1 Pet. 5:8). But we have an *Advocate, Jesus Christ (1 John 2:1), who enables us to overcome his temptation, and in Christ, the "greater" One, we are certain to triumph through His blood and the Word (1 John 4:4; Rev. 12:9–11).

ADVOCATE—one who pleads another's cause before a tribunal or judicial court. The word advocate occurs in 1 John 2:1. The Greek word translated "advocate" is also found four times in the Gospel of John, all referring to the Holy Spirit (John 14:16, 26; 15:26; 16:7; translated "helper," NKJV).

Christians need an Advocate because of the *Adversary, the devil or Satan, who accuses us before God (1 Pet. 5:8; Rev. 12:10). If Satan is the "prosecuting attorney," Christ and the Holy Spirit are the legal advocates, the "defense attorneys," who help, defend, counsel, and comfort us. They plead the Christian's case before God day and night, providing a continuing remedy for sin, as well as energize for triumph in advancing Christ's kingdom on earth, daily through our lives and strategically through our prayer, intercession, and witness.

AGE. (Matt. 28:20) *aion* (ahee-*ohn*); *Strong's #165:* Denotes an indefinitely long period, with emphasis on the characteristics of the period rather than on its duration. In idiomatic usage it designates "forever" or "forever and ever" (21:19; Rom. 16:27; Eph. 3:21). The word is also used as a designation for the present age (Matt. 12:32; 13:22; 1 Tim. 6:17) and for the time after Christ's Second Coming (Mark 10:30; Luke 20:35).

AGREE. (Matt. 18:19) *sumphoneo* (soom-foe-*neh*-oh); *Strong's #4856:* From *sum*, "together," and *phoneo*, "to sound." *Sumphoneo* is to sound together, be in accord, be in harmony. The word "symphony" comes from *sumphoneo*. Metaphorically, the word means to agree together in prayer that is concordant.

AHAB—see ch. 55, §2.3.

AKKADIAN—see ch. 55, §2.2.

ALLEGORY—a symbolic representation of a truth about human conduct or experience.

The Greek word *allegoreo* is in Galatians 4:24, translated "symbolic" in the NKJV.

As a literary device, an allegory may consist of only a few lines or it may be sustained through an entire book. Traditional Jewish and Christian interpretation has often seen the Song of Solomon as an allegory of covenant love between God and His wife, Israel (Jewish) or Christ and His bride, the church (Christian). Other examples of allegory in the Old Testament are Psalm 80:8–19 and Ecclesiastes 12:37. In Psalm 80 the pronouns we and us identify the vine as Israel (vv. 18–19).

In the New Testament, Jesus' parable of the wheat and the tares (Matt. 13:24–30, 36–43) is a good example of allegory. The apostle Paul also used allegories when writing. In Ephesians 6:11–17 he urges his readers to "put on the whole armor of God" and then gives the symbolic spiritual designation for each article worn by the Christian soldier. And in 1 Corinthians 10:14, Paul gives an allegory which compares the experience of Moses and the Israelites to Christian baptism and the Lord's Supper.

The most pronounced of Paul's allegories is in Galatians 4:21–31, where Hagar and Sarah, Ishmael and Isaac are compared and a lesson drawn. Ishmael, born to the bondwoman Hagar, Paul reveals as symbolic of the Old Covenant: the law from Mount Sinai that brings all flesh into bondage. Whereas Isaac, born to a freewoman (Sarah), is symbolic of the New Covenant: the gospel of grace from Mount Calvary that gives spiritual freedom. The apostle concludes "we are not children of the bondwoman but of the free [woman]," urging his readers to reject the bondage of religious legalism.

ALMIGHTY. (Ps. 91:1) *shadday* (shad-dye); *Strong's #7706:* All-powerful; when it appears as *'El Shadday*, it is "God Almighty." This name occurs about fifty times in the Old Testament. It was a name by which God was known to the patriarchs (Gen. 17:1; Ex. 6:3). Some scholars trace its origin to the verb *shadad*, meaning "mighty, unconquerable." Others relate its origin to the Akkadian word for "mountain," indicating God's greatness, strength, or His everlasting nature. Another explanation is that *Shadday* is a compound of the particle *sheh* (which or who) and *day* (sufficient). *Sheh-day* or *Shadday* is therefore the all-sufficient God, eternally capable of being all that His people need.

ALTAR—an elevated place, a table or platform on which a person or priest placed a sacrifice as an offering to God. The nature of altars changed considerably during the several centuries from Old Testament times to New Testament days. In addition to describing altars dedicated to God, the Bible speaks frequently also of pagan altars, particularly those associated with the false worship of the Canaanites.

Altars in the Old Testament. The first altar in the Bible was the one built by Noah after the Flood (Gen. 8:20). Several altars also appear in connection with Abraham. His first altar served as a symbol of his possession of the land (Gen. 12:7). At altars mentioned in Genesis 12:8 and Genesis 13:18, he called upon the name of the Lord. His most dramatic altar was on Mount Moriah (Gen. 22:9). Isaac built an altar at Beersheba (Gen. 26:25), and while Jacob built no new altars, he restored those which Abraham had built at Shechem (Gen. 33:20) and Bethel (Gen. 35:1, 3).

The Hebrew word for altar means "a place of slaughter or sacrifice." But the altars of the Old Testament were not restricted to offerings of animals as sacrifices. Joshua 22:26–29 indicates that altars were occasionally used to remind the Israelites of their heritage or to call attention to a major event. Sometimes an altar might even be used as a place for refuge (1 Kin. 1:50–51; 2:28).

In the *Tabernacle of Moses, two priestly altars assumed important roles in worship: the altar of burnt offering and the altar of incense.

The altar of burnt offering (Ex. 27:1–8) was placed in front of the entrance to the tabernacle (Ex. 40:6, 29), where it was used for the daily burnt offering and meal offering. This altar declared that entry into the presence of God must be preceded by sacrificial *atonement for sin. The altar of burnt offering was made of acacia wood, overlaid with bronze.

The altar of incense (Ex. 30:1–10) stood just before the veil inside the holy place within the tent of the tabernacle (Ex. 40:26–27). Priests burned incense on this altar every day so its fragrance would fill the tabernacle when the sacrificial blood was sprinkled on the altar of burnt offering.

Saul, the first king of Israel, built an altar during his conquest of the Philistines (1 Sam. 14:35). Later, King David erected an altar at the threshing floor of Araunah (2 Sam. 24:15–25), a site David purchased and which became the location for the temple built by Solomon, David's son and successor. Most scholars identify this site with the large rock structure in the city of Jerusalem now seen under the famous mosque known as the Dome of the Rock.

After building the temple in Jerusalem, Solomon constructed an altar (2 Chr. 4:1)

larger than the one Moses had built, probably adapting it to the size of the temple. This was the altar restored later by King Asa (2 Chr. 15:8). Still later, King Ahaz had Solomon's altar moved to the northern part of the temple courtyard (2 Kin. 16:14–15). This was also the same altar cleansed by Hezekiah (2 Chr. 29:18) and rebuilt by Manasseh (2 Chr. 33:16).

When the captives returned to Jerusalem following their years of captivity in Babylon, one of their first acts was to build an altar (Ezra 3:3).

The incense altar of the tabernacle was also replaced by Solomon's altar made of cedar and overlaid with gold (1 Kin. 6:20, 22; 7:48). Incense was burned every morning and evening on this altar. The priest also sprinkled the blood of a sacrificial animal on the incense altar to make atonement for his sins and the sins of the people. The incense altar was also symbolic of prayer. It is the only altar that is mentioned in the heavenly temple (Is. 6:6; Rev. 8:3).

Altars in the New Testament. In addition to the temple of the Jewish people with its altars, the New Testament refers to the altar in Athens that was dedicated "TO THE UNKNOWN GOD" (Acts 17:23). But no physical Christian altar appears in the New Testament. The statement "we have an altar" (Heb. 13:10) refers to the sacrifice of Christ. The altar of incense mentioned in Revelation 8:3 belongs to the heavenly temple. In this heavenly temple there is no need for an altar of burnt offering since atonement for our sins is now complete through the death of Jesus Christ.

Canaanite altars. Archaeology has turned up many Canaanite altars from all periods of Old Testament history.

Canaanite altars were constructed of earth, stone, or metal, and were dedicated to pagan gods other than the one true God. Canaanite altars were devoted to the Baals (2 Chr. 33:3) and various other Canaanite gods and goddesses (Deut. 12:3)—Chemosh the god of Moab, Ashtoreth of the Sidonians, and Molech of the Ammonites (1 Kin. 11:5–7)—and were used in a highly immoral and perverted practice of sex-worship, as well as for infant sacrifices. The Lord gave specific instructions that these pagan altars should be torn down and destroyed before altars dedicated to His worship were built (Deut. 12:2–3).

ALTAR. (2 Kin. 12:9) *mizbeach* (meez-beh-ahch); *Strong's* #4196: Altar, place of sacrifice. The root of *mizbeach* is *zabach*, which means "to slay, to sacrifice, to offer an animal." The word *mizbeach* occurs more than four hundred times. Altars were of great importance in the lives of Noah and the three patriarchs. In the Levitical system and in Solomon's temple, the altar was the center of daily activity, without which the rest of Israel's worship could not take place. The "altar of sacrifice" was also crucial in God's revelation of true worship for joyful times, such as feasts.

AMARNA LETTERS—see ch. 55, §2.2., 3.4.a., 3.7.a.

AMBASSADOR. (Eph. 6:20) *presbeuo* (pres-byoo-oh); *Strong's #4243:* Literally "to be the elder," and later "to be an ambassador," a representative of a ruling authority. Ambassadors would be chosen from the ranks of mature, experienced men. To be an ambassador for Christ necessitates spiritual maturity.

AMORITES—see ch. 55, §3.6., 3.6.d.

ANCIENTS. (Ps. 119:100) *zaqen* (zah-kayn); *Strong's #2205:* An elder, old man, aged person. The verb means "to become old." *Zaqan* means "beard," something that grows with age. Older persons are respected in Scripture because their experience in life has brought them wisdom. Hence, the elders who accompanied Moses (Ex. 24:9–14) or counseled kings (1 Kin. 12:6–8) were older, mature men. In this reference, the psalmist has been schooled by the Lord to such a degree that he knows much more than the old men know (see also v. 99). Young and old should equally hear from God in the outpouring of the Holy Spirit (Joel 2:28).

ANGEL—a member of an order of heavenly beings who are superior to man in power and intelligence. By nature angels are spiritual beings (Heb. 1:14). Their nature is superior to human nature (Heb. 2:7), and they have superhuman power and knowledge (2 Sam. 14:17, 20; 2 Pet. 2:11). They are not, however, all-powerful or all-knowing (Ps. 103:20; 2 Thess. 1:7).

Artistic portrayals of angels as winged beings are generally without basis in the Bible. Rarely is an angel so described. (For exceptions, compare the *cherubim and seraphim and the living creatures—Ex. 25:20; Ezek. 1:6; Rev. 4:8.)

The position of angels. Angels were created by God (Ps. 148:2, 5) and were present to rejoice when He created the world (Job 38:47). In their original state they were holy, but before the creation of the world some of the angelic order rebelled against God and lost their exalted position. The leading angel in this revolt became the devil, also known as *Satan (Gen. 3:4, 14; Ezek. 28:12–16; Rev. 12:4, 7– 9). Another of the fallen angels is named Abaddon

or Apollyon (Rev. 9:11), "the angel of the bottomless pit" [abyss]. The lord or prince of these fallen angels is Satan (Rev. 12:7–9). Fallen angels, or messengers, continue to serve Satan, but their power is limited. Judgment awaits them in the future (Matt. 25:41; Rev. 12:9). The fallen angels referred to in 2 Peter 2:4 and Jude 6 are possibly the beings referred to as "sons of God" in Genesis 6:1–4.

Two of the vast company of unfallen angels are named in the Bible. They are the archangels Michael (Dan. 10:13, 21; 12:1; Jude 9; Rev. 12:7) and Gabriel (Dan. 8:16; 9:21; Luke 1:19, 26). Michael seems to have the special task of caring for Israel, and Gabriel's role is seen in his communicating special messages to God's servants.

The vast army of unfallen angels delight in praising the name of the Lord continually (Ps. 103:21; 148:1–2). Large numbers of them remain at God's side, ready to do His every command (1 Kin. 22:19). Angels in God's presence include the cherubim, seraphim, and living creatures (or living beings) (Ex. 25:20; 15. 6:2; Ezek. 1:5–6; Rev. 4:6).

Unfallen angels are known for their reverence for God and their obedience to His will. Angels represent God in making significant announcements of good news (Gen. 18:9–10; Luke 1:13, 30; 2:8–15). On His behalf they also warn of coming dangers (Gen. 18:16–19:29; Matt. 2:13). In some cases they are God's agents in the destruction and judgment of evil (Gen. 19:13; 2 Sam. 24:16).

Of special importance in the Old Testament is the Angel of the Lord (Gen. 16:7; 22:11; 31:11). This angel is depicted as a visible manifestation of God Himself. He has powers and characteristics that belong only to God, such as the power to forgive sins (Ex. 23:20–21). His similarities to Jesus lead most scholars to conclude that He is the preincarnate Word present with God at the creation of the world (John 1:1, 14).

The relation of angels to man. When visible to human beings, angels consistently appear in human form (Gen. 18:2; Dan. 10:18; Zech. 2:1). Sometimes, however, their appearance inspires awe (Judg. 13:6; Matt. 28:3–4; Luke 24:4).

Angels are never known to appear to wicked people—only to those whom the Bible views as good, such as Abraham, Moses, David, Daniel, Jesus, Peter, and Paul. They are charged with caring for God's people and serving them in times of need (Ps. 91:11–12; Heb. 1:14). They also guide and instruct good people (Gen. 24:7, 40; Ex. 14:19). Sometimes their guidance comes to humans through dreams (Gen. 28:12; 31:11).

Angels also protect the people of God (Ex. 14:19–20; Dan. 3:28; Matt. 26:53). They meet a wide variety of human needs, including relieving hunger and thirst (Gen. 21:17–19; Mark 1:13) and overcoming loneliness and dread (Luke 22:43). They sometimes deliver the people of God from danger (Acts 5:19; 12:6–11).

Although angels themselves are not the subjects of salvation, angels are interested in the salvation of human beings (Luke 15:10; 1 Cor. 4:9). They were particularly active in the events surrounding the birth and resurrection of Jesus (Matt. 1:20; 2:13, 19; 28:2; Luke 1:11–38; 2:9–15; 22:43; 24:23; John 20:12).

Jesus spoke frequently of angels, both good and bad (Matt. 13:41; 26:53; Mark 8:38; Luke 12:8–9). Angels are quite real, and clearly play a vital part in God's plan for the church reaching the world today (examples in Acts 8:26; 10:3; 12:7; 27:23).

ANGEL. (2 Chr. 32:21) *mal'ach* (mahl-*ahch*); *Strong's* #4397: A messenger, ambassador; someone dispatched to do a task or relay a message; specifically an "angel" or heavenly messenger from the Lord. Found more than two hundred times, *mal'ach* is usually translated "angel" (though often translated "messengers" when referring to human messengers; see Gen. 32:3; 1 Sam. 16:19; 2 Kin. 7:15). Angels, mentioned extensively in the Old Testament, were sent to assist or inform the patriarchs, Balaam, David, the prophet Zechariah, and others. Not all angels are of the "angelic" sort (*see* Prov. 16:14 [which might have been translated "death angels"], Ps. 78:49, Prov. 17:11). Psalm 104:4 portrays the supernatural qualities (spirit, fire) of the Lord's messengers.

ANGELS. (Matt. 4:11) *angelos* (*ang*-el-oss); *Strong's* #32: From *angello,* "to deliver a message"; hence, a messenger. In the New Testament the word has the special sense of a spiritual, heavenly personage attendant upon God and functioning as a messenger from the Lord sent to earth to execute His purposes and to make them known to humanity. Angels are invisibly present in the assemblies of Christians and are appointed by God to minister to believers (Heb. 1:14).

ANGELS, THE MINISTRY OF. The unseen realm is constantly described in the Bible as immediately present in our midst, not as a distant reality but as a present one. Angels are not occasionally present in the Bible; they are constantly manifest! The word "angel" occurs over 250 times in the pages of God's eternal revelation of the Scriptures, not only describing things they have done but unfolding things they are assigned to do in our day, as well as in the past. This study shows how the force of these invisible servants and warriors is brought to bear upon our present day: "Are they not all ministering spirits sent forth to minister for those who will inherit salvation?" (Heb. 1:14). The answer from the Bible is "Yes," and that means their ministry applies to us—today.

1. Fivefold Ministry of Angels (Ps. 103:20–21). These verses show God's purpose for angels. Angels exist to serve God in five ways: (1) to "bless the LORD" (in worship and service); (2) to "do His word" (concerning activities on earth); (3) to heed the voice of God's word (as it is spoken through the saints on earth); (4) to minister on God's behalf (as described in Heb. 1:14); and (5) to do God's pleasure (as His hosts are at His direction).

2. Variety in the Appearance of Angels (Judg. 13:6). What do angels look like? The appearance of angels is correctly rendered "very awesome." Angels appear in different forms depending upon their order of creation. For example, God's messenger angel, Gabriel, has the appearance of a man (Dan. 9:21). From Ezekiel 28:13–14 we learn that cherubim (plural for "cherub") are exotic and beautiful—covered with precious stones. Ezekiel 1:23 tells us that cherubim have four wings, while seraphim (plural for "seraph") have six wings—two that cover the face, two that cover the feet, and two with which to fly (Is. 6:2).

3. Organized Structure in the Angelic Realm (Col. 1:16). There is an organized structure in the angelic realm. Profoundly influential in humanity's history, angels are involved according to their designated ranks. Though opinion differs as to the placement of angelic offices, it is clear that the angelic host are part of a highly organized world of angel beings. For example, Daniel 10:13 shows that warring angels have a chief prince, Michael, who is also called an archangel, that is, one who rules over others. Seraphim and cherubim seem to be of a slightly lower rank, just ahead of ministering spirits (Heb. 1:14). However, it may also be that the seraphim and cherubim fill a leadership role in worship while Michael leads the warring angels. As to the dark angels, Ephesians 6:12 offers insight into the ranks of the evil angelic realm: principalities, powers, rulers of the darkness of this world, and spiritual wickedness in high places. From the information the Bible gives, we can see that the angelic realm is a distinctly structured society with different levels of authority or power endowed to each according to God's creative order.

4. Angels' Influence over Nations (Dan. 10:13). Some angels have influence over nations. The ruling prince of Persia, an evil angel whose abode is in the heavenlies (the invisible realm), attempted to keep the captive Israelites from returning to their homeland. This gives us insight into the powerful control such principalities and rulers of darkness may exercise over nations and national issues. In this same chapter we see two other angelic "princes" who rule nations: Michael, "one of the chief princes," who rules and guards the activities of Israel (v. 13); and the "prince of Greece" (v. 20), who, as it was prophesied, would eventually come and take predominance over the "prince of Persia" then in control.

5. Angels as Messengers (Acts 8:26). With God's Word as our source of information, we see that angels may be actively involved in assisting the advance of the church on earth through messages. Philip had evangelized in Jerusalem and Samaria, but it was a messenger angel who told him to go into the desert where he met the Ethiopian eunuch. Acts 10 also reveals angelic intervention on behalf of Cornelius, and the church was enlarged to include Gentiles. As with the supernatural gifts of the Spirit, angelic activity did not cease after the time of the apostles. Angels are still actively involved with building God's kingdom on earth. Nevertheless, wisdom teaches we would do well to heed Paul's warning: "But even if we, or an angel from heaven, preach any other gospel to you than what we have preached to you, let him be accursed" (Gal. 1:8). Any angelic message must be judged by God's eternal word of truth.

6. Guardian Angels Watch Over Us (Ps. 91:11–12). Each of us has our own private guardian angels. Dr. Billy Graham, observing the plural in this text, concluded that each believer must have at least two angels whose assigned duty it is to protect them. Psalm 91:4 speaks of God "covering us with His feathers" and mentions that we are under His "wings." Since God has no feathers or wings, some have suggested that these feathers and wings speak of our guardian angels' wings, which protectively cover us to keep us from falling, getting lost, or stumbling into unknown dangers in the unseen realm of the spirit.

7. The Angel of the Lord Receives Worship (Ex. 3:2, 4). One unusual "angel"—the Angel of the Lord—is different from all others in that this angel received worship. How could this be? No angel can receive worship, which belongs to God alone. The angel Lucifer was expelled from heaven for trying to receive such worship. The mystery is solved in this text where the

Angel of the Lord is revealed to be the Lord God (see Acts 7:30–32). But how could Moses and other Old Testament persons have seen God face-to-face and lived since Scripture clearly states the contrary (Ex. 33:20)? The answer: because they saw the Son of God in a preincarnate form, known in the Old Testament as the Angel of the Lord—the "Messenger [Angel] of the covenant" (Mal. 3:1).

8. Jesus and Angels (Rev. 1:1). Jesus was closely associated with angels. This verse reveals that He commissions His angels to do His bidding. An angel was used to announce Jesus' coming birth to the Virgin Mary and her fiance, Joseph (Luke 1:26; Matt. 1:20). Angels also attended Jesus' birth and announced it to the shepherds (Luke 2:8). They protected Him from Herod's jealous wrath (Matt. 2:13, 22); and later in life, at the end of His forty-day fast, they ministered to Him and strengthened Him (Matt. 4:11).

During His agonizing struggle on the night in which He was betrayed, an angel strengthened Jesus in preparation for the Cross (Luke 22:43). These celestial creatures were present at Jesus' resurrection (Matt. 28:2) and ascension (Acts 1:10). Finally, Jesus will return "in the glory of His Father with His angels" (Matt. 16:27), and we will meet them in the air! (1 Thess. 4:16, 17).

9. Fallen Angels (Rev. 12:7, 9). The Scriptures reveal both good angels and evil angels. The evil entities are those angels who rebelled with Lucifer and were cast out of heaven with him. Their minds and understanding have been covered with the horrible darkness of deception—the same tactic Satan still uses to lead his victims astray. They were created in God's original order to do His will, as those angels who continue in obedience to His throne. But these "did not keep their proper domain" (Jude 6) and are now agents of the Adversary, bound under his dark dominion and serving Satan's rebellious enterprises.

10. Ministering Spirits (Heb. 1:14). Surprisingly enough, there are more direct references to angels in the New Testament than in the Old Testament. A careful study will reveal that the New Testament activity of angels usually revolves around the ministry of Jesus and the establishment of His church on earth. They "minister" (Greek *diakonia*), referring to their "serviceable labor, assistance." They are ministering spirits, or heavenly assistants, who are continually active today in building the body of Christ—advancing the ministry of Jesus and the building of His church.

11. Seraphim (Is. 6:2). The ministry of the seraphim is closely related to the throne and the praises of God. They are seen constantly glorifying God—extolling His nature and attributes, and apparently supervising heaven's worship. It is possible the seraphim are the praising angels of Psalm 148:2 though they are not specifically identified as such. Whereas cherubim are positioned beside and around the throne of God (Ps. 99:1; Rev. 4:6), the six-winged seraphim are seen as hovering above the throne as they minister in worship.

12. The Cherubim (Gen. 3:24). Cherubim are the created beings assigned to guard the throne of God (Ps. 99:1) as well as the ark of the covenant and the mercy seat (Ex. 25:18–22; 37:7–9). Cherubim (plural for cherub) guarded the Tree of Life to keep man from eating of it and, therefore, living forever in his sins. Thus, contrary to popular belief, more than one angel guarded the entrance to Eden. The fullest description of cherubim is in Ezekiel 10, where they are closely related to the glory of God and have a part in its presence and its withdrawal, moving at the Almighty's direction.

13. Archangels (Jude 9). The word "archangel" means "to be first (in political rank or power)," indicating that this is the highest rank of heavenly hosts. The only archangel specifically mentioned in the Scriptures is Michael. It is likely his shout we will hear at the Second Coming (1 Thess. 4:16). Because Gabriel is prominent in the Bible and also because his name is derived from a root word meaning "strength" or "chief" (politically), which is characteristic of archangels, some conclude that he is also an archangel. This opinion, although not supported by Scripture, was popularized by the poet John Milton.

Many scholars hold that Lucifer was an archangel before his fall (Ezekiel 28). However, this is only speculation based on the position and influence he held over the angels who fell with him.

14. Lucifer (Is. 14:12–14). Satan was once an angel called Lucifer, who, in love with his own beauty, fell into pride and self-centeredness. His rebellion manifests in five "I will" statements addressed against God (vv. 13–14). With five utterances he declares he will take the place of the Most High God. But verses 15–20 reveal that God has the last word, as the Most High makes five responses: "Satan, you will (1) be thrown into hell; (2) be gazed upon (that is, made a spectacle); (3) be talked about (mocked, scorned); (4) be cast out of your grave like a carcass; and (5) be alone." God's "last word" on Satan is still applicable to any challenge he attempts to bring against any of the people of God.

15. Believers Accompanied by Angels (Luke 16:22). The Bible indicates angels in the future of all believers, at death or at Jesus' Second Coming. Should death occur, at our transition between this life and the next, it will not be a lonely, dreadful experience. Rather, angels will accompany us into everlasting joy just as they carried the beggar to the resting place appointed for him by God. For us, that will be Jesus' presence (2 Cor. 5:1–8). However, if Christ returns before our death, at the Second Coming the angels will gather us to Christ "from the farthest part of earth to the farthest part of heaven" (Mark 13:26–27).

ANGER. (Judg. 10:7) *'aph* (*ahf*); *Strong's* #639: Anger; face, nostril, nose. This noun occurs approximately 250 times. Translated as "anger" in the great majority of occurrences, "wrath," "nose," and "nostril" may also translate *'aph*. (*See* Ps. 2:5; Song 7:4.) The connection between nose and anger exists through the verb *'anaph* "to be angry"), from which *'aph* is derived. The Hebrew figure of speech, which means "to grow angry," may be translated "his anger burned" or "his nose grew hot." (*See* also Ps. 2:12; Prov. 22:24; Is. 42:25; 65:5.) The idea is that anger is observable in the fierce breathing through the nose of an angry person. *Also* (1 Kin.16:2) *cha'as* (*kah*-ahs); *Strong's* #3707: To grieve, exasperate, vex, provoke, make angry. This word portrays the kind of anger that results from repeated irritation, and not the anger that suddenly explodes for no apparent reason. Thus *cha'as* is closer to "exasperation" than to "wrath." The verb *cha'as* is usually translated "provoke to anger."

ANOINT, ANOINTING—to authorize, or set apart, a person for a particular work or service (Is. 61:1). In the Old Testament, the anointed person belonged to God in a special sense. The phrases, "the Lord's anointed," "God's anointed," "My anointed," "Your anointed," or "His anointed" are used of Saul (1 Sam. 26:9, 11), David (2 Sam. 22:51), and Solomon (2 Chr. 6:42). In the New Testament, all who are Christ's disciples are said to be anointed; they are God's very own, set apart and commissioned for service (2 Cor. 1:21).

Priests, kings, and prophets were anointed. Oil was poured on the head of the person being anointed (Ex. 29:7). Kings were set apart through the ritual of anointing, which was performed by a prophet who acted in God's power and authority (1 Sam. 15:1). The Old Testament also records two instances of the anointing of a prophet (1 Kin. 19:16; Is. 61:1).

Jesus is described as "anointed," which is the meaning of the Hebrew-based word "Messiah" or the Greek-based word "Christ".

In the New Testament, anointing was frequently used in connection with healing. The Holy Spirit's activities in a believer's life are pictured in terms associated with anointing. Jesus' disciples anointed the sick (Mark 6:13), and James instructed the elders of the church to anoint the sick with oil (James 5:14). This anointing was for the purpose of healing.

Anointing in the New Testament also refers to the anointing of the Holy Spirit, which brings understanding (1 John 2:20, 27). This anointing is not only for kings, priests, and prophets; it is for everyone who believes in the Lord Jesus Christ. The anointing occurs physically with a substance such as oil, myrrh, or balsam. But this is also a spiritual anointing, as the Holy Spirit anoints a person's heart and mind with the love and truth of God.

When there is a special sense of Christ's presence or the Holy Spirit's working, people will often say, "there was a real 'anointing' present." These words are not technically biblical, but convey the idea of Christ's presence "with power," as in Mark 5:30; Luke 5:17; and Acts 4:33; 6:8; 8:6–8.

ANOINTED. (Is. 61:1) *mashach* (mah-*shahch*); *Strong's* #4886: To anoint, to rub with oil, especially in order to consecrate someone or something. Appearing almost seventy times, *mashach* refers to the custom of rubbing or smearing with sacred oil to consecrate holy persons or holy things. Priests (Lev. 8:12; 16:32) and kings (2 Sam. 2:4; 5:3; 1 Kin. 1:39) in particular were installed in their offices by anointing. In Exodus 40:9–14, the tabernacle was to be anointed, as well as the altar, the laver, and the high priest's sons. The most important derivative of *mashach* is *mashiyach* (Messiah), "anointed one." As Jesus was and is the promised Anointed One, His title came to be "Jesus the Messiah." Messiah was translated into Greek as *Christos*, thus His designation, "Jesus Christ."

ANOTHER. (John 14:16) *allos* (al-loss); *Strong's* #243: One besides, another of the same kind. The word shows similarities but diversities of operation and ministries. Jesus' use of *allos* for sending another Comforter equals "one besides Me and in addition to Me but one just like Me. He will do in My absence what I would do if I were physically present with you." The Spirit's coming assures continuity with what Jesus did and taught.

ANTHROPOMORPHISM—the practice of describing God in human terms, as if He has feet (Ex. 24:10), hands (John 10:29), a face (Matt.

18:10), a heart (Hos. 11:8), and so forth. Although the Old and New Testaments deny any literal similarity of form between God and His creatures (Job 9:32; John 4:24), the Bible frequently uses such human language to help us understand the direct and personal care and activity of God toward His creation and His redeemed people.

However, the appearance of Jesus of Nazareth, God's Son, incarnate in a human body, is the literal, physical revelation of God to us in the form of man. Jesus was "in the form of God," but He took "the form of a servant," the "likeness" and "appearance" of man (Phil. 2:6–8), to save us and reveal the depth of God's love (John 14:9; 1 John 1:1–2). Therefore, with reference to Jesus, we can literally speak of God in human form. Also see God.

ANTICHRIST, THE—a false prophet and evil being who will set himself up against Christ and the people of God in the last days before the *Second Coming. The term is used only in the writings of John in the New Testament. It refers to one who stands in opposition to all that Jesus Christ represents (1 John 2:18, 22; 4:3; 2 John 7). John wrote that several antichrists existed already in his day—false teachers who denied the deity and the Incarnation of Christ—but that the supreme Antichrist of history would appear at some future time.

The Antichrist's primary work is deception, which also characterizes *Satan in his attempts to undermine the work of God in the world. Satan's deception began in the Garden of Eden (Gen. 3) and will continue until the end of time. The Dragon (or Serpent) of Revelation 12 is Satan, the Serpent mentioned in Genesis 3. Thus the thread of Satan's deceptive work may be traced from Genesis through Revelation. That work reaches its climax in the Antichrist—a kind of "incarnate evil"—who will receive his authority and power from the dragon, Satan (Rev. 13:4).

The idea of Satan working through the Antichrist is clearly rooted in the prophecies of Daniel. Daniel spoke of a dreadful beast with ten horns and one little horn (Dan. 7:7–8). The Ancient of Days will kill the beast and throw it in the fire (Dan. 7:11). Then, according to Daniel, one like the Son of Man will receive the everlasting kingdom (Dan. 7:13–14).

The Antichrist will be the sum total of the beasts referred to in Daniel 7 (Rev. 13:1–4). He will speak arrogant, boastful words; and will be aided by a False Prophet, who will make the entire earth worship him (Rev. 13:11–12) and receive his mark (Rev. 13:16–17). The number of the beast, says John, is 666—a mysterious code name.

Those who worship the Antichrist will experience certain doom through the wrath of God (Rev. 14:9–11). The Antichrist makes war against Christ and His army, but he is captured and is "cast alive into the lake of fire burning with brimstone" (Rev. 19:20). He is later joined by the *devil; together they "will be tormented day and night forever and ever" (Rev. 20:10). The devil, the Beast (or Antichrist), and the False Prophet form a kind of unholy trinity, counterfeiting Father, Son, and Holy Spirit. After much wickedness and suffering have been loosed against Christ and His people, the satanic rebellion will be crushed by the power of God.

Although the apostle Paul does not use the term Antichrist, Antichrist seems to be in mind when he writes of the great "falling away" preceding the return of Christ (2 Thess. 2:1–12). The Antichrist is also called the lawless one (v. 9) who, empowered and inspired by Satan, will lead the final rebellion against God (v. 3) but will be destroyed at the coming of the Lord. Paul urges believers to stand firm in the faith and not be deceived by the Antichrist's counterfeit miracles, signs, and wonders (v. 9). The Bible discusses Antichrist not to encourage idle speculation as to *who* he may be, but to avoid *what* he will do. Believers are warned not to be misled by his deceit (Matt. 24:4–5, 23–24). The times when the Antichrist will appear will be very hard for the faithful, and will require discernment and true devotion to Jesus—the true Christ.

ANTITYPE [AN tih type]—derived from the word *tupos* (Greek) "to mark," a *type* is an early picture or figure of a truth or person in the Bible, and the antitype is the answering fulfillment or completion of that earlier truth or person. Baptism in the New Testament, for example, as an expression of one's salvation, fulfills the function served by Noah's ark in the Old Testament. Thus, Noah's ark was a type, and baptism was an antitype (1 Pet. 3:21).

APOCRYPHA, THE [a POCK rih fuh]—a group of books written during a time of turmoil in the history of the Jewish people, from about 200 B.C. to about A.D. 100. These books fall into two main divisions, Old Testament apocryphal books and New Testament apocryphal books.

The Old Testament books, fifteen in number, were written during the period from about 150 B.C. to about A.D. 70, when the Jewish people were in rebellion against the repression of foreign military rulers. These books were excluded from some early versions of the Old Testament but included in others. This explains why Bibles used by Roman Catholics contain the Old Testament Apocrypha, while they are not included in most Protestant editions of the Bible.

The New Testament Apocrypha was written during the second and third centuries A.D., long after the death of the apostles and other eyewitnesses to the life and ministry of Jesus. None of these books were included in the New Testament, judged as not authoritative by officials of the early church. None of these are in either Protestant or Roman Catholic editions of the Bible.

The Old Testament Apocrypha. The series of events that led to the writing of the Old Testament apocryphal books began in 167 B.C., when the Jews revolted against the king of Syria, Antiochus IV Epiphanes. A pious Jewish priest, Mattathias, and his sons led the rebellion. Mattathias refused to obey Antiochus's command that the Jews worship his gods and offer a pagan sacrifice. Mattathias killed the Syrian official as well as a fellow Jew who was offering the sacrifice and declared: " 'Follow me, every one of you who is zealous for the law and strives to maintain the covenant.' He and his sons took to the hills, leaving all their belongings behind in the town" (1 Macc. 2:27–28, NEB).

Guerrilla warfare against the Syrians followed, until the Jews established control of Palestine. Early in the revolt one of the sons of Mattathias, Judas Maccabeus (Maccabeus means "hammer"), cleansed the temple in Jerusalem from the pollution of the Syrian sacrifices. This day has been celebrated annually by the Jews since that time in the festival known as Chanukah (or Hanukkah), the Feast of Dedication (John 10:22).

These events helped stir the Jewish people to rededicate themselves to the Law of Moses. In the fight to establish their independence and uphold their traditions, some Jewish authors wrote to encourage their own people.

This brief historical sketch provides the background for the Old Testament apocryphal writings. Following are brief descriptions of the Old Testament apocryphal collection.

Baruch—This book is a collection of materials written during the period from 150 B.C. to 60 B.C. Set in the period of the prophet Jeremiah and his secretary Baruch around 585 B.C.

Bel and the Dragon—This book is an addition to the Old Testament's Book of Daniel and was written by a Jew in Palestine around 50 B.C., to declare that the God of the Hebrews can outwit the pagan priests of Babylon.

Ecclesiasticus, or the Wisdom of Jesus, Son of Sirach—This is a book of wisdom teachings in the Apocrypha. It should not be confused with the Book of Ecclesiastes in the Old Testament. The word Ecclesiasticus means "The Church Book" in Latin. But the title of the Book of Ecclesiastes comes from a Greek word which means "assembly" or "gathering."

Esdras, Books of—The First Book of Esdras is a historical narrative taken from 2 Chronicles 35:1; 36:23; Ezra 1:1–11; 2:1—3:13; 4:1—10:44; and Nehemiah 7:73—8:12 of the Old Testament.

The Second Book of Esdras was probably written during the same period as the Book of Revelation in the New Testament, around A.D. 95, by a Palestinian Jew who was disillusioned over the destruction of the temple of Jerusalem in A.D. 70.

Esther, Additions to the Book of—The Old Testament Book of Esther does not mention the name of God or any worship rituals, though clearly His sovereignty and the power of vital faith in Him is evident. Most scholars agree that these apocryphal additions to the Book of Esther were an attempt to connect Esther to the traditions of Israel's faith in a more explicit way.

Jeremiah, Epistle of—This letter is a sermon against idolatry, calling its readers to beware of false gods. The date of its writing is uncertain.

Judith—This book contains the story of a wise and intelligent Jewish woman who was devoted to observing the Law of Moses. It was probably written during the Hasmonean period (142–63 B.C.). Judith emphasized the importance of faithfulness to the Law of Moses and the power of God in the lives of His people.

Maccabees, Books of—The First Book of Maccabees is a history of the struggle of the Jews in Judea under the leadership of one family, the Hasmoneans, from about 165 to 76 B.C. Judas Maccabeus was the family's most famous leader. The theme of the book is that faithful obedience to the law brings success by God's standards.

The Second Book of Maccabees is a two-part work that, in a sense, serves as a prelude to the Book of 1 Maccabees. The first part of the book (1:1—2:18) consists of two letters. The second section of the Second Book of Maccabees (2:19—15:40) describes events in Judea from 191 to 162 B.C. A good description of the celebration of Chanukah (Hanukkah) appears in 10:19. The entire book is important because of its teaching that the world was created "out of nothing" (7:28), and its clear statement of belief in the resurrection of the dead (7:9, 14, 23, 29).

Prayer of Azariah and the Song of the Three Young Men—This brief book is included in the Apocrypha because it represents an addition to the Old Testament Book of Daniel. It probably was written about 150 B.C. by a pious Jew who expanded the famous story in Daniel 3 about the three young Hebrews and the fiery furnace.

Prayer of Manasseh—This book is an addition to the Old Testament Book of 2 Chronicles. Manasseh, one of Judah's most wicked kings, repented of his sin, and God forgave him (2 Chr. 33:10–13).

Song of the Three Young Men (see *Prayer of Azariah*).

Susanna—This book is an addition to the Old Testament Book of Daniel. It is full of suspenseful tragedy and wisdom. Written around 110 to 60 B.C. by a Jew in Palestine, the story is about a woman named Susanna, who was nearly sexually abused, brought to court, and sentenced to death until Daniel defended and vindicated her.

Tobit—This book is a narrative about a Jew who was taken captive to Nineveh after the defeat of Israel in 722 B.C. It teaches that God breaks into human history, using His angels to rescue people.

Wisdom of Solomon—This book, along with the Book of Ecclesiasticus in the Apocrypha, is similar to the Book of Proverbs in the Old Testament. It contains proverbs written centuries after Solomon, attributed to him, but probably composed around 100 to 50 B.C.

The New Testament Apocrypha. The New Testament Apocrypha contains several writings that are similar to New Testament books but which were not included as a part of the New Testament. These writings were greatly influenced by the philosophies and religions of the cities or nations out of which they came. Some of the apocryphal gospels were written to replace the Gospels of the New Testament but were declared false writings by officials of the early church. Others present stories and legends meant to fill in information about the apostles and Jesus that is not in the New Testament.

While some are interesting and informative, none are considered authoritative. For various reasons, these books were judged unworthy and were not accepted when the New Testament took its final form in the third century A.D. Thus, God has worked throughout history not only to inspire the Bible but also to preserve its authenticity and integrity so it can serve as a standard and guide for all believers.

APOSTASY—a falling away from the faith. The nation of Israel fell into repeated backslidings (Jer. 5:6, RSV). The prophet Jeremiah predicted the judgment of God upon such disloyalty: "Your wickedness will chasten you, and your apostasy will reprove you" (Jer. 2:19, RSV).

Some of the noted apostates in the Bible are: King Saul, who turned back from following the Lord (1 Sam. 15:11); Hymenaeus and Alexander, who "suffered shipwreck" of their faith (1 Tim. 1:19–20); Demas, who forsook the apostle Paul because he loved this present world (2 Tim. 4:10).

Second Thessalonians 2:3 declares that the day of Christ "will not come unless the apostasy comes first" (NASB). This great apostasy will be the time of "the final rebellion against God, when wickedness will be revealed in human form" (2 Thess. 2:3, NEB).

Apostasy is generally defined as the determined, willful rejection of Christ and His teachings by a Christian believer (Heb. 10:26–29; John 15:22). This is different from false belief, or error, which is the result of ignorance. Some Christian groups teach that apostasy is impossible for those persons who have truly accepted Jesus as Savior and Lord, while others contend the possibility is present as long as one is alive.

APOSTLE—a special messenger of Jesus Christ; a person to whom Jesus delegated authority for certain tasks. The word apostle is primarily used of the twelve disciples Jesus first called "sent" (Mark 3:14, 6:30). These (excepting Judas Iscariot) were recommissioned by Jesus after His resurrection to be His witnesses throughout the world (Luke 24:46–49; Acts 1:8). After the *ascension of Christ, the Eleven brought their number to twelve again as they prayerfully placed Matthias in their ranks (Acts 1:23–26).

The word apostle is also used in the New Testament when delegates of Christian communities were "sent" into extended ministry (2 Cor. 8:23). Jesus also used the word this way when He quoted the proverb, "A servant is not greater than his master; nor he who is sent [literally, "an apostle"] greater than he who sent him" (John 13:16). Jesus Himself is called "the Apostle . . . of our confession" (Heb. 3:1), a reference to His function as God's special Messenger to the world.

The word apostle has a wider meaning in the letters of the apostle Paul. It includes people who, like himself, were not included in the Twelve, but who saw the risen Christ and were specially commissioned by Him. Paul's claim to be an apostle was questioned by others. He based his apostleship, however, on the direct call of the exalted Lord who appeared to him on the Damascus Road and on the Lord's blessing of his ministry in winning converts and establishing churches (1 Cor. 15:10).

Apparently, James, the Lord's brother, was also regarded as an apostle (Gal. 1:19). This James was not one of the Twelve; in fact, he was not a believer in Jesus before the Crucifixion (John 7:5). It was the resurrected Lord who "was seen by James" (1 Cor. 15:7) and presumably commissioned him for his ministry. When Paul says Jesus was seen not only by James but also by "all the apostles" (1 Cor. 15:7), he seems to be describing a wider group than the Twelve to whom Jesus appeared earlier (1 Cor. 15:5).

In 1 Corinthians 12:28 and Ephesians 4:11, apostles are listed along with prophets and other saints as part of the foundation of the household of God. In this strictly New Testament sense, apostles are confined to the first generation of Christians.

In a thoroughly biblical sense, the term apostle is used today of people who are providentially gifted for broader leadership, or who minister as pioneers in the work of making converts and planting churches. However, the authority committed to the first-century apostles by the Lord Jesus Christ was clearly unique, especially with reference to the instrumentality of those who were used to give us the scriptures, their writings which are contained in the closed canon of the New Testament.

APOSTLES. (1 Cor. 12:28) *apostolos* (ap-*os*-tol-oss); *Strong's* #652: A special messenger, a delegate, one commissioned for a particular task or role, one who is sent forth with a message. In the New Testament the word denotes both the original twelve disciples and prominent leaders outside the Twelve. Marvin Vincent records three features of an apostle: (1) one who has had a visible encounter with the resurrected Christ; (2) one who plants churches; (3) one who functions in the ministry with signs, wonders, and miracles.

APPEARS. (Col. 3:4) *phaneroo* (fan-er-*ah*-oh); *Strong's* #5319: To lay bare, reveal, uncover, make visible, make known what has been hidden or unknown, make clear. *Phaneroo* tells us of Christ's appearing, when we see Him in the full expression of His glorious character.

APPOINTED TIME. (Num. 9:2) *mo'ed* (mo-*ed*); *Strong's* #4150: A fixed time, appointment, appointed season, festival, feast, solemn assembly, appointed place. The root of *mo'ed* is the verb *ya'ad*, which means to "set" or "fix," as in setting a time, or fixing a date, or appointing a place for meeting. The first occurrence of *mo'ed* is Genesis 1:14, where the stars and heavenly bodies are created to serve for "seasons" (*mo'adim*) and as "signs." The books of Moses frequently refer to the tent of "meeting"; the best translation of *mo'ed* in those contexts might be "meeting place." *Mo'ed* is used for the seven "feasts" of the Lord (Lev. 23:2), actually Yahweh's seven sacred appointments, the times He meets with Israel. The entire plan of redemption is revealed in the progression of the seven mileposts, which unfold yearly in the Hebrew calendar. Furthermore, every major event in the life of Jesus occurred during one of Israel's seven feasts.

ARAMAIC—see ch. 55, §3.2., 4., 4.2., 4.3.

 ARK OF THE COVENANT—a sacred portable chest which—along with its two related items, the mercy seat and *cherubim—was the most important sacred object of the Israelites during the wilderness period. It was also known as the ark of the Lord (Josh. 6:11), the ark of God (1 Sam. 3:3), and the ark of the Testimony (Ex. 25:22).

The ark of the covenant was the only article of furniture in the innermost room, or Most Holy Place, of Moses' tabernacle and of Solomon's temple. From between the two cherubim that were on the ark of the Testimony, God spoke to Moses. Once a year the high priest could enter the Most Holy Place, but only with sacrificial blood that he sprinkled on the mercy seat for the atonement of sin.

Description. The ark of the covenant was a chest 2½ cubits long, 1½ cubits wide, and 1½ cubits deep (or, in inches, about 45 by 27 by 27), made of acacia wood and overlaid with gold. It had four rings of gold through which carrying poles were inserted (Ex. 37:1–9). These poles were never removed from the rings, apparently to show that the ark was a portable sanctuary. Even when the ark was placed in Solomon's temple, the poles stayed in place, and they could be seen from a certain point outside the inner sanctuary (1 Kin. 8:8).

The ark had a gold cover known as the "mercy seat" (Ex. 25:17–22). The Israelites regarded the ark as the place of God's enthronement in their midst. The mercy seat was a slab of pure gold which fit exactly within the crown of the ark, so the mercy seat would not slide during transportation.

Of one piece with the mercy seat were two angelic figures called cherubim. They stood at opposite ends of the mercy seat, facing each other with wings outstretched above and their faces bowed toward the mercy seat. They marked the place where the Lord said His presence would dwell. It was the place where the Lord communicated with Moses.

Contents. Within the ark were the two stone tablets containing the Ten Commandments (Ex. 25:16, 21), considered to be the basis of the covenant between God and His people Israel. Thus the ark was often called the ark of the covenant or Testimony. The golden pot of manna, which God miraculously preserved as a testimony to future generations (Ex. 16:32–34), was also deposited in the ark. The third item in the ark was Aaron's rod that budded to prove that Aaron was God's chosen (Num. 17:1–11).

While the New Testament states that the ark contained these three items (Heb. 9:4), by the time of the dedication of Solomon's temple, only the tablets remained. "There was nothing in the ark except the two tablets of stone which Moses put there at Horeb" (1 Kin. 8:9).

History. The ark was carried by the sons of Levi during the wilderness wanderings (Deut. 31:9). Carried into the Jordan River by the priests, the ark caused the waters to part so Israel could cross on dry ground (Josh. 3:6—4:18). During the conquest of the land of Canaan, the ark was carried at the fall of Jericho (Josh. 6:4); later it was deposited at Shiloh, which had become the home of the tabernacle (Josh. 18:1).

Superstitiously trusting some magic power of the ark, rather than truly trusting God, some Israelites took the ark into battle against the Philistines and suffered a crushing defeat (1 Sam. 4:1–11). The Philistines captured the ark, but later sent it back when disaster struck their camp (1 Sam. 5–6). It remained at Kirjath Jearim until David brought it to Jerusalem (1 Chr. 13:3–14; 15:1–28). Solomon established it in the Most Holy Place of the temple which he built.

Nothing is known of what became of the ark. It disappeared when Nebuchadnezzar's armies destroyed Jerusalem in 586 B.C., and was not available when the second and third temples were built. In the many synagogues that arose after the captivity, a chest or ark containing the *Torah (scrolls of the Law) and other sacred books was placed in an area shut off from the rest of the building, just as the original ark was placed in the Most Holy Place of the temple.

ARMAGEDDON [ar mah GED un] (*mountain of Megiddo*)—the site of the final battle of this age in which God intervenes to destroy the armies of Satan and cast Satan into the bottomless pit (Rev. 16:16; 20:13). Scholars disagree about the exact location of this place, but the most likely possibility is the valley between

Mount Carmel and the city of Jezreel. This valley (known as the Valley of Jezreel and sometimes referred to as the Plain of Esdraelon) was the crossroads of two ancient trade routes and thus was a strategic military site. Armageddon is the Greek word for this area, which was the scene of many ancient battles.

Because of this history, Megiddo became a symbol of the final conflict between God and the forces of evil. According to the Book of Revelation, at Armageddon "the cup of the wine of the fierceness of His [God's] wrath" (Rev. 16:19) will be poured out, and the forces of evil will be overthrown and destroyed.

ARTAXERXES II—see ch. 55, §3.2.

ASCENSION OF CHRIST—the dramatic departure of the risen Christ from His earthly, bodily ministry among His followers. Since His birth in Bethlehem by the miracle of the *Incarnation, Jesus had lived physically on earth. But forty days after the Resurrection, His earthly ministry ceased with His ascension into heaven (Mark 16:19; Luke 24:50–51; Acts 1:9–11). To a large extent the Ascension was for the benefit of Jesus' followers. They could no longer expect His physical presence. They must now wait for the promised Holy Spirit through whom the work of Jesus would continue.

Jesus' departure into heaven was a literal, physical, bodily ascension in His resurrected body. Stephen and Paul both reported seeing Jesus in bodily form after His ascension (Acts 7:56; 9:27; 1 Cor. 15:8).

The Ascension marked the beginning of Christ's intercession for His followers at the right hand of God. There He makes continual intercession for all believers (Rom. 8:34; Heb. 4:14; 6:20; 7:25). Although Christ is not physically present with His people today, He is no less concerned for them or less active on their behalf. Christians enjoy peace, hope, and security because Christ is their advocate with the Father (1 John 2:1).

It is as the exalted Lord that Jesus sent or "poured out" the Holy Spirit upon His church, with His gifts for believers (John 14:16–18, 26; 16:7–15; Acts 2:23; Eph. 4:11–12). Heaven's strategy determined that the presence of Jesus would be replaced by the presence of the Holy Spirit, who could be everywhere at the same time. Since Pentecost (Acts 2) until today, Jesus' followers now enjoy the presence of the Spirit and the operation of the Spirit's gifts through them, as the church pursues the mission Jesus ordered (Matt. 28:18–20; Acts 1:8).

As a result of His ascension, Jesus exercises His heavenly reign at the right hand of the Father as Lord of the church (1 Cor. 15:20–28). This reign will last until His *Second Coming, when He will return to the earth as the reigning Messiah (Acts 3:20–21), announced as King of kings and Lord of lords (Rev. 19:16).

Finally, the ascension of Christ is the pledge of His Second Coming: "This same Jesus, who was taken up from you into heaven, will so come in like manner as you saw Him go into heaven" (Acts 1:11). Jesus will return to earth—literally and physically—in bodily form just as He ascended into heaven.

Also see Resurrection.

ASHAMED. (Ezek. 16:63) *bush* (*boosh*); *Strong's* #954: To be ashamed, shamed, disappointed, or embarrassed. This verb occurs approximately one hundred times. Among its derivatives are *busha* (shame) and *boshet*, which is translated "shame," but refers to an idol. The idol itself was considered a shame or an embarrassment. An idol also guaranteed that its worshipers would eventually be shamed and greatly disappointed in their choice of an object of worship. *Bosh* is used for the sense of disappointment one experiences when one's hope fails in an embarrassing way; but those who trust in the Lord shall never be ashamed (Ps. 25:2–3; Joel 2:26–27). In the present reference, being ashamed is the result of remembering the path we walked before coming into God's covenant (v. 62) and realizing that our deeds necessitated the atonement.

ASHURBANIPAL—see ch. 55, §2.2.

ASIA MINOR—see ch. 55, §3.4.a.

ASK. (Matt. 7:7) *aiteo* (ahee-*teh*-oh); *Strong's* #154: To request, petition. The word usually describes a suppliant making request of someone in higher position, such as an individual asking something from God (21:22), a subject from a king (Mark 6:25), a child from a parent (Luke 11:11), or a beggar from a person of substance (Acts 3:2). The word denotes insistent asking without qualms, not "commanding" God, but solidly presenting a requisition whose items He longs to distribute.

ASSEMBLY. (Lev. 16:17) *qahal* (kah-*hal*); *Strong's* #6951: A congregation, assembly, company; a multitude that has been "called together." The verb *qahal* which means "to call together, to assemble, to gather together, to convoke." *Qahal* is used in reference to the whole congregation of Israel nearly thirty times in Exodus through Deuteronomy. While the people comprised an actual family or nation, they were also a spiritual congregation. The New Testament word *ekklesia* (a congregation "called together") parallels *qahal*. *Ekklesia* is translated as "church," but "assembly" or "congregation" is more accurate. God's dealing with the *qahal* in the Old Testament prefigures His dealings with His assemblies in the New Testament. Thus the earliest pattern of congregational life is the "church" in the wilderness.

ASSURANCE—the state of being assured; freedom from doubt and uncertainty. As a theological concept, assurance is one of the richest doctrines of the Bible. It refers to the believer's full confidence and conviction that the penalty of his sins has been paid and that heaven has been secured as his eternal destiny by Christ's death and resurrection.

Assurance means that the Christian not only possesses salvation, but that he also knows what he possesses—he is *assured* of this salvation. First John 5:12 speaks of security ("He who has the Son has life") and the following verse speaks of assurance ("you may know that you have eternal life").

The basis of assurance must be beyond our own subjective experience, which can waver with fear, doubt, and uncertainty. True assurance is ultimately founded on the Word of God alone—the Holy Spirit bearing witness to our spirits that the Word of God is true and reliable. When the believer, by faith, stands upon the Word of God (such passages as John 10:27–29 and Romans 8:35–39 speak clearly of the assurance of our faith), he gains a joyous freedom to live the Christian life. He has been forgiven by God in Christ and is now free to forgive others, to love as he has first been loved by God.

Assurance, then, is not only a theological concept but a practical matter. As long as a person is uncertain about his own standing before God, he is defensive and self-centered. But fully assured of God's salvation, the believer can begin to walk in the footsteps of Christ (1 John 4:17–19), and live effectively as a Spirit-filled, living evidence of the vital life of Jesus Christ—ministering to others we meet (Rom. 8:11; Philem. 4–7).

ASSYRIA—see ch. 55, §2.1., 2.2., 3.6., 3.7.d.

ATONEMENT—the act by which God restores a relationship of harmony and unity between Himself and human beings. The word can be broken into three parts which express this great truth in simple but profound terms: "at-one-ment." Through God's atoning grace and forgiveness, we are reinstated to a relationship of restored unity with God, in spite of our sin.

Human Need. Because of Adam's sin (Rom. 5:18; 1 Cor. 15:22) and our own personal sins (Col. 1:21), no person is worthy of relationship with a holy God (Eccl. 7:20; Rom. 3:23). Since we are helpless to correct this situation (Prov. 20:9) and can do nothing to hide our sin from God (Heb. 4:13), we all stand condemned by sin (Rom. 3:19). It is human nature (our sinfulness) and God's nature (His holy separateness from sin) which makes us "enemies" (Rom. 5:10).

God's Gift: Atonement. God's gracious response to the helplessness of His chosen people, the nation of Israel, was to give them a means of *reconciliation through Old Testament covenant Law. This came in the sacrificial system, where the death or "blood" of the animal was accepted by God as a substitute for the death (Ezek. 18:20) which the sinner deserved: "For the life of the flesh is in the blood, and I have given it to you upon the altar to make atonement for your souls" (Lev. 17:11).

The Law required that the sacrificial victims must be free from defect, and giving them always involved some cost to the sinner. But an animal's death did not automatically make a person or the people right with God in some simplistic or mechanical way. The separation between God and man because of sin was and is a dynamic and personal matter. God for His part personally gave the means of atonement in the sacrificial system; humans, for their part, personally were expected to (1) recognize the seriousness of their sin (Lev. 16:29–30; Mic. 6:6–8); and (2) identify themselves personally with the victim that substituted for them (Lev. 1:4). Thus, under the Old Testament, God Himself brought about atonement by graciously providing the appointed sacrifices. The priests represented Him in the atonement ritual, and the sinner received the benefits of being reconciled to God in forgiveness and harmony.

Although Old Testament believers were truly forgiven and received genuine atonement through animal sacrifice, the New Testament clearly states that during the Old Testament period God's justice was not served: "For it is not possible that the blood of bulls and goats could take away sins" (Heb. 10:4). Atonement was possible "because in His forbearance God had passed over the sins that were previously committed" (Rom. 3:25). However, God's justice was served in the death of Jesus Christ as a substitute who "not with the blood of goats and calves, but with His own blood He entered the Most Holy Place once for all, having obtained eternal redemption" (Heb. 9:12). "And for this reason He is the Mediator of the new covenant" (Heb. 9:15).

Our Response. The Lord Jesus came according to God's will (Acts 2:23; 1 Pet. 1:20) "to give His life a ransom for many" (Mark 10:45), or "for all" (1 Tim. 2:6). Though God "laid on Him the iniquity of us all" (Is. 53:6; also 2 Cor. 5:21; Gal. 3:13), yet Christ "has loved us and given Himself for us, an offering and a sacrifice to God" (Eph. 5:2), so that those who believe in Him (Rom. 3:22) might receive atonement and "be saved from [God's] wrath" (Rom. 5:9) through "the precious blood of Christ" (1 Pet. 1:19).

No believer who truly understands the awesome holiness of God's nature or the justice of His wrath for sin, nor any who even slightly fathom the terrible helplessness and hopelessness of man due to our personal sins, can fail to be overwhelmed by the deep love of Jesus for each of us and the wonder of God's gracious gift of eternal atonement through Christ. Through Jesus His Son, God will present us "faultless before the presence of His glory with exceeding joy" (Jude 24).

ATONEMENT (MAKE). (Num. 15:25) *chaphar* (kah-*far*); *Strong's* #3722: To cover, make atonement, make reconciliation; to pacify or appease; to clear, purge, or cleanse. This verb occurs one hundred times. The primary meaning of *chaphar* may be "to cover." The verb is used in Genesis 6:14, where Noah was instructed to cover the ark with pitch. An important derivative is the word *kippur* (atonement), a familiar term due to its use in *Yom Kippur*, the Day of Atonement (*see* Lev. 23:27–28). "Appease" and "make reconciliation" translate *chaphar* in Genesis 32:20 and Daniel 9:24, respectively.

AUTHORITY—the power or right to do something, particularly to give orders and see that they are followed. The word authority as used in the Bible usually means a person's right to do certain things because of the position or office he holds. This word emphasizes the legality and right, more than the physical strength, needed to do something.

The two basic forms of authority are intrinsic authority (belonging to one's essential nature) and derived authority (given to one from another source). Since "there is no authority except from God" (Rom 13:1), every kind of authority other than that of God Himself is derived and therefore secondary to God's power (John 19:11).

God's authority is absolute and unconditional (Ps. 29:10; Is. 40). He has authority over nature (Job 38), governments (Dan. 4:17, 34–35), and history (Acts 1:7; 17:24–31); and He has the power to send people to eternal judgment (Luke 12:5). Jesus Christ has the same intrinsic authority as the Father (John 10:25–30), although this authority is said to

be given to Christ from His Father, just as the authority of the Holy Spirit is given to Him from the Father and the Son (John 14:26; 15:26; 16:13–15). Christ has the authority to forgive sins (John 5:26–27), to lay down His life and take it up again (John 10:17–18), and to give eternal life (John 17:2).

In addition to the intrinsic authority of God, the Bible speaks of many kinds of derived power. Some of the most important of these are the authority of civil governments (Rom. 13:1–7), parents (Eph. 6:1–4), employers (Eph. 6:5–9), church leaders (Heb. 13:7, 17), angels (Luke 1:19–20), Satan (Luke 4:6), and evil spirits other than Satan (Eph. 6:11–12). There are vast differences among these kinds of authority. Some are permitted by God only for a time.

One derived authority is above every other kind of derived authority, and that is the Bible. Because the Bible is inspired by God (2 Tim. 3:16; 2 Pet. 1:20–21), it has divine power and authority. God did not give the Scriptures to be read only, but to be believed and obeyed, and obedience to them releases the holy power within the Word to operate within the believer (James 1:21; 2 Pet. 1:2–4).

Christians are often given certain authority to exercise. This includes the authority of a parent, a church leader, or of the individual believer who ministers in Jesus' name. People were astonished at the authority which Jesus exercised when He taught and performed miracles during His ministry (Matt. 7:28–29, 8:27; Luke 4:36). This same ministry He delegated to His disciples, both during His ministry on earth and beyond it, even until today (Matt. 10:7, 8; John 14:12–14; Mark 16:15–20). The concept of the authority of the believers is rooted in Christ's authority and lordship in the Christian's life. The most noble use of authority is for serving others. "Let . . . he who governs," Jesus said, be "as he who serves. . . . I am among you as the One who serves" (Luke 22:26, 27). The Christian who seeks to follow Christ's example will learn to use authority with others more than over others. The humble believer will remember that all derived authority will one day be returned to the God who gave it and will always function in praiseful dependence (1 Cor. 15:24–28). The rewards of such faithful service will endure throughout eternity (Matt. 25:14–46; 1 John 2:17).

AUTHORITY. (Acts 8:27) *dunastes* (doo-*nahs*-tace); *Strong's* #1413: A high official, an important personage, a court official, one invested with power, a ruler, a sovereign, a prince, a royal minister, a potentate. (Compare "dynasty.") Luke 1:52 suggests that the *dunastes* of the world systems will be replaced by the Prince of Peace. In Acts 8:27, the *dunastes* only exists during the reign of Candace, queen of Ethiopia. Jesus' kingdom is a perpetual *dunastes* without end.

 BAAL. (Hos. 2:8) *ba'al* (*bah*-ahl); *Strong's* #1167: *Ba'al,* literally lord or master; also, possessor, owner, obtainer, and husband. The Israelites sometimes became contaminated with the worship of a false deity of the Canaanites named Baal. *Ba'al* was also the regular word for "husband" or "master," and was used throughout the Old Testament for human husbands or property-owning men (see Ex. 21:22, 28; 22:8; Deut. 22:22; Judg. 9:6–7, 18; Prov. 31:11; Is. 1:3). Because of its use for Canaanite deities and because it implied ownership rather than relationship, God disassociated Himself from use of the term *ba'al,* asking rather to be called *'ishi,* "My Husband" (Hos. 2:16–17). *Also* see ch. 55, §3.4.

 BABBLER. (Acts 17:18) *spermologos* (spermol-*og*-oss); *Strong's* #4691: Athenian slang for: (1) a bird that picks up seeds; (2) men lounging around the marketplace, making a living by picking up whatever falls from the loads of merchandise; (3) a babbler, chatterer, or gossip retailing bits and pieces of misinformation; (4) a pseudo-intellectual who insists on spouting off. Tragically, the super-intellectuals on Mars' Hill failed to see in Paul all the necessary ingredients for being a truth-bringer.

BABYLON, BABYLONIA—see ch. 55, §2.1., 2.2., 3.4.a., 3.6., 3.6.c., 3.7., 3.7.d.

 BABYLON, CITY OF [BAB uh lon]—ancient walled city between the Tigris and Euphrates Rivers and capital of the Babylonian Empire. The leading citizens of the nation of Judah were carried to this city as captives about 586 B.C. after Jerusalem fell to the invading Babylonians. Biblical writers often portrayed this ancient capital of the Babylonian people as the model of paganism and idolatry (Jer. 51:44; Dan. 4:30).

Babylon was situated along the Euphrates River about 485 kilometers (three hundred miles) northwest of the Persian Gulf and about forty-nine kilometers (thirty miles) southwest of modern Baghdad in Iraq. Its origins are unknown, though some associate it with Nimrod's Babel (Gen. 10:9–10). According to Babylonian tradition, it was built by the demon-god Marduk. The city must have been built some time before 2300 B.C., because it was destroyed about that time by an invading enemy king. This makes Babylon one of the oldest cities of the ancient world.

During its early history Babylon became a small independent kingdom, its most famous king being Hammurabi (about 1728–1676 B.C.) who was known for his revision of a code of law. The dynasty which he established came to an end with the conquest of Babylon by the Hittites about 1595 B.C. The Assyrians plundered Babylon about 1250 B.C., but it recovered and flourished for another century until about 1100 B.C.

In 625 B.C. Nabopolassar seized the throne of Babylon. He was succeeded by Nebuchadnezzar II (605–562 B.C.), the greatest king of Babylon, who enlarged the capital city to an area of six square miles and beautified it with magnificent buildings. This period of the city's development has been the focal point of all archaeological research done in ancient Babylon. The city's massive double walls spanned both sides of the Euphrates River. Set into these walls were eight major gates. One of the numerous pagan temples in the city was that of the patron god Marduk, flanked by a *ziggurat or temple-tower.

Babylon's glory reflected the king's imperial power. Captured kings were brought to his court at Babylon. These included the Judean kings Jehoiachin (2 Kin. 24:15) and Zedekiah (2 Kin. 25:7). During the reign of Nabonidus (555–539 B.C.), while Belshazzar was co-regent (Daniel 5), the city surrendered to the Persians without opposition.

Eventually the balance of power passed from the Persians to Alexander the Great of Greece, to whom Babylon willingly submitted in 331 B.C. Alexander planned to refurbish and expand the city and make it his capital, but he died before accomplishing these plans.

In the Old Testament the prophetic books of Isaiah and Jeremiah predicted the downfall of the city of Babylon. This would happen as God's punishment of the Babylonians because of their destruction of Jerusalem and their deportation of the citizens of Judah (Is. 14:22; 21:9; 43:14; Jer. 50:9; 51:37). Today the ruins of this ancient city stand as an eloquent testimony to the passing of proud empires and to the providential hand of God in history.

In the Book of Revelation, Babylon is the term used to describe the carnal, corrupt and

---

 This icon beside an entry indicates a Word Wealth feature.

 This icon beside an entry indicates a Kingdom Dynamics feature.

 This icon beside an entry indicates an important biblical or doctrinal term.

demonically dominated systems of the world, politically, economically, morally, and spiritually, all of which comes to eventual judgment and destruction (Revelation 17—18).

 BACKSLIDE—to revert to sin or wrongdoing; to lapse morally or in the practice of spiritual obedience and responsibility. "Backsliding" is a term found mainly in the Book of Jeremiah (2:19; 31:22; 49:4), where the prophet refers to the lapse of the nation of Israel into paganism and idolatry. These texts stand as a timeless reminder of the capacity of God's people to forget His grace and neglect His ways.

BACKSLIDINGS. (Jer. 5:6) *meshubah* (meh-shoo-*vah*); *Strong's* #4878: Turning back, turning away; defecting; faithlessness, apostasy, disloyalty; reverting, backsliding. This noun is found twelve times in the Old Testament, nine times in Jeremiah alone. The three other references are in Proverbs 1:32 and Hosea 11:7 and 17:4. The root word is *shub*, a verb which means to "turn, return, or repent." If repentance is a "turning around," backsliding is a "turning back," or "turning away" from God. God gave a merciful invitation to the backslider in Jeremiah 3:12–15, 22. In this latter verse, God regards backsliding as a condition that requires healing.

BAPTISM—a ritual commanded by Christ to be practiced in the church (Matt. 28:18–20; Mark 16:15–16). It is applied in various forms by different denominations and branches of the Christian church. Baptism involves the application of water to the body of a person. It is essentially an action of obedient response to Christ's lordship, following repentance and faith (Acts 2:38–39). It is frequently seen as the act by which the believer enters the fellowship of the church. While widely differing interpretations of the act exist among Christian groups who have different views on the nature of baptism, the importance of this practice should never be minimized in the light of Christ's command.

The nature of baptism. Four positions on the nature of baptism and the early church's practice (Acts 2:41; 8:12, 36–39; 9:18; 10:48; etc.) exist among Christian groups.

The sacramental view—According to this belief, baptism is a means by which God conveys grace. By undergoing this rite, the person baptized receives remission of sins, and is regenerated or given a new nature and an awakened or strengthened faith. Both Roman Catholics and Lutherans have this view of the nature of baptism, born of their interpretation of John 3:5.

The traditional Roman Catholic belief emphasizes the rite itself—that the power to convey grace is contained within administration of the sacrament of baptism. The Lutheran view concentrates on the faith that is present in the person being baptized; awakened faith due to the preaching of the Word of God.

The convenantal view—Some other Christian groups view baptism as a sign and seal of God's covenant, or God's pledge to save man. That is, because of what He has done and what He has promised, God forgives and regenerates. Thus, on the one hand, baptism is a sign of the covenant; on the other, it is the means by which people enter into that covenant and its benefits are obtained.

In the covenantal view, baptism serves the same purpose for New Testament believers that circumcision did for Old Testament believers, these two procedures being linked in Colossians 2:11–12.

The symbolical view—This view stresses the symbolic nature of baptism by emphasizing that baptism does not cause an inward change or alter a person's relationship to God in any way, but is a token or outward indication of an inner change already occurred in the believer's life. It serves as a public testimony.

This position explains that the church practices baptism and the believer submits to it because Jesus commanded that this be done and He gave us the example by being baptized Himself. Thus, baptism is an act of obedience, commitment, and proclamation (Matt. 28:18–20; Mark 16:15, 16).

The dynamic view—Increasing numbers of Christians see elements of truth in other viewpoints, but find their focus on the power (dynamic) inherent in the Holy Spirit's presence at baptism. While repentance and faith must precede the moment, and new birth has been experienced, water baptism is seen as a moment (1) at which a breaking of past bonds to sin may be severed, as Israel's oppressors were defeated—1 Cor. 10:2; (2) when a commitment to separate from the past life of carnal indulgence is made, as circumcision symbolized—Col. 2:11–15; and (3) when the fullness or overflowing of the Holy Spirit's power may be added to enhance the believer's power for witness and ministering (Acts 2:38, 39). This position sees baptism as both a witness and as an encounter. It is symbolic (burial to the past—Rom. 6:3–4) but it is also releasing and empowering for the future.

The subjects of baptism. Christian groups differ as to who should be baptized. Should only those who have come to a personal, conscious decision of faith be baptized? Or, should children be included in this rite? And if children are proper subjects, should all children, or only the children of believing parents, or only children professing personal faith, be baptized?

Infant baptism—Groups that practice baptism of infants baptize not only infants but also adults who have come to faith in Christ. An argument in favor of baptizing infants is that entire households were baptized in New Testament times (Acts 16:15, 33). Some conclude these households must have included children; consequently this practice should be extended to the present day.

A second argument cited is Jesus' treatment of children. Jesus commanded the disciples to bring the children to Him. When they did so, He blessed them (Mark 10:13–16). Because of this example from Jesus, it would seem inconsistent to deny baptism to children today. Interestingly, this same text is the grounds quoted by those who will baptize a child, but only one old enough to have made a personal profession of faith in Jesus.

A third argument put forth by covenant theologians is that children were participants in the Old Testament covenant (Gen. 17:7). Since baptism has now replaced circumcision, these say it seems proper that it should be administered to children, according to those who practice infant baptism.

Those who believe in baptismal regeneration (Catholics especially) argue that baptism of infants is necessary. In traditional Roman Catholic teaching, unbaptized infants who die cannot enter heaven in this state, but are instead consigned to a state of limbo. If this fate is to be avoided, they must be baptized in order to remove the guilt of their sins and receive new life.

Most of the Lutheran tradition would apply baptism only to children of believers, and are careful to emphasize that this whole area of belief is a mystery, known only to God.

Regarding the matter of baptizing infants, the most generous Christian view seems to be in the willingness of many to (1) honor the concerns that prompt infant baptism, and not denigrate the practice, and (2) emphasize the need for personal faith in Jesus Christ, at the earliest possible age of understanding, faith, and repentance.

Believer's baptism—Those who hold to this view believe that baptism should be restricted to those who actually exercise faith. This approach excludes babies or infants, who could not possibly have such faith, but in many cases receives children. The proper candidates for baptism are those who have already experienced the new birth on the basis of their personal faith and who give evidence of this salvation in their lives.

Both positive and negative arguments are advanced in support of this view. The positive approach argues from evidence in the New Testament. In every instance of New Testament baptism in which the specific identity of the persons was known, the persons being baptized were adults. Further, the condition required for baptism was personal, conscious faith; without this, adherents of believer's baptism point out, baptism was not administered. This is especially evident in the Book of Acts (2:37–41; 8:12; 10:47; 18:8; 19:4–5), as well as Matthew 3:2–6 and 28:19. In the New Testament church repentance and faith came first, followed by baptism.

The form of baptism. A final major issue is the method or form of baptism—whether by immersion, pouring, or sprinkling. On this issue, Christian groups organized into two major camps—those which insist upon the exclusive use of immersion, and those which permit and practice other forms.

The immersionist position—This group insists that immersion is the only valid form of baptism. Their position revolves around the Greek word for baptism in the New Testament. Its predominant meaning is "to immerse" or "to dip," implying that the candidate was plunged beneath the water. In addition, the circumstances involved in some of the biblical descriptions of baptism imply immersion. Thus, John the Baptist was baptizing in Aenon near Salim, "because there was much water there" (John 3:23). Jesus apparently went down into the water to be baptized by John (Matt. 3:16). The Ethiopian said, "See, here is water. What hinders me from being baptized?" (Acts 8:36).

The symbolism involved in baptism also seems to argue that immersion was the biblical mode, according to those groups that practice immersion exclusively. Romans 6:4–6 identified baptism with the believer's death (and burial) to sin and resurrection to new life, as well as the death and resurrection of Christ. Only immersion adequately depicts this meaning, according to the immersionist position.

Further strong evidence suggests that immersion was the form of baptism used in the early church. The *Didache*, a manual of Christian instruction written in A.D. 110–120, stated that immersion should be used generally and that other forms of baptism should be used only when immersion was not possible.

The pluralistic position—Holders of this view believe that immersion, pouring, and sprinkling are all appropriate forms of baptism. They point out that the Greek word for baptism in the New Testament is sometimes ambiguous in its usage. While its most common meaning in classical Greek was to dip, to plunge, or to immerse, it also carried other meanings as well. Thus, the question cannot be resolved upon linguistic grounds.

These groups also argue from inference that immersion must not have been the exclusive method used in New Testament times. For example, could John have been physically capable of immersing all the persons who came to him for baptism? Did the Philippian jailer leave his jail to be baptized? If not, how would he have been immersed? Was enough water for immersion brought to Cornelius' house? Or, did the apostle Paul leave the place where Ananias found him in order to be immersed?

Those groups that use sprinkling or pouring also point out that immersion may not be the best form for showing what baptism really means. They see the major meaning of baptism as purification. They point out that the various cleansing ceremonies in the Old Testament were performed by a variety of means—immersion, pouring, and sprinkling (Mark 7:4; Heb. 9:10). Others note the close association between baptism and the outpouring of the Holy Spirit, which was from above. Thus, in their view, true baptism required the symbolism of pouring rather than immersion.

Again, the most generous-spirited among Christians accept the validity of baptism when living faith in Christ is present, irrespective of the form of baptism employed. *Also* see ch. 55, §5.5., 6.

BAPTISM. (Matt. 21:25) *baptisma* (*bap*-tis-mah); *Strong's #908:* From the verb *baptizo*, "to dip, immerse." *Baptisma* emphasizes the result of the act rather than the act itself. In Christian baptism the stress is on the baptized person's identification with Christ in death, burial, and resurrection. The word describes the experience of a convert from initial acceptance of Christ to initiation into the Christian community.

BAR KOCHBA—see ch. 55, §4.3.

BEAUTY. (Ezek. 28:12) *yophi* (yoh-*fee*); *Strong's #3308:* Beauty, splendor, brightness, fairness; perfect in physical form; flawless in symmetry. *Yophi* is derived from the verb *yaphah*, "to be beautiful, lovely, fair, and graceful." *Yophi* occurs eighteen times in the Old Testament, and one-half of these occurrences are in Ezekiel. In the present reference, the king of Tyre is described as being "perfect in beauty" at his origin. In Ezekiel 16:14–15, the beauty that God bestowed upon Israel was so extraordinary that it became famous throughout the world. Zion is called "the perfection of beauty" (Ps. 50:2). The most beautiful sight in Scripture is the messianic King's enjoying His rightful reign without end (Is. 33:17).

BEEN DONE. (John 3:21) *ergazomai* (er-gad-zom-ahee); *Strong's #2038:* Compare "energy." To work, be busy, accomplish something, carry on a trade, produce things, be engaged in, toil, perform, to do business. *Ergazomai* is the opposite of idleness, laziness, or inactivity.

BEHISTUN INSCRIPTION—see ch. 55, §2.2., 3.2.

BELIEVE, BELIEVERS—to place one's trust in God's truth; one who takes God at His word and trusts in Him for salvation. According to the Bible, mere intellectual assent to God's truth does not in or of itself constitute saving faith. (John 8:31–46; Acts 8:13–24; James 2:14–26). Neither is it the human action of "total commitment" to Jesus as Lord that is the essence of saving faith. Each of the above rely too much on the *act* of belief, as opposed to the *object* of belief—Jesus Christ. These observations also reach beyond the biblical call for faith as the means of receiving the "gift" of salvation (John 4:1–42; Eph. 2:8–10). The mind, the will, and the actions are certainly important in responding to God, but in the final analysis, it is the *heart* that believes (Rom. 10: 9–10). The belief that saves is one that rests in the finished work of Jesus Christ; it trusts God alone for salvation (John 3:16). Believers are those who have trusted God with all their "heart"—that is, the affection, devotion and desire (Rom. 10:10; Mark 12:30). Such simple faith, trust, and belief receive of and enter into the provision of "the power of God unto salvation." (Rom. 1:16; 3:21–22). Some of the classic New Testament references dealing with belief, or faith, are John 3:16, 36; Acts 16:31; Rom. 3:25—5:1; Gal. 2:16; Eph. 2:8–10; and 1 John 5:1. Such delineative analysis as made here is an effort at focusing a clear understanding on the fact that faith in Christ is centered in *HIM*; acknowledging Him, loving Him, resting in Him. Let all rejoice in *His* gift of life.

BELIEVE. (2 Chr. 20:20) *'aman* (ah-*mahn*); *Strong's #539:* To be firm, stable, established; also, to be firmly persuaded; to believe solidly. In its causative form *'aman* means "to believe," that is, to "consider trustworthy." This is the word used in Genesis 15:6, when Abraham "believed" in the Lord. Here in 2 Chronicles *'aman* appears three times in one verse and could be translated: "Be established in the LORD, . . . and you will be established." From *'aman* comes *'emunah*, "faith." The most famous derivative is "amen," which conveys this idea: "It is solidly, firmly, surely true and verified and established." *Also* (Rom. 10:9) *pisteuo* (pist-*yoo*-oh); *Strong's #4100:* The verb form of *pistis*, "faith." It means to trust in, have faith in, be fully convinced of, acknowledge, rely on. *Pisteuo* is more than credence in church doctrines or articles of faith. It expresses reliance upon and a personal trust that produces obedience. It includes submission and a positive confession of the lordship of Jesus.

BENEDICTION—a prayer of blessing, that God may bestow certain kindnesses upon His people. In Old Testament times, a regular part of the Temple service was pronouncing the benediction. The form of the priestly benediction was prescribed in the Law:

> "The LORD bless you and keep you;
> The LORD make His face shine upon you,
> And be gracious to you;
> The LORD lift up His countenance upon
>   you,
> And give you peace" (Num. 6:24–26).

The so-called apostolic benediction is often used at the conclusion of a Christian worship service: "The grace of the Lord Jesus Christ, and the love of God, and the communion of the Holy Spirit be with you all. Amen" (2 Cor. 13:14).

BIBLE, INTERPRETATION OF, OR HERMENEU-TICS—the science, art, spiritual practice of biblical study and interpretation. Correct Bible study interpretation should answer the question, "How do I understand what this particular passage means?" Because there are rules which govern its use, it is a science. Because knowing the rules is not enough, it also is an art. Because the Bible is not a mere *human* resource, it is a *spiritual practice*. This practice needs to be applied to learn how to use the rules of Bible study and interpretation.

The question of how to interpret the Bible is not a minor issue. If Satan has a list of what he does not want us to do, Bible study is at the top, along with prayer and worship. Through study of Scripture we learn who Jesus is and are enabled to become like Him. How can we become like Him, if we do not know what He is like? Devotional studies are important, but they must result from a serious study of Scripture. The apostle Paul prayed that the Colossians might be "filled with the knowledge of His will in all wisdom and spiritual understanding" (Col. 1:9).

Knowing Scripture and obeying it are the twin foundations of a godly life. A Holy Spirit-filled life produces the further desire to study God's Word. Bible study and the application of its meaning, therefore, takes the student from study to application, back to study, and on to further application, in a mounting spiral toward God in devotion and toward mankind in service and witness. Satan's attempt to take away our desire to study Scripture is nothing less than an attempt to remove the basis of our spiritual growth and stability.

The basic principles of Bible study. Four basic principles are at the heart of a sound method of biblical interpretation.

1. Because Scripture is a divine Book, and because of our limitation as humans, prayer is an absolute necessity as we study the Bible. Paul teaches that the non-Christian and the spiritually immature Christian are limited in their ability to know Christian things (1 Cor. 2:14–3:3). Therefore, we must pray that God will bridge the gap that separates us from understanding spiritual things, by having the Holy Spirit teach us (John 14:26; 16:13). Without this illumination or insight from God's Spirit, we cannot learn. This need for insight was the concept Paul referred to when he told Timothy to "reflect on what I am saying, for the Lord will give you insight into all this" (2 Tim. 2:7, NIV).

2. The Bible is also a human book and, to a degree, must be interpreted like any other book. This brings us to the principle of common sense. For example, the grammatical-historical method of studying the Bible instructs us to look at the passage carefully to see what it says literally, and to understand a biblical statement in light of its historical background. We understand a historical statement as a straightforward statement and do not change its literal, grammatical sense. This is "common sense." Using the common sense principle, under the control of the Holy Spirit, is a valid principle of interpreting the Bible.

3. The primary rule of biblical interpretation is "context." The context refers to (1) the setting of the verse or passage, the surrounding verses and their subject matter, and (2) the historical or social setting in which the event happened or the words were spoken. When allowed to speak for itself within the context of the paragraph, chapter, or book, the Bible itself will prevent the majority of all possible errors in interpretation.

A challenge at this point is avoiding our own bias, or our subjectivity. We might be tempted to approach a passage thinking we already understand it, and in the process read our own meaning *into* the passage. (This is called *eisegesis*—*Eis* is a Greek preposition meaning "into.") But to interpret the Bible correctly is to humbly seek the Lord and listen to what the Holy Spirit Himself has breathed into the text—to find what the text itself is saying, and then draw the meaning *out of* the passage. (This is called *exegesis—Ex* is a Greek preposition meaning "out of.") If we allow a passage to be basically defined by what it and the surrounding verses say, then we have taken a large step toward interpreting the Bible properly.

4. Four key words—*observation, interpretation, evaluation,* and *application*—are the heart of all approaches to finding out what the Bible means. They provide the structure of what questions you ask of the text, and when. *Observation:* Do I understand the basic facts of the passage such as the meaning of all the words? *Interpretation:* What did the author mean in his own historical setting? *Evaluation:* What does this passage mean in today's culture? *Application:* How can I apply what I have learned to how I live my life?

We should remember that just as a biblical passage can be set in its culture, so the interpreter is likewise controlled to some extent by his own culture. Many people today do not believe that the biblical accounts of miracles are true. For example, some scholars argue that miracles were a part of first century culture and were believed by people in Jesus' day. But this is the 20th century and people do not believe in miracles in this culture. But these scholars' views on the impossibility of the supernatural are likewise influenced by the materialistic, science-oriented culture in which they live. We must be careful about allowing our own culture to influence our view of Scripture.

Above all, humility and an openness to the Holy Spirit are fundamental to "hearing the Word of God" when you read and study it. Rules of interpretation are *not* to inhibit this, but to help us avoid the mistakes of those who, through history, have used the Bible recklessly unto their own shipwreck of faith and holy living; or to guard against any who would mishandle the Word and submit themselves to error.

In interpreting the Bible, we must remember from Whom it comes. We are handling the Lord's message, given by the Holy Spirit for our illumination. This calls for an attitude of humble respect and for our willingness to subject ourselves to its truth, its authority, and its call to holiness and love.

BIBLICAL CRITICISM—the application of one or more techniques of literary analysis in the scientific study of the Bible. These techniques are not only used to examine the Bible; they would be equally helpful in the study of any ancient writings—for example, Homer or Shakespeare. The primary intention in literary criticism is to validate the authenticity of the text—that is, to verify the trustworthiness of ancient manuscripts—and to assist our understanding of the meaning and use of ancient words. For that reason biblical criticism examines the Greek and Hebrew texts (textual criticism), the historical setting of the various parts of the Bible (historical criticism), and various literary questions regarding how, when, where, and why the books of the Bible were first written (literary criticism). These methods of study, when done with reverence for Scripture, should assist a student's appreciation for the *inspiration of the Bible.

Generally, two schools of approach are acknowledged—lower criticism and higher criticism. Neither are superior in scholarship, but higher criticism tends to take a lower view of the spiritual source of the Bible, while lower critics stand for the divine inspiration of the Scriptures. Thus, higher critics introduce seemingly endless speculations about the Bible's source and meaning, contributing to cynicism and doubt about the authority of God's Word. In contrast, scholars of the lower school (unwilling to vaunt human pride above the Spirit of God's Word) study with equal skill and diligence. Their pursuits bear the fruit of an accurate text distilled from carefully examined manuscripts, and they also provide insight, evidence, and an intellectually sound defense against the irreverent judgments of some higher critics.

There are three areas of biblical criticism: textual, historical, and literary.

Textual criticism: the attempt to determine, as accurately as possible, the wording of the text of the Bible as first written down under the inspiration of the Holy Spirit. Since none of the original documents has survived and the text is available only in copies, it is necessary to compare the early copies with each other. This allows the textual critic to classify these early copies into groups exhibiting certain common features and to decide why any differences occurred and what the original wording most likely was.

The early copies on which textual critics work consist mainly of manuscripts in the original languages, translations into other languages, and biblical quotations made by Jewish and Christian writers. (Also see Bible, Interpretation of.)

Historical criticism: the examination of the Bible in light of its historical setting. This is particularly important because the Bible was written over a period of more than one thousand years. The story the Bible records extends from the beginning of civilization in the ancient world to the Roman Empire of the first century A.D.

Historical criticism is helpful in determining when the books of the Bible were written. It is also helpful in determining a book's "dramatic date"—that is, when the people it describes lived and its events happened. The dramatic date of Genesis, for instance, is much earlier than the date when it was written. Historical criticism asks if the stories of the patriarchs—Abraham, Isaac, Jacob, and Joseph—reflect the conditions of the times in which they lived.

The consensus is positive; these stories better reflect their dramatic date than the dates of their writing, just as the picture presented in the New Testament best reflects what is known about the early part of the first century A.D.

Literary criticism: the study of how, when, where, and why the books of the Bible were written. Literary criticism may be divided into questions concerning sources, tradition, redaction, and authorship.

1. *Source criticism* attempts to determine whether the writers of the books of the Bible used earlier sources of information and, if so, whether those sources were oral or written. Some biblical books clearly indicate their dependence on earlier sources: 1 and 2 Chronicles, Luke, and Acts. Some of the sources for the Chronicles are still available to us in 1 and 2 Samuel and 1 and 2 Kings, which were written earlier. The author of Luke and Acts says that much of his information was handed on by "those who from the beginning were eyewitnesses and ministers of the word" (Luke 1:2).

However, these sources usually have not survived independently and their identification and reconstruction cannot be certain. It is fairly clear, however, that the Gospels of Matthew, Mark, and Luke draw on common sources; their two most widely agreed sources are one that related the story of Jesus and one that contained a collection of His teachings.

2. *Tradition criticism* (including form criticism) studies how information was passed from one generation to another before it was put in its present form. Tradition is simply that which is handed down; it may be divinely authoritative, or it may be merely "the tradition of men" (Mark 7:8; Col. 2:8). Sometimes a tradition was handed on by word of mouth for several generations before it was written down, as in the record of the patriarchs in Genesis. Sometimes a tradition was handed on by word of mouth for only twenty or thirty years, as in the records of the works and words of Jesus before the Gospels were written.

Tradition criticism attempts to trace the stages by which these traditions were handed down, the forms which they took at those various stages, and the forms in which they reached the people who committed them to writing.

Classifying sections of the Bible according to the form they take can provide an additional perspective from which one can better understand the text of Scripture. However, this method must be used with great caution and restraint to avoid imposing the critic's own assumptions on the Bible.

3. *Redaction criticism* attempts to understand the contribution to the finished manuscript made by the person who finally committed the oral or written traditions to writing. This may be illustrated from the Gospel of Luke. Luke makes no claim to have been an eyewitness of the events of Jesus' ministry; everything he records in the Gospel was received from others. Tradition criticism studies what Luke received and the state in which he received it. Redaction criticism studies what he did with what he received. Luke (and the same can be said of the other evangelists) was a responsible author who set the stamp of his own personality on what he wrote.

It is important to remember that an author's personal contribution to the finished book was no less reliable (and, hence, no less authoritative) than the tradition which he received. Unfortunately, some redaction critics make the error of assuming that the author's work is inauthentic, ignoring the work of the Holy Spirit in inspiriting the writers of the Bible.

4. *Authorship and destination criticism* involve the attempt to determine the authorship of a work, as well as the person, group, or wider public for whom it was written. Sometimes there is no need for inquiry into these matters; Paul's letter to the Romans, for example, is clearly the work of the apostle Paul and was sent by him to the Christians in Rome. But the judicious use of literary criticism will throw further light on the circumstances which led to the writing of the book and the purpose for which Romans was sent. When, however, a work is anonymous, critical inquiry may help us to discover what sort of person the author was. For example, we do not know for certain who wrote the letter to the Hebrews. However, by looking critically at Hebrews we can learn much about the character of the author and a little about the character and situation of the people to whom the letter was written.

In all, the field of biblical criticism is an honest enterprise serving the health of the believing community. The passing of centuries and the study of Bible texts, transmitted from generation, has only deepened the evidence for the fact that we have in hand a trustworthy text, divinely protected from error or human confusion.

BIBLICAL ETHICS—the study of the Word of God to examine the revelation of Scripture and the logical reasoning undergirding its call to live righteously; to do what is good and to refrain from what is evil, in accordance with the will of God. The term refers not to human theories or opinions about what is right and wrong but to God's revealed truth about these matters. Questions of human conduct prevail throughout the Bible. God's revelation through His written Word narrates the story of man's ethical failure, God's redeeming grace, and the ethical renewal of His people.

God's people are called to holiness because they are God's people: "You shall therefore be holy, for I am holy" (Lev. 11:45). The New Testament counterpart to this principle is found in Matthew 5:48: "Therefore you shall be perfect, just as your Father in heaven is perfect."

For the Christian the ultimate standard of ethics is Jesus Christ and His teachings. The Christian is not under the Law of the Old Testament (Eph. 2:14–16). But since the ethical teachings of Jesus sum up the true meaning of the Old Testament Law, following His teachings fulfills the Law. So there is a direct relationship between the concept of righteousness as revealed in the Old Testament and later in the New.

Jesus' commandment to love is the essence of Christian ethics (Matt. 22:37–40; Rom. 13:9–10).

While love is the summary of Christian ethics, the New Testament contains many specific ethical instructions. A basic pattern for this ethical teaching is the contrast between our old existence before faith in Christ and our new existence in Him. Christians are called to leave behind their old conduct and to put on the new (Eph. 4:22–24), to walk in newness of life (Rom. 6:4), and to exhibit the fruit of the Spirit (Gal. 5:22–23).

Although as Christians we are free from the Law, we are not to use that liberty "as an opportunity for the flesh, but though love" to "serve one another" (Gal. 5:13). Love is best expressed through service and self-giving (Matt. 20:26–27). These points lead naturally to the observation that Jesus Himself is the supreme example of righteousness. Christian ethics are summed up not only in His teaching, but in His life as well. Thus true disciple-

ship consists of following Jesus (Eph. 5:2) and being conformed to His image (Rom. 8:29).

The ethics of the Bible are for the people of God. The Sermon on the Mount is for disciples of Christ. As Christians follow biblical ethics, the world will be affected for good by them.

Also see Holy.

BINDING AND LOOSING—a phrase describing the authority and power that Jesus assigned to His disciples, allowing them to forbid or allow certain kinds of conduct.

This phrase occurs only twice in the New Testament. The first is in Matthew 16:19: Jesus gave "the keys of the kingdom of heaven," saying "whatever you (may) bind on earth will be bound [literally, "shall have already been bound"] in heaven, and whatever you (may) loose on earth will be loosed ["shall have already been loosed"] in heaven."

The second is in Matthew 18:18, where the same words are spoken by Jesus to all the disciples, granting them authority in matters of church discipline and administering the spirit of forgiveness (see also John 20:21–23; Matt. 6:12, 14–15).

Three truths are revealed in these texts. (1) The whole of the passage in Matthew 16:13–19 relates this practice to the ministry of the believer through the age-long era during which Christ shall be building His church. The "gates" (power, authorities, strategies) of hell will be encountered, and Jesus is delegating spiritual authority to His own, to quell or to dispatch the enterprises of the Adversary. (2) The grounds of this delegated authority are established in the finished work of the Cross. The tense of the verbs reveal that what we may exercise of authority is based on something that has already been accomplished (see Matt. 28:18; Col. 2:14, 15; Rev. 1:18). (3) Hereby, the privileged-by-grace responsibility of the believer is magnified. Jesus has conferred authority which, righteously exercised through prayer, intercession, and godly relationships, become the "keys" of introducing God's divine will (kingdom) into earthly situations. The Savior's words made clear that "heaven's" side of these issues is settled and determined, but for the "earth" side of many matters to realize heaven's intent, the humble yet authoritative action of believers must be effected to appropriate God's divine will.

BIRTHRIGHT, ESAU'S, AND JACOB—see ch. 55, §3.5.b.

BISHOP—in New Testament usage, an overseer, elder, or pastor charged with the oversight—*cpi* (over) *scopos* (see)—or responsibility of spiritual leadership in a local church.

Before the church was founded, the Greek word for bishop was used in a general sense to refer to pagan gods as those who watched over people or countries. The word later was applied to men, including those who held positions as magistrates or other government offices, and eventually was extended to refer to officials in religious communities with various functions, including those who supervised the revenues of pagan temples.

The Septuagint (Greek translation of the Old Testament) uses bishop to refer to those who exercise power; sometimes it indicates those who hold positions of authority. It represents a Hebrew term that refers to those who are overseers or officers (Num. 4:16; Neh. 9:9).

In Acts 20:17, 27 and Titus 1:5, 7, the terms bishop and elder are used synonymously. Also the word bishop, or its related words, appears to be synonymous with the word shepherd, or its equivalents (Acts 20:28; 1 Pet. 2:25; 5:2). In the New Testament, Jesus is called the "Overseer of your souls" (i.e. Bishop) (1 Pet. 2:25). In this passage the word is associated with the term shepherd. It is also used in Acts 20:28 to identify the elders of the church at Ephesus summoned to meet Paul. Their responsibility, given by the Holy Spirit, was "to shepherd the church of God." In Philippians 1:1, bishops are acknowledged with deacons, and the qualifications of these two offices are outlined in 1 Timothy 3:2–7 and Titus 1:7–9. Included are standards for his personal and home life, as well as the bishop's relationships with non-believers.

In his work, the bishop was to oversee the flock of God, to shepherd his people, to protect them from enemies, and to teach, exhort, and encourage. He was to accomplish this primarily by being an example to his people. He was to do this willingly and with an eager spirit, not by coercion or for financial gain. To desire a position as bishop, the apostle Paul declared, was to desire a good work (1 Tim. 3:1). Also see Elder.

BLASPHEMOUS. (Acts 6:11) *blasphemos* (*blas*-fay-moss); *Strong's #989:* Compare "blasphemy" and "blasphemous." From *blapto*, "to injure," and *pheme*, "speech"; hence, slanderous, abusive speech.

BLASPHEMY—the act of cursing, slandering, reviling, or showing contempt or lack of reverence for God. In the Old Testament, blaspheming God was a serious crime punishable by death (Lev. 24:15–16). It was a violation of the Third Commandment, which required that the name and reputation of the Lord be upheld (Ex. 20:7).

The unbelieving Jews of Jesus' day charged Him with blasphemy because they thought of Him only as a man while He claimed to be God's Son (Matt. 9:3). Actually, the lawlessness of the Jews themselves was causing God's name to be blasphemed among the Gentiles (Rom. 2:24). By their bitter opposition to Jesus and His gospel, they themselves were guilty of blasphemy (Acts 18:6). Jesus condemned as blasphemy their attributing the work of the Holy Spirit to Satan (Matt. 12:31–32).

Christians are commanded to avoid behavior that blasphemes the Lord's name and teaching (1 Tim. 6:1).

BLEMISH (WITHOUT). (Lev. 23:12) *tamim* (tah-*meem*); *Strong's #8549:* Unblemished, perfect, complete, full, upright, sincere, spotless, whole, healthy, blameless. This word first appears in Genesis 6:9: Noah was "perfect" in his generations. In Genesis 17:1, God tells Abram to walk before Him and be "blameless." *Tamim* is also used to describe animals fit for sacrifice, without blemish. The root verb *tamam* means "to finish, use up, accomplish, be spent, be completed." The dominant thought in all ninety occurrences of *tamim* is of someone or something complete, unblemished, and upright.

BLESS, BLESSING—the act of declaring, or extending-through-pronouncement, God's favor and goodness upon others. The significance in a righteously administered blessing is not only the good effect of words upon the hearer, but in the fact that the Holy Spirit will endow the words with the power to bring them to pass. In the Bible, important persons blessed those with less power or influence. The patriarchs pronounced benefits upon their children, often near their own deaths (Gen. 49:1–28). Even if spoken by mistake, once a blessing was given it could not be taken back (Genesis 27).

Leaders often blessed people, especially when getting ready to leave them. These included Moses (Deuteronomy 33), Joshua (Josh. 22:6–7), and Jesus (Luke 24:50). Equals could bless each other by being friendly (Gen. 12:3). One can also bless God, showing gratitude to Him (Deut. 8:10) in songs of praise (Ps. 103:1–2).

God also blesses people by giving life, riches, fruitfulness, or plenty (Gen. 1:22, 28). His greatest blessing is turning us from evil (Acts 3:25–26) and forgiving our sins (Rom. 4:7–8).

Cases of the opposite of blessing, or cursing, are often cited in the Bible (Deut. 27:11–26). Although the natural reaction to a curse is to curse back, Christians are called instead to bless—to ask for the person's benefit (Matt. 5:44).

BLESS. (Ps. 145:2) *barach* (bah-*rahch*); *Strong's* #1288: To bless; to salute, congratulate, thank, praise; to kneel down. *Barach* is the root word from which *baruch* ("blessed one") and *barachah* ("blessing") are derived. *Berech*, "knee," is probably the source of those words. In Old Testament times, one got down on his knees when preparing to speak or receive words of blessing, whether to God in heaven, or to the king on his throne. From God's side, He is the Blesser, the One who gives the capacity for living a full, rich life. The first action of God the Creator to the newly created man and woman was to bless them (Gen. 1:28). The Aaronic Benediction (Num. 6:22–27) epitomizes God's promise of blessing to His people. In Jewish worship, God is frequently called *ha-Qodesh baruch hu*, or literally, "the Holy One, blessed is He!" *Also* (Luke 6:28) *eulogeo* (yoo-log-*eh*-oh); *Strong's* #2127: Compare "eulogy" and "eulogize." From *eu*, "well" or "good," and *logos*, "speech" or "word." *Eulogeo* is to speak well of, praise, extol, bless abundantly, invoke a benediction, give thanks. *Eulogeo* can be from humans to God, from person to person, and from God to His people. When God blesses individuals He grants them favor and confers happiness upon them.

BLESSED. (Prov. 31:28) *'ashar* (ah-*shar*); *Strong's* #833: Happy, blessed, prosperous, successful, straight, right, contented. Its original meaning is "be straight." Note the use of the word in Genesis 30:13; Leah gave birth to a son and said, "I am happy, for the daughters will call me blessed." She named this son "Asher" (from *'ashar*), meaning "Happy One." Both the Messiah and the nation of Israel will be called "blessed" (*'ashar*) by the whole world: "Men shall be blessed in Him; all nations shall call Him blessed" (Ps. 72:17). "And all nations will call you blessed, for you will be a delightful land" (Mal. 3:12). *Also* (Matt. 5:3) *makarios* (mak-*ar*-ee-oss); *Strong's* #3107: From the root *mak*, indicating large or of long duration. The word is an adjective suggesting happy, supremely blessed, a condition in which congratulations are in order. It is a grace word that expresses the special joys and satisfaction granted the person who experiences salvation.

BLINDNESS. (Rom. 11:25) *porosis* (*po*-row-sis); *Strong's* #4457: Hardening, callousness. The word is a medical term describing the process by which extremities of fractured bones are set by an ossifying, or calloused petrifying. Sometimes it describes a hard substance in the eye that blinds. Used metaphorically, *porosis* denotes a dulled spiritual perceptivity, spiritual blindness, and hardness.

BLOOD—the red fluid circulating in the body that takes nourishment to the body parts and carries away waste. The word blood is often used literally in Scripture. Sometimes the word refers to the blood of animals (Gen. 37:31); at other times it refers to human blood (1 Kin. 22:35). The word is also used figuratively in the Bible. It may mean "blood red" (Joel 2:31) or "murder" (Matt. 27:24). The phrase "flesh and blood" means humanity (Heb. 2:14).

But the most important biblical concept in regard to blood is the spiritual significance of the blood of sacrificial animals. Some scholars see the blood as primarily referring to the animal's *life*, while others see it as referring to its *death*. The one is noting the pouring out of "life" *unto* death while the other is emphasizing the extinguishing of life *through* death. As these sacrifices represent Christ's sacrifice, both aspects are biblical: He gave "His *life* a ransom for many" (Mark 10:45), and He died, "even the *death* of the cross" (Phil. 2:8).

The essential focus of the Scriptures is on the central place of the blood of the sacrifice as the key to the redemptive transaction. The Bible makes it clear that the satisfaction or payment for human sins was made by the blood of a specified substitute: "For the life of the flesh is in the blood, and I have given it to you upon the altar to make atonement for your souls; for it is the blood that makes atonement for the soul" (Lev. 17:11).

In the New Testament, this Old Testament idea of sacrifice is applied to Christ's blood. References to the "blood of Christ" always mean the sacrificial and substitutionary gift of Jesus on the Cross, pouring out His life unto death. References to the blood of Christ were made by Paul (Rom. 3:25), Peter (1 Pet. 1:19), John (Rev. 1:5), and the author of Hebrews (Heb 9:14). Although all have sinned, "we have redemption through His blood, the forgiveness of sins" (Eph. 1:7).

The blood of Christ is also mentioned in Revelation 12:7–12 as a means or resource employed by Christians engaged in spiritual witness and warfare. The merit, as well as the abiding and sustaining power of Calvary's victory over the powers of darkness, is hence declared as an effectual means of overcoming the work of hell, even unto this day.

BLOOD. (Lev. 17:11) *dam* (*dahm*); *Strong's* #1818: Blood (human or animal). This highly significant word appears 360 times in the Old Testament, starting with the introduction of sacrifice (Gen. 4:4), continuing through the Law of Moses with the offering of the blood of sacrifices (appearing in Leviticus about sixty times), and culminating in the sacrifice of God's sinless Lamb. Thus atonement through shed blood is an inescapable scriptural teaching. This text teaches the value of blood: it is the "life" of man and animal; therefore, sacrifice is a life for a life. God has provided blood to cover sin. Finally, the blood actually makes atonement for the "soul," that is to say, a human life. Accordingly, verse 12 shows that blood, being for these vital purposes, is much too sacred to be misused, especially by drinking it. *Also* (1 John 1:7) *haima (hahee-*mah); *Strong's #129:* The technical word for the blood of animals and of people, but in the New Testament text used particularly for the atoning blood of Christ. His sacrificial blood is the agency for cleansing, forgiveness, and redemption.

BLOOD OF THE COVENANT, THE. From the Garden of Eden to the garden in heaven's paradise, the blood of sacrifice is the constant testimony of God's grace. As fallen man was clothed with skins of animals sacrificed by God Himself for such provision (Gen. 3:21), so the blood of the Lamb was shed to clothe in the righteousness of God every member of mankind who will receive His gift. This is the song of those who make this covenant with God "by sacrifice." Thus God will gather to Himself "those who have made a covenant with Me by sacrifice" (Ps. 50:5), and forever they shall sing the song of the redeemed: "To Him who loved us and washed us from our sins in His own blood" (Rev. 1:5).

1. God the Covenant-Maker (Gen. 1:3–5). From the beginning, God is revealed as the covenant-maker. Jeremiah referred to God's activity in creation as acts of covenant (Jer. 33:20), speaking of God's "covenant with the day" and "covenant with the night." Thereby, the unchangeable character of God's nature is emphasized as His relationship with all of His creation is portrayed as an immutable bond under His sovereign administration.

2. "Covenant" First Appears with Noah (Gen. 8:20). Prior to Noah, covenant is presented in the Bible only by inference. The use of the term "covenant" appears first in God's dealings with Noah (6:18; 9:9) and is tied to and established by his sacrificial offering after the Flood. In gratitude for his deliverance, Noah built an altar and offered blood sacrifices. There is no direct command specifically instructing Noah to offer a blood sacrifice, clearly suggesting the precedent had been established, reaching back through Abel to the

lessons of the Garden, where a blood sacrifice was required for the clothing of Adam and Eve. Noah's sacrifice was pleasing to God, and in response, God covenanted not to destroy creation again by flood. This is the first instance in biblical history where the term "covenant" is applied to the relationship between God and an individual, as well as his descendants; and it is established in blood.

3. Isaac, the Result of Covenant (Gen. 22:13). Isaac was born to Abraham and Sarah as a result of covenant promise (17:1). God's requirement of Abraham to sacrifice Isaac was the supreme test that would demonstrate both Abraham's reverence for God and his confidence in God's faithfulness to keep His covenant promise. He prepared to offer up Isaac with the assurance that God would raise him from death itself (Heb. 11:19). God made a timely intervention and provided a ram to be sacrificed instead of Isaac. This is a dramatic foreshadowing of God's offering His only begotten Son to die in our place (John 3:16). God's covenant love gave Abraham a son, and covenant love provided a substitutionary sacrifice to save that son. Centuries later covenant love would cause God to give His own Son as a blood sacrifice for the sons of men.

4. Circumcision's Significance (Gen. 17:10). The act of circumcision was required as a sign of the covenant previously established with Abraham. This was not a new covenant but an external sign that Abraham and his descendants were to execute to show that they were God's covenant people. The fact that this was performed upon the male reproductive organ had at least a twofold significance: (1) the cutting away of the foreskin spoke of the cutting away of fleshly dependence, and (2) their hope for the future posterity and prosperity was not to rest upon their own ability. Circumcision was a statement that confidence was being placed in the promise of God and His faithfulness rather than in their own flesh.

5. The First Blood Sacrifice Covenant (Gen. 15:10). The direct requirement of a blood sacrifice as the means of establishing covenant first appears in this episode (vv. 1–21) and God's instruction to Abraham. The animals to be offered were selected, cut in halves, and arranged in proper order opposite one another. The covenant parties then passed between the halves indicating that they were irrevocably bound together in blood. The cutting in halves of the sacrifice spoke of the end of existing lives for the sake of establishing a new bond or covenant. The sacred nature of this bond was attested to by the shedding of lifeblood. In this instance, only God passed between the pieces, indicating that it was His covenant and He would assume responsibility for its administration. Present in this account of covenant-making are three essential ingredients: (1) a bond that originates from God's initiative, (2) the offering of a blood sacrifice as a requirement of covenant, and (3) God's sovereign administration of the outcome of His oath.

6. No Blood, No Atonement (Lev. 17:11). This is the clearest statement of the necessity of blood as it relates to sacrificial offerings: the life is in the blood. Life and blood were given upon the altar for the specific purpose of making atonement, or attaining reconciliation with God. Apart from the shedding of blood or giving a life, there was no atonement. This established ordinance is reaffirmed in the New Covenant in Hebrews 9:22. The New Covenant in Christ's blood fulfilled the requirements of the Old Covenant for redemption. The blood of Christ is seen as surpassing the blood sacrifices of the Old Covenant and eternally satisfying the requirements of a holy God (Heb. 9:12).

7. Developing the Importance of Blood Sacrifice (Ex. 12:13). Exodus gives a more developed understanding of the importance of blood sacrifices. Sacrifice is seen as the means of deliverance for the individual, the family, and the nation. The blood of sacrificial animals was used regularly as an offering for sins as well as to consecrate the instruments of worship (20:24). It is first called "the blood of the covenant" in 24:5-8. It is in the Mosaic covenant and the Levitical priesthood that we see the most detailed administration of the blood of sacrifices. This developed significance of the role of the blood points toward the blood of Christ and its application for our redemption, justification, and sanctification (Heb. 9:14).

8. The Blood, Essential for Right Standing Before God (Gen. 4:1-10). The issue of blood sacrifice as being essential for right standing with God is conveyed through the offerings of Cain and Abel. Pursuant upon the founding lesson God gave in dealing with Adam and Eve's sin (3:21), Cain's vegetable offering, the fruit of his own efforts, was an offering of self-righteous refusal to live under God's revealed covenant. As Adam's attempt to use fig leaves for a covering was rejected, so was Cain's offering; but Abel's offering of a blood sacrifice was pleasing to God. God's sacrifice of animals in the Garden had established the blood sacrifice as necessary for approaching Him. Right standing before a covenant-making God was shown to be a matter of life and death, not merely a matter of one's good efforts.

9. The Issue of Blood Is Right Relationship (Is. 1:11). The ultimate issue in blood sacrifice is the attitude of the heart. To be acceptable, the sacrifice must represent sincere devotion. Isaiah stated that God had had more than enough of animals that were insincerely offered. Indeed God's holiness required the blood for cleansing, but right relationship was the ultimate goal of His covenant. David reflected this understanding in Psalm 51 when he stated that God's delight was not in animal sacrifices but rather in a broken and contrite spirit. Right relationship, not mere ceremony and sacrifice, is the goal of God's covenant-making activity. Therefore, sacrifices without a sincere desire for relationship with God pervert the real purpose of the sacrificial system and are unacceptable to God.

10. Christ's Sacrifice, Permanent Relief (Heb. 9:12). The Hebrew epistle contrasts the covenants of God through Moses and Christ. The Mosaic covenant provided animal sacrifices that brought temporary relief to man's guilt and demonstrated the lessons of God's justice. The covenant through Moses provided a bond in the blood of animals. These sacrifices, however, had to be repeated annually at the tabernacle, which was only symbolic of God's eternal, heavenly altar. However, Jesus Christ came into history as an eternal priest to offer an eternal sacrifice for sin. The shedding of His blood provided a permanent sacrifice and a permanent covenant bond between God and man. His blood was applied not merely to an earthly altar, but to the very altar of God in heaven, where once and for all it obtained redemption from sin for those who receive Him. The immutable bond that is established through the New Covenant in Christ's blood is the ultimate fulfillment of God's covenant-making nature.

11. The Blood, the Covering (Gen. 3:21). The covenant love of God required that innocent animals be sacrificed to provide garments of skin as a covering for Adam and Eve. This early foreshadowing of substitutionary atonement points toward the necessity of judgment upon the innocent to provide a covering for the guilty. Adam and Eve made a vain attempt to cover themselves with their own efforts by sewing together fig leaves. However, God's order provided covering by means of a sacrifice. Under the New Covenant, we are required to be clothed with Christ rather than with our good works (Gal. 3:27).

12. God Sovereignly Inaugurates the New Covenant (Matt. 26:28). Jesus used the occasion of the Passover meal to inaugurate the New Covenant. The symbolism of the Passover meal under the Old Covenant was about to be fully satisfied through Christ's crucifixion. In this historic moment, Jesus transformed the meaning of the elements of the Passover meal into New Covenant thought. The bread now represented His body, which would be given, and the cup His blood, which would be shed for the forgiveness of sins. The holy requirements of God and the Old Covenant were about to be forever satisfied. A new and living way into the presence and provision of God was being prepared through Christ, the Lamb of God. A new and eternal bond was being established by the blood of Jesus Christ. God was sovereignly inaugurating the new and ultimate covenant.

13. Right Relationship with God Through Blood (Rom. 3:25). God presented Jesus as the sacrifice for atonement or reconciliation with separated mankind. Fellowship with a holy God could only be realized through atoning for the sins that separated mankind from God and His covenant promises. It is the shed blood of Christ that ultimately satisfied the requirements of God's justice. God's judgment was fully put upon Christ, the blameless sacrifice, for all sins both past and present. It is through faith in the blood of Christ that mankind is justified in God's eyes. The blood of Christ then also becomes the bond that joins people to God and entitles them to God's covenant provisions. The blood of Christ is forever the only means of right relationship with the holy God.

14. Gentiles Embraced by Christ's Sacrifice (Eph. 2:13). Prior to the New Covenant, Gentiles were excluded from citizenship in the commonwealth of Israel and were foreigners to the covenant promises of God. There was no hope in this life and no ability to know God's presence in the world. The covenant sacrifice of Christ's blood took Gentile believers who were far from God and joined them together with the Jews in the New Covenant. Gentiles were grafted in to enjoy the covenants of promise through the New Covenant and were included as heirs with the patriarchs of all of God's promises.

15. Bought Back By the Blood (1 Pet. 1:18–19). "Redeemed" means "bought back." The redeemer pays a worthy price to reclaim something previously owned. Mankind was once God's by creation, but became lost through sin. The blood of Christ is the price of our purchase, or redemption. God offers Christ's blood to us as our substitutionary sacrifice and accepts it when we offer it back to Him. Our transaction with God is therefore not a gold-and-silver economy; it is a life-and-death economy. Christ gave His life's blood to buy us out of sin and death. His blood is a worthy price and provides an imperishable bond between God and man.

16. Partaking in the Blood (John 6:53–54). Partaking in the covenant blood of Christ is the means of being joined to God and receiving the benefits of His life. Christ is the covenant sacrifice and is God's provision for our sustenance. When we feed on Him through faith, we become partakers of the divine nature (2 Pet. 1:4), which is life eternal. Through the Holy Spirit's work, we receive His life and partake of His promises (John 6:63). Those who share in this mystery of relationship with Christ are assured of being raised up at the last day into eternal life.

17. Christ's Blood Satisfies Holiness, Thereby Making Peace (Col. 1:20). Mankind was separated from God because of sin and had no acceptable offering to satisfy the demands of God's holy nature. God sent Christ to provide an acceptable sacrifice for sin, establishing a bond with those who received Him, thereby making peace. It was specifically the blood Jesus Christ shed on the Cross that satisfied the demand of God's holiness, established a peace bond or covenant with those who received Him, and provided the means for all of creation to be reconciled to God. Lev. 17:11 declares that sin cannot be forgiven without the shedding of blood. Because sin takes life, life is required to repay sin's debts. Jesus Christ gave divine life in blood to satisfy all of mankind's sin debts and to restore covenant peace between God and man.

18. The Blood, Reconciliation, and Victorious Living (Rom. 5:9). Romans 3:10 establishes that all people are unrighteous and therefore deserving of judgment. The covenant love of God reaches beyond the satisfaction of justice to establish a bond of fellowship in the blood of Jesus Christ. Faith in His blood not only brings our deliverance from the wrath of God, but also is the means of victorious living through participation in His life: (1) the blood of Christ deals with the legal issue of separation from God, reconciling us to Him; and (2) faith in His blood infuses divine life and provision for our continuing triumph over sin.

19. The Weapon of the Blood (Rev. 12:11). This passage portrays Satan as cast down to the earth, confronting and accusing the citizens of the kingdom of God. The primary weapon of the people of God against Satan is the blood of the Lamb. The blood of Christ, the Lamb, causes the people of God to prevail because it answers all of the Enemy's accusations. Satan controls and defeats humankind through guilt and accusations. He is a "blackmailer." However, the saints know that the blood has satisfied all of the charges against them, joined them to God, and provided them with every necessary provision to defeat Satan. The blood has established an unassailable bond with a sovereign God that prevents Satan from separating the embattled Christian from God's eternal and complete resources. God has declared us righteous and victorious through the blood of Christ.

20. The Significance of Communion's Covenant (1 Cor. 10:16). The Passover celebration was to be the last meal that Christ would share with the disciples before His death (John 16:28). It was also the setting in which He chose to transform the meaning of the cup and the bread into New Covenant thought. Now receiving the cup is a participation in the blood of Christ, and the breaking of bread is a participation in His body. The mystery involved in the covenant meal extends beyond Christ's relationship to the individual. Partakers of the covenant meal are also joined together in the body and blood of Christ. The blessings and responsibilities of the covenant are therefore extended laterally among those who partake of Christ together, as certainly as they are vertically between God and the believer in Christ. C.S.

 BODY—the material or physical part of man whether alive or dead. Some religions consider the body evil or inferior to the soul, but the Bible teaches that the body is God's good gift to man (Gen. 2:7). It is a necessary ingredient for a fully human existence. In the Old Testament the word body sometimes means "corpse" (Num. 6:6). Occasionally the reference is to the body as that part of man that is involved in reproduction (Deut. 28:4).

In the New Testament these Old Testament meanings are carried forward but new insights appear. Paul teaches that the body is often the instrument of sin (1 Cor. 6:18); that the body must die as a penalty for sin (Rom. 7:24); and that sin dishonors a person's body (Rom. 1:24). On the other hand, believers in Christ may "put to death the deeds of the body" (Rom. 8:13) and present their bodies as holy sacrifices which please God (Rom. 12:1).

Since human life requires a body, sometimes the term body symbolizes the whole person. Both Jesus and Paul used the word in this way (Matt. 6:22–23; Phil 1:20). The Bible reveals only introductory ideas regarding our state or existence after the death of our human body, but the real promise of an eternal body is given. At death we do not become wandering souls or "unclothed" spirits (2 Cor. 5:1–8). However, the fullest completion of salvation's purpose, in terms of our physical bodies, will be realized at the return of Christ (1 Thess. 4:13–18). Then we shall receive our "glorified" bodies—i.e., eternal bodies like unto Christ's after His resurrection (Phil. 3:21; 1 Cor. 15:35–58; 1 John 3:2).

Also see Body of Christ; Spiritual.

BODY OF CHRIST—a phrase used in three senses in the Bible:

1. The phase refers to the physical body of Jesus. God became fully human, and to lessen that belief—Christ had a truly human body—was and is deemed as heresy (1 John 4:3). He was crucified and died physically for our sins; he rose again in a resurrected, literal, physical, glorified body (Luke 24:36–43).

2. "Body of Christ" is used of the bread of the Lord's Supper (1 Cor. 10:16), for this is the terminology Jesus used to introduce this practice of commemorating His death for us and His promise of triumph in us (Matt. 26:26; John 6:63).

3. The Bible also uses the phrase as a symbol of the church. In Romans 12:14–15 and 1 Corinthians 12:12–27, Paul emphasizes the church's unity, even though there are varied gifts, ministries, and personalities, whereas Ephesians 4:4–12 and Colossians 1:18–24 emphasize Christ's place as the Head of the church, which is His body.

BOLDNESS. (Acts 4:31) *parrhesia* (par-rhay-see-ah); *Strong's #3954:* Outspokenness, unreserved utterance, freedom of speech, with frankness, candor, cheerful courage, and the opposite of cowardice, timidity, or fear. Here it denotes a divine enablement that comes to ordinary and unprofessional people exhibiting spiritual power and authority. It also refers to a clear presentation of the gospel without being ambiguous or unintelligible. *Parrhesia* is not a human quality but a result of being filled with the Holy Spirit.

BREATH. (Ps. 150:6) *neshamah* (ne-sha-*mah*); *Strong's #5397:* Breath, breath of life, breathing person, living soul. This word first appears in Genesis 2:7, where God breathed into man's nostrils the *nishmat chayim*, "breath of life," and man became a living being. This is the tender account of how man took his first breath, aided entirely by the Creator, who shared His own breath with him. God literally taught man how to breathe. The psalmist here counsels everyone and everything that has *neshamah* (breath) to praise the Lord.

BRETHREN. (Ps. 133:1) *'ach* (ahch); *Strong's* #251: Brother, especially an immediate relative, but also any fellowman; countryman, companion. *'Ach* occurs more than 740 times in the Old Testament. Genesis 4:9 illustrates the narrowest usage of *'ach*, referring to sons of the same two parents. Isaiah 41:6–7 presents the wider usage of *'ach*, speaking of the neighbors or fellow workers of craftsmen.

BRIDE—a woman who has recently been married or is about to be married. In the ancient context of biblical times, it was customary for fathers to select wives for their sons (Gen. 38:6). Occasionally, a son might express his preference for a bride to his father, and his father would negotiate with the parents or guardians of a young woman (Gen. 34: 4, 8). The father of the young woman also might initiate wedding proposals (Ex. 2:21). On her wedding day, the bride bathed and put on white robes, often richly embroidered. She put her bridal girdle around her waist, covered her face with a veil, and adorned her head with a garland. The bridegroom, attended by his friends, set out from his house to the house of his bride's parents. The procession was a happy occasion, often accompanied by singers and musicians. He took his bride back to his own (or his parents') house accompanied by singing, the playing of musical instruments, and dancing. The wedding festivities continued for one or two weeks (Judg. 14:12).

In the Old Testament, the word marriage is used to describe God's spiritual relationship with His chosen people, Israel (Ps. 45; Is. 54:6). When God's people fell into sin, especially idolatry, the sin was likened to adultery on the part of a wife (Jer. 3:1–20).

In the New Testament, the analogy is continued: Christ is the bridegroom (John 3:29), and the church is His bride (Eph. 5:25–33). The apostle Paul counsels husbands and wives to imitate the spiritual closeness and love which Christ has for His bride, the church (Eph. 5:22–33).

BRIDEGROOM—a man who has recently been married or is about to be married. The term is applied symbolically to the *Messiah. John the Baptist called Jesus the "bridegroom" (John 3:29). Jesus referred to Himself as the "bridegroom" (Matt. 9:15). Jesus' bride, of course, is the church—those who are spiritually united with Him by faith.

BROTHERLY LOVE—the love of brothers (or sisters) for each other; the love of fellow Christians for one another, all being children of the same Father in a special sense. Occasionally the New Testament uses the word brother to refer simply to another human being, whether

a Christian or not (Matt. 25:40), or to one's fellow countryman (Rom. 9:3). Usually, however, it is used of a fellow believer in Christ. This is true of all places where the concept of brotherly love, or brotherly kindness, appears.

In the Old Testament, Israelites were taught not to hate their brothers: "You shall not hate your brother in your heart . . . but you shall love your neighbor as yourself" (Lev. 19:17–18). This emphasis is continued and is made even more positive in the New Testament. Believers are exhorted to "be kindly affectionate to one another with brotherly love" (Rom. 12:10), to "let brotherly love continue" (Heb. 13:1), to "love the brotherhood" (1 Pet. 2:17), and to "love as brothers" (1 Pet. 3:8). Brotherly love is to be the badge, or hallmark, of a Christian (John 13:35). Also see Love; Love, Brotherly.

BROTHERLY LOVE. (Heb. 13:1) *philadelphia* (fil-ad-el-*fee*-ah); *Strong's* #5360: From *phileo*, "to love," and *adelphos*, "brother." The word denotes the love of brothers, fraternal affection. In the New Testament it describes the love Christians have for other Christians.

BROTHERLY LOVE. Perhaps no wiser warning of the danger to experiencing the power of God is that registered in Paul's epistle to the Corinthians. Here is a people he at once commends and then strongly corrects. As much as he welcomes their experience in the gifts of the Spirit, he commands that they learn the grace of the Spirit—love. Foundational to every other value and goal in Christian life is the call to grow in love. First Corinthians 13 charts the way, noting the absence of value in any accomplishment, gifts, or sacrifice unless love is the fountainhead and the flavor of it all. Such brotherly love is to be nurtured and becomes a proven source of joyful service.

1. Responsibility for One Another (Gen. 4:9). The theme of brotherhood emerges early in Scripture; and from the very beginning, it is clear that God places a high priority on how brothers treat each other. In this passage the question of responsibility for one another first emerges. Cain asks, "*Am I my brother's keeper?*" The word used for "keeper" (Hebrew *shamar*) means "to guard, to protect, to attend, or to regard." Are we responsible? "Absolutely," is God's answer. Not only are we our brother's keeper, we are held accountable for our treatment of and our ways of relating to our brothers (blood and spiritual).

For Cain's sins against his brother, God curses him throughout the earth, takes away his ability to farm, and sentences him to a life as a fugitive and a vagabond (v. 12). This clearly indicates that unbrotherliness destines one to fruitlessness and frustration of purpose.

2. Love Embraces Those Who Have Wronged Us

(Gen. 45:4). The story of Joseph is an early account of the forgiving nature God expects us to display in our treatment of those who have wronged us. It is a founding example of Christ-like love. Though Joseph's brothers sold him into slavery and deceived his father into thinking him dead, when he confronts his brothers during their time of need, his forgiveness and love burst forth from his heart. With uncanny faith in the overriding providence of God, he even professes his belief that God has used his brothers' betrayal of him as a means to deliver his family during the time of famine (v. 7). Joseph's forgiveness of his brothers' sin is so complete that he kisses all of them and weeps with joy at being united with them once again. Brotherly forgiveness is expressive, self-giving, and offered in a way that assists its being received.

3. Unselfish Christian Love Toward Strangers

(Lev. 19:34). In the timeless words of this text, God's Word clearly establishes definite guidelines on how to interact with strangers. The spirit of these guidelines recurs throughout both the Old and New Testaments. God indicates that He expects us to relate to strangers in deep, unselfish, servant-spirited, Christian love. He reminds His people that they, who once were foreigners in the land of Egypt, should above all others remember how it feels to be treated as outsiders.

Lesson 1: Remember how rejection feels, and never manifest it. His further instructions on the treatment of strangers are opposite to normal, worldly standards. The Lord says that when strangers come into our homes, they are to be treated as "one born among you," that is, as blood relatives! Since the Jews placed great emphasis upon bloodlines and lineage, God's use of this terminology had an extremely high impact, underscoring the significance of strangers in God's eyes.

Lesson 2: All humanity is one family. Treat others that way.

4. To Get Closer to God, Love Others (Ps. 15:3).

In Psalm 15, David is asking God the necessary qualifications to abide in His tabernacle (v. 1). God's reply emphasizes that to "abide" in God's presence and purpose first requires a will to exhibit a strong relationship with others. To expect to have a strong relationship with God, determine to conduct life in right relationship with others! God tells David (1) to speak kindly of his neighbors; (2) never to gossip or say anything to destroy another's reputation; (3) to do nothing to hurt another

person in *any* way; and finally (4) God warns David not to "reproach" his neighbor. "Reproach" (Hebrew *cherpah*) means "blame, discredit, disgrace, or shame." If the Old Testament teaches that one desiring to get closer to God must prioritize love toward others, the New Testament commandment "Love your neighbor as yourself" (Rom. 13:9) is surely vital to our relationship with the heavenly Father today.

5. Abundantly Forgiven, Abundantly Forgive

(Ps. 86:5). These words are basic, yet their impact is intended to be life-changing at both points: (1) in our *receiving* God's love and merciful forgiveness and (2) in our *giving* it just as we have received it. Two virtues—goodness and forgiveness—are attributes birthed by our heavenly Father and expected to be found in our own lives. He expects us to be like Him—to stand ready to forgive our brother's transgressions in the same abundance of mercy He shows. "Abundant" is from the Hebrew *rab*, meaning "aboundingly, exceedingly." God does not want us to portion out our mercy and forgiveness with teaspoons. He is looking for people who portion out their forgiveness and mercy with huge, unlimiting shovels.

6. Love Those Who Have Animosity Toward You

(Matt. 5:44). The word "enemy" does not suit any limited, convenient meaning, as though merely referring to those whom we may not particularly like. The command to love our enemies means much more than simply changing our feelings about people with whom we do not get along. Rather, "enemy" (Greek *echthros*) means "adversary or foe" and refers to those whose actions and words manifest hatred for you: the in-law who will not speak to you, the associate who tried to get you fired. We are called to love those filled with animosity toward us. Jesus leaves no room for speculation in this passage, commanding love for those who hate, despise, and persecute us. Such love is only possible through the power of Jesus Christ, who Himself loved in that way and now seeks vessels through whom to love again the hate-filled who assail Him as they oppose you.

7. God's Love Loves the Unlovable (Luke

6:31–35). To love the unlovable is to separate ourselves from the world's self-serving kind of love—to share Christ's love with people who have no apparent ability to return anything at all. Jesus calls us to love as He did—to love those who finish last, those who are ugly, those who are poor, or who are powerless to help us. This response is only possible by a supernatural transformation that begets in us a different order of response than is usual to mankind. Just as the human mind separates man from animals, so Christian love is to be so dramatically different that it separates the believer from the world. It is to remove us from animal responses that snarl, attack, or retaliate. It is to transcend human responses that expect an earthly reward for service or kindness. Such love will become a beacon light, drawing the worldling to us, to question what causes us to radiate love in the midst of unlovable, unloving people. Stephen exemplifies this love (Acts 7:59, 60), and Saul (Paul) reflects the impact of such love (Acts 9:5). Note "the goads" of conviction that had begun piercing him, doubtless through Stephen's love. The perfection of God's love in us can gain a curious and attentive audience.

8. Love Is Servant-Spirited (John 12:26). Love is servant-spirited. The world-mind will never understand or accept this call. A servant is one who accepts and acknowledges a place beneath those whom he serves, one willing to forsake the systems of social status on our human scale of values. Servants are viewed as performing the unworthy tasks considered beneath those whom they serve. But Jesus says that those who function as His servants—serving the world in His name—will be honored by the heavenly Father. Every true servant will ultimately be honored by the One whom they serve and who has promised them honor for that service!

If we follow and serve our King, in that act of service we are elevated to a place of honor!

9. The Priority and Pathway of Brotherly Love (John 15:12–13). Here is summarized the entire duty and direction of the disciple of Jesus. The direct simplicity of this statement establishes the priority and the pathway we are to pursue: (1) Our priority is to love one another. (2) Our pathway is to love as Christ loved us, "laying down His life." Who can measure this love? Christ gave up the comforts, joys, and adoration of heaven to be sullied by the soil of earth and to carry the sins of sinners. His bearing of agonizing pain through beatings, nails in His hands, the spear in His side, the thorns on His head, all exemplify the measure of His love. We find His love, but we also see His manner of loving and are called to bear with others' sins, with inflicted pain, with stabbing, cruel remarks and treatment. Impossible? Yes, to human nature; but as new temples of the Holy Spirit, who has poured out the love of God into our hearts, we can ask for and receive the grace and guidance to love as Jesus loved.

10. Brotherly Love Flows from the Divine Nature (2 Pet. 1:7–8). In 1:4 Peter describes God's "great and precious promises" intended to enable us (1) to be "partakers" in His divine nature and (2) to allow us to "escape the corruption *that is* in the world." These graces are necessary to lift us above the decay of human nature and unto "brotherly kindness" and "love" (v. 7). Brotherly kindness dissolves personal infighting and ungracious ignoring of one another. It allows refocusing on our real enemy—Satan. Further, to master love is to receive and release *agape* love: that Christlike, unconditional gift that is full of affection, bursting with benevolence, and that provides a love feast to all to whom we minister in the name of Jesus. This text is a promise for those yielded enough to let these gifts flow: we can actually participate in the divine nature of God, which is elevated above the corrupt, divisive spirit of the world. D.S.

BROTHERS, LORD'S—Jesus' half-brothers, sons of Mary and Joseph. In 1 Corinthians 9:5 Paul mentions in passing the ministry of "the brothers of the Lord." Also, in Galatians 1:19, Paul calls James "the Lord's brother." The Gospels list four brothers in all—"James, Joses (or Joseph, NASB, NEB, NIV, RSV), Simon, and Judas" (Matt. 13:55), in addition to unnamed sisters.

Some have questioned whether "brothers" should be understood in a literal sense. Those who argue that Mary remained a virgin throughout her life take the word brothers to refer either to sons of Joseph by a prior marriage or to cousins of Jesus, but there is no biblical or theological reason to constrain this stretch of credulity. Both of these possibilities are unlikely.

The Gospels do not suggest that Mary was a perpetual virgin. The designation of Jesus as Mary's "firstborn Son" implies that she had other sons as well (Matt. 1:25). No evidence supports "sons of Joseph" theory, and no New Testament confirms the possibility they were Jesus' cousins. Other words in the Greek language are generally used to indicate "cousin" (Col. 4:10), "sister's son" (Acts 23:16), or the more general "relatives" (Mark 6:4). The Gospels would not likely have called these four the "Lord's brothers" if, in fact, they were really cousins.

Finally, the incident recorded in Matthew 12:46–50 is decisive. Here, as elsewhere (Mark 3:31–35; Luke 8:19–21; John 2:12; Acts 1:14), Jesus' mother is mentioned along with His brothers as if they were all in one family. Jesus grew up in a typical family of the time. This formed part of His training as one who was fully human as well as fully divine.

BUILT. (Zech. 1:16) *banah* (bah-*nah*); *Strong's #1129:* To build, construct, found, set up; obtain children ("build" a family). *Banah* is generally translated "build" in the English versions; its object is usually a city, house, temple, room, gate, or an altar. Occasionally it means "to build up" something, as in Psalm 102:16, "The LORD shall build up Zion; He shall appear in His glory." It is thought that *banah* is the root of *ben* (son) and *banim* (children), as if the linguistic suggestion is that sons are the builders or building blocks of future generations.

CALL, CALLING—an important theological idea with several different meanings in the Bible:

1. God's call of individuals to *salvation, made possible by the sacrifice of Jesus Christ on the Cross (Rom. 8:28–30; 1 Thess. 2:12).

2. God's call to salvation also involves the believer in the high calling of living his life in service to others (1 Cor. 7:20). This is to say, one's vocation or profession or life enterprise is a "calling" to be also lived under Christ's lordship.

3. To call on God for help, or to pray. The Bible contains numerous examples of people who, in their distress, called upon the name of the Lord (Gen. 4:26). God is portrayed as a compassionate, concerned, and personal Deliverer who hears the prayers of His people.

4. To name or to call by name (Gen. 17:5; Luke 1:13). Man has been given the right to name because he is created in the image of God. His role as namer is one of the ways in which he exercises his dominion over the world (Gen. 1:26; 2:19, 23).

CALL. (Jer. 33:3) *qara'* (kah-*rah*); *Strong's #7121:* To call out to someone; cry out; to address someone; to shout, or speak out; to proclaim. *Qara'* often describes calling out loudly in an attempt to get someone's attention (Is. 58:1), or calling upon the Lord or upon His name. (See Is. 55:6; Joel 2:32.) Sometimes *qara'* means "to name something," that is, to call it by its name, as God did when He called the light Day and the darkness Night (Gen. 1:5). Similarly, *qara'* involves the naming of places, holidays, or children; for example, Leah praised the Lord for the birth of her son, and "called his name Judah" (Gen. 29:35). (Compare Gen. 21:31; Esth. 9:26.) *Qara'* appears more than seven hundred times in the Bible.

CALLED. (Gal. 1:6) *kaleo* (kal-*eh*-oh); *Strong's #2564:* From the root *kal*, the source of the English words "call" and "clamor." The word is used to invite or to summon, and is especially used of God's call to participate in the blessings of the kingdom (Rom. 8:30; 9:24–25).

CANAAN, CANAANITES—see ch. 55, §2.1., 3.4., 3.4.c., 6.2.

CARE. (1 Pet. 5:7) *merimna* (*mer*-im-nah); *Strong's #3308:* From *meiro*, "to divide," and *noos*, "the mind." The word denotes distractions, anxieties, burdens, and worries. *Merimna* means to be anxious beforehand about daily life. Such worry is unnecessary, because the Father's love provides for both our daily needs and our special needs.

CAUGHT UP. (1 Thess. 4:17) *harpadzo* (har-*pad*-zoe); *Strong's #726:* To seize, snatch away, catch up, take by force. The word describes the Holy Spirit's action in transferring Philip from one location to another (Acts 8:39) and Paul's being caught up to Paradise (2 Cor. 12:2, 4). It suggests the exercise of a sudden force.

CHARGE. (Acts 16:24) *parangelia* (par-ang-gel-*ee*-ah); *Strong's #3852:* A chain-of-command word, denoting a general order, instruction, command, precept, or direction. It is used in a way that makes the word self-explanatory. The prison authorities charge the jailer to imprison Paul and Silas (v. 24). The apostles were given a charge not to preach by the authorities at Jerusalem (5:28). Paul gives a charge to the Thessalonians (1 Thess. 4:2). *Parangelia* is the charge Paul gave to Timothy (1 Tim. 1:5, 18).

CHASTISEMENT—an infliction of punishment (as by whipping or beating). In the Bible the term chastisement usually refers to corrective punishment or discipline inflicted by God for the purpose of (1) education, instruction, and training (Job 4:3; Ps. 6:7); (2) corrective guidance (2 Tim. 2:25); and (3) discipline, in the sense of corrective physical punishment (Prov. 22:15; Heb. 12:5–11; Rev. 3:19). The most dramatic use of this word in the Bible is in Isaiah 53, in Isaiah's portrait of the Suffering Servant: "He was wounded for our transgressions, He was bruised for our iniquities; the chastisement for our peace was upon Him, and by His stripes we are healed" (Is. 53:5). The New Testament reveals that Isaiah was speaking of Jesus Christ, who (a) died in our place, and for our sins, and who (b) bore the pain of our sick-

---

nesses in our behalf as well as the punishment for our sinning (Matt. 8:16–17; 1 Pet. 2:24).

CHEERFUL. (2 Cor. 9:7) *hilaros* (hil-*ar*-oss); *Strong's #2431:* Willing, good-natured, joyfully ready. The word describes a spirit of enjoyment in giving that sweeps away all restraints. The English word "hilarious" is a transliteration.

CHEERFULNESS. (Rom. 12:8) *hilarotes* (hil-ar-ot-ace); *Strong's #2432:* Compare "hilarious" and "hilarity." Graciousness, joyfulness, gladness, benevolence, amiability, cheerfulness, gaiety, affability. In primitive lands Bible translators define *hilarotes* as, "The heart is laughing and the eyes are dancing." The word was often used for the cheerful demeanor of those visiting the sick and infirm and of those giving alms. The person who exhibits *hilarotes* is a sunbeam lighting up a sickroom with warmth and love.

CHEMOSH—see ch. 55, §2.3.

CHERUBIM [CHER oo beam]—the biblical term for winged angelic beings: creatures often associated with the worship and praise of God. The cherubim are first mentioned in the Bible in Genesis 3:24. When God drove Adam and Eve from the Garden of Eden, He placed cherubim at the east of the garden, "and a flaming sword which turned every way, to guard the way to the tree of life."

According to the prophets, cherubim belong to the category of unfallen angels. However, at one time, Satan or Lucifer was the leader-cherub (Ezek. 28:14, 16), until he rebelled against God (Is. 14:12–14; Ezek. 28:12–19).

Symbolic representations of cherubim were used in the *tabernacle in the wilderness. Two cherubim made of gold were stationed at the two ends of the mercy seat, above the *ark of the covenant in the Most Holy Place (Ex. 25:17–22; 1 Chr. 28:18; Heb. 9:5). Artistic designs of cherubim decorated the ten curtains (Ex. 26:1; 36:8) and the veil (Ex. 26:31; 2 Chr. 3:14) of the tabernacle, as well as Solomon's temple (1 Kin. 6:23–35; 7:29, 36; 8:67; 2 Chr. 3:7–13; 5:7–8).

A careful comparison of their physical description in Ezekiel 1 and 10 shows clearly that the "four living creatures" (Ezek. 1:5) were the same beings as the cherubim (Ezekiel 10). Revelation 4:6–9 seems to be inspired, at least in part, to reveal the same beings, who, throughout the Bible, sing God's praises and testify to God's glory and His abiding presence with His people. In some ways, the cherubim are quite similar to the seraphim of Isaiah 6, but some features of their appearance suggest

they may be another order or form of angelic being. The "im" ending of the words cherubim and seraphim are the Hebrew plural of these two untranslated terms, cherub and seraph.

CHERUBIM. (Ex. 25:18) *keruvim* (keh-roo-*veem*), plural of *keruv*; *Strong's #3742:* A heavenly being represented by carved gold figures on the ark of the covenant. *Keruv* may be related to an Akkadian verb, meaning "to bless, praise, adore." *Keruvim* are mentioned ninety times in the Old Testament, in Genesis, Exodus, Numbers, 1 and 2 Samuel, 1 and 2 Kings, 1 and 2 Chronicles, Psalms, Isaiah, and especially Ezekiel (more than thirty times). *Keruvim* were observed from Adam's time to Ezekiel's time. See the description in Ezekiel 10. The idea persists that *keruv* means "covering angel" (Ezek. 28:14). A *keruv* does cover, as Exodus 25:20 states. (Compare the two angels facing each other, who covered and guarded the Lord of Glory, as His body lay quietly in death: John 20:12.)

CHOSE. (1 Kin. 11:34) *bachar* (bah-*char*); *Strong's #977:* To choose, select, elect; to determine to have one in particular. *Bachar* describes the kind of choosing that is made when more than one item is examined, with only one (or a few) being selected. *Bachar* is used primarily with the idea of God's making significant choices. In this reference, God chose David to be ruler over Israel. The right of God to choose whomever He wishes is well established in Scripture. He chose Abraham to pioneer, Moses to instruct, Israel to bring salvation to the world, and He chose believers before the world began (Eph. 1:4).

CHOSEN. (1 Pet. 2:9) *eklektos* (ek-lek-*toss*); *Strong's #1588:* Compare "eclectic." From *ek*, "out of," and *lego*, "to pick, gather." The word designates one picked out from among the larger group for special service or privileges. It describes Christ as the chosen Messiah of God (Luke 23:35), angels as messengers from heaven (1 Tim. 5:21), and believers as recipients of God's favor (Matt. 24:22; Rom. 8:33; Col. 3:12). The New Testament traces the source of election to God's grace.

CHRIST. (2 Tim. 4:22) *Christos* (Khris-*toss*); *Strong's #5547:* The Anointed One. The word comes from the verb *chrio*, "to anoint," referring to the consecration rites of a priest or king. *Christos* translates the Hebrew *Mashiyach*, "Messiah." Unfortunately, the transliteration of *Christos* into English, resulting in the word "Christ," deprives the word of much of its meaning. It would be better to translate *Christos* in every instance as "the Anointed One" or "the Messiah," denoting a *title*. "Jesus Christ" actually means Jesus the Messiah, or Jesus the Anointed One, emphasizing the fact that the man Jesus was God's Anointed One, the promised Messiah.

CHRISTIAN—an adherent or follower of Christ. The word occurs three times in the New Testament.

The designation of the early followers of Christ as Christians was initiated by the non-Christian population of Antioch (Acts 11:26), and originally it was probably a term of mocking or derision—"little Christs." Eventually, however, Christians used it of themselves as a name of honor, not of shame (Acts 26:28; 1 Pet. 4:16). Prior to their adoption of the name, the Christians called themselves believers (Acts 5:14), brothers (Acts 6:3), or saints (Acts 9:13), names which also continued to be used.

In many modern societies, the original character of the name Christian has been emptied of its meaning as a biblical disciple of Christ. To some Christian refers to (a) a political system void of love, (b) a religious structure void of life, or (c) a tradition without vital faith in the Savior. In this regard, it can be said that Jesus did not come to found "Christianity." He came to reveal the Father to humankind, to die to redeem humankind, and thereby to bring humanity back to God through His work of redemption. All who believe this and receive Jesus Christ as Savior and Lord may be called Christians, but most essentially the ones called believers, or redeemed children of the living God.

CHURCH—a local assembly of believers as well as the redeemed of all the ages who follow Jesus Christ as Savior and Lord.

In the four Gospels of the New Testament, the term church is found only in Matthew 16:18 and 18:17. This scarcity of usage in those books that report on the life and ministry of Jesus is perhaps best explained by the fact that the church as the body of Christ did not begin until the Day of Pentecost after the *ascension of Christ (Acts 1:14).

That the church began on the Day of Pentecost may be demonstrated in various ways: (1) Christ Himself declared the church to be yet future; (2) it was founded upon the death, resurrection, and ascension of Christ, and such an accomplished fact was not possible until Pentecost (Gal. 3:23–25); and (3) there could be no church until it was fully purchased with Christ's blood (Eph. 1:20).

Nature. The Greek word for church is *ekklesia*, an ancient Greek term for the people of a kingdom who are *called* to take their role as responsible citizens. This word is used 115 times in the New Testament, mostly in the Book of Acts and the writings of the apostle

Paul and the General Epistles. At least ninety-two times this word refers to a local congregation. The other references are to the *whole* church, or to all believers everywhere in all ages, to all who follow Christ, without respect to locality or time. Most such general reference to the church occurs in Ephesians 1:22, 3:10–21, 5:23–32. The assembly of all the redeemed in one place will become a reality only after the return of Christ (Heb. 12:23; Rev. 21–22). Most of the New Testament emphasis on the church is on the idea of the local church or congregation, the visible operation of the church in a given time, place, or community.

Commission. After His resurrection, Jesus commissioned His followers to make disciples and teach them what He had taught (Matt. 28:16). The Book of Acts begins this process as the early church pursues this commission under the leadership of the Lord Himself, by the presence and power of the Holy Spirit through whom Jesus continues to direct and empower His church.

Gatherings. The early church met in the temple and Jewish synagogues, as well as private homes of believers (Acts 5:42). Later, in recognition of Christ's resurrection on the first day of the week, Sunday became the principal time for assembled worship (1 Cor. 16:2). Through these worship and fellowship gatherings, believers were discipled and nurtured for practical living, faithful service, and an abiding witness in Jesus' name.

Organization. The early church's organization was flexible to meet changing needs. Offices included the *apostles, *prophets and *prophetesses, *evangelists, *elders and elder women, *bishops, *ministers or teachers, *deacons, and deaconesses (Eph. 4:11; 1 Tim. 3:1–13; Titus 2:1–3; Acts 21:9; Rom 18:1).

Although church organization varies from denomination to denomination today, the pattern and purpose of the New Testament remains a model for churches as they pursue their mission in the world.

CHURCH. (Acts 8:1) *ecclesia* (ek-klay-*see*-ah); *Strong's #1577:* Used in secular Greek for an assembly of citizens and in the Septuagint for the congregation of Israel. The New Testament uses the word in the former sense in 19:32, 39, 41, and in the latter sense in 7:38 and Heb. 2:12. The dominant use in the New Testament is to describe an assembly or company of Christians in the following ways: (1) the whole body of Christians; (2) a local church constituting a company of Christians gathering for worship, sharing, and teaching; or (3) churches in a district. Other related terms are:

"spiritual house," "chosen race," and "God's people." (Compare "ecclesiastic" and "ecclesiastical.") The survival of the Christian church against all its opponents is assured in Jesus' words from Matthew 16:18, "On this rock I will build My church, and the gates of Hades shall not prevail against it."

CHURCH GOVERNMENT—the organization

pattern by which a church movement or congregation governs itself. The concept of church organization and government in the New Testament was flexible, geared to meet changing needs. In the earliest days, the *apostles directed the work of the church. Then seven men were chosen to assist the needs (Acts 6). Later, *prophets, *evangelists, *elders, *bishops, and *deacons were chosen.

No single or conclusive pattern of government can be mandated by reading the New Testament. Thus, various forms of church government are employed by different groups today, to provide order and structure for the work of their churches. Most expressions of church government can be classified in the six following forms.

Congregational. This form of organization focuses on a local congregation's retaining entire freedom to determine what it considers the will of Christ as it governs its own affairs.

Presbyterian. This form of church government also focuses on Christ as Head of the church, and that He will guide His church through elders (Greek, *presbuteros*) who seek to serve the congregation's interests in leading the church.

Episcopalian. This system of church government views the bishop as the principal officer. Decisions are made at levels higher than the local congregation, but common sense often dictates that the will of God and the opinions of members should be given prayerful consideration.

Roman Catholic. Roman Catholic clergy—priests, bishops, etc.—forms a hierarchy that governs the church. The Pope, as the "bishop" of Rome, is the highest authority, and the authority of the papal office is believed to have originated with Peter as the first pope.

National Church Government. This form of church government (found mostly in Europe) recognizes the state's authority as decisive over church matters.

Quakers. The Quakers refuse any type of church official or organization, depending on the inner light which any believer has the right and power to receive directly from God. Decisions are arrived at by mutual agreement among the believers.

CIRCUMCISION—the surgical removal of the foreskin of the male sex organ. This action served as a sign of God's *covenant relation with His people.

Circumcision was practiced in some parts of the ancient world but performed at the beginning of puberty (about age twelve) as an initiation into manhood. In contrast, the Hebrews performed circumcision on infants. This rite had an important ethical meaning, signifying their responsibility to serve as the holy people whom God had called as His special servants in the midst of a pagan world.

The Bible's first mention of circumcision is when God instructs Abraham to circumcise every male in his household (Gen. 17:11). Then, the ritual was ongoingly to be performed on the eighth day after birth (Gen. 17:12), at the time the child was named (Luke 1:59; 2:21).

Circumcision of the Jewish male was required as a visible, physical sign of the covenant between the Lord and His people. Any male not circumcised was to be "cut off from his people" (Gen. 17:14) and regarded as a covenant-breaker (Ex. 22:48).

Moses and the prophets used the term circumcised as a symbol for purity of heart and readiness to hear and obey. Through Moses the Lord challenged the Israelites to submit to "circumcision of the heart," a reference to their need for repentance. "If their uncircumcised hearts are humbled, and they accept their guilt," God declared, "then I will remember My covenant" (Lev. 26:41–42, also Deut. 10:16). Jeremiah characterized rebellious Israel as having "uncircumcised" ears (6:10) and being "uncircumcised in the heart" (9:26).

In the New Testament circumcision was faithfully practiced by devout Jews as recognition of God's continuing covenant with Israel. Both John the Baptist (Luke 1:59) and Jesus (Luke 2:21) were circumcised.

A problem erupted in that, by New Testament times, the tradition had become a badge of spiritual superiority, and some early Jewish believers in Jesus as the Messiah had difficulty relating to Gentile believers who had received Christ but were not circumcised. Gentile believers regarded their Jewish brethren as eccentric because of their dietary laws, Sabbath rules, and circumcision practices. Jewish believers tended to view their uncircumcised Gentile brothers as unenlightened and disobedient to the Law of Moses.

A crisis arose in the church at Antioch when believers from Judea (known as Judaizers) taught the brethren, "Unless you are circumcised according to the custom of Moses, you cannot be saved" (Acts 15:1–2). In effect, the Judaizers insisted that a believer from a non-Jewish background (Gentile) must first become a Jew ceremonially (by being circumcised) before he could be admitted to the Christian brotherhood.

A council of apostles and elders was convened in Jerusalem to resolve the issue (Acts 15:6–29). Among those attending were Paul, Barnabas, Simon Peter, and James, pastor of the Jerusalem church. To insist on circumcision for the Gentiles, Peter argued, would amount to a burdensome yoke (Acts 15:10). This was the decision handed down by the council, and the church broke away from the binding legalism of Judaism.

Years later, reinforcing this decision, the apostle Paul wrote the believers at Rome that Abraham, "the father of circumcision" (Rom. 4:12), was saved by faith rather than by circumcision (Rom. 4:9–12). He declared circumcision to be of no value unless accompanied by an obedient spirit (Rom. 2:25–26).

Paul also spoke of the "circumcision of Christ" (Col. 2:11), a reference to His atoning death which "condemned sin in the flesh" (Rom. 8:3) and nailed legalism "to the cross" (Col. 2:14). In essence, Paul declared that the new covenant of Christ's shed blood has provided forgiveness to both Jew and Gentile and has made circumcision totally unnecessary. All that ultimately matters for both Jew and Gentile, Paul says, is a changed nature—a new creation that makes them one in Jesus Christ (Eph. 2:14–18).

CLAP. (Ps. 47:1) *taqa'* (tah-*kah*); *Strong's* #8628: To clatter, clang, sound, blow (trumpets), clap, strike. This verb occurs more than sixty-five times. "Strike" may be the truest one-word definition; "sound" is also a possibility. *Taqa'* describes pitching a tent or fastening a nail, probably due to the striking of the hammer used for both tasks. In other references, *taqa'* describes blowing a trumpet or sounding an alarm. Thus *taqa'* indicates energy and enthusiasm. Here all nations are commanded to clap their hands and shout triumphantly to God. Formalistic religion seeks to discourage this kind of worship, although God has built into the human being an almost instinctive urge to clap and shout when victory is experienced.

CLEANSED. (Lev. 14:31) *taher* (tah-*hehr*); *Strong's* #2891: To make clean, to purify; to be pure, clean, uncontaminated. This verb and its related adjective *tahor* are used for cleansing physically, ceremonially, and morally, and thus can refer to pure gold (Ex. 25:11), pure

offerings (Lev. 14:4), and a pure heart (Ps. 51:10).

CLEARS. (Num. 14:18) *naqah* (nah-*kah*); *Strong's* #5352: To clear, acquit, cleanse, make clean; to make blameless; to free, exempt; also, to empty by pouring out the contents of something. This verb may have originally meant to "empty out a cup," then developed the meaning of "emptying any charges" against one, thus leaving him clean and clear. Most of the forty references to *naqah* have the suggestion of clearing or declaring one innocent. The adjective *naqi* means "innocent, blameless, and guiltless." *Naqi* occurs forty-two times and refers to innocent people, innocent blood, and to those who are exempt from an oath.

COMFORT. (Ps. 23:4) *nacham* (nah-*chahm*); *Strong's* #5162: To comfort, console, extend compassion, sigh with one who is grieving; to repent. *Nacham* originally may have meant "to breathe intensely because of deep emotion." In some references, the word is translated "repent," the idea being that regret causes deep sighing. In its sense of comfort, *nacham* does not describe casual sympathy, but rather deep empathy. It is like "weeping with those who weep," or actually "sighing with those who sigh." From *nacham* are derived the names "Nahum" ("Comforting") and Nehemiah ("Comfort of Yahweh"). *Also* (Acts 9:31) *paraklesis* (par-*ak*-lay-sis); *Strong's* #3874: A calling alongside to help, to comfort, to give consolation or encouragement. The *paraklete* is a strengthening presence, one who upholds those appealing for assistance. *Paraklesis* (comfort) can come to us both by the Holy Spirit (v. 31) and by the Scriptures (Rom. 15:4).

COMING. (1 Cor. 15:23) *parousia* (par-oo-*see*-ah); *Strong's* #3952: The technical term signifying the second advent of Jesus, never used to describe His first coming. *Parousia* originally was the official term for a visit by a person of high rank, especially a king. It was an arrival that included a permanent presence from that coming onward. The glorified Messiah's arrival will be followed by a permanent residence with His glorified people.

COMMANDMENT—a law, edict, or statute; specifically, one of the Ten Commandments given by God through Moses (Ex. 20:3–17; Deut. 5:7–21). Also see Commandment, New; Commandments, Ten.

COMMANDMENT, NEW—a commandment given by Jesus to His disciples, which is the commandment of Christian love—"that you love one another" (John 13:34).

COMMANDMENTS. (Ps. 119:35) *mitsvah*, plural *mitsvot* (mits-*vah*, mits-*voht*); *Strong's* #4687: Command, ordinance, precept, law; a charge; an order; a directive. *Mitsvah* is derived from the verb *tsavah*, "to command, charge, or appoint" something. *Tsavah* may have involved "marking down" orders since one of its derivatives (*tsiyun*) means "signpost" (Ezek. 39:15). God marked down the commandments, which He gave Israel upon stone tablets. *Mitsvah* occurs 180 times in the Old Testament, forty-three times in Deuteronomy, twenty-two times in Psalm 119, honoring God's multifaceted instructions to His servants. While *mitsvah* sometimes describes a king's "orders" (2 Chr. 9:14), it most often refers to God's commands. The term *Bar Mitsvah* ("Son of the Commandment") marks the coming of age for a young Jewish male who accepts his duties relating to the Law of Moses.

COMMANDMENTS, TEN—the ten laws given by God as guidelines for practical, fruitful, daily living. They are part of a covenant between God and His people (Ex. 34:28; Deut. 4:13; 10:4). These laws are often called the *Decalogue*, from the Greek word which means "ten words."

Although God gave the Ten Commandments to His people through Moses at Mount Sinai more then three thousand years ago, they are still relevant today. They have an abiding significance, for God's character is unchangeable. These laws originate from God and from His eternal character; therefore, their moral value cannot change.

About 1,300 years after God gave the laws, Jesus upheld them, calling them the "commandments" and listing five of them for the rich young ruler (Matt. 19:16–22). And in the Sermon on the Mount, Jesus showed that His coming had not cancelled the Commandments. He specifically mentioned the laws against killing (Matt. 5:21) and committing adultery (Matt. 5:27).

Jesus actually placed these laws on a higher plane by demanding that the spirit as well as the legal aspects of the law be kept. Jesus placed His eternal stamp of approval on the law by declaring, "Do not think that I came to destroy the Law or the Prophets. I did not come to destroy but to fulfill" (Matt. 5:17–19).

The holy God uttered His Commandments from the top of Mount Sinai amid smoke and fire—visible expressions of His power, majesty, and authority (Ex. 19:16–20:17). Later the Commandments were engraved on two tablets of stone, "written with the finger of God" (Ex. 31:18). The awesome nature of the events surrounding the giving of the Law is mentioned a number of times in the Bible, perhaps to emphasize the solemnity of the occasion (Ex. 19:16–19; Deut. 4:11–12).

God never intended for the Ten Commandments to be a set of regulations by which the people of Israel would earn salvation. God's favor had already been freely granted, as overwhelmingly demonstrated by His deliverance of Israel from Egyptian bondage (Deut. 4:37). Thus, at the heart of this covenant relationship, even within the Law, lay an act of divine *grace. God even prefaced the Ten Commandments with a reminder of His deliverance (Ex. 20:2).

The Ten Commandments are still relevant today. The world desperately needs to see the name and character of God displayed in the lives of Christians who still take His Word seriously. These Commandments, particularly coupled with the teachings of Christ, are still the best guidelines for practical daily living known to man.

Jesus enlarged on the ideas prevalent in the Ten Commandments by emphasizing the heart attitude: "Blessed are the pure in heart, for they shall see God" (Matt. 5:8). The Christian has blessed joy on earth when his priorities are straight, and a knowledge and application of the Ten Commandments is a wholesome and desirable practice for spiritually-minded New Testament believers in Christ.

COMMIT. (Prov. 16:3) *galal* (gah-*lahl*); *Strong's* #1556: To roll, roll down, roll away, remove. In Genesis 29:3, *galal* refers to rolling the stone from the well's mouth. In Joshua 5:9, the reproach of Egypt is rolled off from Israel. In this text, the reader is encouraged to roll his works into God's care (see also Ps. 37:5). The picture is of a camel, burdened with a heavy load; when the load is to be removed, the camel kneels down, tilts far to one side, and the load rolls off. From *galal* numerous words are derived, among which are *galgal* ("wheel" or "whirlwind"), *galil* (Galilee, literally, "Circuit" or "District"), *gulgolet* (Golgotha, "Skull" or "Head"), and *megillah* ("scroll").

COMMITED FORNICATION. (Rev. 17:2) *porneuo* (porn-*yoo*-oh); *Strong's* #4203: Compare "pornographic" and "pornography." To engage in illicit sexual intercourse, be unfaithful, play the harlot, prostitute oneself. The word is used literally (Mark 10:19; 1 Cor. 6:18; 10:8; Rev. 2:14, 20) and metaphorically to describe spiritual fornication, that is, idolatry (Rev. 17:2; 18:3, 9).

COMPANION. (Ps. 119:63) *chaber* (chah-*vehr*); *Strong's* #2270: A friend, companion, partner, associate; someone joined together or knit together with another person. *Chaber* comes from the verb *chabar*, "to join together, fellowship, associate with." The plural *chaberim* refers to "friends" who are closely bonded together in love or in a common purpose. In this reference, the psalmist states, "I am a friend of anyone and everyone who reveres the Lord," or to greatly paraphrase it, "Any friend of God's is a friend of mine."

COMPANY. (Ps. 68:11) *tsaba'* (tsah-*vah*); *Strong's #6635:* An army, a company, host, battalion, throng; a division of soldiers. This noun pictures a great mass of people or things. *Tsaba'* appears more than 425 times in the Old Testament. The hosts (armies) of heaven are the innumerable heavenly bodies, which God has created (Gen. 2:1; Ps. 33:6). A title by which God is frequently known is "the LORD of hosts," *Yahweh tsaba'ot* (in English this is sometimes inadequately spelled "Lord Sabaoth"). The Lord of hosts is the God of the armies of Israel, who also has great spiritual armies at His command (*see* Rev. 19:14).

COMPASSION (MOVED WITH). (Matt. 14:14) *splanchnizomai* (splångkh-*nid*-zom-ahee); *Strong's #4697:* To be moved with deep compassion or pity. The Greeks regarded the bowels (*splanchna*) as the place where strong and powerful emotions originated. The Hebrews regarded *splanchna* as the place where tender mercies and feelings of affection, compassion, sympathy, and pity originated. It is the direct motive for at least five of Jesus' miracles.

COMPELS. (Matt. 5:41) *angareuo* (ang-ar-*you*-oh); *Strong's #29:* A verb derived from the Persian, where it described a courier with the authority to impress people into public service. The word carried the same idea in New Testament times, referring to the privilege of Roman officials and soldiers to press into service a person, his horses, his equipment, and his family members, usually without advance notice. *Also* (2 Cor. 5:14) *sunecho* (soon-*ekh*-oh); *Strong's #4912:* From *sun*, "together," and *echo*, "to hold"; hence, "to hold together," or "to grip tightly." The word describes people who are afflicted with various diseases and pains (Luke 4:38) or paralyzed by fear (Luke 8:37), crowds hemming Christ in (Luke 8:45), an army surrounding Jerusalem (Luke 19:43), and soldiers arresting Jesus and holding Him fast (Luke 22:63). In every use of the word, there is a sense of constraint, a tight grip that prevents an escape. The love of Christ leaves us no choice except to live our lives for Him.

COMPLETE. (2 Cor. 13:9) *katartisis* (kat-*ar*-tis-is); *Strong's #2676:* An improving, equipping,

training, disciplining. It includes making the necessary adjustments and repairs. The related verb, *katartizo*, is used for the disciples' mending their nets (Matt. 4:21).

COMPREHEND. (John 1:5) *katalambano* (kat-al-am-*ban*-oh); *Strong's #2638:* The word is capable of three interpretations: (1) To seize, lay hold of, overcome. As such, verse 5 could read, "The darkness does not gain control of it." (2) To perceive, attain, lay hold of with the mind; to apprehend with mental or moral effort. With this meaning the verse could be translated, "The darkness is unreceptive and does not understand it." (3) To quench, extinguish, snuff out the light by stifling it. "The darkness will never be able to eliminate it." Light and darkness essentially are antagonistic. The Christian's joy is in knowing that light is not only greater than darkness but also will outlast the darkness.

CONDEMN, CONDEMNATION—to declare a person guilty and worthy of punishment. Condemn and condemnation are judicial terms, the opposite of justify and *justification (Matt. 12:37; Rom. 5:16, 18). God alone is the judge of humanity; in the face of His demand for righteousness, sin leads invariably to condemnation and death.

The mission of Jesus was not to condemn to world but to save it by bearing on the cross the sin that belonged to His people (John 3:17–18). There is no condemnation for sinners who repent and believe in Him. Jesus not only bore the consequences of sin, but also condemned (destroyed) sin itself so that believers are released from its power (Rom. 8:1, 3). Since they have experienced a gracious pardon, believers are directed to practice forgiveness and to avoid vindictiveness: "Condemn not, and you shall not be condemned" (Luke 6:37).

CONFESSION—an admission of sins and the profession of belief in the doctrines of a particular faith. In the Bible most of the uses of the word confession fall into one of these two categories. Examples of confession of sin may be found in Joshua's words to Achan (Josh. 7:19), in the confession during the Passover during Hezekiah's reign (2 Chr. 30:22), and in Ezra's call to the people to admit wrongdoing in marrying pagan wives (Ezra 10:11).

The Bible also uses the word confession to describe an open, bold, and courageous proclamation of one's faith. The apostle Paul wrote: "If you confess with your mouth the Lord Jesus and believe in your heart that God has raised Him from the dead, you will be saved. For with the heart one believes to righteousness, and with the mouth confession is made to salvation" (Rom. 10:9–10). Some also note the value of a believer's "confessing" God's Word or promises, as a declaration of faith in His trustworthiness. Such a practice can be edifying and fulfilling of the biblical directive in Joshua 1:8, if it is kept free from legalistic, loveless, or superstitious forms.

CONFIDENCE. (2 Thess. 3:4) *peitho* (*pie*-tho); *Strong's #3982:* As an intransitive verb, the word means to be convinced, be confident, have inward certainty, trust (Rom. 2:19; 2 Cor. 2:3). In its transitive use, it means to win over, prevail upon, persuade, induce a change of mind by the use of arguments (Acts 18:4; 19:8, 26; 2 Cor. 5:11).

CONFIRM, CONFIRMATION—to establish, ratify, or strengthen a covenant. In the Bible the word confirm or confirmation is used of a vow or binding oath (Num. 30:13–14), words (Ezek. 13:6), a transaction of redeeming or exchanging (Ruth 4:7), a covenant or statute (Dan. 9:27; Gal. 3:15, 17), a person (Dan. 11:1), promises (Rom. 15:8), the testimony of Christ (1 Cor. 1:6), the gospel (Phil. 1:7), and salvation (Heb. 2:3). The expression is often used to describe the certifying or verifying of a word of prophecy given or received in the name of the Lord. (*See* Elizabeth's confirmation of what the angel had told Mary, Luke 1:45.)

CONFIRMING. (Mark 16:20) *bebaioo* (beb-ah-*yah*-oh); *Strong's #950:* To make firm, establish, secure, corroborate, guarantee. The miracles that accompanied the disciples' preaching confirmed to the people that the messengers were telling the truth, that God was backing up their message with supernatural phenomena, and that a new dispensation, the age of grace, had entered the world.

CONFORMED. (Rom. 12:2) *suschematizo* (soos-khay-mat-*id*-zoe); *Strong's #4964:* Compare "scheme" and "schematic." Refers to conforming oneself to the outer fashion or outward appearance, accommodating oneself to a model or pattern. *Suschematizo* occurs elsewhere in the New Testament only in 1 Peter 1:14, where it describes those conforming themselves to worldly lusts. Even apparent or superficial conformity to the present world system or any accommodation to its ways would be fatal to the Christian life.

CONGREGATION. (Josh. 22:17) *'edah* (ay-dah); *Strong's #5712:* Assembly, crowd, swarm, family, multitude, company. *'Edah* is from the verb *ya'ad,* "to appoint," thus implying a group assembled together by appointment, or acting together. The word occurs more than 140 times in the Old Testament,

most often in reference to the congregation of Israel.

CONQUERORS (MORE THAN). (Rom. 8:37) *hupernikao* (hoop-er-nik-*ah*-oh); *Strong's #5245:* From *huper,* "over and above," and *nikao,* "to conquer." The word describes one who is super-victorious, who wins more than an ordinary victory, but who is overpowering in achieving abundant victory. This is not the language of conceit, but of confidence. Christ's love conquered death, and because of His love, we are *hupernikao.*

CONSCIENCE—a person's inner awareness of conforming to the will of God or departing from it, resulting in either a sense of approval or condemnation.

The term does not appear in the Old Testament but the concept does. David, for example, was smitten in his heart because of his lack of trust in the power of God (2 Sam. 24:10). But his guilt turned to joy when he sought the Lord's forgiveness (Psalm 32). Such passages as Psalm 19 indicate that God is discernible to the human conscience, and is accountable therefore (Rom. 1:18–20).

In the New Testament "conscience" is found most frequently in Paul's epistles. However, the conscience is by no means the final standard of moral goodness (1 Cor. 4:4). Under both the old and new covenant the conscience is only trustworthy when formed by the Word and will of God. The law given to Israel was inscribed on the hearts of believers (Heb. 8:10; 10:16), so the sensitized conscience is able to discern God's judgment against sin (Rom. 2:14–15).

The conscience of the believer has been cleansed by the work of Jesus Christ; it no longer accuses and condemns (Heb. 9:14; 10:22). Believers are to maintain pure consciences or not encourage others to act against their consciences. To act contrary to the urging of one's conscience is wrong, for actions that go against the conscience cannot arise out of faith (1 Cor. 8; 10:23–33).

CONSECRATION—the act of setting apart, or dedicating, something or someone for God's use. In the Old Testament, the temple and its trappings were the most important objects consecrated to God (2 Chr. 7:5–9; Ezra 6:16–17), and Aaron and his sons were consecrated to the priesthood (Exodus 29; Leviticus 8). Even such items as the spoils of battle (Josh. 6:19; Mic. 4:13) and cattle could be consecrated (Lev. 27:28). Before the beginning of the priesthood in Israel's history, the firstborn of men and beasts alike were consecrated (Ex. 13:2; Num. 13:12).

In the New Testament, the supreme example of consecration is Christ himself (John 17:19, Heb. 7:28; 10:10), though believers are also consecrated by Christ (John 17:17; 1 Pet. 2:9), and are urged to consecrate themselves as well (Rom. 12:1; 2 Tim. 2:21).

CONTINUALLY. (Ex. 28:30) *tamid* (tah-*meed*); *Strong's* #8548: Constantly, always, evermore, perpetually. It is assumed that this adverb comes from a root, meaning "to stretch out to eternity," "to extend forever." *Tamid* occurs more than one hundred times in the Old Testament with the primary idea of something permanent and unceasing. In 29:42, *tamid* describes the burnt offering as "continual"; "permanent," "daily," or "regular" may also fit here. *Tamid* occurs in several well-loved verses: "My eyes are *ever* toward the LORD" (Ps. 25:15). "His praise shall *continually* be in my mouth" (Ps. 34:1). "The LORD will guide you *continually,* and satisfy your soul in drought" (Is. 58:11).

CONVERSION—the initial change of attitude and will that brings a person into right relationship with God.

Conversion involves turning away from evil deeds and false worship and turning toward serving and worshiping the Lord. Conversion marks a person's entrance into a new relationship with God, forgiveness of sins, and his new life as a part of the fellowship of the people of God.

Closely related to conversion are repentance and faith. Repentance is turning from sin; faith is turning to God. Thus, conversion is more than the exchange of one set of beliefs for another; it is a wholehearted turning to God (Acts 15:3).

The inward experience of conversion is sometimes referred to as the new birth (John 3:38). This phrase was used by Jesus in His conversation with Nicodemus. New birth refers to a change so radical that it can be described only by the figure of birth into a new life. As an infant enters the physical world with a totally new existence, so conversion opens the way for a totally new beginning in a person's relationship to God and his life and responsibilities toward man.

The experience of conversion may differ with various individuals. The apostle Paul's conversion was sudden and radical, while the conversion of Lydia (Acts 16:14–15) was apparently gradual or over a brief period of time. But the results of conversion are always a clear change of attitude and a new direction for life.

CONVICTION—the Holy Spirit's process in dealing with one's own conscience, alerting and sensitizing us to God's Word and demands. The idea of conviction is a major theme of Scripture, though the word is rarely used (Psalm 32; 51; Acts 2:37; Rom. 7:7–25). The agent of conviction is the Holy Spirit (John 16:7–11). His means of convicting is either through the Word of God (Acts 2:37), or by holding before us God's general revelation of His demands through nature and man's inborn consciousness of right and wrong (Rom. 1:18–20; 2:15). The purpose of conviction is to lead a person to repent of his sins (Acts 2:37–38; Rom. 2:14) and to turn to God for salvation and eternal life. Even beyond one's new birth, the Spirit of God still will deal with or convict us as our senses and sensibilities are refined through the Holy Spirit's sanctifying process in our lives.

CORRECT. (Jer. 10:24) *yasar* (yah-*sar*); *Strong's* #3256: To chasten, correct, instruct; to reform someone. This verb refers to the discipline and correction necessary to moral training. Moses told Israel in Deuteronomy 8:5, that "as a man chastens his son, so the LORD your God chastens you." Some individuals cannot be corrected by words alone (Prov. 29:19). *Yasar* may involve tough measures, as with whips (1 Kin. 12:11), or teaching technique by itself, as in the case of the music director who instructed the Levitical musicians (1 Chr. 15:22). From *yasar* is derived the noun *musar*, "instruction."

COUNSEL. (Zech. 6:13) *'etsah* (ayst-*ah*); *Strong's* #6098: Advice; plan; counsel; purpose. This noun comes from the verb *ya'ats*, "to counsel, to advise." *'Etsah* occurs about eighty-five times, referring both to the Lord's counsel (Ps. 73:24; Jer. 32:19) and the counsel of a true friend, or a group of wise persons (2 Chr. 10:8; Prov. 27:9). The superiority of divine counsel is shown in Psalm 33:11, "The counsel of the LORD stands forever." The present reference refers ultimately to the Lord Jesus, who shall sit as King and Priest on His throne. The counsel of peace (an agreement, plan, and purpose that results in wholeness) shall exist between His kingly and priestly roles. Someday, by God's plan or advice, all powers will be laid on the Messiah's shoulder.

COURTESY. (Acts 24:4) *epieikeia* (ep-ee-*eye*-ki-ah); *Strong's* #1932: Graciousness, gentleness, clemency, moderation, sweet reasonableness, mildness, fairness, kindness, forbearance, what is right or fitting. In 2 Corinthians 10:1, *epieikeia* is an attribute of God. Here it is an appeal to Felix to show the customary graciousness befitting his high office. Christians can display *epieikeia* in virtue of their divine calling.

COURT OF THE GENTILES—see ch. 55, §6.

COVENANT—an agreement between two people or two groups that involves promises on the part of each to the other. The concept of covenant between God and His people is one of the most important theological truths of the Bible. By making a covenant with Abraham, God promised to bless His descendants and to make them His special people. Abraham, in return, was to remain faithful to God and to serve as a channel through whom God's blessings could flow to the rest of the world (Gen. 12:1–3).

Before Abraham, God made a covenant with Noah, assuring him that He would not again destroy the world by flood (Genesis 9). Another covenant was between God and David, in which David and his descendants were established as the royal heirs to the throne of the nation of Israel (2 Sam. 7:12; 22:51). This covenant agreement realized its complete fulfillment when Jesus the Messiah, a descendant of the line of David, was born in Bethlehem about a thousand years after God made this promise to David the king.

A covenant, in the biblical sense, implies much more than a contract or simple agreement. A contract always has an end date, while a covenant is a permanent arrangement. Further, a contract generally involves only one aspect of a person's life, such as a skill, or a portion of one's money. However, a covenant covers a person's total being, and embraces all features of their life, purpose, and destiny.

The Old Testament word for covenant gives insight into this important word. It is derived from a Hebrew root meaning "to cut." This explains the ancient practice of two people passing between the cut portions of slain animals to seal an agreement with each other (Jer. 34:18). Some ritual or ceremony such as this always accompanied the making of a covenant in the Old Testament: (a) some entered into a covenant sharing a holy meal (Gen. 31:54); (b) Abraham and his children were commanded to be circumcised as a sign of their covenant with God (Gen. 17:10–11); (c) Moses sprinkled the blood of animals on the altar and upon the people who entered into covenant with God at Mount Sinai (Ex. 24:38).

The Old Testament contains many examples of covenants between people who related to each other as equals. For example, David and Jonathan entered into a covenant because of their love for each other. This agreement bound each of them to certain responsibilities (1 Sam. 18:3). The striking thing about God's covenant with His people is that God is holy, all-knowing, and all-powerful, but He consents to enter into covenant with man, who is weak, sinful, and imperfect.

In the Old Testament, God's chosen people confirmed their covenant with God with oaths or promises to keep the agreement. At Mount Sinai, the nation of Israel promised to perform "all the words which the Lord has said" (Ex. 24:3). When the people later broke this promise, they were called by their leaders to renew their oath (2 Kin. 23:3). By contrast, God does not break promises. His oath to raise up believing children to Abraham (Gen. 22:16–17) is an "everlasting" covenant (Gen. 17:7).

The New Testament makes a clear distinction between covenants of Law and covenants of Promise. The apostle Paul spoke of these "two covenants," one originating "from Mount Sinai," the other from "the Jerusalem above" (Gal. 4:24–26). Paul also argued that the covenant established at Mount Sinai, the Law, is a "ministry of death" and "condemnation" (2 Cor. 3:7, 9)—a covenant that cannot be fulfilled from man's side because of human weakness and sin (Rom. 8:3).

But the "covenants of promise" (Eph. 2:12) are God's guarantees that He will provide salvation in spite of mankind's inability to keep our side of the agreement because of our sin. The provision of a chosen people through whom the Messiah would be born is the promise of the covenants with Adam and David (Gen. 3:15; 2 Sam. 7:14–15). The covenant with Noah is God's promise to withhold judgment on nature while salvation is occurring (Gen. 8:21–22; 2 Pet. 3:7, 15). In the covenant with Abraham, God promised to bless Abraham's descendants because of his faith.

These many covenants of promise may be considered as tributaries to one grand covenant of grace, which was fulfilled in the life and ministry of Jesus. His death ushered in the new covenant under which we are justified by God's grace and mercy rather than our human attempts to keep the law. And Jesus Himself is the Mediator of this better covenant between God and humanity (Heb. 9:15).

Jesus' sacrificial death, His body "broken" as with the ancient sacrifices forecasting His coming, has allowed us a place to "pass through"—into covenant with God. His death served as the oath, or pledge, which God made to us to seal this new covenant. He is determined to give us eternal life and fellowship with Him, in spite of our unworthiness. As the Book of Hebrews declares, "The word of the oath, which came after the law, appoints the Son who has been perfected forever" (Heb.

7:28). This is still God's promise to any person who turns to Him in repentance and faith.

Also see Covenant, New.

COVENANT. (Gen. 17:7) *berit* (beh-*reet*); *Strong's #1285:* A covenant, compact, pledge, treaty, agreement. This is one of the most theologically important words in the Bible, appearing more than 250 times in the Old Testament. A *berit* may be made between individuals, between a king and his people, or by God with His people. Here God's irrevocable pledge is that He will be God to Abraham and his descendants *forever*. The greatest provision of the Abrahamic covenant, this is the foundation stone of Israel's eternal relationship to God, a truth affirmed by David (2 Sam. 7:24), by the Lord Himself (Jer. 33:24–26), and by Paul (Rom. 9:4; 11:2, 29). All other Bible promises are based on this one. *Also* (Mark 14:24) *diatheke* (dee-ath-*ay*-kay); *Strong's #1242:* A will, testament, pact, contract, an agreed upon plan to which both parties subscribe. While the word may signify an agreement between two parties, with each accepting mutual obligations, most often it is a declaration of one person's will. In the Bible, God initiated the whole action, set the conditions, and defined as a decree a declaration of purposes. God covenanted with Noah, Abraham, Moses, and Israel. In the New Testament Jesus ratified by His death on the Cross a new covenant, termed in Hebrews 7:22 "a better covenant."

COVENANT, BOOK OF THE—a name for the code of laws in Exodus 20:22—23:33, given to Moses at Mount Sinai immediately after the Ten Commandments. The Book of the Covenant was discovered in the temple during the reign of King Josiah of Judah (641—609 B.C.), who used it in his restoration of true worship (2 Kin. 23:2–3, 21; 2 Chr. 34:30–31).

COVENANT, NEW—the new agreement (or new testament) God has made with mankind, based on the death and resurrection of Jesus Christ. The concept of a new covenant originated with the promise of the prophet Jeremiah that God would accomplish for His people what the old covenant had failed to do (Jer. 31:31). Under this new covenant, God would write His Law on human hearts. This promised action suggested a new potential for obedience, a new dimension of knowing the Lord, and a fully accomplished provision of forgiveness for sin. The redeeming work of Jesus Christ has brought the promised new covenant into being. In Luke 22:20, Jesus presented the cup as "the new covenant in My blood," which understanding has continued in the church (1 Cor. 11:25). The Epistle to the

Hebrews elaborates this. It quotes the entire "new covenant" passage from Jeremiah 31:31–34 (Heb. 8:8–12; also 10:16–17), and declares Jesus as "the Mediator of the new covenant" (Heb. 9:15; 12:24), a "better covenant . . . established on better promises" (Heb. 8:6).

Also see Covenant.

COVETOUS. (1 Cor. 6:10) *pleonektes* (pleh-on-*ek*-tace); *Strong's #4123:* Literally "to have more." This word regresses from good to bad. *Pleon* is the basic word for more in quantity, quality, and number. *Pleonazo* means to do more, make more, or increase. *Pleonekteo* means to overreach. *Pleonexia* is avarice. *Pleonektes* means a greedy covetousness so eager for gain that it will defraud others. A person consumed with *pleonektes* will violate laws for unlawful gain. He will cunningly forge ahead at others' expense. Ephesians 5:3 tells us covetousness is idolatry. Idolatry is an aggravated form of self-love motivated by ego-drive. (Compare "pleonasm" or "pleonastic.")

CRAFTINESS. (1 Cor. 3:19) *panourgia* (pan-oorg-*ee*-ah); *Strong's #3834:* Versatile cleverness, astute knavery, sophisticated cunning, unscrupulous conduct, evil treachery, deceptive scheming, arrogant shrewdness, and sly arrogance. Used only five times in the New Testament, it refers to Satan's deceiving Eve (2 Cor. 11:3); the Pharisees' trying to trick Jesus (Luke 20:23); the deception of false teachers (Eph. 4:14); the self-entrapment of the worldly wise (1 Cor. 3:19); and the improper method of presenting the gospel (2 Cor. 4:2).

CREATED. (Gen. 1:1) *bara'* (bah-*rah*); *Strong's #1254:* To form or fashion, to produce, to create. Originally this verb carried the idea of "carving" or "cutting out," and that concept is still expressed by the intensive verbal form in Joshua 17:18, referring to "cutting" down trees to "clear out" the land. This suggests that creating is similar to sculpturing. Thus *bara'* is a fitting word to describe both creating by bringing into existence and creating by fashioning existing matter into something new, as God did in "creating" man (Gen. 1:27) out of dust from the ground. God is always the subject of the verb *bara'* in its standard form; creating is therefore a divine capacity.

CREATION—God's action in creating the natural universe out of nothing. The New Testament Epistle to the Hebrews declares, "By faith we understand that the world was framed by the word of God, so that the things which are seen were not made of things which are visible" (Heb. 11:3).

God is the Creator—the only being capable of making something from nothing. Yet, on a lesser level, man also has been given the capacity to be creative and procreative. While God is the universe's ruler, man has been told to "have dominion" over the realm of his responsibility. God is holy, a moral and ethical God who is completely righteous. So, man is also called and held accountable to be morally and ethically responsible and righteous before God. Human experience and the biblical record suggest that these are some ways in which man reflects the image of God.

Many of the pagan nations of the ancient world had their own creation stories. But in these stories, their gods evolved out of natural processes connected with the world itself. They believed the material universe was eternal, and it brought their gods into being. But Genesis declares that God existed before creation and is in full control of the physical universe. He called the world into being by His word. His power is absolute. He does not have to conform to nature and cannot be threatened by it. God is sovereign and does not have to share His power with other supernatural beings. The account of His act of creation is found in the first two chapters of the Book of Genesis.

Since God created the universe out of nothing, it is His and will always serve His purpose. As He shaped creation without the assistance of anyone, He will bring creation to its desired end. No power can frustrate God in His purpose to complete the process started in creation and revealed in Scripture. Our hope rests in the sovereign power of Him who created the world and who recreates us through the saving power of His Son, Jesus Christ.

CREATION. (Col. 1:15) *ktisis* (*ktis*-is); *Strong's #2937:* A founding, establishing, settling, formation. The word is used to denote both the act of creating and the product of the creative act. Salvation gives a person the status of being a new creation (2 Cor. 5:17; Gal. 6:15).

CREATION AND FLOOD STORIES, BABYLONIAN—see ch. 55, §2.2.

CREATURE—any created being, including man, brought into existence as a result of God's power and authority. The Bible declares that the Redeemer God is the sovereign Creator of all things. Through His might and power He brought the universe into existence (Gen. 1:3–24; Ps. 33:6; Heb. 11:3). Therefore, all beings, including angels, are His creatures (John 1:3; 1 Cor. 8:6). The creaturely status of all finite beings and things reveals the sovereign rule of God and the dependence of man and the world on Him.

Man, the pinnacle of God's creation, was created to have dominion in the world (Gen. 1:26–28; Ps. 8:38). But man "exchanged the truth of God for the lie and worshiped and served the creature rather than the Creator" (Rom. 1:25). God's plan for man to rule His creation is now being fulfilled in Christ (1 Cor. 15:20–28; Phil. 2:5–11). He is establishing God's kingdom.

Redemption involves being made new creatures (2 Cor. 5:17), members of the new creation in Christ that God is bringing about through His power (Rom. 8:19). This universal kingdom of righteousness, peace, and joy will be fully revealed when Christ returns in triumph over all rebellious creatures and God creates a new heaven and earth (1 Cor. 15:20–28).

CREATURE. (Rev. 5:13) *ktisma* (*ktis*-mah); *Strong's #2938:* The created thing, formation, product, the thing founded. In nonbiblical Greek it described founding a town, building it, and then colonizing it. The word comes from *ktizo,* "to build." *Ktisma* denotes the component parts of creation. The creator called every one of them into existence. In verse 13, heaven as well as earth's creatures exist only to glorify God and the Lamb of God.

CREED—a brief, authoritative, formal statement of religious beliefs. The word creed comes from the Latin word *credo* ("I believe"), the first word of both the Nicene Creed and the Apostles' Creed.

The following are the three classic, or most historically important, creeds of the church:

The Nicene Creed. A creed adopted by the First Council of Nicaea (A.D. 325) and revised by the First Council of Constantinople (A.D. 381). The First Council of Nicaea, convened by the Roman emperor Constantine the Great (ruled A.D. 306–337), rejected a heresy known as Arianism, which denied the divinity of Jesus. The Nicene Creed formally proclaimed the divinity and equality of Jesus Christ, the Son of God, in the Trinity.

The Athanasian Creed. A Christian creed originating in Europe in the fourth century and relating especially to the doctrines of the Trinity and the bodily *incarnation of Christ. This creed was originally ascribed to Saint Athanasius (A.D. 293?—373), but it is now believed to be the work of an unknown writer of the time.

The Apostles' Creed. This well-known creed lies at the basis of most other religious statements of belief. Although it bears the name of the apostles, it did not originate with them. It was written after the close of the New

Testament, and it held an important place in the early church. This creed has been appealed to by all branches of the church as a test of authentic faith.

CRUCIFIXION OF CHRIST—the method of torture and execution used by the Romans to put Christ to death. At a crucifixion the victim usually was nailed or tied to a wooden stake and left to die.

Crucifixion was used by many nations of the ancient world, including Assyria, Media, and Persia. Alexander the Great of Greece crucified 2,000 inhabitants of Tyre when he captured the city. The Romans later adopted this method of execution and used it often throughout their empire. Crucifixion was the Romans' most severe form of execution, reserved only for slaves and criminals. No Roman citizen could be crucified.

Crucifixion involved attaching the victim with nails through the wrists or with leather thongs to a crossbeam attached to a vertical stake. Sometimes blocks or pins were put on the stake to give the victim some support as he hung suspended from the crossbeam. At times the feet were also nailed to the vertical stake. As the victim hung dangling by the arms, the blood could no longer circulate to his vital organs. Only by supporting himself on the seat or pin could the victim gain temporary relief.

Gradually exhaustion set in, and death followed, although usually not for several days in cases where the victim was tied, not nailed. If the victim had been severely beaten, he would not live this long. To hasten death, the executioners sometimes broke the victim's legs with a club. Then he could no longer support his body to keep blood circulating, and death followed quickly. Usually the dead bodies were left to rot or be eaten by scavengers.

To the Jewish people, crucifixion represented the most disgusting form of death: "He who is hanged (on a tree) is accursed of God" (Deut. 21:23). Yet the Jewish Sanhedrin sought and obtained Roman authorization to have Jesus crucified (Mark 15:13–15). As was the custom, the charge against Jesus was attached to the Cross; He was offered a brew to deaden His senses, but He refused (Mark 15:23). There was no need for the soldiers to break His legs to hasten death. By the ninth hour (Mark 15:34, 37), probably 3:00 P.M.—in only six hours—Jesus was already dead (John 19:31–33). Jesus' body was not left to rot; the disciples were able to secure Pilate's permission to give Him a proper burial.

The apostle Paul summed up the importance of the crucifixion best: "We preach Christ crucified, to the Jews a stumbling block and to the Greeks foolishness, but to those who are called, both Jews and Greeks, Christ the power of God and the wisdom of God" (1 Cor. 1:23–24). Out of the ugliness and agony of crucifixion, God accomplished the greatest good of all—the redemption of sinners.

CRUSH. (Rom. 16:20) *suntribo* (soon-*tree*-bow); *Strong's #4937:* To trample upon, break in pieces, shatter, bruise, grind down, smash. This statement in verse 20 alludes to Genesis 3:15. Our victory is a continuation of Christ's victory when He bruised the head of the serpent at Calvary. *Suntribo* points to present victories over the powers of darkness as well as to the ultimate destruction of Satan's kingdom at the Second Coming of Christ.

CUNEIFORM—see ch. 55, §2.2.

CURES. (Luke 13:32) *iasis* (*ee*-as-is); *Strong's #2392:* The act of healing, curing the sick. *Iasis* is akin to *iaomai*, "to heal," and *iatros*, "a physician." By the second century A.D., *iasis* included bodily healing, forgiveness of sins, and deliverance from demonic possession. The gospel frees the entire person.

CURSE—a prayer or conjuration for injury, harm, or misfortune to befall someone. Noah, for instance, pronounced a curse on Canaan (Gen. 9:25). Isaac pronounced a curse on anyone who cursed Jacob (Gen. 27:29). The soothsayer Balaam was hired by Balak, king of Moab, to pronounce a curse on the Israelites (Numbers 22—24). Goliath, the Philistine giant of Gath, "cursed David by his gods" (1 Sam. 17:43).

In biblical terms, a curse is more than a mere wish that evil will befall one's enemies. A curse is revealed as possessing the power to bring about the evil the cursor speaks.

In the account of the temptation and Fall, God Himself is described as cursing the serpent (Gen. 3:14–15), as well as the ground (Gen. 3:17). Although the word curse is not used directly of Adam and Eve, the woman is sentenced to pain in childbirth and the man is condemned to earn his living by the sweat of his face. In the New Testament, Jesus cursed the fig tree, saying, " 'Let no fruit grow on you ever again.' And immediately the fig tree withered away" (Matt. 21:19; Mark 11:14). He also taught Christians how to deal with curses: "Bless those who curse you" (Luke 6:28), revealing the power of faith and love to neutralize the power of evil assault.

The apostle Paul spoke of the Law as a curse because it pronounces a curse upon everyone "who does not continue in all things which are written in the book of the law, to do them" (Gal. 3:10). By the grace of God, however, "Christ has redeemed us from the curse of the law, having become a curse for us (for it is written, 'Cursed is everyone who hangs on a tree')" (Gal. 3:13). The by-product of this redemptive truth opens the doorway to blessing. Many see the essence of the blessings of Deuteronomy 28:1–14 being reinstated for believers in Christ; while the curses of Deuteronomy 28:15–19 as being broken before the power of the full flow of Christ's work on the Cross. Finally, the Bible promises that the day is coming when "there shall be no more curse" (Rev. 22:3), and all the redeemed inscribed in the Lamb's Book of Life will enjoy the abundant blessings of God eternally.

CUSTOMS AND MANNERS OF THE BIBLE— see ch. 55, §1.

DAGON—see ch. 55, §3.4., 3.6.

DAISPORA—see ch. 55, §3.2.

DAMASCUS GATE—see ch. 55, §6.1.

DANCING—rhythmic movement of the body, usually done to musical accompaniment. Among the Jews, dancing generally occurred as a way of celebrating joyous occasions. Indeed, dancing became a symbol of joy, the opposite of mourning (Ps. 30:11; Eccl. 3:4; Luke 15:25).

The Bible gives several examples of dancing. Groups of women danced at celebrations of military victories (1 Sam. 18:16). The dancing of the virgins at Shiloh was probably part of a religious celebration (Judg. 21:19–23). Occasionally, children imitated the dance in their play (Job. 21:11; Matt. 11:17). David "danced before the Lord with all his might" (2 Sam. 6:14) when the *ark of the covenant was brought up to Jerusalem from the house of Obed-Edom.

Dancing by the Israelites was usually accompanied by the rhythmic beating of timbrels—or tambourines (Judg. 11:34). On great national occasions, Israel also praised the Lord with stringed instruments, flutes, and cymbals (Ps. 150:4).

Salome's infamous dance, which won her John the Baptist's head on a platter, was in the tradition of Greek dancing, a sensual art form rather than an act of worship (Matt. 14:6). This order of individual or group sensuality is implicitly disapproved of by the example of God's response through Moses on the occasion of the dancing and festivities surrounding the golden calf episode. (*See* Ex. 32:1–34; v. 19.)

DARIUS THE GREAT—see ch. 55, §2.2., 3.2.

DARKNESS—the absence of light. Darkness existed before the light of creation (Gen. 1:2). Since darkness was associated with the chaos that existed before the creation, it came to be associated with evil, bad luck, or affliction (Job 17:12; 21:17). Darkness also was equated with death. In *sheol, the land of the dead, there is only darkness (Job 10:21–22; 38:17). Darkness symbolizes man's ignorance of God's will and, thus, is associated with sin (Job 24:13–17).

Darkness also describes the condition of those who have not yet seen the light concerning Jesus (John 1:4–5; 12:35; Eph. 5:14) and those who deliberately turn away from the light (John 3:19–20). Hating the light will bring condemnation (Col. 1:13; 2 Pet. 2:17). Living in extreme darkness describes those who at the end of time have not repented (Rev. 16:10; 18:23).

DARKNESS. (Luke 11:35) *skotos* (*skot-*oss); *Strong's #4655:* From the root *ska,* "to cover." The word is used literally for physical darkness and metaphorically for spiritual, moral, and intellectual darkness. The darkness arises from error, ignorance, disobedience, willful blindness, and rebellion. Darkness is an evil system absolutely opposed to the light. *Also* (John 12:46) *scotia* (skot-*ee*-ah); *Strong's #4653:* Darkness, gloom, evil, sin, obscurity, night, ignorance, moral depravity. The New Testament especially uses the word in a metaphorical sense of ignorance of divine truth, man's sinful nature, total absence of light, and a lack of spiritual perception. Light equals happiness. *Scotia* equals unhappiness. *Scotia* as spiritual darkness basically describes everything earthly or demonic that is at enmity with God.

DAY—the twenty-four-hour period between two successive risings of the sun. The Hebrew people reckoned their day from evening to evening, the period of time between two successive sunsets (Gen. 1:5, 8; Ex. 12:18; Lev. 23:32).

The Bible also uses the word day in a symbolic sense, as in "the day of His wrath" (Job 20:28), and "the day of the Lord" (Is. 2:12; 13:6, 9; Amos 5:18–20). The same phrase is used in the New Testament (1 Thess. 5:2; 2 Pet. 3:10), meaning "the day of the Lord Jesus" (1 Cor. 5:5), or His Second Coming. To those who scoff at the delay of the Lord's return, Peter declared, "With the Lord one day is as a

---

 This icon beside an entry indicates a Word Wealth feature.

 This icon beside an entry indicates a Kingdom Dynamics feature.

 This icon beside an entry indicates an important biblical or doctrinal term.

thousand years, and a thousand years as one day" (2 Pet. 3:8).

DAY. (Zeph. 1:7) *yom* (*yoam*); *Strong's* #3117: Day; daylight; a day consisting of nighttime and daytime; also, a certain period of time. *Yom* occurs more than 2,200 times with a variety of meanings. *Yom* occurs first in Genesis 1:5, where God called the light "Day"; the remainder of the verse shows that day is not only the period of light, but also a period consisting of evening and morning. (Because God placed evening before morning throughout the week of creation, the Jewish day begins at sundown.) *Yom* may represent a time period or the occasion of a major event. "Day of trouble" (Zeph. 1:15) is thus a troubled time. In Genesis 3:5 and Isaiah 12:4, *yom* expresses an indefinite future time. *Yom Yahweh* ("day of the LORD") may refer to a time when God reveals Himself through judgment and supernatural events. "The day of the LORD" may also refer to the return of the Lord Jesus to judge and rule the world.

DAY OF THE LORD, THE—a special day at the end of time when God's will and purpose for mankind and His world will be fulfilled. Many Bible students see the day of the Lord as a longer period of time rather than a single day—a period when Christ will reign throughout the world before He cleanses heaven and earth in preparation for the eternal state of all mankind.

Amos 5:18–20 is probably the earliest occurrence in Scripture of the phrase, "day of the Lord." According to Amos, that day would be a time of great darkness for any in rebellion against God, whether Jew or Gentile. The day would be a time of judgment (Is. 13:6, 9; Jer. 46:10), as well as restoration (Is. 14:1; Joel 2:28–32).

DEACON—a servant or minister; an ordained lay officer in many Christian churches.

The general concept of deacon as a servant of the church is well established in both the Bible and church history. But the exact nature of the office is hard to define, because of changing concepts and varying practices among church bodies through the centuries. Bible passages associated with deacons are interpreted differently by various church groups, and applied to different duties or roles and with widely varied levels of local authority.

The term deacon occurs in only two passages in the NKJV (Phil. 1:1; 1 Tim. 3:8–13). But the Greek word *diakonos* from which it is taken is found thirty times. In most cases *diakonos* is translated as "servant" rather than "deacon." In the Greek world, *diakonos* was used to describe the work of a servant—a person who waited on tables or ministered as a religious official. When the office of deacon was established in the New Testament church, it clearly implied a "servant spirit" was important to the attitude of a deacon.

The origin of the office of deacon is usually related to the events described in Acts 6:1–6. The young Christian church in Jerusalem was experiencing growing pains, and it had become increasingly difficult for the apostles to effectively distribute charitable gifts to its needy members. To meet this critical need, seven men were chosen by the congregation and presented to the apostles. Although these men were not called deacons at that time, the word used to describe their work comes from the same Greek root for deacon.

The list of qualifications for deacons given in 1 Timothy 3 shows that this servant of the church was to be equipped for a spiritual ministry to serve with the bishop or pastor: "Likewise deacons must be reverent, not double-tongued, not given to much wine, not greedy for money, holding the mystery of the faith with a pure conscience. But let these also first be tested; then let them serve as deacons, being found blameless" (1 Tim. 3:8–10). The biblical deacon is expected to have an exemplary home life (3:11–12), to be a proven leader, and to possess flawless character.

Paul wrote that the reward for faithfulness in the office of deacon is that they "obtain for themselves a good standing and great boldness in the faith which is in Christ Jesus" (1 Tim. 3:13). The selfless deacon may also feel close kinship with his Master who walked the earth as "One who serves" (Luke 22:27). According to Jesus, the true heroes in the kingdom of God are those who assume the role of diakonos—a servant (Matt. 20:26).

DEAD, THE—those no longer alive; the deceased. Death is introduced in Genesis 2:17. God created man to live forever, both physically and spiritually. By man's disobedience, however, death became his lot (Rom. 5:12). The day Adam ate the forbidden fruit, he did not die physically but lived on and reached the age of 930 years (Gen. 5:5). However, with that act of disobedience he died spiritually and was separated from God's fellowship (Gen. 3:24). When the breath leaves the body, the body is dead. When man sins, he is spiritually separated from God and his spirit is "dead" toward God (Eph. 2:1–3, 12).

The Bible speaks of both types of death, physical (Heb. 9:27) and spiritual (Eph. 4:18).

The Bible also speaks of eternal, or everlasting, death. Those who persist in their unbelief remain forever in spiritual death—eternal separation from God—which Scripture calls the "second death" (Rev. 2:11; 21:8).

Also see Hell.

DEAD SEA SCROLLS—see ch. 55, §4., 4.1., 4.2., 4.3.

DEATH—a term which, when applied to the lower orders of living things such as plants and animals, means the end of life. With reference to human beings, however, death is not the end of life. The Bible teaches that man is more than a physical creature; he is also a spiritual being. For man, therefore, physical death does not mean the end of existence but the end of life as we know it and the transition to another dimension in which our conscious existence continues.

Various attitudes toward death are expressed in the Bible, from dread to anticipation. The ancient Hebrews regarded death as entrance into *sheol, where they were cut off from everything dear in life, including God and loved ones. But God revealed to the psalmist that the Redeemer God is both in heaven and in Sheol (Ps. 139:78), and He is able to bring a person out of Sheol ("the grave"; 1 Sam. 2:6).

Because "all have sinned and fall short of the glory of God" (Rom. 3:23), all people are spiritually dead—separated from God who is the Source of spiritual life. By reason of such deadness toward God, sin makes a person hate the light and despise the truth; it causes one to break God's laws and to become insensitive to holy things. Everyone who has not been redeemed by Christ is spiritually dead (Luke 15:32; Eph. 2:13; Col. 2:13).

The Bible also speaks of "the second death" (Rev. 2:11), which is eternal death, the everlasting separation of the lost from God in *Hell. The "second death" is equated with "the lake of fire" (Rev. 20:14); "the lake which burns with fire and brimstone . . . is the second death" (Rev. 21:8).

The apostle Paul speaks of death as an enemy: "The last enemy that will be destroyed is death" (1 Cor. 15:26). In His resurrection, Jesus conquered death—physical, spiritual, and eternal. Through fear of death, humans are subject to bondage (Heb. 2:15); but "our Savior Jesus Christ . . . has abolished death and brought life and immortality to light through the gospel" (2 Tim. 1:10).

DEATH, SECOND—the state of final condemnation and punishment to which unbelievers are condemned by God at the Last Judgment (Rev. 2:11; 21:8). To Smyrna, the persecuted church, the crucified and risen Christ declared, "Be faithful unto death, and I will give you the crown of life . . . He who over-comes shall not be hurt by the second death" (Rev. 2:10–11). The meaning of this verse is that a person without Christ when he faces God's judgment will be condemned to eternal punishment in hell or "the second death." Also see Eschatology.

DEDICATE, DEDICATION—a religious ceremony in which a person or a thing is set aside or consecrated to God's service. In Bible times, many different things were included in such services: the temple (2 Chr. 2:4), a field (Lev. 27:16), a house (Lev. 27:14), articles of precious metal (2 Sam. 8:10), even spoils won in battle (1 Chr. 26:27).

In one of the most beautiful passages in the Bible, Hannah presented her young son Samuel to God in an act of child dedication (1 Sam. 1:19–28). Hannah's prayer of thanksgiving to God (1 Sam. 2:1 10) is a model of praise and dedication for all who seek to honor God through their lives. This is much the same thing that was being done when Joseph and Mary presented Jesus in the temple as an infant (Luke 2:27).

DELIGHTS. (Ps. 112:1) *chafets* (chah-*fayts*); *Strong's* #2654: To be delighted in something; to take pleasure in; to be bent or inclined toward; to cherish; to be favorably disposed toward someone; to love and desire. From *chafets* comes the noun *chefets*, "delight" or "pleasure." A well-known biblical name derived from this word is "Hephzibah" (literally "My Delight Is in Her"), a prophetic name for the land of Israel (Is. 62:4), for God will find His people and His land a delight, that is, very attractive in His view. Here a blessed individual finds God's commandments pleasurable, attractive, delightful, pleasing, and desirable.

DELIVERED. (Luke 23:25) *paradidomi* (par-ad-id-oh-mee); *Strong's* #3860: From *para*, "alongside," and *didomi*, "to give." The verb is quite common in the New Testament and is used in a variety of ways, usually reflecting the root meaning of to give over or deliver. It is used in the sense of to hand over to another (Matt. 25:14; Luke 4:6); to commit or commend (Acts 15:40; 1 Pet. 2:23); to deliver up to prison or judgment (Matt. 4:12; 2 Pet. 2:4); to betray (Matt. 10:4; Mark 13:12); to hand down, such as traditions (Mark 7:13; Acts 6:14); and to permit (Mark 4:29).

DEMONS—another name for fallen angels who joined the kingdom of Satan in rebellion against God.

Origin. The origin of demons is not explicitly discussed in the Bible. But the New Testament speaks of the fall and later imprisonment of a group of angels (1 Pet. 3:19–20; 2 Pet. 2:4; Jude 6). The group that participated in the fall apparently followed one of their own number, *Satan. The fall occurred before God's *creation of the world. In retaliatory hatred for God, Satan and his angels tirelessly seek to contaminate the human race with wickedness (Genesis 3; Matt. 25:41; Rev. 12:9).

A symbolic view of this "initial" fall appears in Revelation 12:34 where the dragon (a symbol for Satan) "drew a third of the stars of heaven" (a symbol for fallen angels) and "threw them to the earth." Thus, Satan has his own "angels," who most students see as the demons of this era (Matt. 25:41; Rev. 12:9).

Demons in the Old Testament. Because the Jews believed God's power was unlimited, the Old Testament contains little information about demons. The primitive status of the understanding of demons during this time is perhaps reflected in the way the Old Testament relates the fallen angels to God. It was a "distressing (or evil) spirit from God" (1 Sam. 16:15–16, 23) that brought great distress to Saul the king. It was a "lying spirit" from the Lord about whom Micaiah, the prophet of the Lord, spoke (1 Kin. 22:21–23). In short, this is not to say God *willed*, but rather *allowed* the evil spirit to do its work. The Bible reveals also that all pagan worship is a fountainhead of demon activity (Lev. 17:7; Ps. 106:37). Demons function with greater freedom to work their bondage wherever human activities open to their "worship"—that is, participate in carnal activities that disobey God's Word, indulge the flesh, and cooperate with hell's agenda of sin, lust, and self-indulgence.

Demons in the New Testament. The New Testament accepts the Old Testament teaching about evil spirits and advances the doctrine significantly. Demons are designated in a number of different ways in the New Testament. They are called "unclean spirits" (Matt. 10:1; Mark 6:7), a "wicked (or evil) spirit" (Luke 7:21; Acts 19:12–13), "deceiving spirits" (1 Tim. 4:1), and a "spirit of error" (1 John 4:6). The Bible warns against occult involvements, showing demon activity proliferates in such an evil spiritual environment. Luke describes one demon as a "spirit of divination" (Acts 16:16). Isaiah 8:19–22 and 47:9–15 clearly reinforce the danger-avoiding direction of Leviticus 17:7, in the spirit of the truth inherent in Deuteronomy 18:9–14 and 32:15–18. Paul clearly held this understanding (1 Cor. 10:20–21) and warns against believers conceding any territory in their souls to the devil or his cohorts (Eph. 4:25–32; *see* v. 27).

A prime purpose of Jesus' earthly ministry was to overcome the power of Satan. This included His conquest of the demonic realm (Matt. 12:25–29; Luke 11:17–22; John 12:31;

1 John 3:8). This explains the fierce conflict between Jesus and these evil spirits while He was on earth, and why Jesus promises His people—the redeemed—authority over and power to cast out demons (Matt. 10:8; Mark 16:17).

Following the resurrection of Jesus and His return to heaven, these demonic principalities and powers have continued their warfare against those who are His followers (Rom. 8:38–39; Eph. 6:12). Yet Satan and his allies will finally be overthrown by God. After Christ returns, the devil and his angels will be defeated and thrown into the lake of fire and brimstone (Matt. 25:41, Rev. 20:10). This is a doom with which demons are quite familiar (Matt. 8:29). God will achieve the ultimate victory in this conflict which has been going on since the beginning of time.

DEMON POSSESSION—"Demonized" would be the more accurate word for that affliction of persons who are controlled by demons (Matt. 4:24; 8:33; demoniac, NASB).

The New Testament gives graphic descriptions of the effect of demons on people. Some of the diseases which they caused included muteness (Matt. 12:22; Mark 9:17, 25), deafness (Mark 9:25), blindness (Matt. 12:22), and bodily deformity (Luke 13:10–17). But the Bible does *not* teach that demons are responsible for all physical ailments or even every human case of the above-referenced maladies. The Gospel writers frequently distinguished between sickness and and demon possession (Matt. 4:24; Mark 1:32; Luke 6:17–18). Sometimes a problem caused by demons appears to have another cause in another situation (Matt. 12:22; 15:30).

Demons are shown as responsible for some mental problems (Matt. 8:28; Acts 19:13–16). The ranting and raving that they produce might be included with some mental disorders (Mark 1:23–24; John 10:20). Uncontrolled fits were another form of demonic affliction (Luke 9:37–42; Mark 1:26). Sometimes a demon also causes a person to behave in an antisocial manner (Luke 8:27, 35).

The method of Jesus and His disciples in casting out demons differed radically from the magical methods so often used in that time. Through His authoritative command Jesus expelled them (Mark 1:25; 5:8; 9:25). His disciples did the same, by the authority of Jesus' name (Luke 10:17; Acts 16:18). In some instances prayer with fasting is necessary before a demon can be cast out (Mark 9:29).

By casting out demons, Jesus showed that the *kingdom of God—God's rule in the affairs of mankind—is a present reality. Unto this day, it is a clear demonstration of His power over Satan and the demonic forces of sin and evil in the world.

DESCENT INTO HADES—Christ's journey to the place of the dead on our behalf following His crucifixion. Some interpreters see this descent in Paul's reference to "lower parts of the earth" (Eph. 4:9). Both Peter (Acts 2:27) and Paul (Acts 13:35) quote Psalm 16:10, declaring that Jesus experienced death, but that He was kept from the corruption of the grave (Acts 2:27). From the heights of heaven's throne Jesus descended to earth and even to death itself to provide for our *redemption.

The Bible does not teach this "descent" as a part of completing salvation's provision or plan. "It is finished," announced at Calvary, reveals Jesus' blood and death perfected full victory over sin, death, and hell (Heb. 2:14–15).

DESIRE. (1 Cor. 14:1) *zeloo* (dzay-*low*-oh), *Strong's #2206:* To be zealous for, to burn with desire, to pursue ardently, to desire eagerly or intensely. Negatively, the word is associated with strong envy and jealousy (Acts 7:9; 17:5; 1 Cor. 13:4; James 4:2).

DESIRED. (Matt. 13:17) *epithumeo* (ep-ee-thoo-*meh*-oh); *Strong's #1937:* To set one's heart upon, eagerly long for, covet, greatly desire, lust after. The word emphasizes the intensity of the desire rather than the object desired. It describes both good and evil desires.

DESPISED. (Amos 2:4) *ma'as* (mah-*ahs*); *Strong's #3988:* To reject, refuse, abhor, despise, disregard; spurn, disdain; to regard as unimportant or worthless. This verb occurs seventy-five times. It represents the opposite of choosing something, thus rejecting, casting away, or having aversion to something. *Ma'as* is translated "rejected" in Psalm 118:22, speaking of the stone that the builders threw away as unfit. *Ma'as* also appears in 1 Samuel 8:7, where the people rejected God. Compare the use of *ma'as* in 1 Samuel 16:1, 7; Isaiah 5:24; Ezekiel 20:16; and Hosea 4:6. In the present reference, Jerusalem's citizens disregarded God's written instructions.

DESTROY. (Luke 9:56) *apollumi* (ap-*ol*-loo-mee); *Strong's #622:* To lay waste, destroy utterly, disintegrate. The New Testament often uses the word to describe spiritual destitution. Destruction for the sinner does not result in annihilation or extinction. It is not the loss of being, but of well-being.

DEVIL (accuser)—the main title for the fallen angelic being who is the supreme enemy of God and man. Satan is his name, and devil is what he is—the accuser or deceiver. The title "devil" appears thirty-five times in the NKJV. In every case it is preceded by the article "the," indicating a title rather than a name. The term comes from a Greek word that means "a false witness" or "malicious accuser." Satan (the devil) is also called:

The Wicked or Evil One (Matt. 6:13; 13:19, 38; 1 John 2:13), who "walks about like a roaring lion, seeking whom He may devour" (1 Pet. 5:8);

The Enemy (Matt. 13:25, 28, 39), who opposes Christ, the church, and the gospel (2 Cor. 10:4–5);

A murderer (John 8:44), who motivated the killing of Abel and the prophets, and who wanted to kill Jesus before His time (8:40);

The Deceiver (Rev. 20:10), who animates evil men who under his power continue to deceive (2 Tim. 3:13);

Beelzebub, Prince of Demons (Matt. 9:34; 12:24), for though there are many demons but only one devil, Beelzebub is their leader.

The Ruler of This World (John 12:31; 14:30; 16:11). Three times Jesus called the devil the "ruler of this world." When the devil offered the world to Jesus if He would worship him (Luke 4:5–8), our Lord refused ("Get behind me Satan") but did not deny Satan's right to make the offer (see 1 John 5:19). However, at Calvary, God dealt a death blow to this world ruler, and it is only a matter of time before His final victory will be revealed through Christ (Matt. 25:41; 1 John 3:8; Rev. 12:7).

The devil is strong, but Christians are stronger through the Lord (Eph. 6:11). They have the protection needed to withstand his assaults. The devil tempts, but God provides a way of escape (1 Cor. 10:13); the devil tries to take advantage of people (2 Cor. 2:11), but he will flee if fought (James 4:7). The devil should not be feared, for Christ in us is more powerful than this deceiving prince of the demons (1 John 4:4).

Also see Satan.

DIRECT. (Prov. 3:6) *yashar* (yah-*shar*); *Strong's* #3474: To be straight, right, upright, pleasing, good. *Yashar* appears in an intensive form here and means to "make straight and right." God will "straighten out" the path of His devoted, trusting servants. From this verb comes the noun *yosher*, "uprightness" (Ps. 119:7). Job is described as blameless and upright (Job 1:1). God's promise to Cyrus was that the crooked places would be made straight (Is. 45:2). Finally, from *yashar* comes the poetical name *Jeshurun* ("Upright One"), a name always applied to Israel as God's righteous nation (Deut. 33:5; Is. 44:2).

DISASTER. (Acts 27:10) *hubris* (*hoo*-bris); *Strong's #5196:* Hurt, loss, injury arising from violence, damage caused by the elements, hardship, detriment, trouble, and danger. In 2 Corinthians 12:10, where Paul described the reproaches he endured for the Lord's sake, *hubris* denotes insolence, impudence, a haughty attitude, insult, injury, outrage, persecution, and affront. The word is definitely adversarial. (Compare "hubristic" and "hybrid.")

DISCIPLES. (Matt. 10:1) *mathetes* (math-ay-tace); *Strong's #3101:* From the verb *manthano*, "to learn," whose root *math* suggests thought with effort put forth. A disciple is a learner, one who follows both the teaching and the teacher. The word is used first of the Twelve and later of Christians generally.

DOCTRINE—a term commonly used today to refer to a body of beliefs about God, man, Christ, the church, and other related concepts. Members of the early church, however, first saw "sound doctrine" as faithful behavior (Titus 2:1–10).

Christ condemned the doctrine of the Pharisees because their lives violated their creeds (Matt. 15:9; Mark 7:7). By contrast, Jesus' teaching was practical and pure, not ideals without corresponding actions; thus, it was fresh and new (Matt. 7:28; Mark 1:22, 27; Luke 4:32).

After Pentecost, Christian doctrine as a creed began to be systematized (Acts 2:42). Doctrinal instruction was given by special teachers (1 Cor. 12:28–29; Gal. 6:6) to those who had responded to the gospel (Rom. 6:17). The earliest doctrine of the Christian church declared: (1) that Jesus was the Messiah, the Christ (Acts 3:18); (2) that God had raised Him from the dead (Acts 1:22; 2:24, 32); and (3) that salvation was by faith in His name (Acts 2:38; 3:16). These three truths were presented as a clear fulfillment of the promises of the Old Testament. Paul taught that true doctrine—both behavior as well as belief—is essential for Christian growth (Eph. 4:11–16; 1 Tim. 4:6; 6:3; Titus 1:9) and that the opposite destroys the church (Eph. 4:14; 2 Tim. 4:3).

DOMINION. (Zech. 9:10) *moshel* (moh-*shel*); *Strong's #4915:* Dominion, sovereignty, jurisdiction, rulership. This noun comes from the verb *mashal*, meaning "to rule, to govern, to reign, have dominion, exercise authority." This verb conveys the thought of a strong sovereign ruling over one's subjects. (Note its use in Gen. 37:8; Deut. 15:6; 1 Chr. 29:12; Ps. 8:6; 103:19.) The noun *moshel* thus refers to the realm of rulership (both geographical and governmental) that belongs to a sovereign authority. In the present reference, the Messiah's dominion is described as universal, extending to the ends of the earth.

DONE NO WRONG (I HAVE). (Acts 25:10) *adikeo* (ad-ee-*keh*-oh); *Strong's #91:* To do an injustice, to act criminally or unrighteously, to violate any human or divine law, to do wrong, to mistreat others. The word is a compound of *a*, "without," and *dike*, "right"; hence, an illegal action. *Adikeo* consists of offending legally, general wrongdoing, social injustice, and inflicting hurt or damage on individuals. In his appeal to Caesar, Paul declares his innocence.

DORMITION ABBEY—see ch. 55, §6.1.

DOUBTING NOTHING. (Acts 11:12) *diakrino* (dee-ak-*ree*-no); *Strong's #1252:* Has two definitions. (1) To judge thoroughly; to decide between two or more choices; to make a distinction; to separate two components, elements, or factors; to render a decision; to evaluate carefully. (2) The word also connotes a conflict with oneself, in the sense of hesitating, having misgivings, doubting, being divided in decision-making, or wavering between hope and fear. This is its use here.

DOWNCAST. (2 Cor. 7:6) *tapeinos* (tap-eye-noss); *Strong's #5011:* Literally "low to the ground." Metaphorically, the word signifies low estate, lowly in position and power, humble.

DREAMS. (Joel 2:28) *chalom* (kah-*lohm*); *Strong's #2472:* A dream; a vision in the night. The root of this noun is the verb *chalam*, "to dream." Dreams of various types are mentioned in Scripture, ranging from the product of one's imagination to the vehicle of God's communication with a person (compare Eccl. 5:3 and Gen. 20:6; see also "false dreams," Jer. 23:32). Many biblical figures, such as Jacob, Laban, Pharaoh, Solomon, Nebuchadnezzar, are known for having dreams (see 1 Kin. 3:5; Dan. 2:1). Joseph and Daniel are the biblical champions of dream-revelation; each not only received his own dreams but also interpreted the dreams of others.

DWELL. (Jer. 42:17) *gur* (goor); *Strong's #1481:* To lodge somewhere, to temporarily reside; to dwell as a stranger among other people; to sojourn; to be a guest or alien in a particular land. *Gur* means to have a temporary resident's status. Here Jeremiah warns his countrymen to avoid plans to lodge temporarily in Egypt, for this would meet with tragic failure. From *gur* comes the noun *ger*, "stranger, alien, resident foreigner." This word occurs about ninety times, mostly in the Law of Moses, where God repeatedly outlines the rights of "alien" residents. Exodus 23:9 indicates the empathy His people were to feel toward sojourners. Note also David's perceptive and humble words in 1 Chronicles 29:15.

DWELLINGS. (Is. 32:18) *mishchan* (meesh-*kahn*); *Strong's #4908:* A tabernacle, a dwelling place; a place of residence, a habitation. *Mishchan* appears more than 130 times in the Old Testament, nearly one hundred of these in Exodus—Numbers, for the tabernacle at Shiloh, and even the dwelling places of the wicked (Ps. 78:60; Job 18:21). The root of *mishchan* is *shachan*, meaning "to dwell, reside, remain, abide, stay." Thus, *mishchan* means literally "place of dwelling." Also from the root *shachan* is *Shekinah*, or "abiding presence and glory" of the Lord. *Shekinah* is not found in the Old Testament, but comes from later Jewish writings.

EAGER. (Gal. 2:10) *spoudazo* (spoo-*dad*-zoe); *Strong's #4704:* To exert oneself, make every effort, give diligence, make haste, be zealous, strain every nerve, and further the cause assiduously. *Spoudazo* combines thinking and acting, planning and producing. It sees a need and promptly does something about it. The word covers inception, action, and follow-through.

EARTH—the planet on which mankind lives. "The earth is the Lord's," wrote the psalmist, "and all its fullness" (Ps. 24:1). God is sovereign over the earth. All its living creatures, including mankind, are subject to His rule. The Israelites were promised that if they obeyed God's will and kept His laws, the earth would produce fruitful harvests; if they were disobedient, however, the crops would fail and famine would come (Deuteronomy 28).

The Bible reveals that the whole creation—including the earth and mankind—was "subjected to futility" and groans to "be delivered from the bondage of corruption" (Rom. 8:20–21). At the end of the age, however, the earth will be given renewed life, fertility, and productivity (Rev. 21:1).

EASTER—a feast or festival of the Christian church that commemorates the resurrection of Christ. It is observed and celebrated on the first Sunday following the full moon that occurs on or after March 21—or one week later if the full moon falls on Sunday. In other

words, Easter falls between March 22 and April 25.

EASY. (Matt. 11:30) *chrestos* (khrase-*toss*); *Strong's #5543:* From the verb *chraomai*, "to use." The word denotes that which is useful, pleasant, good, comfortable, suitable, and serviceable. The legalistic religious system was a severe burden, but service to Jesus does not chafe, because it is well-fitting and built on personal relationship with God by the indwelling Spirit.

EBLA—see ch. 55, §6.2.

EFFECTIVELY. (1 Thess. 2:13) *energeo* (en-erg-*eh*-oh); *Strong's #1754:* One of the four big energy words: *energeo, energes, energeia,* and *energema.* The words all stem from *en,* "in," and *ergon,* "work," and have to do with the active operation or working of power and its effectual results.

EGYPT—see ch. 55, §1., 2.1., 2.2., 3.2., 3.3., 3.4.a., 3.7.a., 3.7.b.

EL—see ch. 55, §3.4.c.

ELAMITE—see ch. 55, §2.2.

ELDER—a term used throughout the Bible but designating different ideas at various times in biblical history. The word may refer to age, experience, and authority, as well as specific leadership roles.

In the Old Testament those leaders associated with Moses in governing the nation of Israel were called "the elders of Israel" (Ex. 3:16; 24:1), "the elders of the people" (Ex. 19:7), or the "seventy elders" (Ex. 24:1).

Later, after the wilderness wandering, bodies of elders ruled in each city. The term elder eventually came to be applied to those who governed in the local communities, tribes, or over all of Israel. These leaders were responsible for legal, political, and military guidance and supervision.

During the years of Israel's captivity in Babylon and the following centuries, elders again appeared as leaders who were responsible for governing in the Jewish communities. Later in this period, a council of elders of seventy-one members, called the Sanhedrin, emerged. This council had both religious and political authority among all the Jewish people in Palestine, particularly in New Testament times. The high priest was the chairman of the Sanhedrin. Local Jewish synagogues, which emerged in the period between the Old and New Testaments, also were governed by a council of elders.

 This icon beside an entry indicates a Word Wealth feature.

 This icon beside an entry indicates a Kingdom Dynamics feature.

 This icon beside an entry indicates an important biblical or doctrinal term.

A governing structure similar to the ruling elders among the Jews was followed in the early church. The title elder was continued, but the significance of the office changed. Thus, later on the term elder is used in the New Testament to refer to certain persons who held office in the church (1 Tim. 5:2; 1 Pet. 5:5).

Elders were associated with James in Jerusalem in the local church's government (Acts 11:30; 21:18) and, with the apostles, in the decision of the early church council (Acts 15). Elders were also appointed in the churches established during the apostle Paul's first missionary journey (Acts 14:23). Paul addressed the elders at Ephesus (Acts 20:17–35). Elders played an important role in church life through their ministry to the sick (James 5:14–15). They also were apparently the teachers in a local congregation. In addition to ministering to the sick, their duties consisted of ministering the Scriptures (1 Tim. 5:17; 1 Pet. 5:5). Thus, they are called to meet high standards of character and fidelity (Titus 2:1–2; see also 1 Tim. 3:1–13; 1 Pet. 5:1–3 equates "elder" with "overseer"—i.e., "bishop"—and "shepherd"—i.e., "pastor").

ELDERSHIP. (1 Tim. 4:14) *presbuterion* (pres-boo-*ter*-ee-on); *Strong's* #4244: A body of elders (literally aged men), composed of men of dignity, wisdom, and maturity. The word is used both of the Sanhedrin (Luke 22:66; Acts 22:5) and of Christian presbyters (1 Tim. 4:14).

ELEPHANTINE PAPYRI—see ch. 55, §3.2.

ELIEZER—see ch. 55, §3.5.b.

ENDURANCE. (Heb. 10:36) *hupomone* (hoop-om-on-*ay*); *Strong's* #5281: Constancy, perseverance, continuance, bearing up, steadfastness, holding out, patient endurance. The word combines *hupo*, "under," and *mone*, "to remain." It describes the capacity to continue to bear up under difficult circumstances, not with a passive complacency, but with a hopeful fortitude that actively resists weariness and defeat.

ENDURE. (2 Thess. 1:4) *anechomai* (an-*ekh*-om-ahee); *Strong's* #430: From *ana*, "up," and *echo*, "to hold." The word carries the idea of persevering, tolerating, bearing with, putting up with, standing firm, and not losing courage under pressure.

ENDURES. (Matt. 24:13) *hupomeno* (hoop-ahm-*en*-oh); *Strong's* #5278: To hold one's ground in conflict, bear up against adversity, hold out under stress, stand firm, persevere under pressure, wait calmly and courageously. It is not passive resignation to fate

and mere patience, but the active, energetic resistance to defeat that allows calm and brave endurance.

ENEMY—one who opposes or mistreats another. This word occurs more frequently in the Old Testament than in the New Testament. The reason for this is that the Old Testament is concerned primarily with the existence of Israel as a nation over against the other countries of the ancient world. Before Israel could serve as the channel of God's grace to the world, its existence as a nation had to be securely established. The enemies of the Hebrew people were thus regarded as God's enemies, and the reverse was also true (Ps. 139:20–22). In the New Testament, by contrast, the enemies to be overcome are primarily spiritual in nature.

While the Old Testament does refer to charity toward one's enemy (Ex. 23:4–5; Prov. 24:17), the New Testament goes further by commanding love for one's enemy (Matt. 5:44; Rom. 12:20). The New Testament looks toward a day when all enemies of good and righteousness will be overcome because of the redemptive work of Christ (1 Cor. 15:25).

ENRAGED. (Rev. 12:17) *orgizo* (or-*gid*-zoe); *Strong's* #3710: Compare "orgy" and "orgiastic." To provoke to anger. In the New Testament the verb is always in the passive, "to be provoked to anger." The word describes a passion that is furious and raging with a desire for revenge. It is so intense a passion that it will terminate by attempting to kill. Christians are to avoid that kind of intense wrath (Matt. 5:22; Eph. 4:26).

EPHOD. (Ex. 35:27) *'ephod* (ay-*phode*); *Strong's* #646: Ephod, a vest or robe, a priestly garment probably extending from the shoulders to the waist; an extended piece called the "robe of the ephod" attached to the upper part, thus making a full-length garment. The ephod was ornately woven and decorated with attached pieces, such as the breastplate. The ephod consisted of intricate linen work, a woven waistband, and two gold chains, which securely fastened the two onyx stones on which were written the names of the tribes of Israel. The breastplate itself contained twelve precious stones, each stone representing one of the tribes. Thus the high priest carried the names and the concerns of Israel's twelve families over his heart (28:29).

EPISTLE—a letter of correspondence between two or more parties; the form in which several books of the New Testament were originally written. Epistle is generally synonymous with letter, although epistle sometimes is regarded as more formal correspondence, and letter as more personal.

There is no real precedent for the New Testament epistles in the Old Testament or Jewish literature. Rather, its twenty-one epistles (Romans through Jude) follow the general custom and form of letters, which became an important form of communication in the Greek-speaking world about three hundred years before the birth of Jesus.

Ancient letters were written with a reed pen on either papyrus or parchment (scraped animal skins). A sheet of papyrus normally was about ten to twelve inches in size, and accommodated about two hundred words. For sending, it was folded or rolled, tied, and often sealed to insure privacy.

Private letters had to be sent by special messengers or friendly travelers. Letters normally were sent to designated parties, although some were "open" or circular letters. Paul's letters, with the possible exception of Ephesians, were addressed to specific congregations; but the non-Pauline letters, usually called "general" epistles, included some letters which were circulated to several churches.

Most ancient letters were dictated to a secretary or scribe; for example, in Romans 16:22, Paul's secretary identifies himself as Tertius.

Ancient letters normally followed a pattern which included: (1) an introduction, listing the names of sender and recipient, followed by a formal greeting; (2) a body, or purpose for writing; and (3) a conclusion, consisting of appropriate remarks and a farewell.

The Pauline epistles are arranged in the New Testament according to length, from the longest (Romans) to the shortest (Philemon), and not by importance or the dates when they were written.

EQUIPPING. (Eph. 4:12) *katartismos* (kat-ar-tis-*moss*); *Strong's #2677:* A making fit, preparing, training, perfecting, making fully qualified for service. In classical language the word is used for setting a bone during surgery. The Great Physician is now making all the necessary adjustments so the church will not be "out of joint."

ERROR—deviation from the truth or an accepted code of behavior (Job 4:18; Eccl. 5:6; 10:5; Dan. 6:4). In the New Testament the Greek word translated as error means "a wandering from the way," "a straying from the path" (Rom. 1:27; 1 John 4:6). In the NKJV the same Greek word is also translated as "deception" (Matt. 27:64), or "deceit" (1 Thess. 2:3). James 5:19–20 indicates that it is possible to wander from the truth. Since the Bible sees truth as moral in nature, error is more than incorrect thinking. It is a wrong way of life.

ERROR. (Jude 11) *plane* (*plan*-ay); *Strong's #4106:* Originally, a wandering; hence, the English word "planet." Metaphorically, the word denotes a going astray, an error. In the New Testament the straying is always in respect to morals and doctrine.

ESAU—see ch. 55, §3.5.b.

ESCHATOLOGY [es cuh TOL ih gih]—a theological term that designates the study of what will happen at the end of history, particularly the event known as the *Second Coming of Christ. The word comes from two Greek words, *eschatos* (last) and *logos* (study)—thus its definition as "the study of last things."

Eschatology reveals the end of history and how God reverses the curse sin brought upon the world, as He separates the good from the bad.

This "end," or "the day of the Lord," is shown as a day when all the world will be brought back under God's rule (Amos 5:18–20; Joel 2:31). The final preparation for that rule was the elevation of Jesus to God's right hand (Ps. 110:1; Acts 2:34–35). We are now under the spiritual rule of Christ, awaiting His earthly rule and the defeat of all His enemies when He returns to reign.

The future judgment of the earth will take place by fire (2 Pet. 3:5–9). The first heaven and earth will eventually fall away and be replaced with the new heaven and earth. This falling away will be a violent burning of the universe (2 Pet. 3:10–13). Jesus Himself thus defined the end-time judgment (Matt. 24:36–44).

Final Judgments. In the end times, a basic order of judgment will prevail as the conflict between God and Satan comes to an end. There will be a time of great *tribulation (Matt. 24:4–26), followed by the *Second Coming (Matt. 24:27–30) and the judgment of the nations (Matt. 25:31–46; 1 Cor. 15:20–24).

The day of the Lord will reverse the curse upon the world by bringing judgment to all of God's enemies. The world will be judged by fire (Is. 66:16), and all nations will be included in this judgment (Amos 1:3—2:3, Ezek. 25:1–17). When the Lord spoke of the judgment of the people living at His arrival (Matt. 25:31–46), He pictured humanity as sheep or goats who inherit either everlasting punishment or *Eternal Life. This concept of separation is expressed also through the figures of reaping harvest (Matt. 13:38–43; Rev. 14:14–20) and sorting out the good and the bad catch from a fishing net (Matt. 13:47–50).

Another judgment is portrayed in Revelation 20:11–15, commonly called the "Great White Throne" Judgment. This judgment is called the second death (Rev. 20:14). Those who are judged will be thrown into the lake of fire if their names are not found in the Book of Life.

The judgments of God at the end of history are preceded by resurrections of the just (Luke 14:13–14; Rev. 20:6) and the unjust (John 5:29; Rev. 20:5). Two specific resurrections are mentioned in the Bible, described as being separated by an interval of 1,000 years (Dan. 12:2–3; Rev. 20:4–6).

Eschatology shows how God's Redeemer will establish His kingdom upon a rebellious earth. The long process through which God selected a righteous group to serve Him on earth came to a climax in the person of Christ. He is indeed "God with us" (Matt. 1:23). This phrase from Isaiah 7:14 spoke of God's presence in Jesus in order to save (Is. 9:6–7) and to judge (Is. 7:17; 8:6–8).

Christ's first coming was to save (Mark 10:45); His second will be primarily to rule. But His return will also spell relief to His faithful remnant. Eschatology shows that God's presence for the redeemed will be fully realized at Jesus' return, when He will dwell among all the redeemed in the new heavens and earth (Rev. 21:3).

Above all, the victory of Christ's Cross is the decisive eschatological event. In it the curse was reversed, and ever since, God has been progressively accomplishing His judgment against the forces of wickedness in heaven and earth.

Psalm 110:1 is a key verse for understanding the redemptive side of eschatology. The King will reign until He defeats His enemies. As He returns to begin the final preparations for His reign, He will gather His own to Himself. They will be evaluated by the Lord (Rom. 14:10; 1 Cor. 3:14–15) and will receive their reward of eternal life and will live in eternal fellowship with the Father and His Christ.

The point of eschatology throughout the Bible is to provide encouragement to believers in their witness for Jesus Christ (Matt. 24:14, 1 Cor. 15:58). It is not mentioned to encourage idle speculation or controversy. The reason God grants us a view of the future is to encourage us to witness for Christ and serve Him in the present.

ESSENE QUARTER—see ch. 55, §6.1.

ESSENES—see ch. 55, §4.2., 5., 5.6., 6.1.

ESTEEMED. (Acts 5:13) *megaluno* (meg-al-*oo*-no); *Strong's #3170:* To make great, to enlarge, to magnify, to increase, to make conspicuous,

to extol, to show respect, to hold in high esteem. When Ananias and Sapphira were judged, many shrank from associating with the apostles and their services. Despite all this, the public looked at the new Christian worshipers favorably (*megaluno*).

ESTHER, BOOK OF—see ch. 55, §4.2.

ETERNAL LIFE—a person's new and redeemed existence in Jesus Christ which is granted by God as a gift to all believers. Eternal life refers to the quality or character of our new existence in Christ as well as the unending character of this life. The phrase, everlasting life, is found in the Old Testament only once (Dan. 12:2). But the idea of eternal life is implied by the prophets in their pictures of the glorious future promised to God's people.

The majority of references to eternal life in the New Testament are oriented to the future. The emphasis, however, is upon the blessed character of the life that will be enjoyed endlessly in the future. Jesus made it clear that eternal life comes only to those who make a total commitment to Him (Matt. 19:16–21; Luke 18:18–22). The Pauline letters refer to eternal life relatively seldom, and again primarily with a future rather than a present orientation (Rom. 5:21; 6:22; Gal. 6:8).

The phrase, eternal life, appears most often in the Gospel of John and the Epistle of 1 John. John emphasizes eternal life as the present reality and the present possession of the Christian (John 3:36; 5:24; 1 John 5:13). John declares that the Christian believer has already begun to experience the blessings of the future even now, *before* their fullest expression (John 17:3).

ETERNITY—infinite or unlimited time; time without beginning or end. The Bible speaks of the eternity of God (Ps. 90:2; Is. 57:15; Rev. 1:4). As Creator, He brought the world into being, even before the beginning of time itself (Gen. 1:1). He also will bring the world to its ultimate conclusion, in accordance with His will and purpose.

EUPHRATES—see ch. 55, §2.1., 2.2.

EVANGELISM, WORLD. From the earliest expression of God's intent to redeem fallen man, He has appointed a "Seed" that would accomplish the task (Gen. 3:15). That "Seed of the woman" fulfilled in Jesus Christ, was destined to become the "Seed of Abraham" though whom all the nations of the earth are intended to be blessed (Gal. 3:29; Gen 12:3). When the Lord says to Israel, just delivered from Egypt, "All the earth is Mine," He links it to a mission: "You shall be to Me a kingdom of priests" (Ex. 19:5–6). There is no question as to their call being from bondage and into mission. So it is, from the beginning of the Bible story of redemption, the redeemed are assigned to world evangelization. This study intends to lead believers in living this truth: (1) receiving God's grace and then (2) sending God's truth; in (1) being filled with the Sprit and then (2) going to the uttermost part of the earth.

1. God's Promise to His Messiah (Ps. 2:8). This great messianic psalm discloses the heart of God toward His own Son. "Ask of Me . . . I will give You the nations for Your inheritance." This conversation introduces an amazing declaration, that all the nations of the world are intended to come under the aegis of His Son's rule. However, the qualifier is, "Ask." In John 17, through His High Priestly Prayer, Jesus does exactly this (John 17:1–28). However, His request involves our response. We must unite (John 17:21) and we must receive the authority "manifest" in God's name and glory, which Jesus, as the Interceding Messiah of Psalm 2, has conferred upon us—His church. In this name we pray, and by this glory we triumph—receiving the inheritance of nations as God has promised.

2. Committed Action to Our Generation (Prov. 24:11–12). There are just two groups of people in the world: those who have heard the gospel and those who have not. If those who have heard (and believed) refuse to tell those who have not heard, God will render to each according "to his deeds." Sobering! We are responsible to our generation. While people often debate over those who have died without hearing the gospel, this passage reveals the soul-stirring importance of seeking those who are alive and have not heard! A practical guideline from Acts 13:36 can teach us: "David . . . served his generation by the will of God." We cannot go back to the last generation, nor can we reach the next generation, but we can serve this one. The only generation God expects us to be vitally concerned about is our own!

3. Spread the Good Tidings—Fearlessly (Is. 40:8–11). The prophet declares the eternal reminder: "The word of our God stands forever," and then anticipates the spread of that word. The world needs a sound foundation upon which to build life, just as surely as it needs a sure salvation to redeem it. "Zion"—the people of God—have that word and are privileged to bring these "good tidings"—the pleasant, happy, and wholesome news of life now and hope forever. Thus (1) "Lift up your voice" (v. 9). The message is to proclaim good tidings, for nothing will happen until that declaration is made. (2) "Be not afraid" (v. 9); for

God will manifest Himself as the proclaimer says, "Behold your God!!" (v. 9). (3) Our message of One who has strength to rule ("a strong hand") and a reward to give ("is with Him," v. 10) will be confirmed. Answering our call to spread "good tidings," we are wise to be fearlessly obedient, believing God to confirm His word (Mark 16:20). Jesus tells of the servant who buried his talent, saying, "I was afraid!!" Let God's perfect love and powerful promise cast out fears, and speak "Behold" to those He allows us to address with His Good News. He will confirm His word with proving power.

4. His Field—A Promise of Harvest (Matt. 13:37–38). To the farmer, the field is a promise of harvest. This area of land prompts his vision of a yielding crop. Having given the parables of the sower (vv. 3–9) and the wheat and the tares (vv. 24–30), Jesus interprets the parabolic picture: "The field is the world." Christ's own imagery points to the process of world evangelism: Go and sow. The field may or may not appear fertile; the field may be ravished by drought (spiritual need) or insect (spiritual opponents), but in either case the field is itself the summons. Lift up your eyes (Prov. 29:18; John 4:35–37).

5. The Gospel and "The End" (Matt. 24:14). In these words, Jesus linked the worldwide witness of the gospel to His Second Coming. The text contains: (1) an anticipation of ministry—"this gospel . . . will be preached," involving the declaration of the kingdom message of grace for forgiveness and power for deliverance; (2) an arena of effort—"to all the nations," including every group of people; (3) a certainty of "signs" for a witness (see Mark 16:15–20), insuring "proof" of Christ's resurrection life and present power to save and heal. How pointedly Jesus' words speak of the Father's desire toward the nations of the world: God cares for all people; Jesus died for every person; and the Word of God is for every nation—before "the end."

6. Commissioned Under the King's Call (Matt. 28:18–20). Since Matthew's theme is Christ as King, it is unsurprising Jesus' final commission to His disciples reflects His global perspective. In teaching kingdom life and principles ("kingdom" appears over fifty times in Matthew), Jesus leads His followers to think, live, and pray that His kingdom come to our entire planet (6:10). In chapter 13, His parables illustrated the kingdom's global expansion (v. 33). As His disciples began to minister, He told them to preach everywhere: "The kingdom of God is at hand." Then, before His ascension, the King gave the Great Commission. This climaxing command to go to all nations directed that their teaching and preaching seek to bring all nations into His kingdom (28:18–20). Prophetically, He forecast that the end would come only as "this gospel of the kingdom" was preached "in all the world as a witness to all nations" (24:14). "Nations" (Greek *ethne*) means "people groupings"—today, about 22,000 on this globe.

7. Commissioned in Christ's Servant Spirit (Mark 16:15–18). To understand the Great Commission in Mark, we must capture the spirit of Mark's focus on Jesus as the Servant. Messianic prophecies, such as Isaiah 42: 1–21, 49:1–7, 50:4–11, and 53:12, forecast Jesus' servant-character would do a specific work and act with unqualified and unsullied obedience.

Mark shows Christ's servant-character by omitting His genealogy (by which other Gospels establish His identity), showing that, as servants of Christ, we, too, might learn the servant-spirit essential to fulfilling the Great Commission. Christ seeks those who will serve without seeking recognition, selflessly and obediently seeking to exalt Christ and make Him known. Such servants establish their personhood and ministries by their devotion and obedience to Jesus, their disposition to serve unselfishly—their only exercise of power being to extend the love of God—ministering His life to the lost, the sick, and those in bondage. They do so wherever and however God sovereignly directs, whether it be through their giving, their going, or their prayerful intercession. The Servant Jesus' love and obedience compel His servants to loyal and unreserved service.

8. Commissioned to Go with Christ's Compassion (Luke 24:45–48). Luke's emphasis in the Great Commission is consonant with his theme: Christ, the Son of Man—showing Jesus' humanity and divinity in balance. The beauty and uniqueness of His character—both divine and human—is revealed as this Divine One brings sinful man to a holy God. In His perfect holiness of life, Jesus reflects compassion for sin-stained and suffering mankind—brokenhearted, sick, mistreated, and bereaved. Our fulfillment of the Great Commission requires such a worldwide scope in ministering compassion and human concern. Jesus' style—sensitive and touchable—is a summons to His followers to speedily answer His command and to answer with His compassion. No geographic boundary, no sin barrier, no ethnic, political, or economic partisan interest is ever to restrict our reach or penetration with the gospel.

9. Commissioned with a Mandate and a Message (John 20:21–23). John's Gospel presents the deity of Jesus—the Son of God. As God He has created all things (1:1–3), and as God He has come to redeem all—to bring the fullness of forgiveness. This aspect of His mission is conveyed to His disciples as their commission as well: Go with forgiveness. It is stated here as both a mandate and a mission: (1) "I also send you." Precisely as the Father sent the Son to bring salvation as an availability to every human being (3:16), so we are sent to insure that availability is understood by everyone. (2) "If you forgive" indicates the conditional nature of His provision. It cannot be responded to unless it is delivered. There is no escape from the awesome nature of His terminology here. We are not only sent with the substance of the message—salvation; we are sent to bring the spirit of its truth—forgiveness. Only the breath of His Spirit, which He breathed upon those who first heard these words, can enable us to go obediently and to reach lovingly. The message (salvation) and its meaning (forgiveness) are ours to deliver, and we need to receive the Holy Spirit to do both.

10. Christ's Final Charter and Promise (Acts 1:8). In five New Testament references, Jesus directly charges His disciples to go and preach the gospel to all the world (Matt. 28:18–20; Mark 16:15–18; Luke 24:45–48; John 20:21–23; Acts 1:8). Here His Great Commission is preceded by His promise of the outpouring of the Holy Spirit. Empowerment for world evangelism is tied inseparably to this promise. There is obvious need for power if people are to fully perceive the gospel. But prior to that, another issue awaits resolution. The Spirit has come to convince us to *go*. We need power to serve effectively, to heal the sick, and to deliver those possessed of unclean spirits. But let us first receive the Holy Spirit's first anointing—power to *act*—to go. Then, He will give (1) power to find the lost; (2) authority to boldly declare Jesus as the Son of God; and (3) power to establish His church—locally and worldwide. The intended borders of expansion are clear: Jerusalem (local), Judea (national), Samaria (cross-cultural) and "the end of the earth" (international). Jesus' last earthly command points to His power and His pathways for global evangelism.

11. The Sole Avenue of Salvation (Acts 4:12). The call to take the gospel to the nations is founded in these basic assumptions: (1) that humankind without Christ is lost, whether the entire race or the individual is concerned; (2) that there is "no other name under heaven given among men by which we must be saved"; that is, that no other authority, no other personality, no other system or philosophy can effect the rescue of the human soul. While some propose possibilities for human hope other than personal trust in Jesus Christ, God's Word preempts such propositions. In 2 Corinthians 5:17 to be "in Christ" is the only way to enter the "new creation" of God's present promise and His eternal salvation.

12. Christ—The Absolute Need of Every Man (Rom. 3:23). World evangelism requires that we see all people as God sees them—as sinners: (1) by nature (3:10); (2) by choice (3:23); and (3) by practice (6:23). Casual attitudes and blinded minds have lured some believers in Christ to overlook the desperate state of the lost: "The wages of sin *is* death" (6:23). Universalism or ultimate reconciliation are terms describing the erroneous belief of some that eventually even the eternally lost will be granted a reprieve from eternal judgment. But Paul said, "We judge that if One died for all, all died" (2 Cor. 5:14). Because he saw the lost as God sees them, he said God's love "constrained" him to world evangelism. The nations—all people—need the gospel desperately and are lost without it. A clear-eyed look into the Word of God will help us capture and retain the conviction that humankind needs the gospel.

13. The Absolute Need for a Messenger (Rom. 10:13–15). Paul asks, "How will they hear without a preacher?" (v. 14). This does not mean we must enter public ministry to "preach" the gospel. The Greek word used here for "preacher" means "one who heralds, proclaims, or publishes." Clearly, every believer is assigned a personal "pulpit"—in the home, the community, at the office, or in school—from which to show and tell others the Good News.

In 1:14 Paul declares, "I am a debtor," pointedly noting his sense of obligation. Why? He answers in Ephesians 2: Man is dead, needing life (v. 1); man is walking a course of destruction, needing deliverance (v. 12); man is hopeless, needing God (v. 13); man is separated from God, needing Christ (v. 14). Jesus concludes the evidence of man's need: he is lost, needing to be found (Luke 19:10). The answer is clear: someone must be sent to preach so that people will hear and believe. There is no other way.

14. The Continuing Call "Beyond" (2 Cor. 10:15–16). Paul's words of "having hope . . . to preach the gospel in the regions beyond you" reveal he was never content to keep the message within the Christian community. As John Wesley said, "The world is my parish." This text models the church's mandate to reach "beyond you." Christ's orders are clear: "Make disciples of all the nations" (Matt. 28:19); "preach the gospel to every creature" (Mark 16:15); "[preach] repentance and remission of sins" (Luke 24:47); and go "as the Father has sent Me" (John 20:21) "to the end of the earth" (Acts 1:8). When the full command is obeyed, the full promise will be fulfilled.

15. The Seedtime of Our Lifetime (Gal. 6:7–8). The law of sowing and reaping is at the heart of world evangelism. In John 4, Jesus declares a divine *Now* to the time for our laboring for the harvest of souls (vv. 35–38). Here, we are reminded that our lifetime is our "seedtime," and our life's harvest will yield multiplied times the fruit of the seed sown—if we sow wisely. This truth calls us to cast off reserve and to give God the finest "soil" of our lives in which He may beget a rich harvest. Hosea 8:7 presents the same principle, contrasting the power of "sowing" for evil rather than for God. The truth is amplified by this comparison. If sowing to evil (the flesh) may reap a whirlwind, how much more may righteous sowing (to the Spirit) make room for God's almightiness! He came as a rushing, mighty wind at Pentecost. Might He not work in holy hurricane power if He can find us sowing to the Spirit? A God-possessed life guarantees partnership with God in worldwide increase.

16. Destined for Victory (Rev. 5:8–10). The Book of Revelation prophetically describes the depth of penetration the gospel will have on the nations. (1) In verses 8–10 John's vision assures people out of every tribe, tongue, people and nation will be redeemed by the blood of Christ; and (2) that they will learn their role of intercession and authority as believers as they function as kings and priests, reigning "in Christ" while on earth, in His kingdom authority (vv. 8, 10). Further, Rev. unveils the fact that the spiritual war will continue until "the kingdoms of this world have become *the kingdoms* of our Lord and of His Christ, and He shall reign forever and ever" (11:15). The messenger (the evangel) is to go to all who dwell on earth—to every nation, tribe, tongue, and people (14:6–7). Revelation 7:9–12 forecasts the ultimate consummation of the Great Commission at work as a countless number from every people gather at God's eternal throne. Let this profound prophetic vision motivate us as we embrace Jesus. We are destined for triumph! G.C.

EVANGELIST—a person authorized to proclaim the gospel of Christ. In a more narrow sense, the word refers to one of the Gospel writers: Matthew, Mark, Luke, or John. Literally, however, the word means, "one who proclaims good tidings" (Eph. 4:11, 2 Tim. 4:5).

The evangelist is a gift of God to the early church (Eph. 4:11). The early disciples were also called evangelists (Acts 8:4) because they proclaimed the gospel. Spiritual leaders are called to "do the work of an evangelist" even if that is not their appointed office (2 Tim. 4:5).

All believers today may continue the witness of the evangelists, Matthew, Mark, Luke, and John. As the evangelists spoke and wrote of Jesus, so are we to bring His message to others.

EVER. (Mic. 4:5) *'ad* (*ahd*); *Strong's* #5703: Everlastingness, perpetuity; eternity, evermore, forever; time passing on and on; world without end; for all time forward; continually. This noun appears nearly fifty times in the Old Testament. Its first occurrence is in Exodus 15:18: "The LORD shall reign forever and ever" (compare Ps. 10:16; Is. 45:17). God dwells eternally in Zion (Ps. 132:14). God inhabits "eternity" (Is. 57:15). In Micah 4:5, Israel vows that they will own Him as their God *Le'Olam Ve'Ad*, "forever and ever." In Psalm 132:11–12, *'ad* describes the length of time that the throne of David shall be occupied by his royal seed: "forevermore." In Isaiah 9:6, Messiah is called "Everlasting Father," which in Hebrew is *'Abi-'Ad*, literally "Father of Eternity," that is, the architect, builder, begetter, producer, and creator of the ages to come.

EVERLASTING—lasting forever; eternal. The Greek word translated as everlasting in the New Testament means "age-lasting," as contrasted with that which is brief and fleeting. The Bible speaks of the everlasting God (Is. 40:28), Father (Is. 9:6), King (Jer. 10:10), and Redeemer (Is. 63:16). The Lord is a God of everlasting kindness (Is. 54:8), love (Jer. 31:3), and mercy (Ps. 100:5; 103:17) who has established an everlasting covenant with His people (Heb. 13:20). His kingdom is everlasting (2 Pet. 1:11), as is His salvation (Ps. 45:17).

EVERLASTING. (Rev. 14:6) *aionios* (ahee-oh-nee-oss); *Strong's* #166: Compare "eon." Perpetual, unchanging, of unlimited duration, eternal, age-long, unending. The word may denote that which is without either beginning or end (Rom. 16:26; Heb. 9:14); without beginning (Rom. 16:25; 2 Tim. 1:9); without end (Luke 16:9; 2 Cor. 5:1; Rev. 14:6).

EVIL—a force that opposes God and His work of righteousness in the world (Rom. 7:8–19), and which is personalized in Satan himself— "the evil one" (1 John 5:19; Matt. 6:13). The word also is used for any disturbance to the harmonious order of the universe, such as disease (Ps. 41:8). But the Bible makes it plain that even these so-called "physical evils" are the result of a far more serious moral and spiritual evil that was given place to with the *Fall of Adam and Eve in the Garden of Eden (Genesis 3). There, mankind not only disobeyed God, but through the act of disobedience submitted themselves to Satan's rebellious intent. The tragic implications of this are that thereby man not only was severed from relationship with God, but the "dominion over the earth" which had been given to humans (Gen. 1:26, 28) was now conveyed into the hand of the Serpent. Thus, Jesus refers to the Adversary as "the prince of this world" (John 12:31; 14:30; 16:11), and John further notes "the whole world lies under the sway of the wicked (or evil) one" (1 John 5:19).

The ultimate source of evil in the world is Satan, also called "the devil" (Luke 8:12) and "the wicked one" (Matt. 13:19). The Christian believer can rest assured that Jesus will triumph at the end of time, when Satan will be cast into a lake of fire and brimstone and evil will be overcome (Rev. 20.10).

Evil also comes from the hearts of people (Mark 7:20–23). It never comes from God, "for God cannot be tempted by evil, nor does He Himself tempt anyone" (James 1:13).

EVIL. (Ps. 5:4) *ra'* (*rah*); *Strong's* #7451: Something bad, evil; badness, tragedy, trouble, distress, wickedness, something of poor quality. Ra' occurs more than six hundred times in the Old Testament. *Ra'* means "badness," but not necessarily evil in the sense of something being inherently wicked, insidious, morally rotten, and so forth. Malnourished cows are described as "evil in appearance" (Gen. 41:27), that is "bad looking." In other references, evil is contrasted with good (Gen. 2:17) and is to be hated (Ps. 97:10).

EXALTED. (Ps. 18:46) *rum* (*room*); *Strong's* #7311: To elevate, raise, bring up, exalt, lift up, hold up, extol; to make high and powerful. Since God is in the highest, and is the Most High ('El 'Elyon), He cannot be higher than He is already; however, He can be raised and exalted in our understanding of Him. Related to *rum* are the words *'Abram* (Abram) and *terumah*. Abram's name means "Father of Height," that is, "Exalted Father," or "Man of Stature." *Terumah* means "heave offering," a gift that evidently was tossed upward while being offered.

EXALTED (HIGHLY). (Phil. 2:9) *huperupsoo* (hoop-er-oop-*sah*-oh); *Strong's* #5251: From *huper*, "over," and *hupsoo*, "to lift up." Thus, the word suggests an exaltation to the highest position, an elevation above all others. The context contrasts humiliation and resulting honors. Jesus' obedience to death is followed by a super-exalted position of honor and glory.

EXAMPLE. (1 Pet. 2:21) *hupogrammos* (hoop-og-ram-*moss*); *Strong's #5261:* From *hupo,* "under," and *grapho,* "to write"; hence, an underwriting. The word referred to tracing letters, copying the writings of the teacher. Then it came to denote an example to be followed. The example of Christ enables us to endure when we suffer for our faith.

EXCELLENCE. (2 Cor. 4:7) *huperbole* (hoop-er-bol-*ay*); *Strong's #5236:* From *huper,* "beyond," and *ballo,* "to throw"; hence, a throwing beyond. The primary idea is that of excellence, superiority, excess, preeminence.

EXCOMMUNICATION—the expulsion of a member from the church because of a divisiveness, doctrinal abberation, or moral lapse.

The process of excommunication from the church was spelled out by Jesus (Matt. 18:15–18). The errant believer should first be confronted about his behavior. If he refuses to heed the warnings, a representative of the church should return with witnesses. If that, too, is ineffective, the person should be brought before the church, which is to excommunicate him: "Let him be to you like a heathen or a tax collector" (Matt. 18:17). The apostle Paul also used the phrase "deliver to Satan" (1 Cor. 5:5; 1 Tim. 1:20), which seems to imply excommunication.

Several purposes stood behind this extremely disciplinary tool. Primarily it was to protect the church from blatant evil in its midst (1 Cor. 5:6). It also had a redemptive function—to force the member to realize the seriousness of his offense and to return to Christ (1 Cor. 5:5).

EXODUS—see ch. 55, §2.1.

EZRA—see ch. 55, §3.2.

FAITH—a belief in or confident attitude toward God, involving commitment to His will for one's life.

According to Hebrews 11, faith was already present in the experience of many people in the Old Testament as a key element of their spiritual lives. In this chapter the various heroes of the Old Testament (Abel, Enoch, Noah, Abraham, Sarah, Isaac, Jacob, Joseph, and Moses) are described as living by faith. In addition, the Old Testament itself makes the same point. Abraham "believed in the Lord" (Gen. 15:6); the Israelites "believed" (Ex. 4:31,

14:31) and the prophet Habakkuk taught that "the just shall live by his faith" (Hab. 2:4).

In the New Testament, "faith" describes various levels of personal commitment: (1) Mere *intellectual agreement* to a truth is illustrated in James 2:19, where even demons are said to believe that there is one God. Obviously, however, they are not saved by this type of belief. (2) Genuine *saving faith* is shown as a personal attachment to Christ, best thought of as a combination of two ideas—reliance on Christ and commitment to Him.

Saving faith involves personally depending on the finished work of Christ's sacrifice as the only basis for forgiveness of sin and entrance into heaven. But saving faith is also a personal commitment of one's life to following Christ in obedience to His commands: "I know whom I have believed and am persuaded that He is able to keep what I have committed to Him until that Day" (2 Tim. 1:12).

Faith is the essence of the believer's life from beginning to end. As the instrument by which the gift of salvation is received (Eph. 2:8–9), faith is thus distinct from the basis of salvation, which is grace, and from the outworking of salvation which is good works. The apostle Paul declared that salvation is through faith, not through keeping the works of the law (Eph. 2:8, 9).

Finally, in the New Testament, faith can refer to the convictions, teachings, and ministry first established in the church—the "faith" which was once for all delivered to the saints (Jude 3). In modern times, faith has been weakened in meaning so that some people use it to mean self-confidence. But in the Bible, true faith is confidence in God or Christ, not in oneself.

FAITH. (Mark 11:22) *pistis* (*pis*-tis); *Strong's #4102:* Conviction, confidence, trust, belief, reliance, trustworthiness, and persuasion. In the New Testament setting, *pistis* is the divinely implanted principle of inward confidence, assurance, trust, and reliance in God and all that He says. The word sometimes denotes the object or content of belief (Acts 6:7; 14:22; Gal. 1:23).

FAITHFUL. (Prov. 28:20) *'emunah* (eh-moo-nah); *Strong's #530:* Firmness, stability, faithfulness, fidelity, conscientiousness, steadiness, certainty; that which is permanent, enduring, steadfast. *'Emunah* comes from the root *'aman,* "to be firm, sure, established, and steady." "Amen," derived from this same root, means, "It is firmly, truly so!" *'Emunah* occurs forty-nine times. It is often translated "faithfulness" or "truth," as truth is considered something ultimately certain, stable, and unchangingly fixed. This word appears in Habakkuk 2:4, the great verse so influential to New Testament thought and Reformation history: "The just shall live by his *'emunah*," that is, his firmness, steadiness, and solid belief.

 FAITHFULNESS—dependability, loyalty, and stability particularly as it describes God in His relationship to human believers. The faithfulness of God and His Word is a constant theme in the Bible. It is particularly prominent in Psalms 89 and 119. God is "the faithful God who keeps covenant" (Deut. 7:9) and chooses Israel (Is. 49:7); great is His faithfulness (Lam. 3:23).

It is not surprising that this aspect of God's nature should also belong to the Messiah, who would be clothed with faithfulness (Is. 11:5) and who is described as the Faithful one (Rev. 19:11), the "faithful witness" (Rev. 1:5; 3:14), and the "faithful High Priest" (Heb. 2:17; 3:2).

God's faithfulness is the source of the Christian's deliverance from temptation (1 Cor. 10:13), assurance of salvation (Heb. 10:23), and forgiveness of sins (1 John 1:9). He is faithful to His children because He is first of all faithful to Himself (2 Tim. 2:13).

God's faithfulness should be so deeply reflected in the lives of His people (Gal. 5:22) that they can be called simply "the faithful" (Ps. 31:23). The New Testament speaks of the faithfulness of Paul (1 Cor. 7:25), Abraham (Neh. 9:8), and Moses (Heb. 3:5).

Faithfulness is also expected in Christian believers. Faithfulness to one's fellowman is seen especially in relation to fulfilling an office. A steward must be found faithful (1 Cor. 4:2), just as Daniel and other persons in the Bible exercised their faithfulness toward God (Dan. 6:4; 2 Tim. 2:2).

FAITH'S CONFESSION OF GOD'S WORD. Jesus Himself established the importance of understanding how faith operates, when He said, "According to your faith let it be to you" (Matt. 9:29). Faith that believes is called to become faith that appropriates. The present day has seen a rise of understanding on this subject, but mixed with a confusing and distracting flurry of ideas that have often brought misunderstanding and criticism. Is there a biblically balanced approach to "confessiong God's Word in faith"? This study is an examination of Scripture that may bring hope for such balance.

1. The Words We Speak (Gen. 17:5). One of the explicit teachings of the Bible is the importance of the words we speak. In this text God changes Abram's name to Abraham and promises Abraham that he will become the father of many nations. "Abram" means "High Father" or "Patriarch." "Abraham" means "Father of a Multitude." Thus, God was arranging that every time Abraham heard or spoke his own name, he would be reminded of God's promise. Adam Clarke's Commentary states it well: "God [associates] the patriarch more nearly to Himself, by thus imparting to him a portion of His own name," noting God added this to Abraham "for the sake of dignity." The principle: Let God's words, which designated His will and promise for *your* life, become as fixed in your mind and as governing of your speech as God's changing Abraham's name was in shaping his concept of himself. Do not "name" yourself anything less than God does.

2. Faith When Facing Delays (Num. 13:30; 14:6–9). Caleb saw the same giants and walled city as the other spies, but the ten spies brought back an "evil report" of unbelief. Caleb's words declared a conviction—a "confession"—before all Israel: "We are well able to overcome." He had surveyed the land, a reminder that faith is *not* blind. Faith does not deny the reality of difficulty; it declares the power of God in the face of the problem.

There is a message in the spirit of Caleb's response to the rejection of his faith-filled report. Some use their confession of faith to cultivate schism, but Caleb stood his ground in faith and still moved in partnership and support—for forty years—beside many whose unbelief delayed his own experience. What *patience* as well as faith! His eventual actual possession of the land at a later date indicates that even though delays come, faith's confession will ultimately bring victory to the believer.

3. Silencing Unbelief (Josh. 6:10). Many texts in God's Word instruct us to "wait on God," to stand still, to be silent before Him (Moses, Ex. 14:13–14; Jehoshaphat, 2 Chr. 20:15–17; David, Ps. 37:7–8). In this text, Joshua commands the children of Israel to maintain total silence as they walk around the city of Jericho. The memory that Israel's forty-year punishment in the wilderness was a result of the people's murmuring in unbelief was doubtless in Joshua's mind. At that time, the spies had returned with a report motivated by what man sees without Holy Spirit-given vision. Their unbelief that they could take the land had sealed their fate in the wilderness.

Now, with the lessons of history in mind, Joshua's directive to keep silent is a precaution that teaches us. When facing great challenges, do not permit your lips to speak unbelieving words. Prohibit demoralizing speech from your lips. Words can bind up or set free, hence the order to silence! Later, they would *see* the salvation of the Lord pursuant upon their *shout* of triumph (6:20).

We cannot help what we see and hear, but our refusal to *speak* doubt and fear will keep our hearts more inclined to what *God* can do, rather than to what we cannot (*see* Prov. 30:32).

4. The Meaning of "Faith's Confession" (2 Chr. 6:24–31).

In Solomon's prayer of dedication, he points to the importance of confessing the Lord's name (v. 24). The power-packed word "confess" opens a great truth concerning God's hearing and answering prayers. It is an appropriate word in Christian tradition, historically used to describe a position-in-faith or belief, as, for example, "The Augsburg Confessions." To confess belief is to say, "I openly receive God's promise and choose to take my stand here, humbly, *on* God's promises and in worship of His Person."

Yadah, the Hebrew word for "confess," contains and supports this idea. Derived from *yad*, meaning "an open or extended hand," the focus is on reaching to take hold of. Just as a closed hand or fist may represent struggle or rebellion, an open hand indicates peace, submitted service or surrender. As Solomon comes with lifted, open hands (v. 12), he comes in peaceful submission to God. *Yadah* also involves worship, with open, extended hands, in a worship-filled confessing of God's faithfulness with thanksgiving and praise. This is the true spirit of the idea of "faith's confession of God's Word": (1) to take a stand on what God says; (2) to speak what is believed with worship and praise; and (3) to do so in the humble spirit of faith in God's Person and promise. Such a stance will never be loveless or arrogant, and neither earth nor hell can successfully protest this confession of faith in heaven's power.

5. "Acceptable" Speech Before God (Ps. 19:14).

This oft-quoted verse attests to the importance and desirability of our words and thoughts being consistent with God's Word and will. The text literally says, "Let what I *speak* and what my heart murmurs to itself be a delight to You, Lord." Clearly, the acceptability of our words in God's sight is dependent upon their being consistent with what our hearts feel or think. The truth of this text urges us to always speak the kind of words that confirm what we believe or think in our hearts about God, His love, and His power. If we believe, yet contradict that belief with careless words from our mouth, it is not acceptable in God's sight. Remember the lesson of Cain's sacrifice (Gen. 4:1–7): what is unacceptable is not only faithless and fruitless; it may also become deadly.

6. Wise Words Bring Health (Prov. 16:23–24).

This text reveals what God's wisdom (His Word) has taught our hearts: those truths and promises are to influence our speech—to transmit that learning to our lips. The Word in our hearts is to teach or control our speech and conduct. The "sweetness" and "health" such speech promotes are desirable, whether in our human relationships or in the release of divine grace in our daily living. It leads the believer to an overcoming, victorious life, through a consistent acknowledgment of the power and might of God with both mouth and manner.

7. Keeping Your Confession Without Hypocrisy (Matt. 15:7–9).

Jesus quotes from Isaiah 29:13 in charging the Pharisees with setting aside God's Word by their traditions. Jesus dismisses their worship because their hearts were not aligned with their lips. Living faith—true worship—requires that the mouth and the heart be together to avoid Jesus' charge of hypocrisy.

Praises and true faith emanate from lips that draw from the depths of the heart. As a living principle, faith's confession is not a ritual recitation of slogans; otherwise, it is only acting out a human tradition and, as Jesus notes, is potentially hypocritical.

Just as we are called to genuine praise and worship, not as pretenders or ritual performers, so let our confessing of God's promises be without hypocrisy. Let us speak what God's Holy Spirit has truly birthed in our hearts, thereby bringing us to faithfully speak with our lips.

8. Jesus on "Faith's Confession" (Mark 11:22–24).

From Jesus' own lips we receive the most direct and practical instruction concerning our exercise of faith. Consider three points: (1) It is to be "in God." Faith that speaks is first faith that seeks. The Almighty One is the Source and Grounds of our faith and being. Faith only flows *to* Him because of the faithfulness that flows *from* Him. (2) Faith is not a trick performed with our lips, but a spoken expression that springs from the conviction of our hearts. The idea that faith's confession is a "formula" for getting things from God is unbiblical. But the fact that the faith in our hearts is to be spoken, and thereby becomes active and effective toward specific results, is taught here by the Lord Jesus. (3) Jesus' words "whatever things" apply this principle to every aspect of our lives. The only restrictions are (a) that our faith be "in God" our living Father and in alignment with His will and word; and (b) that we "believe"—not doubting in our hearts. Thus, "speaking to the mountain" is not a vain or superstitious exercise or indulgence in humanistic mind-science, but instead becomes an applied release of God's creative word of promise.

9. Jesus' Name: Faith's Complete Authority (Acts 3:6). In this first recorded miracle performed by the disciples, we are given the key for use by all believers in exercising faith's authority. When commanding healing for the lame man, Peter employs the full name/title of our Lord: "Jesus Christ [Messiah] of Nazareth." "Jesus" ("Joshua" or "Yeshua") was a common name among the Jews and continues to be in many cultures today. But the declaration of His full name and title, a noteworthy practice in Acts, seems a good and practical lesson for us (see 2:22; 4:10). Let us be complete when claiming our authority over sickness, disease, or demons. In our confession of faith or proclamation of power, confess His deity and His lordship as the Christ (Messiah); use His precious name, as Jesus (Savior). Call upon Him as Lord Jesus, or Jesus Christ, or Jesus of Nazareth, there being no legal or ritual demand intended in this point. But it is wise to remember, just as we pray "in Jesus' name" (John 16:24), so we exercise all authority in Him—by the privilege of power He has given us in His name (Matt. 28:18; Mark 16:12; John 14:13–14).

Many other compound names for Him are found in the Word of God. Let us declare them in faith, with prayer and full confidence.

10. Calling for "Great Grace" (Acts 4:33). Most believers know the common definition of the beautiful word "grace" as "the unmerited favor of God." This is wonderfully true and clearly relates to our salvation apart from the works or energy of our flesh (Eph. 2:7–9).

But "grace," as used in this text ("great grace") and texts such as Luke 2:40 and Acts 11:23, also refers to "operations of the power of God." Just as God in mercy saves us by His grace, so that grace is manifested in great dynamic where the Holy Spirit is at work in power. Zechariah 4:7 provides an Old Testament illustration of this truth. The prophet instructed Zerubbabel to speak "grace" to the "mountain"—the hindrance he faced in the trying task of rebuilding God's temple. Speaking "grace" to obstacles we face is an action of faith, drawing on the operations of God's great power. We only speak: the work is entirely His—by His gracious power and for His great glory.

When we accept salvation, we receive it only through the power of His grace. Likewise, we can trust that His same grace will operate in us and through us, as it has been shown to us. As with the early disciples, great authority and power in other issues flowed through them and in their midst. As we call upon the name of the Lord, speaking His grace into the face of our mountainous impossibilities, we have every reason to expect "great power" and "great grace" today, too.

11. Continuing in Faith As We Have Begun (Rom. 10:9–10). Here is the most foundational lesson in the importance and power of faith's confession found anywhere in the Bible. The principle is established at the very beginning of our life in Christ. Just as salvation (God's righteous working in our behalf) is appropriated by heart belief and spoken confession, so His continuing working in our lives is advanced by the same means.

The word "confess" (Greek *homologeo*) has the connotation of "a binding public declaration by which a legal relation is contractually established" (Kittel). Thus, as our words "contract" from *our* side the salvation God has fully provided from *His* by Christ's saving work and power, so we have a principle for all of life. Beginning in this spirit of *saving* faith, let us grow in *active* faith—believing in God's mighty power for all our needs, speaking with our lips what our hearts receive and believe of the many promises in His Word. Let us accept God's "contracts" for all our need by endowing them with our confessed belief—just as when we were saved.

12. Faith at the Lord's Table (1 Cor. 11:23–26). Just as the act of water baptism outwardly declares or confesses an inward experience of salvation through the blood of the Lord Jesus, each observance of the Lord's Table is a powerful occasion for faith's confession. In the ordinance, the Christian confesses before all heaven that he not only has believed, but that he has not forgotten. "In remembrance" involves more than just memory; the word suggests an "active calling to mind" (Wycliffe).

The word "for" introduces the reason the Supper is continually repeated. It is an acted sermon, for it "proclaims" the Lord's death. The outward act of faith, as the bread and cup are taken, is explicitly said to be an ongoing, active confession—literally "you are *proclaiming*" (v. 26). Each occasion of partaking is an opportunity to say, proclaim, or *confess* again: "I herewith lay hold of all the benefits of Jesus

Christ's full redemption for my life—forgiveness, wholeness, strength, health, sufficiency." The Lord's Supper is not to be simply a ritual remembrance, but an active confession, by which you actively will to call to memory and appropriate *today* all that Jesus has provided and promised through His Cross.

13. Faith Exalting Jesus' Lordship (Phil. 2:9–11). Scholars note that the word "confess" means "to acknowledge openly and joyfully, to celebrate and give praise" (Thayer/Wycliffe). This eloquently and beautifully stated text is a great point of acknowledgment for all who would learn the power of faith's confession. The exalting and honoring of our Lord Jesus Christ is our fountainhead of power in applying faith. The Father honors Him first, then those who confess His Son as well (John 12:26). All humans, angels, and demon spirits will ultimately bow the knee to Jesus, rendering complete and final homage. That confession of every tongue will one day be heard by every ear as He receives ultimate and complete rule. But until that day, our confession of Jesus Christ as Lord invites and receives His presence and power over all evil whenever we face it now. And as we declare His lordship—in faith—His rule enters those settings and circumstances today.

14. Understanding *Rhema* and *Logos* (Heb. 4:11–13). This text is among the foremost in understanding faith's call to "confess" the Word of God. The lesson relates to Israel's renunciation of God's promise, which resulted in a whole generation's dying in the wilderness and failing to possess the inheritance God intended for them. In this context, the Bible describes itself: "The word of God is living and powerful." The term for "word" here is the Greek word *logos*, which commonly indicates the expression of a complete idea and is used in referring to the Holy Scriptures. It contrasts with *rhema*, which generally refers to a word spoken or given. This recommends our understanding the difference between *all* the Bible and the *single* promise or promises the Holy Spirit may bring to our mind from the Word of God. When facing a situation of need, trial, or difficulty, the promises of God may become a *rhema* to you; that is, a weapon of the Spirit, "the word of God" (Eph. 6:17). Its authority is that this "word" comes from the Bible—God's Word—the completed *logos*. Its immediate significance is that He has "spoken" it to your soul by His Spirit and is calling forth faith just as He did from Israel when He pointed them toward their inheritance. Faith's confession receives God's "words" (*rhema*) and stands firm upon these promises. However, faith's

confession is strong not in human willpower, but in the divine will revealed in the whole of the Scriptures—the Holy Bible—the *logos* (completed Word) from which the *rhema* (present "word of promise") has been received.

15. Faith's Confession Is Steadfast (Heb. 11:13–16). This chapter records glorious victories of faith's champions, yet verses 13–16 speak of those who died, "not having received the promises." Even then, the Bible says "these all died in faith," being content to confess that they were only strangers and pilgrims traveling, as it were, through the land: "For true believers, to live by faith is to die by faith" (Wycliffe).

The key to the "confession" (v. 13) of this admirable group in Heb. 11 is that when given a promise by God, as were Abraham and his descendants, they became "fully persuaded" that the promise was true. Thus they embraced (literally "greeted") that promise in their hearts.The word "confess" helps us to understand how easily these of the gallery of faith established their ways before God and left the testimony, which His Word records with tribute. While each of these persons did receive *many* victories through faith, the text says that none of them received *everything* that was promised. Whether or not we receive what we "confess" (ask, pray, or hope for) does not change the behavior or the attitude of the steadfast believer. Faith's worship and walk do not depend on answered or unanswered prayers. Our confession of His lordship in our lives is to be consistent—a daily celebration, with deep gratitude.

16. Declaring the Ultimate Victory in Christ (Rev. 12:11). There is no greater biblical declaration of faith's confession. Those facing the cataclysmic travail of the last days endure it with a constant statement of the overcoming power of the blood of the Lamb and of the word of their transforming faith in Christ. Some of those declaring Christ's ultimate victory with their own lips (6:9; 11:7) face the fury of Satan's most vicious and personal attacks against them. Yet, their faith is unwavering, the result of an abiding relationship with Jesus Christ. This is the heart of faith's confession, based in God's Word and the blood of the Lamb, whose victory has provided the eternal conquest of Satan.

With Christ's victory over Satan, we see these who have maintained their confession of faith and thereby share in His victory. With their sins blotted out and their declaration of Jesus' redemptive work in their lives, they silence the attempts of the prince of darkness to intimidate God's children. His accusing voice of condemnation and guilt is swallowed up in the triumph of Calvary. Declare your abiding faith in the accomplished work of the Cross, and constantly participate in Jesus' ultimate victory, overcoming Satan by the power of the Cross and the steadfastness of your confession of faith in Christ's triumph. R.H.

FAITH, SEED, PRINCIPLES OF. Jesus is called "The Seed" (Gen. 3:15), the Word of God is designated as "Seed" (Luke 8:11; 1 Pet. 1:23), the growth of the believer is likened to a plant (John 15), and the evangelism of the world to a harvest (Matt. 13:30). This only begins the imagery of "seed faith" in the Bible, a theme that is biblically developed in this study. It is altogether desirable to capture a firm grasp of this truth, the essence of which is that the little we have to bring to God is not a limit to faith's possibilities. When we bring Him the smallest of our strength, faith resource, and ability, when it is placed in Him—sown like a seed—there is a guaranteed fruitfulness and harvest forthcoming. It is within the laws of God's creation—both the natural and the spiritual realm—and worthy to be applied in practical living.

1. The Principle of the Seed; the Law of Seedtime and Harvest (Gen. 8:22). Noah's first acts after the Flood were to build an altar and sacrifice to the Lord. God was pleased and made promises to the human family through the faith of Noah. He also instituted *the Law of Seedtime and Harvest*: "While the earth remains, seedtime and harvest . . . shall not cease" (v. 22).

When God created the first living thing, He gave it the ability to grow and multiply. How? Through the *Seed*. Your life began by the seed principle. Every act of your life since your birth has operated by the seed principle—springing from good seeds or bad seeds you have sown—whether or not you were consciously aware of your seed-planting. The principle continues today. To overcome life's problems, reach your potential in life, see your life become fruitful, multiplied, replenished (that is, in health, finance, spiritual renewal, family, or your entire being), determine to follow God's law of seedtime and harvest. Sow the seed of His promise in the soil of your need.

2. Expecting God's Best (2 Sam. 24:24). David had sinned; and, as a result, a plague came on the people. To atone for this sin, the Lord told King David to build an altar on the threshing floor of Araunah and offer a burnt offering so that the plague might be stayed. Araunah tried to give David the land, the oxen, and other items to sacrifice. But David insisted on paying Araunah, saying that he could not present to God an offering that cost him *nothing*.

The very heart of Seed Faith is that unless you experience some sacrifice, you have not truly *given*. Unless your giving costs you something—something that represents a portion of your very life—then it is not a living gift and will not yield a good harvest. Our giving to the Lord must bear these three qualities.

First, it should be our *best*. When we give God our best, we are in a position to expect His *best* back into our lives.

Second, we should give to God *first*. The very first thought in our minds after we have received something should be how we can give a portion of our harvest to the work of the Lord.

Third, our giving should be *generous*, freely from our heart and without expecting anything back from the one to whom we give. As Jesus said to His disciples, "Freely you have received, freely give" (Matt. 10:8).

3. God's Desire for You (Ex. 15:26). In promising His continuing, healing presence as our Covenant Healer, God places two great conditions before His people.

First, God asks us to heed Him. He wants us to listen for His voice, to have a hearing ear so we will hear Him. God has always spoken to His people and He will speak to you today, but you must cultivate an attitude of listening for His voice. He speaks in many ways: through His Word, through His anointed servants, and through direct revelation in your inner man (Eph. 1:17–18). He is seeking a people who will *listen* for His voice and not try to run and hide from Him (see Gen. 3:8).

Second, God asks us to "do what is right in His sight." He is seeking people who will not only *hear* His words, but will take them to heart and *act* on them—people who will obey His word and not be hearers only (see James 1:22–25).

God's goodness is abundantly promised. It awaits those who "[sow] to the Spirit" (Gal. 6:7–9), hearing His voice and doing what He tells us to do.

4. Giving God an Opportunity (1 Kin. 17:8–16). This episode teaches us to invite God to work by His unlimited power within our limited circumstances and resources. Two important principles for our giving are illustrated by this passage of Scripture.

First, we must give something out of our *need*. That is the kind of giving that involves our *faith*. This woman had a need for herself and her family, but she gave to sustain the ministry and life of God's prophet, Elijah. Then God multiplied her giving back to her.

Second, this woman gave *first*. Her giving *activated* the miracle supply of God flowing back into her life. For perhaps as long as three years God multiplied her seed sown.

Your giving causes something to happen according to God's eternal principles of seed-time and harvest. There is an old saying that bears repeating: "Without God, you cannot; without you, God will not." God has already given from His side. Now we must step out in our giving to Him. Doing so will release His flow of provision on our earth-side of things. Sow! Give Him something to multiply!

5. God's Unlimited Resources (2 Chr. 25:9). In man's economy, the law of supply and demand regulates the price paid for goods and services. In times of oversupply, the prices go down; in times of shortage, the prices rise. Man's economy fluctuates with the times and the seasons.

God's economy, however, has no shortages. God's supply always equals our need. He does not want any of His people to have any lack, but rather, to "increase more and more" (see 1 Thess. 4:10–12). Do you think that if you give something to God, you will have less? Not according to God's law of Seed Faith. When you give, you have just put yourself into the position for increase!

We can never outgive God. No matter what we give to Him, He will multiply it back to us in an amount greater than we gave! Our ability to receive the harvest, however, is *not* automatic. Expecting to receive, not from the person to whom we give, but from God our Source, is an act of our faith also. As a farm-boy I learned that to plant means to *do* something, and receiving the harvest likewise requires *doing* something! Both are *acts* of our faith.

6. God Has a Way (Matt. 17:19–20). When you plant a seed, God changes the nature of that seed so that it becomes a plant; and the power of life surges in that tender young plant to such a great extent that even a mountain of earth cannot stop it from pushing upward!

Jesus says our faith in God is like a seed. When we put our faith into action, that is, when we release it to God, it takes on a totally new nature. It takes on the nature of a miracle in the making.

What is the mountain in your life? Loneliness, loss of a job, disease, a wounded relationship, trouble in your home? Something else? Be encouraged! Jesus shows the way to see that mountain removed!

First, God says that you have a measure of faith (Rom. 12:3). It is resident within you. Second, God says that this faith comes alive by "hearing . . . the word of God" (Rom. 10:17). Third, God says that you can *apply* your faith to see your daily needs met. How? You *do* something as an act of your faith. You sow the mustard-seed smallness of your faith into an action of love (Matt. 17:20). Then, when your faith has been planted and is growing, *speak* to your mountain and watch God set about its removal.

7. Biblical Abundance (John 10:10). As you give your total self to God, God gives His total self to you. That is the supreme message of the Bible. Inherent in God's "total self" of His own Person is true, Bible-based prosperity—the real possibility of health for your total being (body, mind, emotions, relationships), of your material needs being met. Above all, His prosperity brings eternal life. Stop to think about it. What else is there worth having?

Jesus said that He came to give life—not just ordinary existence, but life in fullness, abundance, and prosperity (3 John 2). On the other hand, the Enemy (Satan) comes only to steal, kill, and destroy. The line is clearly drawn. On one side is God with goodness, life, and "plenty" of all that is necessary for life (see Joel 2:26 and 2 Pet. 1:3), and on the other side is the Enemy of our souls, who comes to rob us of God's blessings, to oppress our bodies through disease and accidents, and to destroy everything that we love and hold dear.

Your first step toward experiencing full biblical prosperity is to believe that it is God's highest desire for you. The next step is to line up your highest desire with His.

8. Receiving a Harvest; Expecting a Miracle (Luke 6:38). Jesus opened up a whole new way of giving. He gave Himself totally to and for the needs of the people. We can no longer pay or sacrifice our way into God's mercy. Jesus Christ has paid our debt before God, and His Cross is a completed work in our eternal interest. Our giving, then, is no longer a debt that we owe, but a seed that we sow! The life and power source is from Him. Ours is simply to act on the power potential in that seed-life He has placed in us by His power and grace!

Notice that when Jesus said, "Give," He also said, "and it will be given to you." Giving and receiving belong together. Only when we give are we in a position to expect to reach out and receive a harvest. And Jesus said the harvest will be "good measure, pressed down, shaken together, and running over."

We give as to God, and we receive as from God; but we should remain sensitive at all times to the different ways in which God may deliver our harvest. I often say, "A miracle is either coming toward you or going past you all the time. Reach out and take it! Do not let it pass by!" (*see* Matt. 9:20–22). God's miracle for you may be coming as an idea, an opportunity, an invitation, or a previously unknown or unidentified association. Watch expectantly for the ways in which God may choose to deliver your miracle to you in His "due season" (which, for you, may be *today*).

9. A Due Season for All Seeds (Gal. 6:7–9). God has a timetable for every seed we plant. His timetable is not always our timetable. Sometimes the "due season" means a quick return. Sometimes it means a process or a slow return that may take years—even a lifetime. But we can count on three things. First, God will cause a harvest to come from our seeds. Second, God is never early or late—He is always right on time with our best interests at heart. Third, our harvest will have the same nature as our seeds sown: good seeds bring good harvests, bad seeds bring bad harvests.

What are we to do during the growing time of our seeds? (1) Refuse to become discouraged. (2) Determine to keep our faith alive and active. (3) Give and keep on giving; love and keep on loving. Know this—His harvest is guaranteed. Continue in an attitude of expectancy.

10. The Importance of Giving (Mal. 3:10–11). In this passage of Scripture, God actually invites people to *try* (prove) Him—to verify His trustworthiness with their giving. He says that by withheld giving we rob Him of the privilege of pouring out great and overflowing blessings. He calls for renewed giving with this promise. First, there will be "food" or resources for God's work ("in My house"). Second, He says those who give will be placed in position to receive great, overflowing blessings. You can experience the windows of heaven actually opening with blessings you will not be able to "receive" or contain! Third, God says that He will "rebuke the devourer" *for your sakes*. He will cause every blessing that has your name written on it to be directed to you, and Satan himself cannot stop it. Do not be afraid to *prove* God with your giving; He is God and He will stand the test every time.

11. The Key to Receiving (Mark 11:22–24). Believing can take opposite forms. It can be faith or it can be doubt. When you believe that God exists and that He loves you and wants to meet your needs, then your believing creates faith in your heart.

On the other hand, doubt is just as real. The reverse of faith, doubt tells you that God does not exist or that He is unloving and uncaring about your needs. Doubt gives rise to fear, which brings torment, not peace. Fear actually keeps you from receiving the good things God desires to send your way. Capture this truth: Doubt, and do without; with faith believe, and receive. I have said for years, "Expect a miracle!"

Expectancy opens your life to God and puts you in a position to receive salvation, joy, health, financial supply, or peace of mind—everything good your heart longs for, and more!

12. Giving Back to Our Source (Matt. 25:34–40). Whenever you and I give, or plant our seeds of faith, we are doing it for Jesus. The person we feed becomes as Jesus to us. The person we visit in prison or in the sickbed becomes as Jesus to us. How may we know our Lord? We know Him in doing His works and in doing them as much to Him as for Him. We know Him in putting our arms around those who are desperate or alone. He said that when we do this we are putting our arms around Him—Jesus Christ, our blessed Savior.

Although our giving is to take on very real and tangible forms as we reach out to people, as we give through individuals and churches and ministries to meet great needs around the world, the focus of our faith is to be on Jesus and Jesus alone. He is God—and He is our Source. He is the object of our worship and our love. He alone is worthy of our lives, and He alone can supply our needs.

We give to others, but let us keep our vision clear. We look past them, with our faith directed to God and offered as a service of love for Him.

13. Selecting Good Soil for Sowing (Mark 4:1–20). We are not only responsible to plant seeds of our faith through actual acts of giving as to the Lord; we are also responsible for selecting the soil in which we plant. It is the quality of the soil that determines the quantity of our harvest. Jesus clearly outlines how we should direct our giving.

First, we must take charge of our giving. We plant our seeds of faith. We do so with patience and diligence (see Luke 8:15).

Second, we must look for places where the Holy Spirit is at work. Look for places alive with the Word of God—where spiritual results are found; where miracles, signs, and wonders confirm the preaching of the Word. Plant your seeds of faith there!

Third, look for people whose ministries already bear fruit for the kingdom of God. Are souls being saved? Are the sick being healed? Are people being delivered? Plant there!

Our Savior Himself tells you what you can expect when you follow His principles for planting: a multiplied harvest! You can look for 30-, 60-, and 100-fold returns when seed is sown wisely.

14. Multiplying Your Seed (Luke 5:1–11). Jesus taught a great lesson about seed-sowing and the importance of sowing in good soil (see Mark 4:1–20). Then, as if to illustrate His point, He told this group of discouraged and tired fishermen to launch out with their faith for a miracle catch.

These men had just planted their boat as a seed into the ministry of Jesus. They had given Him their greatest possession as a platform from which to preach the gospel. They had served the greatest need Jesus had at that moment, and here Jesus multiplied that gift into the means that met the greatest need they had at that moment in their lives. As commercial fishermen, they had a need for fish in order to make a living. They also had a need to see God working in their lives—to see both that Jesus was who He claimed to be and that their faith was operating effectively. Jesus met both of those needs!

When you give something to God, He will give it back in a way that is even better—plus He will be in it with all His grace and power!

15. Giving What's in Your Hand (2 Cor. 9:8–10). Note especially these three things as you study this passage: First, God is the One who makes all grace abound toward you and provides you sufficiency in all things. All things beneficial for our lives come from God's hands. Second, we are given sufficiency—even "bounty" so that we might do good works. We are blessed in order to be a blessing to others! (see Gen. 12:2). The word "sufficiency" means "self-satisfaction," "contentedness," or "competence"—earmarks of the believer whose life is truly blessed by these characteristics as God increases him (also see Gen. 12:2). And third, the God who gave you seed in the first place is the One who meets your basic needs, multiplies your seeds sown into an abundance you can share with others, and increases you spiritually with love, joy, peace, and all of the other fruit of the Holy Spirit flowing freely in your life ("the fruits of your righteousness").

How great is our God! We have no lack in Him—only potential!

16. A Seed of Prayer, Forgiveness, and Love and Joy (James 5:15–16). Do you ever feel you have absolutely nothing to give to God? Well, you can always plant a seed of faith-believing, love-motivated prayer in another person's life!

What does this type of prayer do? It saves the sick. Now "save" and "heal" are virtually interchangeable words in the Greek language; and "sickness" may broadly refer to any weakness or inability, disease or sin—anything that is "wrong" in life. In other words, the prayer of faith works to do good in whatever area life has gone bad.

And when people pray this kind of prayer, they are healed *as they pray!* Jesus also said that we are forgiven *as we forgive* (see Matt. 6:14–15). We experience love *as we give love away.* We are blessed *as we bless others.* God gives to us *as we give to others.*

We can always plant a faith-believing prayer in the life of another person. Do it with love . . . with joy . . . with a spirit of forgiveness . . . and expect God to multiply that seed in your own life!

17. God's Model for Giving and Receiving (John 3:16). Do you find it difficult to believe that you should expect to receive back from your giving? Read again this most famous verse in all the Bible and notice these things: (1) *God so loved.* God's motivation for giving was love. Ours must be, too. (2) *God gave.* God's love was turned into an act of giving. (3) *God gave His only begotten Son.* He gave His very best! So must we also give our best. (4) *God gave for a specific reason*—to get man back from Satan. God's deepest desire is to have man restored to Himself. And to get that need met, He gave. What is your need? Your giving—as an act of your deepest love and strongest faith—is the key to your having that need met. (5) *God gave sacrificially.* Our salvation cost Jesus His life (see John 12:24). It also costs us—full repentance and the giving of our lives to God. (6) *God's plan works!* Souls are saved because God gave His best, gave first, and gave expecting to receive! God Himself is our role model for giving . . . and receiving! O.R.

FALL, THE—the disobedience and sin of Adam and Eve that caused them to lose the state of innocence and the realm of dominion in and for which they had been created. This event plunged them and all of mankind into a state of sin and corruption, and allowed the loss of their intended rule and purpose. The account of the Fall is found in Genesis 3.

Adam and Eve were created by God in a state of sinless perfection so they could glorify God, reflecting His righteousness on the earth, and enjoy fellowship and union with Him. Their calling was to exercise dominion, or control, over God's creation through their own labors and those of their offspring in faithful response to the word of God. As a specific test of this loyalty, God commanded them not to eat of "the tree of the knowledge of good and evil" (Gen. 2:17). Adam and Eve were to demonstrate their willingness to live "by every word that proceeds from the mouth of the Lord" (Deut. 8:3; Matt. 4:4). God warned them clearly that their disobedience would result in death.

The fall from their original state of innocence and intended purpose occurred when Satan approached Eve through the serpent, who tempted her to eat of the forbidden fruit. Satan called into question the truthfulness of what God had spoken about the tree and its significance. He urged Eve to discover, through trial and error, whether it was in her best interest to do what God had forbidden. Eve's sin did not consist of being tempted, but in believing and acting on Satan's lie. Her rejection of God's command occurred when she was deceived and ate of the forbidden fruit. The New Testament holds the man at least equally if not more responsible, in that his action was consciously disobedient—taking and eating the fruit as an assertive decision, not as the result of deception (1 Tim. 2:14; Rom. 5:17–18). The term Fall should not be interpreted to suggest that their sin was accidental. The temptation was purposeful, and their submission to it involved their willing consent.

The immediate consequence of the Fall was death—the death of their union with God, the death of their dominion under His rule and the setting in motion of the death process in their physical bodies. For the first time, Adam and Eve experienced fear in the presence of the Lord God, and they hid when He approached (Gen. 3:8–10). Because of their unbelief and rebellion, they were driven from the garden that God had provided as their home.

From that time on, man would experience pain and encounter resistance as he worked at the task of earning his daily bread. Physical death, with the decay of the body, is not a natural process. It entered the human experience as God's curse upon sin.

Further, God's Word reveals that Adam did not sin simply as a private person, but as the representative of all members of the human race (Rom. 5:12–21). His sin set loose the death syndrome as a genetic reality, transmitting to all in successive generations, and through the Fall, all persons receive a fallen, corrupt nature. It is this nature that inevitably asserts itself through the actions of every human being, and stands as the root which begets all personal violations of God's commandments. For this reason, the fall of Adam is in actuality the fall of the the whole human

race, whose one hope is in Christ who, as the second Adam, came to recover those who have been birthed of and sinned in the likeness of the old, sinful Adam. Through His plan of redemption and the gift of salvation the reversal of the impact of the Fall has been made possible: "As in Adam all die, even so in Christ all shall be made alive" (1 Cor. 15:22).

FAMILIES. (Gen. 12:3) *mishpachah* (meesh-pah-*chah*); *Strong's* #4940: A family of people, a type, class, or kind of people or things; a species of animals, a group of related individuals (a tribe), or a group of related things (a category). The main concept of *mishpachah* is that people, animals, or things that share a kinship or similarity of kind form a family, clan, or species. Thus its scope can be as narrow as an immediate family, or as broad as a whole nation (10:31–32; Amos 3:2). Genesis 12:1–3 indicates that God separated Abraham from his idolatrous family in order to make him and his descendants the messianic nation, which would bring salvation to *all* earth's families.

FAMILY—a group of persons related by marriage and blood ties and generally living together in the same household. In the created order, the family appears to have been conceived in the mind of God as a man and his wife and their children. However, in the plan of God's redemptive workings, the family clearly takes on varied shapes and sizes and constituencies (Ps. 68:6).

In the ancient world, the extended family could include any or all of the following relationships: the man and his wife or wives; his concubines or female slaves; his sons and unmarried daughters; the wives of the sons; grandchildren; aged parents and grandparents. Others living in the same home and considered as part of the family could include servants and their children and aliens, or strangers, who attached themselves to the family for a time before moving to another location. When Jacob's "family" moved to Egypt from the Promised Land, he was accompanied by at least sixty-six people (Gen. 46:26).

God's design for the family. The concept of the family as the basic social unit reaches back into the *creation account found in Genesis 1—2. A man was to be the husband of one wife and was to leave his father and mother and be joined to his wife.

However, not everyone in the Old Testament measured up to God's ideal. Sometimes a man married more than one wife. Solomon is a marked example. He had seven hundred wives and three hundred concubines (1 Kin. 11:3).

After God created Adam, He declared, "It is not good that man should be alone" (Gen. 2:18). Then He created woman and united the couple; and they became "one flesh" (Gen. 2:24). Thus the family was designed by God to provide companionship for the various members of the family. In addition, the institution of marriage was approved and sanctioned by the Lord (Matt. 19:4–6).

God's ideal for the family is that it be a harmonious unit, where love for God and neighbor are in stilled into each member (Deut. 6:6–9). If the couple is divided, especially by unbelief, harmony as God desires is less probable. Old Testament believers were instructed not to marry those who would bring unbelief to the marriage (Ex. 34:13–16; Deut. 7:3–4), even as the New Testament declares, "Do not be unequally yoked together with unbelievers" (2 Cor. 6:14).

Prophets ministered to restore the family. Micah confronted the breakdown of the home (Mic. 7:5–6). Ezra took steps to remedy the family problems of his day (Ezra 9–10), and the prophet Malachi condemned the men of his generation for being faithless to the wives of their youth (Mal. 2:14–15).

The exalted position of the father. The social structure described in the Old Testament is known as "patriarchal," meaning the "rule of the father." The Old Testament father held a high and responsible position in the family. The Hebrew word translated into English as husband actually means "lord," "master," "owner," or "possessor" (Gen. 18:12; Hos. 2:16). Because of his position, shared to some degree with his wife, the father was to be treated with respect by his family. The fifth commandment declares this idea including the mother: "Honor your father and your mother" (Ex. 20:12). The word honor often refers to one's response to God, thus this commandment suggests that the parents should receive a recognition similar to that given to God, because within their role they are appointed leaders of their home in the eyes of His throne.

With the honor of the position as head of the family, the father had clear responsibilities in three categories: spiritual, social, and economic.

The father was to be responsible for the spiritual well-being of the family, and its individual members (Gen. 12:8; Job 1:5). Later, after the priesthood was established, the father continued to be the religious leader of the family. This involved the training of the children in godliness (Ex. 12:3, 26–27; Prov. 22:6; Eph. 6:4).

The father's social responsibility was to see that no one took advantage of any member of his family. Those not protected by a father were disadvantaged—the "fatherless," as with widows and orphans. (Jewish writings show four specific duties of a father toward his son: to circumcise him; to give his inheritance to his firstborn; to find his son a wife; and to teach him a trade.)

Economically, the father was to provide for family needs. The lazy man is mocked to shame him to do what was expected of him (Prov. 6:6–11). The apostle Paul rebuked those called "Christian" but who did not look after the needs of their families (1 Tim. 5:8).

From this background we can appreciate God as the believer's Father. He knows all about His child, even numbering the hairs on his head (Matt. 10:30). He protects His child and rescues him when he gets into trouble (Is. 63:15–16). He teaches him the way that he should go (Hos. 11:1–3) and supplies all of his needs (Matt. 6:33). In turn, the Father deserves honor from His child, as Jesus taught (Matt. 6:9–10).

The family of God. Biblical writers used other analogies from the family to describe various aspects of the gospel. To be brought into God's family, the believer must be "born from above" or "born again" (John 3:3, 5). Because a person has God as his Father, he must realize that other believers are his "fathers," "mothers," "brothers," and "sisters" (1 Tim. 5:12). The body of believers known as the church is also referred to as the "household of God" (Eph. 2:19) and the "household of faith" (Gal. 6:10). In addition, the concepts of *adoption and *inheritance are used to describe the position of believers in God's family (Gal. 4:5; 1 Pet. 1:4).

FAMILY LIFE, GOD'S ORDER FOR. No theme is more likely to touch God's heart than that which is capturing the renewed attention of every sensitive Spirit-filled person today: The Priority of the Family. As redeemed souls walk in renewed relationship with God through Christ, it is consistent with the whole of Scripture that they prioritize their learning of the biblical pathway to fulfilling and divinely ordered family living. The Bible unfolds its story with a dual display of health in family relationships. Most obviously, the first pair (Adam and Eve) are at peace, in union, and experiencing the perfect intention of God's creative design as the "two shall be made one" married relationship. But another family is clearly present, as God—the heavenly Father of all earth and heaven's family (Eph. 3:14–15)—is seen in His foundational role as Giver, Nourisher, Protector of mankind's destiny. This study intends to offer believers help toward the recovering of the pristine pattern of divine design for relationships—in the home and with the loving Father God of all.

1. God Created Man (Male/Female) in His Own Image (Gen. 1:26–28). These verses introduce a phrase that is the cornerstone of the biblical understanding of man: *image of God*. The *image of God* is presented first and foremost in relation to *a unique social or community concept of God*. "Then *God* [singular] said, 'Let *Us* [plural] make man in *Our* [plural] image.'" Many scholars interpret this use of both the singular and the plural as an allusion to the Trinity: one God, yet a community of Persons.

God then proceeds to create man in His own image. At this all-important beginning point, Scripture highlights a particular aspect of man's nature, namely, that which corresponds to the social or community aspect of God's nature: God creates man *as male and female*—not a solitary individual, but two people. Yet, as we read on, we discover that the two are, nevertheless, "one" (see 2:24).

The "community" that reflects God's image is a special community: the community of a man and a woman. *When God chose to create man in His own image, He created a marriage, a family.* The community of the family is a reflection of the community in the Godhead. Its identity, life, and power come from God.

2. The Identity of Family Is in God (Eph. 3:14–15). Humanly speaking, we link the identity of a husband, wife, and children to their particular family-name. This, however, is only a surface identification. Family identity has a deeper root.

"Family" is a word that is rooted in God: God is *Father*—the Father of our Lord Jesus Christ. In Himself, God is a "divine family." This also expresses itself in the way that God relates to people. The Bible reveals this aspect of God's nature in rich and varied use of family imagery: God is our Father, God is Husband to His people, God is like a nurturing mother, Christ is the Bridegroom of the church.

When a man and a woman come together in marriage, God extends to them this name that in essence belongs to Him—the name of *family*. Husband, wife, and children live up to the true meaning of this name as they reflect the nature and life of the divine family in their human family.

3. Jesus and the Father Model Relationship for Marriage (1 Cor. 11:3). The relationship between God as "Head" and Christ as Son is given as a model for the relationship between husband and wife. When the Bible reveals how the Father and the Son relate to each other, it also tells us something about the way that husbands and wives should relate to each other.

The following principles for the husband-wife relationship are illustrated in the relationship of Jesus and the Father: (1) Husband and wife are to share a mutual love (John 5:20; 14:31). (2) Husband and wife have different *roles* and accomplish different *functions* in the marriage (John 10:17; 14:28; 17:4). (3) Though having different roles, husband and wife are *equal*; they live in *unity* (John 10:30; 14:9, 11). (4) Husband and wife *esteem* one another (John 8:49, 54). (5) Husbands express love for their wives through *care, shared life and ministry, attentiveness* (John 5:20, 22; 8:29; 11:42; 16:15; 17:2). (6) Wives express love for their husbands by being of one will and purpose with them; by exercising authority entrusted to them with humility and meekness, not striving or competing; in a word, by showing *respect* both in attitude and action (John 4:34; 5:19, 30; 8:28; 14:31; 15:10; Phil. 2:5–6, 8; see also Gen. 3:16; 1 Tim. 2:8–15).

4. Christ and the Church Model Husband/Wife Relationships (Eph. 5:22–33). The specific instructions that the apostle Paul gives to husbands and wives are a glimpse of *the* Bridegroom and bride—a heavenly model for every marriage on earth.

As a husband, how should I behave toward my wife? Look to Christ, the divine Bridegroom, in His relationship with the church: love her, sacrifice for her, listen to her concerns, take care of her; be as sensitive to her needs and her hurts as you are to those of your own body.

As a wife, how should I behave toward my husband? Look to the chosen bride, the church, in its relationship with Christ: respect him, acknowledge his calling as "head" of the family, respond to his leadership, listen to him, praise him, be unified in purpose and will with him; be a true helper (see Gen. 2:18).

No husband and wife can do this by mere willpower or resolve, but since you (including your marriage) are "His workmanship" (Eph. 2:8–10), God will help bring this about.

5. Attitudes Toward God Determine Attitudes Toward Mates (1 Pet. 3:1–7). Our attitudes toward our mates are governed by our attitudes toward God. A husband may fall short of a wife's expectations and of God's ideal for a husband. Nevertheless, she seeks in every way to be a good wife, modeling her behavior on Christ, who obeyed and trusted the Father even when His own people rejected Him (John 1:11). Or, a wife may disappoint her husband, disregard his authority, or withhold her respect. Nevertheless, a husband honors his wife, cares for her, and prays for her, modeling his behavior on the Father, who "knows our frame" (Ps. 103:14).

6. Husbands and Wives Called to Operate in God's Order

(Col. 3:18–19, 23–24). A Christian renders service to others *as a way of serving the Lord Christ*. In these verses the relationship to which this truth is specifically applied is the husband-wife relationship. The role and admonition that God assigns to a husband is meant to be a way of serving his wife. Likewise a distinctive role and direction is given to the wife, according to which she serves her husband.

These roles are not self-chosen, nor are they assigned by the culture in which one lives: they are given by God as a means of manifesting the life of Christ on earth. In this setting the word *submission* acquires its full biblical significance for family life: husband and wife alike are submissive to God in fulfilling the roles that He has given them. In serving one another, husband and wife serve and honor Christ. The word "submit" (Greek *hupotasso*) is formed from *hupo* ("under") and *tasso* ("to arrange in an orderly manner"). In this context it describes a person who accepts his or her place under God's arranged order. Also, remember that God's directive to submit is not limited to wives. In James 4:7 and Ephesians 5:21 we see the directive applied to every believer—in his or her relationships with others—and with God.

7. Forgiveness Can Save and Transform a Marriage

(Hos. 2:16–17, 19–20). Through the tragic story of Hosea and Gomer, God reveals *both* the depth and power (1) of His love for Israel and (2) of the marriage bond. God describes His suffering the pain and humiliation of Israel's unfaithfulness; and in obedience to God, Hosea suffers the same pain and humiliation of his own wife's unfaithfulness. But God shows him how the marriage can be saved: through *suffering* and *forgiveness*.

This is one of the most profound revelations about marriage found anywhere in Scripture. Successful marriage is not a business of perfect people living perfectly by perfect principles. Rather, marriage is a state in which very imperfect people often hurt and humiliate one another, yet find the grace to extend forgiveness to one another, and so allow the redemptive power of God to transform their marriage.

8. Three Sides of Sex: Unity, Symbol of Love, Reserved for Marriage

(1 Cor. 7:3–4). Sexual intercourse is an intimate expression of affection between a husband and wife. The apostle underscores its importance in marriage by declaring that it is in fact a *duty*: a husband is to be available for his wife at her request, and a wife for her husband at his request.

It is more than an act of biological mating. The Bible calls it a privileged "mystery" by which two people, a man and a woman, become one (Eph. 5:32; *see* Gen. 2:24). The privilege is abused when people not married to each other have intercourse (*see* 1 Cor. 5:1; 6:16); then that which God meant for blessing becomes a cause of judgment (*see* Eph. 5:5).

Marriage is the one and the only place that God has provided for sexual union to take place. In that setting it becomes a powerful symbol of the love between Christ and the church, a pure sharing of joy and delight in one another that is a gift from the hand of God. Outside those boundaries, it eventually becomes destructive.

9. The Husband, Protector and Provider

(Is. 54:5). God reveals Himself by the title *husband* to disclose how deeply He loves His people and how effectively He cares for them. In so doing, He unveils an important dimension of human family life with particular reference to husbands: a husband is to love and take care of his wife and children. God is a *Protector* and a *Provider*. Husbands who open themselves to God's direction will find both the inspiration and the power to be those things for their families, for those attributes of God's being will flow into and fill their lives.

10. God Backs Up the Covenant of Marriage

(Mal. 2:13–14, 16). When two people marry, God stands as a witness to the marriage, sealing it with the strongest possible word: *covenant.* "Covenant" speaks of faithfulness and enduring commitment. It stands like a divine sentinel over marriage, for blessing or for judgment.

Divorce is here described as *violence*. To initiate divorce does violence to God's intention for marriage and to the mate to whom one has been joined.

Yet, where husband and wife live according to their marriage vows, all the power of a covenant-keeping God stands behind them and their marriage. What a confidence, to know that *God backs up our marriage.* His power and authority stand against every enemy that would violently threaten it from without or within.

11. Divorce Is a Case of a Heart Hardened Toward God (Matt. 19:1–9). In this text Jesus frankly addresses a pivotal issue: the cause of divorce is *hardness of heart.* Behind every broken marriage is a heart hardened against God, then hardened against one's mate. From the very beginning, God's intention for marriage was that it be for life. Realizing this, believers should exercise care in choosing a life mate (*see* 2 Cor. 6:14). Yet no marriage will be so free of differences and difficulties that it could not end up in divorce if husband and wife were deceived into following their natural inclinations.

The devil will exaggerate your mate's failures and inadequacies, sow suspicion and jealousy, indulge your self-pity, insist that you deserve something better, and hold out the hollow promise that things would be better with someone else. But hear Jesus' words, and remember: God can change hearts and remove all hardness if we will allow Him.

12. Divine Appointment Places People in Families (Ps. 68:5–6). We sometimes speak about difficult circumstances into which people are born as "an accident of birth." Viewed from a divine perspective, however, our placement in a human family is no accident at all: it is a divine appointment. "*God* sets the solitary in families." Indeed, the protection and care that one receives in a family is so essential to human life that God says He will personally intervene on behalf of widows and orphans who lose the normal protection of a husband and father. When we are tempted to complain about our family, or suppose that our birth-circumstance would be better somewhere else, we need to regain this divine perspective. This is not to become passive or fatalistic about one's situation, nor is it to say this will cause an escape from sorrow or suffering. Nevertheless, we are reminded that the ultimate well-being of our human families rests upon the promise and care of our Father in heaven and that His sovereign and loving purpose will intervene for our benefit.

13. God's Nurturing Heart in Parents Flows to Children (Hos. 11:1, 3–4). God reveals Himself as a Father who is tender, close to His children, and sensitive to their needs—teaching, encouraging, helping, and healing them. Growing up is not something that He leaves to chance. He is a God who conscientiously *nurtures* His children. God's heart toward His children is tenderly portrayed in the meaning behind Hosea's name. *Hoshea* means "Deliverer" or "Helper." The Hebrew root *yasha* indicates that deliverance or help is freely and openly offered, providing a haven of safety for every child of God.

This is the biblical model for parents: God entrusts children to parents, allowing His own nurturing heart to flow through them to the children.

14. Loving and Caring for Children Honors God (Ps. 127:3–5). God's covenant with Adam and Eve contained two interdependent provisions: *descendants* and *dominion.* Two people alone could not take dominion of the earth. It would require descendants.

For believers, having children is a response to the command, "Be fruitful and multiply; fill the earth and subdue it" (Gen. 1:28). In this psalm, children are called "a heritage from the LORD." This means that children belong to God; they are "ours" only in a secondary sense. God gives children to parents, as a man entrusts his fortune to his heirs. Jesus wants us not to despise "one of these little ones," and He holds up their faith in God as an example for adults (Matt. 18:1–5, 10).

When a couple enters into marriage, they make themselves available to love, serve, and sacrifice for the next generation. To love and care for children is one of the principal ways that we honor God and share in building His kingdom.

15. Parents Responsible to Raise Children (Eph. 6:4). God holds parents responsible for the upbringing of children—not grandparents, not schools, not the state, not youth groups, not peers and friends. Although each of these groups may influence children, the final duty rests with parents, and particularly with the father, whom God has appointed "head" to lead and serve the family. Two things are necessary for the proper teaching of children: a right *attitude* and a right *foundation.* An atmosphere reeking with destructive criticism, condemnation, unrealistic expectations, sarcasm, intimidation, and fear will "provoke a child to wrath." In such an atmosphere, no sound teaching can take place.

The positive alternative would be an atmosphere rich in encouragement, tenderness, patience, listening, affection, and love. In such an atmosphere parents can build into the lives of their children the precious foundation of knowledge of God. (*See also* Deut. 6:6–7; Prov. 22:6.)

16. Corrective Discipline for the Rebellious (Prov. 13:24). Discipline is the other side of teaching. A child with a teachable spirit will still need thorough explanation, much patience, opportunity to try and experiment, including the right to fail and to learn by failure. A child, however, who is caught up in willful disobedience (Prov. 29:15), rebellion (1 Sam. 15:23), or stubborn foolishness (Prov. 22:15), closes off effective teaching and disrupts the harmony of the family. God's answer to this is firm and loving discipline.

The Bible makes a clear distinction between discipline and physical abuse. Discipline may be painful but not injurious. We are never to inflict harm on a child (Prov. 23:13), but at times pain may be a part of effective correction. God describes Himself as a strict disciplinarian. Although He always disciplines us out of love and for our own benefit, His correction may cause us pain (Heb. 12:5–11). Likewise, God requires that parents properly correct their children. Even a child's eternal destiny can hinge upon the godly discipline provided by parents (Prov. 23:14).

17. Receiving One Another Is the Way to Oneness (Rom. 15:5–7). It has been said that most teaching on family life is simply an application of what it means to live as a Christian. These verses in Romans are directed to the Christian community at large, yet they are a frequently used wedding text, for they present a beautiful and fitting description of Christian marriage.

The key word is "receive" (Greek *proslambano*), which means "to take to oneself." Its root indicates strong action toward us—that in Christ, God literally came to us and *took hold of us* "while we were still sinners" (5:8). By that act of acceptance He released the grace of God and set in motion the powers of redemption.

When that power is allowed to work in a family, it will transform the lives of two imperfect people into one life, lived to the praise of God's glory. Therefore, the Lord sets this word like a banner over marriage from the first day until the last, "Receive one another, just as Christ also received us, to the glory of God." L.C.

FAST, FASTING—The Bible reveals fasting as a fully desirable, non-"religious" spiritually dynamic means for intensified seeking of God in prayer. To fast is to go without food or drink voluntarily, and generally was for the purpose of humbling the soul before God (Ps. 35:13; 69:10). Fasting was sometimes done as a sign of distress, grief, or repentance. The Law of Moses specifically required fasting for only one occasion—the Day of Atonement—resulting in this day being called "the day of fasting" (Jer. 36:6) or "the Fast" (Acts 27:9).

A few Old Testament instances of fasting are seen in Exodus 34:28, Judges 20:26, 1 Samuel 7:6, and 1 Kings 21:9, 12.

The most notable Old Testament fasts in spiritual significance would be Jehoshaphat's call for a fast (2 Chr. 20:3); the reaction to Jonah's preaching at Nineveh (Jon. 3:5); the fast Ezra called prior to returning from the captivity (Ezra 8:21, 23); and Esther's call to fast when facing the destruction of her people (Esth. 4:3, 16; 9:31).

Is fasting for the New Testament disciple? The evidence is clearly affirmative. Jesus taught fastings by His own word and example, and said that in the era following His earthly ministry, after His ascension, fasting would be among the disciplines of His people (Matt. 4:2; 6:16; Mark 2:20).

Because it is Christ's will and a clear New Testament discipline when prompted by the Holy Spirit, many still observe fasts. There are two basic kinds of fasts: (1) the general discipline and (2) the special call. Some fast whole or part days each week (as with John Wesley). Special "calls" are also seen in such texts as Daniel 9:3; Joel 2:14; 2 Samuel 1:1; Acts 13:2–3; 14:23; and 2 Corinthians 11:27.

The Bible nowhere suggests that fasting is to be thought a means of earning God's favor or of improving one's status with God. Therefore, one should not fast as a religious or as a superstitious exercise, hoping thereby to gain God's special attention or to tip invisible scales of blessing in their direction. Every good thing that comes from God is a gift (James 1:17) and is the product of His grace, not human endeavor (Eph. 2:8–9).

Nonetheless, Christ's people do partner with God's almightiness through the acceptance and application of certain disciplines as the Holy Spirit directs. Scriptures teach by both precept and example a number of means by which believers may enter into the exercise of spiritual dominion through simple obedience to disciplines shown there. Fasting in prayer stands as one of these along with such commonly acknowledged ones as (a) receiving of the Lord's Table, (b) anointing with oil, (c) tithing with offerings, (d) worship and song, and (e) the reading and study of God's Word. It is also true that prayer joined with fasting is a proven means of advancing spiritual objectives. In knowing that we earn nothing, avoid falling prey to the erroneous notions of historic asceticism; i.e., the belief that a higher spiritual state is attainable through rigorous self-discipline. In contrast to this, however, by fasting we can learn something. The believer may learn a simple, dynamic pathway to spiritual conquest. The Bible makes clear that it is effective and important, that Jesus directed it as a part of His church's life, and to learn to fast when the Holy Spirit gives prompting or direction.

Jesus showed fasting as an effective means of spiritual assault on the power of darkness. What does it do? No direct answer is given, but it accomplishes something that allows for liberty from spiritual bondage and oppression. *See also* Mark 9:29 and note "The authorization for omitting 'and fasting' (because of absence in some ancient manuscripts) is not sufficient. But even if it were, overwhelmingly, fasting would, in its essence be implied." (*See also* Dan. 10:3, 12–13.)

What does one experience through fasting? Many testify today to a harvest of practical and visible results. See Isaiah 58:6–12, which shows fasting is not a mystical, ascetic exercise of piety. It is a normal and powerful participation point in seeing the release of God's purposes and benevolent intent toward mankind: (1) food made available to the needy (v. 7); (2) genuine service and concern for those without (v. 7; *see* 1 John 3:17); (3) life and health-giving ministry begins to flow from believers (v. 8); (4) personal answers to prayer begin to be released (v. 9); (5) a removal of the spirit of criticism graces ones own life (v. 9); (6) God-directed and fruitful living ensues (v. 11); and (7) an edifying, uniting life follows (v. 12).

FAST. (John 3:5) *tsom* (*tsohm*); *Strong's #6685:* A fast; a day of fasting; a time set aside to mourn or pray with no provision for one's normal food needs. This noun comes from the verb *tsum,* "to fast." The verb occurs twenty-two times and the noun twenty-six times. Fasting is a voluntary denial of food. In the Old Testament, the verb "fast" is sometimes coupled with the words "weep," "mourn," or "lay in sackcloth," all expressing intensity. Fasting is an action contrary to that first act of sin in the human race, which was eating what was forbidden. Fasting is refusing to eat what is allowed. (Compare Dan. 1:8–16; 9:3–23; Joel 2:12–19.)

FATHER. (Ps. 68:5) *'ab* (*ahv*); *Strong's #1:* Father; forefather; producer of a certain thing. A very simple word, *'ab* is supposed to be one of the first words a baby can speak. The Aramaic form of *'ab* is *'abba,* which has become common in modern Hebrew as the word Israeli children use for "daddy." Jesus applied this toddler's word to His divine Father (Mark 14:36). The Holy Spirit teaches us to call God "Abba" (Rom. 8:15). *'Ab* is found in many compound names in the Bible; for example, *'Abraham* (Abraham), "Father of a Multitude"; *'Abimelech* (Abimelech), "My Father Is King"; *Yoab* (Joab), "Yahweh Is a Father"; and *'Abshalom* (Absalom), "Father of Peace." Sometimes *'ab* does not mean physical father so much as it does architect, builder, creator, and

the one who causes something to be. Hence, a "father of evil" is someone who produces evil. Jesus described Satan as the "father of lies." *'Ab* as "creator" and "producer" is applied to the Lord Jesus who is *'abi-'ad,* the "Everlasting Father," or more literally, the "Father of Eternity" (Is. 9:6).

FAVOR. (Deut. 33:23) *ratson* (rah-*tzoan*); *Strong's #7522:* Pleasure, desire, delight, favor. The noun *ratson* comes from the verb *ratsa,* which means "to be pleased with" or "to be favorable toward something." *Ratson* refers especially to what is pleasing and desirable to God. The idea here is that Naphtali is to be satisfied with the pleasure, delight, and favor of God.

FEAR—a godly emotion, feeling of reverence, awe, and respect toward the Almighty, or an unpleasant emotion caused by natural circumstance of supernatural assault. Fear may be either healthy or harmful.

A healthy fear is reverence or respect, and older translations use this word in this way (Lev. 19:3; Eph. 5:33; 6:5).

The Scriptures declare that "the fear of the Lord is the beginning of knowledge" (Prov. 1:7) as well as "the beginning of wisdom" (Prov. 16:16) and thereby indicate the propriety and righteousness of a sense of awe before God and His Word.

A harmful fear is a sense of terror or dread. Believers are not to fear the persecution of others, even unto death, because they cannot ultimately harm us (Matt. 10:28, Phil. 1:28). The wicked men, however, often fear others; especially the righteous (Prov. 28:1; Matt. 14:5; Rom. 13:3–4). Such fear causes deceitful acts and efforts at hiding their sins (2 Samuel 11; Matt. 28:4–15).

It would be unnatural if no fear is present at thoughts of God's judgment, for all outside Christ stands condemned before Him (Matt. 10:28; John 3:18). This kind should lead to repentance, but often leads to a feeble attempt to hide from God (Gen. 3:8; Rev. 6:15–17) or worse, to a denial of God's existence and His claim on a person's life (Ps. 14:1; Rom. 1:18–28).

There is a bondage to fear that truth can break (Prov. 29:25; John 8:36). Satan spawns fear to torment human souls, but the power of Jesus Christ is greater when applied with prayer and the Word (Heb. 2:14–15; 2 Tim. 1:7).

FEAR. (Is. 8:13) *morah* (moh-*rah*); *Strong's #4172:* Fear, reverence, terror, awe; an object of fear, respect, or reverence. *Morah* is derived from *yare',* "to be afraid of, to fear, to reverence." *Morah* occurs a dozen times in the Old

Testament, beginning with Genesis 9:2, which speaks of the fear and dread Noah's descendants would inspire in all animals after the Flood. The Lord also inspires fear, as in Psalm 76:11. In the present reference, Isaiah is admonished never to fear human threats, but to let God alone be the object of his reverential fear. *Also* (Hos. 3:5) *pachad* (pah-*chad*); *Strong's #6342:* To be startled, to tremble; to stand in awe, to revere, or fear; be amazed. *Pachad* concerns a person's reaction to something sudden and startling to the point of trembling. The verb appears twenty-four times. The noun *pachad*, which refers to something dreadful and awe-producing, occurs more than forty times. Here Israel will tremble because of God's startling, sudden, amazing goodness showered upon them in the latter days! This verse shows how positive the Hebrew concept of fear, trembling, and reverence can be, as does Proverbs 28:14, "Happy is the man who is always reverent [*pachad*]." *Also* (Matt. 10:26) *phobeo* (fob-*eh*-oh); *Strong's #5399: Phobeo* is defined as a panic that grips a person causing him to run away, be alarmed, scared, frightened, dismayed, filled with dread, intimidated, anxious, and apprehensive. (Compare "phobia.") Jesus is urging His followers not to have a *phobeo* of men, which is destructive, but a reverential awe or fear of God, which is constructive. Proverbs 29:25 addresses the fear syndrome: "The fear of man brings a snare, but whoever trusts in the LORD shall be secure." The New Testament upgrades this thought with 1 John 4:18, "Perfect love casts out fear." Being filled with God's Spirit will cause you to become fearless (2 Tim. 1:7). *Also* (1 John 4:18) *phobos* (*fob*-oss); *Strong's #5401:* In classical Greek the word signified flight. Later it came to denote that which causes flight; hence, fear, terror, dread. In the New Testament, *phobos* denotes both the fear of terror and the fear of reverence toward God. The English word "phobia" transliterates the Greek word.

FEARED. (Ex. 1:17) *yare'* (yah-*ray*); *Strong's #3372:* To fear, be afraid of someone or something; to stand in awe of something or someone possessing great power; to revere someone. The verb *yare'* and its derivatives occur more than four hundred times. While there is some variation in the meaning of this word, its basic meaning is primarily "to be afraid." (*See* 3:6; 14:13; 1 Sam. 18:12; 2 Sam. 6:9.) The fear of God is not a terror that He is against us or will strike without cause or warning. Rather, the fear of the Lord produces wise, healthy actions, as in the present reference: the midwives were more afraid of anger-

ing God by destroying innocent babies than they were afraid of disobeying Pharaoh.

FEED. (Is. 40:11) *ra'ah* (rah-*ah*); *Strong's #7462:* To shepherd, feed, tend; to pasture; to cause one's herd or flock to graze. *Ra'ah* has to do with tending and caring for one's animals, particularly by providing them with good pasture. This verb occurs more than 170 times in the Old Testament. David's early duty to feed his father's flocks (1 Sam. 17:15) is followed by his later task of shepherding the heavenly Father's flock, Israel (Ps. 78:71). The participial form of *ra'ah* is *ro'eh*, "shepherd, tender of sheep, caretaker." *Ro'eh* appears in "The LORD is my shepherd; I shall not want" (Ps. 23:1). (*See also* "Shepherd of Israel" in Ps. 80:1.) Ezekiel 34:23 and Micah 5:4 describe Messiah's responsibility as one of feeding and shepherding.

FELLOWSHIP—sharing things in common with others. In the New Testament, fellowship has a distinctly spiritual meaning. Fellowship can be either positive or negative.

Positively, believers have fellowship with the Father, Son, and Holy Spirit (John 17:21–26; Phil. 2:1; 1 John 1:3), as well as with other believers (Acts 2:42, 1 John 1:3, 7). We have been welcomed warmly to fellowship with God, in the sense of sharing things in common with Him, for He has raised our status through the death and resurrection of Christ (Eph. 2:4–7). Believers are invited to share in common with God (1) a relationship as sons and daughters (John 1:12–13); His own holy character (1 Pet. 1:15), and the privileges of partnership with all things in Christ (Rom. 8:16; Eph. 2:6).

All who have fellowship with Christ also need to nurture fellowship with other believers (Heb. 10:25), a fellowship that illustrates the very nature of God Himself (John 13:35; Eph. 5:1–2; 1 John 1:5–10).

Conversely, believers are not to have fellowship with unbelievers. This means to not share in the world's sinful lifestyle (2 Cor. 6:14–18). It does not mean to withdraw from society, for all believers are called to live and share the gospel with a blinded, unbelieving world (2 Cor. 4:1–7; Phil. 2:14–16).

FELLOWSHIP. (Acts 2:42) *koinonia* (koy-nohn-ee-ah); *Strong's #2842:* Sharing, unity, close association, partnership, participation, a society, a communion, a fellowship, contributory help, the brotherhood. (Compare "coin," "cenobite," "epicene.") *Koinonia* is a unity brought about by the Holy Spirit. In *koinonia* the individual shares in common an intimate bond of fellowship with the rest of the Christian society. *Koinonia* cements the believers to the Lord Jesus and to each other.

FERVENT. (Acts 18:25) *zeo* (*dzeh*-oh); *Strong's #2204:* Compare "zeal," "zeolite," or "seethe." Living fervor, fiery hot, full of burning zeal. It is the opposite of dignified, cold, and unemotional. In a Christian context it signifies a high spiritual temperature, inflamed by the Holy Spirit. Apollos was a complete man, articulate in Scripture, and full of spiritual fervency.

FILL. (Jer. 23:24) *male'* (mah-*lay*); *Strong's #4390:* To fill, fill up, be full; to fulfill. *Male'* is the source of Hebrew words relating to fullness and fulfillment: filling something up to the brim (2 Kin. 4:6); causing something to be thoroughly saturated (as was Naphtali, "full" of the blessings of the Lord, Deut. 33:23); fulfilling one's word, that is, to declare that one will do something, and then to do it (1 Kin. 2:27). God promises to fill all the earth with awareness of His glory (Num. 14:21; Hab. 2:14). *Male'* is the word used in the Old Testament to describe being filled with the Spirit of God (Ex. 31:3; Mic. 3:8). *Also* (Matt. 15:33) *chortazo* (khor-*tad*-zoe); *Strong's #5526:* Originally, to feed or fatten animals. Stoic philosophers began to hold the common people in contempt and transferred *chortazo* from the agriculture field to the dinner table. The word came to signify being satisfied with food in abundance.

FIRSTFRUITS—the firstborn of the flocks and the first vegetables and grains to be gathered at harvest time. The Hebrew people thought of these as belonging to God in a special sense. They were dedicated or presented to God on the day of the firstfruits, a part of the celebration of Pentecost (Num. 28:26; 2 Chr. 31:5). The counterpart today is the "first" of our income or profit, and may be expressed in the worshiping of God with our tithes.

FLESH—the physical bodies of humans or animals. When God removed a rib from Adam with which he created Eve, he closed up the place with flesh (Gen. 2:21). The apostle Paul spoke of the flesh of men, beasts, fish, and birds (1 Cor. 15:39).

The imagery of flesh expresses several different ideas in the Bible. Besides the physical body, the word also refers to "the flesh" as the fallen nature of man, representing lusts and desires (Eph. 2:3). The flesh is contrary to the Spirit (Gal. 5:17). Those who are in the flesh cannot please God (Rom. 8:8). Galatians 5:19–23 contrasts works of the flesh with the fruit of the Spirit. Hope for "all flesh" is given in Christ (Isa. 40:5), as the Savior came "in the flesh" (1 John 4:2). He alone has become our salvation, since by the works of the law "no

flesh shall be justified" (Gal. 2:16), but in Him "the flesh" may now be filled with God's grace, goodness, and glory (Rom. 8:1–11) and God's will for true humanity can be realized (Gal. 5:19–25; Rom. 6:5–14).

FLESH. (Job 19:26) *basar* (bah-*sar*); *Strong's #1320:* Flesh, body, human being. *Kol basar,* "all flesh," means all humanity together. *Basar* refers to the human body, and in some instances, to the bodies of animals as well. Occasionally, *basar* means "meat," that is, the cooked or uncooked pieces of animal flesh, as in Numbers 11:33. The first occurrence of *basar* is in Genesis 2:21, where God closed up the sleeping man's "flesh" after extracting one rib. The simplest meaning is "the visible part of man or animal," that is, the skin, muscle, flesh, and so on. *Also* (Matt. 26:41) *sarx* (sarks); *Strong's #4561:* In its literal sense, *sarx* refers to the substance of the body, whether of animals or persons (1 Cor. 15:39; 2 Cor. 12:7). In its idiomatic use, the word indicates the human race or personhood (Matt. 24:22; 1 Pet. 1:24). In an ethical and spiritual sense, *sarx* is the lower nature of a person, the seat and vehicle of sinful desires (Rom. 7:25; 8:4–9; Gal. 5:16–17).

FOLLOW. (John 13:36) *akoloutheo* (ak-ol-oo-*theh*-oh); *Strong's #190:* To accompany, go along with, go the same way with, follow one who precedes. *A* is in union with, and *keluethos* is a road. *Akoloutheo* is being on the same roadway with someone. Since the word was used for soldiers, servants, and pupils, it can easily be transferred to the life of the Christian. In seventy-eight Gospel occurrences it is used seventy-seven times of following Christ. Metaphorically, it is used for discipleship (Matt. 9:9; Mark 9:38).

FOOT-WASHING—an expression of hospitality extended to guests in Bible times. People traveling dusty roads in Palestine needed to wash their feet for comfort and cleanliness, and foot-washing was generally performed by the lowliest servant in the household (Luke 7:44). Thus, foot-washing became a sign Jesus used to teach humility as He washed His disciples feet. He explained this act as an example of the spirit they must always be ready to show one another (John 13:5–17). First Timothy 5:10 suggests that the early church followed Christ's example in observing the ritual of foot-washing, and some today— either ritually or on sporadic occasion—practice foot-washing as a ministry of humility.

FOREIGNERS. (Eph. 2:19) *paroikos* (par-*oy*-koss); *Strong's #3941:* From *para*, "beside," and *oikeo*, "to dwell"; hence, "dwelling near." The word came to denote an alien who dwells as a sojourner in a land without the rights of citizenship. The word describes Abraham and Moses, sojourners in a land not their own (Acts 7:6, 29), and the Christian who is traveling through this world as an alien whose citizenship and ultimate residence are in heaven (1 Pet. 2:11).

FOREKNOWLEDGE—a fact of God's omniscience which enables Him to know all events, including the free acts of man, before they happen.

In Romans 8:29 and 11:2, the apostle Paul's use of the word foreknew means "to choose" or "to set special affection on," but is clearly shown not as a premptive "knowledge" which judges in advance against some and for others. His predestination and salvation is persuant upon His foresight of human action—not the cause but the effect of His electing love in Christ (Rom. 8:29–33). This same idea is used to express the nation of Israel's special relationship to God (Acts 2:23; Rom. 11:2; 1 Pet. 1:2, 20).

FOREVER. (Ps. 136:1) *'olam* (oh-*lahm*); *Strong's* #5769: Eternity; the ages; infinity; the universe, the world. Derived from the verb *'alam* ("veil from sight" or "conceal"), *'olam* refers to that infinite and everlasting expanse God has created. It is both an unending expanse of space (universe) and time (eternity), indicating the limitless dimensions in which God's sovereignty is displayed. The word sometimes refers to the remotely distant past (93:2) and sometimes to the remotely distant future (Jer. 25:5). God is called *'El 'Olam*, "the Everlasting God" (Gen. 21:33; Is. 40:28). As God is eternal, so is His mercy *le-'olam*, that is, "unto the forever."

FORGIVENESS—the act of excusing or pardoning another in spite of his slights, shortcomings, and errors. As a theological term, forgiveness refers to God's pardoning or passing away of the sins of human beings and His releasing them from the implications and effect of those deeds.

No religious book except the Bible teaches that God completely forgives sin (Ps. 51:1, 9; Is. 38:17; Heb. 10:17). The initiative comes from Him (John 3:16; Col. 2:13) because He is ready to forgive (Luke 15:11–32). He is a God of grace and pardon (Neh. 9:17; Dan. 9:9).

Sin deserves divine punishment because it is a violation of God's holy character (Gen. 2:17; Rom. 1:18–32; 1 Pet. 1:16), but His pardon is gracious (Ps. 130:4; Rom. 5:6–8). In order for God to forgive sin, two conditions are necessary. A life must be taken as a substitute for that of the sinner (Lev. 17:11, 14; Heb. 9:22), and the sinner must come to God's sac-

rifice in a spirit of repentance and faith (Mark 1:4; Acts 10:43; James 5:15).

Forgiveness in the New Testament is directly linked to Christ (Acts 5:31; Col. 1:14), His sacrificial death on the Cross (Rom. 4:24), and His resurrection (2 Cor. 5:15). He was the morally perfect sacrifice (Rom. 8:3), the final and ultimate fulfillment of all Old Testament sacrifices (Heb. 9:11—10:18). Since He bore the law's death penalty against sinners (Gal. 3:10–13), those who trust in His sacrifice are freed from that penalty. By faith sinners are forgiven—"justified" (Rom. 3:28; Gal. 3:8–9). Those who are forgiven sin's penalty are also freed to live beyond its controlling power in their lives (Rom. 6:1–23).

Christ's resurrection was more than proof of His deity or innocence; it was related in a special way to His forgiveness. Christ's resurrection was the act by which God demonstrated to all the incapability of sin to win over Him, or for the guilt He bore in our place to remain. It was God's declaration of the perfect righteousness of His Son, the Second Adam, representing us—declaring His acceptance of Christ's sacrifice (1 Tim. 3:16). Thus, in Him all who believe are acquitted and declared righteous, and thus, Christ's resurrection was a necessary action to the forgiveness of man's sins (1 Cor. 15:12–28), for it not only verified His dominion over sin and death, but certified the same to all His redeemed. To be forgiven is to be identified with Christ in the full triumph of His crucifixion and resurrection.

Christ has the authority to forgive sins (Matt. 1:21; Heb. 9:11—10:18). This forgiveness is an essential part of the gospel message (Acts 2:38; 5:31). But blasphemy against the Holy Spirit (attributing to Satan a deed done by Jesus through the power of God's Spirit) is an unpardonable sin (Mark 3:28–29)—not because God cannot or will not forgive such a sin but because such a hard-hearted person has put himself beyond the possibility of repentance and faith.

God's forgiveness of us demands that we forgive others, because grace brings responsibility and obligation (Matt. 18:23–35; Luke 6:37). Jesus placed no limits on the extent to which Christians are to forgive their fellowmen (Matt. 18:22, 35; Luke 17:4). A ceaselessly forgiving spirit shows that we are truly living as followers of Jesus the Lord (Matt. 5:43–48; Mark 11:25).

FORGIVES. (Ps. 103:3) *salach* (sah-*lahch*); *Strong's* #5545: To forgive, pardon; spare someone; to relieve someone of the burden of their offense. This verb and its derivatives occur fifty times in the Old Testament. In every occurrence God does the forgiving; never does *salach* represent a man's forgiving anyone. This alone explains the shock of Jesus' listeners when they heard Him say "your sins are forgiven" (Luke 5:20). They responded, "Who can forgive sins but God alone?" (Luke 5:21). These scribes knew that forgiveness is God's prerogative. In Isaiah 55:7, *salach* is intensified by a helping verb: "He will abundantly pardon." Jeremiah 33:8 proclaims God's eagerness to forgive His people.

FORGIVING. (Col. 3:13) *charizomai* (khar-id-zahm-ahee); *Strong's #5483:* To do a favor, show kindness unconditionally, give freely, grant forgiveness, forgive freely. The word is from the same root as *charis,* "grace."

FORMED. (Gal. 4:19) *morphoo* (mor-*fah*-oh); *Strong's #3445:* To form. *Schema* and *morphoo* are in bold contradistinction. *Schema* (English "scheme") signifies external form or outer appearance. *Morphoo* and *morphe,* its related noun, refer to internal reality. Galatians 4:19 speaks of a change in character, becoming conformed to the character of Christ in actuality, not merely in semblance.

FORNICATION [for nih KAY shun]—sexual relationships outside the bonds of marriage. The technical distinction between fornication and *adultery is that adultery involves married persons while fornication involves those who are unmarried. But the New Testament often uses the term in a general sense for any unchastity. Of the seven lists of sins found in the writings of the apostle Paul, the word fornication is found in five of them and is first on the list each time (1 Cor. 5:11; Col. 3:5). In the Book of Revelation, fornication is symbolic of how idolatry and pagan religion defiles true worship of God (Rev. 14:8; 17:4).

FORNICATIONS. (Matt. 15:19) *porneia* (por-*ni*-ah); *Strong's #4202:* Compare "pornography," "pornographic." Illicit sexual intercourse, including prostitution, whoredom, incest, licentiousness, adultery, and habitual immorality. The word describes both physical immorality and spiritual, signifying idolatry (Rev. 2:21; 14:8; 17:2).

FRAMED. (Heb. 11:3) *katartizo* (kat-ar-*tid*-zoe); *Strong's #2675:* To arrange, set in order, equip, adjust, complete what is lacking, make fully ready, repair, prepare. The word is a combination of *kata,* "down," and *artios,* "complete," "fitted." It is used for the disciples' mending their nets (Matt. 4:21) and for restoring a fallen brother (Heb. 13:21).

FREE. (Jer. 40:4) *patach* (pah-*tahch*); *Strong's #6605:* To open, open wide, loosen; set free, release, untie, unshackle, liberate. This verb occurs about 150 times. Often referring to opening one's hand, eyes, or mouth, or opening a book, door, gate, or window, occasionally, *patach* means "to free or loose" (Ps. 102:20). The related noun *petach,* "door," "gate," or "entrance," is applied to the door of the tabernacle and the entrance to a house, cave, or city. Hosea 2:15 promises that the Valley of *Achor* (trouble) will be renamed the door of hope, or *petach tiqvah.* In the present reference, great freedom was granted to Jeremiah through the release from all his chains. Also (Rev. 6:15) *eleutheros* (el-*yoo*-ther-oss); *Strong's #1658:* Freeborn, exempt from legal obligation, unconstrained. It is the opposite of enslaved. The word is derived from the verb *eleuthomai,* "to come, go," thus describing the freedom to go where one chooses.

FREE (MADE). (Rom. 8:2) *eleutheroo* (el-yoo-ther-*ah*-oh); *Strong's #1659:* To liberate, acquit, set free, deliver. In the New Testament the word is used exclusively for Jesus' setting believers at liberty from the dominion of sin.

FRIEND. (Prov. 17:17) *re'a* (*ray*-ah); *Strong's #7453:* Friend, companion, neighbor, fellowman; a familiar person. This noun occurs more than 180 times. Its root is the verb *ra'ah,* "associate with," "be a friend of." The present reference is a prescription for a healthy friendship: a friend should love at all times. The responsibility to one's neighbor (*re'a*) is outlined in Psalm 101:5, Proverbs 24:28, and Zechariah 8:17. Also (John 11:11) *philos* (*fee*-loss); *Strong's #5384:* Compare "philosophy," "philology," "philharmonic." An adjective used as a noun, denoting a loved one, beloved, affectionate friend. The verb is *phileo,* which describes a love of emotion and friendship. *Philos* thus has a congeniality about it.

FULLNESS. (Eph. 3:19) *pleroma* (*play*-row-mah); *Strong's #4138:* Full number, full complement, full measure, copiousness, plenitude, that which has been completed. The word describes a ship with a full cargo and crew, and a town with no empty houses. *Pleroma* strongly emphasizes fullness and completion.

FUTILE. (Rom. 1:21) *mataioo* (mat-ah-*yah*-oh); *Strong's #3154:* To make empty, vain, foolish, useless, confused. The word describes the perverted logic and idolatrous presumption of those who do not honor God or show Him any gratitude for His blessings on humanity.

GAP. (Ezek. 22:30) *perets* (*peh*-rets); *Strong's* #6556: A break, gap, or breach; especially a gap in a wall. *Perets* comes from the verb *parats*, "to break forth, break open, or break down." *Perets* occurs about twenty-five times. Two verses (Is. 58:12; Amos 9:11) show that gaps or breaches need to be repaired; the former verse refers to the physical and spiritual ruins of Zion, and the latter to the tabernacle of David. In the present reference, standing in the gap is a metaphor for committed intercession. There is a gap between God and man that an intercessor tries to repair.

GATE, CITY—a massive wooden door in a city wall through which traffic passed. Often reinforced with brass or iron for greater security, these gates were opened during the day to allow the city's citizens to come and go. But they were generally closed at night as a safety measure. In the event of attack, the gates were closed and barred to keep out the enemy.

Goods were often bought and sold and important legal matters were discussed just inside the city gate (Ruth 4:11). Because of their central location, gates were often spoken of in the Bible as symbols of power and authority. God promised Abraham that his descendants would possess the gates of their enemies (Gen. 22:17).

The use of this word by Jesus in saying His church would prevail over the "gates of hades" indicates that He saw gates as representative in the spiritual realm of what they were in the natural realm of that day. As the seat of counsel, training, commerce, and strategy for combat, the gates were the "city hall" of ancient days. Jesus' purpose in building His church is to break the evil hold on these arenas of life which hell perpetrates to human confusion and destruction.

GENEALOGY [gene ee AL o gih]—a list of a person's ancestors that normally contains the members of each generation in succession. When compiled in the form of a "family tree," it begins at the bottom with the root stock from which the family came, then advances and branches out as the "tree" grows. When the genealogy records descent from ancestors by generations, the originating stock is listed first and all subsequent descendants are derived from it.

A technical term that means "family history," "record," or "genealogy" occurs in eleven places in the Book of Genesis in the phrase, "These are the generations of." This phrase divides the book in such a way as to suggest that the units thus formed were the actual sources from which the first thirty-seven chapters of Genesis were compiled. These "family records" sometimes included genealogies (Genesis 10) in much the same way that tablets from ancient Babylonia would occasionally have "family trees" written on the back. This practice helped to date these tablets since they would obviously belong to the last generations to be mentioned.

Genealogies proved very useful in deciding who was qualified by birth to act as priests (Neh. 7:64). By the time of Christ, everyone who was a priest was expected to prove his descent from the tribe of Levi and the house of Aaron. For this purpose a proper written genealogy was of the greatest importance. This procedure was equally vital for the verification of the royal succession in the kingdom of Judah, which traced its descent from the house of David. When the prophets proclaimed that the Messiah would also come from the stock of Jesse (Is. 11:1), the father of David, even greater precautions were taken to preserve the pattern of descent. The genealogies of Christ in the Gospels show the way in which the details of our Lord's descent from the house of David was preserved through the centuries (Matt. 1:1–17; Luke 3:28–38).

Modern readers of biblical genealogies should be instructed of the way such terms as "father," "mother," "son," and "daughter" were sometimes used in the ancient Near East. A "father" could denote a learned, older man who was not even a relative: "Mother" could even be used of a woman who exercised the love and care normally given by mothers, such as the wise woman of Abel (2 Sam. 20:19). A father might be a grandfather or even a remote ancestor; a son actually could be a grandson or a great-grandson; brothers might not be siblings, but men bound together by a treaty. Words such as son and daughter seem to have been used in the ancient world almost as widely as they are now. Thus carefulness in study should be exercised in some cases where such words appear.

The main purpose of genealogies was to establish the broad line of descent without furnishing all the details. Most biblical genealogies occur in the Old Testament: the descent from Adam to Noah (Gen. 5:1–32); the descendants of Noah (Genesis 10); and the line from Shem to Abraham (Gen. 11:10–26). The

---

longest Old Testament genealogy lists persons from Adam to the time of Saul (1 Chronicles 1—9). The house of David was reckoned back to Judah (Gen. 46:12), an important genealogy because of the promises of the prophets about the Messiah.

GENERATION—a word with three distinct meanings in the Bible:

1. A body of people who live at the same time in a given period of history. Example, Deuteronomy 32:5, as Moses calls his contemporaries "a perverse and crooked generation." In this use, "generation" is synonymous with "age," as "Our age (generation) abounds with advances in technology."

2. A quality or kind of people, characterized by certain traits that virtually evidence a spiritual "genetic bond." John the Baptist's "brood of vipers" described a satanic quality among the religious leaders he addressed (Matt. 3:7. *See also* Matt. 10:16; Luke 9:41).

3. A single succession, made up of a set of individuals who share a common ancestor, in the line of descent. (Examples: Gen. 17:7; Ex. 1:6; Matt. 1:17).

"Generation" sometimes indicates a more or less specific span of time (Gen. 15:16), and at others is applied in an indefinite way. It is not possible to force a twenty-five to thirty-year time span upon the word in all its uses in the Bible.

GENERATION. (Esth. 9:28) *dor* (*doar*); *Strong's* #1755: A generation; an age; a revolution of time; a life span, or some portion of one's lifetime. This noun occurs about 160 times. From the verb *dur*, "to dwell," or "to circle," *dor* describes what a generation is: a coming full circle in life (whether from birth to death or from the time one is conceived until he himself produces offspring). Thus *dor* does not represent a fixed number of years. God's design that "one generation shall praise Your works to another" (Ps. 145:4) may be accomplished by fathers who teach their children, or by the writers of Scripture, who keep praising God's deeds to each generation of believers (Ps. 78:5–8).

GENTILES. (Ps. 106:47) *goyim* (go-*yeem*); *Strong's* #1471: Nations, heathen, peoples, Gentiles. This is the plural form of *goy*, which means "nation" or "Gentile." Generally *goy* designates a defined group of people viewed from outside the group. Although *goy* occasionally refers to Israel, usually Israel is sharply contrasted with the *goyim*. It was prophesied that Israel was not to be reckoned among the nations, but rather was to dwell alone (Num. 23:9). This does not mean that there is no ethnic or racial continuity among

Jacob's descendants; it does mean that Israel is not merely one more "nation," but rather a people uniquely known as the Lord's inheritance.

GENTLE. (1 Tim. 3:3) *epieikes* (ep-ee-eye-kace); *Strong's* #1933: From *epi*, "unto," and *eikos*, "likely." The word suggests a character that is equitable, reasonable, forbearing, moderate, fair, and considerate. It is the opposite of harsh, abrasive, sarcastic, cruel, and contentious. The person with *epieikes* does not insist on the letter of the law.

GENTLENESS. (1 Tim. 6:11) *praotes* (prah-*ot*-ace); *Strong's* #4236: A disposition that is even-tempered, tranquil, balanced in spirit, unpretentious, and that has the passions under control. The word is best translated "meekness," not as an indication of weakness, but of power and strength under control. The person who possesses this quality pardons injuries, corrects faults, and rules his own spirit well.

GEZAR CALENDAR—see ch. 55, §2.3.

GIFT. (1 Cor. 1:7) *charisma* (*khar*-is-mah); *Strong's* #5486: Related to other words derived from the root *char*. *Chara* is joy, cheerfulness, delight. *Charis* is grace, goodwill, undeserved favor. *Charisma* is a gift of grace, a free gift, divine gratuity, spiritual endowment, miraculous faculty. It is especially used to designate the gifts of the Spirit (12:4–10). In modern usage, a "charismatic" signifies one who either has one or more of these gifts functioning in his life, or who believes these gifts are for today's church.

GIFT OF TONGUES (*See* Tongues, Gift of).

GIVE. (Acts 20:35) *didomi* (*did*-oh-mee); *Strong's* #1325: Granting, allowing, bestowing, imparting, permitting, placing, offering, presenting, yielding, and paying. *Didomi* implies giving an object of value. It gives freely and is unforced. Acts 20:35 indicates that the giver takes on the character of Christ, whose nature is to give. Jesus did not say it would be more natural or easier to give than to receive, but that it would be more blessed.

GIVE REST. (Ex. 33:14) *nu'ach* (noo-*ahch*); *Strong's* #5117: To rest, settle down; to be soothed or quieted; to be secure; to be still; to dwell peacefully. This verb occurs about sixty-five times, first in Genesis 8:4, which states that the ark rested on the mountains of Ararat. *Nu'ach* is the verb that describes the Spirit of God resting upon the Messiah (Is. 11:2), or upon the seventy elders of Israel (Num. 11:25). The name "Noah" ("Rest-Giver" or "Comforter") is derived from *nu'ach* (see Gen. 5:29). In the present reference, God's presence will give rest to His people, that is, His presence soothes, comforts, settles, consoles, and quiets us.

GLORY—beauty, power, or honor; a quality of God's character that emphasizes His exceeding greatness and authority. The word is used in three senses in the Bible:

1. God's excellence, moral beauty and perfection of character. This divine quality is beyond man's understanding (Ps. 113:4). All people "fall short" of it (Rom. 3:23).

2. God's moral excellence, beauty and perfection as a visible presence. While God's glory is not a substance, at times God does reveal Himself to man in a visible way. Such a display of the presence of God is often seen as fire or dazzling light, and sometimes as an act of power. Some examples from the Old Testament are the pillar of cloud and fire (Ex. 13:21), the Lord's deliverance of the Israelites at the Red Sea (Exodus 14), and especially His glory in the tabernacle (Lev. 9:23–24) and temple (1 Kin. 8:11).

The glory of God has been ultimately and most gloriously shown in the Person of Jesus (Luke 9:29–32; John 1:14–18; 2:11) and in the members of His church (Eph. 1:22–23; 2:19–22; 3:20–21).

Christ now shares His divine glory with His followers (John 17:5–6, 22), so that in their lives Christians are being transformed into the glorious image of God (2 Cor. 3:18). Believers will be fully glorified at the end of time in God's heavenly presence (Rom. 5:2; Col. 3:4). There the glory of God will be seen everywhere (Rev. 21:23).

3. Praise. At times God's "glory" may mean the honor and audible praise which His creatures give to Him (Ps. 115:1; Rev. 5:12–13).

GLORY. (Is. 60:1) *chabod* (kah-*vohd*); *Strong's #3519:* Weightiness; that which is substantial or heavy; glory, honor, splendor, power, wealth, authority, magnificence, fame, dignity, riches, and excellency. The root of *chabod* is *chabad*, "to be heavy, glorious, notable," or "to be renowned." In the Old Testament, "heaviness" represented honor and substance, while "lightness" was equated with vanity, instability, temporariness, and emptiness (*see* Judg. 9:4; Zeph. 3:4). *Chabod* is God's glory—not only His honor, renown, and majesty, but also His visible splendor, which filled Solomon's temple and will someday fill the earth (1 Kin. 8:11; Num. 14:21). From *chabod* are derived the names Jochebed ("Yahweh Is Glory") and Ichabod ("Where Is the Glory?"). *Also* (John 2:11) *doxa* (dox-ah); *Strong's #1391:* Compare "doxology," "paradox," "heterodoxy," and "orthodoxy." Originally, an opinion or estimation in which one is held. Then the word came to denote the reputation, good standing, and esteem given to a person. It progressed to honor or glory given to peoples, nations, and individuals. The New Testament *doxa* becomes splendor, radiance, and majesty centered in Jesus. Here *doxa* is the majestic, absolute perfection residing in Christ and evidenced by the miracles He performed.

GOD—the creator and sustainer of the universe who has provided humankind with a revelation of Himself through the natural world, through His Word, and through His Son, Jesus Christ.

The Bible does not seek to prove the existence of God; it simply affirms His existence by declaring, "In the beginning God . . ." (Gen. 1:1). God has revealed Himself through the physical universe (Ps. 19:1; Rom. 1:19–20). Honest observation of the universe requires acknowledgment of a transcendent power exercised by transcendent wisdom. Creation reveals the results of a universal mind that devised a master plan and executed it. It takes less faith to accept the idea of God as Creator of the universe than to suppose the magnificence of our orderly universe came into existence by chance and from no source—that is, apart from a wise and powerful divine being.

The revelation of God is further given in the Bible, which not only reveals His personal nature and His intent for mankind, but also prophesies the coming of His greatest revelation—His Son, Jesus Christ. As God incarnate, Jesus stated, "He that has seen me, has seen the Father" (John 14:9). Yet even though the full redemptive revelation of God was in Jesus Christ, the finite human mind cannot fully grasp the glory of the infinite God.

Although we cannot fully understand God, we still can know Him. We know Him through the ministry of the Holy Spirit who makes a personal relationship with Christ, and a growing knowledge of Him, possible by faith (John 15:26–27; 16:7–15). We also learn of Him through a study of His revealed Word—the Bible.

God may be described in terms of His *attributes*, the inherent characteristics of His person or being. The Bible reveals both natural and moral attributes of God.

The natural attributes:

God Is Spirit. Jesus taught that "God is Spirit" (John 4:24). God has no body, no physical or measurable form. Thus, God is invisible. He became visible in human form in the person of Jesus Christ, but His essence is invisible.

God Is Changeless. Progress and change may characterize some of His works, but God Himself remains unchanged (Heb. 1:12). He does not change; otherwise, He would not be perfect or complete. Thus, what we know of God can be known with certainty. He is not different from one time to another.

God Is All Powerful (Omnipotent). God's power is unlimited. He can do anything that is not inconsistent with His nature, character, and purpose (Gen. 17:1; 18:14). The only limitations on God's power are imposed by Himself (Gen. 18:25). "Impossible" is not in God's vocabulary. God creates and sustains all things; yet He never grows weary (Is. 40:27–31).

God Is All-knowing (Omniscient). God possesses all knowledge (Job 38:39; Rom. 11:33–36). Because God's presence reaches everywhere at one and the same time, He knows everything simultaneously—past, present, and future. God even knows the thoughts and motives of every heart, as is evident from many Scripture passages (*see* Job 37:16, Ps. 147:5, Heb. 3:13).

God Is Everywhere (Omnipresent). God is not confined to any part of the universe but is present in all His power at every point in space and at every moment in time (Ps. 139:7–12). God does not belong to any one nation or generation. He is the God of all the earth, the heavens, and beyond the universe itself (Gen. 18:25).

God Is Transcendent. Though He has created all things and His presence pervades the entirety of His creation, He is beside and beyond it, unlimited to it and uncontained by it. Thus *pantheism*, which makes God a life force within all things, is in error, as is any system which reduces Him to a "force" rather than a Person.

God Is Eternal. Eternity refers to God's relation to time. Past, present, and future are known equally to Him (2 Pet. 3:8; Rev. 1:8). Time is like a parade that man sees only a segment at a time. But God sees time in its entirety.

The second is moral attributes, describing God's character—His essential nature.

God Is Holy. The word holy comes from a root word that means "to be apart from, different than, separate." Thus, it refers to God as separated from or exalted above all other things (Is. 6:13). Holiness refers to God's moral excellence or absolute completeness. Being holy, God calls for holiness in His own children, and what He calls for, He supplies. Holiness is God's gift that we receive by faith through His Son, Jesus Christ (Eph. 4:24).

God Is Righteous. Righteousness as applied to God refers to His affirmation and administration of what is right as opposed to what is wrong. His righteousness infuses His moral laws in the Ten Commandments, laid down to guide the conduct of humankind. Righteousness also refers to God's administration of justice. He brings equity to the violated and punishment upon the disobedient (Gen. 18:25; Deut. 32:4; Rom. 2:6–16). Finally, God's righteousness is redemptive, as in His declaring the believer to be in a state justified in Christ through His death and resurrection (Rom. 1:16–17; 3:24–26).

God Is Love. Love is the central, quintessential description of the nature of God. God's love for man seeks to awaken a responsive love of man for God. Divine love runs like a golden thread through the entire Bible. There we discover God giving Himself and all He possesses to His creatures, in order to win their response and to possess them and share Himself with them.

God loved and gave; He loved and sought—just as a shepherd seeks his sheep. God loved and suffered, providing His love by giving His all on the Cross for the redemption of humanity. God, in His love, wills only ultimate good for all His creatures (Gen. 1:31; Ps. 145:9, Mark 10:18).

God Is Truth. All truth, whether natural, physical, or spiritual, is grounded in God. Thus, any seemingly inconsistent teaching between natural and physical sciences and God's revelation of Himself is only a temporary misconception of man's based on his limited perspective and incomplete knowledge. Fullness of truth ultimately will be verified and magnified in alignment with God's revelation.

God Is Wisdom. God's wisdom is revealed in His doing the best thing, in the best way, at the best time, for the best purpose.

Some people have knowledge, but little wisdom, while at times it seems the most wise have little knowledge. In contrast, God is "the only wise God" (1 Tim. 1:17), being *all* wise as well as *all* knowing.

In creation, history, human lives, redemption, and finally and ultimately in Christ, His divine wisdom is revealed. The promise of James 1:5 affirms our human privilege of asking for and renewing wisdom from God.

However complete our effort at describing God through His attributes, our understanding of Him will continue to increase throughout our earthly pilgrimage, finally to be completed in eternity when we stand in His presence.

GOD. (2 Kin. 19:15) *'Elohim* (eh-loh-*heem*); *Strong's* #430: God; God in His fullness; also "gods," that is to say, the gods of the idolatrous nations. The word *'Elohim* appears more than 2,500 times in the Old Testament. Its first occurrence is in the first verse of the Bible. The majority of times *'Elohim* occurs it refers to God the Creator, but sometimes it refers to heathen gods or idols. Most scholars believe that the root is *'el* or *'elah*, meaning "strong," "mighty." Christians have long maintained that *'Elohim*, which is a plural form in Hebrew, reveals that God has more than one part of His being. We call those distinct parts "the Father," "the Son," and "the Holy Spirit." Nevertheless, we have *one* God, not three gods.

GODHEAD—an old English term that is a synonym for God, with an emphasis on that which makes the triune God essentially one (Rom. 1:20; Col. 2:9).

In Romans 1:20 the term Godhead describes what mankind ought to see in nature as a result of God's creative handiwork. Colossians 2:9 declares that in Christ "dwells all the fullness of the Godhead bodily."

GOD, NAMES OF—the titles or designations given to God throughout the Bible. In the ancient world, knowing another's name was a special privilege that offered access to that person's thought and life. God favored His people by revealing Himself by several names which offered special insight into His love and righteousness.

Jehovah/Yahweh. The most frequent name used for God in the Old Testament is Yahweh, or Jehovah, from the verb "to be," meaning simply but profoundly, "I am who I am," and "I will be who I will be." The four-letter Hebrew word (called the tetragrammaton) YHWH was the name by which God revealed Himself to Moses at the burning bush (Ex. 3:14). This bush itself was a vivid symbol of the inexhaustible dynamism of God, who burns like a fire with love and righteousness, yet remains the same and never diminishes. English translations of the Bible translate the word as Lord Jehovah, or Yahweh.

As the author of life and salvation, God's "I am" expresses the fact that He is the infinite and original personal God who is behind the existence of everything and to whom everything must finally be traced. This name, "I am who I am," signals the truth that nothing else defines who God is but God Himself. What He says and does is who He is. The inspired Scriptures are the infallible guide to understanding who God is by what He says about Himself and what He does.

Moses was called to proclaim deliverance to the people and was told by God, "Thus you shall say to the children of Israel, 'I AM has sent me to you'" (Ex. 3:14). In the deliverance of the Hebrew people from slavery in Egypt, God revealed a deeper significance to His name. But He had already disclosed Himself to Abraham, Isaac, and Jacob as Yahweh. Each of them had called on the name of the Lord (Yahweh) (Gen. 12:8; 13:4; 26:25; Ex. 3:15) as the God who protects and blesses. Yet Exodus 6:3 shows that Abraham, Isaac, and Jacob did not know the fuller meaning of Yahweh, which was to be revealed to Moses and the Hebrew people in the Exodus experience.

The divine name Yahweh is usually translated Lord in English versions of the Bible, because it became a practice in late Old Testament Judaism not to pronounce the sacred name YHWH, but to say instead "my Lord" (Adonai)—a practice still used today in the synagogue. When the vowels of Adonai were attached to the consonants YHWH in the medieval period, the word Jehovah resulted. Today, many Christians use the word Yahweh, the more original pronunciation, not hesitating to name the divine name since Jesus taught believers to speak in a familiar way to God.

The following are other names in honor of the Lord in the Old Testament that stem from the basic name of Yahweh:

Jehovah-jireh. This name is translated as "The-LORD-Will-Provide," commemorating the provision of the ram in place of Isaac for Abraham's sacrifice (Gen. 22:14).

Jehovah-nissi. This name means "The-LORD-Is-My-Banner," in honor of God's defeat of the Amalekites (Ex. 17:15).

Jehovah-shalom. This phrase means "The-LORD-Is-Peace," the name Gideon gave the altar which he built in Ophrah (Judg. 6:24).

Jehovah-shammah. This phrase expresses the truth that "The-LORD-Is-There," referring to the city which the prophet Ezekiel saw in his vision (Ezek. 48:35).

Jehovah-tsebaoth. This name, translated "The-LORD-of-hosts," was used in the days of David and the prophets, witnessing to God the Savior who is surrounded by His hosts of heavenly power (1 Sam. 1:3).

Jehovah Elohe Israel. This name means "LORD-God-of-Israel," and it appears in Isaiah, Jeremiah, and the Psalms. Other names similar to this are *Netsah Israel*, "The Strength of Israel" (1 Sam. 15:29); and *Abir Yisrael*, "The Mighty One of Israel" (Is. 1:24).

El. El, by itself, refers to a God in the most general sense. In the Bible the word is often defined properly by a qualifier like Jehovah: "I, the LORD (Jehovah) your God (Elohim), am a jealous God (El)" (Deut. 5:9).

Elohim. Elohim is the plural form of El, but it is usually translated in the singular. Some scholars have held that the plural represents an intensified form for the supreme God; others believe it describes the supreme God and His heavenly court of created beings. Still others hold that the plural form refers to the triune God of Genesis 1:13, who works through Word and Spirit in the creation of the world. All agree that the plural form Elohim does convey the sense of the one supreme being who is the only true God.

GODS, PAGAN—the false gods and idols worshiped by people during Bible times—especially the false gods of Egypt, Mesopotamia (Assyria and Babylon), Canaan, Greece, and Rome.

Though these were sincerely worshiped according to the religions of each area, this idol worship was not only erroneous, it was spiritually destructive. In general, the pagan civilizations of Bible times which worshiped many gods were in fact worshiping demon deities (Lev. 17:7; Deut. 32:17; 2 Chr. 11:15; Ps. 106:37). Paul acknowledges this still to be true in New Testament times (1 Cor. 10:20; 1 Tim. 4:1) and John discloses such demonic confusion present on the earth until the end of time (Rev. 9:20).

Baal. The Canaanite god most often referred to is Baal, which means "lord" or "master." The word could be used as a title for any person who owned something, or any god considered to be a lord or master. But *Baal* soon became identified with various regional gods that were thought to provide fertility for crops and livestock. As a god who symbolized the productive forces of nature, Baal was worshiped with much sensuality (Num. 22:41; Judg. 2:13; 1 Kin. 16:31–32).

Baal appeared in many forms and under many different names. The Bible often makes reference to the Baalim (the plural of Baal; KJV) or to the Baals (NKJV; Judg. 2:11; 1 Kin. 18:18; Jer. 2:23).

Baal-Zebub, which means "lord of the fly," was "the god of Ekron" (2 Kin. 1:23, 6, 16)—the name under which Baal was worshiped by the Philistines.

Among the other frequently mentioned demon gods Israel was surrounded and tempted by were:

The goddess *Asherah* (1 Kin. 15:13; 2 Chr. 15:16; *Asherahs,* Judg. 3:7) was portrayed as the wife of El (or sometimes Baal) in Canaanite mythology, and was a favorite deity of women.

The word *asherah* also refers to a wooden pole or cult pillar that stood at Canaanite places of worship—perhaps the trunk of a tree with the branches chopped off—and associated with the worship of the goddess Asherah.

Other pagan gods in addition to Baal and his companions were worshiped by the Canaanites. *Molech* was the national deity of the Ammonites (Lev. 18:21; Jer. 32:35), whose worship was accompanied by the burning of children offered as a sacrifice by their own parents. The god *Molech* also appears in the Old Testament as *Milcom* (2 Kin. 23:13; Zeph. 1:5; *Malcham,* KJV) and in the New Testament as *Moloch* (Acts 7:43).

Chemosh (Judg. 11:24; 2 King. 23:13) was the national god of the Moabites and Ammonites. This deity was apparently compounded with *Athtar,* the Venus star, and so is thought to be a pagan god associated with the heavenly bodies. Chemosh has been identified with Baal of Peor, Baal-Zebub, Mars, and Saturn, as the star of ill omen. Dibon (Num. 21:30), a town in Moab north of the River Arnon, was the chief seat of its worship. Like Molech, Chemosh was worshiped by the sacrifice of children as burnt offerings. Solomon sanctified Chemosh as a part of his tolerance of pagan gods (1 Kin. 11:7), but Josiah abolished its worship (2 Kin. 23:13). Mesha, king of Moab, offered his eldest son as a burnt offering on the wall of Kir Hareseth, the ancient capital of Moab.

Ashtoreth (1 Kin. 11:5, 33; 2 Kin. 23:13) was the ancient Syrian and Phoenician goddess of the moon, sexuality, sensual love, and fertility. In the Old Testament Ashtoreth is often associated with the worship of Baal. The KJV word *Ashtaroth* is the plural form of Ashtoreth; the NKJV has *Ashtoreths* (Judg. 2:13; 1 Sam. 12:10).

Remphan (Acts 7:43; *Rephan,* RSV, NIV, NEB; *Rompha,* NASB) was an idol worshiped by Israel in the wilderness. This may be the same pagan god as *Chiun* (Amos 5:26; *Kiyyun,* NASB; *Kaiwan* your star-god, RSV), or Saturn.

Nehushtan, literally "bronze serpent-idol," was the contemptuous name given by King Hezekiah to the bronze serpent made by Moses in the wilderness (Num. 21:8–9), when people began to worship it (2 Kin. 18:4).

Gad (Is. 65:11; Fortune, RSV, NIV, NASB; Fate, NEB) was a heathen deity worshiped along with *Meni* (Is. 65:11; Destiny, RSV, NIV, NASB; Fortune, NEB). Scholars are uncertain about the exact identity of these pagan gods.

The pagan gods of Greece and Rome. Only a few of the ancient Greek and Roman gods are mentioned in the New Testament.

Zeus (Acts 14:12–13: 19:35; Jupiter, KJV) was the supreme god of the ancient Greeks. According to Greek mythology, Zeus was the ruler of heaven and father of other gods and mortal heroes. He was identified by the Romans as *Jupiter.*

Hermes (Acts 14:12; Mercurius, KJV; Mercury, NEB) was the Greek god of commerce, science, invention, and cunning. He also served as messenger and herald for the other gods. Hermes was identified by the Romans with *Mercury.*

Diana (Acts 19:24, 27–28, 34–35), in Roman mythology, was the goddess of the moon, hunting, wild animals, and virginity. Diana is the same as the Greek goddess *Artemis* (RSV, NIV, NASB).

In both the Old Testament and the New Testament the people of God were surrounded by pagan gods. Today, as then, these invisible powers and principalities are being overthrown from their influence in the regions of peoples they have blinded and bound spiritually (Eph. 6:10–20). The triumph over them Christ accomplished through His Cross (Col. 2:14–15) has brought these forces under His authority (Eph. 1:20–23).

Only the sovereign Lord God has the ultimate right to rule the world; and the Lord Jesus Christ has claim to cast out all principalities and powers as His church advances against hell's dark powers (Matt. 16:18–19).

GOOD. (Ezek. 34:14) *tob* (*tohv*); *Strong's #2896:* Good, goodness; whatever is right, pleasant, or happy; opposite of sorrow or evil. This adjective occurs more than five hundred times, with a much wider range of meaning than the word "good" has in English. In its first occurrence (Gen. 1:4), the Creator evaluates His product: "God saw the light, that it was good." Shortly thereafter, *tob* is used in contrast with its antonym *ra'* (bad or evil) in the phrase "good and evil" (Gen. 2:17; see also Gen. 31:24; Is. 5:20; 7:15). In the present reference, God assures His flock that He will rescue them from their cruel leaders; He will find good pasture to nourish them and will provide a fold where they can rest in safety. *Also* (Matt. 13:48) *kalos* (kal-*oss*); *Strong's #2570:* A descriptive word signifying that which is beautiful, pleasing, acceptable, excellent, serviceable, attractive, honest. Its synonym is *agathos*, good in a physical and moral sense. *Also* (Phil. 1:6) *agathos* (ag-ath-*oss*); *Strong's #18:* Good, in a physical and moral sense, and which produces benefits. The word is used of persons, things, acts, conditions, and so on. A synonym of *agathos* is *kalos*, good in an aes-

thetic sense, suggesting attractiveness, excellence.

GOODNESS. (Rom. 15:14) *agathosune* (ag-ath-oh-soo-nay); *Strong's #19:* Compare "Agatha" and possibly "agate." Beneficence, kindness in actual manifestation, virtue equipped for action, a bountiful propensity both to will and to do what is good, intrinsic goodness producing a generosity and a Godlike state or being. *Agathosune* is a rare word that combines being good and doing good.

GOSPEL—the joyous Good News of salvation in Jesus Christ. The Greek word translated as gospel means "a reward for bringing good news" or simply "good news." In Isaiah 40:9, the prophet proclaimed the "good tidings" that God would rescue His people from captivity. In His first sermon in Nazareth, Jesus used a passage from the Old Testament to characterize the spirit of His ministry: "The Spirit of the Lord is upon Me, because He has anointed Me to preach the gospel to the poor" (Luke 4:18).

The gospel is not a new plan of salvation; it is the fulfillment of God's eternal plan of salvation which was conceived before time, established in Abraham's seed (Israel), completed in Jesus Christ, and now made known by the living church.

The gospel is the saving work of God in His Son Jesus Christ and a call to faith in Him (Rom. 1:16–17). Jesus is more than a messenger of the gospel; He is the gospel. The Good News of God was incarnate in His life, teaching, and atoning death. Therefore, the gospel is both a historical event and a personal relationship. (Also see Gospel of the Kingdom; Kingdom of God.)

GOSPEL. (Mark 1:1) *euangelion* (yoo-ang-*ghel-ee*-on); *Strong's #2098:* Compare "evangel," "evangelize," "evangelistic." In ancient Greece *euangelion* designated the reward given for bringing good news. Later it came to mean the good news itself. In the New Testament the word includes both the promise of salvation and its fulfillment by the life, death, resurrection, and ascension of Jesus Christ. *Euangelion* also designates the written narratives of Matthew, Mark, Luke, and John.

GOSPEL OF THE KINGDOM.

Editor's Note: The most essential idea for each believer to grasp is found in the words of Jesus: "This gospel of the kingdom will be preached in all the world as a witness to all the nations, and then the end will come" (Matt. 24:14). After coming to know

continued on next page

continued from preceding page

salvation through Jesus Christ, God's Son, it is essential for us to gain a practical perspective on all that is included in this one verse in the Bible. This perspective will help us recognize and grow into a fully developing, biblical lifestyle that distinguishes between traditionalized Christianity and dynamic, Christ-honoring life, growth, and ministry. The "gospel of the kingdom" points not only to a message, but to a mindset—to a recognition that Jesus Christ wants to fill every one of His disciples with His life, love, and power, to make them a ministering member of His body (Eph. 1:15–23).

This Handbook is distinctive in its focus on "Spirit-filled, New Testament living"—helping each believer to know God's Word, so as to become an increasingly effective agent of the kingdom of God. This comes as a divinely natural by-product to those who become filled with Jesus' love and enabled by His power, equipped to represent Him in every part of their daily life, without religious fanfare or contrived spirituality.

The truth of "the kingdom of God" studied in its fullness opens the door to a life (1) growing in the truth of God's Word, (2) revealing the love of God's Son, and (3) serving in the power of God's Spirit. This Handbook's central features elaborate this kind of ministry-minded, Holy Spirit-filled "living out" of the Word of God. JWH

Judging from the emphasis of Jesus' ministry and the clear commission He gave His followers, the gospel of the kingdom is the most important message in the Bible. Jesus declared that "this gospel of the kingdom will be preached in all the world as a witness to all the nations, and then the end will come" (Matt. 24:14).

Nothing is to be more central to the understanding or personal mission of each follower of the Lord Jesus than the truth of this gospel and our assignment to bear it to the world. That is why *Hayford's Bible Handbook* centers on the truth of "the kingdom of God"— both the heart of Jesus' message and the divine vision and objective for redemption.

The Content: The Gospel Is Both Word and Deed: There is no gospel other than the gospel of the kingdom of God (or "of heaven"; Matt. 3:2; 4:17; Acts 28:23; Gal. 1:8–9). The gospel of the kingdom is the same as the gospel of Jesus Christ. Jesus Himself used the former

expression frequently, while His followers rightly saw in Jesus both the coming of God's kingdom and the place of Jesus as King of the kingdom. Within a short time, the revelation of Jesus as Lord and Christ turned the popular way of referring to God's gospel toward the form most familiar to us: "the gospel of Jesus Christ."

"Gospel," of course, means "good news"; but what is "the kingdom of God"? Despite using this phrase frequently in the Gospels, Jesus nowhere defines it in dictionary fashion. He points toward it and describes it through parables, and He emphasizes that He must preach it. But what exactly is this kingdom? The connection of "good news of" to "the kingdom" points us in the right direction. News always refers to events or actions that can be reported. What is the "good news" pertaining to "the kingdom"?

First, the good news is that this kingdom has arrived: it was "at hand" and had "come upon" the generation to whom Jesus ministered (Matt. 3:2; 4:17; 10:7; Luke 10:9). The kingdom was present among them; it had happened to them (Luke 17:21).

Second, the good news refers to the divine acts that make the kingdom evident. John the Baptist, discouraged and languishing in Herod's prison, struggled with doubts about having invested his adult life in preparing the way for Jesus. He sent someone to ask Jesus point-blank: Are You the One we've been looking for, the Messiah of God? Is this the time for God's kingdom to arrive, just as we have wanted and hoped? (Luke 7:19–20). Jesus answered "yes" by reminding the inquirers what they themselves had witnessed: "the blind see, the lame walk, the lepers are cleansed, the deaf hear, the dead are raised, the poor have the gospel preached to them" (Luke 7:22). Jesus described what was actually occurring in His ministry, using the prophetic language of Isaiah 35:5–6 and 61:1.

These prophetic passages, along with many others from the Old Testament, look forward to the day of the Lord. In that day, God Himself would perform true justice throughout the earth, save His people from their enemies, and inaugurate a new day of *shalom*—righteous well-being throughout all of creation. Prophets saw the details differently, but they were clear that one day God Himself would do directly what generations of priests and prophets and kings operating under His authority had been unable to do—govern completely and righteously. Evil in all its forms would be vanquished, and righteousness—that which is good and true—would fill the earth.

The "good news of the kingdom," then, announces that this righteous, saving, and restoring rule of God is present through the words and deeds of Jesus, including the ministry to which Jesus commissions His followers. The core concept of the "kingdom of God" is God's saving *action* and the new life His acts bring to believers. Like any news, the "gospel of the kingdom" is expressed in words, but in addition to the *words* that announce and explain salvation, it reports the *deeds* that are themselves enactments or instances of salvation. Jesus not only teaches about the kingdom of God, but He also actuates God's saving reign when He heals the blind, lame, deaf, and leprous; when He casts out demons; when He raises the dead; when He expresses God's tender affection for the underclass and outcasts. In Jesus, that crucial part of the "day of the Lord" known as the "day of salvation" has arrived.

The coming of God's kingdom in and through Jesus unleashed a divine revolution against all manner of evil, benefiting all who would receive Him and His work. Much of Jesus' ministry assaulted the forces of Satan directly and set humanity free from demonic torture. Jesus also forgave sin, and He demonstrated reconciliation between God and humanity, as well as among humanity's striving factions and races, by extending fellowship at the Father's table to all who would receive Him. These acts culminated in the ultimate saving acts of the rejection and suffering of Jesus, His sacrificial death, and His resurrection from the dead. His death paid the penalty for sin and broke its power, while His rising from the dead broke death's power. All the enemies of humanity and of all of God's good creation are defeated: The triumph of God's revolution is assured! Through Christ, believing humanity is now redeemed and in the process of being restored to full participation in God's kingdom plan and purpose.

The earliest followers of Jesus understood that this glorious gospel was never limited to only a verbal message about what had happened in the past. They knew that the gospel included God's past, present, and ongoing *acts* of saving power. In the Book of Acts we find words about what God did through Jesus, along with the saving deeds Jesus continues to perform through the Holy Spirit. This understanding of the gospel as a unity of divine word and deed is expressed also by the apostle Paul when he reminds the Thessalonians that the "gospel did not come to [them] in word only, but also in power, and in the Holy Spirit and in much assurance" (1 Thess. 1:5).

The Promise: The gospel of the kingdom incorporates, first, the promise of eternal life for all who receive God's King as Lord and Savior (John 3:16–19, 33–36). Second, it also contains the promise of the Holy Spirit's indwelling (Acts 2:38; Rom. 8:9–11) and empowering (John 7:38–39; Acts 1:8). With the Spirit's enabling, each "witness" (agent or representative of the kingdom) can minister the gospel in the power of the Lord, assured that the gospel proclaimed will be confirmed by the gospel demonstrated through "signs following" (Mark 16:15–20).

Finally, the gospel of the kingdom promises that ultimately the King shall come again to consummate the rule of God upon the earth (Rev. 19:11–16; 20:1–6). Then all who believe and follow Him shall dwell forever in the eternal kingdom with Christ and the Father (John 14:1–6; Rev. 20:7—21:27).

The gospel of the kingdom of God as a message of power and promise lies at the center of the witness of the early church as it spread from Jerusalem to Samaria to the world (Acts 8:12; 20:24–25; 28:23, 31). It also provides the central conviction that has governed the preparation of the *Handbook*: When Scripture is understood in light of the centrality of this gospel, all Bible students will experience a greater breadth of vision and a more dynamic and practical focus in their study and application of God's Word.

Seeing the centrality of the kingdom of God in Scripture, in the gospel, and in each believer's call to ministry opens the way to fruitful, Holy Spirit-filled living. This life is the gift our Lord Jesus gave through His dying and rising—not only that we would be "saved and gain heaven," but also that we might be present-day agents of His kingdom, daily touching others with God's grace, love, and power, in His name. (*See* "The Essential Message of God's Word," pages x–xi; "Keys to the Scriptures," page 1; "The Kingdom in the New Testament," page 275.)

GOSPEL OF THOMAS—see ch. 55, §7.

GOSPELS—the four accounts at the beginning of the New Testament about the saving work of God in His Son Jesus Christ. The writers of the four Gospels introduced a new literary category into literature. The Gospels are not exactly biographies, because apart from certain events surrounding His birth (Matthew 1—2; Luke 1—2), and one from His youth (Luke 2:41–52), they record only the last two or three years of Jesus' life.

Moreover, the material included is not written as an objective historical survey of Jesus' ministry. The Gospels present Jesus in such a way that the reader realizes that God acted uniquely in Him. The authors of the Gospels wrote not only to communicate knowledge about Jesus as a Person, but also to call us to commitment to Him as Lord.

The Gospels produce four distinctive portraits of Jesus rather than an exact photographic likeness. Thus, there are four Gospels (accounts) of the one gospel (the Good News of salvation in Jesus Christ).

The church adopted symbols for the Gospels—Matthew a lion, Mark an ox, Luke a man, John an eagle (or variations thereof)— from the fourfold witness to God in Scripture (Ezek. 1:5; 10:14; Rev. 4:7). At an early date the church realized that the combined witness of the four Gospels was required to declare the full significance of Christ.

The synoptic Gospels. If one sets the four Gospels side by side, it becomes apparent that Matthew, Mark, and Luke have much in common. Each Gospel arranges its material in a similar fashion, and each Gospel casts the life of Jesus within the framework of a Galilean ministry that extended from Jesus' baptism to His death, with emphasis on His final days in the flesh.

The similarity of the Gospels also includes their content. The first three Gospels recount many of the same incidents or teachings, and often in the same or related wording. A glance, for example, at the baptism of Jesus as related by Matthew (3:13–17), Mark (1:9–11), and Luke (3:21–22) will quickly demonstrate their agreement. Because of this similarity in arrangement, content, and wording, the first three Gospels are called synoptic gospels (from the Greek *synopsis,* "a seeing together"). The Gospel of John presents a more independent account of Christ.

For Mark, Jesus is the Suffering Servant who reveals His divine Sonship on the Cross. Matthew's major concern is to present Jesus as a teacher who is greater than Moses and continually present with the disciples. For Luke, Jesus is the keystone in the history of salvation, beginning with Israel, fulfilled in Jesus, and communicated by the church. The fourth Gospel writer penetrates the mystery of the Incarnation, Jesus as God in human form (John 1:14), who brings life to the world through trust in Him.

The Synoptics and the Gospel of John. All four Gospels portray Jesus Christ through selected events in His life, climaxing in His death and resurrection. But John features an independent, unique presentation of Jesus.

In the Synoptics, Jesus' ministry lasts less than a year, and is conducted mainly in Galilee; in John it extends to three or more years and centers more often in Judea. The Synoptics present Jesus as a man of action who paints word pictures for His hearers; John, however, portrays longer, less picturesque, and more complex discourse coming from Jesus, and comparatively little action. In the Synoptics, Jesus teaches in parables— nearly sixty in all—but in John no parables exist. In the Synoptics, Jesus teaches mainly about the kingdom of God, whereas in John He teaches about Himself. In the Synoptics, Jesus often demands silence of those who behold His miracles, but in John the miracles are related as signs revealing Jesus and His mission.

These facts are sufficient to indicate that the Synoptics present basically one perspective on the life of Jesus and that the Gospel of John presents another perspective, achieved most probably by profound meditation on the meaning of Jesus Christ.

The importance of the Gospels for the early church may be indicated by noting that these four, which were collected perhaps as early as A.D. 125, were the first books of the New Testament to be accepted as authoritative by the early church. Today the four Gospels remain our only reliable source of information about the central figure of the human race.

GOVERNMENT—earthly authority; those who rule over others in order to keep society stable and orderly. Only God is the sovereign ruler of all. When human governments exalt themselves above God, they go beyond their legitimate function in society (Dan. 5:32).

Jesus taught that earthly governments exist by God's will (John 19:11) and are legitimate as long as they do not take over the role reserved for God alone (Mark 12:13–17). Romans 13 discusses human government as ordained by God. Revelation 13, on the other hand, discusses it as degenerate and demonic. Christians live in the tension created by the fact that governments can be good (Romans 13) or evil (Revelation 13). When governments promote good and suppress evil, they fulfill their God-given function (1 Pet. 2:11–12). But if government exalts itself as sovereign over all life, then it has overstepped its bounds and is a handmaid of evil.

Believers are commanded to prioritize their place amid a society by praying for those in power (1 Tim. 2:1–7). Jesus said His church was not to seek political control (John 18:36) but was and is to flavor the society with righteousness (Matt. 5:13–16).

GRACE—favor or kindness shown without regard to the worth or merit of the one who receives it and in spite of what that same person deserves. Grace is one of the key attributes of God. The Lord God is "merciful and gracious, long-suffering, and abounding in goodness and truth" (Ex. 34:6). Therefore, grace is almost always associated with mercy, love, compassion, and patience as the source of help and with deliverance from distress.

In the Old Testament, the supreme example of grace was the redemption of the Hebrew people from Egypt and their establishment in the Promised Land. This did not happen because of any merit on Israel's part, but in spite of their unrighteousness (Deut. 9:5–6). Although the grace of God is always free and undeserved, it must not be taken for granted. Grace is only enjoyed within the *covenant— the gift is given by God, and the gift is received by man through repentance and faith (Amos 5:15). Grace is to be humbly sought through the prayer of faith (Mal. 1:9).

The grace of God is supremely revealed and given in the person and work of Jesus Christ. Jesus was not only the beneficiary of God's grace (Luke 2:40), but He was also its very embodiment (John 1:14), bringing it to mankind for salvation (Titus 2:11). By His death and resurrection, Jesus restored the broken fellowship between God and His people, both Jew and Gentile. The only way of salvation for any person is "through the grace of the Lord Jesus Christ" (Acts 15:11).

The grace of God revealed in Jesus Christ is applied to human beings for their salvation by the *Holy Spirit, who is called "the Spirit of grace" (Heb. 10:29). The Spirit is the One who binds Christ to His people so that they receive forgiveness, adoption to sonship, and newness of life, as well as every spiritual gift or grace (Eph. 4:7).

The theme of grace is especially prominent in the letters of the apostle Paul. He sets grace radically over against the law and the works of the law (Rom. 3:24, 28). Paul makes it abundantly clear that salvation is not something that can be earned or merited; it can be received only as a gift of grace (Rom. 4:4). Grace, however, must be accompanied by faith; a person must trust in the mercy and favor of God, even while it is undeserved (Rom. 4:16). Grace (*charis*) is also the fountainhead of the power-gifts and operations of the Holy Spirit (*charismata*, 1 Cor. 12:1–11). These gifts in manifestation reveal nothing of the merit of the human agency through which they are "delivered" as gifts under the Spirit's distribution process (1 Cor. 12:11). They are grace-works, and so are all mighty movings of the Spirit. (*See* Barnabas's summary view of the revival at Antioch: "He came and had seen the grace of God" (Acts 11:19–24).

The Law of Moses revealed the righteous will of God in the midst of pagan darkness; it was God's gracious gift to Israel (Deut. 4:8). But His will was made complete when Jesus brought the gospel of grace into the world (John 1:17).

GRACE. (Zech. 12:10) *chen* (*chayn*); *Strong's* #2580: Favor, grace, graciousness, kindness, beauty, pleasantness, charm, attractiveness, loveliness, affectionate regard. The root *chanan* means "to act graciously or mercifully toward someone; to be compassionate, to be favorably inclined." God's grace poured out upon Jerusalem enables them to look longingly and beseechingly toward their pierced King. God's grace will result in Israel's seeing Jesus as someone of infinite beauty. His goodness enables them to repent. The Holy Spirit is called "the Spirit of grace" in Hebrews 10:29, a title no doubt inspired by this reference in Zechariah. *Also* (2 Cor. 12:9) *charis* (*khar*-ece); *Strong's #5485:* From the same root as *chara*, "joy," and *chairo*, "to rejoice." *Charis* causes rejoicing. It is the word for God's grace as extended to sinful man. It signifies unmerited favor, undeserved blessing, a free gift.

GRACIOUS (BE). (Mal. 1:9) *chanan* (chah-nahn); *Strong's* #2603: To be graciously inclined toward someone; to have compassion on someone; to bestow favor on a person in need. This verb, which occurs eighty-one times, speaks of an attitude marked by compassion, generosity, and kindness. Note the use of *chanan* in Genesis 33:5, 11; Psalm 119:132; 123:3. "Have pity on me," Job repeatedly and pathetically cries out to his friends (Job 19:21). *Chanan*, as it appears in that context (vv. 14–22), denotes the kind of compassion, kindness, and consideration that will cause one to refrain from further wounding any individual who is bruised and suffering. God is very merciful, by His own choice (Ex. 33:19) and by His very nature (Is. 30:18–19).

GRAIN OFFERING. (Num. 29:6) *minchah* (min-khah); *Strong's* #4503: An offering, gift, tribute, present, sacrifice, portion, or donation. Although the offerings of Cain and Abel are termed *minchah* in Genesis 4:4–5, *minchah* is usually translated "grain offering" (Lev. 6:14). Elsewhere, it is translated "gifts," "presents," or "tribute," as in 1 Kings 4:21. The *minchah* is primarily a religious offering, but may also be a personal gift that one gives to his ruler.

GRAVE. (Hos. 13:14) *she'ol* (sheh-*oal*); *Strong's* #7585: The grave; the abode of the dead; the netherworld; hell. This noun occurs sixty-five times, its use broad enough to include the visible grave that houses a dead body and the abyss, that unseen world to which the soul departs in death. The meaning of "grave" is seen in Genesis 37:35; 42:38; and 1 Kings 2:6. *She'ol* speaks of the realm of departed souls in such verses as Psalms 9:17; 16:10; 55:15; 139:8; Is. 14:9–11; Ezek. 31:15–17; 32:21. The assumed root of *she'ol* is *sha'al*, "to ask, demand, require." Thus "hell" is a hungry, greedy devourer of humanity, is never full or satisfied, but is always asking for more (*see* Prov. 27:20). God's promise in the present verse is that He will save His people from the power of *she'ol* and that He will actually destroy *she'ol* in the end!!

 GREAT. (Ps. 31:19) *rab* (*rahv*); *Strong's* #7227: Great, abundant, many, large in number; of major importance; chief, weighty, significant, noble, princely. *Rab* appears more than four hundred times in the Old Testament. It is derived from the verb *rabab*, "to become numerous or great." The title *rabbi* is a derivative of *rab*. While *rabbi* has been defined as "my teacher," a more exact explanation is that it means "my great one" (full of knowledge) or "my master" (great instructor). Thus our Lord did not allow His followers to be called by this lofty title: He stressed that we can have but one *Rabbi*, and that must be the Messiah only (Matt. 23:8).

GREEK—see ch. 55, §4.2., 4.3.

 GROANING. (John 11:38) *embrimaomai* (em-brim-*ah*-om-ahee); *Strong's* #1690: Derived from *en*, "in," and *brime*, "strength." The word is used to express anger (Mark 14:5), to indicate a speaking or acting with deep feeling (John 11:33, 38), and for stern admonishment (Matt. 9:30; Mark 1:43).

 GUARANTEE. (2 Cor. 1:22) *arrabon* (ar-hrab-ohn); *Strong's* #728: A business term that speaks of earnest money, a part of the purchase price paid in advance as a down payment. *Arrabon* is the first installment, which guarantees full possession when the whole is paid later. Sometimes this transaction was called "caution money," "a pledge," "a deposit," "a guarantee." *Arrabon* describes the Holy Spirit as the pledge of our future joys and bliss in heaven. The Holy Spirit gives us a foretaste or guarantee of things to come.

 GUILTY. (Lev. 4:13) *'asham* (ah-*sham*); *Strong's* #816: To be guilty, to be conscious of guilt; to become an offender, to trespass. In most instances, *'asham* means "guilt offering," "trespass offering." *'Asham* is similar to

chata'ah, which may mean "sin" or "sin offering," depending on context. *'Asham* can portray the condition of guiltiness, guilt itself, the shame of being guilty, the punishment that guilt brings, and the offering that removes guilt. By far the most significant reference is Isaiah 53:10, where *'asham* appears in the description of the Messiah's atoning death. Jesus' death was the ultimate trespass offering for the sins of the whole world. *See* 1 John 2:2.

HABIRU—see ch. 55, §2.2., 3.6.b.

HADES [HAY dees]—Greek word for *hell.

HAGAR—see ch. 55, §3.5.b.

HAMMURABI, CODE OF—see ch. 55, §3.1., 3.5.b., 3.6.a., 3.6.c.

HAND—the end of the arm that serves as a grasping and handling tool for man. The hand enables humans to use tools and to act in ways that are impossible for animals. The Bible speaks often of hands in the literal sense. In the ancient world hands were decorated with bracelets and rings (Gen. 24:22; Ezek. 23:42).

Because hands are involved in almost all of man's activity, the word is often used symbolically in the Bible. The "hand" of someone or some group can mean power. This gives rise to such expressions as "the hand of Saul," "the hand of the Egyptians," and "the hand of my enemies" (Ex. 3:8; 1 Sam. 23:17; Ps. 31:15). Because hands do the will of the entire person, hands may represent someone's "whole being" (Ps. 24:4; Acts 2:23).

The physical position of the hands suggest a person's attitude. Uplifted hands symbolize either praise and petition to God or violence against another person (1 Kin. 11:27; Ps. 63:4; 1 Tim. 1:8). Drooping hands mean weariness (Is. 35:3). To lay one's hands on another's head conveys blessing (Gen. 48:17). In the churches of the New Testament, the ordination of church officials regularly involved this custom (1 Tim. 5:22).

The expression "hand of God" refers to His great power (Deut. 2:15; Ezek. 1:3). Often the emphasis of this expression is on God's power in creation (Ps. 8:6; Is. 64:8). Sometimes His power in judgment is emphasized, especially in the phrase "His hand is outstretched" (Ruth 1:13; Is. 9:12, 17). However, God may also extend His hand to express His mercy and forgiveness (Ps. 37:24).

 This icon beside an entry indicates a Word Wealth feature.

 This icon beside an entry indicates a Kingdom Dynamics feature.

 This icon beside an entry indicates an important biblical or doctrinal term.

HAND. (Josh. 4:24) *yad* (*yahd*); *Strong's #3027:* The hand; means by which a work is accomplished; strength, power. This noun occurs more than 1,500 times in the Old Testament and is found in a great number of figures of speech. For instance, to be "given into the hands" of someone denotes coming under his authority; being rescued "out of the hands" of someone is descriptive of deliverance and freedom. A "high hand" may describe either haughtiness or triumphant rejoicing. One interesting derivative of this noun is the verb *yadah*, generally translated "thank" or "praise"; its original meaning was probably "to praise by lifting up the hand."

HANDS, LAYING ON OF—the placing of hands upon a person by a body of believers in an act of conveying the blessing or purpose of God unto specific ends.

The practice of laying on of hands occurs frequently in the Old Testament. It was an act of identifying with one's sacrifice of worship in the laying of hands on the head of an animal intended for sacrifice. On the Day of Atonement, the priest laid his hands on the scapegoat (Lev. 16:12), probably symbolizing the transfer of any of the sins and guilt of the people to the goat, which was taken away into the wilderness.

The act of laying on of hands in the Old Testament was also dynamically associated with blessing (Gen. 48:18), installation to office (Deut. 34:9), and the setting apart of Levi (Num. 8:10). These passages seem to express the idea of transferral of God's authority and the quality of His holiness to serve His purpose.

In the New Testament Jesus laid his hands on children (Matt. 19:13, 15) and on the sick when he healed (Matt. 9:18). In the early church the laying on of hands was also associated with healing, and with ministering the fullness of the Holy Spirit (Acts 9:17). It is also attended by the setting apart of persons to particular offices and work in the church with prayer (Acts 13:3; 6:6; 1 Tim. 4:14; 2 Tim. 1:6).

The laying on of hands was never practiced as a magical or superstitious rite, but expressed the idea of God's purpose and blessing being transmitted through His people by His power.

HARDENED. (Mark 8:17) *poroo* (po-*rah*-oh); *Strong's #4456:* To petrify, form a callous, make hard. The word is used metaphorically of spiritual deafness and blindness. Hearers of the gospel who repeatedly resist its convicting truth become insensitive and dull and lose the power of understanding.

HEAD—the upper part of the human body containing the face and brain. In the Bible the head is more the center of sense experience (sight, hearing, etc.) than the center of thinking. To wound an enemy's head was to show his utter defeat, and to cut off someone's head was the ultimate disgrace (Ps. 68:21; Mark 6:14–28). Both priests and kings of Israel were initiated into office by having their heads anointed with oil (Lev. 8:12; 1 Sam. 10:1). In the New Testament those who were sick were also anointed (Mark 6:13; James 5:14). This custom apparently symbolized joy and well-being (Ps. 23:5; 45:7).

The position of a person's head symbolized various emotions. Wagging the head meant derision; bowing the head showed grief; covering the head with one's hand suggested shame (2 Sam. 13:19; Is. 58:5, Mark 15:29). To lift up a person's head was to elevate him to higher rank (Gen. 40:20; Jer. 52:31). For blood to be on the head of someone meant for that person to bear responsibility and guilt for some specified action (Josh. 2:19; Acts 18:6). To heap coals of fire on someone's head meant to make an enemy ashamed by treating him well (Rom. 12:20).

The word head is often used of inanimate objects such as rivers to designate a beginning point or top part of the object (Gen. 2:10; Ps. 24:9). In this sense, several important messianic prophecies refer to Christ as the "head cornerstone" (Ps. 118:22; Luke 20:17; 1 Pet. 2:7).

HEAD. (Gen. 3:15) *rosh* (*rohsh*); *Strong's #7218:* Head, the head (of the human body), the head of a line; what is principal or supreme; first, top, prince, the highest part, summit, beginning, foremost, leader, and chief. Just as the "head" of a company refers to its chief person, *rosh* is used to show headship. In 3:15, the promise is that the Seed of woman would someday crush the Serpent's head, that woman in particular would play a part in undoing the effects of the Fall. In its most specific sense the Lord Jesus has trampled Satan at the Cross. In its wider sense, the human race will eventually completely triumph over the Evil One (Rom. 16:20).

HEALED. (Matt. 12:22) *therapeuo* (ther-ap-*yoo*-oh); *Strong's #2323:* Compare "therapy" and "therapeutic." Originally, to serve in a menial way, such as household domestics attending to the members of a family. Since their duties included the care of sick family members, the word took on a medical connotation in the sense of taking care of, tending, and providing for the sick. From there it came to mean to heal, restore to health, cure.

HEALING—the process of applying preventive and remedial practices to maintain good health. In the ancient world health was a highly prized possession. The Hebrews tended to think of health primarily in terms of physical strength and well-being. The land of Palestine apparently provided a relatively healthy environment, as compared to Egypt and Mesopotamia—probably because of its location as well as the various laws and practices prescribed by the Law of Moses.

Regulation of diet. Most of the laws about food consumption are included in the first five books of the Old Testament. The restrictions involving meats were based on two simple tests. Only animals with separated hooves and that chewed the cud were suitable for eating (Lev. 11:3). This meant that pigs and rabbits were unsuitable for eating. Modern medicine has demonstrated that these animals are especially liable to infections with parasites; they are safe only if well-cooked. Thus, the prohibition of these animals for food among the Hebrew people was beneficial to their health.

Rituals. Several rituals were observed among the Hebrew people to maintain sanitary conditions and to promote good health. One of these involved bodily discharge. Although not all bodily discharges are infectious, many are. Since the Hebrew people lacked ways to determine which bodily discharges were infectious, all were treated as potentially infectious. For example, sputum is mentioned as a possible cause of infection (Lev. 15:8)—a fact that was not positively validated until the 19th century.

Another good example of this principle is the instruction given in Deuteronomy 23:12 about the disposal of human excrement. A place was set off outside the camp for this purpose. The Hebrew people were required to carry a spade, dig a hole for the excrement, and cover it (Deut. 23:12–13).

Hygiene. The Law of Moses required that the body and clothes be washed after contact with a diseased or dead person. The regulations about contact with dead bodies specified a period of uncleanness lasting seven days. During this time, the person involved was isolated from other people and required to perform certain acts, including bathing his body and washing his clothes (Num. 19:1–22).

Sexual perversion. The strict laws about sexual morality among the Hebrew people also promoted the prevention of venereal disease. *Circumcision of males was not only a religious rite, but also a hygienic measure that reduced infection and cancer.

Medicine and physicians. The first medicines probably were introduced to the Hebrews by the Egyptians while they were in bondage. In biblical times medicines were made from minerals, animal substances, herbs, wines, fruits, and other parts of plants. The Bible mentions numerous examples of these primitive medicines—notably the "balm of Gilead," which was probably an aromatic substance taken from an evergreen tree. Wine mixed with myrrh was used to relieve pain by dulling the senses. This remedy was offered to Jesus when He was on the Cross, but He refused to drink it (Mark 15:23).

The Bible refers to the work of physicians (Gen. 50:2, 2 Chr. 16:12; Jer. 8:22). In the New Testament, Luke is mentioned as the "beloved physician" (Col. 4:14).

Medical treatment in the ancient world often included the use of *magic, sorcery, and divination. Such practices were prohibited by the Mosaic Law; they were seen as dangerous and entirely inconsistent with the nature of the all-powerful God. The same dangers were present in New Testament times, and in every age magic and true medical aid must be discerned separately.

The ministry of Jesus. The people of Old Testament times tended to think of sickness as punishment for sin. But Jesus firmly declared that His Father's purpose for humankind was health, wholeness, and salvation. He did not teach that disease was a punishment sent by God. And while He was always concerned to heal the sick in body, He also paid close attention to the mind and the spirit of those who suffered.

James 5:14–16 indicates an abiding ministry of healing was practiced by the early church, caring for its own by means of anointing with oil (a symbol of the Holy Spirit) and the prayer of faith.

Healing ministry. The ministry of Jesus established the evidence that it is God's will to recover human beings from every expression of sin and Satan's works. Even a cursory reading of the Gospels makes clear that Jesus' ministry was not complete with preaching and teaching alone. He constantly healed the sick and cast out demons as a complementing part of His ministry (Matt. 4:23–25; 8:14–16; 9:35–38; 10:1–8, et al.). He trained His disciples to minister exactly as He did, and when He commissioned the church to go to all the world, the ministry of healing was contained within the commission (Mark 16:15–18).

Increasingly large sectors of the believing church today see the restoration of Christ's ministry of healing through His church as an extension of the progressive recovery of vital New Testament life that has been being renewed since the beginning of the Reformation. A nearly equal sector sees the grounds for such healing ministry as rooted in the full redemptive provisions of the atonement achieved through the Cross of Christ.

Healing and Christ's Atonement. This position motivates both the proclamation of the healing message—for mind, body, and soul, as a part of the full gospel. Contrary to opponents of this view, it does not presume an unhealed person is any less saved, if the individual has received Christ but not been physically healed through prayer. That position is no more proposed than the empty proposition that a person without a perfectly complete life of holiness (fully sanctified) was therefore unregenerate. Salvation rests completely on faith with Christ's finished work, not on evidences of holiness or health.

However, benefits within the atoning work of Christ do await proclamation and appropriation. Thus, the ministry of healing finds its authority in more than merely the compassion of those ministering. It is a ministry rooted in the heart of God for suffering humanity (as much as for sinful humanity), and revealed in the Word of God as having been illustrated in Jesus' ministry and consummated as a divine availability though His suffering, death, and resurrection.

The Bible teaches that Jesus' suffering was redemptive, too—that His suffering was substitutionary. He suffered in our stead, absorbing in Himself the horrible implications of sin's impact on the human frame.

The Rotherham translation, though clumsy in its technical rendition of the Hebrew text of Isaiah 53:4–5, nonetheless conveys the biblical truth with power. "Yet surely our sicknesses he carried, and as for our pains he bare the burden of them. But we accounted him stricken, smitten of God and humbled. Yet was he pierced for transgressions that were ours, was crushed for iniquities that were ours. The chastisement for our well-being was upon him, and by his stripes there is healing for us."

That text, joined to Matthew 8:17 and 1 Peter 2:24, shows solid biblical reason for ministering the Lord Jesus Christ's deliverance from suffering and sickness. The Holy Spirit's voice speaks to us through the Word of God: "Forget not all His benefits: who forgives all your iniquities, who heals all your diseases" (Ps. 103:2–3).

Healing and faith. Biblically sound ministries of God's healing grace differentiate sharply between divine healing and faith healing.

In this day "faith healing" has become a catch-all phrase generally used by the media and others who are without discernment. Peo-

ple cannot tell the crucial differences between spiritual phenomena which emanate from the human spirit, or the Holy Spirit, or some hellish spirit. The differences between faith healing and divine healing are vast.

Divine healing has as its focus the Person of Jesus Christ, while faith healing looks inwardly to human potential or outwardly to some human agent. Looking unto Jesus, the Author and Finisher of our faith (Heb. 12:2), sound ministry makes Him the center and source of healing gifts and miracles from God. Faith healing finds its energy in self-generated, personal dynamism which claims to tap hidden resources within the individual or released through the "healer." But divine healing is ministered by the power of the Holy Spirit through divinely ordained promises, provision, and providence.

God's healing grace and goodness span the realm of the medical as well as the miraculous, yet because God's Word holds forth resources of health, healing, and deliverance, it is not fanaticism to make one's first point of appeal to Him when sickness strikes. Divine healing need never be a last resort for a final crisis—but a first resort to request and receive the Father's touch and wholeness in Jesus' name.

Healing ministry and medicine. Biblically sound healing ministry recognizes the blessing of God's providence in medical resources. God is viewed as having provided multiple havens of refuge from suffering, sickness, and pain: through natural recuperative processes; through climate and diet; through the charitable efforts of humankind by hospitals, doctors, and medicine; and through the divine means of healing gifts distributed by the Holy Spirit and ministered in the name of Jesus. Thus, to contact a human physician is not seen as rejecting the Great Physician. Spiritual wisdom requires the view that the full balance of God's healing providences flow from His love, through natural, medical, and miracle means. Thus, any or every healing should culminate in adoration and worship with thanksgiving being given to Him.

HEALING. (Mal. 4:2) *marpe'* (mar-*peh*); *Strong's* #4832: Restoration of health, remedy, cure, medicine; tranquility, deliverance, refreshing. Occurring thirteen times, *marpe'* comes from the verb *rapha'*, "to heal, cure, repair." Salvation is God's rescue of the entire person, and healing is His complete repair of that person, as *marpe'* illustrates. Compare the application of *rapha'* in Psalms 41:4 and 147:3, referring to the healing of a soul that has sinned and the healing of a broken heart.

In the present reference, the Messiah is compared to a rising sun, which has visible, radiant beams of sunlight streaming outward in all directions. From each of these beams of glorious light, healing flows.

 HEALING, DIVINE, THE MINISTRY OF. The dynamic ministry of Jesus not only revealed God's heart of love for mankind's need of a Redeemer, but unveiled God's compassionate heart of mercy for mankind's need of a Healer. The will of God was perfectly disclosed in His Son; we are to seek ways to fully convey that perfect revelation. Just as the Fall of man introduced sickness as a part of the curse, the Cross of Christ has opened a door to healing as part of salvation's provision. Healing encompasses God's power to restore broken hearts, broken homes, broken lives, and broken bodies. Suffering assumes a multiplicity of forms, but Christ's blood not only covers our sin with redemptive love; His stripes release a resource of healing at every dimension of our need.

1. The Old Testament Healing Covenant (Ex. 15:26). This verse is widely referred to as the Old Testament Divine Healing Covenant. It is called a "covenant," because in it God promises He will keep His people free from disease, and He conditions the promise upon their diligent obedience.

The words used here for "diseases" (Hebrew *makhaleh*) and "heals" (Hebrew *rapha*) are used regularly for physical sickness and bodily healing. This is not only a spiritual concept, but also an intensely physical one. The covenant is made absolutely certain by the fact that God joins His mighty name to the promise, calling Himself *Yahweh-Rapha*, meaning "the LORD who heals." *Yahweh-Rapha* is one of the compound names by which God revealed His attributes to Israel. Here His very name declares that it is His nature to be the Healer to those who obey His word—to recover *to* health and to sustain *in* health.

While sin and disobedience are not always the direct causes of sickness, man's fall into sin is the original and underlying cause of all disease. Those who seek healing will benefit by looking to Christ Jesus our sin-bearer, along with pursuing renewed consecration. (*See* James 5:14–16; 1 Cor. 11:29–32.)

2. Healing Repentance and Humility (Num. 12:1–16). This passage relates how Moses' sister, Miriam, was healed of leprosy. She received physical healing through the intercession of Moses. However, her healing was delayed seven days because of her sin in defying the God-given leadership of Moses.

Is it possible that delays in receiving answers to our prayer may sometimes be the result of a sinful attitude? Is there instruction in the fact that the progress of the whole camp was delayed until Miriam was restored? Repentance and humility will not earn healing, but they may—as with Miriam—clear the way for God's grace to be revealed more fully (*see* 1 Cor. 12:20–27).

3. The Focus of Divine Healing (Num. 21:5–9). The plague of fiery serpents sent upon God's people was, in reality, a self-inflicted punishment, resulting from their frequent murmuring. God allowed what their own presumption invited, and many died from the bites of the serpents. In answer to the repentance of His people, God prescribed the erecting of a bronze serpent to which any might look in faith and be healed. Jesus referred to this account in John 3:14–15. He clearly implied that the bronze serpent typified His being raised upon the Cross. Our healing, both spiritual and physical, comes from looking to and identifying with Christ crucified, "by whose stripes you were healed" (1 Pet. 2:24).

4. Lessons in Sharing Healing Hope (2 Kin. 5:1–15). Naaman, the Syrian general, was a good man, and apparently his leprosy was not the result of his wrongdoing. Thus, this episode furnishes us with some practical insights into God's healing process when the sick person is innocent of known disobedience or action exposing them to their affliction. (1) Notice the importance of our sharing the hope of God's healing with others. The door to Naaman's healing was opened by a Jewish maid who recommended he seek out the prophet Elisha. Believers do good when they witness to others of *both* the *saving* and *healing* power of Jesus. (2) See how God knows how to deal with each person. Naaman was instructed to dip seven times in the Jordan River, and this displeased him. His human brashness and hidden pride were exposed, but his obedience and submission opened the way to health. A similar call may face any of us, as healing often awaits obedient action. For example, Jesus instructed ten lepers to show themselves to the priest, and they were healed after taking that first step of obedience (Luke 17:12–14). People who have received prayer for healing sometimes give up when they do not see immediate healing, rather than seek God for a possible faith-building step of submission. (See also 2 Kin. 20:1–11.)

5. Healing by Miracle or Medicine? (2 Kin. 20:1–11). This story of Hezekiah's miraculous healing begins with his being informed by the prophet Isaiah that he will die of his illness. He immediately begins to pray and seek God earnestly, not accepting the fate of death. God's addition of fifteen years to his life suggests that prayer in the face of terminal illness is never inappropriate. But Isaiah also directs Hezekiah to apply a poultice of figs to his boil. Some scholars point to the figs as a medical prescription, and attribute the healing power to the poultice. The Bible does not condemn resorting to medical remedies; but, in this case, to think that such a poultice, by itself, could cure a terminal illness seems absurd. God is the Author of all healing benefit; however the application of the poultice appears to suggest that human medical aid is never inappropriate. God alone can heal: He does so by miracle means, by natural means, and by human means. None should be demeaned as unworthy. This text shows clearly that Hezekiah's deliverance from death came from God, not man. (See James 5:14–16.)

6. Job's Affliction and Total Recovery (Job 42:10–13). Some point to Job to prove that sickness is God's will for many people. It is true that God permitted Job's illness to show Satan that Job would not turn from his Lord in the face of adversity. However, it is important to see that the affliction was a direct work of the devil (2:2). Further, illness was only one of Job's adversities. When God later healed him and restored all his losses two times over, the Hebrew text literally refers to his recovery as a return from captivity, an evidence that *all* his restoration was a driving back of evil, a recovering of something that had been "captured from him" (42:10). This complex case, however, requires the additional acknowledgment that Job's healing appears to coincide with repentance for his attitude. Chapter 29 seems to reveal that Job was extremely self-centered, and he repented later (see 42:5, 6). Job's changed attitude and God's restoration are linked.

Before we philosophize about "God's will" in sicknesses, we should note how God corrected Job's friends who had argued that his afflictions were a judgment from God (42:7–9). Job's spirit of forgiveness toward his friends, however, became pivotal for his own well-being and for theirs.

7. A Promise of Divinely Protected Health (Ps. 91:9–10). This passage promises protection from sickness as a blessing of the redeemed life. The word "plague" (Hebrew *nehgah*) is used of something "inflicted" on a body, and specifically was used to refer to "spots of leprosy." Here the Lord describes an abiding defense against "inflicted" disease, but the promise is conditioned upon making the Lord

our true refuge and habitation. How can we do this? Two Hebrew words in verse 9 give us the answer. The word *makhseh*, translated "refuge," means "a shelter," "a place of trust," and derives from the root *khawsaw*, meaning "to flee for protection," "to confide in." *Maween*, translated "dwelling place," indicates "a retreat." It comes from the root `onah*, which describes the security of intimately "dwelling together as in marriage." These key words elaborate a principle. When we make the Lord our refuge and habitation by trusting Him— taking our cares, fears, and needs to Him, seeking His counsel, spending times of refreshing with Him, and loving Him and walking closely with Him through every day—we enter into a sheltered place of promise regarding health. This truth safeguards against our making prayer for healing a recourse only for emergencies, although some do, in sickness or emergency, find repentance and renewed fellowship with God and discover His mercy.

8. God's Saving and Healing Benefit (Ps. 103:3). This is a definite Old Testament promise of bodily healing based upon the character of Yahweh as the Healer. It is clear that the dimension of healing promised here specifically includes physical wholeness. The text reinforces the healing covenant, since the Hebrew word *tachawloo* (diseases) is from the same root (*chawlah*) as the word for "disease" in Exodus 15:26 (*makhaleh*). Further, the words for "heal" are the same in both passages (Hebrew *rapha'*), the distinct meaning involving the idea of mending or curing. The two texts form a strong bond (Deut. 19:15; 2 Cor. 13:1). These two verses bear witness from the Old Testament that the Lord not only forgives iniquities; He heals our diseases. If under the former covenant bodily healing was pointedly included with the Father's many other benefits, we can rejoice and rest in faith. The New Covenant "glory" exceeds everything of the Old (2 Cor. 3:7–11), and we can be certain that God, in Christ, has made a complete provision for the well-being of our total person.

9. Deliverance from Our "Destructions" (Ps. 107:20). In this psalm, sickness is the punishment for transgression. To transgress is to willfully violate known boundaries of obedience. The punishment, then, is not so much a direct action of God's will as an indirect result of our having violated the boundaries of His will, and thus having exposed ourselves to the judgments outside it. However, deliverance may come with genuine repentance. Too often people do not call upon God until calamity strikes. Storms come upon us all; sudden difficulty or severe sickness may arrest us from our unperceived or willful spiritual decline. The text implies that if we seek the Lord with a contrite heart, crying for deliverance, the calamity may be reversed and we may receive *both* spiritual and physical healing. The Lord will hear such a cry; and when He does, He heals us with "His word" (v. 20). (A beautiful example of this is seen in Jesus' healing of the centurion's servant in Matthew 8:8.)

10. Healing Prophesied Through Christ's Atonement (Is. 53:4–5). Isaiah 53 clearly teaches that bodily healing is included in the atoning work of Christ, His suffering, and His Cross. The Hebrew words for "griefs" and "sorrows" (v. 4) specifically mean physical affliction. This is verified when Matthew 8:17 says this Isaiah text is being fulfilled in Jesus' healing people of human sickness and other physical need.

Further, that the words "borne" and "carried" refer to Jesus' atoning work on the Cross is made clear by the fact that they are the same words used to describe Christ's bearing our sins (see v. 11; also 1 Pet. 2:24). These texts unequivocally link the grounds of provision for both our salvation and our healing to the atoning work of Calvary. Neither is automatically appropriated, however; each provision—a soul's eternal salvation or a person's temporal, physical healing—must be received by faith. Christ's work on the Cross makes each possible; simple faith receives each as we choose.

Incidentally, a few contend that Isaiah's prophecy about sickness was fulfilled completely by the one-day healings described in Matthew 8:17. A close look, however, will show that the word "fulfill" often applies to an action that extends throughout the whole church age. (See Is. 42:1–4; Matt. 12:14–17.)

11. The Extent of Jesus' Healing Ministry and Commission (Matt. 4:23–25). These verses show the large extent of Jesus' healing ministry. Jesus' ministry consisted of teaching, preaching, making disciples, healing the sick, and casting out demons. This passage is the first New Testament record of Jesus healing physical afflictions and bringing deliverance to the demonically tormented. Some argue that Jesus healed during His ministry only in order to demonstrate His deity. Look, however, at such passages as 9:36–37 and 14:14, where it is clear that He healed out of compassion for the suffering multitudes. It seems obvious that Jesus intended healing to be part of the Christian mission of deliverance. His Great Commission includes the promise: "They will lay hands on the sick, and they will recover" (Mark 16:18). He extends this commission on the basis of His Atonement, His compassion, and His promise of power to fulfill His word.

12. The Biblical Grounds for Divine Healing (Matt. 8:16–17). The provision of divine healing must rest on clear grounds. Obviously it is biblically based, but from what source is this great mercy of God derived? Some link it to just that—God's mercy. While this is certainly a truth—for His compassion is great—the question at issue is this: What are the *redemptive* grounds of divine healing? Is healing included in God's saving provision in Christ, or is it simply a loving gesture of His benevolent character? This text, together with our discussion of Isaiah 53:4–5, gives clear evidence that divine healing is provided in the atonement of Christ's redeeming work on the Cross. To avoid this truth, some suggest that Isaiah's prophecy was fulfilled completely by the healings of that one day. Such would be impossible, for the prophecy of Isaiah states that the Servant of Yahweh would bear sickness in the same way that He would bear sins—that is, vicariously (see Kingdom Dynamics at Is. 53:4–5). Furthermore, He was to suffer for our sins and sicknesses. If "our" means *all of us* in regard to our sin and our being given a Savior, then it also means *all of us* in regard to sickness and our having been given a Divine Healer.

13. The Lord's Willingness to Heal (Mark 1:40–45). Here Jesus declares His willingness to heal the sick. Some insist that we must always preface our prayer for healing with, "If it is Your will." How can one have positive faith who begins a request with an "if"? We do not pray for salvation with an "if."

The leper was certain that Jesus was *able* to heal him; he was not sure that it was His will. But Jesus' response settled that question: "I am willing; be cleansed." May we not be certain that it is the Lord's will to do that for which He has made redemptive provision? At the same time, one cannot intentionally be living in violation of God's will and expect His promises will be fulfilled. Where biblical conditions for participation in God's processes are present, they must be met; but let us not avoid either God's readiness or God's remedies by reason of the question of His willingness. "If it is Your will" is more often an expression of fear, a proviso to "excuse God of blame" if our faith or His sovereign purposes do not bring healing. If His will is questioned, leave the issue to His sovereignty and remove it from your prayer. Our faith may be weak or incomplete in some regards. We, in fact, may not be healed at times, which should never be viewed as reason for condemnation (Rom. 8:1). Nevertheless, in all things, let us praise Him for His faithfulness and compassion. This is a great environment for healing to be realized and is consistent with the Scriptures, which reveal that Jesus is *willing* to heal.

14. The Place of Persistent Faith (Mark 5:24–34). This passage relates the account of a desperate woman whose healing was the result of great and persistent faith. Her illness made her ceremonially unclean and disqualified her from mixing with crowds of people, yet she was certain that "if only I may touch His clothes, I shall be made well" (v. 28). Jesus did not rebuke her; instead, He delayed His mission to the home of Jairus, whose daughter was dying, in order to assure her of healing and salvation.

Jesus later raised Jairus's daughter from the dead, but here He took time to minister to one with positive faith. That such persistence is rewarded is not to suggest that healing or any other work of God is earned by human effort. It rather illustrates the need to be bold in what we believe—to not be deterred by circumstance or discouraged by others. "All things *are* possible to him [or her] who believes" (9:23); and this is by God's grace (Eph. 2:8–9).

15. Cultivating a Climate of Faith for Healing (Mark 9:22–23). In this passage Jesus tells us that "believing" is the condition for answered prayer for a healing. The father of the demon-possessed boy answered in tears, "I believe," then added, "help my unbelief!" Since faith is a gift, we may pray for it as this father did. Note how quickly God's grace answered. But there is another lesson. Where an atmosphere of unbelief makes it difficult to believe, we should seek a different setting. Even Jesus' ability to work miracles was reduced where unbelief prevailed (Matt. 13:58). Prayer and praise provide an atmosphere of faith in God. In this text Jesus explained yet another obstacle to faith's victory—why their prayers had been fruitless—"This kind can come out by nothing but prayer and fasting" (Mark 9:29). His explanation teaches: (1) some (not all) affliction is demonically imposed; and (2) some kinds of demonic bondage do not respond to exorcism, but only to fervent prayer. Continuance in prayer, accompanied by praise and sometimes fasting, provides a climate for faith that brings deliverance.

16. Which Is Easier, Pardon or Healing? (Luke 5:16–26). While not all affliction is the result of a specific sin, in this case sin was the cause, for the man was healed when Jesus said, "Your sins are forgiven you." From Jesus' words it is clear that Jesus could have said either, "Rise up and walk," or "Your sins are forgiven you." In many cases prayer for healing should begin with confession of sin and repentance (James 5:16; 1 John 1:8–9).

Jesus' linking of healing with forgiveness is also evidence that human wholeness at every point of need is His concern. Obviously, forgiveness of sins is our greater need, but Jesus does not assert that need for divine forgiveness without affirming His concern for human suffering.

Of further note, this episode teaches how healing often comes when a group unites to pray in one accord (v. 16; also Matt. 18:19). The paralytic's healing came by means of men who cared, their faith overcoming all obstacles.

17. The Healing of Spirit, Soul, and Body (Luke 8:36). The Greek word *sozo* ("heal, save, make well or whole") appears in this chapter, offering Luke's unique perspective as a physician. A full range of encounters demonstrates Jesus' healing power: (1) The Gadarene, delivered from the demonic powers dominating him, is "healed," freed of evil powers that countermanded his own rational mind and physical actions. (2) The woman with the issue of blood (vv. 43–48) touches the hem of Jesus' garment, and Jesus says, "Your faith has made you well." (3) In verse 50, after being told the little girl is dead, Jesus declares: "Only believe, and she will be made well." (4) In verse 12, as Jesus explains the parable of the sower, the word "saved" is used of one's restored relationship with God through faith. Luke's precise account offers a complete picture of the Savior's concern to restore every part of man's life: (a) our relationship with God the Father; (b) our broken personalities and bondages; (c) our physical health; and (d) ultimately our rescue from death itself at the Resurrection. Jesus Christ is the Savior of the whole person.

18. The Disciples Instructed to Heal (Luke 10:8–9). Jesus' instructions to the seventy sent out in the surrounding countryside are direct and clear: "Heal the sick there, and say to them, 'The kingdom of God has come near to you.' " The coming of God's kingdom and the ministry of healing are not separated. The same point is made with the twelve disciples in 9:1–2. The authority to heal has been given to Jesus' disciples as they are willing to exercise the privileges of being messengers and participants in the kingdom of God. This ministry should not be separate from the declaration of the coming of the kingdom. The Holy Spirit delights to confirm the presence of the kingdom by glorifying the King's power, verifying Jesus Christ's work through the ministry of healing. This ministry of healing is experienced throughout the Book of Acts, and in James 5:13–16 is declared as a responsibility of eldership in a local congregation.

19. Healing as They Went (Luke 17:12–19). The nature of some healing as "progressive" is noted in the words "as they went, they were cleansed." The ten lepers' healing affords several lessons: (1) Not all healing occurs at the moment of prayer. Instant healings are often expected, whereas this illustrates a healing "in process" over a period of time following prayer. (2) Jesus' directive "Go . . . to the priests" indicates more than His affirmation of the Law (Lev. 13:1–59). Since the priests were the physicians of that culture, it also indicates that He approves of persons who have received healings seeing their physicians for confirmation of the healings. (3) The lepers' obedience to Jesus' command also is important. As they went in obedience, they were healed. When healing is not instantaneous, one ought not to doubt, but find a possible path of obedience. (4) Of that group of lepers healed by Jesus, only one returned to express gratitude. When healing comes, we should express thanks with praise and worship, and not be as the nine who failed to return with thanksgiving.

20. Divine Healing Never Outdated (John 8:58). Jesus' critics challenged His miracle ministry (5:16–18), His paternity (8:41), His integrity (7:12), and His spiritual purity (8:48). Their resistance was not unlike that often raised today against the reality of healing/miracle ministry. A foundational answer to such doubt is found in Jesus' assertion to His critics: "Before Abraham was, I AM." Christ's answer ties *all* facets of His Person and ministry to His own unchanging timelessness. This is a timeless message for us today as well. Jesus is not the great "I was" of yesteryear; He is the great "I AM"—"the same yesterday, and today, and forever" (Heb. 13:8). Some wish to confine miraculous healings to Bible times, but church history annuls that theory. Nothing in Scripture ever indicates that there will be any diminution in the work of Christ or the New Testament church during the whole church age. Jesus said that His church would do greater works than He had done, because He was going to the Father (John 14:12). Jesus healed through the power of the Holy Spirit, and the same Holy Spirit still operates in the church (Acts 2:38–39).

21. Healing in Jesus' Incomparable Name (Acts 3:16). Immediately after the Spirit's outpouring at Pentecost, it is stated, "many wonders and signs were done through the apostles." Chapter 3 gives the account of the healing of a man lame from birth, a fact well known by everyone in Jerusalem. Peter attributed the healing to no unique human powers, but to faith in the name of Jesus (v. 16).

Note how the invoking of the name of "Jesus Christ of Nazareth" (v. 6; 4:10) rings from the apostles' lips. The appeals to Jesus' name as the unmistakable Messiah (Christ), who walked as a Man among men (of Nazareth), establishes His Person, His character, and His kingly office as the authoritative grounds for extending healing grace. The use of another person's name to declare legal rights is called "the power of attorney." Jesus has delegated to us this privileged power to confront the retreating rule that sickness and Satan seek to sustain over mankind.

22. Paul's Healing Ministry in Malta (Acts 28:8–9). Here is a reference to divine healings in spite of the fact that Luke, a physician, accompanied Paul. This fact is so troublesome to critics of modern healing that some propose that the healings mentioned in verse 9 were the work of Luke, who used medical remedies, although Luke is not mentioned by name. This theory is based on the use of *therapeuo*, the Greek word for "healing" (v. 8), which some insist refers to medical therapy.

In fact, however, this word occurs thirty-four times in the New Testament. In thirty-two instances it clearly refers to divine healing; in the other cases the use is general. Both words (*iaomai* and *therapeuo*) are used in reference to the same healing in Matthew 8:7–8, indicating the terms are used interchangeably in the Bible.

This observation is certainly not to oppose medical treatment or to say medicine or medical aid is wrong. It is not. However, it does clarify that this text is not grounds for the substitution of medical therapy for prayer. God heals by many means: the prayer of faith, natural recuperative powers, medical aid or medicine, miracles.

23. The Gift of Healing (1 Cor. 12:9, 28). In order that the church's mission might not be limited to mere human abilities, the Holy Spirit provides specially designed, distributed, and energized gifts. Among them are "gifts of healings." The clear intent is that the supernatural healing of the sick should be a permanent ministry established in the church alongside and abetting the work of evangelizing the world. This is for today—timeless—for "the gifts and the calling of God *are* irrevocable" (Rom. 11:29).

24. The New Testament Divine Healing Covenant (James 5:13–18). Just as Exodus 15:26 is called the Old Testament Divine Healing

Covenant, James 5:13–18 is viewed as the New Testament Divine Healing Covenant. The inspired apostle affirms that sick persons whom the elders of the church anoint with oil, and for whom they pray, will be healed.

Some critics of healing for today contend that oil was a medicinal remedy with which the sick were to be massaged, but it is clear that the oil is intended as a symbol of the work of the Holy Spirit, who is present to glorify Jesus in healing works (John 16:14, 15). The text plainly states that "the Lord [not the oil] will raise him up" (v. 15). This practice probably was intended to be a sacrament, even as baptism and the Lord's Supper are continually observed today. (This should not be confused with "last rites," which some Christians observe when no recovery is possible.)

Here is an abiding healing covenant to be held as such and practiced today. (1) The sick are to exercise faith in calling for the "elders," that is, for pastoral leadership (v. 14). (2) Confession of sin and preparation of the heart are important, since our physical well-being is never separate from or made primary above our spiritual health (vv. 15–16). (3) Healing may come as a result of corporate, group, or personal prayer. (4) The anointing with oil is not a superstitious exercise, but a prophetic action, declaring dependence upon the Anointed One—Christ Jesus—whose power is ministered by the work of the Holy Spirit in our midst. N.V.

HEALS. (Ex. 15:26) *rapha'* (rah-*phah*); *Strong's* #7495: To cure, heal, repair, mend, restore health. Its participial form *rophe'*, "one who heals," is the Hebrew word for doctor. The main idea of the verb *rapha'* is physical healing. Some have tried to explain away the biblical teaching of divine healing, but all can see that this verse speaks of physical diseases and their divine cure. The first mention of *rapha'* in the Bible (Gen. 20:17) refers unquestionably to the cure of a physical condition, as do references to healing from leprosy and boils (Lev. 13:18; 14:3). Scripture affirms, "I am Yahweh your Physician."

HEALTH. (3 John 2) *hugiaino* (hoog-ee-*ahee*-no); *Strong's* #5198: Compare "hygiene" and "hygienic." To be sound in body, in good health. Metaphorically, the word refers to sound doctrine (1 Tim. 1:10; 2 Tim. 4:3; Titus 2:1); sound words (1 Tim. 6:3; 2 Tim. 1:13); and soundness in the faith (Titus 1:13; 2:1).

HEART—the inner self that thinks, feels, and decides. In the Bible the word heart has a much broader meaning than it does to the modern mind. The heart is that which is central to a person. Nearly all the references to the

heart in the Bible refer to some aspect of human personality.

In the Bible all emotions are experienced by the heart: love and hate (Ps. 105:25; 1 Pet. 1:22); joy and sorrow (Eccl. 2:10; John 16:6); peace and bitterness (Ezek. 27:31; Col. 3:15); courage and fear (Gen. 42:28; Amos 2:16).

The thinking processes of man are said to be carried out by the heart. This intellectual activity corresponds to what would be called mind in English. Thus, the heart may think (Esth. 6:6), understand (Job 38:36), imagine (Jer. 9:14), remember (Deut. 4:9), be wise (Prov. 2:10), and speak to itself (Deut. 7:17). Decision-making is also carried out by the heart. Purpose (Acts 11:23), intention (Heb. 4:12), and will (Eph. 6:6) are all activities of the heart.

Finally, heart often means someone's true character or personality. Purity or evil (Jer. 3:17; Matt. 5:8); sincerity or hardness (Ex. 4:21; Col. 3:22); and maturity or rebelliousness (Ps. 101:2; Jer. 5:23)—all these describe the heart or true character of individuals. God knows the heart of each person (1 Sam. 16:7). Since a person speaks and acts from his heart, he is to guard it well (Prov. 4:23; Matt. 15:18–19). The most important duty of man is to love God with the whole heart (Matt. 22:37). With the heart man believes in Christ and so experiences both love from God and the presence of Christ in his heart (Rom. 5:5; 10:9–10; Eph. 3:17).

HEART. (Ps. 37:4) *leb* (*lehv*); *Strong's* #3820: Heart, intellect, awareness, mind, inner person, inner feelings, deepest thoughts, inner self. As in English, the Hebrew concept of "heart" encompasses both the physical organ (2 Kin. 9:24) and a person's inner yearnings (Ps. 37:4). Perhaps the noblest occurrence of *leb* is Deuteronomy 6:5, commanding Israel to love the Lord "with all your heart" (Jesus laid great emphasis on this sentence; see Mark 12:29–30). Jeremiah 17:9 states that the human heart can be the most deceitful thing in the world, but verse 10 shows that the Lord is still able to sort out and analyze what lies within the heart.

HEARTS. (Rev. 2:23) *kardia* (kar-*dee*-ah); *Strong's* #2588: From a root word meaning "to quiver" or "to palpitate" (compare "cardiac" and "pericardium"). The physical organ of the body, the center of physical life, the seat of one's personal life (both physical and spiritual), the center of one's personality, the seat of one's entire mental and moral activity, containing both rational and emotional elements. It is the seat of feelings, desires, joy, pain, and love. It is also the center for thought, understanding, and will. The human heart is the dwelling place of the Lord and the Holy Spirit. In verse 23, the omniscient Lord sees into the innermost being where all decisions concerning Him are made.

HEAVEN—a word that expresses several distinct concepts in the Bible:

1. As used in a physical sense, heaven is the expanse over the earth (Gen. 1:8). The Tower of Babel reached upward to heaven (Gen. 11:4). God is the possessor of heaven (Gen. 14:19). Heaven is the location of the stars (Gen. 1:14; 26:4) as well as the source of dew (Gen. 27:28).

2. Heaven is also the dwelling place of God (Gen. 28:17; Rev. 12:7–8). It is the place of the New Jerusalem (Rev. 21:2, 10). Because of the work of Christ on the Cross, the kingdom of heaven is, in part, present with believers on earth as they obey God's commands (John 14:2, 23).

3. The word heaven is also used as a substitute for the name of God (Luke 15:18, 21; John 3:27). The kingdom of God and the kingdom of heaven are often spoken of interchangeably (Matt. 4:17; Mark 1:15).

At the end of time a new heaven will be created to surround the new earth. This new heaven will be the place of God's perfect presence (Is. 65:17; 66:22; Rev. 21:1). Then there will be a literal fulfillment of heaven on earth.

4. The heavenly city is a place prepared and built by God for those who are faithful to Him (John 14:1–2; Heb. 11:10, 16). Known as the heavenly Jerusalem (Heb. 12:22), this is the city that is to come (Heb. 13:14). These references in Hebrews find their fulfillment in Revelation 21—22. The New Jerusalem is illuminated by the glory of God. It serves as the dwelling place of God among His redeemed forever.

HEAVEN. (1 Kin. 8:23) *shamayim* (shah-*my*-yeem); *Strong's* #8064: Sky, skies; heaven, heavens. The word *shamayim* is plural in form, because the Hebrews knew the great expanse above the earth (the heavens) to be immeasurably vast, and its stars to be uncountable (Jer. 33:22). In the heavens, the dwelling place of God is located. However, even such an expanse does not hold God in, for Solomon stated, "Behold, heaven and the heaven of heavens cannot contain You. How much less this temple which I have built!" (2 Chr. 6:18). Since God spoke "from heaven" (Ex. 20:22), and is "in heaven" (Eccl. 5:2), Jews naturally came to say "heaven" as a euphemism for "God." Thus, "the kingdom of heaven" in Matthew is called "the kingdom of God" in other Gospels. *Also* (Rev. 21:1) *oura-*

nos (oo-ran-*oss*); *Strong's* #3772: Compare "uranography," "uranometry," "Uranus." A word, often used in the plural, to denote the sky and the regions above the earth (Heb. 1:10; 2 Pet. 3:5, 10) and the abode of God (Matt. 5:34; Rom. 1:18), Christ (Luke 24:51; Acts 3:21), angels (Matt. 24:36; Mark 12:25), and resurrected saints (2 Cor. 5:1). By metonymy the word refers to God (Matt. 21:25; Luke 15:18) and to the inhabitants of heaven (Rev. 18:20).

HEAVENS, NEW—a term which, when used with *new earth*, refers to the perfected state of the created universe and the final dwelling place of the righteous. The phrase is found in Isaiah 66:22, 2 Peter 3:13, and in a slightly modified form in Revelation 21:1.

Rooted deep in Jewish thought was the dream of a new heaven and a new earth, a recreation of the universe that would occur following the day of the Lord (Is. 13:10–13; Joel 2:1–2, 30–31). The concept of a recreated universe is closely related to the biblical account of the Creation and the Fall (Gen. 1:1) and the sin of Adam and Eve in the Garden of Eden (Genesis 3). Because of their sin, "the creation was subjected to futility . . . [and] the bondage of corruption" (Rom. 8:19, 21). The need for a new heaven and a new earth arises from man's sin and God's judgment, not from some deficiency or inadequacy on God's part.

The apostle Paul referred to the Old Testament doctrine of the day of the Lord and applied it to the events that will occur at the Second Coming of Christ (2 Pet. 3:10, 13). When Christ returns, this present evil age, which has intruded itself in the wake of man's Fall, will give way to the age to come. The universe will be purified and cleansed by the power of God. This will be reminiscent of the purging of the earth in the days of Noah, but on a universal scale.

HEBREW—see ch. 55, §3.7.e., 4., 4.2., 4.3., 6.2.

HEBREWS—see ch. 55, §3.6.b.

HEIRS. (Heb. 11:9) *sunkleronomos* (soong-klay-ron-*om*-oss); *Strong's* #4789: From *sun*, "with," *klero*, "a lot," and *nemomai*, "to possess." The word denotes a joint participant, co-heir, fellow heir, one who receives a lot with another.

HELL—the place of eternal punishment for the unrighteous. The NKJV and KJV use this word to translate *sheol* and *hades*, the Old and New Testament words, respectively, for the abode of the dead.

Hell as a place of punishment translates *Gehenna*, the Greek form of the Hebrew word that means "the vale of Hinnom"—a valley just south of Jerusalem. In this valley the Canaanites worshiped Baal and the fire-god Molech by sacrificing their children in a fire that burned continuously. Even Ahaz and Manasseh, kings of Judah, were guilty of this terrible, idolatrous practice (2 Chr. 28:3; 33:6).

The prophet Jeremiah predicted that God would visit such destruction upon Jerusalem that this valley would be known as the "Valley of Slaughter" (Jer. 7:31–34; 19:2, 6). In his religious reforms, King Josiah put an end to this worship. He defiled the valley in order to make it unfit even for pagan worship (2 Kin. 23:10).

In the time of Jesus the Valley of Hinnom was used as the garbage dump of Jerusalem. Into it were thrown all the filth and garbage of the city, including the dead bodies of animals and executed criminals. To consume all this, fires burned constantly. Maggots worked in the filth. When the wind blew from that direction over the city, its awfulness was quite evident. At night wild dogs howled and gnashed their teeth as they fought over the garbage.

Jesus used this awful scene as a symbol of hell. In effect he said, "Do you want to know what hell is like? Look at the valley of Gehenna." So hell may be described as God's "cosmic garbage dump." All that refuse to be made fit for heaven will be turned away into hell.

The word *Gehenna* occurs twelve times in the New Testament. Each time it is translated as "hell." With the exception of James 3:6, it is used only by Jesus (Matt. 5:22, 29–30; 10:28; 23:15, 33; Mark 9:43, 45, 47; Luke 12:5). In Matthew 5:22, 18:9; and Mark 9:47, it is used with "fire" as "hell fire." So the word hell *(Gehenna)* as a place of punishment is used in the New Testament by Him who is the essence of infinite love.

In Mark 9:46 and 48, hell is described as a place where "their worm does not die and the fire is not quenched." Repeatedly Jesus spoke of outer darkness and a furnace of fire, where there will be wailing, weeping, and gnashing of teeth (Matt. 8:12; 13:42, 50; 22:13; 24:51; 25:30; Luke 13:28). Obviously this picture is drawn from the valley of Gehenna.

The Book of Revelation describes hell as "a lake of fire burning with brimstone" (Rev. 19:20; 20:10, 14–15; 21:8). Into hell will be thrown the beast and the false prophet (Rev. 19:20). At the end of the age the devil himself will be thrown into it, along with death and hades and all whose names are not in the Book of Life. "And they will be tormented day and night forever and ever" (Rev. 20:10).

Because of the symbolic nature of the language, some people question whether hell consists of actual fire. Such reasoning should bring no comfort to the lost. The reality is greater than the symbol. The Bible exhausts human language in describing heaven and hell. The former is more glorious, and the latter more terrible, than language can express.

HELPER—a word used by Jesus to describe the *Holy Spirit (John 14:16, 26; 15:26; 16:7). The Greek word has been translated into English by various versions of the Bible as comforter, advocate, and counselor, as well as helper. This Greek word is so filled with meaning that it is difficult to translate it with one English word. The basic meaning, however, is "helper."

The Holy Spirit is the one called to our side by Jesus to help us, to stand by us, to strengthen us and give assistance when needed. The Holy Spirit is the "other" helper (John 14:16). Just as Jesus was the Great Helper while on earth, the Holy Spirit is now our Helper, if we desire His help.

HELPER. (Heb. 15:26) *parakletos* (par-*ak*-lay-toss); *Strong's #3875:* From *para*, "beside," and *kaleo*, "to call," hence, called to one's side. The word signifies an intercessor, comforter, helper, advocate, counselor. In nonbiblical literature *parakletos* had the technical meaning of an attorney who appears in court in another's behalf. The Holy Spirit leads believers to a greater apprehension of gospel truths. In addition to general help and guidance, He gives the strength to endure the hostility of the world system. *Also* (John 13:6) *boethos* (bah-ay-*thoss*); *Strong's #998:* From *boe*, "a cry for help," and *theo*, "to run." *Boethos* is one who comes running when we cry for help. The word describes the Lord as poised and ready to rush to the relief of His oppressed children when they shout for His assistance.

HERESIES. (Heb. 2:1) *hairesis* (hahee-res-is); *Strong's #139:* Compare "heresy" and "heretical." From *haireomai*, "to choose." The word originally denoted making a choice or having an option. Progressing to having a preference because of an opinion or a sentiment, it easily slipped into a mode of disunity, choosing sides, having diversity of belief, creating dissension, and substituting self-willed opinions for submission to the truth. The dominant use in the New Testament is to signify sects, people professing opinions independent of the truth.

HEROD THE GREAT—see ch. 55, §6., 6.1.

HEZEKIAH—see ch. 55, §3.7.b.

HIGH PLACES. (Ezek. 6:3) *bamah* (bah-*mah*); *Strong's* #1116: A height; high place, mountain, hilltop, crest, ridge, summit; a shrine upon a lofty site. Geographically speaking, *bamah* refers to any hilltop or elevated place. The high places were often those hilltops upon which idolaters offered sacrifices to pagan gods. These places became a snare for the Israelites, who mixed the worship of Yahweh with the worship of idols. In Numbers 33:52, the Lord commands: "Demolish all their high places." He is not a God who endorses mixture.

HITTITES—see ch. 55, §2.1., 3.3., 3.4.a.

HOLINESS. (1 Thess. 3:13) *hagiosune* (hag-ee-ah-*soo*-nay); *Strong's* #42: The process, quality, and condition of a holy disposition and the quality of holiness in personal conduct. It is the principle that separates the believer from the world. *Hagiosune* consecrates us to God's service both in soul and in body, finding fulfillment in moral dedication and a life committed to purity. It causes every component of our character to stand God's inspection and meet His approval.

HOLY—moral and ethical wholeness or perfection; freedom from moral evil. Holiness is one of the essential elements of God's nature required of His people. Holiness may also be rendered "sanctification" or "godliness." The word holy denotes that which is "sanctified" or "set apart" for divine service; that which has been or is being brought to God's divine state of completion and wholeness—different from the broken or sheltered condition of fallen man.

God instructed Moses to "consecrate Aaron and his sons" (Ex. 29:9) to the priesthood. The children of Israel were admonished to "remember the Sabbath day, to keep it holy" (Ex. 20:8). The "Most Holy Place" (or "Holiest of All") was the most sacred place in the desert tabernacle and in the temple at Jerusalem (Ex. 26:33; Heb. 9:19). Elisha was called a "holy man of God" (2 Kin. 4:9). Herod feared John the Baptist, "knowing that he was a just and holy man" (Mark 6:20).

While holy is sometimes used in a ceremonial sense, the main use is to describe God's righteous nature or the ethical righteousness demanded of His followers (Is. 1:10–14; Matt. 12:7). Originating in God's nature, holiness is a unique quality of His character. The Bible emphasizes this divine attribute. "Who is like You, O LORD?" (Ex. 15:11). "No one is holy like the LORD" (1 Sam. 2:2). "Who shall not fear You, O Lord. . . . For You alone are holy" (Rev. 15:4). God's high expectations of His people flow out of His own holy nature: "You shall be to me a kingdom of priests and a holy nation" (Ex. 19:6); "consecrate yourselves therefore, and be holy, for I am the LORD your God" (Lev. 20:7).

The theme of sanctification, or growing into God's likeness and being consecrated for His use, is prominent throughout the Bible. Like Jesus, the apostles taught that sanctification, or true holiness, expressed itself in patient and loving service while awaiting the Lord's return (1 Pet. 1:15). Paul's prayer "that He may establish your hearts blameless in holiness" is of the same genre (1 Thess. 3:12–13).

HOLY. (Lev. 19:2) *qadosh* (kah-*dosh*); *Strong's* #6918: Set apart, dedicated to sacred purposes; holy, sacred, clean, morally or ceremonially pure. The verb *qadash* means "to set apart something or someone for holy purposes." Holiness is separation from everything profane and defiling; and at the same time, it is dedication to everything holy and pure. People or even objects, such as anointing oil or vessels, may be considered holy to the Lord (Ex. 30:25; Jer. 2:3; Zech. 14:20, 21). Leviticus stresses "holy" and "holiness" most thoroughly. Leviticus 10:10 shows that God desired that the priests be able to distinguish "holy" and "unholy" and teach Israel to do likewise. God is entirely holy in His nature, motives, thoughts, words, and deeds so that He is called *Qadosh*, "the Holy One" or *Qedosh Yisrael*, "the Holy One of Israel." Thus 19:2 can say, "You shall be *qedoshim* [holy ones] for I . . . am holy." *Also* (Acts 7:33) *hagios* (hag-ee-oss); *Strong's* #40: Compare "Hagiographa" and "hagiography." Sacred, pure, blameless, consecrated, separated, properly revered, worthy of veneration, Godlikeness, God's innermost nature, set apart for God, reserved for God and His service. Since nothing that is polluted could be *hagios*, purity becomes a big part of *hagios*. A holy God calls for a holy people.

HOLY SPIRIT—the third person of the Trinity, who exercises the power of the Father and the Son in creation and redemption. Because the Holy Spirit is the source of the power by which believers come to Christ and see with new eyes of faith, He is closer than any word short of "within us" can describe, yet He focuses on another than Himself. Like the eyes of the body through which we see physical things, He is seldom in focus to be seen directly because He rather shows us Christ—the One through whom all life is to be seen in its new light.

The Holy Spirit appears in the Gospel of John as the power by which Christians are brought to faith and helped to understand their walk with God. He brings a person to new birth: "That which is born of the flesh is flesh, and that which is born of the Spirit is spirit" (John 3:6); "It is the Spirit who gives life" (John 6:63). The Holy Spirit is the Paraclete, or Helper, whom Jesus promised to the disciples after His ascension. The triune family of Father, Son, and Holy Spirit are unified in ministering to believers (John 14:16, 26). It is through the Helper that Father and Son abide with the disciples (John 15:26).

This unified ministry of the Trinity is also seen as the Spirit brings the world under conviction of sin, righteousness, and judgment. He guides believers into all truth with what He hears from the Father and the Son (John 15:26). It is a remarkable fact that each of the persons of the Godhead serves the others as all defer to one another: The Son says what He hears from the Father (John 12:49–50); the Father witnesses to and glorifies the Son (John 8:16–18, 50, 54); the Father and Son honor the Holy Spirit by commissioning Him to speak in Their name (John 14:16, 26); the Holy Spirit honors the Father and Son by helping the community of believers.

Like Father and Son, the Holy Spirit is at the disposal of the other persons of the Godhead, and all three are one in graciously being at the disposal of the redeemed family of believers. The Holy Spirit's attitude and ministry are marked by generosity. His chief function is to illumine Jesus' teaching, to glorify His Person, and to work in the life of the individual believer and the church.

This quality of generosity is prominent in the Gospels of Matthew, Mark, and Luke, where the Holy Spirit prepares the way for the births of John the Baptist and Jesus the Son (Matt. 1:20; Luke 1:15, 35, 41). At the baptism of Jesus, the Spirit of God is manifest in the form of a dove. This completes the presence of the Godhead at the inauguration of the Son's ministry (Matt. 3:16–17; Mark 1:9–11; Luke 3:21–22; John 1:33). Jesus is also filled with the Holy Spirit as He is led into the wilderness to be tempted (Luke 4:1). He claims to be anointed by the Spirit of the Lord in fulfillment of Old Testament prophecy (Is. 61:1; Luke 4:18–19).

During His ministry, Jesus refers to the Spirit of God (Matt. 12:28–29; Luke 11:20) as the power by which He is casting out demons, thereby invading the stronghold of Beelzebub and freeing those held captive. Accordingly, the Spirit works with the Father and Son in realizing the redeeming power of the kingdom of God. God's kingdom is not only the reign of the Son but also the reign of the Spirit, as all share in the reign of the Father.

The person and ministry of the Holy Spirit in the Gospels is confirmed by His work in the early church. The baptism with the Holy Spirit (Acts 1:5) is the pouring out of the Spirit's power in missions and evangelism (Acts 1:8). This prophecy of Jesus (and of Joel 2:28–32) begins on Pentecost (Acts 2:1–18). Many of those who hear of the finished work of God in Jesus' death and resurrection (Acts 2:32–38) repent of their sins. With this act of repentance, they are open to receive the gift of the Holy Spirit (Acts 2:38), becoming witnesses of God's grace through the Holy Spirit.

Paul's teaching about the Holy Spirit harmonizes with the accounts of the Spirit's activity in the Gospels and Acts. According to Paul, it is by the Holy Spirit that one confesses that Jesus is Lord (1 Cor. 12:3). Through the same Spirit varieties of gifts are given to the body of Christ to ensure its richness and unity (1 Cor. 12:4–27). The Holy Spirit is the way to Jesus Christ the Son (Rom. 8:11) and to the Father (Rom. 8:14–15). He is the Person who bears witness to us that we are children of God (8:16–17). He "makes intercession for us with groanings which cannot be uttered" (Rom. 8:26–27).

The Holy Spirit also reveals to Christians the deep things of God (1 Cor. 2:10–12) and the mystery of Christ (Eph. 3:3–5). The Holy Spirit acts with God and Christ as the pledge or guarantee by which believers are sealed for the day of salvation (2 Cor. 1:21–22), and by which they walk and live (Rom. 8:3–6) and abound in hope with power (Rom. 15:13). Against the lust and enmity of the flesh Paul contrasts the fruit of the Spirit: "Love joy, peace, longsuffering, kindness, goodness, faithfulness, gentleness, self-control" (Gal. 5:22–23).

Since the Holy Spirit is the present avenue on earth of expressed power of the Godhead, it is imperative that one not grieve the Spirit, since no further appeal to the Father and the Son on the day of redemption is available (Eph. 4:30). Jesus made this clear in His dispute with the religious authorities, who attributed His ministry to Satan rather than the Spirit and committed the unforgivable sin (Matt. 12:22–32, John 8:37–59).

In Paul's letters Christian liberty stems from the work of the Holy Spirit: "Where the Spirit of the Lord is, there is liberty" (2 Cor. 3:17). This is a process of "beholding as in a mirror the glory of the Lord," and "being transformed into the same image from glory to glory, just as by the Spirit of the Lord" (2 Cor. 3:18). The personal work of the Holy Spirit is accordingly one with that of the Father and the Son, so Paul can relate the grace, love, and communion of the Godhead in a trinitarian benediction: "The grace of the Lord Jesus Christ and the love of God, and the communion of the Holy Spirit be with you all. Amen" (2 Cor. 13:14).

Among the other New Testament writings the Spirit's ministry is evident in the profound teaching of Hebrews 9:14, which shows the relationship of God, Christ, and the eternal Spirit. The Holy Spirit's work in the Old Testament in preparation for the coming of Christ is explained in this and other passages in Hebrews (3:7; 9:8; 10:15–17).

This leads us to consider the working of the Spirit in the Old Testament in light of His ministry in the New Testament. The Spirit is the energy of God in creation (Gen. 1:2; Job 26:13; Is. 32:15). God endows man with personal life by breathing into his nostrils the breath of life (Gen. 2:7). The Spirit strives with fallen man (Gen. 6:3), and comes upon certain judges and warriors with charismatic power (Joshua, Num. 27:18; Othniel, Judg. 3:10; Gideon, Judg. 6:34; Samson, Judg. 13:25; 14:6). However, the Spirit departs from Saul because of his disobedience (1 Sam. 16:14).

In the long span of Old Testament prophecy the Spirit plays a prominent role. David declared, "The Spirit of the Lord spoke by me, and His word was on my tongue" (2 Sam. 23:2). Ezekiel claimed that "the Spirit entered me when He spoke to me" (Ezek. 2:2). The Spirit also inspired holiness in the Old Testament believer (Ps. 143:10). It also promised to give a new heart to God's people: "I will put My Spirit within you, and cause you to walk in My statutes" (Ezek. 36:27).

This anticipates the crucial work of the Spirit in the ministry of the Messiah. The prophecy of Isaiah 11:15 is a trinitarian preview of the working of the Father, the Spirit, and the Son, who is the branch of Jesse. Looking forward to the ministry of Jesus Christ, the Holy Spirit inspired Isaiah to prophesy: "The Spirit of the Lord shall rest upon Him" (Is. 11:2). The Holy Spirit inspired Jesus with wisdom, understanding, counsel, might, knowledge, fear of the Lord, righteousness, and faithfulness. Thus we come full cycle to the New Testament, where Jesus claims the fulfillment of this prophecy in Himself (Is. 61:12; Luke 4:18–19).

Isaiah 42:1–9 summarized the redeeming work of the Father, Son, and Spirit in the salvation of the lost, as God spoke through the prophet: "Behold! My Servant whom I uphold, My Elect One in whom My soul delights! I have put My Spirit upon Him; He will bring forth justice to the Gentiles" (Is. 42:1). No clearer reflection of the intimate interworking of the Godhead and the Spirit's powerful role can be found in the Old Testament than in this prophecy. It ties God's grace in Old and New together in remarkable harmony.

HOLY SPIRIT GIFTS AND POWER. Without a doubt, the Pentecostal revival of the early 1900s and the charismatic renewal, which had its beginning in the late 1950s, together constitute one of the most innovative and impactive spiritual renovations in history. But when we investigate this phenomenon we must ask: (1) Why has this happened? (2) What is this doing? and (3) How can spiritual integrity be maintained?

Why Has This Happened?

The first reason has been an evident need for renewal of mission and purpose throughout the church and among its individual members.

Second, in view of this need for renewal, there has been a definite movement on the part of sincere believers to recover the dynamic power of the Holy Spirit, which transformed and empowered the early Christians. Emerging from this movement has been an inbreaking of the Holy Spirit, accompanied by speaking in tongues, among believers in every major denomination, demonstrating that the baptism in the Holy Spirit is not a denomination or a movement but an experience that brings enduement of spiritual power for intensified service.

Third, this inbreaking of the Holy Spirit has linked both the mainline Protestant and the traditional Pentecostal movement to the worship practices of the first century through what has appropriately been referred to as the charismatic movement (derived from *charismata*, the Greek word used, for example, in 1 Cor. 12:4, 30 for the gifts of the Holy Spirit).

What Is This Doing?

Renewal then raises the question, What really happens when the gifts go to church? In attempting to answer, attention must be given to the scriptural foundation, the traditional context, and the contemporary witness.

The Scripture is being fulfilled. First the Bible unequivocally declares, "Be filled with the Spirit" (Eph. 5:18). An analysis of the Greek verb translated "be filled" shows that it is in the present tense, indicating that this blessing is one that we may experience and enjoy now. The fact that the verb is a command (imperative mood) does not leave the responsive disciple an option in the matter. Since the verb is in the passive voice, however, being filled with the Spirit clearly is not something the Christian achieves through his own efforts, but is something done for him and to which he submits. Hence, the Scriptures depict a theocentric view of the Holy Spirit's filling, in which the Higher reaches down to gather up the lower into ultimate communion. Clarity on this point dismisses the criticism or misunderstanding of some who seem to see this experience as something merely conjured up by human suggestion, proposition, or excitement.

The Person of the Holy Spirit is at work. Second, the Bible reveals that the Person of the Holy Spirit has been the primary agent in all of the ministry of the Word throughout the centuries. The Scripture states clearly that the triune Godhead operates coequally, coeternally, coexistently, as one unit. We also might view this unity of activity with an eye toward the special function of each member of the Trinity: the executive is the Father, the architect is the Son, and the contractor is the Holy Spirit.

The Scriptures show the Holy Spirit uniquely and distinctly at work in these roles: (1) He is the Author of the Old Testament (2 Sam. 23:2; Is. 59:21; Jer. 1:9; 2 Tim. 3:15–17; 2 Pet. 1:21) and the New Testament (John 13:25, 26; 1 Cor. 2:13; 1 Thess. 4:15; Rev. 1:10–11; 2:7). (2) He is the Old Testament Anointer. The Scriptures name no less than sixteen Old Testament leaders in Israel who received this anointing: Joseph (Gen. 41:38); Moses (Num. 11:17); Joshua (Num. 27:18); Othniel (Judg. 3:10); Gideon (Judg. 6:34); Jephthah (Judg. 11:29); Samson (Judg. 14:6, 19; 15:14–15); Saul (1 Sam. 10:10; 11:6); David (1 Sam. 16:13); Elijah (1 Kin. 8:12; 2 Kin. 2:16); Elisha (2 Kin. 2:15); Azariah (2 Chr. 15:1); Zechariah (2 Chr. 24:20); Ezekiel (Ezek. 2:2); Daniel (Dan. 4:9; 5:11; 6:3); and Micah (Mic. 3:8).

The Holy Spirit, as contractor, anointed the Old Testament prophets Isaiah and Joel to write—to prophesy of the day when He would be outpoured and when His gifts would be exercised in the church, throughout the whole church age (Joel 2:28–32; Acts 2:17–21). In Isaiah 28:11–12, God used Isaiah to tell Judah that He would teach them in a manner they did not like and that He would give them knowledge through the language of foreigners as a sign of their unbelief. Centuries later the apostle Paul expands the intent of this passage, referring it to the gift of speaking in tongues in the church as a manifestation or sign to unbelievers (1 Cor. 14:21, 22). This sign could be in languages either known or unknown to human beings (compare 1 Corinthians 14 with Acts 2:1–11; 10:45–46).

In all these respects, we see the Holy Spirit as one who operates in the church as a definite personality—a Person given as a gift to the church to assure that the continued ministry of the resurrected Christ is expressed and verified. The Holy Spirit, then, has all the characteristics of a person:

1. He possesses the attributes of mind (Rom. 8:27), will (1 Cor. 12:11), and feeling (Eph. 4:30).

2. He engages in such activities as revealing (2 Pet. 1:21), teaching (John 14:26), witnessing (Heb. 10:15), interceding (Rom. 8:26), speaking (Rev. 2:7), commanding (Acts 16:6–7), and testifying (John 15:26).

3. He has a relationship with human persons: He can be grieved (Eph. 4:30), lied to (Acts 5:3), and blasphemed (Matt. 12:31–32).

4. The Holy Spirit possesses the divine attributes of the Godhead: He is eternal (Heb. 9:14), omnipresent (Ps. 139:7–10), omnipotent (Luke 1:35), and omniscient (1 Cor. 2:10–11).

5. He is referred to by such names as the Spirit of God, the Spirit of Christ, the Comforter, the Holy Spirit, the Holy Spirit of promise, the Spirit of truth, the Spirit of grace, the Spirit of life, the Spirit of adoption, and the Spirit of holiness.

6. He is illustrated with such symbols as fire (Acts 2:1–2), wind (Acts 2:1–2), water (John 7:37–39), a seal (Eph. 1:13), oil (Acts 10:38), and a dove (John 1:32).

All this unfolds something of the vast realm or sphere of the operation of the Holy Spirit in the Old and New Testament and in the contemporary church.

Accounts in Acts are being rediscovered and applied. Third, the Book of Acts provides five accounts of people receiving the fullness or infilling or baptism in the Holy Spirit (Acts 2:4; 8:14–25; 9:17–20; 10:44–48; 19:1–7). In these accounts five factors are manifest: (1) There was an overwhelming inbreaking of God's presence experienced by all who were present. (2) There was an evident transformation in the lives and witness of the disciples who were filled. (3) That which was experienced became the impetus for the growth of the church, as "daily in the temple, and in every house, they did not cease teaching and preaching Jesus as the Christ" (Acts 5:42). (4) The immediate evidence in three of the five accounts was glossolalia: "For they heard them speak with tongues and magnify God" (Acts 10:46). (*Glossolalia* is a coined term derived from the Greek *glossa* ["tongue"] and *laleo* ["to speak"].) (5) The ultimate purpose of this experience was empowered witnessing (Acts 1:8) and a deeper dimension of Christian commitment for the achievement of happiness (Eph. 5:19), gratitude (Eph. 5:20), humility (Eph. 5:21), and fruitfulness (Gal. 5:22–23).

Together, the above facts demonstrate what the present Pentecostal/charismatic renewal is experiencing through the Holy Spirit at work in the church. The problem is that too frequently the elements of this renewal are misunderstood or misapplied for lack of a biblical understanding of "tongues" and the function of the gifts of the Spirit. Although there are varying theological and ethical viewpoints among some in the Neo-Pentecostal/charismatic movement, a common bond of unity in the Spirit-filled renewal is the practice of "speaking with tongues" in prayer and worship, together with an acceptance and welcoming of the operation of the Holy Spirit's gifts in their midst. Thus, to fully understand this phenomenon, it is necessary to see the Pentecostal/charismatic view as they have learned to implement the Book of Acts' manifestations of the Holy Spirit's power-workings, applying the controls taught in 1 Corinthians 12—14.

How Can Spiritual Integrity Be Maintained?

Establishing our perspective. First, the Pentecostal or charismatic sees the baptism or infilling of the Holy Spirit as an experience subsequent to Christian conversion: one that comes about through a process of yielding the complete person into the guidance and indwelling of the Holy Spirit. We agree that the Holy Spirit is operative in *every* believer and in the varied ministries of the church. Still every believer must answer the question of Acts 19:2, "Have you received the Holy Spirit since you believed?"

Two expressions should be qualified here:

1. It should be understood that by "baptism in the Holy Spirit" the traditional Pentecostal/charismatic does not refer to that baptism *of* the Holy Spirit accomplished at conversion, whereby the believer is placed *into* the body of Christ by faith in His redeeming work on the Cross (1 Cor. 12:13). Thus, nonbiblically oriented charismatic ever views a non-charismatic as "less saved" or less spiritual than himself. The baptism in or with the Holy Spirit (John 1:33; Acts 1:5) was and is directed by the Lord Jesus to be "received" (John 20:22; Acts 1:8) as a "gift" given following His ascension (John 7:39: Acts 2:38–39). However, should any prefer to dismiss this terminology, we contend that to experience the Holy Spirit's fullness in the spirit of unity is more important than to separate company or diminish our passion for His fullness over differences in theological wording or practice.

2. By "a process of yielding the complete person" the Pentecostal/charismatic does not mean either (a) a passivity of mind or (b) a self-hypnotic or trancelike state. Rather, this terminology refers to an assertive, prayerful, heartfelt quest for God. The *mind* is active, worshiping Jesus Christ, the Baptizer with the Holy Spirit (John 1:33). The *emotions* are warmed, as the love of God is poured forth into our hearts (Rom. 5:5). One's *physical* being participates, as worship is spoken and expressed, with upraised voice in prayer (Acts 4:24) or upraised hands of adoration (Ps. 63:1–5).

The twofold function of the gift of tongues. In regard to those who have "received," the Bible describes two basic functions of "tongues": it is for personal edification and for public exhortation.

In the experience of the baptism in or infilling of the Holy Spirit, "tongues" functions as a sign of the Holy Spirit's presence. Jesus prophesied it as a sign (Mark 16:17), Paul referred to it as a sign (1 Cor. 14:22), and Peter noted its uniformity as a sign-gift in confirming the validity of the Gentiles' experience in the Holy Spirit. (Compare Acts 10:44–46 with 11:16–17 and 15:7–9). Thus, speaking with tongues is a properly expected sign, affirming the Holy Spirit's abiding presence and assuring the believer of an invigorated living witness. It is not viewed as a *qualification for* fullness of the Holy Spirit, but as one *indication of* that fullness.

Tongues for personal edification. First, "speaking in tongues" is a private affair for self-edification (1 Cor. 14:2–4). Thus, glossolalia is practiced devotionally by the believer in his most intimate and intercessory moments of communication with God as he is moved upon by the Holy Spirit. This "devotional" application may also be practiced by corporate agreement, in group gatherings where no unbelievers or uninformed people are present (1 Cor. 14:23). In line with this understanding, the following reasons are propounded for speaking with tongues:

1. Speaking with tongues as the Holy Spirit gives utterance is the unique spiritual gift identified with the church of Jesus Christ. All other gifts, miracles, and spiritual manifestations were in evidence during Old Testament times, before the Day of Pentecost. This new phenomenon came into evidence and became uniquely identified with the church and was ordained by God for the church (1 Cor. 12:28; 14:21).

2. Speaking with tongues is a specific fulfillment of prophecies by Isaiah and Jesus. (Compare Is. 28:11 with 1 Cor. 14:21, and

Mark 16:17 with Acts 2:4; 10:46; 19:6; and 1 Cor. 14:5, 14–18, 39.)

3. Speaking with tongues is a proof of the resurrection and glorification of Jesus Christ (John 16:7; Acts 2:26).

4. Speaking with tongues is an evidence of the baptism in or infilling of the Holy Spirit (Acts 2:4; 10:45–46; 19:6).

5. Speaking with tongues is a spiritual gift for self-edification (1 Cor. 14:4; Jude 20).

6. Speaking with tongues is a spiritual gift for spiritual edification of the church when accompanied by interpretation (1 Cor. 14:5).

7. Speaking with tongues is a spiritual gift for communication with God in private worship (1 Cor. 14:15).

8. Speaking with tongues is a means by which the Holy Spirit intercedes through us in prayer (Rom. 8:26; 1 Cor. 14:14; Eph. 6:18).

9. Speaking with tongues is a spiritual means for rejoicing (1 Cor. 14:15; Eph. 5:18–19).

10. Paul's application of Isaiah's prophecy seems to indicate that speaking with tongues is also intended as a means of "rest" or "refreshing" (Is. 28:12; 1 Cor. 14:21).

11. Tongues follow as one confirmation of the Word of God when it is preached (Mark 16:17, 20; 1 Cor. 14:22).

Tongues for public exhortation. Turning to the second function of "tongues"—public exhortation—1 Corinthians 14 bases the gifts of the Spirit on the one sure foundation of love (1 Cor. 14:1). Public "tongues" also calls for integrity in practice as the key for the preservation of order in our fellowship and the worship services. Conceding that there have been those who have abused the gift as an occasion for fleshly pride, we must recognize that it can be a vital and valuable part of worship when placed in its proper setting for the edification of the body (1 Cor. 14:12–13).

The sincere Spirit-filled believer will not be preoccupied with this gift alone, for he sees it as only one of many gifts given for the "wholeness" of the church; therefore, he does not worship or meet with others just to speak in tongues for the mere sake of the practice itself. Such motivation would be immature, vain, and idolatrous. Rather, sincere believers gather to worship God and to be thoroughly equipped for every good work through the teaching of His Word (2 Tim. 3:16–17). Consequently, the scripturally sensitive believer recognizes the following New Testament direction regarding spiritual gifts:

1. Speaking in "tongues" only edifies public worship when it is interpreted; thus, the worshiper is to pray for the interpretation, and if it is withheld, he keeps silent, unless some-

one who functions in the gift of interpretation is known to be present (1 Cor. 14:5, 28).

2. The Spirit works only to edify; thus, whenever He is truly present all things are in order and devoid of embarrassment or uneasiness (1 Cor. 14:26, 40).

3. The "spirits of the prophets are subject to the prophets" (1 Cor. 14:32). That is, each truly Spirit-filled person *can* exercise self-control; thus, confusion can and should be avoided so that decency with unity may prevail (1 Cor. 14:40).

4. The basis of all gifts is love. *Love*, not the experience of a gift, is the qualifying factor for those who would exercise spiritual gifts. Thus, in the administration of spiritual authority in the local congregation, the Word demands that we "judge" (1 Cor. 14:29) to confirm that those who exercise gifts actually do "pursue love, and desire spiritual *gifts*" (1 Cor. 13:1–13; 14:1).

5. The Author and Dispenser of the gifts is the Holy Spirit, who divides them as He wills; thus, no gift becomes the exclusive possession of any believer for his personal edification and pride. Rather, the gifts are placed in the church to be exercised by the body for the mutual edification of the believers (1 Cor. 12:1–11) and as a means for expanded ministry.

6. The exercise of tongues is to be limited to sequences of two or three at the most (1 Cor. 14:27). While many hold this to be a rigid number, others understand it to be a guideline to keep the worship service in balance. In actuality, the Holy Spirit rarely moves beyond these limitations; however, on occasions, for special reasons to meet special needs, there may be more than one sequence of two or three appropriately spaced apart in a given service. The overarching guideline is, "Let all things be done decently and in order" (1 Cor. 14:40).

The Contemporary Witness

Moving beyond one's fullness in the Holy Spirit, it is important to understand the impact of the Spirit's full operation of gifts in and through the life and witness of the church.

The Spirit-filled experience is more than just "speaking in tongues." In reality it is coming into the fullness of the gifts and fruit of the Spirit as outlined in the New Testament (1 Cor. 12:7–11; Gal. 5:22–23). It also encompasses the broader scope of exercising God's gifts of spiritual enablement described in Romans 12:3–8 and Ephesians 4:7–12.

The Greek word *charisma* (singular) or *charismata* (plural) is used to designate spiritual gifts, and in the most technical sense mean "gifts of holy grace." In Ephesians 4:11–13 the words *dorea* and *doma* are also used to designate "gifts," referring to these gifts as "enablers" or "equippers" for personal service in the kingdom of God. Also, the word *pneumatika* employed in 1 Corinthians 12:1 is used to describe the gifts as "things belonging to the Spirit." The point is that each of these words gives a contemporary meaning to the supernatural work of the Spirit in our lives as He prepares us for kingdom service and growth in grace. For this to happen we are called upon to "earnestly desire the best gifts" (1 Cor. 12:31). Thus removing the cloak of passivity and ardently seeking to understand the operation of and appropriate response to *all* spiritual gifts is biblically proper.

In speaking of the gifts, however, exclusivism is never implied. The gifts are placed in the church as resources to be utilized at the point of need for ministry in the body. This means that not every believer will have the same gifts as every other believer. Rather, the Holy Spirit is the Author and Dispenser of the gifts to bring about integrity in worship and kingdom expression.

The gifts of the Godhead. For many, clarification of the distinct role each member of the Godhead plays in giving gifts to mankind is helpful. Foundationally, of course, our existence—human life—is given by the Father (Gen. 2:7; Heb. 12:9), who also gave His only begotten Son as the Redeemer for mankind (John 3:16). Redemptively, Jesus is the giver of eternal life (John 5:38–40; 10:27–28): He gave His life and shed His blood to gain that privilege (John 10:17–18; Eph. 5:25–27). Further, the Father and Son have jointly sent the Holy Spirit (Acts 2:17, 33) to advance the work of redemption through the church's ministry of worship, growth, and evangelism.

In sequence, then, we find Romans 12:3–8 describing gifts given by God as Father. They seem to characterize basic "motivations," that is, inherent tendencies that characterize each different person by reason of the Creator's unique workmanship in their initial gifting. While only seven categories are listed, observation indicates that few people are fully described by only one. More commonly a mix is found, with different traits of each gift present to some degree, while usually one will be the dominant trait of that person. It would be a mistake to suppose that an individual's learning to respond to the Creator's gifting of them in one or more of these categories fulfills the Bible's call to "earnestly desire the best gifts" (1 Cor. 12:31). These gifts of our place in God's created order are foundational.

Second, in 1 Corinthians 12:7–11 the nine gifts of the Holy Spirit are listed. Their purpose is specific—to "profit" the body of the church. ("Profit," Greek *sumphero*, means "to bring together, to benefit, to be advantageous," which is experienced as the body is strengthened in its life together and expanded through its ministry of evangelism.) These nine gifts are specifically available to *every* believer as the Holy Spirit distributes them (1 Cor. 12:11). They are not to be merely acknowledged in a passive way, but rather are to be actively welcomed and expected (1 Cor. 13:1; 14:1).

Third, the gifts which the Son of God has given are pivotal in assuring that the first two categories of gifts are applied in the body of the church. Ephesians 4:7–16 indicates the "office gifts" Christ has placed in the church, along with their purpose. The ministry of these leaders is to "equip" the body by assisting each person: (1) to perceive the *place* the Creator has made him to fill, by His creative workmanship in him, and the possibilities that salvation now opens to his realization of what he was made to be; and (2) to receive the *power* of the Holy Spirit, and begin to respond to His gifts, which are given to expand each believer's capabilities *beyond* the created order and toward the redemptive dimension of ministry, for edifying the church and evangelizing the world.

In this light, we examine these clearly designated categories of giftings: the Father's (Rom. 12:6–8), the Son's (Eph. 4:11), and the Holy Spirit's (1 Cor. 12:8–10). While the study expands beyond those listings and beyond the above outlined structure of the gifts of the Godhead, this general outline will help in two ways. First, it assists us by noting the distinct interest and work of each member of the Trinity in providing for our unique purpose and fulfillment. Second, it prevents us from confusing our foundational motivation in life and service for God with our purposeful quest for and openness to His Holy Spirit's full resources and power for service and ministry.

Romans 12:3–8: Gifts of the Father (Basic Life Purpose and Motivation)

1. PROPHECY

a. To speak with forthrightness and insight, especially when enabled by the Spirit of God (Joel 2:28).

b. To demonstrate moral boldness and uncompromising commitment to worthy values.

c. To influence others in one's arena of influence with a positive spirit of social or spiritual righteousness.

NOTE: Because all three categories of gifts involve some expression of "prophecy," it is helpful to differentiate. In this category (Romans 12) the focus is *general,* characterized by that level of the prophetic gift which would belong to *every* believer—"all flesh." The Holy Spirit's "gift of prophecy" (1 Corinthians 12) refers to supernatural prompting, so much so that tongues with interpretation is equated with its operation (1 Cor. 14:5). The office-gift of the prophet, which Christ gives to His church through individual ministries, is yet another expression of prophecy: those holding this office must meet *both* the Old Testament requirements of a prophet's accuracy in his message, and the New Testament standards of life and character required of spiritual leadership.

2. MINISTRY
a. To minister and render loving, general service to meet the needs of others.
b. Illustrated in the work and office of the deacon (Matt. 20:26).

3. TEACHING
a. The supernatural ability to explain and apply the truths received from God for the church.
b. Presupposes study and the Spirit's illumination providing the ability to make divine truth clear to the people of God.
c. Considered distinct from the work of the prophet who speaks as the direct mouthpiece of God.

4. EXHORTATION
a. Literally means to call aside for the purpose of making an appeal.
b. In a broader sense it means to entreat, comfort, or instruct (Acts 4:36; Heb. 10:25).

5. GIVING
a. The essential meaning is to give out of a spirit of generosity.
b. In a more technical sense it refers to those with resources aiding those without such resources (2 Cor. 8:2; 9:11–13).
c. This gift is to be exercised without outward show or pride and with liberality (2 Cor. 1:12; 8:2; 9:11–13).

6. LEADERSHIP
a. Refers to the one "standing in front."
b. Involves the exercise of the Holy Spirit in modeling, superintending, and developing the body of Christ.
c. Leadership is to be exercised with diligence.

7. MERCY
a. To feel sympathy with the misery of another.
b. To relate to others in empathy, respect, and honesty.

c. To be effective, this gift is to be exercised with kindness and cheerfulness—not as a matter of duty.

1 Corinthians 12:8–10, 28: Gifts of the Holy Spirit

1. WORD OF WISDOM
a. Supernatural perspective to ascertain the divine means for accomplishing God's will in given situations.
b. Divinely given power to appropriate spiritual intuition in problem-solving.
c. Sense of divine direction.
d. Being led by the Holy Spirit to act appropriately in a given set of circumstances.
e. Knowledge rightly applied: wisdom works interactively with knowledge and discernment.

2. WORD OF KNOWLEDGE
a. Supernatural revelation of the divine will and plan.
b. Supernatural insight or understanding of circumstances or a body of facts by revelation: that is, without assistance of any human resource but solely by divine aid.
c. Implies a deeper and more advanced understanding of the communicated acts of God.
d. Involves moral wisdom for right living and relationships.
e. Requires objective understanding concerning divine things in human duties.
f. May also refer to knowledge of God or of the things that belong to God, as related in the gospel.

3. FAITH
a. Supernatural ability to believe God without doubt.
b. Supernatural ability to combat unbelief.
c. Supernatural ability to meet adverse circumstances with trust in God's messages and words.
d. Inner conviction impelled by an urgent and higher calling.

4. GIFTS OF HEALINGS
a. Refers to supernatural healing without human aid.
b. May include divinely assisted application of human instrumentation and medical means of treatment.
c. Does not discount the use of God's creative gifts.

5. WORKING OF MIRACLES
a. Supernatural power to intervene and counteract earthly and evil forces.
b. Literally means a display of power giving the ability to go beyond the natural.
c. Operates closely with the gifts of faith and healings to bring authority over sin,

Satan, sickness, and the binding forces of this age.

6. PROPHECY

a. Divinely inspired and anointed utterance.

b. Supernatural proclamation in a known language.

c. Manifestation of the Spirit of God—not of intellect (1 Cor. 12:7).

d. May be possessed and operated by all who have the infilling of the Holy Spirit (1 Cor. 14:31).

e. Intellect, faith, and will are operative in this gift, but its exercise is not intellectually based. It is calling forth words from the Spirit of God.

7. DISCERNING OF SPIRITS

a. Supernatural power to detect the realm of the spirits and their activities.

b. Implies the power of spiritual insight—supernatural revelation of plans and purposes of the Enemy and his forces.

8. DIFFERENT KINDS OF TONGUES

a. Supernatural utterance in languages not known to the speaker: these languages may be existent in the world, revived from some past culture, or "unknown" in the sense that they are a means of communication inspired by the Holy Spirit (Is. 28:11; Mark 16:17; Acts 2:4; 10:44–48; 19:1–7; 1 Cor. 12:10, 28–31; 13:1–3; 14:2, 4–22, 26–32).

b. Serve as an evidence and sign of the indwelling and working of the Holy Spirit.

9. INTERPRETATION OF TONGUES

a. Supernatural power to reveal the meaning of tongues.

b. Functions not as an operation of the mind of man but as the mind of the Spirit.

c. Does not serve as a translation (interpreter never understands the tongue he is interpreting), but rather is a declaration of meaning.

d. Is exercised as a miraculous and supernatural phenomenon as are the gift of speaking in tongues and the gift of prophecy.

Ephesians 4:11 (Also 1 Cor. 12:28): Gifts of the Son (To Facilitate and Equip the Body of the Church)

1. APOSTLES

a. In apostolic days referred to a select group chosen to carry out directly the ministry of Christ; included the assigned task given to a few to complete the sacred canon of the Holy Scriptures.

b. Implies the exercise of a distinct representative role of broader leadership given by Christ.

c. Functions as a messenger or spokesman of God.

d. In contemporary times refers to those who have the spirit of apostleship in remarkably extending the work of the church, opening fields to the gospel, and overseeing larger sections of the body of Jesus Christ.

2. PROPHET

a. A spiritually mature spokesman/proclaimer with a special, divinely focused message to the church or the world.

b. A person uniquely gifted at times with insight into future events.

3. EVANGELIST

a. Refers primarily to a special gift of preaching or witnessing in a way that brings unbelievers into the experience of salvation.

b. Functionally, the gift of evangelist operates for the establishment of new works, while pastors and teachers follow up to organize and sustain.

c. Essentially, the gift of evangelist operates to establish converts and to gather them spiritually and literally into the body of Christ.

4. PASTOR/TEACHER

a. The word "pastor" comes from a root meaning "to protect," from which we get the word "shepherd."

b. Implies the function of a shepherd/leader to nurture, teach, and care for the spiritual needs of the body.

5. MISSIONARY (some see "apostle" or "evangelist" in this light)

a. Implies the unfolding of a plan for making the gospel known to all the world (Rom. 1:16).

b. Illustrates an attitude of humility necessary for receiving a call to remote areas and unknown situations (Is. 6:1–13).

c. Connotes an inner compulsion to lead the whole world to an understanding of Jesus Christ (2 Cor. 5:14–20).

Special Graces

1. HOSPITALITY

a. Literally means to love, to do, or to do with pleasure.

b. Illustrates Peter's notion of one of the two categories of gifts: (1) teaching, and (2) practical service (1 Pet. 4:10–11).

c. Was utilized in caring for believers and workers who visited to worship, work, and become involved in the body of Christ.

d. Illustrated in the teaching of Jesus concerning judgment (Matt. 25:35, 40).

2. CELIBACY (Matt. 19:10; 1 Cor. 7:7–9, 27; 1 Tim. 4:3; Rev. 14:4).

a. The Bible considers marriage to be honorable, ordained of God, and a need for every person.

b. Implies a special gift of celibacy, which frees the individual from the duties, pressures, and preoccupations of family life, allowing undivided attention to the Lord's work.

3. MARTYRDOM (1 Pet. 4:12–13)

    a. Illustrated in the spirit of Stephen (Acts 7:59–60).

    b. Fulfilled in the attitude of Paul (2 Tim. 4:6–8). P.W.

HOLY SPIRIT, SIN AGAINST—a sin that is often referred to as the "unpardonable sin" because, in the words of Jesus, "He who blasphemes [speaks evil] against the Holy Spirit never has forgiveness, but is subject to eternal condemnation" (Mark 3:29).

The context of Jesus' words about the sin against the Holy Spirit provides a clue to its nature. When a demon-possessed man came to Jesus, He was healed. The multitudes were amazed. But the scribes and Pharisees said He was healing through Satan's power (Matt. 12:24). Jesus had cast out the demons by the power of the Holy Spirit; His enemies claimed He cast them out by the power of the devil.

Such slander of the Holy Spirit, Jesus implied, reveals a spiritual blindness, a warping and perversion of the moral nature, that puts one beyond hope of repentance, faith, and forgiveness. Those who call the Holy Spirit Satan reveal a spiritual cancer so advanced that they are beyond any hope of healing and forgiveness.

HONOR. (Ps. 8:5) *hadar* (hah-*dar*); *Strong's* #1926: Splendor, honor, glory, adornment, magnificence, beauty. This noun comes from the verb *hadar*, "to honor, to glorify, to make splendid." *Hadar* speaks of the splendor that belongs to God, to His creation, to His kingdom, and to man made in God's image. The biblical view of man is higher and more worth-affirming than any of the alternate views; in this reference God has actually crowned man with splendor in spite of his smallness relative to the vast heavens! Another well-known use of *hadar* is in the phrase "the beauty of holiness" (96:9; 110:3). The splendor of holiness is a greater beauty than even the glory of nature.

HOPE—confident expectancy. In the Bible, the word hope stands for both the act of hoping (Rom. 4:18; 1 Cor. 9:10) and the thing hoped for (Col. 1:5; 1 Pet. 1:3). Hope does not arise from the individual's desires or wishes but from God, who is Himself the believer's hope: "My hope is in You" (Ps. 39:7). Genuine hope is not wishful thinking, but a firm assurance about things that are unseen and still in the future (Rom. 8:24–25; Heb. 11:1, 7).

Hope distinguishes the believer from the unbeliever, who has no hope (Eph. 2:12; 1 Thess. 4:13). Indeed, a believer is one in whom hope resides (1 Pet. 3:15; 1 John 3:3). In contrast to Old Testament hope, the believer's hope is superior (Heb. 7:19).

Christian hope comes from God (Rom. 15:13) and especially His calling (Eph. 1:18; 4:4), His grace (2 Thess. 2:16), His Word (Rom. 15:4), and His gospel (Col. 1:23). Hope is directed toward God (Acts 24:15; 1 Pet. 1:21) and Christ (1 Thess. 1:3; 1 Tim. 1:1). Its appropriate objects are eternal life (Titus 1:2; 3:7), salvation (1 Thess. 5:8), righteousness (Gal. 5:5), the glory of God (Rom. 5:2; Col. 1:27), the appearing of Christ (Titus 2:13), and the resurrection from the dead (Acts 23:6; 26:6–7).

HOPE. (Hos. 2:15) *tiqvah* (teek-*vah*); *Strong's* #8615: Hope; expectation; something yearned for and anticipated eagerly; something for which one waits. *Tiqvah* comes from the verb *qavah*, meaning "to wait for" or "to look hopefully" in a particular direction. Its original meaning was "to stretch like a rope." *Tiqvah* occurs thirty-three times. In Joshua 2:18, 21, it is translated "line" or "cord"; Rahab was instructed to tie a scarlet *tiqvah* (cord or rope) in her window as her hope for rescue. Yahweh Himself is the hope of the godly (Ps. 71:5). Here God's blessing on His land will transform the Valley of Achor ("trouble") into the "door of hope." *Also* (1 Thess. 1:3) *elpis* (el-*peece*); *Strong's #1680:* Hope, not in the sense of an optimistic outlook or wishful thinking without any foundation, but in the sense of confident expectation based on solid certainty. Biblical hope rests on God's promises, particularly those pertaining to Christ's return. So certain is the future of the redeemed that the New Testament sometimes speaks of future events in the past tense, as though they were already accomplished. Hope is never inferior to faith, but is an extension of faith. Faith is the present possession of grace; hope is confidence in grace's future accomplishment.

HORITES—see ch. 55, §3.5.

HORN. (Ezek. 29:21) *qeren* (keh-ren); *Strong's* #7161: A horn of an animal; a flask or cornet; a symbol of strength, power, and victory. This noun occurs more than seventy-five times. Horned animals, such as oxen, goats, and rams, are symbols of strength. Thus Hebrew speakers refer to a person's horn's being exalted (Ps. 89:24; 112:9; 148:14), or contrarily, picture defeat as the breaking of the horn (Lam. 2:3). The "horns of the altar" (Lev. 4:7; 9:9; Ps. 118:27) are symbolic of the powerful presence of God. The root from which *qeren* comes is *qaran*, "to have horns," "to shine." In Exodus 34:29–30, 35, Moses' face shone, speaking of the projecting rays of glory that streamed from Moses' face.

HOSPITALITY—the practice of entertaining strangers graciously. Hospitality was considered important in Bible times. In the Old Testament, Abraham was the host to angels unaware; he invited strangers into his house, washed their feet, prepared fresh meat, had Sarah bake bread, and later accompanied them as they left (Gen. 18:1–15). Even today a traditional greeting to the guests among the Bedouin people of the Middle East is "You are among your family."

Hospitality was specifically commanded by God (Lev. 19:33–34; Luke 14:13–14; Rom. 12:13). It was to be characteristic of all believers (1 Pet. 4:9), especially bishops (Titus 1:78; 1 Tim. 3:2). Jesus emphasized the importance of hospitality by answering the question of who should inherit the kingdom: "I was a stranger and you took Me in" (Matt. 25:35).

Several Old Testament personalities set a good example for all believers in the practice of hospitality. These included Abraham (Gen. 18:1–8); David (2 Sam. 6:19); the Shunammite woman (2 Kin. 4:8–10); Nehemiah (Neh. 5:17–18); and Job (Job 31:17–20).

Psalm 23 concludes with a portrait of a host who prepares a table for the weary, anoints the head of the guest with oil, and shows every kindness so that the guest's cup runs over. The psalmist sees the Lord Himself as Host; His hospitality exceeds all others.

The New Testament also gives examples of gracious hospitality: Mary (Matt. 26:6–13); Martha (Luke 10:38); the early Christians (Acts 2:45–46); Lydia (Acts 16:14–15); and Priscilla and Aquila (Acts 18:26). The Greek word translated as hospitality in the New Testament literally means "love of strangers."

HOST OF HEAVEN—heavenly beings created by God and associated with Him in His rule over the world, or aligned against His rule as fallen angelic beings marshalled in opposition to His will on earth (Ps. 82:1–8).

As Creator, God has brought other families than man into being, and has implanted His divine image in them. The families of earth bear this image (Ps. 19:1–6; Rom. 1:19–20), as does the host of heaven (Is. 45:12). At the angel's announcement to the shepherds of the birth of Jesus, a multitude of the heavenly host praised God (Luke 2:13). They served as a great choir of created heavenly beings who glorified their Creator and participated in the background of the new age of salvation.

God is also called "the Lord of hosts" (Is. 1:9; 10:23; Rom. 9:29, RSV). The host of heaven consists of angelic beings and celestial bodies whom God has created and whose principal role, like ours, is to serve and glorify Him (1 Kin. 22:19; Ps. 103:19–21; Is. 40:26).

But some of the host of heaven have become demonic, rebelled against God, and come under His judgment (Is. 24:21; 34:4). Mankind is forbidden to worship the host of heaven—a practice yielded to in pursuit of astrology and the occult (Deut. 4:19; 17:3; cf. Is. 8:19–22). Scripture warns of God's judgment upon those who love and serve created things like the host of heaven (2 Kin. 23:5; Acts 7:42; Gal. 4:3, 9). All things are created by God to demonstrate His glory and should be enjoyed as such, but these must never displace God the Creator.

HOUSE. (2 Sam. 7:11) *bayit* (*by*-yeet); *Strong's* #1004: House, household, family, clan; temple, building, home. *Bayit* occurs about two thousand times in the Old Testament. *Bayit* may refer to a dwelling (Ruth 2:7) or a family (Gen. 7:1), and is also the word for the temple, the house of God at Jerusalem (2 Chr. 7:16).

HUMAN WORTH. Fallen though he be, man is still deemed by the Almighty to be of inestimable worth. Though incapable of saving himself, man—as creature—represents God's highest and best, made in His image and intended for His glory. In the light of Christ's will to spend His own life for man's redemption, an eternal insight into the worth of man from God's viewpoint is gained (1 Pet. 1:18–19). Thus, in our understanding, essential to personal growth and relational development with both God and man is a biblical perspective on the fundamental value of the individual, both in God's sight and in your own. Having created man in His image, God has invested unmeasurable worth in each being. His quest for the redemption of sinful, fallen man is evidence not only of God's love but of His wisdom in working to retrieve that which is of infinite value to Him. This study hopes to influence Christians toward a biblical balance in humility before our Creator-Redeemer, joined to a holy learning of mutual esteem for one another as members of Christ's body. May we learn how personal worth may be learned and recovered on God's terms.

1. Man's Intrinsic Value (Gen. 1:26–28). Man is distinct from the rest of creation. The Divine Triune Counsel determined that man was to have God's image and likeness. Man is a spiritual being who is not only body, but also soul and spirit. He is a moral being whose intelligence, perception, and self-determination far exceed that of any other earthly being.

These properties or traits possessed by mankind and his prominence in the order of creation imply the intrinsic worth, not only of the family of mankind, but also of each human individual.

Capacity and ability constitute accountability and responsibility. We should never be pleased to dwell on a level of existence lower than that on which God has made it possible for us to dwell. We should strive to be the best we can be and to reach the highest levels we can reach. To do less is to be unfaithful stewards of the life entrusted to us. (*See* Ps. 8:4–5; 139:13–14.)

2. Man's Dominion over Creation (Ps. 8:4–8).
Not only was man intrinsically distinct from the rest of creation, he was given authority over the earth and everything upon it. Man was made to rule (v. 6). Our ability to exercise authority over the earth is dependent on our willingness to submit to, serve, and obey the living God who holds authority over us. Our authority over the earth makes us accountable for the earth. The mineral resources of the earth, the earth's water and air, the species of animal life beneath and upon the earth (and in the waters of the earth) should all be the concern of every government and individual. Can we allow to pass from the earth forms of life which the Creator has placed here and committed to our care? Do we dare to pollute and corrupt God's creation? "For everyone to whom much is given, from him much will be required" (Luke 12:48).

3. Man's Critical Role in the Affairs of the Earth
(Gen. 3:17). From the perspective of man's strategic role we must assume him to be more valuable than anything on earth. No other form of earthly life plays such a cosmic role as mankind. The world literally stands or falls based on the actions of human beings. Only man has the power to deplete the earth's resources and to pollute its atmosphere. The sin of one man, Adam, corrupted the world. The continued sinfulness of mankind caused the Flood (6:12–13). In contrast, the obedience of one Man, Jesus Christ, brought justification and righteousness to many (Rom. 5:18–19). If redeemed men were to walk in that justification and righteousness, could they not cause the world to bloom and blossom? God wants to reveal His truth and beauty to the world only through redeemed mankind. Each believer has strategic significance in his own sphere. He or she must strive to maximize the impact of the good and encourage others to do the same.

4. The Sacredness of Life (Gen. 9:5–6). Life was
breathed into man by God. Man was made in the "image" of God, and after God's "likeness" (1:26; 9:6). Man was God's unique, spiritual, immortal, intelligent creation. Thus, God commands, "You shall not murder" (Ex. 20:13). To take human life is to assault the image of God in man. Human life should be respected and reverenced. Life, even prenatal life, is always a miracle; and no one should feel he has the right to shed the blood of an innocent human being. The word "require" (Gen. 9:5) indicates that God was doing more than simply stating a rule. He was saying that He will actually "pursue" (Hebrew *darash*) or "seek" a man's life in payment for the innocent life he has taken. Let no disrespect for human life invade any mind. Let us proclaim the value and the sacredness of life.

5. The Unity of the Human Race (Acts 17:26).
Here the unity of the human race is clearly stated, for through Adam and Eve (Gen. 3:20), and then the sons of Noah (Gen. 9:19), all races and nationalities of men came forth. We all proceed from one blood, both figuratively and literally, for the same blood types are found in all races. Humankind is a universal family. "Have we not all one Father? Has not one God created us?" (Mal. 2:10). We live in a single world community. No race or nation has the right to look down on or disassociate itself from another. The apostle Peter said, "God has shown me that I should not call any man common or unclean. . . . In truth I perceive that God shows no partiality. But in every nation, whoever fears Him and works righteousness is accepted by Him" (Acts 10:28, 34–35). There are only two divisions of humankind: the saved and the unsaved. Other differences are merely skin deep or culturally flavored, but all people are relatives.

6. All Believers Are Members of the Body of Christ (1 Cor. 12:12). The human body is an
exquisite organism. Scientists cannot duplicate it or even fully understand it. It is a synthesis of many parts all working together in a comprehensive whole. What affects one part of the body affects the whole. Each member of the body relates to and depends upon other parts of the body. Each contributes to the welfare of the entire body. So are all believers as members of the body of Christ. We should function in Christ's body as the parts of the human body function. The amputation of a limb handicaps the entire body. There is no Christian brother whom we do not need. The word "body" (Greek *soma*) is related to *sozo*, meaning "to heal, preserve, be made whole." This clearly shows how our lives are inextricably woven together within the body of Christ, and how our well-being depends upon the well-being of others (Rom. 14:7). Let us allow Christ to knit us together in His church.

7. Love—The Testing of Discipleship (John 13:34–35). That Christ would command us to love indicates that love is not just a feeling or a preference; it is what one does and how one relates to others—a decision, a commitment, or a way of behaving. Jesus states that the world will know that we are His disciples if we behave lovingly toward one another. Schisms, disputes, unkind criticisms, and defamation of character are contrary to the spirit of Christ. His love was a sacrificial love. It was unconditional love. His love is constant and self-sustaining. His love provides for the best interests of the beloved, and He commands that we should love one another as He has loved us.

8. Christ Mandates Social Concern (Matt. 25:37–40). Christ mandates social consciousness and concern (vv. 31–46). Here are the principles by which individuals will be judged: their treatment of those who are hungry, homeless, poor, diseased, and imprisoned. Social concern cannot biblically be divorced from the Christian walk. "He who has pity on the poor lends to the LORD, and He will pay back what he has given" (Prov. 19:17). Jesus equates our treatment of those who are destitute or distressed with our treatment of Himself. What we do for them, we do for Him. We must not allow the Christian walk to be only a spiritual enterprise, unrelated to the service of humanity. When we fail to care for social need, we fail to place proper value on others, decreasing our own merit in the eyes of the Lord and inviting His condemnation (*see* James 2:14–17).

9. One Should Not Think Too Highly of Himself (Rom. 12:3–5). Because the Bible teaches that human beings are made in God's image, we are to respect the position of each individual under God. This text does not teach that believers should think of themselves as worthless or insignificant beings, but rather that none should consider himself to be more worthy, more important, more deserving of salvation, or more essential than anyone else. Possession of different talents or gifts does not denote differences in worth, for all belong to the one body, to one another, and all are interdependent (vv. 4–5). To think otherwise is to distort reality. Each individual has intrinsic value and worth, as we are all equal before God and in Christ.

10. Respect of Persons (James 2:1–9). Human value cannot be equated with race, wealth, social standing, or educational level. All are significant and valuable in God's order. To regard a race, group, or individual as less important than another is sin in view of the fact that Christ died for all people and for each one in particular. At the foot of the Cross we are equal, both in our worth to God (He sent His Son to die for each of us) and in our need to accept His gift of salvation. Let us learn to respect and honor every person and each people regardless of their station or color. Christ said, "Inasmuch as you did it to one of the least of these My brethren, you did it to Me" (Matt. 25:40).

11. Help from a Despised Source (Luke 10:33). There was distinct racial strain between Jews and Samaritans (John 4:9). They did not frequently interact with one another; and in some cases, outright hostility and hatred existed. But Jesus, early in His ministry, taught the Samaritans the truth of God. He ministered to the "woman of Samaria" and to the people of Samaria (John 4:4–42). Here in this parable the source of assistance was not a kinsman or fellow citizen of Israel but a despised Samaritan. We are reminded that one of the great tragedies of prejudice is that it may separate one from a potential source of assistance. The compassion of the Samaritan was all the more commendable in that the person he assisted, under normal circumstances, probably would not have even spoken to him. Christ has come to break down such division.

12. The Cross-cultural Nature of God's Word and Work (Matt. 27:32). This text reminds us that different cultures were represented at Calvary and in the church. (1) Wise men of all ages would be honored to be allowed to perform the task that was conferred upon Simon of Cyrene, a black man from northwestern Africa. Whether it was voluntary or by force, in any case, black hands were extended to help the Savior bear His Cross. (2) The Ethiopian eunuch from Africa (Acts 8:26) was the first Gentile convert mentioned by name in the Book of Acts. History reports that he returned to Ethiopia to found the Abyssinian Christian Church, which exists until this day.

13. Man's Greatest Need Is for Salvation (1 Pet. 1:18–19). The value of the human being can be inferred from the price paid to redeem man (John 3:16; 1 Cor. 6:20). God the Son, the Divine One through whom the worlds were created, became flesh and died for the sins of humanity. That He willingly shed His blood and died for us reveals not only the value of the human personality, but also the importance of salvation. Through Christ, believers are forgiven, reckoned to be righteous, and by New Birth are renewed in the image of God. Fallen men and women can only produce the works of the flesh. Only the Spirit, by the New Birth, can renew and recover that which was destroyed by the Fall (John 3:5–6). To reach our highest human potential, to have abundant life, we must accept Jesus Christ by faith.

14. Abundant Life (John 10:10). Christ came to earth in defense of life. By His words and actions He opposed any thing, force, or person that might diminish it. Likewise, He calls us to do everything within our power to preserve and enhance the lives of those around us. In addition to evangelizing, we are to work to reduce poverty, disease, hunger, injustice, and ignorance.

Beyond His defense of life, however, Jesus also came to deliver from death and to introduce abundant living. By His death and resurrection, Christ has opened a new dimension of life for all mankind, that "all things become new" (2 Cor. 5:17). C.B.

HUMBLE. (Jer. 13:18) *shaphel* (shah-*fail*); *Strong's* #8213: To make low, depress, sink, lower, debase, set in a lower place, lay low, descend, humble, abase. *Shaphel* occurs twenty-nine times and is generally translated "humble," "bring down," or "make low." *Shaphel* is illustrated by Isaiah 2:11; 5:15. Notice the irony of Proverbs 29:23, "A man's pride will bring him low, but the humble in spirit will retain honor." In Psalm 113:6, God, who dwells on high, humbles Himself to watch what is occurring in heaven and on earth. The most important derivative of *shaphel* is *shephelah*, "low country," or "low hills and plains," referring to the rolling hill country west of the Judean mountains.

HUMBLES. (Matt. 18:4) *tapeinoo* (tap-eye-*nah*-oh); *Strong's* #5013: Literally, "to make low," used of a mountain in Luke 3:5. Metaphorically, the word means to debase, humble, lower oneself. It describes a person who is devoid of all arrogance and self-exaltation—a person who is willingly submitted to God and His will.

HUMILITY. (Acts 20:19) *tapeinophrosune* (tap-eye-nof-ros-*oo*-nay); *Strong's* #5012: Modesty, lowliness, humble-mindedness, a sense of moral insignificance, and a humble attitude of unselfish concern for the welfare of others. It is a total absence of arrogance, conceit, and haughtiness. The word is a combination of *tapeinos*, "humble," and *phren*, "mind." The word was unknown in classical nonbiblical Greek. Only by abstaining from self-aggrandizement can members of the Christian community maintain unity and harmony.

HURRIANS—see ch. 55, §3.5., 3.5.a.

HUSBAND—a woman's marriage partner. In Hebrew society, the husband was the absolute authority in the home. The apostle Paul called on husbands to temper their authority with the higher value of love: "Husbands, love your wives" (Eph. 5:25). He compared the relationship between Christ and the church to the union of husband and wife (Eph. 5:23); this requires caring, tenderness, patience, and understanding to characterize the husband's leadership in the home. There is no biblical justification for chauvinistic notions of male authority over women as such. The husband's role toward his wife is to be one of leadership, which so relates (as Christ) that a loving partnership is nourished and realized. Also see Family.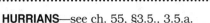

HYKSOS—see ch. 55, §3.7.b.

HYPOCRITE. (Gal. 2:13) *hupokrisis* (hoop-ok-ree-sis); *Strong's* #5272: Literally "a reply." The word came to denote a theatrical performer who spoke in dialogue. Then it was used of playacting, role-playing, pretending; hence, acting insincerely, hypocrisy.

HYPOCRITES. (Matt. 6:2) *hupokrites* (hoop-ok-ree-*tace*); *Strong's* #5273: In Bible days actors wore masks, which included mechanisms for amplifying the voice. Since the dramas were questions and answers, the word describing the dialogue was *hupokrinomai*, "to reply" or "to answer." *Hupokrites* is one who is playacting, reading a script, or one who puts on an act. The *hypocrite* conceals his true motives under a cloak of make-believe.

IDLE TALK. (1 Tim. 1:6) *mataiologia* (mat-ah-yol-og-*ee*-ah); *Strong's* #3150: A combination of *mataios*, "vain," and *logos*, "word." The word denotes futile talk, worthless, empty, meaningless babble, and idle prattle. Here it describes would-be teachers who love to hear themselves speak but have nothing of substance to say.

IDLE TALKERS. (Titus 1:10) *mataiologos* (mat-ah-yol-*og*-oss); *Strong's* #3151: From *mataios*, "idle," "useless," and *lego*, "to speak." *Mataiologos* is speaking that lacks reason and worth and that gives evidence of an undisciplined life-style. The counterpart is men speaking as they are moved by the Holy Spirit (2 Pet. 1:21).

IDOL, IDOLATRY, IMAGE—a representation or symbol of an object of worship; a false god. In a few places in the Bible, the word image

---

 This icon beside an entry indicates a Word Wealth feature.

 This icon beside an entry indicates a Kingdom Dynamics feature.

 This icon beside an entry indicates an important biblical or doctrinal term.

appears in a neutral sense, not referring to a man-made object of worship. Adam, created in the image of God (Gen. 1:26), or Christ, the visible image of the invisible God (2 Cor. 4:4; Col. 1:15) are examples of this.

Most of the time, however, image refers to a statue or something of human manufacture which people have substituted and submitted themselves to instead of the true and living God. Occasionally it appears in the same sentence with idol (Lev. 26:1; 2 Chr. 33:7). As surely as the idols were made of inert, material objects, they became suffused or surrounded by demonic presences when worshiped.

In showing the meaninglessness of idolatry, Isaiah provided considerable detail about the making of idols (Is. 44:9–20). He described the smith with his tongs and hammer and the carpenter with his ruler, line, planes, and compass. Isaiah also ridiculed the idolmakers by noting that such a statue has to be nailed down "that it might not totter" (Is. 41:7). But these material objects are not without an attending invisible presence, Paul warns (1 Cor. 10:19–21). Note in verses 14 and 20 that the spirit of the world is more than an attitude. It is a composite of hell's dark powers seeking to control attitudes and to devastate lives (Eph. 2:1–3).

Perhaps the best definition of an idol is some thing, person, or structure that a person submits themselves to as a god—a ruling, dominant force or value in their life. It may not be a statue or a tree as in ancient times; it can be a system, a preference, or a pursuit that opposes God's rule and will in your life.

Idolatry can take many forms, and it has persisted from the earliest times. Joshua 24:2 states that Abraham's father served idols. Perhaps the earliest reference in the Bible to idols is the "household idols" or teraphim (small clay figurines) which Rachel stole from her father Laban (Gen. 31:34).

Hosea's prophecy summarizes the problems of Israel with idolatry during the monarchy and the divided kingdom. Under the figure of speech of divorcing the Lord and marrying Baal, he tied together the ideas of idolatry, spiritual adultery, and literal adultery (Hos. 2:2; 4:2, 13; 7:4; 8:5; 13:2). Bad kings invariably fell to idolatry, prompting most of the prophets to ridicule, condemn, and warn against idolatry. A sampling of courageous declarations from these courageous preachers would include Isaiah 2:8; Jeremiah 50:2; Ezekiel 6:4–6; Micah 1:7; Habakkuk 2:18; and Zechariah 13:2.

In the Gospels there is virtually nothing about idolatry, but in the letters of Paul and the other New Testament books Christians are frequently warned against idolatry. The Christians lived in a world filled with idols. Both the Romans and the Greeks used them. Paul's observation about Athens in Acts 17:16 tells it well: "He saw that the city was given over to idols."

In the New Testament period the term idolatry began to be used as an spiritual concept. Idolatry became not the actual bowing down before a statue but the replacement of God in the heart or mind of the worshiper: "Put to death . . . covetousness, which is idolatry." (See Col. 3:5; Eph. 5:5.) Today believers must understand the vicious nature of idolatry and the potential bondage inherent in submission to the spirit of the world. Besides material objects such as houses, land, and cars, idols can be people, popular heroes, or those whom we love. Objects of worship can even include things like fame, reputation, hobbies, pride, and deeds done in the name of the Lord. Further, fetishes and paraphernalia related to worldly or occult practice, as well as surrender to abusive or obscene practices—promiscuity, drugs, alcohol, pornography, demonically inspired music—all give place to the devil (Eph. 4:26) and are idolatry.

IMMEDIATELY. (John 6:21) *eutheos* (yoo-*theh*-oce); *Strong's #2112:* From the adjective *euthus*, "straight." Speedily, straightway, immediately, directly, presently, suddenly, quickly. The word describes what is happening right now in contrast to what happened before this time.

IMPART. (Rom. 1:11) *metadidomi* (met-ad-*id*-oh-mee); *Strong's* #3330: To give, share, impart, distribute, grant. The word implies liberality or generosity. It is used to exhort those with two outer tunics to give one to someone who has none (Luke 3:11); to encourage people to give with cheerful outflow (Rom. 12:8); and to urge workers to labor with industry in order to give to him who has a need (Eph. 4:28).

IMPUTATION—charging or reckoning something to a person's account. An example of the concept of imputation is in Philemon, where Paul tells him to "put on my account" (v. 18) any wrong or debt caused by Onesimus. Three distinct biblical truths relate to imputation:

1. *The Imputation of Adam's Sin to His Descendants.* Romans 5:12–19 declares that God imputes the guilt of Adam's sin to all other members of the human race: "By one man's disobedience many were made sinners . . . *judgment* came to all men . . . death reigned through the one." (See also 1 Cor. 15:21–22.)

2. *The Imputation of the Believer's Sin to Christ.* In addition to guilt imputed or inherited from Adam's sin, each individual also stands guilty for his or her personal sin (2 Cor. 5:19). But the Lord Jesus, whose supernatural conception and birth and sinless life kept Him from both personal guilt and from Adam's sin, had no sin counted against Him. When He died as our substitute, God "made Him who knew no sin to be sin for us" (2 Cor. 5:21; 1 Pet. 2:24). Our sin was imputed to Him (Is. 53:6).

3. *The Imputation of Christ's Righteousness to the Believer.* "The blessedness of the man to whom God imputes righteousness" is the theme of the fourth chapter of Romans (also 1 Cor. 1:30; 2 Cor. 5:21; Phil. 3:9). As Jesus became the Holy and Just One (Acts 3:14) through His perfect obedience to God's Law (Rom. 5:19), these qualities are imputed in turn "to us who believe in Him who raised up Jesus our Lord from the dead" (Rom. 4:24). Because of this the believer will appear before God "faultless" (Jude 24). We are welcomed and can stand in God's presence because Jesus has imputed His righteousness and holiness to us through His sacrificial death on the Cross.

INCARNATION—a theological term for the coming of God's Son into the world as a human being. The term itself is not used in the Bible, but it is based on clear references in the New Testament to Jesus as a person "in the flesh" (Rom. 8:3; Eph. 2:15; Col. 1:22).

Jesus participated fully in all that it means to live a human life. If Jesus were merely a man, however, no matter how great, there would be no significance in drawing attention to His bodily existence. The marvelous thing is that in Jesus, God Himself began to live a fully human life: "The Word (Christ) become flesh and dwelled among us" (John 1:14). The capacity of Jesus to reveal God to us and to bring salvation depends upon His being fully God and fully man at the same time.

Unassisted human minds cannot understand how Jesus can be both fully God and fully man, but the Bible reveals this mystery in clear, practical terms.

No person may see God and live (Ex. 33:20), for He dwells in unapproachable light (1 Tim. 6:16). Can we, therefore, only know Him from a distance? No! God has come near in the person of Jesus (Matt. 1:23). He has taken on a form in which He can be seen, experienced, and understood by us as human beings (John 1:14, 18). Jesus reveals God to us perfectly since in His human life He is the image of God (2 Cor. 4:4), exhibiting full likeness with the Father (John 14:7–11). Jesus' godhood revealed within His manhood is the key to our intimate knowledge of God.

This does not mean, however, that Jesus' humanity is only a display case for His divinity. Jesus lived out His human life by experiencing all the pressures, temptations, and limitations that we experience (Heb. 2:18; 4:15; 5:2, 7–8). That is why Jesus' life is truly the supreme human success story (Heb. 5:8). Jesus was a pioneer (Heb. 2:10, RSV), showing in practical terms the full meaning and possibility of human life, lived in obedience to God. In this respect, Jesus is a kind of second Adam (Rom. 5:14–15), marking a new beginning for the human race.

Jesus would have performed a great work if He had done no more than set a perfect example. But His full humanity is also the basis on which it is possible for Him to represent us—indeed, take our place—in dying for us. The Bible makes this clear when it speaks of "the Man Christ Jesus, who gave Himself a ransom for all" (1 Tim. 2:5–6).

When He ascended to glory after His resurrection, Jesus left behind some of the human restrictions experienced during His earthly life. He received at that time His original divine glory (John 17:5). But the joining together of deity and humanity that marks His incarnation did not come to an end with His ascension. Jesus took His resurrected body with Him back to heaven (Luke 24:51; Acts 1:9). In heaven now He is our divine Lord, our human leader, and the Great High Priest who serves as a mediator between God and man (Heb. 3:1).

INHERITANCE—the receipt of property as a gift or by legal right, usually upon the death of one's parent.

In ancient Israel the property of a deceased person was usually distributed according to law or tribal custom. The real and personal property of a father normally was divided among his sons. A larger amount, usually a double portion, went to the eldest son, who assumed the care of his mother and unmarried sisters.

The birthright of the firstborn son could be denied only because of a serious offense against the father, as in the case of Reuben (Deut. 21:15–17; 1 Chr. 5:1). The sons of concubines normally received presents of personal property. If there were no surviving sons, the inheritance went to daughters. The daughters had to marry within the tribe, however, or lose their inheritance. If a man died childless, his estate was received by his brothers or his father's brothers (Num. 27:9–11).

To the Hebrew mind, the term inheritance had strong spiritual and national associations extending far beyond the family estate. The land of Canaan was regarded as an inheritance from the Lord because God had promised the land to Abraham and his descendants (Num. 33:53). Both Moses and Joshua were told by the Lord to divide the land of Canaan among the tribes "as an inheritance" (Num. 26:52–53, Josh. 13:6). God directed that the land be distributed to each tribe by lot according to its population.

Each family, in turn, was assigned a parcel that was to remain in the family's possession. This sense of sacred birthright probably accounted for Naboth's refusal to sell his vineyard to King Ahab: "The Lord forbid that I should give the inheritance of my fathers to you!" (1 Kin. 21:3).

The Greeks relied more on wills for distributing an inheritance than did the Israelites. If a citizen died without a will, his sons in good standing inherited the property in equal parts, the eldest receiving the same as his brothers. Daughters received dowries, which reverted to other heirs if the daughter was divorced or remained childless. If a man had no sons, he usually adopted one to continue the family. If he had daughters, he would arrange for one of them to marry the adopted son. In that instance the major share of the inheritance fell to the daughter and her husband. If only daughters survived, the estate passed to them. If a man died without a will and left no natural or adopted heirs, his closest male relatives received his property.

According to Roman law, the property of a man who died without a will went to his wife and children. But married daughters living with their husbands or children who had been emancipated from their father's authority did not share in the inheritance. If a man left no wife and children, the inheritance passed to his male relatives. The Romans held that a child became his father's heir the moment he was born and that the deceased lived through his heirs. Legally adopted children had full inheritance rights.

The biblical concept of a spiritual inheritance for believers is primarily of Jewish origin. But the analogy used to reveal this concept was adapted to and influenced by Greek and Roman inheritance practices. Three of these influences were: (1) inheritance was regarded as immediate as well as ultimate, (2) all legitimate heirs usually shared the inheritance equally and jointly rather than a division favoring a firstborn son, and (3) legally adopted children enjoyed full inheritance rights along with natural offspring.

The Christian's spiritual inheritance is based strictly on our relationship to Christ. "For you are all sons of God through faith in Jesus Christ. . . . And if you are Christ's, then you are Abraham's seed, and heirs according to the promise" (Gal. 3:26, 29). This spiritual birthright cannot be inherited by sinners (1 Cor. 6:9–11). The present possession of the spiritual inheritance as well as its future glory is emphasized in Romans 8: "The Spirit Himself bears witness with our spirit that we are the children of God, and if children, then heirs—heirs of God and joint heirs with Christ, if indeed we suffer with Him, that we may also be glorified together" (Rom. 8:16–17).

The Holy Spirit's indwelling power is both the sign and seal that we are heirs of God's promise: "Having believed, you were sealed with the Holy Spirit of promise, who is the guarantee of our inheritance" (Eph. 1:13–14). Those who are redeemed, including the Gentiles, become God's adopted sons with full inheritance rights (Gal. 4:17).

Other New Testament teachers present the idea of our spiritual inheritance: Jesus (Matt. 25:34); Peter (1 Pet. 1:3–4; 3:9); and James (James 2:5).

INHERITANCE. (Zech. 2:12) *cheleq* (*chay*-lek); *Strong's* #2506: A portion, part, inheritance, allotment. This noun occurs more than sixty times. It comes from the verb *chalaq*, "to be smooth." From this root are derived such words as "smooth stones" and "flattery," which is smooth words. Perhaps because smooth stones were used for casting "lots," *chalaq* came to mean "to apportion, deal out, divide up, allot." Thus a *cheleq* is an apportionment, allotment, a parcel of land that a person receives as an inheritance. David calls the Lord "my portion" (Ps. 73:26; 142:5). The present reference indicates that Yahweh's portion (allotment, share, inheritance) is the people of Judah in the Holy Land.

INIQUITIES. (Ps. 130:3) *'avon* (ah-*voan*); *Strong's* #5771: Evil, fault, sin, iniquity, guilt, blame; moral illness, perversion, crookedness. *'Avon* is derived from *'avah*, to "bend" or "distort." Thus iniquity is the "evil bent" within human beings, or the "crooked" direction or "warped" deeds of sinners. *'Avon* occurs more than 220 times in the Old Testament. Its first mention is in Genesis 4:13, where Cain finally understands the enormity of his deed and states, "My punishment [iniquity] is greater than I can bear." Knowing that iniquity is something too heavy to be borne by fallen humanity, God promised that His Suffering

Servant would bear the iniquities of His people (Is. 53:11; *'avon* also appears in vv. 5–6).

INSPIRATION—a biblical term for the Holy Spirit's supernatural guidance of those who received special revelation from God as they wrote the books of the Bible. Second Timothy 3:16–17 uses this word which literally says the Scriptures were "breathed by God"—that is, the breath or Spirit of God infused the minds of the writers with His perfect will and truth (2 Pet. 1:20–21). The end result of this inspiration is that the Bible reveals the truths which God wants His people to know and communicate to the world.

Evangelical Christians agree that the primary purpose of the Bible is to lead people to a personal relationship with God as Savior. But everything taught by the Bible on any subject is helpful and instructive for a complete life (2 Tim. 3:16–17). Because Christianity does relate to the real world, the Bible's declarations about the earth and history are completely trustworthy.

Two terms often used in any discussion of the inspiration of the Bible are plenary and verbal. "Plenary" inspiration is a term meaning "full" or "complete," declaring that each book, chapter, and paragraph of the Bible is equally derived from God. Verbal inspiration emphasizes the truth that the wording of the text, as well as the ideas conveyed, is supernaturally inspired by God through the Holy Spirit.

Inerrancy is a term used along with plenary verbal inspiration to convey the view that the Bible's teaching is true on everything of which it speaks. The Bible is not merely a useful body of human ideas. It makes clear the mind of God Himself. Inerrancy is also a term used to assert that the Bible text in its original form (called "autograph" form, or the first time written before copied or printed) was without any error on any subject addressed.

Infallibility is a term often used as a synonym for inerrancy. However, the root meaning of infallibility is "not liable to fail in achieving its purpose." So inerrancy affirms the content of the Bible, while infallibility refers to the fact that no word is without power to fulfill God's purpose (Is. 55:11), and no word of truth or promise within God's Holy Word can be "broken" or violated by being unkept or disregarded by Him (John 10:35).

The fact of biblical infallibility joins to biblical inerrancy to explain why the Holy Spirit so fully anoints and works through the ministry of God's Word. He directed its production from the beginning, and He confirms and certifies its anointed proclamation or communication with evidences of His presence and power.

Inspiration, then, is a statement about God's greatness. God is intelligent and able to communicate with man, whom He created in His image. God knows everything about all reality in creation and is absolutely faithful and true (Rev. 3:7; 21:5). It follows that ideas communicated by divine revelation are true and conform to reality as God knows it. God overruled human limitations and sinful biases so that His spokesmen were able to write what He wanted written. God guided the thought conveyed so that it was without error, accomplishing the objectives He intended.

Exactly what role did the human writers of the Bible play in their transmission of God's message? They were not totally passive, as those whose hands move automatically in an unconscious state. Their distinctive ways of writing stand out, as in the four Gospels, which describe the life and ministry of Jesus Christ. Luke, the beloved physician, used many medical terms not found in Matthew, Mark, or John. Some biblical writers like Moses and Paul were highly educated; others were not.

Although some passages of Scripture may have been received by audible dictation (Ex. 4:12; 19:3–6; Num. 7:89), many were guided by a silent activity of the Holy Spirit (Luke 1:1–4). To err is human and the conscious participation of finite, sinful authors would have led to error if not for this supernatural guidance by the Holy Spirit.

God gave these people the distinctive functions of prophets and apostles, originated what they wrote, and kept them from error in all the writing processes. All of Scripture has prophetic authority, and none of God's Word originated with the will of men. It came about through the will of God (2 Pet. 1:20–21). All Scripture was given by inspiration of God (2 Tim. 3:16).

Clear standards tested whether a person who claimed to speak for God was a true prophet or a false prophet (Deut. 13:15; 18:20–22). People who spoke out of their own hearts and by their own independent wills were subject to the death penalty (Deut. 13:6–10). But genuine prophets were inspired by the Holy Spirit as authentic spokesmen for God.

Although the Bible does not tell exactly how God inspired its writers, it was certainly not in a mechanical way. The Holy Spirit's work in the Virgin Mary's conceiving of Jesus might be an example of how the Spirit worked with the biblical writers. A fully human woman of Adam's sinful race bore a sinless child who would be called the Holy One, the Son of God (Luke 1:35). How could that be? The power of the Highest "overshadowed" her so that she conceived Jesus. Likewise, the power of the Highest "overshadowed" the biblical writers so that what they wrote could be called the Holy Bible, the Word of God.

Followers of Jesus Christ as Savior and Lord will follow Him in His view of the Old Testament Scriptures and the entire Bible. He endorsed all three sections of the Hebrew Bible: the Law, the Prophets, and the Psalms (Writings). He accepted as fact some of today's most controversial passages: Adam and Eve at the beginning of time (Matt. 19:4), Abel's murder of Cain (Luke 11:51), Noah, the ark, and the Flood (Matt. 24:37–39), the destruction of Sodom and Gomorrah and of Lot's wife (Luke 17:28–30), and Moses' authorship of the Pentateuch (John 5:46). That fact sets them forward as conclusively affirmed by God, a settled issue for biblical believers.

The view that God's great mind had to accommodate itself to human errors in the production of the Bible does not fit the high view of Scripture which Jesus had. God certainly adapted His truth to a human level of understanding, but, for example, a person can adapt truth about the origin of human life to a child's level of understanding without teaching errors about "storks." In a similar way, God adapts His truth in part to our limited understandings, but neither He, nor His Son, nor His Spirit taught error in the name of God.

Belief in the plenary verbal inspiration of the Bible, and in its inerrancy and infallibility, best fits the claims of Jesus about the Bible and the claims which the Bible makes for itself.

Also see Bible, Interpretation of.

INSTRUCTION. (Prov. 4:13) *musar* (moo-*sar*); *Strong's* #4148: Correction, chastisement, instruction, discipline; an admonition, rebuke, or warning. *Musar* comes from the verb *yasar*, "to reform, chastise, discipline, instruct." *Musar* appears fifty times in the Old Testament, thirty of these in Proverbs. *Musar* is broad enough to encompass chastening by words and by punishments (1:3; 22:15). Isaiah 53:5 states, "The chastisement for our peace was upon Him, and by His stripes we are healed." In Proverbs 3:11, we are urged not to "despise the chastening of the LORD," nor to grow weary of His correction. A wicked man may even "die for lack of instruction" (Prov. 5:23). Thus *musar* includes all forms of discipline intended to lead to a transformed life.

INSULTED. (Luke 18:32) *hubrizo* (hoo-*brid*-zoe); *Strong's* #5195: Compare "hubristic" and "hybrid." To insult; to treat arrogantly, insolently, sarcastically, and injuriously; to commit an outrage against. It is abuse that runs riot, acts wantonly, shamefully, and with affront. Jesus not only received this treatment from His enemies, but He warned His followers not to be surprised when they received the same treatment (Matt. 22:6).

INTERCESSION—the act of petitioning God or praying on behalf of another person or group. The sinful nature of this world separates human beings from God. It has always been necessary, therefore, for righteous individuals to go before God to seek reconciliation between Him and His fallen creation.

Examples of intercession occur in classic instances. In Genesis 18, where Abraham speaks to God on behalf of Sodom, his plea is compassionate; it is concerned with the well-being of others rather than with his own needs. Such selfless concern is the mark of all true intercession.

Moses was also effective in petitioning God on behalf of the Hebrew people (Ex. 15:25). Even the pharaoh asked Moses to intercede for him (Ex. 8:28). But just as righteous men often succeeded in reconciling Creator and creation, the Bible also reminds us that the ongoing sinfulness of a people can hinder the effects of intercession (1 Sam. 2:25; Jer. 7:16).

The sacrifices and prayers of Old Testament priests (Ex. 29:42; 30:7) were acts of intercession which point forward to the work of Christ. Christ is, of course, the greatest intercessor. He prayed on behalf of Peter (Luke 22:32) and His disciples (John 17). Then in the most selfless intercession of all, He petitioned God on behalf of those who crucified Him (Luke 23:34). His work on the Cross is His ultimate expression of intercession (Is. 53:12).

Christ's intercessory work did not cease when He returned to heaven. He still intercedes for His church (Heb. 7:25), and the Holy Spirit pleads on behalf of the individual Christian (Rom. 8:26–27). Finally, because of their unique relationship to God through Christ, Christians are urged to intercede for all people (1 Tim. 2:1). The latter text shows intercessory prayer is a primary ministry of the church.

INTERCESSION. (Heb. 7:25) *entunchano* (en-toong-*khan*-oh); *Strong's* #1793: To fall in with, meet with in order to converse. From this description of a casual encounter, the word progresses to the idea of pleading with a person on behalf of another, although at times the petition may be against another (Acts 25:24; Rom. 11:2).

INTERCESSION (MAKE). (Jer. 27:18) *paga‘* (pah-*gah*); *Strong's* #6293: To reach; to meet someone; to pressure or urge someone strongly; to meet up with a person; encounter, entreat; to assail with urgent petitions. This verb occurs forty-six times. In some passages it is translated "meet," as in Joshua 2:16. In Joshua 19:27, *paga‘* refers to the extent to which a tribal boundary is reached. Sometimes the verb refers to "falling upon" someone in battle, that is, to meet up with the enemy with hostile intent (1 Kin. 2:29). *Paga‘* is also translated "make intercession," the idea being that a supplicant catches up with a superior, and reaches him with an urgent request. Thus, intercession involves reaching God, meeting God, and entreating Him for His favor.

INTERMEDIATE STATE—the period between a person's death and the final resurrection at the end of time. The Bible does not have a great deal to say about the intermediate state; its emphasis is upon the return of Christ, the final judgment, and the eternal state of man. What it does say is sketchy and open to various interpretations.

The New Testament sometimes describes the act of dying as a "falling asleep" and the state of death as a "sleeping" (Matt. 9:24; 11:11; 1 Cor. 15:20, 51). In 1 Thessalonians 4:13–15, the apostle Paul speaks of "those who have fallen asleep," "those who sleep in Jesus," and "those who are asleep." This should not be understood as "soul-sleeping"—a reference to the dead in an unconscious state. Death as sleep is a widely used biblical concept signifying rest from earthly care and labor, as is true of natural sleep (2 Pet. 3:4).

Jesus' description of the rich man and Lazarus (Luke 16:19–31) presents the rich man as conscious and tormented in Hades and Lazarus the beggar as conscious and blessed in "Abraham's bosom" (the Jewish term for the abode of the righteous dead). The text indicates that immediately after death the righteous are rewarded and the unrighteous receive punishment. The final degrees of both reward and punishment, however, are determined only at the final judgment (Rev. 20:11–15).

On the cross Jesus said to the repentant thief, "Today you will be with Me in Paradise" (Luke 23:43). The word *paradise* is of Persian origin. It suggests an orchard, park, or garden. The apostle Paul spoke of being "caught up into Paradise" (2 Cor. 12:4), evidently equating heaven and Paradise. In the Book of Revelation the crucified and resurrected Christ declared, "To him who overcomes I will give to eat from the tree of life, which is in the midst of the Paradise of God" (Rev. 2:7). The overall sense of these references identifies Paradise with heaven, to which the righteous go immediately after death.

A clear treatment of the intermediate state is found in 2 Corinthians 5:1–8: "For we know that if our earthly house, this tent, is destroyed, we have a building from God, a house not made with hands, eternal in the heavens" (v. 1). This passage anticipates more than an unconscious, or even subconscious, state after death: "We are confident, yes, well pleased rather to be absent from the body and to be present with the Lord" (v. 8). No in-between or intermediate state exists, but those "who sleep in Jesus" (1 Thess. 4:14) are with Jesus now.

INTERPRETATION (*see* Bible, Interpretation of).

IN VAIN. (Is. 45:18) *tohu* (*toh*-hoo); *Strong's* #8414: A formless, chaotic mess, a waste, a worthless thing, emptiness and desolation, for no purpose, for nothing. This word first occurs in Genesis 1:2, "The earth was without form [*tohu*], and void [*bohu*]." *Tohu* and its rhyming synonym *bohu* are coupled to describe a scene of disorder, confusion, and lack of arrangement. However, the Lord brought order out of chaos, as Genesis (and our present earth) testifies. Elsewhere *tohu* refers to a howling waste, a trackless wilderness, a scene of utter disarray, desolation, and barrenness. *Tohu* suggests "sheer emptiness" as opposed to order and balance.

ISAAC—see ch. 55, §3.5.b.

ISAIAH—see ch. 55, §3.7.d.

ISAIAH, BOOK OF—see ch. 55, §4.2.

ISHTAR, TEMPLE OF—see ch. 55, §3.6.

JACOB—see ch. 55, §3.5.b.

JEALOUSY. (2 Cor. 11:2) *zelos* (*dzay*-loss); *Strong's* #2205: The root of the English word "zeal." It signifies eagerness, enthusiasm, intense desire, passionate commitment. The word carries both the idea of zeal (7:11; 9:2; Phil. 3:6) and jealousy (Acts 5:17; 13:45; Rom. 13:13).

JEHOIKIM—see ch. 55, §3.7.

JEREMIAH—see ch. 55, §3.7., 3.7.c., 3.7.d.

JEREMIAH, BOOK OF—see ch. 55, §3.7.e.

 This icon beside an entry indicates a Word Wealth feature.

 This icon beside an entry indicates a Kingdom Dynamics feature.

 This icon beside an entry indicates an important biblical or doctrinal term.

JERUSALEM—see ch. 55, §3.3., 3.7.b., 6.

JERUSALEM COUNCIL, THE—a conference held in about A.D. 49 between delegates from the church at Antioch of Syria and delegates from the church at Jerusalem. This council met to settle a dispute over whether Gentile converts had to be circumcised (Acts 15:1–29).

According to Luke, "Certain men came down from Judea and taught the brethren, 'Unless you are circumcised according to the custom of Moses, you cannot be saved'" (Acts 15:1). They insisted that Gentiles could not be received into the church unless they were circumcised and brought under the rules of the Mosaic Law. The apostle Paul, champion of Gentile freedom, said that all people—both Jews and Gentiles—are saved by grace through faith in Jesus Christ, apart from the works of the Law. To require circumcision, he argued, would destroy the Good News of God's grace.

The conclusion of the Jerusalem Council, which determined that Gentiles did not have to be circumcised, was a decisive moment of the Holy Spirit's opening the door to world evangelism. Speaking for the council, the apostle Peter declared, "We believe that through the grace of the Lord Jesus Christ we [Jews] shall be saved in the same manner as they [the Gentiles]" (Acts 15:11).

Why was the decision of the Jerusalem Council so important? A decision that circumcision is necessary for anyone to become a Christian would have compromised the truth of the gospel. Instead of a gospel based on salvation by grace through faith in Jesus Christ, it would have become one based on salvation by works (the Law).

The Jerusalem Council decreed, therefore, that the Gentiles should make four reasonable concessions of their own: "We write to them to abstain from things polluted by idols, from sexual immorality, from things strangled, and from blood" (Acts 15:20, also 15:29, 21:25). The council was both a theological and a practical success. The concessions it called for were not "compromises"; indeed, they reaffirmed the integrity of the gospel of salvation by faith alone. They also affirmed the spiritual importance of sexual purity and certain tradition. This first great threat to the unity of the church ended instead with rejoicing and encouragement (Acts 15:31).

JERUSALEM, FALL OF, 586 B.C.—see ch. 55, §3.7., 3.7.d.

JERUSALEM, FALL OF, 70 A.D.—see ch. 55, §5.3.

JERUSALEM, NEW—the holy city described by John in Revelation 21—22; God's perfect and eternal order of the future. This New Jerusalem is not built by human hands; it is a heavenly city—one built and provided by God Himself (Rev. 21:2).

The New Jerusalem and the new Garden of Eden (symbols of righteousness, peace, and prosperity) are the dwelling place of God, Christ, and the church. John saw no temple in New Jerusalem, "for the Lord God Almighty and the Lamb are its temple" (Rev. 21:22).

In the Book of Revelation John draws a graphic contrast between the harlot city called "Babylon the Great" (Rev. 14:8; 16:19; 17:1—18:24), the earthly and temporal city of man, and the "New Jerusalem" (Rev. 21:2—22:5), the heavenly and eternal city of God. John also identifies "the great city, the holy Jerusalem" (Rev. 21:10) as the church, which he calls "the bride, the Lamb's wife" (Rev. 21:9).

JESUS. (Phil. 4:23) *Iesous* (yay-*soos*); *Strong's #2424:* The Greek transliteration of the Hebrew *Yeshua*, "He Shall Save," which is the shorter form of *Yehoshua* (Joshua), "Yahweh Is Salvation." It was a common male Jewish name. Ten men in the Old Testament were named *Yeshua*, and three men in the New Testament, in addition to the Lord, were so named.

JESUS CHRIST—the human-divine Son of God, supernaturally incarnate being born of the Virgin Mary; the Lamb of God who died for mankind's sin, Lord of Life who rose from the dead, and the Ascended Lord—our Great High Priest, who intercedes now for His people at the right hand of God's throne from which He will come to earth a second time to receive His redeemed church and judge the earth in righteousness; Founder of the Christian church and the central figure of the human race.

To understand who Jesus was and what He accomplished, students of the New Testament must study: (1) His life, (2) His teachings, (3) His person, and (4) His work.

The life of Jesus. The twofold designation Jesus Christ combines the personal name Jesus and the title Christ, meaning "anointed" or "Messiah." The significance of this title became clear during the scope of His life and ministry.

Birth and upbringing. Jesus was born in Bethlehem, a town about ten kilometers (six miles) south of Jerusalem, toward the end of Herod the Great's reign as king of the Jews (37–4 B.C.). Early in His life He was taken to Nazareth, a town of Galilee. There He was brought up by His mother, Mary, and her husband, Joseph, a carpenter by trade. Hence He was known as "Jesus of Nazareth" or, more fully, "Jesus of Nazareth, the son of Joseph" (John 1:45).

Jesus was His mother's firstborn child; he had four brothers (James, Joses, Judas, and Simon) and an unspecified number of sisters (Mark 6:3). Joseph apparently died before Jesus began His public ministry. Mary, with the rest of the family, lived on and became a member of the church of Jerusalem after Jesus' death and resurrection.

The only incident preserved from Jesus' first thirty years (after his infancy) was His trip to Jerusalem with Joseph and Mary when He was twelve years old (Luke 2:41–52). Since He was known in Nazareth as "the carpenter" (Mark 6:3), He may have taken Joseph's place as the family breadwinner at an early age.

Beginnings of Jesus' ministry. Jesus began His public ministry when He sought baptism at the hands of John the Baptist. John preached between A.D. 27 and 28 in the lower Jordan Valley and baptized those who wished to give expression to their repentance (Matt. 3:13–17; Mark 1:9–11; Luke 3:21–22; John 1:29–34). The descent of the dove as Jesus came up out of the water was a sign that He was the One anointed by the Spirit of God as the Servant-Messiah of His people (Is. 11:2; 42:1; 61:1).

A voice from heaven declared, "You are My beloved Son; in You I am well pleased" (Luke 3:22). This indicated that He was Israel's anointed King, destined to fulfill His kingship as the Servant of the Lord described centuries earlier by the prophet Isaiah (Is. 42:1; 52:13).

Jesus' baptism was followed immediately by His temptation in the wilderness (Matt. 4:1–11; Mark 1:12–13; Luke 4:1–13). This testing confirmed His understanding of the heavenly voice and His acceptance of the path which it marked out for Him. He refused to use His power as God's Son to fulfill His personal desires, to amaze the people, or to dominate the world by political and military force.

Apparently, Jesus ministered for a short time in southern and central Palestine, while John the Baptist was still preaching (John 3:22—4:42). But the main phase of Jesus' ministry began in Galilee after John's imprisonment by Herod Antipas. This was the signal, according to Mark 1:14–15, for Jesus to proclaim God's Good News in Galilee: "The time is fulfilled, and the kingdom of God is at hand. Repent, and believe in the gospel." The character of this kingdom and how He taught it was to be established are developed in articles on the kingdom of God (*see* Kingdom of God).

Jesus' proclamation of the kingdom of God was accompanied by works of mercy and power, including the healing of the sick, par-

ticularly those who were demon-possessed. These works also proclaimed the arrival of the kingdom of God. The demons that caused such distress to men and women were signs of the kingdom of Satan. When they were cast out, this proved the superior strength of the kingdom of God.

For a time, Jesus' healing aroused great popular enthusiasm throughout Galilee. But the religious leaders and teachers found much of Jesus' activity disturbing. He refused to be bound by their religious ideas. He befriended social outcasts. He insisted on understanding and applying the Law of God in the light of its original intention, not according to the popular interpretation of the religious establishment. He insisted on healing sick people on the Sabbath day. He believed that healing people did not profane the Sabbath but honored it, because it was established by God for the rest and relief of human beings (Luke 6:6–11).

This attitude brought Jesus into conflict with the scribes, the official teachers of the law. Because of their influence, He was soon barred from preaching in the synagogues. But this was no great inconvenience. He simply gathered larger congregations to listen to Him on the hillside or by the lakeshore. He regularly illustrated the main themes of His preaching by parables. These were simple stories from daily life which would drive home some special point and make it stick in the hearer's understanding.

The mission of the Twelve and its sequel. From among the large number of His followers, Jesus selected twelve men to remain in His company for training that would enable them to share His preaching and healing ministry. When He judged the time to be ripe, Jesus sent them out two by two to proclaim the kingdom of God throughout the Jewish districts of Galilee. In many places, they found an enthusiastic hearing.

On the return of His twelve apostles, they withdrew under Jesus' leadership from the publicity that surrounded them in Galilee to the quieter territory east of the Lake of Galilee. Even here Jesus and His disciples found themselves pursued by enthusiastic crowds from Galilee. He recognized them for what they were, "sheep without a shepherd." Jesus gave these people further teaching, feeding them also with loaves and fishes. This only stimulated them to try to compel Him to be the king they wanted, and not the king He was prepared to be. Even many of His disciples stopped following.

He took the Twelve further north, into Gentile territory. Here He gave them special training to prepare them for the crisis they would have to meet shortly in Jerusalem.

When Peter declared that He was the Messiah, Jesus recognized He could now make a beginning with the creation of a new community—the church.

Jerusalem: the last phase. At the Feast of Tabernacles in the fall of A.D. 29, Jesus went to Jerusalem with the Twelve. He apparently spent the next six months in the southern part of Palestine. Jerusalem, like Galilee, needed to hear the message of the kingdom. But Jerusalem was more resistant to it even than Galilee. The spirit of revolt was in the air; Jesus' way of peace was not accepted. This is why He wept over people there, realizing their way was bound to lead to their destruction.

During the week before Passover in A.D. 30, Jesus taught each day in the temple area, debating with other teachers of differing beliefs.

On His entry into Jerusalem on a donkey the religious leaders became alarmed. When he cleared the temple of traders and money-changers, this "prophetic action" to the priestly establishment was so disturbing, the priestly party decided to arrest Jesus as soon as possible. Judas Iscariot, one of the Twelve, offered to deliver Jesus into their power without the risk of a public disturbance. Arrested on Passover Eve, Jesus was brought first before a Jewish court of inquiry, over which the high priest Caiaphas presided.

The Jewish leaders attempted first to convict Him of being a threat to the temple, but failed. Then Jesus accepted their charge that He claimed to be the Messiah, which gave the leaders occasion to hand Him over to Pilate on a charge of treason and sedition.

While "Messiah" was primarily a religious title, it could be translated into political terms as "king of the Jews." Anyone who claimed to be king of the Jews, as Jesus admitted He did, presented a challenge to the Roman emperor's rule in Judea. On this charge Pilate, the Roman governor, finally convicted Jesus. This was the charge spelled out in the inscription fixed above His head on the Cross. Death by crucifixion was the penalty for sedition by one who was not a Roman citizen.

With the death and burial of Jesus. the narrative of His earthly career came to an end. But with His resurrection on the third day, He lives and works forever as the exalted Lord. His appearances to His disciples after His resurrection assured them He was "alive after His suffering" (Acts 1:3).

The supreme example. In the teaching of Jesus, the highest of all incentives is the example of God. This was no new principle.

The central section of Leviticus is called "the law of holiness" because of its recurring theme: "I am the Lord your God . . . Be holy; for I am holy" (Lev. 11:44). This bears a close resemblance to Jesus' words in Luke 6:36, "Be merciful, just as your Father also is merciful." The children of God should reproduce their Father's character. He does not discriminate between the good and the evil in bestowing rain and sunshine; likewise, His followers should not discriminate in showing kindness to all. He delights in forgiving sinners; His children also should be marked by a forgiving spirit.

The example of the heavenly Father and the example shown by Jesus on earth are one and the same, since Jesus came to reveal the Father. Jesus' life was the practical demonstration of His ethical teaching. To His disciples He declared, "I have given you an example, that you should do as I have done to you" (John 13:15).

This theme of the imitation of Christ pervades the New Testament letters. It is especially evident in the writings of Paul, who was not personally acquainted with Jesus before he met Him on the Damascus Road. Paul instructed his converts to follow "the meekness and gentleness of Christ" (2 Cor. 10:1). He also encouraged them to imitate Him as he himself imitated Christ (1 Cor. 11:1). When he recommended to them the practice of all the Christian graces, he declared, "Put on the Lord Jesus Christ" (Rom. 13:14). Throughout the New Testament, Jesus is presented as the One who left us an example, that we should follow in His steps (1 Pet. 2:21).

The Person of Christ. The doctrine of the Person of Christ, or Christology, is one of the most important concerns of Christian theology. The various aspects of the Person of Christ are best seen by reviewing the titles that are applied to Him in the Bible.

Son of Man—The title Son of Man was Jesus' favorite way of referring to Himself. He may have done this because this was not a recognized title already known by the people and associated with popular ideas. This title means essentially "The Man," but as Jesus used it, it took on new significance.

Jesus applied this title to Himself in three distinct ways:

First, He used the title in a general way, almost as a substitute for the pronoun "I." (Luke 7:33–34; 9:58).

Second, Jesus used the title to emphasize that "the Son of Man must suffer" (Mark 8:31; 9:12).

Third, Jesus used the title *Son of Man* to refer to Himself as the one who exercised exceptional authority—authority delegated to Him by God. "The Son of Man has power [authority] on earth to forgive sins . . . and is also Lord of the Sabbath" (Mark 2:10, 28).

The Son of Man appeared to speak and act in these cases as the representative man. If God had given man dominion over all the works of His hands, then He who was the Son of Man in this special representative sense was in a position to exercise that dominion.

Near the end of His ministry, Jesus also spoke of His authority as the Son of Man at the end of time. Men and women "will see the Son of Man coming in the clouds with great power and glory," He declared (Mark 13:26; 14:62).

Messiah—When Jesus made His declaration before the high priest and His colleagues, He did so in response to the question: "Are You the Christ the Son of the Blessed?" (Mark 14:61). He replied, "I am" (Mark 14:62), "It is as you said" (Matt. 26:64).

The Christ was the *Messiah, the Son of David—of the royal family of David. For centuries the Jewish people had expected a Messiah who would restore the fortunes of Israel, liberating the nation from foreign oppression and extending His rule over Gentile nations. But Jesus Himself was slow to make messianic claims. The reason was that ideas associated with the Messiah by the Jewish people were quite different from the character and purpose of His ministry. Thus, He refused to give them any encouragement. After His death and resurrection, the concept of His messiahship was transformed by what He was and did. He was proclaimed as Messiah, God's Anointed King, resurrected in glory to occupy the throne of the universe.

Son of God—Jesus was acclaimed as the Son of God at His baptism (Mark 1:11). He also was given this title by the angel Gabriel at the annunciation: "That Holy One who is to be born will be called the Son of God" (Luke 1:35). The Gospel of John especially makes it clear that the Father-Son relationship belongs to eternity—that the Son is supremely qualified to reveal the Father because He has His eternal being "in the bosom of the Father" (John 1:18).

When Jesus is presented as the Son of God in the New Testament, two aspects of His person are emphasized: His eternal relation to God as His Father and His perfect revelation of the Father to the human race.

Word and Wisdom—Jesus' perfect revelation of the Father is also expressed when He is described as the Word *(logos)* of God (John 1:1–18). In the New Testament Christ is portrayed as the personal wisdom of God (1 Cor.

1:24, 30)—the one through whom all things were created (1 Cor. 8:6; Col. 1:16; Heb. 1:2).

The Holy One of God—This title was given to Jesus by Peter (John 6:69, RSV). This was a name belonging to Him as the Messiah—especially set apart for God.

The Lord—"Jesus is Lord" is the ultimate Christian creed. "No one can say that Jesus is Lord except by the Holy Spirit" (1 Cor. 12:3). A true believer, therefore, is a person who confesses Jesus as Lord. Several words denoting lordship were used of Jesus in the New Testament. The most frequent, and the most important in relation to the doctrine of His person, was the Greek word *kurios,* spoken of Him as "The Lord" or "The Master."

God—Jesus is called God in the New Testament. Thomas, convinced that the risen Christ stood before him, abandoned his doubts with the confession, "My Lord and my God!" (John 20:28).

But the classic text is John 1:1. John declared that the Word existed not only "in the beginning," where He was "with God," but also actually "was God." This is the Word that became incarnate as real man in Jesus Christ, without ceasing to be what He had been from eternity.

The Bible thus presents Christ as altogether God and altogether man—the perfect mediator between God and mankind because He partakes fully of the nature of both.

The work of Christ—The work of Christ has often been stated in relation to His threefold office as prophet, priest, and king. As *prophet,* He is the perfect spokesman of God to the world, fully revealing God's character and will. As *priest,* Jesus has offered to God by His death a sufficient sacrifice for the sins of the world. Now, on the basis of that sacrifice, He exercises a ministry of intercession on behalf of His people. As *king,* He is "the ruler over the kings of the earth" (Rev. 1:5)—the one has already introduced that kingdom of God to earth, and whose rule over the whole world will ultimately be revealed.

The work of Jesus can be discussed in terms of past, present, and future.

The finished work of Christ—By the "finished" work of Christ is meant the work of atonement or redemption for the human race which He completed by His death on the Cross. This work is so perfect in itself that it requires neither repetition nor addition. Because of this work, He is called "Savior of the world" (1 John 4:14) and "the Lamb of God who takes away the sin of the world" (John 1:29).

Further, His finished work broke hell's powers. Colossians 2:15 speaks of the "principalities and powers" as those evil powers which have controlled humanity. There was no hope of successful resistance against them until Christ confronted them, when it looked as if death and hell had conquered Him too. But on the Cross He conquered death itself, along with all other hostile forces. In His victory all who believe in Him have a share: "Thanks be to God, who gives us the victory through our Lord Jesus Christ" (1 Cor. 15:57).

Thus, the saving work of Christ includes the reconciliation of sinners to God (2 Cor. 5:19; Col. 1:20). It also brings them together as human beings. Hostile divisions of humanity have peace with one another through Him (Eph. 2:14).

The present work of Christ—The present work of Christ begins with His exaltation by God, after the completion of His "finished" work in His death and resurrection.

The first aspect of His present work was the sending of the Holy Spirit to dwell in His people (John 16:7). The fulfillment of this promise was announced by Peter on the Day of Pentecost (Acts 2:33), a promise that can be traced back to John the Baptist, who prophesied that Jesus would "baptize you with the Holy Spirit" (Mark 1:8).

The present work of Christ that receives the main emphasis in the New Testament is His intercession. Paul, quoting what appears to be an early Christian confession of faith, spoke of "Christ who died, and furthermore is also risen, who is even at the right hand of God, who also makes intercession for us" (Rom. 8:34; Heb. 7:25).

Jesus' presence with God as His people's representative provides the assurance that their requests for spiritual help are heard and granted. To know that He is there is a powerful incentive for His followers. No good thing that Jesus seeks for them is withheld by the Father.

The exaltation of Christ is repeatedly presented in the New Testament as the fulfillment of Psalm 110:1: "Sit at My right hand, till I make Your enemies Your footstool." This means that Christ reigns from His present place of exaltation and must do so until all His enemies are overthrown. Those enemies belong to the spiritual realm: "The last enemy that will be destroyed is death" (1 Cor. 15:26).

The future work of Christ—During His earthly ministry, Jesus declared that He had even works to do in the future: the raising of the dead and the passing of final judgment. To raise the dead and to judge the world are prerogatives of God, but He delegated these works to His Son, to discharge at the time of the end.

The raising of the dead and the passing of judgment are associated with the Second Coming of Christ. When Paul dealt with this subject, he viewed Christ's appearing in glory as the occasion when His people would share His glory and be displayed to the universe as the sons and daughters of God, heirs of the new order. He added that all creation looks forward to that time, because then it "will be delivered from the bondage of corruption into the glorious liberty of the children of God" (Rom. 8:21).

Both the present work of Christ and His future work are dependent on His "finished" work. That "finished" work was the beginning of God's "good work" in His people. This work will not be completed until "the day of Jesus Christ" (Phil. 1:6), when the entire universe will be united "in Christ" (Eph. 1:10). *Also* see ch. 55, §2.1., 5.2., 6.

JESUS, BURIAL OF—see ch. 55, §6.1.

JESUS, TEMPTATIONS OF—see ch. 55, §6.

JOHN THE BAPTIST—see ch. 55, §5.2.

JOINED. (Mark 10:7) *proskollao* (pros-*kol*-lah-oh); *Strong's #4347*: To glue or cement together, stick to, adhere to, join firmly. The word in the New Testament primarily describes the union of husband and wife. The addition of *pros* to *kollao* intensifies the relationship of husband and wife. *Proskollao* includes faithfulness, loyalty, and permanency in relationships.

JOSEPH—see ch. 55, §2.1.

JOSEPHUS—see ch. 55, §5.6., 6.1.

JOSHUA—see ch. 55, §2.2.

JOY. (Ps. 30:5) *rinnah* (ree-*nah*); *Strong's #7440*: A shout of rejoicing; shouting; loud cheering in triumph; singing. *Rinnah* describes the kind of joyful shouting at the time of a great victory. In Proverbs 11:10, *rinnah* describes the jubilation of the righteous when the wicked are eliminated. Zephaniah 3:17 literally says that God will dance over His beloved people with singing or a shout of joy. *Rinnah* may best be illustrated by the testimony of the redeemed, returning to Zion from captivity. *Rinnah* is the word for both singing and joy. *Also* (Hab. 3:18) *gil* (geel); *Strong's #1523*: To joy, rejoice, be glad, be joyful. *Gil* contains the suggestion of "dancing for joy," or "leaping for joy," since the verb originally meant "to spin around with intense motion." This lays to rest the notion that the biblical concept of joy is only "a quiet, inner sense of well-being." God dances for joy over Jerusalem and because of His people (Is. 65:19; Zeph. 3:17). The righteous Messiah shall rejoice in God's salvation with an intensity that the psalmist cannot find words to describe (Ps. 21:1). In turn, His redeemed citizens are joyful in their King; they praise Him with dances, with instruments, and with singing (Ps. 149:2–3). Although everything is wrong in Habakkuk's external world, he is leaping for joy over his fellowship with Yahweh.

JOYFUL. (2 Chr. 7:10) *samech* (sah-*meh-*ahch); *Strong's* #8056: Happy, joyful, cheerful, rejoicing, festive. *Samach* comes from the root *samach*, "to rejoice," "to get happy," or "to be joyful." *Sameach* appears as an adjective twenty-three times in the Hebrew Bible, and more than 150 times in its verbal form, usually translated "rejoice" or "be glad." *Sameach* is a word that is increasingly being used in Christian circles, as pilgrims return from Israel using the phrase *chag sameach*, which roughly compares to the English phrase "happy holidays," but is literally, "joyous festival."

JUBILEE [JOO bah lee] *(blowing the trumpet)*— the fiftieth year, after seven cycles of seven years, when specific instructions about property and slavery took effect (Lev. 25:8–55).

The word jubilee comes from the Hebrew *yobel*, which means to be "jubilant" and to "exult." The word is related to the Hebrew word for ram's horn or trumpet. The Jubilee year was launched with a blast from a ram's horn on the Day of Atonement, signifying a call to joy, liberation, and the beginning of a year for "doing justice" and "loving mercy."

The fiftieth year was a special year in which to "proclaim liberty throughout all the land" (Lev. 25:10). Specifically, individuals who had incurred debts and had sold themselves as slaves or servants to others were released from their debts and were set at liberty. Since all land belonged to God (Lev. 25:23), land could not be sold, but land could be lost to another for reasons of debt. In the Year of Jubilee such land was returned to the families to whom it was originally given.

Like the sabbatical years, the Year of Jubilee was a year for neither sowing nor reaping (Lev. 25:11). The fiftieth year became important in Israel's economic life. If anyone wished to redeem a person in debt, the price for doing so was calculated on the basis of the number of years remaining until the Jubilee.

Part of the reason why God established the Jubilee Year was to prevent the Israelites from oppressing one another (Lev. 25:17). One effect of the Jubilee Year was to prevent a permanent system of classes. The Jubilee Year had a leveling effect on Israel's culture; it gave everyone a chance to start over, economically and socially. The Jubilee Year reminds one of God's interest in liberty; God wants people to be free (Luke 4:18–19). It also stands as a witness to God's desire for justice on earth and calls into question any social practices that lead to permanent bondage and loss of economic opportunity.

JUDAISM, FIRST CENTURY—see ch. 55, §4.2., 5., 5.6., 6.

JUDGE. (Deut. 32:36) *din* (*deen*); *Strong's* #1777: Rule, govern, legislate, judge, strive, plead the cause of someone; contend with someone, contend for something. The noun derived from this word is translated as "plea," "judgment," or "cause." *Dayan* is another derivative and means "a judge." Finally, from *din* comes *medinah*, meaning "state," "province," or "government"; it is literally "place of judgment or justice." *Also* (Judg. 2:18) *shaphat* (shah-*faht*); derived from *Strong's* #8199: One who judges, governs, passes down judgment, pronounces sentence, and decides matters. The root is *shaphat*, to "judge," "decide," and "pronounce sentence." In English, both "to judge" and "judgment" have negative associations, but not so in Hebrew. Judgment is the balance, ethics, and wisdom, which, if present in a ruler's mind, enables him to govern equitably and to keep the land free from injustice. Judgment, when used of God, is that divine faculty whereby He runs the universe righteously, handing down decisions that will maintain or bring about a right state of affairs. Abraham described God as the Judge of the whole earth (Gen. 18:25). In the Book of Judges, God raised up human judges (*shophtim*) who governed Israel, executed justice, and handed down decisions. *Also* (John 18:31) *krino* (*kree*-no); *Strong's* #2919: Compare "criterion" and "critic." To separate, decide, examine, question, select, choose, resolve, make an opinion, determine, decide favorably or unfavorably, pronounce judgment.

JUDGMENT—discernment or separation between good and evil. The essence of the idea of judgment is that by this means God delivered—overthrowing evil. (This is why Israel's judges were called that, as they were instruments of God's judgment against oppression and evil, but deliverance for God's people of covenant.)

As Judge, God judges among people and their actions according to the standards of His *law. Judgment can refer either to this process of discernment or to the punishment meted out to those who fall under His wrath and condemnation (John 5:24).

In the Bible the most important judgment is the final judgment, the ultimate separation of good and evil at the end of history. The precise time of this judgment is appointed by God (Acts 17:31), but it remains unknown to man (Matt. 24:36).

From earliest times it has been recognized that God Himself is the Judge of mankind (Gen. 18:25), and that He has the power and wisdom to judge with righteousness, truth, and justice (Ps. 96:13; 98:9). The final judgment is a task given specifically to God's Son (John 5:22; Acts 17:31) to conclude His work as mediator, deliver His people from sin, and destroy all God's enemies. God's people are associated with Christ in the exercise of this judgment (1 Cor. 6:2–3; Rev. 20:4).

The final judgment will be comprehensive in scope, it will include all people and nations from the beginning of the world to the end of history (Matt. 25:31–46; Rom. 14:10–12), as well as fallen angels (2 Pet. 2:4).

The death of Jesus Christ is unique among these judgments of history. Through His death God paid the judgment price demanded by mankind's sin. The death and resurrection of Jesus are the foundations on which sinners are saved (Is. 53:5) through their trust in Him as Lord and Savior.

God's role as judge is reflected in the leadership functions of political officials, who uphold order in society and execute judgment on evildoers (Rom. 13:1–7). The rulers of Israel bore special responsibility in this respect (Deut. 16:18–19), as do the leaders of the church today (Matt. 18:17–18). Believers also have a responsibility to judge matters of wrongdoing among themselves (Matt. 18:15), but this should always be done fairly and with compassion. Believers are never to take over the task of judgment that belongs to God alone (Heb. 10:30).

JUDGMENT. (Matt. 5:22) *krisis* (*kree*-sis); *Strong's #2920:* Compare "crisis." Carries the idea of a separating, the process of distinguishing and selecting, making a decision. The New Testament uses the word primarily in a forensic sense, especially of the divine judgment. Time is heading for the event when all sin will be confronted, dealt with, and judged accordingly. Because of the atoning work of Christ, believers will stand uncondemned. *Also* (Rev. 20:4) *krima* (*kree*-mah); *Strong's #2917:* Compare "crime" and "criminal." A legal term describing the judicial process of deciding guilt or innocence. The word is used chiefly for the verdict itself, reached after an investigation. The Lord forbids fault-finding decisions in Matthew 7:2, while in 1 Corinthians 6:7, Paul discourages lawsuits against fellow Christians. *Krima* is used frequently of the

judgment of God against wrongdoing.

JUDGMENT SEAT. (Matt. 27:19) *bema* (*bay*-mah); *Strong's #968:* From *baino,* "to go," the word described a step or a stride (Acts 7:5). Then it was used for a raised platform reached by steps, especially from which orations were made. Later it denoted the tribune or tribunal of a ruler where litigants stood trial. In the New Testament it mostly refers to earthly magistrates (Acts 18:12, 16–17), but twice is used of the divine tribunal before which believers will stand (Rom. 14:10; 2 Cor. 5:10).

JUDGMENTS. (Num. 36:13) *mishpat* (meesh-*paht*); *Strong's #4941:* Decision, determination, judgment; a personal cause or right; justice, rectification, correction, punishment. Occurring more than four hundred times, *mishpat* is from the verb *shaphat,* "to decide, decree, judge, rule, determine." Judgment is that faculty (found always in God and sometimes in man) that produces decisions based on justice, rightness, truth, fairness, and equity. Judgment rectifies imbalance and sets things right again. If punishment is what is required to rectify things, then judgment brings punishment. Princes are expected to rule with justice or judgment (Is. 32:2). God Himself is called "a God of judgment" (Is. 30:18). In Isaiah 26:9, God's just decisions fill the earth and instruct the peoples in righteousness.

JUST. (Matt. 1:19) *dikaios* (*dik*-ah-yoss); *Strong's #1342:* Upright, blameless, righteous, conforming to God's laws and man's. The word was originally used to describe people who lived in accordance with *dike,* "rule," "custom." In the New Testament it is used primarily of persons who correspond to the divine standard of right made possible through justification and sanctification.

JUSTICE—the practice of what is right and just. Justice (or "judgment," KJV) specifies what is right, not only as measured by a code of law, but also by what makes for right relationships as well as harmony and peace.

The English term justice has a strong legal flavor. But the concept of justice in the Bible goes beyond the law courts to everyday life. The Bible speaks of "doing justice" (Ps. 82:3; Prov. 21:3), whereas we speak of "getting justice." Doing justice is to maintain what is right or to set things right. Justice is done when honorable relations are maintained between husbands and wives, parents and children employers and employees, government and citizens, and man and God. Justice refers to brotherliness in spirit and action.

Kings, rulers, and those in power are to be instruments of justice (Ps. 72:1), as exemplified by David (2 Sam. 8:15) and Josiah (Jer. 22:15–16). The prophet Micah declared, "He has shown you, O man, what is good; and what does the Lord require of you but to do justly, to love mercy, and to walk humbly with your God?" (Mic. 6:8). During those days, justice was often perverted through bribery and favoritism or partiality (Deut. 1:17; Prov. 17:23). But God's rewards come to those who practice justice in all their dealings with others. In the words of the prophet Amos, "Let justice run down like water, and righteousness like a mighty stream" (Amos 5:24).

 JUSTIFICATION—the process by which sinful human beings are made acceptable to a holy God.

Justification by Grace. Christianity is unique because of its teaching of justification by grace (Rom. 3:24). Justification is God's declaration that the demands of His Law have been fulfilled in the righteousness of His Son. The basis for this justification is the death of Christ. Second Corinthians 5:19 says, "God was in Christ reconciling the world to Himself, not imputing their trespasses to them." This reconciliation covers all sin: "For by one offering He has perfected forever those who are being sanctified" (Heb. 10:14). Justification, then, is based on the work of Christ, accomplished through His blood (Rom. 5:9) and brought to His people through His resurrection (Rom. 4:25).

When God justifies, He charges the sin of man to Christ and credits the righteousness of Christ to the believer (2 Cor. 5:21). Thus, "through one Man's righteous act, the free gift came to all men, resulting in justification of life" (Rom. 5:18). Because this righteousness is "the righteousness of God" which is "apart from the law" (Rom. 3:21), it is thorough; a believer is "justified from all things" (Acts 13:39). God is "just" because His holy standard of perfect righteousness has remained unlowered, but has been entirely fulfilled in Christ. Further, He is the "justifier," because this righteousness is freely given to the believer (Rom. 3:26; 5:16).

Justification by faith. Although the Lord Jesus has paid the price for our justification, it is through our faith that He is received and His righteousness is experienced and enjoyed (Rom. 3:25–30). Faith is considered righteousness (Rom. 4:3, 9), not as the work of man (Rom. 4:5), but as the gift and work of God (John 6:28–29; Phil. 1:29).

The New Testament sometimes seems to speak of justification by works. For example, Jesus spoke of justification (and condemnation) "by your words" (Matt. 12:37). Paul said, "the doers of the law will be justified" (Rom. 2:13). And James concluded that "a man is justified by works, and not by faith only" (James 2:24).

These statements seem to conflict with such warnings as "by the deeds of the law no flesh will be justified in His sight" (Rom. 3:20), and that the attempt to be justified through law is equivalent to being "estranged from Christ" and "fallen from grace" (Gal. 5:4).

The solution to this apparent conflict lies in the distinction between the works of the flesh and the fruit of the Spirit (Gal. 5:16–25). Not only is Christ's righteousness legally accounted to the believer, but Christ also dwells in the believer through the Holy Spirit (Rom. 8:10), creating works of faith (Eph. 2:10). Certainly God's works may be declared righteous (Is. 26:12). Thus, the order of events in justification is grace, faith, and works or, in other words, by grace, through faith, resulting in works (Eph. 2:8–10).

The results of justification. The negative result of justification is what we are saved from: "Having now been justified . . . we shall be saved from wrath" (Rom. 5:9). The positive result is what we are saved to: "Whom He justified, these He also glorified" (Rom. 8:30).

Paul also notes "peace with God" (Rom. 5:1) and access to God's grace (Rom. 5:2) as positive benefits. The believer in Christ may look forward to the redemption of his body (Rom. 8:23) and an eternal inheritance (Rom. 8:17; 1 Pet. 1:4).

JUSTIFIED. (Matt. 12:37) *dikaioo* (dik-ah-*yah*-oh); *Strong's #1344:* A legal term signifying to acquit, declare righteous, show to be righteous. In this passage Jesus refers to the day of judgment as the day of His determining condemnation or justification, based on our hearts' response to the Spirit.

 KEEP A FEAST. (Ex. 23:14) *chagag* (cha-*gahg*); *Strong's #2287:* To celebrate, keep a feast, be festive, dance, assemble for rejoicing and celebration. This verb occurs fifteen times. It is translated as "dancing" in 1 Samuel 30:16, and "kept a pilgrim feast" in Psalm 42:4. An important derivative is *chag,* "feast," especially referring to the seven feasts God gave to Israel. The name "Haggai" comes from *chagag* and means

"Festive One" or "Celebrating One." The Old Testament abounds in feasts and celebrations, ordained by God and resulting in human happiness.

KENOSIS [keh NOE sis]—a theological term used in connection with the dual nature of Jesus as fully human and fully divine. The word comes from a Greek verb which means "to empty" (Phil. 2:7). The NASB translates this passage, "He emptied Himself," but the KJV and NKJV express it, "He made Himself of no reputation."

The Bible teaches that our Savior was both fully divine and completely human during His earthly life. But nowhere does Scripture explain exactly how Jesus' two natures co-existed. Theologians have struggled for years to explain this mystery. "The Kenosis" describes the fact that, according to Philippians 2:7, when God's divine Son became human He voluntarily laid aside His divine rights to function as God. Jesus did not stop being God, but He chose not to exercise His powers as God, choosing instead to become fully dependent upon the Holy Spirit for His power to live and minister. It is this great truth which underscores the fact that Jesus not only lived a sinless life on human terms (yet retaining His nature as God), but He provided a model for His call to us to minister in His name (as mere humans). It is an effective model not because He was "merely human," but because He chose to minister in the Spirit's might, voluntarily confining Himself to those resources.

Thus, in commissioning His own to prayer and ministry, Jesus says of His follower, "The works that I do he will do also; and greater than these he will do, because I go to My Father" (John 14:12).

Jesus has lived out the pathway for redeemed humans to live in the resources of the Holy Spirit and minister in His Name with supernatural expectations—not in their strength or wisdom, but His—a wisdom and grace He demonstrated in His ministry.

KEPT. (1 Pet. 1:5) *phroureo* (froo-*reh*-oh); *Strong's #5432:* A military term picturing a sentry standing guard as protection against the enemy. We are in spiritual combat, but God's power and peace (Phil. 4:7) are our sentinels and protectors.

KEYS, POWER OF—a phrase used by Jesus to describe the authority given by Him to His disciples. In ancient times a key expressed the idea of authority, power, or privilege. Even today, keys represent access, privilege and enfranchisement. So Jesus' words to Peter

that He would give "the keys of the kingdom of heaven" (Matt. 16:19), indicate more than a gift to Peter of authority or the power to bind or loose. These words speak to all saints for all time who know and confess that Jesus is the Christ. The idea in "to bind and loose" stems from Aramaic words which relate to excommunication and reinstatement, or the determining of objects as being either clean or unclean. In essence, they have to do with access and acceptability, or the opposite.

The general Protestant view of this text is that the church is the agent of this power or authority to bind or loose, either through its official leaders or through all believers. This authority or power awaits appropriation, not with arrogance or smugness, but with a humble yet bold spirit of faith. We have been given access to kingdom authority through Christ the King. This awaits application in prayer and ministry, in faith and forgiveness—advancing the church against hell's dark powers and seeing the church built up by the release of divine grace and power.

KIDRON VALLEY—see ch. 55, §6.

KINDNESS, LOVINGKINDNESS—God's loyal love and favor toward His people. In the Old Testament, the word translated as "kindness" or "lovingkindness" refers to God's long-suffering love—His determination to keep His promises to His chosen people in spite of their sin and rebellion (Deut. 7:12; Hos. 2:14–23). This attribute of God was shown through His divine mercy and forgiveness toward sinners when payment of sins through the sacrificial system was no longer effective (Ps. 51:1).

In the New Testament, the Greek word translated as "grace" best represents the idea of God's kindness or lovingkindness. Because God has been gracious toward us, we should treat all people with kindness or grace (Luke 6:35). All people are created in God's image and should be treated accordingly, no matter how badly they have twisted and deformed that image (James 3:9). Kindness is not an apathetic response to sin, but a deliberate act of revealed grace in hopes of bringing people back to God (Hos. 2:14–23; Rom. 2:4).

KINDNESS. (Acts 28:2) *philanthropia* (fil-an-thro-*pee*-ah); *Strong's #5363:* Compare "philanthropist" and "philanthropy." Love for mankind, hospitality, acts of kindness, readiness to help, human friendship, benevolence, and taking thought of others. The word is a compound of *philos*, "love," and *anthropos*, "man." In Titus 3:4, *philanthropia* is used to describe God's lovingkindness toward men. *Also* (Gal. 5:22) *chrestotes* (khray-*stot*-ace);

Strong's #5544: Goodness in action, sweetness of disposition, gentleness in dealing with others, benevolence, kindness, affability. The word describes the ability to act for the welfare of those taxing your patience. The Holy Spirit removes abrasive qualities from the character of one under His control.

KINGDOM OF GOD, KINGDOM OF HEAVEN— God's rule of grace in the world, a future period foretold by the prophets of the Old Testament and identified and ministered by Jesus as beginning with His public ministry and continuing today through His ministry in the church, until that Day it is consummated with His Coming and rule on earth. The kingdom of God is the experience of blessedness, like that of the Garden of Eden, where evil is fully overcome and where those who live in the kingdom know only happiness, peace, and joy. This was the main expectation of the Old Testament prophets about the future.

John the Baptist astonished his hearers when he announced that this expected and hoped-for kingdom was "at hand" in the person of Jesus (Matt. 3:2). Jesus repeated this message (Matt. 4:17; Mark 1:15), but He went even further by announcing clearly that the kingdom was already present in His ministry: "If I cast out demons by the Spirit of God, surely the kingdom of God has come upon you" (Matt. 12:28). Jesus was the full embodiment of the kingdom.

The entire ministry of Jesus is understood in relation to this important declaration of the presence of the kingdom. His ethical teachings, for example, cannot be understood apart from the announcement of the kingdom. They are ethics of the kingdom; the perfection to which they point makes no sense apart from the present experience of the kingdom. Participation in the new reality of the kingdom involves a follower of Jesus in a call to the highest righteousness (Matt. 5:20).

The acts and deeds of Jesus likewise make sense only in the larger context of proclaiming the kingdom. When John the Baptist asked whether Jesus was "the Coming One," or the Messiah, Jesus answered by recounting some of His deeds of healing (Matt. 11:5). The reference in these words to the expectation of a *messiah, especially of the prophet Isaiah (Is. 29:18–19; 35:5–6; 61:1), could not have been missed by John. At the synagogue in Nazareth, Jesus read a passage from Isaiah 61 about the coming messianic age and then made the astonishing announcement, "Today this Scripture is fulfilled in your hearing" (Luke 4:21).

All that Jesus did is related to this claim that the kingdom of God has dawned through His ministry. His healings were manifestations of the presence of the kingdom. In these deeds there was a direct confrontation between God and the forces of evil, or Satan and his demons. Summarizing His ministry, Jesus declared, "I saw Satan fall like lightning from heaven" (Luke 10:18). Satan and evil are in retreat now that the kingdom has made its entrance into human history. This is progressing now (1 John 2:17), and we live in anticipation of the final age of perfection that will be realized at Christ's return.

Although the Gospels of Matthew, Mark, Luke, and John focus on the present aspect of the kingdom of God, it is also clear that the kingdom will be realized perfectly only at the *Second Coming. The kingdom that comes through the ministry of Jesus dawns in the form of a mystery. Although it is physically present in the deeds and words of Jesus, it does not overwhelm the world. The judgment of God's enemies is postponed. The kingdom that arrived with Jesus did not include the triumphal victory so longed for by the Jews. It arrived secretly like leaven, inconspicuously like a mustard seed, or like a small pearl of great value that can be hidden in one's pocket (Matt. 13:31–46).

The demons reflect this oddity when they ask Jesus, "Have you come here to torment us before the time?" (Matt. 8:29). The future kingdom will bring the present age to an end and usher in the perfect age promised in the prophets. The present kingdom is both an anticipation and a guarantee of this future bliss.

The expression kingdom of God occurs mostly in the Gospels of Matthew, Mark, and Luke. The Gospel of John and the epistles of the New Testament refer to the same reality but in different language, using phrases such as eternal life or salvation. The apostle Paul identified the kingdom of God as "righteousness and peace and joy in the Holy Spirit" (Rom. 14:17). Perhaps one reason he described it this way is that the kingdom of God was a Jewish expression unfamiliar and possibly misleading to Gentiles.

Some interpreters of the Bible have described the phrase kingdom of God as a more comprehensive term referring to both heaven and earth. Likewise, some believe kingdom of God is a more restricted term referring to God's rule on earth, especially in relation to the nation of Israel. In this view Jesus offered the literal kingdom of heaven to Israel, but the Jews refused to accept it. Thus, it has been postponed until the Second Coming of Christ.

A careful study of the Gospels, however, shows that the two phrases are used interchangeably. In parallel passages, Matthew uses "kingdom of heaven" while Mark and Luke has "kingdom of God" (Matt. 4:17; Mark 1:15; Luke 13:28). Even in Matthew the two phrases are sometimes used interchangeably, as in Matthew 19:23–24, where they are used one after the other in the same connection.

KINGDOM OF GOD, THE. The whole of Jesus' own preaching, teaching, and ministry centered in these words: "The kingdom of God is at hand" (Mark 1:15). He came as the Savior-Lamb to rescue and redeem mankind to know his original estate in the divine order. The dynamic of Christian life and ministry is found in understanding the kingdom of God, which is not in "eating and drinking" (that is, ritual performance), but in "righteousness and peace and joy in the Holy Spirit" (Rom. 14:17). In a thoroughgoing development constituting 39 brief articles under eight headings, the (1) foundations, (2) terminology, (3) message, (4) character, (5) ministry, (6) conflict, (7) worship, and (8) prophecy of the kingdom are elaborated. Here is a wealth of material to establish a full-orbed perspective on the kingdom of God, the essence of the church's message and life. This study unfolds the balance that calls us to kingdom life and power in the present, while still anticipating the kingdom's final fullness and consummation in the future.

Foundations of the Kingdom

1. God's Sovereignty (Gen. 1:1). The necessary beginning point in studying the theme of "the kingdom of God" is the Bible's opening verse. Here we meet the Sovereign of all the universe, whose *realm*, *reign*, and *regency* are described at the outset. (1) His *realm* (or scope of His rule) is transcendent; that is, not only does it include the entire physical universe, it exceeds it. He existed before all creation, He expands beyond it, and by virtue of having begotten it, He encompasses all that it is. (2) His *reign* (or the power by which He rules) is exercised by His will, His word, and His works. By His own will He creatively decides and designs; by His own word He speaks creation into being; and by His own works, His Spirit displays His unlimited power. (3) His *regency* (or authority to rule) is in His preexistence and holiness. He is there *before* creation "in the beginning." Thus, as its Creator, He deserves to be its Potentate. His benevolent intent in creating things "good" reveals His holy nature (that is, complete and perfect), and thus His moral

right to be creation's King. All kingdom power and authority flow from Him.

2. Man's Delegated "Dominion" (Gen. 1:26–28; 2:16–17). In creating man, the Sovereign of the universe makes a choice to delegate to man "dominion . . . on the earth" (v. 28). Man's power and authority for exercising this rule originate in God's intent to make man in His own image and likeness. Man's ability to sustain his role as delegated ruler of earth will rest in his continued obedience to God's rule as King of all. His power to reign in life will extend only as far as his faithfulness to obey God's law. (See also 1 Chr. 29:10–16.)

3. Before the Fall (Gen. 1:31). The original order of man's environment on earth must be distinguished from what it became following the impact of man's Fall, the Curse, and the eventual Deluge (Is. 45:18; Rom. 8:20; 2 Pet. 3:4–7). The agricultural, zoological, geological, and meteorological disharmony to which creation became subject must not be attributed to God. The perfect will of God, as founding King of creation, is *not* manifest in the presence of death, disease, discord, and disaster any more than it is manifest in human sin. Our present world does not reflect the kingdom order He originally intended for man's enjoyment on earth, nor does it reflect God's kingdom as it shall ultimately be experienced on this planet. Understanding this, we should be cautious not to attribute to "God's will" or to "acts of God" those characteristics of our world that resulted from the ruin of God's original order by reason of man's Fall.

4. Impact of the Fall (Gen. 3:16–24). Through disobedience to the terms of his rule, man "falls," thus experiencing the loss of his "dominion" (vv. 22–23). Everything of his delegated realm (earth) comes under a curse as his relationship with God, the fountainhead of his power to rule, is severed (vv. 17–18). Thus man loses the "life" power essential to ruling in God's kingdom (vv. 19, 22). Beyond the tragedy of man's loss, two other facts unfold. First, through his disobedience to God and submission to the Serpent's suggestions, man's rule has been forfeited to the Serpent. Revelation 12:9 verifies that the spirit employing the snake's form was Satan himself. The domain originally delegated to man now falls to Satan, who becomes administrator of this now-cursed realm. The Serpent's "seed" and "head" indicate a continual line (seed) of evil offspring extending Satan's rule (head) (v. 15). However, a second fact offers hope. Amid the tragedy of this sequence of events, God begins to move redemptively, and a plan for recovering man's lost estate is promised (v. 15) and set in motion with the first sacrifice (v. 21).

5. After the Flood (Gen. 8:20—9:17). Following the Deluge, a renewed order is established. Noah's faith, which occasioned his deliverance, is now manifest in an expression of worship to God as he disembarks from the ark (8:20–22). God declares His covenant with Noah (9:8–17) after restating His purpose to make man to be fruitful and multiply, as at the beginning. However, other factors are not as at the beginning; notably the relationship of God with man, as well as of man with creation. The Flood has not reversed the loss of man's original dominion. He is still fallen, though thankfully a recipient of God's mercy. Further, the animals will fear mankind from this time on (9:2), which was not characteristic of their relationship prior to this. In the ultimate restoration of God's kingdom on earth, the original fearless order will be regained (Is. 11:6–9). Notwithstanding these deficiencies, a cleansed realm for seeking God's kingdom first is newly available to man, and again God asserts man's responsibility for administrating earth with an accountability to Him (9:1–7). The Flood has not neutralized the influence of the Serpent, nor has it changed mankind's capacity for rebellion against God's rule. Nevertheless, new hope dawns with promise for the eventual recovery of what was lost of his first estate.

6. Prototype "Kingdom" Person (Gen. 12:1–3). Abraham is shown in both Old and New Testaments as the prototype of all who experience God's processes of seeking to reinstate man through redemption, first and foremost, in his relationship to God by faith, without works (Rom. 4:1–25). But too seldom is the second facet of redemption noted. Abraham is also shown as a case of God's program to recover man's "reign in life" (Rom. 5:17). Abraham is designated as the "father" of all who walk his pathway of faith (Rom. 4:12). As such, he is God's revealed example of His plan to eventually reestablish His kingdom's rule in all the earth through people of His covenant. Through Abraham, whom He wills to become "a great nation" (restoring rule) and to whom He chooses to give a "great name" (restoring authority), God declares His plans to beget innumerable children who will be modeled after this prototypical "father of faith." This truth is confirmed in Romans 4:13, where Abraham's designation as "heir of the world" parallels Jesus' promise that His followers, who humble themselves in faith, shall also be recipients of "the kingdom" and shall "inherit the earth" (Matt. 5:3–5).

7. Patriarchal Examples (Gen. 26:1–5; 28:1–22). The promise of God to Abraham that he would be "heir of the world" (Rom. 4:13) is repeated to his offspring, Isaac and Jacob, in succession. God's words and dealings in the lives of the patriarchs reveal that His unfolding program of redemption is dual: (1) restoring relationship *to* God to establish fellowship with Him and (2) restoring rulership in life *under* God to reestablish human ability to "rule" in life's practical details of family and business. Thus, under His covenant, God promised these patriarchs both *progeny*—a family line—and *property*—an economic base. This illustrates God's progressive processing of His redemptive promise. He not only provides for restored fellowship with Himself (relationship), but covenants for human fulfillment and personal fruitfulness in life. This plan is geared not only to bless His people, but to make them a blessing to others. Joseph's life elaborates this principle. God redeems him from the pit by His merciful providence, then raises him to rulership in Egypt, for the saving of nations (Genesis 37—50).

The "kingdom" concept of God's delegating His rule on earth to be administrated through those who walk with Him is birthed at creation. Although damaged at man's Fall, it is progressively being reinstated as a redemptive goal and is demonstrated in those who accept His covenant.

8. Human Responsibility (1 Chr. 29:10–16). No text in the Bible more magnificently declares God's sovereign power: there is no one like the Lord, the Almighty One, whose glory fills the universe. And yet, in the center of this grand anthem of acknowledgment to that towering truth, David asserts that although the kingdom is God's (v. 11), God gives resources that are man's to administrate. Verse 14 literally reads, "Everything that exists is from You, and we administer it from Your hand." God is the fountainhead of all life and power; man is the appointed heir for its management. Psalms 8:6 and 115:16 affirm that while the created universe and the glory of the heavens are God's and God's alone, He has delegated the stewardship of earth's affairs to mankind. Noble views of God's sovereignty must be balanced with a complementary view of man's duties and redeemed capacities. Neglect of this balance, while seeming to extol God's greatness, can produce apathy or irresponsible attitudes. For example, God does not predestine mismanaged resources, families, politics, and so on, any more than He does human sinning. Man is responsible and accountable for earth's problems and—reinstated under God—is intended to become the agent for their solution. He can only become such by drawing on God's sovereign wisdom, power, and resource—that is, on God's "kingdom." Just as man's sin and Fall have damaged the potential partnership between the Creator and His appointed heir to this planet, redemption has set the recovery in motion. Renewed under God, the redeemed may, in fact, partner with God and thereby decisively assist in the reestablishment of God's rule over circumstances and situations on earth. But this only operates under the divine order within redemption's plan under divine grace and through man's receiving divine power by God's Spirit.

Terminology of the Kingdom

9. Defining the Hope (Matt. 3:1–2). The New Testament records 137 references to "the kingdom," and over one hundred of these are during Jesus' ministry, as His entire teaching and approach as Messiah—the Savior-King—center on this theme. To what does "the kingdom" refer? It refers to God's sovereign rule in the universe—He is the King of the heavens. (See Gen. 1:1.) But more specifically, here it refers to the entry of God's long-anticipated Anointed One—the prophesied Messiah, the promised Son of David who would not be the Savior, Deliverer, and King of only Israel, but of all mankind. "The Gentiles" (or all nations)—*all flesh*—were promised recipients of this hope (Is. 9:6–7; 11:10; 40:5). Declaring the kingdom "at hand," that is, "drawing near," John was announcing that the rule of God's King was about to overthrow the power and rule of all evil—both human and hellish. The "kingdom" was near because the King was here. And His presence, introducing the power of "the kingdom of God," meant a new world of potential hope to mankind. Man would no more need be held hostage to either the rule of *death* over mankind, resultant from human sin and sinning, or to the *deadening* rule of oppressive human systems, political or otherwise. Further, the kingdom of darkness would be confronted and the death, deprivation, disease, and destruction levied by satanic power would begin to be overthrown. As God's King, Jesus offers the blessing of God's rule, now available to bring life to every human experience, as well as deliverance from the dominance of either flesh or the Devil.

10. Synonymous Expressions (Matt. 19:23–24). This text uses the phrases "kingdom of heaven" and "kingdom of God" interchangeably. In doing so, it sufficiently demonstrates that the two terms are meant to refer to one and the same thing: the kingdom. Although some make a labored distinction between them, this text and ten others in the Gospels clearly show that the "kingdom of heaven" and "kingdom of God" are verifiably synonyms. Matthew is the only New Testament writer who used the term "kingdom of heaven." In doing so, he showed a sensitivity toward his originally intended audience of Jewish readers, for whom too frequent a use of the name of "God" would have seemed irreverent. By a variety of terms Matthew refers to "the kingdom" fifty times in his Gospel: thirty-two times as "kingdom of heaven"; five times as "kingdom of God"; four times as the "Father's" kingdom; and twice as the kingdom of "the Son of Man." The remaining seven references are simply to "the kingdom" without other designation. This variety in the usage, made by the only one using the phrase "kingdom of heaven," surely shows these terms to be synonyms for the kingdom.

11. John's Writings (John 18:36). John is the only Gospel writer who records these words of Jesus: "My kingdom is not of this world." Near the end of the first century, when John was writing his Gospel, Christians were often assailed with the accusation that their goals were not spiritual, but political. The Roman Empire was being filled with reborn citizens of a heavenly kingdom, but their "kingdom of God" terminology could be misunderstood. Thus, John adopts the phrase "eternal life," as much to show the new *quality* of life Jesus Christ has brought as to describe its *quantity*. The idea of "eternal life" describes a divine *dimension* of life available to mankind, as well as a destined *duration* of "everlasting" endlessness. The words "eternal life" occur fifteen times in John's writings, "the kingdom of God" only six. Some have thought John's relatively infrequent use of "kingdom of God" suggested this message application was confined only to the time of Jesus' ministry and the birth of "the church age." Notwithstanding the fact that the birth of the church did introduce a new era in human history, the message of "the gospel of the kingdom" was not changed. For example, see the thrust of its being taught and preached throughout Acts (20:25; 28:23, 30–31).

12. Paul's Writings (Col. 1:27–28). "In Christ" is the expression Paul most frequently uses to designate the new life potential through the gospel. The Messiah (Christ) being King, the term clearly places the believer in the circle of all that is represented and contained in the King, His salvation conquest, and His personal rule. The essential truth is that the

Savior-King has come, and in Him the rule of God has altered the limits sin has heretofore placed on individuals. People no longer need be ruled by their carnality (flesh) or controlled by evil (the devil). Being freed, that is, transferred to a new kingdom, they can know the joy of a relationship with God through the power of the Cross and can realize a beginning reinstatement of their rulership under God, through the power of the Holy Spirit. Thereby, living in the King's kingdom brings a dual hope: eternity with Christ and the promise of grace to begin "reigning in life." Now, "in Christ" designates the new life that may be lived in the benefits of, and by the power of, the King Jesus, "who has brought life [reigning in life presently in Christ—Rom. 5:17] and immortality [reigning forever with Christ—Rev. 22:5] to light through the gospel" (2 Tim. 1:10).

The Message of the Kingdom

13. The Gospel of the Kingdom (Mark 1:14–15). The synoptic Gospels and Acts make at least twenty direct references to the preaching of "the gospel of the kingdom" from John the Baptist (Matt. 3:1–2), throughout Jesus' ministry (Mark 1:14–15), in the disciples' ministry during Jesus' ministry (Luke 9:1–2), and throughout Acts. Jesus prophesied this same message shall be taken to the ends of the world (Matt. 24:14), commissioning His disciples to do this and promising the Holy Spirit's power for the task (Mark 16:15–18; Acts 1:3–8).

It is clear that the early church proclaimed the same message Jesus preached, that is, "the gospel of the kingdom of God" (Acts 8:12; 19:8; 20:25; 28:23, 30–31). Also, they experienced the same confirming evidences present in His ministry.

There is only one gospel: Jesus preached it, transmitted it to His disciples, and has committed it to His church. Paul warned against ever receiving any other gospel. "Any other" may be either a message of outright error or an argument for a diluted message, devoid of power though nominally Christian. Jude 3 urges us always to contend for the original, "the faith which was once for all delivered to the saints." Hold to the full "gospel of the kingdom," and expect the Lord to confirm that "word" with the signs He promised (Mark 16:15–18).

14. Repentance (Matt. 3:1–2; 4:17). The first call of the kingdom is to repentance. The implications of biblical repentance are threefold: (1) renunciation and reversal, (2) submission and teachability, and (3) continual shapeability. There is no *birth* into the king-

dom without hearing the call to salvation, renouncing one's sin, and turning from sin toward Christ the Savior (Acts 3:19).

There is no *growth* in the kingdom without obedience to Jesus' commandments and a childlike responsiveness as a disciple of Jesus, yielding to the teaching of God's Word (James 1:21–25).

There is no lifelong increase of *fruit* as a citizen of the kingdom without a willingness to accept the Holy Spirit's correction and guidance (Eph. 5:30).

15. New Birth (John 3:1–5). Upon repentance, a new order of life opens to the believer in Jesus Christ. Jesus used the figure of "new birth" to dramatically indicate three things: (1) Without new birth, there is no life and no relationship with God (14:6). (2) In new birth, new perspective comes as we "see the kingdom of God" (3:3), God's Word becomes clear, and the Holy Spirit's works and wonders are believed and experienced—faith is alive. (3) Through new birth we are introduced—literally we "enter" (v. 5)—to a new realm, where God's new kingdom order can be realized (2 Cor. 5:17). New birth is more than simply being "saved." It is a requalifying experience, opening up the possibilities of our whole being to the supernatural dimension of life and fitting us for a beginning in God's kingdom order.

16. A Present and Future Kingdom (Matt. 13:1–52). In this chapter, Jesus introduces parables as a means of teaching "kingdom" truths (vv. 10–11). Of the forty parables Jesus gave, He made direct references to the kingdom in nineteen. These stories clearly relate to different time frames. Some impact the present, teaching (1) the need for kingdom people to have hearing ears (vv. 3–23); (2) the breadth of the kingdom's spread (vv. 31–35); and (3) the cost of the kingdom's acquisition (vv. 44–46). Others relate to the future, teaching (1) the final disposing of the fruit of the Adversary's hindrance (vv. 36–43) and (2) the final disposition of the mixed ingathering from kingdom outreach (vv. 47–51). In mixing these two aspects of the "kingdom," Jesus helps us appreciate the kingdoms as both present and prospective. The message of the kingdom is two-edged and relates to two frames of *time*: First, God, in Christ, is *now* recovering man from his double loss—relationship *with* God and of rulership *under* God. He promised this at man's Fall, illustrated it in the patriarchs and Israel's history, and *now* the King has come to begin fully bringing it about. The kingdom is being realized *presently*, in partial and personal ways, as it is spread *through* all the earth by the Holy Spirit's power in the church.

Second, the kingdom will be realized *finally* in consummate and conclusive ways only at the return of Jesus Christ and by His reign *over* all the earth. What we experience of His triumph now, in part, will then be fully manifest (1 Cor. 13:9–10; 15:24; Rev. 11:15). This complete view allows for our understanding and applying the principles of "kingdom come" without falling into the confusion of expecting *now* what the Bible says will only be *then.*

17. People of the Kingdom (Col. 1:13). The "transference" of the believer, from under Satan's authority to Christ's, is described as movement into another "kingdom." Ensuing verses describe Christ's redemption as bringing us to a place of "completeness," that is, of spiritual adequacy, authority, or ability to live victoriously over and above the invisible powers of darkness (vv. 14–16; 2:6–10). This becomes functionally true, as opposed to merely theoretically so, when we (1) live and love as *citizens* of the heavenly kingdom (Phil. 3:20); (2) utilize this kingdom's *currency,* which is of irresistible value (Acts 3:6); (3) operate as *ambassadors* authorized to offer kingdom peace and reconciliation to those yet unrenewed in Christ (2 Cor. 5:20); and (4) serve as the kingdom *militia,* girded for prayerful conflict against the dark powers controlling so much of this present world (Eph. 6:10–20). The terminology of "the kingdom" holds more than poetic pictures. It is practically applicable to all our living.

18. Kingdom within You (Luke 17:20–21). Fundamental to New Testament truth is that the kingdom of God is the spiritual reality and dynamic available to each person who receives Jesus Christ as Savior and Lord. To receive Him—the King—is to receive His kingly rule, not only *in* your life and *over* your affairs, but *through* your life and *by* your service and love. "The kingdom of God is within you," Jesus said.

This will never be possible if we operate independently of God's power and grace. The possibility of reinstatement to rulership is brought about only through the forgiveness of sins and full redemption in Christ through the Cross. The Bible never suggests either (1) that there exists in man a divine spark, which may be fanned to flame by noble human efforts, or (2) that godlikeness is somehow resident in man's potential, as though human beings are or may become "gods." To the contrary, man is lost in darkness and alienated from God (Eph. 4:18; 2:12).

However, full salvation brings restored relationship to God and a full potential for His kingdom's ruling "within us" as we walk with Him. Jesus has sent the Holy Spirit to cause the anointing of His messiahship to be transmitted to us (Is. 61:1–3; Luke 4:18; John 1:16; 1 John 2:20, 27; 4:17). So it is only on these terms that a human being can say, "The kingdom of God is within me."

Character and the Kingdom

19. Basic Traits (Matt. 5:1—7:27). In the Sermon on the Mount, Jesus outlines the primary attributes of people who receive the rule of the kingdom He brings. Nine direct references to "the kingdom" are in this sermon, calling for: humility (5:3), willingness to suffer persecution (5:10), earnest attention to God's commandments (5:19), refusal to substitute false piety for genuinely right behavior (5:20), a life of prayer (6:10, 13), prioritizing spiritual over material values (6:33), and above all, acknowledging Christ's lordship by obeying the revealed will of God (7:21). Clearly, the authority Christ hopes to delegate to His own is intended to be exercised by disciples willing to accept renewal in soul and behavior, as well as rebirth through forgiveness of sin. To these, obviously, the call to "kingdom" living and ministry includes the expectation that Holy Spirit-begotten fruit and gifts will develop in the believer. The same Spirit that distributes gifts of power for kingdom service also works in us to beget kingly qualities of life, love, and a holy character (John 15:1–17; Gal. 5:22–23).

20. Childlikeness (Matt. 18:1–4). Jesus confronts the tendency of humanity to associate authority with an exercise of dominance over others. The dominion or authority in kingdom life God wants to reinstate in us is for victorious, fruitful living and for the overthrow of hellish powers, not for gaining control of others or for serving our own interests. His call to childlike humility and a servantlike heart (John 13:1–17) establishes the spirit and style by which the authority of the believer is to be exercised as an agent of God's kingdom power. (*See* Matt. 19:14; Mark 10:14–15; Luke 18:16–17.)

21. Forgiveness (Matt. 18:18–35). Jesus' prefacing words make this "kingdom" parable of the unforgiving servant especially crucial. He warns against the human capacity to forget God's gracious gift of forgiveness and allow smallness of soul to breed unforgiveness. (1) Jesus showed how unforgiveness can restrict what God would do in others. (Note: The jailed fellow-servant is still in prison at the story's end, revealing the power of unforgiveness to "bind" circumstances to an undesirable level of perpetual problem.) (2) Jesus teaches how the spirit of unforgiveness (the torturers, literally "bill collectors") exacts its toll on our bodies, minds, and emotions. Finally, every "kingdom" person is advised to sustain a forgiving heart toward all other persons. Kingdom privileges and power must not be mishandled. The "binding" power of unforgiveness is potentially dangerous to any of us.

Matthew 18:18–19 is frequently quoted to assert the believer's authority in prayer. But the power to "bind and loose" is quickly shown to be as much of a liability as an asset if unforgiveness remains in the people of God's kingdom.

22. Integrity and Morality (1 Cor. 6:9–10). The privilege of becoming an authorized and empowered representative of God's kingdom and of ministering Christ's life and the Holy Spirit's gifts to others is not the heritage of the unholy. Twice the text says certain people will not "inherit the kingdom of God," and then designates broad categories of people who are excluded from enjoying the resources and rewards of righteousness. (See also Gal. 5:19–21; Eph. 5:5.)

Although our righteousness before God is through Christ's work alone, and while it remains timelessly true that we cannot earn any spiritual gift or right to function in the power of the Holy Spirit, integrity and morality of character are nonetheless essential to the "kingdom person."

Holiness of heart and life keeps the lines of communication with God unjumbled, by keeping any private or carnal agenda out of the way. They also insure the Holy Spirit free access for distributing His gifts and fulfilling the Father's will in any situation.

Ministry of the Kingdom

23. The Holy Spirit (Mark 1:15). Jesus' ministry did not begin until He received His "anointing" as Messiah—the empowering that came through the descent of the Holy Spirit upon Him (v. 10). Though conceived and born by the Spirit's power (Luke 1:35) and sinless His whole lifetime (John 8:46), He did not attempt ministry without the Spirit's power. He insisted John baptize Him, not for repentance, but because He knew the Holy Spirit would come upon Him at that time (Matt. 3:13–17). From that time, He is led of the Spirit (v. 12) and moves into ministry—declaring the presence of God's kingdom and manifesting its miracles, signs, and wonders (Luke 4:14–15; Matt. 4:23–25).

This pathway points each believer to the need for power, if kingdom ministry is to be advanced through us—His church. Like Him, we, too, are "born of the Spirit" (John 3:5–6).

Though our spiritual birth is not as His biological Virgin Birth, the point remains. Spiritual rebirth saves, but spiritual enduement is needed for ministering in kingdom power. Similarly, our justification in Christ—being declared sinless (2 Cor. 5:21)—does not qualify for kingdom power in ministry. In His incarnation Jesus' Person and perfection exceeded ours in every way, yet Jesus still acknowledged the need for His *own* receiving of the power of the Holy Spirit to pursue His ministry. What more needs to be said? Let each of us *personally* hear His command: "Receive the Holy Spirit!" (John 20:22).

24. Authority for Ministry (Luke 9:1–2). Luke shows the flow of power of Jesus the King, who extends the delivering and benevolent rule of the kingdom of God over hell's works (demon power) and human hurt (disease). The order of ministry that began with Jesus (8:1) continues to be exercised by His disciples as He trained them for ministry (9:1–2), and later will issue in the same type of ministry in the church as it spreads the gospel message (Acts 8:4–12). This Gospel throbs with confidence in the full transparency of power and authority for ministry by Jesus to His disciples, then and now:

• We may expect victory over the powers of darkness and their operations (10:19).

• We are assigned to "do business" as authorized representatives of our Lord until He returns (19:13).

• We are promised the Father's pleasure "to give" us the kingdom, that is, to supply us with His peace and power (12:32).

Dominion over evil has been given, but we can expect to see spiritual breakthrough to the degree we receive and apply that authority in prayer, preaching, teaching, and personal ministry.

25. Prayer and Intercession (Luke 11:2–4). Jesus' words "Your kingdom come" are more than a suggestion to pray for a distant millennial day, for everything in this prayer is current. This prayer is not a formula for repetition so much as it is an outline for expansion. Worship is to be longer than a sentence. Petitions are not confined to bread. Forgiveness is to be requested in specifics, not generalities, and prayer for the entry of God's kingdom into present earthborn situations is not accomplished in a momentary utterance. The verb mood and tense of "Your kingdom come" essentially says, "Father, let Your kingdom come here and now!"

Such prayerful *intervention* is called *intercession*. Motivation toward such prayer occurs when we recognize the importance Jesus placed on prayer in helping us serve in our roles as "kingdom administrators." Without the intervention of God's kingdom rule through prayer, earth's circumstances will succumb to inevitable consequences. Earthly scenes of need must be penetrated by God's "will here as in heaven." Either the weakness of man's rule (the flesh) or the viciousness of hell's works (the devil) will prevail. God's power alone can change things and bring heaven's rule (kingdom) instead, and the honor and the glory for prayer's answers are His. However, the praying is ours to do: unless we ask for the intervention of His kingdom and obey His prayer-lessons, nothing will change. All kingdom ministry begins with, is sustained by, and will triumph through prayer.

26. Casting Out Demons (Luke 11:20). Jesus indicates that one signal of a true ministry of the kingdom includes the casting out of demons. He models this in His ministry and promises it as a timeless sign confirming the preaching of the gospel of the kingdom (Mark 16:17). He also balances this aspect of ministry for His disciples, who at first were amazed to experience such power, exclaiming, "Lord, even the demons are subject to us in Your name" (Luke 10:17). While affirming the place and value of this ministry (vv. 18–19), Jesus still reminds them of a foundational truth. Power over demons is not the central reason for rejoicing; rather, their salvation has registered them as heaven's representatives. That is the real grounds for authority in the spiritual realm.

27. Receiving Kingdom Power (Acts 1:3–8). As Jesus presented post-Resurrection teaching "pertaining to the kingdom of God" (v. 3), His disciples asked if now—with the Cross behind—the ultimate messianic kingdom would come. "It is not yours to know the future," He says, "but it is yours to receive the Spirit's power!" With those words, He makes three points: (1) The Holy Spirit is the Person and the power by which assistance and ability are given for serving, for sharing the life and power of God's kingdom with others. (2) The Holy Spirit's power must be "received"; it is not an automatic experience. As surely as the Holy Spirit indwells each believer (Rom. 8:9), so surely will He fill and overflow (John 7:37–39) each who receives the Holy Spirit in childlike faith. (3) When the Holy Spirit fills you, you will know it. Jesus said it and the disciples found it true (Acts 1:5; 2:1–4). Have you received the Holy Spirit? (19:1–6). You may, for the promise is as fully yours today as at any time in the past (2:38–39).

Conflict and the Kingdom

28. Earth's Evil "Ruler" (Luke 4:14–32). As Jesus confronts Satan, He dramatically exposes the Adversary's relationship to this present world. Note the significance in Satan's offer to Jesus of "all the kingdoms of the world." Here we see the Adversary as administrator of the curse on this planet, a role he has held since man's dominion was lost and forfeited at the Fall. Because of this, Jesus does not contest the devil's right to make that offer of this world's kingdoms and glory, but He pointedly denies the terms for their being gained. Jesus knows He is here to regain and ultimately win them, but He will do so on the Father's terms, not the Adversary's. Still, the present world systems are largely grounded by the limited but powerful and destructive rule of the one Jesus calls "the ruler of this world" (John 12:31; 16:30). Understanding these facts, we are wise not to attribute to God anything of the disorder of our confused, sin-riddled, diseased, tragedy-ridden, and tormented planet. "This present evil age" (Gal. 1:4) "lies *under the sway of* the wicked one" (1 John 5:19). But Jesus also said that Satan's rule "will be cast down," and that he "has nothing in Me," that is, no control over Christ or Christ's own. "He who is in you is greater than he who is in the world" (1 John 4:4).

29. Taking It by Force (Matt. 11:12). Jesus asserts the "violence" of the kingdom. The unique grammatical construction of the text does not make clear if the kingdom of God is the victim of violence or if, as the kingdom advances in victory, it does so through violent spiritual conflict and warfare—but the context does. Jesus' references to the nonreligious style of John and the confrontive, miraculous ministry of Elijah teach that the kingdom of God makes its penetration by a kind of violent entry opposing the human status quo. It transcends the "softness" (v. 8) of staid religious formalism and exceeds the pretension of child's play (vv. 16–17). It refuses to "dance to the music" of society's expectation that the religious community provide either entertainment ("We played the flute") or dead traditionalism ("We mourned").

Jesus defines the "violence" of His kingdom's expansion by defining the "sword" and "fire" He has brought as different from the battle techniques of political or military warfare (compare Matt. 10:34–39 and Luke 12:49–53 with John 18:36). The upheaval caused by the kingdom of God is not caused by political provocation or armed advance. It is the result of God's order, shaking relationships, households, cities, and nations by the entry of the

Holy Spirit's power working in people. (See also Luke 16:16.)

30. Grounds of Authority (Col. 2:13–15). Jesus Christ's triumph over sin and evil powers was accomplished in "*it*"—that is, in *the Cross*. This text, joined to and studied beside others (Eph. 2:13–16; Gal. 3:13–14; 2 Cor. 5:14–17; Rom. 5:6–15; and Rev. 12:10–11), firmly establishes Jesus' suffering, shed blood, sacrificial death, and resurrection triumph as the only adequate and available grounds for ransom from sin, reconciliation to God, redemption from slavery, and restoration. The Cross is the sole hope and means for full reinstatement to relationship with God and rulership under Him— to "reign in life" (Rom. 5:17). To avoid presumption or imbalance regarding the message and ministry of the present power of the kingdom of God, we must focus on and regularly review two points: the source and the grounds for the delegation of such authority and power. (1) God's sovereign authority and almighty power is the *source* from which mankind derives any ability to share in the exercise of God's kingdom power. (2) But even more important, seeing sinful, fallen man had lost all claim to his early privilege of rulership under God, let us remember the *grounds* upon which all kingdom privilege or power may be restored and by which such spiritual ministry with authority may be exercised.

31. Pressing In (Luke 16:16). Jesus declares the advance of the kingdom of God is the result of two things: *preaching* and *pressing in.* He shows the gospel of the kingdom must be proclaimed with spiritual passion. In every generation believers have to determine whether they will respond to this truth with sensible minds and sensitive hearts. To overlook it will bring a passivity that limits the ministry of God's kingdom to extending the terms of truth and love—that is, teaching or educating and engaging in acts of kindness. Without question, we must do these things. However, apart from (1) an impassioned pursuit of prayer, (2) confrontation with the demonic, (3) expectation of the miraculous, and (4) a burning heart for evangelism, the kingdom of God makes little penetration in the world.

At the same time, overstatement of "pressing" is likely to produce rabid fanatics who justify any behavior in Jesus' name as applying the boldness spoken of here. Such travesties in church history as the Crusades and various efforts at politicizing in a quest to produce righteousness in society through earth-level rule are extremes we must learn to reject. "Pressing in" is accomplished first in prayer warfare, coupled with a will to surrender one's life and self-interests in order to gain God's kingdom goals.

32. Suffering, Tribulation (Acts 14:21–22). Paul not only taught the joy and peace of the kingdom of God (Rom. 14:7), its power (1 Cor. 14:20), and its present authority to cause the believer to triumph over evil (2 Tim. 4:8; Rom. 16:20). He also taught that "kingdom people" experience trial, suffering, and not always an "instant victory" (2 Thess. 1:5). Triumph and victory may characterize the attitude of each citizen of the kingdom of God, and Holy Spirit-empowered authority is given to be applied to realize results. Yet, God did not promise life without struggle. The "dominion" being recovered through the presence of the King within us and ministered by the Holy Spirit's power through us is never taught by the apostles as preempting all suffering.

This text reminds us that victory only comes through battle, and triumph only follows trial. Only a weak view of the truth of the kingdom of God pretends otherwise. Another weak view surrenders to negative circumstances on the proposition that we are predestined to problems and therefore should merely tolerate them. The Bible teaches that suffering, trial, and all order of human difficulty are unavoidable; but God's Word also teaches they may all be overcome. The presence of the King and the power of His kingdom in our lives make us neither invulnerable nor immune to life's struggles. But they do bring the promise of victory: provision in need, strength for the day, and healing, comfort, and saving help.

Worship and the Kingdom

33. A Kingdom of Priests (Ex. 19:5–7). In these verses the Lord indicates His objective for His delivered people. His purpose for their destiny requires their understanding His essential priority for them: worship—His redemptive goal and kingdom reinstatement. As they learn to worship as a nation of priests, they will discover His foundational means for their possessing their future victories (as ones whose domain, or "kingdom," He has promised). Their restored rule, from sharing to "kingdom" possession, extends from their walk before God in worship. Israel's deliverance from Egypt is not only a triumphant testimony; it is God's timeless type, showing His plans and methods for the church's deliverance and intended conquest (1 Cor. 10:11).

34. "Establishing" God's Throne (Ps. 22:3). The Psalms were the praise hymnal of the early church, and as such are laden with principles fully applicable for New Testament living today. Few principles are more essential to our understanding than this one: the *presence* of God's kingdom power is directly related to the practice of God's *praise*. The verb "enthroned" indicates that wherever God's people exalt His name, He is ready to manifest His kingdom's power in the way most appropriate to the situation, as His rule is invited to invade our setting.

It is this fact that properly leads many to conclude that in a very real way, praise prepares a *specific* and *present* place for God among His people. Some have chosen the term "establish His throne" to describe this "enthroning" of God in our midst by our worshiping and praising welcome. God awaits the prayerful and praise-filled worship of His people as an entry point for His kingdom to "come"—to enter, that *His* "will be done" in human circumstances. (*See* Luke 11:2-4 and Ps. 93:2.) We do not manipulate God, but align ourselves with the great kingdom truth: *His* is the power, ours is the privilege (and responsibility) to welcome Him into our world—our private, present world or the circumstances of our society.

35. Inviting God's Rule (Ps. 93:2). "Your throne is established from of old." The notion that kingdom advance "establishes" God's throne needs clearer understanding. It is foolish to think man could add to or diminish the power or glory of God's kingdom rule. However, it is equally unwise to overlook the responsible place the redeemed have been given. We are to *welcome* the kingdom and administer situations on earth by inviting the overarching might of God's Spirit to move into difficult or impossible circumstances and transform them. This is done by praise: "In everything [not "for" everything] give thanks [fill the situation with praise], for this is God's will for you" (1 Thess. 5:17). Thus we welcome the overruling power of God's presence into any situation we face. Pray, "Your kingdom come, Your will be done—here." Then, set up a place for God's throne to enter by filling your life's settings with praise. As Gideon's trumpeters (Judg. 7:17-22) and Jehoshaphat's choir (2 Chr. 20:20-22) confounded their enemies and paved the way for the victory the Lord said He would give, so praise brings the same entry of the King's kingdom today.

36. Worship and Praise (Rev. 1:5-6). In the opening of Revelation, John introduces himself as a brother and companion in the struggle we all face (v. 9). His words "in the kingdom and patience of Jesus Christ" point to the dual facts of Christ's present kingdom triumph and the ongoing presence of evil and warfare that

exact the patience of the church as the kingdom advances among and through us. In prefacing the broad arenas of prophecy about to be unfolded, John addresses two very important *present* truths: (1) We, Christ's redeemed, are loved and are washed from our sins—a present state (v. 6). (2) We, through His glorious dominion, have been designated "kings and priests" to God—also a present calling. Thus, these dual offices give perspective on our authority and duty and how we most effectively may advance the kingdom of God.

First, we are said to be kings in the sense that under the King of kings we are the new breed—the reborn, to whom God has delegated authority to extend and administer the powers of His rule. Of course, this involves faithful witness to the gospel in the power of the Spirit and loving service to humanity in the love of God. But it also involves confrontation with dark powers of hell, assertive prayer warfare, and an expectation of the miraculous works of God (2 Cor. 10:3-5; Eph. 6:10-20; 1 Cor. 2:4.). Further, this authority is only fully accomplished in the spirit of praiseful worship, as we exercise the office of "priests." Some translations read, "a kingdom of priests," which emphasizes that the rule is only effective when the priestly mission is faithfully attended. Worship is foundational to kingdom advance. The power of the believer before God's throne, worshiping the Lamb and exalting in the Holy Spirit of praise, is mightily confounding to the Adversary. (*See* Ex. 19:5-7 and Ps. 22:3.)

37. Priority of Worship (1 Pet. 2:9). As a "royal" priesthood, the kingly nature of the redeemed worshiper is noted. This passage is rooted in God's call to ancient Israel (see Ex. 19:5-7). Peter and John (Rev. 1:5-6) draw this truth to full application and prophetic fulfillment in the New Testament believer. As with Israel, deliverance through the blood of the Lamb is but the beginning. As promised, dominion and destiny will unfold as their priestly duty is fulfilled. True authority is always related to a walk in purity and a constancy in worship. The spirit of worship is essential to all advance of the kingdom. Just as ancient Israel will only take the Promised Land while doing battle from a foundation of righteous worship before the Lord, so with the contemporary church. We will only experience promised power for evangelism and spiritual victories as we prioritize and grow in our worship of the living God. Kingdom power is kept from pollution this way, as kingdom people keep humbly praiseful before the King—and witness His works of power with joy. (See also Rev. 1:5-6.)

Prophecy and the Kingdom

38. Old Testament: Possessing the Kingdom

(Dan. 7:21–22). Daniel's prophecy in chapter 7 not only spans the spiritual struggle covering the ages through Messiah's First and Second Coming, but it uses two terms important to perceiving the biblical truth of the kingdom of God: "dominion" and "possess." "Dominion" (from Chaldee, *shelet*, "to govern, prevail, dominate") is in the hands of world powers (vv. 6, 12) until the Coming of the Son of Man, at which time it is taken by Him forever (vv. 13–14). But an interim struggle is seen between the First and Second Coming of Messiah. During this season, the saints "possess" (Chaldee, *chacan*, "to hold on or occupy") the kingdom. This communicates a process of long struggle as the redeemed ("saints") "possess" what they have "received" (v. 18). The scenario reads: (1) After the "judgment was made in favor of the saints" (a forecast of the pivotal impact of Christ's Cross upon which hinged both man's redemption as well as his reinstatement to the potential of his rule under God), an extended struggle ensues. (2) This struggle is described as the "time [which] came for the saints to possess the kingdom." They do battle against sinister adversaries and experience a mix of victories and apparent defeats (v. 25). The prophecy unveils the present age of the kingdom, which is one of ongoing struggle—with victory upon victory for the church. Yet it withholds its conclusive triumph until Christ comes again.

This prophecy also balances the question of divine sovereignty and human responsibility. (1) God's sovereignty accomplishes the foundational victory (v. 22) and in the Cross achieves the decisive victory allowing the saints new dimensions for advance and conquest. (2) He entrusts the responsibility for that advance to His own to "possess the kingdom," entering into conflict with the adversary, at times at the expense of their apparent defeat (v. 26). (3) However, movement toward victory is theirs as they press the "judgment" of the "court" (vv. 22, 26) and seize realms controlled by evil. They wrestle the dominion from hellish powers, continuing in warfare until the ultimate seating of the Son of Man (vv. 14, 27).

Prophetic systems vary as to how and when these words unfold on the calendar of church history, for the passage is subject to different schemes of interpretation, each with different projected chronologies. But the foundational fact remains that an agelong struggle between "the saints" and the power of evil in the world calls each believer to a commitment to steadfast battle, a mixture of victories with

setbacks, and a consummate triumph anticipated at Christ's Coming. In the meantime, we "receive" the kingdom and pursue victories for our King, by His power, making intermittent gains—all of which are based on "the judgment" achieved through the Cross.

39. New Testament: Agelong Warfare

(Rev. 12:10–11). John's prophecy in chapter 12 conveys the same essential message as Daniel 7, the primary difference being that John writes *after* Christ's *first* coming, victorious death, resurrection, and ascension (v. 5). Verses 1–17 relate: (1) the ongoing warfare on earth (v. 9); (2) the overcoming ability of the redeemed because "the kingdom" has come (v. 10); (3) the two-edged truth that their victories often cost martyrdom (v. 11); and (4) the basis of their triumph: the Cross ("the blood of the Lamb") and the authority of God's Word ("the word of their testimony"—v. 12). Various interpretive systems see this at different times within redemptive history. The mixture of pre-, a-, and postmillennial viewpoints has often fragmented the church, rather than providing a common base of wisdom for each group to receive while embracing one another as we all face a common Adversary (v. 9). Seeing that no complete interpretive scheme will be verified until after Christ comes, our wisdom is to embrace the Cross as our salvation and our source of overcoming victory. Then we can enter the conflict in confidence, knowing we shall triumph even though circumstances temporarily set us back. In the time of conflict, it will make no difference who was "right," but only that we were on the Messiah's side in this agelong spiritual struggle.

The text provides two indisputable facts: (1) the kingdom of God has already established triumph over the Serpent (vv. 9–10) and (2) still, those engaged in conflict in the name of the Lamb sometimes are vanquished to death (v. 11). Breadth and balance are given to our perspective. The *presence* of the kingdom at this time calls each believer to responsible spiritual warfare and anticipated victories. Yet, at the same time, the presence of evil struggles for survival; though "cast down," the Serpent writhes viciously. Thus our temporal situation is often a fierce and sometimes painful struggle, seeming to issue in an indeterminate standoff before our Enemy. But he only has "a short time," until finally the kingdom *to come* (v. 10) shall become the kingdom *accomplished* (Revelation 19—22). Let us do battle in faith and with faithfulness and, looking to that day of His ultimate kingdom, know the Holy Spirit is preparing us for kingdom victories *today*. J.W.H.

KINSMAN-REDEEMER. There were four specific tasks that the kinsman-redeemer (*go'el*) was to perform as his help was needed: (1) If his kinsman sold his property to pay his debts, the kinsman redeemed or bought back the property (Lev. 25:25; Ruth 4:1–6; Jer. 32:6–15); (2) the person who was captured, enslaved or sold into slavery had every right to expect his kinsman to redeem him and set him free (Lev. 25:47–49); (3) if a person died childless, the redeemer married the dead man's widow and raised up a son to carry on the family line and to honor the deceased person, in a custom known as levirate marriage (Deut. 25:5–10). There also appears to be a role of a kinsman-redeemer to track down the killer in vengeance. In passages noting that custom, *go'el* is translated as "avenger of blood" (Deut. 19:12).

The term kinsman-redeemer is used of God to express His intimate relationship with His people (Is. 41:14; 43:14; 44:24). He is their "next of kin" who ransoms them from bondage (Is. 43:1–3); He pays the price to set them free. Paul reminded the believers at Corinth that God had bought them at a price; therefore, they were to glorify God (1 Cor. 6:19–20).

KNOW. (Ex. 3:7) *yada'* (yah-*dah*); *Strong's* #3045: To know, to perceive, to distinguish, to recognize, to acknowledge, to be acquainted with; in a few instances to "know intimately," that is, sexually; also to acknowledge, recognize, esteem, and endorse. When Scripture speaks of God's making known His name, it refers to His revealing (through deeds or events) what His name truly means. Thus, in 6:3, "I appeared to Abraham, to Isaac, and to Jacob as *'El Shaddai*, but by My name *Yahweh* I was not known to them." God did not mean that the patriarchs had never heard the name *Yahweh*, but rather that He did not reveal the full meaning of His name *Yahweh* until the time of Moses and the Exodus. *Also* (John 8:32) *ginosko* (ghin-*oce*-koe); *Strong's* #1097: Compare "prognosis," "gnomic," "gnomon," "gnostic." To perceive, understand, recognize, gain knowledge, realize, come to know. *Ginosko* is the knowledge that has an inception, a progress, and an attainment. It is the recognition of truth by personal experience.

KNOWLEDGE—the truth or facts of life that a person acquires either through experience or thought. The greatest truth that a person can possess with the mind or learn through expe-

rience is truth about God (Ps. 46:10; John 8:31–32). This cannot be gained by unaided human reason (Job 11:7; Rom. 11:33). It is acquired only as God shows Himself to man—in nature and conscience (Psalm 19; Rom. 1:19–20); in history or providence (Deut. 6:20–25; Dan. 2:21); and especially in the Bible (Psalm 119; Rev. 1:1–3).

Mental knowledge by itself, as good as it may be, is inadequate; it is too capable of only producing pride (1 Cor. 8:1, 13:2). Moral knowledge affects a person's will (Prov. 1:7; Phil. 3:11–12; 1 John 4:6). It is knowledge of the heart, not the mind alone. The Book of Proverbs deals primarily with this kind of knowledge. Experiential knowledge is that gained through one's experience (Gen. 4:1; 2 Cor. 5:21; 1 John 4:7–8).

The apostle Paul's wish for the church at Colosse was that they might increase in the "knowledge of God" (Col. 1:10).

KNOWLEDGE (Mal. 2:7) *da'at* (*dah*-aht); *Strong's* #1847: Knowledge; knowing, understanding, intelligence, wisdom, discernment, skill. *Da'at* comes from the verb *yada'*, "to know." Occurring more than ninety times, its first mention is in Genesis 2:9, describing the tree of knowledge of good and evil. Hosea 4:6 states that the lack of knowledge destroys God's people. In Exodus 31:3, *da'at* refers to craftsmanship and artistic abilities; God gave Bezalel knowledge to design artistic works. Isaiah 53:11 ("By His knowledge My righteous Servant shall justify many") can be taken to mean that knowledge of Him (that is, knowing Him) justifies them, or that He uses His knowledge and skills to obtain their justification: that is, He, by His priestly intercession, knows how to justify believers.

LACHISH, LACHISH OSTRACA—see ch. 55, §3.7., 3.7.a., 3.7.b., 3.7.c., 3.7.d., 3.7.e.

LACK. (Luke 22:35) *hustereo* (hoos-ter-*eh*-oh); *Strong's* #5302: To come late, be behind. With reference to persons, to fail (Heb. 4:1), be inferior to (2 Cor. 11:5), to be in want, to come short of (Matt. 19:20; Rom. 3:23).

LAMB. (Rev. 6:1) *arnion* (ar-*nee*-on); *Strong's* #721: Originally, a little lamb, but the diminutive force is largely missing in the New Testament. In John 21:15, *arnion* is used of young believers, while twenty-nine times in Revelation it is the title of the exalted Christ. *Arnion* is in direct contrast to the beast. The beast is

This icon beside an entry indicates a Word Wealth feature.

This icon beside an entry indicates a Kingdom Dynamics feature.

This icon beside an entry indicates an important biblical or doctrinal term.

savage, cruel, hostile, and destructive. By contradistinction our Lord as a lamb is gentle,
compassionate, loving, and kind, innocently
suffering and dying to atone for our sins. In
Revelation, lion and lamb combine the two elements of majesty and meekness.

LAMB OF GOD—a phrase used by John the
Baptist to describe Jesus (John 1:29, 36).
John publicly identified Jesus as "the Lamb of
God who takes away the sin of the world!"
Elsewhere in the New Testament Jesus is
called a lamb (Acts 8:32; 1 Pet. 1:19; Rev. 5:6).
The Book of Revelation speaks of Jesus as a
lamb twenty-eight times.

John's reference to Jesus as the Lamb of
God calls to mind the Old Testament sacrificial
system. In the sacrifice God accepted the
blood of animals as the means of atonement
for sin. It is likely that John had many themes
from the Old Testament in mind when he
called Jesus the Lamb of God. These themes
probably included the sin offering (Leviticus
4), the trespass offering (Leviticus 5), the sacrifice on the Day of Atonement (Leviticus 16),
and the Passover sacrifice (Exodus 12).

But the strongest image from the Old Testament is the suffering servant who "was led
as a lamb to the slaughter" (Is. 53:7) and who
"bore the sin of many" (Is. 53:12). Thus, this
vivid description of Jesus was a pointed
announcement of the *Atonement He would
bring about on man's behalf.

Also see Jesus Christ.

LAND. (Ex. 32:13) *'eretz* (*eh*-retz); *Strong's*
#776: Earth, land, ground. This noun occurs
more than 2,500 times in the Old Testament.
Its broadest meaning refers to the whole earth,
and especially to the dry ground, as in Genesis 1:1, 10. Less specifically, it refers to any
particular land; *'eretz mitzraim* is the land of
Egypt, *'artzot* (the plural form) *goyim* are the
lands of the Gentiles, and so forth. The most
specific use concerns the "land of Israel," *'eretz
Yisrael*, which is the Promised Land. God's
promises concerning the land of Israel are
emphasized throughout the Old Testament.

LANGUAGES OF THE BIBLE—the languages in
which the Bible was originally written. The
most famous of these are Hebrew, the original
language of the Old Testament, and Greek,
used in the writing of most of the New Testament. But several other ancient languages
also had an important bearing on the writing
or transmission of the original texts of the
Bible.

Aramaic. Spoken from at least about 2000
B.C., Aramaic eventually replaced many of the
languages of the ancient world in popularity

and usage. Parts of the Book of Daniel were
written in Aramaic. Aramaic was the common
language spoken in Palestine in the time of
Jesus. While the New Testament was written
in the Greek language, the language which
Jesus spoke was probably Aramaic. "Talitha,
cumi" (Mark 5:41) and "Ephphatha" are two
Aramaic phrases spoken by Jesus which have
been preserved in English versions of the New
Testament. Another name for the Aramaic
dialect used in the early churches throughout
Asia Minor is Syriac.

Latin. The New Testament also refers to
Latin, the language which sprang from ancient
Rome (Luke 23:38; John 19:20). Most of the
Roman Empire also spoke Greek in Jesus'
day, but as Roman power spread throughout
the ancient world, Latin also expanded in use.
The influence of Latin on the Mediterranean
world in the time of Jesus is shown by the
occurrence of such Latin words as *denarii*
(Matt. 18:28) and *praetorian* (Phil. 1:13, RSV,
NASB) in the New Testament.

Persian. This language was spoken by the
people who settled the area east of the Tigris
River in what is now western Iran. When the
Jewish people were taken as captives to Babylon in 586 B.C., they may have been exposed to
this distinctive language form, which used a
combination of pictorial and phonetic signs in
its alphabet. Scholars are uncertain if Persian
was used in the writing of any parts of the Old
Testament.

LAST SUPPER—see ch. 55, §6.1.

LAUGH. (Eccl. 3:4) *sachaq* (sah-*chahk*);
Strong's #7832: To laugh; to rejoice; to play; to
be amused about something; to mock, tease,
ridicule, or laugh at something. While *sachaq*
primarily means "to laugh," it occasionally
means "to play," whether as exuberant, leaping animals (Job 40:20), or as persons do
when dancing, laughing, and playing music
during a celebration (2 Sam. 6:5, 21). In its
negative sense, *sachaq* refers to the behavior
of rowdy, mocking crowds who come together
to ridicule someone for sport and entertainment, as in Jeremiah 15:17. *Sachaq* is the root
of the name "Isaac," "He Causes Laughter"
(Gen. 21:5–7).

LAW—an orderly system of rules and regulations by which a society is governed. In the
Bible, particularly the Old Testament, a
unique law code was established by direct revelation from God to direct His people in their
worship, in their relationship to Him, and in
their social relationships with one another.

Israel was not the only nation to have a
law code. Such collections were common

among the countries of the ancient world. These law codes generally began with an explanation that the gods gave the king the power to reign, along with a pronouncement about how good and capable he was. Then came the king's laws grouped by subject. The code generally closed with a series of curses and blessings.

The biblical law code, or the Mosaic Law, was different from other ancient near eastern law codes in several ways. Biblical law was different, first of all, in its origin. Throughout the ancient world, the laws of most nations were believed to originate with the gods, but they were considered intensely personal and subjective in the way they were applied. Even the gods were under the law, and they could suffer punishment if they violated it—unless, of course, they were powerful and able to conquer the punishers. The king ruled under the god whose temple and property he oversaw. Although he did not live under a written law code, he had a personal relationship to the god. Therefore, law was decided ultimately case by case and at the king's discretion. For most of a king's lifetime, his laws were kept secret.

By contrast, the biblical concept was that law comes from God, issues from His nature, and is holy, righteous, and good. Furthermore, at the outset of God's ruling over Israel at Sinai, God the great King gave His laws. These laws were binding on His people, and He upheld them. Furthermore, His laws were universal. Ancient oriental kings often tried to outdo their predecessors in image, economic power, and political influence. This was often their motivation in setting forth law codes. God, however, depicts His law as an expression of His love for His people (Ex. 19:5–6).

In Israel all crimes were crimes against God (1 Sam. 12:9–10). Consequently, He expected all His people to love and serve Him (Amos 5:21–24). As the final judge, He disciplined those who violated His law (Ex. 22:21–24; Deut. 10:18: 19:17). The nation or community was responsible for upholding the law and insuring that justice was done (Deut. 13:6–10; 17:7; Num. 15:32–36).

God's law, unlike those of other nations of the ancient world, also viewed all human life as especially valuable, because man is created in God's image. Thus, biblical law was more humane. It avoided mutilations and other savage punishments. Victims could not inflict more injury than they had received. Neither could criminals restore less than they had taken or stolen simply because of a class distinction. Everyone was equal before God's law.

The "eye for eye" requirement of the Mosaic Law was not a harsh statement that required cruel punishment. Instead, it was a mandate for equality before the law (Ex. 21:24). Each criminal had to pay for his own crime (Num. 35:31). Under the law codes of some pagan nations, the rich often could buy their way out of punishment. God's law especially protected the defenseless orphan, widow, slave, and stranger from injustice (Ex. 21:2, 20–21; 22:21–23).

Some scholars refer to Leviticus 17—26 as the "holiness code." Although it does not contain all of God's directions for ceremonial holiness, it does set forth much of what God requires. These chapters contain moral and ritual specifications regarding the tabernacle and public worship as well as the command to love one's neighbor as oneself (19:18). The nation of Israel was to be characterized by separation from other nations. Several of these laws prohibited pagan worship. Because God is holy (21:8), Israel was to be holy and separated from other nations (20:26).

The Book of Deuteronomy is sometimes called the Deuteronomic Code. This book contains the command to love God with all one's heart, soul, and might (Deut. 6:5) as well as a second record of the Ten Commandments (Deuteronomy 5).

Biblical law is more than a record of human law. It is an expression of what God requires of man. It rests on the eternal moral principles that are consistent with the very nature of God Himself. Therefore, biblical law (the Ten Commandments) is the summary of moral law. As such it sets forth fundamental and universal moral principles.

What is often called the civil law includes those specific laws in the Pentateuch (first five books of the Old Testament) that regulate civil and social behavior. All such laws are fundamentally religious since God is the lawgiver and ruler over everything. There are eight distinct categories of civil law in the Old Testament: (1) laws regulating leaders, (2) laws regulating the army, (3) criminal laws, (4) laws dealing with crimes against property, (5) laws relating to humane treatment, (6) laws about personal and family rights, (7) laws about property rights, and (8) laws regulating other social behavior.

LAW. (Is. 42:21) *torah* (toh-*rah*); *Strong's* #8451: Instruction, teaching, direction, law, precept. This noun occurs 217 times in the Old Testament. Usually *torah* refers to the Law of Moses, or a portion of the Law. Sometimes *torah* refers to the rules or instructions of a human parent, or of some other wise person

(Prov. 1:8; 3:1; 13:14). The root of *torah* is *yarah*, meaning "to shoot, to cast down in a straight manner, to direct, to rain down." The idea is that God's instructions to Israel (the Torah) were given to them in a straightforward, direct manner. For Israel the new covenant, by the power of the Spirit of God, will cause the Torah to be written in their hearts (Jer. 31:33–34; Ezek. 36:25–26).

LAYERS. (Amos 9:6) *ma'alah* (mah-ah-*lah*); *Strong's* #4609: Steps, stairs, upper chambers; ascents, lofts. This noun occurs forty-five times and is derived from the verb *'alah*, "to ascend," "to go up." Often it is translated "steps" as in 1 Kings 10:19. In 2 Kings 20:9–11, *ma'alah* is translated "degrees," referring to the ten steps the shadow regressed on the king's sundial. Fifteen psalms are labeled songs of "ascents" (Ps. 120—134). These were probably sung by the Levites as they proceeded up the steps to the temple. In the present reference, the Lord has built His staircase in the sky, a picture of His vast palace through which He walks.

LEADERSHIP, TRAITS OF SPIRITUAL. The apostolic directive laid the groundwork for the role of the leader: (1) equip the saints or assist them to fruitful life and service (Eph. 4:11–12) and (2) transmit the truth to each successive "generation" of converts—that is, discipling those whom you touch, that they may in turn disciple those they touch (2 Tim. 2:2). That directive is only effective in its multiplying the life of the gospel through others as it is obeyed by leaders who first live the truth in the purity and power of the gospel! This study contends for godliness in leadership, that godly offspring may be multiplied. Thus, each new echelon of believers and leaders in the body of Christ will retain the likeness of the Founder—Jesus, whose life and character are not only preached but are present in those who lead in His name.

1. Call of God (Is. 6:8–9). One of the tasks of the Holy Spirit is to call godly leaders in the kingdom. All men and women are "called" to God (Rom. 8:28, 30); yet only a few respond (Matt. 7:13–14; 22:14; John 15:16). Leaders, however, experience a different kind of call and are called in different ways. (1) Many are called *sovereignly.* Moses was singled out by God who spoke to him from a burning bush (Ex. 3:1—4:17). The child Samuel was called while he was asleep (1 Sam. 3:1–18). Young Isaiah was worshiping in the temple when called by God (Is. 6:1–9). (2) Others are called through *men.* Samuel went to David and anointed him with oil (1 Sam. 16:1–13). Paul

instructed Titus to appoint elders in the churches of Crete (Titus 1:5). There is a difference between being a "man of God"—as all are called to be—and being "God's man"—one called to leadership.

2. Hearing God (Matt. 16:13–20). The godly leader "hears" God; that is, his or her spirit is tuned to the promptings and lessons of the Holy Spirit. At Caesarea Philippi, a stronghold of the ancient demon-gods of Syria, Greece, and Rome, Jesus deliberately set Himself against the background of the world's religions' error and confusion; and here He inquired of His disciples about His identity. Peter's answer (v. 16) is set apart from and beyond human reason, as Jesus commended his having heard from God (v. 17). Then Jesus emphasized that leadership in His church would always lead and be based not on man's ability to reason things out as much as on his readiness and receptivity to hear God through "revelation knowledge," the things that God unfolds by the work of the Holy Spirit (Eph. 1:17–18; 3:14–19).

3. Faith (Gen. 12:1–20; 17:1–27; 22:1–19). Abraham's ability to lead was tested in three areas of faith. (1) *Faith to risk* (12:1–5): A wealthy man, Abraham risked all to follow God. The godly leader is willing to risk everything on God's faithfulness and venture into the unknown. (2) *Faith to trust* (17:1–27): Abraham and Sarah were long past the child-bearing age. The godly leader does not rely on facts alone, but goes beyond facts to faith. (3) *Faith to surrender* (22:1–19): Abraham knew the sacrifice of his son would destroy any hope of fulfilling God's promise that he would father many nations. The godly leader is willing to sacrifice all things precious in order to please God.

4. The High Standard for Leadership (James 3:1). Leaders are judged with a higher standard than those who follow. First Timothy 3 and Titus 1 give great attention to details, but here James reminds that those in leadership will be held accountable for exemplifying Jesus Christ in their spirit and behavior, as well as in their words and duties. Government, military, and business leaders are seldom judged on their personal lives. Leaders in the kingdom, however, are judged not so much by what they accomplish as by the character they reveal—who they *are* before what they *do*. This high standard applies not so much to the leader's achievements as to the condition of his or her heart and spirit. It is possible to have grand accomplishments and even orthodox behavior but still manifest a loveless, ungodly spirit. If first the leader's heart is right, godly behavior will always follow and good leadership will be manifested.

5. Character Qualifications (1 Tim. 3:1–13). Most New Testament leaders held that the ministry belonged to the whole believing community. The ordination of leaders was primarily the selecting of individuals of proven maturity and character to lead so the whole church could function effectively in worship, service, outreach, and the fulfillment of individual spiritual gifts. The qualifications for church leaders are carefully outlined in verses 1–13 and in Titus 1:5–9. They do not emphasize family line or some past rite as did the Old Testament priesthood. Instead the focus is on the leader's certified and sustained ethical character. There are over a dozen significant qualities expected, which include spiritual preparedness, self-control, social graciousness, domestic order, and holy living. The basis for continual ministry is continual commitment to character. If a leader falls from these ethical standards, he or she should accept removal from leadership until an appropriate season of reverifying of character can be fulfilled (Gal. 6:1–2).

6. Total Commitment (Acts 26:19). Paul was totally committed to his call to spread the gospel and establish churches throughout the known world. He lived what he wrote, that "the gifts and the calling of God are irrevocable" (Rom. 11:29). His life demonstrated three basic concepts of leadership: (1) He was committed to the goals and spirit of his call (Phil. 3:7–8). (2) He translated his objectives into the lives of his followers (2 Tim. 2:1–2) and bore with all necessary hardship in pursuing that end (2 Cor. 4:8–11; 11:23–33). (3) He was alert to change. He adapted to cultural, social, and political changes and thus never lost his relevancy (1 Cor. 9:19–22).

7. Humility (Judg. 6:1—8:35). Gideon demonstrates seven traits of godly leadership: (1) he declines to lead unless God calls (6:36–40); (2) he depends on God at every turn (7:1–8); (3) he turns faith into action (6:25–27; 7:15–22); and (4) he uses the gifts God had given him to lead others, telling the three hundred who stuck with him to watch him and follow his example (7:17); (5) he gives God glory before and after his victory (7:15; 8:3, 23); (6) he humbly gives others credit that belongs to him (8:1–3); and (7) he refuses to establish a dynasty after he has fulfilled God's charge (8:22–23).

8. A Teachable Spirit (Acts 13:22). Only one man in the Bible enjoys the designation of being a man after God's own heart—David. To outward appearance, David is more readily remembered as a gross sinner. He committed adultery, murdered, lied, betrayed his nation, made severe mistakes in judgment, was a poor manager, and was unable to manage his home. Yet God said, "I have found David the son of Jesse, a man after My own heart, who will do all My will" (v. 22). Almost every time we read about David, he was doing something wrong, yet God commended the *heart* of his leadership. How do we explain it? The answer is in the fact that with every mistake, David repented; and of equal importance, he learned from his mistakes. Not only was he humble and teachable, but he listened to his critics and his enemies as well; and, most significantly, he heeded the prophets of God. This teachable spirit is the trait that caused God to classify him as Israel's finest leader.

9. Vulnerability (Matt. 26:47–54; Luke 22:47–51; John 18:10–11). Being vulnerable as a leader means to stand totally open as a human being, hiding nothing and refusing to defend oneself. Few things elicit more of a response from people than the sense that they are dealing with someone who feels their pain and understands their need, which they discover only if the leader is vulnerable enough to disclose as much. When Jesus refused to defend Himself the night of His arrest, Peter's protective action severed the ear of the high priest's bodyguard. Immediately, Jesus reached out to heal His enemy, making Himself vulnerable to a return sword thrust, since His reaching for the man's head easily could have been interpreted as another hostile move. Vulnerability may expose one to misunderstanding, but it also will bring healing.

10. Secure (John 13:1–17). As Jesus takes the towel and basin to wash His disciples' feet, His assuming a servant's role exhibits more than humility; it evidences the psychological security essential to a leader. Jesus' lifestyle and lessons establish the mode for a new kind of leader—the servant leader (Matt. 20:26–28). The servant leader leads from a position of personal security—that is, knowing who God has made him or her to be, and resting in the peaceful awareness and confidence that God's hand is ordering his or her personal destiny (see this in v. 3, of Jesus). The godly leader is one who stoops to help another, who counts others better than himself (Phil. 2:3–4), who lays down his life for others (John 10:11), who seeks to serve rather than to be served (Luke 22:27). Until a person is ready to wash feet he is not qualified to be a kingdom leader.

11. Leading God's Way (Judg. 8:22–23; 9:1–57). Although Gideon wisely refused to serve as king of Israel (8:23), upon his death, his son

Abimelech hired assassins to murder his brothers, in hope of seizing rule for himself. His youngest brother, Jotham, who escaped, climbed Mt. Gerizim and prophesied that a kingdom founded on sin would soon shatter; within three years this happened. Gideon understood that God intended Israel to be a theocracy (God is King); but Abimelech, though possessing a natural charisma, did not have the mind of God, His appointment, or His anointing. Godly leaders do things God's way. Wickedness disqualifies from leading. The leader who seeks to benefit himself at the expense of others is on a path to self-destruction. Unlike his humble father, Abimelech was ambitious, believing the end justified the means. God judges leaders not on how much they accomplish, but on whether they do things His way.

12. Resisting Popular Opinion (Num. 13:1—14:45; Josh. 6:1–27; 10:1–43). Joshua was continually faced with choices, and most of his decisions went against popular opinion. Yet in each instance he called on the people to increase their faith in God's promises rather than look at the impossible circumstances. The leader does not condition his appeal to the sentiment or mood of the times. Spiritual advance requires faith, and unbelief will never see beyond the difficulties. Unbelief sees "walled cities and giants" rather than the presence and power of God. Unbelief looks at obstacles; faith looks at God. Joshua and Caleb were willing to do the unpopular thing and call the people to positive faith. They led the way into the future by confronting a negative report and helping a new generation rise to serve God in faith.

13. Fasting and Prayer (Acts 13:1–3). Leaders of the early church arrived at decisions only after fasting and prayer. In Antioch the prophets and teachers fasted and prayed, seeking God's direction for the church. While they waited on God, the Holy Spirit gave direction (v. 2), thus beginning the missionary ministry which eventually took the gospel to the whole world. Godly leaders rely on God for the direction and empowerment of their lives and ministry. Disciplined fasting and constant prayer are proven means for this and, as such, are mandatory in the lives of leaders (Matt. 9:15).

14. Dreams and Visions (Acts 16:6–10). On his missionary journey Paul planned a northward turn into Bithynia. That night, however, he dreamed of a man begging him, "Come over to Macedonia and help us" (v. 9). On the basis of the dream, Paul altered his direction, thus exemplifying a trait of Holy Spirit-guided leaders. While ungodly leaders consult horoscopes

and diviners for direction in their lives, godly leaders hear from God (1) through the written Word, the Bible, and (2) through dreams and visions (2:17). Their thought channels are cleansed of impurity (2 Cor. 10:5). They are not conformed to the pattern of this world but are transformed by the renewing of their minds (Rom. 12:2). Their affections are on things above, not on earthly things (Col. 3:2). Therefore, when the Holy Spirit chooses to speak to them through visions (daytime mind pictures) and dreams (sleeping revelations), they hear clearly (see also Ps. 16:7; Acts 9:10; 10:3, 17; 18:9).

15. Miracles, Signs, and Wonders (Acts 2:22). Without exception, miracles, signs, and wonders accompanied the ministry and preaching of early church leaders. Here Peter reminded the people that Jesus' credibility was based on His miracle ministry. This same credibility accompanied those set apart in leadership, such as Stephen, Philip, Barnabas, Silas, and Paul, as well as the original apostles (6:8; 8:6; 15:12; 19:11–12).

Miracles, signs, and wonders were commonly accepted in the early church; and leaders led the way in giving place to such ministry. Also, the early church leaders prayed for miracles (Acts 4:30), seeing them not as random, occasional events, but as worthy evidences of God's anointing, continually glorifying Christ through the church, and therefore to be sought and welcomed.

16. Unity and Harmony (Acts 1:14). Being "of one accord" is a dominant trait of New Testament leadership. Whenever the early church leaders gathered in Jerusalem, it is said they were in unity and harmony, with each other and with God (2:46; 4:24; 5:12; 15:25). Their agreement was spiritual and practical, not only theological, for they shared their lives and possessions. Acts 2:42–47 gives a description of New Testament leadership: meeting together, studying together, sharing their material possessions (2:45; 4:32–37; 6:1). They met often to pray, revealing not only their relationship with each other but their total reliance on God (2:42; 4:31; 12:5; 13:3).

17. Taking Charge (Ex. 27:1—28:43). God called Moses with a direct command to "take charge" (Hebrew *veatta*). (1) "You shall command" (Hebrew *veatta tezave*, 27:20). The overseer must step in and take charge any time he feels his delegated leader is moving in the wrong direction or confusion is beginning to find entrance. (2) "You shall bring close" (Hebrew *veatta hakrev*, 28:1). At times the leader leads by merely putting an arm around his subordinate's shoulder, to affirm, identify with, or encourage. (3) "You shall speak to all who are gifted artisans [the leaders]" (Hebrew *veatta tedeber*, 28:3). The literal statement is "*speak to the wise in heart.*"

Occasionally, in order to avoid misunderstanding, an overseer needs to "take charge" by directly addressing the entire cadre of the workers rather than by speaking through delegated leadership. The wise leader knows when to let the reins of authority hang slack that his delegates may learn, but he should not relinquish full control until God tells him to do so.

18. Authority (Ex. 28:1–2). Moses' authority came from God with direct revelation (33:11), while Aaron's came from his office, through God's appointment. Moses had no special garments, but Aaron needed "holy garments," which endowed him with glory and beauty (28:2). Aaron's office and his attire were essential to designate his authority over the people, while Moses had none of these trappings. He was humble and self-effacing, yet at crucial moments of decision he was powerful and authoritative. This dual type of spiritual authority causes misunderstanding and, at times, even conflict. However, there is no confusion in God's order if we will see that there are both types of leaders in the Bible, and both are necessary in a healthy, balanced church or organization. Every strong-willed, highly popular visionary or prophetic type needs an Aaron—a priest-type who will minister more directly to the needs of the people. The level of apparent authority should not be held in competition, but should be seen as complementary.

19. Inspiration (Judg. 4:1—5:31). Godly leaders lead by inspiration. Deborah convinced her followers to extend themselves beyond their own vision. The inspirational leader provides a model of integrity and courage and sets a high standard of performance. He gives his followers autonomy and not only treats them as individuals, but encourages individualism. There is no better way to develop leadership than to give an individual a job that involves responsibility and let him work it out. Deborah did this with young Barak. She appointed him as her field commander and assigned him the task of recruiting an army to defeat Sisera. She was not afraid to set the example of courage and heroism by using herself as bait for the ambush.

20. Boldness (Luke 3:1–20). John the Baptist began his prophetic ministry not only with the positive message announcing the coming Messiah, but in confrontively calling the people to repentance. It would have been much safer to simply proclaim good news, but John was obedient to the prophetic ministry that challenged human carelessness and sin. His ministry was marked by boldness, daring to preach what was unpopular. He rebuked the religious (v. 8), called to unselfishness (vv. 10–11), denounced dishonesty (vv. 12–13) and required equitable administration of authority (v. 14). Later, he confronted immorality tolerated in leadership (Mark 6:18), and for this he eventually was arrested and beheaded. Jesus' tribute to John's ministry (Matt. 11:11) abides as a testimony to faithfulness and boldness as worthy traits for leaders.

21. The Administrative Leader (1 Cor. 12:28). The New Testament seems to recognize three basic types of administrative leadership: (1) the servant leader or deacon: Greek *diakonia* means "service or ministry" (2 Cor. 8:19–20; 9:1, 12). These "deacons" were patterned after the men set apart in Acts 6:1–6 to serve the widows in Jerusalem. (2) The steward leader or manager: Greek *oikonomos* or *oikonomis* means "steward," such as today's pastor. The word literally means "household manager," a slot often held by a slave in the first century. It refers to those who "manage" the church (1 Cor. 4:1–2; 2 Tim. 1:7). (3) The steersman leader or overseer is found in the office of apostle or bishop. *Kybernesis* is a Greek term borrowed from seafaring, and is used to designate the steersman or pilot who holds the ship on course. The word is rendered "governments" (1 Cor. 12:28) where Paul speaks of the spiritual gift of administration. J.B.

LEFT. (Mark 1:20) *aphiemi* (af-*ee*-ay-mee); *Strong's #863:* A compound of *apo*, "away from," and *hiemi*, "to send." *Aphiemi* has three main categories of meanings: (1) To let go, send away, remit, forgive. In this sense the word is used in connection with divorce (1 Cor. 7:11–13), debts (Matt. 18:27), and especially sins (Matt. 9:2; 1 John 1:9); (2) To permit, let (Matt. 3:15; 5:40; 19:14); and (3) To neglect, forsake, leave alone (Matt. 4:11; Mark 7:8; Luke 13:35; John 4:3).

LEWDNESS. (1 Pet. 4:3) *aselgeia* (as-elg-*eye*-ah); *Strong's #766:* Total debauchery, unashamed indecency, unbridled lust, unrestrained depravity. The person with this characteristic has an insolent defiance of public opinion, sinning in broad daylight with arrogance and contempt.

LIBERTY. (Lev. 25:10) *deror* (deh-*ror*); *Strong's #1865:* Freedom, liberty, release, setting free. Leviticus 25:10 is the verse inscribed on the Liberty Bell. *Deror* is also the Hebrew word for "swallow," a bird swift in flight. In this reference, the details about the Year of Jubilee are given (vv. 8–17 and 39–55), indicating that *deror* is a technical term for the release of slaves and property every fifty years. The Lord Jesus in His first sermon quoted Isaiah 61:1, which states that the Messiah's anointing and divine commission enable Him to "proclaim liberty to the captives" (Luke 4:17–19). *Also* (1 Cor. 10:29) *eleutheria* (el-yoo-ther-*ee*-ah); *Strong's #1657:* Freedom from slavery, independence, absence of external restraint, a negation of control or domination, freedom of access. Paul exulted in the liberty there is in Christ Jesus. Legalistic believers were critical of his new lifestyle, but he responded: "I am free from religious bondage. Why does anyone want me to go back to it?" We are free to serve the Lord in all the ways that are consistent with His word, will, nature, and holiness.

LIFE—the physical functions of people, animals, and plants. In physical terms, life is the time between birth and death. Because God is the source of life, it is a gift from Him. He first filled Adam with the breath of life (Gen. 2:7), and He continues to be the source of all life. The psalmist sang to God "For with you is the fountain of life" (Ps. 36:9).

The New Testament expanded on the Old Testament idea of life. The word life began to refer to more than physical existence. It took on a strong spiritual meaning, often referring to the spiritual life that results from man's relationship with God.

Eternal life means more than eternal existence. Eternal life refers to eternal fellowship with God (John 14:3), and an endlessly unfolding purpose in partnership with Him (Eph. 2:6). "This is eternal life," Jesus declared, "that they may know You, the only true God, and Jesus Christ whom You have sent" (John 17:3).

Eternal life is the highest quality of life. According to Romans 6:21–23, it is freedom from sin, holiness, and a positive relationship with God. This is in contrast to spiritual death, which results from a life of sin.

Eternal life comes through faith in Jesus Christ. He taught, "He who believes in Me has everlasting life" (John 6:47). This symbolic meaning of life appears frequently in the Gospel of John. Of Jesus, John wrote, "In Him was life, and the life was the light of men" (John 1:4).

LIFE. (1 John 5:20) *zoe* (dzo-*ay*); *Strong's #2222:* Compare "zoology," "zoological," "Zoe." Refers to the principle of life. In the New Testament *zoe* denotes not only physical life, but spiritual life, which one can possess only

through faith in Jesus Christ. Eternal life refers not only to duration of life, but to quality of life. It is a present life of grace and a future life of glory.

LIFT UP. (James 4:10) *hupsoo* (hoop-*sah*-oh); *Strong's #5312:* Related to the noun *hupsos,* "height," the verb signifies to lift or raise up. It is used literally (John 3:14; 8:28; 12:32, 34); figuratively, of spiritual privileges given to a city (Matt. 11:23; Luke 10:15); and metaphorically, in the sense of exalting or uplifting (Acts 2:33; 5:31; 13:17). The Bible warns us that exalting ourselves will result in a disgraceful fall, but humbling ourselves leads to exaltation in this and the next world.

LIGHT—illumination; the opposite of darkness. The Bible also speaks of light as the symbol of God's presence and righteous activity.

Light has been associated with the presence, truth, and redemptive activity of God since creation. Before man was created, light was brought into being by the Creator: "Then God said, 'Let there be light'; and there was light. And God saw the light, that it was good" (Gen. 1:3–4). Throughout the Bible, light represents truth, goodness, and God's redemptive work. Darkness, on the other hand, symbolizes error, evil, and the works of Satan (Gen. 1:4).

God or God's Word, the Bible, are frequently represented as lights or lamps to enlighten and guide the believer (1 John 1:5). "Your word is a lamp to my feet and a light to my path" (Ps. 119:105). The psalmist also declared, "The Lord is my light and my salvation; whom shall I fear?" (Ps. 27:1). Light is also used as a symbol of holiness and purity. Paul counseled the Christians at Rome to "put on the armor of light" (Rom. 13:12).

The New Testament presents Jesus as the personification of light or divine illumination: "I am the light of the world" (John 8:12). Jesus plainly stated that those who rejected this divine light would bring judgment upon themselves (John 3:19–21). Jesus and the New Testament writers extended the figure of light to include faithful Christian witnesses, who were called "children of light" (Eph. 5:8).

LISTEN. (1 Kin. 20:8) *shama'* (shah-*mah*); *Strong's #8085:* To hear; to listen, consider, pay attention; to listen carefully and intelligently, to obey. The word conveys a sense of intensity. The most famous reference containing *shama'* is Deuteronomy 6:4, which states, "Sh'ma Yisrael! Hear, O Israel! The LORD our God, the LORD is one!" These words are called the *Sh'ma,* which is the central creed of

Judaism. Moses was calling Israel to listen attentively and very carefully with a mind to obey what God would say. The verb *shama'* also appears in the name *Shmuel* (Samuel), "Heard of God." Samuel was so named after his mother asked for a son, and the Lord listened to her (1 Sam. 3:20).

 LITTLE FAITH. (Matt. 8:26) *oligopistos* (ol-ig-*op*-is-tus); *Strong's #3640:* From *oligos*, "small," and *pistis*, "faith," describing a faith that lacks confidence or trusts too little. Jesus used the word in various situations as a tender rebuke or corrective chiding (6:30; 8:26; 14:31; 16:8; Luke 12:28). Another way to term it is "underdeveloped faith" as opposed to outright unbelief or distrust (*apistis*).

LOOKED. (Heb. 11:26) *apoblepo* (ap-ob-*lep*-oh); *Strong's #578:* A graphic word combining *apo*, "away from," and *blepo*, "to see." The word literally means "to look away from everything else in order to look intently on one object." Moses looked away from the wealth of world systems toward a messianic future.

LOOKING. (Heb. 12:2) *aphorao* (af-or-*ah*-oh); *Strong's #872:* From *apo*, "away from," and *horao*, "to see." The word signifies undivided attention, looking away from all distractions in order to fix one's gaze on one object. *Aphorao* in Hebrews 12:2 is having eyes for no one but Jesus.

LORD. (Mic. 4:13) *'adon* (ah-*don*); *Strong's #113:* Owner, master, lord, sir. The primary meaning is "master." It may refer both to a human master and the divine Lord. A citizen may address his king or any other noble person as *'adon*. It was the title applied to Joseph repeatedly by his brothers in Egypt. *'Adon* is used in modern Hebrew to convey the meaning of "mister" or "sir." The intensive form is *'Adonai*, a kind of plural form that is used only in reference to the glorious Lord in all His powers and attributes. *Also* (John 6:68) *kurios* (*koo*-ree-oss); *Strong's #2962:* Originally, an adjective signifying authority or having power. As a noun the word designates the owner, master, controller, one in authority. In direct address, *kurios* is a title of respect given to masters, teachers, and so on. *Kurios* in the Old Testament was Yahweh, while in the New Testament the title is transferred to Jesus. *Also* (Jude 4) *despotes* (des-*pot*-ace); *Strong's #1203:* The origin of the English word "despot." The word signifies owner, master, one who has absolute dominion, supreme authority, and unlimited power arising from ownership. *Despotes* includes total submission on our part to God's will, not out of slavish fear or bondage, but joyfully and willingly.

LORD'S DAY—the first day of the week, or Sunday; the day especially associated with the Lord Jesus Christ.

A special honor was reserved for Sunday, the first day of the week. This was the day on which Jesus was raised from the dead; every Lord's Day, therefore, is a weekly memorial of Christ's resurrection. Clearly the early church assembled for worship and religious instruction on Sunday, the Lord's Day (1 Cor. 16:2).

The Lord's Day is not to be confused with the *Sabbath, the Jewish day of rest. The Jewish Sabbath corresponds with our Saturday, the seventh or last day of the week. This special day to the Jews commemorated the day on which God rested after the creation of the world.

Under the new dispensation of grace, Christians are not to be trapped by a legalism mandating days or seasons (Col. 2:16–17). Note that the *Jerusalem council did not include a demand for Sabbath observance in its rules for Gentile Christians (Acts 15:20, 28–29). Some members of the early church "esteemed every day alike"; they made no distinction between days, including Jewish festivals and Sabbaths and possibly also Sunday. The apostle Paul said they were not to be judged if they were acting in good conscience out of the fear of God (Rom. 14:1–6).

Some Jewish believers continued then, and some now continue to observe the Sabbath and/or Jewish festivals. According to the Word, they should not be judged for "esteeming one day above another." If their behavior is guided by conscience in the fear of God, such observance is a matter of Christian liberty, so long as the believer does not regard the observance as a necessary qualification for salvation (Rom. 14:5–6; Gal. 4:10; Col. 2:16–17).

Paul's principle of Christian liberty about holy places and holy days comes from the Lord Jesus Christ Himself. Jesus described Himself as one who is greater than the temple (Matt. 12:6) and said, "The Son of Man is Lord even of the Sabbath" (Matt. 12:8; Luke 6:5). When accused by the Pharisees of breaking the Sabbath, Jesus replied, "The Sabbath was made for man, and not man for the Sabbath. Therefore the Son of Man is also Lord of the Sabbath" (Mark 2:27–28).

The phrase the Lord's Day occurs only once in the New Testament, in Revelation 1:10, where John declared, "I was in the Spirit on the Lord's Day." In Asia Minor, where the churches to which John wrote were situated, the pagans celebrated the first day of each month as the Emperor's Day. Some scholars also believe that a day of the week was also called by this name.

When the early Christians called the first day of the week the Lord's Day, this was a direct challenge to the emperor worship to which John refers so often in the Book of Revelation. Such a bold and fearless testimony by the early Christians proclaimed that the Lord's Day belonged to the Lord Jesus Christ and not to the emperor.

LORD'S SUPPER—the biblical practice, usually during a worship service, in which Christians partake of bread and wine (or grape juice) with the purpose of remembering Christ, receiving strength and healing from Him, and being renewed to serve His cause. It is one of two sacraments or ordinances instituted by Christ to be observed by His church until He returns (the other is water baptism).

The term the Lord's Supper is used only in 1 Corinthians 11:20. The practice is also known as Communion (from 1 Cor. 10:16), the Lord's Table (from 1 Cor. 10:21), and the Eucharist (from the Greek word for "giving thanks"; Luke 22:17, 19; 1 Cor. 11:24). The expression breaking of bread (Acts 2:42, 46; 20:7, 11) probably refers to receiving the Lord's Supper with a common meal known as the *love feast (2 Pet. 2:13; Jude 12).

The institution of the Lord's Supper (Matt. 26:17-30; Mark 14:12-26; Luke 22:1-23; 1 Cor. 11:23-25) took place on the night before Jesus died, at a meal commonly known as the Last Supper. Although there is considerable debate over the issue, the Last Supper probably was the Jewish Passover meal, first instituted by God in the days of Moses (Ex. 12:1-14; Num. 9:1-5).

Many of Jesus' actions and words at the Last Supper, such as the breaking and distributing of the bread, were part of the prescribed Passover ritual. But when Jesus said, "This is My body" and "This is My blood" while distributing the bread and the cup, He did something totally new. These words, which were intended for our blessing, have been the focus of sharp disagreement among Christians for centuries. In what sense are the bread and wine Christ's body and blood? What should the Lord's Supper mean to us? The answers to these questions are often grouped into four categories, although there are variations within these four broad views.

The transubstantiation view. The first view is that of the Roman Catholic Church (especially before the Second Vatican Council of 1962-1965). This view holds that the bread and wine become the actual body and blood of Christ when the words of institution are spoken by the priest. This doctrine, known as transubstantiation, holds that while the physical properties (taste, appearance, etc.) of the bread and wine do not change, the inner reality of these elements undergoes a spiritual change.

While this view may help to foster a serious attitude toward the Eucharist, it fails to grasp the figurative nature of Jesus' language. Jesus could not have been holding His actual body and blood in His hands. He probably meant, "This bread represents My body" and "This wine represents My blood." Jesus often used figurative language (Luke 8:11, 21), just as a person does today when showing someone a photograph and saying, "This is my father."

The consubstantiation view. The second viewpoint, developed by Martin Luther, is that Christ's body and blood are truly present "in, with, and under" the bread and wine. The elements do not actually change into Christ's body and blood. But in the same way that heat is present in a piece of hot iron, so Christ is present in the elements. The Lutheran position is often called consubstantiation.

This position can encourage the recipient of the Eucharist with the realization that Christ is actually present at the Supper. But it also misses the figurative use of Jesus' words. It also may tend to draw more attention to the bread and wine than to Christ Himself.

The symbolic view. The third position, known as the symbolic or memorial view, is derived from the teachings of the Swiss reformer, Ulrich Zwingli. Although his teaching is not completely clear, he basically held that the bread and wine were only symbols of the sacrificed body and blood of Christ. He taught that the Lord's Supper is primarily a memorial ceremony of Christ's finished work, but that it is also to be an occasion when God's people pledge their unity with one another and their loyalty to Christ. This is the viewpoint held by most Baptist and independent churches. While Zwingli's ideas are basically sound, this position tends to place more emphasis on what the Christian does and promises in the Supper than on what God does.

The dynamic view. Finally, there is the view of John Calvin and the Reformed and Presbyterian churches which follow his teachings. Known as the dynamic or spiritual presence view, it stands somewhere between the positions of Luther and Zwingli.

Calvin agreed with Zwingli that the bread and wine are to be understood symbolically. Christ is not physically present in the elements, because His risen, glorified body is in heaven (Heb. 10:12-13). Still, He is dynamically and spiritually present in the Lord's Supper through the Holy Spirit.

In the worship service (but not at any one precise moment), when the Word of God is proclaimed and the Lord's Supper is received, the glorified Christ actually gives spiritual nourishment from His own glorified body to those who receive it. As bread nourishes the physical body, so Christ's glorified body enlivens the soul. Because of the organic union between Christ, the risen Head, and the members of His body, the church (Eph. 1:18–23; 4:15–16; 5:23), this nourishment is conveyed to Christians by the Spirit who dwells in them (Rom. 8:9–11). Calvin admits that the way the Spirit does this is a genuine mystery. Yet, it is not contrary to reason—simply above reason.

Calvin seemed at times to place more emphasis on Jesus' glorified flesh and blood than the Scripture's focus, but his position helps to explain why the Eucharist is so important for the Christian to observe and why it is such a serious offense to misuse it. His view also corresponds well with those Scriptures that speak of God's nourishing and empowering work in His people (Eph. 3:14–21; Col. 2:6–10, 19).

Biblical teachings. In 1 Corinthians 10:16 the apostle Paul rebuked the Corinthians for their involvement with idolatry. He referred to the cup as "the communion of the blood of Christ" and the bread as "the communion of the body of Christ." The Greek word for communion has the meaning of "fellowship, participating, and sharing." From the context it appears that Paul is saying that when Christians partake of the cup and the bread, they are participating in the benefits of Christ's death (referred to as His blood) and resurrection life (His glorified body). The most important of these benefits are the assurance of sins forgiven (through Christ's blood) and the assurance of Christ's presence and power (through His body).

The "one body" (the universal church) in 1 Corinthians 10:17 connects with the "body of Christ" in verse 16 in the sense that the entire church of Christ is organically related to the living, glorified human body of Christ now in heaven. The "one [loaf of] bread" (v. 17), representing Jesus the "bread of life" (John 6:35), is eaten by all believers at the Supper, symbolizing their unity and common participation in the one body of Christ. The great discourse of Jesus on the bread of life (John 6:25–68), while not intended to be a direct theological explanation of the Lord's Supper, helps to explain how receiving the Eucharist can be one way in which Christians "feed" on the Lord (John 6:55–57). Other important ways are by prayer and the hearing of God's Word through the Scriptures.

In 1 Corinthians 11:17–34 Paul rebuked the Corinthians for their pride and greed during the meal that accompanied the Eucharist (vv. 17–22). Then (vv. 23–25) he described the institution of the Lord's Supper and emphasized the need for Christians to partake in a worthy manner. Many of them who had not been doing so were weak and sick, and many had even died as a result of misappropriating or neglecting the purpose of the Table (vv. 27–34).

Why does Paul use such strong language when speaking of the abuse of the Lord's Supper? The Corinthians were not properly discerning or recognizing the Lord's body. The wealthy Corinthians who shamed their poorer Christian brothers and sisters by their selfish eating practices (vv. 21–22) were not discerning the true nature of the church as Christ's body in which all distinctions such as social class and race were blotted out (Gal. 3:28).

On the other hand, Christians who received the bread and the cup after behaving disgracefully were failing to discern that Christ would not automatically bless and empower those who received the sacrament in this manner. Such persons were guilty of sin against the body and blood of Jesus (v. 27).

Meaning for today. When we ask how the Lord's Supper should be meaningful to the Christian today, three concepts—relating to the past, present, and future—can be helpful.

First, the Lord's Supper is a time of remembrance and Eucharist. Jesus said, "Do this in remembrance of Me" (Luke 22:19; 1 Cor. 11:24–25). This is not to be so much our dwelling on the agonies of the Crucifixion as it is to be our remembering the marvelous life and ministry of our Savior. The Eucharist is to be an occasion for expressing our deepest praise and appreciation for all Jesus Christ has done for us.

Just as one step in the Jewish Passover meal was to proclaim the Hebrews' deliverance from Egyptian bondage (Ex. 12:26–27), so in the Supper Christians proclaim their deliverance from sin and misery through the death of "Christ, our Passover" (1 Cor. 5:7; 11:26).

Second, the Supper is a time of refreshment and communion. As we participate in the benefits of Jesus' death and resurrection life (Rom. 5:10; 1 Cor. 10:16), we are actually being nourished and empowered from the risen Christ through the Spirit.

John Wesley knew of this strengthening. On the average, he received communion every four or five days throughout his long and fruitful ministerial career. It is not that God cannot empower us without the Lord's Supper, but that He has instituted the Supper for us, even as He has designated prayer and the hearing of Scripture as means of communicating His grace. While the Bible does not tell us how often to observe the Eucharist, Wesley's guideline—"as often as you can"—deserves our serious consideration.

Third, the Supper is a time of recommitment and anticipation. We are to examine (literally "prove" or "test") ourselves and partake in a worthy manner (1 Cor. 11:28–29). In so doing we renew our dedication to Christ and His people, in hopeful anticipation "till He comes" (1 Cor. 11:26). After Christ's return we shall partake with Him—in His physical presence—in the kingdom (Matt. 26:29).

LOVE—the high esteem which God has for His human children and the high regard which they, in turn, should have for Him and other people. Because of the hundreds of references to love in the Bible, it is certainly the most remarkable book of love in the world. It records the greatest love story ever written—God's unconditional love for us that sent His Son to die on the Cross (John 3:16; 1 John 4:10).

Love is not only one of God's attributes; it is also an essential part of His nature. "God is love," the Bible declares (1 John 4:8, 16)—the personification of perfect love. Such love surpasses our powers of understanding (Eph. 3:19). Love like this is everlasting (Jer. 31:3), free (Hos. 14:4), sacrificial (John 3:16), and enduring to the end (John 13:1).

Two distinct Greek words for love appear in the Bible. The word *phileo* means "to have ardent affection and feeling"—a type of impulsive love. The other word *agapao* means "to have esteem" or "high regard." In the memorable conversation between Jesus and Peter, there is a play upon these two words (John 21:15–17).

The warm word *agape* is the characteristic term of Christianity. This word for love is used several different ways in the Bible.

1. *Agape* love indicates the nature of the love of God toward His beloved Son (John 17:26), toward the human race generally (John 3:16; Rom. 5:8), and toward those who believe in the Lord Jesus Christ (John 14:21).

2. *Agape* love conveys God's will to His children about their attitude toward one another. Love for one another was a proof to the world of true discipleship (John 13:34–35).

3. *Agape* love also expresses the essential nature of God (1 John 4:8). Love can be known only from the actions it prompts, as seen in God's love in the gift of His Son (1 John

4:9–10). Love found its perfect expression in the Lord Jesus. Christian love is the fruit of the Spirit of Jesus in the believer (Gal. 5 :22).

Love is like oil to the wheels of obedience. It enables us to run the way of God's commandments (Ps. 119:32). Without such love, we are as nothing (1 Cor. 13:3). Such Spirit-inspired love never fails (1 Cor. 13:8) but always flourishes.

LOVE. (Ps. 97:10) *'ahab* (ah-*hahv*); *Strong's* #157: To love, to have affection for someone; to like, to be a friend. *'Ahab* is remarkably similar to the English word "love" in that its range of meanings covers the same ideas. *'Ahab* can refer to loving God, loving one's friend, romantic love, love of ideals, love of pleasures, and so on. The participial form, *'oheb,* refers to a friend or lover. The first mention of love in the Bible is in Genesis 22:2, where Abraham loved his son Isaac. *Also* (John 21:15) *phileo* (fill-*eh*-oh); *Strong's #5368:* Compare "philharmonic," "philosophy," "philology." To be fond of, care for affectionately, cherish, take pleasure in, have personal attachment for. Jesus asked Peter twice if he had *agape* love. Peter answered with *phileo,* which at that moment was all he had to give. Later, when the Holy Spirit imparted to him the fuller understanding of *agape* love, Peter used the *agape/agapao* words nine times in his writings. *Also* (Rom. 5:5) *agape* (ag-*ah*-pay); *Strong's #26:* A word to which Christianity gave new meaning. Outside of the New Testament, it rarely occurs in existing Greek manuscripts of the period. *Agape* denotes an undefeatable benevolence and unconquerable goodwill that always seeks the highest good of the other person, no matter what he does. It is the self-giving love that gives freely without asking anything in return, and does not consider the worth of its object. *Agape* is more a love by choice than *philos,* which is love by chance; and it refers to the will rather than the emotion. *Agape* describes the unconditional love God has for the world.

LOVE, BROTHERLY—love of brothers for each other (Rom. 12:10; Heb. 13:1; 2 Pet. 1:7). The phrase is used in a symbolic sense to express love of Christians for one another, since all are sons of the same Father. The Greek word translated as brotherly love implies more than love for one's "blood brothers," as in pagan writings; it means love for the broader brotherhood of true believers, for the members of the church, the "household of faith" (Gal. 6:10) and "of God" (Eph. 2:19; also 1 Pet. 2:17; 3:8; 5:9).

Believers in Christ are a brotherhood in the service of Christ (Matt. 23:8), a family made up of those who do the will of God (Matt.

12:50; Mark 3:35, Luke 8:21). "A new commandment I give to you," Jesus said to His disciples, "that you love one another; as I have loved you, that you also love one another. By this all will know that you are My disciples, if you have love for one another" (John 13:34–35).

A Christian's love should extend beyond the circle of faith, however, to all people. "If you greet your brethren only," said Jesus in the Sermon on the Mount, "what do you do more than others?" (Matt. 5:47). The believer is called not only to love his neighbor and his brother but also to love his enemy (Matt. 5:44). (See also Brotherly Love.)

LOVED. (John 3:16) *agapao* (ag-ah-*pah*-oh); *Strong's #25:* Unconditional love, love by choice and by an act of the will. The word denotes unconquerable benevolence and undefeatable goodwill. *Agapao* will never seek anything but the highest good for fellow mankind. *Agapao* (the verb) and *agape* (the noun) are the words for God's unconditional love. It does not need a chemistry, an affinity, or a feeling. *Agapao* is a word that exclusively belongs to the Christian community. It is a love virtually unknown to writers outside the New Testament.

LOVE FEAST—a meal shared by the early Christians when they met together for fellowship and the Lord's Supper. The term love feast is clearly used only in Jude 12 (feasts of charity; KJV), but some Greek manuscripts support "love feasts" instead of "deceptions" in 2 Peter 2:13. The love feast is also referred to in 1 Corinthians 11:17–34, and probably in Acts 6:1–3, although the term does not appear in either passage in English versions of the Bible. The Greek word for love feast also is the main New Testament noun for love, indicating that the meal was originally intended to be a rich experience of God's love. The purpose of the love feast was to remember Christ, to encourage His disciples, and to share God's provisions with the needy.

LOWLY. (Matt. 21:5) *praus* (prah-*ooce*); *Strong's #4235* and *#4239:* A humility that is considerate, unassuming, gentle, mild, meek. The Zealots were looking for a warlike Messiah who would use force. Jesus showed a greater power than armed might, the power of humble wisdom and penetrating love. Meekness is not weakness, but power under perfect control.

LUSTS. (2 Tim. 2:22) *epithumia* (ep-ee-thoo-mee-ah); *Strong's #1939:* A strong desire and intense craving for something. Three times it applies to good desires (Luke 22:15; Phil. 1:23; 1 Thess. 2:17). Its other uses are negative, such as gratifying sensual cravings, desiring the forbidden, longing for the evil, coveting what belongs to someone else, and striving for things, persons, or experiences contrary to the will of God.

MADE. (Ex. 34:27) *karat* (kah-*rat*); *Strong's #3772:* To cut, cut down, cut off, cut in pieces; to cut a covenant. This verb appears almost three hundred times in the Old Testament. Frequently the meaning is cutting something off, or cutting something down. The most important use of *karat* is in the often used phrase "cut a covenant," translated "make a covenant." *Karat* was the most fitting verb to use due to the "cutting up" of sacrificial animals when a covenant was inaugurated. *See* especially Genesis 15:7–21 for a good illustration of "cutting" a covenant. Circumcision, another instance of cutting, is the covenant that admits a Hebrew male into the congregation of the Lord. In the New Testament, the everlasting covenant was made when God's Lamb was pierced to death for His people. (*See* Heb. 9:15; 10:10–22.)

MAGIC, SORCERY, AND DIVINATION—occult practices, such as fortune-telling and witchcraft, which were common among the pagan nations of the ancient world. Such attempts to control evil spirits were expressly forbidden to the Hebrew people. Deuteronomy 18:10–11 mentions the following specific occult practices which were forbidden by the Law of Moses.

Passing a son or daughter through the fire. This phrase refers to the practice of child sacrifice. This seems incredible to some today, but the very fact that it was outlawed by God indicates it was done in the ancient world (Deut. 18:10). Second Kings 16:3 records that King Ahaz sacrificed his son in this way. No doubt he thought that such a sacrifice would appease some pagan god. His grandson, King Manasseh, sacrificed his sons two generations later (2 Kin. 21:6; 2 Chr. 33:6). Second Kings 23:10 reveals that it was mainly the pagan god Molech who required this awful sacrifice, but other false gods apparently also demanded it (2 Kin. 17:31; Jer. 19:5).

Witchcraft. The practice of witchcraft, or

 This icon beside an entry indicates a Word Wealth feature.

 This icon beside an entry indicates a Kingdom Dynamics feature.

 This icon beside an entry indicates an important biblical or doctrinal term.

divination, was a means for extracting information or guidance from a pagan god. The word describes the activity of Balaam the soothsayer, or professional prophet, who was hired to curse Israel (Num. 22:7; 23:23; Josh. 13:22). It also describes the woman at En Dor who brought up the spirit of Samuel. All the major prophets condemned divination (Is. 44:25; Jer. 27:9; 29:8; Ezek. 13:9).

All these forms of superstition, of course, were forbidden among the Hebrew people, notably because they were seen as more than merely empty ideas, but because their practice invited demonic involvement and workings.

Soothsaying. Soothsaying is a relatively rare word in the Bible which describes some form of divination, the practitioner of which is also described by the KJV as "observer of times" (Deut. 18:10). Because it sounds like a Hebrew word for cloud, some scholars believe it refers to cloud reading. This may have been similar to tea leaf reading or astrology, which is a reading of the stars. God forbids the practice (Deut. 18:10, 14; Lev. 19:26). Wicked King Manasseh was also guilty of this sin (2 Kin. 21:6; 2 Chr. 33:6). The prophets of the Old Testament also condemned this occult practice (Is. 2:6; 57:3; Jer. 27:9; Mic. 5:12).

Interpreting omens. Behind this phrase, also rendered as enchantments (KJV), lie four different Hebrew words. The most common of the four occurs in Genesis 30:27, in reference to Laban's "experience"; in Genesis 44:5 and 15, referring to Joseph's cup; and in Numbers 23:23 and 24:1, describing Balaam's activity. Leviticus 19:26 and Deuteronomy 18:10 specifically outlawed this practice as well. Another of the words used for the practice seems to mean "whisper," and it may indicate the way the enchanter lowered his voice, or the result of a demonic presence utilizing the speaker's voice. In Ecclesiastes 10:11 interpreting omens is connected with snake charming.

Sorcery. Sorcery or witchcraft is forbidden in the Law of Moses (Ex. 22:18, Deut. 18:10). Sorcery was apparently practiced by the worst of the kings of Israel and Judah (2 Kin. 9:22; 2 Chr. 33:6), but it was denounced by the prophets (Nah. 3:4).

Conjuring spells. This phrase, also translated as charm, appears in Deuteronomy 18:11, once in the Psalms (58:5), and twice in Isaiah (47:9, 12). Sometimes it is rendered as enchantments. A different Hebrew word lies behind this translation in Isaiah 19:3. Because it is related to a word for bind, it may mean casting a spell ("spellbinding"). One scholar suggests it has to do with tying a magic knot.

Consulting mediums. This phrase may refer to the same thing as practicing wizardry. The word describes the witch at En Dor whom Saul engaged to conduct a seance and bring up the spirit of Samuel (1 Sam. 28:3, 9; familiar spirits, KJV). The woman succeeded either by the power of God or the power of the devil. As with other practices in this list, it was forbidden by the Law of God, practiced by bad kings, and condemned by the prophets. In two places the prophet Isaiah hinted that consulting mediums may be a kind of evil ventriloquism (8:19; 29:4), the voice in such a case being demonic in source.

Spiritism. The word for spiritist always appears with witch. The root of the word in Hebrew is the verb "to know." In modern English wizard means someone very wise or inventive, a very clever or skillful person, but in the Bible it is always a forbidden thing, a kind of black magic. This is why most modern versions translate the word as spiritist, fortune-teller, or sorcerer.

Calling up the dead. Necromancy is another word used for this practice. The phrase occurs only in Deuteronomy 18:11, although this is exactly what an Old Testament witch did. The Bible shows that such a possibility is unavailable today. Christ has emptied "Abraham's bosom," and taken the Old Testament redeemed to Paradise and the unredeemed dead have no ability to communicate with the living (Luke 16:26–28). Any voices people claim to hear today from beyond the grave are demons—familiar spirits who mime and deceive.

Magic. The Hebrew word translated as magic appears only in connection with Egyptian and Babylonian magicians. The first cluster of verses relates to Joseph in Egypt (Gen. 41:8, 24); the second appears in connection with the plagues (Ex. 7:11—9:11); and the third deals with Daniel and the various government-supported magicians of Babylon (Dan. 1:20; 2:2, 10, 27; 4:7, 9; 5:11).

Magic actually comes from a Greek word which appears several times in the New Testament. Simon the sorcerer is one example (Acts 8:9–25), and Elymas the sorcerer is another (Acts 13:6–8). They may have been something like the "itinerant Jewish exorcists," also mentioned in the Book of Acts (Acts 19:13), who attempted to drive evil spirits out of people in the name of Jesus.

Still another New Testament word translated sorcery comes from the same Greek word as our English word, pharmacy. Quite obviously this has to do with drugs; and no more relevant or contemporary application could be found. The denunciations contained in Revelation 9:21; 18:23; 21:8; and 22:15 apply to those who use drugs to bring on trances during which they claim to have supernatural knowledge or power.

MAJESTY. (1 Chr. 29:11) *hod* (*hoad*); *Strong's #1935:* Glory, honor, majesty, beauty, grandeur, excellence in form and appearance. Found in twenty-four Old Testament references, *hod* refers to whatever or whoever is royally glorious. The word "splendor" may best define *hod*. Here David states that the splendor and glory belong to God. Compare with Jesus' words in Matthew 6:13. *Also* (Luke 9:43) *megaleiotes* (meg-al-eye-ot-ace); *Strong's #3168:* Compare "megalomania." Sublimity, grandeur, glory, magnificence, splendor, superbness, greatness. In Acts 19:27, the silversmith Demetrius expressed a fear that the preaching of Paul would destroy the *magnificence* of the goddess Diana. Here and in 2 Peter 1:16 the word magnifies the Lord and His far-surpassing greatness.

MAMMON [MAM mun] (*riches*)—a word that speaks of wealth (Matt. 6:24; Luke 16:9, 11, 13), especially wealth that is used in opposition to God. Mammon is a transliteration of the Aramaic word *mamon*, which means "wealth, riches," or "earthly goods." It is related in ancient lore to a Babylonian deity. Modern Bible versions have "money," "gold," and "material possessions," and would probably best leave the word as Mammon, because it carries more than the material significance of money in its meaning. Jesus said that no one can serve two masters—God and money—at the same time, and makes Mammon a potential "master"; thus, great spiritual consequence is here. Mammon (money) cannot purchase security (see Jesus' parable of the rich fool in Luke 12:13–21). "For what is a man profited if he gains the whole world, and loses his own soul?" (Matt. 16:26; Mark 8:36; Luke 9:25).

MAN—God's highest creation, made in God's own image.

The origin of man. The Bible states that man was created by God. This truth is found especially in Genesis 1:26–31 and 2:7–25. These passages teach that God did not use any previously existing living creature in bringing man into being.

The age of man. Some early students believed that by tracing the genealogies in the Bible and adding up the ages of the persons involved in the several generations, it was possible to establish a date for the creation of man. While it is unlikely that man was created in 4004 B.C. (a date not required by Scripture), it is most likely that he is not only the product of an unevolved, special creation event which began the Adamic race, but that this event is relatively recent—perhaps ten to fifteen thousand years ago.

The makeup of man. The Bible reveals man created as a tripartite being—spirit, soul, and body (1 Thess. 5:23). "Trichotomy" is the term describing this apparent fact of human makeup, an idea which avoids the confusion that is inevitable when the human mind and spirit are made synonymous, which they are not (Heb. 4:12).

MAN. (Gen. 1:26) *'adam* (ah-*dahm*); *Strong's #120:* Man, mankind, Adam the first man, or humanity at large. *'Adam* is translated as "Adam" (the proper name) about twenty times in the Old Testament, and as "man" more than five hundred times. When referring to the whole human race, the Bible often uses the phrase *b'nay 'adam*, the "children of Adam." As with English "man," *'adam* in its general sense has nothing to do with maleness and everything to do with humanness. For example, in one case *'adam* refers exclusively to women! (Num. 31:35). *'Adam* is probably related to the verb *'adom*, to be red, referring to the ruddiness of man's complexion. *'Adamah*, "soil" or "ground," may also be derived from this verb. Thus Gen. 2:7 says, "The LORD God formed *'adam* of the dust of the *'adamah*." Paul sees Adam as earth man or earthy man in 1 Corinthians 15:47. *'Adam* is one of the four major Hebrew words for "man" used in the Bible. See also *'enosh*, *'ish*, and *geber*. *Also* (Is. 32:2) *'ish* (*eesh*); *Strong's #376:* A man, a husband, a male, an individual person. This is one of the four main Hebrew words for "man" in the Old Testament. Unlike the generic term *'adam*, which means "human," *'ish* portrays maleness and so is logically paired with its feminine form, *'ishah*, "wife" or "woman." In Genesis 2:23, Adam says, "She shall be called *'ishah* because out of *'ish* she has been taken." *'Ish* often conveys a sense of nobility, dignity, strength, and especially social standing, as does the word "gentleman"; as in Psalm 62:9, *bnay 'adam*, "sons of men," is translated "men of low degree," whereas *bnay 'ish*, "sons of men," is translated "men of high degree." It is also used with another noun to describe a person; as *'ish 'Elohim*, or "man of God"; other such phrases include "man of blood," "man of the field," "man of words." *Also* (Jer. 31:22) *geber* (*geh*-vehr); *Strong's #1397:* A champion, hero, warrior, mighty man; a man in all his strength. *Geber* is one of the four outstanding words for "man" in the Old Testament. This word describes a man of strength or bravery, and is derived from the verb *gabar*, "to be strong." An intensive form of *geber* is *gibbor*, meaning "champion" or "mighty man of valor," as in Judges 6:12. The word also appears in the phrase *'El Gibbor* ("the Mighty God"), which might be translated "God the Champion"; this title appears in Isaiah 9:6 in reference to the Messiah.

MANHOOD, GOD'S DESIGN FOR. The desperate need in our modern times is for men: men who will *strike a blow of courage* to be what God purposed them to be and *leave an impression of character* on a disintegrating society.

Observing the overwhelming confusion that has been brought about by the lack of distinctive masculinity that has plagued our world, the biblical model of manhood ushers in a breath of fresh air to an age suffocating from the humanistic approach to manhood, which has resulted in a society spiraling out of control (2 Tim. 3:13). If we ever hope to recover what God had in mind regarding living as a human race, biblical manhood must be revisited and its spiritual principles must be lived out in our lives amid a world that is crying out for help. Men who are children of God dare not do otherwise.

1. God's Original Design (Gen. 1:26–27). Underscoring the purpose in God's creating human life as He did is very needful. His majestic plan was to create *distinctiveness within oneness*. This is described by the words, "Let us make man in our image, after our likeness" (v. 26). Although a human being is a creature with features similar to those of other living creatures, distinctive marks of the divine set him apart from other living beings (Gen. 2:7).

This *distinctiveness* is also seen in man's *uniqueness*. God created man "male and female" (v. 27). Although man was created in harmony with woman, they bear differences that are nontransferable. These differences provide for, among other things, the procreation of human life and the orderliness of human existence. Men have been given an essential role in society. Any deviation from God's purpose or trivialization of men's distinctiveness in uniqueness will result in catastrophe. (Compare Rom. 1:22–32.)

2. Leadership Through Headship (1 Cor. 11:3). For a man to serve in his God-appointed role as leader he must understand how he functions in that role. He functions through being "head" of the woman (v. 3). One of the root meanings of the word "head" as rendered in this passage is "woman's source" or "her reason for being" (compare Gen. 2:21–24). First Corinthians 11:3 suggests that men's leadership role in the smallest governmental unit of society—the family—was God's idea. This decision was not arbitrary but was employed to display a divinely functional plan for social order. It places squarely on a man's shoulders the obligation of leadership. This does not mean he is to lord it over the woman; rather, he is to serve as her protector under God's authority. Nor does it mean that the man is superior to the woman; rather, it is that they have different roles.

The case for real manliness is settled here and provides the source for a symphonic society. Therefore, as men apply the biblical principle of godly leadership, harmony and peace will be experienced in the home as well as in the world (1 Pet. 3:7)

3. Responsibility under God (Gen. 3:16). Along with a man's role as God's appointed leader in society comes responsibility. In Genesis 3:16 we are told that the man is to "rule over" the woman. This does not imply dominion in the sense of authoritarian or dictatorial rule but rather responsibility in the sense of providing care and protection. Although this decree was given as a consequence of humanity's rebellion against God, it should not be understood primarily in a negative sense. Understood properly, we see the restoring grace of God's adopting a plan for an orderly society.

At least three areas of responsibility are woven into the social fabric of biblical manhood: (1) *material provision*, which includes food, clothing, and shelter; (2) *emotional provision*, which involves love, security, and understanding; and (3) *spiritual provision*, which stresses guidance, maturity, and sensitivity (Eph. 5:23, 25–27; 1 Tim. 5:8).

If hurtful and chaotic conditions are to be avoided in our world, men must take seriously their essential role of responsibility.

4. Governing Through Authority (Rom. 13:1). The word "authority" as used in the Bible usually means a person's right to do certain things based on the position he holds. Since the family is the smallest unit of governmental authority, this suggests that men represent God's authority to govern.

Just as the physical body needs a head for life, so it also needs a *source* of authority to function properly. Paul described Christ as "Head" of the church (Eph. 5:23), and Christ declared that His *source* of authority was from above (John 6:38; 7:16, 18). Therefore, as God's representative, a man's source of authority is God. However, it is the same kind of authority that Christ demonstrated when He gave His life for the church. The husband is "head" of the wife as Christ is "head of the church" (Eph. 5:23). Jesus Christ was always motivated by love and served the church. In the same way, the husband's authority is based on servanthood.

The same God who gave men authority gave them the right and responsibility to exercise it. For men to refuse this role is to disobey God. For them to misunderstand it is to destroy their manhood.

5. The Risk of Obedience (Heb. 11:8). Obedience stand out as one of the premier qualities of biblical manhood. It requires faith to obey God when all the facts regarding a matter may be unknown (Gen. 12:1–4; Heb. 11:8). Carrying out this day-to-day trust, this matter-of-fact belief, this down-to-earth reliance, is probably the most difficult to achieve of all the models of biblical manhood (Matt. 26:39, 42, 44).

The frightening aspect of obedience is very real because it carries with it uncertainties which, if realized, will result in agonizing consequences. It also carries with it real pain that is generated through conflict—whether human or circumstantial. However, God has called men to obedience. If they do not shrink from this call, they will experience miraculous and glorious results and enjoy the evidence of true manhood (Rom. 4:13–25).

6. The Valor of Self-Discipline (Dan. 6:1–5). The lack of resolve in Christlike living primarily stems from hesitation to apply the spiritual principles of self-discipline. Quite often, biblical principles and society's standards for right living do not match up.

It is conceded that in living out biblical principles there will inevitably be confrontational assaults made upon believers by those who reject Scripture's mandates. Therefore, if one is to exhibit true manhood, he must discipline himself in thought and deed to stand firm in his commitment to his God.

As a man practices standing in right relationship to God, he will find that God provides the strength necessary to move forward in the self-disciplined life. God will reward his courageous efforts as he draws upon the Spirit's resources, for in the final analysis, spiritual discipline can only be produced by a deliberate yielding to the Spirit's power (2 Chr. 19:11).

7. The Blessedness of Self-Giving (Acts 2:45). The worth of a man is defined not by how much he acquires [greed] but by how much he gives away [liberality]. The true greatness of a man is found in his capacity to share himself without any thought of what he will receive in return (John 3:16). Selfishness shrivels the soul and lessens its capacity to demonstrate

the true nature of God, which is love. Man is never diminished by giving himself away. Instead, he proves correct the principle that God has set forth in Scripture: giving supersedes receiving (Acts 2:45; Luke 6:38). Nothing produces more relational harmony than the act of giving one's self away. By the same token, nothing creates more relational breakdown than the act of selfishness—the act of exclusive acquisition for the purpose of personal gain and indulgence (1 Sam. 18:5–11). The unpalatable product of selfishness is fear, but the boundless joy of self-giving is openness characterized by love (1 Sam. 18:12–16).

8. The Purpose of Love (Eph. 5:25). Self-giving, characterized by love, demands the highest degree of sacrifice (John 3:16). Love is not manifested in syrupy sentimentalism but in true affection. Man is provided the capacity to love as Christ loved His church (Eph. 5:25). This a demanding task. The more Christlike a man is, the more it will cost him to be a man of love.

Love demands perfection in the object of its love. However, that perfection is not primarily achieved through the demands made upon the one who is loved but through the sacrifice of the one who loves (Eph. 5:25–28). To love does not stop with who or what the "loved-one" is but seeks to produce in the one "loved" what he may become.

This will be the burning passion of the man who is disciplined in his walk with God— to love in such a way that the object of his love becomes as he is—a true lover.

9. The Wholeness of Integrity (Eccl. 7:29). A world influenced by the ever-mounting ills of humanistic philosophies and situation ethics fights against integrity. It is evident that today's moral values derive their source from the human experience with little to no concern for divine principles. Mankind has been given a command to walk with God in singleness of purpose (Mic. 6:8). Doing this, a man will bring glory to his Creator and find genuine peace (Is. 43:7).

An individual may attain worldly acclaim, social standing, and financial prominence through honest means, but if his emotions, mind, and will are not submitted to the Holy Spirit, he risks being pulled away from the wholeness of life and ultimately becoming a disastrous failure.

The battle lines are drawn: if a man is to be complete, he must walk with God in total integrity of heart (Ps. 7:8, Prov. 11:3).

10. The Standard for Moral Courage (Josh. 1:6–7, 9). Our society is declining morally at an alarming rate. While giving in to the overwhelming decadence in our world is generally far easier than standing against the tidal wave of indifference, the man of God has been given power to withstand the flood of evil. To take a moral position in a quiet yet steadfast way is a thoroughly "manly" act (John 18:4). The courage to do this comes from a conviction that God is sovereign and in control, no matter how bad things may look.

Moral choices fall to all of us. The man who is willing to accept the consequences of his stand is courageous indeed. Although he may seem to stand alone, God has promised to be with him (2 Chr. 19:11).

11. The Strength of Humility (Matt. 11:29). One of the most *remarkable* yet *perplexing* qualities of manhood is humility. It is remarkable because of what it can develop in the soul of an individual, yet it is perplexing because of what the term has come to imply about one who possesses it—that one is weak of resolve or character.

Society's idea of a real man is the blustering *take-charge* type. From the world's perspective, any show of yieldedness is not only a sign of weakness but serves a *death-blow* to all that *is* considered manly. However, the way in which a man shows his true strength is simply to submit himself to another through Christ's love in genuine humility (John 13:4, 13–17). In doing so, he models the example Christ left for us.

12. The Freedom Forgiveness Brings (Eph. 4:32). Forgiving those who have wronged us brings us freedom. When one has been hurt or humiliated, it may seem impossible to believe that letting the perpetrator "off the hook" can be freeing, but it can be. In reality, forgiveness frees the one who forgives and releases him from the tyranny of the one who has acted against him. On the other hand, not to forgive holds one in slavery and produces psychological and physical distress; but, even more tragically, it blocks spiritual growth. The results of this resistance to "let go" are evidenced by the myriad of social and personal strains in relationships.

In our Lord's model guide to prayer, we are instructed to forgive those who have sinned against us as we ask our heavenly Father to forgive us (Luke 11:4). The glory of biblical manhood is the ability to set others free from their indebtedness to us, thereby liberating ourselves (Matt. 18:21–35).

13. The Force of Faithfulness (Gal. 5:22). Faithfulness is a quality of biblical manhood that represents the very nature of God. Scripture is replete with examples of God's faithfulness to His people (for example, see Deut. 7:9). The term speaks of dependability, loyalty, and stability. It carries a far greater impact upon human relationships than appears on the surface, for it is the bridge that links us with those around us. This quality in our lives tells others that we are solid, consistent, and trustworthy.

The man of the world depends upon the scaffolding of power, prestige, intimidation, and the like to support the world order and not upon the true structure provided through faithfulness. Because he has disdained faithfulness, our very institutional base for an orderly society—family, interpersonal, social, national, and global relationships—is being destroyed. But hope reigns supreme for every man who remembers God's faithfulness and honors Him through his manner of life (1 Thess. 5:24; 1 Pet. 4:19).

14. The Peace of Patience (James 1:4). Trusting God in the face of adversity challenges our faith while we wait for His answer. It is human nature to respond to crises based upon the information at hand. Yet our Lord teaches us that it is in our patience that we possess our souls (Luke 21:19). In other words, as we stand firm in the quietness of our hearts during the stressful conditions of life and wait for God's timing, we then lay hold of true peace.

Our Lord, in the face of overwhelming circumstances, endured His real-life trial, so greatly trusting His Father's wisdom and promise that He did not even attempt to avoid His trouble (Heb 12:1–3). Trusting God in troublesome times is another way we live out Christ's example of biblical manhood (2 Tim. 2:3).

15. The Ultimate in Biblical Manhood (Phil. 2:5–8). All qualities of biblical manhood come full circle in the life of our Lord (Phil. 2:5). The sum total of true biblical manhood rests in submission—an act of obedience to the will of another. This submission is borne out of reverence to God. Our Lord demonstrated this by His complete submission to the will of His Father in thought and deed (John 5:19, 30).

Man's search for himself culminates in submission to his Creator. If he rejects this submission, he is separated from God and no longer experiences communion with Him that he was meant to have. Not only is he alienated from his Creator, but also from himself and others, which ultimately ends in a complete breakdown in human relationships. A man finds his manhood not in *self-sufficiency*, but in total acceptance of *self-insufficiency* in order that he may become more than sufficient in God (2 Cor. 2:16; 3:5). Only in this way can the image and likeness of God be reflected in man (Gen. 1:26–27). R.P.A.

MANIFEST. (John 14:21) *emphanidzo* (em-fan-id-zoe); *Strong's #1718:* A combination of *en*, "in," and *phaino*, "to cause to shine," thus, to appear, come to view, reveal, exhibit, make visible, present oneself to the sight of another, be conspicuous. In verse 21, *emphanidzo* is the self-revelation of Jesus to believers. A secondary meaning of the word is to declare, make known (Acts 23:15, 22; 24:1; 25:2, 15).

MANIFOLD. (Eph. 3:10) *polupoikilos* (pol-oo-poy-kil-oss); *Strong's #4182:* From *polus*, "much," and *poikilos*, "varied," "many-colored." The word pictures God's wisdom as much varied, with many shades, tints, hues, and colorful expressions. As a God of variety, He is still entering the human arena displaying many-sided, multicolored, and much variegated wisdom to His people and through His people.

MARDUK—see ch. 55, §3.6.c.

MARI, MARI TEXTS & ROYAL PALACE—see ch. 55, §3.1., 3.4.a., 3.6., 3.6.a., 3.6.b., 3.6.c., 3.6.d.

MARRIAGE—the union of a man and a woman as husband and wife, which becomes the foundation for a home and family.

Origin of marriage. Marriage was instituted by God when He declared, "It is not good that man should be alone; I will make him a helper comparable to him" (Gen. 2:18). So God fashioned woman and brought her to man. On seeing the woman, Adam exclaimed, "This is now bone of my bones and flesh of my flesh; she shall be called Woman, because she was taken out of Man" (Gen. 2:23). This passage also emphasizes the truth that "a man shall leave his father and mother and be joined to his wife, and they shall become one flesh" (Gen. 2:24). This indicates that God's original ideal is for a man to be the husband of one wife and for the marriage to be permanent.

Legislation. God's desire for His people was that they marry within the body of believers. The Mosaic Law clearly stated that an Israelite was never to marry a Canaanite. The Israelite would be constantly tempted to embrace the spouse's god as well (Ex. 34:10–17; Deut. 7:3–4). Likewise, the apostle Paul commanded the members of the church at Corinth, "Do not be unequally yoked together with unbelievers" (2 Cor. 6:14).

Marriages between Israelites were directed by law, and all incestuous relationships were outlawed (Lev. 18:6–8; 20:19–21). In addition, priests were forbidden to marry prostitutes and divorced women (Lev. 21:7,

13–14). Daughters who inherited their father's possessions had to marry within their tribe or lose their inheritance (Num. 27:8; 36:24).

Choosing the bride. In Old Testament times, the parents chose the mate for their son. The primary reason for this was that the bride became part of the clan. Although they were married and became "one flesh," the couple remained under the authority of the bridegroom's father. The parents chose someone who would best fit into their clan and work harmoniously with her mother-in-law and sisters-in-law.

Sometimes the parents consulted with their children to see if they approved of the choice of mates being made for them. For example, Rebekah was asked if she wanted to marry Isaac (Gen. 24:58). Samson demanded that a certain girl be acquired for him. Although his parents protested, they completed the marriage contract for Samson (Judg. 14:14).

Frequently people married at a young age, a fact which made the parents' choice a practical matter. By New Testament times, the Jewish leaders had established minimum ages for which a marriage contract could be drawn up. The age was set at thirteen for boys and twelve for girls.

Even if the young wife lost her husband in war or accident, she remained within the clan and was wed to her brother-in-law or next of kin. This arrangement is known as levirate marriage. It is the basis for the story of Ruth and Boaz (Deut. 25:5–10; Ruth 3:13; 4:1–12).

Concept of love. Although romance before marriage was not unknown in Old Testament times, it played a minor role in the life of teenagers of that era. They did not marry the person they loved; they learned to love the mate they married. Love began at marriage. When Isaac married Rebekah, the Bible records that "she became his wife, and he loved her" (Gen. 24:67).

Marriage customs. A number of customs and steps were involved in finalizing a marriage in Old Testament times. The first was agreeing on a price to be given to the father of the girl. The payment was compensation for the loss of a worker. The sum was mutually agreed upon (Gen. 34:12; Ex. 22:16–17). It could consist of services instead of money. For example, Jacob agreed to work for seven years for Rachel (Gen. 29:18–20). The giving and receiving of money was probably accompanied by a written agreement. After this agreement was made, the couple was considered engaged.

In biblical times, a betrothal for marriage was a binding agreement that set the young woman apart for the young man. The agreement was voided only by death or divorce; one could not get out of the betrothal in any other way. When Joseph discovered that Mary was pregnant, he did not want to make a "public example" of her; instead, he decided to divorce her secretly. However, he did not carry out the divorce, because an angel of the Lord convinced him that the baby to be born to Mary would be the Son of God (Matt. 1:18–25).

During the engagement period, the bridegroom had certain privileges. If war was declared, he was exempt from military duty (Deut. 20:7). He also knew that his bride-to-be was protected by Mosaic Law. If another man raped her, the act was treated as adultery; and the offender was punished accordingly (Deut. 22:23–27). This was considered a more serious crime than the rape of a girl not yet betrothed (Deut. 22:28–29).

The length of engagement varied. Sometimes the couple was married the same day they were engaged. Usually, however, a period of time elapsed between the betrothal and the marriage ceremony. During this time the young man prepared a place in his father's house for his bride, while the bride prepared herself for married life.

On the day of the wedding, the groom and his friends dressed in their finest clothes and went to the home of the bride. Together the couple went back to the groom's house. Their friends sang and danced their way back to his house. Once at the groom's house, the couple was ushered into a bridal chamber. The marriage was consummated through sexual union as the guests waited outside. Once that fact was announced, the wedding festivities continued, with guests dropping by for the wedding feast. Usually the wedding party lasted for a week.

New Testament teaching about marriage. The New Testament does not contradict the teachings about marriage in the Old Testament. Most marriage teaching in the New Testament comes from Jesus and the apostle Paul.

Jesus' first miracle occurred in Cana in Galilee when He and His disciples were attending a wedding (John 2:1–11). Our Lord gave His blessing and sanction to the institution of marriage.

On another occasion, when Jesus was asked about marriage and divorce, He quoted two passages from Genesis. "Have you not read that He who made them at the beginning 'made them male and female,' and said, 'For this reason a man shall leave his father and mother and be joined to his wife, and the two shall become one flesh'? So then, they are no

longer two but one flesh. Therefore what God has joined together, let not man separate" (Gen. 1:27; 2:24; 5:2; Matt. 19:4–6). He taught that marriage was the joining together of two people so they become "one flesh." Not only did God acknowledge the marriage; He also joined the couple.

The church at Corinth struggled over a number of issues, including the proper view of marriage. In response to their questions, Paul gave an answer about marriage. From his answer, it seems that three faulty ideas about marriage were prominent among some believers in the church. The first was that marriage was absolutely necessary in order to be a Christian; another was that celibacy was superior to marriage; the third was that when a person became a Christian, all existing relationships such as marriage were dissolved. When chapter 7 of 1 Corinthians is read with that as background, the following teaching emerges.

First, Paul stated that celibacy is an acceptable lifestyle for a Christian; not all people need to marry. In fact, Paul declared that he himself preferred not to marry for the sake of mobility in his ministry. He counselled, however, that the single life can be lived for God's glory if God has given the gift of singlehood. If one does not have that gift, he should marry (and apparently Paul expected most people to marry).

Next, Paul spoke to the problem faced by a Christian believer whose spouse does not believe. He taught that if the unbelieving partner is willing to live with the Christian, then the Christian should not dissolve the marriage. Remaining with the unbelieving partner could result in his or her salvation (1 Cor. 7:14).

In his letter to the Ephesians, Paul showed how a marriage relationship can best function. First, he said, "Wives, submit to your own husbands, as to the Lord" (Eph. 5:22). The model for the wife's submission is the church, which is subject to Christ (Eph. 5:24). Second, husbands are to love their wives, and to do so in the way manifest by Jesus Christ, who loved His bride, the church, so much that He died for her (Eph. 5:25), and lives in patience, understanding, and forgiveness with her.

MEDIATOR. (Gal. 3:19) *mesites* (mes-*ee*-tace); *Strong's #3316:* From *mesos*, "middle," and *eimi*, "to go"; hence, a go-between, umpire, reconciler, arbitrator, intermediary. In this passage, the word refers to Moses' bringing the Law to the people, along with angelic assistance. In its other occurrences, *mesites* speaks of Jesus' accomplishing salvation by His vicarious death (1 Tim. 2:5) and guaranteeing the terms of the new covenant (Heb. 8:6; 9:15; 12:24).

MEDITATES. (Ps. 1:2) *hagah* (hah-*gah*); *Strong's* #1897: To reflect; to moan, to mutter; to ponder; to make a quiet sound such as sighing; to meditate or contemplate something as one repeats the words. *Hagah* represents something quite unlike the English "meditation," which may be a mental exercise only. In Hebrew thought, to meditate upon the Scriptures is to quietly repeat them in a soft, droning sound, while utterly abandoning outside distractions. From this tradition comes a specialized type of Jewish prayer called "davening," that is, reciting texts, praying intense prayers, or getting lost in communion with God while bowing or rocking back and forth. Evidently this dynamic form of meditation-prayer goes back to David's time.

MEDITATION—the practice of reflection or contemplation. The word meditation or its verb form, *to meditate,* is found mainly in the Old Testament. The Hebrew words behind this concept mean "to murmur," "a murmuring," "sighing," or "moaning." This concept is reflected in Psalm 1:2, where the "blessed man" meditates on God's Law day and night. The psalmist also prayed that the meditation of his heart would be acceptable in God's sight (Ps. 19:14). Joshua was instructed to meditate on the Book of the Law for the purpose of obeying all that was written in it (Josh. 1:8).

The Greek word translated as meditate occurs only twice in the New Testament. In Luke 21:14 Jesus instructed His disciples not "to meditate beforehand" in answering their adversaries when the end of the age comes. The word may be understood in this passage as the idea of preparing a defense for a court appearance. Paul, in 1 Timothy 4:15, urged Timothy to meditate on, or take pains with, the instructions he gives. The idea of meditation is also found in Philippians 4:8 and Colossians 3:2.

Meditation is a lost art for many Christians, but the practice needs to be cultivated again. This form of meditation is not to be confused with either the cultish or oriental practices of mindless abandonment or focused mind control. This might better be described as "waiting on God" and "thinking on His Word or His love."

MEEKNESS—an attitude of humility toward God and gentleness toward people, springing from a recognition that God is sovereign Creator and in control. Although weakness and meekness may rhyme and look similar, they

are not the same. Weakness is due to negative circumstances, such as lack of strength or lack of courage. But meekness is due to a person's conscious choice. It is strength and courage under control, coupled with kindness.

The apostle Paul once pointed out that the spiritual leaders of the church have great power, even leverage, in confronting a sinner. But he cautioned them to restrain themselves in meekness (Gal. 6:1; 5:22–23). Even toward evil men, the people of God should be meek, knowing that God is in control.

Meekness is a virtue practiced and commended by our Lord Jesus (Matt. 5:5; 11:29). As such it is part of the equipment which every follower of Jesus should wear (2 Cor. 10:1; Gal. 5:23; 6:1; Eph. 4:1–2).

MEMORIAL. (Ex. 39:7) *zikron* (zeek-*roan*); *Strong's* #2146: A memorial, remembrance, record, memento; a written record; a momentous event, which is long to be remembered. Occurring twenty-four times, *zikron* is derived from the verb *zakar,* "to remember." The first occurrence of *zikron* in Scripture concerns the Passover; the day, the ceremony, and the meal constitute a memorial of God's mighty deeds (12:14). In the present reference, the stones representing the twelve tribes were placed on the ephod, which served to remind the high priest of each tribe by name. (Compare Josh. 4:7.) In Malachi 3:16, God made up a book of "remembrance," where those who think often of Him are listed, and will someday be like the jewels over Aaron's heart (v. 17).

MENTION (MAKE). (Is. 62:6) *zachar* (zah-*char*); *Strong's* #2142: To remember, bring into mind, recollect; also, to mention, meditate upon, mark down, record, recall, and retain in one's thoughts. To remember something or someone is to approve of, to acknowledge, and to treat as a matter of importance, whereas to forget something or someone is to dismiss or abandon as unimportant. God remembered Noah, Abraham, Rachel, and His covenant (Gen. 8:1; 19:29; 30:22; Ex. 2:24). In the new covenant, God promises never again to remember Israel's sin (Jer. 31:34).

MERCIFUL. (Matt. 5:7) *eleemon* (el-eh-*ay*-mone); *Strong's* #1655: Related to the words *eleeo* (to have mercy), *eleos* (active compassion), and *eleemosune* (compassion for the poor). *Eleemon* is a kind, compassionate, sympathetic, merciful, and sensitive word, combining tendencies with action. A person with this quality finds outlets for his merciful nature. The English word "eleemosynary" or charitable philanthropic relief, finds its origin in this word.

MERCY—the aspect of God's love that causes Him to help the needy or those in miserable, rejected or unfortunate situations just as grace is the aspect of His love that moves Him to forgive the guilty. Those who are miserable may be so either because of breaking God's law or because of circumstances beyond their control.

God shows mercy upon those who have broken His law (Dan. 9:9; 1 Tim. 1:13, 16). God's mercy on the needy or miserable extends beyond punishment that is withheld (Eph. 2:4–6). Withheld punishment keeps us from deserved judgment, but it does not necessarily grant blessing beside. God's mercy is greater than this.

God also shows mercy by actively helping those who are needy or in miserable straits due to circumstances beyond their control. We see this aspect of mercy especially in the life of our Lord Jesus. He healed blind men (Matt. 9:27–31; 20:29–34) and lepers (Luke 17:11–19). These acts of healing grew out of His commitment to reveal the will of God through acts of mercy.

Finally, because God is merciful, He expects His children to be merciful (Matt. 5:7; James 1:27).

MERCY. (Mic. 6:8) *chesed* (*cheh*-sed); *Strong's #2617:* Kindness, mercy, lovingkindness; unfailing love; tenderness, faithfulness. *Chesed* occurs 250 times in the Bible. It may best be translated "kindness"; however, faithfulness is sometimes the main idea. Most often in Scripture, *chesed* is used for God's mercy. In Psalm 136, the phrase "His mercy endures forever" occurs twenty-six times. Jesus quotes Hosea 6:6 ("I desire mercy and not sacrifice") in Matthew 9:13 and calls mercy one of "the weightier matters of the law" (Matt. 23:23). A derivative is *chasid*, generally translated "merciful," "saint," "godly," "holy," or "good" man (Pss. 4:3; 16:10; 18:25; 97:10; Prov. 2:8; Jer. 3:12). Kindness is thus a trait that God expects man to possess. *Also* (2 Tim. 1:16) *eleos* (*el*-eh-oss); *Strong's #1656:* Compassion, tender mercy, kindness, beneficence, an outward manifestation of pity. The word is used of God (Luke 1:50, 54, 58; Rom. 15:9; Eph. 2:4); of Christ (Jude 21); and of men (Matt. 12:7; 23:23; Luke 10:37).

MERCY (HAVE). (Hos. 2:23) *racham* (rah-chahm); *Strong's #7355:* To feel or show compassion, to love deeply, to show pity or mercy; to tenderly regard someone; to tenderly love (especially as parents love their infant child). *Racham* is the origin of the Hebrew word for "womb" (*rechem*). In Isaiah 49:15, God asks, "Can a woman forget her nursing child, and not have compassion on [*racham*] the son of her womb [*rechem*]?" Fathers, too, can show this feeling for their offspring (Ps. 103:13). God wants parents to tenderly love their offspring and to show compassion toward all who are weak and defenseless. God sets the example by His constant compassion for the helpless and undeserving (Is. 54:8, 10). *Also* (Rom. 9:15) *eleeo* (el-eh-*eh*-oh); *Strong's #1653:* Compare "eleemosynary," supported by charities. To show kindness and concern for someone in serious need, feel compassion for, have pity. Those who take care of the sick are called *eleeo*, or showers of mercy. In the New Testament the word is often used of Christ's gracious faithfulness and proof of His benevolence. Mercy is not merely a passive emotion, but an active desire to remove the cause of distress in others.

MERCY SEAT. (Heb. 9:5) *hilasterion* (hil-as-*tay*-ree-on); *Strong's #2435:* Although used only here and in Romans 3:25 in the New Testament, the word is quite common in the Septuagint, where it primarily denotes the mercy seat, the lid of gold above the ark of the covenant. In this verse it has that meaning, indicating the place of atonement. The root meaning of *hilasterion* is that of appeasing and placating an offended god. Applied to the sacrifice of Christ in that regard, the word suggests that Christ's death was propitiatory, averting the wrath of God from the sinner.

MESHA STONE—see ch. 55, §2.3.

MESSIAH [meh SIGH uh] *(anointed one)*—the one anointed by God and empowered by God's Spirit to deliver His people and establish His kingdom. In Jewish thought, the Messiah would be the king of the Jews, a political leader who would defeat their enemies and bring in a golden era of peace and prosperity. In Christian thought, the term Messiah refers to Jesus' role as a spiritual deliverer, setting His people free from sin and death.

The word Messiah comes from a Hebrew term that means "anointed one." Its Greek counterpart is *Christos,* from which the word Christ comes. Messiah was one of the titles used by early Christians to describe who Jesus was.

In Old Testament times, part of the ritual of commissioning a person for a special task was to anoint him with oil. The phrase anointed one was applied to a person in such cases. In the Old Testament Messiah is used more than thirty times to describe kings (2 Sam. 1:14, 16), priests (Lev. 4:3, 5, 16), the patriarchs (Ps. 105:15), and even the Persian King Cyrus (Is. 45:1). The word is also used in connection with King David, who became the model of the messianic king who would come at the end of the age (2 Sam. 22:51; Ps. 2:2). But it was not until the time of Daniel (sixth century B.C.) that Messiah was used as an actual title of a king who would come in the future (Dan. 9:25–26). Still later, as the Jewish people struggled against their political enemies, the Messiah came to be thought of as a political, military ruler.

From the New Testament we learn more about the people's expectations. They thought the Messiah would come soon to perform signs (John 7:31) and deliver His people, after which He would live and rule forever (John 12:34). Some even thought that John the Baptist was the Messiah (John 1:20). Others said that the Messiah was to come from Bethlehem (John 7:42). Most expected the Messiah to be a political leader, a king who would defeat the Romans and provide for the physical needs of the Israelites.

According to the Gospel of John, a woman of Samaria said to Jesus, "I know that Messiah is coming." Jesus replied, "I who speak to you am He" (John 4:25–26). In the Gospels of Matthew, Mark, and Luke, however, Jesus never directly referred to Himself as the Messiah, except privately to His disciples, until the Crucifixion (Matt. 26:63–64; Mark 14:61–62; Luke 22:67–70). He did accept the title and function of messiahship privately (Matt. 16:16–17). Yet Jesus constantly avoided being called "Messiah" in public (Mark 8:29–30). This is known as Jesus' "messianic secret." He was the Messiah, but He did not broadcast it publicly.

The reason for this was that Jesus' kingdom is not political but spiritual (John 18:36). If Jesus had used the title "Messiah," people would have thought he meant to be a political king. But Jesus understood that the Messiah, God's Anointed One, was to be the Suffering Servant (Is. 52:13—53:12). The fact that Jesus was a suffering Messiah—a crucified deliverer—was a "stumbling block" to many of the Jews (1 Cor. 1:23). They saw the Cross as a sign of Jesus' weakness, powerlessness, and failure. They rejected the concept of a crucified Messiah.

But the message of the early church centered around the fact that the crucified and risen Jesus is the Christ (Acts 5:42; 17:3; 18:5). They proclaimed the "scandalous" gospel of a crucified Messiah as the power and wisdom of God (1 Cor. 1:23–24). John wrote, "Who is a liar but he who denies that Jesus is the Christ [the Messiah]?" (1 John 2:22).

As the Messiah, Jesus is the divinely appointed king who brought God's kingdom to earth (Matt. 12:28; Luke 11:20). His way to victory was not by physical force and violence, but through love, humility, and service.

MESSIAH. (Dan. 9:25) *mashiach* (mah-*shee*-ahch); *Strong's* #4899: Anointed one, messiah. Found thirty-nine times in the Old Testament, *mashiach* is derived from the verb *mashach*, "to anoint," "to consecrate by applying the holy anointing oil to an individual." *Mashiach* describes the high priest (Lev. 4:3, 16) and anointed kings, such as Saul (2 Sam. 1:14) and David (2 Sam. 19:21; Ps. 18:50). In Psalms and in Daniel, *mashiach* is particularly used for David's anointed heir, the king of Israel and ruler of all nations (see Ps. 2:2; 28:8; Dan. 9:25–26). When the earliest followers of Jesus spoke of Him, they called Him Jesus the Messiah, or in Hebrew, *Yeshua ha-Mashiach.* "Messiah" or "Anointed One" is *Christos* in Greek and is the origin of the English form "Christ." Whenever the Lord is called "Jesus Christ," He is being called "Jesus the Messiah."

MESSIANIC PROMISES AND CHRIST'S COMING.

Two prophetic stars shine brightest in God's Word: the "Morningstar" and the "Daystar." The first heralds the coming of the new day (Rev. 22:16—Greek, *astar*) fulfilled in our Lord Jesus Christ who has already fulfilled the promised coming Messiah, heralding a yet future day when He shall come again. He who fulfilled the Old Testament prophecies has been announced as the other "Morningstar" (2 Pet. 1:19—Greek, *phosphoros*), the rising sun that not only heralds the coming day but rules it! In the New Testament, Jesus promises, "I will come again," and with that promise He holds in form a cluster of attendant promises to be fulfilled when He does. This study offers the development of both the above truths through a systematic study of the Bible.

1. The Gospel's First Proclamation (Gen. 3:15). This verse contains the first proclamation of the gospel. All of the richness, the mercy, the sorrow, and the glory of God's redeeming work with man is here in miniature. God promises to bring a Redeemer from the Seed of the woman; He will be completely human yet divinely begotten. "That serpent of old, called the Devil," would war with the Seed (see Revelation 12) and would smite Him. But even as the Serpent struck at His heel, His foot would descend, crushing the Serpent's head. In Christ's life and death this scripture was fulfilled. Divinely begotten, yet fully human, by His death and resurrection He has defeated and made a public spectacle of the powers of hell (Col. 2:15). This first messianic promise is one of the most succinct statements of the gospel to be found anywhere.

2. Jesus, the Prophet of the Greater Covenant

(Deut. 18:18–19). To the religious Jews of Jesus' time, no one was greater than Moses. Through Moses God had given the Law; he was the person God used to transmit their whole religious system. But they were also aware that God said He would send another Prophet like Moses. When the Pharisees inquired of John the Baptist whether he was "the Prophet" (John 1:21), they were referring to this passage of Scripture.

As Moses gave the Old Covenant so Jesus came to bring the New Covenant. John says, "For the law was given through Moses, *but* grace and truth came through Jesus Christ" (John 1:17). The writer of Hebrews tells us that Christ became the Mediator of a better covenant (Heb. 8:6). Jesus, as the Prophet, came to fulfill the requirements of the Old Covenant so that a New Covenant could be established between God and man.

3. Messiah's Becoming a Man

(Is. 9:6). In this scripture we have one of the most beautifully poetic promises of the Messiah's coming reign. Yearly we recite this verse and hear it sung as we celebrate Christmas. Yet this verse also contains a reference to one of the great, incomprehensible truths in the Bible: the Incarnation—"a Child is born, . . . a Son is given." God would become a man. A newborn baby would be called "Mighty God, Everlasting Father." We can accept that truth by faith, but we cannot fully grasp what it meant for the Second Person of the Godhead to shed His eternal state and put on flesh. But Paul tells us that He took the form of a servant and came as a man. "Therefore God also has highly exalted Him and given Him the name which is above every name" (Phil. 2:7, 9).

4. Christ Birthed by a Young, Virgin Woman

(Is. 7:14). The prophecy of the Virgin Birth has been a source of considerable controversy due to the use of the Hebrew word *'almah*, which can be translated "young woman," as well as "virgin." Isaiah used *'almah* under the inspiration of the Spirit, because the Lord was making a dual prophecy in this passage. The Lord was giving the sign of a child to King Ahaz, and the conception and birth of that child is recorded in chapter 8. But the Holy Spirit was also speaking of the Messiah who would come, and that Child would literally be born of a virgin. The fact that Christ was virgin-born is indisputable from Matthew and Luke's use of the Greek word *parthenos*, which definitely means "virgin" (Matt. 1:23; Luke 1:27).

5. Messiah Born at Bethlehem

(Mic. 5:2, 4–5). Bethlehem—the name means "House of Bread," and at the "House of Bread" the Bread of Life was born into the world.

The scribes knew that Messiah was to be born there. When the wise men inquired about the birth of the new King, the scribes referred to Micah's prophecy (Matt. 2:1–12). Yet none of the theologians bothered to accompany the wise men to see if, indeed, the Messiah had come. The "little town of Bethlehem" is now a point of pilgrimage for thousands yearly. But let us learn from those who did not make that first pilgrimage: Neither our orthodoxy, biblical knowledge, nor religious status guarantees that we will see what God is doing in our midst today. We must be willing to follow the leading of God and His Word if we wish to see the promise fulfilled.

6. The Lord of Lords or a Rabbi on a Colt?

(Zech. 9:9). This is the prophecy of the Lord's Triumphal Entry. We find accounts of its fulfillment in Matthew 21:1–11; Mark 11:1–11; Luke 19:28–44; and John 12:12–19. In this verse we see again how much God's ways differ from man's. Men looked for a conquering king, high and exalted, to come and deliver Jerusalem with an army of mighty men. What they saw was a meek and lowly Rabbi, riding upon a donkey's colt, and attended by a crowd of rejoicing peasants. He did not look like a conqueror. Yet one week later He had risen from the dead, having conquered death and hell.

7. Detailed Account of the Betrayal of the Messiah

(Ps. 41:9; Zech. 11:12–13). David, who wrote Psalm 41, lived about five hundred years before Zechariah; and Zechariah lived more than five hundred years before Christ. Yet the words of these two men form a single prophecy which was fulfilled in detail. David prophesied that a trusted friend would be the Lord's betrayer; and Judas Iscariot, one of the Twelve, betrayed Him (Matt. 26:14–16; Luke 22:1–6). Zechariah went even further, specifying the amount that would be paid to the traitor, predicting that it would be cast into the house of the Lord, and stating that it would be used to buy a potter's field. Every point was fulfilled in detail: The chief priests gave Judas thirty pieces of silver (Matt. 26:15); Judas, in remorse, returned the money and threw it down in the temple (Matt. 27:5); and the priests used the money to buy a potter's field (Matt. 27:6–10). The detailed fulfillment of this prophecy is truly a testimony to God's sovereign working in the affairs of humankind.

8. Details of Messiah's Death

(Ps. 22:1–31). Within this psalm are many prophecies that

were fulfilled in the death of Jesus; let us look at four. First, the ridicule of the people is predicted (vv. 7–8). The same expressions of ridicule were actually spoken by the chief priests at the Cross (Matt. 27:36–44). Second, verse 16 specifically predicts that His hands and feet would be pierced. This was fulfilled at the death of Jesus (see John 20:25). Further, the casting of lots for Jesus' clothing (John 19:23–24) was prophesied in verse 18. But perhaps the most significant statement in the entire psalm is verse 1, which Jesus quoted from the Cross (Matt. 27:46). In that word we see God Himself turning away from His beloved Son who is bearing the sin of the world. Jesus is bearing man's judgment, not only the judgment of death but also the judgment of separation from God. At that moment Jesus is experiencing the darkest moment of His life, and He bore it—for us.

9. Purposes of the Crucifixion, Atonement, and Abundant Life (Is. 53:1–12). This is the best-known prophecy of the Crucifixion in the Bible, and both Matthew (Matt. 8:17) and Peter (1 Pet. 2:24) quote from it. Writing eight centuries before Christ, Isaiah made incredibly accurate statements concerning the facts of the Crucifixion; but more importantly, he spoke of the purpose of the Cross.

In Christ's suffering and death, He bore more than our sins. The penalty for sin *is* death, but Christ did not need to suffer as He did to provide atonement. This chapter tells us why He suffered: He suffered to bear our griefs and sorrows (v. 4), and He suffered for our peace and healing (v. 5).

Surely atonement for sin is our greatest need; yet God, sending His Son to suffer and die, provided more than an escape from judgment; He provided for abundant life beginning today (see John 10:10).

10. "Declared to Be the Son of God with Power" (Ps. 16:10). The apostles clearly recognized this verse as forecasting the resurrection of Jesus. Peter quotes this verse in his sermon on the Day of Pentecost (Acts 2:27), and Paul quotes this verse in his early preaching at Antioch of Pisidia (Acts 13:35).

The sufficiency of Christ's work of atonement is declared in the Resurrection (Rom. 6; 2 Tim. 1:10; Heb. 2:9–18; 1 Pet. 2:18), and by the Resurrection Jesus was "declared *to be the* Son of God with power" (Rom. 1:4). He has completed the work He came to do and has ascended to the right hand of the Father. Now we look forward in hope, for having broken the power of death, He has introduced the promise of eternal life to all who receive Him as Messiah (John 6:40).

11. Messiah's Peace, Place, and Promise for His People (John 14:1–3). These are among the most comforting words in all of Scripture; from Jesus' own lips, we receive the promise of His return. He spoke these words during His most intimate time with His disciples, and they echo down to us as a precious promise to the bride of Christ.

In this text Jesus tells us of a *peace*, a *place*, and a *promise*. He begins with a comforting exhortation: do not be troubled; be at peace. Our peace is based on our belief in God and Christ. We know that He is trustworthy and that gives us a foundation of peace upon which to build our lives. Second, Jesus spoke of a place. He has promised to prepare for us a place where we will have eternal fellowship with Him. Finally, we have His personal promise that He is returning for us. Think of it! His personal signature is on our salvation; as we have received Him, He is coming to receive us. We look forward to that day in expectation, preparing ourselves for it, for "everyone who has this hope . . . purifies himself" (1 John 3:3).

12. Confirmed: Jesus Will Return (Acts 1:10–11). Before Jesus left His disciples He promised them that He would return (John 14:1–3). Here, at the Ascension of Jesus, the promise is reiterated. In essence, the angels say to the disciples, "Do not stand here looking at the sky! Jesus will return, but now you go and do what He told you to do." We frequently need to be reminded of these words. Often we get so caught up in the precious promise of the Lord's return that we forget that His promise should also affect how we behave toward the world. Jesus has given each of us an assignment, and "blessed is that servant whom his master, when he comes, will find so doing" (Matt. 24:46).

13. The Threefold Announcement of the Lord's Coming (1 Thess. 4:15–18). This is one of the most beloved passages about the Second Coming, and it is also one of the most detailed. We are told that there will be a threefold announcement of the Lord's coming: a shout, the voice of an archangel, and the trumpet of God (v. 16). In addition, there is a threefold promise to believers: (1) the dead in Christ shall rise; (2) we who are alive will be caught away with them; and (3) we shall always be with the Lord (vv. 16–17).

It is important to note as well that this is the key text where the idea of a Rapture is taught. The word "Rapture" is not used in the Bible, but the idea of the saints' being "caught up" and gathered together at the Second Coming of the Lord is clearly spoken of here and in

Matthew 24:30–31. The hope of His coming is to be a source of comfort for us who await Him (v. 18).

14. Only the Father Knows When Christ Will Return (Matt. 25:13). This is a critical verse to remember whenever one considers the Second Coming. Throughout history believers have mistakenly tried to determine when the Lord will return, and an ignorance of the history of this folly has led some in every decade to presume to pinpoint the time of Jesus' coming. But here, as well as in 24:36 and Mark 13:32, Jesus tells us directly that no one but the Father knows the time of His return. People have interpreted the expression "hour or day" to mean that we may discover the month or year, but this is incorrect. We cannot be sure that it will be in any particular year, decade, or even in our lifetime.

However, Jesus began His sentence with the command, "Watch." The challenge the Lord gives us is to be constantly and eagerly waiting for His return. Therefore, our duty is twofold: to prepare ourselves for His coming, so that the Lord will receive a bride without "spot or wrinkle" (Eph. 5:27), and to "do business" until He returns, so that the kingdom of God is preserved and extended on the earth (Luke 19:11–27). Let us be about the Father's business, live in expectation of the Master's return, and be done with all idle speculation or superstitious date-setting regarding the time of His coming.

15. "Surely I Am Coming Quickly" (Rev. 22:20). Among the very last words of the Bible is this promise from the Lord Jesus, "Surely I am coming quickly." This blessed hope, which was declared by angels and spoken of by the apostles, is tenderly reiterated by the Lord at the very end of His Word. It is as if He wished to say, "There is much in My Word that you need attend to, but do not let this hope be overshadowed: I am coming back soon." Together with John, let us say, "Even so, come, Lord Jesus!" J.H.

 MIGHT. (Zech. 4:6) *chayil* (cha-yeel); *Strong's #2428:* Strength, power, force, might (especially an army); valor, substance, wealth. *Chayil* occurs more than 230 times. Its basic meaning is force, especially military strength. It may refer to the power of accumulated goods, that is, "wealth," as in Deuteronomy 8:17. Occasionally *chayil* is translated "valor," especially when describing a military man (Judg. 3:29). It is translated "army" in such references as Deuteronomy 11:4 and 2 Chronicles 14:8. In the present reference, God informs the rebuilder of the temple that the task would not be accomplished through the

force of an army (*chayil*) nor through the muscular power or physical stamina of the workmen; rather, it would be accomplished by the empowering of the Spirit of God.

MIGHTY. (2 Cor. 13:3) *dunateo* (doo-nat-*eh*-oh); *Strong's #1414:* To be able, powerful, mighty. The power at work in believers is that of the same Spirit that raised Jesus from the dead.

MILLENNIUM, THE—the thousand-year period mentioned in connection with the description of Christ's coming to reign with His saints over the earth (Rev. 19:11–16; 20:1–9). Many Old Testament passages refer to the Millennium (Is. 11:4; Jer. 3:17; Zech. 14:9).

These and many other Old Testament passages are often taken to refer only to the thousand-year period itself. However, it is often difficult in these passages to see a clear dividing line between the earthly period of the millennium and the eternal state of new heavens and earth. Therefore, it is best to let one's teaching about the Millennium be drawn specifically from the words in Revelation 20. The other great promises to Israel, while they have a temporary fulfillment in the thousand years, still await the fullness of the new heavens and new earth and the unhindered presence of Israel's king and the church's husband—Jesus Christ our Lord.

During that thousand-year period, Satan will be bound in the bottomless pit so he will not deceive the nations until his short period of release (Rev. 20:3, 7–8). The faithful martyrs who have died for the cause of Christ will be resurrected before the Millennium. They will rule with Christ and will be priests of God and Christ (Rev. 5:10; 20:4). The unbelieving dead will wait for the second resurrection (Rev. 20:5). After the thousand years, Satan will be released and will resume his work of deceit (Rev. 20:7–8).

The most important aspect of the Millennium is the reign of Christ. Peter taught that Christ now rules from the right hand of God (Acts 2:33–36). That rule will last until His enemies are made His footstool (Ps. 110:1). The apostle Paul also understood Christ to be presently reigning in a period designed to bring all of God's enemies underfoot (1 Cor. 15:25–27). Thus the impact of Christ's present rule over the earth from God's right hand must not be seen as unrelated to His future reign during the Millennium.

The Millennium is viewed by interpreters in several different ways. One position holds that the Millennium only refers to Christ's spiritual rule today from heaven. This symbolic view is known as the amillennial interpretation. Another position views Christ's spiritual rule as working through preaching and teaching to bring gradual world improvement leading up to Christ's return. This is the post-millennial view.

The position that holds to an actual thousand-year period in the future is known as the premillennial view. This interpretation does not diminish the power of Christ's present rule from heaven or limit that rule to the church only. That position sees the need for a thousand-year place in history for an earthly fulfillment of Israel's promises of land and blessing. It stresses that the one thousand years in Revelation 20 are actual years and are not symbolic.

MIND—the part of a person that thinks and reasons. Although the Hebrew language had no word for mind, several Hebrew words are sometimes translated as "mind." The word for *heart frequently means "mind" (Deut. 30:1; Jer. 19:5). The word for *soul is sometimes used similarly (1 Chr. 28:9), as is the word for *spirit (Ezek. 11:5). No Hebrew word is translated as brain in English versions of the Bible.

Four separate Greek words account for nearly all instances of "mind" in the New Testament. They all mean much the same thing: understanding, thought, mind, reason. While today we think of a person's mind in a morally neutral way, in the New Testament the mind was clearly thought of as either good or evil. Negatively, the mind may be "hardened" (2 Cor. 3:14), "blinded" (2 Cor. 4:4), "corrupt" (2 Tim. 3:8), and "debased" (Rom. 1:28). On the positive side, humans may have minds which are renewed (Rom. 12:2) and pure (2 Pet. 3:1). They may love God with all their minds (Matt. 22:37; Mark 12:30; Luke 10:27) and have God's laws implanted in their minds (Heb. 8:10). Since Christians have "the mind of Christ" (1 Cor. 2:16), they are instructed to be united in mind (Rom. 12:16; 1 Pet. 3:8).

MIND. (Mark 12:30) *dianoia* (dee-*an*-oy-ah); *Strong's #1271:* Literally, "a thinking through." *Dianoia* combines *nous*, "mind," and *dia*, "through." The word suggests understanding, insight, meditation, reflection, perception, the gift of apprehension, the faculty of thought. When this faculty is renewed by the Holy Spirit, the whole mindset changes from the fearful negativism of the carnal mind to the vibrant, positive thinking of the quickened spiritual mind.

MIND (RIGHT). (Mark 5:15) *sophroneo* (so-fron-*eh*-oh); *Strong's #4993:* To be of sound mind, sane, self-controlled, serious, moderate, sober-minded, restrained, disciplined, able to reason. From *sozo*, "to save," and *phren*, "the mind." The word describes our behavior and

attitude as we approach the ending of the age (1 Pet. 4:7).

MIND (SOUND). (2 Tim. 1:7) *sophronismos* (so-fron-is-*moss*); *Strong's #4995:* A combination of *sos*, "safe," and *phren*, "the mind"; hence, safe-thinking. The word denotes good judgment, disciplined thought patterns, and the ability to understand and make right decisions. It includes the qualities of self-control and self-discipline.

MINISTER, MINISTRY—a distinctive biblical idea that means "to serve" or "servant." In the Old Testament the word servant was used primarily for court servants (1 Kin. 10:5; Esth. 1:10). During the period between the Old and New Testaments, it came to be used in connection with ministering to the poor. This use of the word is close to the work of the seven in waiting on tables in the New Testament (Acts 6:1–7).

In reality, all believers are "ministers." Ephesians 4:11–12 shows the fivefold office ministries—pastor, teacher, apostle, prophet, evangelist—as given to "equip the saints" so they can minister to one another and to the world (Eph. 4:11–12). The model, of course, is Jesus, who "did not come to be served, but to serve" (Mark 10:45). His service is revealed in the fact that He gave "His life a ransom for many" (Matt. 20:28).

Jesus' servanthood radically revised the ethics of Jew and Greek alike, because He equated service to God with service to others. When we minister to the needs of the hungry or the lonely, we actually minister to Christ (Matt. 25:31–46). And when we fail to do so, we sin against God (James 2:14–17; 4:17). In this light, all who took part in the fellowship of service were ministers.

The concept is strengthened when the use of the Greek word *doulos* is noted. This was the term for a bondslave, one who was offered his freedom but who voluntarily surrendered that freedom in order to remain a servant. This idea typified Jesus' purpose, as described by Paul in Philippians 2:7. This passage alludes to the "servant of God" teaching of Isaiah 52—54. Truly Christ fulfilled this exalted calling, because His life was dedicated to the needs of others.

Following our Savior's example, all believers are bondslaves of God (Rom. 1:1; Gal. 1:10; Col. 4:12). We are to perform "good deeds" to all people, with a responsibility especially to fellow Christians (Gal. 6:10; Heb. 10:24).

Our unselfish service should especially be rendered through our spiritual gifting, which is given by God to the saints in order that they might minister to one another and others outside the body (1 Pet. 4:10). These gifts consist of both spiritual gifts—Holy Spirit "charisms"—as well as practical abilities (1 Cor. 12:1–11, 28). They are distributed to various members of the church so that the union of believers can be expressed in loving service.

In Ephesians 4:7–11 the offices of apostles, prophets, evangelists, etc., are described as divine "gifts" to the church. This is the one place where the officers of the church might be linked with the term minister. In a special way these officers do "minister" to the church—the apostles through their inspired leadership; the prophets through their inspired preaching and even foretelling; the evangelists through their traveling missionary work; and the pastor and teachers through their service in local congregations. Yet the primary service of all is to equip all saints for ministry.

The concepts of minister and ministry must be broadened today to include all the members of a church. The heirarchal concept of the pastor as a professional substitute for the ministry of the body must be discarded, because the biblical pattern is for him to be the one who trains the body for ministry. All the saints are responsible for loving and ministering in various ways to one another, using the giftings the Father has given them (Romans 12) and the gifts distributed to each by the Holy Spirit (1 Corinthians 12).

MINISTER. (1 Chr. 15:2) *sharat* (shah-*raht*); *Strong's #8334:* To wait on, to serve, to minister, to attend. *Sharat* refers to the tasks to which the closest servants of God or the king are assigned. The priests and Levites in their ministry in the tabernacle and the temple served God. Examples of significant positions of service to important persons include Joseph to Potiphar (Gen. 39:4), Joshua to Moses (Ex. 33:11), and Elisha to Elijah (1 Kin. 19:21). In today's usage the title "minister" conveys austerity and self-authority, while the scriptural use of the term conveys yieldedness, servanthood, and obedience.

MINISTERED. (Acts 13:2) *leitourgeo* (lie-toorg-*eh*-oh); *Strong's #3008:* Performing religious or charitable acts, fulfilling an office, discharging a function, officiating as a priest, serving God with prayers and fastings. (Compare "liturgy" and "liturgical.") The word describes the Aaronic priesthood ministering Levitical services (Heb. 10:11). In Romans 15:27, it is used for meeting financial needs of the Christians, performing a service to the Lord by doing so. Here the Christians at Antioch were fulfilling an office and discharging a normal function by ministering to the Lord in fasting and prayer.

MINISTERS. (Heb. 1:7) *leitourgos* (lie-toorg-oss); *Strong's #3011:* From *laos*, "people," and *ergon*, "work"; hence, working for the people. The word first denoted someone who rendered public service at his own expense, then generally signified a public servant, a minister. In the New Testament it is used of earthly rulers (Rom. 13:6); the apostle Paul (Rom. 15:16); Epaphroditus, who attended to Paul's needs (Phil. 2:25); angels (Heb. 1:7); and Christ (Heb. 8:2).

MIRACLES—historic events or natural phenomena which appear to violate or transcend natural laws but which reveal God to the eye of faith at the same time. A helpful way of understanding the meaning of miracles is to examine the various terms for miracles used in the Bible.

Both the Old Testament and the New Testament use the word sign (Is. 7:11, 14; John 2:11) to denote a miracle that points to a deeper revelation. Wonder (Joel 2:30; Mark 13:22) emphasizes the effect of the miracle, causing awe and even terror. A work (Matt. 11:2) points to the presence of God in history, acting for mankind. The New Testament uses the word power (Mark 6:7) to emphasize God's acting in strength. These terms often overlap in meaning (Acts 2:43). They are more specific than the more general term "miracle."

Miracles in the Old Testament. The readers of the Old Testament recognized that God is the Creator and sustainer of all life (Ex. 34:10; Ps. 33:6–7; Is. 40:26). This assumption permitted the Israelites the possibility of miracles. They thought of the world as God's theater for displaying His glory and love (Pss. 33:5; 65:6–13). Thus, the miracle was not so much a proof for God's existence as a revelation to the faithful of God's covenant love.

When God parted the water for the Israelites, or when He saved Israel in Egypt through the Passover, God revealed His character; and the Israelites were convinced that God was working for their salvation (Ex. 12:13–14). Miracles were expressions of God's saving love as well as His holy justice.

Miracles in the Old Testament are connected especially with the great events in Israel's history—the call of Abraham (Gen. 12:1–3), the birth of Moses (Ex. 1:1—2:22), the Exodus from Egypt (Ex. 12:1—14:31), the giving of the Law (Ex. 19:1—20:26), and entry into the Promised Land (Josh. 3:1—4:7). These miracles are for salvation or deliverance, but God also acts in history for judgment (Gen. 11:1–9).

The plagues of the Exodus showed God's sovereign power in judgment and salvation

(Ex. 7:3–5). In parting the water, God showed His love and protection for Israel as well as His judgment on Egypt for its failure to recognize God (Ex. 15:2, 4–10). During the wilderness journey, God demonstrated His love and protection in supplying the daily manna (Ex. 16:1–36). Another critical period in Israel's history was the time of Elijah, the champion of Israel. Elijah controlled the rain and successfully challenged the pagan priests of Baal (1 Kin. 17:1; 18:1–40). God revealed Himself as Lord, as Savior of Israel, and as punisher of the nation's enemies.

Miraculous wonders do not appear as frequently during the days of the later prophets. But one unusual miracle was the recovery of Hezekiah (2 Kin. 20:1–21; Is. 38:1–21) as well as the miracles in Jonah and Daniel. Prophecy itself can even be interpreted as a miracle. God revealed Himself during this time through the spoken and written Word.

Miracles in the New Testament. As with the Old Testament, the New Testament miracles are essentially expressions of God's salvation and glory.

Why did Jesus perform miracles? Jesus answered this question Himself. When in prison, John the Baptist sent some of his disciples to Jesus to see if He was the "Coming One" (Matt. 11:3). Jesus told them to inform John of what He had done: "The blind see and the lame walk; the lepers are cleansed and the deaf hear; the dead are raised up and the poor have the gospel preached to them" (11:5). With these words, Jesus declared that His miracles were the fulfillment of the promises of the Messiah's kingdom as foretold by Isaiah (24:18–19; 35:5–6; 61:1). Jesus' miracles were signs of the presence of the kingdom of God (Matt. 12:39).

This theme of the miracles pointing to the kingdom of God was developed and deepened especially in the Gospel of John. John presented the miracles of Jesus as "signs" on seven occasions: John 2:1–11; 4:46–54; 5:1–18; 6:1–15; 6:16–21; 9:1–41; and 11:1–57. He thought of these miracles as pointing to deep spiritual truth, demanding obedient faith (John 2:11, 23–25). Thus, Jesus' feeding miracle (6:1–15) was Jesus' presentation of Himself as the True Manna, the One who gives life and sustenance.

Jesus also understood His miracles as evidences of the presence of the kingdom in His ministry (Matt. 11:2–5; 12:28). Every miracle story was a sign that God's salvation was present. But not only did the kingdom come; it came in great power, because the dead were raised (Is. 26:19; Luke 7:11–15) and Satan was bound (Mark 3:27).

Jesus' miracles were also performed upon the most unlikely people. Jesus consciously brought the salvation of God to those who were rejected. He healed the lame (Matt. 9:1–8), the dumb (Matt. 9:32–33), and lepers (Luke 17:11–19). Jesus brought the kingdom to all, regardless of their condition.

But Jesus' miracles were not theatrical sensations. He demanded faith of others (Matt. 9:2). The hemorrhaging woman was healed because of her faith (Matt. 9:18–26). Furthermore, Jesus expected the disciples to do miracles and rebuked them for their "little faith" and unbelief (Matt. 17:20).

Jesus' call to trust in Himself led regularly to opposition by Jewish leaders. John drew this out when he recorded Jesus' healing of a man born blind. Jesus' salvation comes even on the Sabbath, overturning Pharisaic legalism (John 9:16) and resulting in their blindness (John 9:39–41). Similarly the Pharisees broke into a charge of blasphemy when Jesus healed the paralytic and pronounced him forgiven of sins (Mark 2:1–12). The miracles of Jesus, being God's offer of salvation, demanded a decision. As a result, a division of the Pharisees occurred (Matt. 9:32–34).

Finally, we gain a deeper understanding of Jesus in His miracles. He is Lord over nature (Mark 4:35–41) and death (Luke 8:41–56; John 11:1–44). He is the Suffering Servant who bears the infirmities of others (Matt. 8:16–17). He is the Messiah who was to come (Matt. 11:2–6). He fights the battle against evil (Mark 3:23–30; Luke 11:18–23).

Jesus did not work miracles to prove His deity or His messiahship. In fact, He clearly refused to work miracles as proofs (Matt. 12:38–42; Luke 11:29–32). His death was the proof to Israel. However, Jesus' miracles do give evidence that He was the Son of God, the Messiah.

The Acts of the Apostles is a book of miracles. Again, these miracles are a continuation of the miracles of Jesus, made possible through the Holy Spirit. The miracles of the apostles were done in the name of Jesus and were manifestations of God's salvation (Acts 3:11). This thread of continuity is seen in Peter's miracles which paralleled those of Jesus (Luke 7:22; 5:18–26; 8:49–56; Acts 3:1–16; 9:32–35, 36–42).

God began His church with a powerful display of miracles. At Pentecost, the Holy Spirit came on the people with great power (Acts 2:1–13), leading to conversions (Acts 2:41). When Philip went to Samaria, the Spirit of God anointed him with power (Acts 8:4–40), and the same happened with Peter and Cornelius (Acts 10:1–48). These powerful wonders were designed to convince the apostles and the Palestinian church that other cultures were to be part of the church. To these were added the stunning act of God through Peter when Ananias and Sapphira acted in hypocrisy (Acts 4:32—5:11), the church's power in prayer (Acts 4:23–31), and Paul's transforming vision (Acts 16:6–10).

Miraculous powers were also present in the apostles. Peter healed a lame man (Acts 3:1–6), a paralytic (Acts 9:32–35), and raised the dead (Acts 9:36–42). The apostles performed mighty miracles (Acts 5:12–16), and Peter was miraculously released from prison (Acts 12:1–11). Paul's conversion was a startling incident (Acts 9:1–19). Ability to work miracles was taken as a sign for apostleship by Paul (Rom. 15:18–19; 2 Cor. 12:12). Thus, this ability to work miracles is not only an expression of God's salvation but also God's way of authenticating His apostles.

The lists of the gifts of the Spirit in the New Testament show miracles were one of the means by which believers ministered to others (Rom. 12:6–8; 1 Cor. 12:8–10, 28–30; Eph. 4:11–12). This is sufficient evidence to verify that the working of miracles by the power of the Holy Spirit and to the glory of Jesus Christ is (1) still intended in the church today, and (2) available for ministry through any believer the Spirit may choose to use.

MOAB—see ch. 55, §2.3.

MOABITE STONE—see ch. 55, §2.3.

MOMENT. (1 Cor. 15:52) *atomos* (*at*-om-oss); *Strong's #823:* Compare "atomizer" and "atomic." Uncut, indivisible, undissected, infinitely small. The word is a compound of *a*, "un," and *temnos*, "to cut in two." When used of time, it represents an extremely short unit of time, a flash, an instant, a unit of time that cannot be divided. A second can be calibrated to one-tenth, one one-hundredth, and one one-thousandth of a second. But how do you calibrate an atomic second? Christ's return will be in an atomic second.

MORTAL. (Job 4:17) *'enosh* (eh-*noash*); *Strong's #582:* A man, a mortal; man in his frailty, limitation, and imperfection. Derived from the verb *'anash*, *'enosh* means "to be frail, sick, weak, and sad." *'Enosh* is one of the four primary Hebrew words for man. If *'adam* is man as a species, *'ish* is man as an individual citizen, and *geber* is man at the height of his manly power, then *'enosh* is man as a basically weak creature. *'Enosh* occurs more than 550 times in the Old Testament and often is simply an alternate term for *'adam*. Yet sometimes the original connotation persists, such as in the question in Psalm 8:4, "What is man

[*'enosh*] that You are mindful of him?" In Daniel 7:13, the Aramaic equivalent *bar'enash* (Son of Man) is a messianic term. The Lord Jesus repeatedly called Himself "the Son of Man." He identified with the human race in its weaknesses, yet rises to a position of everlasting strength.

MOSES—see ch. 55, §2.1.

MOST HIGH. (Gen. 14:18) *'elyon* (el-*yohn*); *Strong's #5945:* Most High, uppermost; pertaining to the heights, in the highest; highness; supreme, lofty, elevated, high in rank, exalted. *'Elyon* is derived from the verb *'alah* meaning "to ascend." It appears as an adjective more than twenty times, describing exalted rulers and even the highest rooms in the wall of the temple (Ezek. 41:7). It becomes a divine title when paired with one of the names of God, such as *'El 'Elyon* or *'Elohim 'Elyon*, "God Most High." Compare the angels' declaration at the birth of Jesus: "Glory to God in the highest, and on earth peace, goodwill toward men!" (Luke 2:14).

MOTHER—the female parent of a household. In the Hebrew family, the mother occupied a higher position than that enjoyed by women in many other nations. The mother's duties were primarily domestic, but she was held in high regard by her family and Hebrew society.

The concept of mother was sometimes used in other, more figurative ways. Nations were sometimes thought of as mothers. The prophet Ezekiel used mother as a metaphor for Israel. After being nurtured and cared for by their "mother," the "princes of Israel" brought shame upon her by their idolatrous practices (Ezek. 19:1–14). Jeremiah used the concept of Israel as mother to personify the nation's sin (Jer. 50:12–13), while Hosea made it a continuing theme of his prophecies.

The word mother was sometimes used to describe large and important cities. The city of Abel of Beth Maachah was called "a mother in Israel" (2 Sam. 20:19). A city was also a mother in terms of its influence. Babylon was called "the mother of harlots and of the abominations of the earth" (Rev. 17:5).

The figurative meaning of "mother" also included ancestry. Eve was the "mother of all living" (Gen. 3:20). God blessed Sarah by declaring, "She shall be a mother of nations" (Gen. 17:16). Rebekah was blessed to become "the mother of thousands of ten thousands" (Gen. 24:60).

The love and nurturing of God is sometimes compared to the love and caring a mother gives to a newborn child. Paul referred to new Christians as "babes in Christ" (1 Cor. 3:1), implying a connection to a maternal quality in the Godhead as well as paternal character (1 Thess. 2:7).

MOURN. (Joel 1:9) *'abal* (ah-*vahl*); *Strong's* #56: To weep, lament, mourn, droop, sink down, languish. This verb occurs nearly forty times and describes mourning over a death, over sin, or over the tragedies of Jerusalem (Is. 66:10). In the present reference, *'abal* describes the reaction of godly priests to the plight of the Lord's people. *Also* (Rev. 18:11) *pentheo* (pen-*theh*-oh); *Strong's* #3996: Compare "nepenthe," a drug that removes grief. To grieve, lament, mourn. In verses 11, 15, and 19, *pentheo* is used of merchants who mourn the destruction of Babylon. The ungodly will experience great sorrow at the overthrow of the world system.

MOURNING—the experience or expression of grief, as at a time of death or national disaster, or in cases of repentance for sin or passionate quest for God. In biblical times, the customs of most cultures encouraged a vivid expression of grief. The people of that time would be puzzled by our more sedate forms of mourning, though psychological study suggests our repressed form may be far less healthy in the long term for our emotions.

The Old Testament has many Hebrew words for mourning. These words range in meaning from anger and indignation to the more common idea of grief over a calamity or death. In addition to wailing and weeping, outward forms of mourning included tearing the clothes and wearing sackcloth (Gen. 37:34), fasting (Ps. 35:13), and throwing dust upon the head (Lam. 2:10).

The period for mourning varied. The Egyptians mourned for Jacob seventy days (Gen. 50:3); Israel for Aaron and Moses thirty days (Num. 20:29; Deut. 34:8); Jacob for Joseph "many days" (Gen. 37:34). According to one Jewish tradition, mourning was to take place on the third, seventh, and fortieth days after burial, and on the anniversary of the burial.

Mourning began at the moment a person died. The family would begin its wailing, and neighbors would rush to the bereaved household. If the family could afford them, hired mourners were employed to add their chants to lamentations. Such hired mourners were probably present scorning Jesus at Jairus' household.

In the New Testament only three Greek words are rendered as mourn (Matt. 9:15; 11:17; 24:30). The few references to mourning suggests that Christ's work removed the dread and pain of death (1 Cor. 15:55). Christians

are not to "sorrow as others [unbelievers] who have no hope" (1 Thess. 4:13).

MURDER—the unlawful killing of one person by another, especially with premeditated malice. After the Fall in the Garden of Eden (Gen. 3:1–24), it was not long before the first murder occurred (Gen. 4:8), as Cain killed Abel, his brother.

According to the Book of Genesis, humankind is created in God's image (Gen. 1:26–27). Murdering a human being, therefore, is a serious crime and must be punished (Gen. 9:6). One of the Ten Commandments states, "You shall not murder" (Ex. 20:13; Deut. 5:17). This commandment is quoted several times in the New Testament (Matt. 19:18; Luke 18:20; Rom. 13:9).

In the New Testament, Jesus deepened the Old Testament commands against and laws of retribution for murder by giving it a spiritual dimension. Whoever harbors anger and hatred against his brother is in danger of God's judgment (Matt. 5:21). Murder begins in the heart—one's thoughts and meditations—and proceeds out of the heart (Matt. 15:19; Mark 7:21).

But even murder can be forgiven (Matt. 12:31; Mark 3:28). Before his conversion, Saul of Tarsus launched "threats and murder" (Acts 9:1) against the church. But by the grace of God he was converted and became Paul the apostle, missionary to the Gentiles.

MUSIC—vocal or instrumental sounds with rhythm, melody, and harmony. Music was part of everyday life for the ancient Hebrew people. Music was a part of family merrymaking, such as the homecoming party for the prodigal son (Luke 15:25). Music welcomed heroes and celebrated victories. Miriam and other women sang, danced, and played timbrels when the Israelites miraculously escaped the Egyptians (Ex. 15:20), and the Song of Moses in Exodus 15 is the earliest recorded song in the Bible. Jephthah's daughter greeted him with timbrels to celebrate his victory over the Ammonites (Judg. 11:34). David's triumph brought music (1 Sam. 18:6).

Music was used in making war and crowning kings (Judg. 7:18–20; 1 Kin. 1:39–40; 2 Chr. 20:28). Wartime music-making was apparently little more than making noise, as in the fall of Jericho (Joshua 6). There was music for banquets and feasts (Is. 5:12; 24:8–9) and royal courts and harems (Eccl. 2:8). The Bible gives examples of occupational songs (Jer. 31:4–5), dirges and laments (Matt. 9:23), and worship chants (Ex. 28:34–35; Josh. 6:4–20).

David introduced music into the sanctuary worship. His son and successor Solomon later retained it after the temple was built (2 Sam. 6:5; 1 Kin. 10:12). Music must have been considered an important part of the service, since Hezekiah and Josiah, the two reform kings, saw to it that music was included in the reformation (2 Chr. 29:25; 35:15).

Our greatest clue to Hebrew music lies in the Book of Psalms, the earliest existing hymnbook. As hymns, these individual psalms were suitable for chanting and singing in the worship of God.

The Bible gives a glimpse of musical terminology in the headings of the psalms which appear in the Hebrew language. Meanings are to a large extent obscure, apparently lost as early as 250 B.C.

Categories of psalm headings include the following:

Titles—These include titles such as "A Psalm [Hebrew, *Mizmor*] of" (Psalm 87) and "A Contemplation [Hebrew, *Maschil*] of" (Psalm 78). *Mizmor* seems to mean "to play, sing"; *Maschil* may indicate a meditation.

Directions for performance—*Alamoth* (Psalm 46) may mean "for the flutes" or for soprano voices. *Sheminith* (Psalms 6; 12) suggests a melodic pattern, perhaps an octave lower than Alamoth and, therefore, tenor or even bass. The NKJV translates, "On an eight-stringed harp." *Neginoth* (Pss. 4; 6; 54; 55; 61; 67; 76) is translated "stringed instruments" (NKJV), but in reference to most psalms it probably means simply "a song." *Mahalath* (Psalm 53) was probably a choreographic direction. In Psalm 88 *Mahalath* is coupled with *Leannoth*, the uncertain meaning of which has been interpreted as "for singing antiphonally."

Shiggaion (plural, *Shiggionoth*), a part of the Hebrew heading of Psalm 7 probably referred to an erratic, enthusiastic ode or a psalm of lamentation. *Higgayon* (Ps. 9:16) refers to a solemn sound and may indicate soft music. The meaning of *Muth Labben* (Hebrew heading, Psalm 9) is a mystery. It may be a scribal error. If not, it may refer to a soprano melody for masculine voices.

Cue words—The majority of the psalm titles contain cue words. They direct the practice of setting new words to an old tune, an aspect of hymnology still practiced today. *Shoshannim*, a Hebrew word which means "lilies," occurs in the titles of Psalms 45 and 69 and in Psalm 80 as *Shoshannim Eduth*, "Lilies of testimony" and in Psalm 60 as *Shushan Eduth*, "Lily of the testimony." These expressions may have indicated the melody to which these songs were to be sung. These kinds of cue words appear before Psalms 22; 56—59; and 75, among others.

The heading *Shir-hammaloth* ("A Song of Ascents"; Latin, *cantus graduum)* above Psalms 120—134 has several interpretations. The most common are: (1) These fifteen psalms were sung by Levites standing on the fifteen steps between the court of the women and the court of the Israelites; and (2) these fifteen psalms were sung at three pilgrimage festivals. The second explanation is more probable.

Selah—This word occurs seventy-one times in the Book of Psalms (also Hab. 3:3, 9, 13). Scholars agree that the term is a musical direction of some sort, but they are not agreed on what the direction is. It may mean: (1) an interlude—a pause in the singing while the orchestra continues; (2) the equivalent of today's "Amen"; as such it would separate psalms or sections of psalms which have different liturgical purposes; and (3) an acrostic which means "a change of voices" or "repeat."

Music in the New Testament. The New Testament contains little information about music. But it does give some additional hymns to add to the Old Testament hymns—those of Mary (Luke 1:46–55) and Zacharias (Luke 1:68–79)—the Magnificat and the Benedictus. Early Christians sang Hebrew songs accompanied by music (2 Chr. 29:27–28). The apostle Paul refers to "psalms and hymns and spiritual songs" (Eph. 5:19; Col. 3:16). Matthew 26:30 records that Christ and His disciples sang a hymn after the Passover supper, probably the second half of the Hallel, or Psalms 115—118.

The New Testament also contains accounts of the early Christians singing hymns for worship and comfort (Acts 16:25; Eph. 5:19; Col. 3:16). Some fragments of early Christian hymns also appear in the New Testament (Eph. 5:14; 1 Tim. 3:16).

"*Singing spiritual songs.*" Spiritual songs have sometimes been defined as informal choruses, choral anthems, simpler, more personal statements of faith or brief, uncomplex odes of worship; a growing number see them as a new music form unavailable until the New Testament, until Christ's full redemption allowed the Holy Spirit to dwell in mankind. Clearly, early believers sang spiritual songs of worship. But what were they?

Hodais pneumatikais, the exact words in both Ephesians 5 and Colossians 3, are usually translated "spiritual songs." The first word is simply "ode," the Greek term for any words which were sung. But the second word—*pneumatikais*—seems to be the key to the full meaning of this phrase.

Pneumatikais—a cognate of *pneuma* ("spirit")—is most easily defined and understood noting its use elsewhere in the New Testament. For example, Paul uses this word when introducing the subject of spiritual gifts in 1 Corinthians 12:1 (literally, *pneumatika*, "spiritual things"). Later, in his appeal to the Galatians concerning their duty to restore fallen brethren, the word also appears: "You who are spiritual ones" (*pneumatikoi*) are assigned the task of that restoring ministry. Although *pneumatika* occurs more than twenty times in the New Testament, those two texts give us something of a basic picture. *Pneumatika* seems to indicate Holy-Spirit-filled people of character and charisma. Their character is noted in the Galatian text: "You who are spiritual ones restore the fallen"; their *charism* (in the sense of their functioning in the charisms—gifts of the Holy Spirit) is indicated in their apparent acceptance and response to spiritual things; that is, manifestations of the Holy Spirit's gifts (1 Cor. 12:7).

These factors alone would not finalize a definition, except for the fact that in this same context Paul discusses "singing with the spirit and with the understanding." It is here in this classic passage, 1 Corinthians 12—14, as the apostle corrects their abuse of glossolalia, that he also discusses singing of a distinctly Holy-Spirit-enabled nature:

> For if I pray in a tongue, my spirit prays, but my understanding is unfruitful. What is the conclusion then? I will pray with the spirit, and I will also pray with the understanding. I will sing with the spirit, and I will also sing with the understanding.
>
> 1 Corinthians 14:14–15

His distinguishing singing "with the spirit" from "singing with the understanding" points to what spiritual songs may have meant in the first-century church: an exercise separate from, yet complementary to, the singing of psalms and hymns.

Since the general passage beginning in 1 Corinthians 12:1 and the specific text beginning in 1 Corinthians 14:1 both use *pneumatika* to describe the kind of subject matter being dealt with, it follows that the distinct type of singing referred to as being "with the spirit (*pneuma*)" could be the same as spiritual songs. This proposes that the whole of the New Testament context supports the definition of spiritual songs as being Holy-Spirit-enabled utterances: (1) which were sung rather than spoken; (2) which were most commonly to be a part of one's devotional life; (3) which were explained or interpreted if exercised in corporate gatherings; and (4) which were so desirable as to have Paul assert his personal will to practice them—"I will sing with the spirit" (1 Cor. 14:15). Also see Holy Spirit Gifts.

MYSTERY—the hidden, eternal plan of God that is now being fully revealed to God's people in accordance with His plan.

In the Old Testament, mystery occurs only in the Aramaic sections of Daniel (Dan. 2:18, 27–30, 47; 4:9). Some of God's mysteries were revealed to Daniel and King Nebuchadnezzar.

In the New Testament, mystery refers to a secret that is revealed by God to His servants through His Spirit. As such, it is an "open secret." Mystery occurs three times in the Gospels. Jesus told His disciples, "To you it has been given to know the mystery of the kingdom of God" (Matt. 13:11; Mark 4:11; Luke 8:10). Jesus explained the mystery of God's kingdom to His disciples. But to others He declared, "All things come in parables" (Mark 4:11).

Most of the occurrences of the word mystery are in the Pauline Epistles. Mystery refers to the revelation of God's plan of salvation as that plan focuses in Christ. The gospel itself is a "mystery which was kept secret since the world began" (Rom. 16:25). This mystery was revealed by God through the prophetic Scriptures to Paul and the church (1 Cor. 2:7; Eph. 6:19; Col. 4:3).

Mystery also refers to the future resurrection of Christians (1 Cor. 15:51), the summing up of all things in Christ (Eph. 1:9), the inclusion of Gentiles in the church (Eph. 3:3–9), the future salvation of Israel (Rom. 11:25), the phenomenon of lawlessness (2 Thess. 2:7), and the godliness revealed in Christ (1 Tim. 3:16).

MYSTERY. (Mark 4:11) *musterion* (moos-*tay*-ree-on); *Strong's #3466:* From *mueo,* "to initiate into the mysteries," hence a secret known only to the initiated, something hidden requiring special revelation. In the New Testament the word denotes something that people could never know by their own understanding and that demands a revelation from God. The secret thoughts, plans, and dispensations of God remain hidden from unregenerate mankind, but are revealed to all believers. In nonbiblical Greek *musterion* is knowledge withheld, concealed, or silenced. In biblical Greek it is truth revealed (see Col. 1:26). New Testament *musterion* focuses on Christ's sinless life, atoning death, powerful resurrection, and dynamic ascension.

NAG HAMMADI—see ch. 55, §7.

NAME—a label or designation that sets one person apart from another.

In the Bible a name is much more than an identifier, as it tends to be in our culture. Personal names (and even place names) were formed from words that had their own meaning. Thus, the people of the Bible were very conscious of the "prophetic" meaning of names. They believed there was a vital connection between the name and the person it identified, for a name somehow represented the nature of the person.

This means that the naming of a baby was very important in the Bible. In choosing a name, the parents could reflect the circumstances of the child's birth, their own feelings, their gratitude to God, their hopes and prayers for the child, and their commitment of the child to God. The name Isaac reflected the "laughter" of his mother at his birth (Gen. 21:6). Esau was named "hairy" because of his appearance. Jacob was named "supplanter" because he grasped his brother Esau's heel (Gen. 25:25–26). Moses received his name because he was "drawn out" of the water (Ex. 2:10).

A popular custom of Bible times was to compose names by using the shortened forms of the divine name El or Ya (Je) as the beginning or ending syllable. Examples of this practice are Elisha, which means "God is salvation"; Daniel, "God is my judge"; Jehoiakim, "the Lord has established"; and Isaiah, "the Lord is salvation."

Sometimes very specialized names, directly related to circumstances of the parents, were given to children. The prophet Isaiah was directed to name one of his children Maher-Shalal-Hash-Baz, meaning "speed the spoil, hasten the prey." This name was an allusion to the certain Assyrian invasion of the nation of Judah (Is. 8:3–4). Hosea was instructed to name a daughter Lo-Ruhamah, "no mercy," and a son Lo-Ammi, "not my people." Both these names referred to God's displeasure with His people (Hos. 1:6–9).

The change of a name can also be of great importance in the Bible. Abram's name was changed to Abraham in connection with his new calling to be "a father of many nations" (Gen. 17:5). God gave Jacob the new name Israel ("God strives") because he "struggled with God and with men, and . . . prevailed" (Gen. 32:28; 35:10).

In the giving or taking of new names, often a crucial turning point in the person's life has been reached. Simon was given the name Peter because, as the first confessing apostle, the faith he expressed was the "rock" upon which the new community of the church would be built (Matt. 16:18). Saul was renamed Paul, a Greek name that was appropriate for one who was destined to become the great apostle to the Gentiles.

The New Testament writers also emphasized the importance of names and the close relationship between names and what they mean. A striking illustration of this is Acts 4:12: "For there is no other name under heaven by which we must be saved." In this instance the name is again practically interchangeable with the reality which it represents.

Jesus taught His disciples to pray, "Hallowed be Your name" (Matt. 6:9). Christians were described by the apostle Paul as those who "name the name of the Lord" (2 Tim. 2:19). A true understanding of the exalted Jesus is often connected with a statement about His name. Thus, Jesus "has by inheritance obtained a more excellent name" than the angels (Heb. 1:4). According to Paul, "God also has highly exalted Him and given Him the name which is above every name" (Phil. 2:9).

NAME. (Deut. 18:5) *shem* (*shem*); *Strong's* #8034: Name, renown, fame, memorial, character. Possibly *shem* comes from a root that suggests "marking" or "branding." Thus a person was named because of something that marked him, whether physical features, or accomplishments he had made or was expected to make. *Shem* appears more than eight hundred times in the Old Testament, its most important use being in the phrase "the name of the LORD," sometimes abbreviated to *hashem* ("the name," that is, *Yahweh*). See Leviticus 24:11, where one man blasphemed "the name," meaning that he blasphemed the Lord. Thus, in Judaic tradition, *Yahweh* God is often simply called *hashem.* Also (John 12:13) *onoma* (*on-om-ah*); *Strong's* #3686: Compare "anonymous," "synonym," "onomancy," "onomatology." In general, the word signifies the name or term by which a person or thing is called (Matt. 10:2; Mark 3:16; Luke 1:63). However, it was quite common both in Hebrew and Hellenistic Greek to use *onoma* for all that the name implies, such as rank or authority (Matt. 7:22; John 14:13; Acts 3:6; 4:7), char-

---

acter (Luke 1:49; 11:2; Acts 26:9), reputation (Mark 6:14; Luke 6:22), representative (Matt. 7:22; Mark 9:37). Occasionally, *onoma* is synonymous for an individual, a person (Acts 1:15; Rev. 3:4; 11:13).

NATIONS—countries other than the nation of Israel. In the Bible the word nations means the Gentiles, in contrast to the Jews. God promised that He would make Abraham and his descendants a great nation. Thus, God's elect people were kept clearly distinct and separate from all other nations. The nations were regarded by the Hebrew people as godless and corrupt. Yet God intended ultimately to bless the nations through His people Israel: "And in you all the families of the earth shall be blessed" (Gen. 12:3). Israel was thus meant to be "a light to the Gentiles" (Is. 42:6; 49:6)

The prophecy that "the Gentiles shall come to your light" (Is. 60:3) was fulfilled in the Gentile response to Christ in the New Testament. The Great Commission refers to "all the nations" (Matt. 28:19); Cornelius, the first Gentile convert, was brought to faith through the preaching of Peter (Acts 10). The apostle Paul repeatedly quoted the Old Testament to justify the preaching of the gospel to the nations (Rom. 15:9–12; Gal. 3:8).

NEBUCHADNEZZAR—see ch. 55, §3.7., 3.7.a., 3.7.b., 3.7.d.

NEEDY. (Ps. 70:5) *'ebyon* (ehv-*yoan*); *Strong's* #34: One in need; a destitute, lacking, or poor individual. This adjective occurs about sixty times in the Old Testament. In the Law, God required that the poor should be treated justly (Ex. 23:6). The prophets strongly denounced those who crush or oppress needy persons (Amos 4:1; Ezek. 22:29–31). God is the special Protector of the needy (Is. 25:4). Jesus noted, "The poor have the gospel preached to them" (Matt. 11:5). Thus one of the earliest groups of Jewish followers of Jesus adopted the name "Ebionites" (*'ebyon*-ites), that is, "the poor ones." They delighted in the fact that their needy state prepared them to see the riches of the gospel and the treasure that is the Lord Jesus.

NEHEMIAH—see ch. 55, §3.2.

NEIGHBOR—a friend, close associate, or a person who lives nearby. The Abrahamic Covenant (Gen. 12:1–3) established moral obligations among the Israelites. They were commanded to show concern for their neighbors. The ninth and tenth commandments (Ex. 20:16–17; Deut. 5:20–21) prohibited the defaming or slandering of a neighbor and condemned the envying of a neighbor's wife, servant, livestock, or other possessions.

A person was not to cheat or rob from his neighbor (Lev. 19:13). The maiming or disfigurement of a neighbor was punishable by "eye for eye, tooth for tooth" retribution (Lev. 24:19–20). Despising one's neighbor was sin (Prov. 14:21), as was leading him morally astray (Prov. 16:29–30) or deceiving him, then saying, "I was only joking" (Prov. 26:19). A person was not even permitted to think evil of his neighbor (Zech. 8:17).

Jesus extended the concept of neighbor to include strangers, as in the parable of the Good Samaritan (Luke 10:25–37), and hence all mankind. The apostle Paul declared that "love your neighbor as yourself" was a supreme commandment (Rom. 13:9–10).

NEW. (2 Cor. 5:17) *kainos* (kahee-*noss*); *Strong's* #2537: New, unused, fresh, novel. The word means new in regard to form or quality, rather than new in reference to time, a thought conveyed by *neos*.

NEW BIRTH—inner spiritual regeneration or renewal as a result of the power of God in a person's life. The phrase new birth comes from John 3:3, 7, where Jesus told Nicodemus, "Unless one is born again, he cannot see the kingdom of God." Jesus meant that all people are so sinful in God's eyes that they need to be regenerated—recreated and renewed—by the sovereign activity of God's Spirit (John 3:5–8).

The activity of God's Spirit that regenerates sinful man comes about through faith in Jesus Christ (John 3:10–21). Without faith there is no regeneration, and without regeneration a person does not have eternal life. Regeneration occurs at the moment a person exercises faith in Christ. At that point, his sins are forgiven and he is born again by the power of the Holy Spirit working on behalf of Christ. The new birth is a decisive, unrepeatable, and irrevocable act of God.

Similar words are used elsewhere in the Bible to describe the same general concept. Paul said, "If anyone is in Christ, he is a new creation" (2 Cor. 5:17). Although our "outward man" is perishing, the Christian's "inward man is being renewed day by day" (2 Cor. 4:16).

NUZI TABLETS—see ch. 55, §3.5., 3.5.a., 3.5.b., 3.5.c.

OBEDIENCE—carrying out the word and will of another person, especially the will of God. In both the Old and New Testaments the word obey is related to the idea of hearing. Obedience is a positive, active response to what a person hears. God summons people to active obedience to His revelation. Man's failure to obey God results in judgment. In the Old Testament covenant between God and man, obedience was the basis for knowing God's blessing and favor (Ex. 19:5; 24:1–8). Samuel emphasized that God's pleasure was not in sacrifice but in obedience (1 Sam. 15:22). Even the promise of a new covenant emphasized obedience as God's gift (Jer. 31:33).

In the New Testament, the obedience of Christ stands in contrast to the disobedience of Adam. The disobedience of Adam brought death, but the perfect obedience of Christ brought grace, righteousness, and life (Rom. 5:12–21).

OBEDIENCE. (2 Cor. 10:5) *hupakoe* (hoop-ak-oh-*ay*); *Strong's #5218:* From *hupo,* "under," and *akouo,* "to hear." The word signifies attentive hearing, to listen with compliant submission, assent, and agreement. It is used for obedience in general, for obedience to God's commands, and for Christ's obedience.

OBEYED. (Rom. 6:17) *hupakouo* (hoop-ak-oo-oh); *Strong's #5219:* To hear as a subordinate, listen attentively, obey as a subject, answer and respond, submit without reservation. *Hupakouo* was used particularly of servants who were attentive to the requests made of them and who complied. The word thus contains the ideas of hearing, responding, and obeying.

OFFENDED. (Matt. 11:6) *skandalizo* (skan-dal-id-zoe); *Strong's #4624:* Originally, to put a snare or stumbling block in the way. The noun to which it is related referred to the bait-stick of a trap. In the New Testament *skandalizo* is always used metaphorically of that which hinders right conduct or thought, hence, "to cause to stumble."

OFFENSE—a word with two distinct meanings in the Bible:

1. That which prompts a person to bristle with indignation or disgust. This type of offense may in fact be from God, according to its usage in the Bible. The apostle Paul spoke of "the offense of the cross" (Gal. 5:11). The Jews were offended because faith without Jewish legal observances was offered as the only means of salvation.

2. Offense also refers to those things which cause a person to do something against his conscience. This type of offense may be from Satan or from other people. Its effect is to entice a person to sin (Matt. 5:29; 17:23; 18:6–9). It is this kind of offense which can be produced by the "grey" areas of the Christian life—those practices which are right for some but wrong for others (Rom. 14:13; 1 Cor. 8:13).

OFFENSE. (Matt. 16:23) *skandalon* (*skan*-da-lahn); *Strong's #4625:* Originally, a trapstick, a

bent sapling, or a movable stick with bait used to catch animals. The word then came to denote a snare or stumbling block. Metaphorically, it signifies that which causes error or sin.

OFFERED. (Heb. 9:28) *prosphero* (pros-*fer*-oh); *Strong's #4374:* From *pros,* "toward," and *phero,* "to bring." In addition to the more literal sense of bringing or leading to (Matt. 4:24; 8:16; 9:2, 32), the word denotes an offering, whether of gifts, prayers, or sacrifices (Matt. 2:11; 5:24; Mark 1:44; Heb. 8:3).

OFFERING. (Acts 21:26) *prosphora* (pros-*for*-ah); *Strong's #4376:* A bringing to, setting before, presenting, sacrificing, a gift, the act of offering, or the thing offered. The word includes giving kindness and bestowing benefit. Paul engaged in the purification ceremony. It was not necessary for his salvation, but was an act of devotion to God. Paul's principle was being all things to all people in order to win them.

OLD PERSIAN—see ch. 55, §2.2.

OMNIPOTENCE [om NIP oh tunce]—a theological term that refers to the all-encompassing power of God. The almighty God expects human beings to obey Him, and He holds them responsible for their thoughts and actions. Nevertheless, He is the all-powerful Lord who has created all things and sustains them by the Word of His power (Gen. 1:1–3; Heb. 1:3).

God reveals in the Bible that He is all-powerful and in the final sense is the ruler of nature and history. Before Him "the nations are as a drop in a bucket, and are counted as the small dust on the scales" (Is. 40:15). Yet He has so fashioned humankind that He graciously appeals to every person to return to Him.

OMNIPRESENCE [om nih PRES ence]—a theological term that refers to the unlimited nature of God or His ability to be everywhere at all times. God is unlike any creature, limited to one place at a time. No being is His equal in this or any other way. God reveals Himself in the Bible as the Lord who is everywhere. God was present as Lord in all creation (Ps. 139:7–12), and there is no escaping Him. He is present in our innermost thoughts. Even as we are formed in the womb, He knows all the days of our future.

God sees in secret and rewards in secret, as Jesus taught His disciples; He looks not only on outward actions, but especially on the inner attitudes of a person's heart (Matt. 6:1–18). Because God is the Creator and Sustainer of time and space, He is everywhere.

Being everywhere, He is our great Comforter, Friend, and Redeemer.

OMNISCIENCE [om NISH unce]—a theological term that refers to God's superior knowledge and wisdom, His power to know all things. God is the Lord who knows our thoughts from afar. He is acquainted with all our ways, knowing our words even before they are on our tongues (Ps. 139:1–6, 13–16). He needs to consult no one for knowledge or understanding (Is. 40:13–14). He is the all-knowing Lord who prophesies the events of the future, including the death of His Son (Isaiah 53) and the return of Christ at the end of this age when death will be finally overcome (Rom. 8:18–39; 1 Cor. 15:51–57).

Only the all-knowing and all-powerful God can guarantee real freedom from sin, decay, and death. He can begin a process of change in believers during the present age; for "where the Spirit of the Lord is, there is liberty" (2 Cor. 3:17).

OMRI—see ch. 55, §2.3.

ONE. (Deut. 6:4) *'echad* (eh-*chahd*); *Strong's* #259: One, a unit; united; unity. *'Echad* comes from the root *'achad,* "to bring together, to unify; to collect one's thoughts." *'Echad* serves to portray the same range of meaning as "one" does in English, from the very narrowest sense (one and one only, as in Eccl. 9:18, "one sinner destroys much good") to the broadest sense (one made up of many, as in Gen. 2:24, where a man and his wife "shall become one flesh"). Deuteronomy 6:4–6 is the most important text in the Old Testament. Jesus called it the greatest commandment of Scripture, and it remains the central confession of Judaism to this day. The foundational truth for world redemption is that there is one God who creates and redeems, and yet the New Testament shows that God is Father, Son, and Holy Spirit. Compare the unity of God to the unity of man made in His image: man is comprised of spirit, soul, and body (1 Thess. 5:23). Man is not three "beings" but "one being" with physical, emotional, and spiritual elements.

OPHEL GARDEN—see ch. 55, §6.

ORDAIN, ORDINATION—the process of "commissioning" a pastor or other officer of the church. This process is seldom mentioned in the New Testament. Some scholars doubt whether the solemn service we know today as ordination was practiced in the time of Christ. However, while the technical sense of the term does not occur in the New Testament, several references do indicate an official commissioning ceremony.

The Twelve were "chosen" and "sent" by Christ (Mark 3:13–19; Luke 6:12–16), but without any formal ordination service, and the same is true of the election of Matthias (Acts 1:26). The seven were commissioned by the "laying on of hands" (Acts 6:6). Paul and Barnabas were commissioned by the Antioch church in the same manner (Acts 13:3). However, the laying on of hands was practiced commonly and does not necessarily point to an ordination service.

The primary evidence of an ordination service comes from 1 Timothy 4:14, where Paul apparently speaks of an official ceremony. Timothy's special spiritual "gift" was given to him "by prophecy with the laying on of the hands of the presbytery." From 2 Timothy 1:6 it would seem that Paul joined with them in this service.

The ordination of a Christian leader is an act of the church by which the responsibility of an office is passed on to an individual. Ordination is a solemn affair for the one who is commissioned and the church which commissions.

OTHER. (Acts 4:12) *heteros* (*het*-er-oss); *Strong's* #2087: Different, generic distinction, another kind, not of the same nature, form, or class. Here *heteros* denotes a distinction and an exclusivity, with no second choices, opinions, or options. "Jesus, You are the One. You are the only One. There is no *heteros*, no other!"

PARACLETE [pair uh KLEET]—a transliteration of the Greek word *parakletos,* which means "one who speaks in favor of," as an intercessor, advocate, or legal assistant. The word appears only in the Gospel of John. Jesus applied the term to the *Holy Spirit, who would be an advocate on behalf of Jesus' followers after His ascension; the Spirit would plead their cause before God (John 14:16, 26; 15:26; 16:7).

PARADISE *(park, garden)*—a place of exceptional blessedness, happiness, and delight; a descriptive name for heaven. Originally paradise was a Persian word meaning "a wooded park," "an enclosed or walled orchard," or "a garden with fruit trees." Traditional Hebrew theology held that the dead descended to *sheol. After the emergence of belief in the

 This icon beside an entry indicates a Word Wealth feature.

This icon beside an entry indicates a Kingdom Dynamics feature.

This icon beside an entry indicates an important biblical or doctrinal term.

resurrection, however, this view was drastically modified. In the period between the Old and New Testaments, the Jews believed that, after the resurrection, the righteous would go to Paradise, a place much like the Garden of Eden before the Fall.

In the NKJV the word paradise occurs only three times (Luke 23:43; 2 Cor. 12:4; Rev. 2:7). To the repentant thief on the cross Jesus said, "Today you will be with Me in Paradise" (Luke 23:43). Various commentators have pointed out that when a Persian king wished to bestow upon one of his subjects a special honor, he made him a "companion of the garden." The subject was chosen to walk in the king's garden as a special friend and companion of the king. Thus, Jesus promised the thief that he would be a companion of the King of kings, walking with Christ in the garden of heaven.

 PAROUSIA [PUH ROO sih ah]—a transliteration of a Greek word that refers to the *Second Coming, or the return of the Lord Jesus Christ at the end of this age to set up His kingdom, judge His enemies, and reward the faithful. The Greek word literally means, "a being alongside," hence "appearance" or "presence." Christians are "looking for the blessed hope and glorious appearing of our great God and Savior Jesus Christ" (Titus 2:13). This blessed hope of the Parousia, or Second Coming, sustains believers in a godless age.

PARTAKER. (1 Cor. 9:10) metecho (met-ekh-oh); Strong's #3348: Literally "to have with." The word connotes a sharing in, participating of, copartnering, working in association with another, and taking part in a joint venture. Here the sowers and the reapers share the same hopes. Hebrews 2:14 describes Jesus, by the Incarnation, sharing flesh and blood with humanity for their redemption. 1 Corinthians 10:17 states that all the redeemed have a joint participation in worshiping the Lord Jesus.

PARTAKERS. (Heb. 3:14) metochos (met-okh-oss); Strong's #3353: A participant, associate, sharer, partner, companion. The word is a combination of meta, "with," and echo, "to have."

PARTIALITY. (Acts 10:34) prosopoleptes (pros-oh-pol-ape-tace); Strong's #4381: A receiver of a face, one who takes sides, showing favoritism, exhibiting bias, showing discrimination, showing partiality, treating one person better than another. While society makes distinctions among people, God's love and grace are available for all and can be received by anyone. Also (Col. 3:25) prosopolepsia (pros-oh-pol-ape-see-ah); Strong's #4382: Favoritism, partiality, distinction, bias, condi-

tional preference. The word denotes a biased judgment, which gives respect to rank, position, or circumstances instead of considering the intrinsic conditions. God shows no partiality in justice, judgment, or favorable treatment when dealing with people, and He expects us to follow His example.

 PARTIALITY (SHOW). (James 2:9) prosopolepteo (pros-oh-pol-ape-teh-oh); Strong's #4380: From prosopon, "a face," and lambano, "to lay hold of." The word denotes making distinctions among people based on their rank or influence, showing preference for the rich and powerful. The impartial God shows to all people the same love, grace, blessings, and benefits of His salvation.

PASSED. (Josh. 3:4) 'abar (ah-var); Strong's #5674: To cross over, go over, go beyond, get over, go through, pass through, pass along, come over, pass beyond, transgress. 'Abar, translated in the KJV by more than sixty English words and phrases, occurs more than five hundred times. One of its meanings is "to pass from one side to the other side," pictured most easily by the crossing of a river, as in the present text. An important derivative is 'Ibri ("Hebrew"), the ethnic description of Abraham and, by extension, of his descendants. (See Gen. 14:13; Ex. 7:16; 1 Sam. 29:3.) 'Ibri has been regarded as a name for Eber's descendants. Eber was the great-grandson of Noah's son Shem, who was the father of all the Semitic peoples and a direct ancestor of Abraham. (See Gen. 11:10–26.) Thus, "Hebrews" would simply be one band or tribe of Semites. 'Ibri may also refer to one who had "crossed over" the Euphrates River from the eastern lands as Abraham did.

PATIENCE—forbearance under suffering and endurance in the face of adversity. Two Greek words are translated as patience: makrothymia (Heb. 6:12; James 5:10) and hypomone (Matt. 18:26, 29). The former word generally expresses patience with regard to people. It is also translated longsuffering as a quality of God (Rom. 2:4; 2 Pet. 3:9) and is listed by the apostle Paul as one of the nine fruits of the Holy Spirit (Gal. 5:22).

The second word, hypomone, generally expresses patience with regard to things. It may be described as the quality that enables a person to be "patient in tribulation" (Rom. 12:12). The Christian has for his example the patience of Jesus, who "endured the cross" (Heb. 12:2). The Christian is challenged to run with endurance the race that is set before him (Heb. 12:1).

PATIENCE. (Heb. 6:12) makrothumia (mak-roth-oo-mee-ah); Strong's #3115: From *makros,* "long," and *thumos,* "temper." The word denotes lenience, forbearance, fortitude, patient endurance, longsuffering. Also included in *makrothumia* is the ability to endure persecution and ill-treatment. It describes a person who has the power to exercise revenge but instead exercises restraint. This quality is a fruit of the Spirit (Gal. 5:22).

PATRIARCHS, PATRIARCHAL NARRATIVES— see ch. 55, §2.1., 3.5.b., 3.6., 6.2.

 PEACE—a word with several different meanings in the Old and New Testaments.

The Old Testament meaning of peace was completeness, soundness, and well-being of the total person. This peace was considered God-given, obtained by following the Law (Ps. 119:165). Peace sometimes had a physical meaning, suggesting security (Ps. 4:8), contentment (Is. 26:3), prosperity (Ps. 122:6–7), and the absence of war (1 Sam. 7:14). The traditional Jewish greeting, *shalom,* was a wish for peace.

In the New Testament, peace often refers to the inner tranquility and poise of the Christian whose trust is in God through Christ. This understanding was originally expressed in the Old Testament writings about the coming *Messiah (Is. 9:6–7). The peace that Jesus Christ spoke of was a combination of hope, trust, and quiet in the mind and soul, brought about by a reconciliation with God. Such peace was proclaimed by the host of angels at Christ's birth (Luke 2:14), and by Christ Himself in His Sermon on the Mount (Matt. 5:9) and during His ministry. He also taught about this kind of peace at the Lord's Supper, shortly before His death (John 14:27). Such peace and spiritual blessedness is a direct result of faith in Christ (Rom. 5:1).

PEACE. (Nah. 1:15) *shalom* (shah-*loam*); *Strong's #7965:* Completeness, wholeness, peace, health, welfare, safety, soundness, tranquility, prosperity, perfectness, fullness, rest, harmony; the absence of agitation or discord. *Shalom* comes from the root verb *shalam,* meaning "to be complete, perfect, and full." Thus *shalom* is much more than the absence of war and conflict; it is the wholeness that the entire human race seeks. The word *shalom* occurs about 250 times in the Old Testament (see Ps. 4:8; Is. 48:18; Jer. 29:11). In Psalm 35:27, God takes delight in the *shalom* (the wholeness, the total well-being) of His servant. In Isaiah 53:5, the chastisement necessary to bring us *shalom* was upon the suffering Messiah. The angels understood at His birth that Jesus was to be the great peace-bringer, as they called out, "Glory to God in the highest: and on earth peace, good-

will toward men!" (Luke 2:14–17; compare Is. 9:7). *Also* (Luke 1:79) *eirene* (eye-*ray*-nay); *Strong's #1515:* Compare "eirenicon," "irenic," and "Irene." A state of rest, quietness, and calmness; an absence of strife; tranquility. It generally denotes a perfect well-being. *Eirene* includes harmonious relationships between God and humanity, individuals and individuals, nations, and families. Jesus as Prince of Peace gives peace to those who call upon Him for personal salvation.

PENTATEUCH—see ch. 55, §2.1., 3.1.

PEOPLE. (Ruth 1:16) *'am (ahm); Strong's #5971:* The people. This word, occurring nearly two thousand times in the Old Testament, refers to a body of human beings unified as a nation. Frequently, Israel is called by God *'ami,* literally "My people," as in Exodus 9:13, or *ha-'am,* "the people," as in Exodus 1:20. *'Am,* people viewed from within the group, contrasts with *goi,* a nation viewed from outside the group.

PERCEIVED. (Luke 5:22) *epiginosko* (ep-ig-in-*oce*-koe); *Strong's #1921: Gnosis* is the noun, "knowledge," and *ginosko* is the verb, "to know." *Epiginosko* is to know fully; to know with a degree of thoroughness and competence; to be fully acquainted in a discerning, recognizing manner.

PERDITION—destruction, ruin, or waste, especially through the eternal destruction brought upon the wicked by God (Heb. 10:39; 2 Pet. 3:7). Jesus contrasted the broad way that leads to destruction with the difficult way that leads to life (Matt. 7:13–14). The apostle Paul contrasted perdition with salvation (Phil. 1:28). The "desire to be rich" may lead one to "destruction and perdition" (1 Tim. 6:9). Peter speaks of "the day of judgment and perdition of ungodly men" (2 Pet. 3:7), a perishing far worse than those destroyed in the Flood.

The New Testament twice uses the phrase *the son of perdition:* once of Judas Iscariot (John 17:12) and once of "the man of sin [or lawlessness]," whom some scholars identify with the Antichrist (2 Thess. 2:3). The phrase portrays the progression of an evil character who produces ruin in others and is headed toward final judgment (Rev. 17:8, 11). Perdition in this passage refers to a place of eternal punishment, the final state of the damned.

PERFECT, PERFECTION—without flaw or error, a state of completion or fulfillment. God's perfection means that He is complete in Himself. He lacks nothing; He has no flaws. He is perfect in all the characteristics of His nature. He is the basis for and standard by which all other perfection is to be measured (Job 36:4; Ps. 18:30; 19:7; Matt. 5:48).

By contrast, man's perfection is relative and dependent on God for its existence. As applied to a person's moral state in this life, perfection may refer either to a relatively blameless lifestyle (Gen. 6:9; Job 1:1; James 3:2) or to a person's maturity as a believer (Phil. 3:15; James 1:4). Because perfection in this life is never reached, man will continue to sin (Phil. 3:12, 15; 1 John 1:8). A believer's perfection in the next life, however, will be without sin (Eph. 5:27; Col. 1:28; 1 Thess. 5:23).

PERFECT. (Ps. 138:8) *gamar* (gah-*mar*); *Strong's #1584:* To end, finish, accomplish, perfect; to come to an end, cease; to perform, fulfill. This verb occurs five times in the Old Testament. Three times it refers to something or someone being cut off or brought to an end (7:9; 12:1; 77:8). Twice it refers to the completing, finishing, and perfecting of God's work in one's life (57:2; 138:8). These two references are Old Testament parallels to Philippians 1:6. The idea is that God begins to work out His purposes in the life of His servant and continues His work until it is absolutely and completely done. *Also* (James 3:2) *teleios* (*tel*-eye-oss); *Strong's #5046:* From *telos,* "end." *Teleios* refers to that which has reached an end, that is, finished, complete, perfect. When applied to persons, it signifies consummate soundness, and includes the idea of being whole. More particularly, when applied to believers, it denotes maturity.

PERFECTED. (1 John 2:5) *teleioo* (tel-eye-ah-oh); *Strong's #5048:* To complete, accomplish, carry through to the end, bring to a successful conclusion, reach a goal, fulfill. In an ethical and spiritual sense, the word signifies a bringing to maturity, a perfecting.

PERILOUS. (2 Tim. 3:1) *chalepos* (khal-ep-*oss*); *Strong's #5467:* Harsh, savage, difficult, dangerous, painful, fierce, grievous, hard to deal with. The word describes a society that is barren of virtue but abounding with vices.

PERISH. (Judg. 5:31) *'abad* (ah-*vahd*); *Strong's #6:* Destroy; be destroyed, perish, be ruined, be lost, fail. *'Abad* appears about 180 times in the Old Testament. Its range of meaning stretches from the destruction of a kingdom (2 Kin. 24:2) to the destruction, punishment, and ruination of the satanic figure in Ezekiel 28:16. *'Abad* is used to describe a "lost" sheep, or "perishing" sheep (Ps. 119:176). From *'abad* is derived "Abaddon." Generally regarded as destruction personified, Abaddon is a demonic prince in Revelation 9:11. In all six occur-

rences in the Old Testament, this word is translated "destruction."

PERSECUTION—the hatred and affliction that follows the witness and holy life of God's people in a hostile world. The concept is stressed in many of the Old Testament prophetic books, such as Isaiah. The New Testament also teaches that God's people will suffer persecution. Jesus taught that God's prophets always faced persecution (Matt. 5:12), so His disciples should expect the same (Matt. 10:23).

In the early church, two ideas were taken over from Judaism to express the meaning of persecution. The Jewish theologians taught that the death of the righteous sufferer had redemptive value. While this idea was applied primarily to Jesus by the early Christians, the persecution of His followers was seen as a participation in Jesus' suffering: filling up "what is lacking in the afflictions of Christ" (Col. 1:24). A good statement of this is that of Tertullian: "The blood of the martyrs is the seed of the Church."

The idea of the coming Messiah held that the suffering of God's people was part of the coming of the kingdom—evidence that a person is truly one of God's own. Therefore they are "blessed" (Matt. 5:10) and should "rejoice" and "glorify God" since "the time has come for judgment to begin at the house of God" (1 Pet. 4:13–17).

Jewish leaders' opposition to Christianity arose primarily among the Sadducees (Acts 4:1; 5:17). At first the common people and the Pharisees did not oppose the church strongly (Acts 5:14, 34; 23:6).

Roman opposition to Christianity also developed gradually. The Book of Acts emphasized Roman tolerance for the new religion. But this began to change with the Jewish riots against Christians in Rome, resulting in the Emperor Claudius banning both groups from Rome in A.D. 49. This set the stage for the intense opposition of later years that allowed Nero to make Christians the scapegoats for the fire which leveled Rome in A.D. 64. During this persecution the apostles Paul and Peter were martyred.

PERSEVERANCE—the steadfast effort to follow God's commands and to do His work. The New Testament makes it clear that faith alone can save. But it makes it equally clear that perseverance in doing good works is the greatest indication that an individual's faith is genuine (James 2:14–26). Indeed, perseverance springs from a faithful trust that God has been steadfast toward His people. Through persevering in God's work, the Christian proves his deep appreciation for God's saving grace (1 Cor. 15:57–58).

As a result of perseverance, the Christian can expect not only to enhance the strength of the church, but also to build up the strength of his own character (Rom. 5:3–4). In short, he can expect to become closer to God. He learns that he can persevere primarily because God is intimately related to him (Rom. 8:25–27) and especially because he has the assurance of a final reward in heaven (1 John 5:13).

PERSIA—see ch. 55, §2.2., 3.2.

PHARISEES—see ch. 55, §5.

PHILO—see ch. 55, §5.6.

PHOENICIA—see ch. 55, §3.4.a.

PHYSICIAN—a person skilled in the art of healing the sick. Both the Old and New Testaments frequently mention the curing of ailments, but specific details about how this was done are few.

In the ancient world, primitive medical practices were performed by magicians or priests. This was especially true in ancient Egypt, where even elementary brain surgery was attempted. Some of the Egyptian procedures were adopted by the Hebrews. These included embalming (Gen. 50:2–3, 26) or obstetrics, as with the midwives Shiphrah and Puah (Ex. 1:15).

Specific medical remedies are often recorded in the Bible. These include the application of bandages (Is. 1:6), oil (James 5:14), roots and leaves (Ezek. 47:12), wine (1 Tim. 5:23), and salves—particularly the balm of Gilead (Jer. 8:22).

In the New Testament, the Good Samaritan treated the wounded traveler's injuries with oil and wine (Luke 10:34). Luke, author of the Gospel of Luke, is called "the beloved physician" by the apostle Paul (Col. 4:14).

PILLAR—a word with several different meanings in the Bible:

1. The word pillar can refer to an architectural element that supports a roof. Use of pillars was common in the Near East long before the time of Abraham. Pillars were usually made of wood or stone. References to pillars as a part of a building occur throughout the Old Testament but not in the New Testament (Ex. 27:11; 1 Kin. 7:6, 15–22).

2. Pillars, or upright standing stones with religious significance, were used by both the Canaanites and the Israelites. In Canaanite worship places, a stone pillar was used as a symbol for the male god, usually Baal (2 Kin. 17:10). Moses erected twelve pillars, representing the twelve tribes of Israel, beside the altar he built to call upon the *covenant (Ex.

24:4). Pillars could also serve as boundary markers (Gen. 31:45) or as tombstones (Gen. 35:20).

3. The Bible also contains many figurative references to pillars. For instance, the physical demonstration of God's presence during the Exodus was described as a "pillar of fire" and a "pillar of cloud" (Ex. 13:21). In other places, the importance of persons or things is emphasized by referring to them as pillars (Gal. 2:9). That which holds something up, either figuratively or literally, can also be called a pillar (1 Sam. 2:8; 1 Tim. 3:15).

PILLAR OF FIRE AND CLOUD—the phenomenon by which God guided the Israelites during their travels through the wilderness after leaving Egypt (Ex. 14:24). The pillar of fire and cloud is first mentioned in Exodus 13:21–22, where some of its characteristics are described. In the form of cloud by day and fire by night, the pillar was constantly visible to the Israelites.

The pillar of fire and cloud was a visible sign or representation of God's presence with His people. In a sense God could be said to be "in" the pillar (Ex. 14:24); in it He led, protected them, and also "came down" to the tabernacle of meeting (Num. 12:5) and "appeared" at the tabernacle (Deut. 31:15).

PINNACLE OF THE TEMPLE—see ch. 55, §6.

PLEROMA [pleh RAUH muh]—a Greek word meaning "fullness." In the New Testament *pleroma* is used with two basic senses: (1) something that fills or completes, such as a patch in Matthew 9:16 or love in Romans 13:10; (2) fullness or the state or fact of being filled, such as the completed number of saved Gentiles (Rom. 11:25) or the "full measure" of Christ's blessing (Rom. 15:29, NIV). In some places in the Bible, distinguishing between these two meanings is difficult.

First Corinthians 10:26 (the earth's fullness) and Galatians 4:4 (the fullness of the time, Eph. 1:10) suggest God's sovereign appointment of events in both space and time. In Romans 11:12 *pleroma* refers to the completion of God's plan for the nation of Israel. The Lord Jesus Christ possesses the complete fullness of God's divine nature and attributes. "In Him dwells all the fullness of the Godhead bodily" (Col. 2:9).

The apostle Paul also used the phrase, "all the fullness of God" (Eph. 3:19), to show that Christ embodied the love of God. In Ephesians 4:13, "the fullness of Christ" means that state of Christian maturity in which believers are no longer "tossed to and fro and carried about with every wind of doctrine, by the trickery of men" (v. 14). There are other practical implications of this idea of the fullness of Christ. Knowing that He has been made full and "complete" in Christ (Col. 2:10), each Christian must be willing to accept whatever edifying suffering may be required to reach others, as Paul said, to "fill up in my flesh what is lacking in the afflictions of Christ, for the sake of His body" (Col. 1:24).

POOR—having little or no wealth and few or no possessions; lacking in financial or other resources. Although the poor will remain a part of society (Deut. 15:11; Matt. 26:11), the Bible instructs the righteous to show concern for them.

God takes up the cause of the poor. The psalms repeatedly emphasize that God helps them. He will "spare the poor and needy" (Ps. 72:13). He promises, "I will satisfy her poor with bread" (Ps. 132:15). The poor of the world can take comfort in the fact that God cares for them.

The divine compassion for the poor is demonstrated by Jesus (Luke 6:20). Luke, who especially emphasizes concern for the poor, relates Christ's mission statement from Isaiah, "He has anointed Me to preach the gospel to the poor" (Is. 61:1; Luke 4:18). The rich young man was instructed by Jesus to sell his possessions and "to distribute to the poor" (Luke 18:22). Jesus' followers cannot remain unconcerned about the poor of the world.

Instructions about considerate treatment of the poor are found in the Law, the Prophets, the Writings, and the New Testament. The Law, as well as the Prophets, warned against oppressing the poor and crushing the needy (Deut. 24:14; Prov. 14:31; Amos 2:6; 4:1). People of means were warned not to take advantage of the poor, especially in court: "You shall not pervert the judgment of your poor in his dispute" (Ex. 23:6; Amos 5:12). Help was to be given to the poor (Deut. 15:7–8; Is. 58:7). Such help was to be motivated by God's own action of providing the underprivileged with food and clothing (Deut. 10:18).

The extent to which God identifies with the poor is clear from Proverbs 19:17 and Matthew 25:34–40. Jesus instructed that the poor should be invited when a feast is prepared (Luke 14:12–14; Gal. 2:10). James warned against discrimination against the poor (Lev. 19:15; James 2:2–4).

POOR. (Ps. 40:17) *'ani* (ah-*nee*); *Strong's* #6041: Poor, afflicted, needy; lowly, humble; low in status. *'Ani* may refer to the person whose outward condition makes him poor, afflicted, or depressed. It may also refer to the person who inwardly is lowly, humble, and absolutely not self-exalting. God maintains the

cause of these afflicted (140:12). In Isaiah 61:1, God commissions the Messiah to preach the Good News specifically to the poor. To be of a lowly status is neither a crime nor an indication of lack of faith, as the testimony of the heroes of faith amply demonstrates (*see* Heb. 11:36–40).

POOR (BECAME). (2 Cor. 8:9) *ptocheuo* (ptokhyoo-oh); *Strong's* #4433: To be destitute, poor as a beggar, reduced to extreme poverty. The word suggests the bottom rung of poverty, a situation in which one is totally lacking in this world's goods.

POOR IN SPIRIT—those who admit their spiritual inadequacy and cast themselves on the mercy of God (Matt. 5:3). The poor in spirit are the opposite of the proud, the arrogant, the self-righteous who boast of their own goodness. Jesus' parable of the Pharisee and the tax collector (Luke 18:9–14) illustrates this contrast.

The Gospel of Luke declares, "Blessed are you poor, for yours is the kingdom of God" (Luke 6:20). The poor in spirit are those who look to the Lord for justice, mercy, and deliverance, and not to themselves.

POSSESS. (Deut. 8:1) *yarash* (yah-*rash*); *Strong's* #3423: To inherit, possess, seize, occupy. This verb occurs more than 250 times in the Old Testament. Its great importance is seen in God's promises to Abraham, Isaac, and Jacob. Repeatedly in Genesis God pledges to give the land of Canaan to Abraham's descendants as an everlasting possession.

POSSESSION. (Josh. 22:9) *'achuzzah* (ahchooz-zah); *Strong's* #272: Something obtained, seized, or held. *'Achuzzah* usually refers to the land of Israel (or any portion of it), which is to be held forever by Jacob's descendants. In Psalm 2:8, God promises His Messiah the remotest parts of the earth (that is, the whole earth) for His possession (*'achuzzah*). The related verb form is *'achaz*, meaning to seize, acquire, lay hold of, get, obtain, catch, take possession, grasp. This word is frequently translated "take hold of," as in Exodus 15:15 and Job 38:13.

POSSIBLE. (Matt. 19:16) *dunatos* (doo-natoss); *Strong's* #1415: Compare "dynasty," "dynamite," "dynamo," and "dynamic." Strong, mighty, powerful. In the neuter form, the word means "possible." The inherent idea is that of having the ability to act and the power to accomplish. Christ gives assurance that however powerless our efforts to make things happen, He can demonstrate the dynamic power that translates people from Satan's realm to God's kingdom.

POVERTY. (Rev. 2:9) *ptocheia* (pto-*khi*-ah); *Strong's #4432:* From a root meaning "to cower." The word indicates a state of abject poverty, destitution, indigence. In the New Testament it describes the voluntary poverty that Christ experienced on our behalf (2 Cor. 8:9); the condition of saints in Macedonia (2 Cor. 8:2); and the extreme want of the church of Smyrna (Rev. 2:9).

POWER—the ability or strength to perform an activity or deed. Power is sometimes used with the word authority. If power suggests physical strength, authority suggests a moral right or privilege. One can have power to perform a task but not authority to do it. Jesus Christ had both power and authority (Luke 4:36), and He bestowed these upon His followers (Luke 10:19).

POWER. (Deut. 8:18) *koach* (*ko*-akh); *Strong's #3581:* Vigor, strength, force, capacity, power, wealth, means, or substance. Generally the word means "capacity" or "ability," whether physical, mental, or spiritual. Here Moses informs Israel that it is God who gives to them the "ability" (power, means, endurance, capacity) to obtain wealth, for material blessings are included in the promises to the patriarchs and their descendants. Moses strictly warns Israel in verse 17 not to falsely conclude that this capacity for success is an innate talent, but to humbly acknowledge that it is a God-given ability. *Also* (Mark 3:15) *exousia* (ex-oo-*see*-ah); *Strong's #1849:* One of four power words (*dunamis, exousia, ischus,* and *kratos*), *exousia* means the authority or right to act, ability, privilege, capacity, delegated authority. Jesus had the *exousia* to forgive sin, heal sicknesses, and cast out devils. *Exousia* is the right to use *dunamis,* "might." Jesus gave His followers *exousia* to preach, teach, heal, and deliver (v. 15), and that authority has never been rescinded (John 14:12). Powerless ministries become powerful upon discovering the *exousia* power resident in the name of Jesus and the blood of Jesus. *Also* (Acts 4:33) *dunamis* (*doo*-nam-is); *Strong's #1411:* Dunamis means energy, power, might, great force, great ability, strength. It is sometimes used to describe the powers of the world to come at work upon the earth and divine power overcoming all resistance. (Compare "dynamic," "dynamite," and "dynamometer.") The *dunamis* in Jesus resulted in dramatic transformations. This is the norm for the Spirit-filled and Spirit-led church. *Also* (1 Tim. 6:16) *kratos* (*krat*-oss); *Strong's #2904:* Dominion, strength, manifested power. The word especially signifies exerted strength, power shown effectively in a reigning authority. (Compare "theocracy," "aristocracy," "democracy.") Although it is used in Hebrews 2:14 of the devil's power of death, *kratos* primarily refers to God's kingdom authority, dominion, and majesty.

POWERFUL. (Heb. 4:12) *energes* (en-er-*gace*); *Strong's #1756:* Comparable in meaning to the English word "energetic," which stems from this word. *Energes,* used elsewhere only in 1 Corinthians 16:9 and Philemon 6, denotes something at work, active, and effective. It is the opposite of *argos,* "idle," "inactive," "ineffective."

PRAISE—an act of worship or acknowledgment by which the virtues or deeds of another are recognized and extolled. Praise is revealed as the means by which God's rule and presence may be invited into the midst of any group or private situation or circumstance: The Lord is "enthroned in the praises of Israel" (Ps. 22:3). The praise of man toward man, although often beneficial (1 Cor. 11:2; 1 Pet. 2:14), can be a snare to man (Prov. 27:21; Matt. 6:1–5). But the praise of God toward man is the highest commendation a person can receive. Such an act of praise reflects a true servant's heart (Matt. 25:21; 1 Cor. 4:5; Eph. 1:3–14).

The praise of man toward God is the means by which we express our joy to the Lord. We are to praise God both for who He is and for what He does (Ps. 150:2). Praising God for who He is is called adoration; praising Him for what He does is known as thanksgiving. Praise of God may be in song or prayer, individually or collectively, spontaneous or prearranged, originating from the emotions or from the will.

The godly person will echo David's words, "My praise shall be continually of You . . . And [I] will praise You yet more and more" (Ps. 71:6, 14).

PRAISE. (1 Chr. 23:30) *halal* (hah-*lahl*); *Strong's #1984:* To praise, to thank; rejoice, boast about someone. *Halal* is the root from which "hallelujah" is formed. The phrase is a command: *hallelu-Jah* (all of you must praise *Jah*). *Halal* usually conveys the idea of speaking or singing about the glories, virtues, or honor of someone or something. *Also* (Ps. 63:3) *shabach* (shah-*vahch*); *Strong's #7623:* To commend, praise; to adore; to glory in something; to still, quiet, or pacify someone. *Shabach* goes in two directions, "praising" and "calming." The verb occurs eleven times in the Old Testament, eight of these having to do with speaking words of praise. The other three references speak either about calming the tumultuous sea (65:7; 89:9) or about hushing up things within one's heart (Prov.

29:11). There appears to be a connection between "praising with words" and "soothing with words," as any aggrieved individual offered words of honor can testify. *Also* (Ps. 100:4) *tehillah* (te-hil-*lah,* or in the plural, te-hil-*lim*); *Strong's #8416:* A celebration, a lauding of someone praiseworthy; the praise or exaltation of God; praises, songs of admiration. The noun *tehillah* comes from the verb *halal,* which means "to praise, celebrate, and laud." The Hebrew title of the Book of Psalms is *Tehillim,* literally the Book of Praises. The Book of Psalms was actually the Psalter or songbook for worship events in the temple in Jerusalem. Suitable for prayer or recitation, but especially designed for singing, the Psalms provide the means for eager hearts to express their praises to Israel's Holy One. *Also* (Eph. 1:6) *epainos* (*ep*-ahee-noss); *Strong's #1868:* Approbation, commendation, approval, praise. *Epainos* expresses not only praise for what God does for us, but also for who He is, recognizing His glory.

PRAISE, THE PATHWAY OF. Man was created to live and breathe in an atmosphere of praise-filled worship to His Creator. The avenue of sustained inflow of divine power was to be kept by the sustained outflow of joyous and humble praise to his Maker. The severance of the bond of blessing-through-obedience that sin brought silenced man's praise-filled fellowship with God and introduced self-centeredness, self-pitying, and complaint (*see* Gen. 3:9–12). But now has come salvation and life in Christ, and now upon receiving Jesus Christ as Savior, daily living calls us to prayer and the Word for fellowship and wisdom in living. Our daily approach to God in that communion is to be paved with praise: "Enter into His gates with thanksgiving, and into His courts with praise" (Ps. 100:4). Such a walk of praise-filled openness to Him will cultivate deep devotion, faithful obedience, and constant joy. The intention of this study is to show believers how praise can bring steadfastness in godly living while teaching a praise-walk that is neither fanatical, glib, nor reduced to mere ritual, but one of life-delivering power available to each believer.

1. "Judah" Means "Praise" (Gen. 29:35). "Judah" means "Praise," and out of this man comes a great tribe of Israel. This is one of the most significant praise verses in the Bible. Observe the following passages: (1) Jacob (49:8–12) speaks important words over Judah, giving him the highest blessing. His brothers will praise him. He will triumph over all his enemies. Verse 10 says Judah will have royal authority (scepter) and legal authority (law-giver) and will bring forth the Messiah. (2) Out of Judah, through David, comes the Christ, who in every action and detail is a praise to the Father (Luke 3:23–33). (3) The tribe of Judah (Praise) led Israel through the wilderness (Num. 2:3, 9). (4) They led in the conquest of Canaan (Judg. 1:1–19). (5) Judah is the first tribe to praise David, making him king (2 Sam. 2:1–11).

2. Praise Cures "Dry Times" (Num. 21:16–17). Praise is the cure for the "dry times" that come to every believer, for here the praise of God caused waters to flow from a well. Note four truths: (1) God's *instruction*—"Gather the people together." There is unity and power in corporate gathering. (2) God's *promise*—"I will give them water [life]." (3) The people's *responsibility*—They sang, "Spring up, O well! All of you sing to it." (4) Our *lesson*—In times of pressure, anxiety, or depression, do not stay alone. Gather with God's people, especially a praising people. Regardless of your personal feelings, join in audible praise, and sing to your well—the living God. Let your song be one of thanksgiving for past blessings and a song of faith in God's promises for the present and the future!

3. Power in Unity of Praise (2 Chr. 5:13). This text demonstrates the power in unity of praise, thanksgiving, and music: (1) the trumpeters and singers were as *one*; (2) to make *one sound* in praise and thanksgiving to the Lord, saying "For He is good, for His mercy endures [lasts] forever"; (3) The house (temple) was filled with a cloud (the glory of God's *presence.*)

Remember, even in praise, thanksgiving, and worship, "God is not the author of confusion" (1 Cor. 14:33). Anything said or done that draws attention to the praiser/worshiper and away from God, Jesus, and the Holy Spirit needs to be reconsidered.

4. Powerful Praise Births Victory (2 Chr. 20:15–22). Here is a great lesson on the power of *praise.* Judah was confronted by mortal enemies, Moab and Ammon. The people sought God in prayer and with faith in His Word (20:1–14). Then came the word of the prophet: "Do not be afraid . . . for the battle is not yours, but God's" (v. 15).

The victory came in a strange but powerful manner. The Levites stood and praised "the LORD God of Israel with voices loud and high" (v. 19). Then some were actually appointed to sing to the Lord and praise Him in the beauty of holiness. These went before the army, saying: "Praise the LORD, for His mercy endures [lasts] forever" (v. 21). The result of this powerful praise was total *victory!*

5. Praise Stops the Advancement of Wicked-

ness (Ps. 7:14–17). This short passage contains two truths about praise.

First, praise is the answer when wickedness and iniquity come against the believer. Temptation to sin and live wickedly will soon disappear in the face of sincere, powerful, and audible praise. This will bring the glorious presence of Jesus, driving out the desire to identify with the sinful act and/or thought.

Second, in verse 17 the writer declares, "I will praise the LORD." Praise is an act of the will. It is not merely an exuberance overflowing with words, but a self-induced declaration of thanksgiving—a sacrifice. The praiser *chooses* to praise.

Learn this about praise: (1) Do not wait until all conditions and circumstances are favorable, but (2) offer a thanksgiving of praise *because* God is *worthy* and it is *right*. (See also Is. 12:1–3 and Jer. 33:11.)

6. Praise Spotlights God (Ps. 18:3). Here is the most basic reason for our praise to God: He is "worthy to be praised [Hebrew *halal*, "praise with a loud voice"]." The most primitive meaning of *halal* is "to cause to shine." Thus, with our praise, we are throwing the spotlight on our God, who is worthy and deserves to be praised and glorified. The more we put the spotlight on Him, the more He causes us to shine. Modern medicine attests to the value of bringing a depressed person into a brightly lighted room, acknowledging that light greatly helps to heal their depression. How much more will praise introduce the light of God and bring us into the joy of the Lord.

7. Praise, the Pathway to God's Presence (Ps. 22:3–4). Unquestionably, one of the most remarkable and exciting things about honest and sincere praise is taught here: *Praise will bring the presence of God.* Although God is everywhere present, there is a distinct manifestation of His rule, which enters the environment of praise. Here is the remedy for times when you feel alone, deserted, or depressed. Praise! However simply, compose your song and testimony of God's goodness in your life. *The result:* God enters! His presence will live (take up residence) in our lives. The word "inhabit" (Hebrew *yawshab*) means "to sit down, to remain, to settle, or marry." In other words, God does not merely visit us when we praise Him, but His presence abides with us and we partner with Him in a growing relationship. Let this truth create faith and trust, and lead to deliverance from satanic harassments, torment, or bondage. Notice how this text ties three words together: "praises," "trusted," and "delivered"!

8. Sing Praises with Understanding (Ps. 47:7).

The word "understanding" (Hebrew *sakal*, "prudent or cautious, and hence, intelligent") is linked to wisdom and prosperity. Proverbs 21:16 provides contrast to such understanding: "A man who wanders from the way of understanding will rest in the assembly of the dead." But when we "sing praises with understanding," we are giving testimony to God's love for us and our love for Him. Life results instead of death. Others, listening to us praise God, hear testimony of our salvation and our joyful relationship with Him, which often leads to their own salvation.

9. Praise, the Road to Success (Ps. 50:22–23). This whole chapter relates God's power, majesty, and glory, and is summed up in these closing verses, which apply to us as well as to the people of Israel. If we leave God out of our lives and live in rebellion, destruction follows. In contrast, the simple road to success is set forth: (1) Offer praise, and we glorify God. The focus of praise is directed toward God, but in His wisdom we are the ultimate beneficiaries. (2) We receive power to order our conduct; thus, our lifestyle comes into obedience to God. (3) *Result:* We receive a revelation (understanding)—that is, insight into God's salvation. Our praise becomes a vehicle for God to come to us and to minister through us.

10. Praise Releases Blessings and Satisfaction (Ps. 63:1–5). This classic passage teaches how *expressed* praise releases the blessings of praise. Notice, this is not a silent prayer: "My mouth shall praise You with joyful lips." And look at the fruit: (1) "O God, You are my God" (affirmed relationship); (2) "Early will I seek You" (clear priorities); (3) "My soul thirsts . . . My flesh longs for You" (deep intensity); (4) "I have looked for You in the sanctuary, to see Your power and glory" (desire for corporate involvement); (5) "Because Your lovingkindness is better than life, my lips shall praise You" (appropriate gratitude); (6) *Result:* "My soul [the real me] shall be satisfied as with marrow and fatness" (personal needs met).

11. Creative Praise Stays Lively (Ps. 71:14). Here the psalmist makes a commitment: "I . . . will praise You [God] yet more and more." The idea expressed is beautiful, saying, "I will find *fresh* and *new* ways to express my praise toward God." This does not mean to abandon the old ways but to become as creative in our praises to God as God is creative in meeting our needs. Thus we will not fall prey to careless praise, which becomes dull and boring and ends in merely mouthing phrases. *God wants us to be creative.*

12. Teach Your Children Praise (Ps. 145:4). This verse emphasizes the importance of passing on the praise of God from one generation to another. Praise is to be taught to our children. The Bible enjoins us to raise a generation of praisers. We must not merely "suppose" that children will grow up and desire God. We must be careful. Whatever we possess of God's blessing and revelation can be lost in one generation. We must consistently praise Him and we must also teach (by example, as well as by words), so our children and our children's children will do the same.

13. A Mighty Appeal to Praise (Ps. 150:1–6).
The Psalms conclude with a mighty appeal to praise the Lord. Some psalms are desperate cries, some filled with thanksgiving, and some have theologically or historically based instructions to "praise the LORD" for His own Person, holiness, power, or goodness. But the climax is a command to praise the Lord. We are to praise God (1) in His sanctuary—that is, His earthly temple and throughout His created universe and (2) for His mighty acts and according to His excellent greatness. Then a list of instruments and ways to praise follows. This list is not exhaustive but demonstrates how creative our praise is to be. Finally, in case even one person feels less than inclined to praise Him, the instruction is clear: If you have God's gift of life-breath, you should praise Him. Hallelujah!

14. The Glorious Garment of Praise (Is. 61:3).
The Hebrew root for "garment" (`atah) shows praise as more than a piece of clothing casually thrown over our shoulders. It literally teaches us "to wrap" or "cover" ourselves—that the garment of praise is to leave no openings through which hostile elements can penetrate. This garment of praise repels and replaces the heavy spirit. This special message of instruction and hope is for those oppressed by fear or doubt. "Put on" this garment. A warm coat from our closet only resists the cold wind when it is "put on." When distressed, be dressed—with praise! Act according to God's Word!

15. Perfected Praise Produces Power (Matt. 21:16).
In response to the criticism levelled against this verbal praise, which was powerful, vocal, and strong, Jesus quotes Psalm 8:2 and reminds us of a great secret. Perfected praise will produce strength! It is powerful! At the very moment Jesus is being rejected by the leaders, these young people are captivated by the full meaning of who Jesus is. Capturing this revelation about Him causes loud and powerful praise to come forth. How heartening this must have been to Jesus as He marched toward the Cross!

16. Praise Springs Open Prison Doors (Acts
16:25–26). Study this example of the power of praise, even in difficult circumstances. Beaten and imprisoned, Paul and Silas respond by singing a hymn of praise—a song sung directly from the heart to God. The relationship between their song of praise and their supernatural deliverance through the earthquake cannot be overlooked. Praise directed toward God can shake open prison doors! A man was converted, his household saved, and satanic captivity overthrown in Philippi. Today, as well, praise will cause every chain of bondage to drop away. When you are serving God and things do not go the way you planned, learn from this text. Praise triumphs gloriously!

17. Encouraging One Another in Praise (Eph. 5:18–19).
This text instructs interaction in our praise. Paul tells the Ephesians to "[speak] to one another," using psalms and hymns and spiritual songs. Entering a gathering of believers, even with a small offering of praise, our worship begins to be magnified as we join with others. Their voices encourage us, and we inspire them. Separation from the local assembly deprives a person of this relationship and its strength. Let us assemble often and praise much—encouraging one another in praise.

18. Praise Releases the Spirit of Prophecy (Heb. 2:11–12).
This text quotes the messianic prophecy in Psalm 22:22, showing how the Spirit of the Christ fills the New Testament church, and how Christ identifies Himself so closely with His people when they sing praises. As they do, two important things happen: (1) He joins in the song Himself, and (2) this praise releases the spirit of prophecy. The latter is in the words "I will declare Your name to My brethren." As we joyfully sing praise to our God, Christ comes to flood our minds with the glory of the Father's character ("name"). There is no doubt about it—the praises of the people in the church service release the spirit of prophetic revelation—the magnifying of God through Jesus Christ. Thus, praise introduces edification, exhortation, and comfort to bless the whole body.

19. The Sacrifice of Praise (Heb. 13:10–15).
Why is praising God a sacrifice? The word "sacrifice" (Greek thusia) comes from the root thuo, a verb meaning "to kill or slaughter for a purpose." Praise often requires that we "kill" our pride, fear, or sloth—anything that threatens to diminish or interfere with our worship of the Lord. We also discover here the basis of all our praise: the sacrifice of our Lord Jesus Christ. It is by Him, in Him, with Him, to Him, and for Him that we offer our sacrifice of praise to God. Praise will never be successfully

hindered when we keep its focus on Him—the Founder and Completer of our salvation. His Cross, His blood—His love gift of life and forgiveness to us—keep praise as a *living* sacrifice!

20. Worshipful Walk with God (1 Pet. 2:9). This text not only appoints praise, but represents *a basic revelation of the Bible*: God wants a people who will walk with Him in prayer, march with Him in praise, and thank and worship Him. Note the progression in Peter's description of the people of the New Covenant: (1) *We are a chosen generation*—a people begun with Jesus' choice of the Twelve, who became 120, to whom were added thousands at Pentecost. We are a part of this continually expanding generation, "chosen" when we receive Christ. (2) *We are a royal priesthood.* Under the Old Covenant the priesthood and royalty were separated. We are now—in the Person of our Lord—all "kings and priests to His God" (Rev. 1:6), a worshiping host and a kingly band, prepared for walking with Him in the light or warring beside Him against the hosts of darkness. (3) *We are a holy nation*, composed of Jews and Gentiles—of one blood, from every nation under heaven. (4) *We are His own special people.* God's intention from the time of Abraham has been to call forth a people with a special mission—to proclaim His praise and to propagate His blessing throughout the earth. C.G.

PRAY. (Ps. 122:6) *sha'al* (shah-*ahl*); *Strong's* #7592: To ask, inquire, request, pray, desire, wish for, demand. *Sha'al* is not the usual Hebrew word for "pray," but it has the suggestion of "asking for" or "inquiring about" something. In this psalm for the sake of God's people and for the sake of the Lord's house (vv. 8–9) we are instructed to seek Jerusalem's good, that is, to inquire earnestly about its welfare, pray for its peace, and ask with true concern about its condition. From *sha'al* comes the proper name *Sha'ul* (Saul), meaning "Asked For" or "Requested," that is to say, a wanted child. *Also* (Matt. 6:6) *proseuchomai* (pros-*yoo*-khom-ahee); *Strong's* #4336: The word is progressive. Starting with the noun, *euche*, which is a prayer to God that also includes making a vow, the word expands to the verb *euchomai,* a special term describing an invocation, request, or entreaty. Adding *pros,* "in the direction of" (God), *proseuchomai* becomes the most frequent word for prayer.

PRAYED. (Job 42:10) *palal* (pah-*lahl*); *Strong's* #6419: To pray, entreat, intercede, make supplication. This verb occurs more than eighty times. *Palal* speaks of prayer as intercession, asking someone with more power and wisdom to intervene in behalf of the one praying. For example, Hannah prayed for a son (1 Sam. 1:12); Hezekiah prayed for an extension of his life (Is. 38:2, 3); and Jonah prayed from within the fish's belly (Jon. 2:1–9). Furthermore, *palal* is found in the promise of 2 Chronicles 7:14, "If My people . . . will humble themselves, and pray . . . I will hear from heaven." See other intercessory examples of *palal* in Genesis 20:7, 17; Numbers 11:2; and 1 Samuel 12:23.

PRAYER—communication with God. Because God is personal, all people can offer prayers.

Believers, recognizing their dependence upon their Creator and Savior, cultivate all forms of prayer: praise, worship, thanksgiving, confession, adoration, holy meditation (waiting on God), petition, supplication, intercession, and spiritual warfare. Kingdom life articles are joined herewith to expand prayer, faith, worship and warfare in great detail.

Prayer should not be thought of as a mystical experience in which people lose their identity in the infinite reality. Effective prayer must be a scripturally informed response of persons saved by grace to the living God who can hear and answer on the basis of Christ's payment of the penalty which sinners deserved. Prayer involves several important aspects.

Faith. The most meaningful prayer comes from a heart that places its trust in the God who has acted and spoken in the Jesus of history and the teachings of the Bible. God speaks to us through the Bible, and we in turn speak to Him in trustful, believing prayer. Assured by the Scripture that God is personal, living, active, all-knowing, all-wise, and all-powerful, we know that God can hear and help us. A confident prayer life is built on the cornerstone of Christ's work and words as shown by the prophets and apostles in the Spirit-inspired writings of the Bible.

Worship. In worship we recognize what is of highest worth—not ourselves, others, or our work, but God. Only the highest divine being deserves our highest respect. Guided by Scripture, we set our values in accord with God's will and perfect standards. Before God, angels hide their faces and cry, "Holy, holy, holy is the Lord of hosts" (Is. 6:3).

Confession. Awareness of God's holiness leads to consciousness of our own sinfulness. Like the prophet Isaiah, we exclaim, "Woe is me, for I am undone! Because I am a man of unclean lips, and I dwell in the midst of a people of unclean lips; for my eyes have seen the King, the Lord of hosts" (Is. 6:5). We must confess our sins to God to get right with Him, and

He promises to forgive us of all our unrighteousness (1 John 1:9).

Adoration. God is love, and He has demonstrated His love in the gift of His Son. The greatest desire of God is that we love Him with our whole being (Matt. 22:37). Our love should be expressed, as His has been expressed, in both deeds and words. People sometimes find it difficult to say to others and to God, "I love you." But when love for God fills our lives, we will express our love in prayer to the One who is ultimately responsible for all that we are.

Praise. The natural outgrowth of faith, worship, confession, and adoration is praise. We speak well of one whom we highly esteem and love. The one whom we respect and love above all others naturally receives our highest commendation. We praise Him for His "mighty acts . . . according to His excellent greatness!" (Ps. 150:2), and for His "righteous judgments" (Ps. 119:164). For God Himself, for His works, and for His words, His people give sincere praise.

Thanksgiving. Thankfulness will flow ceaselessly from the understanding soul. God has forgiven our sins, granted us acceptance as His people, and given us His righteous standing and a new heart and life. What reasons to thank Him! While ingratitude marks the ungodly (Rom. 1:21), the believer lives thankfully, seeing God at work on his or her behalf in countless ways. So, in everything we give thanks (Col. 3:17; 1 Thess. 5:18).

PRAYER. (2 Chr. 6:20) *tephillah* (teh-feel-*lah*); *Strong's* #8605: Prayer, supplication, intercession. *Tephillah* occurs more than seventy-five times in the Old Testament, thirty-two of these in the Psalms. In the present reference, prayer from the temple in Jerusalem was afforded special significance, for day and night God watched over that house of prayer. From *tephillah* comes the word *tephilin,* which refers to the bands wound around the arm of a devout Jew as he prepares for his time of prayer.

PRAYER AND SPIRITUAL DEVELOPMENT. The night before His crucifixion, Jesus underscored the privileged pathway of prayer now being opened to His own through His Cross: "Until now you have asked nothing in My name. Ask, and you will receive, that your joy may be full" (John 15:24). By His own emphasis, Jesus placed prayer at the heart of Christian living. When the pulse is steady and the body exercised in this practice, every other facet of life flows with health as the individual is fed by God's Word. Yet prayer is a puzzle to some who think it too mystical and a problem

for others who find the habit hard to establish. This study seeks to help people to practical, applicable-to-life patterns of prayer, as well as unveiling prayer secrets that help for habits by igniting understanding which prompts believers into dynamic prayer-patterns, rather than merely issuing rules. The result is prayer that builds blessing and fruitfulness in your life.

1. Prayer Principles from God's Conversation with Abraham (Gen. 18:17–33). At least three important principles emerge from God's conversation with Abraham in chapter 18. (1) Wicked Sodom could have been spared for the sake of only ten righteous people. From this we learn that it is not the presence of *evil* that brings God's mercy and long-suffering to an end; rather, it is the absence of *good!* (2) Although God sometimes inspires us to pray by showing us things to come (v. 17), our intercession must be in line with God's character and covenant with humankind. Like Abraham, we may appeal to God to preserve His name, honor, and perfect justice before the world (v. 25). (3) Although we often measure influence by numbers, human arithmetic cannot be used to estimate the impact of the righteous. God saves by many or by few.

2. The Heart of the Intercessor (Ex. 32:11–14, 30–34). Moses' true character was revealed in the response he made in prayer when he learned of Israel's ingratitude and rejection. Focusing on *God's* honor, not his *own,* Moses begged God not to destroy Israel. After renewing Israel's commitment to God, Moses stood in the gap for Israel, offering his life for theirs (Ps. 106:23).

Afterward, Moses returned to the mountain another forty days to receive again God's commandments (Ex. 34:1–28). Israel could not blame God for the delay; their own sins had delayed God's purposes for them. Yet those purposes remained intact because Moses had stood between Israel's sin and God's wrath. Unselfish intercession prevails beyond the otherwise destructive effects of human weakness and sin.

3. Joshua and His Warriors Stand in the Gap (Josh. 10:12–14). Strengthened by God's assurance of victory, but knowing they must *fight* to possess that promise, Joshua's select warriors responded to Gibeon's plea for help. Their struggle illustrates a classic syndrome of spiritual life. No sooner had Joshua and Israel conquered Jericho and Ai than five Amorite kings attacked Gibeon to punish it and block Israel's advance. (In a similar way, Satan forges weapons to war upon those who are moving in conquest for Christ.) The battle was long and fierce. Fearful that the sun would set before the enemy was annihilated, Joshua's prayer of faith touched God's omnipotence: the sun and moon—worshiped by the Amorites—stood still at Joshua's command, not only allowing Israel's success in battle, but demonstrating the ineffectiveness of the demon-gods embraced by their opponents. Joshua and his warriors stood in the gap, contending for God's eternal purposes and teaching the triumph such faith and tenacity may realize in our spiritual warfare!

4. God Intervenes with Power (Is. 36:1—37:40). Hezekiah's being threatened with destruction by Sennacherib's army reminds us that even the righteous are often overtaken by trouble. The Assyrian monarch invaded Judah, took forty-six fortified cities, carried away two hundred thousand people, and shut up Hezekiah in Jerusalem like a bird in a cage. But note how Isaiah and Hezekiah went to prayer, their anguish over Sennacherib's blasphemy of God's name rising above their anxiety for Jerusalem (37:16–17).

Consider the magnitude of the crisis. If Sennacherib had taken Jerusalem, the Jews could have ceased to exist as a nation. The messianic promise of God's kingdom's eventually triumphing on earth was in the balance. But when Hezekiah and Isaiah prayed, God intervened with a demonstration of supernatural power that proved to Assyria that He was God indeed (37:36). From that point on, Assyria, which had enjoyed a two-century span of conquests, began its decline—a lesson in the power of prayer to (1) face troublesome times and (2) break evil powers.

5. Intercessors Link God's Mercy with Human Need (Ezek. 22:30). In Ezekiel's day, Judah was all that remained of God's vineyard, His chosen people. The idolatrous kingdom of Israel had been destroyed and its people exiled under the Assyrian ruler Sargon in 722 B.C. Now, almost a century and a half later, sin had made a horrendous gap in Judah's protective wall. A "gap" was a break in the protective thorny hedge or wall of stones that surrounded a vineyard and invited trouble. To bar intruders, someone had to stand guard until the gap could be repaired. Therefore, the Word employs this figure of speech to describe God's search for an intercessor among Judah's priests, prophets, princes, or people—for those who would stand in the gap, linking God's mercy with man's need. In our day, the protective hedge about families, churches, and nations is often in a state of terrible disrepair. God is still searching for intercessors to stand guard "in the gap" and by prayer to help repair the breaches.

6. Spiritual Leaders: Pray as Well as Teach (Eph. 3:14–21). Spiritual leaders must pray for their people as well as teach them. Paul prayed that his fellow believers might know the strength of the Spirit's reinforcement in the inner person, just as a storm-tossed ship on which he once sailed was strengthened inside by bracings and undergirded outside by cables (Acts 27:17). Knowing that the strength of Christianity is not outward laws but inward character, Paul prayed that Christ might enter through the open door of faith, dwell in their hearts, and imprint His nature upon their minds, wills, and emotions. When Christ enters a life, He brings His life—the very soil in which we take root and blossom, the ground in which our lives are founded. Prayer begets prayer, for the believer in whom Christ's love is bringing the fullness of God will learn to ask and expect great things from Him!

7. Prayer and Fasting Birth Signs and Wonders (Acts 13:1—14:28). The signs-and-wonders ministry of Paul and Barnabas was birthed as church leaders prayed, fasted, and sought the Lord. After the Holy Spirit Himself had called the two men, the leaders laid hands upon them and sent them forth (13:1–4). Later, Paul and Barnabas followed that same pattern, traveling from city to city, strengthening disciples and ordaining elders in the churches (14:22–23). What is that pattern? Every ministry sent forth is God's intercessor, standing between the overflowing abundance of God and the overwhelming need of humanity. Therefore, those who send them must be moved by the Holy Spirit through prayer, not by their own spirits, to send men and women whom God has anointed and appointed. When today's church discovers direction for and advances all ministry in and through prayer, we will see opposition and unbelief bow before us as, once again, God confirms His Word with signs and wonders (14:3).

8. Prayer, the Proving Grounds of Our Faith (Acts 4:1–37). See the early church's response when persecutors tried to shut down the Christian movement? They went to prayer! Often the things that threaten to suffocate or destroy the church turn out to be the means of its preservation and advance. This persecution was sparked by controversy over a miracle, just as skeptics still debate the relationship of miracles to Christianity. These early believers knew that if it could be established that the lame man's healing had been accomplished in the name and power of Jesus, Christ's power and authority would be clearly confirmed. Therefore, they went to prayer. The results? Great grace and boldness. Great power and unity (vv. 32–34). They teach us the pathway to proving the reality of our faith: not debate or argument, but prayer.

9. God's Holy Fire Falls (2 Chr. 6:12–42; 7:1). When Solomon dedicated the temple, which he had built so God could dwell among His people, he brought before the Lord petitions regarding many situations that would concern Israel in the future: sin, enemies, forgiveness, drought, pestilence, war, captivity, and so on. Each petition was followed by a plea that God would hear Israel's prayers and answer.

When Solomon's petitions ended, God dramatically demonstrated His approval of the temple and His acceptance of Solomon's prayer. A bolt of fire came out of heaven, consuming the sacrifices and burnt offerings. Then the glory of the Lord filled the temple.

There are lessons here for us, for God now dwells in the temples of our hearts (see 1 Cor. 3:16). If we seek Him, He is instantly with us. The moment we lay our choicest gifts upon the altar, His holy fire falls. And whenever we make room for God, He always comes and fills!

10. Unceasing Prayer Is a Key to Deliverance (Acts 12:1–17). This conflict is a study in ongoing confrontation with evil. The Herods symbolize Satan's relentless attack on the church. Herod the Great had sought to kill Jesus; his son slew John the Baptist; his grandson beheaded James and now was hiding Peter in prison for execution after Passover. While Peter suffered in chains, the church suffered with him on their knees. Hour after hour they wrestled in prayer; and when they had done all they could do, God began. Suddenly an angel "anesthetized" the sixteen guards and removed Peter's chains. (But neither God nor His angel did what Peter could do for himself. He had to put on his garments and sandals and follow.) Nothing hindered their escape. An iron gate opened by itself; and earnest, unceasing prayers brought deliverance. Curiously, the only place Peter found impassable was his friends' front door! Even those who pray sometimes fail to see or believe the speed with which God works when they pray.

11. The Lord's Prayer (Matt. 6:9–13). The Lord's Prayer is a prayer outline with seven major topics, each representing a basic human need: (1) *The Paternal Need: "Our Father" (v. 9)*. When you pray, all needs are met by the benevolence of a loving Father. (2) *God's Presence: "Hallowed be Your name" (v. 9)*. Enter His presence through praise (Ps. 100:4), and call Him "Father" because of Christ's atoning blood (Heb. 10:19–22; Gal. 4:4–6). (3) *God's Priorities: "Your kingdom come" (v. 10)*. Declare that His kingdom priorities (Rom. 14:17) shall be established in yourself, your loved ones, your church, and your nation. (4) *God's Provision: "Give us" (v. 11)*. Jesus, the need-meeter, told us to pray daily, asking Him to supply all our needs. (5) *God's Forgiveness: "And forgive us" (v. 12)*. You need God's forgiveness, and you need to forgive others. Daily set your will to walk in love and forgiveness. (6) *Power over Satan: "And do not lead us . . . deliver us from the evil one" (v. 13)*. Pray a hedge of protection about yourself and your loved ones (Job 1:9–10; Psalm 91), and verbally put on the armor of God (Eph. 6:14–18). (7) *Divine Partnership: "For Yours is the kingdom" (v. 13)*. Praise God for sharing His kingdom, power, and glory with you (2 Tim. 4:18; Luke 10:19; John 17:22). This is the prayer that teaches you how to pray.

12. Prayer Is Agreeing with God's Will (1 John 5:14–15). Immature faith tries to manipulate God. It looks for spiritual shortcuts and formulas guaranteed to produce an answer to any request. It regards prayer as a weapon we use to force God to make good His promises. But true prayer is not a human effort at persuading God or forcing our will on Him. True prayer is founded upon finding and coming into agreement with God's will (v. 14). We ask according to His will; then we stand in faith, confident that God hears us and that what we ask for is already ours (v. 15). Lessons: (1) To pray with authority and receive answers to your prayers, make sure you ask according to the will of God. If you do not know His will, ask Him (James 1:5). (2) Believe that God hears your petition and has already set the answer into motion. (3) Pray tenaciously and persistently until His will is accomplished. That is true prayer.

13. A Prayerful Quest for God Is the Pathway to Satisfaction (John 4:34). When Jesus refused the food offered by His disciples and declared, "I have food to eat of which you do not know" (v. 32), He was not implying that physical hunger and thirst were sinful (He later made eating and drinking sacramental signs). But His spirit's hunger had priority over physical appetites. He found satisfying food in deep communion with God and in doing His Father's will. Applause and material acquisitions can feed vanity and nourish ambition, but they cannot sustain the spirit. A prayerful quest for God will lead to our finding our food, our spiritual strength and satisfaction in doing God's will. Like Jesus, we shall discover God's will through daily communion with Him; and we shall receive a fresh, daily anointing to achieve it.

14. David Asks for Joy and God's Presence
(Ps. 51:1–19). David's prayer of repentance remains on record as a tear-stained testimony of his brokenness before God and as instruction for all others who sin. His repentance did not stem from fear of punishment or concern of future success. He repented for having violated God Himself, His Person and His nature. David cried out, not just for pardon, but for purity; not just for acquittal, but for acceptance; not just for comfort, but for complete cleansing—*whatever the cost.* Although his heart was crushed by his shame and sorrow over sin, he knew the great breadth of God's mercy. See how, once his sins are confessed, forgiven, and purged, David dares to ask for God's choicest gifts: joy, restoration, God's presence, His Holy Spirit. Then he humbly offers himself to be used as an instrument to show forth God's praise and to teach other transgressors. This psalm evidences that God accepted that offer. L.L.

PREACH. (Ezek. 21:2) *nataph* (nah-*tahf*); *Strong's* #5197: To drop down as water, to fall in drops; to flow, drip, ooze, distill, trickle; to cause words to flow. This verb occurs eighteen times and refers to the dripping or flowing of water, rain, honey, myrrh, sweet wine, and words, especially words in a prophetic discourse. *Nataph* is here translated "preach," but actually means "drop your word." In Micah 2:6, 11, *nataph* is translated "prophesy," or, "let your words flow."

PREACHED. (Acts 9:20) *kerusso* (kay-*roos*-oh); *Strong's* #2784: To herald, tell abroad, publish, propagate, publicly proclaim, exhort, call out with a clear voice, communicate, preach. The herald is to give a public announcement of an official message and issue whatever demands the message entails. The Christian herald is to proclaim the message of salvation through Jesus Christ and issue a summons to repent and receive forgiveness of sins.

PREACHER, PREACHING—one who proclaims the gospel; proclamation of God's saving gift in Jesus Christ.

The Old Testament mentions several prominent preachers. Noah, who warned of the impending flood and proclaimed God's ark of safety, was called a "preacher of righteousness" (2 Pet. 2:5). Solomon described himself as a preacher who taught "words of truth" (Eccl. 1:2; 12:9–10). At God's direction, Jonah made a preaching mission to Nineveh, declaring God's judgment and mercy (Jon. 3:2). Like Jonah, all the prophets of the Old Testament were regarded as preachers, particularly Isaiah, Jeremiah, Amos, and Micah.

In the New Testament, the gospel advanced on the wings of preaching. The zeal generated by Pentecost, coupled with growing persecution of the young church, led the disciples to preach everywhere in the known world (Mark 16:20). With a sense of urgency, Jesus and the apostles preached in homes, by the seaside, on the temple steps, and in the synagogues. John the Baptist called for repentance in preparation for the Messiah's appearance (Matt.3:11–12).

At His home synagogue in Nazareth, Jesus connected His ministry with that of the prophets (Is. 61:1) and identified His mission as one of proclaiming deliverance: "[The Lord] has anointed Me to preach the gospel to the poor . . . to proclaim liberty to the captives" (Luke 4:18–19).

Jesus was under a divine order to spread the gospel by means of preaching (Luke 4:43–44). Philip, the preaching deacon, "preached the things concerning the kingdom of God and the name of Jesus Christ" (Acts 8:12). In sending out the Twelve, Jesus commanded them, "As you go, preach, saying, 'The kingdom of heaven is at hand' " (Matt. 10:7). The apostle Paul proudly declared his credentials as one whom God "appointed a preacher and an apostle" (1 Tim. 2:7).

Virtually all New Testament preaching carries an evangelistic thrust. Paul declared, "It pleased God through the foolishness of the message preached to save those who believe" (1 Cor. 1:21). The redemptive mission of Christ as fulfillment of prophecy—particularly His death and resurrection—was the main theme of apostolic preaching (1 Cor. 1:2–3; 15:14). The preacher's personal testimony to Christ's power in his own life was also featured in many sermons (Acts 4:20). As a consequence of such evangelistic passion, thousands were saved when Peter preached at Pentecost (Acts 2:41).

The distinction between preaching and teaching made in the church today is not evident in the New Testament. Both Jesus and Paul regarded themselves as preacher-teachers and were so regarded by others. Luke reports that Jesus "taught the people and preached the gospel" (Luke 20:1). Paul testified that he was appointed "a preacher, an apostle, and a teacher of the Gentiles" (2 Tim. 1:11). The best New Testament preaching, while aimed at motivating sinners to receive Christ, had a strong element of teaching. Paul charged young Timothy to "preach the word! . . . Convince, rebuke, exhort, with all longsuffering and teaching" (2 Tim. 4:2).

The Great Commission has a broad application that calls all believers to participate in preaching the gospel (Mark 16:15). The piercing question, "How shall they hear without a preacher?" (Rom. 10:14), challenges all Christians to share with others the Good News of the gospel of Jesus Christ.

 PRECEPTS. (Ps. 119:15) *piqud* (pee-*kood*); *Strong's* #6490: A commandment, a precept, statute, mandate; something appointed or authorized by God. This word comes from the root verb *paqad*, "to appoint, oversee, take account, or allocate." The verb contains a strong sense of "counting" and "numbering" one's charges (those for which one is responsible). *Piqud* occurs twenty-four times, all in Psalms (twenty-one are found in Ps. 119; the remainder are located in 19:8; 103:18; 117:7). The Lord's *piqudim* are His appointed statutes, mandates, numbered precepts, and His authorized, listed commandments.

PREDESTINATION—the biblical teaching that declares the sovereignty of God over all things in such a way that the freedom of the human will is also preserved.

Two views of predestination are prominent among church groups today. One view, known as Calvinism, holds that God offers irresistible grace to those whom he elects to save. The other view, known as Arminianism, insists that God's grace is the source of redemption but that it can be resisted by man through his free choice. In Calvinism, God chooses the believer; in Arminianism, the believer chooses God.

Although the term predestination is not used in the Bible, the apostle Paul alludes to it in Ephesians 1:11: "We have obtained an inheritance, being predestined according to the purpose of Him who works all things according to the counsel of His will."

All Christians agree that creation is moving within the purpose of God. This purpose is to bring the world into complete conformity to His will (Rom. 8:28). From the very beginning of time, God predestined to save humankind by sending His Son to accomplish salvation. Thus, God "desires all men to be saved and to come to the knowledge of the truth" (1 Tim. 2:4).

The doctrine of predestination does not mean that God is unjust, deciding that some people will be saved and that others will be lost. Mankind, because of Adam's *Fall in the Garden of Eden, sinned by free choice. Thus, no person deserves salvation. But God's grace is universal. His salvation is for "everyone who believes" (Rom. 1:16).

Paul also declared that he was a debtor under obligation to take the message of the gospel to other people (Rom. 1:14) so they might hear and obey.

Predestination is a profound and mysterious biblical teaching. It focuses our thinking on man's freedom and responsibility as well as God's sovereignty.

PREPARED. (Rev. 21:2) *hetoimazo* (het-oy-mad-zoe); *Strong's* #2090: To make ready, prepare, make arrangements. In addition to its normal use describing preparation for coming events, the word is used of preparation for the Messiah (Matt. 3:3; Mark 1:3; Luke 1:76), of blessings that God has ordained (Matt. 20:23; 25:34), and of judgment (Matt. 25:41).

PRESBYTER—a leader in one of the Jewish communities (especially a member of the Sanhedrin), or of the early Christian churches. The Greek word *presbuteros*, translated elders in most English translations of the Bible, basically means an older person and is sometimes used with that sense (1 Tim. 5:1–2). The word may also refer to the lay members of the Jewish Sanhedrin (Mark 14:43, 53) or to the spiritual leaders in each Christian church (Acts 14:23). A number of presbyters together constitute a "presbytery" (1 Tim. 4:14), a council or assembly of Christian elders. Regardless of what the chief governing body in a local church is called today, the members of that body should have the same high qualifications (Titus 1:5–9) and perform the same essential duties of teaching (1 Tim. 5:17; Titus 1:9), serving (James 5:14), decision-making (Acts 15:2, 6, 22–29), and shepherding (Acts 20:17, 28) as the New Testament presbyters. Also see Elder.

PRESBYTERY—an assembly of elders in one of the early Christian churches (1 Tim. 4:14). The same Greek noun translated presbytery *(presbuterion)* is also used twice in the New Testament to refer to the Jewish Sanhedrin (Luke 22:5, 66). Also see Presbyter.

 PRESERVED. (Job 10:12) *shamar* (shah-*mar*); *Strong's* #8104: To guard, keep, protect, preserve; watch over, care for, safekeep; occurs about 450 times in the Old Testament. *Shamar* first appears in Genesis 2:15, where Adam was to tend and keep the Garden of Eden. People are told to guard the covenant, the Sabbath, or the commandments (Gen. 17:9; Ex. 31:14; Deut. 28:9). The participle *shomer* means "guardian," or "he who watches," that is, a watchman or shepherd. The Lord is called "*shomer Yisrael*," the "One who guards Israel"; this Keeper never slumbers and never sleeps, but is always on duty (Ps. 121:4).

 PRIDE. (Mark 7:22) *huperephania* (hoop-er-ay-fan-*ee*-ah); *Strong's* #5243: Twelfth on the list of thirteen inner vices, the word means haughtiness, arrogance, ostentatious pride bordering on insolence, and a disdainful attitude toward others. It is a pharisaical sin characterized by superiority of attitude. The word is a combination of *huper,* "over," and *phainomai,* "to appear." It is a state of pride that is the very opposite of Jesus' claim for Himself, meek (*praotes*) and lowly (*tapeinos*).

PRIEST. (Lev. 5:6) *kohen* (ko-*hayn*); *Strong's* #3548: A priest; especially a chief priest; a minister, a personal attendant, an officer; specifically the high priest descended from Aaron. The *kohen* was the Lord's "personal attendant," one whose entire life revolved around Yahweh's service, both through ministering in the tabernacle (or temple in later times) and in carrying the burden of the people of Israel (*see* Ex. 28:29). A *kohen* ministers to the Lord as priest (Ex. 28:1). Notice the six appearances of the words "minister," "serve," or "service" in the references to the high priest in Hebrews 8:1—9:10. To this day the Jewish surname "Cohen" identifies a family descended from Aaron the high priest.

PRINCIPALITY—a powerful ruler, or the rule of someone in authority. The word (often found in the plural) may refer to human rulers (Titus 3:1, KJV), demonic spirits (Rom. 8:38; Eph. 6:12; Col. 2:15), angels and demons in general (Eph. 3:10; Col. 1:16), or (especially when used in the singular) any type of rule other than God Himself (Eph. 1:21; Col. 2:10). While Christians must often wrestle against evil principalities (Eph. 6:12), they can be victorious because Christ has achieved dominion over all wicked spirits (Col. 2:15), which triumph awaits application through the church's advance of spiritual ministry in prayer and the Word (Eph. 3:10).

PROMISE. (Acts 13:32) *epangelia* (ep-ang-el-ee-ah); *Strong's* #1860: Both a promise and the thing promised, an announcement with the special sense of promise, pledge, and offer. *Epangelia* tells what the promise from God is and then gives the assurance that the thing promised will be done. Second Corinthians 1:20 asserts, "For all the promises [*epangelia*] of God in Him are Yes, and in Him Amen, to the glory of God through us." *Also* (2 Pet. 3:13) *epangelma* (ep-*ang*-el-mah); *Strong's* #1862: From the same root as *epangelia. Epangelma* signifies a promise made.

PROMISED. (Acts 7:5) *epangello* (ep-ang-el-low); *Strong's* #1861: To engage, to profess, to assert something concerning oneself, to announce what one is about to do (an intention), to render a service, to make a commitment, to pledge to do something. Here *epangello* is God's assurance to Abraham that the

land He showed him was for him and his descendants.

PROPHECIES. (1 Thess. 5:20) *propheteia* (prof-ay-*tie*-ah); *Strong's* #4394: From *pro,* "forth," and *phemi,* "to speak." The primary use of the word is not predictive, in the sense of foretelling, but interpretive, declaring, or forth-telling, the will and counsel of God.

PROPHECY—predictions about the future and the endtime; special messages from God, often uttered through human spokesmen, which indicate the divine will for mankind on earth and in heaven.

The focus of all prophetic truth is Jesus Christ (Heb. 1:2; Luke 24:25–27), who was destined to be the greatest prophet (Deut. 18:15–18). He declared God's truth in this age (John 3:31–33) and the age to come (Is. 2:24). As the embodiment of truth (John 1:1), Christ fully radiated the brilliance of God which the earlier prophets could only have reflected partially.

Earlier prophets anticipated Jesus Christ by reflecting His person and message in their own life and ministry (Ex. 34:29–35; 1 Kin. 19:10; 2 Chr. 24:20–21). Each contributed a portion of the truth, sharing in the Spirit that would be completely expressed in Jesus Christ (John 6:68).

Prophecy was technically the task of the prophet. But all truth or revelation is prophetic, pointing to some future person, event, or thing. The full panorama of God's will takes many forms; it may be expressed through people, events, and objects. Historical events such as the Passover anticipated Jesus Christ (John 1:29), as did various objects in the tabernacle, including manna (John 6:31–35) and the inner veil (Matt. 27:51; Heb. 10:20).

Prophecy may also be expressed in many different forms through the prophet himself, whether by his mouth or some bodily action. The prophets received God's messages from the voice of an angel (Gen. 22:15–19), the voice of God, a dream (Daniel 2), or a vision (Ezek. 40:2ff.). The prophetic speech might range from the somber reading of a father's last will (Genesis 49) to an exultant anthem to be sung in the temple (Ps. 96:1, 13).

Sometimes a prophet acted out his message symbolically. Isaiah's nakedness (Isaiah 20) foretold the exile of the Egyptians and the Cushites. Hosea's marriage symbolized God's patience with an unfaithful wife, or the nation of Israel. Ahijah divided his garment to foretell the division of the monarchy (1 Kin. 11:30–31). Even the names of some of the prophets are symbolic, matching their message. Hosea means "salvation"; Nahum, "comfort"; Zephaniah, "the Lord hides"; and Zechariah, "the Lord remembers."

Prophecy declared God's word for all time, so the time of fulfillment of a prophecy is rarely indicated in the Bible. Exceptions to this rule include the timetable assigned to Daniel's seventy weeks' prophecy (Dan. 9:24–27), the prophecy of Peter's denial (Matt. 26:34), and predictions of someone's death (Jer. 28:16–17). The common problem of knowing the time for the fulfillment of a prophecy is acknowledged by Peter (2 Pet. 1:11). This problem is due to several factors. First, some prophecies appear together, as if they would be fulfilled simultaneously. For example, Isaiah 61:1–2 has already been fulfilled, according to Luke 4:18–19; but Isaiah 61:2, which adjoins it, awaits fulfillment. The same is true of Zechariah 9:9–10. The prophets saw the mountain peaks of prophetic events but not the valleys of time in between.

Another factor that complicates the problem is the ambiguity of tenses in the Hebrew language, which distinguishes *type* of action but not *time* of action. The prophets focused on the reality of their prophecies and not the time of their fulfillment. In their minds their prophecies were already accomplished, primarily because they knew God was in charge of history.

PROPHECY AND THE SCRIPTURES. What should be the believer's stance toward the potential of every Spirit-filled Christian to prophesy (Acts 2:17, 18; 1 Cor. 14:31)? What is the relative authority of the Bible in the giving of "words" of prophecy and in the judging or evaluation of their truth or merit? Here are keys to unlock the potential of this ministry without being detoured to dead-end streets of folly or error. This study teaches a way of balance (1) employing the gift of prophecy as the Holy Spirit appoints and (2) keeping the eternal Word of Scripture central and sovereign in that exercise.

1. The Holy Scriptures and the Spirit of Prophecy (Rev. 19:10). The entire Bible is a product of the Holy Spirit, who is not only "the Spirit of truth" (John 16:13), but "the spirit of prophecy" (Rev. 19:10). The verb "to prophesy" (derived from Greek preposition *pro* and verb *phemi*) means "to speak forth *before*." The preposition "before" in this use may mean "*in advance*" and/or "*in front of.*" Thus, "to prophesy" is a proper term to describe the proclamation of God's Word as it forecasts events. It may also describe the declaration of God's Word forthrightly, boldly, or confrontingly before a group or individual—telling forth

God's truth and will. So, in both respects, the Bible is prophetic: a Book that reveals God's will through His Word and His works, as well as a Book that reveals God's plans and predictions.

This text defines the witness or testimony of Jesus Himself as being synonymous with, or at the heart of, the spirit of prophecy. These words not only define Scripture; they also confine all utterances that claim to be true prophecy: Jesus Christ will be at the center of it all, as He is in the whole Bible. (1) The Old Testament exists to reveal Christ (Luke 24:27; John 5:39; 1 Pet. 1:10–12); and (2) the New Testament is inspired by the Holy Spirit for the same purpose (John 14:26; 16:13–15).

2. Prophecy Not Christ-Centered Is Disqualified (1 John 4:1–6). Since the heart of true prophecy is Christ Himself (Rev. 19:10), the word "prophecy" not only *defines* the Bible, but *confines* all prophesying that claims to be true. This text shows that John distinguished the spirit of truth and error by whether the sinless glory and saviorhood of our Lord Jesus Christ was the focus. Paul pronounced a curse upon anyone who violated this sound word of the gospel (Gal. 1:6–9). Both men were addressing the early church community and confronting the encroachment of teachers or teachings that claimed prophetic authority, but failed to present and honor Jesus Christ in a way consistent with the whole of the Scriptures.

Likewise, we should be cautious regarding groups or individuals who claim a Christian foundation: What place is Jesus Himself given? We should also reject any prophesying that preoccupies itself with mystical ideas or secondary issues. All true prophecy rests in and upon Christ, the Foundation. If that Foundation is soundly built upon, the shape of all that rises will look and sound like Jesus, God's Son.

3. The Spirit of Revelation (Eph. 1:17–19). In this text, Paul says he prays for people to receive "the spirit of wisdom and revelation," with the dual objective of their knowing Christ and understanding God's purpose and power in their lives. Such "revelation" refers to an unveiling of our hearts that we may receive insight into the *way* God's word is intended to work in our lives. It may be used of teaching or preaching that is especially anointed in helping people see the glory of Christ and His purpose and power for them. But in making such a biblical use of the term as it appears here in Ephesians 1, it is wise to understand its alternate and grander use.

The word "revelation" is used in two ways

in the Bible. It is important to distinguish them, not only to avoid confusion in studying the Word of God, but to assure the avoidance of a destructive detour into humanistic ideas and hopeless error. The Holy Scriptures are called "the revealed Word of God." The Bible declares that God's "law" (Deut. 29:29) and the "prophets" (Amos 3:7) are the result of His revealing work, essentially describing the whole of the Old Testament as "*revealed.*" In the New Testament, this word is used of writings as well (Rom. 16:25; Eph. 3:3; Rev. 1:1)—writings that became part of the closed canon of the Holy Scriptures (*see* Word of God, "The Content of God's Word Is Completed").

Wisdom and understanding, as well as sound, practical speech, recommend that today's believer both know and clearly express what is meant when he or she speaks of "revelations." The Holy Spirit does indeed give us *revelation*, as this text teaches. But such prophetic insight into the Word should never be considered as equal to the actual giving of the Holy Scriptures. As helpful as insight into God's Word may be, the finality of the *whole* of the revelation of God's Holy Word is the only sure ground for building our lives (Matt. 7:24–29).

4. The Propriety and Desirability of Prophecy (1 Cor.14:1). The life of the New Testament church is intended to be blessed by the presence of the gift of prophecy. As Paul states here in noting love as our *primary* pursuit, prophecy is to be welcomed for the "edification and exhortation and comfort" of the congregation—corporately and individually (v. 3). Such encouragement of each other is "prophecy," not "words" in the sense of the Bible, which uses the *very words* of God, but in the sense of human words the Holy Spirit uniquely brings to mind.

The practice of the gift of prophecy is one purpose of Holy Spirit fullness (Acts 2:17). It also fulfills Joel's prophecy (Joel 2:28) and Moses' earlier expressed hope (Num. 11:29).

The operation of the gift of prophecy is encouraged by Peter (1 Pet. 4:11), and Paul says that it is within the potential of every believer (1 Cor. 14:31). It is intended as a means of broad participation among the congregation, mutually benefiting each other with anointed, loving words of upbuilding, insight, and affirmation. Such prophecy may provide such insight that hearts are humbled in worship of God, suddenly made aware of His Spirit's knowledge of their need and readiness to answer it (1 Cor. 14:24, 25). Prophecy of this order is also a means by which *vision* and *expectation* are prompted and provided, and

without which people may become passive or neglectful (1 Sam. 3:1; Prov. 29:18; Acts 2:17). There are specific guidelines for the operation of this gift, as with all gifts of the Holy Spirit, to insure that one gift not supplant the exercise of others or usurp the authority of spiritual leadership. Further, all such prophecy is subordinated to the plumbline of God's Eternal Word, the Bible—the standard by which all prophetic utterance in the church is to be judged (1 Cor. 14:26–33).

5. Prophecy and the Sufficiency of God's Word (2 Pet. 1:16–19). When Peter encouraged believers to speak "as the oracles of God" (1 Pet. 4:11), he clearly did not mean this verbalizing of Holy Spirit-prompted words to substitute for the preaching and teaching of the Word of God. This text shows the relative importance of prophetic "words" or experiences we receive compared with the place of the Scriptures themselves. Here the apostle compares his own experience with Jesus on the Mount of Transfiguration to the abiding "prophetic word" of the Holy Scriptures (vv. 19–21). He calls the Word of the Scriptures "confirmed," and thereby makes a dramatic point for our understanding through all church history. If Peter's experience *with Jesus Himself* is said by Peter to be subordinate to the "more sure" Word of the Scriptures, we have both a guideline and an ultimate statement. The guideline is that no experience holds greater authority than the Word of God. This is not to discourage our experiencing the works of God's Spirit in power or blessing, but simply to remind us of the relative place of each type of "word" in our values.

There is an *ultimate* statement here, too. Many raise questions today as to whether we who welcome the operation of the gift of prophecy do so because of a lack of persuasion as to the "sufficiency" of God's Word. In other words, do we believe the Bible contains everything we need for *salvation*, for *faith*, and for *obedient living*? Of course, for the Bible believer this is never in question, for in the spirit and practical truth of Peter's words there is no comparison between the eternal Word of God and the present "words" of prophetic utterance. Prophecies are proper, biblically shown to be desirable (1 Cor. 14:1) and helpful (1 Cor. 14:3, 5). But the teaching of the Holy Scriptures are ultimate, conclusively authoritative, and "more to be desired . . . than gold"—the Eternal Word of God (Ps. 19:7–11).

6. The Issue of Personal Prophecy (Acts 21:11). The Bible clearly allows for personal prophecy. Nathan brought David a confrontive "word" from God (2 Sam. 12:13); Isaiah predicted

Hezekiah's death (Is. 38:1); and in this text Agabus told Paul he faced trouble in Jerusalem. "Personal prophecy" refers to a prophecy ("word") the Holy Spirit may prompt one person to give another, relating to personal matters. Many feel deep reservations about this operation of the gift of prophecy because sometimes it is abused. *True* "words" may be used to manipulate others, or they may be unwisely or hastily applied. This passage reveals safeguards against abusive uses of personal prophecy, allowing us to implement this biblical practice. *First,* the "word" will usually not be new to the mind of the person addressed, but it will confirm something God is already dealing with him about. From Acts 20:22–24 we know Paul was already sensitive to the issue Agabus raised. *Second,* the character of the person bringing the "word" ought to be weighed. Agabus's credibility is related not to his claim of having a "word," but to his record as a trustworthy man of God used in the exercise of this gift (11:28; 21:10). *Third,* remember that the prophecy, or "word," is not to be considered "controlling." In other words, such prophecies should never be perceived as dominating anyone's free will. Christian living is never cultish—governed by omens or the counsel of gurus. Paul did not change his plans because of Agabus's prophecy or because of the urging of others (vv. 12–14); he received the "word" graciously but continued his plans nonetheless. *Fourth,* all prophecy is "in part" (1 Cor. 13:9), which means that as true as that "part" may be, it does not give the whole picture. Agabus's "word" was true, and Paul was bound in Jerusalem. But this also occasioned an opportunity to eventually minister in Rome (Acts 23:11). *Finally,* in the light of a "word," we should prayerfully consider the word as Mary did the shepherds' report (Luke 2:19). A hasty response is never required; simply wait on God. We should then move ahead with trust in God, as Hezekiah did. He had been told that he would shortly die; but he prayed instead of merely surrendering to the prophecy, and his life realized its intended length—unshortened by his diseased condition. Occasional personal prophecy is not risky if kept on biblical footings, but neither is it to become the way we plan or direct our lives.

7. The Office of the Prophet (Acts 11:27–30).

Agabus is an example of the "office" of the "prophet" in the New Testament. This role differs from the operation of the gift of prophecy in the life of the believer, for it entails a Christ-appointed ministry *of* a person rather than the Holy Spirit-distributed gift *through* a person. In the New Testament, this office was not sensationalized as it tends to be today. Such an attitude is unworthy, both in the prophet and in those to whom he ministers, and is certain to result in an unfruitful end. (Apparently Paul was addressing such assumption of the prophetic office when he issued the challenge of 1 Cor. 14:37, calling for submission to spiritual authority rather than self-serving independence.) The office of prophet cannot be taken lightly. There is nothing in the New Testament that reduces the stringent requirements for serving this role, and Deuteronomy 18:20–22 ought to be regarded seriously. Prophecy is nothing to be "experimented" with, for souls are in the balance in the exercise of every ministry.

Further wisdom may be gained by noting that on biblical terms there is more than one type of ministry by a prophet. While a few exercised remarkable predictive gifts (Daniel, Zechariah, John), other traits of the prophetic office are seen: (1) preaching—especially at a national or international level (John the Baptist); (2) teaching—especially when unusual insight is present and broad impact made in serving God's people (Ezra); (3) miracles—as remarkable signs to accompany a prophet's preaching (Elijah); (4) renewal—as with Samuel (1 Sam. 3:21; 4:1), or that called for by the psalmist and by Amos (Ps. 74:9; Amos 8:11–12). The incident of Agabus resulted in effective action by the church's rising to meet a challenging situation. This is a valid test of the prophetic office. It is for edification and not for entertainment—to enlarge and refresh the body, whether locally or beyond.

8. The Purposes of Predictive Prophecies (Deut.

28:1). Promise and prophecy are abundant in the Bible. God gives many assurances of His readiness to bless, and often speaks of things He plans to do in the future. In both cases there are always conditions: God's call to align with His will so His word of promise can bless the obedient. Chapter 28 is a classic study of both God's promises and His prophecies. Compare verses 1–2 and 58–59 to note the blessings that are a promised potential to the obedient, and the judgments that are a predicted certainty for the disobedient.

This exemplifies the purpose of predictive prophecy in the Bible. It is to *teach,* to *warn,* and to *instruct* toward obedience and fruitful living. It is never given to arouse curiosity or promote guesswork. In Matthew 24 Jesus makes several prophecies about things to come, but tells His disciples that His purpose is only to elicit practical responses of obedient living (v. 42), not guessing at the possible schedule of forthcoming events (v. 36).

Elsewhere, our Lord indicates that predictive prophecies are also given to undergird our confidence in God's sovereignty and omniscience—that He *is* in control and that He *does* know the end from the beginning. Note His words in John 13:19, 14:20, and 16:4, where His triple emphasis on this purpose of His prediction occurs—"that when it does come to pass, you may believe that I am He" (that is, God's Son, the Messiah).

9. The Prophecies of Last Things (1 John 2:18). Eschatology is that aspect of biblical doctrine dealing with "last things" (from Greek *eschatos*, "final"). In this text, John describes the times in which he wrote as "the last hour," evidencing that he, as vital Christians in every generation, both lived in immediate anticipation of Christ's Second Coming and saw his era as one in which the present evidence seemed to argue that his was possibly the concluding generation. This is not an unhealthy attitude: Christ Jesus desires that people expectantly anticipate His return (Matt. 25:1–13; 2 Tim. 4:8).

John not only addresses the lateness of the hour of history as he views it; he also addresses the subject of the Antichrist, a commonly discussed theme when eschatology is studied. The spirit of antichrist, the Rapture of the church, the Great Tribulation, the restoration of national Israel, and the millennial reign of Christ on earth are all among the many subjects the Bible describes as "last things." The Bible clearly says these things shall occur. However, it is not clear about the exact time; and in many cases it does not conclusively give the sequence or exact manner of the fulfillment of such events.

The *Spirit-Filled Life Bible* does not embrace any conclusive point of view concerning these popularly discussed subjects. We do affirm these things: (1) God is the Sovereign of the universe and the God of history, which is His-Story. (2) As such, He knows the end from the beginning and at the end of history will have been verified as all-wise and vindicated as all-just. (3) His Son, Jesus Christ, shall come to earth again for His church (John 14:1–3; Acts 1:11; 1 Cor. 15:50–58; 1 Thess. 4:16–17), and shall rule on earth (Is. 9:7; 11:6–9; Rev. 20:1–6). (4) There is a final judgment, with the reward of eternal life in heaven promised to the redeemed and the judgment of eternal loss in hell the portion of the unregenerate (Rev. 20:11–15; 21:22—22:5).

We affirm the value of the study of last things and equally declare our conviction that differences of opinion on such matters as the Rapture, the nature of the Millennium, and so on, neither give us an advantage nor hinder us with reference to our life in Christ, as we choose to serve in His love, walk in His truth, and expect His return.

10. Interpretive Approaches to the Book of Revelation (Rev. 4:1). Many devoted Christians are surprised to discover that other equally dedicated believers view the prophecies of the Book of Revelation differently from them. The book tolerates a wide spectrum of approaches, but the common denominator of all is the ultimate triumph of Jesus Christ, who culminates history with His final coming and reigns with and through His church forever.

The most popularized and widely discussed approach is called the *Dispensationalist* interpretation. This proposes that the Rapture of the church is referred to in verse 1, at which time the redeemed in Christ are translated into heaven at His coming "in the air" (1 Thess. 4:17). Chapters 6—18 are perceived as the Great Tribulation (Matt. 24:21) or the wrath of God (1 Thess. 5:9) from which believers are kept (Rev. 3:10). This approach sees national Israel as God's people on earth at this time (the church having been raptured), restored to Jerusalem, protected by divine seal (7:1–8), worshiping in a rebuilt temple (11:1–3), and suffering at the hand of the Antichrist.

Not as widely published but at least equally widely believed is the *Moderate Futurist* view. This proposes the Book of Revelation as summarizing the conclusion of the church's agelong procession through tribulation and triumph, warfare and victory, and consummating in the climactic return of Jesus Christ for His church. The tribulation is generally viewed as agelong, but increasing in intensity, so that the church is understood as present through much of earth's turmoil until just prior to the outpouring of the "bowls full of the wrath of God" (15:7). This occurs during chapter 16 and culminates in the collapse of the present world order (chs. 17; 18).

Among other views are these: (1) The *Historic* position sees Revelation as a symbolic prophecy of the whole of church history, with the events of the book a picture of the events and movements that have shaped the conflict and progress of the Christian church. (2) The *Preterist* views Revelation as a message of hope and comfort to first-century believers only, offering them an expectation of their deliverance from Roman persecution and oppression. (3) The *Idealist* formulates no particular historical focus or effort at interpreting specifics of the book, rather seeing it as a broad, poetic portrayal of the conflict between the kingdom of God and the powers of Satan.

11. The "Day of the Lord" in Prophecy (Obadiah 15). The "day of the LORD" is a term used by the Old Testament prophets to signify a time in the history of mankind when God directly intervenes to bring salvation to His people and punishment to the rebellious. By it God restores His righteous order in the earth. The terms "that Day" and simply "the Day" are sometimes used as synonyms for the fuller expression "the day of the LORD."

The fulfillment of the Day may be seen in four different ways: (1) In the times of the prophets it was revealed by such events as the invasion of Israel by foreign powers (Amos), the awesome plagues of locusts (Joel), and the return of Israelite exiles from captivity (Ezra-Nehemiah). (2) In that prophetic insight had the quality of merging periods of eschatology so that even the prophets themselves could not always distinguish the various times of the fulfillment of their prophecies, that Day developed into a broad biblical concept. Prophetic fulfillments closest to the prophets' own day were mingled with those reaching as far as the final culmination of all things. Hence, the First Coming of Christ and the church age began another phase of the day of the Lord. As participants in this aspect of the Day, the church can call on the risen Christ to cast down forces that hinder God's work in this present world and to bring about innumerable blessings. This is clear in comparing Isaiah 61:1–2 with Luke 4:18–19 and Joel 2:28–32 with Acts 2:16–21. (3) The Second Coming of Christ will inaugurate the third aspect of the day of the Lord, during which Christ's righteous and universal rule will restore God's order to the earth (Amos 9:13; Is. 11:6–9). (4) The ultimate fulfillment of the day of the Lord awaits the full arrival of the world to come, with its new heaven and new earth. (Compare Ezek. 47:1–12 with Rev. 22:1–5.)

12. Prophecy and the Future of Israel (Ps. 122:6). Theologically, there are two different positions concerning what may be expected with regard to the future of Israel. The difference centers on the question: Does Israel, as the ancient people of God, still hold a preferred place in His economy, or have they lost that place through unbelief?

Many see a continuing and distinctive role for Israel in God's plans until the end of time. These believe that Romans 9—11 indicates that a restoration of Israel will take place ("all Israel will be saved," Rom. 11:26), and that the church needs to recognize its Jewish roots

("The root supports you," Rom. 11:18). This view, however, may also allow for a fulfillment of some Old Testament promises and blessings in individual believers and through the church. The church is to demonstrate what it means to enjoy the full blessing of God so that Israel will be encouraged to return to the One who loves them eternally.

Others, however, have seen the church replacing Israel in the plan of God because the majority of the Jewish people refused to accept Jesus as Messiah. Thus the blessings and promises addressed to Israel may now only rightly be applied to the church. From this view, the modern state of Israel and the Jewish people are simply the same as all other nations and ethnic groups, and God will not deal with them differently than He will with any other peoples.

13. The Church and Present-Day Israel (Rom. 11:19–24). While two basically different prophetic positions exist concerning Israel's future, there is only one biblical view concerning the Christian's attitude toward the Jewish people. First, the Bible calls us to honor the fact that since they were the national avenue by which messianic blessing has come to mankind (9:4–5), there should be a sense of duty to "bless" all Jewry (Gen. 12:3), to "pray" with sincere passion for them (Rom. 10:1), and to be as ready to "bear witness" to any Jew as graciously and sensitively as we would to any other human being (1:16–17).

Second, the biblical directive to "pray for the peace of Jerusalem" (Ps. 122:6) cannot be said to have been rescinded. Even though the text of this psalm centers on the presence of the temple in ancient Jerusalem, this prayer assignment ought not to be withdrawn. Those taking this text seriously see their prayer responsibility for "Jerusalem" to be an assignment of continuing concern for God's providential hand of protection and grace upon the nation of Israel in particular (as distinguished from paragraph 1, which relates to Jews everywhere). It is wise for believers to avoid the presumption of passivity toward Israel, since the evidence of all history is that God has not forgotten this people (Rom. 11:23–24). J.W.H.

PROPHET—a person who spoke or speaks for God, communicating God's message courageously to His people.

The prophet's call. Old Testament prophets received their call or appointment directly from God. Some prophets, like Jeremiah or John the Baptist, were called before birth (Jer. 1:5; Luke 1:13–16), but their privilege was not a birthright. Their authority came from God alone, whose message they bore (Ex.

7:1). The call of the prophet required that he not be intimidated or threatened by his audience (Jer. 1:7–8; Ezek. 2:6).

Prophets sometimes acted out their message. Isaiah went naked and barefoot for three years (Is. 20:2–3). Ezekiel lay on his left side for 390 days and on his right side for forty more (Ezek. 4:1–8). Zechariah broke two staffs (Zech. 11:7–14). Sometimes even humbled to make a spectacle, prophets not only aroused curiosity but also suffered the scorn of their peers (Jer. 11:21).

Except for God's call, prophets had no special qualifications. They appeared from all walks of life and classes of society. They included sheepbreeders and farmers like Amos (Amos 7:14) and Elisha (1 Kin. 19:19) but also princes like Abraham (Gen. 23:6) and priests like Ezekiel (Ezek. 1:3). Even women and children became prophets (1 Sam. 3:19–20; 2 Kin. 22:14). In rare circumstances, God used the hesitant or unruly to bear his message. Balaam prophesied (Num. 22:6—24:24) the Lord's message but was actually an enemy of God (2 Pet. 2:15–16; Rev. 2:14). Saul certainly was not in fellowship with God when he prophesied (1 Sam. 10:23–24).

Some prophets were called for a lifetime. But sometimes prophets spoke briefly and no more (Num.11:25–26). In either case, a prophet spoke with the authority of the Holy Spirit (Num. 11:29; 24:4). One trait characterized them all: a faithful proclamation of God's word and not their own (Jer. 23:16; Ezek. 13:2). Jesus' reference to Himself as a prophet in John 12:49–50 rests upon this standard of faithfully repeating God's word to man.

Many scholars deny that prophecy includes the prediction of future events, but fulfillment was, in fact, the test of a prophet's genuineness (Deut. 18:20–22). Whether a prophet's words were fulfilled within his lifetime or centuries later, they were fulfilled to the letter (1 Kin. 13:3; 2 Kin. 23:15–16). But regardless of the time of fulfillment, the prophet's message applied to his generation as well as to ours.

The main role of the prophet was to bear God's word for the purpose of teaching, reproving, correcting, and training in righteousness (2 Tim. 3:16). Whether warning of impending danger or disclosing God's will to the people, they were similar in function to the modern preacher in the church. Prophets were referred to as messengers of the Lord (Is. 44:26; Hag. 1:13), servants of God (Amos 3:7), shepherds (Zech. 11:4, 7; Jer. 17:16), and watchmen (Is. 62:6).

The ministry of the prophet is still alive in the church, and the requirements are the same as reviewed in the study of this office in the Word (1 Cor. 14:29, 32; Eph. 4:11). To acknowledge the present office of a prophet is not to suggest the individual is a writer of Scripture. Those denying this contemporary office suggest that to affirm prophetic ministry today (other than preaching) is to open us to "adding to the Bible." This is not true, as all who wisely accept this office know. Prophets have no special privileges but do have the heavy requirements of the Bible's standard: if they make a forecast, it must come true or they have disqualified themselves. However, this ministry is primarily for stirring up and building up the church (Eph. 4:11–12), not offering interesting forecasts. Prophetic ministry should have a base of accountability where the person's ministry is nourished, prayed for, and sent forth with accountability (Acts 13:1–3; 14:26–28).

PROPHET. (1 Sam. 3:20) *nabi'* (nah-*vee*); *Strong's* #5030: Prophet; one who proclaims or tells a message he has received; a spokesman, herald, announcer. A prophet is someone who announces a message at the direction of another (usually the Lord God). *Nabi'* occurs more than three hundred times in the Old Testament. Six times the word is in the feminine form, *nebiyah*, and is translated "prophetess"; these six references are to Miriam, Deborah, Huldah (twice), Noadiah, and Isaiah's wife (doubtless a prophetess in her own capacity). In all other references, *nabi'* is masculine, "prophet." The word can refer to false prophets and to prophets of false gods, but nearly always refers to Yahweh's commissioned spokesmen. *Also* (Matt. 2:5) *prophetes* (prof-*ay*-tace); *Strong's* #4396: From *pro*, "forth," and *phemi*, "to speak." A prophet, therefore, is primarily a forth-teller, one who speaks forth a divine message that can at times include foretelling future events. Among the Greeks, the prophet was the interpreter of the divine will, and this idea is dominant in biblical usage. Prophets are therefore specially endowed with insights into the counsels of the Lord and serve as His spokesmen. Prophecy is a gift of the Holy Spirit (1 Cor. 12:12), which the New Testament encourages believers to exercise, although at a level different from those with the prophetic office (Eph. 4:11).

PROPHETESS—a female prophet. Women were also blessed with prophetic abilities in Bible times. Miriam, the sister of Moses, led the women with her chorus in response to the great song of her brother (Ex. 15:20). Deborah joined with Barak in song and exulted in their great victory (Judg. 5:2–31). Hannah's prayer was remarkable, foretelling how David's dynasty would be founded (1 Sam. 2:1–10).

Luke reported the prophetic activity of the elderly Anna in the temple (2:36–38), as well as that of Elizabeth and Mary (1:41–45, 46–55). First Corinthians 11:5 assumes the female role in prophesying, seen again in Philip's four virgin daughters (Acts 21:9); both indicate the present place of a woman's potential in this ministry.

PROPITIATION [pro PISH ih a shun]—the atoning death of Jesus on the Cross, through which He paid the penalty justice required because of man's sin, thus setting mankind free from sin and death. The word comes from an old English word, propitiate, which means "to atone" or "to appease"—to establish grounds for reconciliation. Propitiation (*hilasmos*) in the New Testament finds its meaning illustrated in the Old Testament mercy seat (*hilasterion*). As the blood was poured on the mercy seat, covering the sins of the people, Jesus' blood and death has redeemed us: "He Himself is the propitiation for our sins, and not for ours only but also for the whole world" (1 John 2:2).

PROPITIATION. (1 John 4:10) *hilasmos* (hil-as-moss); *Strong's* #2434: Related to *hileos*, "merciful." Used in the New Testament only in 2:2 and 4:10, the word describes Christ, through His sacrificial death, as appeasing the wrath of God on account of sin. It also pictures His death as expiatory, providing a covering for sin. By means of the atoning death of Christ, God can be merciful to the sinner who believes in Him, and reconciliation is effected.

PROSELYTE [PROS eh lite] *(one who has drawn near)*—a convert from one religious belief or party to another. In the New Testament (Matt. 23:15; Acts 2:10), the term is used in a specific sense to designate Gentile converts who had committed themselves to the teachings of the Jewish faith or who were attracted to the teachings of Judaism. A full-fledged proselyte, or convert, to Judaism underwent circumcision and worshiped in the Jewish temple or synagogue. He also observed all rituals and regulations concerning the Sabbath, clean and unclean foods, and all other matters of Jewish custom.

By the New Testament period, when communities of Jews were widely scattered over the Gentile world, many Gentiles came into contact with Judaism. They found worship of one God and its wholesome ethical teaching attractive. Tired of pagan gods and heathen immorality, the Gentiles came to the synagogues to learn of the one true God and His call to holiness, justice, and mercy. Many of them accepted the religion, morality, and lifestyle of the Jews.

PROSPER. (Eccl. 11:6) *chashar* (kah-*shar*); *Strong's* #3787: To be right, successful, proper, correct; to be correctly aligned with certain requirements. *Chashar* occurs three times in the Old Testament: in this reference; in 10:10, "bring success"; and in Esther 8:5, where the queen presents her request on condition that it "seem right" to the king. *Chashar* thus describes whatever is right, fitting, and proper; furthermore, something will prosper and be successful simply because of its "rightness." Its postbiblical derivative *kosher* means that food is properly prepared according to Jewish dietary laws derived from Scripture and rabbinic specifications.

PROVERB. (Prov. 1:6) *mashal* (mah-*shahl*); *Strong's* #4912: Proverb, parable, maxim, adage; a simile or allegory; an object lesson or illustration. This noun comes from the verb *mashal*, "to compare; to be similar." Based on the Book of Proverbs, it might appear that a proverb is a short saying containing a nugget of truth. Yet Old Testament evidence shows it has broader uses. Balaam's long discourse is termed a *mashal* (Num. 23:7—24:24). In other references, *mashal* suggests a taunt, a byword, or an illustration. In still others, it suggests a person or a nation out of which God has made an example. (Compare 1 Kin. 9:7 with Ps. 69:11.)

PROVIDENCE—the continuous activity of God in His creation by which He preserves and governs. The doctrine of providence affirms God's absolute lordship over His creation and confirms the dependence of all creation on the Creator. It is the denial of the idea that the universe is governed by chance or fate.

Through His providence God controls the universe (Ps. 103:19); the physical world (Matt. 5:45); the affairs of nations (Ps. 66:7); man's birth and destiny (Gal. 1:15); man's successes and failures (Luke 1:52); and the protection of His people (Ps. 4:8).

God preserves all things through His providence (1 Sam. 2:9; Acts 17:28). Without His continual care and activity the world would not exist, for it would be surrendered to the fallibility of mankind and the sinister devices of the devil (John 10:10). God also preserves His people through His providence (Gen. 28:15; Luke 21:18; 1 Cor. 10:13; 1 Pet. 3:12).

God's providence, then, is that divine government which sustains, the continued activity by which He directs all things to the ends He has chosen in His eternal plan. God is King of the universe who has given Christ all power and authority to reign (Matt. 28:18–20; Acts 2:36; Eph. 1:20–23). He governs even in insignificant things (Matt. 10:29–31), apparent accidents (Prov. 16:33), as well as man's good (Phil. 2:13) and evil deeds (Acts 14:16). This does not mean He *causes* all things, but that He is above and beyond all, and available to move into any situation and overthrow its destructive design. Regarding God's providential workings, two facts must be remembered:

1. God acts in accordance with the laws and principles that He has established in the world.

2. Man is free to choose and act independently from God's will and plan. While God is above man's choices and actions (Gen. 45:5; Deut. 8:18; Prov. 21:1), His actions never violate the reality of human choice or negate man's responsibility as a moral being. He may permit sinful acts to occur, but He does not cause man to sin nor is He responsible for sin's results (Gen. 45:5; Rom. 9:22). Still, in mercy, God's providence often overrules evil for good and transcends circumstances in bringing about His benevolent will (Gen. 50:20; Acts 3:13).

PROVISION. (Rom. 13:14) *pronoia* (*pron*-oy-ah); *Strong's #4307:* Foreplanning, foresight, forethought, premeditated plan, making preparation for, providing for. Derived from words *pro,* "before," and *noeo,* "to think," "contemplate." Paul prohibited his readers from planning ahead and making any preparations for gratifying their carnal nature.

PSALM. (Ps. 3:title) *mizmor* (meez-mohr); *Strong's #4210:* An instrumental song; a song with words accompanied by musical instruments. *Mizmor* comes from the verb *zamar,* which means "to play or make music while singing, to sing psalms, sing forth praises." The definitive aspect of a *mizmor* is that it requires musical instruments. It is possible to sing songs (*shirim*) without instruments, or to speak praises (*tehillim*) without any musical accompaniment, but it is not possible to fulfill the many biblical commands (as 98:5; Is. 12:5) that use the verb *zamar,* unless instruments are employed. The beauty of musical instruments as a part of worship was greatly developed by King David.

PTOLEMY—see ch. 55, §2.1.

PUNISHMENT, EVERLASTING—the final judgment of God upon the wicked. The classic Old Testament illustration of what eternal punishment will be like is the conclusive destruction of Sodom and Gomorrah (Gen. 19:15–28). While speaking about wicked angels who are being held in "everlasting chains," the writer of Jude in the New Testament likened these wrongdoers to the wicked men of Sodom and Gomorrah, who "are set forth as an example, suffering the vengeance of eternal fire" (Jude 7).

In his second letter to the Thessalonians, the apostle Paul wrote about the final judgment. He explains that those who do not know God "shall be punished with everlasting destruction from the presence of the Lord and from the glory of His power" (2 Thess 1:9). This same idea was expressed by Jesus in the parable of the sheep and the goats (Matt. 25:31–46). After separating the two, Jesus blessed the sheep—those who have cared for the unfortunate and poor. Then he pronounced judgment upon the goats—those who did not have compassion: "Depart from Me, you cursed, into the everlasting fire" (v. 41).

The essential meaning of the phrase everlasting punishment involves banishment from the presence of God and Christ forever—a fate made vivid by the image of eternal fire (Rev. 19:20; 21:8).

Also see Hell.

PURE. (Matt. 5:8) *katharos* (kath-ar-oss); *Strong's #2513:* Without blemish, clean, undefiled, pure. The word describes physical cleanliness (Matt. 23:26; 27:59); ceremonial purity (Luke 11:41; Rom. 14:20); and ethical purity (John 13:10; Acts 18:6). Sin pollutes and defiles, but the blood of Jesus washes the stains away. *Also* (2 Pet. 3:1) *eilikrines* (eye-lik-ree-nace); *Strong's #1506:* Literally "tested by sunlight." The thought is that of judging something by sunlight to expose any flaws. The word described metals with alloys and liquids unadulterated with foreign substances. In the New Testament it is used in an ethical and moral sense, free from falsehood, pure, and without hidden motives. *Also* (1 John 3:3) *hagnos* (hag-noss); *Strong's #53:* From the same root as *hagios,* "holy." The adjective describes a person or thing as clean, modest, pure, undefiled, morally faultless, and without blemish. Christ's ability to overcome temptation and remain pure makes Him a role model for all believers.

PURITY—the quality or state of being free from mixture, pollution, or other foreign elements. The term purity may refer to things (gold, Ex. 25:17; oil, Lev. 24:2) or people. Purity with reference to people may be racial (Phil. 3:5), ceremonial (Lev. 19:16–33; Luke 2:22), ethical (Prov. 22:11), or spiritual (1 Tim. 1:5; 4:12).

The religious leaders of Jesus' day often took ceremonial purity beyond what Scripture required and became vain in their pursuits. They considered ceremonial purity more valuable than a heart for spiritual purity (Mark

7:3–4; Luke 11:39–41). For this error they were soundly rebuked by Jesus (Mark 7:1–13; Luke 11:39–41). Purity in a believer's life is spiritual at its root, and its fruit will reveal itself in humility and love (Matt. 5:8; James 1:27).

PURPOSE. (Rom. 8:28) *prothesis* (*proth*-es-is); *Strong's #4286:* From *pro,* "before," and *thesis,* "a place," thus "a setting forth." The word suggests a deliberate plan, a proposition, an advance plan, an intention, a design. Of twelve occurrences in the New Testament, *prothesis* is used four times for the Levitical showbread (literally "the bread of setting before"). Most of the other usages point to God's eternal purposes relating to salvation. Our personal salvation was not only well planned but demonstrates God's abiding faithfulness as He awaits the consummation of His great plan for His church.

PUT OUT. (Luke 16:4) *methistemi* (meth-*is*-tay-mee); *Strong's #3179:* Literally, "to set aside." The word indicates a change from one place to another, a removal, a transfer, a relocation. The action involved may be either positive (Col. 1:13) or negative (Luke 16:4).

 QUICK, QUICKEN—KJV translation of several Hebrew and Greek words translated by the NKJV as alive (Ps. 55:15), living (Acts 10:42), revive (Ps. 119:25), and gives life to (John 5:21).

QUMRAN, KHIRBET QUMRAN—see ch. 55, §4.2., 5., 5.1., 5.2., 5.3., 5.4., 5.5., 5.6., 6.1.

RAMSES II—see ch. 55, §3.3.

RAS SHAMRA—see ch. 55, §3.4.

RECONCILIATION—the process by which God and man are brought together again. The Bible teaches that God and man are alienated from one another because of God's holiness and man's sinfulness. Although God loves the sinner (Rom. 5:8), it is impossible for Him not to judge sin (Heb. 10:27). Therefore, the initiative in reconciliation was taken by God—while we were still sinners and "enemies," Christ died for us (Rom. 5:8, 10; Col. 1:21). Reconciliation is thus God's own completed act, something that takes place before human actions such as confession, repentance, and restitution. God Himself "has reconciled us to Himself through Jesus Christ" (2 Cor. 5:18).

Paul regarded the gospel as "the word of reconciliation" (2 Cor. 5:19), and pleaded, "as though God were pleading through us: . . . Be reconciled to God" (2 Cor. 5:20).

REDEEMER—one who frees or delivers another from difficulty, danger, or bondage, usually by the payment of a ransom price. In the Old Testament the redeemer could function in several ways. He could buy back property (and even enslaved people) sold under duress (Lev. 25:23–32). He (usually as owner, not as a relative) often redeemed from the Lord dedicated property and firstborn livestock (Lev. 27:1–33; also Ex. 21:28–30). He could (as "legal avenger") take the life of one who had murdered his relative as a blood price (Num. 35:12–28).

Boaz's function as redeemer for Ruth (Ruth 3:13—4:10) is well known, as is Job's resurrection hope in God, his Redeemer (Job 19:25). God Himself is the Redeemer of Israel, a fact mentioned eighteen times—especially by the prophet Isaiah (Ps. 78:35; Is. 41:14).

In the New Testament, Christ is viewed as the ultimate Redeemer, although the Greek word for redeemer is not used. Jesus gave His life as "a ransom for many" (Mark 10:45). Thus, the apostle Paul speaks of believers as having "redemption through His blood" (Eph. 1:7).

REDEMPTION—deliverance by payment of a price. In the New Testament, redemption refers to salvation's provision which "buys back" what has been lost. In the Old Testament, the word redemption refers to redemption by a kinsman (Lev. 25:24, 51–52; Ruth 4:6; Jer. 32:7–8), rescue or deliverance (Num. 3:49), and ransom (Ps. 111:9; 130:7). In the New Testament it refers to loosing (Luke 2:38; Heb. 9:12; Luke 21:28; Rom. 3:24; Eph. 1:14).

In the Old Testament redemption was applied to the recovery of property, animals, persons, and the whole nation. These things typify the dimensions of recovery and release New Testament believers experience in life through the price Jesus paid. So the Old Testament evidences New Testament promise—God's ability in Christ to redeem from the slavery of sin (Ps. 130:7–8), from enemy oppressors (Deut. 15:15), and from the power of death (Job 19:25–26; Ps. 49:8–9).

The New Testament describes the exact cost of redemption: "the precious blood of Christ" (1 Pet. 1:19; Eph. 1:7), which believers are exhorted to remember as they pursue obedient service, faithful ministry, and personal holiness (1 Cor. 6:19–20; 1 Pet. 1:13–19).

 This icon beside an entry indicates a Word Wealth feature.

 This icon beside an entry indicates a Kingdom Dynamics feature.

 This icon beside an entry indicates an important biblical or doctrinal term.

REGENERATION—New Birth, the begetting of new life, the rebirth of the human spirit to a restored relationship with God by an act of God's Holy Spirit through Jesus Christ. In regeneration a person's sinful nature is changed, and he is renewed to life and salvation in God by faith.

The word regeneration occurs only in the New Testament (Matt. 19:28; Titus 3:5), but the concept or idea is common throughout the Bible. The literal meaning of regeneration is "born again." There is a first birth and a second birth. The first, as Jesus said to Nicodemus (John 3:1–12) is "of the flesh"; the second birth is "of the Spirit." Being born of the Spirit is essential before a person can enter the kingdom of God. Every biblical command to man to undergo a radical change of character from self-centeredness to God-centeredness is, in effect, an appeal to be "born again" (Ps. 51:5–11; Jer. 31:33; Zech. 13:1).

Great religious experiences like that of Jacob at Jabbok (Gen. 32:22–32), Moses at the burning bush (Ex. 3:1), Josiah on hearing the reading of the Law (2 Kin. 22:8–13), or Isaiah in the temple (Is. 6:1–8) might well be regarded as Old Testament pictures of "new birth" to the limits under the Old Covenant. In the New Testament, regeneration extends to the total nature of man, bringing the inner being to life by the resurrection of Jesus Christ. Regeneration changes a person's desires because "newness of life" is begotten in the person (Rom. 6:4; 7:6), as well as a right relationship with God in Christ.

Thus, regeneration is an act of God through the Holy Spirit (Titus 3:5), resulting in an inner, personal resurrection from sin to a new life in Jesus Christ (2 Cor. 5:17).

REPENTANCE—a turning away from sin, disobedience, or rebellion and a turning back to God (Matt. 9:13; Luke 5:32). In a more general sense, repentance means a change of mind (Gen. 6:6–7) or a feeling of remorse or regret for past conduct (Matt. 27:3). True repentance is a "godly sorrow" for sin, an act of turning around and going in the opposite direction. This type of repentance leads to a fundamental change in a person's relationship to God.

In the Old Testament the classic case of repentance is that of King David, after Nathan the prophet accused him of killing Uriah the Hittite and committing adultery with Uriah's wife, Bathsheba. David's prayer of repentance for this sin is found in Psalm 51.

In the New Testament the keynote of John the Baptist's preaching was, "Repent, for the kingdom of heaven is at hand" (Matt. 3:2). To the multitudes he declared, "Bear fruits worthy of repentance" (Matt. 3:8; Luke 3:8). When Jesus began His ministry, He took up John's preaching of the message of repentance, expanding the message to include the good news of salvation: "The time is fulfilled, and the kingdom of God is at hand. Repent and believe in the gospel" (Mark 1:15).

In Jesus' preaching of the kingdom of God is seen the truth that repentance and faith are two sides of the same coin: by repentance, one turns away from sin; by faith, one turns toward God in accepting the Lord Jesus Christ. Such a twofold turning, or conversion, is necessary for entrance into the kingdom (Matt. 18:3). "Unless you repent," said Jesus, "you will all likewise perish" (Luke 13:3, 5). This is the negative, or judgmental, side of Jesus' message. The positive, or merciful, side is seen in these words: "There is joy in the presence of the angels of God over one sinner who repents" (Luke 15:10).

After Jesus' crucifixion and resurrection, His disciples continued His message of repentance and faith (Acts 2:38; 3:19; 20:21; 26:20). Repentance is a turning from wickedness and dead works (Acts 8:22; Heb. 6:1) toward God and His glory (Acts 20:21; Rev. 16:9), eternal life (Acts 11:18), and a knowledge of the truth (2 Tim. 2:25).

Repentance is associated with prayer (1 Kin. 8:47), belief (Mark 1:15), baptism (Acts 2:38), and conversion (Acts 3:19) and is accompanied by humility (Matt. 11:21). Repentance is God's will and pleasure (Luke 15:7–10; 2 Pet. 3:9), as well as His command (Mark 6:12; Acts 17:30). It is a gift of His sovereign love (Acts 5:31; 11:18; Rom. 2:4; 2 Tim. 2:25), without which we cannot be saved (Luke 13:3).

Repentance ought also to be seen as a life-long attitude of availability to the ongoing renewing of our minds (Rom. 12:1–2). The teachable soul never hunkers down in a doctrinaire notion of presumed perfection. Constant and progressive transformation (2 Cor.3:17–18) calls us to a growth in the mind of Christ (Phil.2:1–6), a mindset that necessitates ongoing "repentance" because only a will to be changed will allow that transformation.

RESTITUTION—the act of restoring to the rightful owner something that has been taken away, stolen, lost, or surrendered. Leviticus 6:1–7 gives the Mosaic Law of restitution; this law establishes the procedure to be followed in restoring stolen property.

Full restitution of the property had to be made and a percent of its value added, paid as compensation (Lev. 5:16; Ex. 22:4; Ex. 22:1).

In the New Testament, the word restitution is not used, but the idea is expressed. Zacchaeus, a chief tax collector, said to Jesus, "If I have taken anything from anyone by false accusation, I restore fourfold" (Luke 19:8).

Also see Law.

RESTORATION, THE HOLY SPIRIT AND.

New Testament Prophecy of Restoration (Acts 3:19–21)

Restoration in every dimension of human experience is at the heart of the Christian gospel. It is woven through all the Scriptures and must be at the forefront of our ministry of the truth.

Acts 3:19–21 makes the most pointed reference to restoration in the New Testament. Peter urges a return to God for cleansing from sins. He adds that this returning would pave the way for a period of refreshing renewal that would result from the presence of the Lord with His people. It would also prepare for the return of Christ, whom, Peter said, "heaven must receive [or retain] until the times of restoration of all things, which God has spoken by the mouth of all His holy prophets since the world began" (Acts 3:21).

Many feel it is now, in these last days, that "all things" prophesied will be fulfilled and restoration completed. The ultimate restoration is the return of the church, the bride of Christ, to the majesty and glory God intended for her. To accomplish this restoration, God has begun to release His power and purity without measure through the church. The sifting has begun in order that the unshakable kingdom may be revealed (Heb. 12:27–28).

The Biblical Definition of Restoration (Job 42:10–12)

According to the dictionary, "to restore" means to "bring back to a former or original condition." When something is restored in the Scriptures, however, it is always increased, multiplied or improved so that its latter state is significantly better than its original state (*see* Joel 2:21–26).

For example, under the Law of Moses, if someone stole an ox or a sheep, it was not sufficient for him simply to restore the animal he had taken. He had to pay back five oxen or four sheep (Ex. 22:1). When God restored Job after the terrible trials he endured, He gave him twice what he had lost and blessed him more in his latter days than in the beginning (Job 42:10–12). Jesus told His disciples that anyone who gave up anything to follow Him would have it restored a hundredfold (Mark 10:29–30).

God multiplies when He restores. And so, in His restoration work today, God is not simply restoring the church to the glory it displayed in New Testament times. He is seeking to restore it to a state more powerful, majestic, and glorious than anything the world has yet seen!

Restoration "In the Beginning" (Genesis 1—3)

The beginning of the Bible's restoration theme is found at the beginning of all things—in the Book of Genesis. God created man in His own image—male and female. Man enjoyed the image of God, the intimacy of God, and unbroken fellowship with God.

However, man chose to eat of the tree of the knowledge of good and evil. In so doing, he decided to take his life into his own hands. Instead of living from the wisdom, righteousness, and resources of God, he would live from his own limited resources—working things out for himself.

With that tragic decision, man lost his God-image (that is, godliness), as well as his intimacy and his fellowship with the Lord, his Creator. But God's restoration work began immediately. As the now self-conscious man tried the work of his own hands to make covering for his nakedness, God provided clothing made from an animal skin. This clearly revealed God's plan of redemption and restoration for fallen man. That first sacrifice, providing clothing, pointed toward the ultimate sacrificial Lamb of God—Jesus Himself.

Man's Plunge into Degradation (Genesis 4—12)

After being dismissed from the Garden and barred from the Tree of Life that stood in its midst, Adam begot children that were in his own image of self-centered disobedience, rather than in the image of God. From that point man fell deeper and deeper into depravity, until the Lord deemed it necessary to destroy the race and start over with a single family, that of Noah.

The covenant of the rainbow (Gen. 9:13) was one of the most important of many signs God gave during this period of time—a sign by which He indicated His intent to restore what had been lost through Adam and Eve. It is a timeless reminder of God's plan to bring man beyond judgment into His purpose.

With the call of Abram (Genesis 12), that purpose began to unfold as God's program for man's restoration became expressed through a specific individual. The "great nation" He promised to bring forth through Abram began with Israel, but was destined to become the church, the household of God. Although there are many prophecies concerning Israel, we can rest assured that for their fulfillment God had the church at heart from the beginning. The church is no more an afterthought than was God's promise of His Messiah—Jesus Christ.

Restoration Foreshadowed
(Joseph: Genesis 37—46)

The outline of God's restoration work stands out vividly in the life of Joseph. Joseph was *forsaken, falsely accused,* and *forgotten.* But finally he was *favored* by God and restored to the rule God had ordained for him.

1. *Forsaken.* When Joseph revealed to his brothers that God had called him to rule over them, they reacted with vicious envy, selling him into slavery in Egypt.

2. *Falsely Accused.* God prospered Joseph—even in slavery—so that his master put him in charge of his estate. But then his master's wife falsely accused Joseph of assaulting her, and he was thrown into prison.

3. *Forgotten.* While in prison, Joseph interpreted the dreams of Pharaoh's butler and baker. The butler was elated at hearing he would be set free, and Joseph asked him to speak a good word for him to Pharaoh. But, once out of prison and doing well, the butler forgot Joseph.

4. *Favored.* God did not forget, however. Two years later Pharaoh had a dream. The butler remembered Joseph and told Pharaoh about him. Joseph interpreted the dream, warning Pharaoh of seven years of famine. Grateful for the warning, Pharaoh put Joseph in control of all the wealth of Egypt. Not only was Joseph restored by this act, but, when the drought struck, he was in a position to save his people.

Man's Futile Efforts at Self-Restoration
(Jeremiah 8—10; Lamentations 2)

God promised to send a prophet like Moses to the Israelites to assure their ultimate deliverance. This was necessary because they had refused to hear God for themselves, insisting that He speak directly only to Moses (Deut. 18:15–16). Their fear of listening to Him put them under the letter of the law, where human effort labored to gain and keep divine acceptance. But God, knowing the limits of the law, instituted the Mosaic system of animal sacrifices to atone for their sins. He also placed the law as a schoolteacher to point to the ultimate deliverance through the shed blood of Jesus, the ultimate sacrifice (Heb. 10:10).

The failure of their efforts is presented most graphically in Jeremiah 8—10 and Lamentations 2, in the destruction of Jerusalem and the scattering of the people. These chapters paint a grim picture of human stubbornness, and the rebellion, immorality, idolatry, and general corruption afflicting the entire nation of Israel. They had forced God to such extremes of discipline that He had become like an enemy to them (Lam. 2:5).

Jeremiah 9:3 summarizes their plight, which resembles that of many in today's church: "And they do not know Me." Despite their most determine self-effort, they still did not have a personal relationship with God.

The Corruption of Leadership (Ezek. 34:1–10)

Having chosen to hear men rather than God, the people soon were hearing lies (Jer. 9:3). Ezekiel 34:1–10 exposes the wickedness and depravity into which the leaders had sunk. They used their offices and ministries only for what they could get for themselves, not to serve the people. They did not feed the flock, but rather they fed themselves. In His fury, God set Himself against these evil shepherds, vowing to take the sheep from them and put an end to this ruthless exploitation.

The shepherd analogy is retained in the restoration promise with which God follows these censuring statements. "For thus says the Lord God: 'Indeed I Myself will search for My sheep and seek them out. As a shepherd seeks out his flock . . . so will I seek out My sheep' " (vv. 11–12). God, then and now, wants His people to be directly related to Him, hearing Him, responding to Him, and living from His abundant life. He has never wavered from His commitment to restore the intimate love relationship that was lost in Eden.

The Futility of Religious Ritual (Amos 5:21–23)

Because people consistently have thought to earn God's acceptance by their own performance, they came to think even of their spiritual relationship with God only in terms of externals. They thought that just by observing certain rules and regulations, performing certain rituals, and speaking certain words, they could stay in favor with God.

The Lord set them straight concerning this misconception in the words of the prophets. He let them know that He despised their ritualistic worship and empty sacrifices (Amos 5:21–22), mock solemnity (Is. 58:4–5), and lip-service devotion (Jer 7:4). He had become sick of their singing, in which they only mouthed deceptive words that meant nothing to them (Amos 5:23). He vowed to turn their singing into wailing and cause their songs to become songs of lamentation and mourning (Jer. 7:34).

The Shaking of the Works of Men's Hands
(Heb. 12:26–27)

Everything Israel and Judah built up in generations of self-effort was an abomination to God, and He systematically gave over for destruction all they had accomplished by "the works of their own hands" (Jer. 1:16; 32:29–36).

The message of their misconception speaks to us today, and the apostle Paul summarizes the shaking God is determined to perform (Heb. 12:26–27). Everything built by the hand of man, in the energy and wisdom of the flesh, He was vowed to shake down. Only the things that cannot be shaken—the things built in His eternal power and wisdom—will remain.

The great shaking Paul prophesied has begun and is continuing in the church today. The same evils that plagued Israel—seeking to please God by external performance, lapsing into idolatry and moral decay, corruption in leadership, and worshiping the works of men's hands—are too present even in the church. Their removal is an essential part of the restoration process.

The Place of Repentance in Restoration
(Is. 58:1–14)

After pronouncing fierce judgment and chastisement on the people because of their apostasy, God presents wonderful promises of restoration. He says He will bring forth their righteousness as the noonday, and they will become like a watered garden. He will take away their iniquity, heal their apostasy, and love them freely (see Isaiah 58; Jeremiah 31—34; Hosea 14).

Between His voice of judgment and His promise of restoration, however, God's prophets consistently impose one vital exhortation: Repent! In Isaiah 58 it is indicated: "If you turn from your ritual fasts and submit to the true fast." It is contained in the voice of grieving Ephraim in Jeremiah 31:19: "I turned back, I repented." And in Hosea 14:1, it is couched in the pleading words, "Return, O Israel."

"Repent" did not mean to return to more dedicated efforts to please God by keeping the law or performing better works. The plea has always been simply to *turn to God Himself*—to allow Him to cleanse and restore.

Restoration of the Tabernacle of David
(Acts 15:16–18)

In Acts 15:1–29 a question was raised as to whether Gentiles could be accepted as Christians without submitting to the Law of Moses. Peter responded by noting that neither the Jews nor their fathers had been able to bear the burden of the Law; therefore, it made no sense to burden the Gentiles with it. "We believe that through the grace of the Lord Jesus Christ we shall be saved in the same manner as they [the Gentiles]" (v. 11). James confirmed Peter's statement by quoting a passage from Amos, in which God promises to "rebuild the tabernacle of David . . . so that the rest of mankind may seek the LORD" (Acts 15:16–17).

Many other Scriptures refer to the tabernacle of David, though not always by that name. The name often used is "Zion," Jerusalem's mount where the tabernacle stood and where God dwelt among His people.

Joel 2 begins with the thrilling cry, "Blow the trumpet in Zion, and sound an alarm in My holy mountain!" Hebrews 12:22 says: "But you have come to Mount Zion." Both refer to the tabernacle of David. An understanding of the concept of God's restoration of this tabernacle is essential, for it affords a clear, biblical view of what God is doing in the church today.

The Tabernacle of David:
Origin and Description

The tabernacle of David was established shortly after David succeeded Saul as king. The ark of the covenant, which represented the presence and power of God, had been captured by the Philistines. After a series of plagues, the Philistines returned it to Kirjath Jearim, where it remained at the house of Abinadab (1 Sam. 4:1—7:1). David coveted God's manifest presence with him and the people of Israel, so he sought to return the ark to Jerusalem and place it in a tent on Mount Zion (2 Samuel 6; 1 Chronicles 13—16).

Prior to its capture, the ark had been housed in the tabernacle of Moses—resting in the inner chamber called the Most Holy Place. No one but the high priest was allowed to enter into the presence of the ark, and he only once a year to sprinkle the blood of a sacrificed animal on the mercy seat that covered the ark (Heb. 9:1–7). The people could approach only to the outer court of the tabernacle to present their sacrifices and worship God.

The tabernacle of David marked a revolutionary departure from this system of separating God from the people. Without violating the spirit of the Law of Moses, David cultivated a spirit of intimacy again between the people and the Lord.

The Significance of the Restoration
of the Tabernacle of David

The great significance of the tabernacle of David lay in the fact that the ark, the very presence of God, was back in the midst of the people in Jerusalem. The people were taught by David to worship God with praise, thanksgiving, and rejoicing. Some sixteen ministries were ordained to be performed twenty-four hours a day, seven days a week. None of these ministries were related to guilt or condemnation; all reflected recognition of the mercy and lovingkindness of God and His unconditional acceptance of all who approached Him in faith.

Restoration of the tabernacle of David today means doing away with legalism, judgmentalism, and condemnation, and turning to the hurting people of the church and the world with the open and accepting arms of a loving God (Heb. 10:1–25). The Lord is inviting all to turn to Him, to let Him wipe their sins away, and to receive the refreshing that comes from being in the very presence of the Lord (Acts 3:19).

Restoration of the God-Image (Is. 4:2–3)

Just as the tabernacle of David represents restoration of the fellowship with God that was lost in Eden, so the analogy of the Branch symbolizes restoration of the God-image—godliness and the family tie with God. Isaiah 4:2, 3 speaks of a "righteous Branch of David" that will spring forth. That Branch is Christ, the Head of the true church, consisting of those who have received salvation and the new birth by grace through faith. Jesus identified Himself as the Vine and His disciples as the branches, and He said they would bring forth much fruit if they would abide in Him (John 15:5).

Numerous other Scriptures denote that, in Christ Jesus, God restores His people to the Father-child relationship that was broken by Adam's disobedience. All who believe in Him are brought back into the household of God (Eph. 2:19) and are destined to be conformed to His image (Rom. 8:29).

Restoration of Intimacy with God (Rev. 19:7–9)

The Lord illustrates the restoration of His intimacy with His people through the analogy of the bride and Bridegroom. The passage in Revelation 19:7–9 depicts the wedding feast of the Lamb, Jesus, when He claims His bride, the church, after she has made herself ready for Him. In his letter to the Ephesians, Paul explains how the bride will prepare herself: by submitting to God and allowing herself to be cleansed by the washing of His Word, so that she may be presented to the Bridegroom without spot, wrinkle, or blemish (Eph. 6:25–27).

When the bride is prepared and Jesus returns for her, the intimacy broken in the Garden will be completely restored, and man will again become one with Christ and with God, as Jesus prayed in John 17. But, as in the first "marriage," the bride must be bone of His bones and flesh of His flesh—that is, she must be like Him. He will not return for a defiled, defeated bride. In these days of restoration, God is preparing the bride with beauty and power and dressing her in His glory.

The Holy Spirit: The Agent of Restoration (Joel 2:28–29)

God's work of restoration is a work of the Holy Spirit in and through the lives of those who have believed in Jesus and have been born from above (John 3:3). The prophet Joel foretold a day when God would pour out His Spirit "on all flesh" (Joel 2:28–29). Thus, His power would be shared with all His people and not limited to one chosen individual. This explains why Christ told His disciples it was to their advantage for Him to leave them and go to the Father (John 16:7), because then the Spirit could be sent to indwell each of them, to fill them and to enable the supernatural works of God to be done through them.

Titus 3:5–6 reveals that even salvation—the regeneration of the dead spirit of man and the cleansing that makes the new man acceptable to God—is the work of the Holy Spirit.

Finally, in Acts 1:8, Jesus tells the disciples to do nothing until the Holy Spirit has come. Then, He promises, they will be empowered to witness of Him and their witness will spread the Good News throughout the world.

What Restoration Means to the Individual (John 10:10)

Perhaps the best way to summarize all that restoration means to the individual believer would be to use the simple word God used in both the Old and New Testaments: *life.* In Deuteronomy 30:20, Moses said of the Lord, "He is your life." In Colossians 3:4, Paul speaks of "Christ who is our life." And Jesus said, "I have come that they may have life, and that they may have it more abundantly" (John 10:10). But no words exceed the splendor or completeness of David's when he said of the Lord, "He restores my soul" (Ps. 23:3).

Restoration, to the individual, means the replacing of spiritual death with spiritual life. Ezekiel 36:25–28 graphically describes just such a transplant. Not only do we receive a new type and quality of life, but we must also grow in it. In many verses we see that process of growth as a work of the Holy Spirit (John 16:23; 17:22; Rom. 8:13; Phil. 1:6; 2:13; Col. 1:27). By His Holy Spirit, God continues and perfects the work He began in us at salvation.

What Restoration Means to the Church (John 13:34–35)

To the church as a whole, restoration means more than becoming a reproduction of the New Testament church. It means becoming all God originally intended the church to be. Remember, restoration means the establishment of something more and better than the original.

First, restoration means that the church

will display the kind of love Jesus demonstrated during His ministry on earth. By this love, He said, all men would know His disciples (John 13:34–35). Restoration also means the release of God's power without measure through the church. That restraint or restriction under the direction of the Holy Spirit—and in the holy spirit of God's love.

Through the full operation of the gifts and ministries that God appoints, and operating in the love essential to His own nature, the church will reach a level of maturity and unity that can be measured only in terms of "the stature of the fullness of Christ" (Eph. 4:13). As the church becomes a spiritual house (Eph. 2:20) inhabited by a holy priesthood, offering up spiritual sacrifices acceptable to God through Jesus Christ (1 Pet. 2:5), all people will be drawn to Him; the world will at last see the glory of God through this restored church. J.R.

RESURRECTION—being raised from the dead. Resurrection has three primary meanings in the Bible.

1. *Miraculous resuscitations.* In this usage, resurrection refers to individuals who have been brought back to life (resuscitated) in this present world. Such raisings were performed by Elijah on the Zarephath widow's son (1 Kin. 17:20–24), by Elisha on the Shunammite woman's son (2 Kin. 4:32–37) and the dead man who touched Elisha's bones (2 Kin. 13:21), by Jesus on Jairus' daughter (Mark 5:41–43) and Lazarus (John 11:43–44), by Peter on Dorcas (Acts 9:40–41), and by Paul on Eutychus (Acts 20:9–12). In these raisings there is no suggestion that the person did not later experience natural death.

2. *Our Lord's resurrection.* This resurrection is clearly linked with the overcoming of the powers of evil and death. For Paul, Christ's resurrection is the basis for the doctrine of general resurrection (1 Cor. 15:12–19). (*See* Resurrection of Jesus Christ.)

3. *The hope of a general resurrection.* It was Old Testament belief in the goodness of God that led the Jewish people to believe that the righteous dead would yet see God (Job 19:26; Ps. 49:15). This expectation was the foundation upon which the Jewish ideas concerning the resurrection were built.

By the time of Jesus, two positions were firmly entrenched within Judaism. The Sadducees, who were oriented to this world, rejected any belief in the resurrection. They believed that such an idea was irrelevant to this life and was not part of the revelation which God gave to Moses. Jesus condemned

their misunderstanding of Moses and the Scriptures (Mark 12:18–27).

The Pharisees, in contrast, believed in a resurrection. It was from the ranks of the Pharisees that Paul came (Phil. 3:5), and Luke records that in his defense before the Sanhedrin (Jewish Council), Paul stressed that he was a Pharisee of Pharisaic descent and that he was on trial for affirming the resurrection (Acts 23:6).

Israel's Old Testament concept of a resurrection is noted in Isaiah 26:10–19 and Daniel, who prophesied, "Many of those who sleep in the dust of the earth shall awake, some to everlasting life, some to shame and everlasting contempt" (Dan. 12:2).

The New Testament consistently teaches hope in the resurrection of the believer based upon the resurrection of Christ as the "firstborn from the dead" (1 Cor. 15:12–58; Col. 1:18; 1 Thess. 4:14–18; 1 Pet. 1:3–5). This idea of resurrection is expressed in terms or images such as a transformed body (Phil. 3:21), a new dwelling (2 Cor. 5:2), and new clothing (2 Cor. 5:4; Rev. 6:11). The New Testament also contrasts resurrection to life with resurrection to judgment (John 5:29; Acts 24:15). Apparently a similar contrast lies behind the statements in Revelation 20 about "the first resurrection" (20:5) and "the second death" (20:14).

RESURRECTION OF JESUS CHRIST—a central doctrine of biblical faith which affirms that God raised Jesus from the dead on the third day. Without the Resurrection, the apostle Paul declared Christian preaching and belief are meaningless (1 Cor. 15:14). The Resurrection is the point at which God's intention for Jesus becomes clear (Rom. 1:4) and believers are assured that Jesus is the Christ and our sins are forgiven (1 Cor. 15:17).

The appearances. The post-Resurrection appearances of Jesus are clearly at the heart of early Christian belief. The consistent witness of the New Testament is that in the appearances of Jesus something incredible happened. The two followers in Emmaus, upon realizing it was the risen Jesus, forgot their concern with the lateness of the hour and rushed back to Jerusalem to tell the others (Luke 24:29–33). The doubting Thomas uttered Christianity's greatest confession when he realized that the risen Christ was actually addressing him (John 20:27). Peter left his fishing nets for good when the risen Savior asked him, "Do you love Me?" (John 21:15). And at a later time (1 Cor. 15:8), the persecutor Paul was transformed into a zealous missionary as the result of a special appearance by the risen Lord (Acts 9:1–22).

But what was the nature of these appearances? Some have suggested that the appearance of Jesus to Paul seemed to be of a spiritual nature, similar to the revelation of Jesus to believers today. But since Paul equates all of the appearances together in 1 Corinthians 15:5–8, critical arguments that Jesus' appearances must be "spiritual" in nature must collapse. It is clear that the risen Jesus could be touched (Matt. 28:9; Luke 24:39; John 20:27) or that He could eat (Luke 24:41–42).

The truth of Scripture also countermands the contrived approach advocated by the German theologian Rudolph Bultmann, who spoke of an "Easter faith" of the disciples rather than an actual bodily resurrection of Jesus. He splits the Jesus of history from the spiritual experience of the Christ of faith, suggesting the Resurrection was only a belief, not a historical fact. But this notion is inconsistent with the evidence of the New Testament writers who bore witness *not* to what God did for them (with an idea), but what God did to Jesus (raising Him from the dead—Acts 2:32).

The resurrection of Jesus, His exaltation to the right hand of the Father (Acts 2:33), and the giving of the Spirit (John 20:22) are all to be seen as a single cluster of events verifying the resurrection reality. The summary practical impact of the resurrection of Jesus Christ may be seen in the following statement, and studied phrase by phrase with the supporting references from God's Word.

I Believe in the Resurrection

I believe in the resurrection of Jesus Christ, the Son of God; that He personally, physically, and actually died, and on the third day rose again according to the Scriptures. I believe that by His resurrection He declared His deity and announced His conquest of death and hell, and that all who believe this in their heart may be saved.

Because I believe this, I confess with my mouth the Lord Jesus and worship Him whom I glorify as the Son of God, risen from the grave and ascended upon high in triumph above all the powers of darkness.

(Supporting texts: Ps. 16:8–11; John 19:1—20:31; Rom. 1:4; 10:9–10; 1 Cor. 15:1–8; Eph. 1:19–21.)

I believe in the resurrection of the just, that at Christ's coming we shall all be changed into the likeness of His glorious, resurrected body. I believe that we shall receive eternal, physical bodies which shall not be subject to decay, and that in that glorified state we shall forever be with and serve the living God.

Because I believe this, I live life in hope of the resurrection, without fear of death and

without bondage to the endless grievings of those who have no such hope.

(Supporting texts: Job 19–26; Phil. 3:20–21; 1 Cor. 15:51–58; 1 Thess. 4:13–18; 1 John 3:2.)

I believe in the resurrection of all mankind, that on the last day every creature shall stand before the throne of God and give account for the deeds done in the body. I believe that by His death and resurrection, Christ Jesus has made it possible for every person to anticipate that day with joy, but that all those resistant to His Lordship shall experience endless judgment in bodies intended to know eternal blessing rather than eternal shame.

Because I believe this, I walk in faith and holy sobriety, knowing that my motives as well as my deeds, my thoughts as well as my words constitute the substance of eternal values which I either serve or shirk and according to which I shall be judged before the loving and righteous Father.

(Supporting texts: Luke 16:19–31; 1 Cor. 3:12–15; 2 Cor. 5:9–10; Rev. 20:11–15.)

With such an expectation as this, I can walk in praise to a resurrected Savior who has not only given me an eternal hope, but who can fill me with an eternal quality of life and power to live daily in the resources of His victory.

(Jack W. Hayford, Copyright 1979, Living Way Ministries)

RETRIBUTION—the act of dealing to someone what is deserved of just judgment. While retribution may be used in the sense of a reward for doing good, it usually refers to punishment for doing evil, especially in the world to come. The word retribution is not found in the KJV, and it appears only once in the NKJV (2 Chr. 6:23). Other translations use the word more frequently (Rom. 11:9; Heb. 2:2, RSV; Deut. 32:35; 2 Thess. 1:8, NASB; Rom. 1:18; Rev. 11:18, NEB).

The principle of retribution is found often in the Bible; it is indicated by words such as wrath, vengeance, punishment, judgment, and hell. Retribution is the judgment of a holy God upon sin. Eventually it becomes the eternal punishment of the ungodly—unless as sinners we turn in faith to Christ, who took the punishment we deserved upon Himself on the Cross.

Also see Law.

REVELATION—God's disclosure of Himself to mankind, including His nature, His moral standards, and His plan of salvation.

God is a personal being distinct from and transcendent of creation. Thus, for finite minds to know of and understand Him at all, He must take the initiative. Humankind can never unaided arrive at the truth about God, but He has graciously unveiled and manifested Himself to us. The distinction between biblical faith and other religions, philosophies, and endless human quests for God is at this juncture. Human quests are born of human insights; biblical faith is born of divine revelation.

God has revealed Himself in four unmistakable ways: (1) through human conscience in an inate sense of difference between right and wrong (Rom.2:14–15); (2) through the natural creation (Ps. 19:1–6; Rom 1:20), by which God has displayed His glory to all mankind; (3) through His Word (Mic. 6:8; John 20:31; 2 Tim.3:15); and (4) in His Son (John 14:9).

The fullest and final revelation of God has occurred in Jesus Christ. "God, who at various times and in various ways spoke in time past to the fathers by the prophets, has in these last days spoken to us by His Son, whom He has appointed heir of all things, through whom also He made the worlds" (Heb.1:1–2). Christ has "declared" God to us personally (John 1:18) as Christ gave us the words which the Father gave Him (John 17:8), and in the Cross Jesus supremely revealed God's self-giving love.

REVOLT, JEWISH, 66–70 A.D.—see ch. 55, §5.2.

REVOLT, JEWISH, 132–135 A.D.—see ch. 55, §4.3., 5.4.

ROSETTA STONE—see ch. 55, §2.1., 2.2.

SABBATH [SAB bahth]—the practice of observing one day in seven as a time for rest and worship. This practice apparently originated in creation, because God created the universe in six days and rested on the seventh (Genesis 1). By this act, God ordained a pattern for living— that man should work six days each week at subduing and ruling the creation and should rest one day a week. This is the understanding of the creation set forth by Moses in Exodus 20:3–11, when he wrote the Ten Commandments at God's direction.

History of the Sabbath. The practice of the weekly Sabbath was consecrated at creation (Gen. 2:1–3), even before the Ten Commandments were given.

The formal institution of the Sabbath later became a basic part of the Mosaic Law system. Each division of the law contains spe-

cific sections relating to the practice of the Sabbath: the moral law (the Ten Commandments), the civil law (Ex. 31:14), and the ceremonial law (Lev. 23:3). The keeping of the Sabbath was a sign that God truly ruled Israel. To break His Sabbath law was to rebel against Him (Ex 21:14). His people were not to seek advancement outside of submission to Him; therefore all work except acts of mercy, necessity, and worship were forbidden on the Sabbath (Is. 58:13, Matt. 12:1–13).

The Old Testament prophets recount God's blessings upon those who properly observed the Sabbath (Is. 58:13). They call upon the people to observe the Sabbath (Neh. 10:31; 13:15–22), while soundly condemning those who made much of external observance and ignored the heart and moral issues to which the Sabbath bound them (Is. 1:13; Hos. 2:11, Amos 8:5). During the period between the Old and New Testaments, religious leaders expanded details of Sabbath observance, substituting human traditions for divine wisdom (Matt. 15:9), reducing the Sabbath to little more than an external observance (Matt. 12:8), and making the law a burden rather than a rest and delight (Luke 11:46).

Jesus, like the Old Testament prophets, kept the Sabbath Himself (Luke 4:16) and urged others to observe the day (Mark 2:28). But He condemned the pharisaical attitude that missed the deep spiritual truth behind Sabbath observance (Matt 12:14; Mark 2:23; Luke 6:1–11, John 5:1–18).

The Christian Sabbath. Many believers feel that God still expects His people to set aside one day in seven to Him. Some argue that such an observance is a creation ordinance which is either (a) binding until this creation comes to an end, or (b) given as a blessing to be faithfully received with benefits. Some also strongly see the Fourth Commandment (Keep the Sabbath) as morally binding upon all people for all time.

Historically, most Christians seem to have observed Sunday, the first day of the week, as the New Covenant Sabbath, noting that Christ arose on the first day of the week (Matt. 28:1; Acts 20:7; 1 Cor. 16:2; Rev. 1:10). This day on which Jesus arose was called the *Lord's Day (Rev. 1:10).

Meaning of the Sabbath. The Sabbath is a means by which man's living pattern imitates God's manifest pattern for life on this planet (Ex. 20:3–11). Six days of work is to be fol-

---

This icon beside an entry indicates a Word Wealth feature.

This icon beside an entry indicates a Kingdom Dynamics feature.

This icon beside an entry indicates an important biblical or doctrinal term.

lowed by rest. (The idea inherent in the Hebrew word for Sabbath means "cessation.")

The Sabbath includes the idea and practice of celebrating rest, or salvation. To this end God declared that His Sabbath was a day for public convocation (Lev. 23:3), a special time for His people to gather together in public worship to signify their submission to His lordship over them and their way of living (Ex. 31:13; Ezek. 20:12). The idea of Sabbath celebration includes the Sabbath as a sacrament—a gift of God that allows man to participate in the intent of His salvation—a resting from our own works (Hebrews 4).

SACRAMENT—a formal religious act in which the actions and materials used are the means or avenue by which God's grace is communicated, either actually or symbolically. The word sacrament is not used in most English versions of the Bible. It comes from the Latin *sacramentum*, which was the word for a soldier's oath of allegiance. (In Eastern Orthodox tradition, the word also came to have the idea of "mystery" associated with it.)

Roman Catholics and Eastern Orthodox believers practice seven sacraments: the Eucharist (Lord's Supper), baptism, confirmation, penance (the forgiveness of sins), matrimony, holy orders, and extreme unction (the anointing of those in danger of death). They hold that these sacraments are means of grace through which God imparts spiritual blessedness.

Protestant believers generally prefer to use the word ordinances rather than sacraments, and only regard baptism and the Lord's Supper as the essential sacraments instituted by the Lord Jesus. Their position is based on the fact that these are the only two actions involving visible symbols (the water, the bread and wine) that were clearly observed by Christ (Luke 22:14–20) and commanded by Him (Matt. 28:19–20).

A number of Evangelicals and Pentecostals practiuce footwashing, following the example and instruction of Jesus (John 13:1–17). Some observe footwashing as a third ordinance.

SACRIFICE—the ritual through which the Hebrew people offered the blood or the flesh of an animal to God as a "substitute payment" for their sin. Sacrifice and sacrificing originated in the Garden of Eden immediately following the *Fall of man. Adam and Eve made loincloths of leaves to cover their sinfulness, then hid from God because their provision was inadequate in their own minds. God then killed animals and made larger tunics for Adam and Eve. God's covering covered man adequately, while man's covering was insufficient.

These coverings were declared acceptable by God because they covered more of man's body and they were produced by the shedding of blood. Furthermore, the curses and the promise of a redeemer (Gen. 3:14–19) fell between man's attempt to cover his sin (Gen. 3:7) and God's adequate covering (Gen. 3:21). Man's reaction to God's provision (3:14–19) was faith and hope in the Lord, as His provided coverings symbolized acceptance through faith and His promised redemption (Gen. 3:15).

The principle of sacrifice is confirmed in the account of Cain and Abel (Gen. 4:3–5). Abel offering a better sacrifice than Cain (Heb. 11:4). His sacrifice was "better" because it acknowledged God's gracious provision of an acceptable substitute and accepted the sacrifice of a living creature in his place. Abel received God's approval because he believed God and had faith in what God promised (Gen. 4:45).

Noah's first act was to build an altar upon which he sacrificed animals to God (Gen. 9:20–21); Abraham made sacrifice to God (Gen. 15:8–10) and rejoiced in anticipation of the appearance of a promised redeemer (John 8:56). As Abraham continued in worshiping God, the Lord taught him that the ultimate sacrifice would be the sacrifice of a human being, one of Adam's descendants—an only son provided miraculously by God (Genesis 22).

The expansion of the concept of sacrifice came with the Mosaic Law. In this code sacrifice has three central ideas: consecration, expiation (covering of sin), and propitiation (satisfaction of divine displeasure). But no approach to God could be made without a blood sacrifice offered for sin (Lev. 17:11; Heb. 9:22).

Both Testaments confirm that the Old Testament sacrifices were presented as a representative gesture. These substitutes pointed forward to the ultimate substitute, Jesus Christ (Heb. 10:1–18).

What was depicted in the Old Testament system God commanded was fulfilled in Jesus' life and death: (1) The animal sacrificed had to be physically perfect in age and condition; (2) through the perfection of this animal, perfection was presented to God. Thus, the true Lamb of God, innocent of all sin (1 Pet. 1:18–19) took away sin (John 1:29). (3) When coming to the altar, the worshiper laid his hands on the sacrifice, identifying his transferance of his sin and guilt to the sacrificial animal presented in his place. This pointed to the Savior who would do for us what we could not do for ourselves, taking upon Himself our sin and guilt and accomplishing redemption for us by His saving life and death (Is. 53:4–12; Matt. 1:21).

Nearly the whole of the Book of Hebrews details how Jesus' superior sacrifice has "once for all" attained full salvation for mankind (9:11–28). The remaining sacrifice for today's worshiper is *praise*—for Christ the Lamb (Heb. 13:15–16).

SACRIFICE. (Deut. 16:2) *zabach* (zah-*vakh*); *Strong's* #2076: To slay, slaughter, or sacrifice. From this verb comes the noun *zebach,* "a sacrifice." Whereas sacrifice in English sometimes suggests merely an inconvenience or the giving of a costly gift, in Hebrew it involves the offering of a life. From *zabach* also comes the word for "altar," *mizbeach,* which is literally "place of sacrificing."

SADDUCEES—see ch. 55, §5.

SAFETY. (Deut. 33:12) *betach* (beh-tahch); *Strong's* #983: Securely, in safety, confidently, in peace, trustingly; the state of confidence, security, and safety that belongs to those who trust and rely upon the Lord. *Betach* occurs more than forty times in the Old Testament and is most often translated "in safety," "securely," or "confidently"; occasionally, "boldly" (Gen. 34:25), or "in hope" (Ps. 16:9). From *betach* comes *bittachon,* which means "trust," "confidence," or "hope."

SAINTS—people who have been made holy in God's eyes through Christ's merit alone. Followers of the Lord are referred to by this phrase throughout the Bible, although its meaning is developed more fully in the New Testament. Consecration (setting apart) and purity are the basic meanings of the term. Believers are called "saints" (Rom. 1:7) and "saints in Christ Jesus" (Phil. 1:1) because they belong completely to the One who has provided their sanctification (1 Cor.1:2, 6:9–11).

SALVATION—deliverance from the power of sin, including forgiveness as well as wholeness for the whole personality.

In the Old Testament, the word salvation sometimes refers to deliverance from danger (Jer. 15:20), deliverance of the weak from an oppressor (Ps. 35:9–10), the healing of sickness (Is. 38:20), and deliverance from blood guilt and its consequences (Ps. 51:14). It may also refer to national deliverance from military threat (Ex. 14:13) or release from captivity (Ps. 14:7). But salvation finds its deepest meaning in the New Testament as it is revealed in Christ.

Mankind's universal need for salvation is one of the clearest teachings of the Bible. This need goes back to man's removal from the Garden of Eden (Genesis 3). After the Fall, man's life was marked by strife and difficulty, as well as loss of the divine purpose and oppression by the evil one. Increasingly, corruption and violence came to dominate his world (Gen. 6:11–13). When God destroyed the world with the Flood, He also performed the first act of salvation by saving Noah and his family, an action shown to be a pattern of that full salvation which we may receive in Christ (1 Pet. 3:18–22).

The central Old Testament experience and picture of salvation is the Exodus (Ex. 12:40—14:31), freeing God's redeemed to a destiny beyond their grasp (Ex. 13:3–16).

The prophets, however, declared that the full realization of God's purpose of salvation would involve a coming Savior and the promise of a completely new age (Is. 52:13—53:12; 65:17–25). The doctrine of salvation reached its fulfillment in the death of Jesus Christ on our behalf. His mission was to save the world from sin and the wrath of God (Matt. 1:21; John 12:47; Rom. 5:9), and His completed earthly ministry brought salvation as a promised availability opened to us through His death and resurrection (Mark 10:25; Luke 19:9–10).

Salvation through Jesus Christ is revealed in three tenses: past, present, and future. *Past:* When a person believes in Christ, we may instantly say he has been saved from sin's penalty (Acts 16:31). *Present:* We also are in the process of being saved from the power of sin as the new nature in Christ grows within us (Rom. 8:13; Phil. 2:12). *Future:* We shall be saved from the very presence of sin at the coming of our Lord or our homegoing to Him (Rom. 13:11; Titus 2:12–13). Salvation releases into our lives the overcoming power of Christ's newness of life (Rom. 6:4) and allows us a foretaste of our future life as His children (2 Cor. 1:22; Eph. 1:14). One day our experience of salvation will be complete when Christ returns (Heb. 9:28) and the kingdom of God is fully revealed (Matt. 13:41–43).

Also see Adoption, Atonement, Conversion, Forgiveness, Justification, Reconciliation, Redemption, Regeneration.

SALVATION. (Luke 19:9) *soteria* (so-tay-*ree*-ah); *Strong's* #4991: Compare "soteriology." Deliverance, preservation, soundness, prosperity, happiness, rescue, general well-being. The word is used both in a material, temporal sense and in a spiritual, eternal sense. The New Testament especially uses the word for spiritual well-being. Salvation is a present possession (Luke 1:77; 2 Cor. 1:6; 7:10), with a fuller realization in the future (Rom. 13:11; 1 Thess. 5:8–9). *Also* (Acts 28:28) *soterion* (so-tay-ree-on); *Strong's #4992:* Rescue, deliverance, safety, liberation, release, preservation, and the general word for Christian salvation. *Soterion* only occurs five times. *Soteria*, the generic word, occurs forty-five times. It is an all-inclusive word signifying forgiveness, healing, prosperity, deliverance, safety, rescue, liberation, and restoration. Christ's salvation is total in scope for the total man: spirit, soul, and body.

SANCTIFICATION—the work of God's grace by which the believer is separated from sin and becomes dedicated to God's righteousness. Accomplished by the Word of God (John 17:7) and the Holy Spirit (Rom. 8:34), sanctification results in holiness, or purification from the guilt and power of sin. Sanctification is *instantaneous* before God through Christ (1 Cor. 1:3) and *progressive* before man through obedience to the Holy Spirit and the Word (1 Thess. 4:1–8).

Sanctification as separation from the world and setting apart for God's service is a concept found throughout the Bible. Spoken of as "holy" or "set apart" in the Old Testament were the land of Canaan, the city of Jerusalem, the tabernacle, the temple, the Sabbath, the feasts, the prophets, the priests, and the garments of the priests.

Sanctification in the Atonement. As the process by which God purifies the believer, sanctification is based on the sacrificial death of Christ. In his letters to the churches, the apostle Paul noted that God has "chosen" and "reconciled" us to Himself in Christ for the purpose of sanctification (Eph. 1:4; 5:25–27; Titus 2:14).

Old Testament sacrifices did not take away sin, but they were able to sanctify "for the purifying of the flesh" (Heb. 9:13). The blood of the new covenant (Heb. 10:29), however, goes far beyond this ritual purification of the body. The offering of Christ's body (Heb. 10:10) and blood (Heb. 13:12) serves to purge our conscience from "dead works to serve the living God" (Heb. 9:14). Because our cleansing from sin is made possible only by Christ's death and resurrection, we are "sanctified in Christ Jesus" (1 Cor. 1:2; Acts 20:32; 1 Cor. 1:30; 6:11).

Sanctification: God's work. We are sanctified by God the Father (Jude 1), God the Son (Heb. 2:11), and God the Holy Spirit (2 Thess. 2:13; 1 Pet. 1:2). Perfect holiness is God's command (1 Thess. 4:7) and purpose. As Paul prayed, "Now may the God of peace Himself sanctify you completely" (1 Thess. 5:23). Sanctification is a process that continues during

our lives as believers (Heb. 10:14). Other than through our position before God in Christ, only after death will believers be referred to as "perfect" (Heb. 12:23).

Sanctification: the believer's work. Numerous commands in the Bible imply that believers also have a responsibility in the process of sanctification. We are commanded to "be holy" (Lev. 11:44; 1 Pet. 1:15–16); to "be perfect" (Matt. 5:48); and to "present your members as slaves of righteousness for holiness" (Rom. 6:19). Writing to the church of the Thessalonians, the apostle Paul made a strong plea for purity (1 Thess. 4:35).

These commands imply obedience on our part and dependence upon grace to grow. As we believe in Jesus, we are "sanctified by faith in Him" (Acts 26:18). Through the Holy Spirit we must also "put to death the deeds of the body" (Rom. 8:13). Paul itemized the many "works of the flesh" from which we must separate ourselves (Gal. 5:19–21). Finally, we must walk in the Spirit in order to display the fruit of the Spirit (Gal. 5:22–24).

SANCTIFIED. (John 10:36) *hagiadzo* (hag-ee-ad-zoe); *Strong's #37:* Compare "hagiography" and "Hagiographa." To hallow, set apart, dedicate, consecrate, separate, sanctify, make holy. *Hagiadzo* as a state of holiness is opposite of *koinon*, common or unclean. In the Old Testament things, places, and ceremonies were named *hagiadzo*. In the New Testament the word describes a manifestation of life produced by the indwelling Holy Spirit. Because His Father set Him apart, Jesus is appropriately called the Holy One of God (6:69).

SARAH—see ch. 55, §3.5.b.

SATAN [SAY tuhn] (adversary)—the great opposer, or adversary, of God and man; the personal name of the devil.

Whenever this word is used as a proper name in the Old Testament, it refers to the great superhuman enemy of God, man, and good (1 Chr. 21:1; Job 1—2). This use occurs frequently in the New Testament, so it is consistently clear that the Bible teaches the existence of a personal devil.

The New Testament term "the devil," means "slanderer" or "false accuser." Other titles by which Satan is identified in the New Testament include "the tempter" (1 Thess. 3:5); "Beelzebub" (Matt. 12:24); "the wicked one" (Matt. 13:19, 38); "the ruler of this world" (John 12:31); "the god of this age" (2 Cor. 4:4); "Belial" (2 Cor. 6:15); "the prince of the power of the air" (Eph. 2:2); and "the accuser of our brethren" (Rev. 12:10).

History. Two Old Testament passages—Isaiah 14:12–15 and Ezekiel 28:11–19—furnish a picture of Satan's original condition and the reasons for his loss of that position. These passages, prophetically addressed to the kings of Babylon and Tyre, are seen by most scholars to refer to Satan himself. They tell of an exalted angelic being, one of God's creatures, who became proud and ambitious, determined to usurp God's throne, and thus removed by God—banished to hell from his position of great dignity and honor.

Jesus' words in Luke 10:18, with Revelation 12:3–4, describe further implications of Satan's fall. It appears he led a rebellion which caused one-third of the angels to be cast out with him (Rev. 12:3–4). Throughout the Old Testament period he sought to destroy the messianic line, and when the Messiah became a man, Satan tried to eliminate Him (Matt. 2:13–18; Rev. 12:4–5). During the age-long struggle before the Messiah's Second Coming, Satan, cast out of the heavenly sphere through the triumph of the Cross (Col. 2:14–15; Rev. 12:9–10), directs his animosity toward the Messiah's people (Rev. 12:11–17).

Revelation 20 notes the final phases of Satan's work. He will be bound for a thousand years and then finally cast into the lake of fire (Rev. 20:2, 10).

Characteristics. As a result of his original status and authority, Satan has great power and dignity. So great is his strength that Michael the archangel viewed him as a foe too powerful to independently oppose (Jude 9).

Satan's influence in worldly affairs is also clearly revealed (John 12:31). His various titles reflect his control of the world system: "the ruler of this world" (John 12:31), "the god of this age" (2 Cor. 4:4), and "the prince of the power of the air" (Eph. 2:2). The Bible declares, "The whole world lies under the sway of the wicked one" (1 John 5:19).

Satan is not omnipresent or omnipotent, but he exercises his limited evil powers through demons (Matt. 12:24; 25:41; Rev. 12:7, 9). The outburst of demonic activity seen when Jesus came to earth and the kingdom of God began to confront Satan's kingdom (Matt. 12:28–29; Acts 10:38) continues to be overcome wherever believer's advance the gospel today (Mark 16:15–18; Rom. 16:20).

Satan, as an angelic being, also has high intelligence but is not omniscient. Through his subtlty he deceived Adam and Eve and grasped their rule of the world for himself (Gen. 1:26; 3:1–7; 2 Cor. 11:3). By blinding the moral reasoning capacity of fallen humans, and by assailing the character of God in their eyes, he carries out his deceptive work almost at will (2 Cor. 4:4; 2 Tim. 2:24–26).

Satan's attributes are not limitless. His power is subject to God's restrictions (Job 1:12; Luke 4:6; 2 Thess. 2:7–8).

Satan may succeed in afflicting or hindering God's people (Luke 13:16; 1 Thess. 2:18; 2 Cor. 12:7)), but he is never able to win an ultimate victory over them (John 14:30–31; 16:33).

A part of Satan's continuing ambition to replace God is his passionate yearning to have others worship him (Matt. 4:8–9; Rev. 13:4, 12).

Satan's nature is malicious. His efforts in opposing God, His people, and His truth are tireless (Job 1:7; 2:2; Matt. 13:28). He is always opposed to man's best interests (1 Chr. 21:1; Zech. 3:1–2). Through his role in introducing sin into the human family (Genesis 3), Satan has gained the power of death—a power which Jesus has broken through His crucifixion and resurrection (Heb. 2:14–15).

Methods. Of the various methods used by Satan in carrying out his evil work, none is more characteristic than *temptation (Matt. 4:3; 1 Thess. 3:5). Satan leads people into sin by various means. Sometimes he does it by direct suggestion, as in the case of Judas Iscariot (John 13:2, 27); sometimes through his agents who disguise themselves as messengers of God (2 Thess. 2:9; 1 John 4:1); and sometimes through a person's own weaknesses (1 Cor. 7:5). He tempted Jesus directly, trying to lead Him into compromise by promising Him worldly authority and power (Luke 4:58).

Along with his work of tempting mankind, Satan also delights in deception (1 Tim. 3:6–7; 2 Tim. 2:26). His lying nature stands in bold contrast to the truth for which Christ stands (John 8:32, 44). The great falsehood which he uses so frequently is that good can be attained by doing wrong. This lie is apparent in practically all his temptations (Gen. 3:4–5). As the great deceiver, Satan is an expert at falsifying truth (2 Cor. 11:13–15).

Satan's methods are designed ultimately to silence the gospel. He seeks to stop the spread of God's Word (Matt. 13:19; 1 Thess. 2:17–18). When the gospel is preached, Satan tries to blind people's understanding so they cannot grasp the meaning of the message (2 Cor. 4:3–4; 2 Thess 2:9–10). At times he opposes the work of God by violent means (John 13:2, 27; 1 Pet. 5:8; Rev. 12:13–17). He brings disorder into the physical world by afflicting human beings (Acts 10:38). Individuals may even be delivered into his hands for purposes of correction (1 Tim. 1:20; 1 Cor. 5:4–5).

Defeat. Satan is destined to fail in his continuing rebellion against God. His final defeat is predicted in the New Testament (Luke 10:18; John 12:31; Rev. 12:9; 20:10). The death of Christ on the Cross is the basis for Satan's final defeat (1 John 3:8; Heb. 2:14–15; 1 Pet. 3:18, 22). This event was the grand climax to a sinless life during which Jesus triumphed over the enemy repeatedly (Matt. 4:1–11; Luke 4:1–13). The final victory will come when Jesus returns and Satan is cast into the lake of fire (Rev. 20:1–15).

Strength for a Christian's victory over sin has also been provided through the death of Christ. We have assurance that "the God of peace will crush Satan under your feet" (Rom. 16:20). Such personal victory depends on our will to offer resistance to Satan's temptations (Eph. 4:25–27; 1 Pet. 5:8–9). To help Christians win this battle against Satan, God has provided the power of Christ's blood and the authority of His Word on our lips (Rev. 12:11). We also are assured of the continuing prayer of Christ in heaven supporting us (Heb. 7:25), the leading of the Holy Spirit (Gal. 5:16), and various armor and weapons for spiritual warfare (Eph. 6:13–18).

Reality. Some people have trouble admitting the existence of such an enemy as Satan. But his presence and activity are necessary to explain the problems of evil and suffering. The Bible makes it plain that Satan exists and that his main work is to oppose the rule of God in the affairs of man.

Also see Devil.

SATAN. (Job 1:6) *satan* (sah-*tahn*); *Strong's* #7854: An opponent, or the Opponent; the hater; the accuser; adversary, enemy; one who resists, obstructs, and hinders whatever is good. *Satan* comes from the verb which means "to be an opponent," or "to withstand." As a noun, *satan* can describe any "opponent" (2 Sam. 19:21–22). However, when the form *ha-satan* (the Adversary) occurs, the translation is usually "Satan," not his name, but his accurate description: hateful enemy. Since Satan is the Hater, he is all the more opposed to God, who is love (*see* 1 John 3:10–15; 4:7–8). Mankind did not witness Satan's beginning, but by God's design shall see his end, one of ceaseless torment and humiliation (*see* Is. 14:12–20; Ezek. 28:16–19; Rev. 20:10).

SATISFIED. (Amos 4:8) *sabe'a* (sah-*vay*-ah); *Strong's* #7646: To be filled to satisfaction; to sate, satiate, fill, supply abundantly. This verb occurs about one hundred times. Related words appear in Genesis 41:29, seven years of "plenty"; in Job 42:17, Job died when satisfied with his long life ("full of days"); in Psalm 16:11, "fullness" of joy is found in God's presence; and in Isaiah 23:18, God's people may

eat "sufficiently." The most common usage of *sabe'a* concerns being filled with food or drink until one is satisfied. According to Proverbs 27:20, two things that are never satisfied are hell and man's eyes.

SAVE. (Jer. 17:14) *yasha'* (yah-*shah*); *Strong's* #3467: To rescue, save, defend; to free, preserve, avenge, deliver, help. The verb, found more than two hundred times throughout the Old Testament, is a one-word description of God's response to the needs of humanity. God chose a form of this verb to be His Son's name: *Yeshua*, meaning "He Shall Save." (*See* Matt. 1:21.) The original thought of *yasha'* was "to release," "to open wide." Our Deliverer is the One who opened wide the gates of captivity, released and rescued us, and continually defends and preserves us.

SAVED. (Luke 7:50) *sozo* (*sode*-zoe); *Strong's* #4982: To save, heal, cure, preserve, keep safe and sound, rescue from danger or destruction, deliver. *Sozo* saves from physical death by healing, and from spiritual death by forgiving sin and its effects. *Sozo* in primitive cultures is translated simply "to give new life" and "to cause to have a new heart."

SAVIOR. (John 4:42) *soter* (so-*tare*); *Strong's* #4990: Compare "soteriology," the doctrine of salvation. From the same root as *sodzo*, "to save," and *soteria*, "salvation." The word designates a deliverer, preserver, savior, benefactor, rescuer. It is used to describe both God the Father and Jesus the Son.

SAW. (John 20:14) *theoreo* (theh-oh-*reh*-oh); *Strong's* #2334: Compare "theater," "theory," "theoretical." To behold, view attentively, perceive, look with a prolonged and continuous gaze. *Theoreo* conveys looking with a purpose, with interest, and with close scrutiny.

SCRIPTURE—the Old and New Testaments, which make up the Bible, God's written Word. God gave to the world His living Word, Jesus Christ and His written Word, the Scriptures. Although the Bible was written by prophets and apostles, the Bible originated not with their wills, but with God's (2 Pet. 1:20–21). "All Scripture," Paul wrote, "is given by inspiration of God" (2 Tim. 3:16).

The following is a positive, biblical statement for today's believer.

I Believe the Bible

I believe in the Holy Scriptures, the Bible, the eternal Word of God. I believe in its divine inspiration, its infallible authority, and its completeness in form and content.

Because I believe this, I treasure this Book, for therein is the written will of God revealed by the Holy Spirit. I will appeal to this ultimate

Word from heaven as the conclusive guide for every issue of life, knowing that the Living God who has authored it supports its every word and subscribes its every promise. I reject all attempts of flesh or spirit to add to this written revelation, believing that herein is all I need to understand and to communicate the whole of God's creative and redemptive purposes for man.

(Supporting texts: 1 Kin. 8:54–58; Pss. 19:7–11; 119:1–16, 89; Jer. 1:12; Matt. 24:35; Gal. 1:6–9; 2 Tim. 3:16–17; Rev. 22:18–19.)

I believe in the Bible, given by the Holy Spirit through human agency overseen by the mind of the Eternal Father, and thereby established and sustained in its unity of purpose and message which is the testimony of the Son of God, Jesus Christ.

Because I believe this, I depend upon the Holy Spirit to illumine my understanding in the Word of God. I affirm my commitment to hear this Word with my heart as well as my mind, realizing that unless a spiritual, as well as an intellectual response is made, the full intent of the entrance of God's Word is not being gained. In my open quest to receive all the Word contains and intends in spirit and life, I reject any approach to the Scriptures which seek them for other than the revelation of Christ in the Word and the practical unfolding of God's way of life for us in Him.

(Supporting Scriptures: Luke 24:25–27; John 5:37–38; 6:63; 16:13–14; 1 Cor. 2:12–14; Col. 2:8–23; 1 Tim. 4:15–16; 6:20–21; 2 Tim. 2:15–16, 23; 1 Pet. 1:10–12; 2 Pet. 1:19–21; Rev. 19:10.)

I believe in the Word of God, the source of faith. I believe it is to be preached and taught to every man and that through its words the human spirit may be reborn, instructed in righteousness, and brought to maturity in life and love for God and man.

Because I believe this, I receive the Word with both a commitment and a commission. I commit myself to hear the Word with expectation, available as its truth calls forth repentance and transformation in my life, and believing as its promises summon me to a lifetime pathway of practical faith in God. And I acknowledge my responsibility to all mankind, to communicate the Word of God through my witness, my service, and my resource.

(Supporting Scriptures: Ps. 119:97–112; Rom. 10:13–17; Heb. 4:12–13; James 1:22–25; 1 Pet. 1:23; 2 Pet. 1:4–11.)

With such a foundation as this I am undergirded with promise and established in wisdom for a life of fruitfulness and fulfillment.

(Jack W. Hayford, Copyright 1978, Living Way Ministries)

SCRIPTURES. (John 5:39) *graphe* (graf-*ay*); *Strong's #1124:* Compare "graph," "graphic," "biography," "autograph." A document, anything written, holy writ, the Scriptures. *Graphe* points to the divine author with the idea that what is written remains forever identified as the living voice of God. While some scholars restrict *graphe* to the Old Testament writings, 2 Peter 3:16 includes the New Testament writings.

SECOND COMING—Christ's future return to the earth at the end of the present age. Although the Bible explicitly speaks of Christ's appearance as a "second time," the phrase "second coming" occurs nowhere in the New Testament. Many passages, however, speak of His return. In fact, in the New Testament alone it is referred to over three hundred times.

The night before His crucifixion, Jesus told His apostles that He would return (John 14:3). When Jesus ascended into heaven, two angels appeared to His followers, saying that He would return in the same manner as they had seen Him go (Acts 1:11). The New Testament is filled with expectancy of His coming, even as Christians should be today. Irrespective of differences of opinion, readiness and imminent expectancy are already taught as righteous attitudes toward Christ's return throughout the church age (Matt. 25:13; Mark 13:33–37; 1 Thess. 5:1–11; Rev. 22:7, 12–13, 20).

SECOND KINGS—see ch. 55, §2.3.

SECOND TEMPLE PERIOD—see ch. 55, §6.

SEEK. (Hos. 5:15) *baqash* (bah-*kahsh*); *Strong's #1245:* To seek, to diligently look for, to search earnestly until the object of the search is located. *Baqash* can apply to seeking a person, a particular item, or a goal (such as seeking to destroy a city, 2 Sam. 20:19). *Baqash* occurs more than 210 times in Bible. Peace is to be searched for earnestly (Ps. 34:14). The Lord's face, that is, His presence, must especially be sought (Ps. 27:8).

SEER. (1 Sam. 9:9) *ro'eh* (roh-*ay*); *Strong's #7200, 7203:* A visionary, a seer; one who sees visions; a prophet. *Ro'eh* comes from the verb *ra'ah,* which means "to see," but also has a wide range of meanings related to seeing (such as "perceive," "appear," "discern," "look," "stare," and many other nuances). It was only natural for Hebrew speakers to describe a prophet as a "seer," since prophets frequently received messages from God through visions. However, the word *nabi'* (spokesman) is the preferred Hebrew word for prophet.

SELFISH AMBITION. (Phil. 1:16) *eritheia* (er-ith-*eye*-ah); *Strong's #2052:* A word that regressed from denoting honorable work to suggesting dishonorable intrigue. Originally, it meant a field-worker or reaper, and then anyone working for pay, a hireling. *Eritheia* later described a person who was concerned only with his own welfare, a person susceptible to being bribed, an ambitious, self-willed person seeking opportunities for promotion. From there it became electioneering, a partisan factious spirit that would resort to any method for winning followers.

SENNACHERIB—see ch. 55, §3.7.d.

SENSUAL. (James 3:15) *psuchikos* (psoo-khee-koss); *Strong's #5591:* Belonging to the natural or physical, unspiritual. It is living in the domain of the five senses, concerned with this life only. Being sensual is being in common with lusts, illicit desires, and unclean practices that open a person to the demonic. Galatians 5:16 admonishes, "Walk in the Spirit, and you shall not fulfill the lust of the flesh."

SENT. (John 20:21) *apostello* (ap-os-*tel*-low); *Strong's #649:* Compare "apostolic." To commission, set apart for a special service, send a message by someone, send out with a mission to fulfill, equip and dispatch one with the full backing and authority of the sender.

SERAPHIM. (Is. 6:2) *seraphim,* plural of *seraph* (seh-rah-*feem;* seh-*rahf*); *Strong's #8314:* A burning, fiery, gliding, angelic being; also a fire-colored, agile, gliding desert creature, presumably a fiery serpent. The root is the verb *seraph,* "to set on fire, to burn." Accordingly, the *seraphim* may be angels of a fiery color or appearance, or flamelike in motion or clearness. Only in Isaiah 6:2, 6 does the word appear as "seraphim"; in all the remaining five occurrences (Num. 21:6, 8; Deut. 8:15; Is. 14:29; 30:6), it is translated "fiery serpents" and appears along with scorpions and vipers. Perhaps the color or motion of the earthly fiery serpents resembles that of the fiery angels.

SERVANTS. (Rev. 19:5) *doulos* (*doo*-loss); *Strong's #1401:* From *deo,* "to bind." The word denotes one in bondage to or subject to another, and is usually translated "slave" or "servant." Often the service involved is voluntary, in which a person willingly offers obedience, devotion, and loyalty to another, subordinating his will to him. The word is used of natural conditions (Matt. 8:9; 18:23), and metaphorically to describe servants of Christ (Rom. 1:1; 1 Cor. 7:22), of God (Acts 16:17; Titus 1:1), of sin (John 8:34; Rom. 6:17, 20), of corruption (2 Pet. 2:19), and of evil (Matt. 18:32; 24:48).

SERVE. (Ps. 100:2) *'abad* (ah-*vahd*); *Strong's #5647:* To work for, serve, do labor for someone; to be a servant; to worship. From this verbal root comes *'ebed,* "servant," "slave," or "laborer." "Servant" is generally someone who acts at the bidding of a superior. The most significant bearer of this designation is the messianic "Servant of the Lord" in Isaiah. *'Abad* appears in several names, among which are Obed-Edom ("Servant of Edom"), Abed-Nego ("Servant of Nego"), and Obadiah ("Servant of Yah"). Psalm 35:27 illustrates how much God values and is kindly disposed to His servants. Unlike human overlords and masters, God is deeply concerned with the total well-being of each of His servants.

SERVICE. (Luke 1:23) *leitourgia* (lie-toorg-ee-ah); *Strong's #3009:* Compare "liturgy," "liturgical." From *laos,* "people," and *ergon,* "work." The word was used originally of citizens serving in public office at their own expense. Later it included military service or community participation. In the New Testament *leitourgia* is used both for priestly service and unselfish giving. Here it refers to priestly service in the temple. In 2 Corinthians 9:12, it denotes charitable gifts as a service to the needy. Paul names his service to the Christian church *leitourgia* in Philippians 2:17.

SETTLED DOWN. (Nah. 10:12) *shachan* (shah-chahn); *Strong's #7931:* To dwell, abide, remain, stay, tabernacle. This verb occurs more than 120 times. People dwell in tents (Ps. 120:5) or in a certain land (Jer. 7:7); God dwells in Mt. Zion (Is. 8:18); glory dwells in the Holy Land (Ps. 85:9). *Mishkan,* "tabernacle," God's "place of dwelling," is derived from *shakan.* This term also refers to the tabernacle of Moses and to other dwelling places as well. *Mishkan* occurs more than fifty times in Exodus alone. Another derivative of *shakan* is *shekinah,* the "abiding presence of Almighty God." Sometimes the *shekinah* appears in a visible way. Not found in Scripture, *shekinah* comes to us from Judaic writings.

SEVENTY—a number of great significance in the Bible because it is a multiple of the number seven, considered a sacred number by the Hebrew people (Ex. 1:1–5). Seventy is the number of persons of the house of Jacob who went to Egypt (Gen. 46:27). And when Jacob (Israel) died, he was mourned seventy days (Gen. 50:3). Seventy elders of Israel accompanied Moses to Mount Sinai (Ex. 24:1). Psalm 90:10 says that the days of our lives are seventy. In His teachings, Jesus emphasized that we should forgive others not seven times but "up to seventy times seven" (Matt. 18:22).

SEVENTY, THE—in Luke's Gospel, a group of seventy disciples sent out by Jesus to heal the sick and preach the good news of the kingdom of God (Luke 10:1–17). Jewish writings often spoke of the Gentile nations symbolically as numbering seventy. Among the four Gospels, Luke is known as the one with a universal, worldwide view. By speaking of the seventy disciples, Luke probably wanted to show that the gospel of Christ is not only for Jews, the twelve tribes of Israel, but also for the Gentiles, the "seventy nations" of the world.

SEVENTY WEEKS—a term that the prophet Daniel used in his prophecy of the future (Dan. 9:24–27). In Daniel's vision, God revealed that the captivity of His people in Babylon would come to an end and they would be restored to glory as a nation within a period of seventy weeks of seven years each—or a total of 490 years.

Scholars interpret this seventy weeks prophecy in different ways. Some insist that Daniel is not a book of prophecy at all but that he was writing about events that had already happened. Others believe the 490-year period came to a grand climax with Jesus' death on the Cross. Still others believe this prophecy is yet to be fulfilled in the future.

SEVEN WORDS FROM THE CROSS—the seven different utterances of Jesus while He hung on the Cross:

1. "Father, forgive them, for they do not know what they do" (Luke 23:34). Jesus taught that we should forgive those who sin against us. How appropriate that His first words from the Cross should be words of forgiveness.

2. "Assuredly, I say to you, today you will be with Me in Paradise" (Luke 23:43). As He hung on the Cross, Jesus certainly did not appear to be a king. Yet, what faith the repentant thief displayed when he asked, "Lord, remember me when You come into Your kingdom" (Luke 23:42). Jesus' reply was good news indeed to this dying sinner.

3. "Woman, behold your son! . . . Behold your mother!" (John 19:26–27). In spite of His grief and pain, Jesus continued to think of others. His earthly father, Joseph, probably had died by this time. Jesus asked his beloved disciple, John, to take care of His mother, Mary.

4. *Eli, Eli, lama sabachthani? . . . My God, My God, why have You forsaken Me?"* (Matt. 27:46; Mark 15:34). These words came from Jesus' lips about 3 P.M., after He had hung on the Cross for nine hours. Death was near, and Jesus was feeling the pain and loneliness that sin causes. But the sin in this case was our sin and not His. To express His anguish and grief, Jesus quoted the opening words of Psalm 22, using the same words that King David had used many years earlier (Ps. 22:1).

5. "I thirst!" (John 19:28). The Old Testament had prophesied that Jesus would suffer for the sins of the world. In His death, that prophecy was being fulfilled. Jesus suffered spiritual torment as well as physical agony as He hung on the Cross. His spirit thirsted to win the spiritual battle against evil while His body thirsted for water.

6. "It is finished!" (John 19:30). The word translated "finished" shows clearly that Jesus' victory has been achieved. It carries the idea of perfection or fulfillment. God's plan of salvation had been accomplished through Jesus' sacrifice on the Cross.

7. "Father, into Your hands I commit My spirit" (Luke 23:46; also see Ps. 31:5; Matt. 27:50; Mark 15:37). Jesus did not die a failure. He died a victorious Savior. He finished His work triumphantly and entrusted His spirit to God His Father.

SHALL LIVE. (Hab. 2:4) *chayah* (chah-*yah*); *Strong's* #2421: To live, to stay alive, be preserved; to flourish, to enjoy life; to live in happiness; to breathe, be alive, be animated, recover health, live continuously. The fundamental idea is "to live and breathe," breathing being the evidence of life in the Hebrew concept. Hence the Hebrew words for "living being" or "animal" (*chay*) and "life" (*chayyim*) derive from *chayah*. This verb occurs about 250 times in the Old Testament. Many references contain the suggestion that "living" is the result of doing the right thing (Deut. 4:1; 30:19–20; Prov. 4:4; 9:6; Amos 5:4). The present reference is one of the giant pillars of the faith; not only does it appear several times in the New Testament; it also sparked the Reformation. It literally reads, "The righteous person in (or by) his faithfulness (firmness, consistency, belief, faith, steadfastness) shall live!"

SHAMASH—see ch. 55, §3.1.

SHEMA, THE [shuh MAH] *(hear thou)*—the Jewish confession of faith which begins, "Hear, O Israel: The Lord our God, the Lord is one!" (Deut. 6:4). The complete Shema is found in three passages from the Old Testament: Numbers 15:37–41, Deuteronomy 6:4–9, and 11:13–21.

The first of these passages stresses the unity of God and the importance of loving Him and valuing His commands. The second passage promises blessing or punishment according to a person's obedience of God's will. The third passage commands that a fringe be worn on the edge of one's garments as a continual reminder of God's laws. This collection of verses makes up one of the most ancient features of worship among the Jewish people. According to the Gospel of Mark, Jesus quoted from the Shema during a dispute with the scribes (Mark 12:28–30).

SHEOL [SHE ole] (meaning unknown)—in Old Testament thought, the abode of the dead. Sheol is the Hebrew equivalent of the Greek *hades,* which means "the unseen world."

Sheol was regarded as an underground region (Num. 16:30, 33; Amos 9:2), shadowy and gloomy, where disembodied souls had a conscious but dull and inactive existence (2 Sam. 22:6; Eccl. 9:10). The Hebrew people regarded sheol as a place to which both the righteous and unrighteous went at death (Gen. 37:35; Ps. 9:17; Is. 38:10), a place where punishment is received and rewards are enjoyed. Sheol is pictured as having an insatiable appetite (Is. 5:14; Hab. 2:5).

However, God is present in sheol (Ps. 139:8; hell, NKJV). It is open and known to Him (Job 26:6; Prov. 15:11). This suggests that in death God's people remain under His care, and the wicked never escape His judgment. It is apparent that Jesus emptied that portion of sheol where the righteous were waiting until redemption's completion (Luke 23:43). Sheol gives meaning to Psalm 16:10. Peter saw the fulfillment of this messianic psalm in Jesus' resurrection (Acts 2:27).

Also see Hell.

SHEPHERD—a person who takes care of sheep. Figuratively, the Old Testament pictures God as Israel's Shepherd-Leader (Ps. 80:1; Ezek. 34:14). The New Testament reveals Jesus as the Good Shepherd who gave His life for His sheep. When He said, "I am the good shepherd" (John 10:11), Jesus linked His own divine nature with one of the most ordinary occupations in Israel. New Testament pastors are called shepherds (Greek, *polmenas*), accountable for their flocks (Heb. 13:17) to Jesus the Chief Shepherd (1 Pet. 5:1–4).

Abel is the first shepherd mentioned in the Bible (Gen. 4:2). Kings who led Israel (Jer. 6:3; 49:19) and certain ministers (Jer. 23:4) also are called shepherds. The sons of Abraham, Isaac, and Jacob herded sheep (Gen. 13:7; 26:20; 30:36). Rachel was a shepherdess (Gen. 29:3). David (2 Sam. 5:2; Ps. 78:70–72), Moses (Ex. 3:1), and Amos (Amos 1:1) found herding to be excellent preparation for future leadership roles.

Jesus' life exemplifies these leadership traits. Jesus knows each of His sheep intimately (John 10:3–5). Sometimes several shepherds will pen their sheep together in a cave or a sheepfold at night. The next morning each shepherd calls to his own sheep with his own unique guttural cry. Each sheep knows his shepherd's voice and responds immediately. Even in a large flock, one individual sheep will run to his shepherd when his own pet name is called (John 10:27).

Sheep are curious but dumb animals, often unable to find their way home even if the sheepfold is within sight. Knowing this fault, the shepherd never takes his eyes off his wandering sheep (Ps. 32:8). Often a sheep will wander into a briar patch or fall over a cliff in the rugged Palestinian hills. The shepherd tenderly searches for his sheep and carries it to safety on his shoulder, wrapped in his own long cloak (Luke 15:6).

In water-hungry Syria and Palestine, shepherds have always had to search diligently for water, sometimes for hours every day. Sheep must be watered daily. The shepherd might find a bubbling stream for the sheep that are always on the move and needing fresh pastures every day (Ps. 23:2). An old well with a quiet pool or trough close by might provide the water (Gen. 29:7, 30:38; Ex. 2:16). Often the shepherd carries a small pail with him, patiently filling it many times for the thirsty sheep who cannot reach the available water.

A trusted shepherd also provides loving protection for his flock. Shepherds on the Bethlehem hillsides still use a sling, made of goat's hair or leather and immortalized by David against Goliath (1 Sam. 17:49). At times the shepherd will throw his rod at a stubborn, straying sheep that refuses to hear his voice. At other times he gently nudges the stray with the end of his six-foot staff, crooked at one end to fit his strong hand. Both the rod and the staff work together to protect the sheep (Ps. 23:4).

The presence of the shepherd also offers comfort to the flock. David recognized this in Psalm 23. Sheep are content merely to be in the same field with their shepherd; Christians are comforted by the very presence of the Lord. This thought is especially comforting when darkness overshadows the believer. Jesus is our Door (John 10:1–30). Nothing can touch our lives without touching Him first. This is a perfect picture of the shepherd. He literally becomes the living door of the sheepfold. He curls up in the door or in the entrance of a cave. He puts his body between the sleeping sheep and ravenous animals or thieves.

One day Jesus the Chief Shepherd will return, gather His whole flock into one fold, and divide the sheep from the goats (Matt. 25:31–33). Until that time, Jesus continues

His search for every lost sheep (Matt. 18:12–14). His sheep are to yield themselves to Him for His useful service until, at last, they "will dwell in the house of the Lord forever" (Ps. 23:6).

SHEPHERD. (John 10:2) *poimen* (poy-*mane*); *Strong's #4166:* A herdsman, sheepherder; one who tends, leads, guides, cherishes, feeds, and protects a flock. The New Testament uses the word for a Christian pastor to whose care and leadership others will commit themselves (Eph. 4:11). The term is applied metaphorically to Christ (John 10:11, 14, 16; Heb. 13:20; 1 Pet. 2:25).

SHILOH [SHIGH loe] (meaning unknown)—a city in the territory of Ephraim which served as Israel's religious center during the days before the establishment of the United Kingdom. Shiloh was "north of Bethel, on the east side of the highway that goes up from Bethel to Shechem, and south of Lebonah" (Judg. 21:19). This pinpoints Khirbet Seilun, about sixteen kilometers (ten miles) northeast of Bethel. It also is a term pointing toward the coming heavenly King's rule (Gen. 49:10).

At Shiloh the tabernacle received its first permanent home (Josh. 18:1). This established Shiloh as the main sanctuary of worship for the Israelites during the period of the judges (Judg. 18:31).

Hannah prayed for a son at Shiloh (1 Sam. 1:3, 11), resulting in Samuel's birth and early ministry there (1 Sam. 1:9; 4:3–4).

By Jeremiah's time, Shiloh was in ruin (Jer. 7:12, 14), though some still lived at that site (Jer. 41:5). Shiloh became an inhabited town again in the days of the Greeks and Romans several centuries later.

SHILOH. (Gen. 49:10) *shiloh* (shee-*loh*); *Strong's #7886:* Shiloh was a city where the tabernacle was set up (Josh. 18:1). Here in Genesis it appears to be a proper name or title, which believers generally accept as a messianic designation of Jesus. The derivation is uncertain. One idea is that *shiloh* means "the peaceful one." Another view is that *shiloh* is a noun with a pronominal suffix that should be understood to mean "his son"; thus, lawgivers and princes would not depart from Judah until his son comes. Another possibility is to divide *shiloh* into the two words *shay* and *loh*, which would mean "the one to whom tribute is brought." The most likely meaning of *shiloh* is the one accepted by most of the ancient Jewish authorities who understood *shiloh* to be a word compounded from *shel* and *loh*, meaning "to whom it belongs." *Shelloh* may be expressed by the English phrases: "to whom dominion belongs," "whose is the kingdom,"

"he whose right it is to reign." (*See* especially Ezek. 21:27.)

SHOUT (GREAT). (Ezra 3:11) *teru'ah* (teh-roo-ah); *Strong's #8643:* A shout of joy, a clamor, blast of trumpets; the sounding of an alarm (especially with a trumpet); a cry of jubilee; a victory shout. Occurring thirty-six times, *teru'ah* is derived from the root verb *ru'a,* "to cry out and shout," whether in alarm or for joy. *Teru'ah* is an ear-piercing, great noise, a sound that cannot be ignored. *Teru'ah* describes the shouting of the Israelites when the ark was returning (2 Sam. 6:15). In Leviticus 25:9, *teru'ah* is translated "Jubilee," literally "trumpet of the loud sound." *Teru'ah* is a significant term in Psalms (see Pss. 27:6; 33:3; 47:5; 89:15; 150:5.)

SIGN—something that points to, or represents, something larger or more important than itself. The word is used in this way to refer to a wide variety of things in the Bible. But by far the most important use of the word is in reference to the acts of God. Thus, it is often linked with "wonders." In the Old Testament most references point to the miracles produced by God to help deliver the Hebrew people from slavery in Egypt (Ex. 7:3; Is. 8:18).

In the New Testament the word signs is linked with both "wonders" and "miracles" (Acts 2:22; 2 Cor. 12:12; Heb. 2:4). Signs point primarily to the powerful, saving activity of God as experienced through the ministry of Jesus and the apostles. The word occurs frequently in the Gospel of John, pointing to the deeper, symbolic meaning of the miracles performed by Jesus. Throughout the Bible the true significance of a sign is understood only through faith.

SIGN. (Ps. 86:17) *'ot* (oat); *Strong's #226:* A sign, token, visible illustration, portent, ensign, signpost; a miracle, a mighty deed or event. This noun occurs seventy-eight times in the Old Testament. The rainbow (Gen. 9:12–17), circumcision (Gen. 17:11), and the blood of the Passover lamb (Ex. 12:13) are visible illustrations of something that cannot be seen, that is, an agreement between God and His people. God struck Egypt ten times; these miraculous events are called "signs" (Ex. 10:2). In this reference, David prays for a miracle, a token, or some sort of signboard, which his enemies can read loud and clear.

SIGNS. (Rev. 16:14) *semeion* (say-mi-on); *Strong's #4592:* Compare "semeiology," "semeiotic," "semaphore." A sign, mark, token. The word is used to distinguish between persons or objects (Matt. 26:48; Luke 2:12); to denote a warning or admonition (Matt. 12:39; 16:4); as an omen portending future events

(Mark 13:4; Luke 21:7); to describe miracles and wonders, whether indicating divine authority (Matt. 12:38–39; Mark 8:11–12) or ascribed to false teachers and demons (Matt. 24:24; Rev. 16:14).

SILOAM INSCRIPTION—see ch. 55.

SIN—lawlessness (1 John 3:4) or transgression of God's will, either by omitting to do what God's law requires or by doing what it forbids. The transgression can occur in thought (1 John 3:15), word (Matt. 5:22), or deed (Rom. 1:32).

Mankind was created without sin, morally upright and inclined to do good (Eccl. 7:29). But sin entered into human experience when Adam and Eve violated the direct command of God by eating the forbidden fruit in the Garden of Eden (Gen. 3:6). Because Adam was the head and representative of the whole human race, his sin affected all future generations (Rom. 5:12–21). Associated with this guilt is a fallen nature passed from Adam to all his descendants. Out of this fallen nature, twisted from the original order of God's benevolent intent, arise all the sins that people commit (Matt. 15:19); no person is free from involvement in sin (Rom. 3:23).

Sin is not represented in the Bible as the absence of good, or as an illusion that stems from our human limitations. Sin is portrayed as a real and positive evil. Sin is more than unwise, inexpedient, calamitous behavior that produces sorrow and distress. It is a violation of God's law—the universal standard of righteousness (Ps. 119:160)—occasioned by ignorance, disobedience, or rebellion.

Since God demands righteousness (right alignment with Him and His laws), sin must be defined in terms of mankind's relation to God. Sin is thus the breaking of the creature from the just authority and loving intent of his Creator. Any break shatters the symmetry of the whole relationship; thus, breaking God's law at any point is revealed to involve transgression at every point of His law (James 2:10).

Ongoing violation of the law of God in thought, word, and deed shows the sinfulness of the human heart, and sin is capable of compounding its evil even unto the most depraved actions conceivable. Because sin is actually a contradiction to the holiness of God, whose image mankind bears, even the least severe actions of sin are subject to judgment, because they evidence the original sin's ruination of the divine order. Mankind sins by choice, but also is sinful by birth. Apart from Jesus Christ, all are "dead in trespasses and sins" (Eph. 2:1).

This does not mean that humans behave as wickedly as they might, for God's prevenient grace often restrains the outworkings of the sinful heart. At times He even helps sinners to do things that conform to the law (Gen. 20:6). Thus, the corrupting influence of sin is not developed or expressed to the same degree in every person. Neither is it expressed in the same way in any person at all times.

Sin involves the denial of the living God from whom human beings draw their life and existence (Acts 17:28); the consequence of this revolt is death and the torment of hell. Death is the ultimate penalty imposed by God for sin (Rom. 6:23).

Against this dark background of sin and its reality, the gospel comes as the Good News of the deliverance that God has provided through His Son. Jesus bears the penalty of sin in place of His people (Mark 10:45). He also redeems us from lawlessness and begets an inner desire and ability for good works in service to God and others (Rom. 8:1–16; Titus 2:14).

SIN. (John 1:29) *hamartia* (ham-ar-*tee*-ah); *Strong's #266:* Literally, "missing the mark," failure, offense, taking the wrong course, wrongdoing, sin, guilt. The New Testament uses the word in a generic sense for concrete wrongdoing (John 8:34, 46; 2 Cor. 11:7; James 1:15); as a principle and quality of action (Rom. 5:12–13, 20; Heb. 3:13); and as a sinful deed (Matt. 12:31; Acts 7:60; 1 John 5:16).

SINCERE. (1 Pet. 1:22) *anupokritos* (an-oo-pock-ree-toss); *Strong's #505:* From *a*, "negative," and *hupokrisis*, "hypocrisy"; thus, "without hypocrisy." Since hypocrisy originally denoted the acting in a play, *anupokritos* signifies a sincerity void of pretension and without putting on an act.

SINCERITY. (1 Cor. 5:8) *eilikrineia* (eye-lik-ree-ni-ah); *Strong's #1505:* Literally "judged by sunlight." The word alludes to Oriental bazaars where pottery was displayed in dimly lit rooms. Unscrupulous merchants would patch cracked pottery or cover defects with wax. Intelligent buyers would hold up the pottery to the sun and judge its quality by the sunlight. *Eilikrineia* is transparent honesty, genuine purity, manifested clarity, and unsullied innocence. It describes one who does not fear thorough examination of his motives and intents, because he has nothing to hide.

SING. (Judg. 5:3) *shir* (*sheer*); *Strong's #7891:* To sing. *Shir* refers specifically to the kind of song that is sung with the human voice, as contrasted with an instrumental song. There is another common Old Testament word for "sing," *zamar*, and from this word is derived *mizmor,* usually translated "psalm" or "song." *Mizmor* may be vocal as well as instrumental. *Shir* is found in the Hebrew title of The Song of Solomon: *Shir ha-Shirim,* literally, "The Song of Songs."

SING PRAISES. (Ps. 149:3) *zamar* (zah-*mar*); *Strong's* #2167: To make music, sing praises; to sing songs accompanied by musical instruments. *Zamar* occurs more than forty-five times, mostly in Psalms. There seems to be a special affinity between *zamar* and stringed instruments. The most important derivative of *zamar* is *mizmor* (a psalm, or song accompanied by instruments). Musical instruments are an integral part of praise and worship.

SINNER—any person who sins. Because sin is natural to man, every person sins and must be considered a sinner (Rom. 3:23).

Many times in the Bible the word sinner is contrasted with the term righteous. God told Noah he was righteous (Gen. 7:1), but, by definition, Noah was also a sinner. Although Noah did fall into sin (Gen. 9:21), his attitude toward God and what is right made him a "righteous" man.

Jesus also contrasted sinner with righteous. He said, "I did not come to call the righteous, but sinners, to repentance" (Mark 2:17). In this verse the term sinner refers to those who consciously make a lifestyle of sin, rather than the righteous who occasionally fall into sin. In the Sermon on the Mount, Jesus taught that sin lies within a person's attitude rather than his actions (Matt. 5:21–30). Thus, the person with the sinful attitude has separated himself from God, while those with righteous attitudes and a trust in Christ may be united with God.

SINNER. (James 5:20) *hamartolos* (ham-ar-toe-*loss*); *Strong's* #268: An archer's term for missing the mark or a traveler leaving the familiar road and taking twisted paths that cause him to lose his way. The word denotes one devoted to sin by choice, a transgressor whose thoughts, words, and deeds are contrary to the eternal laws of God.

SINNERS (WORSE). (Luke 13:4) *opheiletes* (of-eye-*let*-ace); *Strong's* #3781: A debtor, one who owes a moral obligation, an offender, a delinquent, a moral transgressor. The debt concept comes from this sequence: we are morally bound to live a life free from violation of God's commandments; failing in performance, we become delinquent transgressors and debtors to divine justice.

SIN OFFERING. (Lev. 9:2) *chatta't* (kah-*taht*); *Strong's* #2403: A sin, an offense, a misdeed, also used to describe the punishment for sin, or the offering for sin. The root verb *chata'*

means "to sin, to be at fault, to harm, to offend." The noun appears more than 270 times in the Old Testament, and 112 times is translated "sin offering."

SLIGHTLY. (Jer. 8:11) *qalal* (kah-*lahl*); *Strong's* #7043: In a superficial or light manner; easy, trifling; having very little weight; also, cursing, reviling, making light of someone; ridiculing another person. *Qalal* occurs eighty-two times. For examples of its use as "curse" or "make light of someone," see Genesis 12:3; 2 Samuel 16:13; Ezekiel 22:7. For examples of its use in reference to matters that are considered "light," or of relatively small weight, see 1 Kings 12:9; 2 Kings 20:10; Isaiah 49:6. In the present reference, Israel's spiritual leaders superficially tended to the deep wounds of the people.

SNARE—a device for trapping birds and small animals; figuratively, anything alluring and attractive that entangles the unwary (Job 18:8–10). In the Old Testament, the demon deities of the Canaanites became a snare to Israel (Judg. 2:3), and in that the believer is warned of a parallel possibility in 1 Timothy 3:7 of being caught by the "snare of the devil." Thus, a snare may be any entrapment that, by whatever device or subtle deception of satanic invention or demonic intrusion, captivates or entrances a human soul and thereby "place" is given to the devil (Eph.4:27). A study of the context of Ephesians 4:17–32 can assist in understanding some of the indulgences of the flesh that (1) in grieving God's Spirit (v.25) may (2) yield ground for the Adversary (4:27) to gain an advantage or point of control in one's personal life (2 Cor. 2:11). See in 2 Timothy 2:21–26 how "cleansing" can keep and free believers from the effects of such entrapment of the "snare of the devil."

SOBERLY. (Titus 2:12) *sophronos* (so-*fron*-oce); *Strong's* #4996: From *sozo,* "to save," and *phren,* "the mind." This word is an adverb signifying acting in a responsible manner, sensibly, prudently, being in self-control and in full possession of intellectual and emotional faculties.

SODOMITE, SODOMY [SAHD um ite, SAHD uh me]—one who practices sodomy, unnatural sexual intercourse between two of the same sex. These English words are derived from Sodom, an ancient city in the land of Canaan noted for such depraved activities.

All the men of Sodom came to Lot's house, demanding that he allow them to have sexual relations with two people inside (Gen. 19:5). But Lot refused. The next day Lot escaped from Sodom and God destroyed the city because of its great sin (Gen. 19). Sodomy was prohibited by the Law of Moses (Deut. 23:17) and is revealed by God's Word as being outside the divinely intended order for humanity. Like any sin, it is condemned in order to draw humankind to turn back to the health and joyous benefits of God's ways and salvation's blessings in Christ (Rom. 1:27; 1 Cor. 6:9).

SON. (Gen. 29:32) *ben* (*behn*); *Strong's* #1121: A son, a child. The plural is not restricted to the meaning "sons," but often means "children" or "descendants" of both genders. An example is the phrase *b'nay yisrael* (literally, "sons of Israel"), generally translated "children of Israel." The root from which *ben* comes is possibly *banah*, meaning "to build up," or "to fortify." The idea is that a son is a builder of future generations.

SON (ONLY). (Gen. 22:2) *yachid* (yah-*cheed*); *Strong's* #3173: An only one, an only child, a precious life. *Yachid* comes from the verb *yachad*, "to be one." *Yachid* describes Abraham's unique miracle child, Isaac. Zechariah describes what the Messiah will one day become to Israel's repentant, weeping citizens: a previous, only son (Zech. 12:10). Here the place where God told Abraham to sacrifice his son Isaac is the same place where God sacrificed *His* own Son: the hills of Moriah in Jerusalem. Equally noteworthy is that the phrase "His only begotten Son" in John 3:16 in the Hebrew New Testament is: "His Son, His *Yachid*."

SONS OF GOD—a phrase with at least these different meanings in the Bible:

1. In the Book of Job the phrase is used for angelic or non-human beings (Job 1:6; 2:1). These "sons of God" presented themselves before God in what might be called a heavenly assembly of responsible, angelic creatures. See also Genesis 6:2, where this reference suggests to many interpreters that these persons are angelic beings who violate their intended place (Jude 6), and Psalm 82:6, which seems to refer to this angelic order.

2. The phrase, *sons of God*, appears in the New Testament as a name for all who are born again into the family of God (Eph. 3:14–15). The classic New Testament passage where this phrase occurs is Romans 8:12–19. The apostle Paul encouraged the Christians at Rome to live not "according to the flesh," but "by the Spirit," because those who "are led by the Spirit of God, these are sons of God" (v. 14). We are "sons" by adoption, and thus an heir of God, a joint-heir with Christ (Gal. 4:5; Heb. 2:10; 12:7). Other passages use the phrase *children of God* with the same basic meaning (John 1:12; Phil. 2:15; 1 John 3:1–2).

SORCERIES. (Rev. 9:21) *pharmakeia* (far-mak-*eye*-ah); *Strong's* #5331: Compare "pharmacy" and "pharmacist." Generally described the use of medicine, drugs, or spells. Later the word was used of poisoning, and then of sorcery, accompanied by drugs, incantations, charms, and magic.

SORROW. (Prov. 22:8) *'aven* (ah-ven); *Strong's* #205: Exhaustion, affliction, wickedness, iniquity, unrighteousness; sorrow, mourning; emptiness; idolatry. *'Aven* occurs about eighty-five times. In Hebrew there is such a link between evil and its certain ill effects, that *'aven* can easily involve both meanings. *'Aven* is one of several Hebrew words in which sin and penalty are inextricably yoked.

SOUL—a word with two distinct meanings in the Bible:

1. That which makes a human body alive. The word used in the New Testament for soul occurs in reference to "life," for example, in Mark 8:35–36: "For whoever desires to save his life [soul] will lose it," Jesus declared, "but whoever loses his life [soul] for My sake and the gospel's will save it. For what will it profit a man if he gains the whole world, and loses his own soul?" The same idea—regarding physical life—is also present in the Old Testament. For example, the soul of a dying person departed at death (Gen. 35:18). The prophet Elijah brought a child back to life by stretching himself upon the child three times and praying that God would let the child's soul come back into him (1 Kin. 17:19–23).

2. Foremost, however, is the use of the word soul as it refers to the inner life of man, the seat of his emotions, and the center of human personality. The first use of the word soul in the Old Testament expresses this meaning: "And the Lord God formed man of the dust of the ground, and breathed into his nostrils the breath of life; and man became a living being (soul)" (Gen. 2:7). This means more than being given physical life, but the statement that man became a "living soul" indicates his uniqueness as a fully conscious, coherent, responsible, moral being with a capacity for a spiritual relationship with God.

The soul is described as the seat of many emotions and desires: the desire for food (Deut. 12:20–21), love (Song 1:7), longing for God (Ps. 63:1), rejoicing (Ps. 86:4), knowing (Ps. 139:14), and memory (Lam. 3:20).

In the New Testament, Jesus spoke of his soul as being "exceedingly sorrowful" (Matt. 26:38). Mary, the mother of Jesus, proclaimed that her soul "magnifies the Lord" (Luke 1:46). John prayed that a believer would "prosper in all things and be in health, just as your soul prospers" (3 John 2).

The chart below may help describe the distinction between the soul and spirit (Heb. 4:12).

SOUL. (Prov. 10:3) *nephesh* (*neh*-fesh); *Strong's* #5315: A life, a living being; soul, self, person, mind, personality; inner desires and feelings. This noun, occurring more than 750 times, is a highly significant Bible term. "Soul" is the word usually chosen in translations for *nephesh*, but "heart," "person," "life," and "mind" are occasionally best suited to a particular context. Unlike the English word "soul," which usually describes only the inner person and is contrasted with the outer person, *nephesh* describes the whole person as a unit, that is a life, a living creation. The first five occurrences of *nephesh* (Gen. 1:20, 21, 24, 30; 2:7) illustrate that the scope of the word is broad enough to include animals as living, breathing creatures, as well as human beings. In Exodus 1:5, seventy "persons" came down to Egypt. God's being or person (self, desires, life) is described as a soul; *nephesh* is used concerning God in Jeremiah 5:9 ("Shall I not avenge Myself [My soul]?") and Amos 6:8 ("The Lord *God has sworn by Himself [His soul]").

SOULS. (Luke 21:19) *psuche* (psoo-*khay*); *Strong's* #5590: Compare "psychology," "psychosis," "psychiatrist," "psychedelic." *Psuche* is the soul as distinguished from the body. It is the seat of the affections, will, desire, emotions, mind, reason, and understanding. *Psuche* is the inner self or the essence of life. The word often denotes person or self (Acts 2:41, 43; 1 Pet. 3:20). *Psuche* is not dissolved by death. Body and spirit may be separated, but spirit and soul can only be distinguished.

SOW. (Hos. 10:12) *zara'* (zah-rah); *Strong's* #2232: To sow; to scatter seed; to plant seed in order to increase the returns; to disseminate. The verb *zara'* appears fifty-five times in the Old Testament for the sowing of grain, as well as the planting and increasing of humans and animals (Ps. 107:37; Jer. 31:27–28). In Psalm 97:11, such unusual seed as "light" and "gladness" is sown for the Lord's saints. From the verb *zara'* is derived the noun *zera'*, "seed," whether it is fruit, grain, a male's fluid, or the line of descendants that proceeds from an individual ("seed of Abraham" in Ps. 105:6). The present reference indicates that those who plant righteousness shall harvest tender kindness. Compare planting tears and harvesting joy (Ps. 126:5).

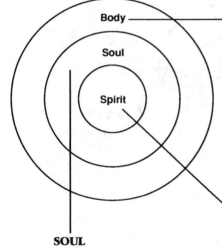

THE STRUCTURE OF A PERSON

Body — **BODY**

Soul

Spirit

BODY

World-consciousness

Senses: see, touch, taste, smell, hear
May yield to indulgence, sensuality.

Well-being: physical systems, strength, disorder.
May become diseased or afflicted.

Appearance, Action: May become self-serving or God-pleasing.

SOUL

Self-consciousness

Intellect: the mind, thoughts, reason.
May yield to unbelief and/or confusion, etc.

Emotion: feelings, temperament, concerns.
May yield to bitterness, lust, anger, etc.

Will: choices, actions
May yield to disobedience.

SPIRIT

God-consciousness

Faith: assurance, stability
Fed by the Word of God.

Hope: confidence expectancy
Sustained by looking unto Jesus.

Love: communication motivation
Nurtured by the flow of the Holy Spirit.

The New Testament reveals human nature as tripartite: spirit, soul, and body (1 Thessalonians 5:23). "Trichotomy" is the term describing this truth; a position which avoids the confusion which is inevitable when the human mind and spirit are made synonomous, which they are not (Hebrews 4:12).

SPECIAL. (Deut. 26:18) *segullah* (seh-goo-*lah*); *Strong's* #5459: Possession, personal property, special treasure. This noun occurs eight times in the Old Testament: in five of those references, it speaks of Israel as God's special treasure; in two references, it speaks of the prized possessions of kings, or "royal treasures"; the one remaining reference is Malachi 3:17, which speaks of the people God will regard as His "jewels." Man's treasure is material objects, but consistently in Scripture God's treasure is human beings!

SPIRIT—a word with three distinct meanings in the Bible:

1. The word is used as a general reference in the New Testament to the spirit of human beings (Matt. 5:3; Rom. 8:16; Heb. 4:12). Jesus made several specific references to His spirit in a human sense (Mark 2:8; John 11:33), as did Paul (Acts 17:16; 2 Cor. 2:13). Paul sometimes referred to the spirits of those to whom he wrote (Gal. 6:18; 2 Tim. 4:22).

2. A second common usage of the word is in reference to good and evil spirits, meaning angelic or demonic beings (Ps. 104:4; Mark 9:25; Acts 19:12–17; Rev. 18:2).

3. The word spirit also is used to refer to the Spirit of God, the Holy Spirit. In the Old Testament, the Spirit occasionally came upon people to give them power to do God's will or to enable them to serve God in a special way. Old Testament examples are Samson (Judg. 14:5–6), Bezaleel (Ex. 31:3), the judges (Judg. 3:10; 11:29), and the prophets (Num. 24:2; Ezek. 11:5).

In the New Testament, the Holy Spirit has an even more active presence: fulfilling Old Testament prophecies (Acts 1:16; 2:16–21; 3:18; 28:25–27); working through prophets and others (Acts 2:4; 19:6); filling, overflowing, or coming upon new Christians (Acts 8:17;

10:44–48; 19:6); purifying and sanctifying believers (2 Cor. 3:18; 2 Thess. 2:13); and guiding missionary ministry (Acts 10:19–20; 16:6–7). In the Gospel of John, He is called the Helper (John 14:16–17, *et al*).

The chart below may help show how the human spirit—dead through sin (Eph.2:1–3)—is brought to life by the power of new life in Christ (2 Cor.5:17).

SPIRIT. (2 Sam. 23:2) *ruach* (roo-ach); *Strong's* #7307: Spirit, wind, breath. This word occurs nearly four hundred times. Job 37:21 and Psalm 148:8 speak about "winds" related to storms. In Genesis 6:17, "the *ruach* of life" is

THE SALVATION OF A PERSON

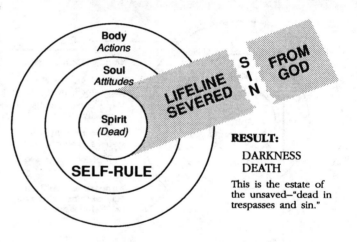

Body
Actions

Soul
Attitudes

Spirit
(Dead)

LIFELINE SEVERED — SIN FROM GOD

SELF-RULE

RESULT:

DARKNESS
DEATH

This is the estate of the unsaved—"dead in trespasses and sin."

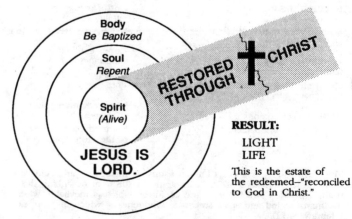

Body
Be Baptized

Soul
Repent

Spirit
(Alive)

RESTORED THROUGH CHRIST

JESUS IS LORD.

RESULT:

LIGHT
LIFE

This is the estate of the redeemed—"reconciled to God in Christ."

translated "the breath of life." Generally *ruach* is translated "spirit," whether concerning the human spirit, a distressing spirit (1 Sam. 16:23), or the the Spirit of God. The Holy Spirit is especially presented in Isaiah: God puts His Spirit upon the Messiah (42:1); He will pour out His Spirit upon Israel's descendants (44:3); Yahweh and His Spirit both send the Anointed One (48:16, a reference to the triune God); the Spirit of God commissions and empowers the Messiah (61:1–3); see also 59:19, 21. *Also* (Rom. 7:6) *pneuma* (*pnyoo*-mah); *Strong's #4151:* Compare "pneumonia," "pneumatology," "pneumatic." Breath, breeze, a current of air, wind, spirit. *Pneuma* is that part of a person capable of responding to God. The Holy Spirit is the third person of the Trinity, who draws us to Christ, convicts us of sin, enables us to accept Christ as our personal Savior, assures us of salvation, enables us to live the victorious life, understand the Bible, pray according to God's will, and share Christ with others.

SPIRIT, HOLY (*see* Holy Spirit).

SPIRITS, FAMILIAR (*see* Magic, Sorcery, and Divination).

SPIRITS IN PRISON—those to whom Jesus preached in connection with His death and resurrection (1 Pet. 3:19).

The most logical explanation of this passage is that Jesus made a proclamation of His victory over death to the rebellious angels who had been placed in prison. His proclamation was also a form of judgment on them because of their sin and rebellion. This idea also seems to be supported by 2 Peter 2:4 and Jude 6.

These texts join to the mention in Ephesians 4:9–10, which references Jesus' descent "into the lower parts of the earth."

He Descended Into Hell

The Apostles' Creed, the universally accepted declaration of Christian truth which for centuries has attested to the foundation stones of biblical belief, included these words which often occasion questions.

"He (Jesus) . . . suffered under Pontius Pilate, was crucified, dead and buried; He descended into hell."

This statement from the larger body of the Creed concentrates the focus of Jesus' passion—His suffering unto death and His paying the price of its mastery. But what actually *accomplished* our salvation must always be kept in bold relief, because there have been tendencies for some novelties of thought or confusing nuances of doctrine to distract from two consummately conclusive facts about the Cross:

(1) Jesus Christ presented His sinless self as a sacrificial offering for our sins, accepting all the weight and penalty of our sins in doing so; and

(2) Jesus Christ literally and physically died, His blood being shed as an atonement for sin and answering fully the requirement for human salvation and the securing of eternal redemption.

These biblically supported propositions clarify an issue raised by some philosophical suppositions which, however sincerely based, find *no foundation* in the Bible and *no basis* in solid theology. Thus, it is incorrect to support the idea that Jesus' "descent into hell" was to secure *any part* of our salvation.

The Bible *does* say "He descended." Ephesians 4:7–10 and 1 Peter 3:18–30 and 4:6 make clear reference to this fact. But what has distracted some has been speculation about what Jesus did "in hell." For the record, this is what the Word of God says He *did* do:

• First, and foundationally, Jesus confronted hell's powers on the Cross and completely broke the hold of sin, Satan, and death through the blood of His Cross (Eph. 2:13–16; Col. 2:13–15).

• Immediately after dying, and because the price of mankind's deliverance from sin was now paid in full through His blood and death, Jesus descended to "the lower parts of the earth" (Eph. 4:9).

• There He "preached to the spirits in prison" (1 Pet. 3:19);

  (a) *declaring* the fulfillment of God's promise of redemption to those temporarily residing "in Abraham's bosom" (Luke 16:19–31—the abode of those who died in faith under the Old Covenant, awaiting the Redeemer-Messiah); and

  (b) *confirming* the faithfulness and judgment of God to those "in torment"; verifying the truth of God's promise and the justice of their consignment to eternal loss.

• Then He finalized His confounding of the powers of darkness, who were completely stunned by the reversal of circumstances they suffered at the Cross (1 Cor. 2:6–8). He freed the forgiven faithful whose salvation He had now accomplished, taking them to Paradise (Luke 23:42–43), then, stripping the keys of death and hell from our Adversary the devil (Rev. 1:18), He concluded any hold which Satan had over human destiny.

These are the things Jesus did in hell, according to the Word of God, *but*:

• He *didn't* suffer there.

His suffering at Calvary accomplished His

procuring of all the prophetic intent of Isaiah 53:5—including those provisions for our healing and our deliverance.

- He *didn't* add to our salvation there.

His blood and death are the completely adequate, fully required, and entirely accomplished price of our forgiveness for all sin, our justification from sin's claim on us, and our release unto eternal life (Rom. 5:6–10).

The Bible calls what Jesus did for us on the Cross "so great salvation" and it is exactly that! As surely as its greatness is due to One Man—Jesus Christ our Savior, the Son of God—so is its completeness derived from One Source—His blood and death as the Sinless Lamb.

(Jack W. Hayford, Copyright 1991, Living Way Ministries)

SPIRITUAL—of the spirit or non-material. The word spiritual refers to non-material things, including a spiritual body (1 Cor. 15:44–46) and spiritual things as distinct from earthly goods (Rom. 15:27; 1 Cor. 9:11). But the most important use of the word is in reference to the Holy Spirit. The Spirit gave the Law (Rom. 7:14) and supplied Israel with water and food (1 Cor. 10:3–4).

The believer's every blessing is from the Spirit (Eph. 1:3), as is his understanding of truth (1 Cor. 2:13–15; Col. 1:9). His songs should be sung in the Spirit (Eph. 5:19; Col. 3:16), and his ability to understand Scripture correctly is given by the Spirit (Rev. 11:8). He is to be so dominated by the Spirit that he can be called spiritual (1 Cor. 2:15; Gal. 6:1), and he is enabled unto prayer and praise with a spiritual language (1 Cor. 14:15).

SPIRITUAL GIFTS—endowments, enablements, and energizings of God,which are given to individuals through which empowerings He grants capacities which allow for each one's serving his or her creative and/or redemptive purpose in the will of God.

The term "spiritual gifts" indicates their supernatural source in the Godhead, thereby begetting a humility from the onset. Each man or woman as a created being is given abilities to various degrees, so that all humanity—each one—is wise to acknowledge the Creator with praise for whatever skills he or she has received, and to seek the Creator in prayer for whatever or wherever He wills those giftings be employed or applied. A multiplicity of gifts from the Godhead are evident in the Bible, from abilities that unenlightened thought might consider "natural" (such as leading or teaching—Rom. 12:7–8) to enablements that appear to be quite more "beyond normal"—

such as working of miracles or different kinds of tongues (1 Cor. 12:10).

These divinely granted resourcings of human vessels are not differentiated in value, and none are to be disregarded for their present validity. While the analogy of the vast difference between the function and prominences of each member of the human body is taught in the Scriptures to explain individuality and varied levels of apparent importance, nothing taught suggests a reduced significance or value of any (Rom. 12:3–5; 1 Cor.12:12–27).

First Corinthians 12:4–6 seems to distinguish between those gifts provided by each member of the Godhead: the (Holy) Spirit—v. 4; the Son (Lord)—v. 4; and the Father (God)—v. 6. Respectively, the Spirit is shown to give "gifts" (*charismata*), the Lord Jesus Christ to provide "ministries" (*diakonia*), and the heavenly Father to grant "activities" (*energemata*). While an elaboration of these distinctives may not be pursued in depth here, the evidence of the New Testament's revelation is that each member of the Godhead is active in providing distinct giftings, qualities and enabling assistance to assure the fulfillment of the divine purpose through the church.

Three primary texts provide the framework for our understanding: Romans 12:1–21; 1 Corinthians 12—14; and Ephesians 4:1–16. Within the longer passages at each reference, the mood or attitude with which the individual should receive and function in their respective gifting is elaborated. The simplest summary of these guidelines is that humility, love and service to others is to characterize one's actions in and exercise of a calling. The objective is clear: that a useful, functional life in the will of God be realized, that the body of Christ be edified, and that the lost be reached and ministered to with a dynamic witness and they be brought to Christ. (*See* Holy Spirit Gifts and Power.)

The subject of the gifts of the Holy Spirit (1 Corinthians 12) cannot be passed without addressing the fact that a small sector of the church today, fearful of or resistant to the contemporaneity of the Holy Spirit's gifts, signs, and wonders, have held that 1 Corinthians 13:10—"when that which is perfect is come"—refers to the completion of the canon of the New Testament Scriptures. In other words, the argument goes, some of these signs and gifts were only immature expressions of God's working; when the text of the Scriptures came to a conclusion (near the end of the first century), then all this "immaturity" ceased.

Rejection of this "ceased now" view is not only the opinion of pentecostals or charismatics. Here is a sampling of other scholars, cited here to show that the "perfect" yet to come refers to the Second Coming of our Lord Jesus Christ, not the completion of the Scriptures.

R. C. H. Lenski: "The aorist subjunctive *elthe* marks the great future moment when the goal shall be reached, namely the Parousia of Christ" (*The Interpretation of St. Paul's First and Second Epistles to the Corinthians* [Minneapolis, Minn.: Augsburg, 1937], 566).

F. W. Grosheide: "[These words refer to a time] when the zenith has been reached. . . . All things hasten to the end, to the culmination point; the Christian must reckon with that fact. Once the acme has been reached and this dispensation comes to an end, then all that belonged to this dispensation, including the charismata, will terminate" (*The First Epistle to the Corinthians*, The International Commentary on the New Testament [Grand Rapids, Mich.: Eerdmans, 1953], 309–10). In related notes, Grosheide uses 1 Corinthians 7:31 and 15:25 to explain that by "this dispensation" he is referring to the church age, which will conclude at Christ's Second Coming.

Henry Alford: "Unquestionably the time alluded to is that of the coming of the Lord" (*The New Testament for English Readers* [Chicago: Moody Press, n.d.], 1058).

Heinrich Meyer: "Both [tongues and prophecy] contain only fragments of the great whole which remains hidden from us as such *before* the Parousia [i.e., Christ's Second Coming]; . . . [but] with the advent of the absolute the imperfect finite ceases to exist, as the dawn ceases after the rising of the sun. . . . What Paul means and says is that these charismata . . . will cease to exist at the Parousia" (*Critical and Exegetical Handbook to the Epistle to the Corinthians* [New York: Funk and Wagnalls, 1894], 305).

More scholarship might be marshalled, but this should be sufficient to assure any inquirer that the notion, touted by a diminishing minority today, that "the perfect" of 1 Corinthians 13:10 equals "the Scriptures when concluded" is by no means a preponderant opinion thoughout the body of Christ.

SPIRITUAL LANGUAGE—a more contemporary term for "speaking with tongues." Even though "tongues" is a biblical expression, it tends to conjure strange images to some people's minds of uncontrolled speech or incoherent, babbling ecstasy, or gibberish—none of which are ever "tongues." The term "spiritual" because its source is the Holy Spirit, or "heavenly" because it comes from God, are words used to describe the supernatural exercise of "speaking with tongues."

The term "ecstasy" is never associated with tongue-speakers in the Bible. Observers, ardent adherents, and antagonists of spiritual language all have used the term "ecstatic speech" for "speaking in tongues," but it isn't biblical. *Ecstasy* is defined as: "A state of being beyond reason and self-control through intense emotional excitement, pain or other sensation." While joy or happiness often attends the experience of the Spirit's overflowing the soul, the exercise of spiritual language isn't "losing control." Neither is this wonder merely a fanning of emotions to induce gibberish. Control may be surrendered to the Holy Spirit in each prayer, but it is not intended to be cast into the air or abandoned by succumbing to some state of mindless oblivion.

Moments of joyfulness or warm emotion are certainly present at times with most who humbly and openly enter the Savior's presence with worship, "praying with the Spirit" (1 Cor. 14:15).

The assocation of "ecstasy" to "tongues" is probably due to the fact that this word's root does appear in Acts 2:12, within the narrative of the Holy Spirit's visitation at Pentecost: "So they were all amazed [*ekistanto*] and perplexed, saying to one another, 'Whatever could this mean?'" The Greek verb *eksistemi* (from which we derive "ecstasy" in English) is in this passage, but *not* used of the ones who spoke with tongues; rather, it's used of the observers, expressing their amazement (ecstasy) which prompted the inquiry they made about tongues-speaking.

The expression "spiritual language" as a more easily accepted description of tongues speaking is precisely biblical. The epistles refer to tongues much more than does Acts. Holy Spirit-assisted language is positively applied in prayer or praise: "Tongues" are said to be (1) "speaking to God" (1 Cor. 14:2), and (2) as "giving thanks" (1 Cor. 14:16–17), as Paul very approvingly speaks of these languages for use in devotion as well as in adoration (1 Cor. 14:5, 18). Notice his terminology in describing his own practice: "I will pray with the spirit . . . I will sing with the spirit" (1 Cor. 14:15), terms similar to those he uses in encouraging all believers to do the same (Eph. 5:18–19; 6:11–18).

The expression "spiritual language" is derived from references where speaking or singing with tongues involved as one is "filled with the Spirit" (Eph. 5:18) or "praying . . . in the Spirit" (Eph. 6:18). The biblical Greek—*en pneumati* "in the Spirit"—literally means, "in the spiritual realm and with the Holy Spirit's aid." In Paul's encouragement to sing "spiritual songs" (Eph. 5:19), the word *pneumatikos* ("spiritual") he uses is defined as "pertaining or relating to the influences of the Holy Spirit, superior in process to the natural course of things, miraculous."

These texts show how accurately—and biblically—prayer and praise which speaks or sings in tongues may properly be described as using "spiritual language," because the root "spirit" (*pneuma*) is common to the words used in describing tongues. Of course, using the word "spiritual" for this prayer language isn't to suggest that spoken prayer or praise in one's native language is unspiritual or semi-spiritual. Each form of prayer is at a different dimension, and neither should be described as unworthy. Also see Tongues, Gift of.

SPIRITUALLY. (Rev. 11:8) *pneumatikos* (pnyoo-mat-ik-*oce*); *Strong's #4153:* Compare "pneumonia," "pneumatic," "pneumatology." An adverb denoting a symbolical or spiritual sense. In 1 Corinthians 2:14, the word is used to describe why natural reasoning cannot comprehend things of the spirit. They are discerned *pneumatikos,* with the aid of the Holy Spirit. Here Jerusalem is called "Sodom" for its gross spiritual perversity and "Egypt" for opposing God's plans and purposes.

SPIRITUAL WARFARE, ADVANCING IN. Few truths have become so pronouncedly vibrant to the renewed church's life in this century as the place and power of prayer warfare. This call in no wise reduces the conviction that the Cross of Jesus Christ has accomplished all victory over the devil (Col. 3:14–15). To the contrary, this order of warfare depends on what He has finished! Just as the mission to evangelize the world is founded in the complete provision of salvation, the mission to precede our evangelistic endeavor with prayer power that paves the way to the overthrow of contemporary works of darkness is founded in the blood of the Lamb (Rev. 12:9–12).

1. Spiritual Warfare (Eph. 6:10–18). Paul admonishes us to put on the whole armor of God in order to stand against the forces of hell. It is clear that our warfare is not against physical forces, but against invisible powers who have clearly defined levels of authority in a real, though invisible, sphere of activity. Paul, however, not only warns us of a clearly defined structure in the invisible realm, he instructs us to take up the whole armor of God in order to maintain a "battle-stance" against this unseen satanic structure. All of this armor is not just a passive protection in facing the enemy; it is to be used offensively against these satanic forces. Note Paul's final directive: we are to be "praying always with all prayer and supplication in the Spirit" (v. 18). Thus, prayer is not so much a weapon, or even a part

of the armor, as it is the means by which we engage in the battle itself and the purpose for which we are armed. To put on the armor of God is to prepare for battle. Prayer is the battle itself, with God's Word being our chief weapon employed against Satan during our struggle.

2. The Invisible Realm and Victorious Warfare (2 Kin. 6:8–17). To believe the impossible one must first see the invisible—the lesson Elisha taught his servant. The text involves war between Israel and Syria, and the prophet Elisha's informing his people of the enemy's tactics through prophetic insight (v. 12). Here is the lesson: Prayer is the key to discerning our adversary's stratagems. Further, the key to dispelling Elisha's servant's panic was his vision being opened to see the invisible. Note these crucial words: "Elisha prayed"! Elisha did not ask God simply to show the servant another miracle; he asked for his servant to see into another dimension. The answer came immediately: "The LORD opened the eyes of the young man, and he saw. And behold, the mountain was full of horses and chariots of fire all around Elisha" (v. 17). Seeing into the invisible is a key to victorious praying—discerning spiritual issues from God's perspective rather than man's, seeing the Adversary's attack plan, and perceiving God's angelic strike-force.

3. Divine Revelation and Spiritual Warfare (Jer. 33:3). God promised Jeremiah that if he would call to Him, not only would He answer him, but He would reveal to him "great and *mighty* things" that could not otherwise be known. The word "mighty" (Hebrew *batsar*) is better rendered "isolated" or "inaccessible." The suggestion is that God would give Jeremiah "revelational insight," revealing things that otherwise would be inaccessible or isolated.

Such "revelational insight" always has been essential for a clear understanding of victorious spiritual warfare. One cannot pray effectively without insight into how to pray, as well as into what things God truly longs for us to seek after in prayer.

4. Intimacy and Spiritual Breakthrough (Prov. 3:5–6). Two words in this passage are especially significant—the words "ways" and "acknowledge."

The word "ways" (Hebrew *derek*) means "a road, a course, or a mode of action." It suggests specific opportunities a person may encounter on a recurring basis. The most common "segment of opportunity" we experience regularly is each new day. It is as if this passage suggests that in all our "days" we should acknowledge God, and in so doing He will direct our paths.

Of equal significance is the word "acknowledge" (Hebrew *yada*). Elsewhere *yada* is translated "know," meaning to know by *observation, investigation, reflection,* or firsthand *experience.* But the highest level of *yada* is in "direct, intimate contact." This refers to life-giving intimacy, as in marriage. Applied to a spiritual context, it suggests an intimacy with God in prayer that conceives and births blessings and victories. Joined to our Proverbs text, we might conclude that if in all our "days" we maintain *yada* (direct, intimate contact with God), God promises to direct our paths toward fruitful, life-begetting endeavors.

5. Faithfulness in Prayer and Spiritual Warfare
(Acts 6:1–4). The early church learned quickly that their prayer had to be continuous because spiritual warfare is continuous. It became their first priority because Satan sought their defeat as his first priority. Thus, their earliest recorded administrative decision after Pentecost places the ministry of prayer (with the Word) as highest in importance.

As the church grew, circumstances required more of the apostles' time. But realizing they needed more prayer, rather than increased activity, the apostles chose seven men to serve as deacons to care for the church. This freed them to focus on prayer and the ministry of the Word. Of the two, prayer, rightfully, is listed first. Faithfulness to prayer recurs throughout Scripture. Paul would later tell the church at Rome to "be kindly affectionate to one another . . . continuing steadfastly in prayer" (Rom. 12:10, 12).

6. Intercession in Spiritual Warfare (Ezek. 22:30).
It is a sad day in Israel's history when God commands Ezekiel to prophesy against the sins of Jerusalem, declaring He has no choice but to judge the land. This chapter describes this condition that deteriorates so shamefully that God finally cries, "Enough!" Then God makes a startling declaration: this could have been avoided if only one intercessor had stood before Him on behalf of the land. He says succinctly, "I sought for a man!"

The text says, "I sought for a man . . . who would . . . *stand . . . before Me on behalf of.*" This clearly identifies this passage with intercession. No single phrase in Scripture more accurately describes the work of an intercessor than the phrase "stand before Me on behalf of." The intercessor always comes "before God" on "behalf of" others.

Also significant is the intercessor's twofold responsibility. Not only would he

"make a wall," which suggests he would restore a breach caused by an enemy, but he would "stand in the gap," or plug up that breach against that enemy throughout the building process.

7. Patterns in Prayer and Spiritual Breakthrough
(Ps. 5:1–3). In this text David builds a case for consistency and order in daily prayer. The repetition of the phrase "in the morning" justifies an alternate translation: "morning by morning." Also significant is the psalmist's selection of the Hebrew word `arak` ("direct") in his declaration that he would "direct" his petitions to God daily. `Arak` is most frequently used in Moses' writings in reference to the priests "setting in order" the sacrifices to be brought to the Lord each day (Ex. 40:4); also to describe an army being "set in array" in preparation for battle (Judg. 20:20–22). Such usage indicates an "ordered strategy" has been prepared for battle. These definitions connote the thought that David's "direct" prayer speaks of a well-thought-out order to his prayers, a *daily prayer strategy* with purpose and meaning.

8. Faith's Victory Through Prayer (Acts 4:31–34).
Following the healing of the lame man (3:1–6), Peter and John were commanded to cease their preaching in Jesus' name (4:18). Recognizing the severity of the situation, they returned to the believers (vv. 23–24) and called for a season of prayer that would release their faith so as to increase the scope of their witness.

Note the progression of events following this prayer (vv. 31–35), resulting in a supernatural shaking. From that moment, further mightiness was manifest: (1) a supernatural fullness—all present experienced the fullness of the Holy Spirit; (2) a supernatural boldness—this prayer led to a baptism of forthright fearlessness to proclaim the Word of God (v. 31); (3) a supernatural unity—the prayer participants were of "one heart and one soul" (v. 32); (4) a supernatural submission; (5) a supernatural fruitfulness—with a new power they went boldly, and fruit was produced for God's glory (v. 33); and (6) a supernatural generosity—they were baptized into a spirit of sacrifice and generosity (vv. 34, 35).

9. Physical Acts in Warfare Prayer (2 Kin. 19:8–19).
King Sennacherib wrote a letter suggesting that God could not stand against him. King Hezekiah, upon receiving the letter, took it and spread it out before the Lord in prayer (v. 14). This is one example where a physical act seems to parallel the establishing of spiritual authority in the invisible realm. In other words, a physical act becomes prophetically

symbolic of a reality that impacts the invisible as action is being taken in the visible realm.

In Hezekiah's case, a physical act of trust—spreading his case (letter) before the Lord—established a foundation for faith upon which Hezekiah prayed. The king was convinced that God would hear his prayer, and the Lord sent an angel that night who destroyed 185,000 enemy troops (2 Kin. 19:35; Is. 37:14–20, 36).

Other physical acts of people recorded in Scripture include vocal praise and shouting (1 Sam. 4:5–6; 1 Kin. 1:40), lifting hands and bowing heads (Neh. 8:6), dancing or leaping (Ps. 149:3; Luke 6:23), groaning in prayer (Rom. 8:26; Gal. 4:19), shaking or trembling (Acts 16:29; Heb. 12:21), intense weeping (Ezra 3:13; Lam. 1:16, 20) and many instances of prostration (Ezek. 1:26–28; Matt. 17:6; Acts 9:1–9; 10:9–14). Prompted by faith and motivated by a genuine intensity of prayer-passion, these are more than superstitious actions. They address the invisible as real—and gain victories.

10. Effectivity in Spiritual Warfare (James 5:13–18).

James pictures a level of prayer that is beyond any believer's normal capacity—it is divinely energized by the direct involvement of the Holy Spirit. The Greek word for "fervent" actually does not appear in the original text. It is an amplification of the word for "effectual" which does appear in the Greek text. The Greek word *energeo* means "effectual, or that which is effective." Yet, to simply say prayer is "effective when offered by a righteous person" was deemed by the translators to be shallow in the context, and therefore "fervent" was rightly added to the text. To fully understand the word *energeo* one needs to examine another passage where the word is used. Paul used the word in describing the power of God's Word as it works special energy in those who believe (1 Thess. 2:13). The foundational premise of the Greek word *energeo* is that something "effectively works." Yet it only works in those who "believe." Applied to this text, this suggests that our praying, when energized by the power of the Holy Spirit, causes things to happen. Our prayers work!

11. Seeking God and Spiritual Warfare (Jer. 29:11–14).

Throughout Scripture we find repeated references to God's people seeking after Him. Implied in these passages is a quest for God that includes a level of intensity beyond what might be termed ordinary prayer. The word "search" along with the phrase "with all your heart" suggests an earnestness that borders on desperation. The word "search" (Hebrew *darash*) suggests a "following after," or close pursuit of a desired objective; it also implies a diligence in the searching process. In 2 Chronicles 15:2, Azariah promises the Lord will be with His people if they "seek" (*darash*) after Him—another indicator of God's emphasis on intensity and diligence in prayer.

12. Fasting to Spiritual Breakthrough (Ezra 8:21–23).

As the exiled Jews prepared to return to Jerusalem, Ezra called for a nation-wide fast (v. 21). The purpose of the fast was threefold. First, they petitioned God to lead them in a "right way." This was the *guidance* focus of their fast. Second, they petitioned God to protect their little ones. This was the *assistance* focus of their fast. Finally, they petitioned God to guard their possessions. This was the *substance* focus of their fast.

Fasting is repeatedly referred to throughout Scripture as a sacrificial form of prayer warfare that produces results available in no other way. This is especially emphasized in the demoniac's deliverance in Christ's day (Matt. 9:14–29). Fasting involves a sacrificial denial of necessary nourishment while turning one's attention to seeking God during that denial. The duration of a fast may be as long as forty days, as in Moses' case (Deut. 9:18–21), or as brief as a portion of a single day, as in Israel's case (2 Sam. 1:11–12).

13. Angelic Activity in Spiritual Warfare (Rev. 12:7–11).

The casting down of Satan results from a great battle between the hosts of heaven and the hordes of hell. In this battle, heaven's warriors force Satan and his demons forever from the heavenly realm. We must note that victory is not achieved solely by the angels, but also by believers' use of spiritual weapons. The angels fight, but God's saints provide the "fire-power." This is clearly shown by verse 11, "They overcame him by the blood of the Lamb and by the word of their testimony." The angels did not overcome the Accuser alone; the saints were in partnership through prayer-warfare; the angels were God's means for administering the victory, which prayer enforced.

Notice the mention of Michael, the archangel (v. 7, one of four places where he is mentioned in Scripture). In each mention, spiritual warfare is clearly implied. This is true in Daniel 10 where Michael's involvement in battle to victory is the direct result of Daniel's fasting and prayer (*see* Dan. 10:1–4, 12–13).

14. Taking Authority and Victorious Warfare (Mark 11:20–24).

Our Savior's action in cursing the fig tree indicates a passion in prayer and faith that we need to learn. When the disciples later noticed with surprise that the tree had withered completely (v. 20), Jesus responded with a sharp command, "Have faith in God." Then, calling His followers to "speak to mountains," He led them to prepare for situations in which they would find it necessary to take direct authority in the spiritual realm to impact things in the natural realm.

15. Trumpets and Spiritual Warfare (Num. 10:1–10). The employing of trumpets has a unique relationship to the exercise of spiritual authority in prayer. Here two silver trumpets were sanctified for use by spiritual leadership in Israel. One was appointed for the calling forth of the assembly and the other for the mobilization of the camps when they were about to journey (v. 2). Thus, the first trumpet's use was primarily to gather the people together, while the second trumpet meant it was time to "move forward," usually in the sense of moving forward into battle. Regarding employment of the second trumpet, note especially the words of verse 9: "you shall sound an alarm with the trumpets . . . and you will be saved from your enemies."

The sounding of trumpets in victorious spiritual warfare is especially significant in God's final plan for the ages (Revelation 8—12). All of the culminating events of Revelation 12 result from the sounding of the seventh trumpet. Further, the sounding of the seven trumpets does not occur until the prayers of God's saints are released with much incense (symbolic of worship) before the throne of God (see Rev. 8:1–6), quite possibly indicating that the prayers of God's people release the final trumpet blasts that herald the coming and establishing of Christ's eternal kingdom on earth. Hearing the clear sound of the trumpet alerts us to the Holy Spirit's call to battle (*see* 1 Cor. 14:8).

16. Tears and Brokenness in Victorious Warfare (Ps. 126:5–6). Tears in Scripture play a unique role in spiritual breakthrough. Here we discover that the planting of seeds accompanied by a spirit of brokenness will not only bring a spiritual harvest of results, but will leave the sower with a spirit of rejoicing in the process. This passage, along with numerous others in Scripture regarding a spirit of brokenness, pictures a variety of purposes and functions related to what might be termed "the ministry of tears," a ministry Charles H. Spurgeon defined as "liquid prayer." First, there are *tears of sorrow* or suffering (2 Kin. 20:5). Second, there are *tears of joy* (Gen. 33:4). Third, there are *tears of compassion* (John 11:35). Fourth, there are *tears of desperation* (Esth. 4:1, 3). Fifth, there are *tears of travail*, or giving birth (Is. 42:14). Sixth, there are *tears of repentance*

(Joel 2:12–13). Passion in spiritual warfare is clearly needed. D.E.

STATUTES. (Neh. 9:13) *choq* (*choak*); *Strong's* #2706: An enactment, engraving, inscription, appointment; a written rule, decreed limit, law, custom, decree. This noun refers to a defined boundary, especially when written into law, but sometimes not in written form, as in God's limits for the sea and for rain (Prov. 8:29; Job 28:26). Here *choq* appears with *mitzvah* (commandment or precept), *torah* (instruction or Law), and *mishpat* (judgment or regulation). *Choq* appears about 220 times. In Psalm 119, *choq* occurs twenty-one times. The messianic decree (*choq*), which the Lord Jesus is destined to declare, is world dominion for God's only begotten Son (Ps. 2:7–9).

STEWARDS. (1 Pet. 4:10) *oikonomos* (oy-kon-om-oss); *Strong's* #3623: Compare "economy." From *oikos*, "house," and *nemo*, "to arrange." The word originally referred to the manager of a household or estate, and then in a broader sense denoted an administrator or a manager in general. In 1 Corinthians 4:1 and Titus 1:7, it refers to Christian ministers; but in 1 Peter 4:10 it denotes Christians in general, using the gifts entrusted to them by the Lord for the strengthening and encouragement of fellow believers.

STEWARDSHIP—the management of another person's property, finances, or household affairs. The believer's stewardship incorporates accountablility for the way in which he or she manages life's affairs as given as a personal oversight (Matt. 25:14–30). The care of the matters of one's "house" (Heb. 3:2) include all the affairs of (1) personal responsibility to private duties, (2) attention to one's family and its obligations, (3) pursuit of vocational tasks and scope of influence, (4) service of God by serving human need, and use of appropriate opportunities to extend the kingdom. These include the stewardship of one's monies, time, abilities, and influence. Notable passages teaching stewardship are: tithing (Mal. 3:8–12); caring (Matt. 25:31–40); unselfishness (Luke 12:13–26); generosity (Luke 6:38); and bold faith in sacrificial giving (2 Cor. 8:1–9, 15).

STEWARDSHIP. The Bible gives us clear guidelines for the wise and careful use of the many gifts God has bestowed upon us. This study focuses on just a few of the many passages that address the importance of being disciplined with regard to our time, material wealth, minds, and bodies.

1. Time Is Short; Use It Well (Ps. 90:1–17). Psalm 90 centers on the brevity of life and the stewardship of time. In meditating upon human frailty, Moses compares life to grass that withers (vv. 5–6). God Himself, on the other hand, is from everlasting to everlasting (v. 2).

Because of sin (vv. 7–9), God has shortened man's time at least twice. The early days of man averaged hundreds of years (Gen. 5:5): Seth, for example, lives 912 years (Gen. 5:8); Cainan, 910 years (Gen. 5:14); and Methuselah, 969 years (Gen. 5:27). After the Flood however, God shortened man's time to 120 years (Gen. 6:3). When we reach the time represented in Psalm 90, man's years have been cut to seventy or eighty years. The final word recorded in James 4:13–16 is that man's life is a vapor, with no guarantee as to the number of his years. Therefore, it is critical that man allow God to teach him to manage well the brief time he has here (v. 12).

2. Take Time to Be Holy (Gen. 2:2–3). God designated the law of the Sabbath to teach man stewardship of time. God Himself labored six days in the creation, but He rested on the seventh day as seen in this passage. From the Hebrew word *Shabat*, "sabbath" means "rest." According to Genesis 3:17–19 and 2 Thessalonians 3:10, we learn that God commanded man to work, but in Exodus 20:8–11 we read that He also commanded man to rest. God emphasized this point when He provided the Israelites with manna in the wilderness (Ex. 6:21–30). The manna was to be gathered every morning, only gathering enough for a two-day supply on the day before the Sabbath. God's law of the Sabbath commanded to the children of Israel was to be obeyed forever. Therefore, as Christians and followers of Jesus Christ, we have accepted our role as stewards of time. We show ourselves to be good stewards by using the Sabbath for worshiping our Lord and Savior and gaining refreshing in His presence.

Because of Jesus' resurrection on the first day of the week (Matt. 28:1–6; Mark 16:1–6; Luke 24:1–3), His disciples began meeting on the first day of the week. The Holy Spirit came upon the church on the Day of Pentecost, which was the first day of the week. The word "Pentecost" means "fiftieth," and it was that day called "the morrow after the seventh sabbath" in Leviticus 23:16.

The early church met twice each day as evidenced in the New Testament, once in the temple and again at a person's house (Acts 2:46), so one day out of seven is the minimum time that Christians are to dedicate to refreshing and renewal in corporate worship and service.

3. Redeem the Time (Eph. 5:15–16). As the apostle Paul expressed in these verses, he considered it foolish to waste time. In fact, he advocated "redeeming," or buying back, every precious wasted minute, because evil days were near at hand. Paul understood that God has made us stewards over our most irreplaceable possession—time. We are to be good stewards of our time, using it wisely, constructively, and in the worship and service of our Lord.

Throughout Old and New Testament scripture, God condemns idleness particularly, saying "an idle soul shall suffer hunger" (Prov. 19:15; see also 2 Thess. 3:10). In Proverbs 31:27, the virtuous woman is described as a busy woman who "eateth not the bread of idleness." The wise king declared in Ecclesiastes 10:18 that the man who does not take time to work in general maintenance will find his house crumbling around him. Similarly, Ezekiel states that the foundation for Sodom's destruction consisted of pride, gluttony, and too much idle time. Our Lord in His parable of the laborers in the vineyard illustrated that God wants our time spent in some worthy endeavor, specifically working in His vineyard (Matt. 20:1–16).

4. Tithing: Managing Material Wealth (Gen. 14:17–24). Tithing, giving ten percent of our income, is the physical manifestation of Christian stewardship. Tithing is important because it is the recognition of God as the sole possessor of heaven and earth (v. 22).

Abram introduce tithing during his encounter with Melchizedek, king of Salem and priest of the most high God. Upon returning from his victorious battle against the kings of Mesopotamia, Abram gives to Melchizedek ten percent of all the spoils. By tithing, Abram recognized that God, the sole possessor of all things, should be given all praise for His mercy to His stewards, the borrowers of time. Tithing preceded the Law as a practice and transcends it as a principle to be applied today. Jesus reinforced the practice of tithing as an "ought to do," and so we should (Matt. 23:23).

King David, one of God's most admired servants, also gave recognition to God as being the only divine king when he accumulated wealth to build the temple. In 1 Chronicles 29:11, David says, "all that is in heaven and in earth is Yours." Verse 12 says, "Both riches and honor come from You," and verse 14 says, "for all things come from You, and of Your own we have given You." Finally, in verse 16, he says, "O Lord our God, all this abundance that we have prepared to build You a house for Your holy name is from Your hand, and is all Your own."

5. Good Stewards of God's Gifts (Hag. 2:8). The

same principle of stewardship King David emphasized in accumulating the wealth to build the original temple (1 Chr. 29:14) was also emphasized in its restoration (Hag. 2:8).

After seventy years of captivity in Babylon, the children of Judah returned to Jerusalem and rushed to the task of rebuilding their own houses. They took the position that the proper time had not come for the Lord's house to be built (Hag. 1:2). The prophet's response was "Is it time for you yourselves to dwell in your paneled houses, and this temple to lie in ruins?" (v. 4), As verse 5 goes on to point out, we must always consider our ways when we seek to use the Lord's money for our purposes and neglect His house and the ministries that seek to accomplish His mission. The children of Judah were made to understand that their lack of material goods was directly related to their unfair and unjust stewardship: "You have sown much, and bring in little; you eat, but do not have enough; you drink, but you are not filled with drink; you clothe yourselves, but no one is warm; and he who earns wages, earns wages to put into a bag with holes" (v. 6).

6. Serving One Another's Need (Acts 4:32–35).
The church at this point was marked by an attitude of stewardship. The people realized that whatever God had placed in their hands was for the good of His people. Each member held in trust material goods and wealth until such time as he was called upon to liquidate his holdings. At the designated time, members sold their property and brought the total proceeds to the place of meetings and laid it at the apostle's feet. The apostles, recognizing their position of stewardship, dared not receive the possessions of the believers as their own personal property, but acted instead as trustees over the repository of the church's total wealth, distributing daily to the individual believer's need.

In this, the early church in Jerusalem was quite different from some today. Members of the early church willingly gave a hundred percent of their lifetime accumulations of wealth, while too many today hesitate even to give ten percent of their weekly incomes.

7. Our Lifestyle and Body (Rom. 12:1). In this
passage the apostle Paul reminds Christians that we are but stewards over our physical bodies. Many Christians live defeated lives by yielding to the flesh, which seemingly has a will of its own. Paul was keenly aware of this fact and dealt with it in passages such as Romans 8:1–13. In recognition of the challenge the flesh poses to the Christian lifestyle, the apostle Paul instructed the believer to "put

on the Lord Jesus Christ, and make no provision for the flesh, to fulfill its lusts" (Rom. 13:14). Paul's insights into the Christian life in Romans 12 are that the Christian lifestyle is possible when (1) Christians present both spirit and body to Christ; (2) Christians recognize that the Christian life is sacrificial; and (3) Christians recognize that the Christian lifestyle is holy—not worldly, but God-conscious and God-centered. Nothing else is acceptable to God.

Christians do not expect to receive citations for a lifestyle that is so different from that of the unsaved. The believer's lifestyle is his reasonable service. Our bodies are not ours to defile with willful acts of sins.

Paul further adds in verse 2 that Christians must be nonconformists to the systems of this world. Christians are not to be conformed to the world, but rather are to be transformed by a renewed mind. The worldly conform to the fads and customs of the times as seen and passed on via mass communication. The believer's mind is renewed by adherence to God's Word.

8. Our Bodies Belong to God (2 Tim. 2:22). The
apostle Paul was concerned that Timothy as a young man live the life of a Christian in such an exemplary manner that he did not bring reproach upon the church. Earlier, Paul had admonished Timothy to live his life in such a way as to not be despised as a Christian youth, but rather be an example of purity (1 Tim. 4:12).

Paul's message was clearly "Total Abstinence" from sexual pleasures until marriage.

Today's youth and young adults should hear this same message. It is a message of stewardship over the body. Many of our youths are dying from sexually transmitted diseases, while parents, teachers, and even some ministers are teaching safe sex. The true danger involved in teaching safe sex goes beyond the possible ill effect of physical disease into the spiritual realm.

The Christian youth must be made to understand that his or her body belongs to God and, therefore, he or she has no right to do anything with it that is not approved by God.

Paul's word is "Flee"; run away from fornication (1 Cor. 6:18). Run also from youthful lusts (2 Tim 2:22), for "the body is not for sexual immorality, but for the Lord, and the Lord for the body" (1 Cor. 6:13).

9. The Temple of the Holy Ghost (1 Cor.
6:13–20). Paul, in an effort to bring the church at Corinth into a right relationship with God,

emphasizes the stewardship of the believer over his or her body.

"The body is . . . for the Lord" (v. 13). "Do you not know that your bodies are members of Christ?" (v. 15). He says the believer's body is not autonomous, self-governing, and self-sustaining, but is a member of Christ; Christ is the believer's life. Jesus said, "I am the vine, you are the branches" (John 15:5). With these facts in mind, He declares that the believer cannot take the body, which is a member of Christ, and join Christ's body to a harlot (1 Cor. 6:15–17).

Paul moves this stewardship of the body into a divine state in verse 19. The believer's body is a temple, the temple of the Holy Ghost. Since the Holy Ghost lives in the believer's body, the believer cannot call the body his or her own.

In verse 20 Paul gives another reason why the believer should not think of the body as his or her own: "You were bought at a price." God purchased the believer's body and spirit with the precious shed blood of Jesus Christ.

10. Judgment on Poor Stewardship of the Body (Rom. 1:18–32). In this passage the apostle Paul tells the fate of those in the past who failed to recognize their position of stewardship over their bodies. They were judged, given over, and given up.

They knew God but did not glorify Him; their imagination was unwholesome; through foolishness their hearts were darkened. They boasted wisdom, while in reality they were fools. As they fell into idolatry, worshiping things created rather than their Creator, God removed the restraints and allowed them to fulfill their lusts and dishonor their bodies.

Once God gave them up, women went against nature to lie with women, and men rejected women to lie with men. This insistence upon doing their own things with their bodies led to a long list of sinful acts, which greatly displeased God. G.E.P.

 STIRRED. (Hag. 1:14) *'ur (oor)*; *Strong's* #5782: To rouse, awaken, stir up, excite, raise up; to incite; to arouse to action; to open one's eyes. Occurring about seventy-five times in the Old Testament, *'ur* is used of an eagle stirring up its nest (Deut. 32:11) and of a musical instrument being awakened or warmed up for playing (Ps. 108:2). In Isaiah 50:4, the Lord awakens the prophet each morning and "awakens" his ear to hear God's message. See also Isaiah 51:9, which speaks of the arm of the Lord being awakened or roused into action. The present reference is similar: God wakes up the spirit of Zerubbabel, inciting him to repair God's temple.

STRANGERS. (Acts 13:17) *paroikia* (par-oy-kee-ah); *Strong's* #3940: Aliens, foreigners, strangers, sojourners, noncitizens dwelling as resident exiles. (Compare "parochial" and "parish.") Israel sojourned in Egypt on a *paroikia* basis. Their permanent home was the land of Canaan. First Peter 1:17 uses *paroikia* in the spiritual sense. Christians live temporarily as aliens in an unfriendly world. The Lord has prepared for them a final home based on permanency, duration, and endless time.

STRENGTH. (Jer. 16:19) *'oz (oaz)*; *Strong's* #5797: Strength, power, security. This noun comes from the verb *'azaz*, "to be firm and strong." Here Jeremiah's description of his God has a poetic quality in Hebrew: *'Uzi u-Ma'uzi* (my strength and my fortress). *'Oz* occurs approximately one hundred times in the Old Testament, often in well-loved verses (see Pss. 8:2; 46:1; 63:2; Is. 12:2). David danced joyfully before the Lord with all his strength (2 Sam. 6:14). Psalm 105:4 sagely counsels us to "seek the LORD and His strength."

STRENGTHENED. (Col. 1:11) *dunamoo* (doo-nam-*ah*-oh); *Strong's* #1412: To make strong, confirm, enable. There is a family of *duna*-power words: *dunamai* (to be able), *dunamis* (power, usually supernatural), *dunamoo* (to strengthen), *dunastes* (sovereign or ruler), *dunateo* (to be mighty), and *dunatos* (powerful). (Compare "dynasty," "dynamic," "dynamite.")

STRONG (BE). (Josh. 1:9) *chazaq* (kah-*zahk*); *Strong's* #2388: Be strong, courageous, valiant, manly, strengthened, established, firm, fortified, obstinate, mighty. Generally the words "strong" or "strengthened" define *chazaq*, but there is a wide range of meaning for this word, which occurs nearly three hundred times in the Old Testament; for example, "to encourage," as when David encouraged himself (literally, "made himself strong") in the Lord (1 Sam. 30:6). *Chazaq* is the root of several Hebrew names, including "Hezekiah," meaning "Strengthened by Yahweh."

SUBJECT. (1 Cor. 14:32) *hupotasso* (hoop-ot-as-so); *Strong's* #5293: Literally "to stand under." The word suggests subordination, obedience, submission, subservience, subjection. The divine gift of prophetic utterance is put under the control and responsibility of the possessor.

SUFFER. (Acts 17:3) *pascho* (*pas*-kho); *Strong's* #3958: Compare "passion," "passive," "pathos." Being acted upon in a certain way, to experience ill-treatment, roughness, violence, or outrage, to endure suffering, and to undergo evils from without. *Pascho* asks the painful question, "What is happening to me?" Of the forty-two times it appears, it is mostly used of Christ's suffering for us.

 SUFFERING—agony, affliction, or distress; intense pain or sorrow. Suffering has been part of the human experience since man's fall into sin (Genesis 3). The Psalms, one-third of which are laments, include graphic descriptions of suffering, including Psalm 22, a prophecy of Christ's suffering.

The Bible makes it clear that some suffering is the result of the evil impact of sin in the world, resultant from the *Fall of man (Gen. 3:16–19). Some suffering is related to persecution and hardship, and a right response can shape and refine the character of the believer (1 Pet. 1:6–7; 5:10). The Book of Hebrews declares that Jesus learned obedience by the things which He suffered (Heb. 5:8) and that His suffering was key to perfecting His full provision for our need (Heb. 2:10).

The experience of suffering can lead to a fresh demonstration of God's power and grace in our lives (2 Cor. 12:7). Those who suffer learn a sensitivity and ability to comfort others who are suffering (2 Cor. 1:3–6).

Suffering often occurs through persecution and tortures people suffer for the sake of Christ and His kingdom (1 Pet. 2:18–22; Phil. 1:29; 2 Thess. 1:5; 2 Tim. 3:12). To do so is to suffer *with* Christ, and to enter into the "fellowship of His sufferings" (Phil. 3:10).

Christ's suffering, endured for the sake of those He redeems, is a promise of available release *from* suffering, with grace and power to go *through* suffering unto deliverance, since "By His stripes we are healed" (see Isaiah's portrayal of the Suffering Servant as both our sin-bearer and sufferer in our place, Is. 53:5).

The believer is not promised exemption from suffering, but we do have God's promise of triumph through trial (Rom. 8:28–37), healing when sick (1 Pet. 2:24; James 5:13–16) and deliverance from evil (2 Pet. 2:9; Matt. 6:13). This confidence is bequeathed to us as a redemptive resource through Christ: "Christ also suffered once for sins, the just for the unjust, that He might bring us to God" (1 Pet. 3:18). He not only has redeemed us from sin, but His redemption affords a resource of victory over or through suffering.

SUMARIA, SUMARIANS—see ch. 55, §6.2.

 SUPPLIES. (Gal. 3:5) *epichoregeo* (ep-ee-khor-ayg-*eh*-oh); *Strong's #2023:* A combination of

epi, intensive, and *choregeo,* "to defray the expenses of a chorus." The word thus means to supply fully or abundantly, generously provide what is needed, to cover the costs completely. (Compare "chorus.") It is used with the strong connotation of great and free generosity. Paul is chiding the Galatians for regressing to the beggarly elements of legalism, which he contrasts with the abounding surplus of God's provision through grace.

SUSA—see ch. 55, §3.1.

SUSTAIN. (Ps. 55:22) *chul* (kool); *Strong's #3557:* To maintain, nourish, provide food, bear, hold up, protect, support, defend; to supply the means necessary for living. Occurring nearly forty times, *chul* primarily suggests "to measure out a provision of food," that is, "to provide." In some references *chul* means "to contain," "to receive," or "to hold" (*see* 1 Kin. 7:26; 2 Chr. 7:7; Jer. 2:13). In Genesis 50:21, Joseph pledges to provide for his brothers and their little children. In the present reference, God will support, nourish, and provide for any person who acknowledges that the burden of cruel treatment (v. 21) is one that only the Lord can handle.

SWORE. (Gen. 26:3) *shaba'* (shah-*vah*); *Strong's #7650:* To swear, to give one's word, to bind oneself with an oath. The origin of this verb is evidently the noun *sheba',* which means "seven." To swear (*shaba'*) meant either to "completely bind oneself" to fulfilling an oath, or to "seven oneself," that is, to repeat some detail of the oath seven times. Perhaps this is why Abraham gave *seven* lambs to Abimelech when entering into an agreement with him (21:28–31). The seven lambs were a witness that Abraham had dug a certain well, and he and Abimelech *swore* to each other to accept the fact that the well was Abraham's. The place was named Beersheba, normally translated "Well of the Oath" but sometimes "Well of the Seven." In 26:3, God by an irrevocable oath assures Isaac that he will have numberless descendants; they will inherit the Promised Land; and Isaac's seed will bless the whole world.

SYRIA—see ch. 55, §3.4., 3.6.

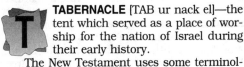 **TABERNACLE** [TAB ur nack el]—the tent which served as a place of worship for the nation of Israel during their early history.

The New Testament uses some terminology and concepts drawn directly from the

---

tabernacle. The supreme event of all the ages is the existence of God's Son in human form. The Bible declares that the Word became flesh and "tabernacled" (Greek word rendered as "dwelt" in the NKJV) among us (John 1:14). In his final speech, Stephen accepted the Old Testament account of the tabernacle as historical (Acts 7:44). In Romans 3:25, Paul used the word propitiation, which might also be translated "mercy seat." Titus 3:5 probably refers to the laver. Revelation 8:35 speaks of the golden incense altar. In Revelation 13:6 and 15:5 reference is made to the heavenly tabernacle. Practically every feature of the tabernacle is found in the Book of Hebrews. (See chart on page 18.)

TAKE. (John 16:22) *airo* (*ahee*-roe); *Strong's #142:* To bear away, take away, carry off, lift from the ground, remove, and take up. The verb is quite common in the New Testament and in addition to a literal use, it is used of Christ's taking away sin (1:29; 1 John 3:5), of believers' putting aside negative attitudes (Eph. 4:31) and taking up a cross (Matt. 16:24), and of the devil's snatching away the word of God from hearers.

TASTE. (Ps. 34:8) *ta'am* (*tah*-ahm); *Strong's #2938:* To taste, eat; discern, perceive; to evaluate. This verb refers to the testing of good by means of the sense of taste. From the primary sense of physical tasting, *ta'am* developed into the idea of evaluative sampling of things other than food. *Ta'am* as a noun came to refer to "discernment," that is, the capacity to choose and delight in good things. Proverbs speaks of a woman who lacks "taste" (11:22), and a woman with good taste, who "perceives" (*ta'am*) that her merchandise is of a high quality (31:18). *Also* (John 8:52) *geuomai* (*ghyoo*-om-ahee); *Strong's #1089:* Compare "gusto" and "disgust." To eat, partake of, feel, experience. *Geuomai* is used both naturally and metaphorically, especially to describe the personal experience of death, whether Christ's (Heb. 2:9) or the believer's (Matt. 16:28; John 8:52).

TEACH. (Ps. 32:8) *yarah* (yah-*rah*); *Strong's #3384:* To instruct, direct, teach; to point, shoot, aim, throw, cast in a straight manner. The primary meaning of *yarah* is "to shoot straight," or "to direct the flow" of something. Hence a derivative of *yarah* is *yoreh*, "rain." *Moreh* is another derivative, and means "teacher," one who aims and throws his directives in a straight way, one who points out the truth. The most important Bible word derived from *yarah* is *Torah*, which refers to the Law. Although *Torah* is often translated as "Law," its meaning is "instruction, teaching." The Law

of Moses is actually the instruction Moses received from God for Israel.

TEACHES. (Is. 48:17) *lamad* (lah-*mahd*); *Strong's #3925:* To instruct, train; prod, goad; teach; to cause someone to learn. The origin of the verb may be traced to the goading of cattle. Similarly, teaching and learning are attained through a great variety of goading, by memorable events, techniques, or lessons. From *lamad* comes *talmid, melammed,* and *Talmud,* being respectively, "scholar," "student," and the "Book of Rabbinic Learning."

TEACHING—the act of instructing students or imparting knowledge and information. As used in the New Testament, the concept of teaching usually means instruction in the faith. Thus, teaching could be distinguished from preaching, or the proclamation of the gospel to the non-Christian world. Teaching in the Christian faith was validated by Jesus, who was called "teacher" (or rabbi).

Since sound instruction in the faith is essential to the spiritual growth of Christians and the development of the church, the Bible contains numerous passages which deal with teaching (Matt. 4:23; Luke 4:14; Acts 13:1–3; Rom. 12:6–8; Gal. 6:6). It also warns against the danger of false teachings (2 Tim. 3:17; 1 Pet. 2:13).

TEMPLE. (Hag. 2:15) *heychal* (hay-*chahl*); *Strong's #1964:* Temple, palace; any splendid building; edifice, citadel, tabernacle, or sanctuary; a spacious, royal building, such as a king would possess. This noun occurs about eighty times, sometimes translated "palace," as in Psalm 45:8, 15 and Isaiah 39:7. However, in the great majority of occurrences, it refers to the Lord's temple in Jerusalem. In several references *heychal* refers to the "inside" aspect of the temple (2 Chr. 29:16; Ps. 11:4; 27:4; Is. 6:1; Jon. 2:7).

TEMPLE MOUNT—see ch. 55, §6.

TEMPLE, SECOND—see ch. 55, §6.

TEMPTATION—an enticement or invitation to sin, sometimes with the implied promise of greater good to be derived from following the way of disobedience (Gen. 3:4–5). In this sense, God does not tempt man, nor can He Himself as the holy God be tempted (James 1:13). God cannot be induced to deny Himself (2 Tim. 2:13). The supreme tempter is Satan (Matt. 4:3; 1 Cor. 7:5; 1 Thess. 3:5), who plays upon the tastes and weaknesses of fallen human nature (James 1:14) to lead people to destruction.

Discipleship as believers in Jesus Christ calls us to resist temptation, promising blessedness to those who do (James 1:12). The gospel also directs us to pray for deliverance from exposure to temptation and from surrender to it (Matt. 6:13; Luke 11:4). The Lord will not allow His people to encounter temptation beyond their Holy Spirit-given ability to resist (1 Cor. 10:13; 2 Pet. 2:9).

In the Old Testament, temptation can best be understood as testing or proving. The context is the covenant relation of mutual love and faithfulness between God and His people. The Lord tests Israel to prove the true nature of her faithfulness to Him (Gen. 22:1; Deut. 8:2, 16). His purpose is not to induce His people to sin but to confirm or verify the true quality of their faith (James 1:2–4).

In the temptation of Jesus (Matt. 4:1–11; Luke 4:1–13), Satan sought to entice Him to forsake His messianic commitment. But Jesus overcame "by the word of God" (Matt. 4:4; Rev. 12:10). Having resisted and mastered satanic temptation Himself, our Savior is able to comfort, aid, and deliver His followers who are tempted in similar fashion (Heb. 2:18; 4:15).

TEMPTATION OF CHRIST—the forty-day period in the wilderness when Jesus was tempted by the devil (Matt. 4:1–13; Mark 1:12–13). Jesus' first temptation (to turn stones to bread) was to use His divine power to satisfy His own physical needs. The second (to jump off the temple) was to perform a spectacular feat so the people would follow Him. The third was to gain possession of the world by worshiping Satan.

One motive lay behind all these temptations: Satan wanted to destroy Jesus' mission. Because Jesus' death would destroy Satan's power, Satan wanted Jesus to pollute His life and ministry. The ultimate issue behind these temptations was the Adversary's quest to head off Christ's eventual rule as Lord of the earth. Satan's offer of that rule *without the Cross*, and through the idolatry of securing Jesus' worship of him instead of God, anticipated the real mission of the Savior. But through refusing to yield to the tempter, not only was His sinlessness maintained and His Saviorhood sustained, but His kingdom mission to restore what Adam lost was secured.

TEMPTED. (Ps. 78:41) *nasah* (nah-*sah*); *Strong's #5254:* To put to the test; to try, prove, tempt. This verb occurs less than forty times in the Old Testament. The basic idea is to put someone to the test to see how he will respond, as in 1 Kings 10:1. Abraham was tested by God (Gen. 22:1) to the utmost degree. David called for God to test his mind and heart, confident that he would pass this test (Ps. 26:2–3). It is God's privilege to test man; it is not man's right to test God. In this

reference, the wilderness generation insulted and grieved the Lord by tempting and limiting Him, as if to test His patience or His power.

TERAPHIM—see ch. 55, §3.5.b.

TESTAMENT—a written document that provides for the disposition of one's personal property after death; a bequest. The word testament occurs only two times in the NKJV (2 Cor. 3:14; Heb. 9:16–17). In the KJV the word appears in several additional places (Matt. 26:28; 2 Cor. 3:6; Rev. 11:19), translated in all these cases as covenant by the NKJV.

The word testament also refers to either of the two main divisions of the Bible: the Old Testament and the New Testament, or, more accurately, the Old Covenant and the New Covenant (2 Cor. 3:14). Thus, testament is generally used to refer to the spiritual *covenant between God and His people.

TESTED. (Rev. 2:10) *peirazo* (pie-*rad*-zoe); *Strong's #3985:* Compare "empirical" and "peirastic." To explore, test, try, assay, examine, prove, attempt, tempt. The word describes the testing of the believer's loyalty, strength, opinions, disposition, condition, faith, patience, or character. *Peirazo* determines which way one is going and what one is made of.

TESTIMONY. (John 19:35) *marturia* (mar-too-*ree*-ah); *Strong's #3141:* Compare "martyr." Witness, historical attestation, evidence, judicial or general certification. The word describes a testimony based on what one has seen, heard, or knows. The English word "martyr" comes from the Greek root, with the implication that a witness is willing to die for his belief. *Also* (Rev. 15:5) *marturion* (mar-*too*-ree-on); *Strong's #3142:* Compare "martyr" and "martyrology." Proof, evidence, witness, proclamation of personal experience. The tabernacle, which evidences God's presence, is a testimony to the covenant between Him and His people.

THANK. (1 Chr. 16:7) *yadah* (yah-*dah*); *Strong's #3034:* To revere or worship with extended hands; to praise, give thanks, acknowledge, declare the merits of someone. *Yadah* is an important word for "praise" or "thanks," and occurs more than one hundred times in the Old Testament, more than half of these in the Book of Psalms. The origin of this verb is the noun *yad* (hand) which developed into the verb *yadah*, suggesting outstretched hands as a means of worship and thanks. Two important related words are *yehudah* and *todah. Yehudah* (Judah) was so named when his mother declared, "Now will I praise [or thank] the LORD" (Gen. 29:35). The word *todah* means "thanks."

THANKS. (John 6:11) *eucharisteo* (yoo-khar-is-*teh*-oh); *Strong's #2168:* From *eu,* "well," and *charizomai,* "to give freely." To be grateful, to express gratitude, to be thankful. Eleven of the thirty-nine appearances of the word in the New Testament refer to partaking of the Lord's Supper, while twenty-eight occurrences describe the praise words given to the Godhead. During the second century, Eucharist became the generic term for the Lord's Supper.

THANKSGIVING—the aspect of praise that gives thanks to God for what He does for us. Ideally, thanksgiving should spring from a grateful heart; but it is required of all believers, regardless of circumstance (1 Thess. 5:18). We are called to be grateful to God for all things (Eph. 5:20; Col. 3:17; 1 Thess. 5:18), especially for His gift of our Savior and our salvation (Rom. 7:25; Col. 1:3–5; 1 Thess. 1:2–7; 2:13). Thank God in anticipation of answered prayer (Phil. 4:6), knowing that His answers are promised to fulfill His perfect will for our lives (Rom. 8:28–29). Also see Praise.

THANKSGIVING. (Ps. 95:2) *todah* (toh-*dah*); *Strong's #8426:* Thanks, thanksgiving, adoration, praise. This word is derived from the verb *yadah,* "to give thanks, to praise." The root of *yadah* is *yad,* "hand." Thus, to thank or praise God is "to lift or extend one's hands" in thanks to Him. *Todah* appears more than thirty times in the Old Testament, a dozen of these in the Psalms (50:23; 100:4). *Todah* is translated "sacrifice of praise" in Jeremiah 33:11.

THEOCRACY [the OCK rih see]—direct government of the nation of Israel by God Himself or His earthly representatives. Although theocracy is not a biblical word, the concept of God's rule on earth is thoroughly biblical. In a theocracy human rulers interpret and carry out the divine ruler's will. In Israel's early days God ruled through men such as Moses, Aaron, and Joshua. Later, He ruled by using a group called the judges.

Deuteronomy 17:14–20 allows for an Israelite monarchy under God and in cooperation with other ruling officials. Later, when Israel finally demanded a king, it was their attitude of being "like all the nations" rather than the request itself that God considered a rejection of His kingship (1 Sam. 8:5). Samuel, the last judge and a great prophet, insisted that having an earthly king did not excuse Israel from obedience to the divine king (1 Sam. 12:1–25). Thus, the human king was not deemed an absolute monarch beyond accountability to God for the stewardship of his rule.

THEOPHANY [the AHF ih knee]—direct, visual manifestation, brief and/or apparent incarnations of the presence of God in the Old Testament. The key word is visual, since God makes His presence and power known throughout the Bible in a variety of ways. But even in a theophany a person does not actually see God Himself (Ex. 33:20; 1 Tim. 6:16; 1 John 4:12).

Theophanies proper are limited to the Old Testament, mostly common in Genesis and Exodus, but they also occur in the writings of the prophets, especially in connection with the calling of a prophet. The most frequent visible manifestation of God's presence in the Old Testament is the "Angel of the Lord." Other theophanies are the burning bush (Ex. 3:1–6), the pillar of cloud and the pillar of fire (Ex. 13:21–22), the cloud and fire of Sinai (Ex. 24:16–18), and the cloud of the glory of the Lord (Ex. 40:34–38).

The Shekinah glory that dwelt in the Most Holy Place in the tabernacle and the temple may also be thought of as a specialized theophany. Theophanies are never given for their own sake, to satisfy a curiosity about God, but to convey some revelation or truth about Him.

In the New Testament Jesus as the physical expression of God is more than a theophany (John 1:14, 18; 14:9), since the uniqueness of the Son of God's incarnation as "God with us" does not make the term theophany appropriate.

The word theophany does not appear in the Bible.

THOUGHTS. (Luke 2:35) *dialogismos* (dee-al-og-is-*moss*); *Strong's #1261:* Compare "dialogue." Inward reasoning, questioning, consideration, and deliberation; turning thoughts over in the mind; reckoning by mental questions, opinions, designs, and disputes. *Dialogismos* is the thinking of a man who is (1) deliberating with himself, (2) settling accounts, or (3) suspicious because of his state of indecision. Through one's acceptance or rejection of Christ, the real thoughts of one's heart toward himself and toward God become clear.

THRONE—the chair of a king. The word may mean either "throne" or "chair" (stool, KJV), depending on the context (2 Sam. 3:10; 2 Kin. 4:10). The throne is a symbol of royal government and may refer to the king's role as a judge (Ps. 122:5; Is. 16:5). Since God alone is the true King, it is natural that the word throne should apply to His royal authority (Ps. 11:4; 45:6), especially His authority as Judge (Ps. 9:4, 7).

The image of God's throne is carried into the New Testament (Acts 7:49; Rev. 4:2). Here God's royal authority is given to Jesus, the heir to David's throne (Luke 1:32; Acts 2:30). Jesus shares this throne with the Father (Rev.

3:21). Believers also will eventually share in Christ's authority and government (Rev. 3:21), and even now are called to be "seated with Him" (Eph. 2:6) in exercising and applying His mastery of all evil powers in the arena of spiritual warfare (Eph.1:17–23).

TIGRIS—see ch. 55, §2.1., 2.2.

TIME. (Col. 4:5) *kairos* (kahee-*ross*); *Strong's #2540:* Opportune time, set time, appointed time, due time, definitive time, seasonable time, proper time for action. *Kairos* describes kind, or quality, of time, whereas *chronos* denotes extent, or quantity, of time.

TIMES. (Is. 33:6) *'et (eht)*; *Strong's #6256:* A particular time; season, age, occasion, or some period of time; current times. Unlike *'olam,* which refers to a vast expanse of time, *'et* is used to describe a small space of time. *'Et* can be a season, such as Passover season, rainy season, harvest season (*see* 2 Chr. 35:17; Jer. 51:33; Zech. 10:1). It may refer to a portion of a lifetime, "time of old age" (Ps. 71:9). (See also "time of trouble," "time of love," and "evil time," Ps. 37:39; Ezek. 16:8; Amos 5:13.) *'Et* occurs 290 times. The present reference speaks of the stabilizing force God will provide to the believers, even in the midst of the uncertain times of this present age (*see* vv. 2–5 for context). *Also* (Acts 1:7) *chronos* (khron-oss); *Strong's #5550:* Compare "chronology," "chronic," "chronicles." Duration of time, which may be a point, a lapse, a span, a period, a stretch, a quantity, a measure, a duration, or a length. *Kairos* ("seasons") suggests kind of time. *Chronos* tells what day it is. *Kairos* tells of special happenings occurring during the time frame of *chronos.*

TITHE—the practice of giving a tenth of one's income or property as an offering to God. The custom of paying a tithe is a timeless practice established as a part of believing worship. The first recorded instance of tithing in the Bible occurs in Genesis 14:17–20. The practice of giving a tenth of income or property was a part of the Mosaic Law (Lev. 27:20). Jacob also, long before the Law of Moses, promised that he would give to the Lord a tenth of all he received (Gen. 28:22).

The Law of Moses prescribed tithing in detailed ways (Lev. 27:30–32) that extended in practices observed in Israel's history (Num. 18:21–32; Deut. 12:5–7, 11–12, 17–18; 26:12–15; 2 Chr. 31:6). Malachi indicated that Israel had robbed God in withholding tithes and offerings, thus the Israelites were exhorted to bring their tithes into the storehouse in order to enjoy the Lord's blessing (Mal. 3:8–12). He also asserted the promise of God's abundance and deliverance as related to believers' obedience with the tithe.

God does not make a legal demand, declaring that if we don't tithe, we will not go to heaven. Salvation's promise transcends legalistic demands. But there is a principle of tithing and giving which God has wrapped into the very structure of creation. Just as the law of gravity manifests predictable responses in the created universe, so does giving or its absence manifest effects in the spiritual realm—and practical outflow of our spiritual responses. Thus, when redeemed humans learn to *let go,* to *give,* to *release,* room is made for life and abundance to flow into their lives according to God's order.

Even though the Bible clearly reveals tithing as a divinely ordered, financial discipline with the wonderful promises attending and guaranteed by God Himself, some still ask: "Isn't tithing only in the Old Testament?" This doubt makes tithing a part of the Law and therefore without meaning to New Testament believers. Some even say to teach tithing will deprive a believer of "liberty" and move him or her "into law and out of grace."

But the truth of the tithe is not only in the Old Testament. The New Testament shows tithing as being as appropriate today as for believers during *all* history. God's Word also reveals that *all* His blessings and covenants are of grace, not law.

Jesus Himself addressed the issue of tithing: "Woe to you, scribes and Pharisees, hypocrites! For you pay tithe of mint and anise and cummin, and have neglected the weightier matters of the law: justice and mercy and faith. These you ought to have done, without leaving the others undone" (Matt. 23:23; see also Luke 11:42). Jesus was dealing with the Pharisees, that cadre of religionists who attended to the letter of the law but neglected its spiritual demands. In observing that they tithed, Jesus was challenging their supposition that obedience to a "ritual" released them from the larger reality of obedience to love's responsibilities.

The "woe" He issued on them was *not* for their tithing, but for their neglect of "weightier matters"—justice, mercy, and faith. If tithing were unimportant to Christ, or meaningless to maintain within the new kingdom order, then as a part of emphasizing that new order He could well have said, "Take care of justice and mercy, and quit bothering with tithing—mint, cummin, or anything else!" But instead Jesus says, "These you ought to have done"—referring to their tithing—"without leaving the others undone"—maintaining righteous attiitudes in righteous works.

In affirming tithing, Jesus employed "the moral imperative"—*ought*. To acknowledge something "ought to be" appeals to a preceding or higher order—to the divine will. Thus, Jesus affirms the timeless practice of tithing.

Tithing as a New Testament practice is even further verified in the Book of Romans. We are specifically admonished to walk "in the steps of faith which our father Abraham" walked (Rom. 4:12). In tracing the footsteps of Abraham, we find "And he gave him [Melchizedek] a tithe of all" (Gen. 14:20). Abraham reveals that tithing was established in the Scripture *before* the Law of Moses. It precedes and transcends the Mosaic code as a principle built into the fabric of the human order of things.

Tithing may have begun in the Old Testament, but its spirit, truth, and practice continue today. God's Word underscores it as ours to believe, rejoice in, worship with, and be rewarded by!

As believers we are also to be generous in sharing our material possessions with the poor and in offerings for the support of Christian ministry. Christ Himself is our model in giving. Giving is to be voluntary, willing, cheerful, and given in the light of our accountability to God. Giving should be systematic and by no means limited to a tithe of our incomes. We recognize that all we have is from God. We are called to be faithful stewards of all our possessions (Rom. 14:12; 1 Cor. 9:3–14; 16:1–3; 2 Corinthians 8—9).

TONGUES, GIFT OF—the Holy Spirit-given ability to speak in languages not learned or known to the speaker, or in another language not normally understood by the speaker or the hearers.

In an appearance to His disciples after His resurrection, Jesus declared, "And these signs will follow those who believe: In My name they will cast out demons; they will speak with new tongues" (Mark 16:17). Later, on the Day of Pentecost, the followers of Christ "were all filled with the Holy Spirit and began to speak with other tongues, as the Spirit gave them utterance" (Acts 2:4).

The people assembled in Jerusalem for this feast came from various Roman provinces representing a variety of languages. They were astonished to hear the disciples speaking of God's works in their own languages. Some have suggested that the miracle was in the hearing rather than in the speaking, but this explanation transfers the miracle from the believing disciples' experience which Jesus promised would be imparted to the multitude. Clearly, the miracle was the disciples'—

"They spoke with tongues." The apostle Peter considered the phenomenon of speaking in tongues that occurred on the Day of Pentecost (Acts 2) as the fulfillment of Old Testament prophecy (Joel 2:28–32). Further, continued New Testament experiences of receiving or being filled with the Holy Spirit were attended by speaking with tongues (Acts 10:44–46; 19:1–6), or some manifestation of equal wonder (Acts 8:14–19).

First Corinthians deals considerably with the phenomenon of tongues: It is affirmed as one of the several valid gifts of the Spirit under the term gifts. Paul declares its frequent use in his own experience (14:18), though he puts it in perspective (14:19) as preferred in private devotional exercise of worship and prayer (14:1–16). As a means of worship, thanksgiving, and prayer, the individual with the gift of tongues addresses God, not man; the result is to intercede (Rom. 8:26–27) as well as to edify (14:4), "building yourselves up on your most holy faith" (Jude 20). The exercise is never intended for self-exaltation but for the praise and glorification of God.

The gift of tongues, which when interpreted is edifying to the congregation (14:5), is to be exercised with restraint and in an orderly way. The regulations for its public use are simple and straightforward. The person who speaks in an unknown tongue is to pray that he may interpret (14:13). Or, someone else is to interpret what he says. Only two or three persons are to speak, with each having an interpretation of what he says. Each is also to speak in turn. If these criteria are not met, they are to remain silent (14:27–28). The gifts of speaking in tongues and their interpretation are to be Spirit-inspired, and as such they may become a sign to unbelievers (14:22). First Corinthians 13 puts the gift of tongues in clearest perspective by affirming that though we "speak with the tongues of men and of angels" (v. 1), if we do not have love, the gift of tongues has no value. If these guidelines are not observed, unbelievers who are present will conclude that the people of the church are out of their minds.

The phenomenon of speaking in tongues described in the New Testament is not some psychological arousal of human emotions that results in strange sounds. This is a genuine, timeless work of the Holy Spirit, and a refreshing, renewing personal resource in prayer. No wonder the church was born with this praise language on its lips! As Paul said, may "all" receive and enjoy this benefit as "at the beginning" (1 Cor.14:5; Acts 2:4; 11:15). Also see Spiritual Language.

TORAH [toe RAH]—Hebrew, meaning guidance or direction from God to His people. In earlier times, the term Torah referred directly to the five books of Moses, or the Pentateuch. Moses told the people, "Command your children to observe to do all the words of this law." While the English word law does not suggest this, both the hearing and the doing of the Law made the Torah. It was a manner of life, a way to live based upon the *covenant that God made with His people.

Later the Hebrew Old Testament included both the books of wisdom and the prophets, but this entire collection was spoken of as the Torah. See Jesus' quotation of Psalm 82:6, calling it a part of the Law (John 10:34). Following the return from Babylon, the development of the synagogue gave rise to interpretations of the Law by leading rabbis, which after a time were collected into 613 precepts. Considered part of the Torah, they were as binding as the Law itself. Jesus referred to these additions to the original Law of Moses as "the traditions of men."

The Torah, to devoted Jews then and now, is to be seen as a total way of life. It requires complete dedication because it is seen as God's direction for living the covenant relationship.

TRANSFIGURATION—a display of God's glory in the person of His Son, Jesus Christ (Matt. 17:1–8; Mark 9:2–8; Luke 9:28–36). Peter cites the Transfiguration as historical proof of the true gospel of Christ (2 Pet. 1:16–18). This event, about six months before His death, discloses the moment the consummate achievement of Jesus in fulfilling the Father's will as a sinless man was verified. The text reveals a glory which radiated not from without but from within Him. The Second Adam had been tested and proven faithful. From this point, He now moves relentlessly toward the Cross (Luke 9:28–31).

TRANSFORM—to change radically in inner character, condition, or nature. In Romans 12:2 the apostle Paul exhorted Christians, "Do not be conformed to this world, but be transformed by the renewing of your mind." Followers of Christ should not be conformed, either inwardly or in appearance, to the values, ideals, and behavior of a fallen world. Believers are called to continually renew their minds through prayer and the study of God's Word, by the power of the Holy Spirit, and be progressively transformed into Jesus' likeness (2 Cor. 3:18). When He returns, Christ will "transform our lowly body that it may be conformed to His glorious body" (Phil. 3:21).

TRANSGRESSION—the violation of a law, command, or duty; the Hebrew word most often translated as transgression in the Old Testament means "revolt" or "rebellion." The psalmist wrote, "Blessed is he whose transgression is forgiven, whose sin is covered" (Ps. 32:1). In the New Testament every occurrence of the word transgression (NKJV) is a translation of a Greek word which means "a deliberate breach of the law" (Rom. 4:15; 1 Tim. 2:14; Heb. 2:2). Also see Sin.

TRANSGRESSION. (Acts 1:25) *parabaino* (par-ab-*ahee*-no); *Strong's* #3845: Abandoning a trust, departing, stepping aside, overstep, violation, rebellion, aberration, apostasy, disobedience, deviation from an original and true direction. In order to go his own way, Judas abandoned his position of service as one of the Twelve.

TRANSGRESSIONS. (Ezek. 18:31) *pesha'* (peh-shah); *Strong's* #6588: Rebellion, transgression, trespass. *Pesha'* comes from the verb *pasha'*, which means "to revolt, rebel, and trespass." Whether as noun or verb, a trespass had to do with revolting against law, God, or government, and was a transgressing, that is, going beyond established limits. "Rebellion," or "breaking out against," might also describe *pesha'*. Isaiah 53:5 shows that the Messiah was wounded on account of our transgressions (*pesha'*), and verse 12 shows Him interceding for transgressors (*pasha'*).

TRANSLATE, TRANSLATION—to remove a person or thing from one condition, place, or state to another. In the Bible, the word translation or the concept of translation is used in three senses: (1) the physical translation of Enoch (Gen. 5:24; Heb. 11:5) and Elijah (2 Kin. 2:11) to heaven without the intervening experience of death; (2) the spiritual translation of believers in their present experience from "the power of darkness" into "the kingdom of the Son of His love" (Col. 1:13); and (3) the future, physical translation and transformation of believers at the *Second Coming of Christ (1 Cor. 15:51–57; Phil. 3:21; 1 Thess. 4:13–18).

TREAD. (Deut. 11:25) *darach* (dah-*rahch*); *Strong's* #1869: To walk, go, tread, trample, march. This word, occurring more than sixty times in the Old Testament, suggests a more forceful activity than mere walking. "Marching" or "treading" would best render *darach*. From this verb comes the noun *derech*, meaning "road," "path," or "way," whether an actual street or the path one habitually treads in life.

TRIBE. (Ex. 38:22) *matteh* (mat-*teh*); *Strong's* #4294: Rod, staff, branch, tribe. Originally *matteh* meant "branch," as in a tree or on a vine. Since a patriarch's rod or staff comes from a branch, *matteh* naturally describes such a rod. Finally, *matteh* is used for a tribe of people, possibly because a tribe was united under a tribal staff, but more likely because it was seen as a "branch" of the family. This is certainly true of the tribes of Israel, which developed from the growing families of Jacob's twelve sons. In English, we also refer to a certain "branch" of one's family. This concept receives further reinforcement in Romans 11:17–24, where Paul speaks of the "branches" as groups of people, showing that the family tree of God's household consists of branches from two sources: the native Jewish branches, and the branches God has chosen from among the Gentiles. Another word for "tribe" is *shevet*, which means "rod, staff, tribe." *Matteh* and *shevet* are used interchangeably in reference to the tribes of Israel.

TRIBULATION—great adversity and anguish; intense oppression or persecution. Tribulation is linked to God's process for making the world right again. His Son underwent great suffering, just as His people undergo a great deal of tribulation from the world (Rom. 5:3; Acts 14:22). This tribulation has its source in the conflict between God and the devil (Gen. 3:15) which will end with the devil being cast into the lake of fire to suffer eternal tribulation (Rev. 20:10).

Also see Tribulation, the Great.

TRIBULATION. (John 16:33) *thlipsis* (*thlip*-sis); *Strong's #2347:* Pressure, oppression, stress, anguish, tribulation, adversity, affliction, crushing, squashing, squeezing, distress. Imagine placing your hand on a stack of loose items and manually compressing them. That is *thlipsis*, putting a lot of pressure on that which is free and unfettered. *Thlipsis* is like spiritual bench-pressing. The word is used of crushing grapes or olives in a press.

TRIBULATION, THE GREAT—a short but intense period of distress and suffering at the end of time. The exact phrase, *the great tribulation*, is found only once in the Bible (Rev. 7:14). The great tribulation is to be distinguished from the general tribulation a believer faces in the world (Matt. 13:21; John 16:33; Acts 14:22) or the agelong difficulties Jesus forecast (Mark 13:7–8, et al). It refers to God's specific wrath upon the unbelieving world at the end of the age (Matt. 24:29–30; Mark 13:24). Those references clearly separate the age-long "tribulation," which increases in intensity throughout, from the final calamities described here and in Revelation 6:12–17 and 16:1–21.

The great tribulation fulfills Daniel's prophecies (Daniel 7—12). It appears to describe a time of evil from false christs and false prophets (Mark 13:22) when natural disasters will occur throughout the world.

Also see Antichrist; Millenium.

TRIMMED. (Matt. 25:7) *kosmeo* (kos-*meh*-oh); *Strong's #2885:* Compare "cosmetic." To beautify, arrange, decorate, furnish, embellish, adorn, put in order. Here is a picture of revival before the Second Coming of Christ.

TRIUMPH—the joy or exultation of victory. In the Bible the word triumph usually refers to God's triumph—in the Old Testament His triumph over Israel's enemies and in the New Testament His victory through Christ on the Cross. Examples of God's triumph over Israel's enemies include the song of Moses (Ex. 15:1) and the song of Miriam (Ex. 15:21). In the Old Testament the word triumph is found most often in the Book of Psalms (25:2; 60:8; 108:9).

In the New Testament the Greek verb which means "to make a show or spectacle of" is twice translated as triumph (2 Cor. 2:14; Col. 2:15). The figure of speech is drawn from the ceremony that greeted a Roman general who had won a decisive victory over a foreign enemy. This ceremony usually featured a display of captives and spoil following the general's chariot.

The apostle Paul used such a triumphal procession as an analogy of Christ's victory on the Cross. By His triumph He conquered supernatural foes and "made a public spectacle of them" (Col. 2:15). Through Christ we also can claim the victory: "Now thanks be to God who always leads us in triumph in Christ" (2 Cor. 2:14).

TROUBLE. (Job 5:7) *'amal* (ah-*mahl*); *Strong's #5999:* Sorrow, labor, toil, grief, pain, trouble, misery, fatigue, exhaustion. This noun occurs fifty-six times in the Old Testament. Its root is the verb *'amal*, "to labor or toil to the point of exhaustion." The verb is used in Psalm 127:1, which pictures the exhausted state of workers who are trying to build God's house without God's cooperation. When Joseph finally obtained happiness after his family's betrayal, his unhappy position as a servant, and his unfair imprisonment, he said, "God has made me forget all my toil and all my father's house" (Gen. 41:51), referring to his anguish, grief, and pain.

TROUBLED. (Luke 24:38) *tarasso* (tar-*as*-so); *Strong's #5015:* To unsettle, stir up, agitate, disturb, trouble. The word is used in a physical sense (John 5:7), but its primary use in the New Testament is metaphorical. It denotes mental agitation from fear or perplexity (Matt.

2:3; 14:26); an upheaval in the spirit (John 11:33; 13:21); stirring up a crowd (Acts 17:8, 13); or confusion resulting from false doctrine (Acts 15:24; Gal. 1:7; 5:10).

TRUE. (Rom. 3:4) *alethes* (al-ay-*thace*); *Strong's #227:* Compare "latent" and "lethargy." Genuine, real, true, ideal, manifest, unconcealed, actual. *Alethes* is the opposite of falsehood, concealment, and human inconsistency. God is faithful to His promises; He is incapable of falsehood. *Alethes* assures us that His utterances agree with reality, are authentic, and harmonize with historical fact.

TRUMPET. (Hos. 8:1) *shophar* (shoh-*fahr*); *Strong's #7782:* A trumpet made from a curved animal horn; a cornet. The *shofar* is mentioned seventy-two times, first in Exodus 19:16, 19 and 20:18, where a trumpet sounded at Mt. Sinai, heralding the Lord's descent (19:20) and the giving of the Law. In the account of the fall of Jericho in Joshua 6:1–20, *shofar* appears fourteen times. In Ezekiel 33:2–9, the sound of a trumpet (which warns a city of danger) is compared to the prophet's voice. The *shofar* was sounded not only as a call to arms but also to herald the Day of Atonement, the Year of Jubilee, and events such as the return of the ark. (*See* Lev. 25:9; 2 Sam. 6:15.)

TRUST. (Zeph. 3:12) *chasah* (chah-*sah*); *Strong's #2620:* To trust; to hope; to make someone a refuge. This verb occurs thirty-six times in the Old Testament. Psalm 57:1 beautifully illustrates the verb, for it pictures David as nestling under God's wings for refuge, in the same manner that a defenseless but trusting baby bird hides itself under its parent's feathers (Ruth 2:12; 2 Sam. 22:3; Ps. 91:4). The middle verse of the Bible is Psalm 118:8, which states, "It is better to trust [*chasah*] in the LORD than to put confidence in man," a fitting centerpiece of the Bible.

TRUTH—conformity to fact or actuality; faithfulness to an original or to a standard.

In the Old and New Testaments, truth is a fundamental moral and personal quality of God. God proclaimed that He is "merciful and gracious, longsuffering, and abounding in goodness and truth" (Ex. 34:6). He is a "God of truth . . . without injustice" (Deut. 32:4). Furthermore, all of His paths are "mercy and truth" (Ps. 25:10). Frequently in the psalms God's mercy and His truth are joined together (Ps. 57:3; 89:14; 115:1). All of God's works,

precepts, and judgments are done in righteousness and truth (Ps. 96:13; 111:8).

Truth is a moral and personal characteristic of God: He is "the God of truth" (Is. 65:16). The psalmist declared, "Your law is truth" (119:142), "all Your commandments are truth" (119:151), and "the entirety of Your word is truth" (119:160). Because of His perfect nature and will God has to speak and act in truth; He cannot lie (1 Sam. 15:29; Heb. 6:18; James 1:17–18).

Jesus is the Word of God who became flesh, "the only begotten of the Father, full of grace and truth" (John 1:14). All Jesus said was true, because He told the truth which He heard from God (John 8:40). He promised His disciples that He would send "the Spirit of truth" (John 14:17; 15:26; 16:13)—a Helper who would abide in Christians forever (John 14:16), testify about Jesus (John 15:26), guide Christians into all truth (John 16:13), and glorify Jesus (John 16:14).

God is truth; the Spirit is truth; and Jesus is truth. Jesus said, "I am the way, the truth, and the life. No one comes to the Father except through Me" (John 14:6). Jesus and the revelation which the Spirit of truth gave through His apostles are the final, ultimate revelation and definition of truth about God, man, redemption, history, and the world. "The law was given through Moses, but grace and truth came through Jesus Christ" (John 1:17).

TRUTH. (Ps. 25:5) *'emet* (eh-met); *Strong's #571:* Certainty, stability, truth, rightness, trustworthiness. *'Emet* derives from the verb *'aman*, meaning "to be firm, permanent, and established." *'Emet* conveys a sense of dependability, firmness, and reliability. Truth is therefore something upon which a person may confidently stake his life. David prayed that God's truth would continually preserve him (40:11). Scripture speaks of "men of truth" (Ex. 18:21), the "law of truth" (Mal. 2:6), and especially the "true God [or God of truth]" (Jer. 10:10). Curiously, *'emet* is spelled with the first, middle, and last letters of the Hebrew alphabet; thus the rabbis concluded that truth upholds the first and the last of God's creation, and everything in between! *Also* (John 4:24) *aletheia* (al-ay-thi-ah); *Strong's #225:* Derived from negative, *a*, and *lanthano*, "to be hidden," "to escape notice." (Compare "latent," "lethargy," "lethal.") *Aletheia* is the opposite of fictitious, feigned, or false. It denotes veracity, reality, sincerity, accuracy, integrity, truthfulness, dependability, and propriety.

UGARIT—see ch. 55, §3.4., 3.4.a., 3.4.b., 3.4.c., 3.4.d., 3.6.d., 6.2.

UNBELIEF—lack of belief or faith in God and His provision. While unbelief does not hinder God's faithfulness (Rom. 3:3), it does affect the individual's capacity to receive the benefits of that faithfulness. The unbelief of many Israelites, for example, kept them from seeing the Promised Land (Heb. 3:19). The unbelief of the citizens of Nazareth prevented them from witnessing Christ's miracles (Matt. 13:58). The skeptic is limited in what he might see or know, while "all things are possible to him who believes" (Mark 9:23).

UNCLEAN. (Lev. 10:10) *tame'* (tah-*may*); *Strong's* #2931: Defiled, contaminated, polluted, unclean. This adjective comes from a root verb, also spelled *tame'*, meaning "to defile" or "to make unclean." The adjective *tame'* occurs more than eighty times (usually translated "unclean"), 75 percent of these in Leviticus, Numbers, and Deuteronomy. The cause for uncleanness is contact with unclean things (7:21). In addition, God restricted Israel from eating a number of species of birds, mammals, fish, and insects, which were to be considered unclean. This emphasis on cleanness or uncleanness was a part of God's design to impress the Israelites with the difference between the two conditions. Not only were the priests to learn to distinguish between holy and unholy, between clean and unclean, but they were to teach that differentiation to all Israel (10:10–11).

UNCTION—KJV word for the act of anointing, referring to the gift of the Holy Spirit (1 John 2:20, anointing, NKJV, RSV, NIV, NASB). In the Old Testament, kings (1 Sam. 10:1), priests (Num. 35:25), and prophets (1 Kin. 19:16) were anointed with holy oil; in the New Testament believers were anointed with the Holy Spirit.

UNDEFILED—unstained, unsoiled, not tainted with evil; clean, pure, faultless. The word undefiled is used of the sinless Christ (Heb. 7:26), of sex in marriage (Heb. 13:4), of a pure and faultless religion (James 1:27), and of our incorruptible inheritance in heaven (1 Pet. 1:4).

UNDERSTAND. (Neh. 8:8) *bin* (*bean*); *Strong's* #995. To understand, discern, perceive, grasp, consider, regard; be perceptive, have insight. This verb occurs more than 165 times and refers to that intelligent process of perception, discernment, and understanding, which all human beings possess in varying amounts. (For biblical range of meaning in the word *bin*, refer to 1 Sam. 3:8; Ps. 92:5–7; Prov. 24:11–12; Is. 40:21; Jer. 30:24; Dan. 10:12.) From *bin* is derived the noun *binah*, meaning "understanding"; this term occurs thirty-seven times. (*See* Prov. 3:5; 4:5; Is. 11:2; Dan. 10:1.) In the present reference, spiritual revival did not come until the people clearly understood the text.

UNDERSTANDING. (Jer. 3:15) *sachal* (sah-*chahl*); *Strong's* #7919: To be wise, behave wisely; to understand, be instructed; to wisely consider; to be prudent and intelligent. *Sachal* describes the complex, intelligent thinking process that occurs when one observes, ponders, reasons, learns, and reaches a conclusion. The word is occasionally translated "prosper." In 1 Kings 2:3, David urged Solomon to be obedient to God's instructions so that he could prosper (literally, "do wisely") in everything he undertook. A derivative of *sachal* is *maschil*, "to give instruction, to make wise and skillful." Thirteen instructive psalms are titled *"Maschil"* (NKJV, "Contemplation"). The *maschil* psalms (32; 42; 44; 45; 52; 53; 54; 55; 74; 78; 88; 89; 142) are designed to make the reader wise. *Also* (Luke 2:47) *sunesis* (*soon*-es-is); *Strong's* #4907: Literally, "a putting together," hence, quickness of apprehension, the critical faculty for clear apprehension, intelligently assessing a situation. Comparable to the modern idiom, "putting two and two together." The New Testament uses two words for understanding, *phronesis* and *sunesis*. *Phronesis* acts, while *sunesis* judges. *Phronesis* is the practical side of the mind, while *sunesis* is the analyzing and discerning side.

UNPARDONABLE SIN (*See* Sin.)

UNRIGHTEOUSNESS. (John 7:18) *Tadikia* (ad-ee-*kee*-ah); *Strong's* #93: Derived from *a*, negative, and the root *dike*, "right." Misdeeds, injustice, moral wrongdoing, unjust acts, unrighteousness, iniquity. It is the opposite of truthfulness, faithfulness, and rightness.

UR—see ch. 55, §3.5.b., 3.6.

URIAH—see ch. 55, §3.3.

USELESSNESS. (Acts 14:15) *mataios* (mat-ah-yoss); *Strong's* #3152: Fruitless, empty, futile, frivolous, hollow, unreal, unproductive, lacking substance, trifling, ineffectual, void of results, devoid of force, success, or utility, and

---

 This icon beside an entry indicates a Word Wealth feature.

 This icon beside an entry indicates a Kingdom Dynamics feature.

 This icon beside an entry indicates an important biblical or doctrinal term.

worthless. The word here describes Greek and Roman mythological ritual. The unregenerate philosophy of that day made Paul and Barnabas urge the people to turn from these useless (*mataios*) things. Their message was "turn from Zeus, who has never lived, to God who has always been alive. As Creator He is worthy to be served, worshiped, and trusted."

 VANITY—emptiness, worthlessness, or futility. The word occurs over thirty-five times in the Old Testament (NKJV), most frequently in Ecclesiastes. The word vanity as used in the Bible does not mean conceit or an attitude of superiority. With reference to people, it means the emptiness, meaninglessness, or futility of natural human life apart from God's life, grace, and fullness (Job 7:3; Eccl. 1:2; 2:1; 4:4; 5:10).

When applied to things, vanity is especially used to describe idols, because there is no abiding substance to them (Is. 41:29). Demonic attractions lure toward emptiness and eventual destruction, thus believers are urged to stay away from vain things and to flow in the Holy Spirit's fullness as He expands the reality of their life in Christ. Anything short of God Himself which a person trusts to meet his deepest needs is vanity (Eph. 4:17–24; 5:19).

VIRGIN BIRTH—the biblical doctrine that Jesus was miraculously begotten by God and born of Mary, who was a virgin. The term virgin birth explains the way in which the Son of God entered human existence; it means that Mary had not had sexual relations with any man when she conceived Jesus.

This unparalleled act of God is described beautifully in Luke 1:26–38. The angel of God appeared to a virgin who was engaged to Joseph. In those days engagement was a legal arrangement in which a woman was betrothed, or pledged, to a man. But engagement did not permit sexual relations.

Since Mary had not "known" Joseph sexually, she wondered how she could bear a child. The angel explained that this would be encouraged by "the power of the Highest" as the Holy Spirit would "overshadow her." There was nothing physical about this divine act; this is emphasized by the statement that the child would be the "Holy One" (Luke 1:35).

The angel also declared that the child would be called "the Son of God." This clearly teaches that it was only through the virgin birth that Jesus, a human being, could also be properly identified as the Son of God. The one person, Jesus, has two natures—divine and human. The eternal, divine nature of the Son

of God was joined, in Mary's womb, with a human nature by the direct act of God.

The parallel account in Matthew 1:18–25 views the virgin birth from Joseph's perspective. Because of the legal nature of engagement, a man who found his fiancee pregnant would normally divorce her. Because Joseph was a fair and just man, he did not want to shame Mary by divorcing her publicly, so he decided to do so privately. But the angel prevented this by assuring him that Mary was still a virgin. Her child was conceived by the Holy Spirit, as predicted in Isaiah 7:14.

After this revelation, Joseph took Mary as his wife but did not unite with her sexually until Jesus was born. This implies (but does not prove) that Joseph and Mary later united sexually and had other children.

Some scholars claim that the reference in Luke 2:27, 33, and 41 to Jesus' parents (Joseph and Mary) implies that the virgin birth was not a part of early Christian tradition. But these words were written by the same writer who described the annunciation of the virgin birth in Luke 1:26–38. Some Bible students also express concern over the lack of reference to the virgin birth elsewhere in the New Testament. However, the other Gospels say nothing about Jesus' birth, so it is not strange that they do not speak of the virgin birth. Since the gospel message concerns the death, burial, and resurrection of Christ (1 Cor. 15:1–3), the virgin birth is not generally a part of its proclamation. But the virgin birth is an essential, wonderful, and powerful truth noted in historic Christian doctrine because it is revealed in the eternal Word of God.

VIRGINS. (Ps. 45:14) *betulah* (beh-too-*lah*); *Strong's* #1330: A virgin; a maiden, a damsel, a grown-up young woman of marriageable age; a fiancee; a newly married bride. *Betulah* is not the only Hebrew word to describe a maiden, a virgin, or a mature young woman; `*almah* also describes a young woman or "lass." Both words come from roots that connote "separation." Nevertheless, *betulah* is used to describe an unfaithful or wayward young woman (Jer. 18:13–15). In Deuteronomy 22:17, *betulah* refers to physical virginity. Generally, the term refers to the vitality and strength of a young woman in a certain age group, whether she is an unmarried maiden or a recently married bride.

VIRTUE. (2 Pet. 1:5) *arete* (ar-*et*-ay); *Strong's* #703: Used in classical Greek to describe any quality that elicited preeminent estimation for a person. Later the word signified intrinsic value, moral excellency, and goodness. It is used both of God (1 Pet. 2:9) and persons (Phil.

4:8; 2 Pet. 1:3, 5). Many scholars feel that in biblical times *arete* was commonly used to refer to manifestations of God's miracle power.

 VISION. (2 Chr. 32:32) *chazon* (cha-*zohn*); *Strong's* #2377: A prophetic vision, dream, oracle, revelation; especially the kind of revelation that comes through sight, namely a vision from God. This noun occurs thirty-five times and is from the root *chazah*, "to see, behold, and perceive." *Chazon* is especially used for the revelation which the prophets received. (*See* Is. 1:1; Ezek. 12:27–28; Dan. 8:1–2; Obad. 1; Hab. 2:2–3.) The prophets understood God's counsels so clearly because He revealed matters to them by visible means. Proverbs 29:18 shows that when a society lacks any revelation from God (divine insight), such a society heads in the direction of anarchy.

VISIONS—experiences similar to dreams through which supernatural insight or awareness is given by revelation. The difference between a dream and a vision is that dreams occur only during sleep, while visions can happen while a person is awake (Dan. 10:7).

In the Bible, people who had visions were filled with a special consciousness of God. The most noteworthy Old Testament examples of recipients of visions are Ezekiel and Daniel. Visions in the New Testament are most prominent in the Gospel of Luke, the Book of Acts, and the Book of Revelation. The Holy Spirit's use of this means of personal prompting was prophesied by Joel (2:28–32) and affirmed at the birth of the church to be an abiding operation of the Holy Spirit's dealings with believers. Visions never supercede Scripture, but like dreams and prophecies are to be tested by the Word (1 Pet. 1:16–21) and judged (1 Cor. 14:29)—that is, evaluated by mature believers.

VOID. (1 Cor. 9:15) *kenoo* (ken-*ah*-oh); *Strong's* #2758: To abase, neutralize, empty, nullify, render void, divest totally, reduce to nothing. The word is used of the incarnation of Christ in Philippians 2:7, which describes His self-emptying of the glories attendant to His deity, but not of deity itself.

VOW—a solemn promise or pledge that binds a person to perform a specified act or to behave in a certain manner. The first mention of a vow in the Bible is of Jacob at Bethel (Gen. 28:20–22; 31:13). Other people who made a vow are Jephthah (Judg. 11:30–31, 39), Han-

nah (1 Sam. 1:11), David (Ps. 132:2–5), and Absalom (2 Sam. 15:7–8).

In the New Testament the apostle Paul, probably at the end of a thirty-day period of abstinence from meat and wine, had his hair cut off at Cenchrea, "for he had taken a vow" (Acts 18:18). The vow that Paul had taken was probably the Nazirite vow (Num. 6:1–21). Samson was an Old Testament hero who had also taken the Nazirite vow (Judg. 13:5, 7; 16:17).

All vows were made to God as a promise in expectation of His favor (Gen. 28:20) or in thanksgiving for His blessings (Ps. 116:12–14). Vowing might be a part of everyday devotion (Ps. 61:8) or the annual festivals (1 Sam. 1:21). Vows must be paid to God in the congregation at the tabernacle or temple (Deut. 12:6, 11; Ps. 22:25).

Vowing was voluntary. But after a vow was made, it had to be performed (Deut. 23:21–23; Eccl. 5:4–6). Vows, therefore, were to be made only after careful consideration (Prov. 20:25) and in keeping with what pleased God (Lev. 27:9–27). Vowing certain deeds is never a means of salvation, only an accepted discipline.

Vowing is joyful worship in faith and love (Ps. 61:4–5, 8), often associated with the proclamation of God's salvation (Ps. 22:22–27; 66:13–20). For this reason, deception in vowing is an affront to God and brings His curse (Mal. 1:14).

 WAIT. (Lam. 3:25) *qavah* (kah-*vah*); *Strong's* #6960: To wait for, look for, expect, hope. This verb is found some fifty times. *Qavah* is the root of the noun *tiqvah*, "hope" or "expectancy." *Qavah* expresses the idea of "waiting hopefully" (Gen. 49:18; Job 30:26; Ps. 40:1; Is. 5:4; 25:9). In the present reference, even in the overwhelming tragedies Jeremiah experienced, he had hope in God's salvation and was willing to wait for it. *Also* (Mic. 7:7) *yachal* (yah-*chal*); *Strong's* #3176: To wait, tarry, hope, trust, expect; be patient; remain in anticipation. *Yachal* appears thirty-eight times in the Old Testament. Its first occurrence is in Genesis 8:10, in the account of Noah's waiting seven days, from the time he first sent out the dove until he sent her out again. *Yachal* is often translated "hope" (Pss. 31:24; 33:18; 130:5, 7; 147:11). The correct way to hope and wait for the Lord is to steadfastly expect His mercy, His salvation, and His rescue, and

---

while waiting, not take matters into one's own hand (compare Gen. 15:1—17:22).

WAR, WARFARE—armed conflict with an opposing military force. From the perspective of the Hebrew people, a war was to be declared by God Himself (Ex. 17:16).

Every warrior considered himself consecrated to God (Is. 13:3). Before and during a war, soldiers abstained from certain activities to sanctify themselves (Judg. 20:26; 2 Sam. 11:11). Those who fought under a divinely ordained leader (Judg. 6:34) had to be single-minded in their devotion to God. Those who were frightened, newly married, or beset by domestic or financial problems were asked to go home (Deut. 20:5–9). The *ark of the covenant, the symbol of God's presence, went with Israel's army into battle (2 Sam. 11:11).

The Israelites determined the right moment to enter into battle and sought guidance in battle by casting the sacred lot or by heeding the words of a prophet (Judg. 1:1; 1 Sam. 23:2; 1 Kin. 22:5). King Ahab was killed when he failed to heed the warning of Micaiah, the Lord's prophet (2 Chronicles 18).

In Numbers 21:14, Moses mentioned a book which has remained a mystery to biblical scholars—"the Book of the Wars of the Lord." This was probably a collection of records or songs celebrating the victories of Israel over its enemies. The Old Testament contains many references to God's role in battle against Israel's foes (Ex. 15:3; Ps. 24:8). God struck Israel's enemies with terror, overtaking and killing all fugitives (Ex. 15:1–27; Josh. 10:10–11). The judge Deborah, in her famous "Song of Deborah," cursed those who did not come to the Lord's aid against mighty Sisera (Judg. 5:23). As Israel's king, David fought "the Lord's battles" (1 Sam. 18:17). The prophet Jeremiah cursed those who refused to fight the Lord's battles (Jer. 48:10).

According to 2 Samuel 11:1, wars were usually waged "in the spring of the year." The trumpet or ram's horn, symbolic of the voice of God, called Israel into battle (Judg. 3:27; 1 Sam. 13:3). The number of soldiers whom Israel mustered for battle made no difference, for God fought alongside them (Judges 7; 1 Sam. 14:6). Indeed, the Israelites were forced to wander forty years in the wilderness because they did not believe God could help them win over the Canaanites, who outnumbered the Israelites in both manpower and equipment (Num. 14:1–12).

The tactics of war were simple. They included surprise, ambush, pretended flight, and surrounding the enemy (Gen. 14:15; Josh. 8:2–7; 2 Sam. 5:23). On occasion a representative of each army met in combat (1 Samuel 17).

According to Deuteronomy 20:10–20, when Israel invaded Canaan three outcomes of war were possible. If the besieged city surrendered, the occupants' lives were spared but all were enslaved. If the city refused to agree to peace terms and had to be taken by force, all males were killed by the sword. An exception to both these policies occurred when the captured city lay within Israel's boundaries. Then all occupants and their possessions were utterly destroyed. Known as the ban, this custom was intended to keep Israel free of any heathen influence (Josh. 6:17; 1 Sam. 15:3).

Besieging a city required elaborate planning. If possible, the city's water supply was cut off. Often the towers and gates of the city were set on fire (Judg. 9:52). In order for armies to use their battering rams and catapults that propelled arrows or stones, mounds were built to raise the weapons to appropriate height. From the mound, scaling ladders were laid against the wall so soldiers could get inside the city. All the while, the city's defenders were using their own similar weapons to kill the enemy and destroy their war machinery (2 Sam. 11:21, 24; 2 Chr. 26:15). (A famous battle using these techniques was the Roman siege of Masada [A.D. 70–73]. A rock fortress about 1.6 kilometers (one mile) west of the Dead Sea, Masada had been considered impregnable. In fact, it took the Romans nearly three years to gain entry into Masada, only to find its some 960 inhabitants, all Jewish Zealots, dead as a result of a suicide pact.)

By the time of Solomon, warfare was the result of national policy set by the ruling king who supposedly was acting at God's direction. Court prophets, when asked about the advisability of entering into war, rarely went against the king's wishes—although Micaiah the son of Imlah did so (1 Kin. 22:8–28; 2 Chr. 18:7–27). Israel entered into international treaties with the great earthly powers rather than relying on God's strength for security (1 Kin. 15:18–19; 2 Kin. 17:4).

Also see Spiritual Warfare.

WATCH—either a group of soldiers or others posted to keep guard (Neh. 4:9; 7:3; 12:25) or one of the units of time into which the night was divided (Ps. 63:6; Lam. 2:19; Luke 12:38).

Because of the mention of the "middle watch" (Judg. 7:19), there must have been three such units in the Old Testament period. The "beginning of the watches" (Lam. 2:19) was apparently the first of these and the "morning watch" was the third (Ex. 14:24; 1 Sam. 11:11). However, by the New Testament period the Roman system of four watches had been adopted (Matt. 14:25; Mark 6:48). These were apparently named as follows: evening, midnight, cockcrow (RSV; the crowing of the rooster, NKJV), and morning (Mark 13:35).

WATCHMAN. (Hos. 9:8) *tsaphah* (tsah-*fah*); *Strong's* #6822: To look out, peer into the distance, spy, keep watch; to scope something out, especially in order to see approaching danger, and to warn those who are endangered. This verb occurs about eighty times. Often it is translated "watchmen," referring to the king's guards (1 Sam. 14:16) or to those who look out from a tower in the city wall (2 Kin. 9:17–18). In other instances, it is spiritual watchmen, or prophets, who look out, see danger, and report to the people. (*See* Is. 52:8; Jer. 6:17; Ezek. 33:2–7.) In Proverbs 31:27, the ideal woman "watches over" the ways of her household.

WATERS. (Is. 43:2) *mayim* (*my*-yeem); *Strong's* #4325: Water; waters, floods, seas. *Mayim* is the Hebrew word for "water," but is always in the plural: "waters." *Mayim* appears 570 times in the Old Testament and has a wide range of use. It occurs as a metaphor for the raging heathen, the chaotic, stormy seas at creation, and vast nations (or seas of people). (*See* Ps. 32:6; 33:7; 46:3; Jer. 46:7–8.) Most significantly, *mayim* speaks of life, sustenance, fertility, blessing, and refreshing. (*See* Ps. 23:2; Is. 12:3; 32:2; 55:1; 58:11; Jer. 17:8.)

WAY—a thoroughfare for travel, such as a path, road, or highway. Figuratively, the word *way* is used in the Old Testament as a synonym for God's divine will and manner of dealing with man (Ps. 1:6). In the New Testament, the word is often used as a metaphor for man's moral course (Matt. 7:13–14; 2 Pet. 21:15).

Jesus reminded His disciples that the single road to God was through Himself: "I am the way, the truth, and the life. No one comes to the Father except through Me" (John 14:6). In the Book of Acts, the phrase *the Way* was a commonly used label for the early movement of believers in Jesus the Messiah. Like the word "Christian" (born as a term of derision), the people of Christ bore the term with pride as the followers of the living Jesus (Acts 9:2; 24:14, 22).

WEALTH—an abundance of possessions or resources. During the times of the patriarchs, wealth was measured largely in livestock—sheep, goats, cattle, donkeys, and camels. This was true of Abraham (Gen. 13:2), Isaac (Gen. 26:12–14), and Jacob (Gen. 30:43; 32:5). People of the ancient world also measured wealth in terms of land, houses, servants, slaves, and precious metals. The prime example is King Solomon, whose great wealth is described in 1 Kings 10:14–29.

Wealth is a major theme in the *Wisdom literature of the Bible (Prov. 10:15; 13:11; 19:4). The most important observation of these writings is that wealth comes from God (Prov. 3:9–10). The possession of wealth is not always the sign of God's favor. "Why does the way of the wicked prosper?" (Jer. 12:1) became a familiar theme to the writers of the Old Testament.

The prophet Amos thundered against the rich and prosperous inhabitants of Israel who sold "the righteous for silver, and the poor for a pair of sandals" (Amos 2:6). Their wealth was corrupt and under a curse because it was founded on exploitation of the poor.

In the New Testament, many warnings are given of the dangers of letting money and things possess a person's heart. In the Sermon on the Mount, Jesus spoke of "treasures on earth" and "treasures in heaven" and called upon His followers to be careful of which treasure they chose (Matt. 6:19–21, 24).

Many of Jesus' parables, such as the rich fool (Luke 12:13–21) and the rich man and Lazarus (Luke 16:19–31), deal with people who made the wrong choice, choosing earthly wealth over heavenly wealth. But the only true and lasting wealth is the spiritual riches of God's grace (Matt. 13:44–46).

Wealth is not deemed unworthy or ungodly in the Scriptures, as long as the person so blessed retains godly priorities and is generous to others, faithful in worship to God with his or her substance, and serves human need.

WENT UP. (Ex. 19:20) *'alah* (ah-*lah*); *Strong's* #5927: To ascend, to go up, to rise. This verb appears more than eight hundred times in the Old Testament. In addition to the obvious meaning of "go up," *'alah* can mean "bring up" or "offer up," when referring to sacrifices. Furthermore, the whole burnt offering is called *'olah* because the smoke from the offering ascended to heaven. In Psalm 24:3, *'alah* refers to ascending God's holy hill by the righteous. *'Alah* is also the root of the word *'aliyah*, "ascension" or "going up," which especially refers to going up to Zion, or to returning to Israel from the lands of dispersion. Finally, *'alah* is the root of *'elyon* (highest), which is part of the divine title *'El 'Elyon* (the Most High God).

WICKED. (Prov. 10:16) *rasha'* (rah-*shah*); *Strong's* #7563: Wicked, wrong, violently disrupted, godless, lawless, guilty, condemned, punishable; vicious, unrighteous, sinful. This noun occurs more than 250 times. It comes from the verb *rasha'* "to be guilty," "wicked," "condemned." Some sense of violent internal disturbance may be conveyed (as if to say that a man is wicked because of unresolved inner turmoil). Often the wicked are contrasted with the righteous, as here and in Genesis 18:23, where Abraham knew that God regarded these two groups of people as requiring separate treatment. *Rasha'* occurs almost eighty times in Proverbs (*see*, for example, 12:10; 15:29; 25:26). In 12:10, we read of a wicked man so far gone that even his "tender mercies" seem cruel.

WILL—a word with two distinct meanings in the Bible:

1. Wishing, desiring, or choosing, especially in reference to the will of God. In the Gospels, primarily in John, Jesus is said to be acting not according to His own will, but according to the will of the heavenly Father (John 5:30; 6:38). Indeed, doing the will of the Father is Jesus' nourishment (John 4:34), and Jesus does nothing apart from the Father's will (John 5:19). Luke confirms this when he quotes Jesus' statement in the Garden of Gethsemane: "Father, if it is Your will, take this cup away from Me; nevertheless not My will, but Yours, be done" (Luke 22:42).

2. A legal declaration of how a person wishes his possessions to be disposed after his death. No written Israelite wills existed until the first century B.C. They were unnecessary because of the strict inheritance customs of the Hebrew people. Land belonged to the family, and it was passed on to the sons, the oldest receiving a double portion. If there were no sons, the land passed in the following order— daughters, brothers, father's brothers, and next of kin (Num. 27:8–11).

WILL. (Matt. 12:50) *thelema* (*thel*-ay-mah); *Strong's* #2307: Used objectively of that which is willed, designed, or desired (18:14; Luke 12:47; John 5:30), and subjectively of the emotion of being desirous (Luke 23:25; John 1:13; 1 Pet. 3:17). The word is used both of the human will and the divine will.

WILLING. (Matt. 8:2) *thelo* (*thel*-oh); *Strong's* #2309: To wish, desire, will, take delight in. It carries the idea of being ready, preferring, and having in mind. A related New Testament word is *boulomai*, a stronger expression of the will, signifying the determinant will deliberately exercised.

WIPED OUT (Col. 2:14) *exaleipho* (ex-al-*eye*-foe); *Strong's* #1813: From *ek*, "out," and *aleipho*, "to anoint"; hence, to wipe out, wipe off, wash. Used metaphorically, the word signifies a removal or obliteration, whether of

sins (Acts 3:19), of writing (Col. 2:14), of a name (Rev. 3:5), or of tears (Rev. 21:4).

WISDOM—ability to judge correctly and follow the best course of action, based on knowledge and understanding. The apostle Paul declared that the message of the Cross is foolishness to the Greeks and a stumbling block to the Jews. But to those who believe, said Paul, this "foolishness of God" is "the wisdom of God" (1 Cor. 1:18–25).

Against the wisdom of God Paul contrasted "the wisdom of this world" (1 Cor. 1:20; 3:19), "human wisdom" (1 Cor. 2:4), "the wisdom of men" (1 Cor. 2:5), "the wisdom of this age" (1 Cor. 2:6), and "man's wisdom" (1 Cor. 2:13).

The biblical concept of wisdom, therefore, is quite different from the classical view of wisdom, which sought through philosophy and man's rational thought to determine the mysteries of existence and the universe. The first principle of biblical wisdom is that man should humble himself before God in reverence and worship, obedient to His commands. This idea is found especially in the Wisdom Literature: the books of Job, Psalms, Proverbs, and Ecclesiastes.

In the Old Testament, the best example of a "wise man" is King Solomon (1 Kin. 10:4, 68; 2 Chr. 1:7–12). And yet the same book that heaps such lavish, warm, and glowing praise upon Solomon for his reputed wisdom (1 Kin. 4:29–34) also points out how Solomon violated his earlier commitment to God's wisdom, and his heart turned away from the Lord (1 Kin. 11:1–13).

WISDOM. (Is. 11:2) *chochmah* (choach-*mah*); *Strong's* #2451: Wisdom; wiseness; skillfulness, whether in the artistic sense (craftsmanship) or the moral sense (skills for living correctly). This noun occurs about 150 times. It is found in all sections of the Old Testament, but is mentioned extensively in Job, Proverbs, and Ecclesiastes. Biblical wisdom unites God, the Source of all understanding, with daily life, where the principles of right living are put into practice. Therefore, one is exhorted to make God the starting point in any quest for wisdom (Ps. 111:10) and to seek wisdom above all else if he would live successfully (Prov. 4:5–9). The present reference shows that wisdom is a permanent characteristic of the Messiah (compare 1 Cor. 1:24). *Also* (Acts 6:10) *sophia* (sof-*ee*-ah); *Strong's* #4678: Practical wisdom, prudence, skill, comprehensive insight, Christian enlightenment, a right application of knowledge, insight into the true nature of things. Wisdom in the Bible is often coupled with knowledge (Rom. 11:33; 1 Cor.

12:8; Col. 2:3). In anticipation of our needing guidance, direction, and knowing, God tells us to ask for wisdom, assuring us of a liberal reception (James 1:5).

WITHDRAWN. (John. 5:13) *ekneuo* (ek-*nyoo*-oh); *Strong's #1593:* Literally "to bend the head aside." To shun, avoid, turn aside, withdraw, retire. Used only here in the New Testament, *ekneuo* describes Jesus leaving the premises after healing the lame man. Although some believe that Jesus slipped away to escape danger, others believe that He was avoiding audience applause or the crisis precipitated with the religious order by healing a man on the Sabbath.

WITHSTAND. (Eph. 6:11) *anthistemi* (anth-*is*-tay-mee); *Strong's #436:* Compare "antihistamine." From *anti,* "against," and *histemi,* "to cause to stand." The verb suggests vigorously opposing, bravely resisting, standing face-to-face against an adversary, standing your ground. Just as an antihistamine puts a block on histamine, *anthistemi* tells us that with the authority and spiritual weapons granted to us we can withstand evil forces.

WITNESS—a person who gives testimony; testimony given for or against someone, often in a law court setting, where there is considerable concern for the truth of the testimony. "You shall not bear false witness against your neighbor" (Ex. 20:16; Deut. 17:6; Prov. 25:18).

A witness can also be a guarantee of the accuracy of a transaction (Jer. 32:10, 12, 25, 44). The Old Testament prophets often pictured God either as bearing witness against Israel (Mic. 1:2) or as challenging Israel to bear witness against Him (Mic. 6:3). God is also seen in the Old Testament as witnessing covenants between individuals (Gen. 31:50) as well as covenants between Himself and the nation of Israel or individuals (Deut. 31:19–26).

In addition to these general uses, witness is also used in connection with the distinctively spiritual message of the Bible. God witnesses to the believer about His assurance of salvation: "The Spirit Himself bears witness with our spirit that we are children of God" (Rom. 8:16).

The Bible also declares that God has not left Himself without witness (Acts 14:17). Witness to Christ is borne by the prophets (Acts 10:43), John the Baptist (John 1:7), the Father (John 5:37; 8:18), the works of Christ (John 5:36; 10:37–38), and Christ Himself (John 8:18).

The believer's life and word also serve as a witness to the world. The essence of this idea is in the fact that a witness is "evidence for the case." True believers become such evidences for the proposition that Jesus is alive! Our witness to the world is in the succession of the faithful who were witnesses of His resurrection (Acts 1:22; 2:32; 10:41; 13:31). Christ's call to witness has implications for all believers and equally calls us all to be filled with the same power of the Holy Spirit as the early believers were (Acts 1:8; 2:1–4), for herein is the power to minister the life and grace of Jesus in a way that verifies He is alive and working today: Jesus Christ, the same yesterday, today, and forever (Heb. 13:8).

WITNESS. (Rev. 1:5) *martus* (*mar*-toos); *Strong's #3144:* Compare "martyr" and "martyrdom." One who testifies to the truth he has experienced, a witness, one who has knowledge of a fact and can give information concerning it. The word in itself does not imply death, but many of the first-century witnesses did give their lives, with the result that the word came to denote a martyr, one who witnesses for Christ by his death (Acts 22:20; Rev. 2:13; 17:6).

WITNESSING. (Acts 26:22) *martureo* (mar-too-*reh*-oh); *Strong's #3140:* Giving evidence, attesting, confirming, confessing, bearing record, speaking well of, giving a good report, testifying, affirming that one has seen, heard, or experienced something. In the New Testament it is used particularly for presenting the gospel with evidence. The English word "martyr" comes from this word, suggesting that a witness is one willing to die for his testimony.

WOMAN—a female adult; the human created co-equal to the male at Creation (Gen. 1:26–28).

In order to understand the Old Testament view of woman, one must turn to the Book of Genesis. When God created mankind, He created both "male and female" (Gen. 1:27; 5:2). Both were created in God's image and both were given the responsibility of exercising authority over God's creation. The man was created before the woman, apparently to accentuate to the man his need for a companion and a helper. God's special act of creation, causing the man to sleep and creating from a part of his body "a helper comparable to him" (Gen. 2:18, 20) clearly introduced to both the original couple the uniqueness of their need for one another. Because the woman was called "helper" does not imply that she was or is inferior to man. (The same Hebrew word translated as helper is used of God in His relationship to Israel—Ps. 33:20; 70:5.)

The influence of the culture that developed around the patriarchs and the Israelites in ancient times seldom had this perspective of woman. Certain Old Testament passages, reporting the events in the cultural context of those in the narrative, reflect the attitude present there that woman was often little more than an object, or intended to be entirely subordinate to man. This attitude was pronounced before the coming of Christ and prevails in much of the world today. (One of the non-biblical, Jewish prayers dating from that era declaimed, "I thank Thee that I am not a woman.")

Jesus lived and taught a better way—the way of returning human dignity at every dimension God intended. This shows in His treatment of women. He allowed women to accompany Him and His disciples on their journeys (Luke 8:1–3). He refused a social taboo and talked with the Samaritan woman at Jacob's Well, leading her to a conversion experience (John 4). Jesus allowed Mary to sit at His feet, assuming the role of a disciple (Luke 10:38–42). Although the Jews segregated the women in both temple and synagogue, the early church did not separate the congregation by sex (Acts 12:1–17; 1 Cor. 11:2–16).

The apostle Paul wrote, "There is neither Jew nor Greek, there is neither slave nor free, there is neither male nor female; for you are all one in Christ Jesus" (Gal. 3:28). Some conclude more severe applications of Paul's statements which restrict women from participating in church leadership as freely as men. A close, unprejudiced look at 1 Corinthians 14:34–35 seems not to disallow verbal ministry in or to the body of the congregation, since women did prophesy as a normative practice in the church (Acts 21:9; 1 Cor.11:5). Rather, it appears Paul was confronting husband-wife bickering in church, and saying, "Settle issues at home!" The passage in 2 Timothy 2:11–12 emphatically refers to husband-wife relationships (Greek, *aner*—husband), and in the context appears to be Paul's call to women to control their remarks and not embarrass their husbands in public. ("Silence" is the same Greek word translated "quiet" in 1 Tim. 2:2—not speechless.)

Some of the finest leaders in Israel were women, in spite of the fact that the culture was male-dominated. Victories were won because of the courage of women (Judges 4—5; 9:54; Esth. 4:16). God revealed His Word through *prophetesses (Judg. 4:4; Luke 2:36; Acts 21:9). God used Priscilla and her husband Aquila to explain "the way of God more accurately" to Apollos the preacher (Acts 18:26). The heroes of faith mentioned in Hebrews 11 include Sarah (v. 11), Moses' mother (v. 23), and Rahab the harlot (v. 31).

These indicate the biblical fact that the church need not yield to the feminist spirit of the world but still may properly acknowledge the place of women in ministry and leadership, while the woman still biblically acknowledges her voluntary submission to her husband (Eph. 5:23–33).

WOMEN, THE WORK AND MINISTRY OF. An inescapably blessed fact fills the Scriptures: God has ordained that every believer realize the significance of their mission and ministry as His servants. Gender is no restriction intended to limit significance or breadth of dimension in living for or serving Christ: "I will pour out My Spirit upon your sons and daughters . . . upon your menservants and your maidservants" (Acts 2:17–18). Sensitive to the need for grace and balance in pursuing this theme, this study unfolds the uniqueness and dynamic of many of the Bible's key women.

1. The First Woman: A Redemptive Instrument—Eve (Gen. 4:25). The Bible reveals that God created male and female, and that all mankind are descendants of that first pair. While Eve was deceived by the Serpent, and the first to violate the divine regulations governing their life (2:16–17; 3:6), the Word of God holds Adam as the disobedient one, who knowingly broke trust with God (Rom. 5:12, 17; 1 Tim. 2:14). This fact does not intimate that the woman was less intelligent or more vulnerable to deception than the man, but that under the circumstances in which the Fall of man occurred, deception of the woman preceded active disobedience of the man.

It is a remarkable token of divine grace that God, in His mercy and in His giving of the first promise of a Deliverer/Messiah (Gen. 3:15), chose to bring this about by Seed of the woman. In short, the one first scarred by sin is selected to be the one first promised to become an instrument of God's redemptive working.

The birth of Seth, the "seed" given to replace the murdered Abel, was the first in the "bloodline" that will trace to the birth of the Lord Jesus Christ. Eve's distinct place in the failure of the first couple becomes the soil in which God's mercy plants the first seed of promise. The message is obvious: God is able to "make all grace abound" toward any of us. However deep the failure, Eve's testimony declares God's grace goes deeper yet.

2. The Submission That Bears Fruit—Sarah (Gen. 16:1). Sarah was originally called "Sarai," which means "Princess." When God changed Sarai's name to "Sarah," He named her *The* Princess" or "Queen," linking her in co-rulership with her husband Abraham (formerly Abram), the "Father of Many Nations," and including her in His covenant promise (17:15–16).

Sarah, the beautiful (12:14) wife of Abraham, was barren (16:1), a condition considered a curse in the ancient world. She is a positive lesson (1) in faith that rises above personal limitations (Heb. 11:11); and (2) in a submitted spirit that responds biblically to her husband, without becoming depersonalized (1 Pet. 3:5–6).

Sarah is also an illustration of the dangers of taking God's promises into our own hands. Her suggestion that Abraham take her handmaid as wife, in view of Sarah's barrenness, resulted in the birth of Ishmael—a child who occasioned jealousy and conflict between the two women, eventually between their two sons, and to this day, among their offspring.

3. The Blessing of an Unselfish Woman—Rebekah (Gen. 24:15–67). Rebekah, the Syrian, was the granddaughter of Nahor, Abraham's brother (22:23). Rebekah's name refers to "tying or binding up," implying that her beauty was so great, it could literally "captivate" or "fascinate" men. She is introduced as a diligently industrious and beautifully sensitive girl. Her willingness to serve Eleazar and her readiness to draw water for all ten of the thirsty camels dramatize this. A lesson in the way God provides surprising rewards for servant-spirited souls is seen in what happened to Rebekah. Little did she know those camels were carrying untold gifts for her and her family. Her will to wait for her family's blessing before accepting the invitation to leave for a marriage to Isaac, who was a wealthy prince of the ancient world, is a model for today. How many marriages today would be different (1) if the Holy Spirit were the guide, (2) if prayer and worship were the order of the day, and (3) if the couple had the blessing of the family?

4. A Godly Quest for Equal Rights—Daughters of Zelophehad (Num. 27:1–11). Zelophehad, of the tribe of Manasseh, had five daughters and no sons. Their names were: Mahlah, meaning "Sickness or Disease"; Noah, meaning "Rest or Comfort"; Hoglah, meaning "Partridge or Boxer"; Milcah, meaning "Queen or Counsel"; and Tirzah, meaning "Pleasantness." If we accept these women's names as pictures of their abilities, natures, or the adversities they had overcome, we see all the qualities necessary for the tenacity, tact, courage, wisdom, and grace they needed to request—and receive—an inheritance for themselves. Their presentation of their case to Moses and the leaders of Israel (v. 2), when the land was being divided to the tribes, is the Bible's first instance of an appeal for equal rights for women. The power of their example is in their wisdom of trusting God to see that they were not denied. All five daughters manifest a balance between a spirit of confrontation and a spirit of cooperation. The former is illustrated by their attack on injustice and the latter by their compliance with the elders' decision (36:2–12) that they should marry within their tribe. God defended them (v. 7) when they allowed Him to be their Deliverer/Provider. They reveal a contemporary pathway to overcoming inequality while sustaining a godly spirit.

5. The Spirit-filled, Multitalented Woman—Deborah (Judg. 4:4–5). Deborah literally means "Bee," reminding us of this woman's wisdom, how she liberally shared with her friends, and how her influence and authority were used by God to "sting" Israel's enemies. Her creative talents and leadership abilities distinguish her. Deborah wrote songs and sang them (ch. 5), and she was a patriotic woman of God who judged (or led) Israel for forty years. She might be called the first woman military commander and first female Supreme Court justice! The keys to Deborah's effectiveness were her spiritual commitment and walk with God, seen in the fact she is called a prophetess. She demonstrates the possibilities for any woman today who will allow the Spirit of God to fill and form her life, developing her full capacities to shape the world around her.

6. Tenacity that Takes the Throne—Ruth (Ruth 1:1—4:22). "Ruth" literally means "Friendship" or "Female Friend." Nowhere else in the Bible do we find a lovelier picture of a true and loyal friend. Ruth's primary virtue is tenacity to purpose: she was a woman who was steadfast. See her constant in her commitment to her mother-in-law (1:16–17) and tireless as she gleans in the fields (2:7, 17). The result of this constancy is her marriage to Boaz and the birth of Obed, who became the father of Jesse, whose son was David the king (4:17). Moreover, since Jesus was born of the seed of David, we see how Ruth, the alien Moabitess, became part of the lineage of the Messiah (Luke 3:31–32).

7. The Woman and Today's Prophetic Possibilities—Huldah (2 Kin. 22:3–20). The name "Huldah" is derived from the Hebrew root *cheled*, which means "to glide swiftly." Perhaps Huldah's name reflects her quickness of mind and her ability to swiftly and rightly discern the things of God. In any case, this woman was used by God in this fleeting moment in history to voice His judgment and His prophecy, and to spark one of the greatest

national revivals in history. She is a case study of the character and the potential of a woman who today will receive the Holy Spirit's fullness and step through whatever open door God provides. It is worth observing how Hilkiah the high priest and Shaphan the scribe sought out Huldah for God's word of wisdom (v. 14). Clearly, she had the complete respect and confidence of these men, a lesson in the truth that spiritual influence flows from a spiritual life-style, not merely from the presence of spiritual gifts. Acts 2:17–18 promises that the church age allows for a proliferation of the Holy Spirit's anointing upon women. Let Huldah's example of respectful, trust-begetting, forthright living teach the grounds for wise and effective spiritual ministry.

8. Rising to Meet Your Destiny—Esther (Esth. 4:1). Esther was a Jewish orphan—a virtual nonentity, raised by her cousin, Mordecai, and with no particular promise. But the account contained in this book unfolds the way God opens destiny to any person who will keep His priorities. Even in the presence of recognition, success, wealth, and luxury—an environment many may covet, but which has so often proven destructive to spiritual commitment— Esther retained her sense of perspective and integrity.

Esther's Hebrew name was "Hadassah," which means "Myrtle," referring to the well-known and beautiful evergreen shrub. She reflected the myrtle in her courage and obedience, which clearly did not wither, even when she faced death! In Persian "Esther" means "Star"; again Esther's beauty, grace, and character shone, bright and unwavering, against the darkness threatening the Jewish people.

Note: (1) Esther's response to Mordecai's call to recognize God's providence in her placement: She believed God, not her beauty, had put her on the throne (4:14). (2) Her respect for the power of prayer and fasting: She recognized the reality of the spiritual realm and the Holy Spirit's resources (4:16). (3) Her unswerving will to lay down her own life for others and her practical good sense and patience in pursuing her enterprise (ch. 5).

9. Faithful Mother: Obedient Disciple—Mary (Luke 1:26–56). There is a wonder surrounding Mary, the mother of Jesus, that transcends traditional religious thought. That she was a privileged vessel, chosen to bear God's Son, is wonder enough, for she is a participant in the miracle of the Incarnation at a level no other human being can comprehend. It is clear that she did not claim to understand it herself, but simply worshiped God in humble acknowledgment of the phenomenon engulfing her existence: "My soul magnifies the Lord," she exclaims (v. 46). We can hardly fathom the bewildering moments she experienced (1) when Simeon prophesied future mental/emotional suffering (2:35); (2) when she and Joseph spoke with Jesus after they thought He was lost in Jerusalem (2:49–50); (3) when Jesus gently rebuffed her at the wedding in Cana (John 2:4); or (4) when Jesus seemed to reject her and His brothers' efforts at helping Him, though they clearly misunderstood Him at that time (Matt. 12:46–50). These instances prompt our learning the wisdom of persistence and obedience in following God's basic directive on our lives, even when the details of the outworking of His will are unclear or mystifying.

Mary is also a study in the pathway forward in God's will. She might have sought elevation in position among those who saw Jesus for who He was—Messiah—but instead (1) she remained steadfast with Him all the way to the Cross, rather than protect herself (John 19:25) and (2) she obediently joined other of Jesus' disciples in the Upper Room, waiting as He commanded for the coming of the Holy Spirit (Acts 1:14).

Mary is a model of responsive obedience, one who lived out her own directive to the servants at Cana—timeless advice for all ages: "Whatever He [Jesus] says to you, do it" (John 2:5).

10. An Effective Older Woman and Widow— Anna (Luke 2:36–38). Anna the prophetess came from Asher, the tribe that was to be blessed and that was to "dip his foot in oil" (Deut. 33:24)—a sign of joy and happiness. But also, Asher's descendants were to have shoes of "iron and bronze," denoting strength (Deut. 33:25). Anna exemplified these qualities of anointing and steadfastness. After being married only seven years, her husband died, and this widow chose a life of fasting and prayer in the temple. She "did not depart from the temple, but served God" (Luke 2:36–37), clearly walking in moral purity and dedicated service.

Her prophetic anointing was untainted by the spirit of the age. Her historic prophecy regarding Jesus called the attention of all present to the uniqueness of the Child just then being brought into the temple for dedication (v. 22).

The name "Anna" means "Favor" or "Grace," and originates from the Hebrew *chanan*, meaning "to bend or stoop in kindness" and "to find favor and show favor." She did find favor in God's eyes, for He revealed the

Messiah, the Hope of Israel, to her aged eyes. Her anointed ministry during later years of life holds forth a promise for older women. There is always ministry awaiting the sensitive, obedient, and pure—ministry that can influence and shape the rising generation (Titus 2:2–5).

11. Freed to Become Fruitful—Mary Magdalene

(Luke 8:2). Mary Magdalene first appears in the Gospels among a number of other women who constitute a part of the support-team assisting Jesus in His ministry. She had been delivered from demonic bondage, the nature of which is not related.

There is an almost indestructible body of myth that has come to surround her, primarily by reason of speakers, writers, novelists, and screenplays, which have created a fantasy that generally suggests three things, *none* of which are in the Bible: (1) that she had been a prostitute, (2) that she was young and attractive, and (3) that she had a romantic affection for Jesus. She has also been frequently confused with the sinful woman forgiven by Jesus (7:36–50) and/or the woman who broke the alabaster box of perfumed ointment (Mark 14:3–9). In fact, all these proposals are speculation, yet through frequent allusion or direct reference have taken on the appearance of fact for multitudes. What *is* true of Mary Magdalene?

First, she was a grateful soul, because she had been freed from terrible torment. This text suggests her service for Christ was motivated by that gratitude. Second, she was a witness of the Crucifixion, though apparently not beside the Cross as were Mary, Jesus' mother, and John the Beloved (Matt. 27:55–56). (The fact that the other women with whom she kept company were all older women supports the reasoning that she was likely their peer in age.) Third, she was present at Jesus' burial (Mark 15:47), among those who came early Easter morning to complete the embalming of Jesus' body (Mark 16:1), among the first to hear the angelic announcement of Jesus' resurrection (Mark 16:6), and the first person actually to talk with Jesus after He was risen (John 20:11–18). It is foolish to conclude that her movement toward greeting Jesus with an embrace following His resurrection suggests anything other than the most logical response of joy at the discovery of His being alive. Jesus' directive that she not do so was not because there was anything unworthy in her approach. His words apparently indicate some yet uncompleted aspect of His post-crucifixion mission.

Mary Magdalene was a steadfast disciple of Jesus and is best seen as a case study of how no dimension of satanic bondage can prohibit any individual's being released to fruitful service for Jesus Christ.

12. Balancing Devotion and Duty—Martha and Mary

(Luke 10:38–42). Martha and Mary were sisters who lived in the village of Bethany, a suburb of Jerusalem. It appears Martha was the elder, for verse 38 speaks of Martha's receiving Jesus "into her house." Thus, Martha felt more keenly the domestic responsibilities of keeping house and the demands of providing hospitality. On the occasion Martha complained to Jesus that Mary was not helping her in the kitchen, Jesus gently reminded her that "Mary has chosen that good part"—sitting at His feet (vv. 39–42). Many have tended to distinguish Martha as "the practical one" and Mary as "the spiritual one." However, the Scriptures indicate that Martha also sat at Jesus' feet (v. 39) and that Mary also served (v. 40). Both of these women reveal unique spiritual gifts with which they lovingly served God. They remind us of the importance of balancing personal devotion with practical duties. These are not irreconcilable facts of believing life and should never be allowed to be pitted against one another.

13. A Radiant Woman "Minister"—Phoebe

(Rom. 16:1). The name "Phoebe" means "Pure or Radiant as the Moon." It is clear that through Phoebe the light of Jesus Christ shone brightly, for Paul calls her not only a servant of the church, but a helper of many (vv. 1–2). Other versions translate the word "servant" as "deaconess." Still others have called her "minister"—inasmuch as in other scriptures where the Greek word *diakoneo* is used, it is translated "minister." According to many scholars it was Phoebe who carried the written book of Romans to the congregation. This is consonant with Psalm 68:11, which declares the place of women in the spread of God's Word: "The Lord gave the word; great was the company [or host of women] . . . who proclaimed it." The inserted words are justified by the Hebrew, and most translators acknowledge this fact. Today multitudes of laywomen and Christian women leaders—licensed or ordained—and prophetesses are helping carry the gospel to the world.

14. Women and New Testament Ministry—Philip's Daughters

(Acts 21:9). This reference to Philip's daughters' each exercising the gifts of prophecy makes clear that women did bring God's word by the power of the Holy Spirit and that such ministry was fully accepted in the early church. This is reinforced by Paul in 1 Cor. 11:5, where he directs (1) that a woman may "prophesy," but (2) that she must be properly "covered," that is, rightly related to her husband or other spiritual authority, a regulation incumbent upon *all* spiritual leaders—male or female (*see* 1 Tim. 3:1–13).

It is puzzling why the place of women in ministry is contested by some in the church. Women had an equal place in the Upper Room, awaiting the Holy Spirit's coming and the birth of the church (Acts 1:14). Then Peter's prophetic sermon at Pentecost affirmed the Old Testament promise was now to be realized: "your daughters" and "maidservants" would now share fully and equally with men in realizing the anointing, fullness, and ministry of the Holy Spirit, making them effective in witness and service for the spread of the gospel.

Though the place of men seems more pronounced in the number who filled leadership offices, there does not appear to be any direct restriction of privilege. Note (1) the direct mention of Phoebe as a deacon ("servant," Greek, *diakonia*, Rom. 16:1); (2) John's letter to an "elect [chosen] lady" with instructions concerning whom she allows to minister in her "house" (a designation for early church fellowships, 2 John); and (3) 1 Cor. 1:11 and Phil. 4:2, where Chloe and Euodia seem to be women in whose homes believers gather. The method of designation suggests they were the appointed leaders in their respective fellowships.

The acceptance of women in a public place of ministry in the church is not a concession to the spirit of the feminist movement. But the refusal of such a place might be a concession to an order of male chauvinism, unwarranted by and unsupported in the Scriptures. Clearly, women did speak—preach and prophesy—in the early church (*see* 1 Tim. 2:8–15).

15. A Word of Wisdom to Wives (1 Pet. 3:1). The spirit of submission, whereby a woman voluntarily acknowledges her husband's leadership responsibility under God, is an act of faith. The Bible nowhere "submits" or subordinates women to men, generically. But this text calls a woman to submit herself to her husband (Eph. 5:22), and the husband is charged to lovingly give himself to caring for his wife—never exploiting the trust of her submission (v. 7; Eph. 5:25–29). This divinely ordered arrangement is never shown, nor was it ever given, to reduce the potential, purpose, or fulfillment of the woman. Only fallen nature or persistent church traditionalism, finding occasion through "proof-texts" separated from their full biblical context, can make a case for

the social exploitation of women or the restriction of women from church ministry.

First Timothy 2:12 and 1 Corinthians 14:34–35, which disallow a woman's teaching (in an unwelcomed manner), usurping authority, or creating a nuisance by public argument, all relate to the woman's relationship with her husband. (The Greek word for "man" in 1 Tim. 2:12 is *aner*, which is as readily translated "husband" as "man." The context clearly recommends "husband," as does the evidence of the rest of the New Testament related to the viability of a woman's public voice in Christian assemblies.)

The Bible's word of wisdom to women seems to be summarized in Peter's word of counsel given to a woman whose husband is an unbeliever. She is told that her "words" are not her key to success in winning her husband to Christ, but her Christlike, loving spirit is. Similarly, this wisdom would apply to any woman with the potential for a public ministry of leadership in the church. Her place will most likely be given when she is not argumentatively insistent upon it, so much as given to "winning" it by a gracious, loving, servantlike spirit—the same spirit that ought to be evident in the life of a man who would lead. F.L./J.W.H.

WONDERS. (Acts 15:12) *teras* (*ter-*as); *Strong's* #5059: Compare "teratology," the science that deals with unexplainable phenomena. *Teras* denotes extraordinary occurrences, supernatural prodigies, omens, portents, unusual manifestations, miraculous incidents portending the future rather than the past, and acts that are so unusual they cause the observer to marvel or be in awe. *Teras* is always in the plural, associated with *semeion* (signs). Signs and wonders are a perfect balance for touching man's intellect, emotions, and will.

WONDROUS SIGN. (Zech. 3:8) *mophet* (moh-*fayt*); *Strong's* #4159: A miracle, sign, token, wonder. Used thirty-six times in the Old Testament, its first occurrence is in Exodus 4:21, where God mentions the "wonders" that Moses will perform before Pharaoh. *Mophet* is translated "miracle" in Exodus 7:9. Generally it is translated "sign" (2 Chr. 32:24) or "wonder" (Ps. 105:27). While *mophet* contains the idea of something miraculous, in some references it seems to connote an illustration or an example. For instance, the psalmist appears to make a complaint when he states, "I have become as a wonder to many" (Ps. 71:7). Ezekiel is described as a "sign" to the house of Israel (Ezek. 12:6, 11; 24:24, 27).

WONDROUS THING (DID A). (Judg. 13:19) *pala'* (pah-*lah*); *Strong's* #6381: To perform a miracle, marvel, wonder, or supernatural deed, that is, something beyond the human ability to grasp, do, or achieve. The verb *pala'* is part of a family of words that includes the noun *pele'* (wonder, marvelous work) and the adjective *pil'iy* (wonderful). Isaiah 9:6 states that one of the Messiah's titles is "Wonderful." The psalmist prays that God will reveal to him "wondrous things" from the law of the Lord (Ps. 119:18), matters beyond normal human perception requiring supernatural insight to see them. For other examples of *pala'*, *see* Exodus 34:10, Psalm 107:8, and Isaiah 29:14.

WORD. (2 Sam. 22:31) *'imrah* (eem-*rah*); *Strong's* #565: Speech; word or words; commandment; dictum; answer; saying. This noun occurs thirty-five times and is derived from the verb *'amar,* "to speak" or "to say." *'Amar* occurs approximately five thousand times in the Old Testament, with many statements introduced by the words "and he said," or "he answered." (*See* Ps. 12:6; 18:30.) In Psalm 119, *'imrah* occurs twenty-one times, including verse 11. "Your word I have hidden in my heart, that I might not sin against You." (Compare vv. 67, 154, 162; Ps. 138:2; Prov. 30:5.) *Also* (Matt. 4:4) *rhema* (*hray*-mah); *Strong's* #4487: That which is said or spoken, an utterance, in contrast to *logos,* which is the expression of a thought, a message, a discourse. *Logos* is the message; *rhema* is the communication of the message. In reference to the Bible, *logos* is the Bible in its entirety; *rhema* is a verse from the Bible. The meaning of *rhema* in distinction to *logos* is illustrated in Ephesians 6:17, where the reference is not to the Scriptures as a whole, but to that portion which the believer wields as a sword in the time of need. *Also* (Acts 19:20) *logos* (*log*-oss); *Strong's* #3056: A transmission of thought, communication, a word of explanation, an utterance, discourse, divine revelation, talk, statement, instruction, an oracle, divine promise, divine doctrine, divine declaration. Jesus is the living *logos* (John 1:1); the Bible is the written *logos* (Heb. 4:12); and the Holy Spirit utters the spoken *logos* (1 Cor. 2:13).

WORD OF GOD, THE. God's Word has been unscrolled in both the Scriptures and in His incarnate Son—Jesus Christ. Jesus, in describing the importance of the eternal Scriptures said, "Man shall not live by bread alone, but by every word that proceeds from the mouth of God" (Matt. 4:4). He also commended the steadfast inquiry into the Word of God: "Search the Scriptures . . . they . . . testify of Me" (John 5:39). There is no such thing as health or growth in Christian living apart from a clear priority on the place of the Bible in the life of the individual or the group. The Scriptures are the conclusive standard for our faith, morals, and practical living and are the nourishment for our rising to strength in faith, holiness in living, and effectiveness in service. The Holy Spirit who comes to fill us is the same Person who has given us the Book to guide and sustain us.

The Source and Nature of God's Word

1. The Divine Inspiration of the Bible (2 Tim. 3:16). The absolute authority of the Bible over our lives is based in our conviction that this Book does not merely contain the Word of God, but that it *is* the Word of God in its sum and in its parts. This text testifies to this, describing the actual process of this inspiration (inbreathing of life): (1) It is the word of the Holy Spirit. *Theopneustos* (Greek), translated "inspiration of God," literally means "God-breathed." This describes the source of the *whole* Bible's derivation (that is, "*all* Scripture") as transcendent of human inspiration. The Bible is not the product of elevated human consciousness or enlightened human intellect, but is directly "breathed" from God Himself. (2) Second Peter 1:20–21 elaborates this truth, and adds that none of what was given was merely the private opinion of the writer (v. 20) and that each writer involved in the production of the Holy Scriptures was "moved by" (literally, "being borne along") the Holy Spirit. This does not mean that the writers were merely robots, seized upon by God's power to write automatically without their conscious participation. God does not override those gifts of intellect and sensitivity that He has given His creatures. (Beware of all instances where individuals claim to "automatically" write anything at any time, for the Holy Spirit never functions that way.) (3) First Corinthians 2:10–13 expands on this process by which the revelation of the Holy Scriptures was given. Verse 13 says that *even the words* used in the giving of the Bible (not just the ideas, but the precise terminology) were planned by the Holy Spirit, who deployed the respective authors of the Bible books to write, "comparing spiritual things with spiritual" (literally, "matching spiritual words to spiritual ideas"). This biblical view of the Bible's derivation is called the *plenary verbal inspiration* of the Scriptures, meaning *every word* is inspired by the Holy Spirit of God.

2. The Complete Trustworthiness of the Bible (Ps. 19:7). That the "law of the LORD is perfect," is direct reference to the absolute, complete, and entire trustworthiness of the Holy Scriptures, which constitute the Bible. The Word of God is *perfect* in its accuracy and *sure* in its dependability. Two terms are generally used to describe these features of God's Word: (1) *Inerrant* (perfect) means that, *in the original copies* of each manuscript written by each Bible book's respective author, there was nothing mistaken or tinged with error. (Further, the excellence of the Holy Spirit's protection of the Scriptures over the centuries has insured that the copies delivered into our hands from generations past are essentially the same. Even literary critics who claim no faith in the *truth* of the Bible attest to its being the most completely reliable of any book transmitted from antiquity, in terms of its actually remaining unchanged and dependably accurate.) (2) *Infallible* refers to the fact that the Bible is unfailing as an absolutely trustworthy guide for our faith (belief in God) and practice (life and behavior). This is so because God is *true* (John 3:33; 17:3), because His Word reveals His truth (John 17:17), and because God cannot lie (Num. 23:19; Titus 1:2; Heb. 6:18).

3. The Content of God's Word Is Completed (Prov. 30:5–6). The word "canon" is the term used to describe the completed number of the books of the Bible—the *closed canon* of the sixty-six books of the Holy Scriptures. It is derived from ancient words meaning "measuring stick," and is applied here to designate those books that meet the requirements of being acknowledged as divinely inspired.

The Bible warns against either adding to or subtracting from its contents. Revelation 22:18 makes a conclusive statement, positional in God's providence and wisdom, at the Bible's end. While it refers directly to the Book of Revelation, most Bible scholars also provide a finalizing footnote on this subject: "Add to or subtract from the Bible at your own risk." (A classic study of the judgment for "taking away" from God's Word is seen in Jer. 36:20–32.)

In this regard, we are wise to understand terms. When we refer to the "revelation of the Scriptures," it is important that we distinguish this consummate order of divine *revelation* from any other use of the term, however sacred. There are many today who do not know the difference between a "revelation" (an insight or an idea that may be of God, of man, or of the devil) and *the revelation* of God, which is in the *closed canon* of the Scriptures.

Because there are many books that claim to be divinely given, a casual or gullible attitude toward them can result in confusion and eventual destruction. It is interesting to note that even in Jesus' time, several books held by some today to be intended for the Old Testament were in existence then. Yet, in the sixty-

four times Jesus quotes from the Old Testament, not once does He quote from any of those books. The Bible is *complete, completely trustworthy*, and sufficient to *completely answer* anything we need to know for eternal salvation or practical wisdom concerning our relationships, morality, character, or conduct.

4. Jesus and the Holy Scriptures (Luke 16:17). As the Resurrected King, God's Messiah and our Savior, our Lord Jesus Christ has given us some of the most important statements concerning the authority and nature of the Word of God. (1) Jesus confirms the truth that *every word* of the Scriptures is given by God. He goes so far as to make direct reference to the smallest letter ("jot," literally *yod*, the Hebrew counterpart to our letter "i" or "j"), and the smallest punctuation point, "tittle." There is no room for debate: Jesus believed and taught the *plenary verbal inspiration* of the Bible— that every word is God-breathed (*see* 2 Tim. 3:16). (2) Jesus also contends that *every truth* the Bible teaches is to be held inviolable. In Matthew 5:17–19 He insists that anyone who teaches anything running at cross-purposes with the Scriptures is not in harmony with His kingdom order. (3) Jesus attests to the indissolubility of the Scriptures (John 10:35). When He says "the Scripture cannot be broken," He literally describes the utter inviolability of God's Word from man's side (do not try to diminish its truth or meaning) and the utter dependability of it from God's side (He will uphold it—His Word will not dissolve or be shaken). Matthew 24:35 is the verse most quoted in this regard. All creation may dissolve: God's Word will stand forever! (4) Jesus affirms the credibility of the Old Testament in general (John 5:39), but also of the miracles recorded in it. He did not see them as superstitiously held beliefs, which He tolerated among those He addressed. Rather, He was the Incarnate Truth; and as the embodiment of truthfulness, His testimony is decisive. Thus, note that Jesus believed the biblical record of: (a) Adam and Eve as the first pair (Matt. 19:4–5); (b) the literal destruction of Sodom and Gomorrah (Mark 6:11; Luke 17:29–30); (c) the actuality of Noah and the Flood (Matt. 24:37–38); (d) the trustworthiness of Daniel's prophecy (Matt. 24:15); (e) the truth of Jonah's being swallowed by the great fish (Matt. 12:39–40); and (f) the miracle of the manna as well as other miracles during the wilderness journey of Moses' time (John 3:14; 6:31–32). Finally, (5) Jesus forecast and authorized the writing of the New Testament Scriptures. In both John 14:26 and 16:12–13, He indicated that the coming ministry of the

Holy Spirit would include His bringing to the apostles' minds the things that should afterward be recorded. His anticipation of that ministry not only places His endorsement upon that facet of their apostolic mission, it also indirectly effects His closure of the canon of Scripture following the completion of this task. (*See* article at Prov. 30:5–6.)

5. The Way God's Word Is to Be Ministered (2 Cor. 3:5–8). Believing in the truthfulness of God's Word does not guarantee that we will minister that truth in the Spirit of God. Ephesians 4:15 describes growth and maturity in the body of Christ as being related to our "speaking the truth in love." In 2 Corinthians 3:6, the apostle Paul warns of the danger of God's Word being ministered *literally* but not *life-givingly*. We need not wonder if this is possible, since the Spirit of Truth (1 John 4:6) and the Spirit of Life (Rom. 8:2) are the same—the Holy Spirit! Blending both will always reveal three things: (1) *A faithfulness to "keep straight"* (2 Tim. 2:15). "Rightly dividing the word of truth" means putting forward the truth, faithfully and forthrightly. (This verse was never intended to refer to "dividing" the Word by *segmenting* it, but rather to a straightforward dealing with *all* the truth and *all* its implications.) (2) *A constant presence of love,* even in the most demanding declarations of correction or judgment. In the texts above (2 Cor. 3:6; Eph. 4:15) we have already discussed this, but human tendencies need this reminder. Urgency may attend our message and passion infuse our delivery; but anger, impatience, and irritation are not of the life-giving Spirit, however literally accurate the interpretation of the Bible or preaching thereof may be. (3) *An expectation of signs to follow the preaching of God's Word.* Jesus promised this, and the early church tasted its beginnings (Mark 16:15–20); Paul described it as normative in his ministry (1 Cor. 2:1–5; 1 Thess. 1:5); and the Book of Hebrews endorsed this as a part of the "so great salvation" we have been provided (Heb. 2:1–4). This last reference shows that the confirmation of God's Word with signs and wonders not only is to verify Christ's living presence where His gospel is preached, but also is to warn us against drifting from the new life to which we have all been called.

The Essential Place and Power of God's Word

6. The Regenerating Power of God's Word (1 Pet. 1:23). Just as we owe our natural existence to the Creator's spoken word and life-giving breath, so we owe our New Birth to the power of God's Word and the Holy Spirit's activation of its power. God's intent for our created being is only completely fulfilled when our spirits are alive toward Him. As sin has produced spiritual death in people (Eph. 2:1–3), so salvation in Jesus Christ has provided spiritual life. This text tells us that the "seed" that has produced new life in us is the *Word* of God, which has begotten us again by the Holy Spirit's power (Titus 3:5) and made us members of God's new creation (2 Cor. 5:17). The power of God's Word—the Holy Scriptures—is in no way more manifest than in this: its power to bring spiritual life to all who open to its truth. James 1:18 elaborates the fact that God's "word of truth" is the means by which He brought us new life, emphasizing that He has done this as a direction of His own will. God's will to save us (2 Pet. 3:9) has been effectively expressed in His Word, which accomplishes that work (John 1:13).

7. The Authority of God's Word over Our Lives (Ps. 119:89–91). This text asserts the all-encompassing, absolutely authoritative Word of God as unchangingly secured in heaven, noting: (1) The timelessness of God's rule by His Word. Though times and seasons change, though social customs, human opinions, and philosophical viewpoints vary, they have no effect on the constancy or authority of God's Word. (2) God is faithful in applying the power, promise, and blessing of His Word, along with its requirements of justice and judgment (v. 90). Just as He spoke and the earth was created and is sustained, so He has spoken regarding His laws for living. The relativism of human thought does not affect His authority or standards. (3) While creation abides by His Word (responding as His "servants," v. 90), man is often a study in contrast to this submission to the Creator's authority. Whatever our past rebellion, however, upon coming to Christ a practical reinstatement of God's Word as the governing principle for all our life is to take place. Not only does Jesus conclusively declare this (John 8:47), but Paul notes that to respond otherwise is to compromise the level of life to which we have been called (1 Cor. 2:13–16). As "spiritual" people we are to refuse the "natural" inclinations of fallen humanity. As we hear and yield to the authority of God's Word, we verify that we are no longer dominated by the world's spirit of error (1 John 4:6).

8. God's Word and Our Soul's Nourishment (Deut. 8:3). Jesus quoted this text in Matthew 4:4, when He faced Satan's snares in the wilderness. The obvious message of the passage is that there is no survival of the soul without God's Word—*daily.* That the parallel is used of Israel's receiving the daily supply of manna makes clear that a regular, daily portion of God's Word is to be sought and fed upon by the believer.

This is not a matter of legal duty, determining one's salvation, but a matter of personal responsibility, determining one's obedience to the pathway of discipleship. Let no one suppose, however, that spiritual survival is possible for long without nourishment from the Word of God. First Peter 2:2 declares that God's Word is as essential to the believer as milk is to a newborn child. But as we come to terms with His Word as key to our survival, let us also see that God has given its pleasantness as a joyful source of sweetness for our living (Ps. 19:10).

9. God's Word and Practical, Fruitful Living (Ps. 119:105).
We are all inexperienced in too much of life to be without a guide. God's Word is that guide. The whole of Psalm 119 unfolds manifold features of God's Word, showing how dynamically it will assist us in life's most practical circumstances. No single verse focuses this more clearly than verse 105, which shows how God's Word lights the way, giving direction for each *step* ("to my feet") and giving wisdom for *long-range* plans ("to my path"). Joshua links the regular application of God's Word to life as the most certain way to both success and prosperity in living (Josh. 1:8). Further, Psalm 119:130 notes the wisdom God's Word gives to the "simple" (Hebrew *pethawee*), a truth specifically pointing toward the avoidance of making decisions based on human delusion or outright senselessness. Also, Proverbs 6:23 reminds us that the "reproofs" or corrections the Bible gives are as much a part of the "light" it provides as any positive or confirming direction we find therein. Let God's Word guide, correct, instruct, lead, teach, and confirm. Do not hasten ahead without it—*ever*.

10. True Spiritual Growth Requires God's Word (1 Cor. 3:1–5).
Beginning in 1 Corinthians 2:10, Paul elaborates our need of Holy Spirit-given wisdom and revelation, and he ties this very firmly to our receiving the "words . . . which the Holy Spirit teaches" (2:13). He immediately turns from these observations to an outright confrontation with the carnality of the Corinthians, attributing it to the shallowness of their intake of God's Word ("not able to receive [solid food]," 3:2; see also Heb. 5:12–15).

The demanding truth of this passage is that no amount of supposed spiritual insight or experience reflects genuine spiritual growth, if it is separated from our basic growth in the knowledge of God's Word in the Bible. Without this rootedness in the Word, we may be deluded about our growth. Such "rootedness" is in *truth* and *love*, not merely in *learning knowledge* or accomplished *study*. In order to experience true spiritual growth, we must spend time in the Word and separate ourselves from the hindrances of lovelessness, competitiveness, and strife.

11. Loving God's Word as Jesus' Follower (John 14:21).
Jesus completely aligned His life and will with the Father's (8:29), which indicates His total allegiance to the Father's Word and commandments. He also said He disapproved of any attitude that would reduce respect for or teach less than full obedience to the entirety of God's revealed Word (Matt. 5:17–19). Thus, in this text, when He explicitly links His disciples' love for Him as Savior with their will to keep His commandments, we conclude Jesus' clear intent: If we love Him, we will love His Father's Word, also.

In John 5:39 our Lord declares that the knowledge of the Scriptures is the pathway to knowing Him well. Further, upon His resurrection, He unveiled the fullness of His own Person as revealed in the Old Testament (Luke 24:27). These texts cluster to teach us that to *follow* Christ, to *know* Him, and to *grow* in insight as people walking with the Resurrected Lord, a basic and continuing requirement is a steadfast commitment to hearing, heeding, and studying the Bible.

12. God's Word: Purifier unto Holy Living (James 1:23–25).
Purity of life is not a quest for perfection as much as it is a quest for liberation from those things that may inhibit effectiveness and reduce power-filled living. This text shows the Word of God as a means of reflection—a mirror into which we are to look and see ourselves. The call is not only to heed what we see and accept the Bible's corrective instruction, but there is an unwritten lesson here. We should avoid the temptation to see (and judge) others in the Word, analyzing what they ought to do, instead of what we need to do. Second Corinthians 3:18 also likens God's Word to a mirror, but describes the image seen as no less than the Lord Jesus Himself. The sum of the two texts: The Bible shows us Christ's likeness in order that we may measure our conduct and character against His and allow God to shape us into Christ's likeness (Rom. 8:29). Other promises for cleansing through God's Word: Jeremiah 29:9 speaks of the "fire" in the Word, which can purge as well as ignite; and Psalm 119:9 holds special promise to the one who wants a pure life of

holy power. God's Word is a powerful, cleansing, delivering agent.

13. God's Word, Evangelism, and Expansion (Is. 55:10–11). Evangelism (the spreading of the Good News) and expansion (the enlarging of life's potential under God) both multiply by the "seed" of God's Word. Jesus described the Word as "seed" also (Luke 8:11), the source of all saving life and growth possibilities transmitted from the Father to humankind. All increase of life within His love comes by His Word, as human response gives place for His blessing. When received, God's word of promise will never be barren. The power in His Word will always fulfill the promise of His Word. We never need wonder how faith is developed or how fruitfulness is realized. Faith comes by "hearing" God's Word (Rom. 10:17), that is, by receiving it wholeheartedly and humbly. Fruitfulness is the guaranteed by-product—whether for the salvation of a lost soul or the provision of a disciple's need— God's Word cannot be barren or fruitless: His own life-power is within it!

14. God's Word: Read It! Study It! Memorize It! (2 Tim. 2:15). The Bible—God's inspired Word— is the only conclusive source of wisdom, knowledge, and understanding concerning ultimate realities. It is a fountainhead of freeing truth (John 8:32) and a goldmine of practical principles (Ps. 19:10), waiting to liberate and/or enrich the person who will pursue its truth and wealth. Thus, Paul's instruction to "be diligent . . . a worker" has been applied by serious Christians through the centuries as a directive to study the Word of God. The only way to healthy, balanced living is through the "rightly dividing" (Greek *orthotomounta*, literally, "cutting straight") of God's Word. Such correct, straight-on application of God's Word is the result of diligent study. The text calls us beyond casual approaches to the Scriptures, telling us to refuse to suit the Bible to our own convenience or ideology.

In his earlier words (1 Tim. 4:13) Paul also told Timothy, "Give attention to reading [God's Word]," but now he emphasizes *studying* like a "worker" (from Greek *ergon*—"toil, effort"). Psalm 119:11 urges memorizing of the Word of God as a mighty deterrent against sin. Memorizing the Scripture also provides an immediate availability of God's "words" as a sword, ready in witnessing and effective in spiritual warfare (Heb. 4:12; Eph. 6:17). J.W.H.

WORDS. (Deut. 1:1) *davar* (dah-*vahr*); *Strong's* #1697: A word, a speech; a matter or thing; a commandment, a report, a message. This multifaceted noun may be translated by dozens of English words, but "word," "speech," and "matter" are most commonly used for *davar*. Frequently in the Old Testament the phrase "the word [*davar*] of the LORD" occurs, particularly in Jeremiah and Ezekiel. The first verse of Deuteronomy explains the contents of the book: "These are the words [speeches, matters, or messages] which Moses spoke to all Israel." The Hebrew title of Deuteronomy is taken from this first sentence, and is *devarim*, or "words." Note the similarity between the Hebrew *davar* and the Greek *logos* (the Word, John 1:1). Jesus is the *davar* of the Old Testament and the *logos* of the New Testament. He is the message of the entire Book.

WORD, THE—a theological phrase which expresses the absolute, eternal, and ultimate being of Jesus Christ (John 1:1–14; 1 John 1:1; Rev. 19:13). The Old Testament spoke of the word of God as the divine agent in the creation of the universe: "By the word of the Lord the heavens were made" (Ps. 33:6). In the New Testament, the Gospel of John declared, "And the Word became flesh and dwelt among us" (John 1:14). Through the incarnation of Christ, God has come to dwell in our midst. Through the life and ministry of Jesus, a unique and final revelation of God has been given—one superior to the revelation given through the Law and the Prophets. In Christ, the word of God's plan and purpose for mankind is clearly revealed (2 Cor. 4:4; Heb. 1:1–3).

Also see Word of God.

WORK—physical or mental activity directed toward the accomplishment of a task; the labor by which a person earns his livelihood.

Man as created was intended to work. One of his primary tasks in the Garden of Eden was to "till [work] the ground" (Gen. 2:5). Although work was ordained by God as a blessing, it became a frustration as the curse resulting from the *Fall took effect (Gen. 3:17–19). The Book of Ecclesiastes teaches that work, no matter how noble and diligently pursued, can become meaningless apart from divine inspiration and grace (Eccl. 4:4). Work in a fallen world is frequently reduced to exploitation and oppression.

Nevertheless, through redemption, work finds meaning. God ordained that six days be spent in work with one day of rest (Ex. 20:9). Much of the Wisdom Literature of the Old Testament praises hard work (Prov. 14:23; 31:27), while it condemns and ridicules laziness (Prov. 6:6–11; 21:25). The same attitude is found in the New Testament. Paul and his associates worked (1 Cor. 4:12; 9:6), and they expected other believers to work and earn their own support (2 Thess. 3:10).

WORKING. (Col. 1:29) *energeia* (en-*erg*-eye-ah); *Strong's #1753:* Working, action, operative power. The English word "energy" comes from this word. *Energeia* usually describes the working of God, but is used of Satan's empowering "the lawless one" (2 Thess. 2:9).

WORKING TOGETHER. (James 2:22) *sunergeo* (soon-erg-*eh*-oh); *Strong's #4903:* Compare "synergist" and "synergism." From *sun*, "together," and *ergeo*, "to work"; hence, to cooperate, help, collaborate, co-labor. There is a practical harmony or synergism between vertical faith in God and horizontal works to a needy world. Faith is both spiritual and practical.

WORKMANSHIP. (Eph. 2:10) *poiema* (*poy*-ay-mah); *Strong's #4161:* From the verb *poieo*, "to make." (Compare "poem" and "poetry.") The word signifies that which is manufactured, a product, a design produced by an artisan. *Poiema* emphasizes God as the Master Designer, the universe as His creation (Rom. 1:20), and the redeemed believer as His new creation (Eph. 2:10). Before conversion our lives had no rhyme or reason. Conversion brought us balance, symmetry, and order. We are God's poem, His work of art.

WORKS. (John 9:4) *ergon* (*er*-gon); *Strong's #2041:* Compare "energy" and "urge." Toil, occupation, enterprise, deed, task, accomplishment, employment, performance, work, labor, course of action. The miraculous accomplishments and deeds of Jesus are works of God implying power and might.

WORKS (WONDERFUL). (Acts 2:11) *megaleios* (meg-al-*eye*-oss); *Strong's #3167:* Conspicuous, magnificent, splendid, majestic, sublime, grand, beautiful, excellent, favorable. Used here and in Luke 1:49. The amazed visitors at Pentecost heard the disciples in their own languages reciting the sublime greatness of God and His mighty deeds.

WORLD—the heavens and the earth which form the universe and the place where man and animals live. Among both the Jewish people and the Greeks the terms world and earth were used interchangeably to mean the created realm, the fruitful and habitable earth. The biblical declaration, "The earth is the LORD's, and all its fullness, the world and those who dwell therein" (Ps. 24:1), denotes the whole of our created planet.

According to the New Testament, the world was created by God's word, identified with Christ in John 1:1–14. John says of Christ in John 1:10, "He was in the world, and the world was made through Him."

World is also associated with mankind.

Christ said of His disciples, "You are the light of the world" (Matt. 5:14). Often world is used to indicate the realm of Satan's control over people (Eph. 2:2) and scope of evil influence (1 John 5:19).

World may also denote the fleeting character of life's riches and pleasures and the folly of making them of central importance in life. "What profit is it to a man if he gains the whole world, and loses his own soul?" (Matt. 16:26).

World also denotes a sphere of habitation. Jesus states, "You are from beneath [of this world]; I am from above [not of this world]" (John 8:23). He lived in this world as a place, but He was separate from its spirit of evil and sin (John 14:30). Jesus also taught His followers to live in the world to work and to witness, but not be trapped by its ungodly ways, pleasures or perversities of life. "I do not pray that You should take them out of the world, but that You should keep them from the evil one" (John 17:15).

The Old Testament world extended from Spain to Persia and from Greece to Ethiopia. The New Testament world also included the southern portions of the Roman Empire. Our world has expanded greatly since biblical times, but the final commands of Jesus to His disciples are as urgent and relevant as ever: "Go therefore and make disciples of all the nations" (Matt. 28:19).

WORLD. (Jer. 51:15) *tebel* (teh-*vel*); *Strong's #8398:* The fruitful earth; the globe, the world, the dry land; earth's substantial material (land); also the entire world (that is, all its inhabitants). *Tebel* occurs thirty-six times. God formed or established the world. (See 1 Sam. 2:8.) The primary idea is land in general, or inhabited land (Prov. 8:31). The root of *tebel* is *yabal*, "to bring," which may imply earth that produces. *Also* (John 18:36) *kosmos* (*kos*-moss); *Strong's #2889:* Compare "cosmic," "cosmogony," "cosmopolitan." Originally, *kosmos* was orderly arrangement, decor, adorning, beauty, symmetry, and the regularity of the world order. *Kosmos* later focused on "the earth" (contrasted with heaven) and the secular world. Often in the New Testament the word describes a world system alienated from and opposed to God, lying in the power of the Evil One.

WORRY. (Matt. 6:25) *merimnao* (mer-im-*nah*-oh); *Strong's #3309:* From *merizo*, "to divide into parts." The word suggests a distraction, a preoccupation with things causing anxiety, stress, and pressure. Jesus speaks against worry and anxiety because of the watchful care of a heavenly Father who is ever mindful of our daily needs.

WORSHIP—reverent devotion and allegiance pledged to God; the rituals or ceremonies by which this reverence is expressed. The English word "worship" comes from the Old English word "worthship," a word which denotes the worthiness of the one receiving the special honor or devotion.

In Old Testament times patriarchs built altars to the Lord and called on His name (Gen. 12:8; 13:18). This worship of God required no elaborate priesthood or ritual. In Moses' time the foundations of Israelite ritual were laid, as God ordered the instructive forms and principles of worship that would govern Israel and typify the coming Redeemer (Exodus 25—31; 35—40).

After the occupation of the Promised Land, Israel's exposure to Canaanite worship corrupted the nation's own worship as the people adopted practices of the pagan world around them. But such idolatry was condemned by God and His special spokesmen, the *prophets of the Old Testament.

New Testament worship was characterized by a joy and thanksgiving because of God's gracious redemption in Christ, as early church worship focused on the presence of God's kingdom grace and power through His saving work in His Son. True worship was defined as that which occurred under the inspiration and animation of the Holy Spirit (John 4:23–24; Phil. 3:3).

The New Testament does not instruct worshipers in a specific procedure to follow in their gatherings, but several elements appear to be component parts of the worship in the early church. First Corinthians 14:26, 1 Timothy 4:13, and 2 Timothy 3:10–4:5 seem to show a combination of participation by the leaders and laity alike.

Of course, other basics are revealed for corporate worship:

1. Prayer apparently had a leading place in Christian worship. The letters of Paul regularly open with references to prayer for fellow Christians who are instructed to "pray without ceasing" (1 Thess. 5:17).

2. Praise, either by individuals or in hymns sung in common, reflects the frequent use of psalms in the synagogue. Also, possible fragments of Christian hymns appear scattered through the New Testament (Acts 4:24–30; Eph. 5:14; 1 Tim. 3:16; Rev. 4:8, 11; 5:9–10, 12–13).

3. Lessons from the Bible to be read, taught, and studied were another part of the worship procedure of the New Testament church. Remember, the Old Testament was their "Bible" at first, and emphasis was probably given to the messianic prophecies which had been fulfilled in Jesus Christ, as well as practical lessons from the rest of the Scriptures (1 Cor. 10:6; Rom. 15:4). Jesus' teachings also received a primary place.

4. The Lord's Table was practiced (1 Cor.11:10–34); prophecies and other gifts of the Spirit in manifestation (1 Cor.12,14); contributions were received (1 Cor. 16:2); and the sick were prayed for (James 5:13–16). Other details about the worship procedures of the early church in the New Testament times are evident, but these elements seem to have been regularly included in their gatherings.

WORSHIP. (Ps. 99:5) *shachah* (shah-*chah*); *Strong's* #7812: To bow, to stoop; to bow down before someone as an act of submission or reverence; to worship; to fall or bow down when paying homage to God. The primary meaning is "to make oneself low." In the present reference, *shachah* is used in contrast to exaltation: exalt the Lord (lift Him up high) and worship (bow yourselves down low before Him) at the place of His feet. *Also* (Rev. 4:10) *proskuneo* (pros-koo-*neh*-oh); *Strong's* #4352: From *pros,* "toward," and *kuneo,* "to kiss." To prostrate oneself, bow down, do obeisance, show reverence, do homage, worship, adore. In the New Testament the word especially denotes homage rendered to God and the ascended Christ. All believers have a one-dimensional worship, to the only Lord and Savior. We do not worship angels, saints, shrines, relics, or religious personages.

WRATH—the personal manifestation of God's holy, moral character in exacting just judgment against sin. Wrath is neither an impersonal process nor is it irrational and fitful like anger. It is in no way vindictive or malicious. It is holy indignation—God's anger directed against sin because of its destructive power and the havoc it wreaks in ruining His benevolent intent for man.

God's wrath is an expression of His holy love. If God were incapable of wrath, His love would be no more than a frail, maudlin sentimentality; the concept of mercy would be meaningless; and the Cross would have been a cruel and unnecessary expense exacted of His Son.

The Bible reveals that all humankind is "by nature children of wrath" (Eph. 2:3) and that "the wrath of God is revealed from heaven against all ungodliness and unrighteousness of men, who suppress the truth in unrighteousness" (Rom. 1:18). Thus, all people— either by nature or calculated enterprise— have earned judgment for sin. But there is promise, since Christ died. We can be "justified by His blood (and) be saved from wrath through Him" (Rom. 5:9). The magnitude of God's love is manifested in the Cross, where God's only Son experienced the wrath of God on sin by bearing it on our behalf.

Ultimately, "The day of the Lord's wrath" (Zeph. 1:18), identical with "the great day of the Lord" (Zeph. 1:14), will come upon this world. "The wrath of the Lamb" (Rev. 6:16) will be manifest through Jesus Christ, as it will fall on the ungodly at His Second Coming (1 Thess. 1:10; 5:9; 2 Thess. 1:7–10).

 WRATH. (Luke 4:28) *thumos* (thoo-*moss*); *Strong's* #2372: Compare "thyme," "dysthymia," "hyperedithumia." Inflammatory rage, exploding anger, turbulent commotion, boiling agitation, impulsive outbursts of hot anger. Another word, *orge*, presents anger as a settled habit.

 WROTE. (Deut. 31:9) *chatab* (kah-*tahv*); *Strong's* #3789: To write, inscribe, engrave, record; to document in written form. *Chatab* refers to inscribing words on some type of material (such as sheepskin), which serves to document and preserve the things written for future reference. Here Moses wrote this Torah and handed it to the Levitical priests for safekeeping. This began the scribal tradition, which has preserved the Scriptures for more than three thousand years. Because of the nature of the Torah, and of all the Word of God, it was essential that the words be kept in written form, as opposed to some other means, such as tribal songs and stories. In John 5:46–47, Jesus stated, "[Moses] wrote about Me. But if you do not believe his writings, how will you believe My words?" Jesus stymied Satan by appealing to the fixedness of the divine record: "It is written!"

 YAH. (Is. 12:2) *Yah (yah)*; *Strong's* #3050: The shorter form of the Lord's holy name *Yahweh*, or Jehovah. This contracted form of the name of the Lord God appears fifty times in the Old Testament. Of these fifty occurrences, forty-four are found in Psalms; the remaining six are found in Exodus and Isaiah. Many of the references in Psalms involve the compound word *Hallelu-Yah*, translated "Praise the LORD"; the word literally means "You must all praise Yah!" This word has spread from Hebrew into many languages and is a beautiful expression suitable for joyous worship.

 YHWH—the Hebrew name of the God of Israel, probably originally pronounced Yahweh. In time Jewish tradition ceased pronouncing it, considering the name too holy for human lips, and instead would say *Adonai*, or "Lord." This oral tradition is reflected in the Greek translation of the Old Testament as *kurios* or "Lord," and is quoted as such in the New Testament (Mark 1:3; Rom. 4:8). English versions of the Old Testament often translate this word as "LORD." There is also a shorter form, YAH (Ps. 68:4; Is. 12:2; 26:4; 38:11). *Also see* ch. 55, §3.7.d.

 ZEALOUS. (Zech. 8:2) *qanah* (kah-*nah*); *Strong's* #7065: To be zealous, filled with zeal, full of emotion; to be passionate; also to be jealous or envious; to be highly possessive of something. *Qanah* and its derivatives appear approximately ninety times in the Old Testament, often in the context of the Lord's becoming provoked to jealousy by the flirtations of His people with false gods. This is not a negative word, though, as it is the zeal of the Lord that will bring about the Messiah's eternal reign (Is. 9:7). In the present reference, God is either zealous with burning zeal for Zion, or jealous with burning jealousy, or perhaps, fanatic over His Jerusalem. Every nation has its plans for Jerusalem; God, too, has His plans (vv. 3–15), which must overrule all human schemes. *Also* (Acts 22:3) *zelotes* (dzay-low-*tace*); *Strong's* #2207: Burning with zeal, having warmth and feeling for or against, deep commitment and eager devotion to something or someone, an enthusiast, uncompromising partisan, admirer, emulator, imitator, follower of anyone. Paul rejected his previous zeal that caused him to become a persecutor of the church, but rejoiced in his *zelotes* for the Lord Jesus Christ.

This icon beside an entry indicates a Word Wealth feature.

This icon beside an entry indicates a Kingdom Dynamics feature.

This icon beside an entry indicates an important biblical or doctrinal term.

BIBLIOGRAPHY
AND
INDEXES

Bibliography

Over the years I have often been asked what study resources have benefited me most. My basic response has included the references listed here. I trust they will prove helpful to readers of this handbook.—*The General Editor*

Apologetics

Answers. Josh McDowell and Don Stewart. Wheaton, IL: Tyndale House Pubs., 1986.

Christian Commitment. Edward John Carnell. Grand Rapids: Baker Book House, 1995.

Evidence that Demands a Verdict. Josh McDowell. Nashville: Thomas Nelson, Inc., 1972, 1979.

He Walked Among Us. Josh McDowell and Bill Wilson. Nashville: Thomas Nelson, Inc., 1988.

Mere Christianity. Clive Staples Lewis. New York: Macmillan Co., 1986.

More Evidence that Demands a Verdict. Josh McDowell. Nashville: Thomas Nelson, Inc., 1975, 1981.

Church Ministry and Leadership

The Church in God's Program. Robert L. Saucy. Chicago: Moody Press, 1972.

The Glorious Body of Christ. Rienk Bouke Kuiper. Carlisle, PA: The Banner of Truth, 1983.

Building Leaders for Church Education. Kenneth O. Gangel. Chicago: Moody Press, 1981.

New Testament Church Organization. Donald L. Norbie. Kansas City, KS: Walterick Pubs., Inc., 1977.

Warnings to the Churches. John Charles Ryle. Carlisle, PA: The Banner of Truth, 1992.

The Holy Spirit

The Beauty of Spiritual Language. Jack W. Hayford. Nashville: Thomas Nelson, Inc., 1996.

God's Empowering Presence. Gordon D. Fee. Peabody, MA: Hendrickson Pub., 1994.

The Holy Spirit: Power from on High. A. B. Simpson. Camp Hill, PA: Christian Pubns., Inc., 1994.

The Holy Spirit and You. Dennis Bennett and Rita Bennett. South Plainfield, NJ: Bridge Pub., Inc., 1971.

The Holy Spirit in the Bible. John Rea. Altamonte Springs, FL: Strang Comms. Co., 1989.

How to Pray for the Release of the Holy Spirit. Dennis Bennett. South Plainfield, NJ: Bridge Pub., Inc., 1985.

I Believe in the Holy Spirit (Revised edition). Michael Green. Grand Rapids: Wm. B. Eerdmans Pub. Co., 1989.

Joy Unspeakable. D. Martyn Lloyd-Jones. Wheaton, IL: Harold Shaw Pubs., 1985.

Keep in Step with the Spirit. J. I. Packer. Grand Rapids: Fleming H. Revell Co., 1987.

The Names of the Holy Spirit. Elmer L. Towns. Ventura, CA: Regal Books, 1994.

A Passion for Fullness. Jack W. Hayford. Dallas: Word, Inc., 1990.

Kingdom of God

Destined for the Throne. Paul E. Billheimer. Fort Washington, PA: Christian Literature Crusade, Inc., 1990.

The Gospel and the Kingdom. George E. Ladd. Grand Rapids: Wm. B. Eerdmans Pub. Co., 1959.

The Kingdom and the Power. Gary S. Greig and Kevin N. Springer. Ventura, CA: Regal Books, 1993.

Prayer

Living and Praying in Jesus' Name. Dick Eastman and Jack Hayford. Wheaton, IL: Tyndale House Pubs., 1988.

Power through Prayer. E. M. Bounds. Minneapolis: World Wide Pubns., 1989.

Prayer Is Invading the Impossible. Jack W. Hayford. South Plainfield, NJ: Bridge Pub., Inc., 1977.

Praying Hyde. Francis A. McGaw et al. Asheville, NC: Revival Literature, (ND).

With Christ in the School of Prayer. Andrew Murray. Springdale, PA: Whitaker House, 1981.

Spiritual Warfare

Churches that Pray. Peter Wagner. Ventura, CA: Regal Books, 1993.

Engaging the Enemy. C. Peter Wagner. Ventura, CA: Regal Books, 1991.

The Handbook for Spiritual Warfare. Ed Murphy. Nashville: Thomas Nelson, Inc., 1992.

Overcoming the Dominion of Darkness. Gary D. Kinnaman. Grand Rapids: Chosen Books, 1990.

Possessing the Gates of the Enemy. Cindy Jacobs. Grand Rapids: Chosen Books, 1991.

Strategic Spiritual Warfare. Ray Beeson and Patricia Hulsey. Nashville: Thomas Nelson, 1995.

Taking Our Cities for God. John Dawson. Altamonte Springs, FL: Strang Comms. Co., 1989.

That None Should Perish. Ed Silvoso. Ventura, CA: Regal Books, 1994.

The Three Battlegrounds. Francis Frangipane. Cedar Rapids, IA: Advancing Church Pubns., 1989.

War on the Saints. Jessie Penn-Lewis. Fort Washington, PA: Christian Literature Crusade, Inc., 1993.

Warfare Prayer. C. Peter Wagner. Ventura, CA: Regal Books, 1992.

Worship

Exploring Worship. Bob Sorge. Canandaigua, NY: Bob Sorge, 1989.

The Heart of Praise. Jack W. Hayford. Ventura, CA: Regal Books, 1992.

Introduction to Christian Worship. James F. White. Nashville: Abingdon Press, 1990.

Mastering Worship. Jack W. Hayford, John Killinger, and Howard Stevenson. Sisters, OR: Questar Pubs., 1991.

People in the Presence of God. Barry Liesch. Grand Rapids: Zondervan, 1988.

Up with Worship. Anne Ortlund. Ventura, CA: Regal Books, 1982.

Worship His Majesty. Jack W. Hayford. Dallas: Word, Inc., 1987.

Worship Is a Verb. Robert E. Webber. Nashville: Thomas Nelson, Inc., 1996.

General Study

The Daily Study Bible Series. William Barclay.

Index

807

Select Bibliography of Publications by Jack W. Hayford

The Beauty of Spiritual Language. Nashville: Thomas Nelson, Inc., 1996.
(A gracious setting forth of the Word of God on the subject of speaking "with tongues.")

The Church On The Way. Grand Rapids: Chosen Books, 1982.
(Learning the principles of New Testament church life.)

Come and Behold Him. Sisters, OR: Questar Publishers, 1995.
(Meditations for Christmas worship.)

Daybreak: Starting Your Day with Christ. Wheaton, IL: Tyndale House Pubs., 1984.
(Insights for building a vibrant life of personal devotion.)

Foundations of Worship. Van Nuys, CA: Living Way Ministries, 1988.
(Twelve principles which undergird vital worship.)

Glorious Morning. Sisters, OR: Questar Publishers, 1995.
(Meditations for Easter worship.)

Glory on Your House. Grand Rapids: Chosen Books, 1991.
(A further revision and expansion of *The Church On the Way* [see above].)

The Heart of Praise. Ventura, CA: Regal Books, 1992.
(Sixty meditations from the Psalms on principles of living worship.)

I'll Hold You in Heaven. Ventura, CA: Regal Books, 1986.
(Comfort for parents in the aftermath of miscarriage, stillbirth, or a past abortion.)

The Key to Everything. Altamonte Springs, FL: Strang Comms. Co., 1993.
(A story-filled, Bible-centered look at giving—life's central "release"-point.)

A Man's Walk with God Series. Nashville: Thomas Nelson Publishers, 1995.
(Six 100-page books geared to point a man toward practical pathways for godly, integrity-filled living:)

A Man's Starting Place
(Explores how men become spiritually mature in Christ through relationships.)

A Man's Confidence
(Studies how men become confident in life by discerning and mastering guilt and condemnation.)

A Man's Walk With God
(Explores the process for faith's progress and practical development.)

A Man's Image and Identity
(Studies a man's pathway to Christlikeness in today's society.)

A Man's Integrity
(Explores how men can develop in godly character.)

A Man's Worship and Witness
(Studies how God's kingdom comes to men and through men.)

The Mary Miracle. Ventura, CA: Regal Books, 1994.

(Appropriating God's miracle possibilites for your life and service.)

Newborn: Your New Life with Christ. Wheaton, IL: Tyndale House Pubs., 1987.
(Introducing the new believer to life in the family of God.)

Outracing the World. Van Nuys, CA: Living Way Ministries, 1994.
(A study guide on racial reconciliation [also available on videotape].)

A Passion for Fullness. Dallas: Word, Inc., 1990.
(A plea for a discerning pursuit for bold and balanced Spirit-filled living and leadership.)

Pastors of Promise. Ventura, CA: Regal Books, 1996.
(A practical and faith-building call to fruitful, fulfilling pastoral ministry.)

The Power and Blessing. Wheaton, IL: Scripture Press Pubns., 1994.
(Dealing with ten primary disciplines of Spirit-filled living.)

Prayer Is Invading the Impossible. South Plainfield, NJ: Bridge Publishing, Inc., 1977.
(A dynamic, insight-filled examination of prayer and the path to effective praying.)

Rebuilding the Real You. Ventura, CA: Regal Books, 1986.
(A study on the personal ministry of the Holy Spirit in the Book of Nehemiah.)

Restoring Fallen Leaders. Ventura, CA: Regal Books, 1988.
(Examining the issue of integrity and spiritual leadership.)

Spirit-Filled: The Overflowing Power of the Holy Spirit. Wheaton, IL: Tyndale House Pubs., 1987.
(A brief guide to receiving and living in the power of the Holy Spirit.)

Taking Hold of Tomorrow. Ventura, CA: Regal Books, 1989.
(Possessing God's promises—a study in Joshua.)

Ten Steps Toward Saving America. Van Nuys, CA: Living Way Ministries, 1994.
(Discerning a believer's role as a citizen.)

Worship His Majesty. Dallas: Word, Inc., 1987.
(A defining study of the purpose, principles, and pathway for worship.)

Other *Spirit-Filled Life Bible* projects on which Pastor Hayford served as General Editor or Executive Editor:

Living the Spirit-Filled Life. Jack W. Hayford and Sam Middlebrook. Nashville: Thomas Nelson, Inc., 1992.

Spirit-Filled Life Bible, New King James Version. Nashville: Thomas Nelson, Inc., 1991.

Spirit-Filled Life Bible, King James Version. Nashville: Thomas Nelson, Inc., 1995.

Spirit-Filled Life Student Bible. Nashville: Thomas Nelson, Inc., 1995.

Spirit-Filled Life Bible Study Series (28, 160-page Study Guides). Nashville: Thomas Nelson, Inc.

Other books to which Jack Hayford has made significant contributions:
A Reader on the Holy Spirit: Anointing, Equipping

and *Empowering for Service.* International
Church of the Foursquare Gospel, 1993.
Mastering Worship. Jack Hayford, John Killinger,
Howard Stevenson. Sisters, OR: Questar Pubs.,
1990.
Seven Promises of A Promise Keeper. 1994 by
Promise Keepers. Published by Focus on the
Family Publishing.

*What Makes a Man? Twelve Promises that Can
Change Your Life.* Bill McCartney with others.
Colorado Springs: NavPress, 1992 by Promise
Keepers.
Who's in Charge? Leith Anderson, Jack Hayford,
Ben Patterson. Sisters, OR: Questar Pubs., 1993.

Index of Illustrations, Charts, and Maps

(Additional charts and maps not listed above
appear in the "Visual Survey of the Bible," on
pages 483–506.)

Index of Kingdom Life Insights by Scripture Reference

Index of Word Wealth Entries by Scripture Reference

Old Testament

Genesis 1:1 **created,** bara'; 1:26 **man** (mankind, humanness), 'adam; 3:15 **head,** rosh; 12:3 **families,** mishpachah; 14:18 **Most High,** 'elyon; 15:6 **accounted,** chashab; 17:7 **covenant** (pledge, treaty, agreement), berit; 22:2 **son** (only; only child, single), yachid; 26:3 **swore,** shaba'; 29:32 **son** (builder of future generations), ben; 49:10 **Shiloh,** shiloh.

Exodus 1:17 **feared,** yare'; 3:7 **know** (perceive, be acquainted with), yada'; 15:26 **heals** (who heals you), rapha'; 16:30 **rested,** shabat; 19:20 **went up,** 'alah; 23:14 **keep a feast,** chagag; 25:18 **cherubim,** keruwim; 28:30 **continually,** tamid; 32:13 **land,** 'eretz; 33:14 **give rest,** nu'ach; 34:27 **made,** karat; 35:27 **ephod,** 'ephod; 38:22 **tribe,** matteh; 39:7 **memorial,** zikron.

Leviticus 4:13 **guilty,** 'asham; 5:6 **priest,** kohen; 9:2 **sin offering,** chatta't; 10:10 **unclean,** tame'; 14:31 **cleansed,** taher; 16:17 **assembly,** qahal; 17:11 **blood,** dam; 19:2 **holy** (set aside for holy purposes), qadosh; 23:12 **blemish** (without), tamim; 25:10 **liberty** (release, set free), deror.

Numbers 9:2 **appointed time,** mo'ed; 10:12 **settled down,** shachan; 13:30 **able,** yakol; 14:18 **clears,** naqah; 15:25 **atonement (make),** chaphar 29:6 **grain offering,** minchah 36:13 **judgments,** mishpat.

Deuteronomy 1:1 **words,** davar; 6:4 **one,** 'echad; 8:1 **possess,** yarash; 8:18 **power** (capacity, ability), koach; 11:25 **tread,** darach; 16:2 **sacrifice,** zabach; 18:5 **name** (marking of fame, memorial, character), shem; 26:18 **special,** segullah; 31:9 **wrote,** chatab; 33:12 **safety,** betach; 32:36 **judge** (rule, legislate, govern), din; 33:23 **favor,** ratson.

Joshua 1:9 **strong (be),** chazaq; 3:4 **passed,** abar; 4:24 **hand,** yad; 22:9 **possession,** 'achuzzah; 22:17 **congregation,** 'edah.

Judges 2:18 **judge** (decide a matter and verdict), shaphat; 5:3 **sing,** shir; 5:31 **perish,** 'abad; 10:7 **anger** (observable, fierce), 'aph; 13:19 **wondrous thing (did a),** pala'.

Ruth 1:16 **people,** 'am; 4:15 **restorer,** shub.

1 Samuel 3:20 **prophet,** nabi'; 9:9 **seer,** ro'eh.

2 Samuel 7:11 **house,** bayit; 8:15 **reigned,** malach; 22:31 **word** (speech, dictum), 'imrah; 23:2 **Spirit** (breath of "life"), ruach.

1 Kings 8:23 **heaven** (expanse above earth), shamayim; 11:34 **chose,** bachar; 16:2 **anger** (from repeated irritation), cha'as; 20:8 **listen,** shama'.

2 Kings 12:9 **altar,** mizbeach; 19:15 **God** (Eternal Creator), 'elohim.

1 Chronicles 15:2 **minister,** sharat; 16:7 **thank,** yadah; 23:30 **praise** (boast about with words and singing), halal; 29:11 **majesty** (royalty, glorious, splendor), hod.

2 Chronicles 6:20 **prayer,** tephillah; 7:10 **joyful,** sameach; 20:20 **believe,** aman; 32:21 **angel,** mal'ach; 32:32 **vision,** chazon.

Ezra 3:11 **shout (great),** teru'ah.

Nehemiah 1:10 **redeemed** (liberate, free, release), padah; 8:8 **understand,** bin; 9:13 **statutes,** choq.

Esther 9:28 **generation,** d'or.

Job 1:6 **Satan,** Satan; 4:17 **mortal,** 'enosh; 5:7 **trouble,** 'amal; 10:12 **preserved,** shamar; 19:26 **flesh** (body), basar; 42:10 **prayed,** palal.

Psalms 1:2 **meditates,** hagah; 3:title **psalm,** mizmor; 5:4 **evil,** ra'; 8:5 **honor,** hadar; 18:46 **exalted** (elevate, lift up, extol), rum; 23:4 **comfort** (console, deep empathy), nacham; 25:5 **truth** (dependability, reliability), 'emet; 30:5 **joy** (laud, cheering in triumph), rinnah; 31:19 **great,** rab; 32:8 **teach,** yarah; 34:8 **taste** (choose and delight in good), ta'am; 37:4 **heart,** leb; 40:17 **poor,** 'ani; 45:14 **virgins,** betulah; 47:1 **clap,** taqa'; 55:22 **sustain,** chul; 63:3 **praise** (to glory in and calm, sooth), shabach; 68:5 **father,** 'ab; 68:11 **company,** tsaba'; 70:5 **needy,** 'ebyon; 78:41 **tempted,** nasah; 86:17 **sign,** 'ot; 91:1 **Almighty,** shadday; 95:2 **thanksgiving,** todah; 97:10 **love** (affection for friend, idea, pleasure, etc.), 'ahab; 99:5 **worship** (stoop as act of submission), shachah; 100:2 **serve,** 'abad; 100:4 **praise** (celebration, lauding, exaltation), tehillah; 103:3 **forgives,** salach; 106:47 **Gentiles,** goyim; 112:1 **delights,** chafets; 119:15 **precepts,** piqud; 119:35 **commandments,** mitsvah; 119:63 **companion,** chaber; 119:100 **ancients,** zaqen; 122:6 **pray** (asking for or inquiring about), sha'at; 130:3 **iniquities** (crooked direction, warped deeds), 'avon; 133:1 **brethren,** 'ach; 136:1 **forever,** olam; 138:8 **perfect** (finish, fulfilled), gamar; 145:2 **bless,** barach; 149:3 **sing praises,** zamar; 150:6 **breath,** neshamah.

Proverbs 1:6 **proverb,** mashal; 3:6 **direct,** yashar; 4:13 **instruction,** musar; 10:3 **soul,** nephesh; 10:16 **wicked,** rasha'; 14:26 **refuge,** machseh; 16:3 **commit,** galal; 17:17 **friend** (companion, neighbor), re'a; 22:8 **sorrow,** 'aven; 28:20 **faithful,** 'emunah; 31:28 **blessed,** 'ashar.

Ecclesiastes 3:4 **laugh,** sachaq; 11:6 **prosper,** chashar.

Isaiah 6:2 **seraphim,** seraphim; 8:13 **fear** (reverence, awe), morah; 11:2 **wisdom** (principals of right living made action), chochmah; 12:2 **YAH,** Yah; 28:12 **rest** (place of stillness, peace, comfort), menuchah; 32:2 **man** (maleness, man, with sense of dignity), 'ish; 32:18 **dwellings,** mishchan; 33:6 **times** (small space of time or season), et; 40:11 **feed,** ra'ah; 42:21 **law,** torah; 43:2 **waters,** mayim; 45:18 **in vain,** tohu; 48:17 **teaches,** lamad; 52:9 **redeemed** (repurchase, buy back), ga'al; 60:1 **glory** (renown and visible splendor), chabod; 61:1 **anointed,** mashach; 62:6 **mention (make),** zachar; 64:5 **rejoices,** sus.

Jeremiah 1:12 **ready,** shaqad; 3:15 **understanding** (intelligent thinking process), sachal; 5:6 **backslidings,** meshubah; 8:11 **slightly,** qalal;

4:10 **propitiation,** *hilasmos;* 4:18 **fear,** (of terror, flight), *phobos;* 5:20 **life,** *zoe.*
3 John 2 **health,** *hugiaino.*
Jude 4 **Lord** (absolute dominion, supreme authority), *despotes;* 11 **error,** *plane;* 24 **able,** *dunamai.*
Revelation 1:5 **witness,** *martus;* 2:9 **poverty,** *ptocheia;* 2:10 **tested,** *peirazo;* 2:23 **hearts,** *kardia;* 4:10 **worship** (prostrate, bow down), *proskuneo;* 5:13 **creature,** *ktisma;* 6:1 **lamb,** *arnion;* 6:15 **free** (freedom to come and go), *eleutheros;* 9:21 **sorceries,** *pharmakeia;* 11:8

spiritually, *pneumatikos;* 12:17 **enraged,** *orgizo;* 14:6 **everlasting,** *aionios;* 14:13 **rest** (cessation from toil, refreshing), *anapauo;* 15:5 **testimony** (proclamation of personal experience), *maturion;* 16:14 **signs,** *semeion;* 17:2 **committed fornication,** *porneuo;* 18:11 **mourn** (over loss of something valuable), *pentheo;* 19:5 **servants,** *doulos;* 20:4 **judgment,** *krima;* 21:1 **heaven** (regions above earth, God's abode), *ouranos;* 21:2 **prepared,** *hetoimazo;* 22:12 **reward,** *misthos;* 22:20 **quickly,** *tachu.*

Index of Kingdom Dynamics Articles by Scripture Reference

Old Testament

Genesis 1:1, *Kingdom of God;* 1:3–5, *The Blood;* 1:26–27, *Manhood;* 1:26–28, *Family Life;* 1:26–28, *Human Worth;* 1:26–28; 2:16–17, *Kingdom of God;* 1:31, *Kingdom of God;* 2:2–3, *Stewardship;* 3:15, *Messianic Promises;* 3:16, *Manhood;* 3:16–24, *Kingdom of God;* 3:17, *Human Worth;* 3:21, *The Blood;* 3:21, *Restoration;* 3:24, *Angels;* 4:1–10, *The Blood;* 4:9, *Brotherly Love;* 4:25, *Women;* 6:5, *Restoration;* 8:20, *The Blood;* 8:20–9:17, *Kingdom of God;* 8:22, *Faith, Seed;* 9:5–6, *Human Worth;* 12:1–3, *Kingdom of God;* 12:1–20; 17:1–27; 22:1–19, *Leadership, Spiritual;* 14:17–24, *Stewardship;* 15:10, *The Blood;* 16:1, *Women;* 17:5, *Faith's Confession;* 17:10, *The Blood;* 18:17–33, *Prayer;* 22:13, *The Blood;* 24:15–67, *Women;* 26:1–5; 28:1–22, *Kingdom of God;* 29:35, *Praise;* 41:42–43, *Restoration;* 45:4, *Brotherly Love.*
Exodus 3:2, 4, *Angels;* 12:13, *The Blood;* 15:26, *Faith, Seed;* 15:26, *Healing, Divine;* 19:5–7, *Kingdom of God;* 27:1–28:43, *Leadership, Spiritual;* 28:1–2, *Leadership, Spiritual;* 32:11–14, 30–34, *Prayer.*
Leviticus 17:11, *The Blood;* 19:34, *Brotherly Love.*
Numbers 10:1–10, *Spiritual Warfare;* 12:1–6, *Healing, Divine;* 13:1—14:45, *Leadership, Spiritual;* 13:30; 14:6–9, *Faith's Confession;* 21:5–9, *Healing, Divine;* 21:16–17, *Praise;* 27:1–11, *Women.*
Deuteronomy 8:3, *Word of God;* 18:18–19, *Messianic Promises;* 28:1, *Prophecy.*
Joshua 1:6–7, 9, *Manhood;* 6:10, *Faith's Confession;* 10:12–14, *Prayer.*
Judges 4:1–5:31, *Leadership, Spiritual;* 4:4–5, *Women;* 6:1—8:35, *Leadership, Spiritual;* 8:22–23; 9:1–57, *Leadership, Spiritual;* 13:6, *Angels.*
Ruth 1:1—4:22, *Women.*
2 Samuel 24:24, *Faith, Seed.*
1 Kings 17:8–16, *Faith, Seed.*
2 Kings 5:1–15, *Healing, Divine;* 6:8–17, *Spiritual Warfare;* 19:8–19, *Spiritual Warfare;* 20:1–11, *Healing, Divine;* 22:3–20, *Women.*

1 Chronicles 29:10–16, *Kingdom of God.*
2 Chronicles 5:13, *Praise;* 6:12—7:1, *Prayer;* 6:24–31, *Faith's Confession;* 20:15–22, *Praise;* 25:9, *Faith, Seed.*
Ezra 8:21–23, *Spiritual Warfare.*
Esther 4:1, *Women.*
Job 40:10–12, *Restoration;* 42:10–13, *Healing, Divine.*
Psalm 2:8, *Evangelism;* 5:1–3, *Spiritual Warfare;* 7:14–17, *Praise;* 8:4–8, *Human Worth;* 15:3, *Brotherly Love;* 16:10, *Messianic Promises;* 18:3, *Praise;* 19:7, *Word of God;* 19:14, *Faith's Confession;* 22:1–31, *Messianic Promises;* 22:3, *Kingdom of God;* 22:3–4, *Praise;* 41:9; 47:7, *Praise;* 50:22–23, *Praise;* 51:1–19, *Prayer;* 63:1–5, *Praise;* 68:5–6, *Family Life;* 71:14, *Praise;* 86:5, *Brotherly Love;* 90:1–17, *Stewardship;* 91:9–10, *Healing, Divine;* 91:11–12, *Angels;* 93:2, *Kingdom of God;* 103:3, *Healing, Divine;* 103:20–21, *Angels;* 107:20, *Healing, Divine;* 119:89–91, *Word of God;* 119:105, *Word of God;* 122:6, *Prophecy;* 126:5–6, *Spiritual Warfare;* 127:3–5, *Family Life;* 145:4, *Praise;* 150:1–6, *Praise.*
Proverbs 3:5–6, *Spiritual Warfare;* 13:24, *Family Life;* 16:23–24, *Faith's Confession;* 24:11–12, *Evangelism;* 30:5–6, *Word of God.*
Ecclesiastes 7:29, *Manhood.*
Isaiah 1:11, *The Blood;* 4:2–3, *Restoration;* 6:2, *Angels;* 6:8–9, *Leadership, Spiritual;* 7:14, *Messianic Promises;* 9:6, *Messianic Promises;* 14:12–14, *Angels;* 28:11–12, *Holy Spirit Gifts;* 36:1—37:38, *Prayer;* 40:8–11, *Evangelism;* 53:1–12, *Messianic Promises;* 53:4–5, *Healing, Divine;* 54:5, *Family Life;* 55:10–11, *Word of God;* 58:1–14, *Restoration;* 61:3, *Praise.*
Jeremiah 8:8–9, *Restoration;* 29:11–14, *Spiritual Warfare;* 33:3, *Spiritual Warfare.*
Ezekiel 22:30, *Prayer;* 22:30, *Spiritual Warfare;* 34:1–10, *Restoration.*
Daniel 6:1–5, *Manhood;* 7:21–22, *Kingdom of God;* 10:13, *Angels.*
Hosea 2:16–17, 19–20, *Family Life;* 11:1, 3–4, *Family Life.*
Joel 2:28–29, *Restoration.*

Index of Kingdom Dynamics Articles by Subtitles